T&T Clark Reader in Political Theology

T&T Clark Reader in Political Theology

Edited by
Elizabeth Phillips,
Anna Rowlands and
Amy Daughton

LONDON • NEW YORK • OXFORD • NEW DELHI • SYDNEY

Bloomsbury T&T Clark
An imprint of Bloomsbury Publishing Plc

50 Bedford Square, London, WC1B 3DP, UK
1385 Broadway, New York, NY 10018, USA
29 Earlsfort Terrace, Dublin 2, Ireland

BLOOMSBURY, T&T CLARK and the Diana logo are trademarks of
Bloomsbury Publishing Plc

First published 2021

Cover design: Eleanor Rose
Cover image © Godong / robertharding

Library of Congress Cataloging-in-Publication Data
Names: Phillips, Elizabeth, 1973– editor.
Title: T&T Clark reader in political theology /edited by Elizabeth Phillips,
Anna Rowlands, and Amy Daughton.
Description: 1 [edition]. | New York : Bloomsbury T&T Clark, 2017. |
Includes bibliographical references and index.
Identifiers: LCCN 2017036902 (print) | ISBN 9780567666970 (hardback : alk.paper) |
ISBN 9780567666963 (pbk. : alk. paper)
Subjects: LCSH:Political theology.
Classification: LCC BT83.59 (ebook) | LCC BT83.59 .T282017 (print) |
DDC 261.7–dc23
LC record available at https://lccn.loc.gov/2017036902

ISBN: HB: 978-0-5676-6697-0
PB: 978-0-5676-6696-3

Typeset by Newgen KnowledgeWorks Pvt. Ltd., Chennai, India
Printed and bound in Great Britain

To find out more about our authors and books visit www.bloomsbury.com
and sign up for our newsletters

Contents

Copyright Acknowledgements viii
About the Editors xiii

General Introduction by *Elizabeth Phillips, Anna Rowlands and Amy Daughton* 1

I The Emergence of Political Theology 7

Introduction by Amy Daughton 7

1 Scriptural Sources 10
  1 Samuel 8; Luke 1:68–79; Luke 23:33–43; Matthew 25:31–46; John 18:33–37
2 Gregory of Nyssa – First Homily on the Love of the Poor, or On Good Works 13
3 John Chrysostom – First Homily on Lazarus and the Rich Man, or On Wealth and Poverty 20
4 Augustine of Hippo – City of God, Book XIX, Chapters 11–28 31
5 Augustine of Hippo – Letters 189, 220 57
6 Thomas Aquinas – Extracts from *Summa Theologiae* 66
7 Thomas Aquinas – Extracts from *De regimine principum* 92
8 Discussion Questions 103

II Approaches to Political Theology 105

Introduction by Anna Rowlands 105

9 Carl Schmitt – Definition of Sovereignty 109
10 Jürgen Moltmann – Covenant or Leviathan? Political Theology for Modern Times 115
11 Johann Baptist Metz – Theology in the New Paradigm: Political Theology 132
12 Dorothee Soelle – Extracts from The Silent Cry: Mysticism and Resistance 140
13 Jürgen Habermas – Faith and Knowledge 151
14 Discussion Questions 161

III The Church and the Political 163

Introduction by Anna Rowlands 163

15 Martin Luther – Extracts from Appeal to the Christian Nobility of the German Nation 168

16 Martin Luther – Extracts from On Secular Authority: How Far Does the Obedience Owed to It Extend? 177

17 John Calvin – Of Civil Government 199

18 John Neville Figgis – Extracts from The Civic Standpoint 225

19 William Temple – What Christians Stand for in the Secular World 230

20 Dietrich Bonhoeffer and Karl Barth – The Aryan Clauses and Further Correspondence 241

21 Dorothy Day – Why 260

22 Dorothy Day – Extracts from We Go on Record 267

23 Discussion Questions 272

IV The Politics of Jesus 273

Introduction by Elizabeth Phillips 273

24 John Howard Yoder – Are You the One Who Is to Come? 276

25 Michael Sattler – The Schleitheim Articles 291

26 Reinhold Niebuhr – The Ethic of Jesus and the Social Problem 297

27 James Cone – Jesus Christ in Black Theology 305

28 Discussion Questions 320

V Violence and Peace 321

Introduction by Elizabeth Phillips 321

29 Tertullian – Extracts from On the Crown 324

30 Ambrose of Milan – Extracts from On the Duties of Clergy, Book I 326

31 Pilgram Marpeck – Concerning the Lowliness of Christ 328

32 Martin Luther King, Jr. – A Time to Break Silence 347

33 William T. Cavanaugh – Violence Religious and Secular: Questioning the Categories 360

34 Rowan Williams – Do Human Rights Exist? 373

35 Discussion Questions 383

VI Liberalism and Democracy 385

Introduction by Anna Rowlands 385

36 Thomas Hobbes – Extracts from Leviathan 389

37 Stanley Hauerwas – The Church and Liberal Democracy 413

38 John Milbank – Liberality versus Liberalism 432

39 Christopher Insole – Theology and Politics: The Intellectual History of
    Liberalism 450
40 Eric Gregory – Love and Citizenship after Augustine 466
41 Aristotle Papanikolaou – The Politics of Divine-Human
    Communion 490
42 Discussion Questions 494

VII Oppression, Marginalization and Liberation 495

Introduction by Amy Daughton 495
43 Leo XIII – Extracts from *Rerum Novarum* 499
44 Jon Sobrino – Extracts from *Extra Pauperes Nulla Salus:* A Short-
    Utopian Prophetic Essay 518
45 Marcella Althaus-Reid – ¿*Bién Sonados?* The Future of Mystical
    Connections in Liberation Theology 539
46 J. Kameron Carter – Interlude on Christology and Race 555
47 Rosemary Radford Ruether – Extracts from Sexism and
    God-Talk: Toward a Feminist Theology 580
48 Musa Dube – Reading for Decolonization (John 4.1–42) 592
49 Discussion Questions 612

VIII Creation, History and Eschatology 613

Introduction by Elizabeth Phillips 613
50 Charles Mathewes – The Republic of Grace; or, the Public Ramifications
    of Heaven 615
51 Oliver O'Donovan – The Political Thought of the Book of Revelation 626
52 Sergii Bulgakov – The Soul of Socialism 650
53 Slavoj Žižek – Extracts from Thinking Backward: Predestination and
    Apocalypse 672
54 Discussion Questions 691

Suggestions for Further Reading 693
Scripture Index 701
Subject Index 709

Copyright
Acknowledgements

Every effort has been made to trace copyright holders and to obtain their permission for the use of copyright material. The publisher apologizes for any errors or omissions and would be grateful if notified of any corrections that should be incorporated in future reprints or editions of this book.

The editors and publishers are grateful for permission to reproduce the following copyright material:

Scripture quotations of 1 Samuel 8, Luke 1.68–79, Matthew 25.31–46, Luke 23.33–43, and John 18.33–37 are from New Revised Standard Version Bible, copyright © 1989 National Council of the Churches of Christ in the United States of America. Used by permission. All rights reserved worldwide.

'First Homily on the Love of the Poor, or On Good Works' (pp. 193–8) by Gregory of Nyssa, edited and translated by Susan R. Holman in *The Hungry Are Dying: Beggars and Bishops in Roman Cappadocia* © Oxford University Press, 2001. Reproduced with permission of the Licensor through PLSclear.

'First Homily on Lazarus and the Rich Man, or On Wealth and Poverty' (pp. 19–88) from *On Wealth and Poverty* by John Chrysostom, translated by Catherine P. Roth © St Vladimir Seminary Press, 1984. Every effort has been made to contact St Vladimir Seminary Press.

Extract (Book XIX, Chapters 11–28) from *City of God* by Augustine of Hippo, translated by Henry Bettenson, Penguin Books, 2003 © Henry Bettenson, 1972. Reprinted by permission of Penguin Random House UK.

'Letters to Boniface', Letters 189 and 220 (pp. 214–25) from *Augustine: Political Writings* by Augustine of Hippo, translated by E. M. Atkins, edited by E. M. Atkins and R. J. Dodaro © Cambridge University Press, 2001. Reproduced with permission of the Licensor through PLSclear.

Extracts (IaIIae 90.1c; 90.2c; 90.3c and ad 1, 2; 90.4c and ad 1; 91.1c, 91.2c and ad 2; 91.3c and ad 1–3; 91.4c and ad 1, 2; 92.1c and ad 1–4; 94.4c; 94.6c; 95.1c; 95.2c, and ad 3; 95.3c; 96.1c; 96.2c and ad 2,3; 96.3c; 96.4c and ad 1–3; 96.5c and ad 1–3; 96.6c and ad 1–3; 97.2c and ad 1; 97.3c and ad 1–3; IIaIIae; 47.10c; 47.11c and ad 3; 47.12c; 50.1c; 50.2c; 57.1c; 57.2c; 58.3c and ad 1 and 4; 58.5c; 58.6c and ad 4; 58.7c and ad 1,

2; 58.8c; 58.11c and ad 1; 58.12c and ad 1–3; 61.1c and ad 1–5; 61.2c and ad 3; 64.3c and ad 3; 64.6c and ad 1,2; 65.1c and ad 2; 65.4 and ad 3; 66.2c and ad 1–3; 66.3c and ad 2; 66.6c and ad 1–3; 66.7c; 68.3c.) from *Summa Theologiae* by Thomas Aquinas, translated and edited by Thomas Gilby, volume 28 © Blackfriars, 1975; volume 36 © Blackfriars, 1974; and volume 37 © Blackfriars, 1975. Every effort has been made to contact The Dominican Council as Trustee for the English Province of the Order of Preachers/Cambridge University Press.

Extracts (pp. 5–15, 17–21, 36–7, 39–41, 42–4) from 'De Regime Principum', in *Aquinas: Political Writings* by Thomas Aquinas, edited and translated by R. W. Dyson © Cambridge University Press, 2002. Reproduced with permission of the Licensor through PLSclear.

'Definition of Sovereignty' (pp. 5–15) from *Political Theology: Four Chapters on the Concept of Sovereignty* by Carl Schmitt, edited and translated by George Schwab. Translation (c) 1985 by George Schwab. Originally published in German as 'Politische Theologie: Vier Kapitel zur Lehre von der Souveranitat'. © 1922, revised edition © 1934 by Duncker & Humblot, Berlin. Reprinted by permission of University of Chicago Press.

'Covenant or Leviathan? Political Theology for Modern Times' (pp. 19–44) by Jürgen Moltmann from *Scottish Journal of Theology* 47 © *Scottish Journal of Theology*, 1994. Reproduced with permission of the Licensor through PLSclear.

'Theology in the New Paradigm: Political Theology' (pp. 355–66) by Johann Baptist Metz, translated by Margaret Köhl from *Paradigm Change in Theology*, edited by Hans Küng and David Tracy © T&T Clark, 1989. Reprinted by permission of Bloomsbury Publishing Plc.

Extracts (pp. 88–93, 191–9) from 'The Journey' and 'As if We Lived in a Liberated World', in *The Silent Cry: Mysticism and Resistance* by Dorothee Soelle, translated by Barbara and Martin Rumscheidt © Augsburg Fortress Press, 2001. Reprinted by permission of Augsburg Fortress via 1517 Media.

'Faith and Knowledge' (pp. 105–15) from *The Future of Human Nature* by Jürgen Habermas, translated by Hella Beister and Max Pensky © Polity Press, 2003. Reprinted by permission of Polity Press/Suhrkamp Insel.

Extracts from 'Appeal to the Christian Nobility of the German Nation' (pp. 403–17) from *Martin Luther: Selections from his writings* by Martin Luther, edited by John Dillenberger, Anchor Books © John Dillenberger, 1961. Reprinted by permission of The Lutterworth Press.

Extracts from *On Secular Authority* (pp. 3–34) by Martin Luther from *Luther and Calvin on Secular Authority*, edited and translated by Harro Höpfl, © Cambridge University Press, 1991. Reproduced with permission of the Licensor through PLSclear.

Of Civil Government (pp. 47–84) by John Calvin from *Luther and Calvin on Secular Authority*, edited and translated by Harro Höpfl, © Cambridge University Press, 1991. Reproduced with permission of the Licensor through PLSclear.

Extracts (pp. 99–106, 125–34) from 'Lecture Three: The Civic Standpoint', in *Churches and the Modern State* by John Neville Figgis. Longmans, Green and Co, 1913. Acknowledging with thanks the sources of the text.

'What Christians Stand for in the Secular World' (pp. 243–65) from *Religious Experience and Other Essays and Addresses* by William Temple © Lutterworth Press, 1958. Reprinted by permission of The Lutterworth Press.

'The Aryan Clauses and Further Correspondence' (pp. 221–49) by Karl Barth and Dietrich Bonhoeffer from *No Rusty Swords: Letters, Lectures and Notes from the Collected Works of Dietrich Bonhoeffer*, translated by E. H. Robertson and John Bowden, edited by E.H. Robertson © William Collins Sons & Co., 1965. Reprinted by permission of Verlagsgruppe Random House GmbH.

'Why?' (pp. 3–18) from *From Union Square to Rome* by Dorothy Day © Orbis Press, 2006. Reprinted by permission of Orbis Books.

Extracts from 'We go on Record' (pp. 311–17) by Dorothy Day from *Dorothy Day: Selected Writings*, edited by Robert Ellsberg, Orbis, 2005 © Robert Ellsberg and Tamar Hennessy, 1983. Reprinted by permission of Orbis Books.

'Are You the One Who is to Come?' (pp. 199–218) from *For the Nations* by John Howard Yoder © Wm B. Eerdmans Press, 1997. Reproduced with permission of the Licensor through PLSclear.

The Schleitheim Articles (pp. 172–80) by Michael Sattler from *The Radical Reformation*, edited by Michael G. Baylor © Cambridge University Press, 1991. Reproduced with permission of the Licensor through PLSclear.

'The Ethic of Jesus and the Social Problem' (pp. 29–40) in *Love and Justice: Selections from the shorter writings of Reinhold Niebuhr*, edited by D. B. Robertson © Westminster John Knox Press, 1957. Reprinted by permission of Westminster John Knox Press.

'Jesus Christ in Black Theology' (pp. 116–36) from *A Black Theology of Liberation* by James H. Cone, Orbis Press, 2010 © James H. Cone 1986, 1990, 2010. Reprinted by permission of Orbis Books.

Extracts from 'On the Crown' (pp. 255–8) from *Disciplinary, Moral, and Ascetical Works by Tertullian*, translated by Rudolph Arbesmann, Sister Emily Joseph Daly and Edwin A. Quain © Catholic University of America Press, 1959. Reprinted by permission of Catholic University of America Press.

Extracts (De Officiis Book 1: Chapters 29, 35, 36) from 'On the Duties of Clergy' by Ambrose of Milan from *De Officiis: Introduction, text and translation*, edited and translated by Ivor Davidson © Oxford University Press, 2001. Reproduced with permission of the Licensor through PLSclear.

Concerning the Lowliness of Christ (pp. 428–63) by Pilgram Marpeck from *The Writings of Pilgram Marpeck*, translated and edited by William Klassen and Walter Klaassen © Herald Press, 1978. Every effort has been made to contact Herald Press.

'A Time to Break Silence' (pp. 231–44) from *A Testament of Hope: Writings and Speeches of Martin Luther King, Jr.* by Martin Luther King, Jr., edited by James Melvin

Washington, Harper Press © Coretta Scott King, 1986. Reproduced with permission of the Licensor through Writers House.

'Violence Religious and Secular: Questioning the Categories' (pp. 55–70) from *Violence, Transformation, and the Sacred* by William T. Cavanaugh © College Theology Society, 2012. Previously published in Margaret R. Pfeil and Tobias L. Winright, eds, *Violence, Transformation and the Sacred: 'They Shall Be Called Children of God'*, the Annual Volume of the College Theology Society 57 (Maryknoll, NY: Orbis Books, 2012) (c) College Theology Society. Reprinted by permission of College Theology Society.

'Do Human Rights Exist?' (pp. 149–59) from *Faith in the Public Square* by Rowan Williams © Bloomsbury Press, 2012. Reprinted by permission of Bloomsbury Publishing Plc.

Extracts (pp. 9–11, 86–100, 245–59) from *Leviathan* by Thomas Hobbes © Cambridge University Press, 1996. Reproduced with permission of the Licensor through PLSclear.

'The Church and Liberal Democracy' (pp. 72–86) from *A Community of Character* by Stanley Hauerwas © University of Notre Dame Press, 1981. Every effort has been made to contact University of Notre Dame Press.

'Liberality versus Liberalism' (pp. 242–63) from *A Future of Love: Essays in Political Theology* by John Milbank, Cascade Books © John Milbank, 2009. Reprinted by permission of Wipf and Stock Publishers.

'Theology and Politics: The Intellectual History of Liberalism' (pp. 173–93) by Christopher Insole from *Theology, University, Humanities: Initium Sapientiae Timor Domini*, edited by Francesca Aran Murphy and Christopher Craig Brittain. © Wipf and Stock, 2011. Reprinted by permission of Wipf and Stock Publishers.

'Love and Citizenship After Augustine' (pp. 79–103) by Eric Gregory from *Polygraph* 19/20 © Polygraph, 2008. Reprinted by permission of Polygraph, affiliated with Duke University.

'The Politics of Divine-Human Communion' (pp. 195–200) from *The Mystical as Political: Democracy and Non-Radical Orthodoxy* by Aristotle Papanikolaou © University of Notre Dame Press, 2012. Every effort has been made to contact University of Notre Dame Press.

Extracts (paragraphs 1–10, 19–23, 31–end) from *Rerum Novarum* by Pope Leo XIII. Acknowledging with thanks the sources of the texts.

Extracts (pp. 48–69) from 'Extra Pauperes Nulla Salus. A Short Utopian-Prophetic Essay' by Jon Sobrino in *No Salvation Outside the Poor* © Orbis Books, 2008. Reprinted by permission of Orbis Books and Darton, Longman, and Todd (UK/EU).

'¿Bién Sonados?: The Future of Mystical Connections in Liberation Theology' (pp. 65–82) in *From Feminist Theology to Indecent Theology* by Marcella Althaus-Reid is © Marcella Althaus-Reid 2004. Published by SCM Press. Used by permission. rights@hymnsam.co.uk.

About the Editors

Elizabeth Phillips is Director of Studies, Westcott House, Cambridge, UK, Research Fellow at the Margaret Beaufort Institute of Theology, Cambridge, UK and an Honorary Fellow of the Department of Theology and Religion, Durham University, UK. She is author of *Political Theology: A Guide for the Perplexed*, and co-editor of *The Cambridge Companion to Christian Political Theology*.

Anna Rowlands is St Hilda Associate Professor of Catholic Social Thought and Practice in the Department of Theology and Religious Studies at the University of Durham, UK and Chair of the UK Centre for Catholic Social Thought and Practice. She is author of *Towards a Politics of Communion: Catholic Social Teaching in Dark Times* and co-editor of the *Oxford Handbook on Religion and Contemporary Migration*, both forthcoming.

Amy Daughton is Lecturer in Practical Theology in the School of Philosophy, Theology and Religion at the University of Birmingham and Research Associate with the Margaret Beaufort Institute of Theology in Cambridge, UK. She is author of *With and For Others*, which considers the work of Paul Ricoeur and Thomas Aquinas for intercultural hermeneutics.

General Introduction

The years during which we have been compiling and editing this book have been years of considerable social and political turmoil, unrest and seemingly unprecedented events. As the book took shape, we saw the UK referendum to leave the EU, the subsequent chaos in British political parties, dramatic instances of hate crime and resurgent antisemitism, the rising tide of populism, nationalism and far right movements in the United States, UK, Europe and beyond, Donald Trump's ascent, the growing Black Lives Matter movement, and backlashes against it, the UK Windrush scandal, reckonings with historic and current gender and sexual abuse and exploitation by individuals and systems, and growing protest movements for climate justice. These headline events are far from being isolated phenomena; rather they are part of a global pattern of social ferment. Terrorist violence, persecution and growing intolerance of ethnic and religious minorities, the internal and external displacement of peoples due to conflict and climate change, the expanding market in human trafficking and the impact of emigration and immigration on local communities are truly global realities. From Sudan and Ukraine, to Aleppo, Australia and Moria, a new struggle for hope in the context of climate crisis and conflict-induced desolation structures our times. Unbelievably, this list does not begin to cover it all.

The study of political theology offers vital and timely resources for the task of interpreting these trajectories. For the political theologian, each of these questions of race, identity, war and violence, polarization over the goods of political community and large-scale displacement is both theological and political. What might such a claim mean? The answer is complex and multilayered. In the first instance, a political theologian will be aware that theological ideas, symbols and practices are being invoked and deployed by actors on every side of these social conflicts: discourses of good and evil, of deserving and undeserving humanity, of suffering and salvation, of justice, sovereignty, judgment and atonement circulate with power and intensity in our contemporary political environment.

Equally, in an increasingly non-religious West where we become less attuned to understanding religion as an embodied practice, we can overlook the ways in which theological resources are used in ordinary and everyday ways to sustain motivation, build resilience and provide grounds for resistance in the face of adversity. While religious institutions are capable of causing as much as responding to various forms of conflict and displacement, and Christians can be found on all sides of increasingly polarized debates about social goods, it is noticeable that church communities have been at the forefront of responsive projects. These include efforts to welcome and settle migrants, to reimagine sanctuary provision and disrupt the increasingly hard borders of the nation-state, to challenge and meet need in the context of food poverty, to provide local mutual aid and new experimental forms of local democratic governance, and to utilize global faith networks in order to identify and rescue the trafficked and to act as peacebuilders. In the face of new social challenges, Christian practices are continuing to be refashioned in ways that are thoroughly and simultaneously ecclesial and political. Nonetheless, religious institutions have been at the heart of a crisis marked by widespread harm and the abuse of power, not limited to sexual abuse crises. The churches have yet to account for the political-theological dimensions of these failures, nor to fully deploy the resources of this theological discipline in the search for a more just and loving expression of Christian-societal life. In sum, questions of the good life and of its absence are integral to the contemporary life of faith communities and theological systems of reasoning as much as they are central to political institutions and sciences.

Our hope as we introduce this collection of readings is at least twofold in the light of the dire possibilities we fear we now may face. It is our hope that we, among many others, hopefully including our readers, will mobilize in the face of these warning signs and prove that the seemingly inexorable may even now be turned back. It is also our hope that this collection is of both intellectual and practical use in these immediately tumultuous times and well beyond them. There are extraordinarily few truly unprecedented political ideas or events. Delving into the ways in which Christians across history have approached, shaped, meditated upon and resisted the politics of their times and places helps us to see patterns as well as possibilities; it gives us realism as well as hope. We gain in these readings both tools and impetus for the practical, reasoning tasks to which political theology summons us. We have not intended to assemble here a history of ideas from the great thinkers on the subjects of theology and politics. Such a project would be a true, if limited, good in its own right. But we hope to have assembled something more provocative (even if not especially radical) – something more like a manual rather than a historical textbook. The selections in this volume can be read as field notes, postings from historical and recent outposts of Christian political praxis, which provoke and inspire readers in their own theopolitical fieldwork.

For those wholly new to political theology, such postings may be reassuringly familiar to the debates of other disciplines. The tasks and questions that political theologians are engaged in share concerns with sociology and anthropology, with political theory and philosophy, with economics, indeed with all the humanities, since these disciplines are ultimately concerned with what human beings are really like. Our entry into political theology is through Christian theology, and scholars from these other disciplines may therefore identify a very different set of texts as core reading in political theology. What we may share in common is the view that political theology seeks to examine our assumptions about what political arrangements are for and the roots and power of our organizing political ideals and structures – though for us as theologians this includes the character both of the church and of the polis as social bodies. Recognizing this teleological and metaphysical level to discussions of politics unearths the implicitly normative weight of conclusions about human institutions and the human person as such. What distinguishes the theological enquiry at both the descriptive and normative levels is its commitment to understanding these questions in their full implications for the human person created by and in relationship with God. Theologians have at their disposal a range of resources from scripture onwards that conceives of human communities in relationship with God, in the light of who God is understood to be. Therefore, theologically speaking, addressing the purpose and shape of political arrangements garners diverse answers through the Christian traditions, throwing into sharp relief the divergence in the visions of human flourishing which political theology depicts.

How to Use This Reader

One way to use this volume is as a companion to Elizabeth Phillips's earlier book, *Political Theology: A Guide for the Perplexed* (London: T&T Clark, 2012). The sections of this reader correspond to the chapters in the *Guide*, and you will find in this reader many of the specific works which are discussed in those chapters, as well as some which are suggested as important further reading. You will also find here some selections which fill notable gaps in that book, particularly from Orthodox authors. Instructors may find that these two volumes together provide a good framework for a course in political theology, and part of our aim was to help those who are already using the *Guide* as a textbook, or may wish to do so if it were not so difficult to gather parallel primary readings. Readers of the *Guide* who are not instructors or students of courses in political theology will hopefully benefit from this collection as well. It would take an extraordinary dedication of time and effort for an individual to select and locate all the central and further readings to which the *Guide* points. We hope to have collected in a single volume an ideal selection of primary readings to accompany that secondary introduction. We have also offered suggestions of discussion questions at the end of each section, which instructors may find helpful.

However, the use of this volume in no way requires the reading or use of the *Guide*. We have constructed it either to stand alone as a collection of readings, gathered for scholars and students of political theology and related disciplines, or to be used as a textbook with instructional frameworks other than the *Guide*. The selection of pieces for this collection arose from our years of experience teaching political theology, sometimes together and sometimes separately, and represents our differing emphases and expertise, making it broader than the *Guide*. We share much in common in our approaches to political theology, but disagree or diverge in some significant places as well. We hope this collection benefits from our collaboration across our similarities and differences, being something better and more significant than any one of us could have produced alone.

In the introduction to each section we outline the theme/s of the pieces included there, and situate them each, briefly, in historical and theological context. We also note intersection and overlap with other sections of the reader, as well as some of the inevitable gaps in what we could include – even a reader of this length is only offering the tip of the iceberg of possible readings. At the end of the volume you will find an annotated list of suggested further readings.

A brief note on footnotes within the selections: some of the pieces included here were, in their original versions, accompanied by extensive critical footnotes written by editors and translators. Although most of these notes are not included here due to space constraints, we have kept those required for understanding a text, for citations and cross references, as well as footnotes original to authors (as opposed to editors and translators).

Section I explores the emergence of political theology in scripture, in patristic sources, and in the two theologians who have been most decisively formative of political theologies in the Christian West, Augustine and Aquinas. Section II explores the emergence of the academic discipline of political theology in relation to the work of Carl Schmitt, in the approach championed by mid-century German theologians who reclaimed the label 'political theology'. In the introduction to this section, public, postliberal, liberationist and postcolonial approaches are introduced as well, and are represented in other sections of the reader.

Sections III–VII explore various treatments of key themes in political theology. Sections III–V address themes which have pervaded historical and contemporary political theologies alike: the relationship between the church and political powers, the politics of Jesus, and issues related to violence and peace. Sections VI and VII address themes which have come into focus more recently, as political theologians have debated the merits of liberalism and democracy (Section VI), and as various twentieth- and twenty-first-century approaches have highlighted pressing concerns of oppression, marginalization and liberation (Section VII).

Finally, Section VIII places all these explorations in the context of overarching questions of how our politics relates to doctrines of creation and eschatology as well as to our understandings and narrations of our place in history between creation and eschaton.

I

The Emergence of Political Theology

Introduction by Amy Daughton

There is the real danger of anachronism when discussing sources from pre-modern eras on questions of politics. Ancient, patristic and medieval sources work within worldviews that do not treat the political as a distinct area of philosophical understanding. Despite this note of caution, any reader engaging with the material drawn together for this section will recognize the kinds of questions, tensions and resolutions with which these sources grappled. These are theologians who encountered social deprivation, were called to leadership roles within their Christian communities, lived in relation to imperial power, and had come to an understanding of God in the light of these political circumstances. Readers will find that many of the dominant quandaries of political theology find their first expression in the works in this section and still resonate for us today.

Those major themes include the nature of the societies humanity may build, and thus the role of authority and kingship; the relationship between the goods of this world and the next and so the role that those with religious convictions may take in public life; and always, necessarily, power – where it lies and how to use it – in the light of the intense and present reality of poverty and exclusion.

The sources of this section cover the widest chronological period of the various collections in this book, beginning with ancient scriptural passages through to the early church, and ultimately into the great medieval systematician Thomas Aquinas. Yet these extracts together represent some of the originary texts of Christian political theology. They offer visions of politics that have been continually reappropriated by the community of interpretation for new circumstances, giving new perspectives on these perennial questions.

A striking example of reinterpretation can be seen intertextually in the choices made from the Hebrew Bible and New Testament scripture, all related to the central concept of kingship. 1 Samuel 8 introduces the advent of the Kings of Israel, granted by God but called for in the face of God's divine sovereignty and subsequently bound by certain expectations. This reveals a scriptural ambiguity at the heart of human leadership. The tension is given a festive resolution in the poetic vision of divine Kingship in Zechariah's canticle of praise (Lk 1:68–9), personified in the messianic horn of salvation arising from the Davidic line and leading Israel out of oppression.

The other three gospel fragments relate to this theme by virtue of their roles in the three-year liturgical cycle of the Catholic Church, where they are given as the gospels for the Feast of Christ the King. The institution of that Feast in *Quas Primus*, Pius XI's 1925 encyclical, gives a striking insight into the Church's expectation for political authority as divinely ordained. Yet that perhaps anachronistic Christendom language is nuanced by the plural gospels spoken at the Feast, which dwell on Christ as a king who confronts entrenched power, may be seen in the face of the poor, and ultimately dies nailed to a cross.

From these earliest beginnings, the sacred stories of the community of interpretation begin to present the tragedy and beauty of earthly governance. There are other texts that are key for drawing out scriptural plurality and appear in this volume through commentators, such as the city in Revelation, reassessed by Oliver O'Donovan (Section VIII: 'Creation, History and Eschatology'), J. Kameron Carter's consideration of Gregory on Ecclesiastes (Section VII: 'Oppression, Marginalization and Liberation'), and Dietrich Bonhoeffer's analysis of Jesus' political witness (Section III: 'The Church and the Political').

Succeeding generations of commentators were also working out their theology under the shadow of the Roman Empire. While Christianity began in persecution, by the time the great fourth-century theologians were writing, religious toleration had been established in the Edict of Milan and the Constantinian shift and reactions to it had begun. Yet in the homilies included here, Gregory of Nyssa and John Chrysostom take up a narrative that is uninterested in Imperial structures but is still radically disruptive to the status quo: rejection of private wealth.

Chrysostom is perhaps the more confrontational of the two, drawing out the story of Lazarus and the Rich Man in graphic language. This homily dates from Chrysostom's time in Antioch, prior to his removal to Constantinople and his closer engagement with ecclesiastical politics, and it is formed by its context (c. 386–98). Perhaps in reaction both to the overindulgence of the previous day's pagan festival and to Antioch's position as a mercantile city, this first of a series of four homilies dwells on the misery of Lazarus, left at the gates in poverty and illness without even a companion in his suffering. Chrysostom proposes that the sight of real starvation and sickness will summon pity and generosity in others, which reveals real hope for human nature. Yet it is this expectation of a natural inclination towards helping others that also prompts him to condemn the rich who do not comfort the poor as 'the worst kind of wickedness, an inhumanity without rival'. That inhumanity calls suffering upon itself in this life and the next, as eternal punishment and as present guilt.

Treatment of the poor as constitutive of one's heavenly destiny is consistent with Gregory's homily as well. For Gregory, the poor themselves are rendered as the 'doorkeepers' of heaven, as the most beloved of God. In this way the Christic presentation of the neglected poor in Matthew is reasserted, sharpened by the contrast with beneficence as the imitation of God, through creativity, invention and generosity. The love of the poor is thus a mature lesson to build on early self-discipline, imagining a 'household of the Word' that draws in those in need. Texts not included in this reader expand on such an image, such as Basil of Caesara's *basileiados* foundation and his advice in his *Asketikon* for forming community.

Both of these sermons seek to erase the difference between rich and poor in the pagan assumption that those who succeed are favoured by the gods. After the sack of Rome in 410, it was this same presumption that prompted Augustine to attempt a reframing of God's relationship to this world in his *City of God against the Pagans*. The extract included in this volume, most likely written in the early 420s, comes from the latter part of the book when Augustine had turned that question back around to consider instead how to relate our doings in this world to God.

This seminal work in the history of political theology identifies peace as the ultimate desire that moves human affairs. This allows Augustine to establish the heavenly city as superior in the way its peace reshapes the order of things fundamentally and forever. The peace achieved in the earthly city reflects this order even while it is by contrast necessarily finite and fallible, associated with the inevitable confrontation with human sinfulness. Thus the political activity of Christians is always in relation to the love of God that offers them true peace and is made sense of within a community of the faithful understood as both present on earth and already with God in heaven. Yet those present on earth remain intermingled with the earthly city and its self-love. It is the desire for peace which shapes the quest of earthly politics and is a task Augustine understood to be shared by all citizens. Christians may be called to roles that uphold the peace of this world.

Augustine's correspondence gives more concrete shape to what this requires of us. Written in 417 to Boniface, Tribune of Africa and so a civic and military leader, letter 189 recognizes the Godly role that such leadership has within the City of God. The war-making to which Boniface is called has its right end in peace, which can, rightly understood, prefigure the divine vision of eternal life with God. By the time Augustine writes letter 220 in 428, Boniface is in open rebellion against Rome, and Augustine's letter represents a call to return to duty. In Augustine's assessment, Boniface is operating from a mistaken beginning, by being committed to a version of security that has more to do with gaining things of this world than gaining those of the next. Augustine rebukes Boniface for using violence without real necessity. Necessity would be the civic power's responsibility to provide peace to its citizens, not for citizens to gain more for themselves from the civic power, however deserved. His concern is not in and of itself political, but rather for Boniface's soul, to exhort him to place his desires in the heavenly city and not in the earthly. A precarious stance, to 'make use of this world as if you were not using it'.

This is still a far cry from the caricature of Augustine offered by too-swift analyses of the origins of political theology. His work is too frequently characterized as pessimistic in contrast with Thomas Aquinas's optimistic account. In fact what ultimately distinguishes Augustine and Thomas's systems of thought is not their assessment of human nature but when they identify the advent of political governance. Augustine sees it as a postlapsarian requirement, while Thomas presents it as always already part of the creative work of human society. Politics is just as necessary for Thomas, but arising from the human condition of interdependence, rather than sinfulness, and in this Thomas reclaims Aristotle's politics for Christian reasoning.

This has certain implications for Thomas's work that are exemplified in the collection of texts drawn together for this section: that law arises from and forms reasoning human activity, without contradicting revelation; that justice reflects the interdependence of human persons by its manifestation in right relationships; that human government has a godly purpose in its pursuit of the common good; that resistance to ungodly or tyrannical authority can therefore be justified if it is a last resort. All these aspects are covered in fragments taken from Thomas's *Summa Theologiae* and *De Regno*, or *De Regimine Principum* (On Kingship, c. 1267), begun at the request of the King of Cyprus. It is this last work that returns this section to the theme of Kingship. Here, Thomas argues that as a singular authority, the King is insulated from the competing interests of democracy, or decision-making solely by popular force of numbers. This allows him to be wholly dedicated to ruling for the common good in the light of God's sovereignty. The need for accountability for that monarch is drawn out in the more sophisticated argument in *Summa*, which allows for an advisory oligarchy.

The leap from Augustine to Thomas allows this section to highlight the key sources of political theology from Christianity's origins through to its Scholastic expression. Inevitably this misses significant commentary, especially from the politically charged period of the Investiture Controversy, which deals with the questions of the relative authority of regal and papal power, a question in which Thomas appeared to have been uninterested. It is also worth noting that the influence of such texts is heightened in the twentieth century, as political theology emerged as a discipline in its own right.

1. Scriptural Sources[1]

1 Samuel 8

[1] When Samuel became old, he made his sons judges over Israel. [2] The name of his firstborn son was Joel, and the name of his second, Abijah; they were judges in Beer-sheba. [3] Yet his sons did not follow in his ways, but turned aside after gain; they took bribes and perverted justice.

[4] Then all the elders of Israel gathered together and came to Samuel at Ramah, [5] and said to him, "You are old and your sons do not follow in your ways; appoint for us, then,

---

[1] All passages of scripture in this section are from the New Revised Standard Version (NRSV)

a king to govern us, like other nations." ⁶ But the thing displeased Samuel when they said, "Give us a king to govern us." Samuel prayed to the LORD, ⁷ and the LORD said to Samuel, "Listen to the voice of the people in all that they say to you; for they have not rejected you, but they have rejected me from being king over them. ⁸ Just as they have done to me, from the day I brought them up out of Egypt to this day, forsaking me and serving other gods, so also they are doing to you. ⁹ Now then, listen to their voice; only—you shall solemnly warn them, and show them the ways of the king who shall reign over them."

¹⁰ So Samuel reported all the words of the LORD to the people who were asking him for a king. ¹¹ He said, "These will be the ways of the king who will reign over you: he will take your sons and appoint them to his chariots and to be his horsemen, and to run before his chariots; ¹² and he will appoint for himself commanders of thousands and commanders of fifties, and some to plow his ground and to reap his harvest, and to make his implements of war and the equipment of his chariots. ¹³ He will take your daughters to be perfumers and cooks and bakers. ¹⁴ He will take the best of your fields and vineyards and olive orchards and give them to his courtiers. ¹⁵ He will take one-tenth of your grain and of your vineyards and give it to his officers and his courtiers.¹⁶ He will take your male and female slaves, and the best of your cattle and donkeys, and put them to his work. ¹⁷ He will take one-tenth of your flocks, and you shall be his slaves. ¹⁸ And in that day you will cry out because of your king, whom you have chosen for yourselves; but the LORD will not answer you in that day."

¹⁹ But the people refused to listen to the voice of Samuel; they said, "No! but we are determined to have a king over us, ²⁰ so that we also may be like other nations, and that our king may govern us and go out before us and fight our battles." ²¹ When Samuel had heard all the words of the people, he repeated them in the ears of the LORD. ²² The LORD said to Samuel, "Listen to their voice and set a king over them." Samuel then said to the people of Israel, "Each of you return home."

Luke 1:68–79

⁶⁸ "Blessed be the Lord God of Israel,
     for he has looked favorably on his people and redeemed them.
⁶⁹ He has raised up a mighty savior for us
     in the house of his servant David,
⁷⁰ as he spoke through the mouth of his holy prophets from of old,
⁷¹ that we would be saved from our enemies and from the hand of all who hate us.
⁷² Thus he has shown the mercy promised to our ancestors,
     and has remembered his holy covenant,
⁷³ the oath that he swore to our ancestor Abraham,
     to grant us ⁷⁴ that we, being rescued from the hands of our enemies,

might serve him without fear, [75] in holiness and righteousness
    before him all our days.
[76] And you, child, will be called the prophet of the Most High;
    for you will go before the Lord to prepare his ways,
[77] to give knowledge of salvation to his people
    by the forgiveness of their sins.
[78] By the tender mercy of our God,
    the dawn from on high will break upon us,
[79] to give light to those who sit in darkness and in the shadow of death,
    to guide our feet into the way of peace."

Luke 23:33–43

[33] When they came to the place that is called The Skull, they crucified Jesus there with the criminals, one on his right and one on his left. [34] Then Jesus said, "Father, forgive them; for they do not know what they are doing." And they cast lots to divide his clothing. [35] And the people stood by, watching; but the leaders scoffed at him, saying, "He saved others; let him save himself if he is the Messiah of God, his chosen one!" [36] The soldiers also mocked him, coming up and offering him sour wine, [37] and saying, "If you are the King of the Jews, save yourself!" [38] There was also an inscription over him, "This is the King of the Jews."

[39] One of the criminals who were hanged there kept deriding him and saying, "Are you not the Messiah? Save yourself and us!" [40] But the other rebuked him, saying, "Do you not fear God, since you are under the same sentence of condemnation? [41] And we indeed have been condemned justly, for we are getting what we deserve for our deeds, but this man has done nothing wrong." [42] Then he said, "Jesus, remember me when you come into your kingdom."

[43] He replied, "Truly I tell you, today you will be with me in Paradise."

Matthew 25:31–46

[31] "When the Son of Man comes in his glory, and all the angels with him, then he will sit on the throne of his glory. [32] All the nations will be gathered before him, and he will separate people one from another as a shepherd separates the sheep from the goats, [33] and he will put the sheep at his right hand and the goats at the left. [34] Then the king will say to those at his right hand, 'Come, you that are blessed by my Father, inherit the kingdom prepared for you from the foundation of the world; [35] for I was hungry and you gave me food, I was thirsty and you gave me something to drink, I was a stranger and you welcomed me, [36] I was naked and you gave me clothing, I was sick and you took care of me, I was in prison and you visited me.' [37] Then the righteous will answer him, 'Lord, when was it

that we saw you hungry and gave you food, or thirsty and gave you something to drink?[38] And when was it that we saw you a stranger and welcomed you, or naked and gave you clothing?[39] And when was it that we saw you sick or in prison and visited you?'[40] And the king will answer them, 'Truly I tell you, just as you did it to one of the least of these who are members of my family, you did it to me.'[41] Then he will say to those at his left hand, 'You that are accursed, depart from me into the eternal fire prepared for the devil and his angels;[42] for I was hungry and you gave me no food, I was thirsty and you gave me nothing to drink,[43] I was a stranger and you did not welcome me, naked and you did not give me clothing, sick and in prison and you did not visit me.'[44] Then they also will answer, 'Lord, when was it that we saw you hungry or thirsty or a stranger or naked or sick or in prison, and did not take care of you?'[45] Then he will answer them, 'Truly I tell you, just as you did not do it to one of the least of these, you did not do it to me.'[46] And these will go away into eternal punishment, but the righteous into eternal life."

John 18:33–37

[33] Then Pilate entered the headquarters again, summoned Jesus, and asked him, "Are you the King of the Jews?"[34] Jesus answered, "Do you ask this on your own, or did others tell you about me?"[35] Pilate replied, "I am not a Jew, am I? Your own nation and the chief priests have handed you over to me. What have you done?"[36] Jesus answered, "My kingdom is not from this world. If my kingdom were from this world, my followers would be fighting to keep me from being handed over to the Jews. But as it is, my kingdom is not from here."

[37]Pilate asked him, "So you are a king?" Jesus answered, "You say that I am a king. For this I was born, and for this I came into the world, to testify to the truth. Everyone who belongs to the truth listens to my voice."

2. Gregory of Nyssa – First Homily on the Love of the Poor, or On Good Works

[453] The president of this church and the ones who teach us perfect piety and the ways of virtue have much in common with the grammarians and primary teachers. When they receive children from their parents, while yet as lisping infants, they do not introduce them to advanced studies but begin by tracing "alpha" in wax, and then the rest of the alphabet; the teacher instructs them on the names of the letters and makes them practice tracing outlines of the letter with their hand. He moves on next to the study of syllables and the pronunciation of words. In the same way, the leaders of the Church begin by teaching the faithful the rudiments of knowledge and only later treating the more advanced concepts.

Over the past two days, I denounced the pleasures of the mouth and the belly. Don't think that today, too, I am going to say the usual things: that it is a fine thing to spurn meat, to abstain from wine, that laughter-loving dionysiac, to moderate the zeal of your cooks and to hold back the weary hand of your cupbearers. I insisted on this point, and your behavior has proven to me that my counsel was not in vain. Since you have learned the elementary lesson, it is now worthwhile to take up next the greater and more mature teachings.

There is an abstinence that is spiritual, and self-control that is immaterial: this is the renunciation of sin that turns toward the soul. It is on this account that abstinence from food was enjoined. Abstain now from evil. *[456]* Practice self-control in your appetite for other people's belongings! Renounce dishonest profits! Starve to death your greed for Mammon. Let there be nothing at your house that has been acquired by violence or theft. What good is it to keep meat out of your mouth if you bite your brother with wickedness? What good does it serve you to observe a strict frugality at home if you unjustly steal from the poor? What kind of piety teaches you to drink water while you hatch plots and drink the blood of a man you have shamefully cheated? Judas, after all, fasted along with the eleven, but failed to master his greed; his salvation gained nothing by fasting. And the devil does not eat, for he is an incorporeal spirit, but he fell from on high through wickedness. Likewise, none of the demons can be accused of gorging themselves, of excessive drinking or getting drunk, for their nature makes feeding unnecessary; nevertheless, night and day, they roam through the air, agents and servants of evil, eager for our loss. They ooze with bitterness and jealousy — things it is well to avoid — at the idea that humans may enter into an intimacy with God, since they have fallen from the supremely worthy dwelling.

Accordingly, let the philosophic way be an instructive model for the Christian life, and let the soul flee from the damaging effect of evil. For if we abstain from wine and meat while clearly and publically yielding to sin, I guarantee and testify to you that the ascetic regime of water and vegetables has no good effect, if the internal disposition is incongruent with external appearance. Fasting was ordained for the soul's purification. If our thoughts and actions degrade it, why force ourselves to drink nothing but water, and why work this filthy quagmire? To what advantage is a fasting of the body if the spirit is not clean? It is no use if the chariot is well-built and the team of horses well disciplined, if the charioteer is insane. What good is a sound ship if the captain is drunk? Fasting is the very foundation of virtue, just as the foundations of a house and keel of a ship are useless and without value, however solidly laid, if the rest is not built with skill. All our austerity likewise does no good unless it nurtures other virtues and receives them as a companion. Let the fear of God teach the tongue to speak only with knowledge, not using idle phrases but only what is moderate and timely, words that are essential and to the point. Let us ponder our terms, not deafening our interlocutors with a verbal shower. This is why the fine membrane that holds the tongue to the lower jaw bears the name of a bridle, so that we might not speak totally at random. Speak praise, not insult: commend, do not blaspheme: bless and do not slander; thus the thought of God stops our heedless hand and holds it as if it were in bonds. This is why we fast, to commemorate the passion of our Lamb *[457]* who, before being nailed to the cross, submitted to insults and brutalities. Let us not imitate the conduct of Judas, we who are disciples of Christ. If we watch our ulterior motives, Isaiah will demand of us, "Why fast during the dispute and quarrel, while you are beating up the lowly with your fist?" (Isa. 58:4) This prophet also teaches us what makes up a pure and sincere fast: "Loose all chains of injustice, send free the oppressed, untie the bonds of forced indenture; share your bread with the hungry, lodge in your (own) house the poor who have no shelter" (Isa. 56:6–7).

We have seen in these days a great number of the naked and homeless. For the most part they are victims of war who knock at our doors. But there is also no lack of strangers and exiles, and their hands, stretched out imploring, can be seen everywhere. Their roof is the sky. For shelter they use porticos, alleys, and the deserted corners of the town. They hide in the cracks of walls like owls. Their clothing consists of wretched rags. Their harvest depends on human pity. For meals they have only the alms tossed at them by those who pass by. For drink they use the springs, as do the animals. Their cup is the hollow of their hand, their storeroom their pocket, or rather whatever part of it has not been torn and cannot hold whatever has been put into it. For a dining table they use their joined knees, and their lamp is the sun. Instead of the public baths, they wash in the river or pond that God gives to all. This life of theirs, wandering and brutal, was not that assigned to them by birth but results from their tribulations and their miseries.

Assist these people, you who practice abstinence. Be generous on behalf of your unfortunate brethren. That which you withhold from your belly, give to the poor. Let a fear of God level out the differences between you and them: with self-control, carefully avoid two contrary evils: your own gorging and the hunger of your brethren. This is how the physician works: he puts some on diets and gives supplementary foods to others, so that by additions and subtractions health can be managed in each individual case. So follow this salutary advice. Let reason open the doors of the rich. Let wise counsel lead the poor to the wealthy.

But dialectic will hardly enrich those in such straits. Let the eternal word of God give also a house and a light and table, by means of the household of the Word. Speak to them with affection and alleviate their miseries with your own substance.

In addition to these are the other poor, very ill and bedridden. Let everyone take care of his neighbors. Don't let someone else treat those in your neighborhood. Don't let another rob you of the treasure laid up for you. Embrace the wretched as gold: take into your arms [embrace] the afflicted as you would your own health, [as you would care for] the safety of your wife, your children, your domestics and all your house. *[460]* The sick who is poor is doubly poor. For the poor who are in good health go from door to door, approaching the homes of the rich or setting up camp at the crossroads and there hailing all who pass by. But those trampled by illness, shut up in their narrow rooms and narrow nooks, are only able, like Daniel in his cistern (Dan. 14:33–39), to wait for you, devout and charitable, as though for Habakkuk. Become a colleague of the prophet with your alms. Nourish those in need, immediately and without hesitating. The gift will not result in loss: don't be afraid. The fruits of merciful acts are abundant. Sow your benefactions and your house will be filled with a plentiful harvest.

You will say, "I am poor; me too!" So it is! Nevertheless, give. Give what you have. God does not demand what is beyond your means. You give bread, someone else a cup of wine, another an outer garment; in this way, through a collective contribution, the misfortunes of one person are eased. Moses did not receive the offerings for the Tabernacle from a single benefactor, but all the people gave him contributions: the rich gave gold, others gave silver, the poor gave animal skins, and the most indigent joined together to offer goat-hair (Ex. 25:1–7). Do you remember how the widow's coin surpassed the liberality of the wealthy? (Luke 21:1–4). She emptied herself of all that she possessed. The rich, for their part, gave only a portion.

Do not despise those who are stretched out on the ground as if they merit no respect. Consider who they are and you will discover their worth. They bear the countenance of our Savior. The Lord in His goodness has given them His own countenance in order that it might cause the hard-hearted, those who hate the poor, to blush with shame, just as those being robbed thrust before their attackers the images of their king to shame the enemy with the appearance of the ruler. The poor are the stewards of our hope, doorkeepers of the kingdom, who open the door to the righteous and close it again to the unloving and misanthropists. These are vehement and good advocates. They defend and prosecute not by speaking, but by being seen by the judge. For the deed done to them cries out to the one who fathoms the heart in a voice clearer than the herald's trumpet.

And it is on account of these that the terrifying judgment of God, which you have often heard, was described in the gospels. There I have seen the Son of man descend from the sky and walking in the air as one walks on earth, and thousands of angels escorting him. Then the throne of glory appeared in the sky, and the king sitting on it, and all the people who ever lived under the sun and breathed this air were separated into two *[461]* camps, and the multitude stood by the tribunal seat. One group, everyone on the right, were called the "sheep." I heard that those in the camp on the left were designated "goats." They deserved this epithet on account of their behavior. The judge interrogated the accused and I listened to their answers. Each received his due: to those who had lived an exemplary life, enjoyment of the kingdom [was granted]; to the misanthropists and wicked, [the judgment was] punishment by fire, and for all of eternity.

The scripture tells this account with such care, and our court of justice has been painted so precisely for no other reason than to teach us the grace and the value of beneficence. For this preserves our life, mother of the poor, teacher of the rich, good nurse, caretaker of the aged, treasury of those in need, universal haven of the unfortunate, who measures out her providential care to all ages and all calamities. As those who mount and preside at the games, the leader proclaims his love of honor by the sound of a trumpet and announces the prizes to all the competitors, and beneficence summons together those who have fallen on hard times and who are in critical circumstances, distributing to those who come forth not blows, but the healing of misfortunes. She is more exalted than every feat of prowess, assisting God, friend of the good man and in close fellowship with him. It is God Himself, who in the first instance manifests Himself to us as the author of good and philanthropic deeds: the creation of the earth, the arrangement of the heavens, the well-ordered rhythm of the seasons, the warmth of the sun, the formation, by cooling, of ice, in short, all things, individually, He created not for Himself — for He had no need of such things — but He maintains them continually on our behalf; invisible farmer of human nourishment, He sows at the opportune moment and waters the earth skillfully. He gives seed to the sower, as Isaiah says (Isa. 55:10), now sprinkling water from the clouds in a gentle shower, later flooding the furrows in a violent downpour. When the delicate buds sprout and green blades appear, He sets the sun over them which, now uncovered, extends its warm and fiery rays so that the ears of grain may become ripe for the harvest. He also causes the clusters on the vine to swell, and in the autumn distills His wine for the thirsty and fattens our various flocks that humankind may have abundant meat. The fleece of some supply us with wool, the skin of others provide us with shoes. You see, God is the original designer of good deeds, nourishing the starving, watering the thirsty, clothing those who are naked, as has been said earlier. *[464]*

And if you wish to know how He eases our sicknesses, hear this: the bee, from whom does she have the secret of wax and honey? Who causes the pine tree, the terebinth, or the mastic tree to produce tears of rosy resin? Who created the land of the Indies, the source of dry fruits and aromatics? Who has made oil to grow, that cures stiffness and bruises? Who has taught us to discern the roots and herbs and the understanding of their properties? Who established the art of healing, medicine? Who caused these thermal springs to gush from the veins of the earth, healing us with cold and hot, by loosening the things that are dry and have been constrained? Yes, we may aptly quote Baruch: "He searched out the entire path to knowledge and gave it to Jacob, his servant" (Baruch 3:36). For this reason we have arts that use fire and those that do not, others that use water and a myriad of practical inventions. And thus God, the founder of good works, provides for our needs with richness and kindness.

But as for us, each letter of the Bible teaches us to imitate our Savior and creator — as much as mortal can try to imitate eternal — yet we monopolize all for our own pleasure in that we spend our fortune on pleasures, in that we accumulate it in capital for our heirs. We do not even give those in distress a single thought, nor do we have any effective concern for those in need. Implacable hardness! A man sees another wanting bread and without nourishment. Instead of promptly caring and reaching out to rescue him, he ignores him as he might a nourishing plant pitifully wilting from lack of water under a parching sun, while at this man's home there is great abundance with the power to relieve many. For as the flow from a single spring nourishes many open fields, the prosperity of a single house can save a crowd of the poor, provided only that the greed and selfishness of the master does not [become] like a rock that, falling into the current of a stream, hinders its flow.

Let us not use everything for the flesh; let us live also for God. For the pleasures of the table assuage only a small part of our flesh, the throat; the food rots in the stomach and ends up in the sewer. Mercy and good deeds are works God loves; they divinize those who practice them and impress [or, stamp] them into the likeness of goodness, that [465] they may become the image of the Primordial Being, pure, who surpasses all intelligence. But what rewards are promised for our efforts? In this life a good hope, an eager expectation of joy. And in the next, when we will have abandoned this fragile flesh and be clothed with immortality, a blessed life, unchangeable and indestructible, prepared among wondrous and as yet unimaginable delights.

Since you have been created with reason, and since you have been endowed with an intelligence that can interpret and inculcate the divine, don't be deceived by ephemeral things. Try to acquire riches that will never abandon their master. Moderate your life's needs. Don't retain everything for yourself, but share with the poor, who are the favorites of God. All belongs to God, our common father. And we are all brothers of the same race. It is best and more just that brothers reap an equal part of the heritage. But since in our imperfect order one or another always monopolizes the greater part of the heritage, at least let the others not be entirely frustrated. One man who wishes to retain all for himself and hinder his brothers from touching a third or even a fifth of the inheritance, this man is a brutal tyrant, an intractable barbarian, a craving beast, eagerly swallowing the whole meal himself, a beast far more ferocious than the entire animal kingdom. Even the wolf tolerates another wolf beside him as he eats, and dogs gather together to devour the same carcass. But such a man, always insatiable, refuses to share his wealth with his own kind. Content yourself with a modest table. Do not suffer shipwreck on the high seas of unbridled banquets, for this wreck is a grievous thing, not just being broken by submerged rocks, but rather being driven out into the shadowy abyss from which no one who falls in ever returns.

Use; do not misuse; so, too, Paul teaches you. Find your rest in temperate relaxation. Do not indulge in a frenzy of pleasures. Don't make yourself a destroyer of absolutely all living things, whether they be four-footed and large or four-footed and small, birds, fish, exotic or common, a good bargain or expensive. The sweat of the hunter ought not to fill your stomach like a bottomless well that many men digging cannot fill. Our gourmands do not, in fact, even spare the bottom of the sea, nor do they limit themselves to the fish that swim in the water, but they also bring up the crawling marine beasts from the ocean bed and drag them to shore. One pillages the oyster banks, one pursues the sea urchin, one captures the creeping cuttle fish, one plucks the octopus from the rock it grips, one eradicates the mollusks from their pedestal. All animal species, those that swim in the surface waters or live in the depths of the sea, *[468]* all are thus brought up into the atmosphere. The artful skills of the hedonist cleverly devise traps appropriate to each.

But what is the ultimate fate of gourmands? It is inevitable that sin, wherever it strikes, like a disease brings on its consequences. Hence those who prepare a delicate and sybaritic table are attracted necessarily to sumptuous dwellings and squander their goods on enormous houses and superfluous ornaments. They also like to rest on magnificent beds covered with flowery hangings, richly embroidered. They have massively expensive silver tables made for them; some are remarkable by the sheen of the metal; on others an artist engraves scenes and one is thus able, during the meal, to delight in beautiful legends. Think further of all the wine bowls, tripods, jars, ewers, platters, all sorts of cups; the clowns, mimes, kithara-players, chanters, poets, male and female musicians, dancers, and all of the equipment of debauchery, boys with effeminate coiffures, shameless girls, sisters to Herodias in their indecency; this is that Herodias who caused the death of John, that is to say, the death of godlike and philosophical intellect in everyone.

While this is going on in the house, a myriad of Lazaruses sit at the gate, some dragging themselves along painfully, some with their eyes gouged out, others with amputated feet, some quite literally creep, mutilated in all their members. They cry and are not heard over the flutes' whistling, loud songs, and the cackling of bawling laughter. If they beg more loudly at the door, the porter of a barbarous master bounds out like a brute and drives them away with strokes of a stick, setting the dogs on them and lashing their ulcers with whipcord. Accordingly they retreat, the beloved of Christ, who embody the essential commandment without having gained one mouthful of bread or meat, but satiated with insults and blows. And in the den of Mammon, some vomit up their meal like an overflowing vessel; others sleep on the table, their wine cups beside them. Twofold is the sin that reigns in this house of shame: one is the excess of the drunkards, the other the hunger of the poor who have been driven away.

If God sees these scenes — and I am sure He does — what fatal catastrophe, do you think, does He hold in store for those who hate the poor? Answer me! Or do you not know that it is to this end that the holy gospel shouts out and testifies with scenes of horror and dread? And thus it describes the deep groaning of the man flung into the pit and held captive in the abyss of the wicked. Another *[469]* of the same type is condemned to a sudden death, such that he plans in the evening his next day's pleasure but does not live to see the first ray of dawn (Luke 16:19; 12:20). Let us not be mortal, fitful, and temporary, in our faith but immortal, boundless, and never-ending in our pleasure. For this is the attitude we cling to, those of us who wish to pander to sensual gratification in everything as though we were rich men without heirs, as though we might be lords of earthly things forever. At harvesttime we worry about sowing and at seed-time we look forward to the joy of the harvest; we plant a plane tree in hopes of sheltering ourself beneath its shade; we bury the seed of the date palm in the wish of savoring its fruits. And often this comes about in our old age, when the late autumn of life has set in, when the winter of death is near, and there remain not a cycle of years but only three or four days.

Let us be realistic, considering these things reasonably: our life is fleeting and flowing, and time cannot be stopped nor held back; it is like a river's current that sweeps everything in its path to final destruction. If only, short-lived and perishable as we are, we would not be called to render account. But such is exactly the peril that looms every hour: we will have to justify all to the incorruptible judge, even the words that we utter. This is why the blessed psalmist meditates on a similar thought and desires to know his own moment of death. He prays that God will tell him how many days he has left, in order to ready himself for his final hour, that he might not be caught unaware, like an unprepared traveler who must seek provisions while he is en route. "Lord," he cries, "Make me to know my end and the measure of my days that I may know in what way I am lacking. See, you have made my days a few hand-breadths, and my lifetime is as nothing in your sight" (Ps. 90:5–6).

Observe the conscientious prudence of this worthy soul, of royal rank though he was. For he perceives the king of kings and judge of judges as clearly as in a mirror, and he seeks to attain the perfect word of the commandments and to die as an intact and flawless citizen of the world to come. May it come to pass that we all attain it by the grace and philanthropy of our Lord Jesus Christ, to whom belongs the glory forever. Amen.

3. John Chrysostom – First Homily on Lazarus and the Rich Man, or On Wealth and Poverty

Yesterday, although it was a feast-day of Satan, you preferred to keep a spiritual feast, receiving our words with great good will, and spending most of the day here in church, drinking a drunkenness of self-control, and dancing in the chorus of Paul. In this way a double benefit came to you, because you kept free of the disorderly dance of the drunkards and you revelled in well-ordered spiritual dances. You shared a drinking-bowl which did not pour out undiluted wine but was filled with spiritual instruction. You became a flute and a lyre for the Holy Spirit. While others danced for the devil, you prepared yourselves by your occupation here to be spiritual instruments and vessels. You allowed the Holy Spirit to play on your souls and to breathe His grace into your hearts. Thus you sounded a harmonious melody to delight not only mankind but even the powers of heaven.

But I have proved sufficiently that we must never desert those who are fallen, even if we know in advance that they will not heed us. Now we must proceed to the condemnation of luxurious living. As long as this feast continues, and the devil goes on wounding the souls of the drunkards with drink, our duty is to go on applying the remedies.

Yesterday we fortified ourselves against the drunkards with Paul's words, "Whether you eat or drink, or whatever you do, do all to the glory of God" (1 Cor. 10.31) Today we will show them Paul's Master, not merely advising and exhorting them to abstain from luxurious living, but actually chastising and punishing one who lived in luxury, for the story of the rich man and Lazarus, and what happened to both of them, demonstrates this very thing. But it will be best if I read you the whole parable from the beginning, to keep us from treating it too carelessly. "There was a rich man, who was clothed in purple and fine linen and who made merry every day. And at his gate lay a poor man named Lazarus, full of sores, who desired to be fed with what fell from the rich man's table; moreover the dogs came and licked his sores" (Luke 16.19-21).

We might ask why the Master speaks in parables, and why He explained some parables but not others, and what in fact a parable is, and many other such questions—but we will save these for another time, so as not to delay this urgent discussion now. We will ask you only this one question, which of the evangelists it is who tells us that Christ told this parable. Who is it? Only Luke. You must also know this, that all four evangelists reported some of Christ's savings, but each of them individually chose others to report. Why is this so? To make us read the other gospels, and to make us realize how remarkable their agreement is. For if all of them told everything, we would not pay careful attention to all of them, because one would be enough to teach us everything. But if everything they tell were different, we would not see their remarkable agreement. For this reason all of them wrote many things in common but each also chose some things to tell individually.

Now, what Christ teaches by the parable is this. There was a rich man, He says, living in great wickedness. The man was not tested by any misfortune, but everything flowed to him as if from a fountain. The very words, "He made merry every day," imply that nothing unexpected happened to him, no cause of distress or disturbance in his life. It is evident that he lived in wickedness both from the end which fell to his lot and, before the end, from his contempt for the poor man. He himself has demonstrated that not only did he neglect that man by the gate but he did not give alms to anyone else either. For if he did not give alms to this man who was continually prostrate at his gate, lying before his eyes, whom he had to see every day once or twice or many times as he went in and out, for the man was not lying in the street nor in a hidden or narrow place, but where the rich man whenever he made his entrance or exit was forced unwillingly to see him, if (I say) he did not give alms to this man, who lay in such grievous suffering, and lived in such destitution, or rather for his whole life was troubled by chronic illness of the most serious kind, whom of those he encountered would he ever have been moved to pity? If we suppose that he passed the man by on the first day, he would probably have felt some pity on the second day; if he overlooked him even on that day, he surely ought to have been moved on the third or the fourth or the day after that, even if he were more cruel than the wild beasts. But he felt no such emotion, but became harder-hearted and more reckless even than that unjust judge who knew neither fear of God nor shame before men (Luke 18.2). For the widow's persistence persuaded that judge, cruel and savage though he was, to grant the favor. He was moved to pity at her supplication; but even persistence could not move this rich man to help the poor man, although his petition was not equivalent to the widow's, but much easier to fulfill and more just. For she besought the judge to aid her against her enemies, but he begged the rich man to release him from hunger and not to ignore him as he lay dying. She pestered the judge with her petition, but he appeared to the rich man many times each day lying in silence. This is enough to soften even the heart of stone. For when we are pestered we often become harder; but when we see those who need help standing by in complete silence, uttering no sound, not complaining though never satisfied, but merely appearing to us in silence, even if we are more insensible than the very stones, we become ashamed at the excess of politeness and are moved to pity. And another fact was not less significant than these, that the very appearance of the poor man was pitiful, as he was overcome by hunger and long illness. Nevertheless none of this tamed that savage man.

This cruelty is the worst kind of wickedness; it is an inhumanity without rival. For it is not the same thing for one who lives in poverty not to help those in need, as for one who enjoys such luxury to neglect others who are wasting away with hunger. Again, it is not the same thing to see a poor man once or twice and pass him by, as to look at him every day and not be aroused by the persistent sight to mercy and generosity. Again, it is not the same thing for one who is troubled in his heart by misfortune and distress not to help his neighbor, as for one who enjoys such happiness and continuous good fortune to neglect others who are wasting away with hunger, to lock up his heart, and not to be made more generous by his own joy. For you surely know this, that even if we are the most savage of men, we usually are made more gentle and kindly by good fortune. But that man was not improved by his prosperity, but remained beastly, or rather he surpassed the cruelty and inhumanity of any beast in his behavior.

Nevertheless he who lived in wickedness and inhumanity enjoyed every kind of good fortune, while the righteous man who practiced virtue endured the extremes of ill fortune. For again in Lazarus' case, we can prove that he was righteous both by his end and, before his end, by his patient endurance of poverty. Do you not seem to see the whole situation as if it were present? The rich man had his ship full of merchandise, and it sailed before the wind. But do not be surprised: he was hastening to shipwreck, since he refused to unload his cargo with discretion. Shall I tell you another wickedness of his? His daily luxurious and unscrupulous feasting. For truly this is extreme wickedness, not only now, when such great wisdom is expected of us, but even at the beginning, under the old covenant, when not so much wisdom had been revealed. Hear what the prophet says: "Woe ... to you who are approaching the evil day, who are drawing near and adopting false sabbaths" (Amos 6.3). What does this mean, "who are adopting false sabbaths?" The Jews think that the sabbath is given to them for idleness. This is not the purpose, but in order that they may remove themselves from worldly cares and devote all their leisure to spiritual concerns. It is evident from the facts that the sabbath is not a subject for idleness but for spiritual work. The priest indeed does double work on that day: while a single sacrifice is offered every day, on that day he is bidden to offer a double sacrifice. If the sabbath were simply for idleness, the priest ought to be idle even more than the rest of the people. Since the Jews, although they were released from worldly activities, did not attend to spiritual matters, such as self-control, kindness, and hearing the divine Scriptures, but did the opposite, gorging themselves, getting drunk, stuffing themselves, feasting luxuriously, for this reason the prophet condemned them. For when he said, "Woe ... to you who are approaching the evil day," and added, "and adopting false sabbaths," he showed by his next words how their sabbaths were false. How did they make their sabbaths false? By working wickedness, feasting, drinking, and doing a multitude of shameful and grievous deeds. To prove that this is true, hear what follows. He reveals what I am saying by what he adds immediately: "Who sleep upon beds of ivory, and live delicately on their couches, and eat kids out of the flocks, and sucking calves out of the midst of the stalls ... who drink filtered wine, and anoint your-selves with the best ointment" (Amos 6.4-6). You received the sabbath to free your soul from wickedness, but you have enslaved it further. For what could be worse than this frivolity, this sleeping on beds of ivory? The other sins, such as drunkenness, greed, and profligacy, provide some pleasure, however small; but in sleeping on beds of ivory, what pleasure is there? What comfort? The beauty of the bed does not make our sleep sweeter or more pleasant, does it? Rather it is more onerous and burdensome, if we have any sense. For when you consider that, while you sleep on a bed of ivory, someone else does not enjoy even sufficient bread, will your conscience not condemn you, and rise up against you to denounce this inequity? But if the accusation is of sleeping on beds of ivory which are also decorated all around with silver, what defense will we have?

Do you wish to see what makes a bed truly beautiful? I will show you now the splendor of a bed, not of a citizen or a soldier, but of a king. For even if you are the most ambitious of all men, I am sure that you will not wish to have a bed more splendid than the king's; and, what is more, I do not refer to any ordinary king, but the greatest king, more kingly than all other kings, who is still honored in song throughout the world: I am showing you the bed of the blessed David. What kind of bed did he have? Not adorned all over with silver and gold, but with tears and confessions. He himself tells this, when he says, "I shall wash my bed every night; I shall water my couch with my tears" (Ps. 6.7). He fixes his tears like pearls everywhere on his bed. And consider with me how he loved God in his soul. Since in the daytime many concerns about rulers, commanders, nations, peoples, soldiers, wars, peace, politics, and troubles in his household or outside or among his neighbors, distracted him and diverted his attention, the time of leisure, which everyone else uses for sleep, he used for confession, prayers, and tears. He did not do this on one night only, ceasing on the second night, nor on two or three nights, omitting the nights in between, but he kept on doing this every night. For he says, "I shall wash my bed every night; I shall water my couch with my tears," revealing the abundance and continuity of his tears. When everyone was quiet and at rest, he met God alone, and the unsleeping eye was with him as he wept and mourned and told of his private sins. You also ought to make a bed like this for yourself. Silver surrounding you awakens jealousy from men and stirs up anger from above; but tears like David's are able to quench the very fires of hell.

Shall I show you another bed? I mean Jacob's. He had the bare ground beneath him and a stone under his head. For this reason he saw the spiritual Rock and that ladder by which angels ascended and descended (see Gen. 28, 1 Cor. 10.4). Let us also set our minds on such beds, so that we may see such dreams as well. But if we lie on silver beds, not only will we not gain any pleasure, but besides we will endure distress. For when you consider that in the most extreme cold, in the middle of the night, when you are sleeping on a bed, the poor man has thrown himself on a pile of straw by the door of the bath-house, wrapping the stalks around him, shivering, stiff with cold, pinched with hunger—even if you are the stoniest of all men, I am sure that you will condemn yourself for providing for yourself unnecessary luxury while not allowing him even what is necessary. "No soldier on service," it is written, "gets entangled in civilian pursuits" (2 Tim. 2.4). You are a spiritual soldier; this kind of soldier does not sleep on an ivory bed, but on the ground. He is not anointed with perfumed oils: these are the concern of those corrupt men who dally with courtesans, of those who act on the stage, of those who live carelessly. You must not smell of perfumes but of virtue. Nothing is more unclean for the soul than when the body has such a fragrance. For the fragrance of the body and the clothes would be a sign of the stench and filthiness of the inner man. When the devil attacks and breaks down the soul with self-indulgence, and fills it with great frivolity, then he wipes off the stain of his own corruption on the body also with perfumes. Just as those who are continually afflicted with a nasal discharge and catarrh will stain their clothes, their hands, and their faces as they continually wipe off the discharge from their noses, so also the soul of this wicked man will wipe off the discharge of evil on his body. Who will expect anything noble and good from one who smells of perfumes and who keeps company with women, or rather courtesans, and who leads the life of a dancer? Let your soul breathe a spiritual fragrance, so that you may give the greatest benefit both to yourself and to your companions.

There is nothing more grievous than luxury. Hear what Moses says about it: Jacob "grew fat, he became thick and broad. The beloved one kicked out" (Deut. 32.15). Moses does not say that Jacob walked out, but that the beloved one kicked out, suggesting how haughty and unbridled he had become. And elsewhere Moses says, when you have eaten and drunk, "take heed to yourself, that you forget not the Lord your God" (Deut. 8.11). In this way luxury often leads to forget-fulness. As for you, my beloved, if you sit at table, remember that from the table you must go to prayer. Fill your belly so moderately that you may not become too heavy to bend your knees and call upon your God. Do you not see how the donkeys leave the manger ready to walk and carry loads and fulfill their proper service? But when you leave the table you are useless and unserviceable for any kind of work. How will you avoid being more worthless even than the donkeys? Why do I say this? Because that is the time when you most need to be sober and wide awake (cf. 1 Thess. 5.6, 1 Pet. 5.8). The time after dinner is the time for thanksgiving, and he who gives thanks should not be drunk but sober and wide awake. After dinner let us not go to bed but to prayer, or we may become more irrational than the irrational beasts.

I know that many will condemn what I say, thinking that I am introducing a strange new custom into our life; but I will condemn more strongly the wicked custom which now prevails over us. Christ has made it very clear that after taking nourishment at table we ought to receive not sleep in bed but prayer and reading of the divine Scriptures. When He had fed the great multitude in the wilderness, He did not send them to bed and to sleep, but summoned them to hear divine sayings. He had not filled their stomachs to bursting, nor abandoned them to drunkenness; but when He had satisfied their need, He led them to spiritual nourishment. Let us do the same; and let us accustom ourselves to eat only enough to live, not enough to be distracted and weighed down. For we were not born, we do not live, in order to eat and drink; but we eat in order to live. At the beginning life was not made for eating, but eating for life. But we, as if we had come into the world for this purpose, spend everything for eating.

Now to make our denunciation of luxury more vehement and more pertinent to those who practice it, let us lead our sermon back to Lazarus. Thus our advice and counsel will be truer and clearer, when you see those who attended to good eating chastised and punished, not in words but in actions. For as the rich man lived in such wickedness, practiced luxury every day, and dressed himself splendidly, he was preparing for himself a more grievous punishment, building himself a greater fire, and making his penalty inexorable and his retribution inaccessible to pardon. The poor man, on the other hand, lay at his gate and did not become discouraged, blaspheme, or complain. He did not say to himself what many people say: "What is this? He lives in wickedness, cruelty, and inhumanity, enjoys everything more than he needs, and does not endure even mental distress or any other of the unexpected troubles (of which many afflict mankind), but gains pure pleasure; but I cannot obtain a share even of necessary sustenance. Everything flows to him as if from a fountain, although he spends all his good on parasites, flatterers, and drunkenness; but I lie here an example for onlookers, a source of shame and derision, wasting away with hunger. Is this the work of providence? Does any justice oversee the deeds of mankind?" He did not say or even think any of these things. How do we know? From the fact that the angels led him away in triumph, and seated him in the bosom of Abraham. If he had been a blasphemer, he would not have come to enjoy such honor.

Many people admire the man for this reason only, that he was poor, but I can show that he endured chastisements nine in number, imposed not to punish him, but to make him more glorious; and indeed this came about. In the first place poverty is truly a dreadful thing, as everyone knows who has experienced it; for no words can describe how great the anguish is which those endure who live as beggars without knowing wisdom. But for Lazarus this was not his only trouble, but illness was yoked to it, and this to an excessive degree. See how he shows both these misfortunes at their height. Christ showed that the poverty of Lazarus surpassed all other poverty at that time, when He said that Lazarus did not even enjoy any of the crumbs which fell from the rich man's table. Again, He showed that Lazarus' illness reached the same measure as his poverty, beyond which it could not stretch out any farther, when He said that the dogs licked his sores. Lazarus was so much weakened that he could not even shoo the dogs away, but he lay like a living corpse, watching them coming without strength to protect himself from them. His limbs were so weak, so much wasted by disease, so far consumed by his trials. Did you see both poverty and disease besieging his body to the extreme degree? If each of these by itself is dreadful and unbearable, when they are woven together, is he not a man of steel who can endure them? Many people are often ill, but do not lack their necessary sustenance; others live in extreme poverty, but enjoy good health; and one good becomes a consolation for the other misfortune. But here both these misfortunes have run together. But, you say, you can tell me of someone who is both ill and poor. But not in such loneliness. For even if not in his own home, at least in public he could receive mercy from those who see him; but for Lazarus the lack of protectors made his two misfortunes more grievous. And this lack itself was made to seem more grievous by his position at the gate of the rich man. For if he had endured such sufferings and been neglected while lying in a desert and uninhabited place, he would not have felt so much distress. If no one had been present, he would have been persuaded even against his will to endure what was happening to him; but since he did not obtain even ordinary concern from anyone although he lay in the midst of so many drunkards and merrymakers, he came to feel his anguish more keenly and to same trials as he had; indeed he could not even hear of so much by our misfortunes when no helper is present as when people are present but unwilling to stretch out a hand; and this was his situation at that time. For there was no one to console him with a word or comfort him with a deed, no friend, neighbor, or relative, not even any onlooker, since the rich man's whole household was corrupt.

In addition to these, the sight of another person in good fortune laid on him an extra burden of anguish, not because he was envious and wicked, but because we all naturally perceive our own misfortunes more acutely by comparison with others' prosperity. In the case of the rich man there was something else which could hurt Lazarus even more. He received a keener perception of his own troubles not only by comparing his own misfortune with the rich man's prosperity, but also by considering that the rich man fared well in all respects in spite of living with cruelty and inhumanity, while he suffered extreme evils with virtue and goodness. Because of this he endured inconsolable distress. For if the man had been just, if he had been good, if he had been admirable, if he had been laden with every virtue, he would not have grieved Lazarus; but since he lived in wickedness, and had reached the height of evil, and was demonstrating such inhumanity, and treated him like an enemy, and passed him by like a stone shamelessly and mercilessly, and in spite of this all enjoyed such affluence: think how he was likely to sink the poor man's soul as if with a series of waves; think how Lazarus was likely to feel, seeing parasites, flatterers, servants going to and fro, in and out, running around, shouting, drinking, stamping their feet, and practicing all other kinds of wantonness. As if he had come for this very purpose, to be a witness of others' good fortune, he lay thus at the gate, alive only enough to be able to perceive his own ill fortune, enduring shipwreck while in the harbor, tormenting his soul with the bitterest thirst so near the spring.

Shall I name another evil in addition to these? He could not observe another Lazarus. We, for our part, even if we suffer a multitude of troubles, can at least gain sufficient comfort and enjoy consolation from looking at him. Finding companions in our sufferings either in fact or in story brings a great consolation to those in anguish. But he could not see anyone else who had suffered the same trials as he had; indeed he could not even hear of anyone among his ancestors who had endured as much. This is enough to darken one's soul. It is possible even to add another evil to these, namely that he could not console himself with any thought of resurrection, but he believed that the present situation was closed within the present life; for he was one of those who lived before the time of grace. But now among us, when so much knowledge of God has been revealed, both the good hope of the resurrection, and the retribution awaiting sinners hereafter, and the rewards prepared for the upright, if some people are so mean-spirited and miserable that they are not upheld even by these expectations, what was he likely to feel, deprived even of this anchor? He could not yet practice any such wisdom because the time had not yet come for these teachings.

There was even something more in addition to these evils, namely that his reputation was slandered by foolish people. For most people, when they see someone in hunger, chronic illness, and the extremes of misfortune, do not even allow him a good reputation, but judge his life by his troubles, and think that he is surely in such misery because of wickedness. They say many other things like this to one another, foolishly indeed, but still they say them: for example, if this man were dear to God, He would not have left him to suffer in poverty and the other troubles. This is what happened both to Job and to Paul. To the former they said, "You have not often been spoken to in distress, have you? Who will endure the force of your words? Whereas you have instructed many, strengthened the hands of the weak, upheld the stumbler with words, and made firm the feeble knees, yet now pain has come to you … and you are impatient. Is not your fear founded in folly?" (Job 4.2-6). What he means is something like this: "If you had done something good, you would not have suffered what you have suffered; but you are paying the penalty of sin and transgression." This was what most distressed the blessed Job. About Paul also the foreigners said the same: for when they saw the viper hanging from his hand, they did not imagine anything good about him, but thought him one of those who have dared the utmost evil. This is clear from what they said, "Though he has escaped from the sea, justice has not allowed him to live" (Acts 28.4). We also often make an extraordinary uproar with words like these.

Nevertheless, although the waves were so great and came so close together, the boat did not sink, but he strengthened himself with wisdom like dew continually refreshing a person lying in a furnace. He did not say to himself anything like what many people are likely to say, that if this rich man, when he departs to the other world, receives punishment and retribution, he has made one for one, but if hereafter he enjoys the same honors as here, he has made two for nothing. Do not you ordinary people use these expressions in the marketplace, and bring the language of the race-course and the theater into the church? I am ashamed, indeed, and I blush to put these expressions before you, except that it is necessary to say these things, to free you from the disorderly humor, the shame, and the harm that comes from such talk. Many people often say these things with a laugh, but even this belongs to the evil methods of the devil, to introduce corrupt teaching into our life in the guise of humorous expressions. Many people use these phrases continually in workshops, in the marketplace, and in their houses: this is a mark of extreme unbelief, of real mania, and of a childish disposition. To say, "If the wicked are punished when they depart," and not to be thoroughly convinced that they surely will be punished, is characteristic of unbelievers and skeptics. To think that, even if this should happen (and it will happen), the wicked will have enjoyed an equal reward with the righteous indicates the height of foolishness.

What do you say? Tell me. If the rich man departs and is punished hereafter, has he made one for one? How would you figure this? How many years do you want to suppose that he has enjoyed his money in this life? Shall we suppose a hundred?

I am willing to say two hundred or three hundred or twice this many, or, if you wish, even a thousand (which is impossible, for, as it is written, "The days of our years … are eighty years" (Ps. 90.10).)—but let us say even a thousand. You cannot show me, can you, a life here which has no end, which understands no limit, like the life of the righteous hereafter? Tell me, if someone in a hundred years should see a good dream on one night, and enjoy great luxury in his sleep, will you be able to say in his case "one for one," and make the one night of those dreams equivalent to the hundred years? You cannot say this. So you must think the same way about the life to come. As one dream is to a hundred years, so the present life is to the future life; or rather the difference is much greater. As a little drop is to the boundless sea, so much a thousand years are to that future glory and enjoyment. What would one need to say more than that it has no limit and knows no end; and as much as dreams differ from the truth of reality, so much this condition differs from that hereafter?

Besides, even before the punishment to come, those who practice wickedness and live in sin are punished in this life. Do not simply tell me of the man who enjoys an expensive table, who wears silken robes, who takes with him flocks of slaves as he struts in the marketplace: unfold for me his conscience, and you will see inside a great tumult of sins, continual fear, storm, confusion, his mind approaching the imperial throne of his conscience as if in a courtroom, sitting like a juror, presenting arguments as if in a public trial, suspending his mind and torturing it for his sins, and crying aloud, with no witness but God who alone knows how to watch these inner dramas. The adulterer, for example, even if he is immensely wealthy, even if he has no accuser, does not cease accusing himself within. The pleasure is brief, but the anguish is long-lasting, fear and trembling everywhere, suspicion and agony. He fears the narrow alleys. He trembles at the very shadows, at his own servants, at those who are aware of his deeds and at those who know nothing, at the woman herself whom he has wronged, and at the husband whom he has insulted. He goes about bearing with him a bitter accuser, his conscience; self-condemned, he is unable to relax even a little. On his bed, at table, in the marketplace, in the house, by day, by night, in his very dreams he often sees the image of his sin. He lives the life of Cain, groaning and trembling on the earth even when no one knows.

Inside he has fire always concentrated. The same happens also to those who practic theft and fraud, to drunkards, and (in a word) to everyone who lives in sin. There is no way to corrupt that court. Even if we do not seek virtue, we still suffer anguish, when we are not seeking it; and if we seek evil, we still experience the anguish when we cease from the pleasure of the sin. Let us not say, about the wicked who are rich here and the righteous who are rewarded hereafter, that one makes one, but that two make nothing. For the righteous, both the life hereafter and this life provide great pleasure; but the wicked and greedy are punished both here and hereafter. They are punished even here by the expectation of the retribution hereafter, and by the evil suspicion of everyone, and by the very fact of sinning and corrupting their own souls. After their departure from here they endure unbearable retribution. In contrast, even if the righteous suffer a multitude of troubles here, they are nourished by good hopes, and have a pleasure that is pure, secure, and permanent; and hereafter the multitude of good things will welcome them, just like Lazarus. Do not tell me that he was afflicted with sores, but consider that he had a soul inside more precious than any gold—or rather not his soul only, but also his body, for the virtue of the body is not plumpness and vigor but the ability to bear so many severe trials. A person is not loathsome if he has this kind of wounds on his body, but if he has a multitude of sores on his soul and takes no care of them. Such was that rich man, full of sores within. Just as the dogs licked the wounds of the poor man, so demons licked the sins of the rich man; and just as the poor man lived in starvation of nourishment, so the rich man lived in starvation of every kind of virtue.

Knowing all these things, let us be wise. Let us not say that if God loved so-and-so, He would not have allowed him to become poor. This very fact is the greatest evidence of God's love: "For the Lord disciplines him whom He loves, and chastises every son whom He receives" (Prov. 3.12, Heb. 12.6). And elsewhere it is written: "My son, if you come forward to serve the Lord, prepare yourself for temptation. Set your heart right and be steadfast" (Sir. 2.1-2). Let us reject from among us, beloved, these frivolous notions and these vulgar expressions. "Let nothing shameful or foolish or ribald," it is written, "come forth from your mouth" (Eph. 5.4, 4.29). Let us not only not say these things ourselves; but even if we see others saying them, let us silence them, let us struggle vigorously against them, let us stop their shameless tongues. Tell me, if you see any robber-chief prowling the roads, lying in wait for passers-by, stealing from farms, burying gold and silver in caves and holes, penning up large herds in his hideouts, and acquiring a lot of clothing and slaves from that prowling, tell me, do you call him fortunate because of that wealth, or unfortunate because of the penalty which awaits him? Indeed he has not yet been apprehended, he has not been handed over to the judge, he has not been thrown into prison, he has no accuser, his case has not come to the vote, but he eats and drinks extravagantly, he enjoys great abundance. Nevertheless we do not call him fortunate because of his present visible goods, but we call him miserable because of his future expected sufferings.

You should think the same way about those who are rich and greedy. They are a kind of robbers lying in wait on the roads, stealing from passers-by, and burying others' goods in their own houses as if in caves and holes. Let us not therefore call them fortunate because of what they have, but miserable because of what will come, because of that dreadful courtroom, because of the inexorable judgment, because of the outer darkness which awaits them. Indeed, robbers often have escaped the hands of men; nevertheless, even knowing this, we would have prayed both for ourselves and for our enemies to avoid that life with its cursed affluence. But with God we cannot say this; for no one will escape His judgment, but all who live by fraud and theft will certainly draw upon themselves that immortal and endless penalty, just like this rich man. Collecting all these thoughts in your minds, therefore, my beloved, let us call fortunate not the wealthy but the virtuous; let us call miserable not the poor but the wicked. Let us not regard what is present, but consider what is to come (cf. Herodotus, *Histories* 1.32). Let us examine not the outer garments but the conscience of each person. Let us pursue the virtue and joy which come from righteous actions; and let us, both rich and poor, emulate Lazarus. For this man did not endure just one or two or three tests of virtue, but very many—I mean that he was poor, he was ill, he had no one to help him. He remained in a house which could have relieved all his troubles but he was granted no word of comfort. He saw the man who neglected him enjoying such luxury, and not only enjoying luxury but living in wickedness without suffering any misfortune. He could not look to any other Lazarus or comfort himself with any philosophy of resurrection. Along with the evils I have mentioned, he obtained a bad reputation among the mass of people because of his misfortunes. Not for two or three days but for his whole life he saw himself in this situation and the rich man in the opposite. What excuse will we have, when this man endured all the misfortunes at once with such courage, if we will not bear even the half of these? You cannot, you cannot possibly show or name any other who has suffered so many and such great misfortunes. For this reason Christ set him before us, so that whatever troubles we encounter, seeing in this man a greater measure of tribulation, we may gain enough comfort and consolation from his wisdom and patience. He stands forth as a single teacher of the whole world, for those who suffer any misfortune whatever, offering himself for all to see, and surpassing all of them in the excess of his own troubles.

For all this let us give thanks to God who loves mankind. Let us gather help from the narration. Let us talk of Lazarus continually in councils, at home, in the marketplace, and everywhere. Let us examine carefully all the wealth which comes from this parable, so that we may both pass through the present troubles without grief and attain to the good things which are to come: of which may we all be found worthy, by the grace and love of our Lord Jesus Christ, with whom to the Father, together with the Holy Spirit, be glory, honor, and worship, now and ever, and unto ages of ages. Amen.

4. Augustine of Hippo – City of God, Book XIX, Chapters 11–28

11. The bliss of everlasting peace, which is the fulfilment of the saints

It follows that we could say of peace, as we have said of eternal life, that it is the final fulfilment of all our goods; especially in view of what is said in a holy psalm about the City of God, the subject of this laborious discussion. These are the words: 'Praise the Lord, O Jerusalem; praise your God, O Sion: for he has strengthened the bolts of your gates; he has blessed your sons within your walls; he has made your frontiers peace' (Ps. 147.12ff.). Now when the bolts of her gates have been strengthened, that means that no one will any more enter or leave that City. And this implies that we must take her 'frontiers' (or 'ends') to stand here for the peace whose finality I am trying to establish. In fact, the name of the City itself has a mystic significance, for 'Jerusalem', as I have said already, means 'vision of peace'.

But the word 'peace' is freely used in application to the events of this mortal state, where there is certainly no eternal life; and so I have preferred to use the term 'eternal life' instead of 'peace' in describing the end of this City, where its Ultimate Good will be found. About this end the Apostle says, 'But now you have been set free from sin and have become the servants of God; and so you have your profit, a profit leading to sanctification, and the end is everlasting life' (Rom. 6.22). On the other hand, the life of the wicked may also be taken to be eternal life by those who have no familiarity with the holy Scriptures. They may follow some of the philosophers in thinking in terms of the immortality of the soul, or they may be influenced by our Christian belief in the endless punishment of the ungodly, who obviously cannot be tortured for ever without also living for ever. Consequently, in order to make it easier for everyone to understand our meaning, we have to say that the end of this City, whereby it will possess its Supreme Good, may be called either 'peace in life everlasting' or 'life everlasting in peace'. For peace is so great a good that even in relation to the affairs of earth and of our mortal state no word ever falls more gratefully upon the ear, nothing is desired with greater longing, in fact, nothing better can be found. So if I decide to discourse about it at somewhat greater length, I shall not, I think, impose a burden on my readers, not only because I shall be speaking of the end of the City which is the subject of this work, but also because of the delightfulness of peace, which is dear to the heart of all mankind.

12. Peace is the instinctive aim of all creatures, and is even the ultimate purpose of war

Anyone who joins me in an examination, however slight, of human affairs, and the human nature we all share, recognizes that just as there is no man who does not wish for joy, so there is no man who does not wish for peace. Indeed, even when men choose war, their only wish is for victory; which shows that their desire in fighting is for peace with glory. For what is victory but the conquest of the opposing side? And when this is achieved, there will be peace. Even wars, then, are waged with peace as their object, even when they are waged by those who are concerned to exercise their warlike prowess, either in command or in the actual fighting. Hence it is an established fact that peace is the desired end of war. For every man is in quest of peace, even in waging war, whereas no one is in quest of war when making peace. In fact, even when men wish a present state of peace to be disturbed they do so not because they hate peace, but because they desire the present peace to be exchanged for one that suits their wishes. Thus their desire is not that there should not be peace but that it should be the kind of peace they wish for. Even in the extreme case when they have separated themselves from others by sedition, they cannot achieve their aim unless they maintain some sort of semblance of peace with their confederates in conspiracy. Moreover, even robbers, to ensure greater efficiency and security in their assaults on the peace of the rest of mankind, desire to preserve peace with their associates.

Indeed, one robber may be so unequalled in strength and so wary of having anyone to share his plans that he does not trust any associate, but plots his crimes and achieves his successes by himself, carrying off his booty after overcoming and dispatching such as he can; yet even so he maintains some kind of shadow of peace, at least with those whom he cannot kill, and from whom he wishes to conceal his activities. At the same time, he is anxious, of course, to be at peace in his own home, with his wife and children and any other members of his household; without doubt he is delighted to have them obedient to his beck and call. For if this does not happen, he is indignant; he scolds and punishes; and, if need be, he employs savage measures to impose on his household a peace which, he feels, cannot exist unless all the other elements in the same domestic society are subject to one head; and this head, in his own home, is himself. Thus, if he were offered the servitude of a larger number, of a city, maybe, or a whole nation, on the condition that they should all show the same subservience he had demanded from his household, then he would no longer lurk like a brigand in his hide-out; he would raise himself on high as a king for all to see – although the same greed and malignity would persist in him.

We see, then, that all men desire to be at peace with their own people, while wishing to impose their will upon those people's lives. For even when they wage war on others, their wish is to make those opponents their own people, if they can – to subject them, and to impose on them their own conditions of peace.

Let us, however, suppose such a man as is described in the verse of epic legends, a creature so unsociable and savage that they perhaps preferred to call him a semi-human rather than a human being. Now although his kingdom was the solitude of a dreadful cavern, and although he was so unequalled in wickedness that a name was found for him derived from that quality (he was called Cacus,[1] and *kakos* is the Greek word for 'wicked'); although he had no wife with whom to exchange endearments, no children to play with when little or to give orders to when they were a little bigger,

---

[1] cf. Virgil, *Aeneid*, 8, 190–305 for the story of Cacus and Hercules.

no friends with whom to enjoy a chat, not even his father, Vulcan (he was happier than his father only in this important respect – that he did not beget another such monster as himself); although he never gave anything to anyone, but took what he wanted from anyone he could and removed, when he could, anyone he wished to remove; despite all this, in the very solitude of his cave, the floor of which, in the poet's description

reeked ever with the blood of recent slaughter (Virgil, *Aeneid.*, 1. 195)

his only desire was for a peace in which no one should disturb him, and no man's violence, or the dread of it, should trouble his repose. Above all, he desired to be at peace with his own body; and in so far as he achieved this, all was well with him. He gave the orders and his limbs obeyed. But his mortal nature rebelled against him because of its insatiable desires, and stirred up the civil strife of hunger, intending to dissociate the soul from the body and to exclude it; and then he sought with all possible haste to pacify that mortal nature, and to that end he ravished, murdered, and devoured. And thus, for all his monstrous savagery, his aim was still to ensure peace, for the preservation of his life, by these monstrous and savage methods. Accordingly, if he had been willing to maintain, in relation to others also, the peace he was so busily concerned to preserve in his own case and in himself, he would not have been called wicked, or a monster, or semi-human. Or if it was his outward appearance and his belching of murky flames that frightened away human companions, it may be that it was not lust for inflicting injury but the necessity of preserving his life that made him so savage. Perhaps, after all, he never existed or, more probably, he was not like the description given by poetic fantasy; for if Cacus had not been excessively blamed, Hercules would have received inadequate praise. And therefore the existence of such a man, or rather semi-human, is discredited, as are many similar poetical fictions.

We observe, then, that even the most savage beasts, from whom Cacus derived the wild-beast side of his nature (he was in fact also called a semi-beast), safeguard their own species by a kind of peace, by coition, by begetting and bearing young, by cherishing them and rearing them; even though most of them are not gregarious but solitary – not, that is, like sheep, deer, doves, starlings, and bees, but like lions, wolves, foxes, eagles and owls. What tigress does not gently purr over her cubs, and subdue her fierceness to caress them? What kite, however solitary as he hovers over his prey, does not find a mate, build a nest, help to hatch the eggs, rear the young birds, and, as we may say, preserve with the mother of his family a domestic society as peaceful as he can make it? How much more strongly is a human being drawn by the laws of his nature, so to speak, to enter upon a fellowship with all his fellow-men and to keep peace with them, as far as lies in him. For even the wicked when they go to war do so to defend the peace of their own people, and desire to make all men their own people, if they can, so that all men and all things might together be subservient to one master. And how could that happen, unless they should consent to a peace of his dictation either through love or through fear? Thus pride is a perverted imitation of God. For pride hates a fellowship of equality under God, and seeks to impose its own dominion on fellow men, in place of God's rule. This means that it hates the just peace of God, and loves its own peace of injustice. And yet it cannot help loving peace of some kind or other. For no creature's perversion is so contrary to nature as to destroy the very last vestiges of its nature.

It comes to this, then; a man who has learnt to prefer right to wrong and the rightly ordered to the perverted, sees that the peace of the unjust, compared with the peace of the just, is not worthy even of the name of peace. Yet even what is perverted must of necessity be in, or derived from, or associated with – that is, in a sense, at peace with – some part of the order of things among which it has its being or of which it consists. Otherwise it would not exist at all. For instance if anyone were to hang upside-down, this position of the body and arrangement of the limbs is undoubtedly perverted, because what should be on top, according to the dictates of nature, is underneath, and what nature intends to be underneath is on top. This perverted attitude disturbs the peace of the flesh, and causes distress for that reason. For all that, the breath is at peace with its body and is busily engaged for its preservation; that is why there is something to endure the pain. And even if the breath is finally driven from the body by its distresses, still, as long as the framework of the limbs holds together, what remains retains a kind of peace among the bodily parts; hence there is still something to hang there. And in that the earthly body pulls towards the earth, and pulls against the binding rope that holds it suspended, it tends towards the position of its own peace, and by what might be called the appeal of its weight, it demands a place where it may rest. And so even when it is by now lifeless and devoid of all sensation it does not depart from the peace of its natural position, either while possessed of it or while tending towards it. Again, if treatment with embalming fluids is applied to prevent the dissolution and disintegration of the corpse in its present shape, a kind of peace still connects the parts with one another and keeps the whole mass fixed in its earthly condition, an appropriate, and therefore a peaceable state.

On the other hand, if no preservative treatment is given, and the body is left for nature to take its course, there is for a time a kind of tumult in the corpse of exhalations disagreeable and offensive to our senses (for that is what we smell in putrefaction), which lasts until the body unites with the elements of the world as, little by little, and particle by particle, it vanishes into their peace. Nevertheless, nothing is in any way removed, in this process, from the control of the laws of the supreme Creator and Ruler who directs the peace of the whole scheme of things. For although minute animals are produced in the corpse of a larger animal, those little bodies, each and all of them, by the same law of their Creator, are subservient to their little souls in the peace that preserves their lives. And even if the flesh of dead animals is devoured by other animals, in whatever direction it is taken, with whatever substances it is united, into whatever substances it is converted and transformed, it still finds itself subject to the same laws which are diffused throughout the whole of matter for the preservation of every mortal species, establishing peace by a harmony of congruous elements.

13. The peace of the universe maintained through all disturbances by a law of nature: the individual attains, by God's ordinance, to the state he has deserved by his free choice

The peace of the body, we conclude, is a tempering of the component parts in duly ordered proportion; the peace of the irrational soul is a duly ordered repose of the appetites; the peace of the rational soul is the duly ordered agreement of cognition and action. The peace of body and soul is the duly ordered life and health of a living creature; peace between mortal man and God is an ordered obedience, in faith, in subjection to an everlasting law; peace between men is an ordered agreement of mind with mind; the peace of a home is the ordered agreement among those who live together about giving and obeying orders; the peace of the Heavenly City is a perfectly ordered and perfectly harmonious fellowship in the enjoyment of God, and a mutual fellowship in God; the peace of the whole universe is the tranquillity of order – and order is the arrangement of things equal and unequal in a pattern which assigns to each its proper position.

It follows that the wretched, since, in so far as they are wretched, they are obviously not in a state of peace, lack the tranquillity of order, a state in which there is no disturbance of mind. In spite of that, because their wretchedness is deserved and just, they cannot be outside the scope of order. They are not, indeed, united with the blessed; yet it is by the law of order that they are sundered from them. And when they are free from disturbance of mind, they are adjusted to their situation, with however small a degree of harmony. Thus they have amongst them some tranquillity of order, and therefore some peace. But they are still wretched just because, although they enjoy some degree of serenity and freedom from suffering, they are not in a condition where they have the right to be serene and free from pain. They are yet more wretched, however, if they are not at peace with the law by which the natural order is governed. Now when they suffer, their peace is disturbed in the part where they suffer; and yet peace still continues in the part which feels no burning pain, and where the natural frame is not broken up. Just as there is life, then without pain, whereas there can be no pain when there is no life, so there is peace without any war, but no war without some degree of peace. This is not a consequence of war as such, but of the fact that war is waged by or within persons who are in some sense natural beings – for they could have no kind of existence without some kind of peace as the condition of their being.

There exists, then, a nature in which there is no evil, in which, indeed, no evil can exist; but there cannot exist a nature in which there is no good. Hence not even the nature of the Devil himself is evil, in so far as it is a nature; it is perversion that makes it evil. And so the Devil did not stand firm in the truth, and yet he did not escape the judgement of the truth. He did not continue in the tranquillity of order; but that did not mean that he escaped from the power of the imposer of order. The good that God imparts, which the Devil has in his nature, does not withdraw him from God's justice by which his punishment is ordained. But God, in punishing, does not chastise the good which he created, but the evil which the Devil has committed. And God does not take away all that he gave to that nature; he takes something, and yet he leaves something, so that there may be some being left to feel pain at the deprivation.

Now this pain is in itself evidence of the good that was taken away and the good that was left. In fact, if no good had been left there could have been no grief for lost good. For a sinner is in a worse state if he rejoices in the loss of righteousness; but a sinner who feels anguish, though he may gain no good from his anguish, is at least grieving at the loss of salvation. And since righteousness and salvation are both good, and the loss of any good calls for grief rather than for joy (assuming that there is no compensation for the loss in the shape of a higher good – for example, righteousness of character is a higher good than health of body), the unrighteous man's grief in his punishment is more appropriate than his rejoicing in sin. Hence, just as delight in the abandonment of good, when a man sins, is evidence of a bad will, so grief at the loss of good, when a man is punished, is evidence of a good nature. For when a man grieves at the loss of the peace of his nature, his grief arises from some remnants of that peace, which ensure that his nature is still on friendly terms with itself. Moreover, it is entirely right that in the last punishment the wicked and ungodly should bewail in their agonies the loss of their 'natural' goods, and realize that he who divested them of these goods with perfect justice is God, whom they despised when with supreme generosity he bestowed them.

God then, created all things in supreme wisdom and ordered them in perfect justice; and in establishing the mortal race of mankind as the greatest ornament of earthly things, he has given to mankind certain good things suitable to this life. These are: temporal peace, in proportion to the short span of a mortal life – the peace that consists in bodily health and soundness, and in fellowship with one's kind; and everything necessary to safeguard or recover this peace – those things, for example, which are appropriate and accessible to our senses: light, speech, air to breathe, water to drink, and whatever is suitable for the feeding and clothing of the body, for the care of the body and the adornment of the person. And all this is granted under the most equitable condition: that every mortal who uses aright such goods, goods designed to serve the peace of mortal men, shall receive goods greater in degree and superior in kind, namely, the peace of immortality, and the glory and honour appropriate to it in a life which is eternal for the enjoyment of God and of one's neighbour in

God, whereas he who wrongly uses those mortal goods shall lose them, and shall not receive the blessings of eternal life.

14. The order and law, earthly or heavenly, by which government serves the interests of human society

We see, then, that all man's use of temporal things is related to the enjoyment of earthly peace in the earthly city; whereas in the Heavenly City it is related to the enjoyment of eternal peace. Thus, if we were irrational animals, our only aim would be the adjustment of the parts of the body in due proportion, and the quieting of the appetites – only, that is, the repose of the flesh, and an adequate supply of pleasures, so that bodily peace might promote the peace of the soul. For if bodily peace is lacking, the peace of the irrational soul is also hindered, because it cannot achieve the quieting of its appetites. But the two together promote that peace which is a mutual concord between soul and body, the peace of an ordered life and of health. For living creatures show their love of bodily peace by their avoidance of pain, and by their pursuit of pleasure to satisfy the demands of their appetites they demonstrate their love of peace of soul. In just the same way, by shunning death they indicate quite clearly how great is their love of the peace in which soul and body are harmoniously united.

But because there is in man a rational soul, he subordinates to the peace of the rational soul all that part of his nature which he shares with the beasts, so that he may engage in deliberate thought and act in accordance with this thought, so that he may thus exhibit that ordered agreement of cognition and action which we called the peace of the rational soul. For with this end in view he ought to wish to be spared the distress of pain and grief, the disturbances of desire, the dissolution of death, so that he may come to some profitable knowledge and may order his life and his moral standards in accordance with this knowledge. But he needs divine direction, which he may obey with resolution, and divine assistance that he may obey it freely, to prevent him from falling, in his enthusiasm for knowledge, a victim to some fata error, through the weakness of the human mind. And so long as he is in this mortal body, he is a pilgrim in a foreign land, away from God; therefore he walks by faith, not by sight (cf. 2 Cor. 5.6f.). That is why he views all peace, of body or of soul, or of both, in relation to that peace which exists between mortal man and immortal God, so that he may exhibit an ordered obedience in faith in subjection to the everlasting Law.

Now God, our master, teaches two chief precepts, love of God and love of neighbour; and in them man finds three objects for his love: God, himself, and his neighbour; and a man who loves God is not wrong in loving himself. It follows, therefore, that he will be concerned also that his neighbour should love God, since he is told to love his neighbour as himself; and the same is true of his concern for his wife, his children, for the members of his household, and for all other men, so far as is possible. And, for the same end, he will wish his neighbour to be concerned for him, if he happens to need that concern. For this reason he will be at peace, as far as lies in him, with all men, in that peace among men, that ordered harmony; and the basis of this order is the observance of two rules: first, to do no harm to anyone, and, secondly, to help everyone whenever possible. To begin with, therefore, a man has a responsibility for his own household – obviously, both in the order of nature and in the framework of human society, he has easier and more immediate contact with them; he can exercise his concern for them. That is why the Apostle says, 'Anyone who does not take care of his own people, especially those in his own household, is worse than an unbeliever – he is a renegade' (1 Tim. 5.8). This is where domestic peace starts, the ordered harmony about giving and obeying orders among those who live in the same house. For the orders are given by those who are concerned for the interests of others; thus the husband gives orders to the wife, parents to children, masters to servants. While those who are the objects of this concern obey orders; for example, wives obey husbands, the children obey their parents, the servants their masters. But in the household of the just man who 'lives on the basis of faith' and who is still on pilgrimage, far from that Heavenly City, even those who give orders are the servants of those whom they appear to command. For they do not give orders because of a lust for domination but from a dutiful concern for the interests of others, not with pride in taking precedence over others, but with compassion in taking care of others.

15. Man's natural freedom; and the slavery caused by sin

This relationship is prescribed by the order of nature, and it is in this situation that God created man. For he says, 'Let him have lordship over the fish of the sea, the birds of the sky … and all the reptiles that crawl on the earth' (Gen. 1.26). He did not wish the rational being, made in his own image, to have dominion over any but irrational creatures, not man over man, but man over the beasts. Hence the first just men were set up as shepherds of flocks, rather than as kings of men, so that in this way also God might convey the message of what was required by the order of nature, and what was demanded by the deserts of sinners – for it is understood, of course, that the condition of slavery is justly imposed on the sinner. That is why we do not hear of a slave anywhere in the Scriptures until Noah, the just man, punished his son's sin with this word (Gen. 9.25); and so that son deserved this name because of his misdeed, not because of his nature. The origin of the Latin word for slave, *servus*, is believed to be derived from the fact that those who by the laws of war could rightly be put to death by the conquerors, became *servi*, slaves, when they were preserved, receiving this name from their preservation.[2] But even this enslavement could not have happened, if it were not for the deserts of sin. For even when a just war is fought it is in defence of his sin that the other side is contending; and victory, even when the victory falls to the wicked, is a humiliation visited on the conquered by divine judgement, either to correct or to punish their sins. We have a witness to this in Daniel, a man of God, who in captivity confesses to God his own sins and the sins of his people, and in devout grief testifies that they are the cause of that captivity (Dan. 9.3-15). The first cause of slavery, then, is sin, whereby man was subjected to man in the condition of bondage; and this can only happen by the judgement of God, with whom there is no injustice, and who knows how to allot different punishments according to the deserts of the offenders.

Now, as our Lord above says, 'Everyone who commits sin is sin's slave' (John 8.34), and that is why, though many devout men are slaves to unrighteous masters, yet the masters they serve are not themselves free men; 'for when a man is conquered by another he is also bound as a slave to his conqueror' (2 Pet. 2.19). And obviously it is a happier lot to be slave to a human being than to a lust; and, in fact, the most pitiless domination that devastates the hearts of men, is that exercised by this very lust for domination, to mention no others. However, in that order of peace in which men are subordinate to other men, humility is as salutary for the servants as pride is harmful to the masters. And yet by nature, in the condition in which God created man, no man is the slave either of man or of sin. But it remains true that slavery as a punishment is also ordained by that law which enjoins the preservation of the order of nature, and forbids its disturbance; in fact, if nothing had been done to contravene that law, there would have been nothing to require the discipline of slavery as a punishment. That explains also the Apostle's admonition to slaves, that they should be subject to their masters, and serve them loyally and willingly (cf. Eph. 6.5). What he means is that if they cannot be set free by their masters, they themselves may thus make their slavery, in a sense, free, by serving not with the slyness of fear, but with the fidelity of affection, until all injustice disappears and all human lordship and power is annihilated, and God is all in all (1 Cor. 15.24, 28).

16. Equity in the relation of master and slave

This being so, even though our righteous fathers had slaves, they so managed the peace of their households as to make a distinction between the situation of children and the condition of slaves in respect of the temporal goods of this life; and yet in the matter of the worship of God – in whom we must place our hope of everlasting

---

[2] A mistaken derivation generally accepted in antiquity.

goods – they were concerned, with equal affection, for all the members of their household. This is what the order of nature prescribes, so that this is the source of the name *paterfamilias,* a name that has become so generally used that even those who exercise unjust rule rejoice to be called by this title. On the other hand, those who are genuine 'fathers of their household' are concerned for the welfare of all in their house holds in respect of the worship and service of God, as if they were all their children, longing and praying that they may come to the heavenly home, where it will not be a necessary duty to give orders to men, because it will no longer be a necessary duty to be concerned for the welfare of those who are already in the felicity of that immortal state. But until that home is reached, the fathers have an obligation to exercise the authority of masters greater than the duty of slaves to put up with their condition as servants.

However, if anyone in the household is, through his disobedience an enemy to the domestic peace, he is reproved by a word, or by a blow or any other kind of punishment that is just and legitimate, to the extent allowed by human society; but this is for the benefit of the offender, intended to readjust him to the domestic peace from which he had broken away. For just as it is not an act of kindness to help a man when the effect of the help is to make him lose a greater good, so it is not a blameless act to spare a man, when by so doing you let him fall into a greater sin. Hence the duty of anyone who would be blameless includes not only doing no harm to anyone but also restraining a man from sin or punishing his sin, so that either the man who is chastised may be corrected by his experience, or others may be deterred by his example. Now a man's house ought to be the beginning, or rather's small component part of the city, and every beginning is directed to some end of its own kind, and every component part contributes to the completeness of the whole of which it forms a part. The implication is quite apparent, that domestic peace contributes to the peace of the city – that is, the ordered harmony of those who live together in a house in the matter of giving and obeying orders, contributes to the ordered harmony concerning authority and obedience obtaining among the citizens. Consequently it is fitting that the father of a household should take his rules from the law of the city, and govern his household in such a way that it fits in with the peace of the city.

17. The origin of peace between the heavenly society and the earthly city, and of discord between them

But a household of human beings whose life is not based on faith is in pursuit of an earthly peace based on the things belonging to this temporal life, and on its advantages, whereas a household of human beings whose life is based on faith looks forward to the blessings which are promised as eternal in the future, making use of earthly and temporal things like a pilgrim in a foreign land, who does not let himself be taken in by them or distracted from his course towards God, but rather treats them as supports which help him more easily to bear the burdens of 'the corruptible body which weighs heavy on the soul' (Wis. 9.15), they must on no account be allowed to increase the load. Thus both kinds of men and both kinds of households alike make use of the things essential for this mortal life; but each has its own very different end in making use of them. So also the earthly city, whose life is not based on faith, aims at an earthly peace, and it limits the harmonious agreement of citizens concerning the giving and obeying of orders to the establishment of a kind of compromise between human wills about the things relevant to mortal life. In contrast, the Heavenly City – or rather that part of it which is on pilgrimage in this condition of mortality, and which lives on the basis of faith – must needs make use of this peace also, until this mortal state, for which this kind of peace is essential, passes away. And therefore, it leads what we may call a life of captivity in this earthly city as in a foreign land, although it has already received the promise of redemption, and the gift of the Spirit as a kind of pledge of it; and yet it does not hesitate to obey the laws of the earthly city by which those things which are designed for the support of this mortal life are regulated; and the purpose of this obedience is that, since this mortal condition is shared by both cities, a harmony may be preserved between them in things that are relevant to this condition.

But this earthly city has had some philosophers belonging to it whose theories are rejected by the teaching inspired by God. Either led astray by their own speculation or deluded by demons, these thinkers reached the belief that there are many gods who must be won over to save human ends, and also that they have as it were, different departments with different responsibilities attached. Thus the body is the department of one god, the mind that of another; and within the body itself, one god is in charge of the head, another of the neck and so on with each of the separate members. Similarly, within the mind, one is responsible for natural ability, another for learning, another for anger, another for lust; and in the accessories of life there are separate gods over the departments of flocks, grain, wine, oil, forests, coinage, navigation, war and victory, marriage, birth, fertility, and so on (cf. Bks. IV, VI, VII of *City of God*). The Heavenly City, in contrast, knows only one God as the object of worship, and decrees, with faithful devotion, that he only is to be served with that service which the Greeks call *latreia*, which is due to God alone. And the result of this difference has been that the Heavenly City could not have laws of religion common with the earthly city, and in defence of her religious laws she was bound to dissent from those who thought differently and to prove a burdensome nuisance to them. Thus she had to endure their anger and hatred, and the assaults of persecution; until at length that City shattered the morale of her adversaries by the terror inspired by her numbers, and by the help she continually received from God.

While this Heavenly City, therefore, is on pilgrimage in this world, she calls out citizens from all nations and so collects a society of aliens, speaking all languages. She takes no account of any difference in customs, laws, and institutions, by which earthly peace is achieved and preserved – not that she annuls or abolishes any of those, rather, she maintains them and follows them (for whatever divergences there are among the diverse nations, those institutions have one single aim – earthly peace), provided that no hindrance is presented thereby to the religion which teaches that the one supreme and true God is to be worshipped. Thus even the Heavenly City in her pilgrimage here on earth makes use of the earthly peace and defends and seeks the compromise between human wills in respect of the provisions relevant to the mortal nature of man, so far as may be permitted without detriment to true religion and piety. In fact, that City relates the earthly peace to the heavenly peace, which is so truly peaceful that it should be regarded as the only peace deserving the name, at least in respect of the rational creation; for this peace is the perfectly ordered and completely harmonious fellowship in the enjoyment of God, and of each other in God. When we arrive at that state of peace, there will be no longer a life that ends in death, but a life that is life in sure and sober truth; there will be no animal body to 'weigh down the soul' in its process of corruption; there will be a spiritual body with no cravings, a body subdued in every part to the will. This peace the Heavenly City possesses in faith while on its pilgrimage, and it lives a life of righteousness, based on this faith (Hab. 2.4, Rom. 1.17), having the attainment of that peace in view in every good action it performs in relation to God, and in relation to a neighbour, since the life of a city is inevitably a social life.

18. The hesitations of the New Academy contrasted with the steadfast certainty of the Christian faith

As for that characteristic which Varro produces as the distinctive mark of the New Academy (cf. Bk. IV), the view that everything is uncertain, the City of God roundly condemns such doubt as being madness. In matters apprehended by the mind and the reason it has most certain knowledge, even if that knowledge is of small extent, on account of the 'corruptible body which weighs down the mind' – as the Apostle says, 'Our knowledge is partial' (1 Cor. 13.9). It also trusts the evidence of the senses in every matter; for the mind employs the senses through the agency of the body, and anyone who supposes that they can never be trusted is woefully mistaken. It believes also in the holy Scriptures, the old and the new, which we call canonical, whence is derived the faith which is the basis of the just man's life, the faith by which we walk on our way without doubting, in the time of our pilgrimage, in exile from the Lord.

So long as this faith is sound and certain we cannot justly be reproached if we have doubts about some matters where neither sense nor reason give clear perception, where we have received no illumination from the canonical Scriptures and where we have not been given information by witnesses whom it would be irrational to distrust.

19. The dress and behaviour of the Christian people

It is completely irrelevant to the Heavenly City what dress is worn or what manner of life adopted by each person who follows the faith that is the way to God, provided that these do not conflict with the divine instructions. Hence, when even philosophers become Christians, they are not obliged to alter their mode of dress or their dietary habits, which offer no hindrance to religion. The only change required is in their false teachings. Thus the peculiar behaviour of the Cynics, which Varro treated as a differentia, is to that city a matter of no importance at all, if there is nothing indecent or immoderate in that behaviour. As for the three kinds of life, the life of leisure, the life of action, and the combination of the two, anyone, to be sure, might spend his life in any of these ways without detriment to his faith, and might thus attain to the everlasting rewards. What does matter is the answers to those questions: What does a man possess as a result of his love of truth? And what does he pay out in response to the obligations of Christian love? For no one ought to be so leisured as to take no thought in that leisure for the interest of his neighbour nor so active as to feel no need for the contemplation of God. The attraction of a life of leisure ought not to be the prospect of lazy inactivity, but the chance for the investigation and discovery of truth, on the understanding that each person makes some progress in this, and does not grudgingly withhold his discoveries from another.

In the life of action, on the other hand, what is to be treasured is not a place of honour or power in this life, since 'everything under the sun is vanity' (Eccl. 1.14) but the task itself that is achieved by means of that place of honour and that power – if that achievement is right and helpful, that is, if it serves to promote the well-being of the common people, for, as we have already argued, this well-being is according to God's intention That is why the Apostle says, 'Anyone who aspires to the episcopate aspires to an honourable *task*' (1 Tim. 3.1). He wanted to explain what 'episcopate' means; it is the name of a task, not an honour. It is, in fact, a Greek word, derived from the fact that a man who is put in authority over others 'superintends' them, that is, he has responsibility for them. For the Greek *skopos* means 'intention' (in the sense of 'direction of the attention'); and so we may, if we wish, translate *epi-skopein* as 'super-intend'. Hence a 'bishop' who has set his heart on a position of eminence rather than an opportunity for service should realize that he is no bishop. So then, no one is debarred from devoting himself to the pursuit of truth, for that involves a praiseworthy kind of leisure. But high position, although without it a people cannot be ruled, is not in itself a respectable object of ambition, even if that position be held and exercised in a manner worthy of respect. We see then that it is love of truth that looks for sanctified leisure, while it is the compulsion of love that undertakes righteous engagement in affairs. If this latter burden is not imposed on us, we should employ our freedom from business in the quest for truth and in its contemplation, while if it is laid upon us, it is to be undertaken because of the compulsion of love. Yet even in this case the delight in truth should not be utterly abandoned, for fear that we should lose this enjoyment and that compulsion should overwhelm us.

20. The fellow-citizens of the saints are in this life made happy by hope

We see, then, that the Supreme Good of the City of God is everlasting and perfect peace, which is not the peace through which men pass in their mortality, in their journey from birth to death, but that peace in which they remain in their immortal state, experiencing no adversity at all. In view of this, can anyone deny that this is the supremely blessed life, or that the present life on earth, however full it may be of the greatest possible blessings of soul and body and of external circumstances, is, in comparison, most miserable? For all that, if anyone accepts the present life in such a spirit that he uses it with the end in view of that other life on which he has set his heart with all his ardour and for which he hopes with all his confidence, such a man may without absurdity be called happy even now, though rather by future hope than in present reality. Present reality without that hope is, to be sure, a false happiness, in fact, an utter misery. For the present does not bring into play the true goods of the mind; since no wisdom is true wisdom if it does not direct its attention, in all its prudent decisions, its resolute actions, its self-control and its just dealings with others, towards that ultimate state in which God will be all in all (1 Cor. 15.28), in the assurance of eternity and the perfection of peace.

21. Scipio's definition of a commonwealth. Was it every a reality at Rome?

This brings me to the place where I must fulfil, as briefly and clearly as I may, the promise I gave in the second book. I there promised that I would show that there never was a Roman commonwealth answering to the definitions advanced by Scipio in Cicero's *On the Republic*. For Scipio gives a brief definition of the state, or commonwealth, as the 'weal of the people'. Now if this is a true definition there never was a Roman commonwealth, because the Roman state was never the 'weal of the people', according to Scipio's definition. For he defined a 'people' as a multitude 'united in association by a common sense of right and a community of interest'. He explains in the discussion what he means by 'a common sense of right', showing that a state cannot be maintained without justice, and where there is no true justice there can be no right. For any action according to right is inevitably a just action, while no unjust action can possibly be according to right. For unjust human institutions are not to be called or supposed to be institutions of right, since even they themselves say that right is what has flowed from the fount of justice; as for the notion of justice commonly put forward by some misguided thinkers, that it is 'the interest of the strongest',[3] they hold this to be a false conception.

Therefore, where there is no true justice there can be no 'association of men united by a common sense of right', and therefore no people answering to the definition of Scipio, or Cicero. And if there is no people then there is no 'weal of the people', but some kind of a mob, not deserving the name of a people. If, therefore, a commonwealth is the 'weal of the people', and if a people does not exist where there is no 'association by a common sense of right', and there is no right where there is no justice, the irresistible conclusion is that where there is no justice there is no commonwealth. Moreover, justice is that virtue which assigns to everyone his due.[4] Then what kind of justice is it that takes a man away from the true God and subjects him to unclean demons? Is this to assign to every man his due? Or are we to say that a man is unjust when he takes an estate from a man who has bought it and hands it over to someone who has no right to it, while we give the name of just to a man who takes himself away from the Lord God who made him, and becomes the servant of malignant spirits?

There is, to be sure, in the same work, *On the Republic,* a most vigorous and powerful argument on behalf of justice against injustice. Earlier in the discussion a plea was put forward for injustice against justice, and it was alleged that a state cannot stand or be governed except by injustice, and it was posited as the strongest point in this case that it was unjust that men should be servants to other men as their masters; and yet an imperial city, the head of a great commonwealth, cannot rule its provinces except by adopting this injustice. Now it was urged in reply on the side of justice, that this situation is just, on the ground that servitude is in the interest of such men as the provincials, and that it is established for their benefit, when rightly established – that is, when unprincipled men are deprived of the freedom to do wrong with impunity. It was also asserted that the subjugated will be better off, because they were worse off before subjugation. In confirmation of this line of reasoning a notable illustration was adduced, ostensibly taken from nature. It was stated thus: 'How is it then that

---

[3] cf. the argument of Thrasymachus in Plato *Republic* 339A–341A.
[4] Aristotle's 'distributive justice' (*Nichomachean Ethics* 5, 5, 2).

God rules man, the soul rules the body, the reason rules lust and the other perverted elements in the soul?' By this analogy it is shown plainly enough that servitude is beneficial for some men, and that servitude to God, at least, is beneficial to all.

Now in serving God the soul rightly commands the body, and in the soul itself the reason which is subject to its Lord God rightly commands the lusts and the other perverted elements. That being so, when a man does not serve God, what amount of justice are we to suppose to exist in his being? For if a soul does not serve God it cannot with any kind of justice command the body, nor can a man's reason control the vicious elements in the soul. And if there is no justice in such a man, there can be no sort of doubt that there is no justice in a gathering which consists of such men. Here, then, there is not that 'consent to the law' which makes a mob into a people, and it is 'the weal of the people' that is said to make a 'commonwealth'. As for the 'community of interest' in virtue of which, according to our definition, a gathering of men is called a 'people', is there any need for me to talk about this? Although, to be sure, if you give the matter careful thought, there are no advantages for men who live ungodly lives, the lives of all. those who do not serve God, but serve demons – demons all the more blasphemous in that they desire that sacrifice be offered to them as to gods, though in fact they are most unclean spirits. However, I consider that what I have said about 'a common sense of right' is enough to make it apparent that by this definition people amongst whom there is no justice can never be said to have a commonwealth.

Now if it is said that the Romans in their commonwealth did not serve unclean spirits but good and holy gods, do we have to repeat, time and time again, the same things that we have already said often enough – in fact, more than often enough? Surely no one who has read the earlier books of this work and has reached this point can doubt that the Romans served evil and impure demons? If he can, he is either excessively dense, or unscrupulously argumentative! But, to say no more of the character of the gods the Romans worshipped with sacrifice, it is written in the Law of the true God, 'Anyone who sacrifices to gods instead of to the Lord only, will be extirpated' (Ex. 22.20). This shows that sacrifice to gods, whether good or bad, was against the will of him who uttered this command with so heavy a threat.

22. The true God, to whom alone sacrifice is due

But it may be asked in reply, 'Who is this God you talk of, and how is it proved that he is the only one to whom the Romans owed obedience, and that they should have worshipped no god besides him?' It shows extreme blindness to ask, at this time of day, who this God is! He is the same God whose prophets foretold the events we now see happening. He is the God from whom Abraham received the message, 'In your descendants all nations will be blessed' (Gen. 22.18). And this promise was fulfilled in Christ, who sprang from that line by physical descent, as is acknowledged, willy nilly, even by those who have remained hostile to this name. He is the same God whose divine Spirit spoke through the lips of the men whose prophecies I have quoted in my previous books, prophecies fulfilled in the Church which we see diffused throughout the whole world. He is the God whom Varro, the greatest of Roman scholars, identifies with Jupiter; although he did not realize what he was saying. Still, I thought this worth mentioning, simply because a man of such great learning could not judge this God to be non-existent or of no worth, since he believed him to be identical with his supreme god. More important still, he is the god whom Porphyry, the most learned of philosophers, although the fiercest enemy of the Christians, acknowledges to be a great god, even on the evidence of the oracles of those whom he supposes to be gods.

23. Porphyry on the oracles about Christ given by the gods

For Porphyry produced a book entitled *Philosophy from Oracles* (cf. Bk VII 25n), a description and compilation of responses, ostensibly divine, on matters of philosophical interest, in which he says (to quote his own words, translated from the Greek), 'The following reply, in verse, was given by Apollo to one who asked what god he should propitiate in order to recall his wife from Christianity.' Then follow these words, purporting to be the utterance of Apollo:

> You might perhaps find it easier to write on water in printed characters, or fly like a bird through the air spreading light wings to the breeze, than recall to her senses an impious, polluted wife. Let her go as she pleases, persisting in her vain delusions, singing in lamentation for a god who died in delusions, who was condemned by right-thinking judges, and killed in hideous fashion by the worst of deaths, a death bound with iron.

Then after those verses of Apollo (here given in a prose translation), Porphyry goes on to say, 'In these verses Apollo made plain the incurability of the belief of Christians, saying that the Jews uphold God more than the Christians.' See how he denigrates Christ in preferring the Jews to the Christians, when he proclaims that the Jews are upholders of God, for he expounds the verses of Apollo, where he says that Christ was slain by right-thinking judges, as if it meant that the Jews passed a just judgement and Christ deserved his punishment. What the lying prophet of Apollo said, and Porphyry believed, or what Porphyry perhaps falsely invented as the utterance of the prophet, is their affair. We shall see later how far Porphyry is consistent with himself, or rather how far he makes those oracles of his agree with one another.

Here, at any rate, he says that the Jews, as upholders of God's rights, passed a just judgement on Christ, in decreeing that he was to be tortured by the worst of deaths. And since Porphyry bears this testimony to the God of the Jews, he ought to have listened to that God when he says, 'Anyone who sacrifices to other gods, instead of to the Lord alone, will be extirpated.' However, let us come to more obvious matters, and hear Porphyry's statement about the greatness of the God of the Jews. For example, in answer to his question, 'Which is better, word (that is, reason) or law?' Apollo, says Porphyry, 'replied in these verses'. Porphyry goes on to quote the verses, from which I select the following, as sufficient: 'in God, the begetter and the king before all things, at whom heaven trembles, and earth and sea and the hidden depths of the underworld and the very divinities shudder in dread; their law is the Father whom the holy Hebrews greatly honour.'[5] In this oracle of his own god Apollo, Porphyry speaks of the God of the Hebrews as so great that the divinities themselves shudder in dread at him. Since, then, this is the God who has said, 'Anyone who sacrifices to other gods will be extirpated', it surprises me that Porphyry himself did not shudder in terror of being rooted out for offering sacrifice to other gods.

Now this philosopher has also some good things to say about Christ, when he appears to have forgotten that insult we have just spoken of, or when it seems as if the malicious remarks his gods had made were uttered in their sleep, while in their waking moments they recognized his goodness and praised him as he deserved. Porphyry, in fact, says, with the air of one on the point of producing some amazing and incredible intelligence, 'What I am going to say may certainly appear startling to some. I mean the fact that the gods have pronounced Christ to have been extremely devout, and have said that he has become immortal, and that they mention him in terms of commendation; whereas the Christians, by their account, are polluted and contaminated and entangled in error; and there are many other such slanders they issue against them.' Then he proceeds to quote some of these supposed slanders of the gods against the Christians, and continues, 'On the other hand, to those who asked whether Christ was God, Hecate replied, "You know that the immortal soul goes on its way after it leaves the body; whereas when it is cut off from wisdom it wanders for ever. That soul belongs to a man of outstanding piety; this they worship because truth is a stranger to them." '[6] Then, after quoting this supposed oracle he adds his own interpretation:

Thus Hecate said that he was a most devout man, and that his soul, like the souls of the other devout men, was endowed after death with the immortality it deserved; and that Christians in their ignorance worship this soul. Moreover, to those who asked: 'Why, then was he condemned?' the goddess gave this oracular

---

[5]Lactantius quotes part of this oracle in Greek (*De Ira Dei*, 2, 312).
[6]Part of the Greek is quoted in Eusebius, *Demonstratio Evangelica*, 3, 6.

reply: 'The body, indeed, is always liable to torments that sap its strength; but the souls of the pious dwell in a heavenly abode. Now that soul of which we speak gave a fatal gift to other souls, those to whom the fates did not grant that they should possess the gifts of the gods or that they should have knowledge of immortal Jupiter; that fatal gift is entanglement in error. That is why they were hated by the gods, because, not being fated to know God or to receive gifts from the gods, they were given by this man the fatal gift of entanglement in error. For all that, he himself was devout, and, like other devout men, passed into heaven. And so you shall not slander him, but pity the insanity of men. From him comes for them a ready peril of headlong disaster.'

Is anyone so dense as to fail to realize that these oracles were either the inventions of a cunning man, a bitter enemy of the Christians, or the responses of demons devised with a like intent? For, surely, their purpose in praising Christ was to ensure that their vituperation of Christians would be accepted as truthful, so that, if possible, they might cut off the way of everlasting salvation, the way by which men and women become Christians. They feel, no doubt, that it is no hindrance to their ingenious and protean maleficence if they are believed when they praise Christ, provided that their vituperation of the Christians is also believed. Their intention is that when a man has believed both praise and slander they may turn him into an admirer of Christ, but an admirer who has no wish to become a Christian; and so Christ, though praised by him, will not set him free from the domination of those demons. And this is particularly true because they praise Christ in such terms that anyone who believes in the kind of Christ they proclaim does not become a genuine Christian but a Photinian heretic, one who acknowledges Christ only as a man, not as God also. That is why such a man cannot be saved by him, and cannot escape or undo the snares of those lying demons.

We, on our side, can approve neither Apollo's vituperation of Christ nor Hecate's praise of him. Apollo, we remember, would have it believed that Christ was an unrighteous man, put to death, he says, by right-thinking judges; Hecate, that he was a man of supreme piety, but only a man. However, the aim of both is the same, to make men refuse to become Christians; for unless they become Christians they cannot be rescued from the power of those false gods. But our philosopher, or rather all those who believe such purported oracles against the Christians, must first, if they can, succeed in harmonizing Hecate and Apollo on the subject of Christ, so that they unite in either his condemnation or his praise. Yet even if they succeeded in this, we should none the less give a wide berth to such delusive demons, whether slanderers of Christ or admirers. And since, in fact, their god and their goddess are in disagreement, and he slanders Christ while she praises him, then surely men in general do not believe them when they vituperate the Christians, if their own thinking is sound.

Now when Porphyry – or Hecate – praises Christ, while adding that he himself gave to the Christians the fatal gift of entanglement in error, he does at the same time reveal, as he supposes, the causes of his error. But before I explain those causes in his own words, I ask first: If Christ gave this fatal gift of entanglement in error, did he do this voluntarily or involuntarily? If voluntarily, how could he be righteous? If involuntarily, how could he be blessed? But now let us listen to the causes of the error. 'There are in a certain part of the world', he says,

> very small earthly spirits, subject to the authority of evil demons. The wise men of the Hebrews (and this Jesus was also one of them, as you have heard from the oracles of Apollo, quoted above) warned religious men against these evil demons and lesser spirits, and forbade them to pay attention to them, telling their hearers rather to venerate the gods of heaven, but, above all, to worship God the Father. But this is what the gods also teach; and we have shown above how they advise us to turn our thoughts to God, and everywhere bid us worship him. Uninstructed and ungodly natures, however, to which fate has not granted the gifts of the gods and the knowledge of immortal Jupiter, have not listened to the gods and to inspired men; and so they have rejected all the gods, while so far from hating the forbidden demons, they offer them reverence. While pretending to worship God, they do not perform those acts by which alone God is adored. For God, as being the father of all, has indeed no lack of anything; but it is well for us when we adore him by means of justice, chastity, and other virtues, making our life itself a prayer to him by imitating him and seeking to know him. For seeking to know him purifies us, while imitation of him deifies us by bringing our disposition in line with his.

Porphyry certainly did well in thus proclaiming God the Father, and in telling of the conduct by which he is to be worshipped; and the prophetic books of the Hebrews are full of such precepts, when the life of holiness is commanded or praised. But in respect of the Christians, Porphyry's mistakes, or his calumnies, are as great as the demons (his supposed gods) could desire. He seems to assume that anyone would have difficulty in recalling the obscenities and indecencies which were performed in the theatre as acts of homage to the gods, and in observing what is read and said and heard in our churches, or what is offered to the true God, and in realizing, from this comparison, where the building up of moral character is to be found, and where its ruin. Who told him or suggested to him such a groundless and obvious lie as that the Christians revere, instead of hating, the demons whose worship was forbidden to the Hebrews? It could only have been a diabolic spirit. For in fact the God whom the wise men of the Hebrews worshipped forbids sacrifices to be offered even to the holy angels and the powers of God, those angels and powers whom we venerate and love, in this mortal pilgrimage of ours, as our completely blessed fellow citizens. He forbids this in a voice of thunder in his Law, which he gave to his Hebrew people, when he said, in words heavy with menace, 'Anyone who sacrifices to other gods will be extirpated' (Ex. 22.20). Now it might be supposed that this precept forbids sacrifice to those most evil demons and the earthly spirits, which Porphyry calls 'least' or 'lesser'; for even these are called 'gods' in the sacred Scriptures – of the Gentiles, that is, not in those of the Hebrews. This is made quite clear by the seventy translators in one of the psalms, where they say, 'For all the gods of the nations are demons' (Ps. 96.5). But to prevent any such supposition that sacrifice, while forbidden to those demons, was allowed to all or some of the heavenly beings, these words immediately follow: 'instead of the Lord alone', that is, 'to the Lord alone'. I say this in case anyone imagines that the words 'to the Lord alone', *Domino soli*, means 'our Lord *the sun*', to whom sacrifice is to be offered. That this is not the meaning can easily be discovered by a reference to the Greek version.

The God of the Hebrews, then, to whom this eminent philosopher gives such impressive testimony, gave to his Hebrew people the Law, written in Hebrew, a Law not obscure and unknown, but by now of wide renown among all nations. And in this Law it is written: 'Anyone who sacrifices to other gods, instead of to the Lord only, will be extirpated.' What need is there for a detailed inquiry on this subject into his Law and into his prophets? Why, the need is not for an inquiry, for the relevant passages are not hard to find or rare; all that is required is the collection and insertion in this discussion of mine of the obvious and frequent passages in which it is made as clear as daylight that the true and supreme God willed that sacrifice should be offered to no other being whatsoever, but to himself alone. Here is one statement, brief, yet certainly impressive, menacing, in fact, but with truth in the menace – a statement of the God whom the most learned of the pagans proclaims in such remarkable terms. It is a warning that must be heard, feared, and acted on, lest the disobedient be rooted out in consequence. 'Anyone who sacrifices to other gods', he says 'instead of to the Lord alone, will be extirpated.' This is not because God stands in need of anything, but because it is to our advantage to belong to him. For it is to him that the psalmist sings, in the holy Scriptures of the Hebrews, 'I have said to the Lord: "You are my God, because you have no need of my goods"' (Ps. 16.2).

And yet it is we ourselves – we, his City – who are his best, his most glorious sacrifice. The mystic symbol of this sacrifice we celebrate in our oblations, familiar to the faithful, as we have maintained in previous books. For the sacrificial victims offered by the Jews, as a foreshadowing of what was to come, were destined to come to an end. This was declared by divine oracles through the lips of the holy prophets, in resounding tones, saying that the nations from the furthest East to the furthest West would offer one sacrifice, as we now see happening. I have extracted as many of those oracles as seemed sufficient, and have already scattered them throughout this work. It follows that justice is found where God, the one supreme God, rules an obedient City according to his grace, forbidding sacrifice to any being save himself alone; and where in consequence the soul rules the body in all men who belong to this City and obey God, and the reason faithfully rules the vices in a lawful system of subordination; so that just as the individual righteous man lives on the basis of faith (Hab. 2.4) which is active in love (Gal. 5.6), so the association, or people, of righteous men lives on the same basis of faith, active in love, the love with which a man loves God as God ought to be loved, and loves his neighbour as himself. But where this justice does not exist, there is certainly no 'association of men united by a common sense of right and by a community of interest'. Therefore there is no commonwealth; for where there is no 'people', there is no 'weal of the people'.

24. An alternative definition of 'people' and 'commonwealth'

If, on the other hand, another definition than this is found for a 'people', for example, if one should say, 'A people is the association of a multitude of rational beings united by a common agreement on the objects of their love', then it follows that to observe the character of a particular people we must examine the objects of its love. And yet, whatever those objects, if it is the association of a multitude not of animals but of rational beings, and is united by a common agreement about the objects of its love, then there is no absurdity in applying to it the title of a 'people'. And, obviously, the better the objects of this agreement, the better the people; the worse the objects of this love, the worse the people. By this definition of ours, the Roman people is a people and its estate is indubitably a commonwealth. But as for the objects of that people's love – both in the earliest times and in subsequent periods – and the morality of that people as it proceeded to bloody strife of parties and then to the social and civil wars, and corrupted and disrupted that very unity which is, as it were, the health of a people – for all this we have the witness of history; and I have had a great deal to say about it in my preceding books. And yet I shall not make that a reason for asserting that a people is not really a people or that a state is not a commonwealth, so long as there remains an association of some kind or other between a multitude of rational beings united by a common agreement on the objects of its love. However, what I have said about the Roman people and the Roman commonwealth I must be understood to have said and felt about those of the Athenians and of any other Greeks, or of that former Babylon of the Assyrians, when they exercised imperial rule, whether on a small or a large scale, in their commonwealths – and indeed about any other nation whatsoever. For God is not the ruler of the city of the impious, because it disobeys his commandment that sacrifice should be offered to himself alone. The purpose of this law was that in that city the soul should rule over the body and reason over the vicious elements, in righteousness and faith. And because God does not rule there the general characteristic of that city is that it is devoid of true justice.

25. True virtues impossible without true religion

The fact is that the soul may appear to rule the body and the reason to govern the vicious elements in the most praiseworthy fashion; and yet if the soul and reason do not serve God as God himself has commanded that he should be served, then they do not in any way exercise the right kind of rule over the body and the vicious propensities. For what kind of a mistress over the body and the vices can a mind be that is ignorant of the true God and is not subjected to his rule, but instead is prostituted to the corrupting influence of vicious demons? Thus the virtues which the mind imagines it possesses, by means of which it rules the body and the vicious elements, are themselves vices rather than virtues, if the mind does not bring them into relation with God in order to achieve anything whatsoever and to maintain that achievement. For although the virtues are reckoned by some people to be genuine and honourable when they are related only to themselves and are sought for no other end, even then they are puffed up and proud, and so are to be accounted vices rather than virtues. For just as it is not something derived from the physical body itself that gives life to that body, but something above it, so it is not something that comes from man, but something above man, that makes his life blessed; and this is true not only of man but of every heavenly dominion and power whatsoever.

26. The peace of the people alienated from God is made use of by God's People on their pilgrimage

Thus, as the soul is the life of the physical body, so God is the blessedness of man's life. As the holy Scriptures of the Hebrews say, 'Blessed is the people, whose God is the Lord' (Ps. 144.15). It follows that a people alienated from that God must be wretched. Yet even such a people loves a peace of its own, which is not to be rejected; but it will not possess it in the end, because it does not make good use of it before the end. Meanwhile, however, it is important for us also that this people should possess this peace in this life, since so long as the two cities are intermingled we also make use of the peace of Babylon – although the People of God is by faith set free from Babylon, so that in the meantime they are only pilgrims in the midst of her. That is why the Apostle instructs the Church to pray for kings of that city and those in high positions, adding these words: 'that we may lead a quiet and peaceful life with all devotion and love' (1 Tim 2.2). And when the prophet Jeremiah predicted to the ancient People of God the coming captivity, and bade them, by God's inspiration, to go obediently to Babylon, serving God even by their patient endurance, he added his own advice that prayers should be offered for Babylon, 'because in her peace is your peace' (Jer. 29.7) – meaning, of course, the temporal peace of the meantime, which is shared by good and bad alike.

27. The peace of God's servants, a perfect tranquility, not experienced in this life

In contrast, the peace which is our special possession is ours even in this life, a peace with God through faith; and it will be ours for ever, a peace with God through open vision (cf. 2 Cor. 5.7). But peace here and now, whether the peace shared by all men or our own special possession, is such that it affords a solace for our wretchedness rather than the joy of blessedness. Our righteousness itself, too, though genuine, in virtue of the genuine Ultimate Good to which it is referred, is nevertheless only such as to consist in the forgiveness of sins rather than in the perfection of virtues. The evidence for this is in the prayer of the whole City of God on pilgrimage in the world, which, as we know, cries out to God through the lips of all its members: 'Forgive us our debts, as we forgive our debtors' (Matt. 6.12). And this prayer is not effective for those whose 'faith, without works, is dead' (James 2.17) but only for those whose 'faith is put into action through love' (Gal. 5.6). For such a prayer is needed by righteous men because the reason, though subjected to God, does not have complete command over the vices in this mortal state and in the 'corruptible body which weighs heavy on the soul' (Wis. 9.15). In fact, even though command be exercised over the vices it is assuredly not by any means without a conflict. And even when a man fights well and even gains the mastery by conquering and subduing such foes, still in this situation of weakness something is all too likely to creep in to cause sin, if not in hasty action, at least in a casual remark or a fleeting thought.

For this reason there is no perfect peace so long as command is exercised over the vicious propensities, because the battle is fraught with peril while those vices that resist are being reduced to submission, while those which have been overcome are not yet triumphed over in peaceful security, but are repressed under a rule still triubled by anxieties. Thus we are in the midst of these temptations, about which we find this brief saying amongst the divine oracles: 'Is a man's life on earth anything but temptation?' (Job 7.1); and who can presume that his life is of such a kind that he has no need to say to God, 'Forgive us our debts', unless he is a man of overwhelming conceit, not a truly great man, but one puffed up and swollen with pride, who is with justice resisted by him who gives grace to the humble, as it says in the Scriptures, 'God resists the proud, but he gives his favour to the humble' (James 4.6, 1 Pet. 5.5).

In this life, therefore, justice in each individual exists when God rules and man obeys, when the mind rules the body and reason governs the vices even when they rebel, either by subduing them or by resisting them, while from God himself favour is sought for good deeds and pardon for offences, and thanks are duly offered to him for benefits received. But in that ultimate peace, to which this justice should be related, and for the attainment of which this justice is to be maintained, our nature will be healed by immortality and incorruption and will have no perverted elements, and nothing at all, in ourselves or any other, will be in conflict with any one of us. And so reason will not need to rule the vices, since there will be no vices, but God will hold sway over man, and the soul over the body, and in this state our delight and facility in obeying will be matched by our felicity in living and reigning. There, for each and every one, this state will be eternal, and its eternity will be assured; and for that reason the peace of this blessedness, or the blessedness of this peace, will be the Supreme Good.

28. The end of the wicked

In contrast with this, however, the wretchedness of those who do not belong to this City of God will be everlasting. This is called also 'the second death', because the soul cannot be said to be alive in that state, when it is separated from the life of God, nor can the body, when it is subjected to eternal torments. And this is precisely the reason why this 'second death' will be harder to bear, because it cannot come to an end in death. But here a question arises; for just as wretchedness is the opposite of blessedness, and death of life, so war is evidently the opposite of peace. And the question is rightly asked: What war, or what kind of war, can be understood to exist in the final state of the wicked, corresponding, by way of contrast, to that peace which is proclaimed with joyful praises in the final state of the good? Now anyone who puts this question should observe what it is that is harmful and destructive in war; and he will see that it is precisely the mutual opposition and conflict of the forces engaged. What war, then, can be imagined more serious and more bitter than a struggle in which the will is so at odds with the feelings and the feelings with the will, that their hostility cannot be ended by the victory of either – a struggle in which the violence of pain is in such conflict with the nature of the body that neither can yield to the other? For in this life, when such a conflict occurs, either pain wins, and death takes away feeling, or nature conquers, and health removes the pain. But in that other life, pain continues to torment, while nature lasts to feel the pain. Neither ceases to exist, lest the punishment also should cease.

These, then, are the final states of good and evil. The first we should seek to attain, the latter we should strive to escape. And since it is through a judgement that the good will pass to the one, and the evil to the other, it is of this judgement that I shall deal, as far as God grants, in the book which follows.

5. Augustine of Hippo – Letters 189, 220

Letter 189 (417 CE)

Augustine sends greetings in the Lord to Boniface, his distinguished, deservedly illustrious, and honoured son.

(1) I had already written to your beloved self;[1] however, when I was looking for the opportunity to get my letter to you, my dearest son Faustus arrived on the scene, on his way to your distinguished self. When he agreed to carry the letter that I had already written to your kind self, he intimated to me that you were very eager to have me write you something that would fortify you for the everlasting security for which you hope in Christ Jesus our Lord. Although I was busy, he pressed me not to postpone doing this, with an urgency that you will recognise, as his affection for you is indeed single-minded. In order therefore to meet his haste, I preferred to write something to you rather hurriedly, than to hamper your eagerness for matters religious, my distinguished and deservedly illustrious and honoured son.

(2) Briefly, then, I am able to say the following: *Love the Lord your God with all your heart and with all your soul and with all your strength, and love your neighbour as yourself* [Mt 22.37, 39; Mk 12.30–1; Lk 10.27; cf. Deut 6.5; Lev 19.18].

That is the saying which the Lord gave us as a summary when he was on earth; as he said in the Gospel: *On these two commandments hang the whole of the Law and the prophets* [Mt 22.40]. Make daily progress, then, in this love, both through prayer and through doing good. Then, with the help of God, who both commanded and granted that love, it may be nourished and grow, until it is perfect, and makes you perfect. For it is charity itself, which (as the apostle says) *is spread in our hearts through the Holy Spirit, who is given to us* [Rom 5.5]. This is also what he referred to in the words, *Charity is the fullness of the Law* [Rom 13.10]. It is charity again through which faith works, to quote the apostle once more: *Neither circumcision nor the foreskin has any value, but faith, which works through love* [Gal 5.6].

(3) In this love all our holy forefathers and patriarchs and prophets and apostles found favour with God. In it all the true martyrs fought against the devil to the point of shedding their blood; and they were victorious just because it neither failed nor *grew cold* [cf. Mt 24.12]. In it all the worthy faithful make daily progress in their desire to reach not a kingdom of mortals but the kingdom of heaven, not a temporary but an everlasting inheritance, not gold and silver but the incorruptible riches possessed by angels, to attain not a few of this world's goods – which cause you fear while you are alive and which you cannot take with you when you die – but rather the vision of God.

---

[1]Probably Letter 185.

The sweetness and delight of the vision of God surpasses in beauty not only earthly bodies, but the heavenly bodies also; it surpasses in splendour every single just and holy soul; it surpasses in loveliness the angels and powers above. It surpasses anything that we can say of it – or rather anything that we can imagine. However, we oughtn't for that reason to lose hope in so great a promise – for it is a great one; rather, because the promise was made by someone very great, we ought to trust that we shall be granted it. As the blessed apostle John said: *We are sons of God, and what we will be has not yet appeared. We know that when it does appear we will be like him, since we shall see him as he is* [1 Jn 3.2].

(4) You must not think that no one who serves as a soldier, using arms for warfare, can be acceptable to God. The holy David was one such, and the Lord offered a great a witness to him. Very many other just men of the same period were also soldiers. So was the centurion who spoke to the Lord as follows: *I am not worthy for you to enter under my roof; however, only say the word, and my boy will be healed. For I am a man placed under authority, and I have soldiers under me; I say to someone 'Go!' and he goes; and to someone else 'Come!' and he comes; I say to my servant, 'Do this' and he does it* [Mt 8.8–10; Lk 7.6–9]. The Lord said of him, *In truth I tell you: I have not found such faith in Israel.*

Cornelius was also a soldier. An angel was sent to him, who said, *Cornelius, your alms have been accepted and your prayers have been heard* [Acts 10.1–33]. The angel advised Cornelius to send for the blessed apostle Peter and to hear from him what he should do. And the man whom Cornelius sent to ask the apostle to come to him was also a devout soldier.

They were also soldiers, who came to be baptised by John, the holy forerunner of the Lord, and *the friend of the bridegroom* [Jn 3.29]. (Indeed, the Lord said of him, *Of those born of woman, none greater than John the Baptist has ever arisen*) [Mt 11.11]. They asked him what they should do; and he replied: *Do not intimidate anyone; do not bring false charges against anyone; and be satisfied with your wages* [Lk 3.14]. He certainly was not forbidding them to live under arms as soldiers when he instructed them to be satisfied with their pay.[2]

(5) It is true that those who abandon all such worldly activities and serve God also through the complete chastity of celibacy hold a higher place with him. However, as the apostle says, *Each one has his own gift from God, one in this way, another in that* [1 Cor 7.7]. So others are fighting invisible enemies on your behalf by praying, while you struggle against visible barbarians on their behalf by fighting. If only everyone shared a single faith, so that the struggle would be less and the devil and his angels more easily vanquished!

However, it is necessary in this age for the citizens of the kingdom of heaven, surrounded as they are by the lost and the impious, to be vexed by temptations, so

---

[2]A. offers parallel scriptural arguments at Letter 138.9–15.

that they can be trained and tested *like gold in a furnace* [Wisd 3.5–6]. We oughtn't therefore before the time is right to wish to live only with the holy and the just; then we might deserve to be granted that in its proper time.

(6) When you are arming yourself for battle, then, consider this first of all, that your courage, even your physical courage, is a gift from God. Then you won't think of using a gift from God to act against God. When one makes a promise, one must keep faith, even with an enemy against whom one is waging a war (Cicero, *De officiis* 3.99–115). How much more so with a friend, for whose sake one is fighting! Peace ought to be what you want, war only what necessity demands. Then God may free you from necessity and preserve you in peace. For you don't seek peace in order to stir up war; no – war is waged in order to obtain peace (*City of God* XIX.12, above). Be a peacemaker, therefore, even in war, so that by conquering them you bring the benefit of peace even to those you defeat. For, says the Lord, *Blessed are the peacemakers, for they shall be called the sons of God* [Mt 5.9]. If, indeed, human peace is so delightful because of the temporary security that belongs to mortals, how much more delightful is divine peace, because of the everlasting security that belongs to the angels. Therefore it ought to be necessity, and not your will, that destroys an enemy who is fighting you. And just as you use force against the rebel or opponent, so you ought now to use mercy towards the defeated or the captive, and particularly so when there is no fear that peace will be disturbed.

(7) Let your character be embellished by marital chastity, by sobriety and by simplicity of life. It is certainly shameful if someone who is undefeated by another human being is defeated by lust, or undefeated by iron, but overwhelmed by wine. If you are short of worldly wealth, don't seek it on earth by doing harm. If you possess it, preserve it in heaven by doing good. Wealth, when it turns up, oughtn't to swell a manly and Christian spirit; when it goes away, it oughtn't to break it. Rather we should reflect on the words of the Lord: *Where your treasure is, there will your heart be also* [Mt 6.21; Lk 12.34]; and when we hear that, we should 'lift up our heart', and we should not be untruthful in making the response which you know that we make.[3]

(8) I know, moreover, that you are very zealous in such matters; I am delighted by your reputation and I congratulate you in the Lord. Consequently, this letter might serve you as a mirror in which you can see what you are like, rather than one from which you learn what you ought to be like. However, if you find in either this letter or in sacred scripture anything you still lack for a life of goodness, then make urgent efforts in prayer and in action to acquire it. Give thanks also for what you do possess to God, as the source of the goodness you have, and in every good deed that

---

[3]During the liturgy of the Eucharist, in response to the bishop's invitation 'lift up your heart', the congregation responded 'we have lifted it up to the Lord', symbolizing their intention of transcending worldly goods and secular motivations for heavenly, eternal ones.

you do, *give* him the *glory* [cf. Ps 115(113b). 1], and yourself the humility. As it is written: *every excellent gift and every perfect present comes down from above from the father of lights* [Jas 1.17].

However much you advance, though, in the love of God or of your neighbour and in true piety, however long you are involved in this life, do not believe that you are sinless. *Surely human life on the earth is a time of testing* [Job 7.1]. Indeed, as long as you are in the body, it is continually necessary for you when you pray to say the words the Lord taught us, *Forgive us our debts, just as we ourselves forgive our debtors* [Mt 6.12; cf. Lk 11.4]. Remember to pardon quickly anyone who sins against you and begs mercy from you, so that you can pray truthfully, and are in a position to obtain mercy for your sins.

I have written this in haste to your dear self, as I was being pressed by our messenger, who is himself in a hurry. However, I give thanks to God that in some way at least I have not failed to satisfy your worthy desire. May the mercy of God ever preserve you, my distinguished, deservedly illustrious and honoured son.

Letter 220 (428 CE)

Augustine greets the lord Boniface, his son, whom he commends to the protection and guidance of the mercy of God for his present and his eternal security.

(1) I could never find a more trustworthy person, nor one who had easier access to your hearing when bringing my letters, than the man whom the Lord has now provided, the deacon Paul, the servant and minister of Christ, a man very dear to both of us. Consequently, I am able to speak to you, not to boost the power and honour that you wield in this unkind age, nor to safeguard your corruptible and mortal flesh – for that is ephemeral and it is always uncertain how long it will last. No, I address you rather on the subject of the security that Christ has promised us, he who was dishonoured and crucified here precisely in order to teach us to disdain rather than love the goods of this world, and to love and hope from him for the future that he revealed in his own resurrection. For *he rose from the dead, and now he does not die and death no longer governs him* [Rom 6.9].

(2) I know that there is no shortage of people who love you as far as the life of this world goes, and offer you advice by its lights, advice that is sometimes beneficial and sometimes not. After all, they are human, and they are wise as far as they can be with regard to the present, when they don't know what will happen the next day. However, as far as God is concerned, it's not easy for anyone to make it their care to prevent the loss of your soul. This is not because there's no one available who might do it; but rather because it's difficult to find a time when they can talk to you about such things. I've always longed to do this myself, but I've never found opportunity or time to discuss such matters with you. But I ought to discuss them with someone I love dearly in Christ.

Moreover, you know what state I was in when you saw me at Hippo, on the occasion on which you were good enough to visit me. I was so tired by my physical weakness that I could scarcely speak. So please listen to me, my son, now that I'm at least conversing with you by letter. I was never able to write to you when you were in a dangerous situation because I was thinking of the risk to the bearer, and also because I was wary of my letter falling into the hands of people I didn't want to have it. I beg your pardon, then, if you think I was more fearful than I should have been; still, I have said that I was afraid.

(3) Listen to me, then; or rather to the Lord our God, through the ministry of my own weak person. Remember what you were like when your first wife (of devoted memory) was still in her body, and when her death was still fresh: how the emptiness of this age made you shudder, and how you longed to be in the service of God! We know about, and we are witnesses to, the conversations you held with us at Tubuna on the soul and on your own intentions. My brother Alypius and I were alone with you.

In my view, indeed, the earthly concerns that fill you at present[4] cannot be powerful enough to blot that out utterly from your memory. Surely you actually desired to abandon all the public activities with which you were busy, and to give yourself instead to sacred leisure by living the life of the servants of God, that is of monks.

What was it that held you back from doing so, except this: you had in mind, and we were pointing out, the degree to which your activities were benefiting the churches of Christ?[5] If, that is, you were acting with the single intention of allowing them to lead a *quiet and peaceful life*, as the apostle says, protected from harassment from the barbarian invasions, *in all piety and chastity* [1 Tim 2.2]. Meanwhile, you yourself would have been looking for nothing from this world, except what you needed to support this present life of yours, and of those dear to you, girded as you would have been with a belt of chaste celibacy, and armed, in the midst of physical weapons, with the safer and stronger weapons of the spirit.

(4) While we were rejoicing that you had make this your purpose, you set sail, and then you married a wife. The sailing you undertook out of the obedience that (according to the apostle) you owed to *higher authorities* [Rom 13.1]. However, you would not have taken a wife had you not been overcome by lust and abandoned the celibacy you had adopted.

I must admit that when I discovered this I was amazed and dumbstruck. My sorrow was eased to some extent by hearing that you wouldn't have been willing to marry her had she not become a Catholic. Despite this, though, the heresy of those who deny the true son of God had so much influence in your household that

---

[4]A. probably refers to Boniface's career ambitions which had progressed in conjunction with his decision to take a wealthy Arian woman, Pelagia, as his second wife, and to allow their daughter and servants to be baptised as Arian Christians. Arianism was the religion of the Goths, whose political and military fortunes in Italy, Gaul, and now also in Africa, were rapidly increasing.

[5]A. and Alypius persuaded Boniface not to join a monastery, but to continue as a soldier defending Roman Africa from long-standing Berber, and from mounting Gothic, threats.

your own daughter was baptised by its adherents. But now, if the rumours that have reached us are not untrue (if only they were!), even maidservants of yours who were consecrated to God have been rebaptised by those heretics! This is a dreadful thing, and we ought to be weeping copious tears over it. People also say that even your wife was not enough for you, and that you defiled yourself by associating with some mistresses or other. Perhaps they are lying.

(5) What am I to say about the many dreadful activities which you pursued after your marriage, and which everybody knew about?[6] You are a Christian; you have a heart; you fear God. Reflect for yourself on the things I am unwilling to mention; and you will discover the number of misdeeds for which you ought to do penance. I believe that God is sparing you for precisely that purpose, and keeping you free of all danger so that you may perform penance as you ought, but on condition that you listen to the words of scripture: *Do not be slow to turn to the Lord, and do not delay from day to day* [Ecclus. 5.7].

You say that your cause is just; I am not judge of it, since I am unable to hear both sides. However, whatever your case is like, there is no need now to examine or debate it; surely you are not able to deny in the presence of God that you wouldn't have reached these straits, if you hadn't been so fond of the goods of this world?[7] Yet as a servant of God, which was how we knew you before, you ought to have disdained them completely, and held them to be worthless. If any were offered you, you ought to have taken them for religious purposes. If any were denied you or merely entrusted to you, you oughtn't to have tried to get them in such a way that they led you to your present straits. For now, even though the things that attract you are valueless, dreadful things are being done, a few by you yourself, and a lot on your behalf. This, even though the things that you're fearing can only harm you for a short time, if at all; but what's being perpetrated can do you genuine harm, and for ever.

(6) If I may say one thing on the subject, it is this: many people associate closely with you in order to preserve your authority and security. Who cannot see that even if all of them are faithful and there is no need to fear treachery from any of them, still, surely, they desire to use you to get hold of goods which they too find attractive not in the light of God, but in the light of the world? As a result you are forced to gratify the desires of others, while you ought to be restraining and checking your own. To achieve this, you need to do a lot of things displeasing to God.[8] Even then, desires like this aren't fully gratified. They are easier to curtail in those who love God than

---

[6]A. refers here to Boniface's open revolt against imperial forces loyal to empress Galla Placidia. Either Flavius Aetius or Flavius Constantius Felix, rival generals under the empress, is thought to have informed Boniface, falsely, that he had been ordered to return to Italy. Boniface seemed aware that a plot was being hatched against him, and defied the orders, subsequently defeating a series of regiments sent to Africa against him.

[7]Whatever the truth of Boniface's version of events, A. locates the source of the spiralling intrigue and violence surrounding Boniface in the latter's personal ambitions.

[8]The implication is that Boniface has had to tolerate acts of plunder and other civil disorder from his troops in order to retain their loyalty.

in those who love the world, and sometimes they can be satisfied. That is why holy scripture says: *Do not love the world, nor the things that are in the world. If anyone does love the world, the father's love is not in him. For everything that is in the world is lust of the flesh, and lust of the eyes, and ostentation of this age, which does not come from the Father, but from the world. And this world and all its lust will pass away. But anyone who does the will of God remains for ever, just as God too remains for ever* [1 Jn 2.15–17].

Faced with so many armed men, whose desires must be fostered and whose ferocity must be feared, when, when, I ask, will you be able, if not to satisfy the lust of those who love this earth (for that can never be done), just to feed it a little, to prevent further destruction of everything? Only, perhaps, if you do things that God forbids and threatens punishment on those who do them. As you can see, the result has been so much damage that now almost nothing, however valueless, can be found to plunder.

(7) Next, what am I to say of the devastation wrought in Africa? The barbarians of Africa are succeeding here without meeting any resistance so long as you are in your present state, preoccupied with your own needs, and are organising nothing to prevent this disaster. When Boniface was appointed in Africa to be *comes* of the Household and of Africa,[9] with high authority and a vast army, a man who as tribune[10] had pacified all the same tribes by attacking them and fighting them with only a few allied troops, would anyone have believed this? Would anyone have feared that by now the barbarians would have become so bold, have advanced so far, have caused so much devastation, have plundered so widely, have made deserts of so many places that were full of people? Surely, anyone would have predicted that whenever you assumed your position as *comes,* the barbarians of Africa would be not only tamed, but even, eventually, tributary members of the Roman empire.[11] Now, though, you can see how human hopes have been turned upside down. I need not discuss this with you at greater length: you will have more thoughts on this topic than I have words.

(8) Perhaps, though, you will reply to this that the blame for such failures must be laid upon various people who have done you harm, and have repaid your dutiful virtues not with corresponding co-operation, but with the opposite. I am not in a position to hear each side of this case or to judge it. Instead, you must look at your own case and examine it, and recognise that it is not between you and some other

---

[9]He was appointed to this post in AD 425. It gave him command of a regiment of the army, the *domestici,* or Household Guard. The *comes* of Africa was field commander of the Roman army in the province of Africa Proconsularis, the capital city of which was Carthage.

[10]A. has in mind a time ten years earlier (417) when Boniface commanded a small unit of troops and defeated tribes of nomadic Berbers who had overrun the southern frontier of the Roman province of Numidia.

[11]A. refers here to the long-standing Roman policy of pacifying migrating tribes of barbarians by offering them military, political and commercial alliances with the empire.

human beings, but between you and God. If you are living faithfully in Christ, you ought to be afraid of offending him.

My own attention, by contrast, is focused on cases of a higher nature; for people ought to be attributing the present sorry suffering of Africa to their own sins. Yet I don't want you to be numbered among the evil and wicked persons who are used by God as a scourge to inflict temporary punishments on whomever he wishes. For God keeps everlasting punishment in store for the wicked, unless they reform; yet he makes just use of their evil purposes to heap temporary troubles upon others.

You, though, attend to God; you, meditate on Christ, who has provided such great goods for us, though he himself endured great evils. All those who desire to reach his kingdom and live for ever in blessedness with him and under him, on top of this *love* their *enemies,* doing *good to those who hate* them and praying for those at whose hands they suffer harassment [Mt 5.44; Lk 6.27–8]; and even if for the sake of discipline they occasionally exercise an unpleasant severity, even in this they don't abandon their single-minded love.

Consequently, if the Roman empire provides you with good things, even if they are ephemeral and earthly (for it is an earthly, not a heavenly, institution and can only provide what is in its power); if then it has bestowed good things upon you, do not return evil for good. However, if it has inflicted evil on you, *do not return evil for evil* [Rom 12.17; 1 Thess. 5.15]. Neither do I wish to debate nor am competent to judge which of the two is the case. I am addressing a Christian: neither *return* evil for good, nor *evil for evil.*

(9) Perhaps you will reply to me: 'What do you want me to do when pressed by such necessity?' Are you asking me to give advice in the light of this world on how to safeguard this ephemeral security of yours, and on how to preserve the power and wealth that you now possess, or even increase it? If so, then I am unable to answer you. There is no secure advice to give for purposes that are so insecure. On the other hand, if you're asking my advice in the light of God, to keep your soul from death, and if you fear the words of Truth when he says, *What does it profit someone if he gains the whole world, but suffers the loss of his soul?* [Mt 16.26; Mk 8.36; Lk 9.25], then I certainly have an answer for you. I have some advice which you may hear from me. But what need is there for me to say anything different from that I quoted above?

> Do not love the world, nor the things that are in the world. If anyone does love the world, the Father's love is not in him. For everything that is in the world is lust of the flesh and lust of the eyes and ostentation of this age, which does not come from the Father, but from the world. And this world and all its lust will pass away. But anyone who does the will of God remains for ever, just as God, too, remains for ever [1 Jn 2.15–17].

Here is my advice. Seize it and act upon it. This will reveal whether you are a brave man. Conquer the passions that lead you to love the world; do penance for your past misdeeds, for the time when, under the sway of such passions, you were being dragged around by empty desires. If you embrace this advice, if you hold to it and keep it, you will attain those goods that are secure, and you will also move freely among those that are not secure, without putting your soul at risk.

(10) Perhaps, though, you will ask me a second question. How are you to achieve this when you are so tangled up in such great earthly needs? Pray with courage; speak to God the word you find in the psalm: *Rescue me from my state of need* [Ps 25(24).17]. These needs of yours will cease when those passions of yours are defeated. He listened to you, and to us on your behalf, when we prayed for your deliverance from the many great dangers of warfare, dangers visible and physical. But in such a case, one's present life alone is at risk (and that has to come to an end at some time); one's soul, however, will not perish unless it is held captive by harmful passions.

He himself will listen to you when you pray to overcome, invisibly and spiritually, your inner and invisible enemies, that is those passions themselves; to make use of this world as if you were not using it; to do good with its good things, rather than to become bad. For they are in themselves good and are given to human beings only by God, who has power over everything in heaven and on earth. They are given to the good people, in case the things are thought to be evil; but they are also given to the wicked, in case they are thought to be great goods, or the greatest of goods. Similarly, they are also taken away from the good, to test them, and also from the wicked, to torment them.

(11) Who is unaware of this? Who is so stupid as not to see that both the good and the wicked are granted good things on earth – the security of their mortal bodies, strength in their limbs, which are destined to decay, victory over human enemies, honour, temporal power and the rest – and also that both the good and the wicked are deprived of them? On the other hand, the security of the soul, together with the immortality of the body, the strength of justice, victory over the hostile passions, glory, honour and peace for eternity, these are given only to the good. It is these then that you must love, these you must desire, these you must seek by any means you can.

Give alms for the sake of winning and keeping these goods; pour out your prayers, practise fasting as you are able without impairing your physical health. But don't love the goods of this earth, however plentifully you may possess them. Make use of them in this way: do much good with them, but no evil for their sake. All such goods will perish, but good works will not perish, even those achieved with goods that are perishable.

(12) If you did not have a wife, I would urge you to live in chaste celibacy, just as I did before at Tubuna. I should also add something that we forbade you to do then: that now, in so far as you might without jeopardising peace in human affairs, you should withdraw from the affairs of war and give yourself leisure for a life in the fellowship of the holy. Previously you were longing to have leisure, which the soldiers

of Christ use for fighting in silence, not to kill people, but to conquer the *rulers and powers and spirits of wickedness* [Eph 6.12], that is, the devil and his angels.

The holy inflict defeat on these enemies, though they cannot see them. Despite this, they conquer the enemy they cannot see by conquering the objects of their senses. Your wife inhibits me from urging you to this way of life, as it is not right for you to live celibately without her agreement. Even if you ought not to have married her after the words you spoke at Tubuna, still she knew nothing of that and married you in innocence and simplicity. Would that you might persuade her to embrace celibacy, so that you could give yourself back to God without obstacle, as you ought to do. However, if you cannot do that together with her, at least preserve decency within marriage; furthermore, ask God to deliver you from your needs, so that you will eventually be able to do what you are at present unable to do. On the other hand, your wife neither prevents you, nor ought to prevent you, from the following: from loving God and not loving the world; from keeping faith even in warfare (if it's still necessary for you to be involved in it) and from seeking peace; from performing good works with worldly goods and from avoiding evil works done for the sake of worldly goods.

It is love, my dearest son, that commands me to write like this to you, the love that makes you dear to me in the light of God, not of this world. For when I think of the words of scripture, *Correct the wise man and he will love you; correct the fool and he will hate you even more* [Prov. 9.8], I certainly ought to consider you not a fool, but a wise man.

6. Thomas Aquinas – Extracts from *Summa Theologiae*

IaIIae – On Law

90.1 REPLY: Law is a kind of direction or measure for human activity through which a person is led to do something or held back. The word comes from *ligando*, because it is binding on how we should act. Now direction and measure come to human acts from reason, from which, as we have shown (IaIIae 1.1 ad 3; 66.1), they start. It is the function of reason to plan for an end, and this purpose, as Aristotle notes (*Physics* II, 9. 200a22. *Ethics* VII, 8. 115Ia16), is the original source of what we do. The originating principle in any class strikes the note for all there comprised, for instance the unit of calculation in a numerical system, or the first motion that sets going a derivative series of motions. We are left with the conclusion, then, that law is something that belongs to reason.

…

90.2 REPLY: To be a principle of human acts, as we have said, is part of the nature of law, since it is for them a rule and measure. As their beginning lies in the reason, so also one phase of its activity is the start of what follows; this first and foremost is where law comes in. Now the deeds we perform, these being the concern of the practical reason, all originate from our last end. We have shown that the last end of human living is happiness or well-being. Consequently law is engaged above all with the plan of things for human happiness.

Again, since the subordination of part to whole is that of incomplete to rounded-off reality, and since a human individual man is part of the full life of the community, it must needs be that law properly speaking deals with this subordination to a common happiness. Thus Aristotle, having explained what he means by 'legal', mentions the happiness of the body politic when he says in the *Ethics* (v, 1. 1129b17) that *we call those acts legally just that tend to produce and preserve happiness and its components for the political community,* the perfect community, according to the *Politics,* being the State (I, 1. 1252a5).

When we speak of 'a-most-of-all' in any class of things then it is the principle and centre of reference for them all, as fire, for instance, which is the hottest thing of all, is the cause of heat in bodies mixed with other elements, and they are called hot in so far as they share its nature. And since we speak of law most of all in terms of the common good, it follows that any other precept about more particular business will not have the nature of law except in so far as it enters into this plan for the common good.

Therefore every law is shaped to the common good.

…

90.3 REPLY: The chief and main concern of law properly so called is the plan for the common good. The planning is the business of the whole people or of their vicegerent. Therefore to make law is the office of the entire people or of the public personage who has care of them. For, as elsewhere to plan for an end belongs to the power matching that end.

Hence: 1. As already observed, law is present not only in the ruling principle but derivatively as well in the subject ruled. In this last manner each is a law unto himself, in so far as he enters into the plan of the governing authority. So St Paul goes on to say that people show *the work of the law written in their hearts* (Rom. 2.15).

2. A private person can persuade, yet he cannot effectively bring another to virtue, for if his advice is not taken he lacks the force, such as a law should possess, to compel good conduct; this is noted by Aristotle (*Ethics* X, 9. 1180a20). This coercive strength resides in the people or public figure who personifies them; such authority can inflict penalties, as will be shown (IaIIae 92.2 ad 3; IIaIIae 64.3), and to it, therefore, the making of law is reserved.

…

90.4 REPLY: It has been already noted that law is laid on subjects to serve as a rule and measure. This means that it has to be brought to bear on them. Hence to have binding force, which is an essential property of a law, it has to be applied to the people it is meant to direct. This application comes about when their attention is drawn to it by the fact of promulgation. Hence this is required for a measure to possess the force of law.

To sum up, from the four foregoing discussions the following definition can be gathered. Law is nought else than an ordinance of reason for the common good made by the authority who has care of the community and promulgated.

Hence: 1. Natural law is promulgated by God's so instilling it into men's minds that they can know it because of what they really are.

...

91.1 REPLY: As stated above, law is nothing but a dictate of practical reason issued by a sovereign who governs a complete community. Granted that the world is ruled by divine Providence, and this we have shown in the *Prima Pars* (Ia 22.1 ad 2), it is evident that the whole community of the universe is governed by God's mind. Therefore the ruling idea of things which exists in God as the effective sovereign of them all has the nature of law.

...

91.2 REPLY: Law is a rule and measure, as we have said, and therefore can exist in two manners, first as in the thing which is the rule and measure, second as in the thing that is ruled and measured, and the closer the second to the first the more regular and measured it will be. Since all things are regulated and measured by Eternal Law, as we have seen, it is evident that all somehow share in it, in that their tendencies to their own proper acts and ends are from its impression.

Hence:...

2. We have stated (IaIIae 10.1) that all activity of reason and will springs from us as being what we are by nature. All reasoning draws on sources we recognize naturally, and all choosing of objectives subordinate to ends is charged with natural appetite for our ultimate end. Accordingly the original directing of our activity to an end should be through natural law.

...

91.3 REPLY: As we have seen, law is a kind of dictate of the practical reason. Now the processes of the theoretic and practical reasons are parallel; both, we have held, start from certain principles and come to certain conclusions. Accordingly we say this, that just as from indemonstrable principles that are instinctively recognized the theoretic reason draws the conclusions of the various sciences not imparted by nature but discovered by reasoned effort, so also from natural law precepts as from common and indemonstrable principles the human reason comes down to making more specific arrangements.

Now these particular arrangements human reason arrives at are called 'human laws', provided they fulfil the essential conditions of law already indicated. Hence Cicero says that *justice took its start from nature, and then certain things became custom by reason of their usefulness; thereafter the things put forward by nature and approved by custom were sanctioned by fear and reverence for the law (De inventione oratoria II.53).*

Hence: 1. The human reason cannot fully grasp the meaning of God's command, but partially holds it after its own fashion. The consequence is that just as the theoretic reason by its nature partakes of divine wisdom, and therefore we have from within an awareness of certain general principles, though not that proper knowledge of every single truth which divine wisdom comprehends, so on the part of the practical reason we enter into the Eternal Law according to some general principles without knowing all individual directives, though these are comprehended in the Eternal Law (Ia 14.11). Hence the need for human reason to proceed further and sanction particular enactments of law.

2. The human reason is not of itself the measure for things (Ia 14.8; 16.1). Yet principles instilled in it by nature provide general rules and measures for what men should do. It is of these human deeds, not of the nature of things, that human law is the measure.

3. The practical reason is concerned with things to be done, which are individual and contingent, not with the necessary things that are the concern of the theoretic reason. That is why human laws cannot have the inerrancy that marks conclusions of demonstrative science. That a measurement should be unerring and exact at every point is not demanded, but only that it should fit to the extent that the matter allows (*Ethics* V, 10. 1129b29).

...

91.4 REPLY: The guidance of human conduct required a divine law besides natural law and human law. And for four reasons.

First, because law directs men to the actions matching what they are made for. Were they destined only to an end not beyond their natural abilities they would need no directive of reason over and above natural law and human law built on it. Yet they are set towards an eternal happiness out of proportion to their natural resources, as we have shown (IaIIae 5.5), and therefore must needs be directed by a divinely given law above natural and human law.

Second, because of the untrustworthiness of human judgment, notably on contingent and particular issues, different people come to differing decisions about human conduct, with the result that diverse and conflicting laws are passed. That men may know without any doubt what should or should not be done there was required a divinely given law carrying the assurance that it cannot be mistaken.

Third, men can make laws on matters on which they are competent to judge. They cannot pronounce on inward motions which are hidden, but only on outward and observable behaviour. Nevertheless full virtue means that a man is right in both. Since human law is not enough, the complement of divine law is needed to check and guide what goes on within us.

Fourth, Augustine remarks that human law cannot forbid or punish all wrongdoing (*De Libero Arbitrio* I.5), for were it to try to do away with all evils it would also take away much that was good, and so hinder what the common good requires in civilized intercourse. Hence the need of a divine law which misses nothing and leaves no evil unforbidden or unpunished.

These four reasons are touched on in the *Psalm* (18.8) which declares, *The law of the Lord is unspotted,* that is allowing no filth of sin, *converting hearts,* that is, directing us within and without, *the testimony of the Lord is sure,* that is, reliably truthful and right, *giving wisdom to little ones,* that is, lifting humanity to a divine and supernatural end.

Hence: 1. Although through natural law the Eternal Law is shared in according to the capacity of human nature, nevertheless in order to be directed to their ultimate supernatural end men have to be lifted up, and through the divine grant of an additional law which heightens their sharing in the Eternal Law.

2. Taking counsel is a sort of investigation, and therefore should progress from some principles. Those imparted to us by nature are not enough, for the reasons given above, and therefore over and above the precepts of natural law some other principles are needed, namely precepts of divine law.

...

92.1 REPLY: We have said that law is nothing other than a decree of reason in the presiding authority whereby subjects are governed. Now the virtue of being a good subject consists in being well-subordinated to the governing principle; thus virtue in our emotional powers of desiring and contending lies in their being well under the reason's control. So Aristotle speaks of a subject's virtue as corresponding to what the ruler requires of him (*Politics* I, 5. 1260a30).

Every law aims at this, to be obeyed by its subjects. It is plain, therefore, that leading its subjects into the virtue appropriate to their condition is a proper function of law. Now since virtue is that which makes its possessor good, the consequence is that the proper effect of law on those to whom it is given is to make them good, either good simply speaking or good in a certain respect.

If the lawmaker's intention bears on true good, namely the common good regulated by divine justice, the consequence will be for men through the law to become quite simply good. If, however, the intention is not for good without reservation, but something that serves his own profit or pleasure, or against divine justice, then keeping the law will make men good, not simply, but relatively, namely amenable to the régime. This manner of being good can be found even in things bad in themselves, as when we speak of a good thief when referring to his skill and success.

Hence: 1. We have pointed out that virtue is twofold, acquired and infused (IaIIae 63.2). Constant practice serves each, but differently, for the first it causes, whereas the second it disposes to, and when possessed keeps it going and growing. And because law is given in order to direct human acts, then how far it makes men good depends on how far these contribute to virtue. Thus Aristotle observes that *legislators make the citizens good by forming habits in them* (*Ethics* II.1. 1103b3).

2. That men obey the law from the fulness of virtue is not always the case; sometimes it is from fear of punishment, sometimes from the prompting of mere reasonableness, which, as we have noticed (IaIIae 63.1), is a beginning of virtue.

3. You assess the goodness of any part in relationship to its whole; so Augustine notes that *any part which does not fit in with the whole is ugly* (*Confessions* 3.8). Since every person is part of a political community he cannot be good unless he be well adjusted to the common good, nor can the community be sound unless its parts are in keeping. Hence the political commonwealth cannot flourish unless its citizens are virtuous, at least those in leading positions: it is enough for the good of the community if others are so far virtuous that they obey the commands of the ruling authorities. That is why Aristotle remarks that *the virtue of a good ruler is the same as that of a good man, but that the virtue of the good citizen and of the good man are not quite the same* (*Politics* III, 2. 1277a20).

4. A tyrannical law is not according to reason, and therefore is not straightforwardly a law, but rather a sort of crooked law. All the same it possesses some quality of law in wanting the citizens to be good. This it does as being the decree of a presiding authority set on rendering its subjects amenable, which is for them to be good from the point of view of the government, not thoroughly good in themselves.

...

94.4 REPLY: As we have shown (IaIIae 94.2-3), the objects to which men have a natural tendency are the concern of natural law, and among such tendencies it is proper to man to act according to reason. Now a characteristic of reason is to proceed from common principles to particular conclusions: this is remarked in the *Physics* (I, 1. 181a16). However the theoretic reason and the practical reason set about this somewhat differently. The business of the theoretic reason is with natural truths that cannot be otherwise, and so without mistake it finds truth in the particular conclusions it draws as in the premises it starts from. Whereas the business of the practical reason is with contingent matters which are the domain of human acts, and although there is some necessity in general principles the more we get down to particular cases the more we can be mistaken.

So then in questions of theory, truth is the same for everybody, both as to principles and to conclusions, though admittedly all do not recognize truth in the conclusions, but only in those principles which are called 'common conceptions' (Boëthius, *De hebdomadibus. Patrologia Latina* 64, 1311). In questions of action, however, practical truth and goodwill are not the same for everybody with respect to particular decisions, but only with respect to common principles; and even those who are equally in the right on some particular course of action are not equally aware of how right they are.

So then it is evident that with respect to general principles of both theory and practice what is true or right is the same for all and is equally recognized. With respect to specific conclusions of theory the truth is the same for all, though all do not equally recognize it, for instance some are not aware that the angles of a triangle together equal two right angles. With respect to particular conclusions come to by the practical reason there is no general unanimity about what is true or right, and even when there is agreement there is not the same degree of recognition.

All hold that it is true and right that we should act intelligently. From this starting point it is possible to advance the specific conclusion, that goods held in trust are to be restored to their owners. This is true in the majority of cases, yet a case can crop up when to return the deposit would be injurious, and consequently unreasonable, as for instance were it to be required in order to attack one's country. The more you descend into the detail the more it appears how the general rule admits of exceptions, so that you have to hedge it with cautions and qualifications. The greater the number of conditions accumulated the greater the number of ways in which the principle is seen to fall short, so that all by itself it cannot tell you whether it be right to return a deposit or not.

To sum up: as for its first common principles, here natural law is the same for all in requiring a right attitude towards it as well as recognition. As for particular specific points, which are like conclusions drawn from common principles, here also natural law is the same for most people in their feeling for and awareness of what is right. Nevertheless in fewer cases either the desire or the information may be wanting. The desire to do right may be blocked by particular factors—so also with physical things that come to be and die away there are occasional anomalies and failures due to some obstruction—and the knowledge also of what is right may be distorted by passion or bad custom or even by racial proclivity; for instance, as Julius Cæsar narrates (*De bello Gallico* VI, 23), the Germans did not consider robbery wicked though it is expressly against natural law.

...

94.6 REPLY: As we noticed when speaking of what belongs to natural law, to begin with there are certain most general precepts known to all; and next, certain secondary and more specific precepts which are like conclusions lying close to the premises. As for these first common principles in their universal meaning, natural law cannot be cancelled in the human heart, nevertheless it can be missing from a particular course of action when the reason is stopped from applying the general principle there, because of lust or some other passion, as we have pointed out (IaIIae 77.2).

As for its other and secondary precepts, natural law can be effaced, either by wrong persuasions—thus also errors occur in theoretical matters concerning demonstrable conclusions—or by perverse customs and corrupt habits; for instance robbery was not reputed to be wrong among some people, nor even, as the Apostle mentions (Rom. 1.24), some unnatural sins.

...

95.1 REPLY: As we have seen (IaIIae 63.1; 94.3), man has an innate bent towards virtue, yet to come to its fulness he needs to be educated. Thus we observe that it is by contrivance that he supplies his necessities, for instance food and clothing: nature starts him off with reason and hands, but not with the complete product, unlike other animals who are sufficiently provided with nourishment and covering. As for human education, it is not easy to find men who are self-sufficient, since to be well adjusted they should be restrained about undue pleasures; to which they are greatly prone, especially the young to whom education is more effectively applied. Hence it is right and proper for them to obtain from others this education which brings them to virtue.

Now for the young apt for deeds of virtue by good natural disposition or by custom or, better still, by divine gift, all that is required is the fatherly discipline of admonition. Not all the young, however, are like that; some are bumptious, headlong in vice, not amenable to advice, and these have to be held back from evil by fear and force, so that they at least stop doing mischief and leave others in peace. Becoming so habituated they may come to do of their own accord what earlier they did from fear, and grow virtuous. This schooling through the pressure exerted through the fear of punishment is the discipline of human law.

Consequently we see the need for men's virtue and peace that laws should be established; as Aristotle says, *man, when perfected by virtue, is the best of animals, but when separated from law and justice, he is the worst* (*Politics* I, 1. 1253a31). For he can use the weapons of reason, which other animals do not possess, to get rid of lusts and brutalities.

...

95.2 REPLY: Augustine observes that *there never seems to have been a law that was not just* (*De libero arbitrio* 1, 5): hence a command has the force of law to the extent that it is just. In human matters we call something 'just' from its being right according to the rule of reason. The first rule of reason is natural law, as appears from what has been stated. Hence in so far as it derives from this, every law laid down by men has the force of law in that it flows from natural law. If on any head it is at variance with natural law, it will not be law, but spoilt law

...

[S]ome commands are drawn like conclusions from natural law, for instance, 'You must not commit murder' can be inferred from 'You must do harm to nobody'. Others, however, are based like constructions on natural law, which, for instance, pronounces that crime has to be punished without deciding whether this or that should be the penalty; the punishment settled is like a determinate form given to natural law.

Both processes are at work in human positive law. Commands, however, that issue according to the first have part of their force from natural law, and not only from the fact of their enactment. Whereas commands that issue according to the second have their force only by human law.

Hence…

3. Owing to the great variety of human affairs the common principles of natural law do not apply stiffly to every case. One outcome is the diversity of positive laws among different peoples.

…

95.3 REPLY: Whatever is for a purpose must needs be adapted to that purpose, thus, to take Aristotle's example, the shape of a saw is such as to fit it for cutting (*Physics* II, 9. 200a10). Again, whatever is right and measured should be configured to what rules and measures it. Human law meets both requirements, for, first, it is something ordered to a purpose, and, second, is a sort of rule and measure itself ruled and measured by a higher. This last, as we have seen (IaIIae 93.3), is twofold, namely divine law and natural law.

The purpose of human law is to be useful to men, as also the Jurist teaches (Ulpian, *Digest* I, III, 25). That is why Isidore starts off by naming three conditions, namely that it is consistent with religion as corresponding with divine law, that it agrees with good discipline as corresponding to natural law, and that it furthers our welfare as corresponding to human usefulness.

…

96.1 REPLY: Whatever is for an end should be proportioned to that end. For law the end is the common good; Isidore remarks that it *should be composed for no private benefit but for the general welfare of the citizens* (*Etymologies* II, 10; V, 21). Therefore human laws should be proportioned to the common good.

Now this comprises many things; hence law should cover all manner of personalities, occupations, and occasions. Many types go to make up the political community, a variety of business serves its common interest, and, as Augustine observes (*City of God* XXII, 6), law is not instituted as a temporary measure but to persist throughout generations of citizens.

…

96.2 REPLY: As we have seen, law is established as a kind of rule or measure for human acts. Now, as noted in the *Metaphysics* (IX. 1053a24), a measure ought to be of the same kind as the thing it measures; different things have different standards. Hence laws should be appointed to men according to their condition; Isidore remarks how law should *be possible both according to nature and the custom of the country* (*Etymologies* II, 10 & V, 21).

The ability of and resource for acting in a certain way spring from an interior disposition or habit; the same course of action is not possible for a man who has a habit of virtue and for a man who lacks it, nor for a grownup and a child: this is why the same laws do not apply, for many things are allowed in the young for which older people are punished, or at least blamed. Likewise many things may be let pass in people of mediocre morals which cannot be countenanced in their betters.

Law is laid down for a great number of people, of which the majority have no high standard of morality. Therefore it does not forbid all the vices, from which upright men can keep away, but only those grave ones which the average man can avoid, and chiefly those which do harm to others and have to be stopped if human society is to be maintained, such as murder and theft and so forth.

Hence:...

2. The purpose of human law is to bring people to virtue, not suddenly but step by step. Therefore it does not all at once burden the crowd of imperfect men with the responsibilities assumed by men of the highest character, nor require them to keep away from all evils, lest, not sturdy enough to bear the strain, they break out into greater wrongs. Thus it is said in *Proverbs, He that violently bloweth his nose bringeth out blood* (Prov. 30.33); and in *Matthew,* that *if new wine be put into old wineskins,* that is into imperfect men, *the skins will burst, and the wine be spilled* (Matt. 9.17), that is the commands will be despised, and from this contempt men will break out into worse evils.

3. Natural law is a kind of sharing by us in the Eternal Law, from which human law falls short. Augustine says, *This law framed for governing the civil community tolerates and leaves unpunished many things which are vindicated by divine Providence; nevertheless because it does not do everything the something it does do should not be disapproved of* (*De Libero Arbitrio* I, 5). So then human law cannot forbid all that natural law forbids.

...

96.3 REPLY: Virtues are specifically differentiated according to their objectives, as we have seen (IaIIae 54.2; 60.1; 62.2). All these objectives involve the private good of the individual person or the common good of the people; thus deeds of courage may defend the rights of a friend or of the State.

Now we have seen that law is ordained to the common good, and consequently there is no virtue of which some activity cannot be enjoined by law. Nevertheless human law does not enjoin every act of every virtue, but those acts only which serve the common good, either immediately, as when the social order is directly involved from the nature of things, or mediately, as when measures of good discipline are passed by the legislator to train citizens to maintain justice and peace in the community.

...

96.4 REPLY: Human positive laws are either just or unjust. If they are just, they have binding force in the court of conscience from the Eternal Law from which they derive, according to *Proverbs, Through me kings reign, and the lawmakers decree just things* (Prov. 8.15).

Now laws are said to be just on three counts; from their end, when they are ordered to the common good, from their authority, when what is enacted does not exceed the lawgiver's power, and from their form, when for the good of the whole they place burdens in equitable proportion on subjects. Since an individual is part of a group, each in all that he is and has belongs to the community, as also is any part what it is because of the whole: nature itself offers hurt upon a part for the health of the whole. Accordingly laws which apportion in due measure the burdens of responsibility are just, legitimate, and oblige at the bar of conscience.

Laws are unjust in two ways, as being against what is fair in human terms and against God's rights. They are contrary to human good on the three counts made above; from their end, when the ruler taxes his subjects rather for his own greed or vanity than the common benefit; from their author, when he enacts a law beyond the power committed to him; and from their form, when, although meant for the common good, laws are inequitably dispensed. These are outrages rather than laws; Augustine remarks, *There never seems to have been a law where justice was not present* (*De Libero Arbitrio* I, 5). Such commands do not oblige in the court of conscience, unless perhaps to avoid scandal or riot; on this account a man may be called to yield his rights, according to the text of *Matthew, If any one forces you to go one mile, go with him two miles, and if any one would sue you and take your coat, let him have your cloak as well* (Matt. 6.40).

Laws can be unjust because they are contrary to God's rights; such are the laws of tyrants which promote idolatry or whatsoever is against divine law. To observe them is in no wise permissible, for as is said in the *Acts, We must obey God rather than men* (Acts 5.29).

Hence: 1. According to St Paul (Rom. 13), *There is no authority,* that is, human authority, *except from God,* and *therefore he who resists the authorities,* that is in what lies within the order of their power, *resists what God has appointed,* and consequently is made guilty in conscience.

2. This argument is put forward about human laws which are directed against God's commandments. They then go beyond the order of power, and are not to be submitted to.

3. This argument is about a law which inflicts an unjust grievance on its subjects; here also it exceeds the power of command divinely granted, and in such cases a man is not obliged to obey, if without scandal or greater damage he can resist.

...

96.5 REPLY: It has been shown that law of its nature has the double rôle of being a guide for human acts and of possessing the power of constraint. Hence a man can be subject to a law on these two counts, first, of being guided by a ruling principle, and second, of being constrained by an enforcing principle.

In the first manner all who are subject to a governing authority are subject to the law it makes. There can be two reasons why a person is not subject, first because he owes no allegiance—thus those who belong to one state or kingdom are independent of the sovereign of another, being subject neither to his dominion nor his laws—and second, because he comes under a higher law; for instance one subject to a proconsul ought to be ruled by his mandate, yet not in matters where he enjoys a dispensation from the emperor; the mandate of an inferior does not bind where a superior mandate directs. And so it happens that somebody who is simply subject to a body of law is not bound by one of its provisions because there he is ruled by a higher law.

In the second manner a person is said to be subject to law as being constrained by an enforcing principle. Thus virtuous and upright men are not bound by law, but only wicked men. What is constrained and forced is contrary to one's own will. The will of good men harmonizes with the law, whereas the will of wicked men clashes with it, and in this sense only the wicked are subject to law, not the just.

Hence: 1. This argument is about subjection by way of constraint. The righteous are not under the law in this way, for they are the law to themselves, and *show that what the law requires is written in their hearts,* as St Paul says (Rom. 2.4). Hence the law exercises no coercion on them, as it does on the unrighteous.

2. The law of the Holy Spirit is higher than any laid down by men. Because spiritual men are led by the Spirit they are not subject to law as regards things inconsistent with the guidance of the Spirit. That they are subject to human laws nevertheless comes from their being led by the Spirit, according to the text in 1 *Peter, Be subject for the Lord's sake to every human institution* (1 Pet. 2.13).

3. A sovereign is described as being exempt from law with respect to its coercive power, for, to be precise, nobody is compelled by himself, and law has its restraining force only from the sovereign's power. That is why he is referred to as being exempt from the law, since no one can pass sentence condemning him if he breaks it. Accordingly on the words of the Psalm, *Against thee, thee only, have I sinned,* a gloss says, *The king has no man to pronounce judgment on his deeds* (*Glossa Lombardi. Patrologia Latina* 191, 486. From Cassiodorus on *Psalms,* 50, 6. *Patrologia Latina* 70, 361).

Yet of his own will a sovereign is subject to the directive power of the law, according to the *Decretals* (Gregory IX, I, II, 6), *Whoever establishes a law for another, the very same he should practise himself.* And a wise authority says, *Be open yourself to the law you produce* (Cato, in Pseudo-Ausonius, *Septem sapientum sententiæ* II, 5. *Patrologia Latina* 19, 876). Our Lord reproaches those who do not practise what they preach, and who *lay heavy burdens on men's shoulders, but they themselves will not stir a little finger to move them* (Matt. 23.3).

Before God's judgment, then, the sovereign is not exempt from the law's directive power, and he ought to fulfil the law, freely not forcedly. Yet he is above the law in that he can change it if expedient, and grant dispensations from it adapted to place and season.

...

96.6 REPLY: As already stated, every law is ordained for the common well-being, and to that extent gets the force and quality of law; in so far as it falls short here it has no binding force. Hence the Jurist says (Ulpian, *Digest* I, III, 25), *No reason in law nor goodwill in equity brooks that we should put harsh interpretations on healthy measures brought in for men's welfare, and take them to a grimness that conflicts with the benefits they bring.*

Now it often happens that it is advantageous to the common welfare for a measure to be observed in the majority of cases, while in some cases this is highly harmful.

Since he cannot envisage every individual case, the legislator frames a law to fit the majority of cases, his purpose being to serve the common welfare. So that if a case crops up where its observance would be damaging to that common interest, then it is not to be observed. Suppose a siege, then a decree that the city gates are to be kept closed is a useful general measure for the public safety. Yet say some citizens among the defenders are being pursued by the enemy, the cost would be heavy were the gates not to be opened to them. So opened they are to be, against the letter of the decree, in order to defend that very common safety the ruling authority had in view.

All the same notice this: if observing the letter of the law does not involve a sudden risk calling for instant decision and to be dealt with at once, it is not for anybody to construe the law and decide what is or what is not of service to the city. This is only for the governing authorities who, because of exceptional cases, have the power to grant dispensations from the laws. If, however, the danger is urgent, and admits of no delay, or time for recourse to higher authority, the very necessity carries a dispensation with it, for necessity knows no law.

Hence: 1. He who acts counter to the letter of the law in case of need is not questioning the law itself, but judging the particular issue confronting him, where he sees that the letter of the law is not to be applied.

2. A man who follows the lawmaker's intention is not interpreting the law simply speaking as it stands, but setting it in its real situation; there, from the prospect of the damage that would follow, it is evident that the lawmaker would have him act otherwise. If he is in doubt then he should follow the letter and consult his superior.

3. Nobody is so wise as to be able to forecast every individual case, and accordingly he cannot put into words all the factors that fit the end he has in view. Even were the legislator able to take every event into consideration, he still should not set them all down in detail, for this would lead to muddle; but he should frame a law according to the usual run of things.

...

97.2 REPLY: The preceding discussion has shown that human law is rightly altered so far as this will provide for the common benefit. Now a change in the law, looked at merely as a change, inflicts a kind of loss on the common well-being, because custom avails much for the observance of law, so much so that breaches of common custom seem so much the graver on that account, though they be light matters otherwise. That is why when law is altered the restraining power of law is weakened in so far as custom is done away with. Hence a human law should never be altered, unless the gain to the common well-being on one head makes up for what has been lost on another.

Such compensation comes either from some highly important and evident gain produced by the new statute; or from the urgent necessity for change, either because of the manifest wrong the old customary law contained or because its observance was highly harmful. So it is said by the Jurist Ulpian (*Digest* I, IV, 2), *In establishing new laws the benefit to be gained by departing from what for ages has been looked upon as equitable should be evident.*

Hence: 1. Human inventiveness alone is responsible for the effectiveness of a work of art, and so an earlier model can be discarded when it can be bettered. Laws, however, get their main strength through custom, and therefore, as Aristotle says (*Politics* II, 5. 1269a20), they should not be too easily changed from old to new.

. . .

97.3 REPLY: All law proceeds from the reason and will of the lawgiver; divine and natural law from the intelligent will of God, human law from the will of man regulated by reason. Man's reason and will in matters of practice are manifested by what he says, and by what he does as well; each carries into execution what he has chosen because to him it seems good.

As manifesting interior concepts and motions of the human mind it is clear that words serve to alter a law as well as express its meaning. So also by repeated deeds, which set up a custom, a law can be changed and explained, and also a principle can be established which acquires the force of law, and this because what we inwardly mean and want is most effectively declared by what outwardly and repeatedly we do. When anything is done again and again it is assumed that it comes from the deliberate judgment of reason.

On these grounds custom has the force of law, and abolishes a law, and is the interpreter of laws.

Hence: 1. Divine and natural law proceed from the divine will, as we have said, and hence cannot be altered by custom proceeding from the will of man; change can come only by divine authority. Accordingly no custom can acquire the force of law against divine or natural law. Isidore says, *Let usage bow to authority, and reason and law prevail over vicious habits* (*Synonyma de lamentatione animæ peccatricis* II, 80).

2. As we have observed, in some cases human laws do not meet a situation. Sometimes therefore it is possible to act beside the law, namely when the law fails to meet the case, and then the act will not be wrong. When such cases are multiplied because of changed human conditions, then custom is an index that a law is no longer serviceable, as would be shown by the verbal promulgation of a law that superseded it. If, however, the reason still holds good which made the law advantageous in the first place, then law prevails over custom, not custom over law. An exception would

be a law that is useless because *not possible according to the customs of the country* (Isidore, *Etymologies* v, 21), which is one of the essential conditions of human law. To set aside the customs of a whole people is impracticable.

3. A human group with its own customs can be in one of two conditions, self-governing or not. If it is a free country, where people are able to make their own laws, their common consensus about a particular observance, expressed in custom, is more important than the authority of the ruler, who has the power of making law only in so far as he represents the people; a whole people can make law, not a single individual. If, however, people are not free to make their own laws, or to put aside a law laid down for them by superior authority, then all the same a prevailing custom among them obtains the force of law when it is allowed by those whose office it is to make laws for them; by this very fact authority seems to approve what has been brought in by custom.

IaIIae – On Justice, Injustice and the Common Good

47.10 REPLY: Some have thought, as Aristotle relates (*Ethics*, VI. 8. 1142a1), that prudence does not reach to the common good, but only to the good of the individual, for that alone, they reckoned, is what a man is bound to seek. This, however, conflicts with Christian charity, which according to the Epistle, *seeketh not her own* (1 Cor. 13.5). And so St Paul speaks of himself as *not seeking mine own profit, but the profit of many, that they may be saved* (1 Cor. 10.33). It conflicts also with right reason, which holds that the common good is higher than the good of the individual. Consequently, since its business is rightly to deliberate, judge, and command about the ways to a due end, prudence clearly regards the common good of the people, not merely the private good of one individual.

...

47.11 REPLY: We have already explained that active qualities or virtues are specifically distinguished by the distinction of the objective interests engaging them (IaIIae 54.2 ad 1; IIaIIae 47.5), which distinction is taken precisely according as they exhibit special forms or meanings. The significance in anything that is done for the sake of an end is looked at, as we have said (IaIIae 1 introduction, 102.1), in the light of that end. Hence from their being related to different ends active dispositions or virtues are rendered specifically distinct. Now the good of the individual, of the family, and of the state or nation are different sorts of end. Consequently there must be a different sort of prudence corresponding to each. One is prudence simply so called, directed to one's own personal good. Another is domestic or 'economic' prudence, directed to the good of the household or family. The third is political prudence, directed to the good of the state or realm.

Hence…

3. Different ends, even when subordinated one to another, set up different interests and disciplines; cavalry training, military art, and statesmanship are specialized occupations even though the aim of one is to serve another. Likewise the good of the individual is subordinate to the good of the people, nevertheless this does not prevent the difference between them setting up a specific difference between the virtues they callfor. What does follow is that the virtue engaged with the furthest end is the superior and commands the other virtues.

…

47.12 REPLY: Prudence is in the reason. Now to rule and govern are proper activities of the reason. And so the more each shares in the responsibilities of ruling and governing so much the more he possesses in the quality of being reasonable and prudent. Clearly subjects and slaves, precisely as such, play no port in ruling and governing, for theirs is rather to be ruled and governed. Consequently prudence is not a virtue for the slave as slave nor for the subject as subject.

Nevertheless because each man, proportionately to his reasonableness, has a share in government through his freely reasoned decisions to that extent political prudence is his. Consequently it is in the ruler in the manner of a master-art, to quote the *Ethics* (VI, 8. 1141b25), yet it is in subjects after the manner of a mechanical art.

…

50.1 REPLY: We have explained that the function of prudence is to rule and command (IIaIIae 47.8;12). Hence wherever in human affairs you find a special kind of ruling and commanding there also you find a special kind of prudence. Clearly in one who is responsible for ruling, not only himself, but also the entire community of the state or kingdom you find a specific and full notion of rulership, which will be more complete the more universal it is, that is, embracing more matters and reaching to a higher purpose. And so the prudence which befits a king, who has charge of a state or kingdom, is of a special and most complete kind. Accordingly the ruling prudence of a polity is set down as a kind of prudence.

…

50.2 REPLY: The slave is moved by the command of his master, and the subject by that of the prince, yet not as non-rational and inanimate things are moved. For these are merely acted upon by a force outside themselves and do not set themselves in motion, for they have no mastery over their actions through free will. Consequently the rightfulness of their governance is in the agents setting them in motion, not them. Now men who are slaves or subjects in some sense are acted on by the command of others, yet in such a way as to be self-acting through freewill. Accordingly this much is required of them, that they possess in themselves a certain rightfulness of governance whereby they direct themselves in obeying their rulers. And this is the concern for that kind of prudence which is called political.

...

57.1 REPLY: The proper characteristic of justice, as compared with the other moral virtues, is to govern a man in his dealings towards others. It implies a certain balance of equality, as its very name shows, for in common speech things are said to be adjusted when they match evenly. Equality is relative to another. The other moral virtues, however, compose a man for activities which befit him considered in himself. So then that which is correct in their working and which is the proper object of their bent is not thought of save in relation to the doer. Whereas with justice, in addition to this, that which is correct is constituted by a relation to another, for a work of ours is said to be just when it meets another on the level, as with the payment of a fair wage for a service rendered.

So then something is said to be just because it has the rightness of justice; it is this that engages the activity of justice, even abstracting from the temper in which it is done; by contrast, the rightness of the other moral virtues is not determined apart from the frame of mind of the person acting. This is why for justice expecially, in comparison with other virtues, an impersonal objective interest is fixed. We call it *the just thing*, and this indeed is a right. Clearly, then, right is the objective interest of justice.

...

57.2 REPLY: As we have seen (IIaIIae 57.1), the right and just is a work that is commensurate with another person according to some sort of fairness. This can be measured in two ways. One, from the very nature of the case, as when somebody gives so much in order to receive as much in return: this is called natural right. The other, the commensurate to the other is settled by agreement or mutual consent, as when a person counts himself content to receive such or such in return. And this may come about in two ways. First, by private engagement, as when the parties bind themselves to a contract without the State entering in; and second, by public agreement, as when the whole civil community or State fixes what is adequate and commensurate or when this is so ordained by the sovereign authority who has charge over and personifies the people: this is called positive right.

...

58.3 REPLY: Since its very name spells an equalization, as we have noted, (IIaIIae 57.1) justice of its nature bears a relationship to another, for something is equal to another, not to itself. And since it is for justice to straighten human acts, as we have also taught (IaIIae 60.2; 61.3;113.1), it must needs be that the otherness required is that between diverse beings capable of acting for themselves. Acts are done by whole and complete substances, not, properly speaking, by parts and forms and powers; except by analogy we do not speak of a hand striking or of heat making hot, but of a man striking with his hand or of fire making hot through its heat. So then justice requires a diversity of persons, and accordingly it is only of one man towards another. Nevertheless in one single man by analogy we can treat various principles of activity as though they were so many diverse agents, such as his reason and his emotional powers of desiring and of coping with difficulties. And so by a figure of speech justice is said to operate within one and the same man in that his reason commands his desirous and spirited emotions and these obey, and also in general that each of his parts is fittingly composed. Aristotle entitles this justice in the metaphorical sense of the term (*Ethics* V, 11. 1138b6).

Hence: 1. The justice that works in us by faith is that through which the ungodly are justified; it lies, as we have seen when treating of justification, in the due order of the parts of the soul (IaIIae 113.1). This belongs to justice in its metaphorical sense, and it can be found even in a man who lives all by himself.

...

4. A man's actions with regard to himself are sufficiently straightened out when his emotions are ruled aright by the other moral virtues. His actions with regard to another, however, call for a special rightfulness in relation to the other on which they bear, not only to his acting self. And so for such actions there is special virtue, and this is justice.

...

58.5 REPLY: As we have seen, justice directs a man in his relations with others. These fall under two heads, those with others considered as individuals and those with others as belonging to the community, inasmuch as he who serves the community serves who all come within it. Consequently justice in its proper meaning can cover both. Now clearly all who are contained in a community are related to it as parts to a whole. A part as such belongs to the whole, so that any good of the part can be subordinate to the good of the whole. Accordingly the value in each and every virtue, whether it composes a man in himself or whether it disposes him in relation to others, may be referred to the common good, to which justice order us. In this way the acts of all the virtues can belong to justice in that it orders a man to the common good. It is in this sense that justice is called a general virtue. And since it is for law to regulate for the common good, as we have seen (IaIIae 90.2), such general justice is called legal justice, for thereby a person accords with law which directs acts of all the virtues to the common good.

...

58.6 REPLY: There are two manners in which something is said to be general, by predication and by power. First, by predication as a genus, thus *animal* is general or generic with respect to man and horse and the like; in this manner the general enters the essence of the subjects that come under the classification, since its genus is part of the essence of a species and falls within its definition. Second, by power or virtually, thus a universal cause is general to all its effects; the sun's energy, for instance, spreads to all bodies lit and transformed by it. The general in this manner does not have to enter the essence of its subjects, since cause and effect are not essentially identical.

To apply the distinction. It is in the second manner that we have spoken of justice as a general virtue, inasmuch as it orders the activities of other virtues to its own end by moving them by its command. For as charity may be called a general virtue because it sets the activities of all the virtues towards the divine good, so it is with legal or general justice which sets them towards the common good. And, to continue the comparison, as charity, which is centered on God's goodness as its proper object, is of its essence a special virtue, so general or legal justice, which regards the common good as its proper object, yet remains a special virtue in essence. As such it resides in the sovereign ruler chiefly and after the fashion of a master-art, and in subjects secondarily and as it were administratively.

All the same, though legal justice, if general by power, is a special virtue in essence, any virtue may be called by its name when ordered to the common good. And to speak in this sense, as Aristotle does, legal justice is one in essence with all virtue though notionally distinct.

Hence...

4. Each virtue, considered in its own specific meaning, directs its activity to its own proper end. That it be directed to a further end, whether always or sometimes, comes from some superior virtue, not from its own special character. Hence the need for one sovereign moral virtue, essentially distinct from the rest of the moral virtues, which orders them to the common good: this is legal justice.

...

58.7 REPLY: We have seen (IIaIIae 58.6) that legal justice, which directly charges a man with the common good, is not essentially identical with all virtue, and that there are other virtues which bear him directly to particular goods. These may relate either to himself or to another individual person. Accordingly, as besides legal justice other particular virtues are called for, which compose a man in himself, namely fortitude and temperance, so also is a particular justice, which orders his dealings with another individual person.

Hence: 1. Legal justice is indeed sufficient to govern us in our dealings with others, immediately when they comprise the common good, yet mediately in the case of the good of one individual person. Hence the need of a particular justice immediately engaged with this.

2. The common good of the State and the particular good of the individual person differ, not just quantitatively as the large and the little, but in kind; the meaning of the common good is other than that of an individual good, as the meaning of a whole is not that of a part. Accordingly Aristotle remarks that *they speak not well who maintain that the State and the home and like communities differ only as the many and the few and not in kind* (*Politics* I, 1. 1252a7).

...

58.8 REPLY: All whatsoever that can be ruled aright by reason are matters for moral virtue, which is defined by right reason, as Aristotle makes clear (*Politics* II, 6. 1107a1). The soul's inner feelings, its outward actions, and the outside things it makes use of, all can be ruled aright by reason. All the same it is through external actions and things, through which men mutually communicate, that the order of one to another is observed, whereas in a man's interior feelings you take note of his uprightness within himself. Since it is directed to others, justice consequently is not about the whole field of moral virtue, but only about external deeds and things, and these under a certain specific aspect, namely of the due co-ordination of one person with another.

…

58.11 ON THE OTHER HAND, there is Ambrose, *It is justice that renders to each what is his and claims not what is another's; it disregards one's own profit in order to maintain a common equity* (*De Officio* I, 24).

REPLY: As we have said (IIaIIae 58.8;10), the subject-matter of justice is what we outwardly do, according as the doing or the thing we employ is proportionate to the other person who lays claim to our justice. Now each person's own is that which is due to him in proportion to making things even. That is why the proper activity of justice is none other than to render to each his own.

Hence: 1. Since justice is a cardinal virtue, other secondary virtues hinge on it, such as mercy, liberality, and the like, as we shall see later (IIaIIae 80). And therefore to succour the needy, which is a work of mercy or compassion, and to be open-handedly beneficent, which is a work of liberality, come back in a sense to justice, which is the main virtue.

…

58.12 REPLY: If we are speaking of general or legal justice, it is evident that justice outshines the other moral virtues, because the common good surpasses the individual good of one person. Accordingly Aristotle declares that justice is the most splendid virtue, and Morning or Evening Star are not so wonderful (*Ethics* V, 1.1129b27).

If we are speaking of particular justice, then it is distinguished among the other moral virtues on two counts. First, as regards its seat; it is in the nobler part of the soul, namely the rational appetite or will, whereas other moral virtues are in the sensitive appetite, the principle of the emotions which are the field of other moral virtues. Second, as regards its objective interest. The other virtues are commended only for the good they do their possessor, justice, however, for the good it does to another; Aristotle remarks how in a sense justice is another's good (*Ethics* V, 1.1130a3). And he also declares that *the greatest virtues must needs be the most decent to others, for virtue is a beneficent power. On this account the greatest honours are accorded the brave and the just; courage serves others in war, yet justice serves others in both war and peace* (*Rhetoric* I, 9. 1366b3).

Hence: 1. Though by liberality one gives from one's own, the emphasis there is on the good of the giver's own virtue, whereas with the justice of rendering to another that which is his, it is on the social good. And furthermore justice is observed towards all, whereas liberality cannot be extended to all. Again, liberality, which gives of one's own, is based on justice, which safeguards the rights of each.

2. When magnanimity is added to justice the goodness of justice is increased. Yet without justice it would not have the character of virtue.

3. The more difficult and the better—fortitude is about the first, not the second. It serves only where there is conflict, whereas justice serves also in peace, as we have mentioned.

...

61.1 REPLY: As we have seen (IIaIIae 58.5;7), particular justice is directed towards the private person, who may be compared to the community as a part to a whole. Now with a part we may note a twofold relationship. First, that of one part to another, and this corresponds to the ordering of private persons among themselves. This is governed by commutative justice, which is engaged with their mutual dealings one with another. Second, that of the whole to a part, which goes with the bearing of the community on individual persons. This is governed by distributive justice which apportions proportionately to each his share from the common stock. And so there are two species of justice, namely commutative and distributive justice.

Hence: 1. A private person is commended for due moderation in his bountifulness, and blamed for squandering it in waste. So likewise should moderation be showed in dispensing community goods, and this is governed by distributive justice.

2. As a part and the whole are identical in a sense, so too in a sense that which is of the whole is also of a part. Accordingly when something is given to each from the goods of the community each in a way receives what is his own.

3. The act of distributing common goods is the office of him who is their guardian. Nevertheless distributive justice is also in subjects in that they are content with the fair sharing out. Yet note that distributive justice may be from the common goods of the family, not the State, and this dispensing can be done by the authority of a private person.

4. A movement gets its character from the term it arrives at. Accordingly general or legal justice aims to conduct the dealings of private persons to the good of the community, whereas the reverse holds when that is brought to private persons; such distribution is a function of particular justice.

5. It is not merely the one and the many that gives rise to the distinction between commutative and distributive justice, it is also the difference between types or kinds of what is due, for somebody is entitled in one manner to what is his own, but in another to what is the community's.

...

61.2 REPLY: We have said that distributive justice gives something to a private person in so far as something belonging to the community is due to a part (IIaIIae 61.1). This is so much the more considerable in correspondence with the greater importance of the part in the whole. Consequently so much the more is given from the common stock as the recipient holds more responsibility in the community. Importance is assessed in an aristocracy by virtue, in an oligarchy by wealth, in a democracy by liberty, and in other régimes variously. So then the virtuous mean is taken in distributive justice, not according to an equality between thing and thing, but according to a proportion between things and persons, and in such a way that even as one person exceeds another so also that which is meted out to him exceeds that which is meted out to the other. Accordingly Aristotle describes the mean here as being *according to geometric proportionality*, in which the even balance or equality lies in a comparative relation, not in a fixed quantity. Thus we reckon that 6 is to 4 as 3 is to 2; in each case the proportion is 1.5, since the greater number is the sum of the smaller plus a half. The excess is not, however, of simple quantity, since 6 exceeds 4 by 2, whereas 3 exceeds 2 by 1.

It is otherwise in exchanges between persons. There something is rendered to an individual person in return for something of his that has been received: this most evidently appears in buying and selling, from which originates the notion of an exchange. There the balance or equalization of thing with thing is called for, so that a man should repay the other as much as he gains in acquiring the thing which belonged to the other. Here the equality will be according to an arithmetical mean, which lies between an equal plus and minus of quantities. Thus 5 is the mean between 6 and 4, since it exceeds the first and is exceeded by the second by 1. If each has 5 to start with, and one receives 1 from what belongs to the other, he will have 6 and the other will be left with 4. Justice will be served when both are bought back to the mean, by 1 being taken from the one who has 6 and given to the other who has 4. Then both will have 5, which is the mean.

Hence...

3. In the give-and-take of action and passion among men the quality of a person involved affects the quantity or size of the thing done; striking a ruler offers greater injury than striking a private person. Yet with distributive justice what counts is the quality or station of a person considered in itself, whereas with commutative justice it lies in a diversification arising from the objective condition of that which is owing.

...

64.3 REPLY: As we have already noted (IIaIIae 64.2), the killing of malefactors is legitimate in so far as it is ordered to the well-being of the whole community. And so this right belongs only to those who are charged with the care of the whole community, just as it is the doctor who has been entrusted with the health of the whole body who may amputate a gangrenous limb. But the care of the whole community has been entrusted to the rulers who exercise public authority, and so it is only they, and not private persons, who may execute malefactors.

Hence...

3. Any private individual may legitimately do anything for the common good provided it harms nobody. On the other hand, anything that does involve harm to

another needs to be judicially decided by whoever is responsible for determining what is to be taken away from the parts for the well-being of the whole.

...

64.6 REPLY: A man can be looked at in two ways—in isolation and in some context. Now, considering man in isolation, it is not legitimate to kill any man. Every man, even the sinner, has a nature which God made, and which as such we are bound to love, whereas we violate it by killing him. It nevertheless remains true, as we have already seen (IIaIIae 64.2), that sin corrodes the common good and so justifies the killing of the sinner, whereas the life of just men preserves and promotes the common good, since they constitute the bulk of the people. There is, therefore, simply no justification for taking the life of an innocent person.

Hence: 1. God has sovereign authority over life and death, for it is in accordance with his ordinance that both sinners and the just die. Therefore, anyone who kills an innocent person in obedience to God's command commits no sin, since God whose order he is executing commits no sin; on the contrary, he is showing his fear of the Lord thereby.

2. In weighing the gravity of sin we have to attend to the intrinsic nature of things rather than to what is incidental to them. And on this criterion, somebody who kills a just man sins more gravely than somebody who kills a sinner. Firstly, because he harms somebody whom he ought to love more, and so he infringes charity all the more. Secondly, because he inflicts injury on somebody who deserves it less, and in this way he also infringes justice all the more. Thirdly, because he deprives the community of a greater good. Fourthly, because he despises God all the more, in accordance with the Lord's saying, *He who rejects you, rejects me* (Luke 10.16). And the fact that a just man who is killed in brought to glory is purely incidental to the killing.

...

65.1 REPLY: A limb is part of the whole body and it therefore exists for the sake of that whole, as the imperfect for the sake of the perfect. The individual limb must therefore be dealt with in the way the benefit of the whole demands. Now the limbs of the human body are as such conducive to the proper functioning of the whole body, though they may also become detrimental thereto, as where a gangrenous limb poisons the whole body. A limb that is healthy and functioning well cannot, therefore, in principle be removed without the whole suffering. At the same time the whole man himself is ordered to the whole community of which he is a part as to his end, as we saw above, and this is why, even though his body may thereby suffer some loss, the community as a whole may benefit from the removal in so far as the penalty is inflicted on him to restrain him from sinning. Therefore, just as the public authority may deprive a person of his life on account of certain major faults, so they may deprive him of a limb for lesser faults. We should, however, note that not any private individual may carry out such an operation, even with the consent of the person concerned, for this involves damage to the community to which a man and his parts belong.

Moreover an organ that is endangering an individual's whole body may legitimately be removed by his own consent for the sake of the well-being of the body as a whole, since each individual is responsible for the well-being of his body as a whole. And the same reasoning applies where it is somebody else's responsibility to look after the person with the infected organ. In any other case it is quite wrong to mutilate another.

Hence…

2. Man's life as a whole is not to be subordinated to any component good of that life; on the contrary, everything that goes to make up a man is for the sake of that life. This is why only the public authorities who are charged with caring for the good of the community may deprive a man of his life. At the same time the removal of an organ can promote the well-being of a single individual, and this is why the decision to have this done may in certain circumstances be his.

…

65.4 REPLY: We can think of the goods of the body in a developmental sequence. First of all, there is simply the physical integrity of the body and this is damaged by killing or mutilation. Secondly, there is the tranquility and delight of the senses, which is affected by blows or any physical pain. And thirdly, there is the use and movement of the limbs, which is inhibited by binding or imprisonment or any kind of detention. To imprison or detain anybody in any sort of way is, therefore, illegitimate unless done according to due process of justice, by way of a penalty or caution to avoid evil.

Hence:…

3. Anybody may indeed detain a man for as long as is necessary to stop him from doing something wrong immediately, such as his throwing himself from a height, or striking another. But only he who has general authority over another's life and actions has a strict right to detain or bind another, for this involves his being restrained not merely from doing wrong but also from doing good.

…

66.2 REPLY: Man has a twofold competence in relation to material things. The first is the title to care for and distribute the earth's resources. Understood in this way, it is not merely legitimate for a man to possess things as his own, it is even necessary for human life, and this for three reasons. First, because each person takes more trouble to care for something that is his sole responsibility than what is held in common or by many—for in such a case each individual shirks the work and leaves the responsibility to somebody else, which is what happens when too many officials are involved. Second, because human affairs are more efficiently organized if each person has his own responsibility to discharge; there would be chaos if everybody cared for everything. Third, because men live together in greater peace where everyone is content with his task. We do, in fact, notice that quarrels often break out amongst men who hold things in common without distinction (*Politics* II, 5, 1262b38).

Man's other competence is to use and manage the world's resources. Now in regard to this, no man is entitled to manage things merely for himself, he must do so in the interests of all, so that he is ready to share them with others in case of necessity. This is why Paul writes to Timothy, *As for the rich of this world, charge them to be liberal and generous* (1 Tim. 6.17-18).

Hence: 1. Community of goods is said to be part of the natural law not because it requires everything to be held in common and nothing to be appropriated to individual possession, but because the distribution of property is a matter not for natural law but, rather, human agreement, which is what positive law is about, as we saw above. The individual holding of possessions is not, therefore, contrary to the natural law; it is what rational beings conclude as an addition to the natural law.

2. A person who arrives at the public games first in order to get things ready for others would not be acting amiss, but only if he stopped them from getting in. And, similarly, a rich man who takes prior possession of something that was common before is not doing anything wrong provided he is ready to share it; he sins only if he unreasonably prevents others from using it. This is why Basil, in the same passage, says, *What point is there in your enjoying plenty whilst the other man is a beggar except for you to gain the merit of managing your wealth well and for him to win the crown of patience?*

3. When Ambrose says, *Let no one say that what is common is his own,* he is talking about the use and management of property in the common interest. That is why he goes on to say, *To charge more than the expenses warrant is violent expropriation.*

. . .

66.3 REPLY: Three things go to make up theft. The first characteristic is that it is contrary to justice, which renders each person his due. Under this aspect theft is the usurping of somebody else's property. The second characteristic of theft is that it is distinguished from sins against the person, like homicide and adultery. In this light theft is, therefore, about possessions. Therefore, if somebody takes something from another that is not exactly a possession, but part of his person, like a limb, as when he amputates it; or like a relative, as when he takes another's daughter or wife, he is not strictly committing theft. But there is a third distinguishing feature of theft which completes its definition, and this is that somebody else's property is taken surreptitiously. It follows that the essence of theft consists in its being the surreptitious taking of somebody else's property.

Hence...

2. Retaining what one owes another does the same sort of harm as taking something from another, and this is why unjustifiable taking must be held to include unjustifiable retention.

. . .

66.6 REPLY: We have already seen (IIaIIae 59.4) that mortal sin consists in cutting oneself off from the charity which is the spiritual life-sap of the soul. But charity consists primarily in loving God, and, secondly, in loving our neighbour which includes wishing him well and acting accordingly. Stealing, however, damages one's neighbour through his property, and human society would perish if everybody started stealing from everybody else. Theft is, therefore, a mortal sin in so far as it is contrary to charity.

Hence: 1. Stealing is said not to be a great fault for two reasons. In the first place, there may be some necessity driving a person to steal, and this would diminish or take away entirely the fault, as we shall be explaining below. This is why the passage quoted continues, *He steals to satisfy his appetite when he is hungry.* Secondly, theft is said not to be a great fault in comparison with adultery, which is punishable by death (Lev. 20.10; Deut. 22.22). And this is why the passage goes on further to say, *And if he is caught, he will pay sevenfold. He who commits adultery destroys himself* (Prov. 6.31-32).

2. Penalties imposed in this life are corrective rather than retributive, for retribution is reserved to God's judgement which *rightly falls on those who do such things* (Rom. 2.2). A man should, therefore, not be sentenced to death in this life for any mortal sin, but only for such mortal sins as cause irreparable damage or else as are particularly perverted. A man is, therefore, not sentenced to death in this life for theft since it causes damage that is reparable, unless there is some aggravating circumstance, as in the case of sacrilege, which is the theft of something sacred, or of peculation, which is the theft of public property, as Augustine explains in his commentary on St John (*Super Joan.* L. on 12.6), or of kidnapping, which *Exodus* makes punishable with death as being the theft of a man (Ex. 21.16).

3. The rational man counts trifles as nothing, and a person will, therefore, not think that he has suffered harm where only such trifles are involved, just as anyone who takes such trifles can presume that he is not acting contrary to the other's will. To this extent, therefore, somebody who takes such trifles from another by stealth can be exonerated of mortal sin. He can, however, commit mortal sin if he intends to steal and to inflict harm, even where such trifles are involved, just as consent to the delight of some sinful act in thought can suffice to constitute mortal sin.

. . .

66.7 REPLY: The dictates of human law cannot derogate from natural or divine law. The natural order established by God in his providence is, however, such that lower things are meant to enable man to supply his needs. A man's needs must therefore still be met out of the world's goods even though a certain division and apportionment of them is determined by law. And this is why according to natural law goods that are held in superabundance by some people should be used for the maintenance of the poor. This is the principle enunciated by Ambrose and repeated in the *Decretum, It is the bread of the poor which you are holding back; it is the clothes of the naked which you are hoarding; it is the relief and liberation of the wretched which you are thwarting by burying your money away* (Gratian, *Decretum,* I, 47 8). At the same time those who suffer want are so numerous and they cannot all be supplied out of one stock, and this is why it is left to each individual to decide how to manage his property in such a way as to supply the wants of the suffering (Aquinas, *Quodlibet.* VIII, 6, 2). If, however, there is so urgent and blatant a necessity that the immediate needs must be met out of whatever is available, as when a person is in imminent danger and he cannot be helped in any other way, then a person may legitimately supply his own needs out of another's property, whether he does so secretly or flagrantly. And in such a case there is strictly speaking no theft or robbery.

...

68.3 REPLY: A complaint is meant to be in the public interest, which is served by the disclosure of crimes, as we have already observed. No one is, however, entitled to injure another unjustly to promote the public interest. A complaint can, therefore, become sinful in two ways. The first way is for the accused to be treated unjustly by being falsely charged, and this is what calumny consists in. The other way is for somebody maliciously to prevent the punishment of the sins, for this impinges on the good of society which is the main raison d'être of complaints. And this in turn takes two forms. One is the use of duplicity in making the complaint, which is what prevarication is, for *prevarication literally means walking crookedly, and so being devious by colluding with the opposing party* (Gratian, *Decretum*, II, 2, 3). The other form is to withdraw from the suit entirely. And this is what abandoning proceedings is, for abandonment involves turning one's back, and to give up what one has started is like turning one's back on it.

7. Thomas Aquinas – Extracts from *De regimine principum*

Book 1

Chapter I: To fulfil this intention, we must begin by explaining how the title 'king' is to be understood. Now in all cases where things are directed towards some end but it is possible to proceed in more than one way, it is necessary for there to be some guiding principle, so that the due end may be properly achieved. For example, a ship is driven in different directions according to the force of different winds, and it will not reach its final destination except by the industry of the steersman who guides it into port. Now man has a certain end towards which the whole of his life and activity is directed; for as a creature who acts by intelligence, it is clearly his nature to work towards some end (Aristotle, *Ethics* I.7, 1098a5). But men can proceed towards that end in different ways, as the very diversity of human efforts and activities shows. Man therefore needs something to guide him towards his end.

Now each man is imbued by nature with the light of reason, and he is directed towards his end by its action within him. If it were proper for man to live in solitude, as many animals do, he would need no other guide towards his end; for each man would then be a king unto himself, under God, the supreme King, and would direct his own actions by the light of reason divinely given to him. But man is by nature a social and political animal, who lives in a community (Aristotle, *Politics* I.2, 1253a2): more so, indeed, than all other animals; and natural necessity shows why this is so. For other animals are furnished by nature with food, with a covering of hair, and with the means of defence, such as teeth, horns or at any rate speed in flight. But man is supplied with none of these things by nature. Rather, in place of all of them reason was given to him, by which he might be able to provide all things for himself, by the work of his own hands (Aristotle, *De partibus animalium* IV.10, 687a19). One man, however, is not able to equip himself with all these things, for one man cannot live a self-sufficient life. It is therefore natural for man to live in fellowship with many others.

...

If, therefore, it is natural for man to live in fellowship with many others, it is necessary for there to be some means whereby such a community of men may be ruled. For if many men were to live together with each providing only what is convenient for himself, the community would break up into its various parts unless one of them had responsibility for the good of the community as a whole, just as the body of a man and of any other animal would fall apart if there were not some general ruling force to sustain the body and secure the common good of all its parts. Solomon is thinking of this at Proverbs 11.14 where he says: 'Where there is no governor, the people shall be scattered.' This accords with reason; for individual interests and the common good are not the same. Individuals differ as to their private interests, but are united with respect to the common good, and such differences have various causes. It is fitting, therefore, that, beyond that which moves the individual to pursue a good peculiar to himself, there should be something which promotes the common good of the many. It is for this reason that wherever things are organised into a unity, something is found that rules all the rest (*Politics* I.5, 1254a28). For by a certain order of Divine providence all bodies in the material universe are ruled by the primary, that is, the celestial, body, and all bodies by rational creatures. Also, in one man the soul rules the body, and, within the soul, the irascible and concupiscible appetites are ruled by the reason. Again, among the members of the body there is one ruling part, either the heart or the head, which moves all the others (Aristotle, *Metaphysics* V.1, 1013a5). It is fitting, therefore, that in every multitude there should be some ruling principle (cf. John of Salisbury, *Policraticus* 5.2).

Chapter II: But where matters are directed towards some end, there may be one way of proceeding which is right and another which not right; and so we find that the government of a community can be directed both rightly and not rightly (*Politics* III.6, 1279a17). Now something is directed rightly when it is led to its proper end, and not rightly when it is led to an end which is not proper to it. But the end proper to a community of free men is different from that of slaves. For a free man is one who is the master of his own actions, whereas a slave, insofar as he is a slave, is the property of another (*Metaphysics* I.2, 982b25). If, therefore, a community of free men is ordered by a ruler in such a way as to secure the common good, such rule will be right and just inasmuch as it is suitable to free men.

…

If just government belongs to one man alone, he is properly called a king. Hence the Lord, at Ezekiel 37:24, says: 'And David my servant shall be king over them, and they all shall have one shepherd.' It is clearly shown by this verse that it is the nature of kingship that there should be one who rules, and that he should be a shepherd who seeks the common good and not his own gain (*Politics* III.7, 1279a25).

Now since it is fitting for man to live in a community because he would not be able to provide all the necessaries of life for himself were he to remain alone, it must be that a society of many men will be perfect to the extent that it is self-sufficient in the necessaries of life. The self-sufficient life is certainly present to some extent in the family of one household, with respect, that is, to the natural activities of nourishment and the procreation of children and other things of this kind; and one locality may be sufficient in all those things belonging to a particular trade; and a city, which is a perfect [i.e. a complete] community, is sufficient in all the necessaries of life (*Politics* I.2, 1252b9). But this is all the more true of a single province, because of the need for common defence and mutual assistance against enemies. Hence, he who rules a perfect community, that is, a city or province, is properly called a king; but he who rules a household is not a king, but the father of a family. He does, however, bear a certain resemblance to a king, and for this reason kings are sometimes called the 'fathers' of their people.

From what we have said, therefore, it is clear that a king is one who rules over the community of a city or province, and for the common good. Hence Solomon, at Ecclesiastes 5:8, says: 'The king commands all the lands subject to him.'

Chapter III:…

This appears also to be borne out by experience. For provinces or cities which are not ruled by one man toil under dissensions and are tossed about without peace, so that the complaint which the Lord made through the prophet (Jeremiah 12:10) may be seen to be fulfilled: 'Many pastors have destroyed my vineyard.' By contrast, provinces and cities governed by a single king rejoice in peace, flourish in justice and are gladdened by an abundance of things. Hence the Lord promises His people through the prophets that, as a great gift, He will put them under one head and that there will be one prince in the midst of them (cf. Jer. 30.21, Ez. 34.23, 37.25).

Chapter IV: …

Again, what renders government unjust is the fact that the private good of the ruler is sought at the expense of the good of the community. The further it departs from the common good, therefore, the more unjust will the government be. But there is a greater departure from the common good in an oligarchy, where the good of the few is sought, than in a democracy, where the good of the many is sought; and there is a still greater departure from the common good in a tyranny, where the good of only one is sought. A large number comes closer to the whole than a small one, and a small one closer than only one. Tyranny, therefore, is the most unjust form of government.

…

The same conclusion is especially apparent if one considers the evils which arise from tyranny. For when the tyrant, despising the common good, seeks his own private good, the consequence is that he oppresses his subjects in a variety of ways, according to the different passions to which he is subject as he tries to secure whatever goods he desires. For one who is in the grip of the passion of greed will seize the property of his subjects; hence Solomon says at Proverbs 29:4: 'The just king makes rich the earth, but the greedy man destroys it.' If he is subject to the passion of wrath, he will shed blood for no reason; hence it is said at Ezekiel 22:27: 'Her princes in the midst thereof are like wolves ravening their prey, to shed blood.' The wise man admonishes us that such rule is to be shunned, saying (Ecclesiasticus 9:13), 'Keep thee far from the man that hath power to kill': that is, because he kills not for the sake of justice, but through power and from the lust of his own will. There will, therefore, be no security, but all things uncertain, when the law is forsaken; nor will it be possible for any trust to be placed in that which depends upon the will, not to say the lust, of another. Nor does such rule oppress its subjects in bodily matters only, but it impedes them with respect to their spiritual goods also; for those who desire to rule their subjects rather than benefit them put every obstacle in the way of their progress, being suspicious of any excellence in their subjects that might threaten their own wicked rule. Tyrants 'suspect good men rather than bad, and are always afraid of another's virtue' (Sallust, *Bellum Catilinae* 7:2). Tyrants therefore endeavour to prevent their subjects from becoming virtuous and increasing in nobility of spirit, lest they refuse to bear their unjust dominion. They prevent the bond of friendship from becoming established among their subjects, and hinder them from enjoying the rewards of mutual peace, so that, for as long as they do not trust one another, they will not be able to unite against a tyrant's rule. For this reason, tyrants sow discord among their subjects, nourish strife, and prohibit those things which create fellowship among men, such as wedding-feasts and banquets and other such things by which familiarity and trust are usually produced among men (*Politics* V.11, 1313a39). They also endeavour to prevent anyone from becoming powerful or rich, because, suspecting their subjects according to their own evil conscience, they fear that, just as they themselves use power and riches to do harm, so the power and wealth of their subjects will be used to do harm to them in return. Hence Job (15:21) says this of the tyrant: 'The sound of dread is ever in his ears, and even when there is peace' – that is, even when no ill is intended towards him – 'he is ever suspicious of treacheries'. For this reason, then, when rulers who ought to cultivate the virtues in their subjects look upon their subjects' virtues with wretched envy and do everything in their power to impede them, few virtuous men will be found under a tyrant. For according to what the Philosopher says, brave men are found among those who honour the bravest (*Ethics* I.3, 1095b28; III.8, 1116a20); and, as Cicero says, 'Things which are despised by everyone always fail and have little strength' (*Tusculanae disputationes* 1:2:4).

It is, indeed, natural that men who are nourished in a climate of fear should degenerate into a servile condition of soul and become fearful of every manly and strenuous act. This is shown by the experience of those provinces which have remained long under a tyrant. Hence the Apostle says at Colossians 3:21: 'Fathers, provoke not your children to anger, lest they be discouraged.' And Solomon is thinking of these harmful effects of tyranny when he says (Proverbs 28:12): 'When the wicked reign, men are ruined': because, that is, subjects fall away from the perfection of virtue through the wickedness of tyrants. And he goes on to say (29:2): 'When the wicked beareth rule, the people mourn'; and again (28:28): 'When the wicked rise, men hide themselves' in order to escape the cruelty of tyrants. And no wonder; for a man who rules without reason according to the lusts of his own soul is no different from a beast. Hence Solomon says (Proverbs 28:15): 'As a roaring lion and a hungry bear, so is a wicked ruler over the poor people.' And so it is that men remove themselves from a tyrant as from cruel beasts, and to be subject to a tyrant seems the same as to be mauled by a ferocious animal.

...

Chapter VII: It is clear from what we have said, therefore, that the rule of one, which is the best, is to be preferred, but that it can turn into a tyranny, which is the worst. It is therefore necessary to labour with diligent care to provide the community with a king who is of such a kind that it will not fall victim to a tyrant. First, then, it is necessary that the character of the man elevated to kingship by those to whom the duty of doing this belongs should be such that it is not probable that he will decline into tyranny. Hence Samuel, commending God's providence in appointing a king, says, at 1 Samuel 13:14: 'The Lord hath sought Him a man after His own heart.' Next, once the king has been appointed, the government of the kingdom should be so arranged as to remove from the king the opportunity of becoming a tyrant; and, at the same time, his power should be restricted so that he will not easily be able to fall into tyranny. How these things can be done will have to be discussed in subsequent chapters. Finally, we must consider what should be done if the king does become a tyrant.

If, however, the tyranny is not excessive, it is more advantageous to tolerate a degree of tyranny for the time being than to take action against the tyrant and so incur many perils more grievous than the tyranny itself. For it may happen that those who take such action prove unable to prevail against the tyrant, and succeed only in provoking the tyrant to even greater savagery. Even when those who take action against a tyrant are able to overthrow him, this fact may in itself give rise to many very grave dissensions in the populace, either during the rebellion against the tyrant or because, after the tyrant has been removed, the community is divided into factions over the question of what the new ruling order should be. Again, it sometimes happens that a community expels a tyrant with the help of some other ruler who, having achieved power, snatches at tyranny himself and, fearing to suffer at the hands of another what he has himself done to another, forces his subjects into a slavery even more grievous than before. It is often true in cases of tyranny that a subsequent tyrant proves to be worse than his predecessor; for, while not undoing any of the troubles inflicted by his predecessor, he devises new ones of his own, out of the malice of his own heart. Thus, at a time when all the people of Syracuse desired the death of Dionysius, a certain old woman continually prayed that he would remain safe and sound and might outlive her. When the tyrant came to know of this, he asked her why she did it. She said to him: 'When I was a girl, we suffered the oppression of a tyrant, and I longed for his death. Then he was slain, but his successor was even harsher, and I thought it a great thing when his rule came to an end. But then we began to have a third ruler who was even more savage: you. And if you were to be taken from us, someone still worse would come instead' (Valerius Maximus, 6:2:2; John of Salisbury, *Policraticus* 7:25).

If, however, a tyranny were so extreme as to be intolerable, it has seemed to some that it would be an act consistent with virtue if the mightier men were to slay the tyrant, exposing themselves even to the peril of death in order to liberate the community. Indeed, we have an example of such a thing in the Old Testament. For a certain Ehud slew Eglon, king of Moab, with a dagger 'fastened to his thigh', because he oppressed the people of God with a harsh bondage; and for this deed Ehud was made a judge of the people. But this is not consistent with apostolic doctrine. For Peter teaches us to be subject with all fear not only to good and gentle masters, but also to those who are ill disposed, 'For this is thankworthy, if a man for conscience toward God endure grief, suffering wrongfully' (1 Peter 2:18f). Thus, when many Roman emperors tyrannically persecuted the faith of Christ, a great part of the community, both nobles and ordinary people, were converted to the faith and are now praised because, offering no resistance, they suffered death for Christ with patience and courage, as appears clearly in the case of the holy legion of Thebes. Moreover, Ehud should be adjudged to have slain an enemy of the people rather than a ruler, albeit a tyrannical one; and so also we read in the Old Testament that those who slew Joash the king of Judah were themselves slain (although their children were spared, according to the teaching of the law) even though he had turned aside from the worship of God (2 Kings 14.5f.). For it would be a perilous thing, both for a community and its rulers, if anyone could attempt to slay even tyrannical rulers simply on his own private presumption. Indeed, the wicked expose themselves to such peril more often than good men do. For the lordship of a just king is usually no less a burden to the wicked than that of a tyrant; for, according to the saying of Solomon at Proverbs 20:26: 'A wise king scattereth the wicked.' What is more likely to come of such presumption, therefore, is peril to the community through the loss of a king than relief through the removal of a tyrant.

It seems, then, that steps are to be taken against the scourge of tyranny not by the private presumption of any persons, but through public authority (cf. ST IIaIIae 42.2 ad 3). First of all, in cases where it belongs by right to a community to provide a ruler for itself, that community can without injustice depose or restrain a king whom it has appointed, if he should abuse royal power tyrannically. Nor should such a community be thought disloyal if it acts to depose a tyrant even if the community has already pledged itself to him in perpetuity; for the tyrant who has failed to govern the community faithfully, as the office of king requires, has deserved to be treated in this way. Thus the Romans who had accepted Tarquin the Proud as their king, then ejected him from the kingship because of his and his sons' tyranny, and substituted a lesser power, that is, the consulate. So also Domitian, who succeeded the mildest of emperors, Vespasian, his father, and Titus, his brother, was slain by the Roman Senate when he exercised tyrannical power, and all the wicked things that he had inflicted upon the Romans were justly and wholesomely revoked and made void by decree of the Senate. Thus it came about that Blessed John the Evangelist, the beloved disciple of God, who had been sent away into exile on the island of Patmos by Domitian, was brought back to Ephesus by special senatorial decree.

If, however, the right to provide a community with a king belongs to some superior, then a remedy against the wickedness of a tyrant must be sought from him. Thus when Archelaus, who began to reign in Judea in place of his father Herod, imitated the wickedness of his father, the Jews made complaint against him to Augustus Caesar, by whom his power was first reduced, the title of king being removed from him and half his kingdom divided between his two brothers; then, when this did not keep his tyrannical behaviour in check, he was banished into exile by Tiberius Caesar to Lyons, a city of Gaul.

If, however, there can be no human aid at all against a tyrant, recourse must be had to God, the King of all, who is 'a refuge in time of trouble' (Ps. 9.9). For it is within His power to turn the heart of the cruel tyrant towards gentleness, according to what Solomon says at Proverbs 21:1: 'The king's heart is in the hand of the Lord: He turneth it whithersoever He will.' He it was Who turned the cruelty of the king of the Assyrians to gentleness when he was preparing death for the Jews (Es. 15.11).

...

Chapter XIII: Following on from what we have said, it is necessary now to consider what the duty of the king is and what sort of person the king should be. And because it is true that art imitates nature (*Physics* II.2, 194a21). and that it is from natural things that we learn how to act according to reason, it would seem best to infer the duties of a king from the forms of government which occur in nature.

Now among natural things there is found both a universal and a particular form of government. The universal form is that according to which all things are contained under the government of God, Who governs all things by His providence. The particular form of government is very similar to the Divine government, and it is found within man, who for this reason may be called a lesser world, because within him is found an example of universal government (*Physics* VIII.2, 252b24; Gregory, *Homilia in evangelia* 29.2). For just as all corporeal creatures and all spiritual powers are contained under the Divine rule, so also the members of the body and the other powers of the soul are ruled by reason; and so the place of reason in man is, in a certain sense, like the relation of God to the world. But because, as we have shown above, man is by nature a social animal who lives in community, this similarity with Divine rule is found in man not only inasmuch as the individual man is ruled by reason, but also inasmuch as a community is ruled by the reason of an individual man; for it is this which belongs especially to the duty of the king. Something similar is found in the case of certain animals who live socially, such as bees, among whom there is said to be a king (Aristotle, *Historia animalium* 5.21, 553b6); but rule of this kind does not come about through reason, but through an instinct of nature implanted in them by the Supreme Ruler.

Let the king understand, therefore, that he has received the duty of being to his kingdom what the soul is to the body and what God is to the world. If he reflects diligently upon this, he will on the one hand be fired with zeal for justice when he considers that he has been appointed to exercise judgment in his kingdom in the place of God; and, on the other, he will acquire kindness and clemency, for he will look upon all those subject to his government as though they were his own members.

Chapter XIV: It is, therefore, necessary to consider what God does in the world; for in this way it will become clear what the king should do. Now God's work in relation to the world must be considered under two general aspects. First, He made the world; second, He governs the world that He has made. Again, the soul has two functions in relation to the body; for, first, the power of the soul gives form to the body, and, second, the body is ruled and moved by the soul. Now it is the second of these activities which more properly belongs to the duty of the king; for the task of governing pertains to all kings, and the title 'king' [*rex*] is derived from the fact that he directs the government [*a gubernationis regimine*] (Isidore of Seville, *Etymologiae* I.29; IX.3). But the first activity does not belong to all kings, for not every king founds the city in which he reigns; many carry on the activity of ruling in a kingdom or city which has been founded already. It must be borne in mind, however, that if there had not been someone in the beginning to found a city or a kingdom, there would be no place in the world for royal government. The founding of a city or kingdom must therefore also be considered as falling within the duty of the king. For some have founded the cities in which they ruled, as Ninus did Nineveh and Romulus Rome (Augustine, *City of God*, XVI.17). Similarly again, it pertains to the duty of government to protect what is governed and to make use of it for the purpose for which it was established.

...

Chapter XV: Just as the foundation of a city or kingdom can fittingly be inferred from the example of the creation of the world, so also can the proper government of the former be inferred from the government of the latter. First of all, however, it must be noted that to govern is to guide what is governed in a suitable fashion to its proper end. Thus a ship is said to be governed when it is steered on its right course to port by the industry of the sailors. If, therefore, something is directed towards an end external to itself, as a ship is to harbour, the duty of its governor will be not only to preserve the thing itself, but also to guide it towards its final end; whereas if there were something with no end outside itself, then the sole task belonging to the ruler would be the preservation of the thing itself in perfect condition.

But nothing of the latter kind [i.e. nothing with no end outside itself] is found in the world [*in rebus*] apart from God, Who is the end of all things; and the care of that which is directed towards an end outside itself is beset with a number of difficulties. For perhaps there is one person whose responsibility it is to preserve the thing itself and another whose task is to lead it towards a higher perfection, as in the case of the ship, from which we have drawn an example of government. For the carpenter has the task of repairing any damage which the ship has sustained, whereas the mariner bears the responsibility for guiding the ship to port. And so it happens also in the case of a man. For the physician has the task of preserving a man's life in a healthy condition; the steward has to supply him with the necessaries of life; the task of the teacher is to see to it that he understands the truth; and that of the moral counsellor is to ensure that he lives according to reason. And if man were not directed towards some good external to himself, the foregoing forms of care would suffice.

But there is a certain extraneous good which awaits man after he has lived this mortal life: namely, the final blessedness to which he looks forward in the enjoyment of God after death. For as the Apostle says (2 Cor. 5:6): 'While we are in the body, we are absent from the Lord.' The Christian man, then, for whom that blessedness has been won by the blood of Christ, and for the attainment of which he has received the earnest of the Holy Spirit, has need of another, spiritual, care by which he is guided towards the harbour of eternal salvation. And this is the kind of care shown to the faithful by the ministers of the Church of Christ.

We must make the same judgment in regard to the end of the whole community as we do of one person (*Politics* VII.2, 1324a5; 1325b31). If the end of man were some good existing only in himself, therefore, the final end of government would similarly be to acquire and preserve that good for the whole community. Thus if that ultimate end, whether of one man or of a community, were the life and health of the body, the physicians would have the duty of governing. And if the final end were abundant wealth, the steward would be king of the community. And if the good were that the community might achieve knowledge of the truth, the king would have the duty of a teacher. But it seems that the end for which a community is brought together is to live according to virtue; for men come together so that they may live well in a way that would not be possible for each of them living singly. For the good is life according to virtue, and so the end of human association is a virtuous life (*Ethics* II.1, 1103b3; *Politics* I.2, 1252b27, III.9, 1280b5).

An indication of this lies in the fact that only those who share with one another in the task of living well are deemed to be parts of a community. For if men came together for the sake of life merely, both animals and slaves would have a part in civil society; if for the sake of acquiring wealth, all those engaged in commerce together would belong to one city (*Politics* III.9, 1280a25). But we see that only those are counted as members of a community who are guided in living well under the same laws and by the same government. But because the man who lives according to virtue is also directed towards a further end, which, as we have already said above, consists in the enjoyment of the Divine, the end of the whole community of mankind must therefore be the same as it is for one man. The final end of a multitude united in society, therefore, will not be to live according to virtue, but through virtuous living to attain to the enjoyment of the Divine. Now if it were possible to achieve this end through natural human virtue alone, it would necessarily belong to the king's duty to guide men to this end; for, as we suppose, it is to the king that the supreme ruling power in human affairs is entrusted, and government is of a higher order according to the finality of the end to which it is directed. For we find that it is always the one who has responsibility for the final end who directs those who carry out the tasks leading to the final end (*Ethics* I.1, 1094a10). For example, the captain whose responsibility it is to direct the navigation of the ship commands him who constructs the ship to make the kind of ship most suitable for his purposes; and the citizen who makes use of arms gives orders to the blacksmith as to what kind of arms he is to forge. But because the enjoyment of Divinity is an end which a man cannot attain through human virtue alone, but only through Divine virtue, according to the Apostle at Romans 6:23: 'The grace of God is eternal life', it is not human but Divine rule that will lead us to this end. And government of this kind belongs only to that King Who is not only man, but also God: that is, to our Lord Jesus Christ, Who by making men sons of God, has led them to the glory of heaven.

...

Chapter XVI: Just as the life that men live here, when they live well, is directed, as to its end, towards the blessed life in heaven for which we hope, so all the particular goods which men obtain, whether wealth or profit or health or skill or learning, are directed, as to their end, to the good of the community. If, therefore, as we have said, he who is responsible for a final end must govern those who are responsible for the things directed towards that end and must direct them by his command, it is clear that the king, just as he must be subject to the lordship and governance administered by the priestly office, must rule over all human occupations and direct them by his own command and rule.

...

The king, therefore, being instructed in the Divine law, must strive with special care to ensure that the community subject to him lives well; and this task may be divided into three parts. First, he must establish the good life in the community subject to him; second, he must preserve it once it is established; third, having preserved it, he must strive to improve it. But the good life for each man requires two things. The first and chief requirement is activity according to virtue, for virtue is that quality by which we live well (Augustine, *De libero arbitrio* 2.19). The other requirement is secondary and, as it were, instrumental: namely, a sufficiency of bodily goods, the use of which is necessary to virtuous conduct (*Ethics* I.8, 1099b1). Man himself is made a unity by natural causation; but the unity of a community, which is called peace, must be brought about by the industry of the ruler. So, then: to establish the good life for a community requires three things: first, that the community be established in the unity of peace; second, that the community united by the bond of peace be guided to act well – for just as a man cannot act well unless we presuppose the unity of his parts, so a multitude of men who are at odds with one another because they lack peace will be prevented from living well; and, third, it requires that, through the industry of the ruler, there be a plentiful supply of those things necessary to living well.

When, therefore, the good life has been established in the community by the duty of the king, he must next consider how to preserve it. Now there are three things detrimental to the permanence of the public good; and one of these arises from the nature of things. For the good of the community should not be established for a particular length of time only, but should be as it were perpetual. But men, because they are mortal, do not endure perpetually; nor, while they are alive, do they always have the same degree of vigour, for human life is subject to many changes, and men are not equally capable of fulfilling the same duties throughout the whole of life. Another obstacle to the preservation of the public good arises from within, and consists in perversity of will; for some people are negligent in carrying out the duties which the commonwealth requires, or even damage the peace of the community when they transgress against justice and disturb the peace of others. And the third obstacle to the preservation of the commonwealth comes from an external cause, when the peace is undone by the invasion of enemies, and sometimes the kingdom or city which has been founded is destroyed. In relation to the three foregoing causes, therefore, the task of the king has a threefold character. The first has to do with the succession of men: that is, with the replacement of those who preside over the various duties. For just as the Divine government ensures that corruptible things, which cannot remain the same for ever, are renewed by the production of others to replace them, and in this way preserves the integrity of the universe, so by the efforts of the king the good of the community subject to him will be preserved when he takes care to ensure that successors take the place of those who are faltering. Second, he should restrain the men subject to him from iniquity by means of laws and commands, penalties and rewards, and lead them to do virtuous works, taking his example from God, Who gave men a law, and Who rewards those who observe it and requites with punishment those who transgress it. Third, it is the king's task to furnish the community subject to him with protection against enemies; for taking measures against internal perils will bring no benefit if it is not possible for it to be defended against external ones.

So, then, a third thing remains as belonging to the duty of the king if he is to ensure the good of the community: he must be careful to secure its improvement. This will be done in each of the ways mentioned above if he corrects what is disordered, if he supplies what is lacking, and if he strives to perfect whatever can be done better. Hence the Apostle, at 1 Corinthians 12:31, admonishes the faithful always to 'covet earnestly the best gifts'.

8. The Emergence of Political Theology: Discussion Questions

What theological role does human government have?

What tools does Christian political theology offer for responding to tyranny?

To what extent should love of the poor characterize the whole project of Christian political theology?

II

Approaches to Political Theology

Introduction by Anna Rowlands

The term 'political theology' was first introduced into the lexicon of modern philosophy and theology in the 1920s by the controversial conservative German legal scholar Carl Schmitt (1888–1985). While the term has ancient, classical and pagan associations, Schmitt redefined the idea to capture his insights into the doctrine of political sovereignty. His was a project in the history of ideas: to understand the development of the idea of the modern state was necessarily to grasp the continuing role of theological ideas in shaping political realities. Schmitt draws an analogy between the idea of the exception in jurisprudence and the miracle in theology. The idea of the sovereignty of monarch or people follows from an earlier theological set of reasoning about the nature of God. In a secularizing era this seemed a counterintuitive thought; however, for Schmitt, the lingering presence of Judeo-Christian religion in the realm of ideas had to be recognized as a constituent part of the political culture of the West.

Schmitt's use of the language of political theology was, however, fraught with difficulties. His intellectual project was connected to a preference for authoritarian forms of politics, and his work tainted by an association with Nazism. Perhaps surprisingly therefore, rather than rejecting out of hand Schmitt's retrieval of the term, in the 1960s a new generation of post-war German theologians chose to reinvent it as the foundation of a new, 'critical' theological approach. This new approach would aim to take seriously the complicity of church practices and theological ideas with the violence of the twentieth century, would place the suffering voice of human subjects at the foundation of theological processes and would challenge the functionalization of religion in a secular age. Jürgen Moltmann is at pains to stress that the project to renew political theology and overturn Schmitt's use of the phrase should not be understood as a re-politicization of church, but rather as the Christianization of political existence based on the nonviolent witness of the Sermon on the Mount. Johann Baptist Metz argues for a paradigm shift in theology, reinventing the tradition of Christian reflection on the political for a post-Holocaust world: moving theology away from both its perceived pre-Enlightenment role as legitimizing political authority and its contemporary role as servant to civil religion denuded of substantial truth claims. The new political theology, typified in the work of Moltmann, Metz and Dorothee Soelle, would necessarily focus on theological interpretation of categories of resistance and suffering. Metz claims boldly that the primary task of all political theology is the deprivatization of religious belief and practice.

Thus the term political theology entered the twentieth-century theological scene as an already contested and plural notion, raising with it as many questions as it posited new answers. Was the appeal to a political theology always fraught with risk of violence? Had the church not always been doing political theology, albeit without self-conscious use of the phrase? Was there really a genuinely 'new' dimension to its operation in the way Moltmann and Metz imagined?

Continuing the conversations begun in Section I, 'The Emergence of Political Theology', we offer the reader some key texts that enable exploration of these contested questions concerning different approaches to the study of Christian political and public theologies.

The first text is taken from the first chapter of Carl Schmitt's treatise *Political Theology*, presenting the argument we have outlined above. The second text is Jürgen Moltmann's seminal and vastly ambitious 1994 article 'Covenant or Leviathan? Political Theology for Modern Times'. Here Moltmann argues that political theology is characterized by two fundamentally different approaches: 'covenant or Leviathan'. Leviathan political theologies, typified in the work of Thomas Hobbes and Carl Schmitt, are rooted in a negative anthropology and tend to emphasize human sinfulness, the distance between Creator and creature, and the formulation of a social contract oriented towards self-determination within a violent social order. By contrast, covenant theologies, typified in forms of Calvinist federalism, tend to adopt a more positive anthropology (although no denial of sin!), a social and relational view of the human person whereby the covenant between creatures emerges both as an analogy of the double covenant between God and his people and as subordinate to the covenant between God and his people. Correspondingly God trusts that we are capable of forming lasting covenants, and God is the ground for creaturely resistance to rule that fails to serve the covenant. Here we hit Moltmann's central concern: a renewed Reformed iteration of a Christian theology of resistance. Moltmann argues that the free person is the one who claims the right of resistance. This way of resistance finds its pattern in the free discipleship of the crucified Christ; it is the cross that Moltmann characterizes as tearing at the political unity of religion and politics.

This articulation of a new, post-war theology of resistance acts as a fascinating shared theme across the Reformed and Catholic theologies produced by Moltmann, Metz and Soelle. Metz's 'Theology in the New Paradigm' poses critical questions about how theology changes, and about how theological ideas and forms of Christian living interrelate. Metz, ahead of current post-secular thinkers, notes the importance of addressing the incompleteness of the secularizing agenda: religion has not been completely privatized and politics has not been entirely secularized. This brings dangers and opportunities for those who wish to discern the political content of Christianity. Metz, like Moltmann, holds onto the necessity of a critical distinction between religion and politics – between spiritual and worldly power. This distinction is necessary in order for theology to be able to engage in criticism of political religion – the co-option or functionalizing of religion by the state, and for it to be able to assert its own public witness for the sake of all. Metz and Moltmann agree that where a real distinction between spiritual and worldly power was upheld there was more resistance to the Nazi 'Leviathan' – but this resistance did not go far enough – tending to limit itself to an assertion of freedom of the church not of the people. While Moltmann asks whether it is possible to reconceive the Christian resistance tradition rooted in a Christian discipleship with a public witness for all, Metz asks whether theology can ground not just a logic or order but also a resistant politics of change.

The theme of resistance takes a decidedly mystical turn in the work of Dorothee Soelle. In this extract from *The Silent Cry* Soelle argues that the task for the post-Holocaust Christian is to live in the world as if a liberated life were possible. Given the contradictions and tensions produced for the human person living in a globalized age programmed towards dehumanizing speed, productivity, consumption and profit, the necessary mode of Christian living will be one of resistance. Our malaise is spiritual, produced by the inner connections between globalization and individualization, and it can only be overcome by a spiritual vision that nourishes resistance. Soelle argues for the presence of mystical movements within the life of the church who have nurtured forms of resistance and dissent. In a parallel way she looks to contemporary movements that resist globalization and individualization as sustained by elements of mysticism. Of what does this mysticism speak, and what is its Christian content and political form? Soelle talks of 'the mysticism of the good beginning and of its re-establishment'. She argues that resistance that maintains the connection between love of truth and love of (persecuted) neighbour requires a revolutionary patience that sets out from 'the experience of what has always been good'. With Metz, Soelle argues for the subjectivity of suffering victims to be allowed to renew theology. With Moltmann, she is conscious of the marketization of all things, including the colonization of the soul by media.

The final text in this section, taken from the work of German social philosopher Jürgen Habermas, belongs to a canon of twentieth-century writings that might be more typically described as public rather than political theology. As Elaine Graham argues in her book *Between A Rock and a Hard Place*, public theology and political theology are distinctive but overlapping theological disciplines.[1] Graham argues that public theology

---

[1] See, Elaine Graham, 'Lost in Translation? The Dilemmas of Public Theology' in *Between a Rock and a Hard Place: Public Theology in a Post-Secular Age* (London: SCM Press, 2013), pp. 69–105

seeks to interpret the moral, metaphysical and theological form of society's economic, cultural and intellectual milieu. She argues that political theology is more narrowly concerned with political processes and institutions. While this definition and distinction perhaps does not take sufficient account of the Schmittian tradition of political theology – tracing the presence of theological ideas put to work in political cultures – nonetheless Graham does note helpfully that public theology tends to be less formally ecclesial in its orientation, drawing its agenda from matters of public policy and discourse and seeks to communicate its substance to a wider societal conversation – it takes 'the public' as its source and as its communicative context. She argues that given the challenges posed by cultural and religious pluralism and new global movements, this distinction between traditions of public and political theology is important to grasp.

Graham argues that engaging in dialogue with the work of Jürgen Habermas is especially important for contemporary public theologians. She proposes that Habermas's writings on the origins of the public square, on post-secularity and on communicative action offer productive theses for stimulating theological engagement. Therefore, our final text in this section is a transcript of Habermas's speech given on the occasion of the award of a Peace Prize in 2001. This speech caused a significant stir at the time of its delivery not long after the events of 9/11 because of its attempt to articulate a different kind of 'post-secular' settlement between religion and the political. It represented a shift in Habermas's own thought towards a re-evaluation of the social and political character of religious forms of solidarity. Habermas outlines what he calls a 'non-destructive secularization' in which religious ideas and communities are able to speak into political processes. Habermas is not arguing that there has been a religious revival, nor that secularization per se has failed, but rather that aspects of the current secular settlement in European societies can be considered flawed. He notes the rather peculiar secular expectation of self-reflection that applies uniquely to religious actors engaging in public speech. He is also attentive to the substantive linguistic voids left where religious concepts previously offered richer ways of describing human experience: sin and evil, resurrection and hope. He notes perceptively that it can feel that we lack a more profound and weighty language for intercultural relations beyond that dictated by the military and the market. Habermas develops a series of criteria for religious contributions to a developed democratic common sense: that religions must first have engaged with the dissonant encounter with other believers, be able to adapt to the insights of the sciences and must accept a constitutional state with a profane morality. However, he is also clear that there are corresponding secular responsibilities incumbent upon the non-religious to listen openly to all traditions of faith and reason in order to develop the best arguments for a genuinely and fully public debate.

In the companion volume to this reader, Elizabeth Phillips describes two 'generations' of political theology, as it has emerged as a distinct theological discipline.

The first generation was characterized by post-war political theologians (including Moltmann, Metz and Soelle), Latin American liberation theologians, the first Black and feminist theologians, and the later emergence of public theology. The second generation has been characterized by postliberalism, radical orthodoxy and newer 'contextual' theologies. We have touched upon post-war and public theologies here, and Section VII will introduce liberation, contextual and postcolonial theologies. Peppered throughout the reader are texts that might be characterized as postliberal. Postliberal theologies arise in the late twentieth century through the work of George Lindbeck and Hans Frei, but with roots in the mid-twentieth-century theology of Karl Barth and the philosophies of Ludwig Wittgenstein and Alistair MacIntyre. Postliberals, often also described as 'narrative' theologians, argue that the political theological task is rooted in reflection on the culture, language, stories and institutions of living traditions of faith and communities of practice. Increasingly postliberal theologies are being drawn into dialogue with forms of postliberal politics, which react against forms of economic and social liberalism to focus on the quality of human relationships forged within communities and institutions. The texts of Stanley Hauerwas and John Milbank in this volume are representative of these trends.

9. Carl Schmitt – Definition of Sovereignty

Sovereign is he who decides on the exception.

Only this definition can do justice to a borderline concept. Contrary to the imprecise terminology that is found in popular literature, a borderline concept is not a vague concept, but one pertaining to the outermost sphere. This definition of sovereignty must therefore be associated with a borderline case and not with routine. It will soon become clear that the exception is to be understood to refer to a general concept in the theory of the state, and not merely to a construct applied to any emergency decree or state of siege.

The assertion that the exception is truly appropriate for the juristic definition of sovereignty has a systematic, legal-logical foundation. The decision on the exception is a decision in the true sense of the word. Because a general norm, as represented by an ordinary legal prescription, can never encompass a total exception, the decision that a real exception exists cannot therefore be entirely derived from this norm. When Robert von Mohl[1] said that the test of whether an

---

[1][Tr.] *Staatsrecht, Völkerrecht und Politik: Monographien*, vol. 2 (Tübingen, 1862), p. 626.

emergency exists cannot be a juristic one, he assumed that a decision in the legal sense must be derived entirely from the content of a norm. But this is the question. In the general sense in which Mohl articulated his argument, his notion is only an expression of constitutional liberalism and fails to apprehend the independent meaning of the decision.

From a practical or a theoretical perspective, it really does not matter whether an abstract scheme advanced to define sovereignty (namely, that sovereignty is the highest power, not a derived power) is acceptable. About an abstract concept there will in general be no argument, least of all in the history of sovereignty. What is argued about is the concrete application, and that means who decides in a situation of conflict what constitutes the public interest or interest of the state, public safety and order, *le salut public,* and so on. The exception, which is not codified in the existing legal order, can at best be characterized as a case of extreme peril, a danger to the existence of the state, or the like. But it cannot be circumscribed factually and made to conform to a preformed law.

It is precisely the exception that makes relevant the subject of sovereignty, that is, the whole question of sovereignty. The precise details of an emergency cannot be anticipated, nor can one spell out what may take place in such a case, especially when it is truly a matter of an extreme emergency and of how it is to be eliminated. The precondition as well as the content of jurisdictional competence in such a case must necessarily be unlimited. From the liberal constitutional point of view, there would be no jurisdictional competence at all. The most guidance the constitution can provide is to indicate who can act in such a case. If such action is not subject to controls, if it is not hampered in some way by checks and balances, as is the case in a liberal constitution, then it is clear who the sovereign is. He decides whether there is an extreme emergency as well as what must be done to eliminate it. Although he stands outside the normally valid legal system, he nevertheless belongs to it, for it is he who must decide whether the constitution needs to be suspended in its entirety. All tendencies of modem constitutional development point toward eliminating the sovereign in this sense. The ideas of Hugo Krabbe and Hans Kelsen, which will be treated in the following chapter, are in line with this development. But whether the extreme exception can be banished from the world is not a juristic question. Whether one has confidence and hope that it can be eliminated depends on philosophical, especially on philosophical-historical or metaphysical, convictions.

There exist a number of historical presentations that deal with the development of the concept of sovereignty, but they are like textbook compilations of abstract formulas from which definitions of sovereignty can be extracted. Nobody seems to have taken the trouble to scrutinize the often-repeated but completely empty phraseology used to denote the highest power by the famous authors of the concept of sovereignty. That this concept relates to the critical case, the exception, was long ago recognized by Jean Bodin. He stands at the beginning of the modern theory of the state because of his work "Of the True Marks of Sovereignty" (chapter 10 of the first book of the *Republic*) rather than because of his often-cited definition ("sovereignty is the absolute and perpetual power of a republic"). He discussed his concept in the context of many practical examples, and he always returned to the question: To what extent is the sovereign bound to laws, and to what extent is he responsible to the estates? To this last, all-important question he replied that commitments are binding because they rest on natural law; but in emergencies the tie to general natural principles ceases. In general, according to him, the prince is duty bound toward the estates or the people only to the extent of fulfilling his promise in the interest of the people; he is not so bound under conditions of urgent necessity. These are by no means new theses. The decisive point about Bodin's concept is that by referring to the emergency, he reduced his analysis of the relationships between prince and estates to a simple either/or.

This is what is truly impressive in his definition of sovereignty; by considering sovereignty to be indivisible, he finally settled the question of power in the state. His scholarly accomplishment and the basis for his success thus reside in his having incorporated the decision into the concept of sovereignty. Today there is hardly any mention of the concept of sovereignty that does not contain the usual quotation from Bodin. But nowhere does one find cited the core quote from that chapter of the *Republic.* Bodin asked if the commitments of the prince to the estates or the people dissolve his sovereignty. He answered by referring to the case in which it becomes necessary to violate such commitments, to change laws or to suspend them entirely according to the requirements of a situation, a time, and a people. If in such cases the prince had to consult a senate or the people before he could act, he would have to be prepared to let his subjects dispense with him. Bodin considered this an absurdity because, according to him, the estates were not masters over the laws; they in turn would have to permit their prince to dispense with them. Sovereignty would thus become a play between two parties: Sometimes the people and sometimes the prince would rule, and that would be contrary to all reason and all law. Because the authority to suspend valid law—be it in general or in a specific case—is so much the actual mark of sovereignty, Bodin wanted to derive from this authority all other characteristics (declaring war and making peace, appointing civil servants, right of pardon, final appeal, and so on).

In contrast to traditional presentations, I have shown in my study of dictatorship that even the seventeenth-century authors of natural law understood the question of sovereignty to mean the question of the decision on the exception. This is particularly true of Samuel von Pufendorf. Everyone agrees that whenever antagonisms appear within a state, every party wants the general good—therein resides after all the *bellum omnium contra omnes.* But sovereignty (and thus the state itself) resides in deciding this controversy, that is, in determining definitively what constitutes public order and security, in determining when they are disturbed, and so on. Public order and security manifest themselves very differently in reality, depending on whether a militaristic bureaucracy, a self-governing body controlled by the spirit of commercialism, or a radical party organization decides when there is order and security and when it is threatened or disturbed. After all, every legal order is based on a decision, and also the concept of the legal order, which is applied as something self-evident, contains within it the contrast of the two distinct elements of the juristic—norm and decision. Like every other order, the legal order rests on a decision and not on a norm.

Whether God alone is sovereign, that is, the one who acts as his acknowledged representative on earth, or the emperor, or prince, or the people, meaning those who identify themselves directly with the people, the question is always aimed at the subject of sovereignty, at the application of the concept to a concrete situation. Ever since the sixteenth century, jurists who discuss the question of sovereignty have derived their ideas from a catalogue of determining, decisive features of sovereignty that can in essence be traced to the points made by Bodin. To possess those powers meant to be sovereign. In the murky legal conditions of the old German Reich the argument on public law ran as follows: Because one of the many indications of sovereignty was undoubtedly present, the other dubious indications also had to be present. The controversy always centered on the question, Who assumes authority concerning those matters for which there are no positive stipulations, for example, a capitulation? In other words, Who is responsible for that for which competence has not been anticipated?

In a more familiar vein it was asked, Who is supposed to have unlimited power? Hence the discussion about the exception, the *extremus necessitatis casus*. This is repeated with the same legal-logical structure in the discussions on the so-called monarchical principle. Here, too, it is always asked who is entitled to decide those actions for which the constitution makes no provision; that is, who is competent to act when the legal system fails to answer the question of competence. The controversy concerning whether the individual German states were sovereign according to the constitution of 1871 was a matter of minor political significance. Nevertheless, the thrust of that argument can easily be recognized once more. The pivotal point of Max Seydel's attempt to prove that the individual states were sovereign had less to do with the question whether the remaining rights of the individual states were or were not subsumable than with the assertion that the competence of the Reich was circumscribed by the constitution, which in principle meant limited, whereas the competence of the individual states was in principle unlimited.

According to article 48 of the German constitution of 1919, the exception is declared by the president of the Reich but is under the control of parliament, the Reichstag, which can at any time demand its suspension. This provision corresponds to the development and practice of the liberal constitutional state, which attempts to repress the question of sovereignty by a division and mutual control of competences.

But only the arrangement of the precondition that governs the invocation of exceptional powers corresponds to the liberal constitutional tendency, not the content of article 48. Article 48 grants unlimited power. If applied without check, it would grant exceptional powers in the same way as article 14 of the [French] Charter of 1815, which made the monarch sovereign. If the individual states no longer have the power to declare the exception, as the prevailing opinion on article 48 contends, then they no longer enjoy the status of states. Article 48 is the actual reference point for answering the question whether the individual German states are states.

If measures undertaken in an exception could be circumscribed by mutual control, by imposing a time limit, or finally, as in the liberal constitutional procedure governing a state of siege, by enumerating extraordinary powers, the question of sovereignty would then be considered less significant but would certainly not be eliminated. A jurisprudence concerned with ordinary day-today questions has practically no interest in the concept of sovereignty. Only the recognizable is its normal concern; everything else is a "disturbance." Such a jurisprudence confronts the extreme case disconcertedly, for not every extraordinary measure, not every police emergency measure or emergency decree, is necessarily an exception. What characterizes an exception is principally unlimited authority, which means the suspension of the entire existing order. In such a situation it is clear that the state remains, whereas law recedes. Because the exception is different from anarchy and chaos, order in the juristic sense still prevails even if it is not of the ordinary kind.

The existence of the state is undoubted proof of its superiority over the validity of the legal norm. The decision frees itself from all normative ties and becomes in the true sense absolute. The state suspends the law in the exception on the basis of its right of self-preservation, as one would say. The two elements of the concept *legal order* are then dissolved into independent notions and thereby testify to their conceptual independence. Unlike the normal situation, when the autonomous moment of the decision recedes to a minimum, the norm is destroyed in the exception. The exception remains, nevertheless, accessible to jurisprudence because both elements, the norm as well as the decision, remain within the framework of the juristic.

It would be a distortion of the schematic disjunction between sociology and jurisprudence if one were to say that the exception has no juristic significance and is therefore "sociology." The exception is that which cannot be subsumed; it defies general codification, but it simultaneously reveals a specifically juristic element— the decision in absolute purity. The exception appears in its absolute form when a situation in which legal prescriptions can be valid must first be brought about. Every general norm demands a normal, everyday frame of life to which it can be factually applied and which is subjected to its regulations. The norm requires a homogeneous medium. This effective normal situation is not a mere "superficial presupposition" that a jurist can ignore; that situation belongs precisely to its immanent validity. There exists no norm that is applicable to chaos. For a legal order to make sense, a normal situation must exist, and he is sovereign who definitely decides whether this normal situation actually exists.

All law is "situational law." The sovereign produces and guarantees the situation in its totality. He has the monopoly over this last decision. Therein resides the essence of the state's sovereignty, which must be juristically defined correctly, not as the monopoly to coerce or to rule, but as the monopoly to decide. The exception reveals most clearly the essence of the state's authority. The decision parts here from the legal norm, and (to formulate it paradoxically) authority proves that to produce law it need not be based on law.

The exception was something incommensurable to John Locke's doctrine of the constitutional state and the rationalist eighteenth century. The vivid awareness of the meaning of the exception that was reflected in the doctrine of natural law of the seventeenth century was soon lost in the eighteenth century, when a relatively lasting order was established. Emergency law was no law at all for Kant. The contemporary theory of the state reveals the interesting spectacle of the two tendencies facing one another, the rationalist tendency, which ignores the emergency, and the natural law tendency, which is interested in the emergency and emanates from an essentially different set of ideas. That a neo-Kantian like Kelsen does not know what to do with the exception is obvious. But it should be of interest to the rationalist that the legal system itself can anticipate the exception and can "suspend itself." That a norm or an order or a point of reference "establishes itself" appears plausible to the exponents of this kind of juristic rationalism. But how the systematic unity and order can suspend itself in a concrete case is difficult to construe, and yet it remains a juristic problem as long as the exception is distinguishable from a juristic chaos, from any kind of anarchy. The tendency of liberal constitutionalism to regulate the exception as precisely as possible means, after all, the attempt to spell out in detail the case in which law suspends itself. From where does the law obtain this force, and how is it logically possible that a norm is valid except for one concrete case that it cannot factually determine in any definitive manner?

It would be consequent rationalism to say that the exception proves nothing and that only the normal can be the object of scientific interest. The exception confounds the unity and order of the rationalist scheme. One encounters not infrequently a similar argument in the positive theory of the state. To the question of how to proceed in the absence of a budget law, Gerhard Anschütz replied that this was not at all a legal question. "There is not only a gap in the law, that is, in the text of the constitution, but moreover in law as a whole, which can in no way be filled by juristic conceptual operations. Here is where public law stops."[2]

---

[2][Tr.] See Georg Meyer, *Lehrbuch des Deutschen Staatsrechts,* 7th ed., vol. 3, ed. G. Anschütz (Munich and Leipzig, 1919), p. 906.

Precisely a philosophy of concrete life must not withdraw from the exception and the extreme case, but must be interested in it to the highest degree. The exception can be more important to it than the rule, not because of a romantic irony for the paradox, but because the seriousness of an insight goes deeper than the clear generalizations inferred from what ordinarily repeats itself. The exception is more interesting than the rule. The rule proves nothing; the exception proves everything: It confirms not only the rule but also its existence, which derives only from the exception. In the exception the power of real life breaks through the crust of a mechanism that has become torpid by repetition.

A Protestant theologian[3] who demonstrated the vital intensity possible in theological reflection in the nineteenth century stated: "The exception explains the general and itself. And if one wants to study the general correctly, one only needs to look around for a true exception. It reveals everything more clearly than does the general. Endless talk about the general becomes boring; there are exceptions. If they cannot be explained, then the general also cannot be explained. The difficulty is usually not noticed because the general is not thought about with passion but with a comfortable superficiality. The exception, on the other hand, thinks the general with intense passion."[4]

10. Jürgen Moltmann – Covenant or Leviathan? Political Theology for Modern Times

1. The Present Question in Europe

FEDERALISM or centralism – this is a decisive question in the political structuring of Europe today. The socialist centralism of the command economy and the ideological surveillance of the people has collapsed. The federal republic with decentralized forms of communication and a diversity of regional, local and personal initiatives proved stronger.

But federalism or centralism is also the problem of the internal unity of Europe. Do we want a democratic Europe with strong citizen participation or a smoothly functioning state machine which takes care of the citizens and takes away their autonomy?

---

[3][Tr.] The reference here is to Søren Kierkegaard.
[4][Tr.] The quote is from Kierkegaard's *Repetition.*

Federalism or centralism – this is not only a practical question of politics, but rather also a question which emerges out of the basic trust and the basic fears of human beings. Don't we expect from the State first of all 'security' and protection from enemies? Didn't chaos break out in the Balkans after the fall of the united Yugoslavian state and a horrible 'struggle of all against all' began? Doesn't history show that human beings act like wolves toward others if they are not tamed by a strong hand?

But who guarantees us that this 'strong state' which offers protection and security will not itself become the wolf and eat up its citizens, moving from the security State to 'State security'? As history also shows, out of the security States have come the dictatorships which disregard and destroy people, to which we have given the names of the well-known animals of prey: the terrible 'Leviathan', the state 'Moloch' and the 'Stasioctopus'. How do we then come to pluralistic freedom without chaos and to peaceful unity without dictatorship?

To answer these present-day questions, I want to offer a contribution out of the history of political theology at the beginning of the modern era in the 16th and 17th centuries. Perhaps we can recognize our own problems in the complex situation of the 16th/17th centuries – and in those beginnings also the possibility of their resolution.

The word 'covenant' stands for the federalistic state idea as it was developed by the so-called Calvinist 'monarchomachians' in the development of the right of resistance against incipient political and religious absolutism in France. These theological-political thoughts are taken from the *Vindiciae contra Tyrannos* (1574, printed 1579) of which Philipp Duplessis Mornay is believed to be the author.

The word 'Leviathan' stands for the influential book of the same title by Thomas Hobbes in 1651 (Latin 1668) about 'The Matter, Forme and Power of a Common Wealth, Ecclesiastical and Civil'. It is the utopia of the security state which unites spiritual and secular power and allows neither the division of powers nor the right of resistance. I speak as a theologian, not as a political scientist, and will look at both schemes according to their theological dimensions and their implicit theological presuppositions. I will then compare them, drawing upon Luther's Circular Disputation of 1539 about the resistance against the apocalyptic 'werewolf'.

I will then leap into the 20th century by analyzing Carl Schmitt's admiration for and his paganizing of 'Leviathan'. Finally, I will offer a thesis about the political theology of democracy and the collapse of the 'Leviathan'.

The famous thesis of Carl Schmitt's political theology is: 'Sovereign is he who can declare the state of emergency' (1922). My thesis is: *Free is whoever claims the right of resistance*. Resistance is the legitimate ending from below of an illegal, tyrannical 'state of emergency' and the beginning and preserving of democracy.

2. The Theology of the Covenant and the Right of Resistance

Calvinism is considered especially political because it is supposed to be theocratically-minded. But this is not so. *Calvin* stated reasons for political resistance in his letters to the Huguenots only within the framework of the existing laws but not according to natural law.[1] Existing laws in France in his time were laws in conflict with the incipient absolutism of the French monarchy and its claim to a state religion: *'Un Roy–une loy–une foy.'* If there are estates in a community – Calvin called them 'ephors' – then it is their duty to stand up for the freedom of the people against a tyrannical ruler. For 'people without office' Calvin suggests suffering resistance and leaving the revenge to God (*Inst.* IV, 20, 31). Natural rights and the sovereignty of the people play no role for Calvin. Resistance against rulers who oppress the faith is for Calvin, however, a religious imperative. As opposed to the medieval discussion about the right of resistance, the Reformation brings with it the novel case of resistance for religious reasons against a change of religion decreed by the State.

On the Night of St Bartholomew, in 1572, the French *'Rex christianissimus'* had the leading Huguenots who were gathered in Paris, among them Admiral de Coligny and the philosopher Petrus Ramus, massacred. This brought about the turning point and called the so-called 'monarchomachian' conflict literature to life.[2] This does not deal with the old problem of 'tyrannicide' but rather with an alternative form of government in the face of incipient absolutism. Out of the confrontation with this 'modern' State form developed a transition from the medieval estate State to the no less 'modern' constitutional State. The transition was accomplished through an increasing democratization of the right of resistance. While *François Hotman* in 1573 defended the estate–related right of resistance according to the image of an aristocratically moderated monarchy, we find *Theodor Beza,* Calvin's successor in Geneva, in 1574 defending the estate–related right to resistance with a view to the rights of the people: 'Everyone can resist those who in the violation of their official duties assume a tyrannical power over the subjects.'[3]

In Presbyterian Scotland, the *Confessio Scotica* was written in 1560. It specified under the 'good works', after the worship of God and love of neighbour, 'tyrannidem opprimere, ab informioribus vim improborum defendere', and with this, elevated the

---

[1]Ernst Wolf, 'Das Problem des Widerstandsrechts bei Calvin', in: A. Kaufmann (Hg), *Das widerstandsrecht,* Darmstadt 1972, 152–169. The older study by *Kurt Wolvendorff, Staatsrecht und Naturrecht in der Lehre vom Widerstandsrecht des Volkes gegen rechtswidrige Ausübung der Staatsgewalt,* Breslau 1916, is weak on the theology of Calvin and Calvinism. Cf. Josef Bohatec, *England und die Geschichte der Menschen- und Bürgerrechte.* hg. Otto Weber, Graz-Köln 1956.

[2]R. Nürnberger, *Die Politisierung des französischen Protestantismus,* Tübingen 1948.

[3]Th. Beza *De jure magistratuum et officio subditorum erga magistratus,* hg. Klaus Sturm, Neukirchen — Vluyn 1965, 12.

resistance against tyrants to a general Christian obligation.[4] The limitation to the estates or Church representatives is no longer mentioned. To the background of this amazing generalization of the right of resistance belongs the old Scottish law which *George Buchanan* in *De jure regni apud Scotos* (1579) explained accordingly: Because both the elected and the inherited monarchy involve the homage of the people, the people are relieved of their obligation of obedience if the ruler damages the contract of rulership.

The most effective and influential document, however, was the famous *Vindiciae contra Tyrannos* which from 1579 onwards was frequently printed under the pseudonym Junius Brutus.[5] Some ascribe it to Hubert Languet, a student of Melanchthon, who as diplomatic representative of the German Protestant estates became an eye-witness of the Bartholomew Night. His student and friend, *Philipp Duplessis Mornay,* one of the spiritual leaders of the Huguenots in the following years of active resistance, seems more likely to be the author.

In this treatise, the traditional right of resistance of the estates against the crown is no longer defended but rather a new federalistic–democratic idea of the State is propagated, although it does not want to abolish the monarchy. Duplessis Mornay was, as far as I know, the first to apply the theological ideas of covenant to the foundation of the right of resistance. Due to the interest in the right of resistance, one usually reads only the third part of the *Vindiciae,* which Carl Bernhard Hundeshagen published in German, and overlooks the theological doctrine of the double covenant which was previously developed in the *quaestio prima* with which Mornay wants to answer four contemporary questions, which are still relevant today:

1. Do subjects owe obedience to a ruler whose decrees contradict the law of God?
2. Is one allowed to resist the ruler if he violates the law of God?
3. Is it allowed to resist a ruler who ruins a state?
4. Are neighbouring rulers allowed to help foreign subjects based on religious or political grounds?

The contract theory which is used in the discussion of the right of resistance in the four named cases is based in accordance with the Old Testament on the theology of the double covenant:[6] God seals the first covenant with the people of Israel on Mt Sinai. The law of this covenant is the Decalogue. 'The people had at first no other king

---

[4]W. Niesel, (Hg), *Bekenntnisschriften und Kirchenordnungen der nach Gottes Wort reformierten Kirche,* Zürich 1938, 97. Cf. Karl Barth, *Gotteserkenntnis und Gottesdienst,* Zürich 1938, 215ff.
[5]C. B. Hundeshagen, *Calvinismus und staatsbürgerliche Freiheit, end* H. Languet, *Wider die Tyranen,* hg. L. Wyss, Zürich 1946. Gerhard Oestreich, 'Die Idee des religiösen Bundes und die Lehre vom Staatsvertrag', in: *Zur Geschichte und Problematik der Demokratie,* FS für Hans Herzfeld, Berlin 1958, 11–32; Charles McCoy/J. Wayne Baker, *Fountainhead of Federalism. Heinrich Bullinger und the covenantal Tradition,* Louisville 1991, 45ff.
[6]G. Oestreich, op. cit. 22.

than God.'[7] The people of God seal the second covenant with their own, God-given King before God. They transfer their sovereignty to him according to the contract of rulership. If a ruler breaks this covenant with the people, then the sovereignty returns to them. He is a tyrant whom the people must resist. But if the ruler breaks God's covenant for the people, then he is a blasphemer whom the people must resist for God's sake. The people install the rulers, transfer the kingdom to them and confirm their calling through their voice. 'Therefore the kings are always to remember that they indeed rule by the grace of God, but through the people and for the people.' This sounds like Abraham Lincoln's Gettysburg Address: 'A government of the people and by the people. . .'[8] The people make the king, not the king the people. The ruler makes his promise in the contract of rulership unconditionally; the people, however, do so only conditionally, because in the case of the non-fulfilment of the contract, they are immediately free from all obligations: *'Populus jure omni obligatione solutus.'* With this sentence a 'sovereignty of the people' is defined almost word by word in the way in which *Jean Bodin* defined the absolute sovereignty of the ruler: *'Princeps legibus solutus est.'*[9]

The *'Vindiciae'* differentiate politically between the tyrant without legal title and the 'tyrant in deed' who rules the kingdom which is entrusted to him against the laws. Private persons are not allowed to raise a sword against him, because he is not appointed by individuals but rather by the whole, so that the representatives of the whole must resist him first. However, against usurpers who gain government power violently and illegally 'all individuals indiscriminately may step forward because no contract is in place'. Against 'blasphemers', finally, resistance in spiritual matters is mandatory.

For Mornay, the Old Testament lives on in the New Testament, the people of Israel in the people of Christ and therefore, also the *Politia Moysi* in the Kingdom of Christ. Therefore, what the Jewish people were commanded is also commanded to the Christian people. Mornay paints the picture as follows: the people and the king are liable for each other against defection from the true God. If the king turns to foreign gods, then the people of God must intervene against him. God gave the people in the covenant contract the authority and the power to intervene against rulers who want to lead the people away from the true faith. Mornay asks with high rhetorical skill: why did God demand the consent of the people? Why did God obligate the people to God's law? And he refers to the prophets whom God calls out of God's people in order to charge the rulers with their sins. On the basis of their covenant with God the people possess authority *in sacris*. Even when the king and a large part of the people defect, the minority must resist because every part of the whole has

---

[7]L. Wyss, 65f.
[8]L. Wyss, 67.
[9]G. Oestreich, 25, points this out.

sworn obedience to God. This was Duplessis Mornay's justification of the resistance of Protestant Christianity which in France was condemned to be a religious minority. For this the most moving example was given by *Marie Durand,* who was imprisoned for 38 years in the Tour de la Constance in Aigues-Mortes and there carved her courageous *'Récister'* into the stone.

From the idea of government we retain the following points, expanding them historically:

1. The foundation of the right of resistance is here not theocratic, nor does it pertain to natural law but rather is derived from a federal theology. Federal theology does not originate with Calvin in Geneva but in Zürich with *Heinrich Bullinger, De Testamento seu Foedere unico et aeterno,* 1534. The covenant of human beings with one another is based on and preserved by God's covenant with them. The 'true citizens of Christ's kingdom' are *confoederati,* explained *Caspar Olevian,* the Heidelberg federal theologian, in 1560.

In this tradition of Reformed federal theology is also *Johann Althusius,* who presented his *'Politica methodice digesta'* (1603) in Herborn and not only developed the contract of rulership based on mutuality out of federal theology, but also a social doctrine of the different social contracts from the family all the way to society.

2. Federal theology presupposed that God considers human beings to be worthy and capable of forming a covenant. Out of this trust of God comes the trust of human beings in their mutual ability to form a covenant.

People are symbiotic, social beings. Their social life is made up of *'consociationes'.* Politics are symbiotic. From this results the famous definition: *'Politica est ars consociandi.'*[10] For this Althusius not only draws upon the history of Israel but also upon the political history of the Hanseatic League and city covenants in Europe and last not least on the political archetype of all federalists in Europe: the Swiss Confederation.

3. Through the emigration of the Puritans from the 'Old World' in England to the 'New World' of America – interpreted as the exodus out of Egyptian theocratic dictatorship to the community of the covenant of the 'free and equal' in the 'new Israel' – the idea of covenant–thinking entered the political history of New England and of the American Revolution.[11] The sermon on the covenant which John Winthrop held in front of the Massachussets Bay Company in 1630 for the first settlers, is generally considered to be the beginning of American political self-confidence. America – a covenanted nation. The church covenant of the free congregations and the social covenant of the colonial confederations mutually reinforced each other. Federalistic

---

[10]Ch. McCoy/J. Wayne Baker, 55ff.
[11]Perry Miller, The New England Mind, I, Cambridge 1954[2], II, Cambridge 1953.

patterns shaped the laws of the individual states as well as their confederation and their Declaration of Independence in 1776.

Charles McCoy recently showed that the famous Federalist *James Madison* was influenced by the federalist theologian *John Witherspoon,* his professor at the College of New Jersey in Princeton.[12] The 'matter of the republic' was realized through the federal principle. The possibility of using the word *covenant* instead of *constitution* was also discussed. This means that the constitution, in Germany, the *Grundgesetz* ('Basic law'), is the contract of the citizens, male and female, 'before God' with which all government has to comply and which obliges all citizens, male and female, to resist all excercise of power which is illegal, illegitimate and contrary to human rights. Resistance against tyrants is obedience towards God and the true test of democracy.

3. Leviathan: The Mortal God and God's Absolute Sovereignty

The political situation in which Thomas Hobbes wrote and published his *'Leviathan'* is generally described as 'civil war': through Calvinism and Puritanism, democratic thought won over the English middle class and the gentry. On the other side, the Catholic Stuarts attempted to rule as absolutistically as Louis XIV in France. The conflicts between parliament and the crown became inescapable. 'Leviathan' appeared in 1651, two years after the execution of Charles I, and as such is also an answer to the state theory and the political result of the 'monarchomachians'.[13] Hobbes, however, thinks differently, his thinking is free from the order of the estates and traditions and as enlightened as the thinking of his contemporary René Descartes. He constructs his State as a human art – product *more geometrico*. It is the ahistoric utopia of a State machine which is directed by a sovereign will and leaves no space for the unforeseen occurrences of legal history. In discussing *Sir Edward Coke* (1552–1632), he denounces English Common Law and makes the Common Law judges responsible for the undermining of royal sovereignty and, with this, for the civil war.[14]

---

[12]Ch. McCoy, 94ff.

[13]Thomas Hobbes, *Leviathan oder Wesen, Form und Gewalt des Kirchlichen und bürgerlichen States,* rororo 187–189, hg. P. C. Mayer-Tasch, I quote from this edition cf. on this. Carl Schmitt, *Der Leviathan in der Staatslehre des Thomas Hobbes. Sinn und Fehlschlag eines politischen Symbols,* Hamburg 1938; Dietrich Braun, *Der sterbliche Gott oder Leviathan gegen Behemoth,* Zürich 1963; Peter Cornelius Mayer-Tasch, *Thomas Hobbes und das Widerstandsrecht,* Tübingen 1965; Winfried Förster, *Thomas Hobbes und der Puritanismus. Grundlagen und Grundfragen seiner Staatslehre,* Hamburg 1969; Jakob Taubes (Hg.), *Der Fürst dieser Welt. Carl Schmitt und die Folgen. Religionstheorie und Politische Theologie* Band I, Müchen 1983.

[14]Thomas Hobbes, *Dialog zwischen einem Philosophen und einem Juristen über das englische Recht.* Hg. Bernard Willms, Weinheim 1992.

But can one therefore say that Hobbes' philosophy is 'the direct reaction to the confessional civil wars on this side and the other of the Channel', as Jakob Taubes believes?[15] I hold it rather to be an Enlightenment State utopia with only limited interest in tradition and religion.

Hobbes begins with the assumption that the natural condition of human beings is wretched, that is, of the 'war of all against all'. He sees the main motive of human being as the insatiable and gnawing 'hunger for power and more power which only ends with death' (77). Therefore 'human coexistence' is 'no pleasure but rather on the contrary, creates much affliction for people as long as there is no superior power which keeps them in check' (98). In addition to the struggle for power, the human being also has the drive to maintain him or herself and the wish for a secure life (131), that is, the desire 'to escape from the miserable condition of the war of everyone against everyone' (131). Human beings therefore seal an original contract in which they transfer their freedom of self-determination to a sovereign, be it a person or an assembly. The State arises in this way.

> When people join to be one person, they form a State;
> in Latin it is called *civitas*. This is the birth of the great *Leviathan,* or rather, (to speak
> more respectfully), of the *mortal*
> *God,* to whom alone we owe protection and peace under the eternal
> God. Through the authority (with which he is granted by every
> individual in the State) and the power which has been transferred
> to him, he is in the position to compel all citizens to peace and
> to mutual help against foreign enemies. He constitutes the essence
> of the State which one can define as a person whose actions are
> acknowledged by a large number as their own through the contract of
> everyone with everyone for the purposes of using this unified
> power at will for the peace and for the defense of all (137).

Nevertheless, the political unity of the many lies not in this original contract but rather in their representative: *'In persona una vera omnium unio.'* So arises out of many individual persons the great macranthropos, the *Leviathan.* The sovereign possesses all power, the wordly and the spiritual. He is the head of the whole; the subjects who have given him their freedom in exchange for their security are his body. The division of powers would threaten the unity, the right of resistance would abolish security. Hobbes also thinks in the categories of covenant and contracts. He grew up in a Presbyterian home. For him, however, there is no covenant of God with the people, which limits the rulership contract, but only the rulership contract of human beings against hostile nature in order to end the war of all against all. The sovereignty of the representative is as absolute as human beings can make it: *'Auctoritas non veritas facit legem'* (cap. 26). His will is itself the law but he stands above the law. He is the

---

[15]Jakob Taubes, 9.

carrier of wordly and spiritual power, that is, the ruler over law and truth, therefore also over miracle and confession. He determines the political religion of the country; only the citizen's inner private belief is, therefore, as untouched and free as his or her thoughts. But politically, the sovereign himself becomes the mythical peace-hero *Leviathan* and must be honoured in an Arian manner as 'mortal God' on earth under the protection of the immortal God in heaven.

Carl Schmitt and Jakob Taubes have rightly pointed to the profound meaning of the symbols on the title page of *Leviathan*: one sees a gigantic person who is made up of many small persons, in the right hand a sword, in the left hand the crozier; both hands are stretched out protectively over a peaceful city. There are a castle, a cannon, lances and a battle; under the crozier, further, a church, a mitre, acts of banishment, and a council.[16] The motto comes from Job 41:24: 'There is no power on earth comparable to him.'

What did Thomas Hobbes want to say with this image of the 'great Leviathan'? On the surface, canonist Hans Barion is right when he points to the medieval theocratic theory of the two swords. Just as the wordly power is awarded according to the '*Dictatus Papae*' by the Pope, according to Hobbes, in the same way the political sovereign has both powers in one hand: the 'enormous, massive person' in charge of protection and peace has a crown on his head. This reminds one of pictures of Henry VIII with a sword in each hand. Jakob Taubes correctly concludes that the actual goal of this political theory is theocracy.[17] The subtitle also confirms this: 'Matter, Forme and Power of a Common Wealth, Ecclesistical and Civil'. The *Leviathan* is the ruler of peace on earth. Hobbes, therefore, repeats 40 times that in his kingdom the confession runs accordingly: 'Jesus is the Christ.' In my opinion, this is only understandable when one interprets Hobbes' State utopia in terms of the Millennium: in the millennial Kingdom of Christ on earth (Rev. 20) spiritual and political power, State and Church coincide.[18] Only this 'Christian State' becomes the 'mortal God' on earth or the 'manifest deity' (Hegel). But why does Hobbes call this political kingdom of peace 'Leviathan'? With this we come to the theological discussion of Thomas Hobbes' political theology:

1. Can the 'war of all against all' be called the natural human condition? Theologically, this is the status *corruptionis,* not the *status naturalis.* Whoever asserts that human beings are evil by nature defames the Creator. With the 'war of all against all', Hobbes, in truth, means the apocalyptic end of the world, endtime anarchy and the drowning of the world in chaos as it was before its creation. He therefore sees in the kingdom of peace of *Leviathan* the power to hold off this end of the world,

---

[16]Carl Schmitt, 25f. J. Taubes, 12f.

[17]Jakob Taubes, 13.

[18]On political Chiliasm cf. Norman Cohn, *Das Ringen um das Tausend Jährige Reich. Revolutionärer Messianismus im Mittelalter und sein Fortleben in den modernen totalitären Bewegungen,* Bern und München 1961; Ernest Lee Tuveson, *Redeemer Nation. The idea of America's Millenial Role,* Chicago 1968.

the apocalyptic 'catechon'. The natural condition is merciless war, only the civil State provides a merciful situation of peace.

These notions are in my opinion based on a disturbed relationship to nature. An artificial, human construction, the Leviathan State, is hence an unnatural, nature-destroying entity. That the human is 'a dangerous being' (C. Schmitt) who only reacts as driven by the mechanics of the will to power and the need for security, only proves true of people who are alienated from nature, as in European modernity. It is an atheistic image as well as an inhumane one.

2. That formation of political will should occur through the surrender of the individual right of self-determination to a sovereign who rules at his own discretion, is also fictitious and counterproductive. Hobbes posed this question himself: 'Where and when is the sovereign power recognized by the subjects?' (163) yet did not answer it. Nor did he write his State doctrine for the citizens but rather for the sovereign, in order to make his real power clear to him and to show him how he could subjugate the people and keep them submissive with the fearful image of the 'struggle of all against all' and through their fear of death. The original contract which Hobbes postulates is nothing other than a contract of submission in exchange for survival.

It is, however, difficult to imagine that human beings with wolf natures can produce a kingdom of peace through relinquishing their freedom and submitting to a sovereign. Does *Leviathan* tame the wolf nature of human beings or does the Leviathan himself become a superwolf?[19] Why should the unquenchable will for power give way on the political level to the need for security instead of being exacerbated until it is overwhelming? Is tyranny really to be preferred to anarchy when tyranny is only an especially disagreeable form of anarchy?

3. Perhaps Hobbes saw these ambiguities himself and therefore chose the image of the Leviathan. Let us return to this mythical image once more. Is the *Leviathan* as peace ruler a Christ figure and as a divine human being a likeness of God become human or is he the Antichrist, the 'animal from the abyss', the 'lord of this world'? As an old man, Hobbes indeed contrasted his good *Leviathan* to the evil *Behemoth*, that is, the English parliament; but he could not have been completely mistaken in the biblical mythology. He only quotes Job 41:24 but he certainly also was familiar with Is 27:1, where the *Leviathan* is named next to the serpent and the dragon as an antidivine chaos-animal whom 'the Lord will come upon at the Lord's time and put him to death in due time'.

He must have also known from the apocalypticism of his time about the biblical development of the Leviathan into dragon, devil, Satan, God or Lord of this perverted world. Also familiar to him would have been the apocalyptic dragon out of the sea, that is, the Roman Empire under Domitian, of which Rev. 13:4 says: 'Who is like the beast, and who can fight against it?'

---

[19]Ernst Bloch, *Naturrecht und menschliche Würde*, Frankfurt 1961, 60f.

Jakob Taubes illustrated his book about 'Carl Schmitt and the Consequences' with the picture of *Leviathan* and gave it the malicious heading 'The lord of this world'. In the gospel of John the 'lord of this world' is called Satan, whose power was first broken through Christ, upon whom he has neither right nor power (Jn 12:31; 14:30; 16:11). Paul calls him 'the god of this world' (2 Cor. 4:4). Hobbes probably based the expression 'the mortal God' on 'lord of this world' and 'god of this world'.

In the apocalyptic imagery of 17th century England, the *Leviathan* is no peace figure but rather a chaotic power which spreads chaos and represents the opposite of the confession 'Jesus is the Christ'.

In order to uncover the *Leviathan,* one could point out that dictatorship against anarchy becomes anarchistic itself. Dictatorship is anarchy from above. Organized crime is indeed the end of individual crime but not of crime altogether. Organized aspiration towards power is indeed the end of 'the struggle of all against all' but not the end of the aspiration towards power. Hobbes' *Leviathan* can also be read as a vision of organized peacelessness. A theologian in the tradition of the Reformation must read Hobbes with this suspicion because the unification of the worldly and the spiritual power in the hands of one single sovereign, be it the Pope or the Emperor, has been considered since Luther a sign of the Antichrist.

4. Martin Luther sent out a circular disputation about the right of resistance against the emperor in the dangerous year 1539.[20] If the Emperor should wipe out the true faith through war against the Protestant State rulers in the service of the Pope, then, for Luther, not only a usurper or a ruler abusing his office appears, but rather the apocalyptic great tyrant. He is the *monstrum* from Daniel 11:36 who rises up against God, and the Antichrist according to 2 Thess 2:3. He is the *tyrannus universalis.* To him indeed applies the principle: 'the power of the ruler is law'. He does not acknowledge natural law or contracts but rather only that law which is given by himself. He has no judicial status himself but rather is the *anomos,* the 'lawless one' of 2 Thess 2:9. Of this end-time tyrant Luther says: '*hoc monstrum lupus est*' and describes him with the animal symbol not of a *Leviathan* or an octopus, but rather of the 'werewolf', that is, a human soul with a wolf's body. How does one recognize him? In that he lifts himself above both kingdoms, the worldly and the spiritual, and destroys all of God's order. Against this apocalyptic monster, everyone must fight, ruler and subjects, rich and poor. 'Under all conditions this monster must be actively resisted by all and by each individual... even when judges or peasants are killed by the monster's persecutors in the great battle, no injustice has been done to them', says Luther in Thesis 65.[21] 'The people have the right and the obligation of revolution against a ruler who supports the world tyrant. It is a revolt for the sake of eternal salvation, not an upheaval of

---

[20]Martin Luther, *Werke,* WA 39 II, 34–91. Dazu E. Wolf, 'Leviathan. Eine patristische Notiz zu Luthers Kritik am Papsttum', in: *Peregrinatio* I, Müchen 1954, 135–145.
[21]Ebd. WA 39/ II, 42.

the State for political aims… Until the danger has passed, natural law rules alone… *Deficiente magistratu plebs est magistratus.* 'Johannes Heckel explains this point in a way which reminds one of federal theology.[22] Luther did not call this monster 'mortal god' but rather a *deus infernalis.* However, not apocalyptic images and the call to resistance are decisive here but rather separation or the unity of spiritual and worldly power.

4. Comparison of Covenant and Leviathan

We will now compare the main theses of the two political theologies at the beginning of modern times not to produce a compromise but rather in order to confront and thus clarify their profiles.

1. The Leviathan image of the State presupposes a negative anthropology in order to legitimate a positive theology of power, authority and sovereignty. Human beings are evil by nature, chaotic, and therefore need a strong State to protect them from other human beings and from themselves. One normally uses Augustine's doctrine of original sin for this negative anthropology.

2. The covenant idea of the State, on the contrary, presupposes a positive anthropology in order to legitimate a critical theology of power as well as democratic institutions for the control of power. 'All men are created free and equal and endowed by their Creator with inalienable rights', as the American Declaration of Independence explains. The political doctrine of the demons, according to which (uncontrolled) power as such is evil (Jakob Burckhardt), is usually cited here.

3. The foundation of the State's power in a negative anthropology is in the end anarchical, because it claims that neither in paradise nor in the Kingdom of God does a State exist. The State is therefore a phenomenon of sin.

4. The foundation of the State's power in the covenant of free citizens recognizes in the polity both a created disposition of humankind and an anticipation of the 'heavenly citizenship' in the Kingdom of God. Although the present State is perverted through political demonism and human sin, it belongs as such to the essence and not just to the alienation of humankind because human beings are social beings.

5. Every positive anthropology is grounded theologically in the experience of God's *proximity.* Every negative anthropology speaks theologically out of God's *distance,* which must be bridged through representative (i.e. mediating) institutions, such as

---

[22]Johannes Heckel, 'Widerstand gegen die Obrigkeit? Pflicht und Recht zum Widerstand bei Martin Luther', in: A. Kaufmann, *Das Widerstandsrecht,* op. cit. 131f.

the Church, as mediator of salvation, and the State, as the mediator of public order. Representative mediators are only necessary when the matter to be mediated is distant and not present everywhere and for every person. Hierarchical churches only exist because the kingdom of God is not yet here. Governmental authority exists only because human beings are not yet free and equal.

6. Positive anthropology replaces representative hierarchy (i.e. Church) through the base-communities of the free and equal, through the covenant of believers. Positive anthropology replaces representative government-authority through the covenant of free citizens and their agreement: Democracy. Positive anthropology begins with the experience that the liberating and life-creating Spirit of God is poured out on 'all flesh' and does not have to be mediated by means of a 'spiritual' institution.

5. Carl Schmitt's Admiration and Paganization of Leviathan

Carl Schmitt, who in 1922 introduced the term 'political theology' for the doctrine of political sovereignty, never made a secret of his admiration for the 'philosopher from Malmesbury' and for the 'Leviathan'. At this point, we will take up only two thoughts from his book: *Der Leviathan in der Staatslehre des Thomas Hobbes. Sinn und Fehlschlag eines politischen Symbols,* Hamburg 1938, because it touches the nerve of Christian faith and thus of Christian theology.

On the one hand there is the distinction of spiritual and political power and on the other private freedom of belief. First, the distinction between religion and politics is for Schmitt a Jewish-Christian distinction. Second, Schmitt claims that Hobbes' preservation of private freedom of religion has led to a Jewish undermining of the State and to the 'castration' of the 'vital Leviathan'. His antisemitism does not interest me here, but rather the threat of the total State which Carl Schmitt rightly perceived in relationship to Jews and Christians.

Calling upon his Jewish discussion partner in the beginning of the 1930s – Leo Strauss[23] – Schmitt contends that Hobbes, in the question of the unity of both powers, stands against 'typically Jewish-Christian doctrines and concretely argues in a pagan-Christian manner' (20). Strauss holds that Hobbes saw the Jews 'as the actual creators of the rebellious differentiation between religion and politics, which is so destructive to the state'. Schmitt corrects: 'the Jewish Christians'. Originally the distinction between the two powers had been foreign to the pagans because 'for them religion was a part of politics'. Leo Strauss contends that the restoration of the original, natural pagan

---

[23]Heinrich Meier, *Carl Schmitt, Leo Strauss und 'Der Begriff des Politischen'. Zu einem Dialog unter Abwesenden,* Stuttgart 1988; Jacob Taubes, *Ad Carl Schmitt. Gegenstrebige Fügung,* Berlin 1987.

unity of politics and religion is the actual meaning of Hobbes' political theory. 'This is true', says Schmitt and adds that it is the question of 'whether or not it (the myth of Leviathan) has stood the test as a political–mythical image in the struggle against the Jewish-Christian destruction of the natural unity, and whether it was a match for the difficulties and malice inherent to such a struggle' (23). From the context of the treatise follows that by 'Jewish-Christian' Schmitt meant Jewish-Christians in the *civitas christiana* (not the early Christian community in Jerusalem), and further the influence of Jewish thought in the Christian realm. The differentiation of the spiritual and political powers which was gained through the investiture struggle, the Lutheran distinction between the two kingdoms and last but not least, the freedom of the church in the constitutional State are considered by him as a Jewish destruction of the original natural and thus vital unity of the all-dominating State. Why this State should be considered 'original', 'natural' and 'vital', he does not reveal.

In my view this means on the contrary that the freedom of the Church from the State and the self-affirmation of the Church vis-à-vis the political religion or the ideology of the State are the best guarantees against the totalitarian State because they do not permit a monstrous Leviathan to arise out of the human State. It is, however, not only the 'Jewish' inheritance in the Christian faith which resists transformation of this faith into religious politics or a political religion even if it is in a Christian State. It is the memory of Christ, who was crucified in the name of the Roman Leviathan. Christianity arose not as a political religion but out of the free discipleship of the Crucified One. Christianity did not arise as a people's religion but as a voluntary community. It is, in the end, always the cross of Christ which stands between the Church and the political unity of religion and politics, tearing this unity.[24] Erik Peterson rightfully explained with regard to Schmitt's Leviathan: 'Whoever renounces the 'Jewish-Christian" division of political unity, ceases to be a Christian and has chosen paganism.'[25]

To Schmitt's regret, Hobbes left a gap in his otherwise tightly knit unity of religion and politics, which later on caused the downfall of the Leviathan: I am referring to the distinction between outward confession and inner faith, of State loyalty in public religion and freedom of thought and of belief in private life. Carl Schmitt sees in this distinction, that is, in this 'individualistic reservation', the starting point for the individual right to freedom in the liberal constitutional systems that followed. From Spinoza to Moses Mendelssohn to Julius Friedrich Stahl, Jews have used this gap in order to take away the 'soul' of the *Leviathan* from the inside (87)

---

[24]This was my thesis in: 'Theologische Kritik der Politischen Religion', in: J. B. Metz, J. Moltmann, W. Oelmüller, *Kirche im Prozeß der Aufklärung*, Müchen-Mainz 1970, 36ff., to which Carl Schmitt, *Politische Theologie II. Die Legende von der Erledigung jeder Politischen Theologie*, Berlin 1970, 118, wrote: 'Im übrigen hat Moltmann recht, wenn er den intensiv politischen Sinn hervorhebt, den die Anbetung eines derartig gekreuzigten Gottes unzerstörbar in sich enthält und der sich nicht ins "rein Theologische" sublimieren läßt.'
[25]Cit. Barbara Nichtweiß, *Erik Peterson. Neue Sicht auf Leben und Werk*, Freiburg 1992, 735.

because what is within now determines what is without and individual freedom of thought becomes the formative principle: 'a small, wavering thought-movement born of Jewish existence, and with simplest logic of consistency, over a few years the decisive turn in the *Leviathan's* fate had come to pass' (89). The *Leviathan's* logical consequence was actually the 'full, undivided absolutism of the state', including the internal sphere: *cuius regio – eius religio*, in which Schmitt saw the 'completion of the Reformation'. But Hobbes had consciously or unconsciously built in an Achilles' heel in his *Leviathan*. Out of belief which is forced to the inside silently grows a reaction because 'as soon as the distinction between the internal and external sphere is acknowledged, the dominance of the internal over the external and with that, that of the private over the public aspect, is at heart already a closed matter' (94). The power of the *Leviathan* becomes exclusively external and thus hollow, empty and sub-human. The distinction between internal and external spheres became a sickness unto death for the 'mortal God'. To demand freedom of religion and conscience from the State is to undermine and weaken its sovereignty. Schmitt discovers in Moses Mendelssohn such a 'paralysis of a foreign (people) in order to make the emancipation of his own Jewish people possible' (93). J. Fr. Stahl was even supposed to have 'ideologically confused and intellectually paralyzed the inner core of the State, royalty, nobility and Protestant Church' (108). Carl Schmitt had a correct insight but in my opinion judged falsely: the affirmation of Christian and Jewish existence in the modern State has secularized it, neutralized it, and made it into the liberal constitutional State. Its re-mythologizing through the *Leviathan* has not succeeded. Hobbes cleverly included mortality for his political god, not because he did not think this theory through, but because he himself believed in a 'Jewish-Christian' manner. Spinoza, Mendelssohn, Stahl and the other emancipated Jews whom Schmitt names, have, therefore, according to Schmitt, saved the culture of liberal democracy from the *Leviathan!*

The socialist Leviathan was obviously also unable to dominate the internal sphere and, lacking a soul, perished. But it is conceivable that through State control of the media the private inner world of the soul is also so dominated by lies and fairy tales, that neither freedom of thought nor freedom of conscience remain, as Noam Chomsky analyzed the situation after the Gulf War in the USA.[26] This destroys democracy. How is the 'individualistic reservation' to defend itself against the political marketing of all things? Perhaps a new *Leviathan* approached us here, against which the Stasi-octopus was a primitive monster.

---

[26]Noam Chomsky, *Media Control. The Spectacular Achievements of Propaganda, Open Magazine Pamphlet Series* 19, Kentfield, Califormina 1991. Cf. also his *Deterring Democracy*, New York; London 1991. P. Mayer-Tasch, op. cit. 296 had already expressed a similar suspicion.

6. The New Political Theology and Democracy

A new political theology arose in Germany after the War under the only gradually perceived shock-effect of *Auschwitz*.[27] Those who came to theology after the war became painfully aware that we must live in the shadow of the Holocaust of the Jews. 'After Auschwitz' became the concrete location of theology for us. The long shadows of this historical guilt became our *locus theologicus*. With the name of 'Auschwitz' we not only associated the moral and political crisis of our people but also a crisis of the Christian faith. Why was there so little resistance against the Nazi *Leviathan* in Christianity? There was no lack of personal courage. We found patterns of behavior in the Protestant and Catholic traditions which obviously led to that failure:

1. The bourgeois opinion, 'religion is a private matter' and has nothing to do with politics, has not taken away the soul of the Leviathan, has not undermined it and has not made it collapse as Carl Schmitt thought, but rather the opposite: inner emigration has allowed for outer crimes and undermined resistance. The 'tendency toward privatization in present day theology' became a reason for *Johann Baptist Metz* to demand and develop a politically critical and publicly responsible theology: 'Deprivatizing is the primary critical task of political theology with regard to theology.'[28] An enlightened person is not someone who thinks in private but rather who has the freedom to make public use of his or her reason. Kant's words are also true for the Christian faith: freedom of religion does not mean being able to foster one's own personal belief but rather making public use of this belief and preaching it.
2. The separation of spiritual and worldly power, of religion and politics, actually led to Church resistance during the years of the German *Leviathan* when the churches were supposed to be 'neutralized'. But it was a resistance of the Church for the sake of its own freedom, not for the sake of the freedom of the people. Through this separation, religion and conscience were limited to the Church and other areas of life were relinquished to unscrupulous power politics.

The new political theology presupposes the public witness of faith and the freedom for political discipleship of Christ which is not only private and not only inside the Church. It does not want to 'repoliticize' the Church as its critics insinuate, but

---

[27]Johann Baptist Metz, *Zur Theologie der Welt*, Mainz-Müchen 1968; Jürgen Moltmann, *Politische Theologie*, Regensburg 1969; also, *Politische Theologie – Politische Ethik*, Mainz-Müchen 1984.
[28]J. B. Metz, *Zur Theologie der Welt*, 101.

rather wants to Christianize the political existence of the churches and of Christians according to the criteria of the discipleship of Christ which are to be found in the Sermon on the Mount: the culture of nonviolence. Politics is the wider context of all Christian theology. It must be critical with respect to political religion and religious politics and affirmative with respect to the concrete involvement of Christians 'for justice, peace and the integrity of creation'. The distinctions of inside and outside, private and political, as well as spiritual and worldly powers do not suffice in restraining the *Leviathan*. The way must – Carl Schmitt also saw this correctly but judged it falsely – lead from the inside to the outside and from faith to political practice.

In closing, I return to the opening question: How do we come to a pluralism of freedom without chaos and to a peaceful unity without dictatorship?

Thomas Hobbes constructed the unity of the *Leviathan* using the idea of representation: 'Unity lies in the representer not the represented.' (Carl Schmitt and Erik Peterson followed him.) Duplessis Mornay and Johann Althusius saw the unity of society in the covenant. 'The crown sits on the constitution, not on the head of a man,' said John Milton. Representative institutions relieve the burden of those who are represented: My political representatives decide for me and through this relieve me of my own political responsibility. Representation is a normal occurrence in all forms of human social life. But this inevitable representation and proxy is always accompanied by the danger of alienation.[29] Political alienation always arises when representatives lord it over those whom they are to represent and when the people submit to their own government. The results are visible in growing political apathy, in the political sulkiness of the citizens and in the separation of the 'political class' from the life of the people. Because their representatives get out of control, the citizens fall back into passivity which then allows the abuse of power. This is not only political alienation but also the beginning of political idolatry. The early Democrats and Federalists saw the connection between representative alienation and political idolatry clearly. Democracy has no monuments. It issues no medals. It does not carry a man's head on its coins. Its true being is 'iconoclasm' said *John Quincy Adams*, the fourth president of the United States. Merely representative democracy does not satisfy this demand. It is necessary but must be supplemented through forms of direct democracy. The 'covenantization' of social life and the federalizing of political life – social covenant – generation covenant – covenant with the Earth – can lead to pluralism without chaos and to peace without dictatorship.

---

[29]J. Moltmann, op. cit.

11. Johann Baptist Metz – Theology in the New Paradigm: Political Theology

1. Paradigm Change in Theology?

1. Let me (incautiously) assume for the moment that there is something like 'progress' in theology. How can this progress be assessed? Perhaps on the basis of paradigm change, in analogy to Kuhn's suggestion? I would hesitate here, and should like to put a number of questions, without aiming at completeness, and without claiming any competence in scientific theory.

What Kuhn understands by progress derives explicitly from an aetiological evolution logic,[1] and is therefore also formulated in neo-Darwinian terms.[2] But is the *logos* of Christian the-ology, with its underlying apocalyptic-eschatological structure, not moulded by a different logic of time, history and development (if indeed we can speak of development here at all)?[3] At all events, for the *logos* of this theology, 'tradition' and 'remembrance', for example, cannot simply be replaced by 'historical reconstruction' on an evolutionistic basis. It is not evident how the evolutionary model could permit a normative use of history, let alone a 'canonical' one.[4]

Is there such a thing as a 'pure' history of theology at all, analogous to the 'pure' history of science and to Kuhn's hermetic scientific community – a history of theology separate from church history, for example, or from political history? Is a new paradigm ever produced internally by theology at all? Is there any such thing as a theological paradigm change independent of reformative processes in the context of the church? Is the history of theological thought not always shaped by the social history of religion and the church?

Who is the conscious subject of theology? What is the place where theology is done? Is this as unequivocally clear for theology as it is when we apply the paradigm theory to scientific history? Does not a change in the subjects of theology and the places where theology is practised perhaps actually belong to the specific theological paradigm change?[5] Finally, are there not always several competing paradigms in theology – constitutionally, and not merely temporarily?[6]

---

[1] In which – to take up a saying of the 'Darwinian' Nietzsche – evolution aims at nothing except – evolution.
[2] *Cf.* Thomas S. Kuhn, *The Structure of Scientific Revolutions* (Chicago & London, 1962), ch. 13. But see also Toulmin's criticism of Lakatos (Popper) taken up by Lamb in his paper. Here the question about time and history could be reconsidered.
[3] On the question about the relation between history and evolution, *cf.* J.B. Metz, *Faith in History and Society,* tr. D. Smith (London & New York, 1980), ch.10.
[4] *Cf.* here Metz, *ibid.* chs. 11 & 12.
[5] Cf. J.B. Metz, *A New Paradigm of Doing Theology?* (Lima, 1983), *Cf.* also *Concilium* (May, 1978): *Doing Theology in New Places.*
[6] In the light of its content (*cf* n.9) and in the light of its subjects and the places where it is pursued (the theology of the religious orders, university theology, basis theology, and so on).

2. I shall therefore use 'paradigm' and 'paradigm change' in theology in a rather broad sense. As *criteria* for a 'new paradigm in theology' I should like tentatively to propose the following:

(*a*) the awareness of crisis and the capacity for dealing with it;

(*b*) the capacity for reduction. I mean this in two ways: first, as a non-regressive reduction of over-complexity and wordiness – language-run-riot (in which the crises of theology are pushed below the surface and covered up);[7] and second, as the non-trivial reduction of doctrine to life, of doxography to biography, because the *logos* of theology always aims at a form of knowledge that is *a form of living*.[8] For the idea of God to which Christian theology is bound is in itself a practical idea. It continually cuts across the concerns of people who try 'merely to think' it. The histories of new beginnings, conversion, resistance and suffering belong to the very definition of this idea of God. The pure concept 'God' is the contraction, the shorthand, so to speak, of histories, in response to which theology must repeatedly decode its terms.[9]

I should like therefore to name the crises which provide the impulse for a paradigm change in theology (section 2); and shall then try to show why, and in what sense, the 'new' theology which is able to absorb these crises productively and tries to achieve the reductions I have described, is a political theology, or has a political dimension (section 3).

2. The Crises

Let me mention three crises which have sparked off new ways of doing theology.[10,11] They are incidentally so constituted that their productive theological absorption is necessarily *ecumenical* in its very approach, not merely in its result.

---

[7]'Reduction' as the criterion of a theological paradigm change must not be confused semantically with the same term as it is employed in system theory.

[8]*Cf.* here my attempt to interpret Karl Rahner's theology as a kind of new paradigm: 'Karl Rahner – ein theologisches Leben', in J. B. Metz, *Unterbrechungen* (Gütersloh, 1981). I should also like in this connection to point to a paradigm discussion in modern Protestant theology which has meanwhile become a classic: the correspondence between Karl Barth and Adolf von Harnack, which was published sixty years ago. Barth stresses over against Harnack the apocalyptically tense crisis structure of faith, and the proclamation character of theology:

The crisis structure of faith|The trust structure of faith
'Proclamation'|'Scholarship'
'dialectical'|'liberal'
Barth|Harnack

[9]In this approach the difference between *logos* and myth, history and histories remains *within* the-ology.

[10]On the following signs of crisis or of the End-time *cf.* among others J. Habermas, *Legitimation Crisis,* tr. T. McCarthy (London, 1976); R Spacmann, 'Die christliche Religion und das Ende des modernen Bewusstseins', *Communio* 8 (1979), pp. 251–270; J.B. Metz, *The Emergent Church,* tr. P. Mann (New York & London, 1981); L. Gilkey, 'The new Watershed in Theology', *Soundings* (1981), pp. 118–131; also Gilkey's paper in the present volume.

[11]*Cf.* here the project of a practical fundamental theology as practical theology: J.B. Metz, *Faith, op.cit.,* chs. 1–4.

1. *Theology in the face of the modern era*: that is, theology after the end of the religious and metaphysical views of the world – views which still provided the context for Reformation theology.
2. *Theology in the face of Auschwitz*: that is, theology after the end of idealism, or all systems of meaning without conscious subjects.
3. *Theology in the face of a socially divided and culturally polycentric worldwide church*: that is, theology at the end of its cultural monocentricism. In my view this 'end' shelters within itself promising signs of a change.

3. The Political Dimension of Theology in the New Paradigm

The 'new' theology which perceives these crises as fundamental crises of theology and which tries to overcome them in productive reduction is a 'political' theology.

1. Theology after the end of the religious and metaphysical views of the world

The theological discernment and absorption of this end – that is, the productive grappling with the processes of the Enlightenment – brings to the fore the political dimension of theology under two aspects. Both these aspects have given rise to misunderstanding and semantic confusion in the past, and still do so today. This is because, on the one hand, people have tried to fit this political theology into the already existing divisions of theological labour. This has led to a misreading of its character as *fundamental theology* (see section (*a*) below). On the other hand, another misunderstanding was due to the fact that, after the Enlightment, this political theology was identified with the legitimizing political theology of the pre-Enlightenment era. Its *critical* character was therefore overlooked (see section (*b*) below).

(*a*) With regard to the first point: the very project of a fundamental theology after the Enlightenment may be termed political theology. The disintegration of the religious and metaphysical world pictures has put an end to the era of theology's cognitive innocence. Theology must now come to terms with the denials of historical innocence through historicism, and with the denials of its social innocence through ideological criticism in both its bourgeois and its Marxist versions. Theology can no longer push the questions invoked here away from its centre into the fringe zones of apologetics. Its very *logos* is affected.

As fundamental theology, it can therefore no longer be content with the usual assignment of historical and social themes in theology to different divisions of labour. As fundamental theology it must be hermeneutics, and its hermeneutics must be political hermeneutics. For it cannot simply leave 'history' to a separate historical theology, as if theology had any foundation without history and without a thinking subject.[12] Nor can it view 'society' as the exclusive domain of social ethics, or the social teachings of the church,[13] as if theology's search for truth and witness to that truth had any foundation completely removed from social concerns and conflicts. Moreover, since the Enlightenment a fundamental theology can no longer simply assume that the relation between theory and practice is, as far as it is concerned, sufficiently settled by way of the customary division of labour between systematic and practical theology. For to assume this would be to conceal from itself the practical foundation of all theological wisdom and the specific form, or *Gestalt,* its theory takes. Fundamental theology, that is to say, must be practical, political hermeneutics.[14] In my view, a fundamental theology of this kind must ultimately again take up the question about the cognitive subjects of theology, and the places where theology is to be done – a question which was supposed to have been dealt with by way of the division of labour in the church.[15]

(*b*) Now of course the disintegration of religious and metaphysical world pictures in the Enlightenment must not be interpreted as if the result were an utterly demythologized and secularized world, with a total divorce between religion and politics.[16] Religion was not completely privatized, and politics was not entirely secularized.[17] Even politically 'enlightened' societies have their political religions, with the help of which they seek to legitimize and stabilize themselves. We are familiar with this political religion in the 'civil religion' of the United States, for example, as well as in what we in Germany call *bürgerliche Religion.* Although linguistically the two phrases 'mean' the same thing (for example, *bürgerliches Recht* = civil law), civil religion and *bürgerliche Religion* can by no means simply be equated, for they derive from very different political cultures.[18] So when in Germany

---

[12]Recent discussions about the narrative structure of theology also belong here.

[13]For criticism of this division of labour see now above all W. Kroh, *Kirche im gesellschaftlichen Widerspruch* (Munich, 1982). Here Kroh carries on the first detailed discussion between the new political theology and the traditions of Catholic social teaching.

[14]H. Peukert, *Science, Action, and Fundamental Theology* (ET Cambridge, Mass., 1984) has developed this approach and carried it further in discussion with contemporary theories of science and action. From the point of view of liberation theology, of particular importance is the epistemological work by C. Boff & F. Castillo, *Theologie aus der Praxis des Volkes* (Munich & Mainz, 1978). Boff includes criticism of J.B. Metz, J. Moltmann and D. Sölle.

[15]*Cf.* the work cited in n. 5.

[16]'The dialectic of Enlightenment' has already taught us how much the notion of the total demythologization or secularization of the world, and the concept of progress moulded by this idea, became the real myth of early modern times.

[17]For important observations here and on the definition of the tasks of a new political theology see F. Fiorenza, 'Religion und Politik', in *Christlicher Glaube in moderner Gesellschaft* 27 (Freiburg, 1982).

[18]*Cf.* J. Habermas, 'Neokonservative Kulturkritik in den USA und in der Bundesrepublik', *Merkur* (November, 1982).

neo-conservatism also recommends the introduction of a 'civil religion',[19], this amounts ultimately to a reproduction of the traditional patterns in which politics is legitimized by religion – in the guise of political theology in its classic form.[20] Of course both political religions, American and German, serve to politicize religion – a politicization which means that religion is assigned a strict social purpose: it is functionalized.

But it is just this politicization of religion which political theology criticizes, and for two reasons. On the one hand, it criticizes it as religion, since political theology contests a religion which acts as legitimation myth and which purchases its discharge from society's criticism of religion through the suspension of its claim to truth. On the other hand, it criticizes the politicization of religion on theological grounds, contesting all theologies which, appealing to their non-political character, become pre-eminently theologies of just this political religion. If we do not want to establish the essence of religion in politics, not even an enlightened politics, we must not suppress theology's political dimension.

Of course this interpretation also provokes questions, and above all this one: if neither civil religion nor its German equivalent is available as the place where, since the Enlightenment, religion and politics can legitimately be reconciled theologically, what then? How then can the universalistic norms of Christianity be brought into harmony with political life at all, since that political life certainly cannot and must not revert to the time before the achievements of the political Enlightenment – the separation of powers, the right to opposition, liberty of opinion, and so forth? Do these universalistic norms make themselves felt when questions about ultimate goals crop up in political life, not merely questions about methods and their application? That is to say, do these norms make their impact when prevailing conditions themselves come under pressure and require legitimation — when a political ethic is required, not merely as an ethic for order but as *an ethic for change*?[21]

2. Auschwitz – or theology after the end of idealism

Here Auschwitz stands for the end of the modern era. In this context we have to notice first of all that the catastrophe of Auschwitz takes on paradigmatic character through its very incomparability. It points theology's historical and political conscience away from the singular 'history' to the plural 'histories of suffering', which cannot be idealistically explained, but can only be recollected in the context of a

---

[19]Recently, above all H. Lübbe, following N. Luhmann.
[20]*Cf.* here the critical comments by J. Moltmann, 'Das Gespenst einer Zivilreligion', *Evangelische Kommentare* (March, 1983). I should like to associate myself specifically with his criticism.
[21]See here as long ago as 1969 J. B. Metz in H. Peukert (ed.), *Diskussion zur 'politischen Theologie'* (Munich & Mainz, 1969). At present this question, for example, is discussed under the heading of 'monotheism and politics'.

practical intent.[22,23] But which theology does not live from a catastrophic background, either by turning its back on it – that is, idealistically – or profoundly chafed and disturbed by it?

There is no meaning which one could salvage by turning one's back on Auschwitz, and no truth which one could thereby defend. Theology therefore has to make an about-turn, a turn which will bring us face-to-face with the suffering and the victims. And this theology is political theology. Its hermeneutics is a political hermeneutics, a hermeneutics in the awareness of danger. It criticizes the high degree of apathy in theological idealism, and its defective sensibility for the interruptive character of historical and political catastrophes.

This political theology after Auschwitz is not a theology in terms of a system. It is theology in terms of human subjects, with a practical foundation. It continually introduces into public awareness 'the struggle for recollection', for the recollecting knowledge which is related to the human subjects concerned. For this theology, the 'system' can no longer be the place of theological truth – not, at least, since the catastrophe of Auschwitz, which no one can ignore without cynicism or can allow to evanesce into an 'objective' system of meaning.

This theology formulates the question about God in its oldest and most controversial form, as the theodicy question, though not in an existentialistic version but in a political one. It begins with the question about the deliverance of those who have suffered unjustly, the victims of our history and the defeated. It continually brings this question anew into the political awareness as indictment, and expounds the concept of a strict universal solidarity, which also includes the dead, as a practical and political idea, on which the fate of human beings as clear and evident subjects depends.

For without this solidarity the life of human beings as subjects tends more and more towards anthropomorphism. The public invitation to apply for the post as successor to the human being as subject has already gone out. The applicant is to have no recollection of past suffering and is to be tormented by no catastrophes. *Time* magazine has already portrayed the successful candidate on its front cover, as the man of the year for 1983: the robot, an intelligence without memory, without feeling and without morals.[24]

3. Theology at the end of its cultural monocentricism

Is our paradigm discussion not too Eurocentrically aligned from the outset? I must ask this, because it is only in the light of this question that I can discuss the political

---

[22]*Cf.* J.B. Metz, *Faith, op. cit.*, ch.9.

[23]Important elements for a 'hermeneutics in the face of danger' may be found in W. Benjamin's work; *cf.* O. John's pertinent dissertation', *… und dieser Feind hat zu siegen nicht aufgehört'. Die Bedeutung Walter Benjamins für eine Theologie nach Auschwitz* (Münster, 1983).

[24]*Cf.* here – in connection with the work of Metz and Peukert – M. Lamb, *Solidarity with Victims* (New York, 1982).

dimension of the 'new' theology adequately. It is a fact that the church no longer merely *has* a third world church but *is* a third world church with, historically, West European origins. What does this fact mean for Catholic theology, for example?

On the one hand it means that the social antagonism in the world is moving to the centre of attention in the church and in theology. Conditions which are directly inconsistent with the gospel, such as exploitation and oppression or racism, are becoming challenges to theology. They demand that faith be formulated in categories of resistance and change. Thus theology is impelled to become political by its own *logos*.

On the other hand, in this new situation in which the church finds itself, a process of theological significance is emerging which we should not fail to take into account in our discussion about a paradigm change. The church is on the move from a culturally more or less monocentric European and North American church to one that is world-wide and culturally polycentric. In order at least to indicate the theological import of this transition, I should like[25] hypothetically to divide the history of theology and the church, up to the present day, into three eras: a first relatively brief founding era of Jewish Christianity; a second, very long era, in a more or less homogeneous cultural area – the age of the Gentile Christianity that grew up on hellenistic soil, the West European culture and civilization that was bound up with that and which lasted down to our own day; and a third era, the era of a world-wide cultural polycentricism in the church and theology, which is emerging at the present time. In this era the modern division between, the churches, for example, appears mainly as an internal fate affecting European Christendom.[26]

Of course the end of cultural monocentricism does not mean disintegration into an arbitrary or random contextual pluralism. Nor does it mean the enthronement of a new, non-European monocentricism in the church and in theology. The church's original western history, which in concrete terms was always also a history of guilt where non-European cultures were concerned, will remain an immanent part of the cultural polycentricism of church and theology. But what is at stake now is mutual inspiration and mutual productive assimilation. This seems to me to be important for our European outlook on the churches and theology of the third world. For I see a reforming impulse coming upon western Christianity from there and, linked with that, the offer of a 'paradigm change' in theology as well. I can do no more than

---

[25]Following a suggestion of Karl Rahner's about the beginnings of a genuinely world-wide church in Vatican II; *cf.* his *Theological Investigations* Vol.20 (London, 1981): 'Concern for the Church'.

[26]Of course, in this hypothesis I have to assume much which I cannot discuss and substantiate here; for example, that there really is such a thing as this cultural polycentricism, and that it has not already been corrupted in germ by the profane Europeanization of the world which we call technology or technological civilization – that is, through the worldwide rule of western rationality, in which far more of the politics, history and anthropology of Europe is concealed than the technocrats of all political colours would have us believe.

indicate that here, in the context of the political dimension of theology which I have been asked to talk about.[27]

With us this new beginning is associated rather abstractly with concepts such as basis church, liberation theology, and so forth. But here the gospel is related in a highly direct and immediate way to the specific political conditions in which people live. This 'application' generally seems to us too naive, too pre-modern, too simplistic, in view of our own over-complex situation, which has been heightened into extreme abstraction, particularly in the context of all the problems of interpretation in Scripture and tradition which have accumulated in our theology ever since the Enlightenment, and which may be summed up under the catchword of 'hermeneutics'. But if we examine the matter more closely, it becomes evident that in this 'application' we see a new form of theological hermeneutics, which I should like to call a political hermeneutics of danger. The awareness of danger as a basic category of a theological hermeneutics has a sound biblical foundation. The flash of danger lights up the whole biblical landscape; danger, present and impending, runs through all the biblical utterances, especially in the New Testament. As we know, the discipleship narratives in the synoptic Gospels are not simply entertaining stories. They are not really even didactic stories. They are stories told in the face of danger: they are dangerous stories. And we have only to read John (15.18f., for instance) or Paul (for example II Cor. 4.8f.): what do we understand about texts like these and their *logos* if, and as long as, the awareness of danger is systematically screened out in our hermeneutics?

Now, this political hermeneutics of danger is certainly reductive – to some degree oversimplifying – and that in the sense of the reductions I named at the beginning as criteria for a paradigm change: practice returns home to pure theory, logic is joined again by mysticism, resistance and suffering once more find their proper place in the theological definition of grace and Spirit. If then there really is 'progress' in theology, and anything like a paradigm change, should we not have to pay particular attention to new impulses like these in the culturally polycentric space for learning offered by the world church and the worldwide Christian faith?[28] Are these things not always bound up with the reformative situations in which Christianity 'returns to its roots'?[29]

---

[27]More detail may be found in my essay 'Aufbruch zur Reformation', *Süddeutsche Zeitung* (April 9–10, 1983). *Cf.* also Metz, 'Toward the Second Reformation', in *The Emergent Church, op. cit.* (*cf.* n. 11).

[28]Of course, this raises the question how Christian universalism can be so understood in the encounter with other religions and cultures that it does not simply, without more ado, 'imperialistically' integrate and subordinate them, but discerns them in their authentic message. I have tried to offer a solution in my reflections on the narrative-practical understanding of Christianity (as distinct from a transcendental-idealistic one) in *Faith, op.cit.,* ch. 9 (*cf.* n.3). It seems to me that this approach also offers an indication of how the deadlocks of a Christian absolutism in the encounter with other religions and cultures could be solved.

[29]Could we not, therefore, after all tentatively include the new paradigm of theology under the heading of 'liberation'? If, for the moment, we start from the assumption that the paradigm that has hitherto moulded modern theology was 'liberty', then the paradigm change in theology would be the change from liberty to liberation. *Cf.* here my reflections in 'Toward the Second Reformation' in *The Emergent Church, op.cit.* (see

12. Dorothee Soelle – Extracts from The Silent Cry: Mysticism and Resistance

As far as possible, we ought to live as we believe we should live in a liberated world, in the form of our own existence, with all the unavoidable contradictions and conflicts that result from this.... Such endeavor is by necessity condemned to fail and to meet opposition, yet there is no option but to work through this opposition to the bitter end. The most important form that this will take today is resistance.

THEODOR W. ADORNO

The Prison We Have Fallen Asleep in: Globalization and Individualization

ONCE AGAIN I TAKE up Rumi's idea of the "prison" in which we humans who have no thought of God have fallen asleep (see chapter 2). I try to describe our First World prison at the end of the millennium. As I see it, this prison is determined by two trends that match perfectly: globalization and individualization.

Since 1989, we live in a standardized, globalized economic order of technocracy that demands and achieves total disposition over space, time, and creation. Its engine runs on, driven by the coercion to produce more and confirmed by technological success of unimaginable proportions. And this engine is programmed for ever more speed, productivity, consumption, and profit, for about twenty percent of humankind. In all of history, this program is more efficient and more brutal than comparable empires and their towers of Babel. Within this super-engine, human beings are not only "alienated" from what they might become, as Karl Marx observed, but they are also addicted and dependent as never before.

One of the spiritual difficulties in our situation is the inner connection between globalization and individualization. The more globally the market economy structures itself, the less interest it demonstrates in the social and ecological webs in which humans live, and the more it requires the individual who is without any relation whatsoever. The partner that our global market economy needs is *Homo oeconomicus*. This is an individual fit for business and pleasure, showing no interest in the antipersonnel mines that his car manufacturer produces, no interest in the water that his grandchildren will use—not to mention interest in God.

---

n. 11), and the references in n.28. In *The Emergent Church*, in the same chapter, I also discuss the dilemma of Catholic theology in the face of the 'liberty' paradigm.

As the agent of justice and protector of the weaker, the old nation state is downsized, dismantled, and disempowered. At the same time, the individual is built up as the being with unlimited capacity for utilization and consumption. By now, choice, purchase, presentation, and enjoyment have long found their own forms of religious staging and production: it is called "cult marketing." The religion of consumerism no longer needs the old and milder forms of the opiate of the people. Much more efficient opiates are for sale everywhere.

Living within the super-engine, I do not find the New Testament and many other items of the religious tradition of humanity mythologically encoded. Instead, I find them enlightening and clarifying. The New Testament describes the normal condition of human beings under Roman imperial rule as being-in-death. "We know that we have passed from death into life" (1 John 3:14). Here, normative submission to the all-governing power is called death. Alienation, sin, and addiction are different names for the spiritual death that masquerades as life, the death that surrounds us. In the same manner, Paul speaks of us having been "enemies" of God (Rom 5:10). This expression also contains nothing that we have to dismiss as mythological projection.

Instead, the tradition of religion helps us to identify correctly our role at the apex of world society: we are enemies of the earth, enemies of more than two-thirds of all human beings, enemies of the sky above us, and enemies of ourselves. Hildegard von Bingen speaks of the "stench" of death that hangs over our earth. Whoever believes that we can evade it subjectively has already made an arrangement with the super-engine. Such a person uses the engine unknowingly, profits from "its positive side," and in so doing experiences the slow death that the engine has planned for the soul.

Within globalization, corporate world dominance collaborates with a novel form of unrelenting individualization that has no attachment to our fellow creatures. This collaboration appears to be beyond hope. Many regard it as a headlong rush toward the apocalyptic end; thoughtful people among them accept it as our unstoppable fate. Can we still live "as we believe we should live in a liberated world?" This would mean insisting on another vision of our life together, a vision that nourishes resistance.

But are such visions not long gone or turned into harmless private eccentricity? Are there any forms of resistance at all; is there any point to protesting or studying civil disobedience in new ways and practicing it? And has not the spirituality of mysticism itself, from which resistance could emerge, already become an aspect of the market against which it promised to offer protection? I struggle with my own fear of the world and the feeling that religion is dying in a spiritless materialism. It is no coincidence that I seek help exactly among those who know the "dark night" of history and of the eclipse of God.

When we only stare at the lords of this world and the mass of individuals rendered harmless, we do not yet have new eyes for seeing. Fear of the world then encircles us and locks us up in the most exquisitely furnished jail that has ever existed. The New Testament offers a new perspective. Its sociological world is neither the masses nor the individual but the groups that set out on a new way. In the course of Christian mysticism, every rebellion appealed to the early churches and their situation in the ancient imperium. They looked back to a time in which it was not a patriarchically ordered hierarchy that decided what belongs to God and what belongs to Caesar. Instead, it was the groups themselves who appealed to the justice of God against that of the emperor. Their understanding of religion was not the performance of rituals that are judged harmless in Rome as in Washington. Religion as a private matter is a contemporary liberal idea. It knows nothing at all of the mystical ardor that another embodiment and reality of life has always needed and which it has always sought.

The early church refused to involve itself in several of the social benefits and obligations of the empire. Christians did not go to the theaters, the public baths, or the circus. They also shunned what Roman culture called *circenses,* games to entertain the masses and divert their attention from real problems. The public executions staged by Rome for deterrence effect were command performances, but Christians still tried to stay away. Every event connected with the military, the swearing of oaths or the offering of incense to the emperor, was seen to be of the devil. In a minority Christian culture, abstinence, separation, dissent, opposition, and resistance flowed one into the other. It was to precisely these forms of negation of the dominant culture that later dissidents looked back upon. Ernst Troeltsch contrasted these dissidents to what in his work are known as "church" and "sect." His understanding of groups working for social reform illumines the sociological location of mysticism. In a third type called "group," he combined the Protestantism of the Radical Reformation and mystical movements.[1]

This thinking presupposes that mysticism enables community even where its manifestation is extremely individualistic. Of necessity, mysticism desires to get away from the privatization of joy, happiness, and oneness with God. The dance of the love of God cannot be danced alone; it brings people together. God's conviviality, of which Ruysbroeck writes, brings people out of the "purely religious" activity that is said to be harmless. The understanding of human dignity, freedom, and the openness for God or the divine spark cannot be reduced to a special religious space where God can be served and enjoyed but not shared with the 80 percent of our superfluous people.

In the present scenario there are global players on one side, and satiated, isolated individuals on the other. But the groups who are committed to voluntary effort, critical openness, and taking their own initiative are the bearers of hope. Politically speaking, these nongovernmental organizations, among which I count those sections of the Christian church that are alive, are the carriers of resistance. From a spiritual perspective, they embody a different subject than the one that has fallen asleep in the prison of consumerism. What sustains those groups? What keeps them awake?

---

[1]See also Bernard McGinn, *The Presence of God: A History of Western Christian Mysticism,* vol. 1: *The Foundations of Mysticism* (New York: Crossroad, 1991), 389–90.

Why do they not give up? I believe that it is elements of mysticism that cannot be extinguished.

God is the nothing that seeks to be everything, says Jacob Böhme. My fear tells me that in the world of globalization this "nothing" is less and less noticeable, that more and more the silent cry is drowned out. But the nothing that wants to be everything generates its own imperturbability, yes, its own mystical defiance. Böhme conceives of God as a movement, as something flowing, growing, driving, as a process. When we engage ourselves in the process we become part of the God-movement and are connected with all others.

When we are part of the movement of nothing, it means that we too live with our nothing, confront our nothing or, as mystics have always put it, that we become annihilated. Without such "disrobing" of faith wherein it becomes stark naked, we cannot take part in the process. Here in the third part of this book I address the ego, possessions, and violence, which are the focus of the disrobing of resistance. To be ego-less, possessionless, and nonviolent is to be identified with the nothing that wants to be everything even among us.

Often tiny, sometimes at a loss as to what to do next, and frequently unorganized, groups of resistance come into being before our very eyes. In order to spot these new hope-bearers, to understand and strengthen them, and protect oneself against one's own fear of the world, it is good to look for the element of mystical resistance in them. The subject that weaves itself into the web of networks and grows into resistance cannot be destroyed. That subject is and remains a "member" (see chapter 6), even if it does not always know it. The nothing that wants to become everything is also at work in and among us.

Out of the Home into Homelessness

"Mysticism *is* resistance." Years ago, a friend said this to me and I wanted to know how to picture the relationship between mysticism and resistance. The experiences of unity in the midst of commotion—hearing the "silent cry"—necessarily puts us in radical opposition to what is regarded as a normal way of life.

At the theological seminary in New York where I used to teach, we were once asked about our religious experiences. There was an embarrassed silence; it was as if we had asked our grandmothers about their sex life. A young woman eventually spoke up and offered to present, in a week's time, an extensive report on her experiences. Accordingly, she told us that as a very young girl in the American Midwest, she had spent many hours reading in bed at night, without permission. One winter's night, she woke up at four in the morning, went outside, and looked at the stars in the clear, frosty sky. She had a once-in-a-lifetime feeling of happiness, of being connected with all of life, with God; a feeling of overwhelming clarity, of being sheltered and carried. She saw the stars as if she had never seen them before. She described the experience in these words, "Nothing can happen, I am indestructible, I am one with everything." This did not happen again until about ten years later when, in a different context, something similar took place. The new context was a huge demonstration against the Vietnam War. There, too, she knew that she was sheltered, a part of the whole, "indestructible," together with the others. Struggling for words and with her own timidity, she brought both experiences together under the rubric of religious experience.

Suppose that this young woman had lived in fourteenth-century Flanders; she would have had at her disposal other traditions of language allowing her to say, "I heard a voice" or "I saw a light brighter than everything else." Our culture confines her to sobriety, self-restriction, and scholarly manners of expression. How she fought these constraints and the very fact that she did so makes her unforgettable.

Mystical experience is bliss and simultaneously it makes one homeless. It takes people out of the home they have furnished for themselves into homelessness, as it did to young Gautama, known later as the Buddha. I sensed a bit of this ascetic homelessness in the student's report and in her feeling of being drawn more and more into a nonviolent life. The least that can be said is that being touched by religion produces a condition that evokes alienation; in terminology that conveys a degree of loathing, the New Testament specifies it as alienation from "this world." Distance from everyday reality does not necessarily legitimate the big word "resistance," but it does point to a different life. Bliss and homelessness, fulfillment and quest, God's presence and the bitterness of God's absence in the everyday, violence-riddled reality belong together.

Is mysticism necessarily connected with this resistance? The thesis can be questioned from two different positions. Observers far removed from mysticism will look upon mysticism more as a flight from the world, an introversion and concentration on the well-being of one's soul. To them the privatization of religion will seem to be the essential aspect within mysticism. They will find the many examples of conflicts included in the first two parts of this book to be beside the point, even though such conflicts arose from mystical sensitivity. Such interpretation strangely flattens out the dimension of the love of God that is essential to every form of religion—as if ritual and being consoled were all there is! Most of the great men and women of mystical movements have also spoken clearly in their theory against a complete withdrawal from the world. For a time being, they indeed practiced the contemplative "way inwards," but their aim was consistently the unity of the contemplative and the active life, of *ora et labora* (work and prayer). The notion of mysticism as a flight from the world is much more a result of the bourgeois idea that religion is a private affair.

But there is also a very different objection to the idea that mysticism is resistance. It comes from a context that is quite far removed from religion and much closer to what political ethics calls resistance. It is represented by postreligious thinkers who concede that in the course of history, mysticism may have on occasion played a part in resisting the numerous forms of barbarism. However, for such thinkers, rational arguments can now provide sufficient support for the refusal to go along obediently with any further barbarization of society. The apparent persuasiveness of this view seems to arise from a certain overestimation of rationality, usually associated with the left. To me it expresses a kind of naive faith in the goddess Reason.

I am personally acquainted with many groups that practice pacifist and ecological resistance and, above all in the world's poorest countries, economic resistance. I learn from them ever anew that experience, analysis, and insight alone are too weak to bring us out of the prison in which we are asleep. We need a different language that keeps awake and shares the memory of liberation and the promise of freedom for all. We need a different hope than that of political strategies and scientific prediction.

For Martin Buber, the difference between secular and religious movements striving for a renewal of society lies in how they relate themselves to what he called the foundational substance of tradition. Is that substance rejected in principle? Is the "axe to be laid at the root" of the existing order, or is there a relation to tradition that does not eliminate tradition as such? In his view, revolutionary movements work with the knowledge of "how it was meant to be; they begin with the hidden spark in every human being and want to wipe clean the mirror of its distortions, bring back again what was lost and repair again what was destroyed."[2] The category of "again" promises liberation from the compulsion to win.

The failure of state socialism perhaps has an in-depth relationship to the totality of its repudiation of received culture, tradition, and religion. It did not invoke the time "when Adam delved and Eve span," nor any memory of the good story of the beginning of life in creation. The new elites were always the authors of their own being; there was no good beginning. They wanted something completely different and not the *renovation* and the renewal of the face of the earth that is promised in Psalm 104:30. What mysticism can contribute today to the substance of resistance movements is this relation to the origin of life that is often expressed in a phrase like "surely, this is not all there is to it, it wasn't meant to be like this." Whoever desires the new needs the memory and the feast that, even now, celebrate the renewing.

The concept of resistance that meets us in many places of mystical tradition is broad and diverse. It begins with our not being at home in this world of business and violence. Abstention, disagreement, and dissent lead on to simple forms of nonconformist behavior. The American Quakers who helped black slaves escape to the North often got into trouble for their love of truth and their deeply rooted preference for plain speech. When asked whether they had seen a slave pass by on the road, they did not say "No," for that would have transgressed the commandment of

---

[2]Martin Buber, *Werke III: Schriften zum Chassidismus* (Heidelberg: Verlag Lambert Schneider, 1963), 803.

truthfulness. Instead, they said, "I saw no slave," staying with the truth that the black person they had seen was a child of God and nothing else. They did not share the implicit belief that such a person could be named a slave. Children of Quakers were sometimes entrusted with hiding refugees so that their parents could truthfully say that they knew nothing about illegal guests.

It is not always easy to keep up this relation between love of truth and protecting the persecuted. In many forms of resistance, there was and is a necessity for secrecy. Whenever possible, the early Quakers preferred to confuse their persecutors "with truth rather than with lies." During the years of the Cold War, Quakers traveled to Poland with aid supplies and were asked by American secret agents what ships they had seen in the harbor. They would reply, "If we had seen any, we would not tell you. It would be deceiving the Polish government to say that we came to help and then spied for the U.S.A." This principle of open and honest talk and disclosure of intentions plays an important role in nonviolent actions. Several Quakers informed the authorities of their acts of civil disobedience, but only after the asylum-seeking refugees had safely crossed the borders.

The broadest notion of resistance assumed here arises from the distance established from what is regarded as the normal world, a world founded on power, possession, and violence. Consequently, in different situations the notion varies between evasion, dissent, abstinence, refusal, boycott or strike, reform or counterproposal, dialogue, or mediation. Yet, however radically mystical consciousness practices and strives for changes in conditions based on possessions and violence, the connection to those who think otherwise is steadfastly maintained. No one is excluded or eliminated. Such consciousness is deeply marked by "revolutionary patience" that sets out from the experience of what has always been good.

I remember an act of civil disobedience when we occupied a nuclear weapons facility in the Hunsrück Mountains in Germany. We spoke the Lord's Prayer together. About forty people faced the huge military vehicles that drove in and out and we said, "Your kingdom come." Never had I heard that petition as I heard it then. Never had I known as clearly how different the kingdom would look without the instruments of death. Never had I felt as I did then what it means to pray. The mysticism of the good beginning and of its reestablishment and resistance against the terror of violence were present to all of us at that moment as genuine forms of life. We knew something that we could not clearly name at the time. Thanks to Jewish mysticism, I see more plainly now. "Every individual in Israel who calls on God in prayer places a crown on God's head, for prayer is an act of crowning God, of acknowledging God as king."[3] The image of the coronation of one who, according to orthodox Christian opinion,

---

[3] Gershom Scholem, *Von der mystischen Gestalt der Gottheit: Studien zu Grundbegriffen der Kabbala* (Frankfurt, 1995), 16.

needs no coronation and certainly not at the hands of ordinary, sinful people shows how far mystics can proceed especially in a situation of resistance.

I have long thought about what verbs go with mysticism and resistance. Which verbs can we can utilize in order to express mysticism and resistance as a unity? Is there such a thing at all as mystical activities? Is praying also a kind of fighting, like weeping, smiling, keeping silent? Years ago, young people in Zürich wrote an ironic mystical slogan on the walls of their city: "We have enough reason to cry even without your tear gas." In this sentence, crying is a mystical activity, a response to the "silent cry."

...

Being Amazed, Letting Go, Resisting: Outline of a Mystical Journey for Today

In this concluding section of a general introduction to mystical thinking, I try to name stations of the way of mysticism for people on the journey today. In this attempt I have been stimulated by the works of Matthew Fox who, particularly in his new reading of Meister Eckhart, depicts quite early in human history the mystical way of creation spirituality.[4]

Fox's way and that of traditional mysticism differ in two aspects. The first is where the way of mysticism is said to begin. In the understanding of mysticism inherited from the Neoplatonists Proclus and Plotinus, purging or purification are always the first step. The beginning of mystical piety is not the beauty and goodness of creation but the fall of human beings from paradise. That this loaded word "fall" does not appear in the Hebraic narrative of the expulsion from paradise seems not to be known. Instead, in this context, marked strongly by Augustine, there is little talk of creation, of the cosmos, and its original goodness. But does this not place the mystical journey at far too late a point in the course of the Christian history of redemption? One of the basic questions Fox asks again and again is whether we ought not refer first of all to the blessing of the beginning, that is, not to original sin but to original blessing? And is it not exactly mystical experience that points us to creation and the good beginning?

The second difference in comparison to the Western tradition of mysticism has to do with the vision of union with God. I agree with Fox on the matter of the *via unitiva*. He defines the goal of the journey differently in this stage; it is more world-related. The goal is creativity and compassion. Creativity presupposes union with the Creator, whose power lives in the oneness with us. Today we understand creativity not only

---

[4]Matthew Fox, *Wrestling with the Prophets: Essays on Creation, Spirituality, and Everyday Life* (San Francisco: HarperSanFrancisco, 1995), 20ff.

as the transformation of an individual soul but of the world as a whole, in which humans could live together. To speak of this *via transformativa* means to embed the mystical project in the context of our life, which is marked by the catastrophe of economic and ecological exploitation.

For me, mysticism and transformation are indissolubly interconnected. Without economic and ecological justice (known as ecojustice) and without God's preferential love for the poor and for this planet, the love for God and the longing for oneness seem to me to be an atomistic illusion. The spark of the soul acquired in private experience may, indeed, serve the search for *gnosis* (knowledge) in the widest sense of the word, but it can do no more. A genuine mystical journey has a much larger goal than to teach us positive thinking and to put to sleep our capacity to be critical and to suffer.

As in the journeys of former times, the stages of today's journey flow one into the other. The three stages are as follows: to be amazed, to let go, and to resist. The first step taken on the way of mysticism is amazement. I relate an experience by way of example: When my oldest son was learning to read numbers, he stood still one day in front of a house's number plate and did not move an inch. When I wanted to move him on with my "come on!" he said, "Look, Mummy, what a wonderful 537!" Naturally, I had never seen it. He spoke the number slowly, tasting it in a mood of discovery. He was submerged in happiness. I think that every discovery of the world plunges us into jubilation, a radical amazement that tears apart the veil of triviality. Nothing is to be taken for granted, least of all beauty!

The first step of this mystical way is a *via positiva,* and it occurs in the primordial image of the rose that blooms in God. The jubilation of my five-year-old responds to the experience of "radical amazement," as Abraham Heschel (1907–1972) calls this origin of our being-in-relation.[5] Without this overwhelming amazement in the face of what encounters us in nature and in history's experiences of liberation, without beauty experienced even on a busy street and made visible in a blue-and-white number plate on the wall of a house, there is no mystical way that can lead to union. To be amazed means to behold the world and, like God after the sixth day of creation, to be able to say again or for the first time, "Look! How very good it all is!"

But it is not enough to describe this amazement as an experience of bliss alone. Amazement also has its bleak side of terror and hopelessness that renders one mute. The ancient Greeks already defended themselves against this bleakness by an injunction against adoring things; Horace summed it up in his motto *nihil admirari* (admire nothing). But this prohibition, with the help of which scientific thinking once was supposed to banish the fear of fear, has succeeded in banishing the demons together with all the angels. Gone is the sensation of paralyzing fright together with the ability to be marvelously amazed. Those who seek to leave behind the terrifying,

---

[5] Abraham Heschel, *God in Search of Man: A Philosophy of Judaism* (New York: Harper & Row, 1955), 45–46.

sinister side of wonderment, the side that renders us dumb, take on, through rational superiority, the role of those who own the world. In my view, to be able to own and to be amazed are mutually exclusive. "What would it help someone, if he gained the whole world but damaged his soul?" (Matt 16:26, in Luther's German translation).

The soul needs amazement, the repeated liberation from customs, viewpoints, and convictions, which, like layers of fat that make us untouchable and insensitive, accumulate around us. What appears obvious is that we need to be touched by the spirit of life and that without amazement and enthusiasm nothing new can begin. Goethe's friend Herder said that "without enthusiasm nothing great and good ever came to be in this world. Those who were said to be 'enthusiasts' have rendered humankind the most useful services." This is exactly the point where the Christian religion—in a world that makes it possible for us human beings, through science, to create cosmic consciousness while, at the same time, through technology, also to undo creation—must learn anew from its own origin in the tradition of Judaism.

What this means in relation to where the journey takes its beginning is that we do not set out as those who seek but as those who have been found. The goodness we experience is there already long before. In an ontological and not necessarily a chronological sense, before the prayers of those who feel abandoned and banished there is the praise without which they would not perceive themselves as banished ones. This ability for wonderment brings about consenting to one's being here, being today, being now. "Being here is magnificent" (Rainer Maria Rilke). Like every form of ecstasy, this ability implies a self-forgetfulness that, as if by magic, lifts us out of ordinary self-forgetfulness and its corresponding triviality.

Amazement or wonderment is a way of praising God, even if God's name is not mentioned. In amazement, whether we know it or not, we join ourselves to the heavens "who declare the glory of the Eternal One" (Ps 19:1). "The beginning of our happiness lies in the understanding that life without wonder is not worth living."[6] Such an understanding of the wonder of being is not dependent on whether the origin of creation is conceived of in personal terms, as in the Abrahamic religions, or in nonpersonal ones. Radical amazement does not have to atrophy as scientific knowledge increases and better explains what is; on the contrary, such amazement grows in the finest scientific minds who frequently feel attracted to mysticism.

Can amazement, the radical wonderment of the child, be learned again? Whatever the badly misused word "meditation" means, it embraces a form of stopping and tarrying wherein individuals or communities intentionally set aside for themselves times and places other than the ordinary ones. Listening, being still, at rest, contemplating, and praying are all there to make room for amazement. "Hear this, O Job, stop and consider the wondrous works of God" (Job 37:14). The unknown name of the mystical rose reminds us of our own amazed blissfulness.

---

[6]Heschel, *God in Search of Man*, 46.

The practice of amazement is also a beginning in leaving oneself; it is a different freedom from one's own fears. In amazement we detrivialize ourselves and enter the second stage of the mystical journey, that of letting go. If to praise God is the first prompting of the journey, then to miss God is another unavoidable dimension of it. The more profound the amazed blissfulness of the *sunder warumbe* (the utter absence of any why or wherefore), the darker the night of the soul *(via negativa)*. The tradition that most often places this way of purification at the beginning and points out ever new ways of asceticism, renunciation, and escape from desires also teaches to discern how far one is from the true life in God.

Letting go begins with simple questions: What do I perceive? What do I keep away from myself? What do I choose? We need a bit of "un-forming" or liberation before we, in the language of Seuse, can be "con-formed" to Christ or transformed. In the world ruled by the media, this "un-forming" has yet a wholly other status than it had in the rural and monastic world of the Middle Ages when life was so much less subject to diversions. For us who today know a hitherto-undreamed abundance of available consumer goods and artificially manufactured new needs, this stage of the journey plays a different role than it does in the cultures of want. We associate rituals of purification and fasting most frequently with such puritanical "giving-up" performances alleged to be necessary in the development of industrial labor morality. In postindustrial consumer society, this ethics works less and less. Our letting go is related above all to our growing dependency on consumerism. We need purification *(purgatio),* both in the coercive mechanisms of consumption and in the addictions of the everyday working world.

The more we let go of our false desires and needs, the more we make room for amazement in day-to-day life. We also come closer to what ancient mysticism called "being apart," which is living out concretely one's farewell to the customs and norms of one's culture. Precisely the fact that our mysticism begins not with banishment but with amazement is what makes the horror about the destruction of wonder so radical. Our relation to the basic realities of ownership, violence, and the self is changing. In this turning away from our rough ways *(Entgröbung),* the road becomes increasingly narrower. Companions and friends take their leave and the initial amazement clouds over. The symbol of the first stage of mysticism's path is the rose, that of the second stage is the dark night.

To miss God is a form of tradition called "suffering from God." To become more and more empty means not only to jettison unnecessary ballast but also to become more lonely. Given the destruction of nature that marks our context, it becomes more and more difficult to turn back to certain forms of our relationship to and with nature and to the original amazement. Mystical spirituality of creation will very likely move deeper and deeper into the dark night of being delivered into the hands of the principalities and powers that dominate us. For it is not only the poor man from Nazareth who is tortured together with his brothers and sisters on the cross, it is also our mother earth herself.

The horizon of ecological catastrophe is the backdrop before which today's road of the mystical journey has to be considered. To praise God *and* to miss nothing so much as God leads to a "life in God" that the tradition called the *via unitiva*. To become one with what was intended in creation has the shape of *cocreation*; to live in God means to take an active part in the ongoing creation.

The third stage leads into a healing that is at the same time resistance. The two belong together in our situation. Salvation means that humans live in compassion and justice cocreatively; in being healed (saved) they experience also that they can heal (save). In a manner comparable to how Jesus' disciples understood themselves to be "healed healers," so every way of union is one that continues onward and radiates outward. Being-at-one is not individualistic self-realization but moves beyond that to change death-oriented reality. Being-at-one shares itself and realizes itself in the ways of resistance. Perhaps the most powerful symbol of this mystical oneness is the rainbow, which is the sign of the creation that does not perish but continues to live in sowing and harvesting, day and night, summer and winter, birth and death.

Being Amazed	Letting Go	Healing / Resisting
via positiva radical amazement bliss	*via negativa* being apart letting go of possession, violence and ego	*via transformativa* changing the world compassion and justice
praising God the rose	missing God the "dark night"	living in God the rainbow

13. Jürgen Habermas – Faith and Knowledge

When restricted in one's choice of a subject by the depressing current events, one is severely tempted to compete with the John Waynes among us intellectuals to see who is the fastest shot. Only the other day, opinions differed about another issue – the question of whether, and how, we should, via genetic engineering, submit to self-instrumentalization or even pursue the goal of self-optimization. The first steps on this path led to a clash between the spokespersons of institutionalized science and those of the churches. One side feared obscurantism and the consolidation, based on skepticism toward science, of remnants of archaic emotions; the other side objected to the crude naturalism of a scientistic belief in progress supposedly undermining morality. But on September 11, 2001, the tension between secular society and religion exploded in an entirely different way.

As we now know from Atta's testament and from Bin Laden himself, the suicidal murderers who made living bombs of civil aircraft, directing them against the capitalist citadels of Western civilization, were motivated by religious beliefs. For them, the symbols of globalized modernity are an embodiment of the Great Satan. And we, too, the universal eyewitnesses of the "apocalyptic" events, were assailed by biblical images as we watched television repeat again and again, in a kind of masochistic attitude, the images of the crumbling Manhattan twin towers. And the language of retaliation – which the President of the United States was not the only one to resort to in response to the unbelievable – had an Old Testament ring to it. As if the blind fundamentalist attack had struck a religious chord in the very heart of secular society, synagogues, churches, and mosques everywhere began to fill. The hidden correspondence, however, failed to induce the civil-religious mourning congregation, gathering in the New York Stadium a week later, to assume a symmetrical attitude of hatred. For all its patriotism, not a single voice was heard calling for a warlike extension of national criminal law.[1]

In spite of its religious language, fundamentalism is an exclusively modern phenomenon and, therefore, not only a problem of others. What was immediately striking about the Islamic assailants was the perceptible time-lag between their motives and their means. This mirrors the time-lag between culture and society, which in their home countries has only come to exist as the result of an accelerated and radically uprooting modernization. What in our countries, under more propitious conditions, could after all be experienced as a process of *creative* destruction was, there, not bound up with the promise of compensation for the pain suffered through the disintegration of traditional forms of life. The prospect of seeing one's material conditions of life improved is but one thing. What is crucial is the shift in mentality, perhaps blocked so far by feelings of humiliation, which in the political realm comes to be expressed in the separation of church and state. Even in Europe, where under similar circumstances history allowed for much more time to be taken in developing a sensitive attitude toward Janus-faced modernity, feelings toward "secularization" are still highly ambivalent, as shown by the dispute over genetic engineering.

Orthodoxies exist in the Western world as well as in the Middle or Far East, among Christians and Jews as well as among Muslims. If we want to avoid a clash of civilizations, we must keep in mind that the dialectic of our own occidental process of secularization has as yet not come to a close. The "war against terrorism" is no war, and what comes to be expressed in terrorism is also the fatally speechless clash of worlds, which have to work out a common language beyond the mute violence of terrorists or missiles. Faced with a globalization imposing itself via deregulated markets, many of us hoped for a return of the political in a different form – not in the original Hobbesian form of the globalized security state, that is, in its dimensions of police activity, secret service, and the military, but as a worldwide civilizing force. What we are left with, for the moment, is little more than the bleak hope for a cunning of reason – and for some self-reflection. The rift of speechlessness strikes home, too.

---

[1]H. Prantl, "Das Weltgericht," *Süddeutsche Zeitung*, Sept. 18, 2001.

Only if we realize what secularization means in our own postsecular societies can we be far-sighted in our response to the risks involved in a secularization miscarrying in other parts of the world. Such is the intention which guides my taking up, once more, the topic of "Faith and Knowledge." I will speak neither on bioethics nor on a new kind of terrorism but on secularization in our postsecular societies. This self-reflection is one among several steps necessary if we want to present a different image of the West to other cultures. We do not want to be perceived as crusaders of a competing religion or as salespeople of instrumental reason and destructive secularization.

Secularization in Postsecular Society

In Europe, the term "secularization" first had the juridical meaning of a forced conveyance of church property to the secular state. This meaning was then extended to cover the rise and development of cultural and social modernity as a whole. Ever since, "secularization" has been subject to contrasting evaluations, depending on whether its main feature is seen as the successful *taming* of clerical authority, or as the act of unlawful *appropriation*. According to the first reading – "taming" – religious ways of thinking and forms of life are *replaced* by rational, in any case superior, equivalents; whereas in the second reading – "stealing" – these modern ways of thinking and forms of life are *discredited* as illegitimately appropriated goods. The replacement model suggests a progressivist interpretation in terms of disenchanted modernity, while the expropriation model leads to an interpretation in terms of a theory of decline, that is, unsheltered modernity. Both readings make the same mistake. They construe secularization as a kind of zero-sum game between the capitalistically unbridled productivity of science and technology on the one hand, and the conservative forces of religion and the church on the other hand. Gains on one side can only be achieved at the expense of the other side, and by liberal rules which act in favor of the driving forces of modernity.

This image is inconsistent with a postsecular society which adapts to the fact that religious communities continue to exist in a context of ongoing secularization. It obscures the civilizing role of a democratically shaped and enlightened common sense that makes its way as a third party, so to speak, amid the *Kulturkampf* confusion of competing voices. To be sure, from the perspective of the liberal state, only those religious communities which abstain, by their own lights, from violence in spreading their beliefs and imposing them on their own members, let alone manipulation inducing suicide attacks, deserve the predicate of "reasonable."[2] This restraint results from a triple reflection of the believers on their position in a pluralist

---

[2] J. Rawls, *Politischer Liberalismus* (Frankfurt am Main, 1998), pp. 132–41, English edition *Political Liberalism* (New York: Columbia University Press, 1993); R. Forst, "Toleranz, Gerechtigkeit, Vernunft," in Forst (ed.), *Toleranz* (Frankfurt am main: Campus, 2000), pp. 144–61.

society. Religious consciousness must, first, come to terms with the cognitive dissonance of encountering other denominations and religions. It must, second, adapt to the authority of the sciences which hold the societal monopoly of secular knowledge. It must, last, agree to the premises of a constitutional state grounded in a profane morality. Without this thrust of reflection, monotheisms in relentlessly modernized societies unleash a destructive potential. The term "thrust of reflection" [*Reflexionsschub*] suggests, however, the misleading image of a process carried out by one side only, and of one that has already come to a close. Actually, this reflection sets in again and again, and continues with each conflict of existential weight.

As soon as an issue of existential relevance makes it to the political agenda, citizens, whether believers or unbelievers, clash over beliefs impregnated by different worldviews; grappling with the strident dissonances of public dispute, they experience the offensive fact of an antagonistic coexistence of competing worldviews. If, aware of their own fallibility, they learn to deal with this fact of pluralism in a nonviolent way, that is, without disrupting the social cohesion of a political community, they realize what the secular grounds for the separation of religion from politics in a postsecular society actually mean. The neutral state, confronted with competing claims of knowledge and faith, abstains from prejudging political decisions in favor of one side or the other. The pluralized reason of the public of citizens follows a dynamic of secularization only insofar as the latter urges equal distance to be kept, *in the outcome,* from any strong traditions and comprehensive worldviews. In its willingness to learn, however, democratic common sense remains osmotically open to *both* sides, science and religion, without relinquishing its independence.

Science as an Agent of Informed Common Sense

Of course, common sense, being full of illusions about the world, needs to be informed, without any reservation, by the sciences. The scientific theories which intrude upon the lifeworld, however, do not essentially touch on the *framework* of our everyday knowledge, which is linked to the self-understanding of speakers and actors. Learning something new about the world, and about ourselves as beings in the world, changes the *content* of our self-understanding. Copernicus and Darwin revolutionized the geocentric and the anthropocentric worldview. As it is, the traces left by the destruction of the astronomical illusion about the orbits of the stars are less profound than those of the biological disillusionment about the position of man in natural history. The closer scientific findings approach our bodily existence, the more disconcerting they seem for our self-understanding. Brain research instructs us on the physiology of consciousness. But does it also change the intuitive awareness of authorship and responsibility which accompanies all our actions?

We realize what is at stake if, with Max Weber, we look at the beginnings of the "disenchantment of the world." To the extent that nature is made accessible to objectivating observation and causal explanation, it is depersonalized. Nature as an object of science is no longer part of the social frame of reference of persons who communicate and interact with one another and mutually ascribe intentions and motives. What, then, will become of these persons if they progressively subsume *themselves* under scientific descriptions? Will common sense, in the end, consent to being not only instructed, but completely absorbed by counterintuitive scientific knowledge? The philosopher Wilfrid Sellars addressed this question in 1960 (in a famous essay on "Philosophy and the Scientific Image of Man"), responding to it by the scenario of a society where the old-fashioned language games of our everyday life are invalidated in favor of the objectivating description of mental processes.

The vanishing point of this naturalization of the mind is a scientific image of man drawn up in the extensional concepts of physics, neurophysiology, or evolutionary theory, and resulting in a complete desocialization of our self-understanding as well. This naturalization of the mind can only be achieved, however, if the intentionality of human consciousness and the normativity of our actions are completely accounted for by such an objectivating self-description. The theories required would have to explain, for instance, how actors may follow, or break, rules, be they grammatical, conceptual, or moral.[3] Sellars's followers misconstrued the aporetic thought experiment of their teacher as a research program.[4] The project of a scientific "modernization" of our everyday psychology[5] led to attempts at a semantics – teleosemantics – explaining the contents of thought in terms of biology.[6] But even these most advanced efforts fail, it seems, because the concept of purposefulness with which we invest the Darwinian language game of mutation and adaptation, selection and survival is too poor to be adequate to the difference of "is" and "ought" which is implied if we violate rules – misapplying a predicate or violating a moral rule.[7]

In describing how a person did something she did not want to do, nor should have done, we *describe* her – but not in the same way as we describe a scientific object. The description of persons tacitly includes elements of the pre-scientific self-understanding of speakers and actors. If we describe an event as being a person's action, we know for instance that we describe something which can be not only

---

[3]W. Sellars, *Science, Perception and Reality* (1963; Altascadero, CA: Ridgeview, 1991), p. 38.

[4]P. M. Churchland, *Scientific Realms and the Plasticity of Mind* (Cambridge: Cambridge University Press, 1979).

[5]J. D. Greenwood (ed.), *The Future of Folk Psychology: Intentionality and Cognitive Science* (Cambridge: Cambridge University Press, 1991), Introduction, pp. 1–21.

[6]W. Detel, "Teleosemantik. Ein neuer Blick auf den Geist?" *Deutsche Zeitschrift für Philosophie*, 49, no. 3 (2001), pp. 465–91. Teleosemantics, based on neo-Darwinian assumptions and conceptual analyses, aims to show how the normative consciousness of living beings who use symbols and represent facts might have developed. According to this approach, the intentional frame of the human mind originates from the selective advantage of certain behaviors (e.g. the bees' dance) which are interpreted as representations by those belonging to the same species. Against the background of normalized copies of this kind, divergent behaviors are, then, supposed to be interpretable as misrepresentations – which provides a natural explanation for the origins of normativity.

[7]W. Detel, "Haben Frösche und Sumpfmenschen Gedanken? Einige Probleme der Teleosemantik," *Deutsche Zeitschrift für Philosophie*, 49, no. 4 (2001), pp. 601–26.

explained like a natural process, but also, if need be, justified. In the background, there is the image of persons who may call upon one another to account for themselves, who are naturally involved in normatively regulated interactions and encounter one another in a universe of public reasons.

This perspective, going along with everyday life, explains the difference between the language games of justification and *mere* description. Even nonreductionist strategies of explanation end up against this dualism.[8] They too, after all, provide descriptions from the observer's perspective. But the participant's perspective of our everyday consciousness – in which the justificatory practices of research are grounded – can neither be easily integrated nor simply subordinated to the perspective of the observer. In our everyday dealings, we focus on others whom we address as a second person. Understanding the yes or no of the other, the contestable statements we owe and expect from one another, is bound up with this attitude toward second persons. The awareness of authorship implying accountability is the core of our self-understanding, disclosed only to the perspective of a participant, but eluding revisionary scientific description. The scientistic belief in a science which will one day not only supplement, but *replace* the self-understanding of actors as persons by an objectivating self-description is not science, but bad philosophy. No science will relieve common sense, even if scientifically informed, of the task of forming a judgment, for instance, on how we should deal with prepersonal human life under descriptions of molecular biology that make genetic interventions possible.

Democratic Common Sense and Religion

Thus, common sense is linked to the awareness of actors who can take initiatives, and make and correct mistakes. Against the sciences, it holds its own by persisting in its perspective. The same awareness of being autonomous which eludes naturalistic reduction is also the reason for keeping a distance, on the other hand, from a religious tradition whose normative substance we nevertheless feed on. By its insistence on rational justification, science seems in the end to succeed in getting on its side an informed common sense which has found its place in the edifice of the constitutional state. Of course, the contractualist tradition, too, has religious roots – roots in the very revolution of the ways of thinking that were brought about by the ascent of the great world religions. But this legitimation of law and politics in terms of modern natural law feeds on religious sources that have long since become secularized. Against religion, the democratic common sense insists on reasons which are acceptable not just for the members of *one* religious community. Therefore, the liberal state makes believers suspect that occidental secularization might be a one-way street bypassing religion as marginal.

---

[8]These research strategies account for the complexity of new properties (of organic life or of man) emerging on higher evolutionary stages by abstaining from describing processes of the higher evolutionary stage in concepts which apply to processes of a lower evolutionary stage.

The other side of religious freedom is in fact a pacification of the pluralism of worldviews that distribute burdens unequally. To date, only citizens committed to religious beliefs are required to split up their identities, as it were, into their public and private elements. They are the ones who have to translate their religious beliefs into a secular language before their arguments have any chance of gaining majority support. In Germany, just to give an example, Catholics and Protestants claim the status of a subject of human rights for the gamete fertilized ex utero; this is how they engage in an attempt (an unfortunate one, I think) to translate man's likeness to God into the secular language of the constitution. But only if the secular side, too, remains sensitive to the force of articulation inherent in religious languages will the search for reasons that aim at universal acceptability not lead to an unfair exclusion of religions from the public sphere, nor sever secular society from important resources of meaning. In any event, the boundaries between secular and religious reasons are fluid. Determining these disputed boundaries should therefore be seen as a cooperative task which requires *both* sides to take on the perspective of the other one.

Liberal politics must abstain from externalizing the perpetual dispute over the secular self-awareness of society, that is, from relegating it only to the religious segment of the population. Democratic common sense is not singular; it describes the mental state of a *many-voiced* public. Secular majorities must not reach decisions in such questions before the objections of opponents who feel that these decisions violate their beliefs have been heard; they have to consider these objections as a kind of dilatory plea in order to examine what may be learned from them. Considering the religious origins of its moral foundation, the liberal state should be aware of the possibility that Hegel's "culture of common sense" ["Kultur des gemeinen Menschenverstands"] may, in view of entirely novel challenges, fail to be up to the level of articulation which characterized its own origins. Today, the all-pervasive language of the market puts all interpersonal relations under the constraint of an egocentric orientation toward one's own preferences. The social bond, however, being made up of mutual recognition, cannot be spelled out in the concepts of contract, rational choice, and maximal benefit alone.[9]

Therefore, Kant refused to let the categorical "ought" be absorbed by the whirlpool of enlightened self-interest. He enlarged subjective freedom [*Willkür*] to autonomy (or free will), thus giving the first great example – after metaphysics – of a secularizing, but at the same time salvaging, deconstruction of religious truths. With Kant, the authority of divine commands is unmistakably echoed in the unconditional validity of moral duties. With his concept of autonomy, to be sure, he destroys the traditional image of men as children of God.[10] But he preempts the trivial consequences of

---

[9]A. Honneth, *The Struggle for Recognition*, trans. J. Anderson (Cambridge: Polity, 1995).
[10]The Preface to the first edition of *Religion within the Limits of Reason Alone* (1793) begins with the sentence: "So for as morality is based upon the conception of man as a free agent who, just because he is free, binds himself through his reason to unconditioned laws, it stands in need neither of the idea of another Being over him, for

such a deflation by a critical *assimilation* of religious contents. His further attempt to translate the notion of "radical evil" from biblical language into the language of rational religion may seem less convincing. The unrestrained way in which this biblical heritage is once more dealt with today shows that we still lack an adequate concept for the semantic difference between what is morally wrong and what is profoundly evil. There is no devil, but the fallen archangel still wreaks havoc – in the perverted good of the monstrous deed, but also in the unrestrained urge for retaliation that promptly follows.

Secular languages which only eliminate the substance once intended leave irritations. When sin was converted to culpability, and the breaking of divine commands to an offense against human laws, something was lost. The wish for forgiveness is still bound up with the unsentimental wish to undo the harm inflicted on others. What is even more disconcerting is the irreversibility of *past* sufferings – the injustice inflicted on innocent people who were abused, debased, and murdered, reaching far beyond any extent of reparation within human power. The lost hope for resurrection is keenly felt as a void. Horkheimer's justified skepticism – "The slaughtered are really slaughtered" – with which he countered Benjamin's emphatic, or rather excessive, hope for the anamnestic power of reparation inherent in human remembrance, is far from denying the helpless impulse to change what cannot be changed any more. The exchange of letters between Benjamin and Horkheimer dates from spring 1937. Both, the true impulse and its impotence, were prolonged after the holocaust by the practice, as necessary as it was hopeless, of "coming to terms with the past" ["Aufarbeitung der Vergangenheit"] (Adorno). They are manifest as well in the rising lament over the inappropriateness of this practice. In moments like these, the unbelieving sons and daughters of modernity seem to believe that they owe more to one another, and need more for themselves, than what is accessible to them, in translation, of religious tradition – as if the semantic potential of the latter was still not exhausted.

Dispute Over a Heritage: Philosophy versus Religion

The history of German philosophy since Kant can be perceived in terms of a trial on this disputed heritage. By the end of the Middle Ages, the Hellenization of Christianity had resulted in a symbiosis of religion and metaphysics. This symbiosis was broken up again by Kant. He draws a sharp line between the moral belief of

---

him to apprehend his duty, nor of an incentive other than the law itself, for him to do his duty" (I. Kant, *Religion within the Limits of Reason Alone,* trans. and introd. T. M. Greene and H. H. Hudson (La Salle, Ill.: Open Court, 1934), p. 3.

rational religion and the positive belief in revealed truths. From this perspective faith had certainly contributed to the "bettering of the soul" [*Seelenbesserung*], but "with its appendages of statutes and observances ... bit by bit ... became a fetter."[11] To Hegel, this is pure "dogmatism of enlightenment" ["Dogmatismus der Aufklärung"]. He derides the Pyrrhic victory of a reason which resembles those barbarians who are victorious, but succumb to the spirit of the conquered nation, in that it holds "the upper hand outwardly" only ["der äußeren Herrschaft nach die Oberhand behält"].[12] So, with Hegel, *delimiting* reason is replaced by a reason which *embraces*. Hegel makes death by crucifixion as suffered by the Son of God the center of a way of thinking that seeks to incorporate the positive form of Christianity. God's incarnation symbolizes the life of the philosophical spirit. Even the absolute must realize itself in its other because it will experience itself as absolute power only if it passes through the agonizing negativity of self-limitation. Thus, religious contents are saved in terms of philosophical concepts. But Hegel sacrifices together with sacred history [*Heilsgeschichte*] the promise of a salvaging future in exchange for a world process revolving *in itself*. Teleology is finally bent back into a circle.

Hegel's students and followers break with the fatalism of this dreary prospect of an eternal recurrence of the same. Rather than save religion in thought, they want to realize its profanized contents in a political effort of solidary praxis. This pathos of a desublimated earthly realization of the Kingdom of God is the driving force behind the critique of religion from Feuerbach and Marx to Bloch, Benjamin, and Adorno: "Nothing of theological content will persist without being transformed; every content will have to put itself to the test of migrating into the realm of the secular, the profane" ["Nichts an theologischem Gehalt wird unverwandelt fortbestehen; ein jeglicher wird der Probe sich stellen müssen, ins Säkulare, Profane einzuwandern"].[13] Meanwhile, it is true, it had become evident from the course of history that such a project was asking too much of reason. As reason was despairing of itself under these excessive demands, Adorno secured, albeit with a purely methodological intention, the help of the Messianic perspective: "Knowledge has no light but that shed on the world by redemption" ["Erkenntnis hat kein Licht als das von der Erlösung her auf die Welt scheint"].[14] What applies to Adorno here is a proposition by Horkheimer aiming at Critical Theory as a whole: "Knowing there is no God, it nevertheless believes in him" ["Sie weiß, dass es keinen Gott gibt, und doch glaubt sie an ihn"].[15]

---

[11] Kant, *Religion within the Limits of Reason Alone*.

[12] G. W. F. Hegel, *Faith and Knowledge*, trans. W. Cerf and H. S. Harris (Albany: Stage University of New York Press, 1977).

[13] T. W. Adorno, *Critical Models: Interventions and Catchwords*, trans. H. W. Pickford (New York: Columbia University Press, 1998), p. 136.

[14] T. W. Adorno, *Minima Moralia: Reflections from Damaged Life*, trans. E. F. N. Jephcott (London: New Left Books, 1974), p. 247.

[15] M. Horkheimer, "Kritische Theorie und Theologie" (Dec. 1968), pp. 507–9 of *Gesammelte Schriften*, vol. 14, p. 508.

Today, Jacques Derrida, from different premises, comes to a similar position – a worthy winner of the Adorno Prize also in this respect. All he wants to retain of Messianism is "messianicity, stripped of everything."[16]

The borders of philosophy and religion, however, are mined grounds. *Reason which disclaims itself* is easily tempted to merely borrow the authority, and the air, of a sacred that has been deprived of its core and become anonymous. With Heidegger, devotion [*Andacht*] mutates to become remembrance [*Andenken*]. But there is no new insight to be gained by having the day of the Last Judgement evaporate to an undetermined event in the history of being. If posthumanism is to be fulfilled in the return to the archaic beginnings *before* Christ and *before* Socrates, the hour of religious kitsch has come. Then the department stores of art open their doors to altars from all over the world, with priests and shamans flown in from all four points of the compass for exclusive exhibitions. *Profane*, but *nondefeatist* reason, by contrast, has too much respect for the glowing embers, rekindled time and again by the issue of theodicy, to offend religion. It knows that the profanation of the sacred begins with those world religions which disenchanted magic, overcame myth, sublimated sacrifice, and disclosed the secret. Thus, it can keep its distances from religion without ignoring its perspective.

The Example of Genetic Engineering

This ambivalence may also lead to the reasonable attitude of keeping one's distance from religion without closing one's mind to the perspective it offers. This attitude may help set the right course for the self-enlightenment of a civil society torn by *Kulturkampf*. Postsecular society continues the work, for religion itself, that religion did for myth. Not in the hybrid intention of a hostile takeover, to be sure, but out of a concern to counteract the insidious entropy of the scarce resource of meaning in its own realm. Democratic common sense must fear the media induced indifference and the mindless conversational trivialization of all differences that make a difference. Those moral feelings which only religious language has as yet been able to give a sufficiently differentiated expression may find universal resonance once a salvaging formulation turns up for something almost forgotten, but implicitly missed. The mode for nondestructive secularization is translation. This is what the Western world, as the worldwide secularizing force, may learn from its own history. If it presents this complex image of itself to other cultures in

---

[16]J. Derrida, "Faith and Knowledge: The Two Sources of 'Religion' at the Limits of Reason Alone," in J. Derrida and G. Vattimo (eds), *Religion* (Cambridge: Polity; Stanford: Stanford University Press, 1998), p. 18; cf. also J. Derrida, "Den Tod geben," in A. Haverkamp (ed.), *Gewalt und Gerechtigkeit* (Frankfurt am Main: Suhrkamp, 1994), pp. 331–445.

a credible way, intercultural relations may find a language other than that of the military and the market alone.

In the controversy, for instance, about the way to deal with human embryos, many voices still evoke the first book of Moses, Genesis 1: 27: "So God created man in his own image, in the image of God created he him." In order to understand what *Gottesebenbildlichkeit*–"in the likeness of God" – means, one need not believe that the God who is love creates, with Adam and Eve, free creatures who are like him. One knows that there can be no love without recognition of the self in the other, nor freedom without mutual recognition. So, the other who has human form must himself be free in order to be able to return God's affection. In spite of his likeness to God, however, this other is also imagined as being God's creature. Regarding his origin, he cannot be of equal birth with God. This *creatural nature* of the image expresses an intuition which in the present context may even speak to those who are tone deaf to religious connotations. Hegel had a feeling for this difference between divine "creation" and mere "coming from" God. God remains a "God of free men" only as long as we do not level out the absolute difference that exists between the creator and the creature. Only then, the fact that God gives form to human life does not imply a determination interfering with man's self-determination.

Because he is both in one, God the Creator and God the Redeemer, this creator does not need, in his actions, to abide by the laws of nature like a technician, or by the rules of a code like a biologist or computer scientist. From the very beginning, the voice of God calling into life communicates within a morally sensitive universe. Therefore God may "determine" man in the sense of enabling and, at the same time, obliging him to be free. Now, one need not believe in theological premises in order to understand what follows from this, namely, that an entirely different kind of dependence, perceived as a causal one, becomes involved if the difference assumed as inherent in the concept of creation were to disappear, and the place of God be taken by a peer – if, that is, a human being would intervene, according to his own preferences and without being justified in assuming, at least counterfactually, a consent of the concerned other, in the random combination of the parents' sets of chromosomes. This reading leads to the question I have dealt with elsewhere: Would not the first human being to determine, *at his own discretion*, the natural essence of another human being at the same time destroy the equal freedoms that exist among persons of equal birth in order to ensure their difference?

14. Approaches to Political Theology: Discussion Questions

What, if anything, does Carl Schmitt's use of the term political theology have to offer to the contemporary political theologian?

Do you think there is a distinctive and genuinely new dimension to the political theology offered by Moltmann, Metz and Soelle? If so, how would you describe this contribution?

Is the term 'post-secular' helpful for exploring the interaction of religion and the political in contemporary societies?

III

The Church and the Political

Introduction by Anna Rowlands

There has never been a period in the history of the church when the question of the relation of the church to the political has been a matter of settled consensus. This question arises for the church from the wellsprings of her own historical experience of migration, mission, persecution and empire. It arises equally as a perennial systematic theological question within a tradition that teaches a complex relation between a relativizing eschatological promise of a future Kingdom of peace and justice and the necessary participation of Christians in the search for a contingent earthly peace. In a contemporary era marked by secularization and post-secularization, these historically particular questions of ecclesial and political forms, discipleship and political membership take on new dimensions and associations.

In one sense the entirety of this Reader is concerned with the question of the church and the political. Section VI, 'Liberalism and Democracy' includes reflections from contemporary political theologians who are reshaping this debate, and we would encourage you to read the two sections together. However, in this section we have focused on a small selection of texts that enter into the heart of debates about this relationship in the context of two vastly different, turbulent historical contexts: the Reformation and the early twentieth century, taking us from 1520 to 1945. Any theological discussion of the church and the political involves addressing the relationship between spiritual and temporal powers, and the purpose of human government set within classical Christian doctrines of creation, Christology and eschatology. While Augustine and Thomas Aquinas had provided a scriptural and doctrinal basis for such reflection (see Section I), it is with the events of the Reformation that we see a major reinvention and break with this earlier tradition: a shift in the political self-perception of the church.

The first text is taken from Luther's appeal *To the Christian Nobility of the German Nation* (1520). Published following the papal bull *Exsurge Dominine* (Arise, o Lord), which rejected the reforms Luther sought, the *Appeal* is a call to the nobility to take up its baptized Christian duty to seek the reform of the Church in the face of the excesses of the Roman Church and its rejection of the means of conciliar self-correction. This text represents an early stage in the development of Luther's political theology, and contrasts (as we shall see) to mid- and later-period Lutheran texts. Despite the shifting sands of Luther's political thought, the text does introduce a series of insights on the relation of the church and the political, which have had an enduring legacy. Luther presents a Pauline theology of the political, focused on the baptism of those in secular authority, and the participation of all persons within the one body of social Christendom according to the different public offices we hold. He reaffirms an Augustinian theology of human government: government is ordained by God as a consequence of sin and as a force for restraining evildoers and rewarding the virtuous. What matters to Luther is the enforcement of law, the act of ruling rather than disputations on the nature of law itself. We are created equal, but in guilt we are subject to each other in relations of hierarchy.

The second text from Luther, *On Secular Authority*, was written in a matter of months between 1522–23, following the edict issued by George, Duke of Saxony, banning Luther's translation of the New Testament in November 1522. It represents a developed and coherent position on the rights and duties of rulers, although not his final position on these questions. While in the *Appeal* Luther had argued for the absence of limits on the interference of secular rulers in the affairs of the church, here Luther revises his position. Luther draws ever more firmly the contrast between the society of the church and the society of the temporal polity: liberty and equality attend the life of the church, hierarchy and subjugation that of the polity. The life of the Christian is a private, inner realm; that of the polity is a public and outer realm. Christians are not in need of formal law for they live according to a gospel of grace; the polity must be ruled by the sword: a sword which is quite intentionally a symbol of both order and violence. Luther can see no real justification for an active involvement of the church *qua* institution in secular affairs in the pages of the New Testament: resistance – the only category other than obedience that might make some sense – is to be passive and interior in focus, although we should note Luther's own followers extend and develop this teaching in notable ways following his death.

Luther's teaching on the sharp distinction between public and private realms, grace and nature, temporal and spiritual powers, and the postlapsarian theology of coercive power and limited resistance continue to form the Christian political imagination in powerful ways between the sixteenth and twenty-first centuries. Johann Baptist Metz and Jürgen Moltmann react to this legacy of thought in the texts included in Section II, 'Approaches to Political Theology'. We also see both William Temple and Dietrich Bonhoeffer tarry with Luther's thought in the context of a twentieth-century world at war later in this section.

However, the Reformation also brought forth Anabaptist and Calvinist streams of thought that produced legacies just as profound and significant as Luther's. Readings in Section IV, 'The Politics of Jesus', and Section V, 'Violence and Peace', explore the Anabaptist legacy; here we include John Calvin's *On Civil Government*. While this text also reflects an intense meditation on Romans 13, and takes authority and obedience as key biblical concepts to guide political thought, Calvin departs from Luther's two kingdoms structure in important ways. While Calvin affirms that all authority in matters of governance stems from God, he emphasizes the delegated and representative character of this authority in new ways. Calvin is careful not to propose a spatial distinction between temporal and spiritual power, rather solely a distinction in the means available for each to exercise governance. He also imagines greater consistency between the theological approach to the governance of the church and the secular realm. Monarchy is to be resisted in both contexts and power is to be dispersed through a form of mixed polity, which combined elements of different forms of representation. This polity requires a church capable of public self-government and a godly magistracy willing to embrace its role in enforcing the moral teaching of the scriptures. It is this tradition of thought that becomes the basis for the federalist and proto-democratic politics of the settlers of New England.

Our second selection of texts in this section catapults us into the context of the challenges posed by conceiving the role of the church and the political in the context of two opposing political movements of the twentieth century: fascism and liberal democracy. They represent the work of thinkers and activists caught up in the historically particular dialogues with the cultural movements of their time: Marxism and atheism, National Socialism and Christian Socialism.

John Neville Figgis (1866–1919) was a leading figure in the turn of the twentieth-century Anglican Pluralist movement. An historian of ideas, political philosopher and theologian, Figgis was also a priest of the Church of England. The text from which this extract is taken is composed of a series of four lectures on the church in the modern state, delivered to Anglican clergy in Gloucester in 1911. The earlier chapters of his text focus on a question which exercised Figgis greatly: in an era of liberal legal and political thought, is it still possible to conceive of an independent social entity named 'church'? Focusing on controversial cases of parliamentary involvement with questions of church marriage and public prayer, Figgis concludes that the law struggles to conceive of a notion of church recognizable to the Christian. Figgis disputes whether 'statesmen and lawyers' are able to recognize the church as a social body with a personality, desiring to develop according to her own inherent spirit.

In this third lecture, Figgis proposes a German social model which views the state as a community of communities, but warns repeatedly of the tendency of the state to frequently overreach the limits of its role, interfering in matters that ought to remain the preserve of smaller-scale communities. We might say Figgis was concerned with the way that the state tends to take initiatives that 'crowd out' civil initiative, colonizing these communities to the detriment of healthy political and ecclesial cultures. Figgis is clear that the Church seeks to claim its rights as a social body within the limits of civil society. The pluralist case is neither a claim for the church as a body outside the law, nor a nostalgic wish to control the state – but rather a call to embrace a way of living a corporate life in the historical conditions of the liberal state. In this regard the church has no power other than the attraction of her way of life and the power of persuasion.

Figgis's work exercised an influence on the young Anglican priest theologian and later renowned Archbishop of Canterbury, William Temple. In the piece we have chosen, Temple argues for a distinction between the spheres and methods appropriate to the church and state based on a distinction between nature and grace, justice and charity. While church and state are composed of the same people, they are differentiated by responsibility and approach. However, Temple was acutely aware of the shifting historical character of the church and in particular sharply aware of the effects of secularization. In this context Temple offers a warning against two different forms of perfectionist political theology. The first temptation stems from not taking sin seriously enough by reducing political theology to discussion of the character-forming function of non-political or ecclesial associations. He calls for a social and political witness able to talk intelligently and realistically about the ways sinful social structures form the soul. The second form of risky perfectionism stems from a desire to return to the catacombs to consolidate a more purely Christian set of practices in opposition to a Godless world. This he condemns as a temptation to evade responsibility: the church cannot choose to flee from conflict, only be pushed reluctantly and with resistance to catacombs.

In this text and in his more famous *Christianity and Social Order*, Temple's writings focus on the struggle for meaning in history and the eschatological mediation of hope. It is God's hopeful action, constantly seeking embodiment in the temporal order, that stops us giving in to our temptation to flee the social conflicts faced by each generation. The unique task of the church is to mediate and embody this hope. He tells his reader: '[w]hat none but utopians can hope for in the secular world should be a matter of actual experience in the Church'.

The third piece in this section explores the theology of German Lutheran pastor and theologian Dietrich Bonhoeffer through the lens of his correspondence with Swiss Reformed theologian and pastor Karl Barth. The two men had been in correspondence about matters theological and political during the 1920s and 1930s, culminating in this intense exchange during 1933. Bonhoeffer died at the hands of the Nazis in Flossenberg jail in 1945. These texts represent both anguished personal reflection and a deep, systematic theological reflection on the changing relationship between the church and the political.

In the crucible of the shattered German polity, Bonhoeffer formulates a revised Lutheran approach, emphasizing that any political theology worth its salt must begin with Jesus Christ. He argues that the crucifixion of Jesus at the hands of human government implies a special relationship between Christ and government. In the crucifixion Christ both submits to the divinely grounded authority of government – its *exousia* or power to act – but also speaks to its failure to be an instrument of God's order in the world. For Bonhoeffer, Christ stands in the place of all victims, and through Him we perceive the grounds for powerful, non-violent resistance.

Forced to confront the need for a new theological grounding for resistance to Nazism, Bonhoeffer reformulates the Reformation tradition of teaching on resistance to rulers, presenting a case for a three-fold process for Christian resistance: the church must address the state, witnessing to the true character and vocation of human government; where the excess or lack of law and order cause suffering, the church must directly aid the victims of state action; and where the first two options are already invoked but have proved ineffective, the Christian may act to put a spoke in the wheels of the state system.

It might be helpful for the reader to know that the first part of the extract we include here is taken from Bonhoeffer's reflections on the Aryan Clauses, a Nazi document that disqualified persons of Jewish origin from holding state positions. The second part is taken from correspondence between Barth and Bonhoeffer concerning Bonhoeffer's ministry in Germany and London, and the final section takes the form of a sermon preached by Bonhoeffer in 1933; much of Bonhoeffer's most powerful political writing is worked out through his sermons. The material is knitted together via E. H. Robertson's editorial notes and textual references marked "G.S." refer to their sourcing from the various volumes of Bonhoeffer's *Gesammelte Shriften* or Collected Works. Shortly after this correspondence, Barth would become the main author of the Barmen Declaration of the Confessing Church before returning to Switzerland; Bonhoeffer would return to Germany to teach in the Confessing Church seminary and later to join the resistance movement which would end with his imprisonment and execution.

We close this section with two texts taken from the journalism and spiritual writing of the twentieth-century Catholic American peace activist and founder of the Catholic Worker Movement (CWM), Dorothy Day. The CWM began in New York in the 1930s and combined direct support for the poorest with non-violent direct political action. Day wrote widely of her experience with CWM through journalism in the Catholic Worker newspaper and in her autobiographical writings. We include an extract from each here. Day, alongside Dorothee Soelle, is one of only a small number of women who have succeeded in being recognized as significant political theologians of the mid-twentieth century. Like Soelle, Day's work crosses the genres of mystical spiritual writing, political polemic, and sacramental and fundamental theology. Both are writers who can be situated within the Radical Christian tradition of opposition and resistance to state processes, and both emphasize the mysticism of the act of political resistance. Day's writings emerge in particular from the crucible of her work among the homeless, addicted and those suffering mental ill health in the Catholic worker household as well as her frequent periods of incarceration. From these experiences emerge theological insights, sometimes lacking from more formally academic political theology.

In these extracts Day explains the grounds of her pacifist objection to the payment of federal taxes. She cleverly weaves a connection between the patristic and scholastic tradition of reflection on Matthew 25, the works of mercy and a programme for pacifist civil disobedience. She describes the works of mercy as a simple programme of direct political action. Reminding her reader of the Christian account of limits to state authority, she notes: 'government has no right to legislate as to who can perform the Works of Mercy', and where it attempts to do so it should be resisted. The refusal to pay taxes is construed as part of a Christian practice that contrasts the works of mercy with the works of war.

15. Martin Luther – Extracts from Appeal to the Christian Nobility of the German Nation

Doctor Martin Luther to His Most Illustrious, Most Mighty and Imperial Majesty, and to the Christians of the German Ruling Class.

Grace and power from God to his Illustrious Majesty, and to you, most gracious and honourable Gentlemen.

It is not due to sheer impertinence or wantonness that I, a lone and simple man, have taken it upon myself to address your worships. All classes in Christendom, particularly in Germany, are now oppressed by distress and affliction, and this has stirred not only me but everyman to cry out anxiously for help. It has compelled me to beg and pray that God will endow someone with His Spirit to bring aid to this unhappy nation. Proposals have often been made at councils, but have been cunningly deferred by the guile of certain men, and matters have gone from bad to worse. Their artifices and wickedness I intend with God's help to lay bare in order that, once shown up, they may never again present such hindrances or be so harmful. God has given us a young man of noble ancestry to be our head[1] and so has raised high hopes in many hearts. In these circumstances, it is fitting for us to do all we can to make good use of the present time and of God's gracious gift to us.

The first and most urgent thing just now is that we should each prepare our own selves in all seriousness. We must not begin by assuming we possess much strength or wisdom, even if we had all the authority in the world. For God cannot and will not suffer a goodly enterprise to be begun if we trust in our own strength and wisdom. God will surely abase such pride, as is said in Psalm 33 [:16], "No king stands by the multitude of his host, and no lord by the greatness of his strength." For this reason,

---

[1] The emperor, Charles V.

I fear, it came to pass in former times that the good princes, emperors Frederick I and II, and many other German emperors, were shamelessly trodden under foot and oppressed by the popes whom all the world feared. Perhaps they relied more on their own strength than on God, and therefore had to fall. And what else, in our day, has raised the bloodthirsty Julius II[2] so high, if it were not, as I fear, that France, Germany, and Venice depended on themselves? The children of Benjamin slew 42,000 Israelites because they relied on their own strength.[3]

Lest we have the same experience under our noble emperor, Charles, we must be clear that we are not dealing permanently with men in this matter, but with the princes of hell who would fill the world with war and bloodshed, and yet avoid letting themselves be caught by the flood. We must go to work now, not depending on physical power, but in humble trust in God, seeking help from Him in earnest prayer, with nothing else in mind than the misery and distress of all Christendom suffering over and above what sinful men have deserved. Otherwise our efforts may well begin with good prospects, but, when we get deeply involved, the evil spirit will cause such confusion as to make the whole world swim in blood, and then nothing will be accomplished. Therefore, in this matter let us act wisely, and as those who fear God. The greater the power we employ, the greater the disaster we suffer, unless we act humbly and in the fear of God. If hitherto the popes and Romanists have been able, with the devil's help, to bring kings into conflict with each other, they will be able to do it again now, if we set forth without God's help, and armed only with our own strength and shrewdness.

The Three Walls

The Romanists have very cleverly surrounded themselves with three walls, which have protected them till now in such a way that no one could reform them. As a result, the whole of Christendom has suffered woeful corruption. In the first place, when under the threat of secular force, they have stood firm and declared that secular force had no jurisdiction over them; rather the opposite was the case, and the spiritual was superior to the secular. In the second place, when the Holy Scriptures have been used to reprove them, they have responded that no one except the pope was competent to expound Scripture. In the third place, when threatened with a council, they have pretended that no one but the pope could summon a council. In this way, they have adroitly nullified these three means of correction, and avoided punishment. Thus they still remain in secure possession of these three walls, and practise all the villainy and wickedness we see to-day. When they have been compelled to hold a council, they

---

[2]Julius II, Pope, 1503–13.
[3]Judges 20:21 says 22,000.

have made it nugatory by compelling the princes to swear in advance that the present position shall remain undisturbed. In addition they have given the pope full authority over all the decisions of a council, till it is a matter of indifference whether there be many councils or none, for they only deceive us with make-believes and sham-fights. So terribly fearful are they for their skins, if a truly free council were held. Further, the Romanists have overawed kings and princes till the latter believe it would be impious not to obey them in spite of all the deceitful and cunning dodges of theirs.

May God now help us, and give us one of those trumpets with which the walls of Jericho were overthrown; that we may blow away these walls of paper and straw, and set free the Christian, corrective measures to punish sin, and to bring the devil's deceits and wiles to the light of day. In this way, may we be reformed through suffering and again receive God's blessing.

i. Let Us Begin by Attacking the First Wall.

To call popes, bishops, priests, monks, and nuns, the religious class, but princes, lords, artizans, and farm-workers the secular class, is a specious device invented by certain timeservers; but no one ought to be frightened by it, and for good reason. For all Christians whatsoever really and truly belong to the religious class, and there is no difference among them except in so far as they do different work. That is St. Paul's meaning, in I Corinthians 12 [:12f.], when he says: "We are all one body, yet each member hath his own work for serving others." This applies to us all, because we have one baptism, one gospel, one faith, and are all equally Christian. For baptism, gospel, and faith alone make men religious, and create a Christian people. When a pope or bishop anoints, grants tonsures, ordains, consecrates, dresses differently from laymen, he may make a hypocrite of a man, or an anointed image, but never a Christian or a spiritually-minded man. The fact is that our baptism consecrates us all without exception, and makes us all priests. As St. Peter says, I Pet. 2 [:9], "You are a royal priesthood and a realm of priests", and Revelation, "Thou hast made us priests and kings by Thy blood" [Rev. 5:9 f.]. If we ourselves as Christians did not receive a higher consecration than that given by pope or bishop, then no one would be made priest even by consecration at the hands of pope or bishop; nor would anyone be authorized to celebrate Eucharist, or preach, or pronounce absolution.

When a bishop consecrates, he simply acts on behalf of the entire congregation, all of whom have the same authority. They may select one of their number and command him to exercise this authority on behalf of the others. It would be similar if ten brothers, king's sons and equal heirs, were to choose one of themselves to rule the kingdom for them. All would be kings and of equal authority, although one was appointed to rule. To put it more plainly, suppose a small group of earnest Christian laymen were taken prisoner and settled in the middle of a desert without any episcopally ordained priest among them; and they then agreed to choose one of themselves, whether married or not, and endow him with the office of baptizing, administering the sacrament, pronouncing absolution, and preaching; that man would be as truly a priest as if he had been ordained by all the bishops and the popes. It follows that, if needs be, anyone may baptize or pronounce absolution, an impossible situation if we were not all priests. The fact that baptism, and the Christian status which it confers, possess such great grace and authority, is what the Romanists have overridden by their canon law, and kept us in ignorance thereof. But, in former days, Christians used to choose their bishops and priests from their own members, and these were afterwards confirmed by other bishops without any of the pomp of present custom. St. Augustine, Ambrose, and Cyprian each became bishops in this way.

Those who exercise secular authority have been baptized like the rest of us, and have the same faith and the same gospel; therefore we must admit that they are priests and bishops. They discharge their office as an office of the Christian community, and for the benefit of that community. Every one who has been baptized may claim that he has already been consecrated priest, bishop, or pope, even though it is not seemly for any particular person arbitrarily to exercise the office. Just because we are all priests of equal standing, no one must push himself forward and, without the consent and choice of the rest, presume to do that for which we all have equal authority. Only by the consent and command of the community should any individual person claim for himself what belongs equally to all. If it should happen that anyone abuses an office for which he has been chosen, and is dismissed for that reason, he would resume his former status. It follows that the status of a priest among Christians is merely that of an office-bearer; while he holds the office he exercises it; if he be deposed he resumes his status in the community and becomes like the rest. Certainly a priest is no longer a priest after being unfrocked. Yet the Romanists have devised the claim to *characteres in delebiles,* and assert that a priest, even if deposed, is different from a mere layman. They even hold the illusion that a priest can never be anything else than a priest, and therefore never a layman again. All these are human inventions and regulations.

Hence we deduce that there is, at bottom, really no other difference between laymen, priests, princes, bishops, or, in Romanist terminology, between religious and secular, than that of office or occupation, and not that of Christian status. All have spiritual status, and all are truly priests, bishops, and popes. But Christians do not all follow the same occupation. Similarly, priests and monks do not all work at the same task. This is supported by Romans 12 [:4f.] and I Corinthians 12 [:12f.], and by I Peter 2 [:9], as I showed above. In these passages, St. Paul and St. Peter say that we are all one body, and belong to Jesus Christ who is the head, and we are all members of one another. Christ has not two bodies, nor two kinds of body, one secular and the other religious. He has one head and one body.

Therefore those now called "the religious", i.e., priests, bishops, and popes, possess no further or greater dignity than other Christians, except that their duty is to expound the word of God and administer the sacraments—that being their office. In the same way, the secular authorities "hold the sword and the rod", their function being to punish evil-doers and protect the law-abiding. A shoemaker, a smith, a farmer, each has his manual occupation and work; and yet, at the same time, all are eligible to act as priests and bishops. Every one of them in his occupation or handicraft ought to be useful to his fellows, and serve them in such a way that the various trades are all directed to the best advantage of the community, and promote the well-being of body and soul, just as all the organs of the body serve each other.

Now let us consider whether it is Christian to affirm and declare that secular authorities do not exercise jurisdiction over religious office-bearers, and should not inflict penalties on them. That is as much as to say that the hand ought to do nothing to help when the eye suffers severely. Would it not be unnatural, or indeed unchristian, for one organ not to help another and not ward off what is destroying it? Rather, the more precious an organ is, the more ought the other to help. Therefore, I maintain, that since the secular authorities are ordained by God to punish evil-doers and to protect the law-abiding, so we ought to leave them free to do their work without let or hindrance everywhere in Christian countries, and without partiality, whether for pope, bishops, pastors, monks, nuns, or anyone else. If, to prevent the exercise of secular authority, it were enough to say that the civil administration was, from the Christian standpoint, a lower function than that of preacher or confessor or the religious status, then surely tailors, shoemakers, stonemasons, carpenters, cooks, menservants, farmers, and all secular craftsmen, being lower still, should be forbidden to make shoes, clothes, houses, things to eat and drink, or pay rents and tributes to the pope, bishops, priests, and monks. But if these laymen are to be allowed to do their work undisturbed, what is the purpose of Romanist writers who make laws by which they exempt themselves from the secular Christian authorities? It is simply that they may do evil unpunished, and fulfil what St. Peter said, "There shall arise false teachers among you, moving among you with false and imaginary sayings, selling you a bad bargain."

Hence secular Christian authorities should exercise their office freely and unhindered and without fear, whether it be pope, bishop, or priest with whom they are dealing; if a man is guilty let him pay the penalty. What canon law says to the contrary is Romish presumptuousness and pure invention. For this is what St. Paul says to all Christians, "Let every soul (I hold that includes the pope's) be subject to the higher powers, for they bear not the sword in vain. They serve God alone, punishing the evil and praising the good" [Rom. 13]. And St. Peter [I Pet. 2:13, 15], "Be subject unto every ordinance of man for God's sake, whose will is that it should be so." He has also proclaimed that such men would come, and would contemn secular authority; and this has, in fact, come about through canon law.

That in my view overturns the first wall—of paper. The reason is that the social corpus of Christendom includes secular government as one of its component functions. This government is spiritual in status, although it discharges a secular duty. It should operate, freely and unhindered, upon all members of the entire corpus, should punish and compel where guilt deserves or necessity requires, in spite of pope, bishops, and priests; and whether they denounce or excommunicate to their hearts' desire. That is why guilty priests, before being handed over to the secular arm, are previously deprived of the dignities of their office. This would not be right unless the secular "sword" already possessed authority over them by divine ordinance. Moreover, it is intolerable that in canon law, the freedom, person, and goods of the clergy should be given this exemption, as if laymen were not exactly as spiritual, and as good Christians, as they, or did not equally belong to the church. Why should your person, life, possessions, and honour be exempt, whereas mine are not, although we are equally Christian, with the same baptism, guilt, and spirit and all else? If a priest is killed, a country is placed under interdict; why not also if a farmer is killed? Whence comes such a great difference between two men equally Christian? Simply from human law and fabrications.

It cannot have been a man of goodwill who devised such distinctions, and made some sins exempt and immune. For it is our duty to strive as much as we can against the Evil One and his works and to drive him away, for so Christ and His apostles bade us. How comes it then that we are told to hold our peace and be silent when the pope or his supporters design impious words or deeds? Are we, on account of certain men, to neglect divine commands and God's truth which we swore at our baptism to defend with life and limb? Of a truth we shall be held responsible for the souls of all who are abandoned and led astray thereby. Surely, it must be the archdevil himself who propounded that canon law which declares, "Even if the pope were so wicked that he led men in multitudes to the devil, nevertheless he could not be deposed." This is the accursed and impious foundation on which they build at Rome, maintaining that we should sooner let all the world go to the devil than oppose their villainy. If a certain person were not to be penalised on the ground that he was superior to the rest, then no Christian may penalise his fellows, since Christ bade us one and all to serve the meanest and humblest.

There is no longer any defence against punishment where sin exists. St. Gregory himself wrote[4] that, while we are all equal, guilt makes one man subject to others. All this shows plainly how the Romanists deal with Christian people, robbing them of their freedom without any warrant from Scripture, but by sheer wantonness. But God and the apostles made them subject to the secular "sword". Well may we fear that Antichrist has been at work, or is completing his preparations.

ii

The second wall is more loosely built and less indefensible. The Romanists profess to be the only interpreters of Scripture, even though they never learn anything

---

[4]Pope Gregory the Great (590–604), in the *Regula pastoralis*, II, 6 (Migne, *Patrol. Ser. Lat., 77,* 34).

contained in it their lives long. They claim authority for themselves alone, juggle with words shamelessly before our eyes, saying that the pope cannot err as to the faith, whether he be bad or good; although they cannot quote a single letter of Scripture to support their claim. Thus it comes about that so many heretical, unchristian, and even unnatural laws are contained in the canon law—matters of which there is no need for discussion at the present juncture. Just because the Romanists profess to believe that the Holy Spirit has not abandoned them, no matter if they are as ignorant and bad as they could be, they presume to assert whatever they please. In such a case, what is the need or the value of Holy Scripture? Let it be burned, and let us be content with the ignorant gentlemen at Rome who "possess the Holy Spirit within", who, however, in fact, dwells in pious souls only. Had I not read it, I should have thought it incredible that the devil should have produced such ineptitudes at Rome, and have gained adherents to them. But lest we fight them with mere words, let us adduce Scripture. St. Paul says, I Corinthians 14 [:30], "If something superior be revealed to any one sitting there and listening to another speaking God's word, the first speaker must be silent and give place." What would be the virtue of this commandment if only the speaker, or the person in the highest position, were to be believed? Christ Himself says, John 6 [:45], "that all Christians shall be taught by God". Then if the pope and his adherents were bad men, and not true Christians, i.e., not taught by God to have a true understanding; and if, on the other hand, a humble person should have the true understanding, why ever should we not follow him? Has not the pope made many errors? Who could enlighten Christian people if the pope erred, unless someone else, who had the support of Scripture, were more to be believed than he?

Therefore it is a wicked, base invention, for which they cannot adduce a tittle of evidence in support, to aver that it is the function of the pope alone to interpret Scripture, or to confirm any particular interpretation. And if they claim that St. Peter received authority when he was given the keys—well, it is plain enough that the keys were not given to St. Peter only, but to the whole Christian community. Moreover the keys have no reference to doctrine or policy, but only to refusing or being willing to forgive sin. Whatever else the Romanists claim in virtue of the keys is an idle invention. But Christ's word to Peter, "I have prayed for thee that thy faith fail not" [Luke 22:32], cannot be stretched to apply to the pope, seeing that the majority of the popes have had no faith, as they themselves are obliged to confess. Therefore, Christ did not pray for Peter only, but for all apostles and Christians. As He said in John 17 [:9, 20], "Father, I pray for those whom Thou hast given me, and not only for them, but for all those who believe on me through their word." Surely these words are plain enough.

Think it over for yourself. You must acknowledge that there are good Christians among us who have the true faith, spirit, understanding, word, and mind of Christ. Why ever should one reject their opinion and judgment, and accept those of the pope, who has neither that faith nor that spirit? That would be to repudiate the whole faith and the Christian church itself. Moreover, it can never be the pope alone who is in the right, if the creed is correct in the article, "I believe in one, holy, Christian church"; or should the confession take the form: "I believe in the pope of Rome"? But this would be to concentrate the Christian church entirely in one man, and that would be in every way an impious, pernicious, error.

In addition, as I have already said, each and all of us are priests because we all have the one faith, the one gospel, one and the same sacrament; why then should we not be entitled to taste or test, and to judge what is right or wrong in the faith? How otherwise does St. Paul's dictum stand, I Corinthians 2 [:15], "He that is spiritual judges all things and is judged by none", and II Corinthians 4 [:13], "We all have the one spirit of faith"? Why then should we not distinguish what accords or does not accord with the faith quite as well as an unbelieving pope? These and many other passages should give us courage and set us free. We ought not to allow the spirit of liberty—to use St. Paul's term—to be frightened away by pronouncements confabricated by the popes. We ought to march boldly forward, and test everything the Romanists do or leave undone. We ought to apply that understanding of the Scriptures which we possess as believers, and constrain the Romanists to follow, not their own interpretation, but that which is in fact the better. In former days, Abraham had to listen to Sarah [Gen. 21:12], who was more completely subject to him than we are to anyone in the world. Similarly, Balaam's ass was more perspicacious than the prophet himself [Num. 22:28]. Since God once spoke through an ass, why should He not come in our day and speak through a man of faith and even contradict the pope? Moreover, St. Paul upbraided St. Peter as a wrongdoer [Gal. 2:11]. Hence it is the duty of every Christian to accept the implications of the faith, understand and defend it, and denounce everything false.

iii

The third wall falls without more ado when the first two are demolished; for, even if the pope acts contrary to Scripture, we ourselves are bound to abide by Scripture. We must punish him and constrain him, according to the passage, "If thy brother sin against thee, go and tell it him between thee and him alone; but if he hear thee not, take with thee one or two more; and if he hear them not, tell it to the church; and if he hear not the church, let him be unto thee as a Gentile" [Matt. 18:15–17]. This passage commands each member to exercise concern for his fellow; much more is it our duty when the wrongdoer is one who rules over us all alike, and who causes much harm and offence to the rest by his conduct. And if I am to lay a charge against him before the church, then I must call it together.

Romanists have no Scriptural basis for their contention that the pope alone has the right to summon or sanction a council. This is their own ruling, and only valid as long as it is not harmful to Christian well-being or contrary to God's laws. If, however, the pope is in the wrong, this ruling becomes invalid, because it is harmful to Christian well-being not to punish him through a council.

Accordingly, we read in Acts 15 [:6] that it was not St. Peter, but all the apostles and elders, who called the Apostolic Council. If that had been the sole right of St. Peter, it would not have been a Christian council, but an heretical *conciliabulum*. Further, the bishop of Rome neither called nor sanctioned the council of Nicea, the most celebrated of all, but the emperor, Constantine. After him, many other emperors did the same, and these councils were the most Christian of all. But if the pope had really had the sole authority, then they would necessarily all have been heretical. Moreover, when I examine decisions of those councils which the pope himself called, I find they did nothing of special importance.

Therefore, when need requires it, and the pope is acting harmfully to Christian well-being, let anyone who is a true member of the Christian community as a whole take steps as early as possible to bring about a genuinely free council. No one is so able to do this as the secular authorities, especially since they are also fellow Christians, fellow priests, similarly religious, and of similar authority in all respects. They should exercise their office and do their work without let or hindrance where it is necessary or advantageous to do so, for God has given them authority over every one. Surely it would be an unnatural proceeding, if fire were to break out in a town, if everyone should stand still and let it burn on and on, simply because no one had the mayor's authority, or perhaps because it began at the mayor's residence. In such a case, is it not the duty of each citizen to stir up the rest, and call upon them for help? Much more ought it to be the case in the spiritual city of Christ, were a fire of offence to break out, whether in the pope's régime or anywhere else. The same argument would hold, if an enemy were to attack a town; that man who called his fellow citizens together at the earliest moment would deserve honour and gratitude. Why then should not honour be accorded to one who makes our infernal enemies known, rouses Christian people, and calls them together?

It is empty talk when the Romanists boast of possessing an authority such as cannot properly be contested. No one in Christendom has authority to do evil, or to forbid evil from being resisted. The church has no authority except to promote the greater good. Hence, if the pope should exercise his authority to prevent a free council, and so hinder the reform of the church, we ought to pay no regard to him and his authority. If he should excommunicate and fulminate, that ought to be despised as the proceedings of a foolish man. Trusting in God's protection, we ought to excommunicate him in return, and manage as best we can; for this authority of his would be presumptuous and empty. He does not possess it, and he would fall an easy victim to a passage of Scripture; for Paul says to the Corinthians, "For God gave us authority, not to cast down Christendom, but to build it up" [II Cor. 10:8]. Who would pretend to ignore this text? Only the power of the devil and the Antichrist attempting to arrest whatever serves the reform of Christendom. Wherefore, we must resist that power with life and limb, and might and main.

Even if some supernatural sign should be given, and appear to support the pope against the secular authority; e.g., if a plague were to strike someone down, as they boast has happened sometimes, we ought only to regard it as caused by the devil on account of our lack of faith in God. It is what Christ proclaimed, "False Christs and false prophets will come in my name, and will do signs and wonders, so as to lead astray, if possible, even the elect" [Matt. 24:24]. St. Paul says to the Thessalonians [II Thess. 2:9] that the Antichrist shall, through Satan, be mighty in false, miraculous signs.

Therefore, let us firmly maintain that no Christian authority is valid when exercised contrary to Christ. St. Paul says, "We can do nothing against Christ, but only for Christ" [II Cor. 13:8]. But if an authority does anything against Christ, it is due to the power of the Antichrist and of the devil, even if that authority makes it rain and hail miracles and plagues. Miracles and plagues prove nothing, especially in these latter days of evil, for specious miracles of this kind are foretold everywhere in Scripture. Therefore, we must hold to God's Word with firm faith. The devil will soon abandon his miracles.

And now, I hope that I have laid these false and deceptive terrors, though the Romanists have long used them to make us diffident and of a fearful conscience. It is obvious to all that they, like us, are subject to the authority of the state, that they have no warrant to expound Scripture arbitrarily and without special knowledge. They are not empowered to prohibit a council or, according to their pleasure, to determine its decisions in advance, to bind it and to rob it of freedom. But if they do so, I hope I have shown that of a truth they belong to the community of Antichrist and the devil, and have nothing in common with Christ except the name.

16. Martin Luther – Extracts from On Secular Authority: How Far Does the Obedience Owed to It Extend?

To the illustrious and noble Prince and Lord, John, Duke of Saxony, Landgrave of Thüringen and Margrave of Meissen, my gracious Lord

Grace and peace in Christ. The force of circumstances, and the fact that many have asked me, but above all your Grace's [express][1] wishes, my most excellent and noble Prince and gracious Lord, oblige me to write once again about secular authority and its Sword: how can a Christian use be made of it and how far do

---

[1]Translator's note: Square brackets indicate words needed to complete the sense in the translation which are not in the original text. They are also used in Luther's scriptural references where, as not infrequently, they are inaccurate or Luther dd not supply them, and to give verse references.

Christians owe it obedience? What disturbs those [who have asked me to write] is Christ's words in Matthew 5 [25,39–40]: 'resist not evil ... but be compliant with your opponent, and the person who takes your coat, let him also take your cloak.' And Romans 12 [19]: 'Vengeance is mine, says the Lord, I will repay.' It is precisely these texts that Prince Volusian long ago used in objection to St Augustine, impugning Christian doctrine for giving evil-doers a free hand, and for being incompatible with the secular Sword.

The sophists at the universities have also found a stumbling-block here, since they could not square the two [the Sword and Christ's words]. So, in order not to put princes outside Christianity altogether, they have taught that these sayings of Christ are not commands, but merely 'counsels of perfection'. In other words, to save the standing and dignity of princes, Christ had to be made out to be saying what was neither true nor right. They could not exalt princes without abasing Christ, blind wretched sophists that they are. This poisonous error has now pervaded the whole world and the common opinion about these sayings of Christ is that they are merely advice for those who want to be perfect, rather than binding commands intended for each and every Christian. [The sophists] have gone so far as to allow the [use of the] Sword and secular authority to the 'perfect' estate of bishops, and even to the 'most perfect' estate of all, that of the pope. In fact, they have not merely allowed them [to make use of what properly belongs only to] this 'imperfect' estate of the Sword and secular authority; on the contrary, they have made them over wholly to the pope, more than to anyone else on earth. The devil has taken complete possession of the sophists and the universities; even they themselves no longer realize what they are saying and teaching.

But my hope is that I may be able to teach princes and secular authorities how they can remain Christians and yet leave Christ as Lord, without reducing Christ's commands to mere 'counsels' for their sake. And I wish to accomplish [this task] as a humble service to Your Grace, as something for all to make use of if they need it, and to the praise and glory of Christ our Lord. And I commend Your Grace and all your kin to God's grace, to keep them in his mercy. Amen.

Wittenberg, New Year's Day, 1523
Your Grace's humble servant
Martinus Luther

Some time ago, I wrote a pamphlet to the German nobility.[2] In it I set out their tasks and duties as Christians. How much notice they took of it is plain for all to see. And so I must turn my efforts in another direction and write instead about what they ought *not* to do, and *desist* from doing. I am confident that they will

---

[2] *An den Christlichen Adel deutscher Nation (Appeal to the Christian Nobility of the German Nation)*, 1520.

pay as little attention this time as they did to my last piece. Long may they remain princes, and never become Christians. For God Almighty has driven our princes mad: they really think they can command their subjects whatever they like and do with them as they please. And their subjects are just as deluded, and believe (wrongly) that they must obey them in all things. It has now come to this, that rulers have begun to order people to hand over books and to believe and think as their rulers tell them. They have had the temerity to put themselves in God's place, to make themselves masters of consciences and belief and to undertake to give lessons to the Holy Spirit from what is in their addled brains. And after all that, they will not allow anyone to dare to tell them [the truth], and still insist on being called 'My gracious Lords'.

They write and issue edicts, [pretending that these] are the Emperor's commands, and that they [themselves] are merely acting as the Emperor's obedient Christian princes, as if they meant it seriously and as if people were incapable of seeing through that sort of subterfuge. If the Emperor were to take away one of their castles or towns, or to command something else that did not seem right to them, we would soon see them finding reasons why they were entitled to resist and disobey him. But as long as it is a question of harassing the poor man and subjecting God's will to their own arbitrary whims, it must be called 'obedience to the Emperor's commands'. In days gone by, people like that were called scoundrels, but now we are to call them 'Christian and obedient princes'. And yet they will allow no one to obtain a hearing or to reply to charges against them, however humbly you plead with them, even though they would think it intolerable to be treated in that way themselves, by the Emperor or anyone else. These are the princes that rule the German territories of the Empire, and it is little wonder that things there are in such a state.

Now, because the raging of these fools tends to the destruction of Christian faith, the denial of God's Word and blasphemy against God's majesty, I can no longer stand idly by and merely watch my ungracious lords and angry princes. I must resist them, even if it is only with words. And since I was not afraid of their idol the pope when he threatened me with the loss of heaven and my soul, I must show the world that I am not afraid of the pope's lackeys either, who threaten me [only] with the loss of my life and worldly possessions. May God let them rage to the end of time and help us to survive their threats. Amen.

1. Our first task is [to find] a firm grounding for secular law and the Sword, in order to remove any possible doubt about their being in the world as a result of God's will and ordinance. The passages [of Scripture] which provide that foundation are these: Romans, 12 [in fact 13.1–2]: 'Let every soul be subject to power and superiority. For there is no power but from God and the power that exists everywhere is ordained by God. And whoever resists the power, resists God's ordinance. But whosoever resists God's ordinance shall receive condemnation on himself.' And again 1 Peter 2 [13–14]: 'Be subject to every kind of human order, whether it be to the king as the

foremost, or governors as sent by him, as a vengeance on the wicked and a reward to the just.'

The Sword and its law have existed from the beginning of the world. When Cain beat his brother Abel to death, he was terrified that he would be killed in turn. But God imposed a special prohibition, suspending [punishment by] the sword for Cain's sake: no one was to kill him. The only possible reason why Cain should have been afraid is that he had seen and heard from Adam that murderers should be killed. Furthermore, God re-instituted and confirmed [this command] in express words after the Flood when he says in Genesis 9 [6]: 'Whosoever sheds man's blood, by man let his blood be shed.' This cannot be interpreted as a reference to God [himself] inflicting suffering and punishment on murderers, since many of them, either because they repent or by favour, remain alive and die [naturally] without the sword. No: it refers to the right of the Sword: a murderer forfeits his life, and it is right that he should be killed by the sword. And if something prevents the law being enforced, or if the sword is dilatory and the murderer dies a natural death, that does not prove Scripture wrong. What Scripture says is that whosoever sheds man's blood, that person's blood ought to be shed by men. It is the fault of men if God's law is not carried out, just as other commandments of God are not obeyed either.

The Law of Moses afterwards confirmed this [command]: 'If a man should kill his neighbour out of malice, him shall you drag from my altar, to kill him' (Exodus 21 [14]). And again: 'A life for a life, an eye for an eye, a tooth for a tooth, a foot for a foot, a hand for a hand, a wound for a wound, a bruise for a bruise.' And what is more, Christ too confirms it when he said to Peter in the garden [of Gethsemane, Matt. 26.52]: 'Whoever takes up the sword shall perish by the sword', which is to be understood in the same sense as Genesis 9[6]: 'Whoever sheds man's blood etc.'; there is no doubt that Christ is here invoking those words, and wishes to have this commandment introduced and confirmed [in the New Covenant]. John the Baptist teaches the same [Luke 3.14]. When the soldiers asked him what they were to do, he told them: 'Do no violence or injustice to anyone and be content with your pay.' If the Sword were not an occupation approved by God, John ought to have commanded them to cease to be soldiers, all the more since [his vocation] was to make the people perfect and to teach them in a true Christian manner. How the secular Sword and law are to be employed according to God's will is thus clear and certain enough: to punish the wicked and protect the just.

2. But what Christ says in Matthew 5 [38–9] sounds as if it were emphatically opposed to this: 'You have heard what was said to your ancestors: an eye for an eye, a tooth for a tooth. But I say to you: resist no evil. Rather, if anyone strikes you on the right cheek, turn him the other cheek. And if someone will dispute with you at law, to take your coat, let him have your cloak also. And if a man should compel you to go with him one mile, go two miles etc.' To the same effect, Paul in Romans 12 [19]: 'Dearly beloved, do not defend yourselves, but rather give place unto the wrath

of God. For it is written: Vengeance is mine; I will repay, says the Lord.' And again, Matthew 5 [44]: 'Love your enemies. Do good unto them that hate you.' And 1 Peter 2 [error for 3.9]: 'No one shall render evil for evil, or insults for insults etc.' These and others of the same sort are hard sayings, and sound as if Christians in the New Covenant were to have no secular Sword.

This is why the sophists say that Christ has abolished the Law of Moses, and why they make [mere] 'counsels of perfection' out of such commands. They then divide up Christian doctrine and the Christian estate into two parts. The one part they call 'those who are perfect', and to this they allot the 'counsels'; the other part they term 'the imperfect' and to them they allot the commands. But this is pure effrontery and wilfulness, without any warrant from Scripture. They fail to notice that in that very place Christ imposes his teachings so emphatically, that he will not have the slightest thing removed from it, and condemns to hell those who do not love their enemies [Matt. 5.22ff]. We must therefore interpret him in another way, so that his words continue to apply to all, be they 'perfect' or 'imperfect'. For perfection and imperfection do not inhere in works, and do not establish any distinction in outward condition or status between Christians; rather, they inhere in the heart, in faith, in love, so that whoever believes more [firmly] and loves more, that person is perfect, irrespective of whether it be a man or a woman, a prince or a peasant, monk or layman. For love and faith create no factions and no outward distinctions.

3. Here we must divide Adam's children, all mankind, into two parts: the first belong to the kingdom of God, the second to the kingdom of the world. All those who truly believe in Christ belong to God's kingdom, for Christ is king and lord in God's kingdom, as the second Psalm [v. 6] and the whole of Scripture proclaims. And Christ came in order to begin the kingdom of God and to establish it in the world. This is why he said before Pilate [John 18.36ff]: 'My kingdom is not of this world, but whoever belongs to the truth hears my voice', and why throughout the Gospel he announces the kingdom of God, saying [Matt. 3.2]: 'Repent, for the kingdom of God is at hand'; and again [Matt. 6.33]: 'Seek first the kingdom of God and its righteousness.' And indeed he calls the Gospel a gospel of the kingdom of God, in that it teaches, governs and preserves the kingdom of God.

Now: these people need neither secular [weltlich] Sword nor law. And if all the world [Welt] were true Christians, that is, if everyone truly believed, there would be neither need nor use for princes, kings, lords, the Sword or law. What would there be for them to do? Seeing that [true Christians] have the Holy Spirit in their hearts, which teaches and moves them to love everyone, wrong no one, and suffer wrongs gladly, even unto death. Where all wrongs are endured willingly and what is right is done freely, there is no place for quarrelling, disputes, courts, punishments, laws or the Sword. And therefore laws and the secular Sword cannot possibly find any work to do among Christians, especially since they of themselves do much more than any laws or teachings might demand. As Paul says in 1 Tim. 1 [9]: 'Laws are not given to the just, but to the unjust.'

Why should this be? It is because the just man [*der Gerechte*] of his own accord does all and more than any law [*Recht*] demands. But the unjust [*Ungerechten*] do nothing that is right [*recht*], and therefore they need the law to teach, compel and urge them to act rightly. A good tree[3] needs no teaching and no law in order for it to bear good fruit; it is its nature to do so without teaching or law. A man would have to be an idiot to write a book of laws for an apple-tree telling it to bear apples and not thorns, seeing that the apple-tree will do it naturally and far better than any laws or teaching can prescribe. In the same way, because of the spirit and faith, the nature of all Christians is such that they act well and rightly, better than any laws can teach them, and therefore they have no need of any laws for themselves.

You will reply: 'Why then has God given all mankind so many laws and why has Christ in the Gospel taught so much about what we ought to do?' I have written at length about this in my 'Postil'[4] and elsewhere and therefore I shall state the matter very briefly. St Paul says that the law is given for the sake of the unjust. In other words, those who are not Christians are constrained by laws to refrain outwardly from wicked deeds, as we shall see below. But since no man is by nature a Christian or just, but all are sinners and evil, God hinders them all, by means of the law, from doing as they please and expressing their wickedness outwardly in actions. And St Paul assigns another task to the law in Romans 7[7], and Galatians 2 [in fact 3.19 and 24]: it teaches how sin may be recognized, so as to humble man into a willingness to accept grace and faith in Christ. Christ teaches the same in Matthew 5[39]: evil is not to be resisted. Here he is explaining the law and is teaching us the nature of a true Christian, as we shall hear below.

4. All those who are not Christians [in the above sense] belong to the kingdom of the world or [in other words] are under the law. There are few who believe, and even fewer who behave like Christians and refrain from doing evil [themselves], let alone not resisting evil [done to them]. And for the rest God has established another government, outside the Christian estate and the kingdom of God, and has cast them into subjection to the Sword. So that, however much they would like to do evil, they are unable to act in accordance with their inclinations, or, if they do, they cannot do so without fear, or enjoy peace and good fortune. In the same way, a wicked, fierce animal is chained and bound so that it cannot bite or tear, as its nature would prompt it to do, however much it wants to; whereas a tame, gentle animal needs nothing like chains or bonds and is harmless even without them.

If there were [no law and government], then seeing that all the world is evil and that scarcely one human being in a thousand is a true Christian, people would devour each other and no one would be able to support his wife and children, feed himself

---

[3]The implicit reference is to the parable in Matthew 7.18.
[4]i.e. *Sermons on the Church's Year,* cf. Weimar edition, 10:2:152–70.

and serve God. The world [*Welt*] would become a desert. And so God has ordained the two governments, the spiritual [government] which fashions true Christians and just persons through the Holy Spirit under Christ, and the secular [*weltlich*] government which holds the Unchristian and wicked in check and forces them to keep the peace outwardly and be still, like it or not. It is in this way that St Paul interprets the secular Sword when he says in Romans 13[3]: 'It [the Sword] is not a terror to good works, but to the wicked.' And Peter says [1 Pet. 2.14]: 'It is given as a punishment on the wicked.'

If someone wanted to have the world ruled according to the Gospel, and to abolish all secular law and the Sword, on the ground that all are baptized and Christians and that the Gospel will have no law or sword used among Christians, who have no need of them [in any case], what do you imagine the effect would be? He would let loose the wild animals from their bonds and chains, and let them maul and tear everyone to pieces, saying all the while that really they are just fine, tame, gentle, little things. But my wounds would tell me different. And so the wicked under cover of the name of Christians, would misuse the freedom of the Gospel, would work their wickedness and would claim that they are Christians and [therefore] subject to no law and no Sword. Some of them are raving like this already.

Such a person must be told that it is of course true that Christians are subject to neither the law nor the Sword for their own sake, and do not need them. But before you rule the world in the Christian and Gospel manner, be sure to fill it with true Christians. And that you will never do, because the world and the many are unchristian and will remain so, whether they are made up of baptized and nominal Christians or not. But Christians, as the saying goes, are few and far between, and the world will not tolerate a Christian government ruling over one land or a great multitude, let alone over the whole world. There are always many more of the wicked than there are of the just. And so to try to rule a whole country or the world by means of the Gospel is like herding together wolves, lions, eagles and sheep in the same pen, letting them mix freely, and saying to them: feed, and be just and peaceable; the stable isn't locked, there's plenty of pasture, and you have no dogs or cudgels to be afraid of. The sheep would certainly keep the peace and let themselves be governed and pastured peaceably, but they would not live long.

Therefore care must be taken to keep these two governments distinct, and both must be allowed to continue [their work], the one to make [people] just, the other to create outward peace and prevent evil-doing. Neither is enough for the world without the other. Without the spiritual government of Christ, no one can be made just in the sight of God by the secular government [alone]. However, Christ's spiritual government does not extend to everyone; on the contrary, Christians are at all times the fewest in number and live in the midst of the Unchristian. Conversely, where the secular government or law rules on its own, pure hypocrisy must prevail, even if it were God's own commandments [that were being enforced]. For no one becomes truly just without the Holy Spirit in his heart, however good his works. And equally where the spiritual government rules over a country and its people unaided, every sort of wickedness is let loose and every sort of knavery has free play. For the world in general is incapable of accepting it or understanding it [i.e. the spiritual government].

You can now see the implication of the words of Christ which we cited earlier from Matthew 5 [39], that Christians are not to go to law or use the secular Sword amongst themselves. This is really only said to the Christians he loves, and it is only they that accept it and act accordingly, rather than reducing it to mere 'counsels', like the sophists. On the contrary, such is the character that the Holy Spirit has imparted to their hearts, that they do harm to no one, but rather suffer it willingly at the hands of anyone else. Now if all the world were Christian, these words would apply to them all and they would all act accordingly. But since they are unchristian, the words have nothing to do with them, and neither do they follow them. Instead they belong under the other [i.e. secular] government, by which the Unchristian are outwardly constrained and forced to behave peaceably and well.

For the same reason Christ did not bear the Sword [in person], or institute it in his kingdom: he is king over Christians and rules by his Holy Spirit alone, without any laws. And even though he confirmed [the legitimacy of] the Sword, he himself made no use of it, for it does not advance his kingdom, which contains none but the just. It is for this same reason that in the old days David was not permitted to build the Temple, for he had borne the Sword and shed much blood. Not that he had done wrong thereby, but he could not prefigure Christ, who will have a peaceful kingdom without the Sword. Instead, Solomon must do it – 'Solomon' in German means peaceable, peaceful – for Solomon had a peaceful kingdom, which could therefore be the emblem of the peaceful kingdom of Christ, the true Solomon. And again, during the whole time the Temple was built, says the Scripture, there was heard no sound of iron; all this because Christ wanted a free, willing people without coercion or constraint, law or Sword [1 Kings 6.7].

This is what is meant by the prophets: Psalm 109 [possibly Ps. 110.3]: 'Thy people shall be those who are willing', and Isaiah 11[9]: 'They shall not kill or harm on all my holy mountain' (in other words the Church). And Isaiah 2[4]: 'They shall make their swords into ploughshares and their spears into sickles; and no one shall raise a sword against another; and they shall study fighting no more etc.' Those who want to extend the meaning of these and similar sayings to make them cover all who call themselves Christians would be perverting [the meaning of] Scripture, for these things are said only of the true Christians, who do in fact act in this way towards each other.

5. You will object here: seeing that Christians need neither the secular Sword nor law, why does Paul in Romans 13[1] say to all Christians: 'Let every soul be subject to power and superiority'? And St Peter [1 Pet. 2.13]: 'Be subject to every human ordinance etc.', as cited above? My answer is: I have already said that Christians among themselves and for themselves need no law and no Sword, for they have no

use for them. But because a true Christian, while he is on the earth, lives for and serves his neighbour and not himself, he does things that are of no benefit to himself, but of which his neighbour stands in need. Such is the nature of the Christian's spirit. Now the Sword is indispensable for the whole world, to preserve peace, punish sin, and restrain the wicked. And therefore Christians readily submit themselves to be governed by the Sword, they pay taxes, honour those in authority, serve and help them, and do what they can to uphold their power, so that they may continue their work, and that honour and fear of authority may be maintained. [All this] even though Christians do not need it for themselves, but they attend to what others need, as Paul teaches in Ephesians 5[21].

In the same way, the Christian performs every other work of love that he does not require for himself. He visits the sick, but not in order to become well himself. He does not feed others because he needs food for himself. And neither does he serve authority because he himself stands in need of it, but because others do, in order that they might enjoy protection, and so that the wicked might not grow even worse. Such service does no harm to him, and he suffers no loss by it, but the world benefits greatly. To omit to do it would not be the act of a Christian; it would be contrary to [the Christian duty of] love, and would give a bad example to [the Unchristian]: they too would refuse to submit to authority, although they are unchristian. And all this would bring the Gospel into disrepute, as if it taught rebellion and created selfish people unwilling to be of use or service to anyone, whereas the Gospel makes the Christian a servant to everyone. Thus Christ in Matthew 17 [27] paid the tax, although he had no need to do so, in order not to give offence.

And so in the words quoted above from Matthew 5[39], you do indeed find Christ teaching that those who are his are to have no secular Sword or law among themselves. But he does not forbid them to serve and be subject to those who do have the secular Sword and laws. On the contrary, precisely because you do not need it and are not to have it, you ought to serve those who have not reached the same [spiritual] level as you and do still need it. Although you yourself do not need your enemy to be punished, your weak neighbour does, and you are to help him to enjoy peace and to see to it that his enemies are kept in check. And that cannot be unless power and superiors are held in honour and awe. The words of Christ are *not*: you are not to serve the power, nor be subject to it; but rather: 'you shall not resist evil', as if to say: so conduct yourself as to suffer all things, so that you have no need for those in power to help or serve or be of use to you; on the contrary, *you* are to help, serve and be indispensable to them. I will have you be of such a noble and honourable status as not to need them; rather they shall need you.

6. You ask whether a Christian can even wield the secular Sword and punish the wicked [himself], seeing that Christ's words 'Do not resist evil' seem so peremptory and clear that the sophists have to water them down into a mere 'counsel'. Answer, 'you have now heard two [conflicting] things. One is that there can be no Sword amongst

Christians. And therefore you cannot bear the Sword over or among Christians. So the question is irrelevant in that context and must instead be asked in connection with the other group [the Unchristian]: can a Christian use be made of it with regard to them? This is where the second part [of what I have said] applies, the one that says that you owe the Sword your service and support, by whatever means are available to you, be it with your body, goods, honour or soul. For this is a work of which you yourself have no need, but your neighbour and the whole world most certainly do. And therefore if you see that there is a lack of hangmen, court officials, judges, lords or princes, and you find that you have the necessary skills, then you should offer your services and seek office, so that authority, which is so greatly needed, will never come to be held in contempt, become powerless, or perish. The world cannot get by without it.

How does this resolve the difficulty? In this way: all such actions would be devoted wholly to the service of others; they would benefit only your neighbour and not you or your possessions and honour. You would not be aiming at revenge [for yourself], at repaying evil with evil, but rather at the good of your neighbours, the preservation, protection and peace of others. As far as you yourself and your possessions are concerned, you keep to the Gospel and act according to Christ's word; you would gladly turn the other cheek and give up your cloak as well as your coat, when it is you and your possessions that are involved. And so the two are nicely reconciled: you satisfy the demands of God's kingdom and the world's at one and the same time, outwardly and inwardly; you both suffer evil and injustice and yet punish them; you do not resist evil and yet you do resist it. For you attend to yourself and what is yours in one way, and to your neighbour and what is his in another. As to you and yours, you keep to the Gospel and suffer injustice as a true Christian. But where the next man and what is his are concerned, you act in accordance with the [command to] love and you tolerate no injustice against him. And that is not prohibited by the Gospel; on the contrary the Gospel commands it elsewhere [cf Romans 13:4].

It is in this way that all the saints have borne the Sword from the beginning of the world: Adam and his descendants, Abraham when he saved Lot, his brother's son, and slew the four kings (Genesis 14[13–16]); and surely Abraham typifies the whole Gospel? This is how the holy prophet Samuel slew King Agag (1 Samuel 15[32ff]) and Elias the prophets of Baal (1 Kings 18[40]). And Moses, Joshua, the Children of Israel, Samson, David and all the kings and princes of the Old Testament acted in the same way. So did Daniel and his companions Ananias, Asarias and Mishael in Babylon; so did Joseph in Egypt and so forth.

Some would claim here that the Old Covenant is abolished and no longer valid and that there is therefore no point in rehearsing these examples to Christians. Not so. For St Paul says in 1 Corinthians 10[3]: 'They have eaten the same spiritual food as we, and have drunk the same spiritual drink from the rock which is Christ.' That is: they had the same spirit and faith in Christ that we have, and were just as much Christians as we are. And what it was right for them to do is right for all Christians, from the beginning to the end of the world. For time and outward changes make no difference among Christians. Nor is it true that the Old Covenant has been abolished, so that it need not be kept, or that it is wrong to keep it – a point on which St Jerome and many others have slipped up. Rather, this is the way in which the Old Covenant has been abolished: doing or omitting are left free, and no longer bind on pain of losing our souls, as they did formerly.

For St Paul says in 1 Corinthians 7[19] and Galatians 6[15]: 'Neither uncircumcision nor circumcision are anything; rather: a new creation in Christ.' That is: it is no sin to be uncircumcised, [contrary to what] the Jews thought, neither is it a sin to be circumcised, as the pagans thought, but both are equally good and equally left to our discretion, as long as whoever does them does not think he will be justified or saved thereby. The same is true of all the other parts of the Old Covenant: it is neither wrong to omit, nor wrong to do, but everything is left as free and good, to be done or omitted. And in fact, were it a question of what is necessary or conducive to the salvation of our neighbour's soul, it would be obligatory to keep them all. Everyone has a duty to do what is necessary for his neighbour, irrespective of whether it is under the Old or the New Covenant, be it something Jewish or pagan, as St Paul teaches in 1 Corinthians 12[13]: 'Love penetrates everything and transcends everything, and looks only to the need and advantage of others, but does not ask whether it is old or new.' The same goes for the examples of the [use of the] Sword. You are free to follow them or not. But when you see your neighbour in need, then love obliges you to do what would otherwise be left free to do or omit. Only do not imagine that your actions will justify or save you, as the Jews had the audacity to think; rather leave that to faith, which makes you into a new creation without works.

But to prove my point from the New Testament as well, we can rely on John the Baptist (Luke 3[15]), whose duty was without a doubt to witness to, show forth, and teach Christ; that is, his doctrine was to be evangelical, the pure New Testament, and he was to lead a perfect people to Christ. John confirms the office of soldier, saying that they are to be content with their pay. If it were unchristian to bear the sword, he should have punished them and told them to throw away both their swords and their pay; otherwise he would not have been teaching them what is fitting for Christians. And when St Peter in Acts 10[34ff] was teaching Cornelius about Christ, he did not tell him to abandon his office, as he should have done if it had been a hindrance to Cornelius' [attaining] the status of a Christian. Furthermore, before [Cornelius] was baptized [Acts 10.44], the Holy Spirit descended on him. And St Luke praised him as a just man [Acts 10.2] before Peter taught him, and did not find fault with him for being a commander of soldiers and a captain of the pagan Emperor. What it was right for the Holy Spirit to leave unchanged and unpunished in Cornelius is equally right for us.

The same example is given to us by the Ethiopian eunuch, a captain, in Acts 8[27ff], whom the evangelist Philip converted and baptized and then allowed to retain his office and return home. [The Ethiopian] could hardly have held such a powerful office under the Queen of Ethiopia without bearing the sword. The same is true of the Governor of Cyprus, Sergius Paulus (Acts 13[7,12]), whom St Paul converted and yet allowed to remain governor among and over pagans. And the same was done by many holy martyrs, who were obedient to the pagan emperors of Rome, went into battle under them and no doubt killed people to keep the peace, as is written of St Maurice, St Achatius and St Gereon, and of many others under the Emperor Julian [the Apostate].

But more important than all these is the clear, strong text (Romans 13[1]), where St Paul says: 'Power is the ordinance of God.' And again: 'Those in power do not bear the sword in vain. For power is the handmaiden of God, his avenger for your good against him that does evil' [Romans 13.4]. My dear brother, do not presume to say that the Christian must not do what is in fact God's own work, ordinance and creation. Otherwise you would also have to say that the Christian must not eat, drink, or marry, for these too are God's works and ordinances. And since they are, they are good, and equally it is good for everyone to make a Christian use of them, as St Paul says in 2 Timothy 4[4]: 'Everything created by God is good, and not to be rejected by the faithful and those who recognize the truth.' And you must count not only food and drink, clothes and shoes, but also power and subordination, protection and punishment, as things created by God.

So to cut a long story short: because St Paul says that power is the handmaiden of God, its use must be allowed not only to pagans but to all mankind. For what can it mean to say that power is the handmaiden of God, if not that it is by nature something which can be used to serve God. It would be wholly unchristian to say that there is anything which serves God and which yet a Christian should not do, for there is no one more suited to serving God than a Christian. In the same way it is right and necessary that all princes should be good Christians. The Sword and power, as a special service rendered to God, are more suited to Christians than to anyone else in the world, and so you should value the Sword and power as much as the married state, or cultivating the soil, or any other trade instituted by God. Just as a man can serve God in the married state, in farming or manual labour, for the benefit of his neighbour, and indeed must do so if his neighbour's need demands it, so too he can serve God by the [exercise of] power, and he ought to do it, when his neighbour needs it. For those are God's servants and labourers who punish evil and protect what is good. But this is to be left to free choice where there is no [absolute] need, just as marrying and engaging in farming are also left to people's choice, where there is no [absolute] need.

If you then ask: why did Christ and the Apostles not exercise power? my answer is: why did not [Christ] take a wife, or become a cobbler or tailor? Are we to think that a status or occupation is not good merely because Christ did not have it himself? In that case, what would happen to every status and occupation except that of preacher, since that was the only one he held? Christ occupied the office and status proper to him, but in doing so he did not condemn any other. It was not fitting for him to bear the Sword, for his only office was to be that of ruling his kingdom and whatever serves that kingdom alone. And it did not pertain to his kingship to become a husband, cobbler, tailor, ploughman, prince, hangman, or beadle; nor again to bear the Sword or [make] secular laws; all that did pertain to it was God's Word and spirit by which his own are governed, inwardly. And the office he held then and continues to hold now is always bestowed by the spirit and God's Word. And the apostles and all spiritual governors were to succeed him in that office. That work, the work of the spiritual Sword, the Word of God, will give them so much to do, if they are to do it properly, that they will have to neglect the secular Sword and leave it to others who do not have to attend to preaching, even though it is not incompatible with their status to do so, as has been said. For everyone must attend to his own calling and work.

And so, even though Christ did not bear or teach the Sword himself, it is enough that he did not forbid or abolish it but rather confirmed it, just as it is enough that he did not abolish the married state but confirmed it, albeit he himself took no wife and taught nothing about it. For the task appropriate to his status was to concern himself wholly with that work which specifically served his kingdom and nothing else, to prevent his example being treated as a binding reason for teaching and believing that God's kingdom could not continue without marriage or the Sword or suchlike outward things, whereas that kingdom subsists by God's Word and spirit alone. (For Christ's example compels imitation.) Christ's own office was and had to be that of the most high king in this same kingdom. And since not all Christians have the same office (even though they could have it), it is right and fitting that they should have some other external [office], by which God may also be served.

From all this it follows that the right interpretation of Christ's words in Matthew 5[39]: 'You shall not resist evil etc.' is that Christians should be capable of suffering every evil and injustice, not avenging themselves, and not going to court in self-defence either. On the contrary they will require nothing at all for themselves from secular authority and laws [Recht]. But they may seek retribution, justice [Recht], protection and help for others, and do whatever they want to that end. And those in power for their part should help and protect them, either on their own initiative, or at the behest of others, even though the Christians themselves lodge no complaint, and do not petition or institute proceedings. Where [the secular authorities] fail to do so, the Christian should allow himself to be abused and maltreated, and should not resist evil, just as Christ's Word says.

But you may be sure of this: this teaching of Christ is not a 'counsel for the perfect', as our blaspheming and lying sophists will have it, but a strict injunction to every Christian. And rest assured that those who avenge themselves and litigate and quarrel in the courts for their goods and honour are mere pagans bearing the name of Christians, and will never be anything else. Pay no attention to the common run of people and what they usually do. Make no mistake about it: there are few Christians on earth. And God's command is something different from what is usually done.

You can see here that Christ did not abolish the Law when he said: 'You have heard how it was said to your ancestors: an eye for an eye. But I say to you: you shall not resist evil etc.' [Matthew 5.38f]. Rather, he is interpreting the meaning of the Law and telling us how it ought to be understood, as if to say: you Jews think that it is right and proper in the sight of God for you to recover what is yours by [recourse to] the law, and you rely on Moses saying 'an eye for an eye etc.' But I say to you that Moses gave this law on account of the wicked, who do not belong to God's kingdom, to prevent them from taking revenge themselves or doing worse. By such externally imposed law they would be compelled to desist from evil, and would be hedged about by outward law and government, and subjected to authority. But you are so to conduct yourselves that you neither need nor seek such law. For although secular authority must have such laws, to judge the unbelieving, and even though you yourselves may make use of it to judge others, all the same for yourselves and in your own affairs you are neither to resort to it nor to use it, for you have the kingdom of heaven and you should leave the earthly kingdom [*Erdreich*] to those who take it from you.

You see, then, that Christ did not interpret his [own] words as abolishing the Law of Moses or as prohibiting secular authority. Rather he withdraws those who are his own from it, so that they will make no use of it for themselves, but leave it for the unbelievers, whom they may indeed serve with such laws, since the Unchristian do exist, and no one can be made a true Christian by compulsion. But it becomes clear that Christ's words are directed to his alone when he says somewhat later that they are to love their enemies and to be perfect, as their heavenly father is perfect [Matt. 5.44,48]. But a man who is perfect and loves his enemy, leaves the law behind; he does not need it to exact an eye for an eye. But neither does he hinder the Unchristian who do not love their enemy and who do want to employ the law; on the contrary, he helps the law to catch the wicked, to prevent them doing still more wickedness.

This, in my view, is how the words of Christ are reconciled with those texts that institute the Sword. What they mean is that Christians are neither to employ nor to call on the Sword for themselves and in their own concerns. But they may and should use it and call on it for the sake of others, so that evil may be prevented and justice upheld. In just the same way the Lord says in the same place that Christians shall not take oaths, but that their speech is to be yea, yea and nay, nay [Matt. 5.34ff]. In other words, they are not to take oaths on their own behalf or of their own will and inclination. But when the necessity, benefit and salvation [of others] or the honour of God demands it, they should take oaths. They make use of the [otherwise] forbidden oath to help others, in precisely the same way that they use the prohibited sword. Indeed Christ and Paul themselves often swear on oath, in order to make their teaching and witness beneficial and credible to mankind, as people do, and are allowed to do, in those treaties and compacts of which the 62nd Psalm [in fact 63 v. 12] speaks: 'They are praised, who swear by his name.'

A further question that arises is whether beadles, hangmen, lawyers, advocates and all the rest of their sort can be Christians and in a state of grace? The answer is that if government [*die Gewalt*] and the Sword serve God, as has been shown above, then everything that government needs in order to bear the Sword, is equally a service to God. There has to be someone to catch the wicked, to accuse them, and execute them, and to protect, acquit, defend and save the good. And therefore if the intention of those who carry out these tasks is not that of looking to their own advantage, but only of helping to uphold the laws and authorities, in order to repress the wicked, then there is no danger in it for them, and they can do it like any other job, and get their living by it. As has already been said, love of one's neighbour has no regard for self, neither does it consider whether what is to be done is important or trivial, so long as it is for the good of one's neighbour or the community.

Finally, you might ask: can't I use the Sword for myself and my own concerns, provided I am not out for my own good, but merely intend that evil should be punished? My answer is that such a miracle is not impossible, but very unusual and dangerous. It may happen where the Spirit is present in great fulness. We do indeed read in Judges 15[11] that Samson said: 'I have done unto them as they did unto me.' But against this is Proverbs 24[29]: 'Do not say: I will do unto him, as he has done unto me.' And Proverbs 20[22]: 'Do not say: I will repay his wickedness.' Samson was required by God to plague the Philistines and save the children of Israel. And even though he used his private concerns as a pretext for declaring war against them, he nevertheless did not do it to avenge himself or to seek his own advantage, but to help [the Israelites] and punish the Philistines. But no one can follow this precedent unless he be a true Christian, filled with the [Holy] Spirit. Where [ordinary human] reason wants to do likewise, it no doubt pretends that it is not seeking its own advantage, but the claim will be false from top to bottom. The thing is impossible without grace. So if you want to act like Samson, then first become like Samson.

Part Two: How Far Secular Authority Extends

We now come to the main part of this sermon. We have learnt that there must be secular authority on this earth and how a Christian and salutary use may be made of it. Now we must establish how long its reach is, and how far it may stretch out its arm without overreaching itself and trenching upon God's kingdom and government. This is something about which we need to be quite clear. When [secular government] is given too much freedom of action, the harm that results is unbearable and horrifying, but to have it confined within too narrow a compass is also harmful. In the one case there is too much punishment, in the other too little. But it is more tolerable to err on the side of the latter: it is always better that a villain should live than that a just man should be killed. There always are, and always must be, villains in the world, but there are few just men.

The first point to be noted is that the two parts into which the children of Adam are divided (as we have said above), the one the kingdom of God under Christ, the other the kingdom of the world under [secular] authority, have each their own kind of law.

Everyday experience sufficiently shows us that every kingdom must have its own laws and that no kingdom or government can survive without law. Secular government has laws that extend no further than the body, goods and outward, earthly matters. But where the soul is concerned, God neither can nor will allow anyone but himself to rule. And so, where secular authority takes it upon itself to legislate for the soul, it trespasses on [what belongs to] God's government, and merely seduces and ruins souls. I intend to make this so unambiguously clear that no one can fail to grasp it, in order that our lords the princes and bishops may see the folly of trying to compel belief in this or that by means of laws and commands.

If someone imposes a man-made law on souls, compelling belief in what he wants to be believed, then there will probably be no word of God to justify it. If there is nothing in God's Word about it, then it is uncertain whether this is what God wants. If he himself has not commanded something, there is no way of establishing that it is pleasing to him. Or rather, we can be sure that it is not pleasing to him, for he will have our faith grounded solely in his divine Word; as he says in Matthew 18 [in fact 16.18]: 'On this rock I will build my church.' And John 10[27]: 'My sheep hear my voice and know me, but the strangers' voice they hear not, but flee from them.' From this it follows that secular authority drives souls to eternal damnation with such blasphemous commands. For this is to compel people to believe that something is certain to please God, when it is not certain at all; on the contrary, it is certain that it displeases God, since there is no clear [text in] God's Word to warrant it. For whosoever believes something to be right, which is in fact wrong or uncertain, denies the truth, which is God himself, and believes lies and error . . .

It is therefore utter folly for them to order us to believe the Church, the [Church] Fathers and the Councils, even though there is no [express] Word of God [for what they tell us to believe]. It is the apostles of the devil that issue that sort of command, not the Church. The Church commands nothing except what it is certain is God's Word. As St Peter says [1 Pet. 4.11]: 'Whoever speaks, let him speak according to God's word.' But they will never be able to show that the decrees of Councils are the Word of God. And what is even more ridiculous is when it is argued that, after all, this is what kings and princes and people generally believe. But, my friends, we are not baptized in the name of kings and princes and people in general, but in the name of Christ and of God himself. And our title is not 'kings' or 'princes' or 'people in general', but Christians. No one can or should lay down commandments for the soul, except those who can point it on the way to heaven. But no human being can do that; only God. And therefore in those things which concern the salvation of souls, nothing is to be taught or accepted except God's Word.

Another important point is this. However stupid they are, they must admit that they have no power over the soul. For no human being can kill the soul or bring it to life, or lead it to heaven or to hell. And if they will not believe us, then Christ will show it clearly enough when he says in Matthew 10[28]: 'Do not be afraid of those that kill the body and after that can do nothing more. Fear rather him who, after he kills the body, has the power to condemn to hell.' Surely that is clear enough: the soul is taken out of the hands of any human being whatsoever, and is placed exclusively under the power of God. Now tell me this: would anyone in his right mind give orders where he has no authority? You might as well command the moon to shine at your behest. What sense would there be in it, if the people of Leipzig were to lay down laws for us here in Wittenberg, or vice versa? Anyone who tried it, would be sent a dose of hellebore by way of thanks, to clear their heads and cure their cold. But this is just what our Emperor and our prudent princes are doing; they let the Pope, the bishops and the sophists lead them, the blind leading the blind, commanding their subjects to believe as they see fit, without God's Word. And then they still want to retain the title of 'Christian Princes', which God forbid.

Another way of understanding this point is that each and every authority can only act, and ought only to act, where it can see, know, judge, adjudicate and change things. What kind of judge would it be that judges blindly in matters where he can neither hear nor see? But tell me this: how can a human being see, know, judge and change hearts? That is reserved to God alone. As Psalm 7[10] says: 'God searches the heart and bowels.' And again [Ps. 7.9]: 'The Lord is judge over the people', and Acts 10 [in fact 1.24; 15.8]: 'God knows the heart.' And Jeremiah 1 [in fact 17.9]: 'Wicked and unsearchable is the human heart. Who can search it? I the Lord, who search hearts and bowels.' A court has to have an exact knowledge of what it is to judge. But people's thoughts and minds cannot be manifest to anyone but God. And therefore it is impossible and futile to command or coerce someone to believe this or that. A different skill is needed here; force will not do. I am surprised at these lunatics, seeing that they themselves have a saying: *De occultis non iudicat ecclesia*; the Church does not judge in secret matters. Now, if [even] the Church, the spiritual government, only rules over matters that are public and open, by what right does secular authority, in its folly, presume to judge a thing as secret, spiritual, hidden as faith?

Each must decide at his own peril what he is to believe, and must see to it that he believes rightly. Other people cannot go to heaven or hell on my behalf, or open or close [the gates to either] for me. And just as little can they believe or not believe on my behalf, or force my faith or unbelief. How he believes is a matter for each individual's conscience, and this does not diminish [the authority of] secular governments. They ought therefore to content themselves with attending to their own business, and allow people to believe what they can, and what they want, and they must use no coercion in this matter against anyone. Faith is free, and no one can be compelled to believe. More precisely, so far from being something secular authority ought to create and enforce, faith is something that God works in the spirit. Hence that common saying which also occurs in Augustine: no one can or ought to be forced to believe anything against his will.

Those blind and wretched people do not realize what a pointless and impossible thing they are attempting. However strict their orders, and however much they rage, they cannot force people to do more than obey by word and [outward] deed; they cannot compel the heart, even if they were to tear themselves apart trying. There is truth in the saying: Thought is free. What is the effect of their trying to force people to believe in their hearts? All they achieve is to force people with weak consciences to lie, to perjure themselves, saying one thing while in their hearts they believe another. And in this way [rulers] load on themselves the horrifying sins done by others, because all the lies and perjuries such [people with] weak consciences utter, when they are spoken under compulsion, fall back on the one who compels their being done. It would be much easier, although it may mean allowing their subjects to fall into error, just to let them err, rather than to force them to lie and profess [with their mouths] what they do not believe in their hearts. And it is not right to prevent one evil by doing another, even worse, one.

Do you want to know why God has ordained that the secular princes must come to grief in this horrible fashion? I'll tell you. God has given them perverse minds, and he means to make an end of them, just as he will make an end of their Spiritual Lordships. For my ungracious lords, the pope and bishops, should be [real] bishops and preach the Word of God; but they have left off doing so and have become secular princes, ruling by means of laws that concern only life and goods. They have managed to turn everything upside down: they ought to rule souls with God's Word, inwardly, and instead they rule castles, towns, countries and peoples, outwardly, and torment souls with unspeakable murders. And the secular lords, who should rule countries and peoples outwardly, do not do so either; instead, the only thing they know how to do is to poll and fleece, heap one tax on another, let loose a bear here, a wolf there. There is no good faith or honesty to be found amongst them; thieves and villains behave better than they do, and secular government is sunk as low as the government of the spiritual tyrants. God has made them to be of perverse minds and has deprived them of their senses, so that they want to rule spiritually over souls, just as the spiritual authorities want to rule in a worldly manner. And [God's purpose in all this is] that they should thoughtlessly pile up on themselves the sins of others, earn his hatred and that of mankind, until they are ruined along with bishops, parsons and monks, all knaves together. And then they blame everything on the Gospel, blaspheming God instead of confessing their guilt, and saying that it is our preaching that has done this, whereas it is their perverse wickedness that has brought it on them, and they deserved it and continue to deserve it; the Romans said just the same, when they were destroyed. And here you have God's judgement on these great men. But they do not realize it, in order that God's grave counsels may not be frustrated by their repentance.

But you will reply: doesn't St Paul say in Romans 13[1]: 'Let every soul be subject to power and superiority'? And Peter, that we are to be subject to every human ordinance? [1 Pet. 2.13]? You are quite right, and this is grist to my mill. St Paul is speaking of superiors and power. But I have just shown that no one has power over the soul except God. St Paul cannot be speaking of obedience where there is no power [entitled to obedience]. It follows that he is not talking about faith and is not saying that worldly authority ought to have the right to command faith. What he is talking about is outward goods, about commanding and ruling on earth. And he makes clear that this is what he means when he lays down a limit to both power and obedience: 'Give to each what is due to him, tax where tax is due, customs duties where customs duties are due, honour where honour, fear where fear' [Romans 13.7]. In other words secular obedience and power extend only to taxes, duties, honour, fear, outward things. To the same effect: 'Power is not a terror to good, but to wicked works' [Romans 13.3]. He is setting a limit to power: it is not to have mastery over faith and God's Word, but over evil-doing.

St Peter means the same when he speaks of 'human ordinance'. Now, human ordinance cannot extend to heaven and the soul, but only to the earth and the outward dealings of men with one another, matters about which men can see, know, judge, pass sentence, punish and acquit.

Christ himself summarizes all this with the admirable distinction [he draws] in Matthew 22 [21]: 'Give to the Emperor the things that are the Emperor's and to God the things that are God's.' If the emperor's power extended to God's kingdom and God's power, and were not something distinct and separate, there would be no point in distinguishing the two. But, as has been said, the soul is not subject to the emperor's power. He can neither teach nor guide it; he cannot kill it or bring it to life; he cannot bind or loose it, judge it or sentence it, hold it or release it. And yet he would need to [be competent to do all of these] if he were to have the power to legislate for it and issue orders to it. But as to goods and honour, here is his proper domain. For such things *are* subject to his power.

David long ago summarized all this in a short, fine saying in Psalm 113 [in fact 115.16]: 'He has given heaven to the Lord of heaven, but the earth he has given to the children of men.' In other words, as regards whatever is on earth, and belongs to the temporal, earthly kingdom, man can have power from God. But whatever belongs to heaven and to the eternal kingdom, is subject to the Lord of heaven alone. And Moses was mindful of this when he says in Genesis 1[26]: 'God said: let us create men, that shall rule over the animals and the fish in the water and the birds in the air.' All this concedes no more than outward rule to men. And in sum, what is meant is, as St Peter says in Acts 4 [in fact 5.29]: 'We must obey God rather than men.' And with this he is evidently setting a limit to secular authority. For if we were bound to do everything those with authority in the world tell us to do, there would be no point in saying 'We must obey God rather than men.'

So, if a prince or a secular lord commands you to adhere to the papacy, to believe this or that, or to surrender books, then your answer should be: it is not fitting for

Lucifer to sit next to God. My good Lord, I owe you obedience with my life and goods. Command me what lies within the limits of your authority, and I will obey. But if you command me to believe, or to surrender my books, I will not obey. For then you [will have] become a tyrant and overreach[ed] yourself, commanding where you have neither right or power. If he then takes away your goods and punishes you for your disobedience, then blessed are you, and you should thank God for counting you worthy to suffer for the sake of his Word. Let the fool rage; he shall surely find his judge. But I say to you: if you do not resist him and let him take away your faith or your books, then you will truly have denied God.

Let me give you an example. In Meissen, Bavaria and the Mark, and in other places too, the tyrants have issued a decree, ordering [all] copies of the New Testament to be surrendered to their offices. What subjects [of these rulers] must do is this: they must not surrender a page, not even a letter, on pain of their soul. Whoever does so, is surrendering Christ to Herod; is a murderer of Christ, as Herod was. They should suffer their houses to be forcibly [*mit Gewalt*] invaded and ransacked, whether it is their books or their goods that are taken. Evil is not to be resisted, but suffered. Of course, you should not approve what is done, or lift a finger or walk a single step to aid and abet them in any way, nor should you obey. These tyrants act as worldly princes are meant to act. Worldly princes is what they are. But the world is God's enemy, and therefore they must do what is at variance with God, but congenial to the world, in order to retain their honour and remain worldly princes. And so you should not be surprised at their raging and stupidity against the Gospel. They must be true to the titles they bear.

You should know that a prudent prince has been a rare bird in the world since the beginning of time, and a just prince an even rarer one. As a rule, princes are the greatest fools or the worst criminals on earth, and the worst is always to be expected, and little good hoped for, from them, especially in what regards God and the salvation of souls. For these are God's jailers and hangmen, and his divine wrath makes use of them to punish the wicked and maintain outward peace. Our God is a mighty lord, and this is why he must have such noble, well-born, rich hangmen and beadles, and will have them receive riches, honour and fear from everyone in heaped measure. It is his divine will and pleasure that we should call his hangmen 'gracious lords', fall at their feet and be subject to them in all humility, so long as they do not over reach themselves by wanting to become pastors instead of hangmen. If a prince should happen to be prudent, just or a Christian, then that is one of the great miracles and a most precious sign of divine favour on the land. But in the ordinary run of things, what Isaiah says in 3[4] holds good: 'I will give them children for princes, and gawpers shall be their lords.' And Hosea 13[11]: 'I shall give you a king in my wrath, and out of disfavour take him away again.' The world is too wicked to deserve princes much wiser and more just than this. Frogs must have storks.

But you will again object that secular authority does not compel belief; it merely, by the use of outward means, prevents people from being led astray by false doctrine.

How else could heretics be restrained? The answer is: it is for bishops to do that; that task has been assigned to them and not to rulers. The use of force can never prevent heresy. Preventing it requires a different sort of skill; this is not a battle that can be fought with the sword. This is where God's Word must fight. And if that does not win, then secular power can certainly not succeed either, even if it were to fill the world with blood. Heresy is a spiritual thing; it cannot be struck down with steel, burnt with fire or drowned in water. God's Word alone can [conquer] here; as St Paul says in 2 Corinthians 10[4f]: 'Our weapons are not carnal ones, but are mighty in God, to destroy all the counsels and eminences that rise up against the knowledge of God, and they take captive all the senses in the service of Christ.'

And indeed neither faith nor heresy are ever stronger than when mere force, rather than the Word of God is used against them. For [in that case] people take it for granted that force is not being used in the cause of right, and that those who use it are acting unjustly, precisely because they are acting without God's Word and because they cannot think of any other way of furthering their aims except by mere force, like animals that have no use of reason. Even in secular matters force cannot be used unless guilt has first been established by reference to the law. And it is all the more impossible to use force without right and God's Word in such high, spiritual matters [as heresy]. What clever princes they are! They mean to drive out heresy, but cannot attack it except with something that gives it new vigour, bringing themselves under suspicion and justifying the heretics. My friend: if you want to drive out heresy, then you must first hit on a way of uprooting it from the heart, and breaking its hold on the will. And you will not do that by using force; you will merely strengthen it. What point is there in reinforcing heresy in hearts, even if you do weaken it outwardly by shutting up people's mouths or forcing them to pretend? God's Word, on the other hand, enlightens the heart and with that all heresy and error will fall away by themselves.

It is of this way of destroying heresy that the prophet Isaiah spoke when he prophesied (Isaiah 11 [4]): 'He will strike the earth with the rods of his mouth, and will kill the godless with the spirit of his lips.' You can see from this that it is words that will bring about the death and conversion of the godless. In short, such princes and tyrants do not know that fighting against heresy is fighting against the devil who takes possession of hearts by means of error. As Paul says in Ephesians 6[12]: 'Our struggle is not against flesh and blood, but against spiritual evil, against the princes that rule this darkness etc.' And therefore as long as the devil is not rejected and driven out of the heart, destroying his instruments by fire and sword has as much effect on him as fighting against it with a straw would have on lightning. Job dealt with all this amply when he said (Job 41[18]): 'The devil looks on iron as mere straw and fears no power on earth.' And experience teaches the same. For even if all Jews and heretics are burnt, no one is vanquished or converted thereby, or ever will be.

But a world such as this one must have this sort of rulers; heaven forbid that anyone should ever do their duty! Bishops must abandon the Word of God and make no attempt to rule souls with it. Instead they must command the secular princes to rule souls by the sword. The secular princes for their part must allow usury, robbery, adultery, murder and other kinds of wickedness to go unchecked, and indeed commit such things themselves, and leave it to the bishops to punish them with letters of excommunication. And in this way everything is stood on its head: souls are ruled by steel, bodies by letters. So worldly princes rule spiritually, and spiritual princes rule in a worldly manner. What else is there for the devil to do in this world, except to play tricks on his subjects and masquerade as in a carnival? These, then, are our 'Christian princes', the 'defenders of the faith' and 'hammers of the Turks'. Able men, on whom we can rely! And they most certainly will achieve *something* by their admirable cleverness: they will break their necks and reduce their lands and subjects to misery and penury.

I have a piece of good advice for these misguided people. Beware of the little saying in Psalm 106 [in fact 107.40]: *Effundit contemptum super principes* [He pours out his contempt on princes]. I swear to God: if you ignore this little text, and it comes into effect against you, you are lost, even if every one of you were as mighty as the Turk; and all your snorting and raving will not help you. To a considerable extent it has happened already. There are few princes whom people do not regard as fools or criminals, and their actions bear out [that judgement]; the common man is becoming knowledgeable and a mighty plague on princes (which God calls *contemptum*) is spreading amongst the common people and the common man. My fear is that there will be no way to stop it, unless princes begin to behave like princes and to rule reasonably and cautiously. People will not put up with your tyranny and arbitrariness any longer; they cannot and they do not want to. My good lords and masters, take heed. God [himself] will not put up with it any longer. This is no longer the world it was when you hunted and drove your people like game. So put aside your blasphemy and violence; take care that you act justly and let God's Word have free passage; it will, it must and it should, and you cannot stop it. If there is heresy, then let it be overcome by God's Word; that is how it should be. But if you go about drawing the sword on every occasion, then beware of someone coming along who will tell you to put your sword away, and not in God's name either.

But what if you were to say: how are Christians to be ruled outwardly, seeing that there ought to be no secular Sword amongst them? [Surely] there must be superiors amongst Christians too? My answer is that there neither can, nor ought to be any superiors amongst Christians. Rather, each is equally subject to all the rest, as St Paul says in Romans 12[10]: 'Each is to regard the next person as his superior.' And Peter (1 Pet. 5[5]): 'Be ye all subject one to another.' And this is what Christ wants (Luke 14[10]): 'If you are invited to a wedding, take the lowest place of all.' Among Christians there is no superior except Christ alone. And how can there be superiority [or inferiority] when all are equal, and all have the same right, power, goods and honour? No one desires to be another's superior, for everyone wants to be the inferior of the rest. How could one establish superiors amongst such people, even if one wanted to? Nature will not tolerate superiors when no one wants to be, or can be, a superior. But where there are no people of [the latter] sort, there are no true Christians either.

What of priests and bishops? Their government is not one of superiority or power, but rather a service and an office. For they are not higher or better than other Christians. And therefore they ought not to impose any laws or commands on others without their consent and permission. Their government, on the contrary, is nothing but furtherance of the Word of God, guiding Christians and overcoming heresy by means of it. As has been said, Christians can be governed by nothing except the Word of God alone. For Christians must be governed in faith, not by outward works. But faith cannot come by human words, only by God's Word. As St Paul says in Romans 10[17]: 'Faith comes by hearing, but hearing comes through the Word of God.' Those who do not have faith are not Christians and do not belong to Christ's kingdom, but to the kingdom of the world, to be coerced and ruled by the Sword and by external government. Christians [on the other hand] do everything that is good, without any compulsion, and have all they need in God's Word. But of this I have written much and often elsewhere.

17. John Calvin – Of Civil Government[1]

1. We have established that there are two governments to which mankind is subject, and we have already said enough about the first of these, which rules over the soul or the inner man, and concerns itself with eternal life. Our order of presentation now demands that we say something about the second, whose province is the establishment of a merely civil and external justice, a justice in conduct. [1559:] What I shall be discussing may seem to be quite divorced from matters of faith and spiritual doctrine, which are my subject. Nevertheless the course of the argument will show that I am right to link the two topics, ⟨and indeed there is no other way but to

---

[1]Translator's note: The text translated here is that of the Latin 1559 edition. Dates in square brackets signal the first appearance of the most substantial additions to the text subsequent to the first edition. [1536:] marks the return to the text of the first edition. The text translated here is that of the Latin 1559 edition. Dates in square brackets signal the first appearance of the most substantial additions to the text subsequent to the first edition. [1536:] marks the return to the text of the first edition. Square brackets indicate words inserted by the translator to complete the sense. (FV:) indicates a minor variation from the Latin in the French versions. More significant variations are noted in the footnotes. ⟨ ⟩ indicates a portion of the Latin text omitted from the French versions.

link them). Especially since on the one side there are (FV: nowadays) madmen and savages bent on overturning this order established by God. And on the other, there are the flatterers of princes, who vaunt the might of princes without [acknowledging] any bounds to it, and do not hesitate to oppose it to the overlordship of God himself. Unless we avoid both these evils, all pure faith will perish. To this should be added that it is of considerable benefit to us to know what merciful care God has taken for the wellbeing of mankind in this respect: it should incite us to a greater zeal for his service, to show that we are not ungrateful.

[1536:] In the first place, before we go any further in this matter, we must hold fast to (FV: recall) the distinction we drew earlier. For if we do not, we will be led into a thoughtless confusion of the two things we distinguished, which are of quite different character. This often happens. For when people hear that the Gospel promises a liberty which acknowledges neither king nor magistrate (FV: master) among men, but relies on Christ alone, they cannot imagine that any benefit can be derived from this liberty as long as they find themselves subject to any authority whatever. And they think nothing will go well, unless the whole world is given a new face, without courts, or laws, or magistrates, or anything else of the same sort, which they imagine obstructs their freedom. But anyone who knows how to distinguish between body and soul, between this present transitory life and the eternal life to come, will not find it difficult to understand that the spiritual kingdom of Christ and civil government are things far removed from one another. It is a Judaic folly to look for the kingdom of Christ among the things that make up this world, and to shut it up among them; our opinion, which is supported by the plainest teaching of Scripture, is that, on the contrary, the fruit we reap from grace is a spiritual fruit. We must therefore take great care to confine that liberty which is promised and offered to us in Christ within its own limits. How can the same apostle command us to stand firm and not to submit to the yoke of servitude (Gal. 5.1), and then in another place tell servants not to be solicitous about their condition, unless it is because spiritual liberty and civil servitude can stand very well together? It is in this same sense that we are to take this other sayings: 'In the kingdom of God there is neither Jew nor Greek, neither male nor female, neither slave nor free' (Gal. 3.28). And again: 'There is neither Jew nor Greek, uncircumcision or circumcision, barbarian or Scythian, ⟨slave or free⟩, but Christ is all in all' (Col. 3.11). He means that what your status or condition in the world is, and under the laws of which nation you live, are a matter of indifference, for the kingdom of Christ in no way inheres in such things.

2. But neither does this distinction [between the two governments] in any way imply that we are to regard everything related to the polity as something unclean, and as having nothing to do with Christians. The fantasts (FV: in our days), [1555:] who delight in unbridled licence, [1536:] rant and boast that, once we have become dead

to this world through Christ, are translated to the kingdom of God and sit amongst celestial beings, it is far beneath our [new] dignity and excellence to trouble ourselves with such profane and tainted matters (FV: related to the business of this world), things quite alien to the proper concerns of a Christian. What use, they ask, are laws without trials and [law] courts? And what has a Christian to do with lawcourts? And if it is not right to kill, what use are laws and lawcourts?

We have just warned that [secular] government and the spiritual and internal kingdom of Christ are quite distinct. But equally we must recognize that they are in no way incompatible with each other. For already, while we are still on earth, Christ's spiritual rule establishes in us some beginnings of the celestial kingdom, and in this mortal and evanescent life, allows us some foretaste of immortal and incorruptible blessedness. The end of secular government, however, while we remain in this world, is [1559:] to foster and protect the external worship of God, defend pure doctrine (FV: and religion) and the good condition of the Church, accommodate the way we live to [the requirements of] human society, [1536:] mould our conduct to civil justice, reconcile us one to another, and uphold and defend the common peace and tranquillity. I admit that all this would be superfluous if the kingdom of God as it now exists among us put an end to this present life. But if it is the will of God that during the time we are still yearning for our [true] home we are on pilgrimage on earth and that such aids are necessary for our journey, then those who deprive men of them take away their human nature. As for their claim that the perfection of the Church of God must be so great as to make all other government and laws redundant, this is stupidity, for it is to imagine a perfection which can never be found in any association of human beings. The effrontery of the wicked is so great, and their evil-doing so incorrigible, that [even] laws of great severity are scarcely enough to hold them in check. If not even force is enough to restrain them from wrong-doing, how would we expect them to act once they [were to] see that they could do what evils they pleased, with impunity?

3. But there will be a more appropriate occasion for speaking about the benefits of civil order. For the present, the one thing that must be clearly understood is that [even] to think about abolishing it is a monstrous barbarity. Mankind derives as much benefit from it as it does from bread, water, sun and air, and its dignity is far greater than any of them. For unlike them all, civil order has not only to do with men's ⟨breathing⟩, eating, drinking and flourishing (although it certainly encompasses all these, in that it makes human association possible). Its concern, I say, is not only with these, but what is more [important], it prevents idolatries, sacrileges against the name of God, blasphemies against his truth, and other scandals to religion from emerging into the light of day and spreading (FV: being sown) among the people; it prevents disturbances of the public peace; it allows each to remain safe and unharmed in the enjoyment of what is his; it makes possible innocent contacts between people; [1539:]

and it sees to the cultivation of upright conduct and decency. [1536:] In short, it upholds a public form of religion amongst Christians, and humanity amongst men. Nor ought it to worry anyone that I am now allotting to the human polity that care for the right order of religion, which I seem earlier to have placed outside [merely] human determination. I approve a political order that makes it its business to prevent true religion, which is contained in the law of God, from being besmirched and violated with impunity by public and manifest sacrilege. But in doing so, I no more allow men to make laws about religion and the worship of God according to their fancy than I did before.

But if we treat the various parts of the subject separately, then the clarity of the order of exposition will itself help the reader to understand better what he is to think about this whole matter of civil government. There are three such parts. The first is the magistrate, the defender and guardian of the laws. The second is the laws themselves, in accordance with which the magistrate governs. The third is the people, who are governed by the laws, and obey the magistrate. Let us therefore first deal with the office of magistracy, and consider whether this is a legitimate vocation approved by God, what the duties of the office are, and how far its authority extends. Then, by what laws a Christian polity must be governed. And finally, what benefit the people derive from laws and what obedience they owe to their magistrate.

4. As regards the office of magistrate: our Lord has not only declared that it is acceptable to him and approved by him, but (what is more) has particularly commended its dignity to us, by adorning it with titles of the highest honour. To cite only a few examples: all those who hold the office of magistrate are called gods (Exodus 22.8; Ps. 82, 1 and 6). This title is not to be reckoned as having little importance, for it shows that they have a commission from God, that they are endowed with divine authority, and that they in fact represent his person, acting in a certain sense in his place. This is not some sophism of mine; rather, it is the interpretation of Christ himself when he says: 'If Scripture has called gods those to whom the Word of God is addressed …' (John 10.35). What else can this mean but that they have received a charge and commission from God to serve him in their office? And, as Moses and Jehoshaphat said to the judges they set over every city in Judah (Deut. 1.16; 2 Chron. 19.6): [they were to] execute justice not in the name of men but of God. What the wisdom of God says by the mouth of Solomon is to the same effect: it is his work that kings reign and counsellors make just decisions; that princes exercise their principate and all the judges of the earth are generous (Prov. 6.15 and 16). Which is as much as to say that it is not at all by the perversity of men that kings and other superiors obtain their power over all things on earth; on the contrary it comes about by the providence and sacred ordinance of God, whose pleasure it is to have mankind governed in this manner. [1539:] ⟨For he is present with them, and indeed presides over them, when they make laws and pronounce equitable judgements⟩. [1536:] This is also clearly what Paul teaches

when he numbers 'positions of authority' amongst the gifts of God which, as they are diversely distributed to men according to the diversity of grace, so they must be used by Christ's servants for building up the Church (Rom. 12.8). [1539:] It is true that he is here referring specifically to the council of grave men which was established in the early Church to supervise public discipline, an office which he terms (kyberneseis) 'government' in the Epistle to the Corinthians (1 Cor. 12.28). However, since we see civil authority tending to the same end, there is no doubt that he is commending all just authority. [1536:] And the point is made even more clearly when Paul addresses precisely this subject. For he teaches that all power exists by divine ordinance and that there is none which is not established by God. [He goes on to say] that princes are ministers of God to honour those who act rightly and to execute the vengeance of his wrath upon evil-doers (Rom. 13.14). In this connection, we may also cite the example of holy men, some of whom ruled as kings, like David, Josiah and Hezekiah, others held high offices of state, like Joseph and Daniel, yet others had the government of a free people, like Moses, Joshua and the Judges; we know that the offices of all of them were acceptable to God, for he declared them to be so. Hence there can be no doubt that in the sight of God civil authority (FV: superiority) is not merely a holy and legitimate vocation, but by far the most sacred and honourable of all human vocations.

5. [1559:] Those who want to introduce anarchy reply that although there were formerly kings and judges (FV: governors) over (FV: the Jews, for they were) a rude and savage people, such a servile manner of government is wholly inappropriate nowadays; it cannot square with the perfection which Christ has brought us in his Gospel. In this they disclose their stupidity as well as their devilish pride, laying claim to a degree of perfection of which we do not see even a hundredth part in them. But, leaving aside their morals and conduct, their contention is easy enough to refute. For when David exhorts kings and all rulers (FV: princes) to kiss the Son of God (FV: as a sign of homage), he does not command them to lay down their power (FV: quit their station) and retire into private life (FV: become private persons), but rather to subject the power vested in them to Christ, so that he alone may have pre-eminence over all. In the same way Isaiah, when he promised that kings would be nursing-fathers of the Church and queens nursing-mothers (Isa. 49.23), does not strip kings and queens of their honour; on the contrary he invests them with the honourable title of protectors of the faithful servants of God. For this prophecy refers to the coming of Christ. I deliberately omit many other testimonies to be found in various places [in Scripture], especially in the Psalms, which assert the right of all superiors. But there is one place in Paul more notable than all the rest. He admonishes Timothy to have public prayers said for kings, and he at once adds the reason: so that we might live peacefully under them, in all godliness and decency (1 Tim. 2.2). With these words, he is committing the well-being of the Church to them, as its custodians and guardians.

6. [1536:] Magistrates ought to ponder this constantly, for it can be a spur to prick them to do their duty, and can bring them marvelous consolation, alleviating the difficulties (FV: and vexations) inherent in their office, which are certainly many and grave. Will they not set themselves the highest standards of integrity, prudence, clemency, moderation and innocence, when they recognize themselves to have been ordained ministers of divine justice? How will they have the effrontery to admit any iniquity to their [judgement-] seat, when they hear that it is the throne of the living God? To pronounce unjust sentence with the mouth they know to be destined to be an organ of God's truth? Will their consciences allow them to sign some evil ordinance with the hand which they know to be ordained for writing God's laws? In sum, if they remember that they are representatives of God, they will have to apply all their energy, zeal and solicitude to the work of representing before men an image, so to say, of the providence, protection, goodness, benevolence and justice of God. Furthermore, they must always keep in mind that if all those are accursed who do the work of executing God's vengeance deceitfully (Jer. 48.10), then all the more are they accursed, if they behave disloyally in so just a vocation. Thus, when it was Moses's and Jehoshaphat's purpose to exhort their Judges to do their duty, they could find nothing better fitted to stir their hearts than [the exhortation) we mentioned earlier: 'Be careful in what you do, for it is by no means in the name of mortal men that you execute justice, but in the name of God, who is beside you when you deliver judgement. May the fear of God therefore be upon you; and see that you act as is fitting, for there is no perversity with the Lord our God' (Deut. 1.16; 2 Chron. 19.6). And in another place it is written that 'God has stood in the assembly of the gods and that in the midst of the gods he renders judgement' (Ps. 82.1). It ought to spur them on to do their duty to hear that they are God's legates and will one day have to render him an account of how they have governed their provinces. And this warning ought to carry great weight with them. For if they are guilty of some dereliction of duty, they not only wrong the people by the crimes they commit against them, but God [himself], whose sacred judgements they defile. On the other hand [magistrates] may derive the amplest consolation from reflecting that theirs is not some profane occupation (FV: vocation) alien to servants of God, but a most sacred commission, for it is a God's legates that they act.

7. As for those who remain unmoved by so much evidence from Scripture and who dare to condemn this holy ministry (FV: vocation) as something entirely contrary to Christian religion and godliness: is this not to insult God himself? It is impossible to despise God's ministers without dishonouring God himself. But in fact it is not magistrates that such people reject, but rather God himself and his rule. For if it was rightly said about the people of Israel when they rejected Samuel's rule (1 Sam. 8.7), that they would not allow [God] to reign over them, why might the same thing not equally well be said today about those who allow themselves licence

to malign all positions of authority instituted by God? But [they claim that] the Lord forbids all Christians to meddle with kingdoms and positions of authority, for he tells his disciples that the kings of the nations lord it over them, but that it is not to be so among [Christians], where he who is first should become the least (Luke 22.25 and 26). What skilful interpreters! A dispute had arisen between the disciples (FV: apostles) about which one of them ought to be accorded pre-eminence. To rebuke such vanity, the Lord declares that their ministry is not like kingship, where one has precedence over all the rest. In what way, may I ask, does this comparison diminish the dignity of kings? In fact, does it prove any thing at all, except that the office (FV: estate) of king is not the [same thing as] the ministry of an apostle? What is more, although there are various sorts and types of magistracy (FV: superiors), they nevertheless do not differ at all in one respect, namely that we are to accept them as orders established by God. Paul includes them all when he says that there is no power but from God (Rom. 13.1). And the form which was least palatable to men has been singled out for commendation above all the rest, namely power exercised by one man. [This] was never acceptable to the heroic and nobler spirits in the old days, because this [form of rule] carries with it the common servitude of all except the one person, to whose will and pleasure all the rest are subjected. But Scripture, to obviate the malignity of such opinions, affirms specifically that it is by the providence of the divine wisdom that kings reign (Prov. 8.15), and particularly commands that kings be honoured (1 Pet. 2.17).

8. It would be [1536: It is] utterly pointless for private men, who have no right to decide how any commonwealth whatever is to be ordered, to debate what would be the best state of the commonwealth [1543:] in the place where they live. [1536:] Besides, it would be rash to [try to] settle the matter without [making] qualifications, seeing that what is crucial to this discussion is circumstances. And even if one compares various forms of government without taking circumstances into account, it is not easy to decide which is the most beneficial [form], so evenly balanced are their respective advantages and disadvantages. Kingship is liable to collapse into tyranny. But aristocracy turns into faction almost as easily. And [the decline from] popular rule into sedition is the easiest of all. [1543:] I readily admit that if the three forms of government which philosophers refer to are considered in themselves, then aristocracy, either pure or a mixed form compounded of aristocracy and polity, greatly excels all the others. [1559:] This however is not because that form is inherently better, but [rather] because it is very rare for kings to exercise such self-control that their will never differs from what is equitable and right. And it is equally rare for kings to be equipped with such prudence and acuity of understanding as to be able [always] to discern what is good and useful. It is therefore the vices or defects of mankind that make it safer and more tolerable that several persons should govern [jointly], all of them assisting, instructing and

admonishing one another; so that if one of them arrogates more to himself than he is entitled to do, there will be others to act as his censors and masters, to curb his licence. [1543:] Experience has always borne this out, and the Lord confirmed it by his own authority when he instituted an aristocracy bordering on a polity among the Israelites, since he wished to keep them in the best possible condition [1559:] until such time as he would bring forth an image of Christ in [King] David. [1543:] I freely admit that no form of government is better than that in which liberty and the right degree of restraint are reconciled, [a government] rightly ordered so as to be durable. Accordingly, I regard those as most fortunate who are allowed to enjoy such a condition; and if they always do their utmost to preserve and maintain it, I admit that this is to do no more than their duty. And what is more, the magistrates [under this form of government] ought to make every effort to prevent any diminution, still less violation, of that liberty of which they have been appointed guardians. If they are slothful or unconcerned in the matter, they are traitors to their office and their country.

But if those whom the Lord has assigned some other form of government were to treat what I _have said as having any relevance to themselves and consequently were to be tempted to bring about some upheaval or change, it would not merely be a foolish and pointless idea, but a pernicious one as well. [1536:] If you do not confine your reflections to just a single commonwealth, but consider either the world as a whole, or at least some regions farther afield, you will find that it was not without a good purpose that divine providence has so disposed that different regions are governed by different sorts of regime. For just as elements only cohere because they are differently proportioned, so [each polity] is most firmly held together only in virtue of a certain inequality. But all this is superfluous for those for whom the will of God is reason enough. For if it has seemed good to him to set kings above kingdoms and senators or other officials over free commonwealths, then we for our part must be obedient and dutiful to whomever he has appointed ruler over the place we inhabit.

9. This is the place to say a word in passing about the duties of magistrates, about what they are and what the Word of God says of them. [1559:] And even if Scripture did not teach us that the magistrate's competence extends to both Tables of the Decalogue, we could still learn it from the pagan writers. For there is not one of them who, when dealing with the duties of magistrates, law-making and the civil order, did not begin with religion and divine worship. By so doing, they all acknowledged that no polity can be well constituted, unless it makes duties [owed] to God its first concern, and that for laws to attend [only] to the well-being of men, while disregarding what is owed to God, is an absurdity. And so, since all philosophers give pride of place to religion, and since the whole human race has always been of one accord in respecting this [primacy], Christian princes and magistrates should be ashamed of any negligence in the performance of this duty. We have already shown that God has made what relates to religion their special business, and it is only right that they should

preserve and assert his honour, whose representatives they are and by whose grace and favour they rule. Certain holy kings are much praised in Scripture for restoring the worship of God when it had been corrupted or overturned, and for making it their chief concern that religion should flourish pure and unimpaired under their rule. By contrast, the sacred history ranks anarchical conditions amongst the evils: since there was no king in Israel, each man did whatever he pleased (Judg. 21.25). Hence those who would confine their efforts solely to doing justice amongst men, without any concern for God, stand convicted of stupidity. As if God had established superiors in his name to decide worldly controversies, but had omitted to provide for what is of far greater moment, namely that he should be worshipped purely, according to the rule laid down in his Law. But such is their passion for innovating in everything with impunity, that these turbulent (FV: spirits) want the elimination of everyone who would defend godliness when it has been violated.

As regards the Second Table, [1536:] Jeremiah tells kings (22.3) that they should render judgement and justice, and deliver the oppressed from the hands of their detractors, neither aggrieving strangers, widows and orphans, nor doing any injustice or shedding innocent blood. To the same effect is the exhortation which we find in Psalm 82 [3, 4], that they should do justice to the poor and needy, relieve those in poverty and want, and snatch the poor and needy from the hand of their oppressor. And Moses (Deut. 1.16) tells the rulers he had appointed to govern as his representatives that they should hear the cause of their brothers, judging between brother and brother, and strangers; that they should be no respecters of persons in their judgements, hearing both the great and the small and fearing no man, because theirs is the judgement of God. I leave aside [what is written elsewhere], that kings should not accumulate horses unto themselves (Deut. 17.16), nor give their minds over to greed, nor rise up in pride over their brothers; that they should be assiduous in meditating upon the Law of God all the days of their life; that judges should be impartial (16.19); that they should accept no 'presents'; and whatever else of the same sort is to be found in Scripture. For in explaining the duty of magistrates, my purpose is not so much to teach magistrates themselves, as rather to teach others what magistrates are and why God has established them. We see, therefore, that they have been appointed protectors and vindicators of public innocence, propriety, decency and tranquillity and that their one endeavour must be to provide for the common peace and well-being. David declared that, once raised to the royal throne, he would show forth these virtues (Ps. 101); that is, that he would not be party to any crimes, but would hate the unrighteous, the calumniators and the proud, and would search everywhere for upright and faithful counsellors (Ps. 101). But since magistrates cannot carry out [their appointed task) unless they protect good men from the injustices of the wicked, and help and protect the oppressed, they have been armed with power, to repress (evil-doers and) malefactors, whose wickedness disturbs and troubles the public peace. We know by experience the truth of Solon's saying that all commonwealths are kept in being by rewards and punishments; take these away and all the discipline of polities collapses and vanishes. For in many hearts a concern for what is right and just grows cold unless honours are assigned to virtue; and the depravity of the wicked cannot be checked except by severity and the knowledge that they will be punished. And these two [rewards and punishments) are included in what the prophet says (Jer. 21.12 and 22.3) when he commands kings and other superiors to render judgement and justice. For justice means placing the innocent under one's protection, cherishing them, safeguarding them, defending and delivering them. And judgement means taking a stand against the effrontery of the wicked, repressing their violence and punishing their crimes.

10. But here, it seems, a difficult and vexing questing arises; if the Law of God (Exod. 20.13; Deut. 5.17; Matt. 5.21) forbids all Christians to kill, and if the prophet (Isa. 11.9 and 65.25) foretells that they shall neither afflict nor harm anyone on God's holy mountain (in other words the Church), then how can magistrates be dutiful to God and shed blood at the same time? But if we understand that when magistrates inflict punishments, it is not any act of their own, but only the execution of God's [own] judgements, we will not be inhibited by any scruple on this score. The Law of God prohibits killing. But in order that murders shall not go unpunished, the Lawgiver himself puts the sword into the hands of his ministers, to be used against all murderers. Afflicting and harming are not the actions of godly men, but to avenge, at God's command the afflictions of the godly is not 'afflicting or harming'. If only this consideration were always present in our minds: in punishing, nothing is done by human presumptuousness but by God's command and authority. (And when that comes first, there is never any straying from the right path.) Unless perhaps divine justice is to be bridled, so as to prevent it punishing crimes. And if it is not permissible to impose a law on God, why do we slander his ministers? They do not bear the sword in vain, says St Paul (Rom. 13.4), for they are God's ministers to execute his wrath and wreak vengeance on evildoers. Therefore, if princes and other superiors know that there is nothing more acceptable to the Lord than their obedience, let them spare no effort in exercising this ministry, if indeed they have any desire to please God by their piety, obedience and justice. Certainly it was this desire that impelled Moses when he slew the Egyptian, knowing himself to be destined by the power of God to be the liberator of his people (Exod. 2.12); and again when he slew three thousand in one day, to punish the idolatry of the people (32.27). And it was the same desire that moved David, when at the end of his life he commanded his son Solomon to kill Joab and Shimei (1 Kings 2.5). This too is why he mentions (Ps. 101.8) 'destroying the wicked of the earth' amongst the royal virtues, so that all who work iniquity might be eliminated from the city of God. Here also belongs the praise which is accorded to Solomon (Ps. 45.7): 'You have loved justice and hated iniquity.' How could Moses, normally of a gentle and peaceable disposition, reach such a pitch of cruelty as to run through the camp eager for further slaughter, when he was already bespattered and dripping with the blood of his brothers? How was it that David, all his life a man

of great gentleness, made this bloodthirsty last will and testament with his dying breath: that his son should not allow Joab and Shimei to go grey-haired and in peace to their graves (1 Kings 2.3; 6.8)? The savagery (FV: if indeed it should be called that) of both Moses and David sanctified those hands which they would have sullied by mercy, for it was the vengeance which God had committed to them that they were carrying out. 'It is an abomination in kings to do-iniquity', says Solomon (Prov. 16.12), 'for the throne is made lasting by justice.' And again (20.8): 'The king who sits in the throne of judgement casts his eye over all malefactors' (FV: that is, to punish them). Again (20.26): 'A wise king scatters the unrighteous and turns [i.e. breaks] them on the wheel'; and (25.4 and 5): 'separate the dross from the silver, and a vessel shall come forth to the man who makes the cast; remove the unrighteous from the king's sight, and his throne shall be established in righteousness'. And again (17.15): 'To acquit the unrighteous and condemn the righteous are both abominations unto the Lord.' And (17.11): 'The rebellious man draws down calamity upon himself and a cruel messenger is sent to him'. (24.24): 'Whosoever says to an unrighteous man, you are just, him the people and the nations shall vilify.' The true justice [of rulers], then, is to pursue the evil-doers and the unrighteous with drawn sword. If [rulers] sheath their sword and keep their hands unsullied by blood, while the wicked roam about massacring and slaughtering, then so far from reaping praise for their goodness and justice, they make themselves guilty of the greatest possible injustice. But let there be no peremptory or savage harshness, nor the sort of court which has been rightly called 'the rock on which accused men founder'. For I am not one of those who favour an insatiable savagery, nor do I think an equitable verdict can be pronounced unless clemency is always in attendance, that 'best counsellor and most certain preserver of royal thrones', as Solomon says (Prov. 20.28). Someone[2] once rightly called it the chief virtue of princes. The magistrate must however exercise care neither to damage more than he mends, by excessive severity, nor to lapse into a most cruel 'humanity' allowing himself to be enervated by a superstitious attachment to clemency into a soft and dissolute indulgence, to the destruction of many. For it was pointedly remarked by someone (when Nerva was emperor), that it is bad to live under a prince who permits nothing, but much worse to live under one who permits everything.

11. From time to time it is necessary for kings and peoples to take up arms in order to carry out this kind of public vengeance. And our previous argument also allows us to conclude that wars engaged in for this purpose are legitimate. For if kings and peoples have conferred on them the power to preserve the tranquillity of their territories, to repress the seditious upheavals fomented by rebellious men, to help, those oppressed by violence and to take measures against the wicked, what better occasion can there be for employing that power, than in order to quell the fury of someone who disturbs the peace and quiet not only of private individuals

---

[2]Seneca, a commentary on whose *On Clemency* was Calvin's first published work.

but of entire communities? Someone who foments sedition and perpetrates violence and oppression and other outrages? If it is the duty [of kings and peoples] to act as guardians and champions of the laws, they must also make every effort to frustrate the enterprises of those whose crimes undermine the discipline of laws. Besides, if they are right to punish criminals by whose misdeeds only a few are harmed, are they to let criminality that afflicts and lays waste an entire region go scot-free? It is of no consequence here whether it is a king or the lowest of the mob who invades a foreign region where he has no jurisdiction, to murder and pillage; all of them are equally to be regarded as criminals and punished accordingly. [1543:] Natural justice and their office equally demand that princes must be armed (FV: use the sword) not only to repress private wrong-doing by means of judicial penalties, but also to defend, by means of war, the territories committed in trust to them when they are invaded by enemies. And wars of this sort the Holy Spirit declares to be legitimate by the testimony of many places in Scripture.

12. If someone here objects; that there is no proof-text or example in the New Testament which shows that war is permissible for Christians, my reply is this: in the first place, the reasons for waging war which existed formerly, still exist today. Conversely, there is nothing which prevents a magistrate from defending his subjects. Furthermore, we are not to seek an explicit discussion of matters of this sort in the apostolic writings (FV: doctrine); their purpose is to teach the spiritual kingdom of Christ, not to shape a polity. In any case, Scripture does indeed offer evidence in passing that Christ by his coming changed nothing in this regard. For if Christian teaching (to use Augustine's term) condemned all wars, the soldiers who sought advice about salvation would have been told to throw away their weapons and to quit the army at once. What they were in fact told, however, was: 'Strike no one, do injustice to no one, and be content with your pay' (Luke 3.14). If Christ commanded them to be content with the pay of soldiers, he was [evidently] not forbidding them to fight as soldiers. [1536:] But all magistrates are to take the greatest care not to give in, however little, to their passions; rather, if penalties are to be inflicted, they are not to allow themselves to be carried away by anger, or hatred, or implacable severity, but to have compassion on our common [human] nature, as Augustine says, even in those whose crimes they punish. And even though arms must indeed [sometimes] be taken up against an enemy, that is an armed criminal, [magistrates] are not to snatch at every casual opportunity: even if an occasion presents itself, they should not avail themselves of it unless compelled by a necessity which permits no escape. For much more is demanded of Christians than was demanded by the pagan[3] who wanted war to be a sort of searching for peace; everything else ought to be tried first before the recourse to arms. And in both kinds of activity [war and punishing criminals], magistrates must not allow themselves to be carried away by any private passion,

---

[3]Cicero, De officiis, 1.23.

but must be guided by a concern for the public good alone. To do anything else is the worst abuse of their authority, which is given to them for the benefit and service of others, and not for their own. On this same right to wage war also hinges the legitimacy of garrisons, alliances and other military provisions. I call 'garrisons' the disposition of soldiers in various cities to protect the borders of a region; 'alliances', those [treaties] which are made by neighbouring princes for mutual assistance against disturbances in their territories, and in order to join forces for the suppression of the common enemies of the human race; and 'military provisions' whatever is used in the art of war.

13. Let me add this last point. Taxes of various kinds are the legitimate revenue of princes. They should employ them in the main to defray the public expenses they incur by virtue of their office, but they may also use them to maintain the splendour of their households, a thing linked in a certain way to the dignity of the high office they bear. Thus we see that David, Hezechiah, Josiah, Jehoshaphat and other holy kings, and equally Joseph and Daniel, in respect of the public person they bore, lived sumptuously from the public purse, without offending against their duties to God in any way. And we read in Ezekiel (48.21) that a most generous tract of land was assigned to kings. [1539:] And although Ezekiel is here depicting the spiritual kingdom of Christ, nevertheless he draws his image or analogy from what is legitimate in earthly kingdoms. [1536:] But again, princes for their part are reminded [by Ezekiel] that the public revenues (FV: domains) are not their private coffers but rather the treasury of the whole people – as Paul tells us (Rom. 13.6) – which they cannot waste or squander without flagrant injustice. This is in fact almost the very life-blood of the people, which it would be the cruellest inhumanity not to use sparingly. As for their imposts, duties, and other sorts of taxes, these they are to regard as assistance rendered them for the sake of public necessity alone; and it would be tyrannical rapacity to vex the poor people with them needlessly. What I say here does not encourage princes to engage in costly extravagance and luxury; there is no need to fan the flames of their desires, which bum brightly enough already without any help from me: But princes must be taught what is permissible for them, since it is of the utmost importance that they should not fall into contempt of God by an impious over-confidence, and that whatever it is they undertake, they should undertake it only when they have a pure conscience before God. And it is not irrelevant that private persons too should be taught about this, so that they do not allow themselves a ⟨rash and thoughtless⟩ reviling of princes for their expenditures, even if these do exceed the ordinary and civil measure.

14. Next in order ⟨in the polity⟩, after magistrates, come the laws, those strongest sinews of the commonwealth or, as Cicero, following Plato, calls them, the soul without which magistracy cannot survive, just as the laws in their turn are quite powerless without the magistrate. And thus nothing could be more true than the saying that the law is a silent magistrate and the magistrate a living law. But although

I have undertaken to say what laws are to establish a Christian polity, there is no reason in that for anyone to expect from me a long disquisition about which laws would be best; that is an interminable topic and not relevant to my subject. I shall merely, as it were in passing, note a few things about what laws [such a polity] can justly employ and by which it can be rightly governed, in the sight of both God and men. And I would have preferred to pass over even this in silence, but for the fact that I see many falling into dangerous errors on this score. For there are some who deny that any commonwealth can be properly ordered if it is governed simply by the laws common to all nations, but without embracing the political laws of Moses. Others may concern themselves, if they wish, with how dangerous and seditious this opinion is; for my purposes it is enough to show that it is a false and stupid one. We must bear in mind here the commonplace division of the whole Law of God, as promulgated by Moses, into moral, ceremonial and judicial parts, and we must consider these parts separately, so as to be certain which of them apply [directly] to us, and which less so. Nor should we allow ourselves to be detained by the quibble that judicial and ceremonial laws also have to do with morality. The old authors who handed down this division knew well enough that ceremonial and judicial laws have a bearing on morality, but did not call them 'moral' laws, because they could be changed and abrogated without danger to morals. They reserved the term 'moral' for the part of the Law on which the true holiness of morals ⟨and the immutable rule of right living⟩ depends.

15. To begin then with the moral law. It has two headings, under the former of which we are commanded to worship God in pure faith and godliness, under the latter to love our fellow man with unfeigned love. This is the true and eternal rule of justice, laid down for all those in every age and of every nation who want to order their lives in accordance with the will of God. It is his eternal and immutable will that he be worshipped by all of us and that we should truly love one another. The ceremonial law was a way of educating the Jews; this is how it seemed good to the Lord to train them while they were their infancy (so to speak), until that time of fulness when he would manifest the totality of his wisdom to the earth, and show forth the truth of those things which he had formerly represented only obscurely and in figures. In the judicial laws which he gave the Jews to serve them as their civil order, he set down certain rules of justice and equity by which they might live together in innocence and tranquillity. But just as this training by means of ceremonies was indeed part of their education in the service of God (in that it made the church of the Jews adhere to God's religion and worship), and yet could nevertheless be distinguished from [the essence of] that service itself, in the same way the [specific] form of their judicial laws is something distinct from the commandment to love, although the sole purpose of these laws was to be the best means of preserving that mutual love which the eternal law of God teaches. And therefore, just as ceremonies could be abrogated without dutifulness to God being in any way impaired, so judicial laws could be abrogated,

and yet leave the perpetual duties and precepts of love intact. And if this is true (FV: and it certainly is), then individual peoples have been left the freedom to make what laws they see to be expedient, but all of these laws must be measured against the law of love. Their form varies, but they must all have the same end. Of course I do not regard as true laws those barbarous and brutish laws by which [for example] robbers were rewarded with honours, or promiscuous intercourse was permitted, and others even more disgusting and absurd; they are abhorrent not only from the point of view of justice but even of humanity.

16. My point will become clear if we consider the distinction to be made in any law between the form and content on the one hand, and equity, which is the end for which it is made and the basis on which it rests, on the other. Equity, in as much as it is natural, must be the same for all, and therefore all laws ought to make it their purpose, although accommodated to the particular subject with which they deal. Because positive laws depend in part on specific circumstances, they can [perfectly well] have the same object, namely equity, even though they differ as to their provisions. Now, the Law of God which we call the moral law is acknowledged to be none other than the testimony of natural law and of that conscience which is engraved (FV: imprinted) in the souls of men by God, and so the whole content of equity is prescribed by it. Hence that equity alone must be the end and rule and boundary of all laws. And there is therefore no reason why we should reject any laws whatever, even though they vary amongst themselves or differ from the Mosaic Law, so long as they have equity for the end at which they aim, the rule by reference to which they are formulated, and the limit which they must not transgress. The Law of God forbids theft. What punishments were prescribed for theft in the polity of the Jews may be seen in Exodus. The oldest laws of other nations punished theft by demanding double restitution; later laws distinguished between open and secret theft. Other laws again went as far as exile, whipping and finally the death penalty. Again (FV: the Law of God forbids bearing false witness), the Jews punished false witness by the *lextalionis*, other people punished it by disgrace only, yet others by hanging or crucifixion. (FV: The Law of God forbids murder.) All laws coincide in avenging murder by shedding blood, but they prescribe different forms of death. ⟨Adultery has been punished in some places by more severe penalties, in others by lighter ones.⟩ But for all these variations, we see that in each case the end envisaged is one and the same. For they all with one accord proclaim punishments for those crimes which the eternal Law of God condemns: murder, theft, adultery, false witness; they merely differ as to what the penalty shall be. And it is not necessary or even expedient that they should [all be identical in that respect]. There are regions which would be immediately ravaged by slaughter and brigandage unless a hideous example were made of murderers. There are times which demand increased severity of penalties. [1559:] If the public order (FV: a country) has been disturbed in some way, the evils that commonly arise out of such disturbances must be remedied by new laws. In time of war, amid the clash

of arms, all humanity would collapse unless unusual punishments were introduced to inspire fear. In times of dearth or pestilence, everything would go to wrack and ruin, unless greater severity were used. [1536:] Some peoples are particularly prone to certain vices, unless they are held in check by great harshness. And therefore those who object to such diversity, when it is in fact highly suited to maintaining the observance of the Law of God, are malicious enemies of the public good. Nor is there any substance at all in the claim sometimes made, that it is to hold God's Law, as declared by Moses, in contempt to abrogate it and to prefer some new law to it. For when other laws are found more acceptable, it is not a question of an [unconditional] preference, but rather of reference to the conditions of time, place and people. Nor can it be called 'abrogating the Law of Moses', when it was never decreed for us in the first place. The Lord did not have Moses promulgate the Law for all peoples and all times. Rather, his will was to be the [sole and] special lawgiver for the Jewish people, whom he had taken under his patronage and protection, and made his clients. And so, in the manner of a good lawgiver, he had regard in all his laws to [the special needs of] this people.

17. It remains for us to consider the topic we proposed to deal with last, namely what benefits accrue to the ⟨general⟩ association of Christians from laws, courts and magistrates. And to this is attached another question, namely how far the obedience and submission which private men owe to magistrate [FV: superiors] extends. Many regard the office of magistrate as irrelevant as far as Christians are concerned. They claim that Christians are not entitled to appeal to magistrates for help, since all vengeance, all appeals to courts and all litigation are prohibited [by God]. But on the contrary, as St Paul plainly declares (Rom. 13.4), [magistrates] are ministers of God for our good. This teaches us that it has been divinely ordained that we should be defended by the hand and protection of the magistrate against the outrages and injustices of the wicked, and so be able to live our lives in peace and safety. God would have accorded us such protection in vain, if we were forbidden to make use of it, and so it is evident enough that we can call on it without any sin. But here I have two sorts of people to contend with. There are many whose passion for litigation is so all-consuming that they can never be at peace with themselves unless they are at war with others. They embark on lawsuits in a spirit of mortal hatred and bitterness, with an insane thirst for revenge and for inflicting suffering, and they pursue their suits with implacable persistency until their adversary is ruined. And all the while, they defend their wickedness with the pretext of legality, so that no one will think of them as doing anything except what is right. But even though it is legitimate to take one's brother to court, it does not follow that it is right to hate him, to be possessed by a rage to do him harm, or to hound him relentlessly (FV adds: without mercy).

18. Let such men learn this (FV: maxim): making use of courts is legitimate if one uses them rightly. And the right way to use them is this: the accused, on being summoned, should appear on the appointed day, and defend his cause by producing

what justification he can without bitterness, and with no other intention but that of safeguarding what is his by right. The plaintiff who has been made to suffer unjustly either in respect of his person or his goods, should put himself in the hands of the magistrate, should explain the charge he has brought and ask for what is just and right. But he should do all this without any thirst for revenge or desire to inflict injury, without bitterness or hate, and without taking pleasure in quarrelsomeness; on the contrary, he should be prepared to yield up his right and suffer any wrong rather than to allow his mind to be filled with enmity towards his adversary. On the other hand, where any particle of [the duty to] love is neglected because minds are suffused with ill-will, corrupted by envy, burning with anger, breathing vengeance, or inflamed by quarrelsomeness, then every legal proceeding must be contrary to our duties to God, however just it might be in itself. It ought to be considered a principle laid down for every Christian that it is impossible for anyone to proceed Justly with a case at law, however good his cause, unless he bears towards his adversary the same love and benevolence [that he would] if the business at issue had already been amicably transacted and settled. Some will perhaps object here that such (FV: moderation and) self-restraint is never in fact to be found in the lawcourts, and that it would be a miracle if ever one saw an instance of it. I admit that, the morals of our times being what they are, one rarely encounters an instance of a virtuous litigant, but the thing itself does not cease to be good and pure, provided it remains untainted by evil. And when we hear that the assistance which the magistrate renders is a sacred gift of God, we must take all the more care not to sully it by our viciousness.

19. As for those who condemn all courts and all litigation absolutely and without distinction; they should realize that they are rejecting a sacred ordinance of God and one of those [divine] gifts which can be pure to those who are pure. Unless, that is, they want to charge St Paul [himself] with a crime. For he rebutted the calumnies of his accusers, exposing their craftiness and malice into the bargain, asserted his privileges as a Roman citizen in the courts, and appealed from a wicked judge to the tribunal of Caesar when the need arose (Acts 22.1, 24.12, 25.10). Nor is the fact that all Christians are forbidden to desire vengeance any objection: we too would have such desires banished from Christian courts (Matt. 5.39; Deut. 32.35; Rom. 12.19). For if the matter is a civil one, there is no right way except that of commending one's case to the judge, as guardian of the public [good], in innocent simplicity and without the least thought of returning evil for evil (that is, without any desire for vengeance); or if it is a more serious or capital case that is to be brought before a court, we require of an accuser that he should not be animated by a thirst for revenge, that his mind should be untouched by rancour for the injustice he has suffered, and that his only intention should be to impede wicked men in their endeavour to damage the commonwealth. For if there is no vengeful intent, there is nothing in all this that goes against the commandment that Christians should not avenge themselves. But here [the rejoinder might be that] Christians are not only forbidden to avenge

themselves, they are also commanded to wait for the hand of God, who has promised to avenge the oppressed and afflicted. And those who call on magistrates to help them or others, forestall the celestial vengeance of their divine protector. But that objection [too] is quite groundless: the magistrate's punishment must be regarded as something inflicted by God, not by men, for it is God who acts in this way for our good by means of the ministry of men, as St Paul says (Rom. 13.4).

20. Nor is there any contradiction between what we teach here and the saying of Christ (Matt. 5.39) which forbids us to resist evil and commands us to turn the right cheek to the person who strikes us on the left, and to allow him who takes our tunic to take our cloak as well. Christ does indeed demand of his followers that any thought of revenge should be so far from their minds that they would rather suffer twice the harm inflicted on them than to retaliate. But we are not discouraging such patience. Christians must be people born to suffer contumely and injustices, and to be exposed to wickedness, deceit and ridicule from the dregs of mankind. And not only this, but they must bear all such evils patiently, that is, with such composure that when they suffer one affliction, they should prepare themselves for more to come, expecting nothing throughout the whole of their lives except a perpetual carrying of their cross. In the mean time, they must do good to those who harm them and pray for those who speak evil against them, and they must seek to overcome evil with good, for this is to be their only victory (Rom. 12.21; Matt. 5.39). If this is how they are disposed, they will not demand an eye for an eye or a tooth for a tooth, seeking revenge, which is what the Pharisees taught their disciples. Rather, following Christ's injunction, they will allow their bodies to be multilated and their goods to be maliciously seized, and yet be ready to forgive the injuries they suffer the very moment they are inflicted. But this equitableness and composure of mind will not inhibit them from making use of the help of magistrates for the preservation of what is theirs, while maintaining complete amity towards their enemies. And their zeal for the public good will [induce] them to demand punishment on a criminal and pestilent man who they know can be reformed in no other way (except by death). [1543:] Augustine rightly interprets all these precepts as intended to prepare a just and upright man to bear patiently every evil from those he hopes will become righteous, so that the number of good men might grow, rather than adding himself to the number of the wicked by more wrong-doing of his own. [He also thinks that] these precepts have more to do with the heart within than with external acts, so that in the secrecy of the soul patience and benevolence prevail, but in outward acts we should see to it that we are able to do what benefits those whom we ought to wish well.[4]

21. [1536:] As for the usual objection that Paul condemns all litigation without exception, it too is false. From his words (1 Cor. 6.1ff) it is easy to see that there

---

[4]Calvin is quoting the *Epistola ad Marcellinum*, translated in M. Dods (ed.), *Works of St Augustine* (Edinburgh: T. and T. Clark, 1875), Vol XIII, Letter CXXXVIII, pp. 203–4.

was a boundless passion for litigation in the Church of the Corinthians; so much so that they exposed the Gospel of Christ and the whole of that religion which they professed to the scoffing and detraction of the ungodly. What St Paul chiefly reproached in them was that their violent dissensions brought the Gospel into disrepute amongst the pagans. He also deplored the fact that it was brothers at variance with brothers. So far from bearing injuries patiently, they in fact coveted each other's goods, and indeed attacked and damaged one another. It is therefore this insane passion for litigation and not every sort legal proceeding that Paul condemns. He declares it to be a vice or a weakness not to prefer to suffer the loss of one's own goods, rather than striving to preserve them, to the point of enmity. [1543:] It was, he says, a sign of a disposition too ready to take offence and not sufficiently inclined to patience, that people were distressed by the slightest loss and were ready to run to the courts for the most trivial reasons. [1536:] The Christian way is always to be prepared to forego one's rights, rather than to go to court. For courts are places hard to leave without minds in turmoil, inflamed with hatred for one's brother. But when someone sees that he can protect what is his without any diminution of love, and when the loss would be grievous to him, he does nothing which is at variance with the teaching of Paul [in resorting to the courts]. Finally, as we said at the beginning, love is every man's best counsellor: all disputes begun without it are unjust and ungodly, and so are all those that go beyond [what love allows]. This seems to us incontrovertible.

22. The first duty of subjects towards their magistrates (FV: superiors) is to hold their office in the highest possible regard; that is, to recognize it as a commission delegated ⟨so to speak⟩ by God, and on this account to revere them as God's ministers and representatives. Now, you will find some who do indeed obey their magistrates, and who would not wish there to be none (FV: no superiors) for them to obey, for they recognize that the public good requires it. Nevertheless, they think of them as a kind of necessary evil. But Peter demands more of us than this (1 Pet. 2.17) when he commands us to honour the king; and so does Solomon (Prov. 24.21) when he commands us to fear God and the king. For Peter includes a sincere and heartfelt esteem in [the meaning of] this word 'to honour'. And Solomon, by linking kings with God, shows a king to be entitled to sacred veneration and dignity. And we also find Paul speaking (FV: of superiors) in terms of high praise (Rom. 13.5): we should be obedient not only on account of the wrath, but for conscience's sake. By this he means that subjects are to hold themselves in subjection to princes ⟨and [other] superiors⟩ not only out of fear, as people submit to an armed enemy, realizing that any failure to obey will be promptly punished, but because in obeying their superiors they are obeying God himself, since their power is from God. [1559:] I am not speaking about the persons of rulers, as if the dignity [of their office) could mask their stupidity, villainy or cruelty, their immorality of life and viciousness, and as if in this way vices could acquire the praise due to virtue. But I do say that their rank itself deserves

honour and reverence; those in authority ought to be valued and venerated by us for the sake of their high office.

23. [1536:] From this it also follows that subjects should show them obedience and well-disposed minds, whether it be in complying with their laws, paying taxes, accepting public offices or burdens related to the public defence, or doing whatever else is demanded of them. 'Let every soul', says Paul (Rom. 13.1), 'be subject to the higher powers, for whoever resists the power resists the ordinance of God.' And he writes to Titus (3.1): 'Exhort them to be subject to principalities and powers; they should obey the magistrates and be ready for every good work.' And Peter says (1 Pet. 2.13): 'Be subject to every human creature ⟨[1545:] (or rather, as I interpret it, every human ordinance)⟩ [1536:] for God's sake, whether it be the king as having pre-eminence, or governors, who are sent by him to punish the wicked, but to give praise to those who act rightly.' What is more, in order to prove that their subjection is not merely feigned subjection, but rather that it is sincere and comes from the heart, Paul adds (1 Tim. 2.1) that subjects are to pray for the well-being and prosperity of those under whom they live. 'I exhort you', he says, 'to offer prayers, petitions and thanksgiving for all men, for kings and for all placed in authority, that we may live peaceful and quiet lives in all godliness and decency.' And make no mistake: it is impossible to resist the magistrate without also resisting God. Even if it appears possible to defy an unarmed magistrate with impunity, God is armed and his vengeance for any contempt shown him is harsh. The obedience [of which I am speaking] also includes that self-restraint which private persons ought to impose on themselves in public [matters], neither meddling in public matters, nor intruding rashly on the magistrate's, preserve, nor undertaking anything whatever of a public nature. If there is something in need of correction in the public order, private men are not to create disturbances, or take matters into their own hands, for these hands ought here to be tied. Instead, they should submit the matter to the cognizance of the magistrate (FV: superior), whose hand alone is free. What I mean is that they should do nothing, unless they have a specific right or command to do so. For where a superior lends them his authority, then they too are invested with public authority. The ruler's advisers are commonly described as his 'eyes and ears'; it would not be inappropriate to call those whom he has commissioned to act for him his 'hands'.

24. Up to this point we have been considering magistrates who live up to the titles given to them: fathers of their country, or ⟨as the poet[5] puts it⟩ shepherds of the people, guardians of the peace, upholders of justice, defenders of the innocent. And anyone who thinks the authority of such persons unacceptable deserves to be considered a madman. But we find in almost every age another sort of prince. Some of them live lives of indolence and pleasure, not in the least concerned about

---

[5]i.e. Homer.

all those duties to which they ought to attend. Others, intent only on their own profit, prostitute every right, privilege, judgement and charter by putting them up for sale. Others again drain the poor people of their money, only to squander it in wild prodigality. Yet others pillage homes, violate wives and maidens, slaughter the innocent; in short, they engage in what can only be called criminality. And there are many people who cannot be convinced that these too ought to be acknowledged as princes, and (as being endowed with an authority which is) to be obeyed, as far as is permissible. For they cannot see any semblance of that image of God which ought to shine forth from magistrates, nor any vestige of that 'minister of God' who is given to the righteous in praise and to the wicked for their punishment. Faced with such lack of dignity and with criminal conduct so remote from the duties of a magistrate, indeed so remote from the duties of ordinary humanity, they cannot recognize the kind of superior whose dignity and authority Scripture commends to us. Mankind has always had an innate hatred and detestation of tyrants, just as it loves and venerate lawful kings.

25. But reflection on the Word of God will carry us beyond [the ordinary sentiments of mankind]. For we are to be subject not only to the authority of those princes who do their duty towards us as they should, and uprightly, but to all of them, however they came by their office, even if the very last thing they do is to act like [true] princes. For even though, the Lord declares that the [office of] magistrate is the greatest gift of his goodness for the preservation of mankind, and although he himself sets the boundaries within which they are to confine themselves, nonetheless he also declares at the same time that whatever they are (FV: and however they govern), it is from him alone that they derive their authority. Those who govern for the public good are true examples (FV: mirrors) and signs of his goodness; those who govern unjustly and intemperately have been raised up by him to punish the iniquity of the people. Both are equally furnished with that sacred majesty, with which he has endowed legitimate authority (FV: superiors). I shall not continue without offering some proof-texts for my point: Job 34.30; Hosea 13.11; Isaiah 3.4 and 10.5; Deuteronomy 28.29. We need not devote much effort to proving that an ungodly king is the wrath of God on the land; there is no one (1 imagine) who will deny it, and in any case this says no more about kings than might equally be said of a robber who steals your goods, or an adulterer who defiles your marriage-bed, or a murderer who encompasses your death; all these calamities are counted by Scripture amongst God's curses (Deut. 28.29). What however does require more proof, because people are much less ready to accept it, is that even the worst of them, and those entirely undeserving of any honour, provided they have public authority, are invested with that splendid and sacred authority which God's Word bestows on the ministers of his justice and judgement. And hence, as far as public obedience is concerned, they are to be held in the same honour and reverence as would be accorded an excellent king, if they had such a one.

26. So that in the first place I would have my readers note and meditate on this: it is not without good reason that Scripture so often reminds us of God's providence and his special operation in distributing kingdoms and setting up such kings as he sees fit. As it says in Daniel (2.21 and 37): 'The Lord changes the times and the diversity of times; he overthrows kings and sets them up.' And again: 'Let the living know that the Most High is mighty in the kingdom of men and gives [the kingship] to whomever he wishes.' The whole of Scripture abounds in such passages, but they are especially frequent in the prophets. Everyone knows what sort of a king Nebuchadnezzar was; the man who took Jerusalem and who was always bent on invading and ravaging other men's lands. And yet in Ezekiel (29.19) the Lord affirms that it was He himself who gave him the land of Egypt, in return for the service he had rendered Him in laying it waste. And Daniel said to him (Ezek. 2.37): 'You O King are the king of kings, to whom the Lord of heaven has given a kingdom powerful, strong and glorious; to you I say he gave it, and all the lands inhabited by the sons of men, the beasts of the forest (FV: wild beasts) and the birds of the air; he gave them into your hand and made you to rule over them.' And again to his son Belshazzar (Dan. 5.18): 'The Lord the Most High gave to your father Nebuchadnezzar kingship and magnificence, honour and glory; and on account of the greatness he conferred on him, all peoples, tribes and tongues were fearful and trembled in his sight.' When we hear that God established such a king, we must also recall to mind the divine ordinances about honouring and fearing kings, nor must we be in any doubt that we must honour [even] the worst tyrant in the office in which the Lord has seen fit to set him. When Samuel proclaimed to the people of Israel what they would have to endure from their kings, he said (1 Sam. 8.11): 'This will be the right (*ius*) of the king who will reign over you: he will take your sons and put them to his chariots to be his horsemen, to work his fields and gather in his harvest, and to make him weapons: He will take your daughters to make perfumes, to cook and to bake. He will take your fields and your vineyards and your best olive groves and give them to his servants. He will take tithes of your seed and your grape-harvest and give them to his eunuchs and servants. He will take your servants, handmaidens and asses and apply them to his work and will take tithes of your flocks besides, and you shall be his servants.' Kings will not indeed do all this by right on the contrary, God's law fully instructs them in temperance and self-restraint. But Samuel calls it a right (*ius*) over the people, because they must obey the king and are not allowed to resist him. It is as if Samuel had said: kings will be carried away by their licentiousness, but it will not be for you to restrain them; all that will remain for you will be to hear what they command, and obey.

27. One passage stands out as especially important and memorable: Jeremiah 27.5ff. I am prepared to quote it because, although it is somewhat long, it resolves the question in the clearest possible fashion. [It reads:] 'The Lord says: I have made heaven, and mankind, and the animals who are on the surface of the earth, in the

greatness of my power and by my outstretched arm, and have handed them over to whoever is pleasing in my sight. And now therefore I have given all these lands into the hands of my servant Nebuchadnezzar; let all the peoples and the ⟨great⟩ kings serve him until the time of his land shall come. And it shall come to pass that every people and kingdom which has not served the king of Babel (FV: and has not bowed the neck under his yoke), I shall visit that people with sword, hunger and pestilence; therefore serve the king of Babel and live.' We see here the degree of obedience and honour the Lord wished to be accorded to that loathsome and cruel tyrant, and merely because he was in possession of the kingship. It was this [possession] alone which showed that he had been placed on the royal throne by divine decree, and had been vested with royal majesty, which must remain inviolate. If we keep firmly in mind that even the very worst kings are appointed by this same decree which establishes the authority of kings [in general], then we will never permit ourselves the seditious idea that a king is to be treated according to his deserts, or that we need not obey a king who does not conduct himself towards us like a king.

28. There is no force either in the objection that this precept was exclusively for the Israelites. We must consider the reason God himself gave to support it. What he says is: 'I have given the kingdom to Nebuchadnezzar; therefore serve him and live' (Jer. 27.17). Thus we cannot doubt that we must serve anyone who has manifestly had kingship conferred on him. In the very act of raising someone to the exalted rank of king, the Lord thereby reveals to us that it is his will that that person should rule. And there are general testimonies to the truth of this to be found in Scripture. In Solomon (Prov. 28.1): 'Because of the iniquity of the land there are many princes.' And Job 12.18: 'He takes away dominion from princes, and then girds them again with a girdle.' When that is admitted, there remains nothing for us but to serve and live. And in the prophet Jeremiah (29.7) we find another command of the Lord. There he orders his people to seek peace in Babylon, to which they had been taken by force as captives, and to pray to him for Babylon, for in its peace would be their peace. Notice how the Israelites, despoiled of all their goods, expelled from their homes, carried off into exile, cast down into a wretched bondage, are [yet] commanded to pray for the prosperity of their conqueror. And not merely in the sense that we are elsewhere commanded to pray for those who persecute us, but rather, to pray for the peace and safety of his reign, so that they too might live prosperously under him. And in the same way David, already designated king by God's ordinance and anointed with his holy oil, when he was persecuted by Saul without having done anything to deserve it, nonetheless treated the person of his ambusher as sacrosanct, because God had honoured Saul with the royal dignity. 'Far be it from me,' he said (1 Sam. 24.6 and 11), 'that I should do this thing to my lord, the Anointed of the Lord, in the sight of the Lord my God: that I should lay my hands on him (FV: to do him harm); for he is (FV: the Christ, that is,) the Lord's Anointed.' And again (1 Sam. 26.9): 'My soul has

spared you and I have said: I shall not lay hands on my lord, since he is the Anointed of the Lord.' And again: 'Who shall lay hands on the Anointed of the Lord and remain guiltless? The Lord lives, and unless the Lord strikes him down, or his day comes and he dies, or is laid low in battle, far be it from me that I should lay hands on the Anointed of the Lord' (1 Sam. 24.7–11; 26.9 and 10).

29. This is the kind of reverence and dutifulness that we all owe to our superiors, whoever they are. I say this often, so that we might learn not to consider the persons and conduct [of rulers], but be content with the person they represent, by the will of God, and with ⟨whose⟩ inviolable majesty ⟨they have been inscribed and stamped⟩. But, you will reply, superiors in their turn reciprocally owe duties to their subjects. I have already acknowledged it. But if you go on to infer that only just governments. (FV: just lords) are to be repaid by obedience, your reasoning is stupid. Husbands and wives owe each other mutual duties; so do parents and children. But what if husbands or parents do not do their duty? What if parents, although forbidden to provoke their children to anger (Eph. 6.4), are instead hard and intractable and weary their children beyond measure by their peevishness? What if husbands treat their wives with great abusiveness, even though they have been commanded to love and spare them, as weak vessels (Eph. 5.25; 1 Pet. 3.7)? Shall children then be less obedient to their parents, or wives to their husbands on that account? But [children and wives] are subject to the wicked and the undutiful just as much [as to the upright and dutiful]. No: all are to act in such a way as not to look at the bag hanging from the backs of other people; that is, they are not to ask about the duties of others, but only to consider their own, and especially when they are placed in subjection to the power of others. Hence, if we are tormented by a cruel ruler, if we are fleeced by a rapacious and extravagant one, if we suffer neglect from an indolent one or are afflicted for [our] godliness by an impious and sacrilegious one, let us first recall to mind our sins, for it is those without a doubt which God is punishing by such scourges. Then humility will bridle our impatience. And let us all summon this reflection to our assistance: it is not for us to remedy such evils; all that is left to us is to implore the help of the Lord, for the hearts of princes and alterations of kingdoms are in his hands (Prov. 21.1). It is God who will stand in the assembly of the gods and will give judgement in their midst (Ps. 82.1). Before his face all kings will fall down and be terrified, and the judges who had not kissed his Anointed (Ps. 2.12); those who wrote unjust laws to oppress the poor by their judgements and to do violence to the cause of the humble; to prey on widows and rob orphans (Isa. 10.1–2).

30. And in all this is revealed God's admirable goodness, might and providence. For sometimes he raises up avengers from amongst his servants, designated and commanded by him to punish the tyranny of vicious men and to deliver the oppressed from their wretched calamities; at other times he turns the frenzy of men who intended something quite different to the same end. In the former manner he freed the people of Israel from Pharaoh's tyranny by means of Moses, from the

violence of Chusan, King of Syria, by Othoniel, and from other servitudes by other kings or judges (Exod. 3.8; Judg. 3.9 and ff chs.). And by the latter means he overcame the pride of Tyre by means of the Egyptians, the haughtiness of the Egyptians by the Assyrians, the ferocity of the Assyrians by the Chaldeans, the overweening pride of Babylon by the Medes and Persians, when Cyrus had already subjugated the Medes. On occasion, he punished the ingratitude shown him by the kings of Israel and Judah for his many mercies, and their contempt to him, by means of the Assyrians, on other occasions by the Babylonians, though in quite different ways. The former [i.e. the avengers] were summoned to punish these crimes by a lawful calling from God; they did not in the least violate the majesty with which kings are endowed by divine ordinance when they took up arms against kings. Armed by heaven, they subjugated a lesser power by a greater, in just the same way that kings are entitled to punish their own officials. The latter, by contrast, did God's work without knowing it, for all that they intended to do was to commit crimes. All the same, it was the hand of God that directed them do to his bidding.

31. But irrespective of what may be thought about the actions themselves, it was the Lord who by these instruments carried out his just purpose, when he broke the bloodstained sceptres of insolent kings and overturned unbearable tyrannies. Let princes hear and be afraid. As for us, however, let us take the greatest possible care never to hold in contempt; or trespass upon, that plenitude of authority of magistrates (FV: superiors) whose majesty it is for us to venerate and which God has confirmed by the most weighty pronouncements, even when it is exercised by individuals who are wholly unworthy of it and who do their best to defile it by their wickedness. And even if the punishment of unbridled tyranny is the Lord's vengeance [on tyrants], we are not to imagine that it is we ourselves who have been called upon to inflict it. All that has been assigned to us is to obey and suffer. Here as always, I am speaking about private persons. It may be that there are in our days popular magistrates established to restrain the licentiousness of kings, corresponding to those 'Ephors' (FV: as they were called), which were set against the authority of the kings of the Spartans, or the Tribunes (FV: defenders) of the People, set over against the Roman consuls, or the 'Demarchs', set up against the Council of the Athenians. And perhaps, in current circumstances, the authority exercised by the three estates in individual kingdoms when they hold their principal assemblies is of the same kind. If there are such [popular magistrates established], then it is no part of my intention to prohibit them from acting in accordance with their duty, and resisting the licentiousness and frenzy of kings; on the contrary, if they connive at their unbridled violence and insults against the poor common people, I say that such negligence is a nefarious betrayal of their oath; they are betraying the people and defrauding them of that liberty which they know they were ordained by God to defend.

32. But there is always one exception to that obedience which, as we have established, is due to (the authority of) superiors, and it is this that must be our

principal concern: we must never allow ourselves to be diverted from our obedience to the one to whose will the desires of every king must be subjected, to whose decrees all their commands give place, and before whose majesty they must lay down their worn insignia. Would it not be an absurdity to give contentment to [mere] men [by obeying them], but thereby to incur the wrath of him on whose account alone [any human being at all] must be obeyed? The Lord is the king of kings. When his sacred mouth has spoken, it alone and no one else is to be heard. We are subject to those who have been placed over us, but only in him. If they command anything against [his will], it must be as nothing to us. And in this instance we must ignore all that dignity that magistrates (FV: superiors) possess. There is no injustice in compelling it to be subordinate to the true, unique and supreme power of God. [1559:] It is for this reason that Daniel (Dan. 6.22) denied that he was guilty of any offence against the king when he disobeyed an ungodly law the latter had made: for the king had transgressed the bounds set to him [by God] and had not only wronged men, but had raised his horns against God, there by abrogating his own power. By contrast, the Israelites are condemned (FV: in Hosea 5.11) for their excessive readiness to submit to an ungodly law of their king. For when Jeroboam had had the golden calves cast, they defected from the temple of God and went over to new superstitions (1 Kings 12.30), in order to please him. Their descendants were just as ready to accommodate themselves to the will and pleasure of their kings. They too were sharply reproved by the prophet for submitting to the king's commands. Thus there is nothing at all to praise in that pretended 'humble submission' which the flatterers at court invoke to cover themselves and deceive the simple, when they claim that it is wrong for them to refuse obedience to anything their kings command. As if God had surrendered his own rights to the mortal men he has placed in authority over the human race. Or as if earthly power suffered diminution by being subjected to God's, who is its author and in whose sight even the celestial principalities tremble in fear (and supplication). [1536:] I recognize full well the gravity and the immediacy of the perils which threaten [those who show) the constancy I demand; I know that kings are not prepared to tolerate any defiance and that their anger is a messenger of death, as Solomon says (Prov. 16.14). But heaven's messenger Peter (in Acts 5.29) proclaims this commandment: 'we must obey God rather than men.' Let us therefore derive consolation from the thought that we are rendering to God the obedience he demands when we rather suffer all things than to depart from our duty to him. And so that our courage may not fail us, Paul (1 Cor. 7, 23) adduces something else to spur us on: our redemption has been purchased at so high a price in order that we might not become slaves to the wicked desires of men; still less should we submit to their ungodliness.

PRAISE BE TO GOD

18. John Neville Figgis – Extracts from The Civic Standpoint

Lecture III

The civic standpoint

So far our course has been clear. We have seen that the essential minimum of any claim we make for the Church must depend on its recognition as a social union with an inherent original power of self-development, acting as a person with a mind and will of its own. All other matters between Church and State are questions of detail; and there is room for mutual concession. What is not a detail but a principle is that which I have put forward, and we have seen that this is not granted; that it is opposed by the prevailing opinion of State omnipotence entrenched in popular thought, and still more so in the opinion of lawyers; that the doctrine to which we are opposed is no novelty, nor is it specifically modern, but that it owes its force to the continuance of age-long traditions, to the survival of the State idea of the ancient world related most completely to the Athens of Aristotle, but developed and heightened with all the majesty of Imperial Rome, and inherent in the Canon no less than the Civil Law. Further, we have seen that this false conception of the State as the only true political entity apart from the individual is at variance not only with ecclesiastical liberty, but with the freedom of all other communal life, and ultimately with that of the individual; moreover, that it is fast breaking down under the pressure of the historical jurists like Dr. Gierke and Maitland, and the fact of the innumerable developments of the associative instinct and of the positive political facts of a modern world-empire. All these developments are facts; although it may not be impossible to harmonise them verbally with the old cast-iron definitions of sovereignty and law, such modification destroys the original conception, while in the treatment of corporate life there arise serious practical dangers. Our first aim, then, must be to endeavour to induce men by persuasion and all means morally legitimate to admit the positive right of societies to exist, and in this we shall follow the example which was the origin of civil freedom. In the seventeenth century it was not the isolated individual but the religious body, the sect with it's passionate assertion of its own right to be, which finally won toleration from the State. By himself apart from religious discords the individual would have secured no freedom. The orgy of State-autocracy which set in with the Renaissance and was developed by the Reformation would have gone on unchecked, as, indeed, it did in those States like France or the German principalities in which uniformity in religion was enforced. It was the competing claims of religious bodies, and the inability of any single one to destroy the others, which finally secured liberty. The rights of man were their recognition of the sense of his duties towards God. Political liberty is the fruit of ecclesiastical animosities.

Now, however, we are but at the threshold of our task. Once it has been realised as a problem of universal importance, a matter which concerns not clerical privilege but the very idea of corporate society, and involving the whole problem of the true nature alike of the State and the persons natural and juristic of which it is composed, we shall see that we are faced by further questions as to our duty as citizens and the limits which this freedom now claimed must place upon our efforts to influence the law of the land. Countless other questions will also arise, which I shall not do more than indicate. The right of the individual to liberty and self-development does not imply his right to do anything he pleases. Even so strong an individualist as Herbert Spencer was wont to guard the security of the liberty of each by reference to the equal liberty of all. If this be the case with individuals, it must still more plainly be so with all societies. For in the nature of things they are more powerful than individuals; the relative disinterestedness they claim from their members may, and often will, lead to methods and claims which cannot be justified; the higher their object, the greater danger there is of their outstepping the bounds of justice in their desire to promote it; and the greater need, therefore, of government regulation and control. Moreover, while the question of the recognition of the individual citizen is one that can be solved with no trouble, the registration of a society and the determination of the marks which indicate its full legal personality are more complex; and however strongly we may assert the naturalness of the corporate life, no one, I believe, would deny the duty of the State to demand proper proofs that it is being formed and supplied with duly constituted organs of its unity; while, further, it must clearly be within the province of the State to prevent bodies of persons acting secretly, and practically as corporations, in order to escape the rightful government control. This, I suppose, is half the difficulty of the trust problem in America. In regard to religion, the State as "a power ordained by God" ought not to allow men so to use the great truth of freedom as to be false to the ends of civil society. No one, I suppose, would now demand that the officers of corporate bodies should not pay their debts, or claim that the State may not use force to compel them.[1] Great as may be this freedom, we have large tracts of life dependent on property and contract, which must come within the control of the civil power. Here, however, there may be one kind of exception. Within any social group, if the members are sufficiently loyal, there may grow up all kinds of ties and arrangements which could not be enforced at law, and yet are practically

---

[1]"Sæculares judices qui, licet ipsis nulla competat jurisdictio in hac parte, personas ecclesiasticas ad solvendum debita, super quibus coram eis contra ipsas earum exhibentur literæ vel prelationes aliæ inducuntur, damnapili præsumptione compellunt, a temeritate hujusmodi per locorum ordinarios censura ecclesiastica decernimus compescendos." — *Corpus Juris Canonici, Sext* II. ii. 2.

restrictive. For instance, at this moment there is no restriction on publication except that provided by the law of libel, yet the bulk of works published by Roman Catholics have on them an *imprimatur*. This is a restriction not legally enforceable, but dependent on the loyalty to their own authorities of the members of the Roman Church. It would, however, be a distinct invasion of the province of that Church if the courts were to interfere with the excommunication of anyone on the ground that he had contravened this regulation. Even now between families and individuals a vast amount of arrangements go on which could not be legally enforced; nor will this ever cease to be needful. Except in a small and highly-undeveloped society, very many transactions must take place which depend for their validity on the character of men, and not on any legal instrument. Another instance is the matter of monastic vows. These are not now a legal obligation, but that they have a very practical effect is not doubtful. Certain exceptions do not prove the contrary, any more than the existence of criminals proves the law to be of none effect.

In regard to the matter of Churches, it is necessary to lay stress on the fact, that what we claim is freedom within the limits of civil society, and that we neither claim to be outside the law nor to exercise control over politics. For the whole question is prejudiced by recollections of the Middle Ages and the seventeenth century. Then, in one sense the Church was free, or seemed to be so; but, as I said last time, she was still under the same notion of State autocracy as that of the ancient world, and consequently she understood by freedom supremacy: she demanded the proscription of all those who did not accept her discipline: she identified citizenship with Churchmanship, and she claimed to dictate on religious grounds the law and policy of the State. Much of the prejudice against the just claims of religious bodies arises from the recollection of these facts, and the evils of clerical immunities. Benefit of clergy in the Middle Ages had more in it's favour than is often supposed; it served to mitigate the barbarity of the ordinary law, and it set limits to a royal authority which was striving by every means to become absolute. Yet it did mean the definite withdrawal, not of all justice, but of the protection afforded by the King's Courts from all persons injured by a clerk, and you know how wide was the interpretation given to this. Boniface VIII, at the close of the thirteenth century, went further, and denied the right of the civil courts to enforce the payment of debts by the clergy, and of the State to tax them in the famous Bull *Clericis Laicos*.

...

Other instances are ready to hand. There is the social question. Moved by the intolerable wrongs and oppressions of our industrial system, with its spectacle of thousands of lives maimed and wasted and born with an evil environment, men are apt to claim that it is the duty of Christians as such to adopt some particular remedy, and to identify the Gospel with some definite organisation of society. That Churchmen ought to have a conscience in these matters is true; that it is the province of all who are teachers in the Church to awaken this conscience and to make their hearers far more uncomfortable than they are with the existing régime is certain. They ought to preach to them the duty of forming political or economic opinions with such regard to justice, such careful inquiry, and disinterested zeal for the whole people, and not merely a class, as they may. They may warn them against the danger of opposition to changes owing to the prejudices of their own environment or the fear of being less well off. They ought to preach, much more than they do, that a Christian ought to be prepared to forego sources of income or methods of business open to others, and to scrutinise the undertakings from which his own income is derived; to be considerate to employés, to servants of every kind; to be less extravagant in clothes or ornaments than those who are not Christians. Of this teaching we have all too little. The average layman of the comfortable class seems to have little notion that his standard ought to be, in any way, higher than that of his neighbours over the way who are not Christians; and his sons, and still more his daughters, have, for the most part, even less. Of course there are exceptions; but I am speaking of the ordinary churchgoer. But, whereas so much is needed here, too little is given. So far as many of those who are concerned with these matters go, an effort is made to indicate that he must, as a Christian, be in favour of this or that scheme, the Minority Report of the Poor Law for instance, or else his attention is directed to vast schemes of social reorganisation which he can do little to forward, and, in any case, are unlikely to be realised, save in a far future. I do not say that he should not be directed to consider the evils of the capitalist system or bidden to seek a solution. I wish our congregations were roused to this more and more. But I do not think any policy ought to be forwarded by the Church as a corporate society, and imposed in its name in a State of which Churchmanship has no longer anything to do with the qualifications of a citizen. Those who take their ethical ideas from Nietzsche or their practice from Gabriele d'Annunzio, are hardly likely to be in favour of Christian solutions; and they have every whit as much a place in the State as you or I. The evils of capitalism are "gross, open, huge as mountains," and the oppression of the poor cries to heaven; what we need to persuade Church people is of their own duty in regard to their own wealth and the means of getting it. Consider how vast would be the change if every regular communicant in the Church of England—we will omit the rest for the moment—were sincerely to embrace the maxim of St. Paul, that "having food and raiment we ought therewith to be content," and, without descending from the legitimate expenses of his station, were for himself or his children to give up thinking of a large income as the one desideratum; were to cease judging occupations at their cash value; were to limit himself severely in the matter of motor–cars, hotels, theatres, and clothes for his daughters and to give the rest in charity, and to spend time saved from amusements in some form of social work. If those who have a competence, whether earned or inherited, were no longer to be driven by the ceaseless desire for more and ambition for their children, there would be a revolution in the face of things, and many of our problems would solve themselves. So much energy would be set free for worthy objects that the tone of the nation and social life would speedily be raised. Now, I do not see how such things can be preached to an agnostic or a hedonist; they are absurd on his principles. But they ought not only to be preached but practised by all communicant members of the Christian Church. If in no age can we expect perfection in these matters, and must always allow for a fringe of those of lower standard, the quiet worldliness of many and the self-complacent enjoyment of position by really devout Christians are perhaps the peculiar evil of the Church of England.

What I am anxious to emphasize is that, primarily, the business of Christians is with the moral standard of their own society and with themselves as its members. The raising of that will gradually bring about the elevation of the great mass of those who do not belong to it. So long as Churchmen do not see, except in a few matters, such as Sunday observance and sexual morality, any real reason why they should have any higher standard than the world at large, so long is the Christian Church failing in its mission. And the attempt to confuse this object with that of securing a better social organisation to be imposed by law on the whole nation seems to me likely to enfeeble the former without ultimately strengthening the latter. We want an enormously heightened public opinion within the Church, and then it is bound to affect the world at large. That is what happened in the early days of the Church. Any attempt to impose the opposite doctrine seems to me partly to be a survival from the régime of the seventeenth century, and from the theocratic ideals which Puritans and Carolines alike inherited from the Middle Ages; and partly due to the definite effort to establish an all-embracing humanitarian Church-State, which would ultimately mean the destruction of all freedom in religious bodies. For the unitary doctrine of the State leads only, in very rare instances, to the establishment of the claims of the Church (which from this standpoint are always illegitimate), and then they only take the form of supremacy. In nine cases out of ten it means the secularising of the Church, and the dominance of Erastianism. We can see this at the present moment. The attempt to force the Church law of marriage on all, the refusal to let the State go her own way provided we can go ours, has led, as a matter of fact, to the strangest indiscretions. Language is sometimes used which appears to mean that the House of Commons as at present constituted is the true interpreter of the words of our Lord about adultery. A recent book by the Dean of Ripon on *Natural Christianity* shows a desire to admit all persons to its privileges on the ground of nationality, apart from any question of religion. Others raise the cry of sectarianism whenever any attempt is made to enforce a rule of the Church, oblivious of the fact that unless you definitely enforce religious belief, the Christian Church, however broadly defined, can be only a sect, a part of the modern nation. Sectarianism, in the sense in which it is condemned by Canon Hensley Henson, the Dean of Ripon, or the Editor of the *Spectator,* is not the evil fruit of High Churchmanship; it is the result of the principle of toleration. Where all beliefs are held, those who profess any one can be no more than a part, and thus unity in belief will ultimately make them a society, *i.e.* a sect. Even if you reduce Christianity to a Unitarian Modernism, Christians will still be distinct from those who have no faith in the other world; and that difference will enormously differentiate their whole life and standards of value. Even if you go further, and identify Christianity with a vague humanitarianism, independent of faith or unbelief in God, still there will be those who do not hold it. For instance, the followers of Nietzsche would certainly have been excluded from any such body; and then even a Positivist Christianity, with the motto of kindness as its one maxim, would have to be ultimately separated off, *i.e.* a sect in a world where no restriction is laid upon opinion.

We cannot escape sectarianism even by sacrificing the creeds; still less by attempting a wholly unreal identification of the Church with the nation, an identification which had ceased to represent all the facts even in the time of Hooker, and has been becoming less true ever since. Neither, on the other hand, in such a world can you without disaster attempt to impose the standards of the Church on the whole mass of your countrymen, except in so far as they still rule in some matters on other grounds. Every attempt to raise the code of the nation to that of the Church leads, if unsuccessful, to an attempt to lower the code of the Church to that of the world, because it proceeds from a notion that at bottom the two are identical. Thus if the lax party gets the upper hand it will compel the Church to conform to its standards, an attempt which is being made on all hands just now. The two societies are distinct—distinct in origin, in aim, and (if you have toleration) in personnel. The smaller is never likely, as things are, to control the larger. If she attempt to do so she will be beaten, and in the process be like to lose her own freedom. The Puritans attempted to raise the nation to their own notions of a high morality. The consequence was seen after the Restoration. It is the essence of the Church to be different from the world, and her mission to proclaim that difference. Whenever men try to sanctify the world by raising it to the level of the Church, they commonly succeed only in lowering the life of the Church to accommodate it to the practice of the world. The two centuries which began with Pope Boniface VIII ended with Alexander VI.

19. William Temple – What Christians Stand for in the Secular World

The distinction between the tasks of Church and of society, of churchmen and citizens, is seldom clearly drawn; and the result is confusion and impotence. Either Christians try to act as churchmen in the world, only to find that the world refuses to be ordered on the principles proper to the Church; or else they look out for the secular policy most congenial to their Christian outlook, only to find that their Christianity is a dispensable adjunct of no practical importance.

Church and State are different, though they may comprise the same people; and each has its own appropriate sphere and method. Churchman and citizen are words with a different connotation even when they denote the same person; and that person, the individual Christian, has to exercise both of these different functions. As long as he acts quite unreflectively he is likely to maintain the distinction and the appropriate balance fairly well, though he is also likely as a citizen to be excessively swayed by currents of purely secular thought and feeling. Moreover, it is almost impossible in these days to retain that naive spontaneity. Reflection or its fruits are thrust upon us, and when once that process has started it must be carried through. It is half-baked reflection which is most perilous.

In the nineteenth century men still assumed a Law of God as universally supreme. In this country, at any rate, it was widely believed that God, whose nature was revealed in the Gospel and proclaimed by the Church, was also the orderer of the world and of life; in only a few quarters was the alienation of the actual order from any subjection to the God and Father of Jesus Christ perceived or stated. The Church was, therefore, free to concentrate its main energies on its distinctive task of proclaiming the Gospel of redemption, without any sense of incongruity with the ordering of life in the world outside. Theologians could undertake the task of showing that Christianity enables us to "make sense" of the world with the meaning "show that it is sense." And those of us who were trained under those influences went on talking like that; I was still talking like that when Hitler became Chancellor of the German Reich.

All that seems remote today. We must still claim that Christianity enables us to "make sense" of the world, not meaning that we can show that it is sense, but with the more literal and radical meaning of making into sense what, till it is transformed, is largely nonsense—a disordered chaos waiting to be reduced to order as the Spirit of God gives it shape. Our problem is to envisage the task of the Church in a largely alien world. Some would have us go back to the example of the primitive Church or of the contemporary Church entering on an evangelistic enterprise in a heathen country; this means the abandonment of all effort to influence the ordering of life in the secular world and concentration of all effort upon what is, no doubt, the primary task of the Church, the preaching of the Gospel and the maintenance among converts of a manner of life conformed to the Gospel. They advocate a spiritual return to the catacombs in the hope that the Church may there build up its strength till, having the shield of faith intact and the sword of the Spirit sharp, it may come forth to a new conquest of a world which has meanwhile returned to a new dark age.

But this is a shirking of responsibility. The Church must never of its own free will withdraw from the conflict. If it is driven to the catacombs it will accept its destiny and set itself there to maintain and to deepen its faith. But it cannot abandon its task of guiding society so far as society consents to be guided. It has a special illumination which it is called to bring to bear on the whole range of human relationships, and if, for lack of this, civilization founders, the Church will have failed in its duty to men and to its Lord.

But if so, it must be active in two distinct ways. It must at all costs maintain its own spiritual life, the fellowship which this life creates, and the proclamation of the Gospel in all its fullness, wherein this life expresses itself. Here it must insist on all those truths from which its distinctive quality is derived—that God is Creator and man with the world His creature; that man has usurped the place of God in an endeavour to order his own life after his own will; that in the Birth, Life, Death, Resurrection and Ascension of Jesus Christ God has Himself taken action for the redemption of mankind; that in the Holy Spirit given by the Father through the Son to those who respond to the Gospel, power is offered for a life of obedience to God which is otherwise impossible for men; that those who are thus empowered by the Spirit are a fellowship of the Lord fitly called the Church; that in that Church are appointed means whereby men may receive and perpetually renew their union with their Lord and with one another in Him, and so increase in the Holy Spirit. All this must be maintained and proclaimed. And unless the Church is firm in its witness to its own faith, it will have no standing-ground from which to address the world.

But standing firm upon its own ground, it can and must address the world. By what convictions constantly in mind will Christians called to such a task direct their actions?

Basic Decisions

There is in fact more widespread agreement than is generally supposed with regard to these basic convictions. I do not mean that they are universally accepted among Christians; there are currents of Christian thought in all denominations which are directly opposed to some of them; and many devout Christians have as yet not turned their attention in this direction at all. But among Christians who have seriously and thoughtfully faced the historical situation with which we are dealing there is, as I have proved by testing, an observable convergence which may be presented in five affirmations; but as these are acts of faith, resting on a deliberate choice and involving a specific determination of the will, I speak of them rather as Decisions.

1. For God who has spoken

A vague theism is futile. The cutting edge of faith is due to its definiteness. The kind of deity established (if any is at all) by the various "proofs"—ontological, cosmological and the like—is completely insufficient; it is usually little else than the rationality of the world presupposed in all argument about the world. The Christian has made a decision for God who has spoken—in nature, in history, in prophets, in Christ.

It follows that the value of man and the meaning of history is to be found in the nature and character of God, who has thus made Himself known. The value of a man is not what he is in and for himself—humanism; not what he is for society—fascism and communism; but what he is worth to God. This is the principle of Christian equality; the supreme importance of every man is that he is the brother for whom Christ died. This is compatible with many forms of social differentiation and subdivision. It is not compatible with any scheme which subjects a man's personality to another man or to any group of men such as the government or administrators of the State.

The purpose of God is the governing reality of history. Progress is approximation to conformity with it and fulfilment of it; deviation from it is retrogression. The nature of God is a righteousness which is perfect in love; His purpose, therefore, is the establishment of justice in all relationships of life—personal, social, economic, cultural, political, international. Many "humanists" share that aim, and Christians may well co-operate with them in practical policies from time to time. But a "decision for God" involves a sharp separation in thought, and, therefore, in the long run in practice, from many dominant tendencies of our time which seek the whole fulfilment of man's life in his earthly existence.

God has given to man freedom to decide for Him or against Him. This freedom is fundamental, for without it there could be only automatic obedience, not the obedience of freely offered loyalty. God always respects this freedom to the uttermost; therefore, freedom is fundamental to Christian civilization.

But though man is free to rebel against God, and can indeed do marvels through science and human wisdom in controlling his own destiny, yet he cannot escape the sovereignty of God. To deviate from the course of God's purpose is to incur disaster sooner or later—and sooner rather than later in so far as the deviation is great. The disaster ensues by "natural laws" as scientists use that phrase—that is by the causal processes inherent in the natural order. But these laws are part of God's creation, and the disasters which they bring are His judgments.

Yet because man has so great a power to shape his own destiny he is responsible for using this. Belief in God is used by many Christians as a means of escape from the hard challenge of life; they seek to evade the responsibility of decision by throwing it upon God, who has Himself laid it upon them. Faith in God should be not a substitute for scientific study, but a stimulus to it, for our intellectual faculties are God's gift to us. Consequently a decision for "God who has spoken" involves commitment to the heroic, intellectual and practical task of giving to spiritual faith a living content over against the immensely effective this-worldliness of Marxism and secular humanism, while absorbing the elements of truth which these movements have often perceived more clearly and emphasized more strongly than Christians in recent times have done.

2. For neighbour

As the first great commandment is that we love God with all our being, so the second is that we love our neighbour as ourselves. Here we are not concerned with that duty, but with the fact that underlies it whether we do our duty or not—not with what ought to be, but with what *is*. This is that we stand before God—that is, in ultimate reality—as bound to one another in a complete equality in His family. Personality is inherently social; only in social groupings can it mature, or indeed fully exist. These groupings must be small enough to enable each individual to feel (not only to think) that he can influence the quality and activity of the group, so that he is responsible for it, and also that it needs his contribution, so that he is responsible to it. He must feel that he belongs to it and that it belongs to him.

It is characteristic of much democratic thought that it seeks to eliminate or to depreciate all associations intermediate between the individual and the State. These, as the foci of local or other departmental loyalties, are nurseries of tradition and, therefore, obnoxious in the eyes of some prophets of progress. But it is in and through them that the individual exercises responsible choice or, in other words, is effectively free. The State is too large; the individual feels impotent and unimportant over against it. In his local, or functional, or cultural association he may count for something in the State, so that through his association he may influence the State itself, as alone he can scarcely do.

Thus the limitless individualism of revolutionary thought, which aims at setting the individual on his own feet that he may, with his fellows, direct the State, defeats its own object and becomes the fount of totalitarianism. If we are to save freedom we must proceed, as Maritain urges, from democracy of the individual to democracy of the person, and recollect that personality achieves itself in the lesser groupings within the State—in the family, the school, the guild, the trade union, the village, the city, the county. These are no enemies of the State, and that State will in fact be stable which deliberately fosters these lesser objects of loyalty as contributors to its own wealth of tradition and inheritance.

Christianity has always favoured these lesser units. The Catholic Church itself is composed of dioceses, in each of which the structure of the Church is complete, representing the family of God gathered about the Bishop as its Father in God. And the civilization which the Church most deeply influenced was characterized by an almost bewildering efflorescence of local and functional guilds of every sort.

The revolutionary and mechanistic type of thought finds its classical and fontal expression in Descartes' disastrous deliverance, *Cogito, ergo sum.* Thus the individual self-consciousness became central. Each man looks out on a world which he sees essentially as related to himself. (This is the very quality of original sin, and it seems a pity to take it as the constitutive principle of our philosophy.) He sets himself to explore this world that he may understand and increasingly control it. In the world he finds a great variety of "things." He studies these in his sciences of physics, chemistry, and biology, according to their observable characteristics. Among the "things" are some which require a further complication of his method of study, giving rise to psychology. But though he is now allowing for instincts, emotions, sentiments, purposes and similar factors, his attitude is the same as toward "things" which lacked these qualities. He organizes these psychological "things" in ways calculated to extract from them the result he desires. He may, for example, as an industrial manager, introduce welfare work because he can in that way increase output. He might even, in an ultimate blasphemy, supply his troops with chaplains with no other object except to keep up military morale.

Now, in all this he is treating persons as things. His relation to them is an "I—it" relation, not an "I—Thou" relation. This latter he only reaches so far as he loves or hates, and only in this relation does he treat persons as they really are. He may do very much what the enlightened man of purely "scientific" outlook does: he provides for the welfare of employees, if he is an employer, and is, of course, glad that it pays; but that is not his motive: his motive is that they are human beings like himself. So he supplies what he would wish to have, and hopes and works for the time when they will not depend on him for what their welfare requires, but will be in a position to supply it to themselves. For he will prefer fellowship to domination.

It is in love and hate—the truly "personal" relationships—that we confront our neighbour as he is, a man like ourselves. Even hate has an insight denied to the egoist who coldly manipulates human beings as his pawns, and men resent it less. Most of us would rather be bullied than mechanically organized. But hate too is blind, partly from its own nature, partly because men hide from an enemy, as they do from a cynic, what is deepest and tenderest in their nature. Only love—the purpose of sheer goodwill intensified by sympathetic feeling—gives real insight and understanding.

We cannot command that love. Those who live with God become increasingly filled with it. But none of us can so rely on feeling it as safely to plan his life on the supposition of its emergence when required; and when we consider secular society as a whole we know that we cannot count on it in volume adequate to the need. Indeed, in the relationships of politics, commerce and industry it cannot find expression and can scarcely arise. To this we shall return. What we have to notice at present is that the primary relation between persons—by which in every generation multitudes of men and women have, consciously or unconsciously, guided their lives—has been relegated to a subordinate place by men's headlong eagerness to explore the secrets and exploit the resources of this wonderful universe. In the concentration on wealth we have tended to overlook the more fundamental and more difficult problems of the adjustment of our personal relations to one another.

It is a question whether it was primarily a false understanding of reality that gave free rein to men's egoisms and ambitions; or whether their inherent selfishness inclined them to misread the true nature of things. To whichever cause we assign the greater weight, men's self-centred aims and a false philosophy have co-operated to bring about a profound misunderstanding of the meaning of human life and to create the state of things which we see today.

Science, which has been perhaps the chief influence in giving its distinctive cast and colour to the modern consciousness, is essentially an expression of the individualistic approach. As scientist, the individual stands over against the world, measuring, weighing, experimenting, judging, deciding. The gains which have resulted from this approach and activity are incalculable. We can today only regret the timidity which led Christians in the past to oppose the advances of science. No enlightened Christian today would question the right of science to investigate everything that it is capable of investigating. It is certain that the problems of our complex society cannot be mastered without a continuous expansion of scientific knowledge, more particularly in the field of the social sciences.

It is none the less vital for the health of society that we should realize that, while man is meant to have dominion—and we cannot, therefore, be too thankful for the gift of science as an instrument, and are under an obligation, to make the fullest use of it—the scientific attitude is only one approach to reality and not the most fundamental and important. As scientist the individual is monarch; he sits in the seat of judgment and asks what questions he will. But the situation is fundamentally changed when he encounters another person who, like himself, is monarch in relation to the world of things. In the encounter with another person or group he is no longer free to ask what questions he will and to order things according to his choice. Questions may be *addressed* to him from a source over which he has no control, and he has to *answer*. He is no longer sole judge, but is subject himself to judgment.

This profound difference between these two approaches to reality, which are uninterchangeable, is often hidden from us, because it is always possible to bring the relations between persons into the framework of the self-centred view. After the collision has taken place we can reflect upon it and fit it into our picture of the world. At any moment we can step out of the arena of conflict and take our place on the spectator's bench. So ingrained has the habit become that, without being aware of it, we continually have recourse to this form of escape. There is an immense deal that we can learn about persons with the aid of science; but so long as we study them medically, psychologically, sociologically, we never *meet* them. And it is precisely in meeting that real life consists.

It will need a strong and sustained effort to emancipate ourselves from the one-sidedness of the individualistic attitude and to penetrate to the full meaning of the truth that the fundamental reality of life is the interplay, conflict and continuous adjustment of a multitude of different finite points of view, both of individuals and of groups.

Acknowledgment of this truth would create a wholly different spiritual and intellectual climate from that which has prevailed in recent centuries. Men would still strive, no doubt, to gratify their desires and seek their own aggrandisement; they would not desist from the attempt to domineer over others. But these tendencies would be kept within bounds by a public opinion more aware than at present that in pursuing these courses men are doing violence both to their own nature and to the true nature of things. It would be recognized that men can live at peace with one another only if each individual and each group renounces the claim to have the final and decisive word. Society would have restored to it the sanity which comes from an understanding of human finitude.

A decision for sociality as the basic truth of human existence would create an outlook and temper so different from that which has been dominant in the modern era now drawing to its close as to create a new epoch in human history.

Between the decision for God and the decision for neighbour there is a most intimate connection. In the New Testament these are always intertwined. We should in all remembrance of God remember also our neighbour, and in all thought of our neighbour think also of God. Our highest act of worship is not a mystic "flight of the alone to the Alone," but a fellowship meal, a Holy Communion. We come before God as "Our Father" to whom all His other children have the same right of access; the truth about God is, among other things, His universal Fatherhood. So too the truth about our neighbour is not only what he is to us nor what he is in himself, but above all what he is to God. His relationship to God is the ultimate fact about him, and if we are to think rightly about him or act rightly towards him, we must have that relationship full in view. We must cease to think and feel either in the vertical dimension wherein we are related to God, or in the horizontal dimension wherein we are related to our neighbours, and substitute the triangular relationship, God—Self—Neighbour, Neighbour—God—Self.

3. For man as rooted in nature

The most important thing about man is his relation to God and to other men. But his life has also been set in a natural order, which is God's creation. A fundamental duty which man owes to God is reverence for the world as God has made it. Failure to understand and acknowledge this is a principal cause of the present ineffectiveness of the Christian witness in relation to the temporal order. It is one of the chief points at which a fundamental change of outlook is demanded from Christians. Our false outlook is most of all apparent in the exploitation of the physical world. As animals we are part of nature, dependent on it and inter-dependent with it. We must reverence its economy and co-operate with its processes. If we have dominion over it, that is as predominant partners, not as superior beings who are entitled merely to extract from it what gratifies our desires.

There are two major points at which failure to recognize that man's life is rooted in nature and natural associations leads to mistaken and vain attempts to solve the problem of society. The first grave error characteristic of our time is a too exclusive occupation with politics to the neglect of other equally important spheres of human life and activity. It is assumed that the ills from which society is suffering can be cured, if only we have the will and the right aims. It is forgotten that man is not a being ruled wholly by his reason and conscious aims. His life is inextricably intertwined with nature and with the natural associations of family and livelihood, tradition and culture. When the connection with these sources from which the individual life derives nourishment and strength is broken, the whole life of society becomes enfeebled.

Recognition of the vital importance of centres of human life and activity that underlie and precede the sphere of politics must not be made an excuse for evading the political decisions which have to be made in the near future. It is not a way of escape from political responsibility. Far-reaching decisions in the political sphere may be the only means of creating the conditions in which the non-political spheres can regain vitality and health; but the recovery of health in those spheres is in its turn an indispensable preliminary to political sanity and vigour.

The present plight of our society arises in large part from the break-down of these natural forms of association and of a cultural pattern formed to a great extent under Christian influences. New dogmas and assumptions about the nature of reality have taken the place of the old. New rituals of various kinds are giving shape to men's emotional life. The consequence is that while their aims still remain to a large extent Christian, their souls are moulded by alien influences. The real crisis of our time is thus not primarily a moral, but a cultural crisis. In so far as this is true, the remedy is not to be found in what the Church is at present principally doing—insisting on ideals—or in efforts to intensify the will to pursue them. The cure has to be sought in the quite different direction of seeking to re-establish a unity between men's ultimate beliefs and habits and their conscious aims.

Christians must free their minds from illusions and become aware of the impotence of moral advice and instruction when it is divorced from the social structures which by their perpetual suggestion form the soul. It must be remembered that when exhortation and suggestion are at variance, suggestion always wins. Christians must take their part in recreating a sound social and cultural life and thereby healing the modern divided consciousness, in which head and heart have become divorced and men's conscious purposes are no longer in harmony with the forces which give direction and tone to their emotional life.

But, secondly, if Christians are to have a substantial influence on the temporal order, it is not only necessary that they should have a clearer and deeper understanding of the positive, character-forming function of the non-political forms of human association, but their whole approach to social and political questions needs to be much more realistic than it has commonly been in the past. The Christian social witness must be radically dissociated from the idealism which assumes men to be so free spiritually that aims alone are decisive. There is need of a much clearer recognition of the part played in human behaviour by subconscious egoisms, interests, deceptions and determinisms imposed by man's place in nature and history, by his cultural patterns and by his sinfulness.

It has to be recognized that society is made up of competing centres of power, and that the separate existence of contending vitalities, and not only human sinfulness, makes the elimination of power impossible. What has to be aimed at is such a distribution and balance of power that a measure of justice may be achieved even among those who are actuated in the main by egoistic and sinful impulses. It is a modest aim, but observance of political life leaves no doubt that this must be its primary concern.

If Christians are to act with effect in the temporal order, it is necessary, as was said at the beginning, to distinguish more clearly than is commonly done between the two distinct spheres of society and Church, or the different realms of Law and Gospel. We also need a clearer and deeper understanding of the difference between justice, human love and Christian charity. The last transcends both justice and human fellowship while it has contacts with each. Associations cannot love one another; a trade union cannot love an employers' federation, nor can one national State love another. The members of one may love the members of the other so far as opportunities of intercourse allow. That will help in negotiations; but it will not solve the problem of the relations between the two groups. Consequently, the relevance of Christianity in these spheres is quite different from what many Christians suppose it to be. Christian charity manifests itself in the temporal order as a supranatural discernment of, and adhesion to, *justice* in relation to the equilibrium of power. It is precisely fellowship or human love, with which too often Christian charity is mistakenly equated, that is *not* seriously relevant in that sphere. When the two are identified, it is just those who are most honest and realistic in their thinking and practice that are apt to be repelled from Christianity.

There is scarcely any more urgent task before the Church than that this whole complex of problems should be thought out afresh, and it is obviously a task which can be successfully undertaken only in the closest relation with the experience of those who are exposed to the daily pressures of the economic and political struggle. The third decision involves a commitment to a new realm in Christian thought and action; the citizen and the churchman should remain distinct though the same individual should be both.

4. For history

It is a question of vital importance whether history makes any fundamental difference to our understanding of reality. The Greek view was that it does not, and through the great thinkers of antiquity the Hellenic view still exercises a powerful influence over the modern mind.

In the Christian view, on the other hand, it is in history that the ultimate meaning of human existence is both revealed and actualized. If history is to have a meaning, there must be some central point at which that meaning is decisively disclosed. The Jews found the meaning of their history in the call of Abraham, the deliverance from Egypt, and the covenant with God following upon it. For Mohammedans the meaning of history has its centre in Mohammed's flight from Mecca. For Marxists the culminating meaning is found in the emergence of the proletariat. The Nazis vainly pinned their hopes to the coming of Hitler. For Christians the decisive meaning of history is given in Christ.

Christianity is thus essentially a continuing action in history determining the course of human development. The Christian understanding of history has much closer affinities with the Marxist view, in which all assertions about the nature of man are inseparably bound up with the dynamics of his historical existence, and with other dynamic views of history, which understand the world in terms of conflict, decision and fate, and regard history as belonging to the essence of existence, than with the interpretations of Christianity in terms of idealistic thought which were lately prevalent.

A decision for history confronts us with two urgent practical tasks. The first is to disabuse the minds of people of the notion, which is widespread, and infects to a large extent current Christian preaching, that Christianity is in essence a system of morals, so that they have lost all understanding of the truth, so prominent in the New Testament, that to be a Christian is to share in a new movement of life, and to co-operate with new regenerating forces that have entered into history.

The second task is to restore hope to the world through a true understanding of the relation of the Kingdom of God to history, as a transcendent reality that is continually seeking, and partially achieving, embodiment in the activities and conflicts of the temporal order. Without this faith men can only seek escape from life in modes of thought which, pushed to their logical conclusion, deprive politics, and even the ethical struggle, of real significance, or succumb to a complete secularization of life in which all principles disintegrate in pure relativity, and opportunism is the only wisdom.

5. For the Gospel and the Church

This understanding brings us face to face with the decision whether or not we acknowledge Christ as the centre of history. He is for Christians the source and vindication of those perceptions of the true nature of reality which we have already considered. In the tasks of society Christians can and must co-operate with all those, Christians or non-Christians, who are pursuing aims that are in accord with the divinely intended purpose of man's temporal life. But Christians are constrained to believe that in the power of the Gospel of redemption and in the fellowship of the

Church lies the chief hope of the restoration of the temporal order to health and sanity.

What none but utopians can hope for the secular world should be matter of actual experience in the Church. For the Church is the sphere where the redemptive act of God lifts men into the most intimate relation with Himself and through that with one another. When this is actually experienced the stream of redemptive power flows out from the Church through the lives of its members into the society which they influence. But only a Church firm in the faith set forth in outline earlier in this essay can give to its members the inspiration which they need for meeting the gigantic responsibilities of this age. Spiritual resources far beyond anything now in evidence will be needed. It may be that the greatness of the challenge will bring home to Christians how impotent they are in themselves, and so lead to that renewal which will consist in re-discovery of the sufficiency of God and manifestation of His power.

20. Dietrich Bonhoeffer and Karl Barth – The Aryan Clauses and Further Correspondence

The Aryan Clauses

Hitler had made no secret of his attitude to the Jews. He had risen to power on a wave of anti-semitism. But before the final solution of the Jewish problem was put into effect, with its hideous massacres, he legalised a series of disabilities. The most important of these were contained in the Aryan Clauses, which disqualified those of Jewish origin, regardless of religious affiliation, from holding office in the state. This disqualification was extended to those married to Jews. The peculiar relation between church and state in Germany, which to an outsider looks like a system which makes ministers into state officials, inevitably imposed the same disqualification on those seeking church appointments. These clauses were immediately attacked by all who saw in them a perversion of the Christian teaching. The German Christians accepted them as a consequence of their conviction that the German church should be truly German. Bonhoeffer was first in the field to lead the attack.

The Church and the Jewish Question

Luther 1546: 'We would still show them the Christian doctrine and ask them to turn and accept the Lord whom they should by rights have honoured before we did.' ... 'Where they repent, leave their usury, and accept Christ, we would gladly regard them as our brothers.'

Luther 1523: 'If the Apostles, who also were Jews, had dealt with us Gentiles as we Gentiles deal with the Jews, there would have been no Christians among the Gentiles. But seeing that they have acted in such a brotherly way towards us, we in turn should act in a brotherly way towards the Jews in case we might convert some. For we ourselves are still not yet fully their equals, much less their superiors.... But now we use force against them ... what good will we do them with that? Similarly, how will we benefit them by forbidding them to live and work and have other human fellowship with us, thus driving them to practise usury?'

The fact, unique in history, that the Jew has been made subject to special laws by the state solely because of the race to which he belongs and quite apart from his religious beliefs, raises two new problems for the theologian, which must be examined separately. What is the church's attitude to this action by the state? And what should the church do as a result of it? That is one question. The other is, what attitude should the church take to its members who are baptised Jews? Both questions can only be answered in the light of a true concept of the church.

I

Without doubt, the Church of the Reformation has no right to address the state directly in its specifically political actions. It has neither to praise nor to censure the laws of the state, but must rather affirm the state to be God's order of preservation in a godless world; it has to recognise the state's ordinances, good or bad as they appear from a humanitarian point of view, and to understand that they are based on the sustaining will of God amidst the chaotic godlessness of the world. This view of the state's action on the part of the church is far removed from any form of moralism and is distinct from humanitarianism of any shade through the radical nature of the gulf between the standpoint of the Gospel and the standpoint of the Law. The action of the state remains free from the church's intervention. There are no piqued or pedantic comments from the church here. History is made not by the church, but by the state; but of course only the church, which bears witness to the coming of God in history, knows what history, and therefore what the state, is. And precisely because of this knowledge, it alone testifies to the penetration of history by God in Christ and lets the state continue to make history. Without doubt the Jewish question is one of the historical problems which our state must deal with, and without doubt the state is justified in adopting new methods here. It remains the concern of humanitarian associations and individual Christians who feel themselves called to the task, to remind the state of the moral side of any of its measures, i.e. on occasions to accuse the state of offences against morality. Any strong state needs such associations and such individuals, and will to some extent take good care of them. It is an insight into the finer arts of statesmanship which knows how to make use of these spokesmen in their relative significance. In the same way, a church which is essentially regarded as a cultural function of the state must at times contact the state with such reminders, and must do so all the more strongly as the state takes the church to itself, i.e. ascribes to it essentially moral and pedagogic tasks.

The true church of Christ, however, which lives solely from the Gospel and realises the character of the state's actions, will never intervene in the state in such a way as to criticise its history-making actions, from the standpoint of some humanitarian ideal. It recognises the absolute necessity of the use of force in this world and also the 'moral' injustice of certain concrete acts of the state which are necessarily bound up with the use of force. The church cannot in the first place exert direct political action, for the church does not pretend to have any knowledge of the necessary course of history. Thus even today, in the Jewish question, it cannot address the state directly and demand of it some definite action of a different nature. But that does not mean that it lets political action slip by disinterestedly; it can and should, precisely because it does not moralise in individual instances, continually ask the state whether its action can be justified as legitimate action of the state, i.e. as action which leads to law and order, and not to lawlessness and disorder. It is called to put this question with great emphasis where the state appears to be threatened precisely in its nature as the state, i.e. in its function of creating law and order by means of force. It will have to put this question quite clearly today in the matter of the Jewish question. In so doing it does not encroach on the state's sphere of responsibility, but on the contrary fathers upon the state itself the whole weight of the responsibility for its own particular actions. In this way it frees the state from any charge of moralising and shows precisely thus its appointed function as the preserver of the world. As long as the state continues to create law and order by its acts, even if it be a new law and new order, the church of the Creator, the Mediator and the Redeemer cannot engage in direct political action against it. It may not of course prevent the individual Christian, who knows himself called to the task, from calling the state 'inhuman' on occasion, but *qua* church it will only ask whether the state is bringing about law and order or not.

Now here, of course, the state sees itself to be limited in two respects. Both too much law and order and too little law and order compel the church to speak. There is too little law and order where a group of men becomes lawless, though in real life it is sometimes extraordinarily difficult to distinguish real lawlessness from a formally permitted minimum of law. Even in slavery a minimum of law and order was preserved, and yet a re-introduction of slavery would mean real lawlessness. It is at any rate worth noting that Christian churches tolerated slavery for eighteen centuries and that a new law was made only at a time when the Christian substance of the church could at least be put in question, with the help of the churches, but not essentially or even solely by them. Nevertheless, a step back in this direction would be to the church the expression of a lawless state. It therefore follows that the concept of law is subject to historical change, and this in its turn once again confirms the state in its characteristic history-making law. It is not the church, but the state, which makes and changes the law.

Too little law and order stands in contrast to too much law and order. That means that the state develops its power to such an extent that it deprives Christian preaching and Christian faith (not freedom of conscience—that would be the humanitarian illusion, which is illusory because any life in a state constrains the so-called 'free conscience') of their rights—a grotesque situation, as the state only receives its peculiar rights from this proclamation and from this faith, and enthrones itself by means of them. The church must reject this encroachment of the order of the state precisely because of its better knowledge of the state and of the limitations of its action. The state which endangers the Christian proclamation negates itself.

All this means that there are three possible ways in which the church can act towards the state: in the first place, as has been said, it can ask the state whether its actions are legitimate and in accordance with its character as state, i.e. it can throw the state back on its responsibilities. Secondly, it can aid the victims of state action. The church has an unconditional obligation to the victims of any ordering of society, even if they do not belong to the Christian community. 'Do good to all men.' In both these courses of action, the church serves the free state in its free way, and at times when laws are changed the church may in no way withdraw itself from these two tasks. The third possibility is not just to bandage the victims under the wheel, but to put a spoke in the wheel itself. Such action would be direct political action, and is only possible and desirable when the church sees the state fail in its function of creating law and order, i.e. when it sees the state unrestrainedly bring about too much or too little law and order. In both these cases it must see the existence of the state, and with it its own existence, threatened. There would be too little law if any group of subjects were deprived of their rights, too much where the state intervened in the character of the church and its proclamation, e.g. in the forced exclusion of baptised Jews from our Christian congregations or in the prohibition of our mission to the Jews. Here the Christian church would find itself *in statu confessionis* and here the state would be in the act of negating itself. A state which includes within itself a terrorised church has lost its most faithful servant. But even this third action of the church, which on occasion leads to conflict with the existing state, is only the paradoxical expression of its ultimate recognition of the state; indeed, the church itself knows itself to be called here to protect the state *qua* state from itself and to preserve it. In the Jewish problem the first two possibilities will be the compelling demands of the hour. The necessity of direct political action by the church is, on the other hand, to be decided at any time by an 'Evangelical Council' and cannot therefore ever by casuistically decided beforehand.

Now the measures of the state towards Judaism in addition stand in a quite special context for the church. The church of Christ has never lost sight of the thought that the 'chosen people', who nailed the redeemer of the world to the cross, must bear the curse for its action through a long history of suffering. 'Jews are the poorest people among all nations upon earth, they are tossed to and fro, they are scattered here and there in all lands, they have no certain place where they could remain safely and must always be afraid that they will be driven out ...' (Luther, *Table Talk*). But the history of the suffering of this people, loved and punished by God, stands under the sign of the final homecoming of the people of Israel to its God. And this home-coming happens in the conversion of Israel to Christ. 'When the time comes that this people humbles itself and penitently departs from the sins of its fathers to which it has clung with fearful stubbornness to this day, and calls down upon itself the blood of the Crucified One for reconciliation, then the world will wonder at the miracle that God works, that he works with this people! And then the overweening Philistines will be like dung on the streets and like chaff on the rooftops. Then he will gather this people from all nations and bring it back to Canaan. O Israel, who is like thee? Happy the people whose God is the Lord!' (S. Menken, 1795). The conversion of Israel, that is to be the end of the people's period of suffering. From here the Christian church sees the history of the people of Israel with trembling as God's own, free, fearful way with his people. It knows that no nation of the world can be finished with this mysterious people, because God is not yet finished with it. Each new attempt to 'solve the Jewish problem' comes to nothing on the saving-historical significance of this people; nevertheless, such attempts must continually be made. This consciousness on the part of the church of the curse that bears down upon this people, raises it far above any cheap moralising; instead, as it looks at the rejected people, it humbly recognises itself as a church continually unfaithful to its Lord and looks full of hope to those of the people of Israel who have come home, to those who have come to believe in the one true God in Christ, and knows itself to be bound to them in brotherhood. Thus we have reached the second question.

II

The church cannot allow its actions towards its members to be prescribed by the state. The baptised Jew is a member of our church. Thus the Jewish problem is not the same for the church as it is for the state.

From the point of view of the church of Christ, Judaism is never a racial concept but a religious one. What is meant is not the biologically questionable entity of the Jewish race, but the 'people of Israel'. Now the 'people' of Israel is constituted by the law of God; a man can thus become a Jew by taking the Law upon himself. But no one can become a Jew by race. In the time of the great Jewish mission to the Gentile world there were different stages of membership of Judaism (Schürer, III 3. 4 1909, pp. 150ff.). In the same way, the concept of Jewish-Christianity has religious, not biological content. The Jewish-Christian mission also stretched to Gentile territory (Paul's opponents in the Epistle to the Galatians). There were Gentile Jewish-Christians and Jewish Gentile-Christians.

Thus from the point of view of the church it is not baptised Christians of Jewish race who are Jewish Christians; in the church's view the Jewish Christian is the man who lets membership of the people of God, of the church of Christ, be determined by the observance of a divine law. In contrast, the Gentile Christian knows no presupposition for membership of the people of God, the church of Christ, but the call of God by his Word in Christ.

This difference in the understanding of the appearance of Christ and of the Gospel alone led to the first division of the church of Christ into Jewish Christianity and Gentile Christianity (Apostolic Council!). This cleavage was regarded on both sides partly as intolerable heresy, partly as tolerable schism.

There would be an analogous situation today where a church group within the Reformation Church allowed membership of the church to be determined by the observance of a divine law, for example the racial unity of the members of the community. The Jewish-Christian type materialises where this demand is put irrespectively of whether its proponents belong to the Jewish race or not. Then there is the further possibility that the modern Jewish-Christian type withdraws from the Gentile-Christian community and founds its own church community based on the law. But it is in that case impossible for the church to exclude from the community that part of the community which belongs to the Jewish race because it destroys the legalistic, Jewish-Christian claim. For that would be to demand that the Gentile-Christian community be made Jewish Christian, and that is a claim which it must rightly refuse.

The exclusion of Jews by race from our German church would bring this latter into the Jewish-Christian category. Such an exclusion thus remains impossible for the church.

The only permissible conclusion from the fact of the presence of foreign French, English, etc. communities in Germany is that there is nothing to hinder a voluntary association of Christians of Jewish race in one church (as happened, say, in London in the Jewish-Christian alliance of 1925). But the forced expulsion of Gentile-Christian Jews from Gentile-Christian congregations of German race is in no case permissible, quite apart from the difficulty of demonstrating that these Jews are not Germans (cf. Stöcker's thesis that the Jew becomes a German through his baptism). Such a forced ejection—even if it did not have a corporal, organised character—would still represent a real split in the church, simply because it would raise the racial unity of the church to the status of a law which would have to be fulfilled as a presupposition for church membership. In doing this the church community which did the excluding would constitute itself a Jewish-Christian community.

What is at stake is by no means the question whether our German members of congregations can still tolerate church fellowship with the Jews. It is rather the task of Christian preaching to say: here is the church, where Jew and German stand together under the Word of God; here is the proof whether a church is still the church or not. No one who feels unable to tolerate church fellowship with Christians of Jewish race can be prevented from separating himself from this church fellowship. But it must then be made clear to him with the utmost seriousness that he is thus loosing himself from the place on which the church of Christ stands and that he is thus bringing to reality the Jewish-Christian idea of a religion based on law, i.e. is falling into modern Jewish Christianity. It then still always remains an open question whether such a separation can or cannot be regarded as a tolerable schism. But one must have an extraordinarily restricted view not to see that any attitude of our church towards the baptised Jews among our church people, other than that described above would meet with widespread misunderstanding.

Luther on Psalm 110. 3: There is no other rule or test for who is a member of the people of God or the church of Christ than this: where there is a little band of those who accept this word of the Lord, teach it purely and confess against those who persecute it, and for that reason suffer what is their due.

G.S. II pp. 44–53

This careful statement is typical of Bonhoeffer. It is no diatribe against German Christians, but a carefully worked out theological objection to the Aryan Clauses, based upon a clearly understood doctrine of the church. The resistance was, as always, theological, not political. This issue led to the second exchange of letters with Karl Barth. In June, Barth had published the first of what was to become a very important series of booklets, with the general title, 'Theological Existence Today'. The first dealt with the Aryan Clauses. Bonhoeffer's correspondence began with a comment on this first booklet on the 9th September 1933.

Berlin, 9th September 1933

BONHOEFFER TO BARTH: In your booklet you said that where a church adopted the Aryan Clauses it would cease to be a Christian church. A considerable number of pastors here would agree with you in this view. Now the expected has happened, and I am therefore asking you on behalf of many friends, pastors and students, to let us know whether you feel that it is possible either to remain in a church which has ceased to be a Christian church or to continue to exercise a ministry which has become a privilege for Aryans. We have in the first place drawn up a declaration in which we wish to inform the church authorities that, with the Aryan Clauses, the Evangelical Church of the Old Prussian Union has cut itself off from the church of Christ. We want to wait for the answer to it, i.e. to see whether the signatories will be dismissed from their posts or whether they will be allowed to say something of this sort unmolested. Several of us are now very drawn to the idea of the Free Church. The difference between our present situation and that of Luther lies in the fact that the Catholic Church expelled Luther under its laws against heretics, while our church authorities can do nothing of the sort because they completely lack any concept of heresy. It is therefore by no means simple to argue directly from Luther's attitude. I know that many people now wait on your judgment; I also know that most of them are of the opinion that you will counsel us to wait until we are thrown out. In fact, there are people who have already been thrown out, i.e. the Jewish Christians, and the same thing will very soon happen to others on grounds which have absolutely no connection with the church. What is the consequence for us if the church really is not just an individual congregation in any one place? How do things stand with the solidarity of the Pastorate? When is there any possibility of leaving the church? There can be no doubt at all that the *status confessionis* has arrived; what we are by no means clear about is how the *confessio* is most appropriately expressed today.

I permit myself at the same time to send you a copy of the draft of a confession of faith which was made in Bethel and will appear in print very soon. I was expressly asked in Bethel to request your view and your comments. Please excuse these two requests, which will make some inroads on your time. But they are matters which affect thousands of our theologians, and all of us here feel inadequate for them. Your help would be most gratefully received.

Barth replied almost by return of post!

Bergh, Oberrieden, 11th September 1933

BARTH TO BONHOEFFER: I would like to send at least a greeting straight away in reply to your friendly letter. The draft of the confession of which you write was not with your letter. But the other questions which you raise are serious enough. I have been following everything that has happened abroad from here. Should one not be almost thankful that everything seems to be heading so forcefully for a crisis? But of course the question of what to do when the crisis comes is still open. Naturally the decision of the General Synod has at least partly realised the possibility which I considered. They do not, or apparently not, want to go as far as excluding non-Aryans from church membership. But even the decree about officials and pastors is intolerable, and I too am of the opinion that there is a *status confessionis*. That will first of all mean this, that the church authorities, or the supposed or real majority of church members represented by them, must be told directly, and at the same time publicly, 'Here you are no longer the church of Christ!' And it is clear that this protest cannot be made just once; it must go on and on until the scandal is done away with—or until the church answers by evicting or muzzling those who protest. So the step you had in mind seems to me to be the right one to begin with. But whatever its success may be, it must be followed by further similar steps. Otherwise I am for waiting. When the breach comes, it must come from the other side. Perhaps it will come straight away in the form of an answer to the protest on behalf of the Jewish-Christian pastors. Perhaps the damnable doctrine which now holds sway in the church must first find vent in other, worse deviations and corruptions; in this connection I have gathered a pile of German Christian literature and can only say that on all sides I am most dreadfully portrayed! It could then well be that the encounter might take place at a still more central point. In any case, the bad decision, now made, must first be allowed to work itself out; the deed, once done, must as it were be allowed to speak.

If people go on in this way, the Free Church will one day simply just be there. But one should not even play with the possibility beforehand. The matter is too serious for one to be justified in canvassing it in any way, in wanting to 'start' it. I suppose that in fact it is already being canvassed in secret in a thousand corners! But we may, must be the last really to leave the sinking ship, if it should come to the point that we see it to be a sinking ship. Perhaps in that case it may not be absolutely necessary to be willing to wait until one is expelled or dismissed. Perhaps one will then really have to 'go out'. But that can only be a last resort for us. We rightly did not allow ourselves to be driven out of the Dibelius Church of the past straight away, despite scandal, very considerable scandal, of a different kind; we made our protest in the church itself. And we are called to do this now, at least to begin with, in the Hossenfelder church as well. We will in no way need to regret at a later date an extremely active, polemical, period of waiting even at this point. I am thinking, of course, that all sorts of intruders may come to us with this or that wild new creation. But it will be worth while if we refuse to think tactically now, but prefer to think spiritually, as well as we can and know how.

I continue to get letters on my pamphlet—almost all in agreement—mostly from quite unknown people, as a rule nontheologians, who very often speak on behalf of 'many others'. From this I conclude that there can be no question of any unanimity of 'church people' towards the present trend. But, we don't just want to answer one rumour with another! So it would certainly not be hopeless to unleash another of them just now. This battle will be won by those who first use their ammunition as sparingly as possible but when they do shoot aim most accurately and shoot most mercilessly. One day, just you depend on it, the whole Hossenfeldery will dissolve into atoms, leaving behind it a considerable stink . . .

I have also just now been reading the *Junge Kirche* on the matter, glad of any information, but really quite distressed by the 'tread softly' and 'take it easy' attitude which holds the field. Can't anyone see that the German Christians will just laugh at opponents who speak and behave like this? God help the German church if the opposition from within the church, which is so badly needed just now, cannot get hold of other viewpoints and other principles and above all a different language, instead of this brave and yet so fearful muddle which is all one can see at the moment. I am curious to see what Herr Lilje has promised to produce against me. At present I am not sorry for any sharp words I have written in this direction. —I write this to you to make it clear that I hold only the sharpest stand on principles to be good enough to justify waiting.

Now then, I am eagerly awaiting your draft declaration of faith. I will not conceal from you the fact that the name 'Bethel' puts me in some disquiet. The middle line which Georg Merz took in the last number of *Zwischen den Zeiten* was intolerable. I could certainly have nothing to do even with a Free Church 'of the middle line', which is the best thing I would expect from there.

Perhaps I will try to write something else sooner or later. But in myself I am not yet at the point of seeing clearly what is really going on now and what had to go on. You will be doing me a great favour if you will let me know from time to time what you know and what you think.

Meanwhile, Bonhoeffer had obtained leave of absence from Germany to become pastor of two German-speaking congregations in London. His next letter to Barth is from England.
London, 24th October 1933

BONHOEFFER TO BARTH: I am now writing a letter to you which I wanted to write six weeks ago and which perhaps at that time would have resulted in a completely different turn to my personal life. Why I did not write to you then is now almost incomprehensible to me. I only know that there were two contributory factors. I knew that you were busy with a thousand other things and in those hectic weeks the outward condition of one person seemed to me so utterly insignificant that I simply could not think it important enough to bother you. Secondly, I believe that there was also a bit of anxiety about it; I knew that I would have to do what you told me and I wanted to remain free; so I simply withdrew myself. I know now that that was wrong, and that I must ask you to forgive me. For I have now made up my mind 'freely' without being able to be free in respect of you. I wanted to ask you whether I should go to London as a pastor or not. I simply believed that you would tell me the right thing, you, and only you (except for a man who has such constant concern for my fortunes that he was drawn up into my uncertainty).

I have always very much wanted to become a pastor; I've already told you that a couple of times before. In July the London business came up. I agreed, with reservations, travelled over here for two days, found the congregation quite neglected, and remained uncertain. When the thing had to be decided in September, I said Yes. The formal contract is easy. Six months' notice. I just took leave from the University. How far the link with the congregation is getting stronger is impossible to detect at this stage. I was offered at the same time a pastorate in the East of Berlin; my election was certain. Then came the Aryan Clauses in Prussia and I knew that I could not accept the pastorate I longed for in this particular neighbourhood without giving up my attitude of unconditional opposition to the church, without making myself untrustworthy to my people from the start and without betraying my solidarity with the Jewish Christian pastors—my closest friend is one of them and is at the moment on the brink; he is now coming to me in England. So the alternative remained, lecturer or pastor, and if pastor, at any rate not in Prussia. I cannot begin to recount to you the abundance of pros and cons; I haven't got through them by a long way— perhaps I never shall. I hope that I did not come purely out of annoyance at the state of affairs in our church and at the attitude of our particular group. It probably would not have been long before I would have had to part formally from all my friends—but I really believe that all this spoke much more strongly against London than for it. If one is going to discover quite definite reasons for such decisions after the event, one of the strongest, I believe, was that I simply did not any longer feel up to the questions and demands which came to me. I felt that I was incomprehensibly in radical opposition to all my friends, that my views of matters were taking me more and more into isolation, although I was and remained in the closest personal relationship with these men—and all that made me anxious, made me uncertain. I was afraid I would go wrong out of obstinacy—and I saw no reason why I should see these things more correctly, better than so many able and good pastors, to whom I looked up—and so I thought that it was probably time to go into the wilderness for a while and simply do pastoral work, with as little demands as possible. The danger of making a gesture at the present moment seemed to me greater than that of going off for some quietness. So off I went. Another symptom was that the Bethel confession, on which I really worked so passionately, met with almost no understanding at all. I think I know for certain that this did not put me personally out of humour; there was really not the slighest occasion for that. I was simply uncertain in my mind.

Then ten days before my departure there came a call from the church Chancellery that there were difficulties about my going away because of my hostile attitude towards the German Christians. Luckily I managed to have a conversation with Müller, to whom I said that I could not of course abandon my position and that I would rather remain here than sail under a false flag; I could not represent the German Christians even abroad. This was all put on the record at my request. Müller made an unspeakably poor impression, and said to soothe me, 'Besides, I have already taken steps for the existing differences to be smoothed out.' But he remained uncertain in my case, and I hoped that the decision would not simply come from outside, and was very glad about it. The next day the news came that I was to go. Worry about the ecumenical movement—tiresome. Now I've been here a week, have to preach every Sunday, and receive news almost daily from Berlin about the state of affairs. That almost tears one apart inside. And now you will soon be in Berlin and I cannot be there. It also occurs to me that I have let you down personally by my going away. Perhaps you will not understand that. But it is a very great reality to me. And despite all this, I am infinitely glad to be among a congregation, even so completely out of things. I also hope that the questions about the ecumenical movement will really clear themselves up for me. I mean to carry on that work over here. Perhaps in this way one can really support the German church once again in something.

I still don't know how long I shall be kept here. If I knew that I was really needed over there—it is so infinitely difficult to know what we should do. 'We know not what we should do, but . . .'

So now this letter is written. They are only personal things, but the sort of thing I would very much like you to know about. It would be good if I were to hear a word from you again. I think of you and your work very often, and where we would be but for it. Would you please let me have your frank opinion on all this? I would be ready, and thankful, I think, even for a sharp word—I might write to you again when I have my typewriter. It's too much bother for you this way.

Barth's reply to that anxious letter was not immediate, but written only after careful thought. When it came, it was all that Bonhoeffer could have hoped or feared!

Bonn, 20th November 1933

BARTH TO BONHOEFFER: You can deduce from the very way in which I address you that I do not think of regarding your departure for England as anything but a necessary personal interlude. Once you had this thing on your mind, you were quite right not to ask for my wise counsel first. I would have advised you against it absolutely, and probably by bringing up my heaviest guns. And now, as you are mentioning the matter to me *post eventum,* I can honestly not tell you anything but 'Hurry back to your post in Berlin!'

What is all this about 'going away', 'the quietness of pastoral work', etc., at a moment when you are just wanted in Germany? You, who know as well as I do that the opposition in Berlin and the opposition of the church in Germany as a whole stands inwardly on such weak feet! That every honest man must have his hands full making it sharp and clear and firm! That now perhaps everything is going down the drain not because of the great power and deceit of the German Christians, but because of the pig-headedness and stupidity, of the desperate shallowness of, of all people, the anti-German Christians! Now, one can on no account play Elijah under the juniper tree or Jonah under the gourd, but must shoot from all barrels! What's the use of the praise you lavish on me—from the other side of the channel! What was the use of the message which your pupil gave me when I was busy having it out with the famous 'council of brethren' of the Emergency League—instead of your being there and supporting me against these brethren? Look, I have now been to Berlin twice in recent weeks and I think that I know quite well what is going on there. I have also honestly tried to snatch round the helm, and I have probably also had some degree of success; but if things had turned out well, I should have had quite, quite different success, and so I went away from the place extremely depressed, particularly the second time. Why weren't you there to draw on the sail with me, the sail that I could hardly shift by myself? Why aren't you always there, where so much could depend on there being a couple of game people on the watch at every occasion, great or small, and trying to save what there is to be saved? Why, why? Look, I gladly suppose, as I have already said, that this departure was personally necessary for you! But I must be allowed to add, 'What does even "personal necessity" mean at the present moment!' I think that I can see from your letter that you, like all of us—yes, like all of us!—are suffering under the quite uncommon difficulty of taking 'certain steps' in the present chaos. But should it not dawn on you that that is no reason for withdrawing from this chaos, that we are rather required in and with our uncertainty, even if we should stumble or go wrong ten times or a hundred times, to do our bit, whether we then help our cause or damage it? I just will not allow you to put such a private tragedy on the stage in view of what is at stake for the German church today, as though there were not time afterwards, when if God wills we have got a little way out of this muddle again, for the study of the different complexes and inhibitions from which you suffer, as indeed others also must. No, to all the reasons or excuses which you might perhaps still be able to put in front of me, I will give only one answer: 'And the German church?' 'And the German church?'—until you are back again in Berlin to attend faithfully and bravely to the machine-gun which you have left behind there. Don't you see yet that an age of completely undialectical theology has dawned, in which it just won't do to keep oneself in reserve with a 'Perhaps—but again, perhaps not!'? Don't you see that any biblical saying you like formally cries out to us that we, lost and damned sinners, should now simply believe, believe, believe?! With your splendid theological armoury and your upright German figure, should you not perhaps be almost a little ashamed at a man like Heinrich Vogel, who, wizened and worked up as he is, is just always there, waving his arms like a windmill and shouting 'Confession! Confession!', in his own way—in power or in weakness, that doesn't matter so much—actually giving his testimony? I cannot really give you the prospect of taking part in a triumph, when I ask you to return to Germany. Here everything is as wretched and as dismal as you could imagine, and as far as one engages in tactical or historical-theological thought even a little bit, one can realise every moment that—the sea rages and will have its victims—in spite of any efforts, the German church is lost. You will see from the continuation of the new series—Booklets 3 and 4 have some of my more or less current things—how much trouble I myself have had in keeping off weariness. But one simply cannot become weary just now. Still less can one go to England! What in all the world would you want to do there? Be glad that I do not have you here in person, for I would let go at you urgently in quite a different way, with the demand that you must now leave go of all these intellectual flourishes and special considerations, however interesting they may be, and think of only one thing, that you are a German, that the house of your church is on fire, that you know enough and can say what you know well enough to be able to help and that you must return to your post by the next ship. As things are, shall we say the ship after next? But I cannot tell you emphatically and urgently enough that you belong to Berlin and not to London.

As all that you really wrote to me was that you are now over there, this time all that I will write to you is that you ought to be in Berlin.

Unfortunately I must first get your address from G. Staewen, so there will be some delay before this letter reaches you. You will understand it in the friendly spirit in which it is intended. If I were not so attached to you, I would not let fly at you in this way. G.S. II pp. 126–37

That last letter from Barth shows how wise Bonhoeffer was not to seek his advice before deciding whether he should go to London. But Barth's utter frankness and his high regard for Bonhoeffer must have been some consolation for the devastating impact of that letter. Bonhoeffer did not reply and he did not return to Berlin, though he must have been sorely tempted to do so. Barth's guns were heavy and his argument still sounds convincing. The 'Bethel Confession' which is referred to in this correspondence was sent out by von Bodelschwingh on 26th August. As the correspondence makes clear, Bonhoeffer had a dominant hand in it.

Here is the section on the Jewish question.

The Church and the Jews

The church teaches that God chose Israel from among all the nations of the earth to be his people. He chose them solely in the power of his Word and for the sake of his loving-kindness, and not because they were in any way pre-eminent (Exod. 19. 5–6; Deut. 7. 7–11). The Sanhedrin and the Jewish people rejected Christ Jesus, promised by the Law and the Prophets, in accordance with Scripture. They wanted a national Messiah, who would bring them political freedom and the rule of the world. Jesus Christ was not this, and did not do this. He died at their hands and for their sakes. The barrier between Jew and Gentile has been broken down by the crucifixion and resurrection of Jesus Christ (Eph. 2). The place of the Old Testament people of the covenant was taken not by another nation, but by the Christian church, called out of and living among all nations.

God abundantly shows his faithfulness by still keeping faith with Israel after the flesh, from whom was born Christ after the flesh, despite all their unfaithfulness, even after the crucifixion. It is his will to complete the salvation of the world, which he began with the election of Israel, through these selfsame Jews (Rom. 9–11). Therefore he continues to preserve a 'holy remnant' of Israel after the flesh, which can neither be absorbed into another nation by emancipation and assimilation, nor become one nation among others as a result of the efforts of Zionist and other similar movements, nor be exterminated by Pharaoh-like measures. This 'holy remnant' bears the indelible stamp of the chosen people. The church has received from its Lord the commission to call the Jews to repentance and to baptise those who believe on Jesus Christ to the forgiveness of sins (Matt. 10. 5f.; Acts 2. 38ff.; 3. 19–26). A mission to the Jews which for cultural or political considerations refuses to baptise any more Jews at all is refusing to be obedient to its Lord. The crucified Christ is to the Jews a stumbling-block and to the Greeks folly (I Cor. 1. 22f.). 'The Crucified One' as little accords with the religious ideal of the Jewish soul as it does with the religious ideal of the soul of any other nation. Faith in him cannot be given by flesh and blood even to a Jew, but only by the Father in heaven through his spirit (Matt. 16. 17).

The community of those who belong to the church is not determined by blood and therefore not by race, but by the Holy Spirit and baptism.

We reject any attempt to identify or confuse the historical mission of any nation with Israel's commission in sacred history.

No nation can ever be commissioned to avenge on the Jews the murder at Golgotha. 'Vengeance is mine, says the Lord' (Deut. 32. 35, Heb. 10. 30). We reject any attempt to misuse the miracle of God's especial faithfulness towards Israel after the flesh as an indication of the religious significance of the Jewish people or of another people.

We oppose the assertion that the faith of Jewish Christians is, as opposed to that of Gentile Christians, affected by their descent and is Judaistic heresy.

We oppose the attempt to deprive the German Evangelical church of its promise by the attempt to change it into a national church of Christians of Aryan descent. This would be to erect a racial barrier against entering the church and would make such a church itself a Jewish Christian community regulated by the Law. We therefore reject the forming of Jewish Christian communities, because the false presupposition for such action is the view that the special element in Jewish Christianity can be appropriately compared with, for example, the historically determined peculiarity of the communities of French refugees in Germany, and that Christians from Judaism must develop a form of Christianity appropriate to their character. The special element in the Jewish Christian does not lie in his race or his character or his history, but in God's special faithfulness towards Israel after the flesh and in that alone. The way in which the Jewish Christian has a special position in the church which is not based on any legal ruling in itself makes him a living memorial of God's faithfulness within the church and is a sign that the barrier between Jew and Gentile has been broken down and that faith in Christ may not be perverted into a national religion or a racially-determined Christianity. It is the task of the Christians who come from the Gentile world to expose themselves to persecution rather than to surrender, willingly or unwillingly, even in one single respect, their brotherhood with Jewish Christians in the church, founded on Word and Sacrament. G.S. II pp. 115–17

The correspondence with Karl Barth has taken us into the London period, but before we look at that time in detail it is necessary to see how Bonhoeffer's attitude to events in Germany itself was shaping before he decided to leave. He had already become aware that the prophetic voice was needed in Germany and his effectiveness in the role of a prophet was one of the reasons why Barth was so angry at his departure. Bonhoeffer's voice had already been heard and it was a voice of judgment. He was no destroyer, he loved his land and his church, but he felt compelled to attack. Typical of his attitude in 1933 was the sermon he preached in the Kaiser Wilhelm Memorial Church in Berlin on 28th May, when he deputised for Jacobi. This sermon shows his longing to find a way of reconciliation for his people.

A Church of the World or a Church of the Word?

Sermon preached in the Kaiser Wilhelm Memorial Church, Exaudi, 28th May 1933. Exodus 32. 1–7, 15, 19f, 30–4.

Priest against prophet, worldly church against the church of faith, the church of Aaron against the church of Moses—this is the eternal conflict in the church of Christ. And it is this conflict and its resolution that we are to consider today.

Moses and Aaron, the two brothers, of the same tribe, of the same blood, sharing the same history, going for part of the way side by side—then wrenched apart. Moses, the first prophet, Aaron, the first priest; Moses, called of God, chosen without regard of his person, the man who was slow of tongue, the servant of God, living solely to hear the Word of his Lord; Aaron, the man with the purple robe and the holy diadem, the consecrated and sanctified priest, who must maintain his service of God for the people. And now, in our story: Moses, called alone into the presence of the living God, high above on the mount of fear, between life and death in the thunder and lightning, to receive the law of the covenant of God with his people—and there down below in the valley, the people of Israel with their priest in his purple robe, sacrificing, far from God.

Why must Moses and Aaron be in conflict? Why cannot they stand side by side in the same service? Why must the church of Moses and the church of Aaron, the church of the Word and the worldly church turn time and again to different ways? The answer to this question is given in our text.

Moses is called up the mountain by God for his people. It is God's will to speak with him up there. The children of Israel know that. They know that up there Moses is standing, fighting, praying, suffering for them. He wears no purple robe, he is no priest; he is nothing at all, nothing but the servant who waits on the Word of his Lord, who is tormented when he is not given to hear this word. He is nothing—nothing but the prophet of his God. But the church of Aaron, the worldly church, cannot wait. It is impatient. Where has Moses got to? Why does he not come back? Perhaps we will not see him again. Where is he, with his God? 'As for this Moses … we do not know what has become of him.' It may be that he no longer exists, that he is dead.

These are the questions which the church of Aaron at all times puts to the church of the Word. 'We cannot see it. Where are its works? What is its contribution? No doubt at all, it is dead.' Do we not then understand that perhaps God himself is keeping Moses up on the mountain, that he is not yet letting him go because he still has something to say to him? Do we not understand that perhaps even today he is not yet letting the church of Moses go, the church whose wish is to hear only the Word of God, because he has still something to say in the quietness? Even God needs time with his prophets and with his church. Is it for us to be impatient? Certainly, the church of the Word is once again on Sinai, and in fear and trembling, amidst the

thunder and lightning, stands up to the Word of God, waits, believes, prays, fights ...
For whom? For the church of Aaron, for the church down there in the valley, for the
worldly church. The unwillingness of the worldly church to wait, its impatience, is
the first stage of its clash with the church of the Word. So it has always been, and so
it will continue to be.

'As for this Moses ... we do not know what has become of him. Up, Aaron, make
us gods, who shall go before us.' That is the second stage, which follows immediately
upon the first. The worldly church, the church of the priests, wants to see something.
Now it will wait no longer. It must go to work by itself, see by itself, do by itself what
God and the prophet are not doing. What is the use of the priest, what is the use of
the church, if they are constantly kept on the watch? No, our church ought to have
something. We want to see something in our church. We will not wait. You priests,
you are sanctified, you are consecrated. You owe us something. Up, Aaron the priest,
do your duty, attend to the divine service. God has left us, but we need gods. We need
religions. If you cannot prevail with the Living God, make us gods yourself!

The concern expressed here is really not as bad as all that. It is even a pious
concern. People are not saying, 'Away with gods!', but, 'We need gods, religions, make
us some!' The priest is not driven out, he is told, 'Do your duty!' They really want to
keep a church with gods and priests and religion, but a church of Aaron—without
God. And Aaron yields. He looks to his office, to his consecration; he looks to the
people. He understands their impatience, their urge to do something, and their pious
tumult only too well—and he yields. Come, you who have been abandoned by your
God and by your prophet, make yourselves a god who will not leave you again, more
splendid, more glorious than the God who has left us. Bring precious adornment,
gold, jewellery, bring it as an offering. And they all come, without exception. They
bring their precious offering to their own image of their god. They tear the ornaments
from their bodies and throw them into the glowing mass from which Aaron now
shapes the glittering, monstrous, golden calf. We hear it said that the people are not
so ready for sacrifice. But those who talk like this do not know the world. The human
race is ready for any sacrifice in which it may celebrate itself and worship its own
work. The worldly church, the church of Aaron, is ready for any sacrifice if it is to
be allowed to make its own God. The human race and the worldly church fall on
their knees joyfully, and with smiles, before the god whom we make as it pleases us.
But *God* finds little readiness for sacrifice. No, the church of Aaron does not stint,
it is not mean, it is lavish with its god. Everything that is precious and valuable and
holy to it is cast into the glow of the image of its god. Everything must contribute
to the glorification of the god, so each one, according to his inclinations and his
capabilities, throws his own ideals into the melting pot—and then the orgy begins.
The worldly church celebrates its triumph, the priest has shown his power, and now
he himself stands in the middle in his purple robe and his holy diadem and worships
the creation of his own hand. And round him the people prostrate themselves in

ecstasy and look up at the god whom they have made in their own strength, at their own sacrifice. Who would want to stand aside from this pious joy, this unparalleled exuberance, this achievement of human will and ability? The worldly church now has its god, come, celebrate him, enjoy yourselves, play, eat, drink, dance, make merry, take yourselves out of yourselves! You have a god again. These are your gods, O Israel, who brought you up out of the land of Egypt! Come, behold, worship!

But there are rumblings on Sinai. For God shows Moses his faithless people. And Moses trembles for his people and comes hastily down from the mountain. He already hears the merrymaking and the shouts of the dance and the tumult and the orgy. He already sees his brother in purple robe and holy diadem, and in the midst the golden god of the worldly church, the worldly god, the god of the priests, the god who is no God. —There he stands amongst them, the unexpected prophet, high in his hands he swings the tables of the law, and they all must see it, the writing engraved by the hand of God, 'I am the Lord your God, you shall have no other gods before me!' Dumb terror, dismay, seizes the worldly church at the sight. The party is over. The living God has come amongst them, he rages against them. What will happen? There—a sight unequalled, a fearful moment—and the tables of the law lie shattered on the idol, and the idol itself is broken in pieces and consumed. That is the end of the worldly church. God has appointed it. God has remained Lord. Lord, have mercy . . .!

Church of the priests against church of the Word, church of Aaron against church of Moses—this historical clash at the foot of Sinai, the end of the worldly church and the appearance of the Word of God, repeats itself in our church, day by day, Sunday by Sunday. Time and again we come together for worship a worldly church, as a church which will not wait, which will not live from the invisible; as a church which makes its own gods; as a church which wants to have the sort of god which pleases it and will not ask how it pleases God; as a church which wants to do by itself what God will not do; as a church which is ready for any sacrifice in the cause of idolatry, in the cause of the divinisation of human thoughts and values; as a church which appropriates to itself divine power in the priesthood. And we should go away again as a church whose idol lies shattered and destroyed on the ground, as a church which must hear afresh, 'I am the Lord your God ..', as a church which is humbled as it is faced with this Word, as the church of Moses, the church of the Word. The impatient church becomes the quietly waiting church, the church anxious to see sights becomes the church of sober faith, the church which makes its own gods becomes the church which worships the One God. Will this church too find such devotion, such sacrifice?

But the rupture is not the end. Once again Moses climbs the mountain, this time to pray for his people. He offers up himself, 'Reject me with my people, for we are still one. Lord, I love my brother.' But God's answer remains dark, fearful, threatening. Moses could not make expiation. Who makes expiation here? It is none other than he who is priest and prophet in one, the man with the purple robe and the crown of thorns, the crucified Son of the Father, who stands before God to make intercession for us. Here, in his cross, there is an end of all idolatry. Here, the whole human race, the whole church, is judged and forgiven. Here God is wholly the God who will have no other god before him, but now also wholly God in that he forgives without limit. As the church which is always at the same time the church of Moses and the church of Aaron, we point to this cross and say, 'This is your God, O Israel, who brought you out of slavery and will lead you evermore. Come, believe, worship!' Amen. G.S. IV pp. 124–9

Before he made his reluctant decision to leave Germany, Bonhoeffer had already started working with Niemöller to organise the League which was to help pastors who had suffered from the Nazi laws. The decision to form this Pastors' Emergency League was taken as soon as the effects of the Aryan Clauses became known. When it was known that the National Synod of the German Evangelical Church was prepared to act upon these Clauses, Bonhoeffer called for a World Alliance protest. He sent an urgent telegram to Henriod in Geneva: 'General Assembly finished. All general superintendents dismissed. Only Teutonic Christians admitted to National Synod. Aryan Clauses now in action. Please work out memorandum against this and inform press at once. Separation at hand. More information at Sofia.'

At about the same time, Bonhoeffer and Niemöller sent out the following declaration, which became the draft for a call to ministers to form the Pastors' Emergency League.

Declaration

According to the confession of our church, the teaching office of the church is bound up with a call in accordance with the order of the church and with that call alone. The 'Aryan Clauses' of the new enactment concerning offices in the church put forward a principle which contradicts this basic clause of the confession. As a result, a position which must be regarded as unjust is proclaimed as church law, and the confession is violated.

There can be no doubt that as long as the ordained ministers affected by the enactment are not dispossessed of the rights which belong to their status as ministers by formal proceedings they have under all circumstances the right to preach the Word and administer the sacraments freely in the Evangelical Church of the Old Prussian Union which rests on the confessions of the Reformation.

Anyone who gives his assent to a breach of the confession thereby excludes himself from the community of the church. We therefore demand that this law, which separates the Evangelical Church of the Old Prussian Unon from the Christian church, be repealed forthwith.

7th September 1933.

Martin Niemöller
Dietrich Bonhoeffer
G.S. II pp. 70–1

21. Dorothy Day – Why

Chapter 1

It is difficult for me to dip back into the past, yet it is a job that must be done, and it hangs over my head like a cloud. St. Peter said that we must give a reason for the faith that is in us, and I am trying to give you those reasons.

This is not an autobiography. I am a woman forty years old and I am not trying to set down the story of my life. Please keep that in mind as you read. While it is true that often horror for one's sins turns one to God, what I want to bring out in this book is a succession of events that led me to His feet, glimpses of Him that I received through many years which made me feel the vital need of Him and of religion. I will try to trace for you the steps by which I came to accept the faith that I believe was always in my heart. For this reason, most of the time I will speak of the good I encountered even amid surroundings and people who tried to reject God.

The mark of the atheist is the deliberate rejection of God. And since you do not reject God or deliberately embrace evil, then you are not an atheist. Because you doubt and deny in words what your heart and mind do not deny, you consider yourself an agnostic.

Though I felt the strong, irresistible attraction to good, yet there was also, at times, a deliberate choosing of evil. How far I was led to choose it, it is hard to say. How far professors, companions, and reading influenced my way of life does not matter now. The fact remains that there was much of deliberate choice in it. Most of the time it was "following the devices and desires of my own heart." Sometimes it was perhaps the Baudelairean idea of choosing "the downward path which leads to salvation." Sometimes it was of choice, of free will, though perhaps at the time I would have denied free will. And so, since it was deliberate, with recognition of its seriousness, it was grievous mortal sin and may the Lord forgive me. It was the arrogance and suffering of youth. It was pathetic, little, and mean in its very excuse for itself.

Was this desire to be with the poor and the mean and abandoned not unmixed with a distorted desire to be with the dissipated? Mauriac tells of this subtle pride and hypocrisy: "There is a kind of hypocrisy which is worse than that of the Pharisees; it is to hide behind Christ's example in order to follow one's own lustful desires and to seek out the company of the dissolute."

I write these things now because sometimes when I am writing I am seized with fright at my presumption. I am afraid, too, of not telling the truth or of distorting the truth. I cannot guarantee that I do not for I am writing of the past. But my whole perspective has changed and when I look for causes of my conversion, sometimes it is one thing and sometimes it is another that stands out in my mind.

Much as we want to know ourselves, we do not really know ourselves. Do we really want to see ourselves as God sees us, or even as our fellow human beings see us? Could we bear it, weak as we are? You know that feeling of contentment in which we sometimes go about, clothed in it, as it were, like a garment, content with the world and with ourselves. We are ourselves and we would be no one else. We are glad that God made us as we are and we would not have had Him make us like anyone else. According to the weather, our state of health, we have moods of purely animal happiness and content. We do not want to be given that clear inward vision which discloses to us our most secret faults. In the Psalms there is that prayer, "Deliver me from my secret sins." We do not really know how much pride and self-love we have until someone whom we respect or love suddenly turns against us. Then some sudden affront, some sudden offense we take, reveals to us in all its glaring distinctness our self-love, and we are ashamed. . . .

I write in the very beginning of finding the Bible and the impression it made on me. I must have read it a good deal, for many passages remained with me through my earlier years to return and haunt me. Do you know the Psalms? They were what I read most when I was in jail in Occoquan. I read with a sense of coming back to something that I had lost. There was an echoing in my heart. And how can anyone who has known human sorrow and human joy fail to respond to these words?

> "Out of the depths I have cried to thee, O Lord:
> Lord, hear my voice. Let thy ears be attentive to the voice of my supplication.
> If thou, O Lord, wilt mark iniquities:
> Lord, who shall stand it.
> For with thee there is merciful forgiveness: and by reason of thy law, I have waited
>   for thee,
> O Lord. My soul hath relied on his word: my soul hath hoped in the Lord.
> From the morning watch even until night, let Israel hope in the Lord.
> Because with the Lord there is mercy; and with him plentiful redemption.
> And he shall redeem Israel from all his iniquities."

> "Hear, O Lord, my prayer: give ear to my supplication in thy truth: hear me in thy
>   justice.
> And enter not into judgment with thy servant: for in thy sight no man living shall be
>   justified.
> For the enemy hath persecuted my soul: he hath brought down my life to the earth.
> He hath made me to dwell in darkness as those that have been dead of old:
> And my spirit is in anguish within me: my heart within me is troubled.
> I remembered the days of old, I meditated on all thy works:
> I meditated upon the works of thy hands.
> I stretched forth my hands to thee: my soul is as earth without water unto thee.
> Hear me speedily O Lord; my spirit hath fainted away.
> Turn not away thy face from me, lest I be like unto them that go down into the pit.

Cause me to hear thy mercy in the morning; for in thee have I hoped.
Make the way known to me, wherein I should walk: for I have lifted up my soul
    to thee."

All through those weary first days in jail when I was in solitary confinement, the only thoughts that brought comfort to my soul were those lines in the Psalms that expressed the terror and misery of man suddenly stricken and abandoned. Solitude and hunger and weariness of spirit–these sharpened my perceptions so that I suffered not only my own sorrow but the sorrows of those about me. I was no longer myself. I was man. I was no longer a young girl, part of a radical movement seeking justice for those oppressed, I was the oppressed. I was that drug addict, screaming and tossing in her cell, beating her head against the wall. I was that shoplifter who for rebellion was sentenced to solitary. I was that woman who had killed her children, who had murdered her lover.

The blackness of hell was all about me. The sorrows of the world encompassed me. I was like one gone down into the pit. Hope had forsaken me. I was that mother whose child had been raped and slain. I was the mother who had borne the monster who had done it. I was even that monster, feeling in my own heart every abomination.

As I read this over, it seems, indeed, over-emotional and an exaggerated statement of the reactions of a young woman in jail. But if you live for long in the slums of cities, if you are in constant contact with sins and suffering, it is indeed rarely that so overwhelming a realization comes upon one. It often has seemed to me that most people instinctively protect themselves from being touched too closely by the suffering of others. They turn from it, and they make this a habit. The tabloids with their presentation of crime testify to the repulsive truth that there is a secret excitement and pleasure in reading of the sufferings of others. One might say there is a surface sensation in the realization of the tragedy in the lives of others. But one who has accepted hardship and poverty as the way im life in which to walk, lays himself open to this susceptibility to the sufferings of others.

And yet if it were not the Holy Spirit that comforted me, how could I have been comforted, how could I have endured, how could I have lived in hope?

The Imitation of Christ is a book that followed me through my days. Again and again I came across copies of it and the reading of it brought me comfort. I felt in the background of my life a waiting force that would lift me up eventually.

I later became acquainted with the poem of Francis Thompson, *The Hound of Heaven,* and was moved by its power. Eugene O'Neill recited it first to me in the back room of a saloon on Sixth Avenue where the Provincetown players and playwrights used to gather after the performances.

"I fled Him, down the nights and down the days;
I fled Him, down the arches of the years;

I fled Him, down the labyrinthine ways
Of my own mind; and in the mist of tears
I hid from Him."

Through all my daily life, in those I came in contact with, in the things I read and heard, I felt that sense of being followed, of being desired; a sense of hope and expectation.

Through those years I read all of Dostoyvsky's novels and it was, as Berdyaev says, a profound spiritual experience. The scene in *Crime and Punishment* where the young prostitute reads from the New Testament to Raskolnikoff, sensing the sin more profound than her own, which weighed upon him; that story, *The Honest Thief*; those passages in *The Brothers Karamazov*; the sayings of Father Zossima, Mitya's conversion in jail, the very legend of the Grand Inquisitor, all this helped to lead me on. The characters, Alyosha and the Idiot, testified to Christ in us. I was moved to the depths of my being by the reading of these books during my early twenties when I, too, was tasting the bitterness and the dregs of life and shuddered at its harshness and cruelty.

Do you remember that little story that Grushenka told in *The Brothers Karamazov*? "Once upon a time there was a peasant woman and a very wicked woman she was. And she died and did not leave a single good deed behind. The devils caught her and plunged her into a lake of fire. So her guardian angel stood and wondered what good deed of hers he could remember to tell God. 'She once pulled up an onion in her garden,' said he, 'and gave it to a beggar woman.' And God answered: 'You take that onion then, hold it out to her in the lake, and let her take hold and be pulled out. And if you pull her out of the lake, let her come to Paradise, but if the onion breaks, then the woman must stay where she is.' The angel ran to the woman and held out the onion to her. 'Come,' said he, 'catch hold, and I'll pull you out. And he began cautiously pulling her out. He had just pulled her out, when the other sinners in the lake, seeing how she was being drawn out, began catching hold of her so as to be pulled out with her. But she was a very wicked woman and she began kicking them. 'I'm to be pulled out, not you. It's my onion, not yours.' As soon as she said that, the onion broke. And the woman fell into the lake and she is burning there to this day. So the angel wept and went away."

Sometimes in thinking and wondering at God's goodness to me, I have thought that it was because I gave away an onion. Because I sincerely loved His poor, He taught me to know Him. And when I think of the little I ever did, I am filled with hope and love for all those others devoted to the cause of social justice.

"What glorious hope!" Mauriac writes. "There are all those who will discover that their neighbor is Jesus himself, although they belong to the mass of those who do not know Christ or who have forgotten Him. And nevertheless they will find themselves well loved. It is impossible for any one of those who has real charity in his heart not to serve Christ. Even some of those who think they hate Him, have consecrated their lives to Him; for Jesus is disguised and masked in the midst of men, hidden among the poor, among the sick, among prisoners, among strangers. Many who serve Him officially have never known who He was, and many who do not even know His name, will hear on the last day the words that open to them the gates of joy. O Those children were I, and I those working men. I wept on the hospital bed. I was that murderer in his cell whom you consoled.'"

But always the glimpses of God came most when I was alone. Objectors cannot say that it was fear of loneliness and solitude and pain that made me turn to Him. It was in those few years when I was alone and most happy that I found Him. I found Him at last through joy and thanksgiving, not through sorrow.

Yet how can I say that either? Better let it be said that I found Him through His poor, and in a moment of joy I turned to Him. I have said, sometimes flippantly, that the mass of bourgeois smug Christians who denied Christ in His poor made me turn to Communism, and that it was the Communists and working with them that made me turn to God.

Communism, says our Holy Father, can be likened to a heresy, and a heresy is a distortion of the truth. Many Christians have lost sight, to a great extent, of the communal aspect of Christianity, so the collective ideal is the result. They have failed to learn a philosophy of labor, have failed to see Christ in the worker. So in Russia, the worker, instead of Christ, has been exalted. They have the dictatorship of the proletariat maintained by one man, also a dictator. The proletariat as a class has come to be considered the Messiah, the deliverer.

A mystic may be called a man in love with God. Not one who loves God, but who is *in love with God.*And this mystical love, which is an exalted emotion, leads one to love the things of Christ. His footsteps are sacred. The steps of His passion and death are retraced down through the ages. Almost every time you step into a Church you see people making the Stations of the Cross. They meditate on the mysteries of His life, death, and resurrection, and by this they are retracing with love those early scenes and identifying themselves with the actors in those scenes.

When we suffer, we are told we suffer with Christ. We are "completing the sufferings of Christ." We suffer His loneliness and fear in the garden when His friends slept. We are bowed down with Him under the weight of not only our own sins but the sins of each other, of the whole world. We are those who are sinned against and those who are sinning. We are identified with Him, one with Him. We are members of His Mystical Body.

Often there is a mystical element in the love of a radical worker for his brother, for his fellow worker. It extends to the scene of his sufferings, and those spots where he has suffered and died are hallowed. The names of places like Everett, Ludlow, Bisbee, South Chicago, Imperial Valley, Elaine, Arkansas, and all those other places where workers have suffered and died for their cause have become sacred to the worker.

You know this feeling as does every other radical in the country. Through ignorance, perhaps, you do not acknowledge Christ's name, yet, I believe you are trying to love Christ in His poor, in His persecuted ones. Whenever men have laid down their lives for their fellows, they are doing it in a measure for Him. This I still firmly believe, even though you and others may not realize it.

"Inasmuch as ye have done it unto one of the least of these brethren, you have done it unto me." Feeling this as strongly as I did, is it any wonder that I was led finally to the feet of Christ?

I do not mean at all that I went around in a state of exaltation or that any radical does. Love is a matter of the will. You know yourself how during a long strike the spirit falters, how hard it is for the leaders to keep up the morale of the men and to keep the fire of hope burning within them. They have a hard time sustaining this hope themselves. Saint Teresa says that there are three attributes of the soul: memory, understanding, and will. These very leaders by their understanding of the struggle, how victory is gained very often through defeat, how every little gain benefits the workers all over the country, through their memory of past struggles, are enabled to strengthen their wills to go on. It is only by exerting these faculties of the soul that one is enabled to love one's fellow. And this strength comes from God. There can be no brotherhood without the Fatherhood of God.

Take a factory where fifty per cent of the workers themselves content, do not care about their fellows. It is hard to inspire them with the idea of solidarity. Take those workers who despise their fellow-worker, the Negro, the Hungarian, the Italian, the Irish, where race hatreds and nationalist feelings persist. It is hard to overcome their stubborn resistance with patience and with love. That is why there is coercion, the beating of scabs and strikebreakers, the threats and the hatreds that grow up. That is why in labor struggles, unless there is a wise and patient leader, there is disunity, a rending of the Mystical Body.

Even the most unbelieving of labor leaders have understood the expediency of patience when I have talked to them. They realize that the use of force has lost more strikes than it has won them. They realize that when there is no violence in a strike, the employer through his armed guards and strikebreakers may try to introduce this violence. It has happened again and again in labor history.

What is hard to make the labor leader understand is that we must love even the employer, unjust though he may be, that we must try to overcome his resistance by non-violent resistance, by withdrawing labor, *i.e.,* by strikes and by boycott. These are non-violent means and most effective. We must try to educate him, to convert him. We must forgive him seventy times seven just as we forgive our fellow-worker and keep trying to bring him to a sense of solidarity.

This is the part labor does not seem to understand in this country or in any country. Class war does exist. We cannot deny it. It is there. Class lines are drawn even here in America where we have always flattered ourselves that the poor boy can become president, the messenger boy, the head of the corporation. The very fact of the necessity of national security laws, old age and unemployment insurance, acknowledges the existence of a proletariat class. The employer much too often does not pay a wage sufficient for a man to care for his family in sickness and in health. The unskilled worker, who is in the majority, does not have enough to lay some by for his old age or enough to buy a home with or to buy his share in partnership. He has been too long exploited and ground down. The line has been fixed dividing the rich and the poor, the owner and the proletariat who are the unpropertied, the dispossessed.

And how to convert an employer who has evicted all his workers because they were on strike so that men, women, and children are forced to live in tents, who has called out armed guards as Rockefeller did in Ludlow, who shot into those tents and fired them so that twenty eight women and children were burnt to death? How to forgive such a man? How to convert him? This is the question the worker asks you in the bitterness of his soul? It is only through a Christ-like love that man can forgive.

Remember Vanzetti's last words before he died in the electric chair. "I wish to tell you I am an innocent man. I never committed any crime, but sometimes some sin. I wish to forgive some people for what they are now doing to me."

He said when he was sentenced: "If it had not been for these things, I might have lived out my life talking at street corners to scorning men. I might have died unmarked, unknown, a failure. Now we are not a failure. This is our career and our triumph. Never in our full life could we hope to do such work for tolerance, for justice, for man's understanding of man, as now we do by accident. Our words, our lives, our pains–nothing! The taking of our lives–lives of a good shoemaker and a poor fishpeddler–all! That last moment belongs to us. That agony is our triumph." He forgave those who had imprisoned him for years, who had hounded him to his death. You have read Mauriac. He was one of those of whom Mauriac was speaking when he said, "It is impossible for any one of those who has charity in his heart not to serve Christ. Even those who think they hate Him have consecrated their lives to Him."

It was from men such as these that I became convinced, little by little, of the necessity of religion and of God in my everyday life. I know now that the Catholic Church is the church of the poor, no matter what you say about the wealth of her priests and bishops. I have mentioned in these pages the few Catholics I met before my conversion, but daily I saw people coming from Mass. Never did I set foot in a Catholic church but that I saw people there at home with Him. First Fridays, novenas, and missions brought the masses thronging in and out of the Catholic churches. They were of all nationalities, of all classes, but most of all they were the poor. The very attacks made against the Church proved her Divinity to me. Nothing but a Divine institution could have survived the betrayal of Judas, the denial of Peter, the sins of many of those who professed her Faith, who were supposed to minister to her poor.

Christ is God or He is the world's greatest liar and imposter. How can you Communists who claim to revere Him as a working class leader fail to see this? And if Christ established His Church on earth with Peter as its rock, that faulty one who denied him three times, who fled from Him when he was in trouble, then I, too, wanted a share in that tender compassionate love that is so great. Christ can forgive all sins and yearn over us no matter how far we fall.

How I ramble on! I do it partly to avoid getting on to the work of this book. It will, no doubt, be disjointed, perhaps incoherent, but I have promised to write it. It entails suffering, as I told you, to write it. I have to dig into myself to get it out. I have to inflict wounds on myself. I have, perhaps, to say things that were better left unsaid.

After all, the experiences that I have had are more or less universal. Suffering, sadness, repentance, love, we all have known these. They are easiest to bear when one remembers their universality, when we remember that we are all members or potential members of the Mystical Body of Christ.

However, one does not like to write about others, thus violating their privacy, especially others near and dear. So, in what follows I have tried to leave out as much as possible of other personalities, those of our own family and those with whom later I associated most intimately.

A conversion is a lonely experience. We do not know what is going on in the depths of the heart and soul of another. We scarcely know ourselves.

22. Dorothy Day – Extracts from We Go on Record

I We Go on Record

As one method of withholding consent from the State's preparation for war, the Catholic Worker has always urged nonpayment of federal income tax. Dorothy's position had been well known to the government since at least the late 1950's, when she was summoned by the Internal Revenue Service to give an accounting. After submitting patiently to a long discourse on personal responsibility and the Fathers of the Church, a young I.R.S. employee asked Dorothy to estimate her personal income for the previous ten years. "I'll tell you what," she is reported to have answered. "You estimate my income for the past ten years, and you estimate what I owe you, and I won't pay it! How's that?"

The subject was not raised again until 1972, when a suit from the Internal Revenue Service threatened to put the Catholic Worker out on the street. Refusing to contest the issue in court, Dorothy trusted instead in her "spiritual weapons." Girded with prayer, she rose with confidence to meet the challenge head on.[1]

---

[1]Editorial note by Robert Ellsberg.

The Catholic Worker has received a letter from the Internal Revenue Service stating that we owe them $296,359 in fines, penalties, and unpaid income tax for the last six years. As the matter stands right now, there might be a legal battle with delays and postponements which may remind us of Dickens' *Bleak House*. Or, since we will not set up a defense committee to campaign for funds, it may terminate swiftly in the confiscation of our property and our bank account (never very large). Our farm at Tivoli and the First Street house could be put up for sale by government agents and our C.W. family evicted.

Perhaps no one here at St. Joseph's House realizes the situation we are in right now as keenly as I do, having seen so many evictions in the Depression—furniture, clothes, kitchen utensils piled up on the streets by landlords' marshals. The Communists used to demonstrate and forcibly move the belongings of the unfortunate people back into the tenements, but our Catholic Worker staff, a handful of us, begged money and rented other apartments for eight to fifteen dollars a month and moved the evicted families there. What a job! It exhausts me to think of it.

I can only trust that this crisis will pass. Just as we believe that God, our Father, has care of us, I am sure that some way will be found either to avert the disaster or for us to continue to care for our old, sick, helpless, hungry, and homeless if it happens.

One of the most costly protests against war, in terms of long-enduring personal sacrifice, is to refuse to pay federal income taxes which go for war. The late Ammon Hennacy, one of our editors, was a prime example of this. He earned his living at agricultural labor, always living on a poverty level so as not to be subject to taxes, though he filed returns. Another of our editors, Karl Meyer, recently spent ten months in jail for what the I.R.S. called fraudulent claims of exemption for dependents. He ran the C.W. House of Hospitality in Chicago for many years, working to earn the money to support the house and his wife and children. Erosanna Robinson, a social worker in Chicago, refused to file returns and was sentenced to a year in prison. While in prison she fasted and was forcibly fed. It will be seen that tax refusal is a serious protest. Wars will cease when we refuse to pay for them (to adapt a slogan of the War Resisters International).

The C.W. has never paid salaries. Everyone gets board, room, and clothes (tuition, recreation included, as the C.W. is in a way a school of living). So we do not need to pay federal income taxes. Of course, there are hidden taxes we all pay. Nothing is ever clear-cut or well defined. We protest in any way we can, according to our responsibilities and temperaments.

(I remember Ammon, a most consistent, brave, and responsible person, saying to one young man, "For the love of the Lord, get a job and quit worrying about taxes. You need to learn how to earn your own living. That is most important for you.")

We have to accept with humility the fact that we cannot share the destitution of those around us, and that our protests are incomplete. Perhaps the most complete protest is to be in jail, to accept jail, never to give bail or defend ourselves.

In the fifties, Ammon, Charles McCormack (our business manager at the C.W.), and I were summoned to the offices of the I.R.S. in New York to answer questions (under oath) as to our finances. I remember I was asked what happened to the royalties from my books, money from speaking engagements, etc. I could only report that such monies received were deposited in the C.W. account. As for clothes, we wore what came in; my sister was generous to me—shoes, for instance.

Our accounts are kept in this way: Contributions, donations, subscriptions that come in daily are entered in one book. The large checkbook tells of bills paid, of disbursements. Since we send out an appeal once or twice a year, we have to file with our state capital, pay a small fee, and give an account of monies received and how they were spent. We always comply with this state regulation because it is local—regional. We know such a requirement is to protect the public from fraudulent appeals and we feel our lives are open books—our work is obvious. And of course our pacifism has always been obvious—a great ideal of nonviolence to be worked toward.

Christ commanded His followers to perform what Christians have come to call the Works of Mercy: feeding the hungry, giving drink to the thirsty, clothing the naked, sheltering the harborless, visiting the sick and the prisoner, and burying the dead. Surely a simple program for direct action, and one enjoined on all of us. Not just for impersonal "poverty programs," government-funded agencies, but help given from the heart at a personal sacrifice. And how opposite a program this is to the works of war which starve people by embargoes, lay waste the land, destroy homes, wipe out populations, mutilate and condemn millions more to confinement in hospitals and prisons.

On another level there is a principle laid down, much in line with common sense and with the original American ideal, that governments should never do what small bodies can accomplish: unions, credit unions, cooperatives, St. Vincent de Paul Societies. Peter Maurin's anarchism was on one level based on this principle of subsidiarity, and on a higher level on that scene at the Last Supper where Christ washed the feet of His Apostles. He came to serve, to show the new Way, the way of the powerless. In the face of Empire, the Way of Love.

And here in small groups we are trying to talk of these things in the midst of the most powerful country in the world, during wartime, with the imminent threat of being crushed by this government, all because of principle, a principle so small and so important! It is not only that we must follow our conscience in opposing the government in war. We believe also that the government has no right to legislate as to who can or who are to perform the Works of Mercy. Only accredited agencies have the status of tax-exempt institutions. After their application has been filed, and after investigation and long delays, clarifications, intercession, and urgings by lawyers— often an expensive and long-drawn-out procedure—this tax-exempt status is granted.

As personalists, as an unincorporated group, we will not apply for this "privilege." We have explained to our donors many times that they risk being taxed on the gifts they send us, and a few (I can only think of two right now) have turned away from us. God raises up for us many a Habakkuk to bring his pottage to us when we are in the lion's den, or about to be, like Daniel of old.

Frankly, we do not know if it is because the government considers us a danger and threat that we are faced by this crisis. I beg the prayers of all our readers, whether they are sympathetic to us or not. I'm sure that many will think me a fool indeed, almost criminally negligent, for not taking more care to safeguard, not just the bank account, but the welfare of all the lame, halt, and blind who come to us.

Our refusal to apply for exemption status in our practice of the Works of Mercy is part of our protest against war and the present social "order" which brings on wars today.

May 1972

II

Last month, I wrote of the crisis we found ourselves in when we received a letter from the Internal Revenue Service stating that we owe them $296,359 in fines and penalties and unpaid income tax for the years 1966 through 1970. This was a very impressive bill, and we wondered what it would be if they started figuring out what they thought we owed them for the years from 1933, when we started, up to 1966!

There is no real news at the moment, nor will there be until I appear before a federal judge on July 3 to explain why the C.W. refuses to pay taxes, or to "structure itself" so as to be exempt from taxes. We are afraid of that word "structure." We refuse to become a "corporation."

Perhaps it is a *structure* which makes for such a scandal as the story which appeared in the press all over the country of a famous charity for children which had millions of dollars in reserve, money which could have been used either for expansions in the work or in working to bring about conditions in housing and education which would make so much "charity" unnecessary. "Charity" becomes a word which sticks in the gullet and makes one cry out for justice!

We repeat—we do not intend to "incorporate" the Catholic Worker movement. We intend to continue our emphasis on personal responsibility, an emphasis we were taught from the beginning by Peter Maurin.

I would like to be able to say to our readers, our family (as I like to think of them), that I am not at all worried about all this mishmash and the outcome. But of course one becomes intimidated in the awesome presence of a judge—not to speak of stenographers, and swearing "to tell the truth, the whole truth and nothing but the truth, so help me, God," and maybe not being allowed to finish a sentence or to explain. Anyone who writes as much as I do is not a "woman of few words." The older I get, the more I have to study and learn—there is no end to it. Of course, the Gospel tells us that when we are called before judges we should not worry about how to answer, what to say. I'll have to do a good deal of praying, doing what in the quaint terminology of the Church was formerly called "making acts of adoration, contrition, thanksgiving, and supplication." A.C.T.S. Easy to remember. Easy to do in those crises in which every family, without exception, finds itself.

O God, make haste to help me. Hear my prayer. Let my cry come unto Thee.

Besides praying, it is also good to distract the mind. In Tolstoy's *War and Peace,* which I read again recently (part of the distraction), Nicolai advises the fearful sixteen-year-old soldier never to think of the battle ahead, or of previous fears.

Actually our tax situation and the threats which hang over us involve nowhere near as much suffering and heartbreak as the moral, physical, and mental illnesses of so many who are dear to us.

It is then that I turn most truly for solace, for strength to endure, to the Psalms. I may read them without understanding, and mechanically at first, but I do believe they are the Word, and that Scripture, on the one hand, and the Eucharist, the Word made Flesh, on the other, have in them that strength which no power on earth can withstand. One of Ammon Hennacy's favorite quotations was "All things work together for good to those who love God."

As Sonya said at the end of *Uncle Vanya,* "I have faith, Uncle. I have fervent, passionate faith."

June 1972

III

Dear fellow workers in Christ,

Good news! On July 11 we received absolution from the U.S. Government in relation to all our tax troubles. We have related the story of the notice we had received—that we owed the government nearly $300,000 in back income taxes including penalties for "late filing and negligence." The examining officer of the Manhattan District had arrived at these figures through the reports we had obediently made to Albany on our appeals for funds. We had accepted this compromise with our local state because we are decentralists (in addition to being pacifists). When we first thought about federal income taxes, most of which go for war or "defense," we simplistically considered ourselves exempt because we had no income; no salaries are paid at the Catholic Worker, nor ever have been since we started in 1933.

But with growing tax resistance throughout the United States the government has become concerned. Telephone calls and official visits made us realize that trouble was impending.

Now we are happy to report the outcome. In a conference in late June with William T. Hunter, litigation attorney from the Department of Justice, one of the Assistant Attorneys General of the United States, we reached a verbal settlement couched in more human and satisfactory terms than the notice we later received.

"They" were willing to recognize our undoubtedly religious convictions in our conflict with the state, and were going to drop any proceedings against us. They had examined back issues of *The Catholic Worker,* they had noted the support we had from the press (the editorials of the *New York Times* and the *New York Post*), and had come to this conclusion that ours was a religious conviction. They had come to the further conclusion that it was not necessary that the federal government seek any other kind of a "conviction" against us.

The conference took place in a law office in Manhattan, 9:30 of a Monday morning. John Coster, our lawyer, Mr. Hunter and Ed Forand, Walter Kerell, Patrick Jordan, Ruth Collins, and I attended. There were no hostilities expressed. As peacemakers we must have love and respect for each individual we come in contact with. Our struggle is with principalities and powers. We cannot ever be too complacent about our own uncompromising positions because we know that in our own way we, too, make compromises. (For instance, in having a second-class mailing privilege from the government we accept a subsidy, just as Mr. Eastland does in Mississippi!)

It was Jesus who said that the worst enemies were those of our own household, and we are all part of this country, citizens of the United States, and share in its guilt.

I think Mr. Hunter (our opponent) shared with us the conviction that you could not kill an idea, and that we would continue to express ourselves and try to live the Catholic Worker positions as best we could, no matter what steps were taken against us by government. To *resist* and to *survive*—these are the growing convictions amongst the best of our youth. Harder for the aged and ill, but many of those among us have had a background of practice through the Depression, unemployment, and war.

It was a good confrontation we had for those three or four hours with the lawyers. We left to celebrate with a lunch at the Automat before we returned to office and work.

Yes, we would survive, I thought to myself, even if the paper were eventually suppressed and we had to turn to leafleting, as we are doing now each Monday against the I.B.M. Wall Street offices, trying to reach the consciences of all those participating in the hideous and cowardly war we are waging in Vietnam.

July–August 1972

23. The Church and the Political: Discussion Questions

What grounds do you think there might be for Christian resistance to rulers/the state?

How do you respond to Figgis's suggestion that a liberal democratic form of government struggles to grasp the social character of the church?

How does the reality of religious and cultural pluralism affect the way that we might think about the relation of the church and the political?

IV

The Politics of Jesus

Introduction by Elizabeth Phillips

Both Christological questions and questions surrounding the historical Jesus play important roles in historical and contemporary political theologies. The issues of relating the church and the political, explored in Section III, are often directly tied to issues of relating Jesus Christ to human politics. Luther's argument for the doctrine of the Two Kingdoms, for example, arose from the question of how the biblical sanctions of human governments and their use of lethal force could be reconciled with Jesus' teachings against retaliation and violence.

For some, particularly in medieval theology, the central questions surround settlements between the sovereignty of the risen and ascended Christ, the authority of his representatives on earth in the church, and the authority of human government. These questions remain central for some contemporary political theologians such as Oliver O'Donovan. For others, particularly in early Christianity and in Anabaptist traditions, the key questions surround the life and teachings of Jesus of Nazareth. Scholars of historical Jesus studies have debated whether Jesus was an apolitical moral/religious figure, a political revolutionary in line with the Zealots of his time, or an apocalyptic prophet whose politics arose from his conviction that the world was nearing its end. Differences in these interpretations lead some to argue for the irrelevance of Jesus to political theology either because he was not political, or because his politics were based on mistaken eschatology. Still other interpreters argue for the political normativity of Jesus, usually either in relation to nonviolence in particular or in relation to a general principle of political subversion and resistance.

Perhaps the most influential work on the subject in the twentieth century was *The Politics of Jesus* by John Howard Yoder. First published in 1972, *The Politics of Jesus* argued against the assumptions, both scholarly and popular, which have prevented Christians from understanding Jesus of Nazareth as ethically normative in the social and political realms. Primarily through tracing the political settings, content, and impact of narratives in Luke's gospel, Yoder offered an interpretation of Jesus as rejecting all the political options expected of and available to him. However, he was not therefore apolitical, but instead embodied a politics of non-violent liberation through suffering service, aligning himself with Isaiah and Jeremiah instead of David. The first essay in this section, 'Are You the One Who Is to Come?', originally a lecture presented in 1984, traces the same argument as *The Politics of Jesus* on a smaller scale.

Yoder was himself an Anabaptist, drawing on a tradition which held the normativity of Jesus of Nazareth at the heart of politics. Sixteenth-century Anabaptism is often considered under the heading of 'the Radical Reformation', which includes all those reformers who broke with the magisterial reformers as well as with Rome. Considered as a separate 'wing' of the Reformation in this way, the politics of the Radical Reformers ranged from apocalyptic theocracy to spiritualist antinomianism to sectarian separatism. Many of these groups, while important historically and in their own right, have little bearing on the pacifist forms of Anabaptism which continued beyond the sixteenth century. Representative of one such form of Anabaptism, *The Schleitheim Articles* (or *Schleitheim Confession*) arose from a gathering of first-generation Swiss Anabaptists in 1527 and sought to distinguish Anabaptist conviction and practice from the magisterial reforms of Luther and Zwingli, while also distancing their form of Anabaptism from other versions as well as from Protestant and Catholic misunderstandings of Anabaptism. Traditionally, Michael Sattler has been considered the main author of the text. Sattler was a key leader in sixteenth-century Swiss Anabaptism, and like so many Anabaptists of the time, he was brutally martyred just a few months after the Schleitheim gathering. The articles address baptism, the ban (a practice of excommunication when admonition has failed), breaking bread, separation from the world, shepherds in the church, the sword (governmental use of violence and coercion) and swearing oaths. Rather than a form of apoliticism, which Anabaptism is often assumed to be due to the separatism of many Anabaptist groups, the *Articles* describe the church as a visible body of committed believers living an alternative politics marked by the centrality of the normativity of Jesus.

John Howard Yoder was both an apologist for and a vocal critic of his Anabaptist tradition, and his relationship to Anabaptism is one of the most important aspects of his work. After centuries of being considered irrelevant to other Christian traditions, particularly in relation to politics, Anabaptism rose to an unprecedented level of theological influence in the late twentieth century, partially due to Yoder's work. One of his main critical interlocutors in this project, both explicitly in some places, and behind the scenes in general throughout his work, was Reinhold Niebuhr. During much of the twentieth century, Reinhold Niebuhr's 'Christian realism' dominated Protestant social ethics, particularly in America. Rejecting the humanistic optimism of the late nineteenth and early twentieth centuries, Niebuhr advanced a form of Augustinianism which focused on accounting for the realities of human sinfulness. For generations many regarded his understandings of sin, responsibility and realism as key sources for social ethics, and for Yoder these concepts were key targets for his arguments against what he saw as the marginalization of Jesus in Christian ethics. More recently, authors such as Eric Gregory and Charles Mathewes have engaged with Niebuhr's form of Augustinianism both critically and constructively (see selections from their work in Sections VI and VIII).

Niebuhr was a true 'public theologian' in his prolific writing for popular periodicals and ability to draw large crowds for public addresses. 'The Ethic of Jesus and the Social Problem' was a periodical essay published in 1932, in which Niebuhr describes why the teachings and example of Jesus must not be applied to politics. Here Niebuhr reinterprets Luther's designation of the sovereignty of Christ over the inward, spiritual kingdom in relation to late modern liberalism. In the social and political realms, Niebuhr argues, the 'pure love ethic' of Jesus can only stand as an impossible standard by which to judge all ethics. Such love cannot, however, shape the social order; justice requiring coercion and force must be the norm of politics.

Yoder's legacy has been called into serious question since his death, and in particular since a coalescing of online conversations and revelations which came to a peak in 2013. It is now clear that Yoder engaged in a consistent pattern of manipulating, violating and abusing women across many years and multiple continents.[1] Although his historical significance is undeniable, many now question whether Yoder's work can be used constructively in light of the facts of his life. Without question, if it is to be of continuing value it must be critically reassessed in relation to what we now know about the life from which the theology arose. All theology comes from somewhere.

The idea that all theology comes from somewhere may seem a truism, too commonsensical to require explicit statement. If indeed that is the case, political theologies of the mid-to-late twentieth century are one of the main reasons (see Section II 'Approaches to Political Theology' and Section VII 'Oppression, Marginalization, and Liberation'). Liberation, feminist, queer and Black theologians brought the context and contingency of all theology into startling relief by explicitly embracing it in their own work. James Cone's pioneering Black theology arose from his experiences of growing up in the segregated South during the decades of the lynching mobs, receiving a theological education which seemed utterly disconnected from the lives of the Black students to whom he tried to communicate it, and coming into his own as a theologian in a moment when Black Americans were torn between the non-violent resistance of Martin Luther King, Jr. and the revolutionary vision of Malcolm X. In 'Jesus Christ in Black Theology', originally a chapter in his ground-breaking 1970 book *A Black Theology of Liberation*, we see some of his most provocative early writing in which he demonstrates the centrality of the politics of Jesus in Black theology, arguing that Jesus 'is black' and that 'to be a disciple of the black Christ is to become black with him'.

---

[1] See Rachel Waltner Goosen, '"Defanging the Beast": Mennonite Responses to John Howard Yoder's Sexual Abuse', *Mennonite Quarterly Review* 89.1:7–80.

24. John Howard Yoder – Are You the One Who Is to Come?[1]

"Prophetism can be defined as that understanding of history that finds its meaning in the concern and purpose of God for that history, and in the participation of God in that history."[2] One might do well, in some context, to invest some time in unpacking the assumptions and implications of this compact and formal way of putting our question. What would be the alternative understandings? Would there be a God who would not care about history and not act in it? Or a God who would act within it without caring about it? Or who would care without acting? Does it make a difference which "history" one is talking about? Is there only one history, namely, something like "history as a whole" or "history as such"? Or is history necessarily particular, so that the God who called the Jews might not be identical with the God of whom the Bantus speak? Is the choice of histories itself a choice of Gods?

For present purposes, however, we need to lean in the other direction. I seek here simply to disengage from the Gospel narrative a description of the specific ways in which Jesus said his "Father" cared for and intervened in the life of people.

If we were conversing with Platonism or with Buddhism, it might be appropriate to discuss *whether* God is interested in history at all. From some religious and philosophical perspectives, the question may be whether God can care about history: whether it is compatible with the nature of Deity to be concerned about the realm of the finite and the particular. Is not Deity, by definition, infinite and incompatible with taking with ultimate seriousness any one time, any one place, any one practical goal, any one set of people?

That is not a question which can be meaningfully addressed to the Gospel accounts; they stand on the shoulders of centuries of Hebrew history, where that question had been resolved with such resounding certainty as not to be a possible question. The question that was evident from the perspective of Greek or Roman antiquity and that in the West became visible again in the age of Enlightenment — "how odd of God to choose the Jews" — did not strike the Gospel writers as odd at all. That YHWH of Hosts cares about a particular people is the specific definition, the identity of YHWH, as the one who chooses to be and to bring into being, more than it is a description of anything meritorious or lucky about the lineage of Abraham. Jesus presupposes and prolongs that understanding of the uniqueness of YHWH as the one who chooses.

---

[1] Initially presented 22 March 1984 as one of six Parker Lectures in Theology and Ministry at the Institute of Religion, which is linked to the Texas Medical Center at Houston, Texas. The series title was "The Pastor as Prophet," which also became the title of the book based on the lecture series, which was published by Pilgrim Press in 1985 (editors Earl E. Shelp and Ronald H. Sunderland).

[2] This phrase was part of the programmatic instructions sent to all the speakers by the series planners.

The story about the Jew Jesus between the Zealots and the Romans, between the Essenes and the Sadducees, does not show him as being tested or tempted at all to conceive of God as not in history. The questions were in *which* history and in which *direction,* toward what end, that caring divine intervention was to be discerned and obeyed.

In this essay I have been asked to discuss the witness of the Gospel texts themselves: It cannot be my task to seek to reach past the specific texts into the critical reconstruction and deconstruction of the events or the redactional processes behind them. A gospel is, by nature, a witnessing document, and it is that dimension of witness that we want to hear. Rather than distill from the Gospel accounts a few timeless generalizations about a vision for history, I propose to review a series of the more dramatic vignettes within the narrative. Each implies and affirms certain deep certainties about God's intention for the human story.

The Promise Is Fulfilled

The private beginning of Jesus' ministry, according to three of the Gospel accounts, was a conversation with Satan in the desert, after Jesus had been baptized (like many other people) by John. What was being tested was his understanding of the way in which he was to proceed to be the liberator-designate. Will he do it as showman, as thaumaturgic welfare distributor, as multiplier of loaves and fishes? Will he do it by appearing suddenly in the temple to claim effective sovereignty, in the style of the Maccabees? Will he enter into a pact with the powers already ruling the globe?

None of these options would take Jesus or his people out of history. None would denature history as unimportant over against some other realm or kind of being. Jesus' answer is in the same world. It is a concrete alternative to those forms of the messianic temptation. His way will be an alternative to the way of the demagogue sweeping crowds along by his unique power, to that of the Zealot seizing the city by surprise violence, and to that of the collaborator scheming his way into the existing structures' domination.

The way of the demagogue, the Zealot, or the Herodian collaborator is not set aside because his goal of serving God's purposes is too concrete or too historical or too "political," but because it is historical differently. It is that differentness for which Jesus was first to live quietly half a lifetime in simple subordination to the Galilean family structure, from which he then emerged as a self-educated rabbi (something of a contradiction in terms) and peripatetic prophet, and finally, by living just as he did, gathering disciples just as he did, dying just as he did, and rising just as he did to plant in the midst of history a new kind of social phenomenon. He reformulated what it means to be the people of God in the world.

The Platform

According to Luke's Gospel, the first milestone of Jesus' public ministry was the time when, in his hometown synagogue, he was given the scroll of Isaiah to read. It was already open, or he turned it open, to chapter 61 (vv. 1–2), where Messiah is speaking:

> The Spirit of the Lord GOD is upon me,
>   because the LORD has anointed me
> to bring good tidings to the afflicted;
>   he has sent me to bind up the brokenhearted,
> to proclaim liberty to the captives,
>   and the opening of the prison to those who are bound;
> To proclaim the year of the LORD's favor. (RSV)

There is no way to take history in general or God in general more seriously than to say of a divine promise, as Jesus did in Nazareth: "Today this word is fulfilled among you."

History is a process in which specific events can be identified as links in the chain leading from God's past to our common future. What it was that was fulfilled, according to this prophetic text, was the promise of a transformed set of human relations involving the forgiveness of debts, the liberation of prisoners, and the renewal of the agrarian economy. What the Authorized Version translated impenetrably by "the acceptable year of the Lord" clearly meant in the Isaiah text the promulgation of the year of Jubilee, the arrangement under which, in the Mosaic order, every family would be reinstated every half-century in the possession of their ancestral land. If their fathers had lost it through bad luck, it would be restored to them; if they had come into wealth because of their fathers' astuteness, they would give it back as a celebration of the year of grace.

Such a vision is obviously not a literal model for other times and places. It presupposed the patterns of kingship and of landholding of ancient Israel, giving no guidance (if taken with picayune literalism) for urban economies or for the landless. Jesus' vision was not antiquarian. It would be equally inappropriate to read with picayune literalism the analogous vision of the book of Micah, according to which all people will be unafraid, owning their own vines and fig trees, and to complain that it would not be an interesting promise for the Wheat Belt. What counts is the simplicity with which both visions use the stuff of common economic reality to concretize the divine presence.

This direct description of liberation as the assignment of Messiah, and as the mark of this present instant, lays claim on the historical moment in a more radical way than do those eschatological visions that project unthinkable cosmic catastrophes in the distant or even the imminent future. Jesus is saying that a new quality of human life is beginning to be operative in his time and place: in Nazareth and, more broadly, in Galilee, and all the way to Jerusalem in those weeks and months when his presence will force decision on his listeners. The decision his presence imposes is for or against a new order that can be likened to the new beginning prescribed by the "year of the Lord's favor." That proclamation was unacceptable in Nazareth: it rejected the insider privilege of those who thought of themselves as especially God's people.

The Precursor's Doubts

The prefaces to all three of the Synoptic Gospels report Jesus' baptism at the hands of John as the beginning of his public ministry. Luke's Gospel reports a more formal crossing of the threshold from the age of John to that of Jesus, when emissaries from John visit Jesus while John is in prison to allay John's doubts about whether what Jesus was achieving was what John had been predicting.

Jesus had been one with John in the confidence that the impact of the promised kingdom was to be a profound reversal: the axe at the root of the tree, the unproductive branches thrown to the fire, the flail attacking the threshing floor, the chaff being blown off to burn.... That is what made of John's question a most fitting challenge: "Are you the one to come, or do we wait for another?" The question makes clear that the framework of historical meaning is a temporal expectation, which a given historical figure can either live up to or fail to live up to. The present moment either is or is not the time of fulfillment. John has earned the right to ask.

Jesus accepted the question but did not answer it with a sentence or a "yes." He answered by pointing to events in process, to miracles of healing. That kind of healing, it appears, should sustain the faith of those who were probably looking for a different kind of liberation.

Detailed biographical or historical reconstruction, to the extent to which scholars can risk it at all, points up differences between contrasting pictures of what various people thought John might have wanted and what Jesus wanted: Was John more like a Zealot or an Essene? Were the connections between the two movements or the two men as direct as Luke says? How do we interpret the difference between the Lucan account, with the appearance of a positive transition from John to Jesus, and the picture that John's Gospel gives of some competitiveness between the two movements, and some need for the disciples of Jesus to disavow John in order to affirm Jesus?

We need to name those questions, as part of the necessary seriousness of real history; yet for the purposes of this essay they do not matter. In any case, the Gospel account affirms a sequence of historic projects in which precursor and successor both understand God to be working in the real world to establish justice. Neither gives an independent value to contemplative or ritual religion, even though both spent long seasons in solitude and both laid claim to immediate understanding of the identity and purpose of God characterized by an immediacy quite different from the religions of tradition and authority. Their witness is not like what the Social Gospel vision of sixty years ago proposed by way of the reduction of religion to ethics. What they bring is not a reduction but a rise to a higher power. They offer not "ethics" in the sense of a set of behavioral imperatives for good people, but the proclamation of a new social possibility for the human story. Both of them affirmed the real alternatives of first-century Palestine as the place where, thanks to a renewed transcendent intervention, God's will is known and achieved.

Jesus both does and does not take over the mantle and the prophetic style of his cousin John. His answer to the emissaries from John who asked whether he is what John was looking for is affirmative; yet the evidence he tells John's disciples to convince their leader is his own ministry of healing, not his projected takeover of the palace. He does not even join John in scolding Herod for his blatant public and probably politically motivated immorality. He does not let his prophetic mission be downgraded into telling rulers what not to do. Yet he is with John in seeing what he is doing as an alternative to the way the elders proceed.

The King in the Desert

The hinge of the public ministry of Jesus, to the extent to which creative historical empathy can reconstitute anything of the way in which that ministry might have developed, is the feeding of the multitude. Until then, the crowds following Jesus were mixed in their composition and their expectations. His closest disciples are described as not yet understanding the core of what he was proclaiming. The miracle of the loaves and fishes had fulfilled in powerful public drama the prediction of the tempter: if Jesus would feed the people, if in the face of the privation and vulnerability that being in the desert has always meant for the human organism Jesus were to provide abundant sustenance for the body, he would be accredited as the coming king. John's Gospel, the most interpretative account, makes that most clear.

This event is the peak of the readiness of the crowds to acclaim Jesus as their anointed liberator. This had to mean (although our habits of interpretation have hitherto not taken it very seriously) that they would also be committed to supporting him in the military defense, against the Romans, of the kingdom they wanted him to set up. Now, for the first time, Jesus directly rejects that prospect. Now, for the first time, he tells his disciples of his coming suffering in ways that they are unable to understand and unwilling to accept. It is not that Jesus withdraws from having a messianic project for his people. It is that that project is defined with increasing clarity in ways that reject the temptations of holy violence. He joins the rabbis who had already decided that the Maccabean experiment had been a mistake. He prefigures a later rabbi like Johanan ben Zakkai, who was to disavow the Zealot rebellion of A.D. 66–70. That did not mean acquiescence in the Sadducean strategy of negotiation with the Romans within the framework of colonial status. It did not mean Essene quietism. For the present, Jesus does not say what alternative social project his message will mean. It has, in any case, meant a renewed claim to the mantle of Moses as the instrument of God's sustaining the people with bread in the desert, at the beginning of a new exodus.

The Disciple's Choice: *Caveat Emptor*

For Luke's account, the most dramatic statement of the alternative way toward which Jesus has been leading his disciples since the episode of the loaves in the desert is chapter 14. The sequence of account that describes Jesus' movement toward Jerusalem (chap. 9) had been marked along the way with reminders of his political vision. At the beginning of chapter 13 are two references to episodes of Zealot violence: the incident of the tower of Siloam and the massacre of some Galileans by Pilate. "Great multitudes" are still following Jesus (14:25); it is to them that he addresses his dramatic warning against a too-easy decision to join his movement.

Any normal notion of wise leadership would have one make the most of a moment of popularity, while it lasted, to enlist more people, to make it easy for them to extend and deepen their commitment to him, to move them from mere awareness to commitment.... We are accustomed to seeing it as the task of leaders, especially of the pastor, to make people's decisions easier. We believe we are serving people when we help them picture life in God's cause as the attainable goal of an easy transition. We assume that loyalty grows through involvement; they should not be frightened off at the outset.

Yet Jesus moves the other way. He warns his listeners against being too willing to follow him. Anyone who will follow him must be ready to jeopardize immediate nuclear family loyalties. The phrase he uses is "hate his own father and mother." Certainly this reference to division within the family does not mean preoccupation with psychic problems of internal family dynamics. It is, rather, that the unity of the family as the basic social cell is sacrificed to the values of the larger social cause to which a follower of Jesus becomes committed.

That cost is also described as the loss of one's own life. The way one might lose one's own life is described as one's "own cross." The "cross" in that connection can obviously not mean what it has come to mean in later Protestant pastoral care: neither the inward suffering of struggle with self nor the outward suffering of personal ill health or difficult social relations.[3] The "cross" could only mean (in the setting that Luke's account means to narrate) what the Romans were wont to do with people threatening their political hegemony. Jesus warns the crowd that to follow him means exposing oneself to the reproach of causing political unrest.

---

[3]Cf. "The Cross in Protestant Pastoral Care," in *The Politics of Jesus*, 2nd ed. (Grand Rapids: Eerdmans, 1994), pp. 129ff.

He goes on to reinforce the warning against a too-easy adhesion to his cause by recounting two anecdotes concerning public figures who found, to their shame, that they could not complete an ambitious project they had undertaken: a building project and a war. King Herod had just done both these things. If he had been speaking in March 1984, Jesus might have referred to a former astronaut who thought he could get himself nominated to the presidency or to a president who thought he could pacify Beirut by sending the Marines. Better not to set out for battle if you are not ready to give your life for the cause. What more dramatic demonstration could there be of the irrevocably historical shape of Jesus' project?

What is the cost one should count? The family is the basic cell of society. Yet in a serious missionary situation, to decide in favor of Jesus may have to be done at the cost of other real values, especially one's commitments to family and ethnic group. Jesus uses the verb "to hate" with regard to the values of family loyalty and one's own life. "Hate" here does not mean a malevolent emotion or a desire to destroy someone; it must however mean a conscious decision to put those values in second place.

The other word for the cost of following is "the cross." By the time Luke wrote his Gospel, he and his readers of course knew about Jesus' own death; yet for the account of Jesus' speaking to the crowd, that meaning cannot be assumed. What the cross *then* had to mean was what the practice of crucifixion by the Roman army already meant in that setting, namely, as the specific punishment for insurrection. Followers of Jesus, he warns them, must be ready to be seen and to be treated as rebels, as was going to happen to him.

The Liberator's Choice

The most outright and overt explanatory statement of what he is doing that Jesus ever gives is probably his word to the disciples in "the upper room." Luke has placed here in the middle of the passion account a word that in Matthew and in Mark is found at other points in Jesus' ministry. It is framed between the breaking of bread, in which Judas's betrayal is foretold, and two other words about rejection: the prediction of Peter's denial and the word about the two swords. Certainly we are not pressing the text when we understand Luke to be illuminating all those conflict words with this one general teaching, and illuminating the teaching with the words of conflict. When Jesus says, "The kings of the Gentiles exercise lordship over them; and those in authority over them are called benefactors" (22:25, RSV), he is describing his own temptation. When he says, "But not so with you; rather let the greatest among you become as the youngest, and the leader as one who serves" (22:26, RSV), he is describing not only his own decision about his own path but also the prophetic perspective on the moral resolution of conflict. He is restating, in the form of a moral teaching, his own choice, which he had been making and renewing weekly since his baptism and day by day from the triumphal entry until that upper room conversation, and which he would be renewing again that night in the garden. It is the choice between violence claiming to be sanctified by the good it promises to do (those in authority calling themselves benefactors) and the authentic good done by one who serves.

Jesus thereby first of all makes clear that the most fundamental decision he had to make in this world was how to be that kind of benefactor. At the dramatic turning point of this passion Passover, he best describes his path by contrasting it — but that also means comparing it — with what the rulers of the peoples claim to do. He does not suggest that he has an alternative way to be a priest, although later Christians rounded out their picture of him by saying that too.[4] He does not claim to be a better prophet, although he acknowledges the line of prophets culminating in John as his precursors. Later Christians have properly also used the language of "prophet," as this book does, to describe his achievement. Yet the comparison and contrast with which he does define his mission are that of kingship. Lords in this world claim to be benefactors; he claims to be benefactor. They claim to be great; he provides an alternative vision of greatness. They dominate; he serves; and there is no more profound description of what he asks of his disciples than that they be servants, with him and in his way.

That contrast is not meant as one moral hint among many, as Luke recounts it. It is not merely one scrap of political wisdom among others. It is a capsule statement of Jesus' own key self-definition, as he was torn between quietistic and Zealot models of the messianic role. The difference is not simply between ways to run a battle or ways to be socially responsible. It is between definitions of salvation.

What we learn from Jesus is not a suggestion about strategy or skill in the discharge of those particular leadership responsibilities ordinarily associated with the pastorate. What the gospel tells us is rather what kind of word we are called to minister in and toward. In a world of greed and self-aggrandizement, whose technology and dominant philosophy foster selfishness more than ever before, the people of God, as a whole, are called to be the firstfruits of an age of redistribution and shared sufficiency. In an age of rampant and in fact renascent nationalisms and of imperialisms whitewashed with the ideology of liberty, we are called to be heralds and instruments of the one word already created at the cross and at Pentecost, whose ultimate triumph we are to proclaim despite its evident present defeats.

Yet what is most striking about the way in which Jesus serves those goals is not the stated ends — which many another sage had dreamed about and many another activist promoted. What is original and redemptive is that he does it with his own blood. The community he creates is the product and not the enforcer of that new

---

[4]When apostolic writers called Jesus a priest, their accent fell on how he differed from ordinary priests; namely, by sacrificing himself. They were not interest [sic] in priesthood, or in the pastoral role, as a fixture in the life of religious institutions.

regime. His followers will live from, not toward, the victory of Christ. Our life is to proclaim, not to produce, the new world.

Our series of vignettes could be extended through the rest of the Gospel accounts and on through Acts; but for now, with this word from the upper room, we may leave the narrative and move to analysis.

Not Engineering, but Doxology

The standard account of the challenge of social concern would have us believe that the most difficult problem is to describe with some precision what kind of world we want: Do we want property to be owned socially or privately? Do we want prices to be set by the marketplace or in some other way? Do we want decisions to be made by an aristocracy or by a referendum? Do we want the races to mix or to live at peace apart? Once those broad goals have been set, the standard account of our social ethical agenda would have us believe that then the rest is only a matter of engineering, of bringing to bear toward that end whatever power we have available. Those who know which way the course of events should go can, with moral propriety, push them in that direction, and the clearer they are about that direction, the more authority they have to take control. The worse the situation is, the more violently they have the right to take over.

Jesus does not reshape the question by choosing a different social goal behind which to place his prophetic authority, and toward which to legitimate the application of power. His social goal is utterly traditional: It is that of the Mosaic corpus, with its bias toward the sojourner, the widow, and the orphan. It is that of Isaiah and Micah, the vision of a world taught the arts of peacemaking because they have come to Jerusalem to learn Torah and to hear the judicial oracles of YHWH. It is the ingathering of the nations in the age of the anointing. What differs about Jesus is not a different goal; it is that he sees, for both himself and his disciples, a different mode of implementation. They are not to be content with the existing order, as if it were close enough to what YHWH wants that one could get from where we are organically to where YHWH wants to take us. It is not the path of the quietists or the Essenes, who went to the desert to wait for God to act, or of the Pharisees, who kept themselves pure within society, disavowing the present world's structures but leaving it to a future divine intervention to set them straight. It is not the path of Zealot presumption, claiming to be the party of righteousness authorized by God to trigger the coming of the new age through a paroxysm of righteous insurrection.

Each of those standard type responses to "the mess the world is in" is a different answer to the question, "How do we get from here to there?" Jesus' alternative is not to answer that question in a new way but to renew, as the prophets had always been trying to do, the insistence that the question is how to get from there to here. How can the lordship of YHWH, affirmed in principle from all eternity, be worthily confessed as grace through faith? How can the present world be rendered transparent to the reality already there, that the sick are to be healed and the prisoners freed? We are not called to love our enemies in order to make them our friends. We are called to act out love for them because at the cross it has been effectively proclaimed that from all eternity they were our brothers and sisters. We are not called to make the bread of the world available to the hungry; we are called to restore the true awareness that it always was theirs. We are not called to topple the tyrants, so that it might become true that the proud fall and the haughty are destroyed. It already is true; we are called only to let that truth govern our own choice of whether to be, in our turn, tyrants claiming to be benefactors.

It is thus a profound misapprehension of the messianic moral choice to think that in his rejection of violence, Jesus was led by methodological purism in moral choice, choosing to be an absolutist about the sacredness of life. It would be an equally profound misapprehension to think that he was the world's first Gandhian, calculating the prospects for a social victory as being in his particular circumstances greater for nonviolent than for violent tactics. Both of those interpretations of what Jesus was doing as a social strategist follow the "standard account of social ethical discernment" that it is precisely the purpose of all the prophets to free us from. Jesus' acceptance of the cross, from which we throw light on his rejection of both pietism and Zealot compulsion, was not, in the first analysis, a moral decision, but an eschatological one. It was dictated by a different vision of where God is taking the world. Or, we may it was an ontological decision, dictated by a truer picture of what the world *really is.*

As a final exercise in clarification, perhaps the originality of the prophetic vision of Jesus can be brought out by an effort to contrast it with the other models that have tended to dominate this discussion and to teach us how to think.

For four centuries now, it has been especially the Lutheran believers who have tirelessly reminded us that in soteriology we are not supposed to achieve, but to trust. Salvation is not a product, but a presupposition. We do not bring it about, but we accept it as a gift of grace mediated through faith. Jesus and the early disciples did not let that understanding dictate for them only what to do about "salvation," in the sense of the present integrity or the ultimate destiny of the soul. They applied it as well to shalom as the social historical purpose of YHWH. We do not achieve it so much as we accept it. It is not as basic to engineer it as to proclaim it.

For still longer than the Lutherans, Roman Catholics, or at least the Schoolmen among them, have been concerned to clarify that nature and grace stand not in opposition but are integrated in a complementary or organic way. The behavior God calls for is not alien to us; it expresses what we really are made to be. Yet, unfortunately, later Catholic strategy has foreshortened the critical potential of that vision by confusing the "nature of things" with the way things are now in the fallen world, especially in ethnic and national definitions of community and patriarchal definitions of order. When society has been defined as the nation and social order as patriarchy, then it is no longer true that grace completes nature; in the face of that definition of "nature," the word of YHWH has to be like a fire, like a hammer that breaks rocks into pieces.

Yet when the "nature of things" is properly defined, the organic relationship to grace is restored. The cross is not a scandal to those who know the world as God sees it, but only to the pagans, who look for what they call wisdom, or the Judaeans, who look for what they call power (1 Corinthians 1.17f). This is what I meant before, when I stated that the choice of Jesus was ontological: it risks an option in favor of the restored vision of how things really are. It has always been true that suffering creates shalom. Motherhood has always meant that. Servanthood has always meant that. Healing has always meant that. Tilling the soil has always meant that. Priesthood has always meant that. Prophecy has always meant that. What Jesus did — and we might say it with reminiscence of Scholastic christological categories — was that he renewed the definition of kingship to fit with the priesthood and prophecy. He saw that the suffering servant is king as much as he is priest and prophet. The cross is neither foolish nor weak, but natural.

A form of Catholic moral discernment older than the Scholastic vision is the culture of the early medieval period, between the old Caesars and the new Carolingians, an age during which civilization had to survive without the support of the preferred vehicle of righteous royalty. If you look at that epoch with the eyes of Justinian or of Charlemagne, it was the "dark ages." If, however, we ask of those ages what kind of light people had to live by, the answer is that it was the culture of the saints. Moral education was a matter of telling the stories of holy people. Holiness included patterns of renunciation and withdrawal, but it was also the age when a hermit would be called from his cave or an abbot from his monastery to be made a bishop. It was an age when the bishop, through his control of the sacrament of absolution, was the community's main moral teacher and, through his administration of the right of sanctuary, was its most solid civil peacekeeper.

It has been one major impoverishment of our Western moral universe that first the Schoolmen and then the Reformers, the former looking for something more intellectually generalizable and the latter denouncing abuses, have robbed us of the place of hagiography in morality. Not only did that mean a loss of the human concreteness of biography as a way to talk about being human. It also led to forgetting wholeness. It predisposed us to pulling love apart from justice, purity from practicality, and leadership from servanthood, dichotomies that have dominated moral analysis ever since. When God chose Jesus as the way to come into the world, when Jesus chose disciples as a way to make his message mobile, and when the disciples chose the "gospel" as preferred literary form of witness, each meant the choice of the story of the holy one as the dominant prototype not only of communicating, but of being good news. Jesus' parables, like his presenting himself as model, did not represent a mere pedagogical choice of "storytelling" as a more understandable way to communicate to illiterate crowds; the story is rather in the order of being and in the order of knowing the more fundamental mode of reality.

Yet older than our teachers from the "dark ages" is the Hebrew heritage which taught generations of Jews and Christians that law is a form of grace. Christians have been busy since the second century weakening that awareness. Hellenistic apologetes felt that the Jewishness of Torah would keep them from reaching nonbelievers. Reformers feared it would let religious performance stand in the way of saving grace. Both of these forms of anti-Judaism have profoundly impoverished us. It is only now, in the shadow — or should we say the light of — the Hitlerian Holocaust, that we are beginning to renew the recognition of all that was lost with the Jewishness of the original meaning of Jesus. Jesus' insistence, at the center of the Sermon on the Mount, which is itself the literary-catechetical center of the Gospel account as structured by Matthew, that the law is fulfilled and not forgotten is indispensable to understanding his claims in his time and even more for our time. Thinking that we are freed from the law instead of *through and for* the grace of Torah is at the root of the anomie of our age, even though regrettably most of the preachers who proclaim that sorry truth seem to be interested in restoring a law that was not fulfilled in the Sermon on the Mount, one that would not relativize the family and favor the outsider.

The point of these side glances at the Lutheran, the Scholastic, the hagiographical, and the nomic visions has been not to reject them as wrong but to englobe and transcend them as true but inadequate. To make the claim with the simplicity of caricature: The prophetic vision does more wholly what each of those other modes seeks to do. Its vision of the priority of grace is more fundamental than that of the Lutheran mode, since it applies justification by grace through faith to morality as well as to "salvation" — or, as I hinted earlier, because its picture of the shalom that is given us by grace is both morality and what used to be called "salvation." It affirms "the nature of things" more profoundly than the Scholastic vision because it reads the substantial definition of nature from the incarnation and holy history, not from medieval culture *or* Greek philosophy. It affirms and transcends the culture of saintliness by planting in our midst the magnetic story of the model of all models, whom to follow is first of all a decision and a path before it becomes goals and principles. It fulfills the vision of the law of God by focusing the deep meaning of not swearing falsely, not committing adultery, loving the neighbor not as a mere holding pattern to save the civil order but as the design for restoring the cosmos.

To confess and to celebrate the healing of the world and to distinguish authentic healing from idolatrous and blasphemous counterfeits, the prophetic community is indispensable. The transformation of the world will proceed sometimes through the conscious exercise of discerning insight by believers, but also by others of good will, and even (despite themselves) by others of good will being providentially used, carrying out the imperatives and skills, of their vocations, i.e., those definable skills and goals of which the social organism is constituted. Yet to discern how those structures can be defined as servants of the "divine purpose" and be rescued from the idolatrous claims that their imperatives are univocal or their value autonomous, which led the apostles to describe them as rebellious principalities and powers, for the faith community is again instrumentally prerequisite. How do we know which vision of the vocation of motherhood is redemptive and which oppressive? How do we know which vision of national dignity or world liberation is true and which tyrannical? A doctrine of the vocation, or an affirmation of the orders of nature or creation, is powerless to answer if abstraction is made from the prophetic.

If then we confess the world as the ontological locus of God's sovereign intentions, and the believing community as its epistemological locus, the imperative is not first to stoke up our motivational devotedness, nor to develop more powerful sociological tools of persuasion or coercion, but to nurture the organic integrity of the community charged with the task of insight. The agents of coordination the apostles called "overseers and elders," the agents of community memory they called scribes, the agents of perception they called prophets, the agents of critical linguistic awareness they called teachers,[5] the agents of more-than-rational sensitivity they called discerners of spirits, the agents of doxology they called speakers in tongues, to say nothing of the healers, the administrators, and the bearers of other forms of charismatic empowerment which did not happen to occur in the apostolic lists but will be needed, and will be provided as need arises — must all be created anew and integrated repeatedly in the ongoing presence of God the Spirit in the body.

Cop-out or *Pars Pro Toto?*

If the gospel logic does not follow the standard account in centering the ends of Christian historical concern in the specific project to be achieved through the prophets' influencing the bearers of power, and if the model of the cross remains normative both in its particular historical orientation to the man Jesus and in its principled renunciation of coerciveness in implementation, is this not some kind of other-worldly quietism?

The possibility has always been open that it could be read that way. It is intrinsically not that. They do not crucify quietists. A more adequate description would be to say that in its most formative stages this view is "apocalyptic"; but to sort out the multiple meanings that that term has in recent usage would be beyond our scope. What can be said most simply is that the future toward which the prophet knows God has already

---

[5]This review of the variety of distinct roles within the community's process of discernment harks back to my listing in my *The Priestly Kingdom* (Notre Dame, Ind.: Notre Dame University Press, 1984), pp. 28ff. It is because of their diversity that the focus of the 1984 Houston conference on just the pastor was counterproductive.

effectively begun to move the world is prefigured in the possibilities offered and to some modest extent fulfilled in the believing community. Sometimes it is the Holy Spirit, sometimes it is the church that the apostolic writings refer to as the *arrabon* (the pledge, or down payment) or as the "firstfruits" of God's impending victory. Here already the lame are healed, here the underdog is honored, here bread is shared and ethnicity is transcended.

The people of God are not a substitute or an escape from the whole world's being brought to the effective knowledge of divine righteousness; the believing community is the beginning, the pilot run, the bridgehead of the new world on the way. Its discourse may be called "apocalyptic" if by that — without disregard for other meanings the term may have — we designate a portrayal of the way the world is being efficaciously called to do that does not let present empirical readings of possibility have the last word.

I have used the phrases "believing community" and "people of God" instead of the other apostolic term *ekklesia,* because one learns from the literature concerned with this theme that reference to the community is often taken pejoratively; that is, the term "church" is often defined not by the apostolic and prophetic vision but by the abuses of sectarian, triumphalist, or ritualistic experience of the past.

None of those abuses is founded in what the prophets, Jesus, and the apostles were talking about. The believing community is the epistemological prerequisite of the prophetic confession. Whether it is God's intent to restore the world does not depend on faith, but faith is an instrumental precondition of knowing the shape of that restoration and defending it from our own foreshortened perspectives, whether foreshortened by selfishness or shame or by a too simple hope or a too weak one. As Yahweh could use famine and pestilence, Midianite merchants, and pagan emperors for his purposes in the Hebrew story, so tomorrow we may be confident that powers beyond the confines of faith can be instruments of judgment and of construction; yet to confess and celebrate that work, the prophetic function of the confessing community is indispensable.

By the nature of the case, the life of this kind of community cannot be cared for only by one specialized functionary named "the pastor"; that understanding of the pastoral task would be a contradiction in terms. How such a community would be appropriately structured, in the diversity of ministries or charismata distributed by the. Holy Spirit, can, however, not be unfolded on the basis of the Gospel texts. For the Gospel texts, Jesus himself is the shepherd.

Nonetheless we do well to recognize that as the messianic community continues to minister to a still not-yet-messianic age, there will be need, in order to maintain and propagate the community and to illuminate its interfaces with "the world," for skills and perspectives that our parlance calls "pastoral," focusing on a style more than an office. The bearer of the prophetic task is the whole people of God. Specific ministerial gifts within that work are to be measured by their congruence with the whole community's calling to be the advance agents of the coming realm. Each of the partial perspectives we have recognized — vocation, nature, sanctification, law — will call for specific people to help articulate the shape of the prophecy needed. Scribes will need to be "pastoral" rather than legalistic. Elders will need to be "pastoral" rather than patriarchal. Prophets will need to be "pastoral" rather than neurotic. Teachers will need to be "pastoral" rather than abstruse. The one who consoles will need to be "pastoral" rather than manipulatively therapeutic. Those who plan and lead assemblies for worship and those who "preach" will need to point beyond themselves to the realm, and beyond the aesthetic to the prophetic. In our age's thought forms, the term most apt to preserve this accent will probably not be "pastor," with its overtones of professionalism and privilege; the place of the cross as a model for ministry will often better be rendered by the language of servanthood. Yet watching our language is not enough; "servicer" or "ministry" can also come to mean privilege.

The closest the Jesus of the Gospel accounts came to projecting the shape of the church was the description in Matthew (18:15–20) and in John (14–16; 20:19–23) of the coming guidance of the Paraclete to empower forgiveness and discernment. That is the warrant for continuing prophetic clarity. It is also the reason that the shape of the ministries contributing to that clarity must be renewed in every age. This is not a blank check for future impulsive, intuitionistic, or situationist "flexibility," for the Spirit's task is to remind the disciples of Jesus. The "more truth" that the Spirit interprets is coherent with its origin. Yet its coherence is not timeless rigidity; it is like that of a plant's organic growth, the implementation of a new regime. For this all the ministries in the body will be drawn on. Yet here I have let Jesus' pointers send us beyond the Gospels to the Epistles, beyond annunciation to unfolding.

The doctrine of the two natures of the divine Son, enshrined in the formulae of Chalcedon, has come to be a metaphysical puzzle. Yet what these notions originally meant, and should still mean, is that God takes history so seriously that there is no more adequate definition of God's eternal purposes than in the utterly human historicity of the Jew Jesus. That same prophetic condescension makes of the believing community—i.e., of the human historicity of those who confess Jesus' normativeness—God's beachhead in the world as it is, the down payment, the prototype, the herald, the midwife of the New World on the way. The ultimate test of whether we truly believe that God's purposes are for the whole world, that they are knowable, that they are surely about to be fulfilled is whether we can accept that in the present age it is the circle of his disciples who by grace are empowered to discern, more visibly and more validly than the Caesars and the Cromwells, what it means when at his command they pray,

> Your kingdom come,
> your will be done
> on earth as in heaven.

25. Michael Sattler – The Schleitheim Articles

The Brotherly Agreement of Some Children of God Concerning Seven Articles

Among all who love God and are children of light may there be joy, peace, and mercy from our father, through the atonement of the blood of Jesus Christ, together with the gifts of the spirit, who is sent by the father to all believers for their strength, consolation, and perseverance through every grief until the end, amen. These children of light are dispersed to all the places which God our father has ordained for them, and where they are assembled with one mind in one God and father of us all. May grace and peace exist in all your hearts, amen.

Beloved in the Lord, brothers and sisters, our first and paramount concern is always what brings you consolation and a secure conscience, which has been misled previously. We are concerned about this so that you may not be separated from us forever, like foreigners, and almost completely excluded, as is just. We are concerned that you might turn, rather, to the truly implanted members of Christ, who are armed with patience and self-knowledge, and so that you may again be united with us in the power of one divine, Christian spirit and zeal for God.

It is also evident that the devil has slyly separated us through a thousand tricks, so that he might be able to destroy the work of God which has partly begun in us through God's mercy and grace. But the faithful shepherd of our souls, Christ, who has begun this work in us, will direct it until the end, and he will teach us, to his honor and our salvation, amen.

Dear brothers and sisters, we who are assembled together in the Lord at Schleitheim, are making known through a series of articles to all who love God that, as far as we are concerned, we have agreed that we will abide in the Lord as obedient children of God, sons and daughters, and as those who are separated from the world – and who should be separated in all that they do and do not do. And may God be praised and glorified in unity, without any brother contradicting this, but rather being happy with it. In doing this we have sensed that the unity of the father and our common Christ have been with us in spirit. For the Lord is the lord of peace and not of dissention, as Paul shows [1 Cor. 14:33]. You should note this and comprehend it, so that you understand in which articles this unity has been formulated.

Some false brothers among us have nearly introduced a great offense, causing some to turn away from the faith because they suppose they can lead a free life, using the freedom of the spirit and Christ. But such people lack truth and are given over (to their condemnation) to the lasciviousness and freedom of the flesh. They have thought that faith and love may tolerate everything, and that nothing will damn them because they are such believing people.

Observe, you members of God in Christ Jesus, faith in the heavenly father through Jesus Christ does not take this form. It does not result in such things as these false brothers and sisters practice and teach. Protect yourselves and be warned about such people, for they do not serve our father, but their father, the devil.

But you are not this kind of people. For those who belong to Christ have crucified their flesh with all its lusts and desires. You certainly know what I mean and the brothers we are talking about. Separate yourselves from these brothers, for they are perverted. Ask the Lord that they acquire the knowledge to repent, and that we have the steadfastness to proceed along the path we have undertaken, following the honor of God and his son Christ. Amen.

The articles which we have discussed and about which we agree are these: baptism, the ban [excommunication], the breaking of bread [Lord's Supper], separating from the abomination [the existing polity], shepherds in the community [ministers], the sword, the oath, etc.

First, concerning baptism, note this. Baptism should be given to all who have learned repentance, amendment of life, and faith through the truth that their sin has been removed by Christ; to all who want to walk in the resurrection of Jesus Christ and to be buried with him in death so that they can be resurrected with him; and to all who desire baptism in this sense from us and who themselves request it. Accordingly, all infant baptism, the greatest and first abomination of the pope, is excluded. You have the basis for this in the testimony of Scripture and the custom of the apostles. Matthew 28[:19]; Mark 16[:6]; Acts 2[:38], 8[:36]; 16[:31ff.], and 19[:4]. We wish to maintain this position on baptism simply, yet firmly.

Second. We have agreed as follows concerning the ban. The ban should be used against all who have given themselves to the Lord and agreed to follow his commandments, and who have been baptized into the one body of Christ, letting themselves be called brother or sister, and who nevertheless sometimes slip and fall into error and sin, and have been unknowingly overtaken. These people should be admonished twice privately and the third time should be punished or banned publicly, before the whole community, according to the command of Christ, Matthew 18[:15–18]. This banning should take place, according to the ordinance of the spirit [Mt. 5:23], before the breaking of bread, so that we are all of one mind, and in one love may break from one bread and eat and drink from one cup.

Third. We are agreed and united about the breaking of bread as follows. All who wish to break one bread in memory of the broken body of Christ, and all who wish to drink from one cup in memory of the blood that Christ shed, should previously be united in the one body of Christ – that is, God's community, of which Christ is the head – namely, through baptism. For as Paul shows [1 Cor. 10:21], we cannot simultaneously sit at the Lord's table and the devil's table. We cannot simultaneously drink from the Lord's cup and the devil's cup. That is, all who have fellowship with the dead works of darkness do not partake of the light. Thus, all who follow the devil and the world have nothing in common with those who are called out of the world to God. All who reside in evil have no part of what is good. And it must be thus. He who has not been called by one God to one faith, to one baptism, to one spirit, and to one body in the community of all the children of God, may not be made into one bread with them, as must be the case if one wants to break bread truly according to the command of Christ.

Fourth. Concerning separation, we have agreed that a separation should take place from the evil which the devil has planted in the world. We simply will not have fellowship with evil people, nor associate with them, nor participate with them in their abominations. That is, all who have not submitted themselves to the obedience of faith, and have not united themselves to God so that they want to do his will, are a great abomination before God. Since this is so, nothing but abominable things can issue from them. For there has never been anything in the world and among all creatures except good and evil, believing and unbelieving, darkness and light, the world and those who are out of the world, God's temple and idols, Christ and Belial, and neither may have anything to do with the other. And the commandment of the Lord is evident – he tells us to become separated from evil [2 Cor. 6:17]. In this way he wants to be our God, and we will be his sons and daughters. Further, he also admonishes us to withdraw from Babylon and worldly Egypt so that we will not participate in the suffering which the Lord will inflict upon them [Rev. 18:4ff.].

From all this we should learn that everything which is not united with our God and Christ is the abomination which we should flee. By this we mean all popish and neo-popish works and divine services, assemblies, ecclesiastical processions, wine shops, the ties and obligations of lack of faith, and other things of this kind, which the world indeed regards highly but which are done in direct opposition to the commandments of God, as is the great injustice in the world. We should leave all these things and have nothing to do with them, for they are vain abominations which make us hated by our Christ Jesus, who has liberated us from the servitude of the flesh and made us suitable for service to God through the spirit, which he has given us.

Thus, the devilish weapons of force will fall from us, too, such as the sword, armor and the like, and all their uses on behalf of friends or against enemies; [such nonviolence is commanded] by the power of the words of Christ, "You should not resist evil" [Mt. 5:39].

Fifth. We have agreed as follows concerning the shepherds in the community of God [i.e. ministers]. According to Paul's prescription [1 Tim. 3:7], the shepherd in God's community should be one who has a completely good reputation among those who are outside the faith. His duties should be to read, to admonish, to teach, to warn, and to punish or ban in the community; to lead all sisters and brothers in prayer and in breaking bread; and to make sure that in all matters that concern the body of Christ, the community is built up and improved. He should do this so that the name of God is praised and honored among us, and the mouths of blasphemers are stopped.

Should this pastor be in need, he should be provided for by the community that chose him, so that he who serves the gospel should also live from it, as the Lord has ordained [1 Cor. 9:14]. But if a shepherd should do something requiring punishment, he should not be tried except on the testimony of two or three people. If they sin [by testifying falsely], they should be punished in front of everybody so that others are afraid.

But if a shepherd is banished or through the cross [execution] brought to the Lord, another should be ordained in his place immediately so that God's little people are not destroyed, but maintained and consoled by the warning.

Sixth. Concerning the sword we have reached the following agreement. The sword is ordained by God outside the perfection of Christ. It punishes and kills evil people and protects and defends the good. In the law the sword is established to punish and to kill the wicked, and secular authorities are established to use it. But in the perfection of Christ the ban alone will be used to admonish and expel him who has sinned, without putting the flesh to death, and only by using the admonition and the command to sin no more.

Now, many who do not recognize what Christ wills for us will ask whether a Christian may also use the sword against evil people for the sake of protecting the good or for the sake of love. Our unanimous answer is as follows: Christ teaches us to learn from him that we should be mild and of humble heart, and in this way we will find rest for our souls. Now, Christ says to the woman taken in adultery [Jn. 8:11], not that she should be stoned according to the law of his father (yet he says, "As the father has commanded me, thus I do" [Jn. 8:22]), but that she should be dealt with in mercy and forgiveness and with a warning to sin no more. And Christ says, "Go and sin no more." We should also hold to this in our laws, according to the rule about the ban.

Secondly, it is asked about the sword, whether a Christian may pass judgment in worldly quarrels and conflicts at law such as unbelievers have with one another. This is the answer: Christ did not want to decide or judge between brother and brother concerning an inheritance, and he refused to do so [Lk. 12:13]. Thus, we should do likewise.

Thirdly, it is asked about the sword, whether a Christian may hold a position of governmental authority if he is chosen for it. This is our reply: Christ should have been made a king, but he rejected this [Jn. 6:15] and did not view it as ordained by his father. We should do likewise and follow him. In this way we will not walk into the snares of darkness. For Christ says, "Whoever wants to follow me should deny himself and take up his cross and follow me" [Mt. 16:24]. Also, Christ himself forbids the violence of the sword and says, "Worldly princes rule," etc., "but not you" [Mt.

20:25]. Further, Paul says, "Those whom God foresaw, he also ordained that they should be equal to the model of his son," etc. [Rom. 8:30]. Also Peter says, "Christ has suffered, not ruled, and he gave us a model, so that you shall follow in his footsteps" [1 Pet. 2:21].

Lastly, it should be pointed out that it is not fitting for a Christian to be a magistrate for these reasons: the authorities' governance is according to the flesh, but the Christian's is according to the spirit. Their houses and dwellings remain in this world, but the Christian's are in heaven. Their citizenship is of this world, but the Christian's is in heaven. Their weapons of conflict and war are carnal and only directed against the flesh, but the Christian's weapons are spiritual and directed against the fortifications of the devil. Worldly people are armed with spikes and iron, but Christians are armed with the armor of God - with truth, with justice, with peace, faith, and salvation, and with the word of God. In sum, what Christ, our head, thought, the members of the body of Christ through him should also think, so that no division of the body [of the faithful] may triumph through which it would be destroyed. Now, as Christ is – as is written about him – so too must the members be, so that his body may remain whole and united for its own benefit and edification.

Seventh. We have reached agreement as follows concerning the oath [i.e. swearing oaths]. The oath is a confirmation among those who are quarreling or making promises. And it has been ordained in the [Mosaic] Law that it should take place truthfully and not falsely, in the name of God alone. Christ, who teaches the perfection of the law, forbids his followers all swearing, either truthfully or falsely, either in the name of heaven or of earth or of Jerusalem or by our own head [Mt. 5:34f.]. And he does this for the reason which he gives afterward: "For you are not able to make a single hair white or black." Notice this! All swearing has been forbidden because we cannot fulfill what is promised in swearing. For we are not able to alter the slightest thing about ourselves.

Now, there are some who do not believe God's simple command. They speak as follows and ask, "Did God not swear to Abraham on his own godhead when he promised that he wished him well and wanted to be his God, if he would keep his commandments? Why should I not swear also when I promise somebody something?"

Our answer is this. Listen to what Scripture says. Because God wanted to prove conclusively to the heirs of the promise that his counsel does not waver, he sealed it with an oath, so that we could rely on the consolation received through two unwavering things [i.e. the promise and the oath; Heb.6:17f.] about which it is impossible for God to lie. Note the meaning of this passage of Scripture: "God has the power to do that which he forbids you. For all things are possible for him" [Mt. 29:26, Mk. 10:27]. God swore an oath to Abraham (Scripture says) in order to prove that his counsel never wavered. That is, no one can resist or hinder his will, and so he was able to keep the oath. But, as has been said above by Christ, we can do nothing to keep or fulfill an oath. Therefore we should not swear at all.

Some now say further, "In the New Testament it is forbidden by God to swear; but it is actually commanded in the Old, and there it is only forbidden to swear by heaven, earth, Jerusalem, and by our head." Our answer is this. Listen to Scripture – "He who swears by the temple of heaven swears by the throne of God and by him who sits on it" [Mt. 23:22]. Notice that it is forbidden to swear by heaven, which is a throne of God. How much more is it forbidden to swear by God himself? You fools and blind people, which is greater, the throne or he who sits on it?

Some say further, "Why is it now unjust to use God as a witness to the truth, when the apostles Peter and Paul have sworn?" Our answer is that Peter and Paul testify only to that which God promised Abraham through the oath. And they themselves promised nothing, as the examples clearly show. For testifying and swearing are two different things. When a person swears, in the first place he makes a promise about future things, as Christ – whom we received a long time later – was promised to Abraham. But when a person testifies, he is testifying about the present, whether it is good or evil, as Simon spoke to Mary about Christ and testified to her, "This child is ordained for the fall and resurrection of many in Israel, and as a sign which will be rejected" [Lk. 2:34]. Christ has also taught us this same thing when he said, "Your speech should be 'yea' or 'nay' for anything else comes from evil" [Mt. 5:37]. Christ says, "Your speech or words should be 'yea' or 'nay'," so that none can understand it in the sense that he has permitted swearing. Christ is simply "yea" and "nay" and all who seek him in simplicity will understand his word. Amen.
Dear brothers and sisters in the lord,

These are the articles about which some brothers have previously been in error and have understood differently from the true understanding. The consciences of many people have been confused through this, as a result of which the name of God has been greatly blasphemed. Therefore it has been necessary for us to reach agreement in the Lord, and this has happened. May God be praised and glorified!

Now, because you have amply understood the will of God, which has now been set forth through us, it will be necessary for you to realize the will of God, which you have recognized, perseveringly and without interruption. For you know well what reward the servant deserves who knowingly sins.

Everything that you have done unknowingly or that you have confessed to having done unjustly is forgiven you through the faithful prayer which is performed by us in our assembly for all our failures and our guilt, through the merciful forgiveness of God and through the blood of Jesus Christ. Amen.

Beware of all who do not walk in the simplicity of the divine truth which is encompassed in this letter from us in our assembly. Do this so that everyone among us may be subject to the rule of the ban, and so that henceforth false brothers and sisters may be prevented from joining us.

Separate yourselves from that which is evil. Then the Lord will be your God, and you will be his sons and daughters.

Dear brothers, keep in mind how Paul admonished Titus. He said this: "The saving grace of God has appeared to all. And it disciplines us so that we shall deny ungodly things and worldly lusts and shall live chastely, justly, and piously in this world. And we shall await our same hope, the appearance of the majesty of the great God and our savior, Jesus Christ, who gave himself to redeem us from all injustice, and to purify a people as his own who would be zealous for good works" [Tit. 2:11–14]. If you think about this and practice it, the lord of peace will be with you.

May the name of God be eternally blessed and highly praised, Amen. May the Lord give you his peace. Amen.

Enacted at Schleitheim on St. Matthew's day [24 February] in the year 1527.

26. Reinhold Niebuhr – The Ethic of Jesus and the Social Problem

Since Walter Rauschenbusch aroused the American church to the urgency of the social problem and its relation to the ethical ideals of the gospel, it has been rather generally assumed that it is possible to abstract an adequate social ethic for the reconstruction of society from the social teachings of Jesus. Dozens of books have been written to prove that Jesus' ideals of brotherhood represented an outline of the ideal society, that his law of service offered an alternative to the competitive impulse in modern society, that guidance for the adjustment of every political and economic problem could be found in his words, and that nothing but a little logic would serve to draw out the "social implications" of his teachings.

Most of this energy has been vainly spent and has served to create as much confusion as light. There is indeed a very rigorous ethical ideal in the gospel of Jesus, but there is no social ethic in the ordinary sense of the word in it, precisely because the ethical ideal is too rigorous and perfect to lend itself to application in the economic and political problems of our day. This does not mean that the ethic of Jesus has no light to give to a modern Christian who faces the perplexing economic and political issues of a technological civilization. It means only that confusion will be avoided if a rigorous distinction is made between a perfectionist and absolute ethic and the necessities of a social situation.

The ethic of Jesus was, to begin with, a personal ethic. It was not individual in the sense that he believed in individual perfection abstracted from a social situation. He saw that wealth tempted to covetousness and that poverty prompted the virtue of humility. He spoke of the Kingdom and not of salvation, and the Kingdom meant an ideal social relationship, even though he might emphasize that it proceeded from internal spiritual forces. His ethic was an ethic of love, and it therefore implied social relationships. But it was an individual ethic in the sense that his chief interest was in the quality of life of an individual. He regarded as a temptation the suggestion that he become a political leader or that he develop the political implications of the Messianic idea, and he resisted the effort to make him king. He was not particularly interested in the Jewish people's aspirations toward freedom from Rome, and skillfully evaded the effort to make him take sides in that political problem. He accepted monarchy on the one hand and slavery on the other, though he called attention to the difference between the ideal of his Kingdom, which measured greatness by service, and the kind of greatness which the "kings of the Gentiles" attained.

His lack of concern for social and political issues is, however, not as important from the perspective of this problem as the kind of ethical ideal which he actually developed. In terms of individual life his ethical ideal was one of complete disinterestedness, religiously motivated. No one was to seek his own. The man who asked him to persuade his brother to divide an inheritance with him was rudely rebuked. Evil was not to be resisted, the borrower was to be given more than he asked for without hope of return. A special premium was placed upon actions which could not be rewarded. In other words, the prudential motive was treated with utmost severity. There are, of course, words in the teachings of Jesus which are not as rigorous as this. He promised rewards. Some of these words belong to a humanist strain in his teachings in which he merely makes a shrewd analysis of the effect of certain actions. The severe judge will be judged severely. The proud man will be abased and the humble man exalted. Here the social rewards of social attitudes are recognized. Other offers of reward occur, but with one or two exceptions they can be placed in the category of ultimate rewards — "in the resurrection of the just," "treasures in heaven," favor with God. On the whole, they do not seriously qualify his main position that moral action must be motivated purely by obedience to God, emulation of God's attributes, and gratitude for the forgiving grace of God. An ulterior motive (desire for social approval, for instance) for a worthy action would destroy the virtue of the action and would result only in the attainment of the object of the ulterior motive — "verily, they have their reward."

Jesus did not deny that disinterested action would result in rewards; "all these things" would be added, and the man who forgot himself completely would find himself most truly. Here is the recognition of the basic ethical paradox that the highest result of an action can never be its desired result. It must be a by-product. If it is desired, the purity of the action is destroyed. If I love to be loved or to be socially approved, I will not be loved or approved in the same way as if my fellow men caught in me a glimpse of pure disinterestedness. Obviously the only way to achieve such pure disinterestedness is to have actions motivated purely by religious motives. But this very emphasis upon religious motives lifts the ethic of Jesus above the area of social ethics. We are asked to love our enemies, not because the social consequences of such love will be to make friends of the enemies, but because God loves with that kind of impartiality. We are demanded to forgive those who have wronged us, not because a forgiving spirit will prove redemptive in the lives of the fallen, but because God forgives our sins. Here we have an ethic, in other words, which we can neither disavow nor perfectly achieve. We cannot disavow it because it is a fact that the prudential motive destroys the purity of every ethical action. We have a right to view the social and personal consequences of an action in retrospect, but if we view it in prospect we have something less than the best. So powerful is the drive of self-interest in life, however, that this ideal is as difficult to achieve as it is to disavow. It remains, therefore, as an ideal which convicts every moral achievement of imperfection, but it is always a little beyond the realm of actual human history.

Though Jesus was as indifferent to the social consequences of pure disinterestedness as he was critical of concern for the personal consequences, it is not difficult to draw conclusions in regard to the social ideal implied by such disinterestedness. In practical terms it means a combination of anarchism and communism dominated by the spirit of love. Such perfect love as he demands would obviate the necessity of coercion on the one hand because men would refrain from transgressing upon their neighbor's rights, and on the other hand because such transgression would be accepted and forgiven if it did occur. That is anarchism, in other words. It would mean communism because the privileges of each would be potentially the privileges of all. Where love is perfect the distinctions between mine and thine disappear. The social ideal of Jesus is as perfect and as impossible of attainment as is his personal ideal. But again it is an ideal that cannot be renounced completely. Whatever justice men attain in the society in which they live is always an imperfect justice. The careful limitation and definition of rights which Stoicism gave to the world as a social ideal always develop into injustice in actual life because every person views rights not from an absolute but from a biased perspective. The result is a society in which the perspective of the strong dictates the conceptions of justice by which the total community operates and necessitates social conflict through the assertion of the rights of the weak before the injustice is corrected. Justice, in other words, that is only justice is less than justice. Only imaginative justice, that is, love that begins by espousing the rights of the other rather than self, can achieve a modicum of fairness.

Whether we view the ethical teachings of Jesus from the perspective of the individual or of society we discover an unattainable ideal, but a very useful one. It is an ideal never attained in history or in life, but one that gives us an absolute standard by which to judge both personal and social righteousness. It is a standard by comparison with which all human attainments fall short, and it may offer us the explanation of Jesus' words, "Why callest thou me good? no one is good save God." Perhaps it ought to be added that an attempt to follow this ideal in a world that is, particularly in its group relationships, hardly human and certainly not divine, will inevitably lead us to where it led Jesus, to the cross.

Valuable as this kind of perfectionism is, it certainly offers no basis for a social ethic that deals responsibly with a growing society. Those of us who believe in the complete reorganization of modern society are not wrong in using the ideal of Jesus as a vantage point from which to condemn the present social order, but I think we are in error when we try to draw from the teachings of Jesus any warrant for the social policies which we find necessary to attain to any modicum of justice. We may be right in believing that we are striving for a justice which approximates the Christian ideal more closely than the present social order, but we are wrong when we talk about achieving a "Christian social order." The Barthians are quite right, I think, in protesting against the easy identification of the Kingdom of God with every movement of social reform and social radicalism that has prevailed in American Christianity in particular and in liberal Protestantism in general. Those of us who dissociate ourselves from the easy optimism of modern liberalism and who believe that a just society is not going to be built by a little more education and a few more sermons on love have particular reason to reorient our thinking in this matter so that we will not come forward with a social ethic involving the use of force and coercion and political pressure of every kind and claim the authority of Jesus for it.

Our confusion is, of course, no worse than that of the conventional teachers of Christian ethics and theology who have a rather complacent attitude toward the present economic society and criticize us for violating the ethic of Jesus in our espousal of the class struggle, for instance. Our confusion is, in fact, not quite as bad as theirs. They have used every kind of exegetical device to prove that the teachings of Jesus are not incompatible with participation in nationalistic wars or, if they have been a little more clearheaded, they have found ethical justification for their actions by proving that the ethic of Jesus does not provide for the responsibilities of politics and economics, and therefore leaves them free to choose a political strategy that is most consonant with their conception of the moral good will which they believe Jesus to idealize. The critics of the former type have no ground to stand upon at all when they accuse radical Christians of violating the ethic of Jesus; for participation in a nonviolent strike action, to choose an obvious example, is certainly not more incompatible with the ethic of Jesus than participation in an international conflict. Critics of the latter type have cut the ground for criticism from under their own feet. They admit that any responsible relationship to political and economic affairs involves compromise, and they ought to have a difficult time proving that the assertion of national interest or the protection of national rights is more compatible with the perfectionist ideal of pure disinterestedness than the assertion of class interests and the protection of class rights.

But the confusion of our critics does not absolve us of the necessity of clear thought for ourselves. The struggle for social justice in the present economic order involves the assertion of rights, the rights of the disinherited, and the use of coercion. Both are incompatible with the pure love ethic found in the Gospels. How, then, do we justify the strategy of the "class struggle"? We simply cannot do so in purely Christian terms. There is in the absolute sense no such thing as "Christian socialism."

We must justify ourselves by considerations of the social situation that we face and the human resources that are available for its solution. What we discover in the social situation is that human life in its group interests moves pretty much upon the basis of the economic interests of various groups. We realize that intelligence and spiritual and moral idealism may qualify economic interest, but they do not destroy it. Whatever may be possible for individuals, we see no possibility of a group voluntarily divesting itself of its special privileges in society. Nor do we see a possibility of pure disinterestedness and the spirit of forgiveness on the part of an underprivileged group shaming a dominant group into an attitude of social justice. Such a strategy might possibly work in intimate personal relationships but it does not work in the larger group relations. The Negro has been forgiving in his subordinate position in society for a long time, but he has not persuaded the white man to grant him larger privileges in society. Whatever place the industrial worker has won in society has been won by the assertion of his rights through his trade-union organizations. Even the most imaginative urban dwellers lack the imagination to envisage the needs of the farmer. The farmer has been forced to exert political pressure for the attainment of even such minimum justice as he is granted in the present economic organization of our country. No one who looks realistically at the social scene can fail to discover that economic, racial, and national groups stand on a moral level considerably lower than that of the most sensitive individuals. They are not easily persuaded to a voluntary sacrifice of privileges, and an attitude of pure nonresistance on the part of those who suffer from their exactions does not produce the spirit of repentance among them. Intelligence, which may create a spirit of justice among individuals by persuading them to grant to their fellows what they claim for themselves, is generally not acute enough to function in similar fashion in group relations. More frequently it does no more than to create rational sanctifications for special group interests. Only rarely does intellectual force rise high enough to create a perspective from which group prejudices and biases have been banished. The relations between groups are so indirect that the consequences of our actions in the life of another group are not easily discerned, and we therefore continue in unethical conduct without the restraint upon our conscience that intimate personal relations create. Very few white men have any conception of the havoc that is wrought in the souls and upon the bodies of Negroes by prevailing race prejudices; and there is not one American in a million who knows what our reparations policy means for starving workers of Germany. This unhappy group seems under the necessity of asserting its interests, not only against the rest of the world, but against the more comfortable middle classes of their own country.

The social struggle involves a violation of a pure ethic of love, not only in the assertion of rights, but in the inevitable use of coercion. Here again one need but state the obvious; but the obvious is usually not recognized by academic moralists. No society can exist without the use of coercion, though every intelligent society will try to reduce coercion to a minimum and rely upon the factor of mutual consent to give stability to its institutions. Yet it can never trust all of its citizens to accept necessary social arrangements voluntarily. It will use police force against recalcitrant and antisocial minorities, and it will use the threat of political force against a complacent and indifferent group of citizens which could never be relied upon to initiate adequate social policies upon its own accord. No government can wait upon voluntary action on the part of the privileged members of a community for an adequate inheritance or income tax. It will use political force created by the votes of the disinherited and less privileged to initiate and enforce taxation policies, designed to equalize privileges. Privileged groups may accept such legislation without violent revolt, but they will probably argue against its justice until the day of their death. An intelligent society will constantly strive toward the goal of a more equal justice by initiating a more rigorous policy just as soon as a previous and more tentative one has been accepted and absorbed into the social standards of the community. If this is not done by gradual process, with the unrealized goal of essential equality beckoning each generation to surpass the approximations of justice achieved in the past, the inequalities of the social order, always increasing through natural process, are bound to grow until an outraged sense of justice (probably spurred by actual physical want on the part of the least privileged members of a community) will produce a violent revolt. In such nations as Germany, for instance, it is really an open question whether any political measures can achieve the desired end of social justice quickly enough to prevent violent revolution.

The necessity of this kind of coercion, based upon the assertion of interest on the part of the less privileged, is such a clear lesson of history that one hesitates to belabor the point and would refrain from doing so were it not for the fact that half of the academic treatises on social ethics and Christian ethics were written as if no such necessity existed. In this respect secular moralists are frequently as naive as religious ones. In the one case it is expected that a change in educational technique will eliminate the drive of self-interest which determines economic life and in the other case there is a naive confidence in the possibility of changing human nature by religious conversion or religious inspiration. It is the thesis of the radical wing of Christian social theorists, whether in England, Germany, or America, that nothing accomplished by either education or religious suasion will be able to abolish the social struggle. We believe that such hopes are corrupted by the sentimentalities of the comfortable classes and are caused by their lack of understanding of the realities of an industrial civilization. In what sense, then, may we call ourselves Christian, or how do we hope to insinuate Christian and ethical values into the social struggle? The simplest answer is that we believe that the highest ethical and spiritual insight may mitigate the social struggle on the one hand and may transcend it on the other.

We believe that it makes some difference whether a privileged group makes a stubborn and uncompromising defense of its special privileges or whether it has some degree of social imagination and tries to view its privileges in the light of the total situation of a community. Education ought to create some of that social imagination, and in so far as it does, it will mitigate the class struggle or the social struggle between races. The religious contribution to the same end may consist of various elements. Real religion produces the spirit of humility and repentance. It destroys moral conceit. Moral conceit is precisely what makes privileged groups so stubborn in the defense of their privileges. The human animal is just moral enough to be unable to act immorally with vigor if he cannot find a moral justification for his actions. If the Christian church used the ethical ideal of Jesus, the ideal of pure disinterestedness, more rigorously, and if the modern pulpit made a more astute analysis of human motives in the light of this ideal, many of the rationalizations that now support the antisocial policies and attitudes of privileged and powerful people would be destroyed. At least they might be qualified. One of the most unfortunate facts about our contemporary moral situation is that the church has ceased to convict men of selfishness at the precise moment in history when human greed is more obvious and more dangerous than at any previous time. Nowhere has the liberal church played more false to its generation than in its optimistic and romantic interpretation of human nature, just when an industrial civilization revealed the drive of self-interest in all its antisocial power. The part of the Christian church that has tried to convict the generation of sin knows too little about the problems of modern life to convict men of their significant sins. Thus religion has on the whole produced moral complacency rather than the spirit of repentance. The number of men who are sufficiently sensitized by religion actually to renounce their privileges must always remain small. But it ought not to be impossible for the church to create enough contrition and consciousness of human selfishness to prompt men to a more willing acceptance of and less stubborn resistance against social policies that aim at the restriction of power and privilege. If we dealt realistically with the facts of human nature, we might be able to create an attitude of complacency toward increasing social restraint, based upon the realization that few, if any, of us are wise enough to restrain our expansive desires voluntarily in a degree sufficient for the needs of our highly interdependent society. If there were a better understanding of human nature in the church today, an understanding that we could acquire by the study of psychology and economics but which we might appropriate just as easily from the insights of great religion, there would be fewer Christian captains of industry who lived under the illusion that they were good enough and wise enough to hold irresponsible power and exercise it for the good of the community. They would know that the very possession of irresponsible power tempts to its selfish use and that the benevolent pretensions of despotism rest either on unconscious self-deception or conscious hypocrisy.

True religion could mitigate the cruelties of the social struggle by its creation of the spirit of love as well as the spirit of repentance. The love ideal which Jesus incarnates may be too pure to be realized in life, but it offers us nevertheless an ideal toward which the religious spirit may strive. All rational idealism creates a conflict between the mind and the impulses, as in Stoicism and Kantian morality. The mind conceives ideals of justice which it tries to force upon recalcitrant selfish impulses. Real religion transmutes the social impulses until they transcend the limits set them by nature (family, race, group, etc.) and include the whole human community. Real religious imagination is able, furthermore, to create an attitude of trust and faith toward human beings, in which the potentialities rather than the immediate realities are emphasized. Through such imagination the needs of the social foe are appreciated, his inadequacies are understood in the light of his situation, and his possibilities for higher and more moral action are recognized. Only the religious spirit which surveys the human scene from the perspective of its presuppositions about the character of life is thus able to disregard present facts and appeal to ultimate possibilities. The fact that in Jesus the spirit of love flowed out in emulation of God's love, without regard to social consequences, cannot blind the eye to the social consequences of a religiously inspired love. If modern religion were really producing it, it would mitigate the evils of the social struggle. It would, to emphasize the obvious once more, not abolish the social struggle, because it would not approximate perfection in sufficiently numerous instances. The fight for justice in society will always be a fight. But wherever the spirit of justice grows imaginative and is transmuted into love, a love in which the interests of the other are espoused, the struggle is transcended by just that much.

It is the fashion among many Christian idealists to criticize the political movements of the disinherited for the spirit of hatred which they generate. The church, so it is said, would espouse their cause much more readily if the spirit of love were manifest in it. What the church fails to realize is that its responsibility is chiefly for the moral and spiritual attitudes of the privileged rather than the disinherited; for it is the former who makes professions of Christian idealism. If the church wants to insinuate the spirit of love into the social struggle, it ought to begin with the privileged groups, not only because it has greater responsibility for them, but because those who hold entrenched positions in the social struggle are obviously under the greater obligation to be imaginative in gauging the needs and discounting the limitations of those who suffer from social injustice. The perfectionist ethic of Jesus allows for no such distinctions; for it demands that love be poured forth whether or not we suffer from injustice. But no one can avow such an ethic from the vantage point of privilege and security. If the portion of society that benefits from social inequality and which is endangered by a rising tide of social discontent attempts to counsel love, forgiveness, and patience to the discontented, it will convict itself of hypocrisy, except it is able first of all to reveal fruits of the Spirit, which it commends, in its own life. Even if it were to reveal some fruits, but too meager to justify a more trusting and a less vehement attitude on the part of the underprivileged, its moral ideals would be regarded as pretensions. The race situation in the South offers interesting commentary upon this point. The fine work which the interracial commission has done has failed to preserve the respect of the more eager young Negroes for it, because they feel that through its efforts of conciliation white men have yielded only inconsequential social advantages in order that they may hold to their major ones. The most perfect love may not ask for social justification, but any love within the capacity of ordinary men and groups does. The disinherited will have their spirits corrupted by hatred and their policies tinctured with violence except they are able to detect some genuinely ethical elements in the policies of the privileged and entrenched social groups. If the spirit of love is to qualify and mitigate the social struggle, the groups that profess to believe in the efficacy of love and who, at the same time, have favored positions in society are clearly under obligation to introduce this Christian element in society. They may be quite sure that any solid ethical achievement among them would result in practically immediate ethical reactions of trust and faith among those who are trying to advance socially. Only the faith and trust of the advancing group will not and ought not ever rise to the point where purely voluntary action toward equality is expected. A degree of ethical insight on the part of the whole community will not abolish the necessity of social conflict, but it may prevent violence and reduce the hatred that must inevitably arise when the disinherited are faced, not only with the stubborn greed of the powerful and comfortable social classes, but also with the protection of their privileges by the covert use of force and their hypocritical pretension of virtue.

A Christian ethical idealism that espouses the cause of proletarian groups and identifies itself with their political movements is, in short, as pure as any Christian movement that assumes a responsible attitude toward society. The compromises that it makes with the pure Christian ethic are inevitable compromises which everyone must make who deals with the social problem from the perspective of society rather than that of the individual. It might claim, in addition, to appropriate the Christian ethical ideal more closely than a type of thought that fears contamination in the social struggle. For the social struggle is a reality in society and we will be contaminated by it except we get out of society. The ascetic may possibly have a vantage point from which to criticize the ethical purity of Christian socialism or Christian radicalism. Those who stay in society have not. If our critics were less confused about the moral and social realities of modern society, they would know that neutrality in a social struggle between entrenched and advancing social classes really means alliance with the entrenched position. In the social struggle we are either on the side of privilege or need. No ethical perfectionism can save us from that choice.

27. James Cone – Jesus Christ in Black Theology

Christian theology begins and ends with Jesus Christ. He is the point of departure for everything to be said about God, humankind, and the world. That is why christology is the starting point of Karl Barth's *Dogmatics* and why Wolfhart Pannenberg says that "theology can clarify its Christian self-understanding only by a thematic and comprehensive involvement with Christological problems."[1] To speak of the Christian gospel is to speak of Jesus Christ who is the content of its message and without whom Christianity ceases to be. Therefore the answer to the question "What is the essence of Christianity?" can be given in the two words: Jesus Christ.

Because Jesus Christ is the focal point for everything that is said about the Christian gospel, it is necessary to investigate the meaning of his person and work in light of the black perspective. It is one thing to assert that he is the essence of the Christian gospel, and quite another to specify the meaning of his existence in relation to the slave ships that appeared on American shores. Unless his existence is analyzed in light of the oppressed of the land, we are still left wondering what his presence means for the auction block, the Underground Railroad, and contemporary manifestations of black power. To be sure, white theology has informed us that Jesus Christ is the content of the gospel, but it has failed miserably in relating that gospel to Nat Turner, Denmark Vesey, and Gabriel Prosser. It is therefore the task of black theology to make theology relevant to the black reality, asking, "What does Jesus Christ mean for the oppressed blacks of the land?"

The task of explicating the existence of Jesus Christ for blacks is not easy in a white society that uses Christianity as an instrument of oppression. White conservatives and liberals alike present images of a white Jesus that are completely alien to the liberation of the black community. Their Jesus is a mild, easy-going white American who can afford to mouth the luxuries of "love," "mercy," "long-suffering," and other white irrelevancies, because he has a multibillion-dollar military force to protect him from the encroachments of the ghetto and the "communist conspiracy." But black existence is existence in a hostile world without the protection of the law. If Jesus Christ is to have any meaning for us, he must leave the security of the suburbs by joining blacks in their condition. What need have we for a white Jesus when we are not white but black? If Jesus Christ is white and not black, he is an oppressor, and we must kill him. The appearance of black theology means that the black community is now ready to do something about the white Jesus, so that he cannot get in the way of our revolution.

The Historical Jesus and Black Theology

Investigation of the question "Who is Jesus Christ?" involves the question about the historical Jesus. Since the appearance of Albert Schweitzer's *The Quest of the Historical Jesus* and the rise of the form-history school, knowledge about the historical Jesus cannot be taken for granted. During the nineteenth century, theologians assumed

---

[1]Wolfhart Pannenberg, *Jesus—God and Man,* trans. by L. L. Wilkins and Duane A. Priebe (Philadelphia: The Westminster Press, 1968), p. 11.

that the real Jesus was accessible to historical investigation, and they attempted to go behind the preaching (kerygma) of the early church in order to find the authentic Jesus of Nazareth. But Schweitzer demonstrated conclusively that the liberal search for the historical Jesus was a failure and only represented creations of the human mind. The nineteenth-century "lives" of Jesus told us more about the investigators than about Jesus himself.

Rudolf Bultmann and the form critics went even further by suggesting that the Gospels (the only source for knowledge about Jesus) are not historical at all. The setting of the narratives is artificial, and their contents were created entirely by the early Christian community in order to meet its own practical needs. It is therefore foolish to imagine that it is possible to find a historical kernel within them. That is why Bultmann says that "we can know almost nothing concerning the life and personality of Jesus, since the early Christian sources show no interest in either, are moreover fragmentary and often legendary."[2]

Bultmann's radical historical skepticism has been questioned by some of his followers. The new quest for the historical Jesus began in 1953 with Ernst Käsemann's lecture, "The Problem of the Historical Jesus." According to Käsemann:

> Only if Jesus' proclamation decisively coincides with the proclamation about Jesus is it understandable, reasonable, and necessary that the Christian kerygma in the New Testament conceals the message of Jesus; only then is the resurrected Jesus the historical Jesus. From this perspective we are required, precisely as historians, to inquire behind Easter. . . .
>
> By this means we shall learn whether he stands behind the word of his church or not, whether the Christian kerygma is a myth that can be detached from his word and from himself or whether it binds us historically and insolubly to him.[3]

Günther Bornkamm, Ernst Fuchs, and Hans Conzelmann joined Käsemann in his concern.[4] Although all agreed that a life of Jesus is impossible, they do not agree that history is irrelevant to the Christian gospel as implied in Bultmann's analysis of New Testament mythology.[5] Bornkamm puts it this way:

> Certainly faith cannot and should not be dependent on the change and uncertainty of historical research. . . . But no one should despise the help of historical research to illumine the truth with which each of us should be concerned.[6]

---

[2]Bultmann, *Jesus and the Word*, trans. by L. P. Smith and F. H. Lantero (New York: Charles Scribner's Sons, 1958), p. 8.

[3]Quoted in Pannenberg, *Jesus*, p. 56.

[4]For an analysis of the new quest, see James Robinson, *The New Quest of the Historical Jesus* (London: SCM Press, 1959).

[5]See Bultmann, "New Testament and Mythology," in H. W. Bartsch, ed., *Kerygma and Myth* (New York: Harper and Row, 1961).

[6]Günther Bornkamm, *Jesus of Nazareth*, trans. by Irene and Fraser McLuskey with James Robinson (New York: Harper and Row, 1960), p. 9.

Like the theologians of the new quest, black theology also takes seriously the historical Jesus. We want to know who Jesus *was* because we believe that that is the only way to assess who he *is*. If we have no historical information about the character and behavior of that particular Galilean in the first century, then it is impossible to determine the mode of his existence now. Without some continuity between the historical Jesus and the kerygmatic Christ, the Christian gospel becomes nothing but the subjective reflections of the early Christian community. And if that is what Christianity is all about, we not only separate it from history, but we also allow every community the possibility of interpreting the kerygma according to its own existential situation. Although the situation is important, it is not the gospel. The gospel speaks *to* the situation.

Christianity believes, as Paul Tillich has suggested, that it has the answer to the existential character of the human condition. It is the function of theology to analyze the changeless gospel in such a way that it can be related to changing situations. But theology must be careful not to confuse the two. If the situation becomes paramount (i.e., identified with the gospel), as it appears in Bultmann's view of the kerygmatic Christ, then there are no checks to the community's existential fancies. Black theology also sees this as the chief error of white American religious thought, which allows the white condition to determine the meaning of Jesus. The historical Jesus must be taken seriously if we intend to avoid making Jesus into our own images.

Taking seriously the New Testament Jesus, black theology believes that the historical kernel is the manifestation of Jesus as the Oppressed One whose earthly existence was bound up with the oppressed of the land. This is not to deny that other emphases are present. Rather it is to say that whatever is said about Jesus' conduct (Fuchs), about the manifestation of the expectant eschatological future in the deeds and words of Jesus (Bornkamm), or about his resurrection as the "ultimate confirmation of Jesus' claim to authority" (Pannenberg), it must serve to illuminate Jesus' sole reason for existence: to bind the wounds of the afflicted and to liberate those who are in prison. To understand the historical Jesus without seeing his identification with the poor as decisive is to misunderstand him and thus distort his historical person. And a proper theological analysis of Jesus' historical identification with the helpless is indispensable for our interpretation of the gospel today. Unless the contemporary oppressed know that the kerygmatic Christ is the real Jesus (as Martin Kähler would put it), to the extent that he was completely identified with the oppressed of his earthly ministry, they cannot know that their liberation is a continuation of his work.

The Character of the New Testament Jesus

What evidence is there that Jesus' identification with the oppressed is the distinctive historical kernel in the gospels? How do we know that black theology is not forcing an alien contemporary black situation on the biblical sources? These questions are important, and cannot be waved aside by black theologians. Unless we can clearly articulate an image of Jesus that is consistent with the essence of the biblical message and at the same time relate it to the struggle for black liberation, black theology loses its reason for being. It is thus incumbent upon us to demonstrate the relationship between the historical Jesus and the oppressed, showing that the equation of the contemporary Christ with black power arises out of a serious encounter with the biblical revelation.

Black theology must show that the Reverend Albert Cleage's description of Jesus as the Black Messiah[7] is not the product of a mind "distorted" by its own oppressed condition, but is rather the most meaningful christological statement in our time. Any other statement about Jesus Christ is at best irrelevant and at worst blasphemous.

1. Birth. The appearance of Jesus as the Oppressed One whose existence is identified exclusively with the oppressed of the land is symbolically characterized in his birth. He was born in a stable and cradled in a manger (the equivalent of a beer case in a ghetto alley), "because there was no room for them in the inn" (Luke 2:7). Although most biblical scholars rightly question the historical validity of the birth narratives in Matthew and Luke, the mythic value of these stories is important theologically. They undoubtedly reflect the early Christian community's *historical* knowledge of Jesus as a man who defined the meaning of his existence as being one with the poor and outcasts. The visit of the shepherds, the journey of the wise men, Herod's killing of the babies, the economic, social, and political unimportance of Mary and Joseph— all these features reflect the early community's image of the man Jesus. For them Jesus is certainly a unique person, but the uniqueness of his appearance reveals the Holy One's concern for the lonely and downtrodden. They are not simply Matthew and Luke's explanation of the origin of Jesus' messiahship, but also a portrayal of the significance of his messiahship.

Jesus' messiahship means that he is one of the humiliated and the abused, even in his birth. His eating with tax collectors and sinners, therefore, is not an accident and neither is it a later invention of the early church; rather it is an expression of the very being of God and thus a part of Jesus' purpose for being born.

2. Baptism and Temptation. The baptism (affirmed by most scholars as historical) also reveals Jesus' identification with the oppressed. According to the synoptic Gospels, John's baptism was for repentant sinners, an act which he believed provided an escape from God's messianic judgment. For Jesus to submit to John's baptism not only connects his ministry with John's but, more importantly, separates him from John. By being baptized, Jesus defines his existence as one with sinners and thus

---

[7]See this book published by Sheed and Ward, 1968. I should point out that my intention is not to suggest that my view of Christ is identical to Reverend Cleage's. Our perspectives do differ at points, but more importantly, we share in common the belief that *Christ is black*. It is also appropriate to express my indebtedness to his excellent work in this area.

conveys the meaning of the coming kingdom. The kingdom is for the poor, not the rich; and it comes as an expression of God's love, not judgment. In baptism Jesus embraces the condition of sinners, affirming their existence as his own. He is one of them! After the baptism, the saying "Thou art my beloved Son; with thee I am well pleased" (Mark 1:11) expresses God's approval of that very definition of Jesus' person and work.

The temptation is a continuation of the theme already expressed in the baptism. As with the birth narratives, it is difficult to recover the event as it happened, but it would be difficult to deny that the narrative is intimately related to Jesus' self-portrayal of the character of his existence. The tempter's concern is to divert Jesus from the reality of his mission with the poor. Jesus' refusal to turn the stone into bread, or to worship the tempter, or to throw himself from the pinnacle of the temple (Luke 4:3–12) may be interpreted as his refusal to identify himself with any of the available modes of oppressive or self-glorifying power. His being in the world is as one of the humiliated, suffering poor.

3. *Ministry.* The Galilean ministry is an actual working out of the decision already expressed in his birth and reaffirmed at the baptism and temptation. Mark describes the implication of this decision: "Now after John was arrested, Jesus came into Galilee, preaching the gospel of God, and saying, 'The time is fulfilled, and the kingdom of God is at hand; repent and believe in the gospel'" (Mark 1:14–15).

New Testament scholars have spent many hours debating the meaning of this passage, which sometimes gives the average person the impression that there is a hidden meaning discernible only by seminary graduates. But the meaning is clear enough for those who are prepared for a radical decision about their movement in the world. Jesus' proclamation of the kingdom is an announcement of God's decision about oppressed humankind. "The time is fulfilled, and the kingdom of God is at hand"—that is, slavery is about to end, because the reign of God displaces all false authorities. To "repent and believe in the gospel" is to recognize the importance of the hour at hand and to accept the reality of the new age by participating in it as it is revealed in the words and work of Jesus. The kingdom is Jesus, whose relationship to God and human beings is defined by his words and work.

From this it is clear that Jesus' restriction of the kingdom to the poor has far-reaching implications for our understanding of the gospel message. It is interesting, if not surprising, to watch white New Testament scholars explain away the real theological significance of Jesus' teachings on the kingdom and the poor. Nearly always they are at pains to emphasize that Jesus did not necessarily mean the economically poor but rather, as Matthew says, "the poor in spirit." Then they proceed to point out the exceptions: Joseph of Arimathea was a rich man (Matthew 27:57) and he was "a good and righteous man" (Luke 23:50). There are also instances of Jesus' association with the wealthy; and Zacchaeus did not promise to give up *all* his goods but only *half.* As one biblical scholar has put it:

It was not so much the possession of riches as one's attitude towards them and the use one makes of them which was the special object of Jesus' teachings and this is true of the biblical teachings as a whole. Jesus does not condemn private property, nor is he a social reformer in any primary sense; he is concerned with men's motives and hearts.[8]

With all due respect to erudite New Testament scholars and the excellent work that has been done in this field, I cannot help but conclude that they are "straining out a gnat and swallowing a camel"! It is this kind of false interpretation that leads to the oppression of the poor. As long as oppressors can be sure that the gospel does not threaten their social, economic, and political security, they can enslave others in the name of Jesus Christ. The history of Christendom, at least from the time of Constantine, is a history of human enslavement; and even today, white "Christians" see little contradiction between wealth and the Christian gospel.

It seems clear that the overwhelming weight of biblical teaching, especially the prophetic tradition in which Jesus stood unambiguously, is upon God's unqualified identification with the poor precisely because they are poor. The kingdom of God is for the helpless, because they have no security in this world. We see this emphasis in the repeated condemnation of the rich, notably in the Sermon on the Mount, and in Jesus' exclusive identification of his ministry with sinners. The kingdom demands the surrender of one's whole life. How is it possible to be rich, seeing others in a state of economic deprivation, and at the same time insist that one has complete trust in God? Again, how can it be said that Jesus was not primarily a social reformer but "concerned with men's motives and hearts," when the kingdom itself strikes across all boundaries—social, economic, and political?

Jesus' teaching about the kingdom is the most radical, revolutionary aspect of his message. It involves the totality of a person's existence in the world and what that means in an oppressive society. To repent is to affirm the reality of the kingdom by refusing to live on the basis of any definition except according to the kingdom. Nothing else matters! The kingdom, then, is the rule of God breaking in like a ray of light, usurping the powers that enslave human lives. That is why exorcisms are so prominent in Jesus' ministry. They are a visible manifestation of the presence of the kingdom. "If it is by the finger of God that I cast out demons, then the kingdom of God has come upon you" (Luke 11:20).

Jesus is the Oppressed One whose work is that of liberating humanity from inhumanity. Through him the oppressed are set free to be what they are. This and this alone is the meaning of his *finality,* which has been camouflaged in debates about his humanity and divinity.

4. Death and Resurrection. The death and resurrection of Jesus are the consummation of his earthly ministry with the poor. The Christian church rightly focuses on these

---

[8]Alan Richardson, "Poor," in Alan Richardson, ed., *Theological Word Book of the Bible* (New York: The Macmillan Co., 1960), pp. 168–69.

events as decisive for an adequate theological interpretation of Jesus' historical ministry. Rudolf Bultmann pointed this out convincingly. Although post-Bultmannians generally do not agree with Bultmann's extreme skepticism regarding history, they do agree on his assessment of the importance of the death-resurrection event in shaping the Christian view of the earthly ministry of Jesus. The Jesus of history is not simply a figure of the past but the Christ of today as interpreted by the theological significance of the death-resurrection event.

Black theology certainly agrees with this emphasis on the cross and resurrection. The Gospels are not biographies of Jesus; they are *gospel*—that is, good news about what God has done in the life, death, and resurrection of Jesus. This must be the focus of christological thinking.

The theological significance of the cross and resurrection is what makes the life of Jesus more than just the life of a good man who happened to like the poor. *The finality of Jesus lies in the totality of his existence in complete freedom as the Oppressed One who reveals through his death and resurrection that God is present in all dimensions of human liberation.* His death is the revelation of the freedom of God, taking upon himself the totality of human oppression; his resurrection is the disclosure that God is not defeated by oppression but transforms it into the possibility of freedom.

For men and women who live in an oppressive society this means that they do not have to behave as if *death* were the ultimate. God in Christ has set us free from death, and we can now live without worrying about social ostracism, economic insecurity, or political tyranny. "In Christ the immortal God has tasted death and in so doing ... destroyed death"[9] (compare Hebrews 2:14ff.).

Christian freedom is the recognition that Christ has conquered death. Humankind no longer has to be afraid of dying. To live as if death had the last word is to be enslaved and thus controlled by the forces of destruction. The free are the oppressed who say no to an oppressor, in spite of the threat of death, because God has said yes to them, thereby placing them in a state of freedom. They can now deny any values that separate them from the reality of their new being.

Moltmann is correct when he speaks of the resurrection as the "symbol of protest":

> To believe in the resurrection transforms faith from a deliverance from the world into an initiative that changes the world and makes those who believe into worldly, personal, social and political witnesses to God's righteousness and freedom in the midst of a repressive society and an unredeemed world. In this, faith comes to historical self-consciousness and to the recognition of its eschatological task within history.[10]

---

[9]Richardson, "Death," in ibid., p. 60.
[10]Moltmann, "Toward a Political Hermeneutics of the Gospel," *Union Theological Seminary Quarterly Review*, vol. 23, no. 4 (Summer 1968), pp. 311–312.

The Black Christ

What is the significance of the historical and resurrected Jesus for our times? The answer to this question must focus on both the meaning of the historical Jesus and the contemporary significance of the resurrection. It is impossible to gloss over either one of these emphases and still retain the gospel message.

Focusing on the historical Jesus means that black theology recognizes *history* as an indispensable foundation of christology. We are not free to make Jesus what we wish him to be at certain moments of existence. He *is* who he *was,* and we know who he was through a critical, historical evaluation of the New Testament Jesus. Black theology takes seriously Pannenberg's comment that "faith primarily has to do with what Jesus was."[11]

To focus on the contemporary significance of the resurrection means that we do not take Pannenberg's comment on the historical Jesus as seriously as he does. No matter how seriously we take the carpenter from Nazareth, there is still the existential necessity to relate his person to black persons, asking, "What is his relevance to the black community today?" In this sense, unlike Pannenberg, we say that the soteriological value of Jesus' person must finally determine our christology. It is the oppressed community in the situation of liberation that determines the meaning and scope of Jesus. We know who Jesus *was* and *is* when we encounter the brutality of oppression in his community as it seeks to be what it is, in accordance with his resurrection.

The christological significance of Jesus is not an abstract question to be solved by intellectual debates among seminary professors. The meaning of Jesus is an existential question. We know who he is when our own lives are placed in a situation of oppression, and we thus have to make a decision for or against our condition. To say no to oppression and yes to liberation is to encounter the existential significance of the Resurrected One. He is the Liberator *par excellence* whose very presence makes persons sell all that they have and follow him.

Now what does this mean for blacks in America today? How are they to interpret the christological significance of the Resurrected One in such a way that his person will be existentially relevant to their oppressed condition? The black community is an oppressed community primarily because of its blackness; hence the christological importance of Jesus must be found in his blackness. If he is not black as we are, then the resurrection has little significance for our times. Indeed, if he cannot be what we are, we cannot be who he is. Our being with him is dependent on his being with us in the oppressed black condition, revealing to us what is necessary for our liberation.

The definition of Jesus as black is crucial for christology if we truly believe in his continued presence today. Taking our clue from the historical Jesus who is pictured

---

[11]Pannenberg, *Jesus,* p. 28.

in the New Testament as the Oppressed One, what else, except blackness, could adequately tell us the meaning of his presence today? Any statement about Jesus today that fails to consider blackness as the *decisive* factor about his person is a denial of the New Testament message. The life, death, and resurrection of Jesus reveal that he is the man for others, disclosing to them what is necessary for their liberation from oppression. If this is true, then Jesus Christ must be black so that blacks can know that their liberation is his liberation.

The black Jesus is also an important theological symbol for an analysis of Christ's presence today because we must make decisions about where he is at work in the world. Is his presence synonymous with the work of the oppressed or the oppressors, blacks or whites? Is he to be found among the wretched or among the rich?

Of course clever white theologians would say that it is not either/or. Rather he is to be found somewhere in between, a little black and a little white. Such an analysis is not only irrelevant for our times but also irrelevant for the time of the historical Jesus. Jesus was not for and against the poor, for and against the rich. He was for the poor and against the rich, for the weak and against the strong. Who can read the New Testament and fail to see that Jesus took sides and accepted freely the possibility of being misunderstood?

If the historical Jesus is any clue for an analysis of the contemporary Christ, then he must be where human beings are enslaved. To speak of him is to speak of the liberation of the oppressed. In a society that defines blackness as evil and whiteness as good, the theological significance of Jesus is found in the possibility of human liberation through blackness. Jesus is the black Christ!

Concretely, to speak of the presence of Christ today means focusing on the forces of liberation in the black community. Value perspectives must be reshaped in the light of what aids the self-determination of black persons. The definition of Christ as black means that he represents the complete opposite of the values of white culture. He is the center of a black Copernican revolution.

Black theology seeks to do in American theology what Copernicus did to thinking about the physical universe. Inasmuch as this country has achieved its sense of moral and religious idealism by oppressing blacks, the black Christ leads the warfare against the white assault on blackness by striking at white values and white religion. The black Copernican revolution means extolling as good what whites have ignored or regarded as evil.

The blackness of Christ clarifies the definition of him as the *Incarnate* One. In him God becomes oppressed humanity and thus reveals that the achievement of full humanity is consistent with divine being. The human being was not created to be a slave, and the appearance of God in Christ gives us the possibility of freedom. By becoming a black person, God discloses that blackness is not what the world says it is. Blackness is a manifestation of the being of God in that it reveals that neither divinity nor humanity resides in white definitions but in liberation from captivity.

The black Christ is he who threatens the structure of evil as seen in white society, rebelling against it, thereby becoming the embodiment of what the black community knows that it must become. Because he has become black as we are, we now know what black empowerment is. It is blacks determining the way they are going to behave in the world. It is refusing to allow white society to place strictures on black existence as if their having guns means that blacks are supposed to cool it.

Black empowerment is the black community in defiance, knowing that he who has become one of them is far more important than threats from white officials. The black Christ is he who nourishes the rebellious impulse in blacks so that at the appointed time the black community can respond collectively to the white community as a corporate "bad nigger," lashing out at the enemy of humankind.

It is to be expected that some whites will resent the christological formulation of the black Christ, either by ignoring it or by viewing it as too narrow to include the universal note of the gospel. It will be difficult for whites to deny the whiteness of their existence and affirm the oppressed black Christ. But the concept of black, which includes both what the world means by oppression and what the gospel means by liberation, is the only concept that has any real significance today. If Christ is not black, then who is he? We could say that he is the son of God, son of Man, messiah, lord, son of David, and a host of other titles. The difficulty with these titles is not that they fail to describe the person of Christ, but they are first-century titles. To cling to them without asking, "What appropriate symbol do these titles refer to today?" is to miss the significance of them altogether.

What is striking about the New Testament names of Jesus is the dimension of liberation embedded in them. For example, Jesus Christ as Lord, a postresurrection title, emphasizes his complete authority over all creation. Everyone is subject to him. The Lord is the "ruler," "commander," he who has all authority. If "Jesus is Lord," as one of the earliest baptismal creeds of the church puts it, then what does this say about black and white relationships in America? The meaning is perhaps too obvious for comment. It means simply that whites do not have authority over blacks. Our loyalty belongs only to him who has become like us in everything, especially blackness. To take seriously the lordship of Christ or his sonship or messiahship is to see him as the sole criterion for authentic existence.

If Jesus is the Suffering Servant of God, he is an oppressed being who has taken on that very form of human existence that is representation of human misery. What we need to ask is this: "What is the form of humanity that accounts for human suffering in our society? What is it, except blackness?" If Christ is truly the Suffering Servant of God who takes upon himself the suffering of his people, thereby reestablishing the covenant of God, then he must be black.

To get at the meaning of this and not get bogged down in racial emotionalism, we need only ask, "Is it possible to talk about suffering in America without talking about the meaning of blackness? Can we really believe that Christ is the Suffering Servant par excellence if he is not black?" Black theology contends that blackness is the only symbol that cannot be overlooked if we are going to take seriously the christological significance of Jesus Christ.

But some whites will ask, "Does black theology believe that Jesus was *really* black?" It seems to me that the *literal* color of Jesus is irrelevant, as are the different shades of blackness in America. Generally speaking, blacks are not oppressed on the basis of the depth of their blackness. "Light" blacks are oppressed just as much as "dark" blacks. But as it happens, *Jesus was not white* in any sense of the word, literally or theologically. Therefore, Albert Cleage is not too far wrong when he describes Jesus as a black Jew; and he is certainly on solid theological grounds when he describes Christ as the Black Messiah.

The importance of the concept of the black Christ is that it expresses the *concreteness* of Jesus' continued presence today. If we do not translate the first-century titles into symbols that are relevant today, then we run the danger that Bultmann is so concerned about: Jesus becomes merely a figure of past history. To make Jesus just a figure of yesterday is to deny the real importance of the preaching of the early church. He is not dead but resurrected and is alive in the world today. Like yesterday, he has taken upon himself the misery of his people, becoming for them what is needed for their liberation.

To be a disciple of the black Christ is to become black with him. Looting, burning, or the destruction of white property are not *primary* concerns. Such matters can only be decided by the oppressed themselves who are seeking to develop their images of the black Christ. What is primary is that blacks must refuse to let whites define what is appropriate for the black community. Just as white slaveholders in the nineteenth century said that questioning slavery was an invasion of their property rights, so today they use the same line of reasoning in reference to black self-determination. But Nat Turner had no scruples on this issue; and blacks today are beginning to see themselves in a new image. We believe in the manifestation of the black Christ, and our encounter with him defines our values. This means that blacks are *free* to do what they have to in order to affirm their humanity.

The Kingdom of God and the Black Christ

The appearance of Jesus as the black Christ also means that the black revolution is God's kingdom becoming a reality in America. According to the New Testament, the kingdom is a historical event. It is what happens to persons when their being is confronted with the reality of God's historical liberation of the oppressed. To see the kingdom is to see a happening, and we are thus placed in a situation of decision—we say either yes or no to the liberation struggle.

The kingdom is not an attainment of material security, nor is it mystical communion with the divine. It has to do with the *quality* of one's existence in which a person realizes that *persons* are more important than property. When blacks behave as if the values of this world have no significance, it means that they perceive the irruption of God's kingdom. The kingdom of God is a *black* happening. It is black persons saying no to whitey, forming caucuses and advancing into white confrontation. It is a beautiful thing to see blacks shaking loose the chains of white approval, and it can only mean that they know that there is a way of living that does not involve the destruction of their personhood. This is the kingdom of God.

For Jesus, repentance is a precondition for entrance into the kingdom. But it should be pointed out that repentance has nothing to do with morality or religious piety in the white sense.

Günther Bornkamm's analysis of Jesus' call to repentance is relevant here. To repent, says Bornkamm, is "to lay hold on the salvation which is already at hand, and to give up everything for it."[12] It means recognizing the importance of the kingdom-event and casting one's lot with it. The kingdom is God's own event and inherent in its appearance is the invitation to renounce everything and join it. That is why Jesus said:

> If your hand or your foot causes you to sin, cut it off and throw it from you; it is better for you to enter life maimed or lame than with two hands or two feet to be thrown into eternal fire. And if your eye causes you to sin, pluck it out and throw it from you; it is better for you to enter life with one eye than with two eyes to be thrown into the hell of fire [Matthew 18:8–9].

According to Bornkamm:

> Repentance comes by means of grace. Those who sit at the table of the rich lord are the poor, the cripples, the blind and lame, not those who are already half-cured. The tax collectors and sinners with whom Jesus sits at meat are not asked first about the state of their moral improvement.... . The extent to which all talk of the conditions which man must fulfill before grace is accorded him is here silenced, as shown by the parables of the lost sheep and the lost coin, which tell only of the finding of what was lost, and in this very manner describe the joy in heaven "over one sinner who repents" (Luke 15:7, 10). So little is repentance a human action preparing the way for grace that it can be placed on the level of being found.[13]

The kingdom is what God does and repentance arises solely as a response to God's liberation.

The event of the kingdom today is the liberation struggle in the black community. It is where persons are suffering and dying for want of human dignity. It is thus incumbent upon all to see the event for what it is—God's kingdom. This is what conversion means. Blacks are being converted because they see in the events around

---

[12]Bornkamm, *Jesus of Nazareth*, p. 82.
[13]Ibid., pp. 83–84.

them the coming of the Lord, and will not be scared into closing their eyes to it. Black identity is too important; it is like the pearl of great value, which a person buys only by selling all that he or she has (Matthew 13:44–46).

Of course, whites can say that they fail to see the significance of this black phenomenon. But loss of sight is characteristic of the appearance of the kingdom. Not everyone recognizes the person from Nazareth as the incarnate One who came to liberate the human race. Who could possibly imagine that the Holy One of Israel would condescend to the level of a carpenter? Only those with eyes of faith could see that in that person God was confronting the reality of the human condition. There is no other sign save the words and deeds of Jesus himself. If an encounter with him does not convince persons that God is present, then they will never know, except in that awful moment when perfect awareness is fatally bound up with irreversible judgment.

That is why Jesus compared the kingdom with a mustard seed and with yeast in dough. Both show a small, apparently insignificant beginning but a radical, revolutionary ending. The seed grows to a large tree, and the bread can feed many hungry persons. So it is with the kingdom; because of its small beginning, some viewers do not readily perceive what is actually happening.

The black revolution is a continuation of that small kingdom. Whites do not recognize what is happening, and they are thus unable to deal with it. For most whites in power, the black community is a nuisance—something to be considered only when the natives get restless. But what white America fails to realize is the explosive nature of the kingdom. Although its beginning is small, it will have far-reaching effects not only on the black community but on the white community as well. Now is the time to make decisions about loyalties, because soon it will be too late. Shall we or shall we not join the black revolutionary kingdom?

To enter the kingdom is to enter the state of salvation, the condition of blessedness. Historically it appears that "salvation" is Paul's translation of Jesus' phrase "kingdom of God." But, oh, how the word "salvation" has been beaten and battered in nineteen centuries of Christian verbiage! What can salvation possibly mean for oppressed blacks in America? Is it a kind of spiritual juice, squirted into the life of the dispirited that somehow enables them to withstand the brutality of oppressors because they know that heaven is waiting for them? Certainly, this is what rulers would like the oppressed to believe.

In most societies where political oppression is acute and religion is related to the state, salvation is interpreted always in ways that do not threaten the security of the existing government. Sometimes salvation takes the form of abstract, intellectual analysis or private mystical communion with the divine. The "hope" that is offered the oppressed is not the possibility of changing their earthly condition but a longing for the next life. With the poor counting on salvation in the next life, oppressors can humiliate and exploit without fear of reprisal. That is why Karl Marx called religion the opiate of the people. It is an open question whether he was right in his evaluation; but he was correct in identifying the intention of oppressors. They promote religion because it can be an effective tool for enslavement.

The history of the black church is a case in point. At first, white "Christian" slaveholders in America did not allow their slaves to be baptized, because Christianity supposedly enfranchised them. But because the white church was having few converts among blacks, it proceeded to assure slaveholders that baptism had nothing to do with civil freedom. In fact, many white ministers assured slave masters that Christianity would make for better slaves. With that assurance, the masters began to introduce Christianity to blacks, confident that it would make blacks more obedient. But many blacks were able to appropriate white Christianity to their own condition by turning it into a religion of liberation. The emergence of the "invisible institution" (secret church) among the slaves of the south, the organization of the African Methodist Episcopal Church (1816) and the African Methodist Episcopal Zion Church (1821), together with other black independent religious institutions, and their involvement in the antislavery movement, show that black religionists did see through the fake white Christianity of the period.

For the pre–Civil War black church, salvation involved more than longing for the next life. Being saved was also a present reality that placed persons in a dimension of freedom so that earthly injustice became intolerable. That was why Nat Turner, a Baptist preacher, had visions of God that involved his own election to be the Moses of his people, leading it from the house of bondage. After his insurrection black preachers were outlawed in many parts of the south.

Unfortunately, the post–Civil War black church fell into the white trick of interpreting salvation in terms similar to those of white oppressors. Salvation became white: an objective act of Christ in which God "washes" away our sins in order to prepare us for a new life in heaven. The resurgence of the black church in civil rights and the creation of a black theology represent an attempt of the black community to see salvation in the light of its own earthly liberation.

The interpretation of salvation as liberation from bondage is certainly consistent with the biblical view:

> In the Old Testament salvation is expressed by a word which has the root meaning of "to be wide" or "spacious," "to develop without hindrance" and thus ultimately "to have victory in battle" (I Sam. 14:45).[14]

To be saved meant that one's enemies have been conquered, and the savior is the one who has the power to gain victory:

---

[14]F. J. Taylor, "Save," in Richardson, *Theological Word Book,* p. 219 .

He who needs salvation is one who has been threatened or oppressed, and his salvation consists in deliverance from danger and tyranny or rescue from imminent peril (I Sam. 4:3, 7:8, 9:16). To save another is to communicate to him one's own prevailing strength (Job 26:2), to give him the power to maintain the necessary strength.[15]

In Israel, God is the Savior par excellence. Beginning with the exodus, God's righteousness is for those who are weak and helpless. "The mighty work of God, in which his righteousness is manifested, is in saving the humble … the poor and the dispirited."[16] The same is true in the New Testament. Salvation is release from slavery and admission to freedom (Galatians 5:1, II Corinthians 3:17), saying no to the fear of principalities and yes to the powers of liberty (I John 4:18). This is not to deny that salvation is a future reality; but it is also hope that focuses on the present.

Today the oppressed are the inhabitants of black ghettos, Amerindian reservations, Hispanic barrios, and other places where whiteness has created misery. To participate in God's salvation is to cooperate with the black Christ as he liberates his people from bondage. Salvation, then, primarily has to do with earthly reality and the injustice inflicted on those who are helpless and poor. To see the salvation of God is to see this people rise up against its oppressors, demanding that justice become a reality *now*, not tomorrow. It is the oppressed serving warning that they "ain't gonna take no more of this bullshit, but a new day is coming and it ain't going to be like today." The new day is the presence of the black Christ as expressed in the liberation of the black community.

28. The Politics of Jesus: Discussion Questions

Should the life and teachings of Jesus be normative in Christian political theology?

Do the historical Jesus and the Christ of theology point to different political theologies? If so, why?

How do you respond to Niebuhr's claim that the way of Jesus applied to politics is irresponsible and doomed to failure?

---

[15]Ibid.
[16]Ibid.

V

Violence and Peace

Introduction by Elizabeth Phillips

Many of the texts in other sections of this reader could also be considered under the heading of 'Violence and Peace'. In discussion of 'The Church and the Political' (Section III), questions of spiritual and temporal authority often include the assumption that temporal authorities can and must use violence while spiritual authorities cannot and should not (although Christian history obviously and tragically attests that the latter conviction was stronger in espousal than in practice). Even in the pacifist traditions arising from sixteenth-century Anabaptism, the historical assumption has been that human governments were ordained by God to use force and coercion in order to maintain order, justice and peace. Where Anabaptists parted with Catholic and Protestant traditions was in the belief that Jesus had invited his followers into a way of ordering themselves without coercion or violence; the way of Christ is necessarily a way of peace which does not exercise force and which calls into question the violence of governments. However, those truly following this way are few, and governments will continue to exist and to exert force so long as people live 'outside the perfection of Christ', as in the Schleitheim document in 'The politics of Jesus' section of this reader (Section IV).

Thus, virtually all Christians have agreed historically that (particularly due to the fall and human sinfulness) governments had God-given duties which required coercion and force; the disagreement has come concerning which, if any, Christians can participate in such violence, and under what conditions. This historic assumption would largely go unquestioned until it faced the challenges of modern humanism, on the one hand, from which arose forms of pacifism based on optimism about humans' ability to end violence; and on the other hand, twentieth-century theological approaches such as in John Howard Yoder and Walter Wink, which denied both that governments must be violent and that humans can create a non-violent world, embracing instead a view that because the violence of governments is part of their fallenness, it is also an object of Christ's redemption; Christians must participate in calling governments to peace, while understanding this calling as work which is necessarily unfinished this side of the eschaton.

Before these options of questioning whether governments must and should be violent arose, conversations in Christian theology were about whether Christians can participate in governmental violence, and if so, when. Many of the earliest theologians taught that no Christians should exercise violence, including the second-to-third-century apologist, Tertullian. Tertullian did not suggest that the Empire could not or should not have its wars, but he did question Christian participation in them. The specific occasion for this piece, 'On the Crown' (c. 211), seems to have been a Christian soldier who was killed for refusing to wear a military crown in a procession honouring the emperor. Some argue that such a piece gives a window into the fact that early Christian rejection of violence may have been more precisely a rejection of imperial idolatry, and thus irrelevant to modern, secular state violence. Others would suggest that there is something always necessarily idolatrous in militarism and warfare, whether that of Rome or that of the modern nation-state. (The latter is a central thread in the work of William Cavanaugh, who is also introduced in this section.) While it is probably anachronistic to label most patristic texts as 'pacifist', many of the earliest Christian theologians, including Justin Martyr, Athenagorus, Tertullian, Origen and Cyprian, wrote about the peacableness of the Christian life and Christian renunciation of warfare and violence.

Christian refusal to participate in governmental violence was likely never universal, and certainly weakened as the Roman Empire's hostility to Christianity waned. Soon the central question of violence and Christian practice would be the conditions under which violence was justifiable. Eventually growing into a tradition of 'just war theory', this discussion begins most clearly in the late-fourth-century work of Ambrose of Milan. In 'De Officiis' (Offices, c. 380s), modelled on the text of the same title by the Roman philosopher Cicero, Ambrose gives an account of the ethical duties of the Christian clergy, seeking both to offer guidance as well as to prove the superiority of Christian morality. In the excerpts included here, he stresses the virtues of justice and fortitude, framing the question in terms of whether a war is just or unjust, and upholding the violence committed by Moses and David (respectively) as models of defense of others against injustice and of prudence in discerning when to go to war.

Augustine would build upon Ambrose to begin developing what would later become criteria for a just war, insisting upon the legitimacy of the authority which commands the war, and that the just war would end or punish lust for power and love of violence, instead of becoming an instance of such evils. Thomas Aquinas would later begin to present these principles more systematically as criteria. During the middle ages, Christian renunciation of violence would largely become understood as the particular calling of some clerics and those in religious orders. Few Christians would argue for the normativity of this renunciation for all Christians until the Anabaptists of the sixteenth century. Pilgram Marpeck was a mining magistrate turned lay leader of Anabaptist groups, whose writings focused on themes including the central importance of free, uncoerced conscience and conversion, freedom of the church from interference from governments, and the active pursuit of love and justice. 'Concerning the Lowliness of Christ', written in 1547, emphasizes themes which were also common in patristic appeals against violence: the example of the humility of Christ and the importance of practising patience.

Scholars today often speak of 'intersectionality'; in political theology, feminists and postcolonial theologians are especially interested in the overlapping and interconnectedness of various modes and systems of oppression and domination. Martin Luther King, Jr. began to address intersectionality long before its existence was theorized or named. His movement of non-violent resistance against segregation and racism eventually widened to a program to defeat poverty, and near the end of his life, the intersectionality of racism, poverty and militarism came into focus as America fought a war in Vietnam. Exactly one year before his assassination, he spoke to a gathering of clergy at the Riverside Church in New York City, saying that it was 'A Time to Break Silence' (1967), to put loyalty to the way of Jesus Christ above loyalty to the cause of the American government, to name the ways in which Vietnam was a further manipulation and victimization of the poorest both at home and abroad, and to demand an end to the war. We will never know whether King, had he lived longer, would have widened his gaze even further to how these forms of oppression intersected with oppression of and violence against women. Feminists and womanists would soon identify the inattention to women and the absence of women's voices and experiences as a serious problem across the first generation of Black theology in America.

Whether or not governments must be violent, whether or not Christians should participate in wars and violence, and when Christians must stand up against particular wars and violent oppression are all longstanding questions within political theology. A more recent set of questions arises from the modern identification of 'religious violence' as a discrete phenomenon. William Cavanaugh's 'Violence Religious and Secular: Questioning the Categories' is something of a precis of his book *The Myth of Religious Violence* (2009), in which he argues that the constructs of 'religion' and 'religious violence' may serve to mystify more than to clarify, and to draw our critical attention away from supposedly 'secular' violence.

A further contemporary question surrounds what can be done in practice to reduce violence, presumably a conversation which can be shared by both pacifists and those who believe violence is sometimes necessary as a last resort and a means to peace and justice. The theory of Just Peacemaking, proposed primarily by Glen Stassen, has been one thread in this conversation. Conversations about limiting and preventing violence often overlap with important conversations surrounding human rights. After Alastair MacIntyre's influential critiques of the framework of human rights, political theologians such as Stanley Hauerwas and John Milbank have made strong arguments against the framework of 'rights' in relation to its philosophical and theological underpinnings and implications (related to their wider critiques of liberalism, which are introduced in Section VI). Different sorts of critiques of human rights have also been found among liberationists and postcolonial theologians (see Section VII), who note how the actual framework, laws and judicial practice of human rights primarily arise from and serve those who already have more power and privilege in the world.

Other theologians defend the framework of human rights and trace its resonance with and historical grounding in Christian convictions (see especially the work of Esther Reed and Ethna Regan, in Further Reading suggestions). In 'Do Human Rights Exist?' (based on a lecture delivered at the London School of Economics in 2008), then Archbishop of Canterbury, Rowan Williams, addresses Alastair MacIntyre's scepticism about 'rights' discourse and draws on New Testament texts on slavery to argue that there can be theological grounding for understandings of universal human dignity and equality which are not beholden to the poverties of Enlightenment philosophy diagnosed by MacIntyre.

29. Tertullian – Extracts from On the Crown

Chapter XI

(1) Now, to come down to the very heart of this question about the soldier's crown, should we not really first examine the right of a Christian to be in the military service at all? In other words, why discuss the merely accidental detail, when the foundation on which it rests is deserving of censure? Are we to believe it lawful to take an oath of allegiance to a mere human being over and above the oath of fidelity to God? Can we obey another master, having chosen Christ? Can we forsake father, mother, and all our relatives? By divine law we must honor them and our love for them is second only to that which we have toward God [Cf. Exod. 20.12]. The Gospel also bids us honor our parents [Matt. 15.4; Mark 7.10; Luke 18.20], placing none but Christ Himself above them [Matt. 10.37; Luke 14.26]. (2) Is it likely we are permitted to carry a sword when our Lord said that he who takes the sword will perish by the sword? [Cf. Matt. 26.52]. Will the son of peace who is forbidden to engage in a lawsuit [Cf. 1 Cor. 6.7] espouse the deeds of war? Will a Christian, taught to turn the other cheek when struck unjustly [Cf. Matt. 5.39; Luke 6.29], guard prisoners in chains, and administer torture and capital punishment? (3) Will he rather mount guard for others than for Christ on station days? And what about the Lord's Day? Will he not even then do it for Christ? Will he stand guard before temples, that he has renounced? Will he eat at pagan banquets, which the

Apostle forbids? [Cf. 1 Cor. 8.10]. Will he protect by night those very demons whom in the daytime he has put to flight by his exorcisms, leaning on a lance such as pierced the side of Christ [on the cross]? [Cf. John 19.34]. Will he bear, too, a standard that is hostile to Christ, and will he ask the watch-word from his commander-in-chief—he who has already received one from God? Moreover, after death, will he be disturbed by the horn of the trumpeter—he who expects to be aroused by the trumpet of the angel? [Cf. 1 Cor. 15.52; 1 Thess. 4.16]. Will his corpse be cremated according to military custom—when he, a Christian, was not permitted to burn incense in sacrifice, when to him Christ remitted the eternal punishment by fire he had deserved?

(4) Yes, these and many other offenses can be observed in the discharge of military duties—offenses that must be interpreted as acts of desertion. To leave the camp of Light and enlist m the camp of Darkness means going over to the enemy. To be sure, the case is different for those who are converted after they have been bound to military service. St. John admitted soldiers to baptism [Cf. Luke 3.14]; then there were the two most faithful centurions: the one whom Christ praised [Cf. Matt. 8.10; Luke 7.9], and the other whom Peter instructed [Cf. Acts 10]. But, once we have embraced the faith and have been baptized, we either must immediately leave military service (as many have done); or we must resort to all kinds of excuses in order to avoid any action which is also forbidden in civilian life, lest we offend God; or, last of all, for the sake of God we must suffer the fate which mere citizen-faith was no less ready to accept.

(5) For, military service offers neither exemption from punishment of sins nor relief from martyrdom. The Gospel is one and the same for the Christian at all times whatever his occupation in life. Jesus will deny those who deny Him and confess those who confess Him [Cf. Matt. 10.32, 33; Luke 12.8,9]; He will save the life that has been lost for His Name's sake, but He will destroy the one that has been gained against His Name [Cf. Matt. 10.39; Mark 8.35; Luke 9.24]. With Him the faithful citizen is a soldier, just as the faithful soldier is a citizen. (6) The state of faith admits no plea of compulsion. Those are under no compulsion to sin whose sole obligation is not to sin. A Christian may be pressed to the offering of sacrifice and to the straight denial of Christ under threat of torture and punishment. Yet, the law of Christianity does not excuse even that compulsion, since there is a stronger obligation to dread the denial of the faith and to undergo martyrdom than to escape suffering and to perform the sacrificial rite required. (7) Moreover, that kind of argument destroys the very essence of our sacramental oath, since it would loosen the fetters for voluntary sins. For, it will be possible to maintain that inclination is a compulsion, too, since there is indeed, some sort of compelling force in it. The foregoing principles I wish to have also applied to the other occasions for wearing crowns in some official capacity (it is with reference to such occasions especially that people are wont to plead compulsion), since for this very reason we must either refuse public offices lest we fall into sin, or we must endure martyrdom in order to sever our connection with them.

30. Ambrose of Milan – Extracts from On the Duties of Clergy, Book I

XXIX

Here is another measure of the greatness of justice: it is never without relevance, no matter what the place, or the person, or the time. Even warring parties maintain its importance: so, if it has been decided with an enemy that battle will take place at a particular place or on a particular day, it is regarded as a violation of justice to arrive at the place in advance or to bring forward the time. It is one thing for a person to be captured in a battle, after a bitter struggle, and quite another if it happens with the help of a favour from on high or some chance occurrence: for on fiercer enemies, those who prove treacherous and those who are guilty of greater crimes, fiercer vengeance is taken. This was what happened with the Midianites. They had caused most of the Jewish people to sin through the way their women had behaved, and the anger of God was poured out on our fathers' people because of it. The result was that when Moses defeated them, he would not allow a single one of them to be spared. In the case of the Gibeonites, however, who had tried our fathers' people by an act of treachery instead of fighting them in war, Joshua would not crush them: instead, he subjected them to the indignity of being reduced to a vassal status. Or take the case of Elisha. The Syrians were besieging the city, and he had struck them with a temporary blindness and led them in while they could not see anything; but he would not give the king of Israel leave to slay them when he wanted to. 'You must not slay those whom you have not captured with your sword and spear,' he said. 'Set bread and water before them; let them eat and drink, and go back to their master.' His aim was that they would be so inspired by this act of humanity that they would show favour in return. And so it turned out: the Syrian raids on the land of Israel stopped from that time on.

If justice is binding like this in war, it is surely all the more necessary to respect it in peacetime. We find that the prophet showed this favour as well, in the way he treated those who had come to seize him. This is what we read. The king of Syria had sent his army to lie in wait for him, for he had discovered that it was Elisha who was thwarting all his schemes and machinations. When Gehazi, the prophet's servant, caught sight of the army, he began to tremble: he was terrified for his life. The prophet said to him: 'Do not be afraid: there are more with us than with them'. Whereupon the prophet prayed that his servant's eyes might be opened, and they were opened. All at once, Gehazi saw the whole mountain filled with horses and chariots, all gathered in a circle around Elisha. As the Syrians came down, the prophet said: 'Lord, strike the Syrian army with blindness.' This prayer was granted, and he then said to the Syrians: 'Come with me, and I will take you to the man you are looking for'. They 'saw'

Elisha, the one they so wanted to seize; but even as they saw him, they were quite unable to take hold of him. So, it is quite clear that good faith and justice need to be respected even in war, and there can be nothing seemly about any situation where good faith is violated.

People of olden times even used a mild name to describe their foes: they spoke of them as *peregrini*, strangers, for there was an ancient custom of designating *hostes*, enemies, as *peregrini*, strangers. We can say with equal confidence that this, too, was taken from our Scriptures. For the Hebrews used to call their foes *allophyloi*, or, in Latin, *alienigenae*, 'those of another race'. So we read in the first book of the Kings: 'And it came to pass in those days, that *alienigenae*, those of another race, mustered for battle against Israel'.

The foundation of justice, then, is faith, for the hearts of the just meditate on faith, and the person who is just, and thus critical of himself, raises the edifice of his justice on the foundation of his faith; indeed, his justice is apparent every time he confesses the truth. This is what the Lord says through Isaiah: 'See, I lay a stone for a foundation in Sion.' That stone is Christ, who is the foundation of the church. For Christ is the faith of us all, and it is the church that reflects the true character of justice. Here, the rights of all are common; the church prays in common, works in common, and is tempted in common. Wherever you find a person who denies himself, there you have one who is just, and there you have one who is worthy of Christ. This was why Paul also placed Christ at the foundation of everything: it was so that we would build our works of justice upon him, with faith as the foundation. When our works are evil, they reflect injustice; but when they are good, it is justice that is seen.

. . .

XXXV

We have now dealt quite fully with the nature and essence of what is honourable from the standpoint of justice. Let us at this point move on to deal with courage. Since it belongs higher up the scale, as it were, than all the other virtues, courage gets divided into two types: one has to do with the business of war, the other with ordinary domestic life. But a taste for the affairs of war appears to be quite alien to the kind of duty which concerns us now, for our interest is in the duty of the soul rather than the body, and our activity has to do not with arms but with the business of peace. All the same, it has to be said that our ancestors, men like Joshua son of Nun, or Jerubbaal, or Samson, or David, won great glory in the affairs of war as well.

Courage belongs higher up the scale than the other virtues, then; but it is a virtue which never comes unaccompanied, for it does not depend purely on its own resources—at any rate, where courage is without justice, it leads only to wickedness, for the stronger it is, the readier it is to crush an inferior party. Even in the business of war, though, it is considered necessary to assess whether a particular war is just or unjust.

David never engaged in war unless he was provoked. This way, he was able to combine courage with prudence when it came to battle. Take the occasion when he was about to go into single-handed combat with Goliath, the man whose physical bulk was so colossal: he spurned the armour offered to him, saying that it would only weigh him down—for bravery depends on its own muscle, rather than on any protection offered by independent resources. Then, remaining at a distance so that he could strike with more deadly force, he felled his foe with the blow of a single stone. From that day forth, he never undertook a war without consulting the Lord first. And so it was that he emerged victorious in every battle he fought, and remained fighting fit and ready to bear arms well into his old age—there he was, engaged in a war against veritable Titans, right in the thick of it, fighting like a true warrior amidst the fierce columns, eager for glory, and quite unconcerned for his own safety.

But this is not the only type of courage to be regarded as remarkable. We learn too of the glorious courage of those who, through faith, and with greatness of spirit, 'stopped the mouths of lions, quenched the force of fire, escaped the edge of the sword, and out of weakness grew courageous'. They were not surrounded by comrades-in-arms or by legions, nor were they winning the kind of victory in which a host of others could claim a share; it was by the bare valour of their spirits that they fought and won their triumphs single-handedly over infidels. Look at Daniel, and how invincible he was! He knew no fear even when the lions were roaring right beside him! The beasts were growling furiously, and he remained intent on his food.

XXXVI

So the glory of courage does not consist merely in physical strength or the power of muscle: it is to be found far more in valour of spirit. And the law of valour consists not in doing people an injury but in protecting them from such things. In point of fact, the person who fails to deflect an injury from his neighbour, when he is in a position to do so, is as much at fault as the one who inflicts it. This was where holy Moses took his earliest steps towards proving his courage in war. For when he saw a Hebrew being ill-treated by an Egyptian, he defended him—and did it so successfully that he finished the Egyptian off and hid him in the sand. Solomon also says: 'Rescue a man who is being taken to meet his death.'

31. Pilgram Marpeck – Concerning the Lowliness of Christ

To all the elect and saints of God in the Grisons, Appenzell, St. Gall, in Alsace, and wherever they are scattered hither and yon, my dearest ones in Christ.

Grace and peace from God our Father, and our Lord Jesus Christ, be and remain with us for ever. Amen.

My dearly beloved in God the Father and the Lord Jesus Christ. Especially in this critical time of great danger, my fervent prayer, wish, and desire, now and always, is that one of these days, before my end, God might open the way to [come to] you all. There, together, we might rejoice in the way, truth, and life which is Jesus Christ, discuss His will, mind, and Spirit which are given in word, deed, and act, and share our delight in the love and truth of the gospel of Christ.

This is the message which Christ in His grace has given, commanded, and delivered to us. It is the costliest and most esteemed treasure, for it is Christ the Lord Himself. In this treasure are hidden all the treasures of the secret will and pleasure of the Father, for no one has seen the Father, much less known Him, except the Son who is in the bosom of the Father. Similarly, no one has known the Son except the Father who sent Him. The Son reveals [His Father] in His holy, external teaching. And the miracle and power of His works on earth are the Father's testimony to His teaching. He to whom the Father has not been revealed cannot, and may not, know the Father of lights. Similarly, no one can know that Jesus Christ is the Son of the living God unless the Father reveals it to him. Thus, the Son is glorified through the Father and the Father through the Son.

He was born to the Father from the race of man, for the sake of man. He was born to liberate man from the power of the devil, sin, death, and hell, that is, from the guilt of Adam into which all men have come. [They have come into it] because of the guilt of sin, and because of the pains of hell and death which were laid on men. Men have been given over to the devil, who has the power of death and torment as well as of sin. And it is sin which causes the wrath of God so that, even among men who possess the salvation given by the Son of God, there can be no cessation of sin. Thus, the wrath of God delivers to sin, death, hell, pain, and the devil. Because of the one sin of disobedience, man in all eternity is no longer able to know his God, Father, and Creator. Even today, man is utterly under the wrath of God and because of sin, man is outside of Christ, the Lord and Savior.

However, because of our sin, the Father did not spare the Son. He has given Him for the sake of man, and delivered Him into the suffering and pain of death, even to condemnation, as a salvation for men. Thus, Christ's sufferings enable men to regain the original purity and innocence in which they were created and to be prepared for their God, Father, Creator, and Maker. The Holy Spirit, who cannot be where sin is, can again find a place and gain a dwelling in men, and then [transfer them] from the earthly to the heavenly. Thus, man is created an earthly creature but, through the incarnation of Christ, the earthly may become heavenly. Had Adam not fallen, there would be no need for suffering. But, because of sin, suffering and death came upon Christ. And, unlike man who experiences suffering and death because of guilt, Christ is without guilt. Grace, and the justification which leads to true devotion and which proceeds from faith, transfers man from the earthly to the eternal, heavenly state. Therefore, all earthly creatures are made subject to man in order that man might be made subject to the Lord Jesus Christ in His heavenly state and glory. Similarly, in true manhood, the Son is subject to the Father.

By the will of the Father, He was born of a virgin from the generation of the fathers. He was born the true Son of God, full of grace and truth and according to the Spirit. He is the eternal Word, and the only born Son of the Father. He is filled with every counsel and knowledge, wisdom, understanding, and perception of the Father's will. As announced in Isaiah 9[6]: "For to us a child is born, a son is given, and the kingship will be upon his shoulder." As Samuel told the people of Israel when, like the Gentiles, they desired a king, the kings of this world rest their kingship as a heavy burden upon the shoulders of the people. Such a king had the right to expect that his kingship should rest on the shoulders of the people, that they should bear the burden of the king. However, this King, the Lord Jesus Christ, has liberated His people from their eternal burden; He has put it on His own shoulders and has fastened it to the cross. Can we conceive of a more glorious kingdom, priesthood, kingship, or king? Isaiah further says that His name is Wonderful Counselor, the mighty God, the everlasting Father, the Prince of Peace. His kingdom shall have no end, and peace will be multiplied [Is. 9:7]. This child has been given to us by the Father with all His treasures and gifts. That same Lord, King, and true God has given Himself with all His treasures and gifts, and He will be the acceptable new year [Lk. 4:19].

These treasures were hidden and locked in the trunk of His body, the ark of the covenant. This ark He destroyed on the cross, and then He pried it open, which was the finishing of His work. The child fulfilled the Father's promise to us. The suffering and death on the cross completed His work on earth. Then, He made the descent into hell, and dwelt with the condemned, with those imprisoned in perdition, and with those held by death. As Christ Himself said: "My God, why have you forsaken me?" [Mk. 15:24]. However, both on earth and in the Pit, Christ was proclaimed. In the depth of death and in the abyss of hell, the Lord of both life and death proclaimed the Word to the dead. Here, the soul of Christ preached the gospel. On earth, Christ's physical suffering and death proclaimed the Word to men living in the body. Just as it was on earth, among the dead in the prison of hell all faith and hope had disappeared. Because of the guilt of the first Adam, death and hell had seized, and held captive, Him who had brought and accomplished salvation on earth, and who had also brought salvation to the prisoners of death and hell in the Pit. Then, all faith and hope disappeared from the earth and from the dead in the Pit.

The parable and prediction of the Prophet Jonah was fulfilled in Christ. Even as Jonah was swallowed by the actual leviathan in the real depth of the sea, so, too, was the Lord, together with the rest of the dead, swallowed and made captive by the spiritual leviathan, the lord of the spiritual sea, of torment and death, who has power eternally. Contrary to the view held by some erring spirits, Christ did not descend in triumph to the dead. Such a fabrication contradicts the true teaching of Christ. Even as Jonah sang a song of triumph in the whale, Christ triumphed in hell and death. And just as Jonah was in the belly of the whale three days and three nights, even so, the Son of Man will be in the middle of the earth three days and three nights. And just as Jonah was in the whale only a short while, Christ remained in death and hell until He had completely paid, for our sake, the guilt of sin.

Thus, the Father did not spare the Son, but gave Him up so that all who believe in Him may have eternal life. The Father sealed the guilt of sin in death and in the prison of hell forever. In His human poverty, the payer of the debt, the true warrantor, went Himself into the depths of hell with our sins, and yet without any sin of His own, through His torment on earth in order to make payment. Moreover, He took the power away from death and from him who has the dominion over pain and death. The whale could not hold Jonah, nor could the Pit hold Him there. Life broke through in its power, which the Lord had had in Himself against all the power of hell. By means of the glory, dominion, and power of life He took life back again out of the midst of death, together with all who have hoped for the Lord and His salvation. Their hope, and also the hope of the apostles on earth, was gone. For their very sakes, the joy, splendor, and glory of Christ has ascended to the heights, not only with all the imprisoned, but with the prison itself. Paul's question is appropriate here: "Death, hell, devil, and sin, where is your power and dominion?"

Thus, death has been swallowed up in victory, and Christ has emerged from death to life with all His chosen ones. To do so, He had both to descend and ascend, for His soul did not remain in hell. Death could not possibly keep the life of all life imprisoned, and darkness could not put out or comprehend the light, even though the light had come into the darkness of hell. Since the light Himself was imprisoned and held by darkness, there were three hours of darkness over the whole earth, not from some natural cause, but from the irruption of the Pit, which is the source of all darkness. The true light, which had the most right to shine, did not assert His power and, since He Himself had commanded all other lights to shine, the natural lights then had to surrender their brilliance. But the Lord, as the true light, has broken out of the darkness of the devil, death, sin, and hell, through the brilliance of His light and clarity and returned alive from death. In His own power He took life back; He ascended, and seated Himself to the right of the majesty of God the Father and in the glorification of the Father, with that eternal, preexistent glory which He had with the Father before the foundations of the world were laid.

The Son conquered the sin of many precisely by this descent into the depths, this greatest humility with which He humbled Himself before the Father, and by which the Father afflicted and humbled the Son. All the saints of God must learn the depths of Christ, these same depths of humility and damnation, into which the leaven of our sin brought Christ. [They must learn] the consequences of sin. Provided the devil completes sin's work in man, sin brings man into death. Here, only the deep humility of Christ brings any possibility of salvation. Whoever does not grasp that he must be condemned with and in Christ in the depths can never understand nor achieve the height of Christ. Indeed, the whole world does not want to grasp this depth of Christ; it does not want to be condemned, to recognize its lostness, and so be saved.

However, almost everyone babbles and boasts deceitfully about the height and divinity of Christ, and uses reason and scriptural subtleties, to find a false sufficiency of joy in themselves. Yet, no one is prepared to go down with Christ into death and be buried with Him. They begin with the height [of Christ], in order to deceive themselves and others. Thus, they must go down to destruction and suffer eternal exclusion from the height of Christ.

Baptism is a secret, severe water which drives all reason down into the depth to die with Christ and be buried in His death. Only then can the soul rise with Christ and become a partaker of His gifts and the treasures of His kingdom, which He distributes to all His chosen ones and gives to His own. Thus, the Son makes the Father known, and the Father makes known and reveals the Son. The elect are glorified in them, just as the Father and Son are glorified in and with themselves.

But all this has been revealed and learned first through His holy humanity. His power and miracles proved that men might believe what He said, did, and accomplished on earth. And He has received His power from the Father. To His honor and glory, He has opened it to us. Thus, our lives are renewed in order that we should eternally honor, praise, and thank the heavenly Father through His beloved Son.

To the honor and glory of the Father, He has sealed us with the Holy Spirit. As the true Prince of Peace, He, through the Holy Spirit, has established eternal, perpetual peace with us in our hearts and consciences. He never ceases to increase the kingdom of His peace, not in the world's manner, but eternally and without end. [He gives], not only peace, but also joy and comfort. Hence, no disaster may come eternally near the dwelling which is God and man eternally, Jesus Christ Himself, in whom all believers dwell and He in them.

[Gloss:] The faithful have their dwelling and safety in the temple of Christ's body. Thus, the Father and Son, after the manner of deity, have their dwelling in the hearts of all the faithful through the action of the Spirit.

After this temple or tabernacle of His body had been broken, He raised it up again on the third day. The hearts of all the faithful ascended with Him, and their hearts were made temples and dwellings of God, in which God, Father, Son, and Holy Spirit live, govern, and reign in righteousness, godliness, faithfulness, and truth, from now until eternity. Thus, all the faithful live and dwell in the risen temple of the body of Christ, which is built, raised, and erected to the right of the majesty of God, the almighty, heavenly Father. The Father Himself has prepared and erected this temple for Himself, for in it the one God, the Father, Word, and Holy Spirit, dwells eternally.

He dwells nowhere else, and God cannot be found, nor comprehended, at any other place or location eternally; nor can He be known, seen, or heard anywhere else.

In this eternal, sublime, and holiest place, God allows Himself to be apprehended, seen, and heard. As the true mercy seat, the place of worship in the Spirit and in truth is now this sole temple. Because of the sharp sword of the Word, which proceeds out of the mouth of Him who sits on the throne, nothing unclean can approach. In this temple all the faithful find pardon and rest for their souls, yes, all that is needful for their life, and all the treasures, glory, and pleasure of the temple, in which God Himself is the highest adornment, treasure, and glory eternally. For this reason, all the faithful, like David, properly demand what they have prayed for: that they may remain in the house of God their whole life and behold the pleasure of His temple. They would rather be doorkeepers than live in the dwellings of the godless.

For your soul, and for my own, I fervently desire an acceptable year, which all the faithful ought properly to explore.

I wish to discuss briefly this acceptable year, in which everything, including the treasures given us, has become new in Christ. We should see and observe the pleasure of the temple of His body and thus comfort and make glad our souls. Indeed, we should fall into wonderment, and thank our God and Father for it. We should frequently contemplate the gifts, for we should pay more attention to the giver than to the gifts. Such is the giver's intention. He who does not contemplate the gifts cannot understand either the gift or the giver. Nor may he love either of them properly, nor can he truly thank the giver.

All gifts are given us by God, and they are given for two reasons. First, in them we can learn to know our Creator, God, and Father and thus, with a pure heart, we may glorify, praise, and thank Him. Second, we are to use the gifts to serve each other, and not to lord it over each other. And, if we accomplish something to the praise of the Lord and the benefit of the neighbor, we do not rejoice over it. Our highest joy shall be that, in heaven, our names are written in the book of life (Lk. 10:20). To show, with unwavering faith and certain hope, love toward our neighbor, and thus prove our love of God, is and shall be our highest joy. Not the work, but love itself, to serve and to be a guardian of the salvation of all the elect of God, is heavenly joy.

Therefore, we are obligated to contemplate, and pay attention to, the treasures and most precious gems of Christ; we are obligated to explore, to fathom, and to observe them diligently, and in the shrine of our hearts to protect them carefully from thieves and murderers. Thus, one may discover what a wonderful, acceptable new year the heavenly Father has given and committed to us to proclaim through His child Jesus Christ. Isaiah 61 speaks about the child and Lord, and His kingdom; he also speaks of the Lord's servants, messengers, and ambassadors and their office, and what they are to accomplish in the power of the Spirit. Therefore, the Lord has also given the Holy Spirit to His ambassadors and servants for this office. Isaiah says: "The Spirit of the Lord is upon me, for the Lord has anointed me and sent me to announce good news to the poor, to bind up wounded hearts, to announce deliverance to the captives, and to open the prison-house of those in bondage. I am to announce the year of the Lord's favor and the vengeance of our God, comfort all who mourn and give beauty instead of ashes to those who lament in Zion. I am to give them a happy anointing instead of a stench, a beautiful garment instead of a heavy heart. They will be called gods of righteousness, a planting of the Lord in which he will exult."

[Gloss:] Christ's garment of innocence for sin. The prisoners and sick and wounded in spirit.

This text describes the service of the Lord Himself and the office of His ambassadors in this time of our mortal life which all ambassadors still have. We should take care that we do not speak evil of this precious treasure. Paul says: "That we may comprehend, together with all the saints of God, the depth and the height, the length and the breadth of Christ, yes, the love which surpasses all understanding and knowledge." To this end, all the chosen of God must strive to follow the pattern and example given to us by the Lord Himself. The servant is not, nor ever will be, above his Lord, nor will the disciple be above his master, or the apostle above Him who sent him. The Lord Himself has tested this principle; so, too, will it also be tested in His servants.

The Lord has opened, given, and revealed His priceless treasure and gift without price. Through His divine skill, He has unlocked and released the Scriptures, the most sublime and learned old and new treasure, written for Himself by the Holy Spirit. All the patriarchs, law, and prophets point to Himself. Then, according to the fullness of understanding and knowledge of the Father, the fullness of Godhead appeared bodily in Christ Himself.

This is the conclusion concerning the old and new treasure.

Moses gives the law, and the prophets have predicted the future grace until as the one who prepared the way of the Lord, John baptized unto repentance and fasting. The old treasure was given because of sin, and it was to point them and to lead them, in faith and hope, to the future grace, accomplished by the Spirit of Christ in the law, the prophets, and John, who pointed with his finger to the Lord as the true Lamb of God that takes away the sin of the world. Through the Lamb, the Lord Jesus Christ, grace and truth have appeared. On the cross, His death and blood, offered up for the remission and forgiveness of sins, fulfilled grace and truth. There, on the cross, the old was completed and there, the new treasure, the grace and truth which Christ brought with Him, was offered. Thus, our greatest scribe and treasurer gave everyone in his time his due.

Similarly, it behooves all the apostles and evangelists, who are the scribes of the Holy Spirit, to give to each in his time his due out of the old and new treasure. The old treasure, the law and the prophets, still minister to the old Adam. They live in his sin and under his sin, for they live only according to the flesh. As His first grace, Christ in His fullness gives to them the old treasure. God's stern wrath, His penalty and vengeance, are proclaimed against him and against all ungodliness. He is shown that he must repent, forsake sin, and show regret and remorse for his sin. A genuine sorrowing is begun in their hearts by which they are bruised, and made captive and ill in their consciences. Thus, they are prepared for the Lord, the true Physician. The old treasure applies solely to the children of the first Adamic birth, and their repentance from sin rightly comes from the old treasure.

Thus, through His preceding Holy Spirit, the Lord Jesus Christ worked in John and the prophets.

In the same way, according to the measure of His will, He fills His servants with His skill, wisdom, and understanding in order that they may administer in the right manner, according to time, measure, and apportionment, His treasures and wealth. The true treasure is Christ Himself. He is the fulfillment of all in all, be it skill, wisdom, understanding or knowledge. His body and true humanity are, moreover, the genuine temple and treasure-house, the true dwelling and abode of God. As the true dwellings, treasure-houses, and temples of God, in which Father and Son themselves, the most sublime treasures, live and remain in the power of the Spirit, the hearts of all the faithful are prepared and built up by Him for [the enjoyment of] these treasures. He adorns and consecrates this temple with all its utensils and glorious gems, the gifts and virtues of the Holy Spirit, and anoints them with the oil of gladness with which the Lord Himself has been anointed by the Father above all His fellows. Thus, He is the High Priest before the Father, and He accomplishes the priestly office in the hearts of the faithful. He establishes His own as fellow priests to rule and reign with Him forever. That is the length and the breadth of Christ, the highest treasure, who is from eternity and who spreads Himself out in the hearts of all the faithful.

In this new and acceptable year, He has been given to us in our earthen vessels. These vessels are easily broken or damaged if we do not take care of ourselves, or if we speak evil of the treasure. If struck, these earthen vessels will break. One must also diligently watch that his own earthen vessels in which the treasure is given, is not exposed to offense; one should not easily become offended by Christ and His own, and thus sustain damage, Moreover, it behooves us not to give offense or scandal to others, or to take it ourselves. Rather, we should cling firmly and immovably to the truth, and preserve from offense the earthen vessel into which the treasure of Christ is laid by God the Father, Son, and Holy Spirit.

Thus, we should allow ourselves neither to be offended nor scandalized by anything. Also, we are to watch diligently that our earthen vessel does not cause offense to anyone else. Otherwise, our own or our neighbor's vessel might be broken. If we carnally attack one another, or fight one another in the spirit of the flesh, in arrogance and conceit, such breakage will occur. It also happens if we give room and place to the lust of the flesh. To do so, under the guise of the liberty of Christ, is to assume that one is free to do anything; such an assumption is contrary to the manner of Christ, and defiles the treasure of the love which is in Christ. In whatever form offense happens and manifests itself, the earthen vessels and containers are easily shattered and destroyed, and the treasures, along with all the gifts of Christ, are defiled and slandered. Yes, in us, Christ Himself is shamed, despised, blasphemed, and crucified anew. What is even worse is if someone is injured by deception and cunning, and polluted by abominable vices. Even in the law of Moses, such vices were condemned; much less may they have room under the grace of Christ.

Therefore, my beloved ones, let us be aware of the High Priest Christ in our hearts, and of His anointment of us, with the oil of gladness, comfort, and peace. This anointing gives us all learning, wisdom, understanding, and comprehension, and then we may understand what is best and most pleasing to the Father of our Lord Jesus Christ.

We should often take the treasures out in one place, and diligently discern what God the heavenly Father has conferred upon and given to each for the service of building up the body of Christ. The gifts in every single member must be heard and seen. There can be no unendowed member who has not been given something of the treasures of Christ, such as virtues and the fruits of the Holy Spirit on the body of Christ. Everything has been given to us by the Father of lights with and in Christ. Always, the gifts of the Father are only good gifts, which He gives to His children who ask Him. There are no stones for bread, nor scorpions for eggs, nor serpents for fish. Thus, the Father does not regret that He gives the gifts to His children. Nor does He give His gifts and treasures to unclean wild animals, for He never throws the pearls before swine nor what is holy to the dogs; the Lord Himself forbade His own to do it. His holiness is the pearls, treasures, precious stones, and gems with which He has sanctified Himself for His own. And these treasures which He gives are given only to the sanctified. Thus, with such sacred treasures, yes, with Christ Himself, His own may cleanse one another and, to the pleasure of their God and Father, sanctify one another with all the virtues and gifts, and with the Holy Spirit's adornment and finery.

The Father of our Lord Jesus Christ desires and expects the mother, the bride of Christ and sanctified by Christ, to nourish, raise, and preserve the children for the Father in all sanctification, adornment, and ornament. Isaiah says: "[Such children] will be the Father's boast, His honor, glory, and majesty, and the mother with her children will express and give eternal praise, laud, honor, and thanks to the heavenly Father forever." Such housekeeping is demanded not only of the mother and the bride of Christ herself, but also of her servants, the highest angels of God, who freely serve. Indeed, the angels desired to see this housekeeping of Christ and His bride. And, unlike Christ's bride and her children, those angels who, because of their willful pride, did not freely surrender themselves to this service, the deep humility of Christ, were eternally cast out and bound in hell. Christ's bride and her children did serve Him and, as He did in the time of His human life, they humbled themselves.

[Gloss:] Jacob was deceived with his first wife, but he served again for the beautiful Rachel. These two wives represent the old and new marriage.

Whoever, therefore, serves from pride or, because of pride, refuses to serve, relates to this housekeeping of Christ and His espoused bride as the whole world does, which wants to rule and not serve, and what it serves it serves from pride. They are all like their ruler, the devil, and the outcast angels.

Therefore, the precious gems, pearls, and sacred things are to be given to all who are washed, cleansed, and redeemed through the blood of the Lamb. They are children of and fellow-heirs to all the treasures of Christ's grace. They are to be adorned and beautified to the honor of their God and Father, and the Lord Jesus Christ. Only for the others are Christ, His riches and treasures a mockery and a derision.

Therefore, my dear ones, let us be aware of our calling. Let us rightly look to our High Priest and forerunner. Let us see the treasure, gems, and ornaments, the fullness of grace and truth, with which He Himself has adorned the temple of His body, and see the glorious, beautiful, and priestly garments, all the virtues and gifts of the Holy Spirit, with which He, as the true God, was clad by His heavenly Father. His faithful ones should learn from His example, and be amazed by it. Just as the whole of the true and chosen ones, the royal priestly generation and God's own people, are clad with the virtues and gifts of the Holy Spirit, so should the faithful ones long to be similarly clad. They are all fellow-priests. Through Jesus Christ and the Holy Spirit, their God and heavenly Father clothes them with the same gifts and virtues.

Moses prepared the figurative temple and the Aaronic or Levitical priesthood. God had showed him the design on Mount Sinai. The temple was to be adorned with glorious ornament and lavishly decorated with gold, silver, copper, bronze, and iron, and all kinds of precious wood and stone. Everything was washed, anointed, sanctified, consecrated, and cleansed. Thus, God was worshiped and honored with great external pomp and splendor. The high priest used no unclean or unconsecrated vessels in his high priestly function.

Much more glorious, however, is the most exalted form, the real manner and way, which is not according to any model, but according to the glory of the true Priest, the Son of God Himself. More glorious is He Himself who came down from the highest eternal God and Father in the Son, and proclaimed the will, pleasure, and commandment of the heavenly Father. That commandment was no longer written in stone tablets, that is, in hardened hearts; it was written by the finger of God in broken hearts of flesh. It is not adorned with earthly gold, but with spiritual gold; it is fired, purified, and cleansed, and made steadfast in all tribulation in the power of faith. This gold is love, that is, God Himself, and it does not pass away, but endures forever.

Similarly, all the other sacred gems of the temple, and of the royal High Priest Christ and His own, are not of earthly production, of elemental or creaturely birth. Given to the Son Himself, to His fellow-priests and the spiritual temple, the Father gives these treasures in the power and working of the Spirit. This compactly built temple is not cleansed, nor is it consecrated with the blood of animals. It is consecrated with the precious blood of Christ Jesus. The washing, cleansing and purifying in baptism are the basis of faith in the forgiveness of sins. They are a co-witness to the belief in the Holy Spirit and the truth of the Father. This temple and its priesthood receive the treasures, gems, and gifts, which are not of silver, gold, or precious stones, nor apparel of silk. Rather, such treasures, gems, ornaments, and honor are spiritual gifts, produced and prepared by the Holy Spirit, of which Saint Paul (Gal. 5 [22, 23]) and John wrote: "The virtues of the Holy Spirit are love, faith, hope, patience, joy, peace, long-suffering, goodness, kindness, gentleness, purity," etc.

Our apparel is justification and chastisement; it is the grace of our heavenly Father, who does not allow His own to appear in the shame of nakedness. Therefore, it behooves us to keep our priestly garments unsullied, unspotted, and clean so that they may not be taken from us, and we be found unclothed in the shame of nakedness. All belongs to our priestly office and priesthood, and to our hearts, the temples of God. In them, God dwells. They are the most precious treasures and gems, given to us by our Father God and Lord with Christ. With them, we may eternally offer thanksgiving, laud, and sacrifices of praise.

No high priest, serving in the temple and spiritual house of God, may ever use an unholy, unclean or unconsecrated utensil. Every utensil must be sprinkled with the blood and the grace of Jesus Christ in the forgiveness of sins. Whenever so-called Christians do use unclean utensils, and it happens today, God's anger flares. The gifts of the Holy Spirit are withdrawn, and the hearts of the faithful destroyed and desecrated. So it happened with the figurative treasures, temple, and priests. The same happens daily before our eyes through deceit. But, in the house and temple of God, no vessel is used in dishonor. In and for His wrath, God uses such unclean and unholy vessels outside of the house. But in the house and temple of the Father, our High Priest uses only pure, holy vessels in all holiness. He has Himself hallowed them in His holiness. In them, and in the hiddenness and patience of their hearts, He conceals His treasure and gems according to the mystery of His will.

Yes, they are hidden from the whole world and all unclean animals. The ark or coffer of the new covenant or testament is the Christ and the patience of faithful saints, who are prepared for the Father's praise in all patience. In this coffer, all the household furnishings of God, the treasures, virtues, and gifts of the Holy Spirit, are safely kept and locked away from all enemies of God and His own. Neither the violence, aggression, pride, and pomp of the world, nor anything else that may rise up against it, will be able to open, destroy or shatter this ark or coffer, which is the patience of Christ itself, bound, mounted, and locked away with the band of love, humility, and surrender. Without this ark or coffer, our treasure, the virtues and gifts of the Holy Spirit, which are placed in our hearts as temples of God, cannot be locked, protected, or preserved. Therefore, as the Lord says, we must arm and prepare our souls with patience, for we will need patience if we wish to preserve the treasures and the true rod of our high priest Aaron which, together with the golden bucket, blossomed in our souls.

In the loving hearts of the faithful is the true bread from heaven, which the father gave us from heaven and which has given us life, kept for a perpetual remembrance. This bread [is] His broken or prepared flesh and blood, given up for our life. The pure flesh and blood of the virgin Mary prepared this flesh and blood for us, and this heavenly bread, which the Word made flesh, raises us from death to life. It is the true food and drink, given for our life; it nourishes and preserves our souls. The true bread of remembrance belongs in the golden bucket, and this bread is kept locked in the ark of the New Testament. In all patience, united with gentleness, humility, and surrender, our High Priest has locked the treasures in the ark. Thus, the temple of His body is preserved in the ark of the covenant of the New Testament so that we have a perpetual remembrance of Him. Had our High Priest not so carefully locked His treasure for us, every covenant and witness of the eternal covenant would be pillaged by the enemy, who steals all divine treasure. Wherever impatience breaks the ark of the covenant, all the treasures of our temple, that is, of our hearts, are lost, pillaged, and stolen, and the temple of God is destroyed and broken down. Therefore, if, indeed, we wish to preserve the treasures of our temples in this new and acceptable year, in this time of grace, and if we wish to save these gems from the Philistines, we need patience.

The ark of the New Testament is not compatible with the Philistines, I mean with the world. The impatience of the Philistines opposes the true patience of Christ. Were they to possess it, and were they to decide to use it, patience would only cause them disaster. If, indeed, it is the ark of the New Testament, and it is truly called patience, tribulation always accompanies the ark. And when tribulation comes, they impatiently send it away again. Ignorant and unbridled animals, soldiers armed with weapons, accomplish for them what patience cannot. In their secret parts, the tribulation of Christ is a plague and a shame to them. Thus along with an offering, which God refuses, they send the ark back to its place. They endure their suffering and death to death in every impatience. If one wishes to, one can see that such is the case these days. There are those who have adopted the gospel, but they only appear to adopt the patience of Christ; the Philistines now send the ark back home again. Are these not truly the unspiritual Philistines who, together with their Goliath, trust only in human power? Such a trust is contrary to the true manner of the patience of Christ; it contradicts the genuine and true David. Armor and sword do not fit Him. He kills all His enemies with their own sword. Under the new David, their own impatience consumes them. As the Lord says: "Whoever fights with the sword will be destroyed by it." Human coercion will destroy all who [support] a human, forcibly imposed faith and all who claim the Word of faith, but who trust and depend upon human protection and power; like Peter, they will be driven to a denial. Peter also thought that Christ would be a temporal and earthly Redeemer who would save them with carnal weapons. Thus, Peter pledged that he was prepared to give his life for the Lord. However, he received no help from the Lord in his carnal fighting; Jesus, for example, helped the one whose ear Peter had cut off. Then, Peter denied the Lord three times, and swore that he had never known the Man.

So it happens to all who know Christ only after the flesh, who know Him only in terms of temporal aid and the saving of temporal life and property. They know nothing of the Holy Spirit's heavenly treasures and gifts, which are given to all faithful believers in Christ. God grant that they fall into no worse denial, or into a betrayal like Judas did, or that they have become thus toward each other. Rather, God grant that they should later confess their sin and repent like Peter, who in his ignorance and fear denied the Lord. Nevertheless, he risked his life and entered the fray with no thought about what might happen to him. He did not, like Judas, betray the Lord for the price of shame.

Would to God, for their sake, that it were not true that today there are worse and even more evil merchants than the Jewish Pharisees, who bought the Lord from Judas out of envy and hate. [But, today], whole lands, armies, and peoples (many hundreds of thousands of people, even though they are not good people) are betrayed, sold, and bought by their loans, finance, and usury. It is done out of avarice, envy, and hate, an attempt to preserve their earthly pomp, pride, and vain honor. Moreover, all the actions, of both the old and new forcers of faith, are done in the semblance of Christ and His gospel. I am concerned that, shortly, the words of James, "Howl and weep, you rich," etc., will be fulfilled in them.

Those who hold a faith which has been forced on them cannot bring forth better fruit. Whatever is preached from the dead letter of Scripture or ancient, idolatrous custom, and whatever is taught under human power, protection, and patronage will also by human coercion and power be destroyed and scattered again in mutual denial and betrayal. Even though all creatures are clean, the riches, treasures, gold and silver, precious stones, pearls, velvet and silk garments can produce no better fruit in the heart than eternal condemnation. I do not intend to judge or condemn the world. The world, along with her prince, the devil, has already been judged before God. Rather, I write this letter as a testimony to Christ that their works are evil. Just as the light is distinguished from darkness, or the riches and treasures of Christ from the treasures of this world, I distinguish them from good works. The children of light always bring forth good from the treasures of their hearts, and the evil bring forth evil from their evil treasures. Where the treasure is, there the heart is also.

Therefore, it behooves us to look again to our calling and to Him who called us from the horrible darkness of this world to His marvelous light. For He called us from the world, not we Him. He has revealed to us the will of His heavenly Father. He has taught and instructed us with full understanding. He has also sent us the teacher in the heart, and the Comforter to comfort, and to teach us with Jesus' own words and teaching. He equips and empowers us with the heavenly, inner, hidden power from above; He leads, instructs, and guides us, and He anoints us, as the Father of lights anointed the Lord Himself, with the oil of gladness.

Our life is hidden with Christ in God; it is not we who live, but Christ who lives in us. We are not taught by the human voice, by the literal, external teaching of Christ and the apostolic preaching of the gospel. We are taught, not by man, but by God, the Holy Spirit Himself. The Spirit takes the treasures and good things of the Father and the Son, and has poured into our hearts the love which is the mind of Christ and the true and only understanding. Only what Christ Himself has said and taught, and no other word, does the Spirit of wisdom bring to remembrance in His own.

Therefore, no matter how holy they may appear, all those who take away and add to this word and teaching are false priests. Nor does God teach those who only hear the Word from the mouth of Christ, the apostles and other saintly people, nor does He teach those who read their writings only according to the letter, without the reminder of truth and teaching of the Holy Spirit. They are thieves and murderers who run before, and lag behind, Christ. With their own inventions and sophistries in Scripture, they either run ahead of the Holy Spirit of Christ, before they have been driven by Him, or else they lag behind Christ, and presume to teach those who are under God's judgment. Thus, without being called, and without any discrimination about who is drawn or sent by the Father, they throw the pearls before the swine and what is sacred only to the dogs. They pay no regard to the admonition the Lord gave to His own to distinguish between people. Instead, these others, without discrimination, dump their teachers and teaching, like the useless salt, in front of all men, so that men trample it underfoot and, as one can now see, mock it. Men, like swine and ravenous dogs, turn around and rend them. These are the clouds without water which are driven by the whirlwind; they are not driven, taught, or reminded by the Holy Spirit, nor are they led by Him in the truth. Those whom the Spirit of God drives, they are the children of God. All these teachers, self-appointed or reestablished by the violence of men, who teach for the sake of carnal gain and self-indulgence under the protection of men, who have not drunk at the streams of living water but have stolen their human sophistry of Scripture from stagnant cisterns, all these, as the prophet says, build with crumbling mortar.

Therefore, their building immediately collapses, and they perish along with it. They are destroyed by the human violence and protection under which they build their edifice. Through the deceit and error of man's teaching, they fall and are overcome by the debris.

Let him who has ears to hear, hear, and him who has eyes to see, see. See what has happened everywhere to these so-called Christians, who have only the semblance of the gospel. Such righteous judgments by the almighty righteous God, our heavenly Father of the Lord Jesus Christ, rightly follow. It is the judgment of the Holy Spirit who now, because of sin, judges the world, together with her prince. With the justice of Christ, the Potentate of heaven and earth, who now sits at the right hand of the majesty of God, the Holy Spirit judges the sin of the unbelief into which they are rejected and thrown. His is the true righteousness. He went to the Father for the sake of exercising this righteousness and judgment of the Holy Spirit. From above, He now creates and effects the same righteousness, which alone is valid before God, and which exists and remains eternally before the Father in His saints.

Prior to this ascension of Christ and access to the Father, no man was justified in the justification of grace. Before His departure to the Father, even the earthly teaching, power, and miracles of Christ could not justify the apostles, nor any other man, to this eternal justification. For this reason, even though the earthly teaching of Christ, the Son of Man, was testified to by His miracles and the divine power which the Father had in Him and He in the Father, the apostles could not bear, understand, nor comprehend the teaching of Christ so that they might have remained steadfast in it. Thus, since only God could do the works He did, the apostles were led to believe and to confess Him as the Lord Jesus Christ, the true God, the Son of the Father. This faith, however, was received from the earthly teachings and miracles. Without the true teacher and reminder, the Holy Spirit who comforts and leads into the truth, and whom Christ promised to send, such faith was not valid. After His resurrection from the dead, He sent Him and made the promise, which still stands, that He would eternally be with all the faithful believers who have been taught, reminded, and led into truth by His Holy Spirit. He comforts man in his repentance and sorrow for sin, and forgives.

Therefore, all external service of Christ, and of those who belong to Him in the time of this mortal life, serves and prepares the way for the Holy Spirit. [This external service consists] of the external preaching, teaching, miracles, baptism, foot washing, the Lord's Supper, discipline, chastisement, and admonition. Such service also includes the ban of exclusion and separation from the fellowship of the body of Christ. In order to preserve the true fellowship of all the faithful, we are commanded to keep the ban, together with the Lord's Supper, in remembrance of the true love of Christ and His gracious deed in His death. In the time of His mortal life, Christ did not rule; He served. Thus, He sent His own to serve, not to rule. Man is to be served by Christ and His own, and man is to be prepared for the Holy Spirit. Some spirits either regard such preparation as unnecessary, or else they regard it too highly. But wherever this service of Christ is not carried out in all its provisions, there the Holy Spirit cannot do His work. To believe, like Peter, that such a Lord should not wash one's feet, and to refuse to have the act performed on the basis of such carnal reasoning, is to rely on private invention rather than the Holy Spirit. Even today, Christ says to these individuals that they can have no part in His kingdom. For the Holy Spirit may not, and cannot, function, nor can it find an abiding place without the preparatory teaching. Service is commanded by Christ, and it is the means by which, according to the command of Christ, men are prepared. Moreover, the Key of David is also a means, for it is the key of understanding with which man's earthly mind is opened. Then, the Holy Spirit, as true God with Father and Son, can move where He will, namely, in those whom the Father draws to Christ, to the same apostolic church and bodily service, preaching and teaching, baptism, foot washing, and the Lord's Supper. Men submit to this service in the obedience of faith in Christ and under the discipline of the Spirit.

When we as men are renewed, and born again of the Holy Spirit, the Holy Spirit becomes the pledge and the third witness of salvation. The apostolic service of the church is properly carried out, in accordance with the commands of Christ, when it prepares, cultivates, fertilizes and, as God's helper, breaks again the hearts of men. When this new breaking occurs, the church seeds and plants, in the heart, the word of truth, which is to be believed, and it waters the heart with the baptism of water. But even if all external service is done according to the command of Christ, the earthly Man, the Spirit still moves in glorious liberty wherever He will, and He gives the increase and the growth to whomever He will. Such is the prerogative, in eternity, of the Godhead, and it belongs to the Father and the Son.

> [Gloss:] Antichrist has destroyed the apostolic service and therefore, Christ moves wherever He is prayed for.

It is sheer fabrication and deception when some insist that the Holy Spirit moves apart from the apostolic service of the church, that such service, commanded by Christ, is unnecessary. On which Holy Spirit, then, did the Lord base His teaching, Word, and work? If not the actual spoken words, commands, and laws of Christ, reminded and taught by the Spirit, what other teaching words or work can, or may, the Holy Spirit teach, remind, and lead us into as the truth? For the Lord Himself promised that the Holy Spirit would remind us of all that Jesus said or commanded. Certainly, a spirit who teaches contrary to the Son of Man, who taught men with a human voice, is a deceiving spirit.

Again, they deceive themselves who think that, when they serve, teach, and baptize, simply because the apostolic service is performed, it follows that the Holy Spirit also moves and teaches. Nor is the church of Christ merely where the external service is properly done. *Not so!* If the inner, through the Holy Spirit, does not witness to the external, through faith, everything is in vain for, where the carcass is, the eagles gather. The true community and gathering of Christ cannot be identified with a place, nor can it be called a human name. Wherever such a gathering is, according to the Word of the Lord, there Christ is with the Father and the eternally abiding Holy Spirit. They love Him who keep His Word and commandment. To them, He and the Father will come and dwell.

Therefore, whoever says that Christ is anywhere else than living on earth, as in heaven, in the power and clarity of the Spirit and in the heart of each faithful believer, he is a deceiver. Whoever does not find Christ dwelling in his own heart, eternally, will not find Him elsewhere.

However, where such hearts as temples and dwellings of God, are built into a spiritual dwelling for the Lord, these places are named and identified only so long as the faithful live there. Thus, that place is holy for the sake of the saints, even as God sanctified the figurative temple. When it was destroyed, its place was profaned. The same is true of a place without saints. Where they do not dwell, it is a curse and malediction; it is desecrated, destroyed, and profaned before God. At this time, we see it clearly in the whole world.

Because of their sectarian, external, coerced religion, by which they deceive themselves, the whole world imagines that it has Christ living here or there. Since the earthly and true service of Christ did not come into force in the hearts of the apostles without the moving of the Holy Spirit, how can the forced and coerced faith, or the faith based on old custom, stand before God? This forced, coerced faith, based as it is on sophistic interpretation of Scripture or on ancient custom, is not from God, nor is it taught by the Holy Spirit and His manner, birth, artistry and wisdom; [it is unrelated to the Spirit's] reminding and leading us into truth. Rather, it is from the generation and will of the flesh of man (Jn. 1[12]), who is steeped in his earthly, fallen nature and human reason, sophistry, and wisdom.

Thus, even if, in the power of the Spirit before man, one should preach the apostolic service and teach the teaching of Christ which flows out of the inmost being of believers as a fountain flowing into eternal life, still, the teaching of the Spirit, which alone reminds and leads us into truth, and which teaches the divine artistry of wisdom, must always accompany it. Those who are thus taught are not taught by any man, but by God.

All the others continually learn from, and are taught by, men. But these others never come to the knowledge of the truth, which is eternal life (Jn. 17 [3]). They never know God the Father as the true God, and Jesus Christ as the One whom the Father has sent. Therefore, the Lord says that not everyone who cries "Lord, Lord" will enter the kingdom of heaven. Only he will enter who does the will of the heavenly Father. Since no one knows the Father but the Son and him to whom the Son reveals the Father (Mt. 11[27]), no one but the Son could do the will and pleasure of the heavenly Father. Thus, no one but the Father knows the Son.

Therefore, Paul writes in 1 Corinthians 12[3] that no one can call Christ Lord except by the Holy Spirit. Thus, no one can do the will of the Father without the Son. It follows that those who are in Christ do not themselves live, but Christ lives in them (Gal. 2[20]). Moreover, whatever they ask the Father, Christ Himself will do and perform in the hearts of all the faithful. Such is the true righteousness, the reason why Christ went to the Father (Jn. 14[13]). Thus, Saint Paul says that everyone should examine to see whether Christ dwells in his heart (2 Cor. 13[5]). If He does not, that individual is cast off. Therefore, whoever calls Jesus "Lord" and God "Father" without the Holy Spirit does not for that reason enter the kingdom of heaven. To such, God says: "You call me Father, but where is my honor? You call me Lord, but where is my fear?" (Mal. 1[6]).

Without the artistry and teaching of the Holy Spirit, who pours out the love, which is God, into the hearts of all the faithful, and which surpasses all reason and understanding, everything is in vain. The Holy Spirit proceeds from the Father and Son, and He witnesses to the Father and Son in the hearts of all the faithful; He copies and repeats the perfect law of the liberty of Christ. The faithful look into this law of liberty in order that they may fervently do what Christ spoke and commanded. They have a blessing, but not a temporal or temporary one as Moses did, who engraved the written literal law through twelve witnesses from the twelve tribes of Israel with earthly blessings and maledictions (Deut. 27:11–13). The Father, as true God, Himself witnesses to the Son and the Son to the Father. Hence, all who believe in the Son have an eternal blessing.

Thus, twelve witnesses are established from the twelve tribes of Israel; they are the twelve apostles of which the Lord speaks in Acts 1[8], where He says that they should be His witnesses to the ends of the earth. They had been with Him from the beginning and, for witness, He gave them the Holy Spirit so that they should announce to all nations repentance and forgiveness of sins through His death and blood. "Whoever believes and is baptized for the forgiveness of sins shall be saved. Whoever does not believe is condemned." The Holy Spirit is the true, complete copier of the law of Christ in the appointed messengers and witnesses of Christ. The Holy Spirit renews and copies Christ's law in the hearts of believers so that all things are rightly understood, recognized, and known, even as the Lord spoke, taught, and intended what He knew and received from the Father. Without this copier of the law of Christ, I mean the Holy Spirit, the apostles could neither understand nor bear the teaching of their Master. He repeated in them again what Christ had said, taught, and commanded. He is the true pledge of our salvation, and the true witness to our faith; He is the true repeater, Teacher, and reminder of our perfect law, no longer written on stone tablets, but in the hearts of the faithful. The Holy Spirit Himself no longer takes from the image or the mediation of angels, nor does he take it in fire, clouds or darkness, as Moses received it and took it from God. He takes it from the Father and the Son, and gives it to the hearts of all the faithful. In them are the laws and new commandments of Christ the Lord written by the finger of God.

That is the true book of replication, for all the faithful, written by the three heavenly witnesses and affirmed by the Father, the Word, and the Holy Spirit. Physical action, the power displayed with signs and wonders, testify to it on earth before men. The Father performed it in the Son, and the Son in the Father. As the Lord says in John 5[17]: "My Father works hitherto and I work also." The Father, the Spirit, and the Word are the three witnesses who witness in the incomprehensible, invisible, heavenly Being, and these three witnesses have also witnessed before actual men on earth in visible, tangible, and bodily form. The bodily miracles of the Son showed the Father. The Son taught the external words, which He Himself was as the Word of the Father, and revealed the Father. Thus, He was glorified before man as true God. The Holy Spirit, in visible form as a dove, testified to the Son that God, the Creator of heaven and earth, was His Father. He also appeared as tongues of fire to the apostles. Although God is, and remains, a Spirit in three persons, Father, Word, and Spirit, and is, eternally, invisible heavenly unity, nevertheless, Father, Son, and Holy Spirit witnessed before men on earth in bodily, visible form (as stated above) as one unitary Spirit, God, Father, and Son.

Thus, with water and blood (1 Jn. 5[7, 8]), the Holy Spirit also witnesses on earth to the Lord Jesus Christ as true man on earth. But there is blood as well as water so that all three serve in the one Lord, Jesus Christ, on earth [and] in heaven. If, with integrity of heart and with the co-witness of the three names and persons, God the Father, Son, and Holy Spirit, one is baptized in exact copy of Christ's command, and if that baptism is witnessed to in heaven as on earth, this witness is the subject of a fine new book of replication written in the hearts of all the faithful. This law and book of replication cause no curse, but only blessing for men. It has not only human witnesses on earth, but also divine witnesses in heaven, for it is witnessed to by Father, Son, and Holy Spirit, along with the co-witnesses of the apostles and servants of Christ. As the Lord said to the Twelve: "You are my witnesses because you have been with me from the beginning." So, too, have the apostles patiently witnessed to the spiritual law of complete liberty and to the book of replication. As the true ark of the covenant of the New Testament, they preserve in patience together with all the other gems of the temple of Christ's body. Their deaths and their lives preserved it from all enemies. To our heavenly Father's eternal praise, they possessed the power of the love that was poured out so that, in this ark of patience, we could bring home the treasures and vessels, and all the gems of our temple, to the heavenly Jerusalem, to the true temple of the body of Christ.

This temple was erected for perpetual worship, and it is [served by] a royal priesthood that is not perishable or destructible, but remains forever. Thus, the Lord Himself, in all gentleness, humility, and patience, determined and has preserved it from all the enemies whom He has overcome in the depth. As they travel through the wilderness of this world, it behooves all faithful believers to exercise the greatest care for this ark of the new covenant, and ensure that it may not be broken and seized by the enemy, and the treasures of Christ robbed. In this ark of patience, if indeed we want to be glorified with Christ and share His joy, all the treasures and gifts of Christ are kept until the last enemy is overcome.

Misery always precedes honor. In the Lord's case, tribulation, sorrowing, and grief were followed by joy, blessing, and glory. Our treasures will then no longer be mocked, nor will they be seized by any enemy. Indeed, the ark is no longer necessary, for all the treasures and gems, as well as the garments of honor, are in discipline and virtue, taken out of the ark of patience to the praise and glory of the heavenly Father, and to the eternal honor and glory of the Lord Jesus Christ. We, in the Holy Spirit, return and offer again [to them] these gifts and virtues. There, before the eternal glory and only majesty of God, they will be used without any fear or care in eternal worship. Only there, with all the angels, will the hallelujah be truly sung and understood. Finally, it will be revealed that the sufferings of this world are not worthy to be compared with the future glory, and that all the tribulation and poverty is worthless by comparison with the unsurpassed riches and glories of the treasures of Christ.

This acceptable new year has been prepared for all the faithful in order that we may fervently rejoice over it and in it, and thank and praise our heavenly Father. We invite all creatures to rejoice with us and to sing praise to our God. Together with David, let us heartily sing the song of praises:

"I will extol you, O King, and praise your name forever and ever. Every day I will bless you and praise your name forever and ever. Great is the Lord and worthy of all praise; His greatness is unfathomable. Children's children will praise your deeds and speak of your power. I will speak of the glory of your praise and of your wonders so that others will speak of the power of your deeds and extol your glory. They shall tell the story of your great goodness, and praise your justice. Gracious and merciful is the Lord, forbearing and of great goodness. The Lord is good to all, and His mercy is over all His works. All your works thank you, and all your saints praise you. They talk of the glory of your kingdom and of your power so that all the children of men know your power and the glorious gifts of your kingdom. Your kingdom endures for all time, and to your dominion there is no end. The Lord preserves all those who fall, and raises up those who have been beaten down. All eyes are lifted up to you, and you give them their food when it is time. You open your hand and fill everything that lives with what is good. The Lord is just in all His ways and holy in all His deeds. The Lord is near to all who call on Him. He does His pleasure to those who fear Him; He hears their cry and helps them. The Lord protects all who love Him, and will exterminate the wicked. My mouth shall announce the praise of the Lord, and all flesh shall praise His name forever and ever." Amen.

For all of you, as for my own soul, I wish fervently that you may sing this song of praise. Pray the Lord faithfully for us, and all the faithful with me, and send to all who are in the Lord from me, and all the faithful, the greeting of peace and love in Christ Jesus our Lord. Amen.

The grace of our Lord Jesus Christ be and remain with us all forever. Amen. Dated at Augsburg, the first day of February, anno domini 1547.

Your servant and comrade in the tribulation which is in Christ.
Pilgram Marpeck.

32. Martin Luther King, Jr. – A Time to Break Silence

I come to this magnificent house of worship tonight because my conscience leaves me no other choice. I join with you in this meeting because I am in deepest agreement with the aims and work of the organization which has brought us together: Clergy and Laymen Concerned about Vietnam. The recent statement of your executive committee are the sentiments of my own heart and I found myself in full accord when I read its opening lines: "A time comes when silence is betrayal." That time has come for us in relation to Vietnam.

The truth of these words is beyond doubt but the mission to which they call us is a most difficult one. Even when pressed by the demands of inner truth, men do not easily assume the task of opposing their government's policy, especially in time of war. Nor does the human spirit move without great difficulty against all the apathy of conformist thought within one's own bosom and in the surrounding world. Moreover when the issues at hand seem as perplexed as they often do in the case of this dreadful conflict we are always on the verge of being mesmerized by uncertainty; but we must move on.

Some of us who have already begun to break the silence of the night have found that the calling to speak is often a vocation of agony, but we must speak. We must speak with all the humility that is appropriate to our limited vision, but we must speak. And we must rejoice as well, for surely this is the first time in our nation's history that a significant number of its religious leaders have chosen to move beyond the prophesying of smooth patriotism to the high grounds of a firm dissent based upon the mandates of conscience and the reading of history. Perhaps a new spirit is rising among us. If it is, let us trace its movement well and pray that our own inner being may be sensitive to its guidance, for we are deeply in need of a new way beyond the darkness that seems so close around us.

Over the past two years, as I have moved to break the betrayal of my own silences and to speak from the burnings of my own heart, as I have called for radical departures from the destruction of Vietnam, many persons have questioned me about the wisdom of my path. At the heart of their concerns this query has often loomed large and loud: Why are *you* speaking about war, Dr. King? Why are *you* joining the voices of dissent? Peace and civil rights don't mix, they say. Aren't you hurting the cause of your people, they ask? And when I hear them, though I often understand the source of their concern, I am nevertheless greatly saddened, for such questions mean that the inquirers have not really known me, my commitment or my calling. Indeed, their questions suggest that they do not know the world in which they live.

In the light of such tragic misunderstandings, I deem it of signal importance to try to state clearly, and I trust concisely, why I believe that the path from Dexter Avenue Baptist Church—the church in Montgomery, Alabama, where I began my pastorate—leads clearly to this sanctuary tonight.

I come to this platform tonight to make a passionate plea to my beloved nation. This speech is not addressed to Hanoi or to the National Liberation Front. It is not addressed to China or to Russia.

Nor is it an attempt to overlook the ambiguity of the total situation and the need for a collective solution to the tragedy of Vietnam. Neither is it an attempt to make North Vietnam or the National Liberation Front paragons of virtue, nor to overlook the role they can play in a successful resolution of the problem. While they both may have justifiable reason to be suspicious of the good faith of the United States, life and history give eloquent testimony to the fact that conflicts are never resolved without trustful give and take on both sides.

Tonight, however, I wish not to speak with Hanoi and the NLF, but rather to my fellow Americans who, with me, bear the greatest responsibility in ending a conflict that has exacted a heavy price on both continents.

Importance of Vietnam

Since I am a preacher by trade, I suppose it is not surprising that I have seven major reasons for bringing Vietnam into the field of my moral vision. There is at the outset a very obvious and almost facile connection between the war in Vietnam and the struggle I, and others, have been waging in America. A few years ago there was a shining moment in that struggle. It seemed as if there was a real promise of hope for the poor—both black and white—through the poverty program. There were experiments, hopes, new beginnings. Then came the buildup in Vietnam and I watched the program broken and eviscerated as if it were some idle political plaything of a society gone mad on war, and I knew that America would never invest the necessary funds or energies in rehabilitation of its poor so long as adventures like Vietnam continued to draw men and skills and money like some demonic destructive suction tube. So I was increasingly compelled to see the war as an enemy of the poor and to attack it as such.

Perhaps the more tragic recognition of reality took place when it became clear to me that the war was doing far more than devastating the hopes of the poor at home. It was sending their sons and their brothers and their husbands to fight and to die in extraordinarily high proportions relative to the rest of the population. We were taking the black young men who had been crippled by our society and sending them eight thousand miles away to guarantee liberties in Southeast Asia which they had not found in southwest Georgia and East Harlem. So we have been repeatedly faced with the cruel irony of watching Negro and white boys on TV screens as they kill and die together for a nation that has been unable to seat them together in the same schools. So we watch them in brutal solidarity burning the huts of a poor village, but we realize that they would never live on the same block in Detroit. I could not be silent in the face of such cruel manipulation of the poor.

My third reason moves to an even deeper level of awareness, for it grows out of my experience in the ghettos of the North over the last three years—especially the last three summers. As I have walked among the desperate, rejected and angry young men I have told them that Molotov cocktails and rifles would not solve their problems. I have tried to offer them my deepest compassion while maintaining my conviction that social change comes most meaningfully through nonviolent action. But they asked—and rightly so—what about Vietnam? They asked if our own nation wasn't using massive doses of violence to solve its problems, to bring about the changes it wanted. Their questions hit home, and I knew that I could never again raise my voice against the violence of the oppressed in the ghettos without having first spoken clearly to the greatest purveyor of violence in the world today— my own government. For the sake of those boys, for the sake of this government, for the sake of the hundreds of thousands trembling under our violence, I cannot be silent.

For those who ask the question, "Aren't you a civil rights leader?" and thereby mean to exclude me from the movement for peace, I have this further answer. In 1957 when a group of us formed the Southern Christian Leadership Conference, we chose as our motto: "To save the soul of America." We were convinced that we could not limit our vision to certain rights for black people, but instead affirmed the conviction that America would never be free or saved from itself unless the descendants of its slaves were loosed completely from the shackles they still wear. In a way we were agreeing with Langston Hughes, that black bard of Harlem, who had written earlier:

O, yes,
I say it plain,
America never was America to me,
And yet I swear this oath—
America will be!

Now, it should be incandescently clear that no one who has any concern for the integrity and life of America today can ignore the present war. If America's soul becomes totally poisoned, part of the autopsy must read Vietnam. It can never be saved so long as it destroys the deepest hopes of men the world over. So it is that those of us who are yet determined that America *will* be are led down the path of protest and dissent, working for the health of our land.

As if the weight of such a commitment to the life and health of America were not enough, another burden of responsibility was placed upon me in 1964; and I cannot forget that the Nobel Prize for Peace was also a commission—a commission to work harder than I had ever worked before "the brotherhood of man." This is a calling that takes me beyond national allegiances, but even if it were not present I would yet have to live with the meaning of my commitment to the ministry of Jesus Christ. To me the relationship of this ministry to the making of peace is so obvious that I sometimes marvel at those who ask me why I am speaking against the war. Could it be that they do not know that the good news was meant for all men—for Communist and capitalist, for their children and ours, for black and for white, for revolutionary and conservative? Have they forgotten that my ministry is in obedience to the one who loved his enemies so fully that he died for them? What then can I say to the "Vietcong" or to Castro or to Mao as a faithful minister of this one? Can I threaten them with death or must I not share with them my life?

Finally, as I try to delineate for you and for myself the road that leads from Montgomery to this place I would have offered all that was most valid if I simply said that I must be true to my conviction that I share with all men the calling to be a son of the living God. Beyond the calling of race or nation or creed is this vocation of sonship and brotherhood, and because I believe that the Father is deeply concerned especially for his suffering and helpless and outcast children, I come tonight to speak for them.

This I believe to be the privilege and the burden of all of us who deem ourselves bound by allegiances and loyalties which are broader and deeper than nationalism and which go beyond our nation's self-defined goals and positions. We are called to speak for the weak, for the voiceless, for victims of our nation and for those it calls enemy, for no document from human hands can make these humans any less our brothers.

Strange Liberators

And as I ponder the madness of Vietnam and search within myself for ways to understand and respond to compassion my mind goes constantly to the people of that peninsula. I speak now not of the soldiers of each side, not of the junta in Saigon, but simply of the people who have been living under the curse of war for almost three continuous decades now. I think of them too because it is clear to me that there will be no meaningful solution there until some attempt is made to know them and hear their broken cries.

They must see Americans as strange liberators. The Vietnamese people proclaimed their own independence in 1945 after a combined French and Japanese occupation, and before the Communist revolution in China. They were led by Ho Chi Minh. Even though they quoted the American Declaration of Independence in their own document of freedom, we refused to recognize them. Instead, we decided to support France in its reconquest of her former colony.

Our government felt then that the Vietnamese people were not "ready" for independence, and we again fell victim to the deadly Western arrogance that has poisoned the international atmosphere for so long. With that tragic decision we rejected a revolutionary government seeking self-determination, and a government that had been established not by China (for whom the Vietnamese have no great love) but by clearly indigenous forces that included some Communists. For the peasants this new government meant real land reform, one of the most important needs in their lives.

For nine years following 1945 we denied the people of Vietnam the right of independence. For nine years we vigorously supported the French in their abortive effort to recolonize Vietnam.

Before the end of the war we were meeting eighty per cent of the French war costs. Even before the French were defeated at Dien Bien Phu, they began to despair of the reckless action, but we did not. We encouraged them with our huge financial and military supplies to continue the war even after they had lost the will. Soon we would be paying almost the full costs of this tragic attempt at recolonization.

After the French were defeated it looked as if independence and land reform would come again through the Geneva agreements. But instead there came the United States, determined that Ho should not unify the temporarily divided nation, and the peasants watched again as we supported one of the most vicious modern dictators—our chosen man, Premier Diem. The peasants watched and cringed as Diem ruthlessly routed out all opposition, supported their extortionist landlords and refused even to discuss reunification with the north. The peasants watched as all this was presided over by U.S. influence and then by increasing numbers of U.S. troops who came to help quell the insurgency that Diem's methods had aroused. When Diem was overthrown they may have been happy, but the long line of military dictatorships seemed to offer no real change—especially in terms of their need for land and peace.

The only change came from America as we increased our troop commitments in support of governments which were singularly corrupt, inept and without popular support. All the while the people read our leaflets and received regular promises of peace and democracy—and land reform. Now they languish under our bombs and consider us—not their fellow Vietnamese—the real enemy. They move sadly and apathetically as we herd them off the land of their fathers into concentration camps where minimal social needs are rarely met. They know they must move or be destroyed by our bombs. So they go—primarily women and children and the aged.

They watch as we poison their water, as we kill a million acres of their crops. They must weep as the bulldozers roar through their areas preparing to destroy the precious trees. They wander into the hospitals, with at least twenty casualties from American firepower far one "Vietcong"-inflicted injury. So far we may have killed a million of them—mostly children. They wander into the towns and see thousands of the children, homeless, without clothes, running in packs on the streets like animals. They see the children degraded by our soldiers as they beg for food. They see the children selling their sisters to our soldiers, soliciting for their mothers.

What do the peasants think as we ally ourselves with the landlords and as we refuse to put any action into our many words concerning land reform? What do they think as we test out our latest weapons on them, just as the Germans tested out new medicine and new tortures in the concentration camps of Europe? Where are the roots of the independent Vietnam we claim to be building? Is it among these voiceless ones?

We have destroyed their two most cherished institutions: the family and the village. We have destroyed their land and their crops. We have cooperated in the crushing of the nation's only non-Communist revolutionary political force—the unified Buddhist church. We have supported the enemies of the peasants of Saigon. We have corrupted their women and children and killed their men. What liberators!

Now there is little left to build on—save bitterness. Soon the only solid physical foundations remaining will be found at our military bases and in the concrete of the concentration camps we call fortified hamlets. The peasants may well wonder if we plan to build our new Vietnam on such grounds as these? Could we blame them for such thoughts? We must speak for them and raise the questions they cannot raise. These too are our brothers.

Perhaps the more difficult but no less necessary task is to speak for those who have been designated as our enemies. What of the National Liberation Front—that strangely anonymous group we call VC or Communists? What must they think of us in America when they realize that we permitted the repression and cruelty of Diem which helped to bring them into being as a resistance group in the south? What do they think of our condoning the violence which led to their own taking up of arms? How can they believe in our integrity when now we speak of "aggression from the north" as if there were nothing more essential to the war? How can they trust us when now we charge them with violence after the murderous reign of Diem and charge them with violence while we pour every new weapon of death into their land? Surely we must understand their feelings even if we do not condone their actions. Surely we must see that the men we supported pressed them to their violence. Surely we must see that our own computerized plans of destruction simply dwarf their greatest acts.

How do they judge us when our officials know that their membership is less than twenty-five percent Communist and yet insist on giving them the blanket name? What must they be thinking when they know that we are aware of their control of major sections of Vietnam and yet we appear ready to allow national elections in which this highly organized political parallel government will have no part? They ask how we can speak of free elections when the Saigon press is censored and controlled by the military junta. And they are surely right to wonder what kind of new government we plan to help form without them—the only party in real touch with the peasants. They question our political goals and they deny the reality of a peace settlement from which they will be excluded. Their questions are frighteningly relevant. Is our nation planning to build on political myth again and then shore it up with the power of new violence?

Here is the true meaning and value of compassion and nonviolence when it helps us to see the enemy's point of view, to hear his questions, to know his assessment of ourselves. For from his view we may indeed see the basic weaknesses of our own condition, and if we are mature, we may learn and grow and profit from the wisdom of the brothers who are called the opposition.

So, too, with Hanoi. In the north, where our bombs now pummel the land, and our mines endanger the waterways, we are met by a deep but understandable mistrust. To speak for them is to explain this lack of confidence in Western words, and especially their distrust of American intentions now. In Hanoi are the men who led the nation to independence against the Japanese and the French, the men who sought membership in the French commonwealth and were betrayed by the weakness of Paris and the willfulness of the colonial armies. It was they who led a second struggle against French domination at tremendous costs, and then were persuaded to give up the land they controlled between the thirteenth and seventeenth parallel as a temporary measure at Geneva. After 1954 they watched us conspire with Diem to prevent elections which would have surely brought Ho Chi Minh to power over a united Vietnam, and they realized they had been betrayed again.

When we ask why they do not leap to negotiate, these things must be remembered. Also it must be clear that the leaders of Hanoi considered the presence of American troops in support of the Diem regime to have been the initial military breach of the Geneva agreements concerning foreign troops, and they remind us that they did not begin to send in any large number of supplies or men until American forces had moved into the tens of thousands.

Hanoi remembers how our leaders refused to tell us the truth about the earlier North Vietnamese overtures for peace, how the president claimed that none existed when they had clearly been made. Ho Chi Minh has watched as America has spoken of peace and built up its forces, and now he has surely heard of the increasing international rumors of American plans for an invasion of the north. He knows the bombing and shelling and mining we are doing are part of traditional pre-invasion strategy. Perhaps only his sense of humor and of irony can save him when he hears the most powerful nation of the world speaking of aggression as its drops thousands of bombs on a poor weak nation more than eight thousand miles away from its shores.

At this point I should make it clear that while I have tried in these last few minutes to give a voice to the voiceless on Vietnam and to understand the arguments of those who are called enemy, I am as deeply concerned about our troops there as anything else. For it occurs to me that what we are submitting them to in Vietnam is not simply the brutalizing process that goes on in any war where armies face each other and seek to destroy. We are adding cynicism to the process of death, for they must know after a short period there that none of the things we claim to be fighting for are really involved. Before long they must know that their government has sent them into a struggle among Vietnamese, and the more sophisticated surely realize that we are on the side of the wealthy and the secure while we create a hell for the poor.

Somehow this madness must cease. We must stop now. I speak as a child of God and brother to the suffering poor of Vietnam. I speak for those whose land is being laid waste, whose homes are being destroyed, whose culture is being subverted. I speak for the poor of America who are paying the double price of smashed hopes at home and death and corruption in Vietnam. I speak as a citizen of the world, for the world as it stands aghast at the path we have taken. I speak as an American to the leaders of my own nation. The great initiative in this war is ours. The initiative to stop it must be ours.

This is the message of the great Buddhist leaders of Vietnam. Recently one of them wrote these words: *Each day the war goes on the hatred increases in the heart of the Vietnamese and in the hearts of those of humanitarian instinct. The Americans are forcing even their friends into becoming their enemies. It is curious that the Americans, who calculate so carefully on the possibilities of military victory, do not realize that in the process they are incurring deep psychological and political defeat. The image of America will never again be the image of revolution, freedom and democracy, but the image of violence and militarism.*

If we continue there will be no doubt in my mind and in the mind of the world that we have no honorable intentions in Vietnam. It will become clear that our minimal expectation is to occupy it as an American colony and men will not refrain from thinking that our maximum hope is to goad China into a war so that we may bomb her nuclear installations. If we do not stop our war against the people of Vietnam immediately the world will be left with no other alternative than to see this as some horribly clumsy and deadly game we have decided to play.

The world now demands a maturity of America that we may not be able to achieve. It demands that we admit that we have been wrong from the beginning of our adventure in Vietnam, that we have been detrimental to the life of the Vietnamese people. The situation is one in which we must be ready to turn sharply from our present ways.

In order to atone for our sins and errors in Vietnam, we should take the initiative in bringing a halt to this tragic war. I would like to suggest five concrete things that our government should do immediately to begin the long and difficult process of extricating ourselves from this nightmarish conflict:

1. *End all bombing in North and South Vietnam.*
2. *Declare a unilateral cease-fire in the hope that such action will create the atmosphere for negotiation.*
3. *Take immediate steps to prevent other battlegrounds in Southeast Asia by curtailing our military buildup in Thailand and our interference in Laos.*
4. *Realistically accept the fact that the National Liberation Front has substantial support in South Vietnam and must thereby play a role in any meaningful negotiations and in any future Vietnam government.*
5. *Set a date that we will remove all foreign troops from Vietnam in accordance with the 1954 Geneva agreement.*

Part of our ongoing commitment might well express itself in an offer to grant asylum to any Vietnamese who fears for his life under a new regime which included the Liberation Front. Then we must make what reparations we can for the damage we have done. We must provide the medical aid that is badly needed, making it available in this country if necessary.

Protesting the War

Meanwhile we in the churches and synagogues have a continuing task while we urge our government to disengage itself from a disgraceful commitment. We must continue to raise our voices if our nation persists in its perverse ways in Vietnam. We must be prepared to match actions with words by seeking out every creative means of protest possible.

As we counsel young men concerning military service we must clarify for them our nation's role in Vietnam and challenge them with the alternative of conscientious objection. I am pleased to say that this is the path now being chosen by more than seventy students at my own alma mater, Morehouse College, and I recommend it to all who find the American course in Vietnam a dishonorable and unjust one. Moreover I would encourage all ministers of draft age to give up their ministerial exemptions and seek status as conscientious objectors. These are the times for real choices and not false ones. We are at the moment when our lives must be placed on the line if our nation is to survive its own folly. Every man of humane convictions must decide on the protest that best suits his convictions, but we must all protest.

There is something seductively tempting about stopping there and sending us all off on what in some circles has become a popular crusade against the war in Vietnam. I say we must enter the struggle, but I wish to go on now to say something even more disturbing. The war in Vietnam is but a symptom of a far deeper malady within the American spirit, and if we ignore this sobering reality we will find ourselves organizing clergy-and-laymen-concerned committees for the next generation. They will be concerned about Guatemala and Peru. They will be concerned about Thailand and Cambodia. They will be concerned about Mozambique and South Africa. We will be marching for these and a dozen other names and attending rallies without end unless there is a significant and profound change in American life and policy. Such thoughts take us beyond Vietnam, but not beyond our calling as sons of the living God.

In 1957 a sensitive American official overseas said that it seemed to him that our nation was on the wrong side of a world revolution. During the past ten years we have seen emerge a pattern of suppression which now has justified the presence of U.S. military "advisors" in Venezuela. This need to maintain social stability for our investments accounts for the counter-revolutionary action of American forces in Guatemala. It tells why American helicopters are being used against guerrillas in Colombia and why American napalm and green beret forces have already been active against rebels in Peru. It is with such activity in mind that the words of the late John

F. Kennedy come back to haunt us. Five years ago he said, "Those who make peaceful revolution impossible will make violent revolution inevitable."

Increasingly, by choice or by accident, this is the role our nation has taken— the role of those who make peaceful revolution impossible by refusing to give up the privileges and the pleasures that come from the immense profits of overseas investment.

I am convinced that if we are to get on the right side of the world revolution, we as a nation must undergo a radical revolution of values. We must rapidly begin the shift from a "thing-oriented" society to a "person-oriented" society. When machines and computers, profit motives and property rights are considered more important than people, the giant triplets of racism, materialism, and militarism are incapable of being conquered.

A true revolution of values will soon cause us to question the fairness and justice of many of our past and present policies. On the one hand we are called to play the good Samaritan on life's roadside; but that will be only an initial act. One day we must come to see that the whole Jericho road must be transformed so that men and women will not be constantly beaten and robbed as they make their journey on life's highway. True compassion is more than flinging a coin to a beggar; it is not haphazard and superficial. It comes to see that an edifice which produces beggars needs restructuring. A true revolution of values will soon look uneasily on the glaring contrast of poverty and wealth. With righteous indignation, it will look across the seas and see individual capitalists of the West investing huge sums of money in Asia, Africa and South America, only to take the profits out with no concern for the social betterment of the countries, and say: "This is not just." It will look at our alliance with the landed gentry of Latin America and say: "This is not just." The Western arrogance of feeling that it has everything to teach others and nothing to learn from them is not just. A true revolution of values will lay hands on the world order and say of war: "This way of settling differences is not just." This business of burning human beings with napalm, of filling our nation's homes with orphans and widows, of injecting poisonous drugs of hate into veins of peoples normally humane, of sending men home from dark and bloody battlefields physically handicapped and psychologically deranged, cannot be reconciled with wisdom, justice and love. A nation that continues year after year to spend more money on military defense than on programs of social uplift is approaching spiritual death.

America, the richest and most powerful nation in the world, can well lead the way in this revolution of values. There is nothing, except a tragic death wish, to prevent us from reordering our priorities, so that the pursuit of peace will take precedence over the pursuit of war. There is nothing to keep us from molding a recalcitrant status quo with bruised hands until we have fashioned it into a brotherhood.

This kind of positive revolution of values is our best defense against communism. War is not the answer. Communism will never be defeated by the use of atomic bombs or nuclear weapons. Let us not join those who shout war and through their misguided passions urge the United States to relinquish its participation in the United Nations. These are days which demand wise restraint and calm reasonableness. We must not call everyone a Communist or an appeaser who advocates the seating of Red China in the United Nations and who recognizes that hate and hysteria are not the final answers to the problem of these turbulent days. We must not engage in a negative anti-communism, but rather in a positive thrust for democracy, realizing that our greatest defense against communism is to take offensive action in behalf of justice. We must with positive action seek to remove those conditions of poverty, insecurity and injustice which are the fertile soil in which the seed of communism grows and develops.

The People Are Important

These are revolutionary times. All over the globe men are revolting against old systems of exploitation and oppression and out of the wombs of a frail world new systems of justice and equality are being born. The shirtless and barefoot people of the land are rising up as never before. "The people who sat in darkness have seen a great light." We in the West must support these revolutions. It is a sad fact that, because of comfort, complacency, a morbid fear of communism, and our proneness to adjust to injustice, the Western nations that initiated so much of the revolutionary spirit of the modern world have now become the arch anti-revolutionaries. This has driven many to feel that only Marxism has the revolutionary spirit. Therefore, communism is a judgment against our failure to make democracy real and follow through on the revolutions that we initiated. Our only hope today lies in our ability to recapture the revolutionary spirit and go out into a sometimes hostile world declaring eternal hostility to poverty, racism, and militarism. With this powerful commitment we shall boldly challenge the status quo and unjust mores and thereby speed the day when "every valley shall be exalted, and every mountain and hill shall be made low, and the crooked shall be made straight and the rough places plain."

A genuine revolution of values means in the final analysis that our loyalties must become ecumenical rather than sectional. Every nation must now develop an overriding loyalty to mankind as a whole in order to preserve the best in their individual societies.

This call for a world-wide fellowship that lifts neighborly concern beyond one's tribe, race, class and nation is in reality a call for an all-embracing and unconditional love for all men. This oft misunderstood and misinterpreted concept—so readily dismissed by the Nietzsches of the world as a weak and cowardly force—has now become an absolute necessity for the survival of man. When I speak of love I am not speaking of some sentimental and weak response. I am speaking of that force which all of the great religions have seen as the supreme unifying principle of life.

Love is somehow the key that unlocks the door which leads to ultimate reality. This Hindu-Moslem-Christian-Jewish-Buddhist belief about ultimate reality is beautifully summed up in the first epistle of Saint John:

> Let us love one another; for love is God and everyone that loveth is born of God and knoweth God. He that loveth not knoweth not God; for God is love. If we love one another God dwelleth in us, and his love is perfected in us.

Let us hope that this spirit will become the order of the day. We can no longer afford to worship the god of hate or bow before the altar of retaliation. The oceans of history are made turbulent by the ever-rising tides of hate. History is cluttered with the wreckage of nations and individuals that pursued this self-defeating path of hate. As Arnold Toynbee says: "Love is the ultimate force that makes for the saving choice of life and good against the damning choice of death and evil. Therefore the first hope in our inventory must be the hope that love is going to have the last word."

We are now faced with the fact that tomorrow is today. We are confronted with the fierce urgency of now. In this unfolding conundrum of life and history there is such a thing as being too late. Procrastination is still the thief of time. Life often leaves us standing bare, naked and dejected with a lost opportunity. The "tide in the affairs of men" does not remain at the flood; it ebbs. We may cry out desperately for time to pause in her passage, but time is deaf to every plea and rushes on. Over the bleached bones and jumbled residue of numerous civilizations are written the pathetic words: "Too late." There is an invisible book of life that faithfully records our vigilance or our neglect. "The moving finger writes, and having writ moves on... ." We still have a choice today; nonviolent coexistence or violent co-annihilation.

We must move past indecision to action. We must find new ways to speak for peace in Vietnam and justice throughout the developing world—a world that borders on our doors. If we do not act we shall surely be dragged down the long dark and shameful corridors of time reserved for those who possess power without compassion, might without morality, and strength without sight.

Now let us begin. Now let us rededicate ourselves to the long and bitter—but beautiful—struggle for a new world. This is the calling of the sons of God, and our brothers wait eagerly for our response. Shall we say the odds are too great? Shall we tell them the struggle is too hard? Will our message be that the forces of American life militate against their arrival as full men, and we send our deepest regrets? Or will there be another message, of longing, of hope, of solidarity with their yearnings, of commitment to their cause, whatever the cost? The choice is ours, and though we might prefer it otherwise we must choose in this crucial moment of human history.

As that noble bard of yesterday, James Russell Lowell, eloquently stated:

Once to every man and nation,
Comes the moment to decide
In the strife of truth with falsehood

For the good or evil side;
Some great cause, God's new Messiah
Offering each the gloom or blight
And the choice goes by forever
Twixt that darkness and that light.
Though the cause of evil prosper
Yet 'tis truth alone is strong
Though her portion be the scaffold
And upon the throne be wrong
Yet that scaffold sways the future
And behind the dim unknown
Standeth God within the shadow
Keeping watch above his own.

33. William T. Cavanaugh – Violence Religious and Secular: Questioning the Categories

When I tell people the title of my book *The Myth of Religious Violence*, they tend to smile if they are polite and laugh if they are not. I can practically hear them thinking "Is this a sequel to your book *The Myth of a Spherical Earth*?" Everyone seems to know that religion has a dangerous tendency to promote violence. This story is part of the conventional wisdom of Western societies, and it underlies many of our institutions and policies, both domestic and foreign, from limits on the public role of churches to efforts to promote secularism in the Middle East.

In my book I challenge the conventional wisdom, but not in the conventional ways it is sometimes challenged. I do not deny that Christians or Muslims who do violence are really true Christians or Muslims. I do not claim that the wars often cited as evidence against religion are really about economics or politics and not about religion. I think that the idea that there is a rigid line between religion and politics, et al., is a questionable assumption, as I will explain later. Indeed, many Muslims, for example, make no such distinction. Finally, I do not deny that faith systems like Christianity and Islam can and do contribute to violence, given certain conditions.

But what is implied in the conventional wisdom is that Christianity, Islam, and other faiths are *more* inclined toward violence than ideologies and institutions that are identified as "secular." In order for the indictment of religion to hold, religion must be contrasted with something else that is inherently *less* prone to violence: the secular. It is *this* story that I will challenge here. I will argue 1) that there is no good reason for thinking that religious ideologies and institutions are more inherently prone to violence than so-called secular ideologies and institutions, and 2) that this is so because there is no *essential* difference between religious and secular to begin with. These are invented categories, not simply the way things are. I will look at the political reasons why these categories were invented in the modern West. I will then show that the idea that something called religion is essentially prone to violence is an ideological justification that can be used to justify the violence of so-called secular orders. The myth of religious violence promotes a dichotomy between *us* in the secular West who are rational and peacemaking, and *them*, the hordes of violent religious fanatics in the Muslim world. *Their* violence is religious, and therefore irrational and divisive. *Our* violence, on the other hand, is secular, rational, and peacemaking. We find ourselves forced to bomb them into the higher rationality.

I. Defining Religious and Secular

Let us start with one of the most famous atheists today, Christopher Hitchens. His bestselling book *God is Not Great* is subtitled – with typical British understatement – *How Religion Poisons Everything*. There he points to histories of abuses by Christians, Jews, Muslims, Hindus, Buddhists, Confucianists, and so on. But he also faces up to the fact that rigidly atheist regimes, like those of Joseph Stalin and Kim Jong-Il, are responsible for tens of millions of deaths and uncounted suffering. Hitchens deals with this little problem by declaring that atheist regimes like Stalin's are religious too. Totalitarianism aims at human perfection, which is essentially a religious impulse, according to Hitchens.[1]

Religion poisons everything because everything poisonous gets identified as religion. At the same time, everything good ends up on the other side of the religious/secular divide. Hitchens says of Martin Luther King Jr., "In no real as opposed to nominal sense, then, was he a Christian."[2] Hitchens bases this remarkable conclusion on the notion that King was nonviolent, while the Bible preaches violence from cover to cover. What is not violent cannot possibly be religious, because religion is *defined* as violent.

Now at this point we could dismiss Hitchens, assume that Stalin is not really religious, and start arguing over who has caused more deaths in the twentieth century, atheists or those who believe in God. But that would be to assume that we really know what religion is and what it isn't. Hitchens is useful because he shows that what counts as religion and what doesn't is very fluid and often depends on the political agenda one is pursuing. Hitchens is by no means alone in this. If you examine arguments that religion causes violence, you find that what counts as religion and what does not is largely incoherent.

---

[1] Christopher Hitchens, *God is not Great: How Religion Poisons Everything* (New York: Twelve, 2007), 231.
[2] Ibid., 176.

Let me give a few examples. In a book on public religion, famed historian Martin Marty argues that religion has a particular tendency to be divisive and therefore violent.[3] When addressing the question "What is religion?" however, Marty is coy. He begins by listing seventeen different definitions of religion, then begs off giving his own definition, since, he says, "[s]cholars will never agree on the definition of religion."[4] Instead Marty gives a list of five "features" that mark a religion. He then proceeds to show how "politics" displays all five of the same features. Religion focuses our ultimate concern, and so does politics. Religion builds community, and so does politics. Religion appeals to myth and symbol, and politics "mimics" this appeal in devotion to the flag, war memorials, and so on down the list.[5] Marty offers five defining features of "religion," and shows how "politics" fits all five. Should one then assume that "politics" is a type of "religion," or vice-versa? If not, what distinguishes the two? The reader can be forgiven for being confused by this display of evasion. Marty nevertheless proceeds in the rest of the book to discuss "religion" as if it were perfectly obvious what he is talking about.

Another example: sociologist Mark Juergensmeyer, whose book *Terror in the Mind of God*, perhaps the most widely influential academic book on religion and violence. According to Juergensmeyer, religion exacerbates the tendency to divide people into friends and enemies, good and evil, us and them, by ratcheting divisions up to a cosmic level. But he is forced to admit the difficulty of separating religious violence from secular violence. In his book *The New Cold War?: Religious Nationalism Confronts the Secular State*, he writes "Secular nationalism, like religion, embraces what one scholar calls 'a doctrine of destiny.' One can take this way of looking at secular nationalism a step further and state flatly… that secular nationalism *is* 'a religion.'"[6] He repeats this claim in his 2008 book *Global Rebellion*, where he also says that "the secular is a sort of advanced form of religion."[7] Here Juergensmeyer acknowledges the work being done to historicize and question the religious/secular distinction. Juergensmeyer's statements are crucial concessions which, taken seriously, would undermine the entire basis for Juergensmeyer's work on the peculiar relationship between religion and violence. To say that the secular is a form of religion is to demolish the distinction between the two. But without the distinction, there is simply no basis for examining religion and violence as a special category, for religion must be contrasted with something—the secular—in order for religion to stand out as a special subject of interest. So Juergensmeyer continues to treat religious and

---

[3]Martin E. Marty with Jonathan Moore, *Politics, Religion, and the Common Good* (San Francisco: Jossey-Bass Publishers, 2000), 25–6.

[4]Ibid., 10.

[5]Ibid., 10–14.

[6]Mark Juergensmeyer, *The New Cold War?: Religious Nationalism Confronts the Secular State* (Berkeley: University of California Press, 1993), 15.

[7]Mark Juergensmeyer, *Global Rebellion: Religious Challenges to the Secular State, from Christian Militias to Al Qaeda* (Berkeley: University of California Press, 2008), 23.

secular as a mutually opposed binary, so that he can continue to make claims about the peculiar relationship of "religion" to violence.

For some religion-and-violence theorists, the confusion around the religious/secular divide is resolved in a functionalist way by openly expanding the definition of "religion" to include ideologies and practices that are usually called "secular." In his book *Why People do Bad Things in the Name of Religion,* Richard Wentz blames violence on absolutism. Religion has a peculiar tendency toward absolutism, says Wentz. But when considering religion, Wentz includes faith in technology, secular humanism, consumerism, football fanaticism and a host of other worldviews. This type of view is called "functionalist" because it expands the category of religion beyond the usual list of "world religions" (a "substantivist" restricts "religion" Christianity, Islam, Hinduism, and a handful of others) to include all those ideologies and symbol systems that function in the same way that the "world religions" do in providing meaning and order to a person's life. Wentz thus expands "religion" so widely that he is compelled to conclude, "Perhaps all of us do bad things in the name of (or as a representative of) religion."[8] If Juergensmeyer is right about nationalism as a religion, for example, then Wentz is simply being consistent by expanding the definition of religion to include such ideologies and institutions. The only problem is that once the definition of religion has been thus expanded, it becomes necessary to ask "Religion, as opposed to what?" Wentz' analysis is really of the violence of absolutism, and the term "religion" adds nothing to the analysis. The conclusion to be drawn from the analysis is simply that worldviews and symbol systems of all kinds can promote violence when taken absolutely.

Wentz, Hitchens, Juergensmeyer, and others are not necessarily wrong to include so-called "secular" things in the category "religion." There is a vast literature on Marxism as a religion, for example. There is an extensive body of scholarship that explores the prevalence of civil religion in the United States which, as Robert Bellah says, "has its own seriousness and integrity and requires the same care in understanding that any other religion does."[9] For Bellah, religion as such is not privatized in the U.S.; traditional faiths like Christianity and Judaism are privatized, while the religion of nationalism occupies the public realm. Carolyn Marvin similarly argues that "nationalism is the most powerful religion in the United States, and perhaps in many other countries."[10] Scholars have explored the peculiar myths, symbols, and sacrifices that surround the flag. In the wake of rolling blackouts in California in 2001, one of the architects of the deregulation of California's electrical utilities was quoted in the *New York Times* expressing his belief that free markets always work better than state

---

[8]Richard E. Wentz, *Why People do Bad Things in the Name of Religion* (Macon, GA: Mercer University Press, 1993), 37.

[9]Robert N. Bellah, "Civil Religion in America" in *American Civil Religion,* ed. Donald E. Jones and Russell E. Richey (San Francisco: Mellen Research University Press, 1990), 21.

[10]Carolyn Marvin and David Ingle. "Blood Sacrifice and the Nation," *Journal of the American Academy of Religion,* Volume LXIV, Issue 4, Fall 1996: 767–780, 767.

control: "I believe in that premise as a matter of religious faith."[11] Scholars who take a Durkeimian functionalist approach take him at his word. A survey of religious studies literature finds the following treated under the rubric "religion": totems, witchcraft, the rights of man, Marxism, liberalism, Freudianism, Japanese tea ceremonies, nationalism, sports, free market ideology, Alcoholics Anonymous and a host of other institutions and practices.[12]

If one objects that religion is really about belief in God or gods, then one would need to eliminate certain belief systems that are usually called "religions", such as Daoism and Confucianism and many forms of Buddhism, which don't have a central concept of God or gods. If the definition of religion is expanded to include such belief systems under the rubric of "transcendence" or some such more inclusive term, then all sorts of practices, including many that are usually labeled "secular," fall under the definition of religion. Many institutions and ideologies that do not explicitly refer to God or gods function in the same way as those that do. Expanding the concept of religion to include godless Buddhism makes it difficult to exclude godless Marxism. Likewise, as Juergensmeyer implicitly acknowledges, nationalism is just as "transcendent" as any of the so-called "world religions." The term "transcendence" is a tool of Western scholars of religion, who borrowed the term from the Judeo-Christian tradition, with its distinction between a Creator God and a created order. To apply this term to Buddhism, which has no such distinction, one needs to define "transcendence" in an exceedingly vague manner. But the vaguer the term becomes, the less justification one has for excluding other systems of belief and practice, such as nationalism. Defining religion in terms of transcendence, the sacred, the supraempirical, and so on just begs the question of what those terms mean. If these terms are made vague enough to be transcultural, then the exclusivity of the term "religion" breaks down very quickly.

This is particularly relevant to the question of violence. Is there any good reason to suppose that people are more likely to kill for a god than for a nation?

Suppose we ask two more specific questions: What percentage of Americans who identify themselves as Christians would be willing to kill for their Christian faith? What percentage would be willing to kill for their country? It seems clear that, at least among American Christians, the nation-state is subject to far more absolutist fervor than Christianity. The majority of American Christians would consider the idea of killing for God or for Christianity abhorrent, and yet most would consider killing and dying for the flag and for the nation as sometimes necessary and often laudable. The fact is that people kill for all kinds of things, and there is no coherent way to isolate "religious" ideologies with a peculiar tendency toward violence from their

---

[11]Philip Romero, quoted in Alex Berenson, "Deregulation: A Movement Groping in the Dark," *New York Times*, February 4, 2001: 4.6.
[12]Timothy Fitzgerald, *The Ideology of Religious Studies* (New York: Oxford University Press, 2000), 17.

tamer "secular" counterparts. So-called "secular" ideologies and institutions like nationalism and capitalism can inspire just as much violence as so-called "religion."

The problem with Hitchens, then, is not just that he thinks Stalinism is a religion. The problem is that, if he is going to use such an expansive definition of religion, he should do so consistently, but he doesn't. For Hitchens, American civil religion is not religion; it is purely secular. The secular/religious distinction is really nothing more than the distinction between the things Hitchens likes and the things he doesn't. Please note that the problem is not simply that the concept of religion has some fuzzy edges. So does every concept, like politics or culture, for example. The problem with the "religion and violence" arguments is not that their working definitions of religion are too fuzzy. The problem is that their implicit definitions of religion are *unjustifiably clear* about what does and does not qualify as a religion. Certain belief systems, like Islam, are condemned, while certain others, like nationalism, are ignored.

My point here is not to argue either for or against an expansive definition of religion. I have no intention of trying to solve, once and for all, the debate between substantivists and functionalists whether or not Confucianism or Marxism or free market capitalism is a religion, for example. I don't think there is a once and for all definition of religion. My point is rather that "religion" is a category constructed in different ways in different places and times, and according to the interests of who is doing the construction. To understand why there is so much confusion around the category of religion, we need to examine its history.

II. History of the Religious/Secular Distinction

The basic problem with the idea that religion causes violence is the category "religion." Those who indict religion assume that religion is a transhistorical and transcultural human activity that is essentially different from secular phenomena. In reality, however, the religious/secular distinction is a relatively recent, Western creation, and what counts as religion and what counts as secular in any given context is determined by certain political configurations of power.

Charles Kimball's book *When Religion Becomes Evil* begins with the following claim: "It is somewhat trite, but nevertheless sadly true, to say that more wars have been waged, more people killed, and these days more evil perpetrated in the name of religion than by any other institutional force in human history."[13] Here we must ask again "Religion, as opposed to what?" As opposed to "politics" perhaps? The problem is that there was no "religion" considered as something separable from politics until the modern era, and then primarily in the West. The Romans had the term *religio*, but there was no religion/politics distinction. How could there be, when Caesar was considered a god? The ancient Romans employed the term *religio*, but it covered all

---

[13]Charles Kimball, *When Religion Becomes Evil* (San Francisco: HarperSanFrancisco, 2002), 1.

kinds of civic duties and relations of respect that we would consider "secular." As St. Augustine says in *The City of God*, "We have no right to affirm with confidence that religion (*religio*) is confined to the worship of God, since it seems that this word has been detached from its normal meaning, in which it refers to an attitude of respect in relations between a man and his neighbor."[14] As Wilfred Cantwell Smith showed in his landmark 1962 book *The Meaning and End of Religion*, "religion" as a discrete category of human activity separable from "culture," "politics," and other areas of life is an invention of the modern West. In the course of a detailed historical study of the concept "religion," Smith concluded that in premodern Europe there was no significant concept equivalent to what we think of as "religion."[15] In the medieval era, the religious/secular distinction was used almost exclusively to distinguish between clergy who belonged to an order and diocesan clergy. (Catholics still refer to joining an order like the Dominicans as entering the religious life). In 1400 the "religions" of England were the various orders. There was no realm of secular pursuits to which God was indifferent, and though there was a distinction between civil and ecclesiastical authorities, there was no distinction between politics and religion as we conceive it.[16]

The religious/secular distinction as we know it today was a creation of the early modern struggles for power between ecclesiastical and civil authorities. In the creation of the modern sovereign state between the fifteenth and seventeenth centuries, "religion" was invented as a universal, essentially interior and private, impulse that is essentially separate from politics and other "secular" concerns. Henceforth the church's proper area of concern would be essentially alien from politics. The idea that "religion" is a transcultural and transhistorical impulse makes the separation of religion and politics appear natural and inevitable, not a contingent arrangement of power in society.

The religious/secular distinction was subsequently exported to non-Western cultures during the process of colonization. Smith's study concludes that there is no "closely equivalent concept [to religion] in any culture that has not been influenced by the modern West"; there was no such concept in ancient Greece, Egypt, China, India or anywhere else in the ancient world.[17] When we ask a question like "Were the pyramids built for religious or political reasons?," we immediately see how anachronistic and nonsensical it is. This remains the case until the rest of the world was colonized by Europeans. In their initial encounters with the non-Western world, European explorers reported, with remarkable consistency, that the natives had no religion at all. Once colonized, however, the category "religion" became a powerful

---

[14]Augustine, *City of God*, trans. Henry Bettenson (Harmondsworth, England: Penguin, 1972), X.1 (p. 373).
[15]Wilfred Cantwell Smith, *The Meaning and End of Religion* (New York: Macmillan, 1962), 18–19.
[16]"Religion," *Oxford English Dictionary,* 2nd ed. (Oxford: Clarendon Press, 1989); see also Cantwell Smith, *Meaning and End*, 31.
[17]Smith, 19.

tool for the classification of native cultures as essentially distinct from the business of government.

"Hinduism," for example, a term first used in 1829, became a religion in the course of the nineteenth century, despite the fact that it encompassed the entire Indian way of life, everything we would include under culture, politics, religion, and economy. Frits Staal has concluded, "Hinduism does not merely fail to be a religion; it is not even a meaningful unit of discourse."[18] This is not an insult to Hindus. Staal simply means that talking about "Hinduism" is like talking about "Americanism"; it encompasses too much of disparate meaning to have much accuracy. Nevertheless, the classification of Hinduism as a religion was useful under British rule, because it was a way to take everything Indian and classify it as essentially private. This is why many contemporary advocates of Hindu nationalism or Hindutva—especially the powerful Bharatiya Janata Party—also refuse to call Hinduism a religion. As Richard Cohen writes, "The proponents of Hindutva refuse to call Hinduism a religion precisely because they want to emphasize that Hinduism is more than mere internalized beliefs. It is social, political, economic, and familial in nature. Only thus can India the secular state become interchangeable with India the Hindu homeland."[19]

For similar reasons, at the same time that European scholars were discovering Chinese religions in the 19th and early twentieth centuries, Chinese scholars like Liang Chichao declared that "there is no religion among the indigenous products of China." Such scholars regarded religion as individualistic and nonprogressive. Despite Western categorization of Confucianism as a religion, Chinese scholars regarded it as unitive, progressive, and therefore emphatically not religious.[20] For similar reasons, the Chinese Communist government today excludes Confucianism from its official list of religions in China. It is seen as an expression of the national character, superior to "religions" such as Christianity and Buddhism, which are private and otherworldly.[21]

In her book *The Invention of World Religions*, Tomoko Masuzawa concludes "This concept of religion as a general, transcultural phenomenon, yet also as a distinct sphere in its own right… is patently groundless; it came from nowhere, and there is no credible way of demonstrating its factual and empirical substantiality."[22] In other words, the religious/secular distinction is not engraved in the nature of things;

---

[18]Frits Staal, *Rules Without Meaning: Ritual, Mantras, and the Human Sciences* (New York: Peter Lang Verlag, 1989), 397.

[19]Richard S. Cohen, "Why Study Indian Buddhism?," in *The Invention of Religion: Rethinking Belief in Politics and History*, ed. Derek R. Peterson and Darren R. Walhof (New Brunswick, NJ: Rutgers University Press, 2002), 27.

[20]Peter Beyer, "Defining Religion in Cross-National Perspective: Identity and Difference in Official Conceptions," in *Defining Religion: Investigating the Boundaries Between the Sacred and the Secular*, ed. Arthur L. Greil and David G. Bromley (Oxford: JAI, 2003), 174–5.

[21]Ibid., 175–7.

[22]Tomoko Masuzawa, *The Invention of World Religions: Or, How European Universalism Was Preserved in the Language of Pluralism* (Chicago: University of Chicago Press, 2005), 319.

it is rather a distinction that is employed in Western or Westernized societies to marginalize certain kinds of beliefs and practices, and to authorize others.

III. Uses of the Argument

If, as we have seen, the idea that religion promotes violence and the very religious/ secular distinction upon which it relies, are not innocent of political use, then we might ask what purposes these ideas have in current discourse.

In domestic life in the United States, the myth of religious violence has played a key role in shifting the dominant mode of jurisprudence from what Frederick Gedicks calls "religious communitarianism" to "secular individualism." Well into the twentieth century, "religion" was cited in Supreme Court cases as having a unifying social effect. Beginning in the 1940s, however, religion came to be seen as a potentially dangerous and divisive social force. The first U.S. Supreme Court decision to invoke the myth of religious violence was *Minersville School District v. Gobitis* (1940), which upheld compulsory pledging of allegiance to the American flag. Writing for the majority, Justice Felix Frankfurter invoked the specter of religious wars in denying the Jehovah's Witnesses the right to dissent from patriotic rituals. "Centuries of strife over the erection of particular dogmas as exclusive or all-comprehending faiths led to the inclusion of a guarantee for religious freedom in the Bill of Rights. The First Amendment ... sought to guard against repetition of those bitter religious struggles by prohibiting the establishment of a state religion and by securing to every sect the free exercise of its faith."[23] One would think that the Jehovah's Witnesses would be entitled to such free exercise. Not in this case, says Justice Frankfurter. Their dissent threatened the "promotion of national cohesion. We are dealing with an interest inferior to none in the hierarchy of legal values. National unity is the basis of national security."[24] Furthermore, the government has the right to impose such unity over against dissenters. "What the school authorities are really asserting is the right to awaken in the child's mind considerations as to the significance of the flag contrary to those implanted by the parent."[25]

The Court would reverse itself three years later, but Frankfurter had succeeded in introducing the idea that First Amendment decisions could be made against a backdrop of some unspecified history of "bitter religious struggles," the antidote to which is the enforcement of national unity. In the succeeding decades, the myth of religious violence would be invoked by the Supreme Court in case after case, in decisions banning school prayer, forbidding voluntary religious instruction on public school property, forbidding

---

[23]*Minersville School District v. Gobitis*, 310 U.S. 586 (1940), 593.
[24]Ibid., 595.
[25]Ibid., 599. For the court to intervene "would amount to no less than the pronouncement of pedagogical and psychological dogma in a field where courts possess no marked and certainly no controlling competence"; ibid., 598–9.

state aid to parochial school teachers, and so on. When the Court banned school prayer in the *Abington* case in 1963, again invoking the specter of religious violence, Justice Potter Stewart dissented, warning of "the establishment of a religion of secularism."[26] Stewart's warning would go unheeded.

Martin Marty discusses the *Minersville v Gobitis* case and cites the many instances of Jehovah's Witnesses who were attacked, beaten, tarred, castrated, and imprisoned in the U.S. in the 1940s because they believed that followers of Jesus Christ should not salute a flag. One would think that he would draw the obvious conclusion that zealous nationalism can cause violence. Astonishingly, Marty concludes "it became obvious that religion, which can pose 'us' versus 'them'... carries risks and can be perceived by others as dangerous. Religion can cause all kinds of trouble in the public arena."[27] For Marty, "religion" refers not to the ritual vowing of allegiance to a flag, but only to the Jehovah's Witnesses' refusal to do so. In this way the myth of religious violence is used to draw attention away from nationalist violence and toward so-called "religious violence," even though in this case the Jehovah's Witnesses suffered rather than perpetrated the violence.

This is only possible, of course, if a strict division is enforced between "religion" on the one hand, and the ritual vowing of allegiance to a nation's flag on the other. In an article cited by the Supreme Court in two more landmark religion-clause cases—*Walz v. Tax Commission* (1970) and *Lemon v. Kurtzman* (1971)—Harvard Law professor Paul Freund discusses the unique dangers of religious questions to public peace. He compares the Jehovah's Witnesses' eventual success in getting themselves excused from having to say the Pledge of Allegiance to the *Abington* case, in which a Unitarian objected to public school prayer and the court banned prayer for everyone. The flag salute continued to be employed in public schools even though the Jehovah's Witnesses found the Pledge of Allegiance "at least as unacceptable and religious in nature"[28] as the Unitarians found the Lord's Prayer. Freund finds the difference in the rulings perfectly justified. "Why? Because the prevailing, dominant view of religion classifies the flag salute as secular, in contravention of the heterodox definition devoutly held by the Witnesses."[29] Freund continues on to declare, *pace* Stewart, that the idea that secularism is a religion is merely a "play on words."[30]

Neither Freund nor the Supreme Court ever offers a definition of religion or offers reasons why the "orthodox" definition of religion should hold. It is simply taken for granted that the ritual pledging of allegiance to a piece of cloth is *not religious*. Religion is divisive; nationalism is unifying. And so the idea that religion has a tendency to promote violence becomes one of the principal ways whereby we

---

[26]*Abington Township School District v. Schempp*, 374 U.S. 203 (1963), 313.
[27]Marty, 24.
[28]Paul A. Freund, "Public Aid to Parochial Schools," *Harvard Law Review* 82 (1969): 1686.
[29]Ibid.
[30]Ibid., 1690.

become convinced that killing and dying for the flag is sweet and fitting: *dulce et decorum est, pro patria mori.*

This dynamic becomes most apparent in foreign policy, especially where the conventional wisdom on religion and violence helps reinforce and justify Western attitudes and policies toward the non-Western world. Muslims are the primary subject here; their primary point of difference with the West is said to be their stubborn refusal to tame religious passions in the public sphere. Hitchens, for example, skewers "religion" for its violence, but has been an enthusiastic supporter of the Iraq War and Western military adventures in the Muslim world. Despite his attempt to recruit Martin Luther King to his side, Hitchens has some approving things to say about killing people. "And I say to the Christians while I'm at it, 'Go love your own enemies; by the way, don't be loving mine... I think the enemies of civilization should be beaten and killed and defeated, and I don't make any apology for it."[31] For Hitchens, the Iraq War is part of a broader war for secularism, and the game is zero-sum. "It is not possible for me to say, Well, you pursue your Shiite dream of a hidden imam and I pursue my study of Thomas Paine and George Orwell, and the world is big enough for both of us. The true believer cannot rest until the whole world bows the knee."[32] The true believer Hitchens has in mind is the Islamist. But Hitchens's message is that the true believer in secularism can also not rest until the whole world has been converted to secularism—by force, if necessary.

Hitchens gives us an example from the right, but the myth of religious violence is also employed by those on the left to support America's wars. An example is Paul Berman's *Terror and Liberalism*, another *New York Times* bestseller, this time by a professor at New York University and a contributing editor to *The New Republic*. Berman, who describes himself as "pro-war and left- wing,"[33] articulates a justification for the U.S. wars in Iraq and Afghanistan based fundamentally on the myth of religious violence, that is, the idea that liberalism has found the solution to the perpetual problem of the inherent violence of religion and we need now to share that solution with the world—by military means if necessary.

For Berman, liberalism is founded in the problem of religious violence.

> The whole purpose of liberalism was to put religion in one corner, and the state in a different corner, and to keep those corners apart. The liberal idea arose in the seventeenth century in England and Scotland, and the philosophers who invented it wanted to prevent the English Civil War, which had just taken place, from breaking out again. So they proposed to scoop up the cause of that war, which was religion, and,

---

[31]Christopher Hitchens, from a public debate in San Francisco, quoted in Chris Hedges, *I Don't Believe in Atheists* (New York: Free Press, 2008), 23.

[32]Hitchens, *God is not Great*, 31.

[33]Paul Berman, *Terror and Liberalism* (New York: W. W. Norton & Company, 2003), 7.

in the gentlest way, to cart it off to another place, which was the sphere of private life, where every church and sect could freely rail at each of the others.[34]

This problem and solution were not just a matter of local and contingent circumstances. Over the course of the nineteenth century, Western liberalism found what Berman calls "the secret of human advancement."[35] That secret is "the recognition that all of life is not governed by a single, all-knowing and all-powerful authority—by a divine force."[36] Therefore each sphere or "slice" of life could operate independently of the others, and especially "religion" could operate independently of politics, science, and so on.

Unfortunately, the twentieth century saw this secret challenged by the atavistic, irrational impulse to impose totality on the social order. Modern totalitarianism, according to Berman, is just a variation on an age-old religious theme derived from the Bible: the people of God, under attack from evil forces, must be united to achieve victory.[37] Thus does Berman, like Hitchens, include even atheistic regimes like the Soviet Union under the rubric "religion." Since the basic battle is liberalism versus religion, any anti-liberal political system counts as religion too. Thus does the explicitly secular Baathi movement end up falling under Berman's indictment of religion, as he lumps secular Baathi socialism and Islamic fundamentalism together as species of totalitarianism, thus justifying Western military intervention in Iraq. "The Baathi and the Islamists were two branches of a single impulse, which was Muslim totalitarianism—the Muslim variation on the European idea."[38]

What seems to be most crucial about the "Islamists and Baathi" totalitarians is their irrationality. "Their ideology was mad. In wars between liberalism and totalitarianism, the totalitarian picture of war is always mad."[39]

In a chapter entitled "Wishful Thinking," Berman excoriates liberals whose own rationality leads them to assume that others are rational too. Because of liberals' rationality they assume, for example, that Palestinians must have some legitimate reasons for using violence against the Israeli occupation. But Berman assures us that the only explanation is "mass pathology" based on crazy religious ideas. The violence of the Israeli response under Ariel Sharon is regrettable, but rational: "this policy of his conformed to an obvious logic of military reasoning. A conventional logic: to smother violence under a blanket of greater violence."[40] Suicide attacks against Israel, on the other hand, are irrational and futile, and only show the madness of the Palestinian ideology.

---

[34]Ibid., 79.
[35]Ibid., 37.
[36]Ibid.
[37]Ibid., 46–7.
[38]Ibid., 60.
[39]Ibid., 182–3.
[40]Ibid.

What is needed, then, is not sympathy with madness, but "a liberal war of liberation, partly military but ultimately intellectual, a war of ideas, fought around the world."[41] The "Terror War" will be fought with guns, but primarily with philosophy, ideas. If the opposition is mad, however, it is hard to see how rational persuasion is going to work. It would seem, given the inherent irrationality of non-liberals, that they will have to be dealt with by force. Although Berman would prefer to deal in lectures and books, he puts his justifications of the Gulf War, the war in Afghanistan, and the Iraq War[42] in the context of a wider argument about the need for liberalism to flex its military might. Berman considers Lincoln's Gettysburg Address in this light. Lincoln spoke about death without glorifying it as a totalitarian would. But nevertheless Lincoln "spoke about death as 'the last full measure of devotion,' which the Union soldiers had given... 'From these honored dead we take increased devotion,' he said. He was explaining that a liberal society must be, when challenged, a warlike society; or it will not endure."[43] Berman continues on to say that a liberal society is different from other societies because it shuns absolutes; "but liberalism does not shun every absolute."[44] The absolute that it does not shun but requires is the "absolute commitment to solidarity and self-government,"[45] even unto death.

IV. Conclusion

Berman's "liberal war of liberation" is just one expression of a foreign policy that is commonly labeled "Wilsonian" after President Woodrow Wilson made its terms explicit. Wilson was convinced that the future peace and prosperity of the world depended on the extension of liberal principles of government—along with open markets—to the entire world. The liberal tradition on which Wilson drew assumes that liberal democratic governments are inherently more peaceable than other types of government, in part because the former have learned to separate religion from politics. In the American tradition which Wilson articulated, it was assumed that America—and in particular American military might—had a special mission of bringing liberal ideals to the rest of the world.[46] This is a remarkably ambitious project. As John Lukács remarked, "If we judge events by their consequences, the great world revolutionary was Wilson rather than Lenin."[47]

---

[41]Ibid., 191.

[42]Ibid., 6–7, 198–9.

[43]Ibid., 170.

[44]Ibid.

[45]Ibid., 171.

[46]Colin Dueck, *Reluctant Crusaders: Power, Culture, and Change in American Grand Strategy* (Princeton: Princeton University Press, 2006), 22.

[47]John Lukács, quoted in Andrew J. Bacevich, *American Empire: The Realities & Consequences of U.S. Diplomacy* (Cambridge, MA: Harvard University Press, 2002), 87.

The situation is not different at the beginning of the 21st century. As political scientist Colin Dueck says, Americans tend to favor military action "either for liberal reasons, or not at all."[48] This is expressed in the Bush Doctrine that America has access to liberal values that are "right and true for every person, in every society," that we must use our power to promote such values "on every continent," and that America will take preemptive military action if necessary to promote such values.[49]

I do not wish either to deny the virtues of liberalism or to excuse the vices of other kinds of social orders. I wish rather to challenge the religious/secular dichotomy that causes us to turn a blind eye to liberal forms of imperialism and violence. A balanced approach will not ignore violence done in the name of *jihad* and the sacrificial atonement of Christ, but neither will it ignore violence done in the name of the flag or capitalism or freedom. The problem is not "religious violence"; the problem is violence, and we need to see clearly, from both eyes, before we can address it.[50]

34. Rowan Williams – Do Human Rights Exist?

Twenty-seven years ago, Alasdair MacIntyre in his seminal work on the foundations of moral discourse, *After Virtue,* declared that human rights did not exist. 'Rights which are alleged to belong to human beings as such and which are cited as a reason for holding that people ought not to be interfered with in their pursuit of life, liberty and happiness' are a fiction: 'there are', he says, 'no such rights, and belief in them is one with belief in witches and in unicorns'.[1] The language of rights emerges, MacIntyre argues, at a time when people need a fresh moral compass in the wake of the dissolution of much traditional morality; like the concept of 'utility', which is another characteristic notion developed in the modern period as a touchstone for moral decision, the idea of 'rights' is meant to act as a trump in moral argument. The trouble is, MacIntyre argues, that rights and utility don't get along very well together in argument: one is essentially about the claims of the individual, the other about the priorities of administration. The result is the familiar modern stand-off between the individual and the bureaucratic state. The state is both the guarantor of rights – more clearly than ever with the emergence of the 'market state' in which the most important

---

[48]Colin Dueck, *Reluctant Crusaders: Power, Culture, and Change in American Grand Strategy* (Princeton: Princeton University Press, 2006), 26.

[49]*The National Security Strategy of the United States of America*, September 2002, prologue and page 15.

[50]This essay is a significantly revised version of my plenary address to the College Theology Society Annual Meeting, June 2, 2011, at Iona College. The essay and lecture are a drastically abbreviated version of my book *The Myth of Religious Violence: Secular Ideology and the Roots of Modern Conflict* (New York: Oxford University Press, 2009).

[1]*After Virtue: A Study in Moral Theory* (London, 1981; 3/2007), pp. 66–7.

reason for recognizing the legitimacy of a state is its ability to maximise your choices, as Philip Bobbitt has demonstrated – and the authority that claims the right to assess and on occasion overrule individual liberties. Hence the tension between the state and civil society which has been so explosive a theme in twentieth-century politics. The lack of mediating concepts to deal with this tension was identified by Hannah Arendt, echoed more recently by Gillian Rose, as one of the roots of totalitarianism. But Rose notes also the same problem identified by MacIntyre, the way in which the stand-off between rights and utility leaves the path open to an exclusively *managerial* account of political life, in which 'expertize' about process is allowed to short-circuit proper discussions of corporate human goals.

MacIntyre's point is not, therefore, to deny the reality of human rights in the name of some kind of absolutism; quite the contrary. He is anxious that the language of rights and the language of utility are, as typically used in the modern world, no more than assertion – stop-gap notions to avoid complete relativism in public morality. This is one of the undoubted complexities in contemporary discussion of rights. On the one hand, 'human rights' is habitually used as a discussion-stopper, as the way in which we speak about aspects of social morality that are not up for negotiation or compromise. 'Human rights abuses' are widely seen as the most damaging weaknesses in a state's claim to legitimacy, and in extreme cases may be used as part of an argument for direct intervention by other states. On the other hand, what is often discussed in connection with both the Universal Declaration of Human Rights and the specifics of current human rights legislation is, in fact, a hybrid mass of claims to be decided by the state through its legislative apparatus; it is a quintessentially bureaucratic or managerial business, weighing various supposed entitlements against each other. If we speak without qualification of the right to life, the right to a fair trial, the right to raise a family and the right to a paid holiday under exactly the same rubric, it is very hard to see how this language can plausibly be understood as dealing with moral foundations. Fundamental issues blend with reasonable contractual expectations in a confusing way, and the idea of a list of entitlements dropped, as it were, into the cradle of each individual is deeply vulnerable to the charge of arbitrariness. MacIntyre's scepticism is well placed.

But if we are to salvage something from this, what do we need? Salvaging is important, if only for the reason that, if the language of rights is indeed the only generally intelligible way in modern political ethics of decisively challenging the positive authority of the state to do what it pleases, the only way of expressing how the state is itself under law, then this language needs to be as robust as it can be. In these remarks, I want to propose two ways in which a particular religious tradition may offer resources for grounding the discourse. There is now an abundant literature on religion and human rights, and a certain feeling in some quarters that there is a tension between rights and religious belief. It has been a good deal discussed in the context of Muslim critiques of the Universal Declaration, but Christian theologians have also voiced some unease about a scheme of ideas that places claims ahead of duties or even dignity. But I do not believe that this supposed tension is as serious as it is made out to be – so long, that is, as there is some recognition that rights have to be more than pure assertion or, as some would now have it, necessary fictions to secure a maximal degree of social harmony.

As Roger Ruston has argued in a very important study of the development of rights language,[2] the idea of irreducible or non-negotiable liberties for human beings has a strong theological basis in medieval thought. Paradoxically, it is in part the result of Christianity's confused and uneasy relationship with the institution of slavery. As is often pointed out, slavery as such is not condemned in Scripture, and is taken for granted, with varying degrees of regret, as an unavoidable social institution by most if not all Christian thinkers of the first millennium and a half of Christian history. However, from the first, the Christian community included both slaves and slave-owners; the letter to the *Ephesians* in the New Testament touches briefly on their relationship (6.5–9), as does *1 Peter* (2.13–25). The slave must give service as if freely to the Christian slave-owner, not as a response to compulsion, and being willing to serve the harsh master as willingly as the kind one; and the slave-owner must remember that s/he and the slave are alike bound in 'slavery' to one master. This last point relates to a passing remark made by St Paul in *Romans* 14.4 about refraining from judging another believer: you are not entitled to assess the satisfactoriness of the behaviour of someone else's slave.

The point is that the slave-owner's relationship to the slave is severely complicated by the baptismal relationship. The slave is no longer simply the property of the master or mistress, but 'belongs' to the one divine Master and is ultimately answerable to him, in exactly the same way as is the Christian slave-owner. As the Christian community develops and reflection about these issues continues, some implications are tentatively spelled out. In a world in which the slave-owner had powers of life and death over the slave, the Church determines that it is sinful to kill a slave (though the penitential tariff for this doesn't seem appropriately high to a modern reader). In a context where the slave-owner was assumed to have unlimited sexual access to slaves, sex with a slave is treated on the same basis as any other sexual misdemeanour; and marriage between a slave and a free person is recognized by the Church.

Stoic writers like Seneca had made it a commonplace that the master had no power over the mind of the slave; but no philosopher attempts to limit what ownership of the body might entail. The Christian attempt to think through the implications of slave and slave-owner as equal members of the same community inevitably qualified what could be said about absolute ownership, and offered minimal but real protection to the body of the slave. So it is not surprising that Thomas Aquinas, discussing the limits of obedience to earthly masters or sovereigns,[3] [says] explicitly that while 'a

---

[2]R. Ruston: *Human Rights and the Image of God* (2004).
[3]*Summa theologiae*: IIa IIae 104.5.

human being is bound to obey another in matters external to the body, in those things that affect the nature of the body, no one is bound to obey another human being, but to obey God alone – for instance, in matters to do with the body's sustenance or the begetting of children.' A slave cannot be commanded, for example, to starve to death; nor can he or she be prohibited from deciding on marriage or celibacy.

The principle that has been established is that the human body cannot in the Christian scheme of things be regarded as an item of property. It is not just that I have an 'ownership' of my body that is not transferable, though some moralists (including a few recent Christian writers) have tried to argue something like this; it is rather that the whole idea of ownership is inappropriate. I may talk about 'my body' in a phrase that parallels 'my house' or 'my car', but it should be obvious that there is a radical difference. I can't change it for another, I can't acquire more than one of it, I cannot survive the loss of it. The body (and this is where Aquinas and the tradition associated with him significantly refuses to accept a separation of 'soul' and 'body' as entities existing side by side) is the organ of the soul's meaning: it is the medium in which the conscious subject communicates, and there is no communication without it. To protect the body, to love the body, is to seek to sustain the means of communication that secure a place within human discourse. And so a claim to control the body absolutely, to the point where you could be commanded to deny your body what is needed for its life, would be a refusal to allow another to communicate, to make sense of themselves. The ultimate form of slavery would be a situation in which your body was made to carry the meanings or messages of another subject and never permitted to *say* in word or gesture what was distinctive for itself as the embodiment of a sense-making consciousness.

My own relation to my body is not that of an owner to an object; and to recognize another material thing as a human body is to recognize that it is not reducible in this way to an object among others. In that it is a means of communication, it cannot be simply instrumental to another's will or purpose. It is significant that Aquinas uses the examples he does. The nurture of the body is, for humans, more than an instinctive business; it requires thought and a measure of liberty. And the sexual involvement or non-involvement of the body is a primary locus for the making of sense; denial of this liberty is the denial of something absolutely fundamental (which is why sexual abuse is indeed a prime instance of rights being violated, the body becoming an instrument for someone else's 'meanings', a tool for the construction of another person's sense-making). The recognition of a body as a human body is, in this framework, the foundation of recognizing the rights of another; and to recognize a body as a human body is to recognize that it is a vehicle of communication. It is not a recondite point. The state of mind in which someone is unable to grasp that another's body is a site of feeling and so of consciousness and so of communication is routinely regarded as seriously distorted, whether we are talking of the difficulties of the extreme end of the autism spectrum or of the plainly psychotic. Our ordinary human interchange simply and straightforwardly depends upon understanding any apparently human body we encounter as in some sense a potential communicator with me. And when in the past people have sought to justify slavery or other forms of institutionalised dehumanizing, it has been necessary to restrict, often expensively and dramatically, their opportunity to communicate and to belittle their ability to do so. In George Steiner's extraordinary story 'The Portage to San Cristobal of A.H.', in which a group of Jewish agents have been given the task of kidnapping an aged Hitler from his South American hideaway, they are strictly instructed not to allow him to speak to them, because that will force them to see him as a human like themselves.

One advantage of putting the issue in these terms is that it takes us away from the more unhelpful aspects of those rights theories that stress the grounding of rights in human dignity, but then associate human dignity with a particular set of capacities. The danger of these is that, by trying to identify a list of essential capacities, it becomes possible to identify criteria according to which full claims to human rights may be granted or withheld. The right of the imperfectly rational person – whether the child or the person with mental disabilities – may be put in question if we stipulate a capacity for reasoned self-consciousness as a condition for acknowledging rights. And to speak of the right of the body as such casts a different light on the sensitive issue of the right of the unborn; the unanswerable question of when embryonic material becomes a 'person', let alone when it acquires a soul, still assumes a basic dualism about the body and its inhabitant or proprietor – where the way in which we ought to be framing the question is in terms of what counts as bodily continuity and what can be said about the 'communicative' dimension of the organic life of the unborn, how even the foetus requires to be seen and understood as expressing something to us in its character as an individual human organism.

But that is a complex set of arguments, and my aim for now is simply to establish that recognizing the human body as a human body, that is as a system of communication, by no means exclusively rational, let alone verbal, is fundamental for understanding why we should want to speak of rights at all, of equal liberties that are rooted in the liberty to 'make sense', that is to engage in communication. As I have said, it is in one way only to spell out the act of faith we make every time we engage in human communication at all. Yet behind that routine act lies something else, given that many human societies have in practice assumed that some human bodies are not worth communicating with or receiving communication from. Hence the point of excavating the theological insights that have moved us irreversibly in the direction that leads towards universal doctrines of right. Grasping that the body cannot be an item of property is one of the things that is established by the Christian doctrine of communion in, and shared obedience to, Christ. The doctrine affirms that the body of every other individual is related to its maker and saviour before it is related to any human system of power. This in turn implies that there is a level of human identity or selfhood that cannot be taken over by any other person's will – a level of human identity both bodily and subjective or interior. And this belongs with the recognition that the body *speaks,* that it is the way I make myself present to myself and to others. This holds true even for the most inarticulate, or those whose communications are hardest to decode: to put it as vividly as I can, they still have *faces.* Over against those who want to locate human dignity in the distinctive structure of the human self, a position which still skirts the risks of setting *conditions* for dignity, I want to propose that the character of the body as the vehicle of language is what is basic here.

Michael Zuckert, in a careful and interesting essay entitled 'Human Dignity and the Basis of Justice: freedom, rights, and the self'[4] makes a strong case for beginning from the character of the self as a mental structure allowing human beings to understand themselves as agents with an identity that continues through time and a capacity for envisaging future situations as resulting from present decisions. This is surely what is most irreducibly unique about us, and thus what grounds a universal moral code. But I believe he weakens his case by speaking of the self (following Locke) as proprietor of its experiences ('The relation of the rights-bearer to his property is remarkably parallel to his relation to his self'[5]). The embodied self as communicator, I suggest, is more than the self-conscious organizer of experience into patterns of continuity through time, past and future; it can survive the absence of this sort of self-awareness without forfeiting its claim to be treated as possessed of equal liberty in the basic sense defined earlier. Given the much-chronicled history of the abuse, psychological, physical and sexual, of the mentally challenged, of small children or sufferers from dementia, it is crucial to clarify our grounds for regarding them as protected from being made the carriers of the desires and purposes of others; if we begin from the recognition of them as embodied in the same sense that we are, we have such a clear foundation, in a way that I am not sure we can have even on so sophisticated a version of capacity-theory as Zuckert's.

If this is correct, the irreducible core of human rights is the liberty to make sense as a bodily subject; which means that the inviolability of the body itself is where we should start in thinking about rights. 'Man is "created equal"', wrote the poet and artist David Jones in the early 1940s, 'in the sense that all men belong to a form-creating group of creatures – and all men have unalienable rights with respect to that equal birth right';[6] and that form-creating character is anchored most simply and primitively in the character of what we mean by the very notion of a body (as opposed to an object). It is true, of course, that while the sort of Christian thinking represented by Thomas Aquinas laid the foundations for this, it still accepted extreme physical punishment, including death, for transgression, and of course did not understand the necessary freedom to determine the pattern of one's sexual life as a charter for

---

[4]*The Hedgehog Review* 9.3 (Fall 2007), pp.32–48 [a special issue on human dignity and justice].
[5]Ibid., p.47.
[6]D. Jones: *Epoch and Artist* (London, 1959), p.90.

everyone to shape their own destinies irrespective of the Church's teaching. The implications of Aquinas's view still allow the state to say that it will limit the bodily freedom of some of its citizens when that freedom threatens the freedom of others – though, centuries on from Aquinas, we have taken on board more fully the need for punishment both to respect the essential physical dignity of the punished, and to be capable of rational communication to the punished. The basic concept of right with which Aquinas works itself puts in question capital punishment or humiliating and damaging physical penalties. It is what grounds the modern refusal of legitimacy to torture, degrading or humiliating punishment or even indefinite detention without charge; significant markers in the age of Guantanamo or Abu Ghraib, and at least a significant part of the argument about the time limits for detention now being discussed in our own legislature. Likewise, this view allows the Church to say that there is a limit on morally acceptable options for sexual life; although we would not now understand this as licensing a restriction by law on the decisions people may make in this area. We are free to make bad or inadequate sense of our bodily lives, and the legal restriction of this, beyond the obvious protections of the vulnerable, would have to be seen as outside the powers of rulers. If the state legislates against sexual violence and abuse, as it must, it is because of the recognition that this is an area in which the liberty to make sense of or with one's own body is most often put at risk by predatory behaviour on the part of others.

So: equal liberty is at root inseparable from the equality of being embodied. Rights belong not to the person who can demonstrate capacity or rationality, but to any organism that can be recognized as a human body, at any stage of its organic development. If the body cannot be property, it will always be carrying meanings or messages that are inalienably its own. And this opens up the second area in which aspects of Christian theology offer a foundation for a discourse of universal rights. Thus far, the emphasis has been upon the view from within, as it were – the body as carrier of the soul's meaning, the body as 'formed', given intelligible shape, by the continuing self called into being by God. But the process by which the body realizes its communicative nature, by which it becomes concretely and actively a locus of meaning, is a process in which the body *receives* and digests communication. The individual communicates meaningfully when s/he is decoding and responding to the meanings that are present to him or her; the full development of the particular body's freedom to communicate is realized in the process of understanding, managing and responding to the communications that are being received.

The human other is thus essential to my own growth as a communicative being, a bearer of meaningful messages that cannot be silenced; my own liberty not to be silenced, not to have my body reduced to someone else's instrument, is nourished by the equal liberty of the other not to be silenced. And, in the framework we have been using, this is identified as the central feature of the community created by the Christian gospel. Slave and owner are not merely bound to a common divine Master, they are bound in a relation of mutuality according to which each becomes the bearer of necessary gifts to the other. The relation of each to the Master is such that each is given some unique contribution to the common life, so that no one member of the community is able fully to realize their calling and their possibilities without every other. Not abusing or killing the slave is, for the slave-owner, the necessary implication of recognizing that the slave is going to be his or her benefactor in ways that may never be visible or obvious, but are nonetheless vital.

The dignity accorded to the human other is not, then, a recognition that they may be better than they seem, but simply a recognition that what they have to say (welcome or unwelcome, intelligible or unintelligible, convergent or divergent) could in certain circumstances be the gift of God. Not every human other is a fellow-member of the Body of Christ in the biblical sense; but the universal command to preach the gospel to all prohibits any conclusion that this or that person is incapable of ever hearing and answering God's invitation, and therefore mandates an attitude of receptivity towards them. Not silencing the other or forcing their communication into your own agenda is part of remaining open to the communication of God – which may come even through the human other who is most repellent or opaque to sympathy. The recognition of a dignity that grounds the right to be heard is the recognition of my own need to receive as fully as I can what is being communicated to me by another being made by God. It compels that stepping back from control or manipulation of the other which we so often seek for our security, so as to hear what we cannot generate for ourselves. And it should be clear, incidentally, that this is an argument that also grounds whatever we might want to say about the 'right' of the non-human world to have an integrity not wholly at the mercy of human planning.

To found human rights on the body's liberty to express its own message, and the need for all embodied human beings to receive each other's meaningful communication in order for them to be who and what they are, removes from the argument those elements of conditionality which can creep in if we speak too glibly about capacities, whether rational or moral. Nicholas Wolterstorff, in the special issue of the *Hedgehog Review* already quoted, notes the way in which some other contributors insist that the discourse of human rights and dignity expresses simply 'an explication of what it is to treat humans as humans'; but he very reasonably goes on to ask why in particular circumstances I should treat *this* human being as a human being, if, for example, I conclude that s/he is a poor or inadequate specimen of humanity. If the appeal to treating humans as humans is not to be purely assertive or tautologous, we need more.[7] Something related to language about the image of God seems called for – but we need also to be aware that this language can't just be 'mentioned' as if it instantly provided a clear rationale for rights as we understand them.[8]

---

[7] *Hedgehog Review,* pp. 68–9.
[8] Ibid., p.65.

My purpose in these reflections has been to suggest precisely what might be involved in doing more than 'mentioning' the biblical themes. Is this, then, to argue that we simply cannot talk about human rights intelligibly if we do not have a religious or even a Christian foundation for doing so? Given that there is already more than one essay in grounding human rights in traditions other than Christianity (Abdulaziz Sachedina's work is a case in point, as seen in his contribution to the *Hedgehog* symposium quoted), it may be rash to make excessive claims for Christianity here. But the fact is that the question of foundations for the discourse of non-negotiable rights is not one that lends itself to simple resolution in secular terms; so it is not at all odd if diverse ways of framing this question in religious terms flourish so persistently. The uncomfortable truth is that a purely secular account of human rights is always going to be problematic if it attempts to establish the language of rights as a supreme and non-contestable governing concept in ethics. MacIntyre's argument, with which we began, alerts us to the anxiety and the tension that is hidden within the classical Enlightenment discourse of rights, the sense of having to manage the effects of a moral bereavement; and the development of that discourse in the ways we have witnessed in the late twentieth century does little to diminish the anxiety or resolve the tension. The question of whether there is anything at all that is quite strictly non-negotiable about human dignity – whether, for example, we might be permitted to revisit the consensus about torture when faced with the 'captured terrorist and ticking bomb' scenario beloved of some political ethicists – is not academic. Our instinct seems to be that something has to be secured over against the claims of *raison d'etat* in the name of a human 'form of life' beyond choice and convenience.

Sabina Lovibond, in her brilliant essay on *Realism and Imagination in Ethics,* has some pertinent reflections on Wittgenstein's remark that 'justification comes to an end': that is, that there comes a point where we have to stop arguing and accept that we have reached a level that is recognized as basic for any kind of human thinking.[9] 'Justification', producing reasons for doing this rather than that, comes to an end, she argues, 'not because we get bored with it, but because rational discourse unfolds within a setting not chosen by ourselves' – a setting which she, with both Wittgenstein and Hegel, associates with the fact of embodiment. When we grasp that our embodied state is the condition of everything else we might want to say about thinking in general and ethics in particular, we have arrived at the point where it no longer makes sense to ask for 'justification'. To speak of non-negotiable rights is to attempt some explication of this 'not chosen' dimension of our reality. And to be able to assess or even prioritize the wildly varied entitlements that are currently called 'rights' means developing some means of seeing how far, in a specific social context, this or that claimed entitlement reflects what is required for participation in any recognizable thing we could call human culture and discourse; how far it is

---

[9]S. Lovibond: *Realism and Imagination in Ethics* (Minneapolis MN, 1983), p.215.

inseparable from the imperative to allow the body the liberty to say what it means to say. We may, for instance, feel instinctively that the right to a paid vacation belongs to a different order from the right to fair trial; yet in certain economic conditions, guaranteed freedom for leisure is an intelligible aspect of possessing adequate bodily/communicative liberty.

The idea of a pattern of embodied interaction in which every body, literally, is equipped to 'say' what it has it in it to say, in intelligible exchange (which means more than a chorus of individual self-expressions), is, for Lovibond, the heart of an ethic that can seriously claim universality and objectivity, 'realism'. I would only add that, while this is an absolutely accurate account of the formal shape of a universal ethic (and thus one that can do justice to the language of inalienable right) it still leaves some unfinished business. I have interpreted the New Testament texts about slavery so as to suggest that the recognition that it is impossible to own a human body is rooted not only in the recognition of how the body works as a communicative organism, but in the conviction that the bare fact of embodied reality 'encodes' a gift to be offered by each to all, a primitive communication by the creator; the inviolability of the body is ultimately grounded in the prior relation of each embodied subject to God. And, as I have hinted here (and developed further elsewhere, as in the essays in this book on environmental issues), this has some application for the rest of the material order as well.

Political and legal philosophy is unlikely to arrive at complete convergence with theology in any imaginable future; but the way in which a theology may propose a frame for political and legal questions is not the less important for that. The theological perspective as I have tried to outline it here is, at least, a way of insisting that we should not pretend that the discourse of universal ethics and inalienable right has a firmer foundation than it actually has. If the Enlightenment has left us in some measure bereaved, it is important to accept that, and to ask what are the most secure foundations that can still be laid for our universalist aspirations. We should beware of looking for easy refuge in bare assertion or brisk functionalism about rights: but it is also important to grasp that universalism itself is not a simple and self-evident idea and that there are various ways of conceiving it outside the strict Enlightenment framework. Among those ways will be the various religious modes of imagining universal destiny or equal human dignity. These, I suggest, need to be engaged with, rather than dismissed as irrational or regressive. It may be that the most important service that can be offered by religious commitment where human rights are concerned is to prevent any overlooking of the issue of how to establish a 'non-negotiable' foundation for the whole discourse. As in other areas of political or social thinking, theology is one of those elements that continue to pose questions about the legitimacy of what is said and done in society, about the foundations of law itself. The secularist may not have an answer and may not be convinced that the religious believer has an answer that can be generally accepted; but our discussion of social and political ethics will be a great deal poorer if we cannot acknowledge the force of the question.

35. Violence and Peace: Discussion Questions

Is the use of violence necessary for the rightful exercise of governmental authority?
What is the significance of eschatology to questions of violence and peace?
Is Christianity inherently violent? Are all 'religions' inherently violent?

VI

Liberalism and Democracy

Introduction by Anna Rowlands

While the first generation of post-war political theologians opted for a dual critique of modernity and the church, the second generation of political theologians have chosen to focus more sharply on the relationship between liberalism, democracy and Christian faith. This focus has produced both starkly critical, even rhetorically oppositional, accounts but also more constructive reappraisals. In the selections below we include a range of voices representing a kaleidoscope of views. At stake in these writings is the basic definitional question: what do we mean when we use the term 'liberalism'? Are we referring pre-eminently to a theory of government, a normative story of what it means to be human, an historical era, an ethical theory, a series of particular political practices? How might we construe the relationship between a liberal political system and a capitalist market system, between freedom, production and consumption? These are hotly disputed questions.

Given Thomas Hobbes's status as the first theorist of the modern state and his frequent and contested invocation by second-generation political theologians, this section begins with an extract from *Leviathan*. *Leviathan* was written in the context of the aftermath of the English civil war (1642–69) and is dominated by the tensions between congregationalist and hierarchical political imaginations. The extracts presented here cover Hobbes's outline of the nature of society and his theory of the state. Hobbes famously posits human origins in a war of all against all, presents self-preservation as a natural desire and a right, and argues that it is through the social contract that individuals negotiate this tension between innate violence and a desire to be at peace. This contract, however, holds only through the rule of an absolute sovereign. While Hobbes retains Luther's pre-liberal focus on the authority of the ruler and offers an extensive account of the remit of temporal power, Hobbes's doctrine is now shorn of true transcendence, and therefore also of any real theory of resistance. The absence of a more conventional doctrine of God does not prevent this text being saturated with religious and theological language and imagery. The extraordinary woodcut made for the front cover of Leviathan portrays this strikingly and with un-mistakable theological resonance: the two swords of ecclesial and secular power are held by the one sovereign, whose very body – rising from the land itself – is made up of the congregation of his people.

A contrasting liberal voice can be found in the writings of Conservative British philosopher Edmund Burke. *Reflections on the Revolution in France*, a text that offers a vision of a society rooted in both a social contract and a tradition that embraces a formal and independent ecclesial dimension, was written in the space of a year following the French Revolution of 1789[1]. We include mention of Burke here (and see reference to the text in the footnote, if you wish to read further) because he has been a critical voice in the development of both conservative and liberal strands of political theology. Having originally suspended judgment on the situation in France, Burke was propelled into action by the events of 5–6 October 1789, and by a sermon given in favour of the Revolution by the English Dissenter Richard Price. Burke makes clear his defence of tradition and convention and his desire to uphold the virtues of a mixed polity. Democracy and monarchy in their undiluted forms were both equally dangerous forms of government, although both might play their part in a balanced, gradually evolving system. Burke argues for a politics of virtue rooted in active intermediate associations, an established relationship between church and state, and a system of prescriptive rather than abstract rights. Burke was alarmed by the rise of what he considered abstract metaphysical accounts of the rights of man and instead argued for maintenance of rights rooted in the legal language of property, inheritance, institution and trust.

In contrast to Hobbes, Burke argues for a dual form of social contract. Burke gradually comes to see that the initial contract that forms the basis for civil society appears more as a form of mysterious covenant, with providential dimensions, than a deliberate human choice, and as such it is best maintained through the practices of convention and tradition. Echoing (perhaps unwittingly) Aquinas's theory of justice, Burke views civil society as an expression of an intergenerational eternal society linking the living, the dead and the not yet born. Nonetheless, Burke conceives the second form of social contract, which founds human government, as a thoroughly human action, rooted in the exercise of human wisdom. Burke was strongly critical of the attempt to remove religious institutions from public roles and warned that theological heterodoxy and doctrinal upheavals brought with them political consequences. Importantly, Burke saw limits to the role of religion in politics; he was deeply suspicious of what he called 'political theology' and theological politicians, especially those who chose to preach politics from their pulpits! Nonetheless, his own work has provided a critical source for later political theologians reflecting on the character of liberalism.

The second grouping of texts in this section are taken from the critical debates about liberalism and democracy that have irrupted within political theology since

---

[1]Edmund Burke, *Reflections on the Revolution in France: A Critical Edition*, ed., J. C. D. Clark (Stanford, CA: Stanford University Press, 2001).

the early 1980s. We begin with two texts from Stanley Hauerwas and John Milbank, the two contemporary political theologians most associated with the Christian theological critique of liberalism. It is worth noting that both contributions would be as much as home in Section III of this volume, 'The church and the political', for both authors have made distinguished contributions to the political theory of the church. Nonetheless they appear in this section because each offers a distinct analysis of failures of liberalism. Hauerwas argues starkly that it is not that liberal democracy has yet to be properly tried but that it has been tried and found wanting. Both authors agree that Christianity and liberalism are antithetical in their account of selfhood, concepts of authority and liberty, and interpretation of concepts of right shorn of concepts of the good. To express this positively, both authors claim that justice requires a concept of the good, the individual is better cast as a dependent and relational person, and freedom is grounded first in the action of a Creator.

Reviving claims for the distinctiveness of Christian theological accounts of the political, both Milbank and Hauerwas draw our attention to the temptation Christianity faces to seek to integrate without contradiction into liberal democracies. Both authors also draw clear connections between liberalism and capitalism, between narratives of freedom and practices of consumption, politics of fear and economic narratives of scarcity. For each author only a distinctive form of Christian ecclesial practice can counter such logic. Hauerwas focuses especially on the complex psychology of liberalism, recognizing that in some sense 'we are all liberals', and on the challenge to practise the church's story: to exhibit the kind of community made possible when trust, and not fear rules. Hauerwas places his focus on the life of the church and is unwilling to be drawn into contributing to the long tradition of Christian reflection on forms of government (see thinkers in Sections I and II especially). Milbank, by contrast, offers a vision of a renewed form of contemporary politics, including forms of government, drawing its inspiration from Anglican, Roman Catholic and Orthodox Catholic social traditions. Grounded in a Pauline theology of gift, Milbank argues for a re-Christianization of politics through a Thomist-inspired mixed polity formed through a combination of monarchic, aristocratic and corporate elements. Rejecting a focus on the nation-state in favour of a theory of subsidiarity, he calls for a renewal of regional and transnational cooperation focused on enacting the common good. Thus a narrow politics of liberalism might give way to a politics of 'liberality' or generosity.

In the final grouping of texts in this section we hear from those who fear that Hauerwas, Milbank and their colleagues have produced accounts of the relationship of liberalism, democracy and Christian faith that are, by turn, a little too coherent, oppositional, singular and purist. By contrast each of the three voices we have selected offer critical rereadings of the relationship between liberalism and Christian theology.

Christopher Insole's 'Theology and Politics: The Intellectual History of Liberalism' draws particular attention to the question of what is at stake in the way that we define 'liberalism'. He outlines his suspicion of both the tendency to focus on singular intellectual histories of liberalism and the corresponding sense of an emerging 'definition tailor made to fit the evaluation'. Deploying a playful image, Insole argues that rather than attempting to find the posed image that can be snapped by the camera in freeze frame and tucked into the album labelled 'liberalism', theologians need to approach liberalism first and foremost as a complex and shifting set of practices. These practices include the restriction in the use of coercive power to sustain peace and justice, a framework of rights and liberties, the separation of powers, provision for a mixed constitution, representation, the rule of law, and accountability and transparency through freedom of speech and association. Arguing for a 'family resemblances' concept of liberalism over and against a single 'liberal' narrative arc, Insole suggests that such a focus on practices is not a denial of the presence of metaphysics, but a way for us to grasp the very complexity and plurality of metaphysical claims that underlie the contradictory manifestations of liberalism as lived reality. He notes that such an approach intensifies the role of the theologian, for the competing normative strands within different strata of liberalism have their ultimate grounding in theological convictions and disputes.

The second critical reappraisal of liberalism and theology is taken from Eric Gregory's writings on the Augustinian civic virtue tradition. Gregory focuses his account less on a reading of 'what Augustine really meant …' and more on a history of Augustine's reception within the twentieth century. He argues for the presence of three main schools of twentieth-century Augustinianism: a realist school focused on sin, pessimism and the morally ambivalent character of liberal democracy and the corresponding virtue of hope; a second school which suspends the category of the good in favour of a concept of justice as fairness; and a third, less dominant, school which has tried to foster a form of civic virtue Augustinianism. Gregory sees his work as a contribution to developing this third stream of thought in new ways. But Gregory is equally aware of the challenging judgements of political philosophers – from Hannah Arendt and Martha Nussbaum to Romand Coles – about the limitations of Augustine for use in a liberal age. Such thinkers view Augustine as a tantalizingly brilliant but ultimately worryingly other-worldly thinker, unable to take citizenship, difference and tolerance seriously enough.

In contrast to Augustinian 'pessimists' and critics alike, Gregory argues for a concept of love and sin in which each category constrains the other. Gregory presents the reader with a political theology capable of speaking of love – and indeed the emotions and virtues more generally – but which understands the way that vice pits love 'against pretty tough odds'. Augustine focuses on the presence of disordered loves, loves which become possessive, excessive and self-absorbed. Gregory asks, might we engage Augustine in service of ways of being political that enable us to forge non-possessive relations to the good? Can we imagine ways to seek the good of self and neighbor, in which coercion is constrained and limited by love? To begin to imagine such a politics requires us to be willing to acknowledge and work with our human dependency and vulnerability. This he sees as the grounds of an Augustinian liberalism that engages rather than refuses the task of social criticism and expands an ever-contracting public space.

Finally, we turn to the (often overlooked) Christian theologies of the East. Addressing the debate about the compatibility between liberalism and democracy in a post-Communist Eastern European and Orthodox context, Aristotle Papanikolaou notes parallels between discussions about the 'clash of civilisations' and the compatibility of Islam with liberalism. He warns that any attempt to argue that Orthodoxy must oppose liberalism should be treated with some suspicion. He is particularly concerned to note the tendencies within Western Christian theology to argue for an absolute incompatibility between liberalism and Christian anthropology, concepts of human being, which can be deployed by unreflective forms of Eastern Orthodoxy to justify worrying forms of ecclesial political hegemony. However, his main target is binary and Gnostic forms of Orthodox thought which spiritualize the central Orthodox idea of *theosis* (divine-human communion) and fail to work through to the full materialist consequences of this mystical teaching. Papanikolaou offers a redefinition of the idea of *theosis*, insisting that all human life, including the political is taken up with the struggle to embody the communion of Creator and creature.

Echoing Eric Gregory's reading of Augustine, and Insole's argument for a greater focus on practices, Papanikolaou suggests that the human task is to learn how to love: fulfilling the love command in a context of sin and struggle requires ascetical discernment and practices. The particular practices that come to define the heart of the political in ways that resonate strongly for the Christian tradition centre on the task of forming relations with strangers. He counters the politics of vice (motivated by fear, anger or hatred) with a call for Christian politics-as-asceticism. This is not to confuse the ecclesial and political but to argue that the truly mystical *is* political: how Christians act in the world affects the political space; practices of Eucharist, truth-telling, forgiveness are ecclesial political practices rooted in the life of communion. This is the more ecclesial side of the political-mystical coin invoked by Dorothee Soelle, discussed in Section II. In making his case, Papanikolaou returns us once again to the mystical and ascetic practices that might ground fresh directions of renewal within political theology.

36. Thomas Hobbes – Extracts from Leviathan

NATURE (the Art whereby God hath made and governes the World) is by the *Art* of man, as in many other things, so in this also imitated, that it can make an Artificial Animal. For seeing life is but a motion of Limbs, the begining whereof is in some principall part within; why may we not say, that all *Automata* (Engines that move themselves by springs and wheeles as doth a watch) have an artificiall life? For what is the *Heart,* but a *Spring*; and the *Nerves,* but so many *Strings*; and the *Joynts,* but so many *Wheeles,* giving motion to the whole Body, such as was intended by the Artificer? *Art* goes yet further, imitating that Rationall and most excellent worke of Nature, *Man.* For by Art is created that great LEVIATHAN called a COMMON-WEALTH, or STATE, (in latine CIVITAS) which is but an Artificiall Man; though of greater stature and strength than the Naturall, for whose protection and defence it was intended; and in which, the *Soveraignty* is an Artificiall *Soul,* as giving life and motion to the whole body; The *Magistrates,* and other *Officers* of Judicature and Execution, artificiall *Joynts*; *Reward* and *Punishment* (by which fastned to the seate of the Soveraignty, every joynt and member is moved to performe his duty) are the *Nerves,* that do the same in the Body Naturall; The *Wealth* and *Riches* of all the particular members, are the *Strength*; *Salus Populi* (the *peoples safety*) its *Businesse*; *Counsellors,* by whom all things needfull for it to know, are suggested unto it, are the *Memory*; *Equity* and *Lawes,* an artificiall *Reason* and *Will*; *Concord, Health*; *Sedition, Sicknesse*; and *Civill war, Death.* Lastly, the *Pacts* and *Covenants,* by which the parts of this Body Politique were at first made, set together, and united, resemble that *Fiat,* or the *Let us make man,* pronounced by God in the Creation.

To describe the Nature of this Artificiall man, I will consider

First, the *Matter* thereof, and the *Artificer,* both which is *Man.*
Secondly, *How,* and by what *Covenants* it is made; what are the *Rights* and *just Power* or *Authority* of a *Soveraigne*; and what it is that *preserveth* and *dissolveth* it.
Thirdly, what is a *Christian Common-wealth.*
Lastly, what is the *Kingdome of Darkness.*

Concerning the first, there is a saying much usurped of late, That *Wisedome* is acquired, not by reading of *Books,* but of *Men.* Consequently whereunto, those persons, that for the most part can give no other proof of being wise, take great delight to shew what they think they have read in men, by uncharitable censures of one another behind their backs. But there is another saying not of late understood, by which they might learn truly to read one another, if they would take the pains; and that is, *Nosce teipsum, Read thy self*: which was not meant, as it is now used, to countenance, either the barbarous state of men in power, towards their inferiors; or to encourage men of low degree, to a sawcie behaviour towards their betters; But to teach us, that for the similitude of the thoughts, and Passions of one man, to the thoughts, and Passions of another, whosoever looketh into himself, and considereth what he doth, when he does *think, opine, reason, hope, feare,* &c, and upon what grounds; he shall thereby read and know, what are the thoughts, and Passions of all other men, upon the like occasions. I say the similitude of *Passions,* which are the same in all men, *desire, feare, hope,* &c; not the similitude of the *objects* of the Passions, which are the things *desired, feared, hoped,* &c: for these the constitution individuall, and particular education do so vary, and they are so easie to be kept from our knowledge, that the characters of mans heart, blotted and confounded as they are, with dissembling, lying, counterfeiting, and erroneous doctrines, are legible onely to him that searcheth hearts. And though by mens actions wee do discover their designe sometimes; yet to do it without comparing them with our own, and distinguishing all circumstances, by which the case may come to be altered, is to decypher without a key, and be for the most part deceived, by too much trust, or by too much diffidence; as he that reads, is himself a good or evil man.

But let one man read another by his actions never so perfectly, it serves him onely with his acquaintance, which are but few. He that is to govern a whole Nation, must read in himself, not this, or that particular man; but Man-kind: which though it be hard to do, harder than to learn any Language, or Science; yet, when I shall have set down my own reading orderly, and perspicuously, the pains left another, will be onely to consider, if he also find not the same in himself. For this kind of Doctrine, admitteth no other Demonstration.

...

Chap. XIII.

Of the Naturall Condition of Mankind, as Concerning Their Felicity, and Misery.

Nature hath made men so equall, in the faculties of body, and mind; as that though there bee found one man sometimes manifestly stronger in body, or of quicker mind then another; yet when all is reckoned together, the difference between man, and man, is not so considerable, as that one man can thereupon claim to himselfe any benefit, to which another may not pretend, as well as he. For as to the strength of body, the weakest has strength enough to kill the strongest, either by secret machination, or by confederacy with others, that are in the same danger with himselfe.

And as to the faculties of the mind, (setting aside the arts grounded upon words, and especially that skill of proceeding upon generall, and infallible rules, called Science; which very few have, and but in few things; as being not a native faculty, born with us; nor attained, (as Prudence,) while we look after somewhat els,) I find yet a greater equality amongst men, than that of strength. For Prudence, is but Experience; which equall time, equally bestowes on all men, in those things they equally apply themselves unto. That which may perhaps make such equality incredible, is but a vain conceipt of ones owne wisdome, which almost all men think they have in a greater degree, than the Vulgar; that is, than all men but themselves, and a few others, whom by Fame, or for concurring with themselves, they approve. For such is the nature of men, that howsoever they may acknowledge many others to be more witty, or more eloquent, or more learned; Yet they will hardly believe there be many so wise as themselves: For they see their own wit at hand, and other mens at a distance. But this proveth rather that men are in that point equall, than unequall. For there is not ordinarily a greater signe of the equall distribution of any thing, than that every man is contented with his share.

From this equality of ability, ariseth equality of hope in the attaining of our Ends. And therefore if any two men desire the same thing, which neverthelesse they cannot both enjoy, they become enemies; and in the way to their End, (which is principally their owne conservation, and sometimes their delectation only,) endeavour to destroy, or subdue one an other. And from hence it comes to passe, that where an Invader hath no more to feare, than an other mans single power; if one plant, sow, build, or possesse a convenient Seat, others may probably be expected to come prepared with forces united, to dispossesse, and deprive him, not only of the fruit of his labour, but also of his life, or liberty. And the Invader again is in the like danger of another.

And from this diffidence of one another, there is no way for any man to secure himselfe, so reasonable, as Anticipation; that is, by force, or wiles, to master the persons of all men he can, so long, till he see no other power great enough to endanger him: And this is no more than his own conservation requireth, and is generally allowed. Also because there be some, that taking pleasure in contemplating their own power in the acts of conquest, which they pursue farther than their security requires; if others, that otherwise would be glad to be at ease within modest bounds, should not by invasion increase their power, they would not be able, long time, by standing only on their defence, to subsist. And by consequence, such augmentation of dominion over men, being necessary to a mans conservation, it ought to be allowed him.

Againe, men have no pleasure, (but on the contrary a great deale of griefe) in keeping company, where there is no power able to over-awe them all. For every man looketh that his companion should value him, at the same rate he sets upon himselfe: And upon all signes of contempt, or undervaluing, naturally endeavours, as far as he dares (which amongst them that have no common power to keep them in quiet, is far enough to make them destroy each other,) to extort a greater value from his contemners, by dommage; and from others, by the example.

So that in the nature of man, we find three principall causes of quarrell. First, Competition; Secondly, Diffidence; Thirdly, Glory.

The first, maketh men invade for Gain; the second, for Safety; and the third, for Reputation. The first use Violence, to make themselves Masters of other mens persons, wives, children, and cattell; the second, to defend them; the third, for trifles, as a word, a smile, a different opinion, and any other signe of undervalue, either direct in their Persons, or by reflexion in their Kindred, their Friends, their Nation, their Profession, or their Name.

Hereby it is manifest, that during the time men live without a common Power to keep them all in awe, they are in that condition which is called Warre; and such a warre, as is of every man, against every man. For WARRE, consisteth not in Battell onely, or the act of fighting; but in a tract of time, wherein the Will to contend by Battell is sufficiently known: and therefore the notion of *Time,* is to be considered in the nature of Warre; as it is in the nature of Weather. For as the nature of Foule weather, lyeth not in a showre or two of rain; but in an inclination thereto of many dayes together: So the nature of War, consisteth not in actuall fighting; but in the known disposition thereto, during all the time there is no assurance to the contrary. All other time is PEACE.

Whatsoever therefore is consequent to a time of Warre, where every man is Enemy to every man; the same is consequent to the time, wherein men live without other security, than what their own strength, and their own invention shall furnish them withall. In such condition, there is no place for Industry; because the fruit thereof is uncertain: and consequently no Culture of the Earth; no Navigation, nor use of the commodities that may be imported by Sea; no commodious Building; no Instruments of moving, and removing such things as require much force; no Knowledge of the face of the Earth; no account of Time; no Arts; no Letters; no Society; and which is worst of all, continuall feare, and danger of violent death; And the life of man, solitary, poore, nasty, brutish, and short.

It may seem strange to some man, that has not well weighed these things; that Nature should thus dissociate, and render men apt to invade, and destroy one another: and he may therefore, not trusting to this Inference, made from the Passions, desire perhaps to have the same confirmed by Experience. Let him therefore consider with himselfe, when taking a journey, he armes himselfe, and seeks to go well accompanied; when going to sleep, he locks his dores; when even in his house he locks his chests; and this when he knowes there bee Lawes, and publike Officers, armed, to revenge all injuries shall bee done him; what opinion he has of his fellow subjects, when he rides armed; of his fellow Citizens, when he locks his dores; and of his children, and servants, when he locks his chests. Does he not there as much accuse mankind by his actions, as I do by my words? But neither of us accuse mans nature in it. The Desires, and other Passions of man, are in themselves no Sin. No more are the Actions, that proceed from those Passions, till they know a Law that forbids them: which till Lawes be made they cannot know: nor can any Law be made, till they have agreed upon the Person that shall make it.

It may peradventure be thought, there was never such a time, nor condition of warre as this; and I believe it was never generally so, over all the world: but there are many places, where they live so now. For the savage people in many places of *America,* except the government of small Families, the concord whereof dependeth on naturall lust, have no government at all; and live at this day in that brutish manner, as I said before. Howsoever, it may be perceived what manner of life there would be, where there were no common Power to feare; by the manner of life, which men that have formerly lived under a peacefull government, use to degenerate into, in a civill Warre.

But though there had never been any time, wherein particular men were in a condition of warre one against another; yet in all times, Kings, and Persons of Soveraigne authority, because of their Independency, are in continuall jealousies, and in the state and posture of Gladiators; having their weapons pointing, and their eyes fixed on one another; that is, their Forts, Garrisons, and Guns upon the Frontiers of their Kingdomes; and continuall Spyes upon their neighbours, which is a posture of War. But because they uphold thereby, the Industry of their Subjects; there does not follow from it, that misery, which accompanies the Liberty of particular men.

To this warre of every man against every man, this also is consequent; that nothing can be Unjust. The notions of Right and Wrong, Justice and Injustice have there no place. Where there is no common Power, there is no Law: where no Law, no Injustice. Force, and Fraud, are in warre the two Cardinall vertues. Justice, and Injustice are none of the Faculties neither of the Body, nor Mind. If they were, they might be in a man that were alone in the world, as well as his Senses, and Passions. They are Qualities, that relate to men in Society, not in Solitude. It is consequent also to the same condition, that there be no Propriety, no Dominion, no *Mine* and *Thine* distinct; but onely that to be every mans, that he can get; and for so long, as he can keep it. And thus much for the ill condition, which man by meer Nature is actually placed in; though with a possibility to come out of it, consisting partly in the Passions, partly in his Reason.

The Passions that encline men to Peace, are Feare of Death; Desire of such things as are necessary to commodious living; and a Hope by their Industry to obtain them. And Reason suggesteth convenient Articles of Peace, upon which men may be drawn to agreement. These Articles, are they, which otherwise are called the Lawes of Nature: whereof I shall speak more particularly, in the two following Chapters.

Chap. XIV.

Of the First and Second Naturall Lawes, and of Contracts.

The RIGHT OF NATURE, which Writers commonly call *Jus Naturale,* is the Liberty each man hath, to use his own power, as he will himselfe, for the preservation of his own Nature; that is to say, of his own Life; and consequently, of doing any thing, which in his own Judgement, and Reason, hee shall conceive to be the aptest means thereunto.

By LIBERTY, is understood, according to the proper signification of the word, the absence of externall Impediments: which Impediments, may oft take away part of a mans power to do what hee would; but cannot hinder him from using the power left him, according as his judgement, and reason shall dictate to him.

A LAW OF NATURE, (*Lex Naturalis,*) is a Precept, or generall Rule, found out by Reason, by which a man is forbidden to do, that, which is destructive of his life, or taketh away the means of preserving the same; and to omit, that, by which he thinketh it may be best preserved. For though they that speak of this subject, use to confound *Jus,* and *Lex, Right* and *Law*; yet they ought to be distinguished; because RIGHT, consisteth in liberty to do, or to forbeare; Whereas LAW, determineth, and bindeth to one of them: so that Law, and Right, differ as much, as Obligation, and Liberty; which in one and the same matter are inconsistent.

And because the condition of Man, (as hath been declared in the precedent Chapter) is a condition of Warre of every one against every one; in which case every one is governed by his own Reason; and there is nothing he can make use of, that may not be a help unto him, in preserving his life against his enemyes; It followeth, that in such a condition, every man has a Right to every thing; even to one anothers body. And therefore, as long as this naturall Right of every man to every thing endureth, there can be no security to any man, (how strong or wise soever he be,) of living out the time, which Nature ordinarily alloweth men to live. And consequently it is a precept, or generall rule of Reason, *That every man, ought to endeavour Peace, as farre as he has hope of obtaining it; and when he cannot obtain it, that he may seek, and use, all helps, and advantages of Warre.* The first branch of which Rule, containeth the first, and Fundamentall Law of Nature; which is, *to seek Peace, and follow it.* The Second, the summe of the Right of Nature; which is, *By all means we can, to defend our selves.*

From this Fundamentall Law of Nature, by which men are commanded to endeavour Peace, is derived this second Law; *That a man be willing, when others are so too, as farre-forth, as for Peace, and defence of himselfe he shall think it necessary, to lay down this right to all things; and be contented with so much liberty against other men, as he would allow other men against himselfe.* For as long as every man holdeth this Right, of doing any thing he liketh; so long are all men in the condition of Warre. But if other men will not lay down their Right, as well as he; then there is no Reason for any one, to devest himselfe of his: For that were to expose himselfe to Prey, (which no man is bound to) rather than to dispose himselfe to Peace. This is that Law of the Gospell; *Whatsoever you require that others should do to you, that do ye to them.* And that Law of all men, *Quod tibi fieri non vis, alteri ne feceris.*

To *lay downe* a mans *Right* to any thing, is to *devest* himselfe of the *Liberty,* of hindring another of the benefit of his own Right to the same. For he that renounceth, or passeth away his Right, giveth not to any other man a Right which he had not before; because there is nothing to which every man had not Right by Nature: but onely standeth out of his way, that he may enjoy his own originall Right, without hindrance from him; not without hindrance from another. So that the effect which redoundeth to one man, by another mans defect of Right, is but so much diminution of impediments to the use of his own Right originall.

Right is layd aside, either by simply Renouncing it; or by Transferring it to another. By *Simply* RENOUNCING; when he cares not to whom the benefit thereof redoundeth. By TRANSFERRING; when he intendeth the benefit thereof to some certain person, or persons. And when a man hath in either manner abandoned, or granted away his Right;

then is he said to be OBLIGED, or BOUND, not to hinder those, to whom such Right is granted, or abandoned, from the benefit of it: and that he *Ought,* and it is his DUTY, not to make voyd that voluntary act of his own: and that such hindrance is INJUSTICE, and INJURY, as being *Sine Jure*; the Right being before renounced, or transferred. So that *Injury,* or *Injustice,* in the controversies of the world, is somewhat like to that, which in the disputations of Scholers is called *Absurdity.* For as it is there called an Absurdity, to contradict what one maintained in the Beginning: so in the world, it is called Injustice, and Injury, voluntarily to undo that, which from the beginning he had voluntarily done. The way by which a man either simply Renounceth, or Transferreth his Right, is a Declaration, or Signification, by some voluntary and sufficient signe, or signes, that he cloth so Renounce, or Transferre; or hath so Renounced, or Transferred the same, to him that accepteth it. And these Signes are either Words onely, or Actions onely; or (as it happeneth most often) both Words, and Actions. And the same are the BONDS, by which men are bound, and obliged: Bonds, that have their strength, not from their own Nature, (for nothing is more easily broken than a mans word,) but from Feare of some evill consequence upon the rupture.

Whensoever a man Transferreth his Right, or Renounceth it; it is either in consideration of some Right reciprocally transferred to himselfe; or for some other good he hopeth for thereby. For it is a voluntary act: and of the voluntary acts of every man, the object is some *Good to himselfe.* And therefore there be some Rights, which no man can be understood by any words, or other signes, to have abandoned, or transferred. As first a man cannot lay down the right of resisting them, that assault him by force, to take away his life; because he cannot be understood to ayme thereby, at any Good to himself. The same may be sayd of Wounds, and Chayns, and Imprisonment; both because there is no benefit consequent to such patience; as there is to the patience of suffering another to be wounded, or imprisoned: as also because a man cannot tell, when he seeth men proceed against him by violence, whether they intend his death or not. And lastly the motive, and end for which this renouncing and transferring of Right is introduced, is nothing else but the security of a mans person, in his life, and in the means of so preserving life, as not to be weary of it. And therefore if a man by words, or other signes, seem to despoyle himselfe of the End, for which those signes were intended; he is not to be understood as if he meant it, or that it was his will; but that he was ignorant of how such words and actions were to be interpreted.

The mutuall transferring of Right, is that which men call CONTRACT.

There is difference, between transferring of Right to the Thing; and transferring, or tradition, that is, delivery of the Thing it selfe. For the Thing may be delivered together with the Translation of the Right; as in buying and selling with ready mony; or exchange of goods, or lands: and it may be delivered some time after.

Again, one of the Contractors, may deliver the Thing contracted for on his part, and leave the other to perform his part at some determinate time after, and in the mean time be trusted; and then the Contract on his part, is called PACT, or COVENANT: Or both parts may contract now, to performe hereafter: in which cases, he that is to performe in time to come, being trusted, his performance is called *Keeping of Promise*, or Faith; and the fayling of performance (if it be voluntary) *Violation of Faith*.

When the transferring of Right, is not mutuall; but one of the parties transferreth, in hope to gain thereby friendship, or service from another, or from his friends; or in hope to gain the reputation of Charity, or Magnanimity; or to deliver his mind from the pain of compassion; or in hope of reward in heaven; This is not Contract, but GIFT, FREE-GIFT, GRACE: which words signifie one and the same thing.

Signes of Contract, are either *Expresse*, or *by Inference*. Expresse, are words spoken with understanding of what they signifie: And such words are either of the time *Present*, or *Past*; as, *I Give, I Grant, I have Given, I have Granted, I will that this be yours*: Or of the future; as, *I will Give, I will Grant*: which words of the future are called PROMISE.

Signes by Inference, are sometimes the consequence of Words; sometimes the consequence of Silence; sometimes the consequence of Actions; somtimes the consequence of Forbearing an Action: and generally a signe by Inference, of any Contract, is whatsoever sufficiently argues the will of the Contractor.

Words alone, if they be of the time to come, and contain a bare promise, are an insufficient signe of a Free-gift and therefore not obligatory. For if they be of the time to Come, as, *To morrow I will Give*, they are a signe I have not given yet, and consequently that my right is not transferred, but remaineth till I transferre it by some other Act. But if the words be of the time Present, or Past, as, *I have given, or do give to be delivered to morrow*, then is my to morrows Right given away to day; and that by the vertue of the words, though there were no other argument of my will. And there is a great difference in the signification of these words, *Volo hoc tuum esse cras*, and *Cras dabo*; that is, between *I will that this be thine to morrow*, and, *I will give it thee to morrow*: For the word *I will*, in the former manner of speech, signifies an act of the will Present; but in the later, it signifies a promise of an act of the will to Come: and therefore the former words, being of the Present, transferre a future right; the later, that be of the Future, transferre nothing. But if there be other signes of the Will to transferre a Right, besides Words; then, though the gift be Free, yet may the Right be understood to passe by words of the future: as if a man propound a Prize to him that comes first to the end of a race, The gift is Free; and though the words be of the Future, yet the Right passeth: for if he would not have his words so understood, he should not have let them runne.

In Contracts, the right passeth, not onely where the words are of the time Present, or Past; but also where they are of the Future: because all Contract is mutuall translation, or change of Right; and therefore he that promiseth onely, because he hath already received the benefit for which he promiseth, is to be understood as if he intended the Right should passe: for unlesse he had been content to have his words so understood, the other would not have performed his part first. And for that cause, in buying, and selling, and other acts of Contract, a Promise is equivalent to a Covenant; and therefore obligatory.

He that performeth first in the case of a Contract, is said to MERIT that which he is to receive by the performance of the other; and he hath it as *Due.* Also when a Prize is propounded to many, which is to be given to him onely that winneth; or mony is thrown amongst many, to be enjoyed by them that catch it; though this be a Free gift; yet so to Win, or so to Catch, is to *Merit,* and to have it as DUE. For the Right is transferred in the Propounding of the Prize, and in throwing down the mony; though it be not determined to whom, but by the Event of the contention. But there is between these two sorts of Merit, this difference, that In Contract, I Merit by vertue of my own power, and the Contractors need; but in this case of Free gift, I am enabled to Merit onely by the benignity of the Giver: In Contract, I merit at the Contractors hand that hee should depart with his right; In this case of Gift, I Merit not that the giver should part with his right; but that when he has parted with it, it should be mine, rather than anothers. And this I think to be the meaning of that distinction of the Schooles, between *Meritum congrui,* and *Meritum condigni.* For God Almighty, having promised Paradise to those men (hoodwinkt with carnall desires,) that can walk through this world according to the Precepts, and Limits prescribed by him; they say, he that shall so walk, shall Merit Paradise *Ex congruo.* But because no man can demand a right to it, by his own Righteousnesse, or any other power in himselfe, but by the Free Grace of God onely; they say, no man can Merit Paradise *ex condigno.* This I say, I think is the meaning of that distinction; but because Disputers do not agree upon the signification of their own termes of Art, longer than it serves their turn; I will not affirme any thing of their meaning: onely this I say; when a gift is given indefinitely, as a prize to be contended for, he that winneth Meriteth, and may claime the Prize as Due.

If a Covenant be made, wherein neither of the parties performe presently, but trust one another; in the condition of meer Nature, (which is a condition of Warre of every man against every man,) upon any reasonable suspition, it is Voyd: But if there be a common Power set over them both, with right and force sufficient to compell performance; it is not Voyd. For he that performeth first, has no assurance the other will performe after; because the bonds of words are too weak to bridle mens ambition, avarice, anger, and other Passions, without the feare of some coercive Power; which in the condition of meer Nature, where all men are equall, and judges of the justnesse of their own fears, cannot possibly be supposed. And therfore he which performeth first, does but betray himselfe to his enemy; contrary to the Right (he can never abandon) of defending his life, and means of living.

But in a civill estate, where there is a Power set up to constrain those that would otherwise violate their faith, that feare is no more reasonable; and for that cause, he which by the Covenant is to perform first, is obliged so to do.

The cause of feare, which maketh such a Covenant invalid, must be always something arising after the Covenant made; as some new fact, or other signe of the Will not to performe: else it cannot make the Covenant voyd. For that which could not hinder a man from promising, ought not to be admitted as a hindrance of performing.

He that transferreth any Right, transferreth the Means of enjoying it, as farre as lyeth in his power. As he that selleth Land, is understood to transferre the Herbage, and whatsoever growes upon it; Nor can he that sells a Mill turn away the Stream that drives it. And they that give to a man the Right of government in Soveraignty, are understood to give him the right of levying mony to maintain Souldiers; and of appointing Magistrates for the administration of Justice.

To make Covenants with bruit Beasts, is impossible; because not understanding our speech, they understand not, nor accept of any translation of Right; nor can translate any Right to another: and without mutuall acceptation, there is no Covenant.

To make Covenant with God, is impossible, but by Mediation of such as God speaketh to, either by Revelation supernaturall, or by his Lieutenants that govern under him, and in his Name: For otherwise we know not whether our Covenants be accepted, or not. And therefore they that Vow any thing contrary to any law of Nature, Vow in vain; as being a thing unjust to pay such Vow. And if it be a thing commanded by the Law of Nature, it is not the Vow, but the Law that binds them.

The matter, or subject of a Covenant, is alwayes something that falleth under deliberation; (For to Covenant, is an act of the Will; that is to say an act, and the last act, of deliberation;) and is therefore alwayes understood to be something to come; and which is judged Possible for him that Covenanteth, to performe.

And therefore, to promise that which is known to be Impossible, is no Covenant. But if that prove impossible afterwards, which before was thought possible, the Covenant is valid, and bindeth, (though not to the thing it selfe,) yet to the value; or, if that also be impossible, to the unfeigned endeavour of performing as much as is possible: for to more no man can be obliged.

Men are freed of their Covenants two wayes; by Performing; or by being Forgiven. For Performance, is the naturall end of obligation; and Forgivenesse, the restitution of liberty; as being a re-transferring of that Right, in which the obligation consisted.

Covenants entred into by fear, in the condition of meer Nature, are obligatory. For example, if I Covenant to pay a ransome, or service for my life, to an enemy; I am bound by it. For it is a Contract, wherein one receiveth the benefit of life; the other is to receive mony, or service for it; and consequently, where no other Law (as in the condition, of meer Nature) forbiddeth the performance, the Covenant is valid. Therefore Prisoners of warre, if trusted with the payment of their Ransome, are obliged to pay it: And if a weaker Prince, make a disadvantageous peace with a stronger, for feare; he is bound to keep it; unlesse (as hath been sayd before) there ariseth some new, and just cause of feare, to renew the war. And even in Commonwealths, if I be forced to redeem my selfe from a Theefe by promising him money, I am bound to pay it, till the Civill Law discharge me. For whatsoever I may lawfully do without Obligation, the same I may lawfully Covenant to do through feare: and what I lawfully Covenant, I cannot lawfully break.

A former Covenant, makes voyd a later. For a man that hath passed away his Right to one man to day, hath it not to passe to morrow to another: and therefore the later promise passeth no Right, but is null.

A Covenant not to defend my selfe from force, by force, is alwayes voyd. For (as I have shewed before) no man can transferre, or lay down his Right to save himselfe from Death, Wounds, and Imprisonment, (the avoyding whereof is the onely End of laying down any Right,) and therefore the promise of not resisting force, in no Covenant transferreth any right; nor is obliging. For, though a man may Covenant thus, *Unlesse I do so, or so, kill me*; he cannot Covenant thus, *Unlesse I do so, or so, I will not resist you, when you come to kill me*. For man by nature chooseth the lesser evill, which is danger of death in resisting; rather than the greater, which is certain and present death in not resisting. And this is granted to be true by all men, in that they lead Criminals to Execution, and Prison, with armed men, notwithstanding that such Criminals have consented to the Law, by which they are condemned.

A Covenant to accuse ones selfe, without assurance of pardon, is likewise invalid. For in the condition of Nature, where every man is Judge, there is no place for Accusation: and in the Civill State, the Accusation is followed with Punishment; which being Force, a man is not obliged not to resist. The same is also true, of the Accusation of those, by whose Condemnation a man falls into misery; as of a Father, Wife, or Benefactor. For the Testimony of such an Accuser, if it be not willingly given, is praesumed to be corrupted by Nature; and therefore not to be received: and where a mans Testimony is not to be credited, he is not bound to give it. Also Accusations upon Torture, are not to be reputed as Testimonies. For Torture is to be used but as means of conjecture, and light, in the further examination, and search of truth: and what is in that case confessed, tendeth to the ease of him that is Tortured; not to the informing of the Torturers: and therefore ought not to have the credit of a sufficient Testimony: for whether he deliver himselfe by true, or false Accusation, he does it by the Right of preserving his own life.

The force of Words, being (as I have formerly noted) too weak to hold men to the performance of their Covenants; there are in mans nature, but two imaginable helps to strengthen it. And those are either a Feare of the consequence of breaking their word; or a Glory, or Pride in appearing not to need to breake it. This later is a Generosity too rarely found to be presumed on, especially in the pursuers of Wealth, Command, or sensuall Pleasure; which are the greatest part of Mankind. The Passion to be reckoned upon, is Fear; whereof there be two very generall Objects: one, The Power of Spirits Invisible; the other, The Power of those men they shall therein Offend. Of these two, though the former be the greater Power, yet the feare of the later is commonly the greater Feare. The Feare of the former is in every man, his own Religion: which hath place in the nature of man before Civill Society. The later hath not so; at least not place enough, to keep men to their promises; because in the condition of meer Nature, the inequality of Power is not discerned, but by the event of Battell. So that before the time of Civill Society, or in the interruption thereof by Warre, there is nothing can strengthen a Covenant of Peace agreed on, against the temptations of Avarice, Ambition, Lust, or other strong desire, but the feare of that Invisible Power, which they every one Worship as God; and Feare as a Revenger of their perfidy. All therefore that can be done between two men not subject to Civill Power, is to put one another to swear by the God he feareth: Which *Swearing*, or OATH, is a *Forme of Speech, added to a Promise; by which he that promiseth, signifieth, that unless he performe, he renounceth the mercy of his God, or calleth to him for vengeance on himselfe.* Such was the Heathen Forme, *Let* Jupiter *kill me else, as I kill this Beast.* So is our Forme, *I shall do thus, and thus, so help me God.* And this, with the Rites and Ceremonies, which every one useth in his own Religion, that the feare of breaking faith might be the greater.

By this it appears, that an Oath taken according to any other Forme, or Rite, then his, that sweareth, is in vain; and no Oath: And that there is no Swearing by any thing which the Swearer thinks not God. For though men have sometimes used to swear by their Kings, for feare, or flattery; yet they would have it thereby understood, they attributed to them Divine honour. And that Swearing unnecessarily by God, is but prophaning of his name: and Swearing by other things, as men do in common discourse, is not Swearing, but an impious Custome, gotten by two much vehemence of talking.

It appears also, that the Oath addes nothing to the Obligation. For a Covenant, if lawfull, binds in the sight of God, without the Oath, as much as with it: if unlawfull, bindeth not at all; though it be confirmed with an Oath.

...

Chap. XXXI.

Of the *Kingdome of God by Nature*.

That the condition of meer Nature, that is to say, of absolute Liberty, such as is theirs, that neither are Soveraigns, nor Subjects, is Anarchy, and the condition of Warre: That the Praecepts, by which men are guided to avoyd that condition, are the Lawes of Nature: That a Common-wealth, without Soveraign Power, is but a word, without substance, and cannot stand: That Subjects owe to Soveraigns, simple Obedience, in all things, wherein their obedience is not repugnant to the Lawes of

God, I have sufficiently proved, in that which I have already written. There wants onely, for the entire knowledge of Civill duty, to know what are those Lawes of God. For without that, a man knows not, when he is commanded any thing by the Civill Power, whether it be contrary to the Law of God, or not: and so, either by too much civill obedience, offends the Divine Majesty, or through feare of offending God, transgresses the commandements of the Common-wealth. To avoyd both these Rocks, it is necessary to know what are the Lawes Divine. And seeing the knowledge of all Law, dependeth on the knowledge of the Soveraign Power; I shall say something in that which followeth, of the KINGDOME OF GOD.

God is King, let the Earth rejoyce, saith the Psalmist. And again, *God is King though the Nations be angry; and he that sitteth on the Cherubins, though the earth be moved.* Whether men will or not, they must be subject alwayes to the Divine Power. By denying the Existence, or Providence of God, men may shake off their Ease, but not their Yoke. But to call this Power of God, which extendeth it selfe not onely to Man, but also to Beasts, and Plants, and Bodies inanimate, by the name of Kingdome, is but a metaphoricall use of the word. For he onely is properly said to Raigne, that governs his Subjects, by his Word, and by promise of Rewards to those that obey it, and by threatning them with Punishment that obey it not. Subjects therefore in the Kingdome of God, are not Bodies Inanimate, nor creatures Irrationall; because they understand no Precepts as his: Nor Atheists; nor they that believe not that God has any care of the actions of mankind; because they acknowledge no Word for his, nor have hope of his rewards, or fear of his threatnings. They therefore that believe there is a God that governeth the world, and hath given Praecepts, and propounded Rewards, and Punishments to Mankind, are Gods Subjects; all the rest, are to be understood as Enemies.

To rule by Words, requires that such Words be manifestly made known; for else they are no Lawes: For to the nature of Lawes, belongeth a sufficient, and clear Promulgation, such as may take away the excuse of Ignorance; which in the Lawes of men is but of one onely kind, and that is, Proclamation, or Promulgation by the voyce of man. But God declareth his Lawes three ways; by the Dictates of *Naturall Reason,* by *Revelation,* and by the *Voyce* of some *man,* to whom by the operation of Miracles, he procureth credit with the rest. From hence there ariseth a triple Word of God, *Rational, Sensible,* and *Prophetique*: to which Correspondeth a triple Hearing; *Right Reason, Sense Supernaturall,* and *Faith.* As for Sense Supernaturall, which consisteth in Revelation, or Inspiration, there have not been any Universall Lawes so given, because God speaketh not in that manner, but to particular persons, and to divers men divers things.

From the difference between the other two kinds of Gods Word, *Rationall,* and *Prophetique,* there may be attributed to God, a twofold Kingdome, *Naturall,* and *Prophetique*: Naturall, wherein he governeth as many of Mankind as acknowledge his Providence, by the naturall Dictates of Right Reason; And Prophetique, wherein having chosen out one peculiar Nation (the Jewes) for his Subjects, he governed them, and none but them, not onely by naturall Reason, but by Positive Lawes, which he gave them by the mouths of his holy Prophets. Of the Naturall Kingdome of God I intend to speak in this Chapter.

The Right of Nature, whereby God reigneth over men, and punisheth those that break his Lawes, is to be derived, not from his Creating them as if he required obedience, as of Gratitude for his benefits; but from his *Irresistible Power.* I have formerly shewn, how the Soveraign Right ariseth from Pact: To shew how the same Right may arise from Nature, requires no more, but to shew in what case it is never taken away. Seeing all men by Nature had Right to All things, they had Right every one to reigne over all the rest. But because this Right could not be obtained by force, it concerned the safety of every one, laying by that Right, to set up men (with Soveraign Authority) by common consent, to rule and defend them: whereas if there had been any man of Power Irresistible; there had been no reason, why he should not by that Power have ruled, and defended both himselfe, and them, according to his own discretion. To those therefore whose Power is irresistible, the dominion of all men adhaereth naturally by their excellence of Power; and consequently it is from that Power, that the Kingdome over men, and the Right of Afflicting men at his pleasure, belongeth Naturally to God Almighty; not as Creator, and Gracious; but as Omnipotent. And though Punishment be due for Sinne onely, because by that word is understood Affliction for Sinne; yet the Right of Afflicting, is not alwayes derived from mens Sinne, but from Gods Power.

This question, *Why Evill men often Prosper, and Good men suffer Adversity,* has been much disputed by the Antient, and is the same with this of ours, *by what Right God dispenseth the Prosperities and Adversities of this life*; and is of that difficulty, as it hath shaken the faith, not onely of the Vulgar, but of Philosophers, and which is more, of the Saints, concerning the Divine Providence. *How Good* (saith *David*) *is the God of Israel to those that are Upright in Heart; and yet my feet were almost gone, my treadings had well-nigh slipt; for I was grieved at the Wicked, when I saw the Ungodly in such Prosperity.* And *Job*, how earnestly does he expostulate with God, for the many Afflictions he suffered, notwithstanding his Righteousnesse? This question in the case of *Job*, is decided by God himselfe, not by arguments derived from *Job's* Sinne, but his own Power. For whereas the friends of *Job* drew their arguments from his Affliction to his Sinne, and he defended himselfe by the conscience of his Innocence, God himselfe taketh up the matter, and having justified the Affliction by arguments drawn from his Power, such as this, *Where wast thou when I layd the foundations of the earth,* and the like, both approved *Job's* Innocence, and reproved the Erroneous doctrine of his friends. Conformable to this doctrine is the sentence of our Saviour, concerning the man that was born Blind, in these words, *Neither hath this man sinned, nor his fathers; but that the works of God might be made manifest in him.* And though it be said, *That Death entred into the world by sinne,* (by which is meant that if *Adam* had never sinned, he had never dyed, that is, never suffered any separation of his soule from his body,) it follows not thence, that God could not justly have Afflicted him, though he had not Sinned, as well as he afflicteth other living creatures, that cannot sinne.

Having spoken of the Right of Gods Soveraignty, as grounded onely on Nature; we are to consider next, what are the Divine Lawes, or Dictates of Naturall Reason; which Lawes concern either the naturall Duties of one man to another, or the Honour naturally due to our Divine Soveraign. The first are the same Lawes of Nature, of which I have spoken already in the 14. and 15. Chapters of this Treatise; namely, Equity, Justice, Mercy, Humility, and the rest of the Morall Vertues. It remaineth therefore that we consider, what Praecepts are dictated to men, by their Naturall Reason onely, without other word of God, touching the Honour and Worship of the Divine Majesty.

Honour consisteth in the inward thought, and opinion of the Power, and Goodnesse of another: and therefore to Honour God, is to think as Highly of his Power and Goodnesse, as is possible. And of that opinion, the externall signes appearing in the Words, and Actions of men, are called *Worship*; which is one part of that which the Latines understand by the word *Cultus*: For *Cultus* signifieth properly, and constantly, that labour which a man bestowes on any thing, with a purpose to make benefit by it. Now those things whereof we make benefit, are either subject to us, and the profit they yeeld, followeth the labour we bestow upon them, as a naturall effect; or they are not subject to us, but answer our labour, according to their own Wills. In the first sense the labour bestowed on the Earth, is called *Culture*; and the education of Children a *Culture* of their mindes. In the second sense, where mens wills are to be wrought to our purpose, not by Force, but by Compleasance, it signifieth as much as Courting, that is, a winning of favour by good offices; as by praises, by acknowledging their Power, and by whatsoever is pleasing to them from whom we look for any benefit. And this is properly *Worship*: in which sense *Publicola*, is understood for a Worshipper of the People; and *Cultus Dei,* for the Worship of God.

From internall Honour, consisting in the opinion of Power and Goodnesse, arise three Passions; *Love,* which hath reference to Goodnesse; and *Hope,* and *Fear,* that relate to Power: And three parts of externall worship; *Praise, Magnifying,* and *Blessing:* The subject of Praise, being Goodnesse; the subject of Magnifying, and Blessing, being Power, and the effect thereof of Felicity. Praise, and Magnifying are signified both by Words, and Actions: By Words, when we say a man is Good, or Great: By Actions, when we thank him for his Bounty, and obey his Power. The opinion of the Happinesse of another, can onely be expressed by words.

There be some signes of Honour, (both in Attributes and Actions,) that be Naturally so; as amongst Attributes, *Good, Just, Liberall,* and the like; and amongst

Actions, *Prayers, Thanks,* and *Obedience,* Others are so by Institution, or Custome of men; and in some times and places are Honourable; in others Dishonourable; in others Indifferent: such as are the Gestures in Salutation, Prayer, and Thanksgiving, in different times and places, differently used. The former is *Naturall*; the later *Arbitrary* Worship.

And of Arbitrary Worship, there bee two differences: For sometimes it is a *Commanded,* sometimes a *Voluntary* Worship: Commanded, when it is such as hee requireth, who is Worshipped: Free, when it is such as the Worshipper thinks fit. When it is Commanded, not the words, or gesture, but the obedience is the Worship. But when Free, the Worship consists in the opinion of the beholders: for if to them the words, or actions by which we intend honour, seem ridiculous, and tending to contumely; they are no Worship; because no signes of Honour; and no signes of Honour; because a signe is not a signe to him that giveth it, but to him to whom it is made; that is, to the spectator.

Again, there is a *Publique,* and a *Private* Worship. Publique, is the Worship that a Common-wealth performeth, as one Person. Private, is that which a Private person exhibiteth. Publique, in respect of the whole Common-wealth, is Free; but in respect of Particular men it is not so. Private, is in secret Free; but in the sight of the multitude, it is never without some Restraint, either from the Lawes, or from the Opinion of men; which is contrary to the nature of Liberty.

The End of Worship amongst men, is Power. For where a man seeth another worshipped, he supposeth him powerfull, and is the readier to obey him; which makes his Power greater. But God has no Ends: the worship we do him, proceeds from our duty, and is directed according to our capacity, by those rules of Honour, that Reason dictateth to be done by the weak to the more potent men, in hope of benefit, for fear of dammage, or in thankfulnesse for good already received from them.

That we may know what worship of God is taught us by the light of Nature, I will begin with his Attributes. Where, First, it is manifest, we ought to attribute to him *Existence*: For no man can have the will to honour that, which he thinks not to have any Beeing.

Secondly, that those Philosophers, who sayd the World, or the Soule of the World was God, spake unworthily of him; and denyed his Existence: For by God, is understood the cause of the World; and to say the World is God, is to say there is no cause of it, that is, no God.

Thirdly, to say the World was not Created, but Eternall, (seeing that which is Eternall has no cause,) is to deny there is a God.

Fourthly, that they who attributing (as they think) Ease to God, take from him the care of Man-kind; take from him his Honour: for it takes away mens love, and fear of him; which is the root of Honour.

Fifthly, in those things that signifie Greatnesse, and Power; to say he is *Finite,* is not to Honour him: For it is not a signe of the Will to Honour God, to attribute to him lesse than we can; and Finite, is lesse than we can; because to Finite, it is easie to adde more.

Therefore to attribute *Figure* to him, is not Honour; for all Figure is Finite:

Nor to say we conceive, and imagine, or have an *Idea* of him, in our mind: for whatsoever we conceive is Finite:

Nor to attribute to him *Parts,* or *Totality;* which are the Attributes onely of things Finite:

Nor to say he is in this, or that *Place:* for whatsoever is in Place, is bounded, and Finite:

Nor that he is *Moved,* or *Resteth:* for both these Attributes ascribe to him Place:

Nor that there be more Gods than one; because it implies them all Finite: for there cannot be more than one Infinite.

Nor to ascribe to him (unlesse Metaphorically, meaning not the Passion, but the Effect) Passions that partake of Griefe; as *Repentance, Anger, Mercy*: or of Want; as *Appetite, Hope, Desire*; or of any Passive faculty: For Passion, is Power limited by somewhat else.

And therefore when we ascribe to God a *Will,* it is not to be understood, as that of Man, for a *Rationall Appetite*; but as the Power, by which he effecteth every thing.

Likewise when we attribute to him *Sight,* and other acts of Sense; as also *Knowledge,* and *Understanding*; which in us is nothing else, but a tumult of the mind, raised by externall things that presse the organicall parts of mans body: For there is no such thing in God; and being things that depend on naturall causes, cannot be attributed to him.

Hee that will attribute to God, nothing but what is warranted by naturall Reason, must either use such Negative Attributes, as *Infinite, Eternall, Incomprehensible*; or Superlatives, as *Most High, most Great,* and the like; or Indefinite, as *Good, Just, Holy, Creator*; and in such sense, as if he meant not to declare what he is, (for that were to circumscribe him within the limits of our Fancy,) but how much wee admire him, and how ready we would be to obey him; which is a signe of Humility, and of a Will to honour him as much as we can: For there is but one Name to signifie our Conception of his Nature, and that is, I AM: and but one Name of his Relation to us, and that is *God*; in which is contained Father, King, and Lord.

Concerning the actions of Divine Worship, it is a most generall Precept of Reason, that they be signes of the Intention to Honour God; such as are, First, *Prayers*: For not the Carvers, when they made Images, were thought to make them Gods; but the People that *Prayed* to them.

Secondly, *Thanksgiving*; which differeth from Prayer in Divine Worship, no otherwise, than that Prayers precede, and Thanks succeed the benefit; the end both of the one, and the other, being to acknowledge God, for Author of all benefits, as well past, as future.

Thirdly, *Gifts*; that is to say, *Sacrifices*, and *Oblations*, (if they be of the best,) are signes of Honour: for they are Thanksgivings.

Fourthly, *Not to Swear by any but God*, is naturally a signe of Honour: for it is a confession that God onely knoweth the heart; and that no mans wit, or strength can protect a man against Gods vengeance on the perjured.

Fifthly, it is a part of Rationall Worship, to speak Considerately of God; for it argues a Fear of him, and Fear, is a confession of his Power. Hence followeth, That the name of God is not to be used rashly, and to no purpose; for that is as much, as in Vain: And it is to no purpose, unlesse it be by way of Oath, and by order of the Common-wealth, to make Judgements certain; or between Commonwealths, to avoyd Warre. And that disputing of Gods nature is contrary to his Honour: For it is supposed, that in this naturall Kingdome of God, there is no other way to know any thing, but by naturall Reason; that is, from the Principles of naturall Science; which are so farre from teaching us any thing of Gods nature, as they cannot teach us our own nature, nor the nature of the smallest creature living. And therefore, when men out of the Principles of naturall Reason, dispute of the Attributes of God, they but dishonour him: For in the Attributes which we give to God, we are not to consider the signification of Philosophicall Truth; but the signification of Pious Intention, to do him the greatest Honour we are able. From the want of which consideration, have proceeded the volumes of disputation about the Nature of God, that tend not to his Honour, but to the honour of our own wits, and learning; and are nothing else but inconsiderate, and vain abuses of his Sacred Name.

Sixthly, in *Prayers, Thanksgiving, Offerings* and *Sacrifices*, it is a Dictate of naturall Reason, that they be every one in his kind the best, and most significant of Honour. As for example, that Prayers, and Thanksgiving, be made in Words and Phrases, not sudden, nor light, nor Plebeian; but beautifull, and well composed; For else we do not God as much honour as we can. And therefore the Heathens did absurdly, to worship Images for Gods: But their doing it in Verse, and with Musick, both of Voyce, and Instruments, was reasonable. Also that the Beasts they offered in sacrifice, and the Gifts they offered, and their actions in Worshipping, were full of submission, and commemorative of benefits received, was according to reason, as proceeding from an intention to honour him.

Seventhly, Reason directeth not onely to worship God in Secret; but also, and especially, in Publique, and in the sight of men: For without that, (that which in honour is most acceptable) the procuring others to honour him, is lost.

Lastly, Obedience to his Lawes (that is, in this case to the Lawes of Nature,) is the greatest worship of all. For as Obedience is more acceptable to God than Sacrifice; so also to set light by his Commandements, is the greatest of all contumelies. And these are the Lawes of that Divine Worship, which naturall Reason dictateth to private men.

But seeing a Common-wealth is but one Person, it ought also to exhibite to God but one Worship; which then it doth, when it commandeth it to be exhibited by

Private men, Publiquely. And this is Publique Worship; the property whereof, is to be *Uniforme*: For those actions that are done differently, by different men, cannot be said to be a Publique Worship. And therefore, where many sorts of Worship be allowed, proceeding from the different Religions of Private men, it cannot be said there is any Publique Worship, nor that the Commonwealth is of any Religion at all.

And because words (and consequently the Attributes of God) have their signification by agreement, and constitution of men; those Attributes are to be held significative of Honour, that men intend shall so be; and whatsoever may be done by the wills of particular men, where there is no Law but Reason, may be done by the will of the Common-wealth, by Lawes Civill. And because a Commonwealth hath no Will, nor makes no Lawes, but those that are made by the Will of him, or them that have the Soveraign Power; it followeth, that those Attributes which the Soveraign ordaineth, in the Worship of God, for signes of Honour, ought to be taken and used for such, by private men in their publique Worship.

But because not all Actions are signes by Constitution; but some are Naturally signes of Honour, others of Contumely, these later (which are those that men are ashamed to do in the sight of them they reverence) cannot be made by humane power a part of Divine worship; nor the former (such as are decent, modest, humble Behaviour) ever be separated from it. But whereas there be an infinite number of Actions, and Gestures, of an indifferent nature; such of them as the Common-wealth shall ordain to be Publiquely and Universally in use, as signes of Honour, and part of Gods Worship, are to be taken and used for such by the Subjects. And that which is said in the Scripture, *It is better to obey God than men,* hath place in the kingdome of God by Pact, and not by Nature.

Having thus briefly spoken of the Naturall Kingdome of God, and his Naturall Lawes, I will adde onely to this Chapter a short declaration of his Naturall Punishments. There is no action of man in this life, that is not the beginning of so long a chayn of Consequences, as no humans Providence, is high enough, to give a man a prospect to the end. And in this Chayn, there are linked together both pleasing and unpleasing events; in such manner, as he that will do any thing for his pleasure, must engage himselfe to suffer all the pains annexed to it; and these pains, are the Naturall Punishments of those actions, which are the beginning of more Harme than Good. And hereby it comes to passe, that Intemperance, is naturally punished with Diseases; Rashnesse, with Mischances; Injustice, with the Violence of Enemies; Pride, with Ruine; Cowardise, with Oppression; Negligent government of Princes, with Rebellion; and Rebellion, with Slaughter. For seeing Punishments are consequent to the breach of Lawes; Naturall Punishments must be naturally consequent to the breach of the Lawes of Nature; and therfore follow them as their naturall, not arbitrary effects.

And thus farre concerning the Constitution, Nature, and Right of Soveraigns; and concerning the Duty of Subjects, derived from the Principles of Naturall Reason. And now, considering how different this Doctrine is, from the Practise of the greatest part of the world, especially of these Western parts, that have received their Morall learning from *Rome,* and *Athens*; and how much depth of Morall Philosophy is required, in them that have the Administration of the Soveraign Power; I am at the point of believing this my labour, as uselesse, as the Common-wealth of *Plato*; For he also is of opinion that it is impossible for the disorders of State, and change of Governments by Civill Warre, ever to be taken away, till Soveraigns be Philosophers. But when I consider again, that the Science of Naturall Justice, is the onely Science necessary for Soveraigns, and their principall Ministers; and that they need not be charged with the Sciences Mathematicall, (as by *Plato* they are,) further, than by good Lawes to encourage men to the study of them; and that neither *Plato,* nor any other Philosopher hitherto, hath put into order, and sufficiently, or probably proved all the Theoremes of Morall doctrine, that men may learn thereby, both how to govern, and how to obey; I recover some hope, that one time or other, this writing of mine, may fall into the hands of a Soveraign, who will consider it himselfe, (for it is short, and I think clear,) without the help of any interessed, or envious Interpreter; and by the exercise of entire Soveraignty, in protecting the Publique teaching of it, convert this Truth of Speculation, into the Utility of Practice.

Part 3
Of a Christian Commonwealth

Chap. XXXII.
Of the Principles of Christian Politiques.

I have derived the Rights of Soveraigne Power, and the duty of Subjects hitherto, from the Principles of Nature onely; such as Experience has found true, or Consent (concerning the use of words) has made so; that is to say, from the nature of Men, known to us by Experience, and from Definitions (of such words as are Essentiall to all Politicall reasoning) universally agreed on. But in that I am next to handle, which is the Nature and Rights of a CHRISTIAN COMMONWEALTH, whereof there dependeth much upon Supernaturall Revelations of the Will of God; the ground of my Discourse must be, not only the Naturall Word of God, but also the Propheticall.

Neverthelesse, we are not to renounce our Senses, and Experience; nor (that which is the undoubted Word of God) our naturall Reason. For they are the talents which he hath put into our hands to negotiate, till the coming again of our blessed Saviour; and therefore not to be folded up in the Napkin of an Implicite Faith, but employed in the purchase of Justice, Peace, and true Religion. For though there be many things in Gods Word above Reason; that is to say, which cannot by naturall reason be either demonstrated, or confuted; yet there is nothing contrary to it; but when it seemeth so, the fault is either in our unskilfull Interpretation, or erroneous Ratiocination.

Therefore, when any thing therein written is too hard for our examination, wee are bidden to captivate our understanding to the Words; and not to labour in sifting out a Philosophicall truth by Logick, of such mysteries as are not comprehensible, nor fall under any rule of naturall science. For it is with the mysteries of our Religion, as with wholsome pills for the sick, which swallowed whole, have the vertue to cure; but chewed, are for the most part cast up again without effect.

But by the Captivity of our Understanding, is not meant a Submission of the Intellectuall faculty, to the Opinion of any other man; but of the Will to Obedience, where obedience is due. For Sense, Memory, Understanding, Reason, and Opinion are not in our power to change; but alwaies, and necessarily such, as the things we see, hear, and consider suggest unto us; and therefore are not effects of our Will, but our Will of them. We then Captivate our Understanding and Reason, when we forbear contradiction; when we so speak, as (by lawfull Authority) we are commanded; and when we live accordingly; which in sum, is Trust, and Faith reposed in him that speaketh, though the mind be incapable of any Notion at all from the words spoken.

When God speaketh to man, it must be either immediately; or by mediation of another man, to whom he had formerly spoken by himself immediately. How God speaketh to a man immediately, may be understood by those well enough, to whom he hath so spoken; but how the same should be understood by another, is hard, if not impossible to know. For if a man pretend to me, that God hath spoken to him supernaturally, and immediately, and I make doubt of it, I cannot easily perceive what argument he can produce, to oblige me to beleeve it. It is true, that if he be my Soveraign, he may oblige me to obedience, so, as not by act or word to declare I beleeve him not; but not to think any otherwise then my reason perswades me. But if one that hath not such authority over me, shall pretend the same, there is nothing that exacteth either beleefe, or obedience.

For to say that God hath spoken to him in the Holy Scripture, is not to say God hath spoken to him immediately, but by mediation of the Prophets, or of the Apostles, or of the Church, in such manner as he speaks to all other Christian men. To say he hath spoken to him in a Dream, is no more then to say he hath dreamt that God spake to him; which is not of force to win beleef from any man, that knows dreams are for the most part naturall, and may proceed from former thoughts; and such dreams as that, from selfe conceit, and foolish arrogance, and false opinion of a mans own godlinesse, or other vertue, by which he thinks he hath merited the favour of extraordinary Revelation. To say he hath seen a Vision, or heard a Voice, is to say, that he hath dreamed between sleeping and waking: for in such manner a man doth many times naturally take his dream for a vision, as not having well observed his own slumbering. To say he speaks by supernaturall Inspiration, is to say he finds an ardent desire to speak, or some strong opinion of himself, for which hee can alledge no naturall and sufficient reason. So that though God Almighty can speak to a man, by Dreams, Visions, Voice, and Inspiration; yet he obliges no man to beleeve he hath so done to him that pretends it; who (being a man) may erre, and (which is more) may lie.

How then can he, to whom God hath never revealed his Wil immediately (saving by the way of natural reason) know when he is to obey, or not to obey his Word, delivered by him, that sayes he is a Prophet. Of 400 Prophets, of whom the K. of *Israel* asked counsel, concerning the warre he made against *Ramoth Gilead,* only *Micaiah* was a true one. The Prophet that was sent to prophecy against the Altar set up by *Jeraboam,* though a true Prophet, and that by two miracles done in his presence appears to be a Prophet sent from God, was yet deceived by another old Prophet, that perswaded him as from the mouth of God, to eat and drink with him. If one Prophet deceive another, what certainty is there of knowing the will of God, by other way than that of Reason? To which I answer out of the Holy Scripture, that there be two marks, by which together, not asunder, a true Prophet is to be known. One is the doing of miracles; the other is the not teaching any other Religion than that which is already established. Asunder (I say) neither of these is sufficient. *If a Prophet rise amongst you, or a Dreamer of dreams, and shall pretend the doing of a miracle, and the miracle come to passe; if he say, Let us follow strange Gods, which thou hast not known, thou shalt not hearken to him, & c. But that Prophet and Dreamer of dreams shall be put to death, because he hath spoken to you to Revolt from the Lord your God.* In which words two things are to be observed; First, that God wil not have miracles alone serve for arguments, to approve the Prophets calling; but (as it is in the third verse) for an experiment of the constancy of our adherence to himself. For the works of the *Egyptian* Sorcerers, though not so great as those of *Moses,* yet were great miracles. Secondly, that how great soever the miracle be, yet if it tend to stir up revolt against the King, or him that governeth by the Kings authority, he that doth such miracle, is not to be considered otherwise than as sent to make triall of their allegiance. For these words, *revolt from the Lord your God,* are in this place equivalent to *revolt from your King.* For they had made God their King by pact at the foot of Mount *Sinai;* who ruled them by *Moses* only; for he only spake with God, and from time to time declared Gods Commandements to the people. In like manner, after our Saviour Christ had made his Disciples acknowledge him for the *Messiah,* (that is to say, for Gods anointed, whom the nation of the *Jews* daily expected for their King, but refused when he came,) he omitted not to advertise them of the danger of miracles. *There shall arise* (saith he) *false Christs, and false Prophets, and shall doe great wonders and miracles, even to the seducing (if it were possible) of the very Elect.* By which it appears, that false Prophets may have the power of miracles; yet are wee not to take their doctrin for Gods Word. St *Paul* says further to the *Galatians,* that *if himself, or an Angell from heaven preach another Gospel to them, than he had preached, let him be accursed.* That Gospel was, that Christ was King; so that all preaching against the power of the King received, in consequence to these words, is by St *Paul* accursed. For his speech is addressed to those, who by his preaching had already received *Jesus* for the *Christ,* that is to say, for King of the *Jews.*

And as Miracles, without preaching that Doctrine which God hath established; so preaching the true Doctrine, without the doing of Miracles, is an unsufficient argument of immediate Revelation. For if a man that teacheth not false Doctrine, should pretend to bee a Prophet without shewing any Miracle, he is never the more to bee regarded for his pretence, as is evident by *Deut.* 18.*v.*21,22. *If thou say in thy heart, How shall we know that the Word* (of the Prophet) *is not that which the Lord hath spoken. When the Prophet shall have spoken in the name of the Lord, that which shall not come to passe, that's the word which the Lord hath not spoken, but the Prophet has spoken it out of the pride of his own heart, fear him not.* But a man may here again ask, When the Prophet hath foretold a thing, how shal we know whether it will come to passe or not? For he may foretel it as a thing to arrive after a certain long time, longer than the time of mans life; or indefinitely, that it will come to passe one time or other: in which case this mark of a Prophet is unusefull; and therefore the miracles that oblige us to beleeve a Prophet, ought to be confirmed by an immediate, or a not long deferr'd event. So that it is manifest, that the teaching of the Religion which God hath established, and the shewing of a *present* Miracle, joined together, were the only marks whereby the Scripture would have a true Prophet, that is to say, immediate Revelation to be acknowledged; neither of them being singly sufficient to oblige any other man to regard what he saith.

Seeing therefore Miracles now cease, we have no sign left, whereby to acknowledge the pretended Revelations, or Inspirations of any private man; nor obligation to give ear to any Doctrine, farther than it is conformable to the Holy Scriptures, which since the time of our Saviour, supply the place, and sufficiently recompense the want of all other Prophecy; and from which, by wise and learned interpretation, and carefull ratiocination, all rules and precepts necessary to the knowledge of our duty both to God and man, without Enthusiasme, or supernaturall Inspiration, may easily be deduced. And this Scripture is it, out of which I am to take the Principles of my Discourse, concerning the Rights of those that are the Supream Governors on earth, of Christian Common-wealths; and of the duty of Christian Subjects towards their Soveraigns. And to that end, I shall speak in the next Chapter, of the Books, Writers, Scope and Authority of the Bible.

37. Stanley Hauerwas – The Church and Liberal Democracy

1. Christian Social Ethics in a Secular Polity

It has become commonplace that we live in a secular world and society. But attempts to describe and assess the significance of being "secular" are notoriously controversial.[1] I have no intention of adding further fuel to that particular debate. Rather I want to concentrate on a more limited, but I think no less important, set of challenges a secular polity, such as liberal democracy, presents for Christian social ethics.[2]

By calling attention to the secular nature of our polity I am not trying to provide or defend a theory about what it means to live in the "modern world" or to be a "modern woman or man." All I mean by secular is that our polity and politics gives no special status to any recognizable religious group.[3] Correlatively such a policy requires that public policies be justified on grounds that are not explicitly religious.

American religious groups have been particularly supportive of this understanding of the secular nature of our polity, in that it seems to allow for the free expression of religious convictions without limiting any one group. Of course particular religious groups have in fact been discriminated against socially and politically, but such discrimination, we feel, is not endemic to how our polity should work. Moreover some interpret the secular nature of our polity, that is, our government's acknowledgment of its noncompetency in religion, as a profound confession of the limits of the state appropriate to a recognition of God's sovereignty or as a realistic understanding of human sinfulness.[4]

---

[1]For an anthology that helps clarify many of the issues surrounding claims about "secularity," see *Secularization and the Protestant Prospect*, ed. James Childress and David Harned (Philadelphia: Westminster Press, 1970). Too often discussions about religion and secularity are attempts, explicitly or implicitly, to make summary judgments, positive or negative, about our culture. I doubt that any one description, whether it be claims about secularity or that this is a post-modem culture, has the power to describe the diverse activities that make up our culture or any other. What we require are discriminating criteria that will let us get a descriptive as well as normative hold on those aspects of our society of particular importance to Christians.

[2]Nor do I intend to enter the debate concerning the existence, meaning, or status of civil religion in America. Robert Bellah is, of course, the primary focus of this debate. See his *Beyond Belief: Essays on Religion in a Post-Traditional World* (New York: Harper and Row, 1970) and *The Broken Covenant, American Civil Religion in Time of Trial* (New York: Seabury, 1975). Equally if not more important is the work of Sidney Mead, for in many ways Mead has argued more forcefully for the significance of a "religion of the republic." See his *The Lively Experiment* (New York: Harper and Row, 1963) and *The Nation with the Soul of a Church* (New York: Harper and Row, 1975). Nor should H. R. Niebuhr's *The Kingdom of God in America* (New York: Harper, 1937) be overlooked.

[3]Some, of course, would question this understanding of "secular" on grounds that a secular society finally in fact, if not as a matter of policy, is biased against religion per se. Whether that is the case remains to be seen. It is certainly true that our country's toleration of "religious" symbols at our state ceremonies may, on a strict enforcement of the Constitution, be illegitimate.

[4]John Courtney Murray bases his defense of democracy primarily on God's sovereignty and Reinhold Niebuhr places the emphasis on sin. There is much to be said for both accounts and neither is exclusive of the other.

This positive evaluation presents a decisive challenge to Christian social ethics that we have seldom understood. Even as Christians recover the profound social significance of the Gospel, they find that the terms of expression and justification of those convictions must be secular. Many Christians assume this presents no problem, as the inherent justice of our secular and democratic polity provides the appropriate means for the expression of Christian social concerns. Most recent Christian social ethics in America has thus derived from the largely unexamined axiom that Christians should engage in politics to secure a more nearly just society. Following the lead of the social gospel, social ethics presumes that the task of Christians is to transform[5] our basic social and economic structures in order to aid individuals in need. Thus political involvement is seen to be the best mechanism to deal with, and perhaps even transform, structures of injustice.

While Christians have sometimes naively overestimated the extent of such transformations, they have also developed extremely sophisticated and influential portrayals of the moral possibilities and limits of our polity. Reinhold Niebuhr took the enthusiasm of the social gospel and made it all the more powerful by suggesting the limits of what love could accomplish through the politics characteristic of our society. Niebuhr saw clearly that love without power is ineffective, but that power must at the same time limit the possibilities of the realization of love. Yet those limits do not lessen the Christian duty to use power to secure the forms of justice possible in our social and political system.[6] To do anything less is to be unfaithful to the Christian's understanding of history and our involvement in it.

Moreover, from this perspective attempts by Christians to avoid political involvement because of the "dirty" nature of politics are rightly condemned as irresponsible, if not unfaithful. Rather it is the task of Christians to be politically involved exactly because we recognize that our politics inherently involves compromise and accommodation.

The primary difference between Niebuhr and Murray is not that Murray had a more optimistic view of man, but that Murray presupposed the necessity of the existence of the church to remind the state of its limits. In a peculiar way Niebuhr was more profoundly an American theologian, as America was his primary community. See Murray's *We Hold These Truths* (New York: Sheed and Ward, 1960) and Niebuhr, *The Children of Light and the Children of Darkness* (New York: Scribner's, 1944).

[5]The popularity of the image of "transformation" in Christian social ethics has had the unfortunate effect of oversimplifying the description of social change and the church's relation to it. For it is assumed that H. R. Niebuhr's "type" or "image" of transformation is clearly normative for Christian social ethics, irrespective of the kind of society in which Christians find themselves. As a result the "image" of transformation is too quickly accepted as entailing a strategy of involvement. What we fail to notice is that Niebuhr's account of the types failed to deal with a crucial problem—namely how to discriminate between different kinds of cultures and different aspects of any culture for what might be transformed and what might be accepted. Niebuhr's uncritical use of the word "culture" allowed him to load his case too simply against the "Christ against Culture" type and to present the "Christ transforming Culture" type in a far too uncritical light. It is not my intention to challenge the heuristic value of Niebuhr's typology, but to remind us that the account of types is not a sufficient argument for a particular social ethic. H. R. Niebuhr, *Christ and Culture* (New York: Harper and Row, 1956).

[6]See, for example, *Reinhold Niebuhr on Politics,* ed. Harry Davis and Robert Good (New York: Scribner's, 1960), pp. 70–130.

To withdraw from the political in order to remain pure is an irresponsible act of despair. Even more, such withdrawal is self-deceptive as it creates the condition by which the political realm may claim unwarranted significance.

It is my contention, however, that Christian enthusiasm for the political involvement offered by our secular polity has made us forget the church's more profound political task. In the interest of securing more equitable forms of justice possible in our society, Christians have failed to challenge the moral presuppositions of our polity and society. Nowhere is the effect of this seen more powerfully than in the Christian acquiescence to the liberal assumption that a just polity is possible without the people being just.[7] We simply accepted the assumption that politics is about the distribution of desires, irrespective of the content of those desires, and any consideration of the development of virtuous people as a political issue seems an inexcusable intrusion into our personal liberty.

The more destructive result is that the church has increasingly imitated in its own social life the politics of liberalism. We have almost forgotten that the church is also a polity that at one time had the confidence to encourage in its members virtues sufficient to sustain their role as citizens in a society whose purpose was to counter the unwarranted claims made by other societies and states. Indeed, only if such people exist is it possible for the state to be "secular." Because the church rarely now engenders such a people and community, it has failed our particular secular polity: Christians have lacked the power that would enable themselves and others to perceive and interpret the kind of society in which we live. Christians have rightly thought that they have a proper investment in making this, and other societies, more nearly just, but have forgotten that genuine justice depends on more profound moral convictions than our secular polity can politically acknowledge.

Christians must again understand that their first task is not to make the world better or more just, but to recognize what the world[8] is and why it is that it understands the political task as it does. The first social task of the church is to provide the space and time necessary for developing skills of interpretation and discrimination sufficient

---

[7]There is no inherent reason that liberalism or secularism should exclude a concern for the development of citizen virtues. I suspect that the past association of "morality" with "religion" accounts for the lack of emphasis on the development of virtuous people. For virtue, like religion, is relegated to the "private" sphere in order to make sure that the "freedom of the individual" is properly safeguarded. For a fascinating account of how these issues were formed in the Renaissance see Quentin Skinner's *The Foundation of Modern Political Thought,* I (Cambridge: Cambridge University Press, 1978), pp. 45, 92–101, 228–236.

[8]The distinction between church and world is a complex one. Even though in some Christian texts "world" simply means those who reject Christ and is thus understood in a negative light, the world is also recognized elsewhere as God's creation. Moreover Christian judgment of the world is always self-referential, as we can never forget that the world is not "out there" but in us. The church must be separated from the world, for without separation we have no way to make discriminating judgments about the negative and positive aspects of the world. But the necessity of separation cannot blind us to the significance of the world for the church. For the church also learns what it should be from the world. The church's task is not to destroy or deny the world, or even to make it Christian, but to be a witness in the world of God's Kingdom.

to help us recognize the possibilities and limits of our society. In developing such skills, the church and Christians must be uninvolved in the politics of our society and involved in the polity that is the church. Theologically, the challenge of Christian social ethics in our secular polity is no different than in any time or place—it is always the Christian social task to form a society that is built on truth rather than fear. For the Christian, therefore, the church is always the primary polity through which we gain the experience to negotiate and make positive contributions to whatever society in which we may find ourselves.

2. A Critique of Our Society

Insofar as many Christians assume that our liberal and secular society is at least neutral to, if not positively an advantage for, the church, we have failed to see and understand the depth of the moral challenge facing this society. Of course we all recognize our society has problems, but we assume our society and politics have the means to deal with them. We have no reason to question fundamentally our "form of government" or the "American way of life." Rather, as Christians we assume we have a stake in America's extraordinary experiment to create a free people through the mechanism of democratic government.[9]

We thus feel puzzled by critiques of our society such as that of Solzhenitsyn. For it is the brunt of his charge that a polity is ultimately judged by the kind of people it produces, and from such a perspective our society can only be found wanting. He suggests that for all the injustice and terror of the Russian and Eastern European societies, they have been through a spiritual training far advanced of the Western experience:

> Life's complexity and mortal weight have produced stronger, deeper, and more interesting characters than those generated by the standardized Western well-being. It is true, no doubt, that a society cannot remain in an abyss of lawlessness, as in our country. But it is also demeaning for it to elect such mechanical legalistic smoothness

---

[9]One of the difficulties of American society and government is that rather than being a people prior to the state, as is true for most European countries, we had to found a state in order to try to make ourselves a people. Therefore where many societies can provide the mechanism for a strong government, knowing that social custom can still act as a limit on government, the United States had to resort to legal means to substitute for the lack of custom. We morally justified our legal arrangements by claiming they were necessary to protect, not society, but the individual from government. Thus the only two entities recognized in our polity became the state and the individual. As a result more traditional political theory that makes the state one agency among others for the protection of the common good of a society, and not just individuals, simply does not apply to America.

In some ways our situation is even more complex, as America was originally a society profoundly underwritten by Protestant presupposition—America was the great experiment in constructive Protestantism. Exactly because our founders, irrespective of their own personal religiosity, could presuppose such a society, they thought all they needed to provide was a framework, a constitution, for our society to work. But as we lost the social presuppositions supplied by Protestantism or as they were increasingly replaced by Enlightenment assumptions, the framework became what it was never meant to be—an end in itself.

as you have. After the suffering of decades of violence and oppression, the human soul longs for things higher, warmer, and purer than those offered by today's mass living habits, introduced by the revolting invasion of publicity, by TV stupor, and by intolerable music.[10]

It is tempting to dismiss such attacks as failing to understand the character of the American people or our form of government. Some have suggested that Solzhenitsyn has confused a social and cultural critique with a political critique.[11] Yet to dismiss Solzhenitsyn in this way is but to manifest the problem he is trying to point out. For we have assumed that we can form a polity that ignores the relation between politics and moral virtue. In contrast, Solzhenitsyn takes the classical view that it should be the function of politics to direct people individually and collectively toward the good.[12]

Thus Solzhenitsyn's critique is radical insofar as it reaches to the roots of our societal presuppositions. In effect he is suggesting that when freedom becomes an end in itself people lose their ability to make sacrifices for worthy ends. The problem with our society is not that democracy has not worked, but that it has, and the results are less than good.[13] We have been freed to pursue happiness and "every citizen has been granted the desired freedom and material goods in such quantity and of such quality as to guarantee in theory the achievement of happiness. In the process, however, one psychological detail has been overlooked: the constant desire to have

---

[10]Aleksandr Solzhenitsyn, address at Harvard University; *Harvard Gazette,* June 1978, p. 2.

[11]Indeed one of the problems with America is the divorce of political consideration from culture. One of the signs of this is the association of politics with issues of power rather than symbols. In such a polity symbolic acts are reduced to issues of maintaining or projecting an "image" rather than the articulation of our profoundest loyalties. Lincoln was one of the few American presidents who appreciated the symbolic role of the political.

[12]As George Will has suggested, "Men and women are biological facts. Ladies and gentlemen—citizens—are social artifacts, works of political art. They carry the culture that is sustained by wise laws, and traditions of civility. At the end of the day we are right to judge a society by the character of the people it produces. That is why statecraft is inevitably soulcraft." *The Pursuit of Happiness and Other Sobering Thoughts* (New York: Harper and Row, 1978), p. 3.

It is important to note that neither Will nor Solzhenitsyn argues (nor do I) that it is the function of the state to *make* people good, but rather to direct them to the good. Politics as a moral art does not entail the presumption that the state is a possessor of the good, but rather that the good is to be found in a reality profounder than the state. In the absence of such a good the temptation is for the state to try to create a cause that can serve as a substitute. Thus it is profoundly and chillingly true that there is nothing wrong with America that a good war could not cure.

[13]Jimmy Carter promised us a government as good as the American people and it may be unfortunately true that is what we have. This does not mean that the American people are particularly bad, as they certainly are not. As many have pointed out, the American people continue to be extraordinarily generous and kind. The difficulty is that we simply do not have any way to understand the political significance of such virtues. Politically we seem caught in a system that reinforces our assumption that our political task is to pursue our self-interests aggressively and fairly. In contrast, George Will argues that "politics should be citizens expressing themselves as a people, a community of shared values, rather than as merely a collection of competing private interests inhabiting the same country. Instead, politics has become a facet of the disease for which it would be part of the cure. The disease is an anarchy of self-interestedness, and unwillingness, perhaps by now an inability, to think of the public interest, the common good. This disease of anti-public-spiritedness is not a candidate's disease. It is a social disease." *The Pursuit of Happiness and Other Sobering Thoughts,* p. 192. Will is one of the few American conservatives who seems to understand that conservatism in America is a radical position vis-à-vis our liberal heritage.

still more things and a still better life and the struggle to obtain them imprints many Western faces with worry and even depression, though it is customary to conceal such feelings. Active and tense competition permeates all human thoughts without opening a way to free spiritual development."[14]

Moreover, one of the great ironies of our society is that by attempting to make freedom an end in itself we have become an excessively legalistic society. As Solzhenitsyn points out, we feel there is little need for voluntary self-restraint, as we are free to operate to the limit of the law. Thus in condemning Richard Nixon, virtues of decency and honesty were invoked, but the legal system offered the only code by which the unacceptableness of those actions could be clearly and cogently expressed. An insightful commentator of the "Talk of the Town" column in the *New Yorker* observed that Nixon's legal gymnastics to claim innocence in his interview with Frost was in a sense truthful—

> truthful in that he honestly did not know of any other moral framework by which to judge himself, truthful in that no other armature of principle was available to him on which to mold an understanding of his character. One searched for a hint of something in his character, some shred of belief or awareness, that might have given him the strength and the foothold—a motive—to act differently; but, save for the misgiving that his strategy might backfire, no such motive was there.... And yet if one asked onself what that foothold of belief might have been, there was no ready answer—only a prickling of dread. Each of us may have a sense of principle which he has generated himself, or has drawn from his particular background, but that is not a satisfactory answer here. What is called for is principles that can be pointed to as the mainstays of the culture, principles of which no disparate individuals but the society is the custodian. What is needed is something that could be called a tradition. Individual ethics can be very fine, but they cannot survive for long if they are not reinforced by the society, and even while they last they can have little public significance if they are not echoed in the general moral awareness of the world in which their possessor lives. Perhaps such an awareness does exist, but, if so, it has become so obscured that we cannot be sure what it is, or even whether it is there at all. Under these circumstances the only way in which we can clearly distinguish ourselves from Richard Nixon is by our view that the legal system is inadequate as a moral tradition. Unlike him, we are not at all comfortable when the legal system is made to assume this role. And we become even more uneasy as it occurs to us that there may be nothing sounder available to us.[15]

That our society has been brought to such a pass is no surprise to Solzhenitsyn, as he thinks it is the inevitable result of a social order whose base is the humanism

---

[14]Solzhenitsyn, p. 1. Though often condemned for being too competitive, competition is one of our most important moral endeavors. For all societies need to provide a sense of participation in an adventure. Insofar as many feel they lack such an adventure, all that is left is beating the next person. Thus the dominance of the comparative mode in American life—we must be the first this or the best of that. It is very hard for us simply to be different and to enjoy that fact as an end in itself.

[15]"Talk of the Town," *New Yorker*, May 23, 1977, pp. 24–25.

of the Enlightenment, which presupposed that intrinsic evil did not exist, nor did man have any higher task than the attainment of his own happiness. "Everything beyond physical well-being and accumulation of material goods, all other human requirements and characteristics of a subtler and higher nature, were left outside the area of attention of state and social system, as if human life did not have any superior sense."[16] But such presumptions are profoundly false and any politics founded on them can only lead men to destruction, for

> if humanism were right in declaring that man is born to be happy, he would not be born to die. Since his body is doomed to die, his task on earth evidently must be of a more spiritual nature. It cannot be unrestrained enjoyment of everyday life. It cannot be the search for the best ways to obtain material goods and then cheerfully get the most out of them. It has to be the fulfillment of a permanent, earnest duty so that one's life journey may become an experience of moral growth, so that one may leave life a better human being than one started it.[17]

Now it must be admitted that for those of us identified with religious traditions the kind of rhetoric Solzhenitsyn used in his Harvard address is a bit of an embarrassment. It is frankly religious rhetoric and somehow we have come to think such condemnations of the political order a bit out of place. Such rhetoric is for matters personal and best left to those institutions that specialize in such matters—that is, the family and the church. Solzhenitsyn seems not to realize that our society's commitment to "religious freedom" is based exactly on the understanding that the church will not challenge the primary assumption of our system. The very materialism and banality of American life that Solzhenitsyn condemns is the price, and not a high price at that, we must pay in order to make the state neutral in matters moral and religious. Solzhenitsyn wrongly assumes that the characteristics of the American people he finds so unappealing are matters of public concern rather than religious concern. Politically we are right to take up a stance of self-interest; morally and religiously we know however that self-interest is not an appropriate form of life for the rest of our lives.

Thus we console ourselves with the idea that Solzhenitsyn has failed to understand the genius of our polity because he fails to see the moral advance represented by the amorality of our politics. His view of us is therefore too myopic and narrow and he fails to appreciate those "non-political" aspects of our lives that should qualify his overly harsh judgments about the shallowness of American life. Yet I think Solzhenitsyn's critique remains accurate,[18] but to demonstrate that, it is necessary to

---

[16]Solzhenitsyn, p. 3.

[17]Ibid.

[18]However I am in profound disagreement with Solzhenitsyn's more positive proposals as well as his understanding of the international situation. His hatred of communism and reliance on the "will of the West" to oppose communism gives far too uncritical support to some of the more reactionary political

pay closer attention to our profoundest political assumptions. For I want to suggest that the moral insufficiencies Solzhenitsyn finds so destructive about our society are necessarily built into the founding assumptions of America and have been reinforced by our best political practices and philosophy.

3. The Moral Assumptions of Political Liberalism

The American political system has been the testing ground for the viability of liberal theory. To be sure, "liberalism" is a many-faced and historically ambiguous phenomenon, and historically and culturally there were many factors in American life that served to qualify its impact.[19] But it is still the case that America, more than any nation before or after, has been the product of a theory of government.[20] Our assumption has been that, unlike other societies, we are not creatures of history,

---

positions in our country. His profound commitment to Orthodoxy, I am afraid, remains still far too tied to Russia and Russian nationalism. For a good critique of Solzhenitsyn's thought on this point, see Andrei Sinyavsky, "Solzhenitsyn and Russian Nationalism," *New York Review of Books,* 26/18 (November 22, 1979), pp. 3–6. For an interesting critique of Solzhenitsyn's inability to understand the moral status of pluralism, see Martin Marty, "On Hearing Solzhenitsyn in Context," *World Literature Today,* Autumn 1979, pp. 578–584. However, also see John Garvey's "In Defense of Solzhenitsyn," *Commonweal,* 105/17 (September 1, 1978), pp. 553–555.

[19]For example, C. B. Macpherson suggests that liberal democracy can mean simply the democracy of a capitalist market society (no matter how modified that society appears to be by the rise of the welfare state), or it can mean a society striving to ensure that all its members are equally free to realize their capabilities. *The Life and Times of Liberal Democracy* (Oxford: Oxford University Press, 1977), p. 1. It has, of course, been the thrust of Macpherson's work to show that liberalism as a political institution was transformed and perverted by capitalism and that now our task is to save liberalism from the perversion. For a critique of liberalism, and in particular Rawls, similar to my own, see George Parkin Grant, *English-Speaking Justice* (Sackville, New Brunswick: Mount Allison University Press, 1974). Grant makes the interesting point that Rawls' theory of justice is abstracted from any consideration of the facts of war and imperialism, pp. 44ff. I am grateful to Paul Ramsey for calling Grant's work to my attention.

A criticism of the following account of liberalism is that I take far too seriously philosophical theories of liberalism—i.e., Rawls, Nozick—and fail to pay appropriate attention to the historical experience of liberalism. For accounts of the latter one should not look to the philosophers but the work of cultural and social historians. Such work shows the American experience often provided a richer sense of history and the common good than the philosophical accounts of liberalism could give expression to. There is much to commend such a strategy, but it is my contention that it is no longer viable. For liberalism has become a self-fulfilling prophecy such that now theories of liberalism are not only descriptively powerful but shape our dominant public policies. Of course, much still occurs in our society that is not explicable from the point of view of liberalism and denotes fragments of other political moralities that have been present in American life and thought.

[20]I am not suggesting that the Constitution was the product of an explicit political theory in some deductive manner. Certainly the American form of society and government, like most governments and societies, was as much the product of historical accidents as theory. But our history has increasingly been interpreted and formed through liberal political philosophy. As Louis Hartz has argued in his now classic study, *The Liberal Tradition in America* (New York: Harcourt, Brace, and Company, 1955), even though life in the Puritan colonies and the South was in some ways deeply antagonistic to liberalism, liberalism became our dominant political tradition because we had no other tradition to which we might appeal. In the absence of any feudal experience, Americans simply have, in Hartz's phrase, a "natural liberalism" which they ironically dogmatically adhere to and defend.

but that we have the possibility of a new beginning.[21] We are thus able to form our government on the basis of principle rather than the arbitrary elements of a tradition.

Our assumptions in this respect profoundly distort our history, but their power is hard to deny. Liberalism is successful exactly because it supplies us with a myth that seems to make sense of our social origins. For there is some truth to the fact that we originally existed as a people without any shared history, but came with many different kinds of histories. In the absence of any shared history we seemed to lack anything in common that could serve as a basis for societal cooperation. Fortunately, liberalism provided a philosophical account of society designed to deal with exactly that problem: A people do not need a shared history; all they need is a system of rules that will constitute procedures for resolving disputes as they pursue their various interests. Thus liberalism is a political philosophy committed to the proposition that a social order and corresponding mode of government can be formed on self-interest and consent.

From this perspective the achievement of the Constitution is not its fear of tyranny, or even its attempt to limit the totalitarian impulses of the majority. Rather the wisdom and achievement of the Constitution comes from the guiding "assumption that only by institutionalizing the self-interest of the leaders, on the one hand, and of the individual citizen, on the other, could tyranny be averted."[22] The ethical and political theory necessary to such a form of society was that the individual is the sole source of authority. Thus Hobbes and Locke, to be sure in very different ways, viewed the political problem as how to get individuals, who are necessarily in conflict with one another, to enter into a cooperative arrangement for their mutual self-interest.

Likewise, Madison assumed that "the causes of faction are sown into the nature of man," and since such causes cannot be eliminated without destroying "freedom," the primary task of government is to control the effects of conflict. He argues in the tenth *Federalist* essay that the chief advantage of an extended republic is that aggregates of self-interested individuals will find it difficult to interfere with the rights of others to pursue their self-interest. Thus, William Hixson argues, Madison justified his understanding of our political character on two suppositions, that

the only possible source of public authority is the private need of the independently situated political actors, each of whom is vested with a right to act according to

---

[21]Macpherson rightly observes that liberalism has "always meant freeing the individual from the outdated restraints of old established institutions." *The Life and Times of Liberal Democracy*, p. 21. This has had a peculiar effect on the form of our political theory, as it tends to be excessively removed from the actual process of our government and society. The latter are treated by political science and history, which often putatively claim to have no normative interests.

[22]William Hixson, "Liberal Legacy, Radical Critique," *Commonweal*, 105/20 (October 13, 1978), p. 649. Thus Americans' paradoxical attitude toward politicians. They want only people of integrity to run for office, but they make them subject to a polity that defines the essence of the political as compromise and a willingness to subject one's own convictions to the interests of one's constituency. Perhaps that is one of the ways we have for devaluing the realm of the political—namely, we have created a system where only the morally compromised can be political actors.

self-defined standards of conscience and interest, and second, that the only legitimate function of "the sovereign" is the preservation of order through the management of conflict between such individuals.[23]

The irony is that our founders thought that the system of competing factions would work only if you could continue to assume that people were virtuous. John Adams in his first year as vice-president under the new constitution said: "We have no government armed with power capable of contending with human passions unbridled by morality and religion. Our constitution was made only for a moral and a religious people. It is wholly inadequate for the government of any other." Yet the very theory that has formed our public rhetoric and institutions gives no sufficient public basis for the development of such people. It was assumed that in making "morality" a matter of the "private sphere"—that is, what we do with our freedom—it could still be sustained and have an indirect public impact. But we know this has not been the case; our "private" morality has increasingly followed the form of our public life. People feel their only public duty is to follow their own interests as far as possible, limited only by the rule that we do not unfairly limit others' freedom. As a result we have found it increasingly necessary to substitute procedures and competition for the absence of public virtues. The bureaucracies in our lives are not simply the result of the complexities of an industrialized society, but a requirement of a social order individualistically organized.[24]

Many of our current political problems and the way we understand and try to solve them are a direct outgrowth of our liberal presuppositions. For example, the American government is often condemned for its inability to develop an economic or energy policy, but such policies must necessarily be public policies. Just as it has been the genius of the American political system to turn every issue of principle into an issue of interest, so it has been the intention of our polity to make impossible the very idea of public policy or public interest. Public policy cannot exist because society is nothing more than an aggregate of self-interested individuals. The policy which is formulated therefore must be the result of a coalescence of self-interests that is then justified in the name of the greatest good for the greatest number (but too often turns

---

[23]Hixson, p. 649.

[24]Alasdair MacIntyre argues further that the "lack of shared moral beliefs in our political culture—which in eighteenth century terms is part, although only part, of our lack of virtue—is a great threat and possibly even the great threat to our liberties. I shall argue toward the conclusion by suggesting that the consequence of a lack of shared moral beliefs tends to be *either* that government acts without the proper assent of the people to its actions, because lack of shared moral beliefs prevents the occurrence of the kind of political dialogue which would enable the people to understand the Proposed acts of government *or* the government connives at the creation of false simulacra of moral consensus, moods either of public hysteria or of public fatigue, which happily are transitory, but which while they last deceive both the government and many of those over whom they rule. And when government fails because its policies lack proper support or because that support derives from false simulacra the temptation to government to act in covert and clandestine ways sometimes becomes overwhelming." "Power and Virtue in the American Republic" (unpublished manuscript), pp. 8–9.

out to be the greatest good for the most powerful). Liberalism thus becomes a self-fulfilling prophecy; a social order that is designed to work on the presumption that people are self-interested tends to produce that kind of people.

It is often pointed out that there is a deep puzzle about the American people, for in spite of being the best off people in the world, their almost frantic pursuit of abundance seems to mask a deep despair and loss of purpose. I suspect that our despair is the result of living in a social order that asks nothing from us but our willingness to abide by the rules of fair competition. We have been told that it is moral to satisfy our "wants" and "needs," but we are no longer sure what our wants and needs are or should be. After all, "wants" are but individual preferences. Americans, as is often contended, are good people or at least want to be good people, but our problem is that we have lost any idea of what that could possibly mean. We have made "freedom of the individual" an end in itself and have ignored that fact that most of us do not have the slightest idea of what we should do with our freedom. Indeed, the idealists among us are reduced to fighting for the "freedom" or "right" of others to realize their self-interests more fully.

Such a system is defended because, whatever its faults, it is at least noncoercive. Therefore our public policies are formed in a manner that avoids as much as possible impinging on anyone's self-interest. As a result we fail to notice that "freedom" can become coercive by the very conception of "choice" it provides. For example, in his remarkable book *The Gift Relationship*, Richard Titmuss compares the blood distribution systems in America and Britain.[25] In Britain the only way one is allowed to obtain blood is through a voluntary donor who does not know to whom his or her blood is given. It is against the law to sell one's blood. In America we rely on diverse ways to obtain blood, ranging from voluntary programs to buying it. We feel that our system is inherently superior to the British because we do not prevent anyone from giving or selling their blood. We have a choice and are therefore free.

What we fail to notice is that by giving a "choice" we also create the assumption that blood, like cars and toothbrushes, can be bought and sold. We thus ignore the fact that the choice of selling blood trains us to see blood as simply one commodity among others. Put differently, what we have overlooked is that social policies should not only be efficient and fair, but they should also train us to have certain virtues as citizens. By concentrating on whether our policies are efficient, we have implicitly trained ourselves to assume that all human relationships should as much as possible take the form of an exchange model.[26] Thus Kenneth Arrow, in criticism of Titmuss' argument in favor of the British system, suggests

---

[25]Richard Titmuss, *The Gift Relationship* (New York: Random House, 1972).

[26]Of course, in many ways there is nothing more human, as it seems to be our nature to deny that our security may rest in the hands of another. Thus it is a characteristic of human society to turn all gift relationships into exchanges. For example, it is very hard for us not to think of gifts as "putting us in debt" and thus at a disadvantage. We, therefore, quickly try to give something in return so that we will not be another's "debt."

I do not want to rely too heavily on substituting ethics for self-interest. I think it best on the whole that the requirement of ethical behavior be confined to those circumstances where the price system breaks down. Wholesale usage of ethical standards is apt to have undesirable consequences. We do not wish to use up recklessly the scarce resources of altruistic motivation, and in any case ethically motivated behavior may even have a negative value to others if the agent acts without sufficient knowledge of the situation.[27]

We should not be too hasty in criticizing Arrow's claim that the economic model should prevail for as many relations as possible, since he is stating the profoundest assumptions of a liberal polity. For liberal polity is the attempt to show that societal cooperation is possible under the conditions of distrust. The very genius of our society is to forge a political and social existence that does not have to depend on trusting others in matters important for our survival. Thus to leave our destiny to the gift of blood from a stranger simply becomes unthinkable.

Of course the more it becomes unthinkable to trust a stranger, the more we must depend on more exaggerated forms of protection. But the human costs of distrust are perhaps the most destructive. For we are increasingly forced to view one another as strangers rather than as friends, and as a result we become all the more lonely. We have learned to call our loneliness "autonomy" and/or freedom, but the freer we become the more desperate our search for forms of "community" or "interpersonal relationship" that offer some contact with our fellows. Even the family is not immune from this development, since we now assume that children should have "rights" against the parents, as if the family itself were but a contractual society.[28]

In spite of our claim that the family is the bedrock of our society, the family has always been an anomaly for the liberal tradition. Only if human beings can be separated in a substantial degree from kinship can they be free individuals subject to egalitarian policies. Thus we assume—and this is an assumption shared by political conservatives and activists alike—that it is more important to be an "autonomous person" than to be a "Hauerwas" or a "Pulaski" or a "Smith." For example, the Supreme Court recently held in *Planned Parenthood* vs. *Danforth* that a husband has no rights if his wife wishes an abortion, because "abortion is a purely personal

---

[27]Kenneth Arrow, "Gifts and Exchanges," *Philosophy and Public Affairs*, 1/4 (Summer 1972), p. 355. The power of the economic model is perhaps no better exemplified than in Arrow's assumption that "altruistic" behavior is a "scarce resource." Moreover, he seems to be right to claim that once you have established a system, that works on the presumption of self-interest, it becomes a disvalue for anyone to act "ethically," since such behavior is not predictable. Thus we have the odd state of affairs where a morally altruistic person must act self-interestedly for not to do so is to act "selfishly."

[28]For a critique of "rights" language in relation to children, see my "Rights, Duties, and Experimentation on Children: A Critical Response to Worsfold and Bartholome," *Research Involving Children: Appendix* (Washington, D.C.: National Commission for Protection of Human Subjects of Biomedical and Behavioral Research Publication, No [OS] 77-0005, 1977), article 5, pp. 1–24.

right of the woman, and the status of marriage can place no limitations on personal rights."[29]

Or, for example, Milton Friedman, the paradigm liberal whom we mistakenly call "conservative," claims that for liberals "freedom of the individual or perhaps the family, is our ultimate goal in judging social arrangements. In a society freedom has nothing to say about what an individual does with his freedom; it is not an all-embracing ethic. Indeed, a major aim of the liberal is to leave the ethical problem for the individual to wrestle with."[30] But Friedman fails to recognize that the kind of freedom gained by the individual in our society is incompatible with freedom of the family. A society that leaves the "ethical problem to the individual" cannot engender or sustain the virtues necessary for providing the individual or the family the power to resist the state.[31]

Shorn of particularistic commitments essential to our public life, we exist as individuals, but now "individuals" is but a name for a particular unit of arbitrary desires. As C. B. Macpherson argues, liberalism's embrace of the market as the dominant institution of society involved a fundamental change in the conception of human nature. The traditional view of man was that of a being whose activity was an end in itself. With the rise of the market society the essence of rational purpose was taken to be the pursuit of possessions—we are what we own. But as soon as you

> take the essence of man to be the acquisition of more *things* for himself, as soon as you make the essential human quality the striving for possessions rather than creative activity, you are caught up in an insoluble contradiction. Human beings are sufficiently unequal in strength and skill that if you put them into an unlimited contest for possessions, some will not only get more than others, but will get control of the means of labor to which the others must have access. The others then cannot be fully human even in the restricted sense of being able to get possessions, let alone in the original sense of being able to use their faculties in purposive creative activity. So in choosing to make the essence of man the striving for possessions, we make it impossible for many men to be fully human.[32]

---

[29]For a spirited argument against this view, see Paul Ramsey, *Ethics at the Edges of Life* (New Haven, Conn.: Yale University Press, 1978), pp. 3–18.

[30]Milton Friedman, *Capitalism and Freedom* (Chicago: University of Chicago Press, 1962), p. 12.

[31]This is also the great dilemma of the "neo-conservatives." As Peter Steinfels points out, "The institutions they wish to conserve are to no small extent the institutions that have made the task of conservation so necessary and so difficult." *The Neoconservatives* (New York: Simon and Schuster, 1979), p. 103. Particularly illuminating is Steinfels' analysis of Daniel Bell's work, for Bell's understanding of the "Cultural Contradictions of Capitalism" clearly makes him the most interesting of those loosely identified as neo-conservatives. Michael Walzer, in a review of Steinfels' book, points out, "What made liberalism endurable for all these years was the fact that the individualism it generated was always imperfect, tempered by older restraints and loyalties, by stable patterns of local, ethnic, religious, or class relationships. An untempered liberalism would be unendurable. That is the crisis the neoconservatives evoke: the triumph of liberalism over its historical restraints. And that is a triumph they both endorse and lament.... Neoconservatives are nervous liberals, and what they are nervous about is liberalism. They despair of liberation, but they are liberals still, with whatever longing for older values." "Nervous Liberals," *New York Review of Books*, 26/15 (October 11, 1979), p. 6.

[32]C. B. Macpherson, *The Real World of Democracy* (Oxford: Oxford University Press, 1972), p. 54. Many who seek to secure a more equitable distribution of goods in our society often fail to see that a "justice" so

Ironically, however, when such a view of man prevails scarcity becomes an ever-present necessity. For scarcity is a necessary social creation when men are defined as having unlimited desires. The genius of liberalism was to make what had always been considered a vice, namely unlimited desire, a virtue. Thus it became legitimate for us to assume that the governing law of human nature is "the insatiable desire of every man for power to render the person and properties of others subservient to his pleasures."[33] Indeed such a view has us so strongly in its grip that we are now unable to think what might sustain a society that did not make scarcity integral to its understanding of man. No matter how great our abundance, we assume it is necessary to make and want more, even if the acquisition of more requires the unjust exploitation of "less developed lands." In truth we have no choice, for in a social order where distrust is primary we can only rely on abundance and technology to be a substitute for cooperation and community.

The recent emphasis on "justice" in the elegant ethical and political theory eleborated by John Rawls might be taken to indicate that liberalism is capable of a profounder sense of justice than I have described. Without going into the detailed argument necessary to criticize Rawls, his book stands as a testimony to the moral limits of the liberal tradition. For the "original position" is a stark metaphor for the ahistorical approach of liberal theory, as the self is alienated from its history and simply left with its individual preferences and prejudices.[34] The "justice" that results

---

secured may well only reinforce a more fundamental unjust view of ourselves. The problem with American egalitarianism, as Michael Walzer has argued, is that egalitarians fail to see that different goods should be distributed to different people for different reasons. We have tried to avoid articulating or institutionalizing the criteria for such differences by making the ability to make money the common denominator for everyone, the assumption being that if everyone has a basic minimum of money, then the distribution of their other talents will take care of itself. But such a system is inherently unjust, since many have no talent for making money. As Walzer suggests, "Equality requires a diversity of principles, which mirrors the diversity both of mankind and of social goods," but as a society we seem to have no way of embodying such diversity in our public policies, for the recognition of diversity seems to result in injustice and envy. "In Defense of Equality," *Dissent,* 20/4 (Fall 1973), pp. 399–408. To avoid envy a society must have a sense of those offices and tasks that receive special favor because of the service they perform for the existence of the community as a whole.

[33]Macpherson, *The Real World of Democracy,* p. 62. Though I am in deep agreement with much of Macpherson's analysis of the dilemma of contemporary liberalism, I am unconvinced by his claim that technology has now freed us from scarcity to the extent that we can now throw off our dependence on the market. Rather, I suspect, as his own analysis suggests, that we can only free ourselves from the coercion of the market when we are morally trained not to think of ourselves as deserving whatever we desire, or perhaps more accurately, when we learn to desire the right things rightly.

[34]This criticism may appear unfair to Rawls, as his own criticism of ideal observer theory and utilitarianism rests on those theories' tendencies to conflate into one, thereby eradicating their individual histories. Rawls' strategy, in contrast, is to try to provide an account of justice that will allow for the development of an appreciation for individual differences without envy. However, his attempt requires him to resort to the device of the original position that seems to entail exactly the loss of individuality he was trying to avoid. *A Theory of Justice* (Cambridge, Mass.: Harvard University Press, 1972), pp. 184–192. Thus Robert Paul Wolff has argued that "Rawls conceives of the moral point of view as an atemporal vantage from which, like Lucretius gazing down upon the plain of battle, we contemplate all time and all space equanimously and isotropically. But human existence is not accidentally temporal; it is essentially temporal. What makes it a matter of justice how a subgroup chooses for the whole society is the fact that in principle that entire group *could* be included in

from the bargaining game is but the guarantee that my liberty to consume will be fairly limited within the overall distributive shares. To be sure, some concern for the "most disadvantaged" is built into the system, but not in a manner that qualifies my appropriate concern for my self-interest. Missing entirely from Rawls' position is any suggestion that a theory of justice is ultimately dependent on a view of the good; or that justice is as much a category for individuals as for societies. The question is not only how should the shares of any society be distributed equitably, but what bounds should individuals set for themselves if they are to be just. In an effort to rid liberalism of a social system built on envy, Rawls has to resort to the extraordinary device of making all desires equal before the bar of justice. As a result he represents the ultimate liberal irony: individualism, in an effort to secure societal cooperation and justice, must deny individual differences.

Perhaps Solzhenitsyn's critique is truer than even he suspected, for his criticisms reach to the basic moral presumptions of our society. Perhaps what he criticizes in us results not from our having been untrue to our best insights, but because we have been true to them. Of course, there have always been richer experiences of trust and community in our polity, but the problem is that such experience and community have no way to find political expression.[35] Thus blacks are encouraged to participate fully in our political process so that their interests might be known, yet there is no

---

the choosing. What makes it seem a matter of justice how parents choose for their children is the human fact that generations overlap, so that the children, the parents, and the grandparents must live for a time in the same world. What makes it manifestly *not* a matter of justice how this generation chooses for a generation far in the future is the certainty that they cannot share the same world, and hence could not even in principle gather together to share the act of choice. The veil of ignorance creates a choice situation in which the *essential* characteristics of human existence are set aside along with accidents of individual variations. What results, it seems to me, is not a moral point of view, but a nonhuman point of view from the perspective of which moral questions are not clarified but warped and distorted." *Understanding Rawls* (Princeton, N.J.: Princeton University Press, 1977), p. 97.

[35]Some have argued, for example, that our American experience, especially as it is understood in terms of the theological notion of covenant, must be taken seriously as an important moment in God's history. Thus Richard Neuhaus' *Time Toward Home: The American Experiment as Revelation* (New York: Seabury, 1975), pp. 46–67. I do not have the space to deal adequately with the challenge of this position. However, without denying the power and profundity often associated with such attempts to understand theologically the American experience, I am often left wondering if they have anything to do with reality.

For a particularly provocative account of the political implications of covenant, see Robin Lovin, "Covenantal Relationships and Political Legitimacy," *The Journal of Religion*, 60/1 (January 1980), pp. 1–16, Lovin argues convincingly that political community interpreted in terms of covenant, in contrast to the contractarian tradition, has the advantage of not treating "the power of the state as some extraordinary menace, to be restrained from infecting the more creative institutions of family and culture. Like all other powers, the state must act in accordance with duty, but it also shares with other powers a creative role in establishing relationships of communication and obligation." Moreover, covenant reminds us that freedom emerges precisely at the point "that it is possible to speak meaningfully about duty as a reminder that covenantal freedom always contains an element of mutuality," pp. 9–10. Lovin also rightly suggests that equality understood covenantally is not, in the first instance, distributive, but rather that it is necessary to insure political participation. What Lovin does not do, however, is to provide an account of whether covenant is really an operative ideal in our polity or, even more important, what is the nature, status, and task of the church for such a polity. Also needing justification is the implicit assumption that the notion of "covenant" adequately sums up the "biblical" understanding of God.

political recognition that the history of their suffering might or should be recognized as a valuable political resource.[36] Such concerns make good political rhetoric, but have little to do with the reality of politics which deals with the satisfaction of interests as articulated through group conflict and cooperation.

4. The Church as a School for Virtue

If this analysis of our society's polity is even close to being correct, then it is by no means clear what the church's stance ought to be. The temptation is to assume that the task of the church is to find a political alternative or ways to qualify some of the excesses of liberalism. But such a strategy is both theologically and ethically problematic, for it fails to recognize that our society offers no ready alternatives to liberalism. We are all liberals. In fact for us in America, liberalism, a position dedicated to ending our captivity to nature, custom, and coercion, ironically has become our fate. The great self-deception is in thinking that the tradition of liberalism gives us the means to recognize that it is indeed a tradition. Instead it continues to promise us new tomorrows of infinite creation. And the more we are convinced we are free, the more determined we become.

For the church to adopt social strategies in the name of securing justice in such a social order is only to compound the problem. Rather the church must recognize that her first social task in any society is to be herself.[37] At the very least that means that the church's first political task is to be the kind of community that recognizes

---

[36]Such a recognition would require white Americans to claim the history of slavery as their history, rather than simply an unfortunate event that can now be forgotten. In effect we are trying to say to the American black community that now that blacks have allegedly the same opportunities as whites, slavery can be forgotten, for after all what is a little slavery between friends. In the face of what cannot be changed, we often think the only thing we can do is forget, but when we forget we lose our own history. What is required is forgiveness, but for forgiveness to work politically we must be the kind of people capable of making another people's history our own. For a remarkable account of the significance of forgiveness as an integral aspect of any political process, see Haddon Willmer, "The Politics of Forgiveness—A New Dynamic," *The Furrow*, 30/4 (April 19, 1979), pp. 207–218; see also my "The Necessity of Forgiveness," *Worldview*, 23/1–2 (January–February 1980), pp. 15–16. See also H. R. Niebuhr's provocative account of the necessity of shared history for community in *The Meaning of Revelation* (New York: Macmillan, 1960), pp. 114–132.

[37]The claim that the first social task of the church is to be herself is not "sectarian" if by that is meant a retreat or withdrawal from the world. Indeed, I am in some respects deeply sympathetic with the social strategy that Max Stackhouse has called "conciliar denominationalism"—that is, the combination of the free church tradition with a concern for the wider social order. However, as Stackhouse denotes, this strategy seems to entail two conflicting motifs: sectarianism and Christendom. Thus, a figure such as Rauschenbush "saw the necessity of the select body of believers anticipating the kingdom in the word and deed in good sectarian fashion, and of taking the world seriously on its own terms, as did all visions of Christendom." "The continuing Importance of Walter Rauschenbush: Editor's Introduction," in Walter Rauschenbush's *The Righteousness of the kingdom*, edited and introduced by Max Stackhouse (Nashville: Abingdon Press, 1968), p. 23. What advocates of this stance often overlooked, however, in their enthusiasm for liberal society was that such a society made the internal discipline necessary to sustain a free church as an independent and socially significant presence appear arbitrary and coercive. Moreover, they failed to see that the kind of "constitutional" democracy of the free church was radically transformed when translated into the language of liberalism. Thus Rauschenbush too readily assumed that his understanding of messianic theocracy could be institutionalized through the

the necessity that all societies, church and political alike, require authority. But for Christians our authority is neither in society itself nor in the individual; it is in God.[38] As a result the church must stand as a reminder to the pretensions of liberalism that in spite of its claims to legitimate authority, some necessarily rule over others as if they had the right to command obedience.

The church also has a constitution that requires consent, but its constitution takes the form of the story of a savior who taught us to deal with power by recognizing how God limits all earthly claims to power.[39] Because we have been so called and formed, Christians should be free from the fear that fuels the power of coercion for liberal and illiberal states alike. The moral adventure represented by liberalism has been to diffuse the coercive nature of the state and society by developing a culture and government that left the individual to his or her own desires. As a result the coercive aspects of our social order are hidden, since they take the appearance of being self-imposed. Yet the distrust of the other inherent in liberal social and political theory cannot help but create powers that claim our loyalties and destructively run our lives.

Ironically, the most coercive aspect of the liberal account of the world is that we are free to make up our own story. The story that liberalism teaches us is that we have no story, and as a result we fail to notice how deeply that story determines our lives. Accordingly, we fail to recognize the coercive form of the liberal state, as it, like all states, finally claims our loyalty under the self-deceptive slogan that in a democracy the people rule themselves because they have "consented" to be so ruled. But a people who have learned the strenuous lesson of God's lordship through Jesus' cross should recognize that "the people" are no less tyrannical than kings or dictators.

In the absence of anyone knowing the truth, it has been the liberal assumption that "the people," particularly as they balance one another's desires, limit the power of

---

increasing democratization of institutions. And he failed to understand that a Christian social order that would "make bad men do good things" is antithetical to the moral presuppositions of a liberal society. The enthusiasm for the American experiment has been one of the primary sources for the failure of Christian social ethicists to appreciate the difficulty of making analogies between church (and kingdom) and our society work. As H. R. Niebuhr has observed, Protestantism was hard put to provide principles for human construction, given the old societies in which it was born. In many ways one of the most healthy aspects of Protestantism was it was always forced to live in a world it has not or could not make. But with America the situation changed, as here Protestantism could finally turn protest to construction and America, in fact, became, as I suggested above, an experiment in constructive Protestantism. See Niebuhr, *The kingdom of God in America* (New York: Harper Brothers, 1937), pp. 28–44. Therefore Christian social ethicists in America have never been clear what the primary object of their work should be—the church or America—since attention to the latter seemed to be the immediate task of the church.

[38]To be sure, many of those active in the founding and development of American democracy assumed that the limits imposed on government were not based on the sovereignty of man, but because all government was subject to the kingdom of God. See H. R. Niebuhr, *The Kingdom of God in America*, pp. 75–87. However, the Enlightenment assumption of the sovereignty of man has increasingly become the more prominent, as a "government under God" simply makes no sense in a pluralist society.

[39]This does not mean that Christians live in a night in which all "cats and/or nations are grey," (Barth). To be sure the church has a stake in developing relative criteria to distinguish between more nearly just and unjust, more violent and less violent, freer and coercive states. Nor would I deny that in many ways pluralist societies, such

falsehood. The church accepted such a strategy because it seemed to express a humility about the status of the state that, if not founded on the confession of God's lordship, at least was appropriate to our conviction that God limits all earthly power. Moreover, such a strategy seemed to offer the church freedom to preach the Gospel in a manner few societies had ever been willing to allow. While reveling in such "freedom" we failed to notice that the church had again been coopted into accepting the assumption that the destiny of a particular state and social order was intrinsic to God's Kingdom.

The challenge of the political today is no different than it has always been, though it appears in a new form. The challenge is always for the church to be a "contrast model" for all polities that know not God. Unlike them, we know that the story of God is the truthful account of our existence, and thus we can be a community formed on trust rather than distrust. The hallmark of such a community, unlike the power of the nation-states, is its refusal to resort to violence to secure its own existence or to insure internal obedience. For as a community convinced of the truth, we refuse to trust any other power to compel than the truth itself.

It is in that connection that the church is in a certain sense "democratic," for it believes that through the story of Christ it best charts its future. We rejoice in the difference and diversity of gifts among those in the church, as that very diversity is the necessary condition for our faithfulness. Discussion becomes the hallmark of such a society, since recognition and listening to the other is the way our community finds the way of obedience.[40] But the church is radically not democratic if by democratic we mean that no one knows the truth and therefore everyone's opinion counts equally. Christians do not believe that there is no truth; rather truth can only be known through struggle. That is exactly why authority in the church is vested in those we have learned to call saints in recognition of their more complete appropriation of that truth.

Put starkly, the way the church must always respond to the challenge of our polity is to be herself. This does not involve a rejection of the world, or a withdrawal from the world; rather it is a reminder that the church must serve the world on her own terms. We must be faithful in our own way, even if the world understands such faithfulness as disloyalty. But the first task of the church is not to supply theories of governmental legitimacy or even to suggest strategies for social betterment. The first task of the church is to exhibit in our common life the kind of community possible when trust, and not fear, rules our lives.

Such a view of the political task of the church should not sound strange to Christians, whose very existence was secured by people who were willing to die rather

---

as America, provide a unique opportunity for the church. It is not pluralism itself that causes the problem but the theories of pluralism that we must reject.

[40]A. D. Lindsay has rightly argued that the key to democracy is discussion, but discussion can only be effective when we have genuinely different points of view. That is why equality is not only compatible with but demands differences. Perhaps the most significant thing the church can do for any society is to be a community capable of sustaining the kind of discussion necessary for the formation of good and truthful arguments and lives. See A. D. Lindsay, *The Modern Democratic State* (Oxford: Oxford University Press, 1962), pp. 249–286.

than conform to the pretentious claims of government. And we must remember that the demand that religion be freed from state control was not simply an attempt to gain toleration, but to make clear that the church represented a polity truer and more just than the state can ever embody. Simply because we live in a society that has institutionalized "freedom of religion" does not mean the church's political task has thereby been accomplished.

This kind of challenge is all the more needed in a society like ours that is living under the illusion that justice can be based on the assumption that man rather than God controls the world. As John Howard Yoder has suggested, "it is more important to know with what kind of language we criticize the structures of oppression than to suggest that we have the capacity to provide an alternative which would not also be a structure of oppression."[41] As Christians we have a language to describe the problems of liberalism, but we have become hesitant and embarrassed to use it. We must take courage from Solzhenitsyn's example and clearly say that the problem with our society and politics is its sinful presumption that man is born to be happy, when he clearly has to die. A truthful politics is one that teaches us to die for the right thing, and only the church can be trusted with that task.[42]

Moreover, by taking seriously its task to be an alternative polity, the church might well help us to experience what a politics of trust can be like. Such communities should be the source for imaginative alternatives for social policies that not only require us to trust one another, but chart forms of life for the development of virtue and character as public concerns. The problem in liberal societies is that there seems to be no way to encourage the development of public virtue without accepting a totalitarian strategy from the left or an elitist strategy from the right. By standing as an alternative to each, the church may well help free our social imagination from those destructive choices. For finally social and political theory depends on people having the experience of trust rather than the idea of trust.

But we must admit the church has not been a society of trust and virtue. At most, people identify the church as a place where the young learn "morals," but the "morals" often prove to be little more than conventional pieties coupled with a few unintelligible "don'ts." Therefore any radical critique of our secular polity requires an equally radical critique of the church.

And it is a radical critique, for I am not calling for a return to some conservative stance of the church. My call is for Christians to exhibit confidence in the lordship of Yahweh as the truth of our existence and in particular of our community. If we

---

[41]John Howard Yoder, "The Christian Case for Democracy," *Journal of Religious Ethics*, 5 (Fall 197), p. 220.

[42]This does not mean, however, that the church expects little from society as a way of enhancing the moral role of the church. On the contrary the church wants whatever society in which it finds itself to live up to its highest aspirations. Even though this paper has been primarily negative, my primary intentions are positive. For it is my central contention that the church will serve our social order best when it is able to form a people who have something to offer our social order. I have tried to suggest that that "something" is nothing less than the virtues and trust necessary to sustain a polity capable of maintaining a rich pluralism of differences.

are so confident, we cannot help but serve our polity, for such confidence creates a society capable of engendering persons of virtue and trust. A people so formed are particularly important for the continued existence of a society like ours, as they can provide the experience and skills necessary for me to recognize the difference of my neighbor not as a threat but as essential for my very life.

38. John Milbank – Liberality versus Liberalism

The recent history of political theory is strange. The welfare of this world has been wrecked by the ideology of neoliberalism and yet its historic challengers—conservatism and socialism—have been mostly in total disarray. Socialism, in particular, appears to be wrong-footed by the discovery that liberalism and not socialism is the bearer of "modernity" and "progress." If the suspicion then arises that perhaps modernity and progress are themselves by no means on the side of justice, then socialists today characteristically begin to half-realize that their own traditions in their Marxist, Social Democratic, and Fabian forms have been themselves too grounded in modes of thought that celebrate only utility and the supposedly "natural" desires, goods, and needs of isolated individuals.

For these reasons, there is no merit whatsoever in the contention of the ageing Left (Habermas, Hobsbaum, etc.) that we have been faced with an abandonment of progress and the enlightenment by a postmodern era. To the contrary, it is clear that what we have experienced is rampant enlightenment, after the failure of secular ideologies derived from the nineteenth century—socialism, positivism, romantic nationalism, communism—that sought to some degree to *qualify* enlightenment individualism and formalism with organicism, distributive justice, and socio-historical substance.

Instead, in the face of the mismatch I have indicated, we need to take the risk of thinking in an altogether new way that will take up the traditions of socialism less wedded to progress, historical inevitability, materialism, and the state, and put them into debate with conservative anti-capitalist thematics and the traditions of classical and biblical political thought which may allow us to see the inherent restrictions of the parameters of modern social, political, and economic reflection. Our perspective may remain basically a "Left" one, but we need to consider the possibility that only a re-alignment of the Left with more primordial, "classical" modes of thinking will now allow it to criticize currently emerging tyranny.

This should include at its center an openness to religion and to the question of whether a just politics must refer beyond itself to transcendent norms. For this reason, in what follows I have undertaken the experiment of thinking through a Catholic

Christian (Roman Catholic, Orthodox, High Anglican) approach to the social sphere in the light of current reality, in the hope that this will have something to offer not just to Christians, but to a degree also to Jews, Muslims, and people of no religious persuasion whatsoever. I do not choose to insult the latter by concealing in any way the religious grounds of what I wish to say, nor my view that a predominantly secular culture will only sustain the neoliberal catastrophe or cause it to mutate (after the credit crunch) into a new form of state-market oligarchy.

The documents of Vatican II, especially *Gaudium et Spes,* appear in retrospect to have been in some ways over-accepting of modern liberal democracy and market economics.[1] This is historically understandable—since the Church needed to move beyond a previous endorsement of reactionary and sometimes absolutist monarchy, and static and hierarchical economic systems linked to unequal landholding.

Today though, we need to recognize that we are in a very different situation. First of all, recent events demonstrate that liberal democracy can itself devolve into a mode of tyranny. One can suggest that this is for a concatenation of reasons. An intrinsic indifference to truth, as opposed to majority opinion, means in practice that the manipulation of opinion will usually carry the day. Then governments tend to discover that the manipulation of fear is more effective than the manipulation of promise, and this is in keeping with the central premises of liberalism which, as Pierre Manent says, are based in Manichean fashion upon the ontological primacy of evil and violence: at the beginning is a threatened individual, piece of property, or racial terrain.[2] This is *not* the same as an Augustinian acknowledgment of original sin, perversity, and frailty—a hopeful doctrine, since it affirms that all-pervasive evil for which we cannot really account (by saying, for example, with Rousseau that it is the fault of private property or social association as such) is yet all the same a contingent intrusion upon reality, which can one day be fully overcome through the lure of the truly desirable which is transcendent goodness (and that itself, in the mode of grace, now aids us). Liberalism instead begins with a disguised naturalization of original sin as original egotism: our own egotism which we seek to nurture, and still more the egotism of the other against which we need protection.

Thus increasingly, a specifically liberal politics (and not, as so many journalists fondly think, its perversion) revolves round a supposed guarding against alien elements: the terrorist, the refugee, the person of another race, the foreigner, the criminal. Populism seems more and more to be an inevitable drift of unqualified liberal democracy. A purported defence of the latter is itself deployed in order to justify the suspending of democratic decision-making and civil liberties. For the

---

[1]See Tracy Rowland, *Culture and the Thomist Tradition after Vatican II.* London: Routledge, 2003.
[2]Pierre Manent, *An Intellectual History of Liberalism.* Translated by Rebecca Balinski. Princeton: Princeton University Press, 1995.

reasons just seen, this is not just an extrinsic and reactionary threat to liberal values: to the contrary, it is liberalism itself that tends to cancel those values of liberality (fair trial, right to a defense, assumed innocence, *habeas corpus,* a measure of free speech and free enquiry, good treatment of the convicted) which it has *taken over,* but which as a matter of historical record it did not invent, since they derive rather from Roman and Germanic law transformed by the infusion of the Christian notion of charity—which, in certain dimensions means a generous giving of the benefit of the doubt, as well as succor, even to the accused or wicked. For if the ultimate thing to be respected is simply individual security and freedom of choice (which is not to say that these should not be accorded penultimate respect) then almost any suspensions of normal legality can tend to be legitimated in the name of these values. In the end, liberalism takes this sinister turn when all that it endorses is the free market along with the nation-state as a competitive unit. Government will then tend to become entirely a policing and military function as J. G. Fichte (favorably!) anticipated. For with the decay of all tacit constraints embedded in family, locality, and mediating institutions between the individual and the state, it is inevitable that the operation of economic and civil rules which no individual has any longer any interest in enforcing (since she is socially defined only as a lone chooser and self-seeker) will be ruthlessly and ever-more exhaustively imposed by a state that will become totalitarian in a new mode. Moreover, the obsessive pursuit of security against terror and crime will only ensure that terror and crime become more sophisticated and subtly effective. We have entered a vicious global spiral.

In the face of this neoliberal slide into despotism, Catholic Christianity needs once more to proclaim with the classical tradition it carries—and which tended to predict just such a slide of a "democratic" ethos into sophistic tyranny—that government is properly mixed. Democracy, which is "the rule of the Many," can only function without manipulation of opinion if it is balanced by an "aristocratic" element of the pursuit of truth and virtue for their own sake on the part of some people whose role is legitimate even if they remain only "the Few," although they should ideally be themselves the Many. Democracy equally requires the "monarchic" sense of an architectonic imposition of intrinsic justice by a transcendent "One," however constituted, that is unmoved by either the prejudices of the Few or those of the Many. (One can think here of the legitimate European outlawing of capital punishment, against the wishes of the people or certain activities of the unelected European commissioners in protecting the minority interests of European Atlantic fishermen.) In addition, the Church needs boldly to teach that the only justification for democracy is theological: since the people is potentially the *ecclesia,* and since nature always anticipates grace, truth lies finally dispersed amongst the people (although they need the initial guidance of the virtuous) because the Holy Spirit speaks through the voice of all. *Vox populi, vox Dei* alone legitimates democracy, not the view that the collective will, simply because it represents a lowest common denominator of arbitration, should always prevail.

But to say this is to ask that we subordinate contract to gift. A government may be contractually legitimate as elected and its laws may be legitimate as proceeding from sovereign power, but such arrangements can be formally correct and yet lead to tyranny—as the Nazi example and now the Bush example so clearly show. So beyond this it needs to be supposed that the truth lies with the people somewhat in the way that truth lies in the Church for St Paul: namely that the body of Christ receives from the Holy Spirit—who is life and gift—a life of circulation which is the exchange of gifts. Different people and groups have different talents and insights—these they share for the good of the whole body. The people give their goods to the head of the Church who is Christ; in like manner the people should give their gifts of insight and talent to the sovereign representative who acts in their name.

Inversely the sovereign power must think of itself as distributing gifts—gifts of good governance and ordering, not simply as imposing a fiat in order to expand the utility and productiveness of a nation-state. This is an outrageous notion—for example New Labour's racist view that Britain should only accept "skilled" immigrants and refugees who can increase the gross national product. A government that gives must rather pursue the intrinsic fulfillment of its citizens. To rule in this way means that the subjects of rule can participate in this ruling, can appropriate its task to themselves. To be ruled renders them indeed "subjects" even in the ontological sense, since thereby something is proposed to them that can form their own integrated good if they respond to it. And no one is self-originated.

This means that to be a subject of a "crown" (in an extended sense) is actually a more radical idea than to be a citizen of a republic possessing "natural rights" in the contractualist sense of Rousseau (not necessarily in the ancient Roman sense). For the citizen is a natural individual before the state comes into being and only a citizen as co-composing the state. This means that he is always implicitly threatened by what Giorgio Agamben calls "the state of the exception": if he lapses back into being a natural individual like the denizens of Guantanamo Bay, he now lacks all human dignity.[3] This will only be granted to him as long as the contractual co-composition of the state holds good. Moreover, since in practice individual freedom of choice must always be limited, an appeal to "human rights" as an unassailable norm will always mean in reality a covert allowance of specific freedoms for some and certain converse inhibitions of specific freedom for others for interested reasons of power-politics.

By contrast, if one has what one may metaphorically describe as "constitutional monarchy" (I am not necessarily advocating it in the literal sense) then according to natural law and not just natural right, the sovereign authority is only "subjecting" men because it is obliged to offer them the gift of good coordination of diverse talents

---

[3]Giorgio Agamben, *State of Exception*. Translated by Kevin Attell. Chicago: University of Chicago Press, 2005.

and needs. St. Paul desacralized and redefined human rule as only concerned with justice and not with the protection of religious power or a domain—hence no human animal can fall outside a beneficent subjecting (in principle) which is in excess of contract.

For this reason, the Christian principles of polity stand totally opposed to any idea of the "nation-state" as the ultimate unit and rather favor at once the natural pre-given "region" on the one hand, and the universal human cosmopolis on the other. Likewise they oppose the manipulative politics of human rights and propose instead the distribution of specific liberties, offices and duties to certain individuals and groups in certain circumstances according to the discernment of what is specifically desirable and has a tendency to cement human solidarity. Such a principle refuses the dangerous double-tendency of the nation-state now becoming a global superstate-cum-global market. This double tendency is on the one hand to exalt the "rights" of many diverse cultural groupings, an exaltation that ultimately encourages the rise of terrorism rooted in particularism, and on the other hand to limit public norms to empty, abstract ones. Since these alone have to do the business of mediating the unmediably diverse interests of multiple cultural sub-groupings, they enjoy unlimited respect which must encourage the growth of a universal tyranny, since such abstract principles have no grounding save in the maintenance of power and some sort of peaceful order (which is in reality but suspended hostility) for their own sakes. Because they cannot really mediate the diverse interest groups, these will continue to be aggrieved against each other and against the central power, which will never be perceived as conceding to them "enough." Thus postmodern terrorism of the particular and the different feeds off modernist terror of the formally universal and vice-versa. In neither secular otherness nor secular universality now resides any hope.

To the contrary, the only ground for hope lies in the rediscovery of a more positive mode of mediation between regional interests and between the regions and the cosmopolis. Such a mediation involves the sense that differences are not valid as such, but are rather valid in their partial but necessary monadic intuitings of an elusive universal. Conversely, universality cannot be valid as a claimed finished grasp of ultimate principles, but only as a very remote intuition of the shape of a global and cosmic community in which all differences are reconciled and mutually flourish. But such a genuine account of unity and difference only makes sense if it appeals to a ground of their blending that is the true universality beyond the human, toward which we may genuinely journey. Transcendence must here be invoked, and indeed it is clear that only the notion of a Trinitarian God who is eternally relation and eternally the expression of unity in difference provides the adequate thought of a grounding for human association that would point us beyond the current mutual complicity of state terror with anarchic terror.

Such an anticipation of Trinitarian transcendence can only be mediated by a mixed government which includes a monarchic concern with unifying charitable synthesis for the sake of its intrinsic justice and not simply because a majority desire it. This positive feature of "monarchy" does not of course mean that the "monarchic" power should not be elected. To the contrary, it should be regarded as able to give rule because it has first been constituted by the mass donation of varied talents and points of view.

This perspective, however, should encourage us to revisit notions of "corporate" authority that are characteristic of Catholic thought and linked with the principle of subsidiarity. Not all bonding and grouping happens at the central level, and there is not first of all an aggregate of isolated individuals. To the contrary, people forever form micro-social bodies, and governments should treat people not according to formal abstraction but as they are—in regions, metiers, local cultures, religious bodies, etc.

To re-insist on monarchic, aristocratic, and corporate dimensions is in one sense conservative. Yet I remain a socialist of sorts. My case is rather that democracy will collapse into sophistic manipulation, as Plato taught, if it is not balanced by the element of "education in time" which requires a certain constantly self-cancelling hierarchy. The hierarchies of liberalism are in fact absolute spatial hierarchies of fixed power: one can climb up the ladder of power but only to displace someone else. The purpose of control here is simply utility and not the sharing of excellence. By contrast, the genuine spiritual hierarchy (after Dionysius the Areopagite) is a hierarchy that for human spiritual beings is endemic to time: in which pupil may overtake master and yet there should be no jealousy by the hierarch of the potential of the temporarily subordinate, because excellence is intrinsically shareable. Today, especially in Britain, all education is being subordinated to politics and economics. But a Catholic view should teach just the reverse: all politics and economics should be only for the sake of *paideia*.

This means: make time equal to space or even primary. Unqualified democracy has a kind of spatial bias—it supposes that we are all contracting individuals within a sort of eternalized *agora*. But this is to deny *life*—indeed it is part of the culture of death of which Pope John Paul II spoke—for life flows as a perpetual *glissando* through time. Life is not simply democratic, because it is both spontaneously creative and giving: with the arrived child, something new emerges. We must give to this child nurture, but from the outset the child reverses this hierarchy by revealing his unique creative power of response. No democratic contract can be involved here. Pure democracy tends to deny the sanctity of life, the importance of the child, the procedure beyond mere political participation to old age and death—its "normal" person is rather the freely choosing and contracting autonomous thirty-one-year-old. But *no* human person is forever like this; it is rather only a moment in a coming to be and passing away.

A politics subordinate to education—and so to the various traditions of wisdom, including religious traditions which can alone undertake a real *paideia*—can be truer to life as such, and also will be bound to ask questions about the final end of life. For only if life is deemed to have such a final end can every moment of life in fact be granted value. At this point it is not, after all, that one is straightforwardly advocating the primacy of the temporal dimension over the spatial one. Nor an aristocracy of *paideia* over a democracy of the *agora*. Indeed there can also be a bad modern, liberal mode for the dominance of time over space. For it is actually the case that pure spatialization will *also* tend to subordinate every given spatial form to the process of time leading towards the future. But not the time of gift: rather the empty time of pointless accumulation of a new spatial hoard of "wealth"—a hoarding of capital whose investment in the real is infinitely postponed.[4] By contrast, time can only be the time of gift where time is providing gradually the way to eternity beyond time. From this perspective every formed spatial stage of the way has an aesthetic value in itself and is not subordinate to future production.

Hence pure contractual democracy is spatial and yet in fact it nihilistically evacuates material space in favor of an abstract time always to come and so always perpetually postponed. On the other hand, a mixed government grounded in eternal law sanctifies local spaces in their actual temporality and does not subordinate them to the pure *glissando* of mere process.

So in the face of the crisis of liberal democracy, Catholic Christian thought needs to return to certain older themes of its critique of liberalism, but for radical and not conservative reasons. The "modernity" of liberalism has only delivered mass poverty, inequality, erosion of freely associating bodies beneath the level of the state and ecological dereliction of the earth—and now, without the compensating threat of communism, it has abolished the rights and dignity of the worker, ensured that women are workplace as well as domestic and erotic slaves, undermined working-class family structure, and finally started to remove the ancient rights of the individual which long precede the creed of liberalism itself (such as *habeas corpus* in Anglo-Saxon law) and are grounded in the dignity of the person rather than the "self-ownership" of autonomous liberal man (sic).

The only creed which tried to challenge this multiple impoverishment—communism—did so only in the name of the subordination of all to the future productivity of the nation (in practice also to the oligarchic power of a few technocrats), and ignored people's need's for an aesthetic and religious relationship to each other and to nature. What must rather challenge liberalism is a truer "liberality" in the literal sense of a creed of generosity which would suppose, indeed, that societies are more fundamentally bound together by mutual generosity than by contract—this

---

[4]See Oscar Guardiola-Rivera, *Being Against the World: Rebellion and Constitution*. London: Birkbeck Law, 2008.

being a thesis anciently investigated by Seneca in his *De Beneficiis* and in modernity again reinstated by Marcel Mauss.

This is not, of course, to deny that merely "liberal" measures of contract are not ceaselessly necessary to safeguard against the worst tyrannies, nor that we do not often have to resort to them in *lieu* of more substantive linkages. For these reasons I am *not* seeking to push a liberal approach altogether off the political agenda. Instead, the argument is that contract can never be the thing that fundamentally brings people together in the first place, nor can it represent the highest ideal of a true distributative justice. So before contract, since it is more socially real, lies the gift, and ahead of contract, since it is more socially ideal, lies, once again, the gift.

But considerations about gift are relevant also to a second context for contemporary social reflection. This concerns the economic realm. Recently, at least up till late 2008, we have lived under the tyranny of an unrestricted capitalist market. We have abandoned the Marxist view that this market must inevitably collapse and evolve into socialism. So we have thereby bid *adieu* to immanent, secular, historicist hope. But we have also largely abandoned the social democratic idea that the capitalist market can be mitigated. Here a Marxist analysis still largely holds good: social democracy was in the capitalistic interest for a phase which required a Keynesian promotion of demand; but it was abandoned when the excessive demands of labor, together with economic competition between nation-states ensured that the generation of profits became problematic. It is nonetheless true that neoliberalism has scarcely solved the problems of relatively slow Western productive growth since the 1950s, and now it faces its own crisis of excessive capital build-up, unable to realize itself in investment and real assets and so transferred to the funding of debts that have now become unpayable. What we now face is the likelihood of a new round of doubtless different Keynesianism, which may this time threaten a new market-state totalitarianism.

Here again, Catholic social thought needs to remain true to its own genius which has always insisted that solutions do not lie either in the purely capitalist market nor with the centralized state. There is in fact no "pure" capitalism, only degrees of this mode of production and exchange, even though one should still aspire eventually to go beyond the capitalist system. Small-scale local capitalist economies are only in truth semi-capitalist, because they often exhibit a competition for excellence, but not a mutually-abolishing drive of companies towards monopoly (as was rightly argued by Fernand Braudel). This is because, in such cases, for example in parts of North Italy and of Germany, a certain local culture of design-excellence ensures that there is *no* pursuit of production *only* to make money, nor any exchange of commodities *only* determined by supply and demand and not also by a shared recognition of quality—such that supply and demand plus the accumulation of capital for the future and offering of loans at interest for reasonable social benefit are themselves involved in an exchange in what is taken to be inherent value and not just formal, market-determined value. (This is not at all to deny that there will be always be a never foreclosed *debate* as to what constitutes intrinsic value.)

Given such a consideration, one can see that an element of "gift-exchange" can remain even within the modern market economy. Producers of well-designed things do not just contract with consumers. The latter give them effectively counter-gifts of sustenance in return for the gifts of intrinsically good things, even though this is mediated by money.

From this example one can suggest that more of the economy could be like this. This requires indeed that one favors local production of locally suitable things linked to local skills. We should import and export only what we have to, or else what truly can only come from elsewhere—for I am not advocating asceticism! Rather the true hedonism of the genuine and its interchange. But if we receive only the exotic from elsewhere, then here, too, there can be a form of gift-exchange in operation. In actual fact, global communications and transport favor this: within a global village those in Europe wishing to receive the good gift of organically-farmed food can in exchange pay a fair price for this which is a counter-gift ensuring that producers should not be exploited. (Nevertheless, one should be on guard against situations where consumers are made to pay excessively in order to compensate for inadequate investment or excessive profit-making on the part of exploiting owners of production.)

It is also likely that Islam and Judaism will be sympathetic to this way of looking at things and in fact the best hope for Europe is the reemergence, beyond the dominance of a worn-out *Aufklärung*, of a certain religiously informed but shared philosophic culture built around a wisdom tradition that re-awakens the old Western fusion of biblical with neoplatonic (Platonic plus Aristotelian and Stoic elements) tradition. This alone will be able to provide ontological grounds for the possibility of a future achievement of social participation that is a real consensus—rather than the liberal semi-suspended warfare of plural co-existence. These adequate grounds concern the affirmation of an ontological participation of the temporal in eternal peace and justice; the "memory" of a pre-fallen and uninterrupted mediation of this eternal peace to time; and finally the hope for an eschatological re-disclosure of this peace here on earth.

Things like the economy of fair-traded food-items may not sound dramatic or decisive and indeed they remain pathetically marginal and often compromised, but nevertheless the extension of such gift-exchange bit by bit is the sure way forward rather than revolution, government action alone, or else capitalistic solutions. Groups linking across the globe can ensure that something is given back to the earth and that genuine goods go into planetary circulation. We need once again to form systematic links between producer and consumer co-operatives and we need to see an emergence of cooperative banking, social credit unions, trade guilds, and voluntary economic courts (perhaps supervised by Church, Islamic, and Jewish bodies) to regulate and adjudicate the interactions between many different modes of cooperative endeavour. Only this will correct the mistake of all our current politics: namely to suppose that the "free market" is a given which should be either extended or inhibited and balanced. For if the upshots of the free market are intrinsically unjust, then "correcting" this through another welfare economy is only a mode of resignation; moreover its task is Sisyphean and periodically doomed to go under with every economic downturn.

Instead, we need a different sort of market: a re-subordination of money transaction to a new mode of universal gift-exchange. This requires that in every economic exchange of labor or commodity there is always a negotiation of ethical value at issue. Indeed, economic value should only be ethical value, while inversely ethical value should be seen as emerging from the supply and demand of intrinsic gifts.

For ethical value is not for Christianity just "virtue": rather it is supremely informed by charity and therefore it is the forging of bonds through giving and receiving. Virtue is here ecstasized and therefore its context ceases to be simply, as for Aristotle, political, but rather becomes, as for St. Paul, also economic—the virtue of a new "social" in the middle realm between *polis* and *oikos* that is equally concerned with political just distribution and with domestic care and nurture (the equality of women, which stems from Paul, even though he could not see how far this must go, has profoundly to do with this). St. Paul does not mention *arête*, though he does talk of the person who is *phronimos*. The latter is now more a giver and receiver of gifts than he is the attainer of a certain inner balance between reason and passion (as for Aristotle), as Philippians especially shows. For St. Paul, in speaking of *ecclesia*, proposes a new sort of *polis*, which can counteract and even eventually subsume the Roman empire—as the heirs of Abraham, Moses, and Plato must today subsume the American one. This new *polis*, as Bruno Blumenfeld shows, as with Philo, is at once monarchic, headed by Christ, and drastically democratic in a participatory sense—the people are the body of the King; the King can only act through the people.[5] Since virtue is now newly to do with the wisdom of love, virtue with Christianity gets democratized, and is indeed dispersed amongst the diverse gifts of the body of Christ which, as talents, also need to be constantly exchanged in order to realize the solidarity of the whole. As much later in Christian history (the seventeenth century) Pierre Bérulle suggested (though too much in the sense of Royal absolutism), human kingly rule is entirely Christological, since it echoes the kenotic and deificatory exchange of worshipping and worshipped (the King manifesting in a faint degree the glory of divine rule as such) that is fused in one corpus by the Incarnation.[6]

The latter event creates a new paracosmic reality—a new order somehow embracing both God and the Creation and a new order which abolishes the previous absolute dominance and semi-universality of the law, of *torah, lex,* and *nomos,* and so of all political process as such. The participation of the creation in God through the newly realized cosmic body of Christ ruled by the new order of love is utterly self-abandoning toward the good of the cosmic community of *esse* (as for Aquinas,

[5]Bruno Blumenfeld, *The Political Paul: Justice, Democracy and Kingship in a Hellenistic Framework.* London: Continuum, 2001.
[6]See Stéphane-Marie Morgain, *La Théologie Politique de Pierre de Bérulle (1598–1629).* Paris: Publisud, 2001.

there is only one divine *esse* in Christ for Bérulle). And it meets all the time with an equivalent divine kenosis: such that God now is—or is also and so is even in himself—simply a sharing of himself with the Creation, and yet this by free gift of love and not by inexorable fate of immanent pantheistic process which would tend always to appropriate the beings of the Creation. No. As created, things exceed both temporal process and fixed form; out of these they constantly weave the exchange of *relation,* and relation persists all the way down, because the created thing is at bottom outside itself as relation to another, namely God who gives it to be. But the God who creates affirms this within himself as generation of the *Logos,* and affirms also the worshipping response of the Creation within himself as the procession of the Holy Spirit.

Yet to this infinite good within the Trinity is added the ecstatic mysterious "extra" of finite dependence and finite worship. God, as both Philo and Bérulle in different eras said, lacks worship of himself, since he does not, as ontological rather than ontic, depend even on himself anymore than he causes himself. Yet in the Incarnation, suggests Bérulle, God ceases to lack even this and in coming to share God's life we are returned by God in Christ always back to specifically finite excellence. The invisible points back to the visible as well as the other way round, as Maximus the Confessor says in his *Mystagogy.*

So with the Incarnation, for all that God, it seems, can receive nothing, it happens that God comes to receive our worship of himself by joining to the personhood of the *Logos* our human worship. Thus in some mysterious way, it is not just that the finite receives unilaterally the infinite, nor that the finite returns to the infinite a unilateral praise. It is now rather true that there is an infinite-finite exchange of gifts—as St. John of the Cross affirmed, was the case in his experience of deification. And in this way Christ is now King upon the earth, so that it follows that there should be always also a secular fusion of democratic dispersal with monarchic liberality and objectivity. Indeed this should run almost in the direction of monarchic anarchy, as clearly recommended by Tolkien in the *Lord of the Rings* (no law in the Shire; but the orderly echo of remote kingship). Or perhaps in the spirit of Robin Hood: like other legendary outlaws of the time of King John he had been declared "civilly dead" (*civile mortuus*) outside the law and therefore outside humanity, with the price on his head equivalent to that of the head of a forest-wolf. He had been declared so by a feudal king who tended to reduce his rule to the self-interested formation of contracts, and so was eventually restrained by the counter-contract of the Baronial *Magna Carta* to which he was forced to submit. But Robin Hood in legend appeals to the King in exile (in later re-tellings this becomes John's brother Richard, away on crusade), the King of natural law from whose legal domain no living human being can possibly be excluded. It is this natural law of fair distribution and generous assistance that Robin in the forest seeks to uphold, under the knowledge that its earthly sovereign representative remains in existence and may mysteriously show up at any time.[7]

---

[7]See A. J. Pollard, *Imagining Robin Hood: The Late-Medieval Stories in Historical Context.* London: Routledge, 2004.

In order for it to be possible that sovereign authority can exercise such a light touch, there must, however, be a collective interest in a sustainable and stable economy in which each person enjoys what is legitimately his own because it meets some of his basic needs and allows sufficient scope for the exercise and marketing of his talents. Property, as Hilaire Belloc taught, needs therefore to be as widely and equally dispersed as possible, in order to ensure that people have real creative liberty, little interest in greed and a tendency spontaneously to form self-regulating mechanisms of exchange of benefits. Today very few people, even middle class "well-off" people, possess any real property as opposed to a mass of temporary commodities that they have been more or less constrained into buying. For all the neoliberal talk of freedom, it is not an accident that so few are allowed the kind of property that permits one to leave a creative mark in the world. This is above all true of land—but we are made to pay most dearly of all and on almost life-time lease for the very space in which it is possible to sleep, make love, be born, die, prepare food, engage in play and in the arts. We should instead seek a way to provide people as widely as possible with real property, commencing with landed property itself.

As I have just indicated, property that is to do with self-fulfilment rather than accumulation is the foundation for a free giving and receiving that begins to compose a wider social household. But here gift-exchange is not just a mode of economy, but also a mode of politics; its spontaneous formation of an ethos and of tacit conventions restricts, without entirely removing, the need for the operation of codified and enforceable law—though this is still somewhat required, especially in order to prevent any breaking of the norms of wide dispersal. Monarchy in some sense, as Belloc like Tolkien taught, enters into the picture here, because mass popular movements along with the centralizing ambitions of the few can—as in fact occurred in the early modern period—tend to subvert the more genuine operation of local participatory democracy that is linked to the dispersal of property, whether in town or countryside. (In the Medieval case, especially in the towns.) Here the function of a somewhat "transcendent" single power should be to secure, uphold, and intervene occasionally in favor of, the subsidiary dispersal of power to its levels of appropriate exercise.

In this way, the function of the rule of "the One" that I am invoking runs against, rather than in support of, the modern doctrinal and practical upholding of an absolute sovereign center, which tends to ensure that even a supposed rule of the Many—"the sovereignty of the people"—is in reality an *over-emphatic* rule of the One.

We have seen that *ecclesia* names a new sort of universal polity, primarily democratic, yet also monarchic, which was invented by Christianity. But just how is this *ecclesia* constituted and how is it supposed to work? For St. Paul it seems to be a kind of universal tribalism of gift-exchange over-against both local polis and universal empire. But how can this be? Gift-exchange is normally of sacred things amongst friends. With relative strangers one needs formal rules of contract to ensure mutual benefit. Things exchanged here get secularized. How can one return to tribalism and exchange gifts with relative strangers? Well, I have already indicated that there may be a virtuous dialectic at work here: the more we become strangers also the more—potentially at least—we become universal neighbors. For when strangeness becomes absolute—as, for example, when Captain Cook encountered the Maoris—then there is no conceptual context for contract and the spontaneous familiarity of gift must once more be resorted to. We cannot today achieve this spontaneous familiarity as isolated individuals, but we can achieve it if across the globe localities and kinship groups still retain identity—as they tend to do, to assert themselves against anonymity—and yet ceaselessly exchange this with other groups: the way for example different folk musics remain themselves and yet constantly borrow from other folk musics.

But there is another and specifically theological point. Christianity renders all objects sacred: everything is a sign of God and of his love. Moreover in Christ this is *shown again,* and he provides the *idiom* for rendering all sacred. Hence there need be no more neutral commodities just as there are no more strangers—not because we are citizens, even of *cosmopolis,* but because we are sons, daughters, and brothers in Adam and now in the new Adam who is Christ. We are literally one kin, as the Middle Ages saw it—one kin both physical and spiritual; one kind under Christ. Thus we live by an exchange of blood, and charity is just this exchanging.

But is it? Is not charity the free one-way gift? But this makes love always sacrifice. But what is sacrifice, the ultimate free one-way gesture of love for? Surely to re-establish exchange. In this way sacrifice by no means escapes an economy, nor should it. And yet in gift-exchange, though there is equivalent return, the same thing does not come back. Something passes never to return at all. And for this reason no counter-gift ever cancels a debt but always inaugurates a new one. In the New Testament one finds both repeated unease (in both the gospels and the epistles) about gift-exchange as something pursued for the power of the benefactor, unlike the grace of God, and yet at the same time a continued insistence that God's grace must be actively received and responded to, and that the mediators of this grace, like St. Paul himself, deserve acknowledgment and support—the tension between these two stresses underlies many tortured passages in his writings.

For this reason the gift is not a straight line, but nor is it a closed circle. Rather it is a spiral or a strange loop. Beyond the law of non-contradiction it is both unilateral and reciprocal. It spirals on and on, and there is no first free gift, because to give to another one must have received at least her presence. Likewise one cannot be grateful without a gesture, which is already a counter-gift.

And when one gives, for that unilateral instance one is a monarch. One stands, as it were, hierarchically above the one who cannot choose what you are going to give to him, say to him, etc. No contractual liberalism can ever bind the oscillating aristocracy of mere conversation. Likewise when one receives, for that instance one is a monarch receiving tribute, even if the roles will be reversed in the next instance. Thus to give, or to receive, is hierarchically and unilaterally to help continue a process that is nonetheless fundamentally democratic and reciprocal. Indeed charity as welfare and justice as equity have always been the prerogative of kings and empires rather than city-states, all the way from Babylon to Elizabethan England. But charity is not just welfare, it is also, as the Middle Ages taught, the festive "between" that binds people, like the state of grace between the beggar who blesses you and you who give your coin to the beggar.

We, today, have totally divided reciprocal market contract from private free giving. And yet the latter remains secretly a contract and the former is also like the crossing of two unilateral gifts whose objects in no way mingle. Our situation therefore has crazy undercurrents that go unrecognized. Giving is, by contrast, only really free and liberal where it respects and helps further to create reciprocal norms. Contract is only really fair where there is a judged equivalence of objects and also a free mutual promotion by donation of the welfare of the exchanging parties.

Judged equivalence of objects. If all objects are sacred then, as for primitives, they possess a kind of animated force. Objects or their equivalents must return to their first owners or primal origins because they have in some sense personality. And this is the ecological dimension of gift-exchange. Humans identify themselves through the production and exchange of things: Marx was right. So inversely things are imbued with the story of human comings and goings. Objects naturally carry memories and tell stories; only commodified ones do not—or they tell shameful tales which they also conceal. In a modest way, even the packet of fair-trade coffee can start again to be a mythical object with personality.

For Catholic Christians, this is as it should be. Everything is sacramental; everything tells of the glory of Christ, and therefore every economy is part of the economy of salvation and every process of production and exchange prepares the elements of the cosmic Eucharist. This was true for St. Paul: his thought about grace is indissociable from his thought about the human exchange of talents and of material benefits. But the latter can only be a just exchange where there are constantly re-negotiated and agreed upon standards concerning the human common good: of what should be produced and with what standards; of whom should be rewarded and to what degree for the sake of further beneficial action by individuals. "To each according to his needs and from each according to his means" should still be our aim; but outside a completely crass materialism the question is about legitimate and desirable needs and means and the ordering of diverse needs and means. Here the crucial paradox so often ignored by socialists (but not by John Ruskin) is that only where there is an agreed hierarchy of values, sustained by the constantly self-cancelling hierarchy of education, can there actually be an equal sharing (according to a continuous social judgement as to who will most benefit from such and such a gift, etc.) of what is agreed to be valuable. Without such an agreement, sustained through the operation of professional guilds and associations as well as cooperative credit unions and banks, there can only be market mediation of an anarchy of desires—of course ensuring the triumph of a hierarchy of sheer power and the secret commanding of people's desires by manipulation.

For where there is no public recognition of the primacy of absolute good as grounded in something super-human, then democracy becomes impossible, for it is no longer supposed that one should even *search* for the intrinsically desirable. It then follows that people can only find out what they "should" desire, or even about the possible objects of desire, from the very "mass" processes that are supposed to represent only the general desires of the people. Liberal democracy is then doomed to specularity: the represented themselves only represent to themselves the spectacle of representation.

Moreover, a *purely* participatory democracy, without representation, is surely an illusion under any conditions, ancient or modern. For prior to the complex decisions made for itself by the multitude lie always persuasions by the Few and the many "ones," while the execution of these sovereignly autonomous decisions involves once again heteronomous interventions by the One and the Few, since all cannot attend to the business of all, for all of the time. If there are no criteria for the legitimate operation of these processes of "aristocratic" and "monarchic" education and mediation, then the covert operation of these processes will corrupt any ventures in democratic participation, which most certainly should be promoted.

Indeed the allowing of the instance of the aristocratic and monarchic moments actually ensures a tempering of any attempted purely representative democracy, because it will tend to balance the element of the passing of the gift of trust to representatives with a return-gift of self-ruling to the people themselves in their diverse regions and smaller groups—a self-ruling exercised directly in terms of an organization of the resources for economic and cultural life, and not primarily through the ballot-box.

For there is simply no truth in the Marxist assumption that, once freed from the shackles of oppression, people will "by reason" choose equality and justice. To the contrary, in the light of a mere reason that is not also vision, *eros*, and faith, people may well choose to prefer the petty triumphs and superiorities of a brutally hierarchic *agon* of power or the sheer excitement of a social spectacle in which they may potentially be exhibited in triumph. This is exactly why the vast numbers of the American poor are not waiting to rise up in revolt.

For the same reason, "pure" democracy would be a *mise en abyme*: one would have to have endless "primaries" before "primaries" in any electoral process. Instead, in reality, at the end of the line always, someone puts herself forward as a "candidate" (in some sense), someone stands up and says something that no one has voted on or contractually agreed that she should say. Gift always precedes both choice and contract, because no formal pre-arrangements can entirely control the content of what we impose upon others in our words and symbolic actions which inevitably sway them in a certain fashion.

In the United States, part of the problem is that there is a yearning for the madness of pure democracy: thus there is no "monarchic" body that organizes boundaries of voting districts, because this would be considered "undemocratic." In consequence this task is left to the reigning political party and the resultant gerrymandering is seen as just a fact of life. Thereby the lure of the democratic abyss abolishes democracy, whereas some admission of aristocratic and monarchic principles (as in Canada, for example) actually secures the space of the possibility of democracy. Similar considerations apply to the dangerous United States practice of systematically replacing all government officials with party-placemen after every change of the party in power. This encourages a subversion of the democratic process by career interest and the narrow perspectives of the professional technocrat and manipulator over the more genuinely mandarin, wide-ranging interest in objective justice and human benefit of the unelected civil servant. It should finally be insisted, as Michael Lind has pointed out in *Prospect,* that the United States' "division of powers," while it was in part inspired by a genuine Harringtonian desire for mixed government, was from the outset contaminated by Montesquieu's modern simulacrum of this principle: namely a division of powers that would permanently pit richer and poorer, federal and more local, urban and landed social forces against each other in a balanced and eternally sterile *agon* that precisely mirrors the stable conflict of the marketplace.

The same abyss exerts its fascination when the New Labour government—as obliquely indicated by Archbishop Rowan Williams in his Dimbleby lecture—obscures the irreducible moment of non-democratic decision which it should be obliged to take responsibility for, in the name of appeal to "opinion-soundings" and the like which purport to gauge not just what the people want, but more crucially what they will permit a government to get away with. Such apparent sensitivity to public opinion in reality subverts democracy, because it fails to acknowledge that democracy operates through a gift-exchange of *trust* that also exceeds an impossible "absolute" democracy. A government has been trusted to take its *own* decisions on the basis of justice and integrity, precisely because the electorate has previously endorsed its general principles, record, and ethical character. No plebiscitory process of whatever kind can displace this "monarchic" need for self-grounded decision taken "under God," for the reason that the people can never collectively be placed in the exact position that an executive power should occupy: of being (ideally) of the right human type, having enjoyed the right experience, receiving the right information, being able as an individual or small-group mind to arrive at a complex conclusion on the basis of complex reasoning.

In consequence, for a government to pretend not to decide, or not to have to decide, will always be in reality to decide in a disguised way through manipulation of opinion, plus the following of the most debased mass-opinion or of the course that it can most easily get away with. And where a government has no sense that it has a duty to decide for justice and the long-term global and national good that is in excess of democratic norms, then its horizon for decision will be only that of increasing its own power and influence to the degree that this is seen to be compatible with remaining in power, retaining the good-will of its temporarily most powerful allies and procuring a sufficient continued popular assent or being able to ride-out temporary public discontent. One can argue that the over-weaning recent power of the British governmental executive, as manifest especially in the lead-up to the invasion of Iraq, is linked not *just* to its contempt for accountability to the elected sovereign body of Parliament, but also to its evasion of a properly executive responsibility which would be to take decisions and guide Parliament on the basis of intrinsic justice and the most long-term legitimate interests of the people on whose behalf it takes decisions. In the case of Iraq, this included the long-term inevitable British relationship to continental Europe, as opposed to its short-term beneficial links to the United States.

One could of course protest here that the problem was rather Blair's "monarchic" commitment to his own judgment of the overwhelming need to overthrow tyranny, even in the face of mass unpopularity. Yet if there was indeed an element of this then it was essentially delusional, since it had earlier ignored the need to remove other tyrannies when this was less clearly in the perceived U.S. interest and the British interest if it wished to remain in American good graces. Such delusional decisionism appears surely as a kind of bastard version of true "monarchic" leadership and itself as an outgrowth of delusions of grandeur fostered precisely by the notion of leadership as the courtship of mass adulation. At a deeper level the latter, evasively non-monarchical logic was surely still in force: Blair aligned himself by instinct with the further advancement of Western neoliberalism and Western global dominance now undertaken by military means in the face of economic and political adversity. Thus he aligned himself in addition with a political culture that necessarily has to seek legitimacy in terms of popularity—in the old times of the secure nation-state in the mode of material and spectacular increase, in new globalized times of uncertain boundaries in the mode of the warding-off of continual threats to human security. Even if the war in Iraq can appear contradictorily to have increased those threats and so to court *un*popularity, by the very fact that it increases global insecurity in the future it helps to sustain the new currency of political legitimation which is fear. And I have already explained why this currency is the extreme outworking of the principles of liberal democracy, not the classical ones of mixed government.

We need then, in the Europe and the World of the future, a new conception of the economy as a non-zero-sum game that is engaged in for mutual benefit: that is to say, as an exchange of gifts in the sense of both talents and valued objects that blend material benefit with sacramental significance. We need also to encourage a new post-liberal participatory democracy that is enabled by the "aristocratic" process of an education that seeks after the common good and absolute transcendent truth. Finally, we need to see that it is equally enabled by a monarchic principle, which permits a unified power at the limit to intervene in the name of non-codifiable equity—the liberal alternative to this being the brutal exclusion of those, like the inmates of Guantanamo Bay, who escape the nets of codes and are therefore deemed to be sub-human.

Does all this sound fantastic? No, the fantastic is what we have: an economy that destroys life, babies, childhood, adventure, locality, beauty, the exotic, the erotic, people, and the planet itself.

Moreover, if we refuse a profound and subtle theological social carapace, we will not in the future necessarily recover secularity: instead we may witness the effective triumph (in power if not in numbers) of religious fundamentalism and especially Protestant fundamentalism, in cynical alliance with a liberal nihilism. For the formal emptiness of the liberal market and bureaucracy is now apparent to all: its heart will be filled with something, and especially with a neo-Calvinistic creed that justifies this emptiness, because cumulative success in the reckoning to oneself of its void sums is seen as a sign of favor with another eternal world that alone really matters—although that, too, is conceived in terms of preferential absolute success in contrast with absolute failure.

Most, including myself, have hitherto supposed that the religious conflicts in Ireland are an anachronistic echo, in a remote corner of Europe, of ancient European conflicts. But then why have they flared up again so recently (the latter half of the twentieth century) and persisted so long? Is not Ireland somewhat like the United States, where a "belated" avoidance of secular ideologies has turned imperceptibly into a foreshadowing of a time when those ideologies are exhausted? Here again, there is no progressive plot to history. What one has seen in the province of Ulster has often been a conflict between a bigoted, puritanical, and hyper-evangelical neo-Calvinism on the one hand, and a largely reasonable, socially and political-aspiring Catholicism on the other—the murderous fanatics on the "Catholic" side have tended to be so for socio-political rather than religious reasons. Moreover, Government responses to this conflict now seem, in retrospect, like dummy-runs for a global suspension of civil liberties in the name of anti-terrorism.

Certainly not in any straightforward fashion, but nonetheless in a real one, it could be that the Irish conflict is in fact a harbinger of a wider, future, and much more complex and many-faceted new struggle for the soul of Christianity itself—which may yet dictate the future of Europe and even of the world.

39. Christopher Insole – Theology and Politics: The Intellectual History of Liberalism

Definitions and Histories of Liberalism

THEOLOGIANS, WHEN DISCUSSING "LIBERALISM" in the context of political philosophy, are apt to pull out of their hat whatever they have stuffed into it before the show began: what sort of creature emerges—cuddly, mingy, or verminous—reveals more about the temperament and prejudices of the theologian than anything else. The definition is already tailor made to fit the evaluation. "Liberalism" is found to be—because in truth it is defined to be—secular, individualistic, and morally corrupt, or ordered to justice and human flourishing. Introducing an historical dimension to the discussion can actually make things worse, in that we can feel more learned, and so become more taken in by our prejudices. True, what we now tailor is a whole intellectual history and narrative, but still this description can be shaped for us, or by us, in such a way that most of the evaluative work has already been smuggled in.

Here, for example, are two rival intellectual histories of liberalism, which feed parasitically off each other's crudity. On the one hand, there is a Whiggish genealogy, which tells the following narrative about the emergence of liberalism. Liberalism arrived not a moment too soon after the Reformation and the Wars of Religion: a wise, gracious, and soothing host, settling down the fractious religious delinquents of warring Europe, Catholic against Protestant. Before the liberal state: warfare, religious fanaticism, oppression, and intolerance (bad). With the liberal state: peace, freedom, and toleration (good). In the wake of William Cavanaugh's influential work,[1] many theologians now set against this a rival history of liberalism, which is much less flattering to its subject. The rise of the liberal state, according to this counter-narrative, is to be understood against the context of the dispute running through the middle ages concerning whether authority and power was held by the Church, or by temporal rulers. Luther's contribution is massively to centralize power in the prince, as opposed to the Pope. The absolutist prince of Lutheranism, opposed to the trans-national claim of the Roman Catholic Church, is secularized by thinkers such as Hobbes, and set on its way to becoming the bureaucratic state of late-capitalism. This totalizing state claims to save us from a category of "violent religion" (which category it largely invents), while actually demanding allegiance to the new religion of nationalism enforced by violence. In both cases we have a

---

[1]See William T. Cavanaugh, "'A Fire Strong Enough to Consume the House': The Wars of Religion and the Rise of the State." *Modern Theology* 2 (1995): 397–420, and *Theopolitical Imagination,* esp. ch.1. For a fuller response to Cavanaugh, see my "Discerning the Theopolitical."

genealogy which is supposed to give us the key to the meaning of "liberalism." By uncovering *the* intellectual history of liberalism, we now know its hidden aspirations and deepest motivations, enabling us to come to judgment about it.[2]

In my view, neither of these narratives is helpful. They do serve though to illustrate the danger in starting with a single definition, or historical narrative, for as complex a phenomenon as liberalism. In reflecting more widely on the interface between "Theology and Politics," I would suggest that our thinking is immeasurably improved when theologians do not *begin* with metaphysically and theologically freighted definitions and narratives. Rather, we should begin with a set of *practices*. These practices, I suggest—whatever we think of them, and however far we think contemporary politics has fallen away from them—make up what we know of as "constitutional liberalism," where and when it exists: the restriction of the use of coercive public power to sustaining peace and justice (giving to each their due), rather than to enforcing ultimate truth or unity of belief; the protection of individuals within a framework of rights and liberties; the separation of powers (between the law-makers, law-enforcers and those who interpret the application of the law), and the mixed constitution (elements of rule of the one, the few and the many). Representation is taken to be the basis of authority, and the rule of law the manifestation of this authority. Such law is established by consent and is oriented to the welfare of the people governed by it. The law protects and enshrines certain rights, which cannot be violated or trumped. The law is understood to have a limited external scope, allowing subjects to pursue their own ends within a tolerant and pluralistic society, inasmuch as they do not put peace or justice at peril. In constitutional liberalism, the law has authority rather than the individual ruler, and the ruler is held accountable for their use of authority: so a further set of practices, such as freedom of speech and association, arise as an expression of the commitment to the accountability and transparency of power. The internal circumscription of the powers of the state, and the limited external scope of the law, means that the state allows and facilitates semi-autonomous public institutions, such as churches and universities, which institutions are protected within a framework of law, but where it is not within the purview of the law to determine, say, the truths of physics or of theology. Only where most or all of these practices are adhered to, more or less well, do we have constitutional liberalism.

If we begin with this fairly loose "family resemblance" concept of constitutional liberalism, we are in a position to illuminate the complexity of the subject. This must be better than having to balance our precarious pile of historical bricolage, just long enough to take our pristine snapshot, to put in the album with the sticker "liberalism" next to it. Thinking of liberalism in terms of this set of practices can help us to understand how some thinkers join us for some of the party, but leave—or storm

---

[2]Pierre Manent, *An Intellectual History of Liberalism.* Translated by Rebecca Balinski. Princeton: Princeton University Press, 1995. Manent, it should be said, does not indulge in unhelpful reductionism, but sets out admirably a range of thinkers and concerns that constitute the diverse liberal tradition.

out—before it really gets going: so, for example, Hobbes is often called a "liberal" thinker because he has something to say about rights and liberties, and about representation and consent. We each have a right to self-preservation, and because of the war against all in the state of nature, we can only secure this right by contracting amongst ourselves to create an absolute sovereign, capable of keeping the peace. The sovereign acts, but as we have created the sovereign from our act of consent, in the ultimate analysis, we are the authors of the sovereign's actions. For this reason, dissent from the sovereign is actually a form of self-contradiction. This is a notion of "representation" in the strongest possible sense. We are the *authors* of the absolute sovereign's actions.

By all means we can talk of Hobbes as a "liberal" thinker, and of Hobbesian liberalism. But we must be sure to be specific. Because we only have the one term "liberalism" where about eleven might suffice, we need to differentiate other strands and traditions of liberalism. Consider: Hobbes deplores the mixed constitution, the separation of powers, freedom of speech and association, and the notion that the law has authority over the ruler. Just as there must be no internal division of sovereignty, for Hobbes, there must also be no external limitation on the authority of the state: with there being no public space not under the control of authoritarian state structures. This immediately reveals the at best partial success of any theological engagement with politics—certainly at work in the Cavanaugh narrative outlined above—which is convinced that Hobbes, and Hobbes' absolute state, is the key to understanding "liberalism" as such.

So we see that some forms of liberalism do not endorse all the practices listed above, or prioritize the practices differently. We can do some of the work of clarification by talking specifically. Just to add the term "constitutional" to our liberalism might help to pick out liberalisms that are committed to constitutional practices. But even where there is agreement on the importance of a practice, it can be capable of a number of quite different metaphysical underpinnings and justifications. History reflects this conceptual complexity by embodying in different thinkers and movements quite opposed justifications for similar practices. The practices, we might say, are over-determined by theory: a number of normative frameworks can and have been offered for them.

The first task of theology in relation to politics, and to political philosophy, should, I would suggest, be this: to avoid reductionism. Theologians should resist the temptation, in themselves and others, to cut intellectual corners by a speedy appeal to the "foundations" of liberalism. As Wittgenstein said, "don't think, but look."[3] Look first of all at the complexity of what might be meant by "liberalism." And then, Wittgenstein again, I'll teach you differences."[4] Theologians have a great deal to offer

---

[3]Wittgenstein, *Philosophical Investigations*, §66.
[4]Rhees, *Recollections of Wittgenstein*, 157.

in separating out the complexity of normative strands in the various geological strata of liberalism, just because so many of these differences have their ultimate grounding in theological convictions and disputes. It is ironic that it is often the very same theologians who pride themselves both on being post-foundationalist and properly attentive to *practices,* who should themselves appeal to the "foundations" of liberalism and neglect a range of concrete practices when thinking about politics. Interesting to reflect also on Wittgenstein's insight that "what it is we believe" is not fixed simply by "mental contents," but is expressed in the full weave of our behavior and practices. This might put a question mark against the not unfamiliar figure of a theologian who announces an opposition to "liberalism" alongside an active and positive engagement and protective instinct towards some or all of the practices listed above.

In case, for some, this begins to smell too hygienically Wittgensteinian—practices *rather than* metaphysics, with metaphysics as a sort of idle wheel in the mechanism—I should say that I do not mean to imply that these practices float free of theory. There should be no dualism in our understanding of practices and theory, as if a practice, such as the preservation of rights, is not already imbued with an anthropology and a metaphysics. This notion that we can have certain practices without any (at least implied) substantial theory or metaphysics is one that the liberal theorist John Rawls himself pedals. If theologians can be too quick to start with metaphysical foundations, secular political philosophers can often be observed nimbly steadying themselves on the branch that they are sawing off, denying that there are any such foundations while patently standing on them. The precise claim I want to make is this: theological and metaphysical premises do a *great deal of work* in framing, constituting and justifying the practices listed above, and the practices are always to some extent framed, constituted, and justified by theological, quasitheological, or metaphysical assumptions and premises. The opposite of good theology is not no theology, but bad theology. That we begin our engagement by discerning practices does not mean that this is where we will stay, or where we will end up. But we must learn to disaggregate, and to discern diversity and nuance before we begin to adjudicate. Aphorisms such as "don't think but look," and "I'll teach you differences," point to the diversity of practices involved in liberalism, and to the range and diversity of theoretical and metaphysical underpinnings for these practices. It is to the speedy and reductive resort to monolithic foundations that I object, rather than a more nuanced, historically curious and theologically sensitive interest in foundations.

For the remainder of this chapter, I intend to take just one of the practices listed above as a lens through which to look at some wider considerations. Focusing on the notion of the mixed constitution will enable us to reflect first of all on the role of democracy. Secondly, it will point us—through a brief encounter with medieval ecclesiology—to the importance of doctrinal themes in the emergence of liberalism. Finally, I will look at the Kantian reconstruction and defense of liberal practices. The only practice that Kant rejects is the mixed constitution. Understanding why Kant does this will take us deeper into some of the very distinctive and theological origins of apparently secular underpinnings for liberal constitutionalism, which are widely understood as hostile to theological reasoning. In particular, it takes us to secular underpinnings such as we find in John Rawls, and Rawlsian reconstructions of the tradition. It is dismaying when the "theology and liberalism" debate just becomes the "theology and John Rawls' debate: as if liberalism was discovered in 1971 with the publication of his *Theory of Justice*. Liberalism was no more discovered in 1971 than sex was in 1963. At the same time, Rawlsian/Kantian liberalism is for many the dominant expression of this tradition. It demands our attention.

There will be distinct changes of gear between the sections of the chapter: from a consideration of democracy, to medieval ecclesiology and then a concluding section on Kant. My hope is that the progression exemplifies the virtues of the methodology of attention and disaggregation before adjudication, which I have been recommending. We discern first of all what the practice is, and its role in constitutional liberalism, and use this to explore two very different theological and metaphysical groundings for constitutional practices (first of all ecclesiology, and then Kantian reason).

The Mixed Constitution
The role of democracy

The specific arrangements of different mixed constitutions can be very complex, but it is clear enough what is being sought. A mixed constitution works between the need to come to political judgment, whilst not trusting any single mechanism for discerning the right course of action. The monarchical mechanism, of course, does not require a King or a Queen: a president of a republic also embodies the principle of "rule by one." In the UK the monarchical mechanism is represented symbolically by the sovereign, but exercised concretely through the Prime Minister's royal prerogative. Monarchy can deliver swift and effective action; but Prime Ministers, Kings and Presidents are only human, and can err. A small group of expert rulers—with, it is hoped, particular capacities or opportunities for political wisdom—incorporates a greater range of experience and perspectives than the monarchical principle, but can itself become beholden to particular interest groups or segments of society. In the UK the House of Lords plays this role made up of life peers with expertise in a range of professions, Anglican Bishops, and hereditary members, who in theory are supposed to have the advantages of stability, independence and historical memory.

Democratic rule, where some part of the people decide directly or through representatives (such as the House of Commons), extends the process of discernment to a wide range of interest groups, and can disrupt the plans of a cozy elite. But it also extends it to those without the means—the time, expertise and experience— of discernment, and is vulnerable to the injustices and preoccupations of the mob. Supporters of the mixed constitution reject pure monarchy, pure aristocracy, and pure democracy, and insist that these three mechanisms act as checks and balances upon one another. This constitutional instinct is concerned to limit the absolutizing pretensions and powers of the state, and the same momentum that supports a mixed constitution will also seek legal protection and relative independence for strong public institutions below the level of the state. It is crucial to constitutionalism that there should be more levels of political reality than the individual and the state.

Concentrating on the mixed constitution has the one distinct advantage that it enables us, immediately and incontrovertibly, to put democracy in its place, and to harness as an ally of liberalism significant contemporary theological critiques of "liberalism" (so-called). One of the most deleterious conflations in political theology is the sense that constitutional liberalism and democracy are either the same thing, or that liberalism gets its normative value by virtue of *being the product of a democratic process*. In fact, democracy is one of the practices supported within the framework of constitutional liberalism; but it is not the framework itself, and it is not the source of constitutional liberalism. As Oliver O'Donovan puts it, "rather than underpinning justice, democracy is a task of justice on the narrow front of political representation," so that "by providing a just settlement to thorny conflicts of representation, democracy adds a further layer to liberal government."[5]

This is not meant to imply that democracy is *the* practice that guarantees representation: all levels of the constitution are *representative,* as is our involvement in voluntary associations. All these mechanisms are intended to represent our true interests, as they meet questions of public power and coercive law. Being properly represented is not like some sort of interactive reality show, where you must "have your say" by phoning in your opinion or your vote. Edmund Burke told his Bristol electorate that it was his duty to "sacrifice his repose, his pleasures" and "his satisfactions, to theirs," and "in all cases, to prefer their interest to his own." The representative owes the represented "his unbiased option, his mature judgment, his enlightened conscience," but "he betrays" instead of serving them if he "sacrifices it to [their] opinion."[6]

Where democracy—as a form of collective autonomy—is seen as the source of normativity, the foundation rather than an implication, then it is more than likely to become a danger to other practices of constitutional liberalism. To put it simply: if democracy is the *source* of truth, rather than one of its protectors, some of the practices of liberalism are put on a very precarious footing: why bother to preserve freedom of speech and association, or certain rights and liberties, if the general will that bestows these things, has determined that they are to be taken away (in the interests of security say)?

---

[5]O'Donovan, *Ways of Judgment,* 174.
[6]Burke, "Speech to the Electors of Bristol," 446–48.

Because democracy is one of the practices of liberalism, and owing to the expansion of both liberalism and democracy in roughly the same places at the same time, their conceptual distinguishability is not widely appreciated. The tradition of reflection about constitutional liberalism—running through Locke, Burke, de Tocqueville,[7] Mill, and Arnold—is a litany of caution about the role and impact of democracy. In 1923 Carl Schmitt goes as far as to identify the essence of democracy as the "assertion of an identity of governed and governing, sovereign and subject … the quantitative (the numerical majority or unanimity) with the qualitative (the justice of the laws)."[8] Schmitt considered democracy to be fundamentally at odds with constitutional liberalism, which he interpreted as resting upon a transcendent conception of truth, alongside a sense that discussion and openness is the best way to approach this truth. Citing the "liberal Burke" as a paradigmatic example, Schmitt argues that "the belief in parliamentarianism … belongs to the intellectual world of liberalism … not to democracy," such that "discussion means an exchange of opinion that is governed by the purpose of persuading one's opponent through argument of the truth or justice of something, or allowing one-self to be persuaded of something as true or just."[9]

Schmitt's observations have some bite when one reflects that he was the leading jurist during the Weimar Republic, attempting during the early 1920s to preserve order against extreme anti-constitutional elements, such as fascism and communism. Schmitt discerned these movements harnessing democracy at the cost of constitutionalism, and became convinced that the incoherence of mixing liberal and democratic grounds for the political was one of the factors pulling the infant Republic apart. His *Crisis of Parliamentary Democracy*, written in 1923, he described later as a "warning and cry for help."[10] Schmitt wanted President von Hindenburg to use extraordinary powers to protect the whole constitution against an overactive democratic gland. In May 1933, in the interests of "order"—as he saw it—Schmitt threw his lot in with the National Socialists. This was because Schmitt was enough of a Hobbesian to think that the greatest political evil was disorder, with order of any sort better than chaos and civil war. Totalitarianism he understood as opposed to liberalism, but as on the same continuum as democracy: the expression of a democratic logic, whereby the general will constructs truth. The question of how the general will is construed (through the ballot box, or through the great man) being a secondary and more technical matter.

If there is a lesson from all this, it is that many critiques of "liberalism" from contemporary theologians are better understood as cultural critiques of democracy, which are in fact part of a liberal tradition as old as liberalism itself.[11]

---

[7]See, for example, Manent, "Tocqueville."
[8]Schmitt, *Crisis of Parliamentary Democracy*.
[9]Ibid., 6–8.
[10]Ibid., xxxviii.
[11]It should be clear that some defenses of democracy in a wider sense are not directly targeted by such cultural critiques of democracy. So, for instance, when Stout defends "democracy" in *Democracy and Tradition* he is

The same anxieties that we find in Edmund Burke, de Tocqueville, and Matthew Arnold tend to surface in figures such as John Milbank and Stanley Hauerwas: the corrosive impact of a homogenizing, permissive, licentious, commercial, and individualistic society, without proper cultural formation, ecclesial involvement, historical memory, social integration, appropriate authority, or social and communal virtues. Only if we have already conflated democracy with liberalism do these critiques look like anything other than a defense of recognizably liberal practices and institutions.

Schmitt, Burke, and warnings about democracy: this might all sound—it might be—rather reactionary. Against this, it should be noted that being aware of the distinction between liberalism and democracy does not always lead to a *critique* of an overactive democratic dimension. Consonant with our methodological principle to look for differences and variety, there are in the liberal tradition a variety of construals of the value of democratic processes, even where the status of democracy as a means to an end, rather than an end in itself, is well understood. We can understand all this, but still think that there is not enough democracy about, or not the right sort of democracy, perhaps because it is insufficiently supported by the virtues and social structures that are necessary for its healthy flourishing. Thinkers more on the left of liberalism understand that equality is a necessary aspect of liberty and the protection of individuals, and understand democracy as a necessary expression and protection of this equality. An anxiety about too thin a theory of the state, which leaves individuals vulnerable to a morally neutral economic sphere, is precisely the concern of nineteenth-century liberals such as T. H. Green, J. S. Mill, and Hobhouse. And then there is the republican model of liberalism, harking back to the Greek city republics, which emphasizes the importance of a virtuous public space, and which highly values democratic traditions (this is a strong tradition in North America, embodied in de Tocqueville, and represented recently by Jeffrey Stout). Again, the point is that when theologians worry about too small a conception of the state, a lack of equality, or the atrocities of global markets, they are not necessarily stepping outside of recognizably liberal traditions: or, at least, they are expressing concerns first and frequently expressed by liberal thinkers.

---

best construed as defending a set of practices and virtues that underpin constitutional liberalism, although as Little insightfully points out, Stout obscures this point by disavowing the term "liberal." Little correctly warns that by abandoning the term "liberalism," Stout risks surrendering "with one hand what he has gained with the other," as "rescuing the word 'liberal' is no trivial undertaking, since the idea of *'liberal* democracy, properly understood, and as opposed to *'illiberal* democracy' is indispensable both to the contemporary worldwide discussion of democracy and, as a matter of fact, to much that Stout himself appears to favor about American Democracy" (288). See Little, "On Behalf of Rights."

Doctrine and the mixed constitution

Now for the first change of gear, to more historical concerns. In this section I will outline very briefly the way in which medieval ecclesiology is one of the main conduits for the practice of the mixed constitution. I say "one of the main conduits" because—again acknowledging differences—there are others: for example, a republican tradition—coming through Machiavelli, Harrington, and Montesquieu—derives an interest in constitutional checks and balances more directly from the classical sources, Aristotle and Polybius. Here again we have case of the same practice being capable of different construals and justifications. My focus here will be on the ecclesial and theological tradition, and the particular way it has construed the practice.

But before that, we need to face a blunt question: who cares? That is, who cares what the genealogy is? Is it simply of academic antiquarian interest to uncover the medieval historical roots of a practice? Well, we should care, for the following reason. Precisely if we want to be attentive to the different textures and possibilities of liberal practices, it helps us to recover some of the motivations and aspirations of the original practices, in their original context. We might find that we have become coarsened and deaf to the history of the present, replacing a rich polyphony with an irritating jingle. As I will show, this is in fact what we find: that when the church meets the liberal tradition, it misunderstands itself and that tradition if it meets it as an alien and secular innovation. Aspects of liberalism are in fact ecclesial traditions, with strong doctrinal support.

This gives the lie to the "Whiggish" of the two narratives I set out at the beginning. The liberal state is not simply a post-Reformation solution to delinquent warring "religions." It would be more true to say that constitutional liberalism finds its roots in strands of medieval ecclesiology. Such debates arise from a profound reckoning with the question of the relationship between salvation and the use of power given that every individual must be, in Augustine's words a "question to themselves before God"[12]—that is to say, that even a pope, prince or sacred college of cardinals can err, for who is without some sin in this life? We find in medieval ecclesiology a sustained meditation on the need to come to political judgment, where some judgments approximate the good more than others, against the backdrop of our inability to make judgments, given imperfection and sin. Sin which is individual, communal and structural, pervasive but not uniform, and which cannot be eliminated from human nature by social formation, virtue, the best of intentions, or any process or mechanism of social engineering or historical progress.

Of particular importance is the conciliar movement of the fourteenth and fifteenth centuries, which sought to contain the monarchical power of the pope within a mixed

---

[12]Augustine *Confessions* X.33.50.

constitution—embodying elements of the one, the few and the many—such that the whole church was perceived to be present most authoritatively in a representative council. The conciliarists made an appeal on three fronts: to the notion of the mixed constitution supported by Aristotle, to representative structures in Roman and canon law where the head is answerable to the collective body, and to the Mosaic polity of the Old Testament, which the conciliarist Jean Gerson characteristically describes as "the best government just as it was under Moses ... mixed from three polities: regal in Moses, aristocratic in the seventy-two elders, and timocratic since the rectors were chosen under Moses from the people and from single tribes."[13] "Timocracy" means here the virtuous form of rule by the many in Aristotle, of which democracy is the corrupt version. Gerson's framing of a mixed constitution for the church is representative of the movement: "we can divide the ecclesiastical polity into papal, collegial, and synodal (that is, of the general council). Papal [rule] imitates regal, the collegial [rule] of the Lord Cardinals imitates aristocracy, general synodal [rule] imitates polity or timocracy; or rather it [ecclesiastical polity] is a perfect polity that results from all."[14]

The causal link between these medieval conciliarists and the emergence of liberal constitutional principles in the sixteenth and seventeenth centuries has been demonstrated beyond question by historians (such as John Neville Figgis, Francis Oakley, Brian Tierney, and James Blythe):[15] the only possible debate is one concerning degrees of emphasis relative to other traditions. Such ecclesiastical constitutionalism enters the political blood stream through early defenses of Anglicanism, which conveniently construe the Church of England as being in continuity with the conciliar medieval Catholic Church. Marsilius of Padua, one of the most important fourteenth-century conciliarists, is translated into English within a year of the break with Rome, and given a preface that explicitly draws attention to the continuity and preservation of constitutional practices.[16] Richard Hooker's *Laws of Ecclesiastical*

---

[13]Gerson, *Oeuvres Completes*, in Blythe, *Ideal Government*, 251.

[14]Gerson, in Blythe, *Ideal Government*, 250.

[15]The classic work here is Figgis' *Political Thought From Gerson to Grotius*. If there were problems with Figgis' approach, they would be the following: first of all, he did not trace the origins of conciliarism far back enough, and secondly, he did not explain how the conciliarist thought of the middle ages fed into "secular" constitutionalism. Since Figgis, much work has been done on both fronts. On the foundations of conciliar thinking Brian Tierney has done groundbreaking work, demonstrating that the roots of conciliar thinking lie in canonistic glosses of the twelfth and thirteenth centuries, and showing the influence of the movement into the early modern period: see his *Religion, Law and Constitutional Thought 1150-1650*, and *The Foundations of the Conciliar Theory*. James Blythe has built on Tierney's work, showing the importance of the notion of the mixed constitution—derived from Aristotle and Biblical/Mosaic models—to a wide range of scholastic thinkers: see his *Ideal Government and the Mixed Constitution*. For the influence of conciliar thinkers on later resistance theories see Oakley, "On the Road." Oakley is putting the flesh on a suggestion made initially by Harold Laski that "the road from Constance to 1688 is a direct one" in "Political Thought in the Later Middle Ages" (41). For useful overviews of the scholarship in this area Burns, *Cambridge History of Medieval Political Thought*, ch.17, and Skinner, *Foundations of Modern Political Thought*, ch.4.

[16]The Act of Supremacy, consolidating the split with Rome and declaring Henry VIII to be governor of the Church of England, was passed in 1534. One year later in 1535, we find the first English translation of Marsilius

Polity is also steeped in such constitutionalism, with explicit parallels drawn between ecclesiastical and temporal governance.

In seventeenth-century debates concerning the resistance, if any, that might legitimately be exerted against the power of a monarch, we find interlocutors on all sides of the question acknowledging—lamenting or celebrating in speeches and pamphlets—the medieval ecclesiological roots of constitutional restrictions on the sovereign's power. In continuity with the medieval tradition, the concern is with the abuse of power. This theologically informed suspicion of power, and the determination to call the state to account in the face of a higher truth and authority, is found powerfully in the eighteenth century in a figure such as Edmund Burke.[17] And it is no accident that a leading nineteenth-century liberal, Lord Acton, should root his constitutionalism in his deeply help Catholic convictions. Commenting that the Christian is "bound by his very creed to suspect evil,"[18] Acton explicitly celebrates the liberal resistance to absolutism and the constitutional protection of the individual. It is against a background of doctrinal commitments, explicitly informed by his interest in medieval ecclesiology, that Acton frames his famous maxim that "power tends to corrupt and absolute power corrupts absolutely."[19] In terms of the narrative put forward by Cavanaugh, we might say that rather than the liberal state weighing in on the side of the prince in the medieval conflict between the pope and the prince, it stands against both, in refusing to locate absolute power anywhere; power is mistrusted, dispersed and held accountable within constitutional frameworks enshrined in law.

Oliver O'Donovan and Joan Lockwood O'Donovan are contemporary theologians who have done a great deal to keep this memory alive. Crude characterizations of Oliver O'Donovan's political theology as a version of "Christendom" hardly do justice to his success in bringing alive a tradition that makes rulers answerable to Christ, and attempts to build in concrete structures by which this answerability is made actual. The lesson for the theologian interacting with political philosophy should be clear. The doctrinal themes at the heart of ecclesiology—creation, fall, redemption, eschatology—are formative influences on the emergence of the structural curbing of power, and the pluralizing of sources of discernment and loyalty.

---

of Padua's radically conciliar treatise *Defensor Pacis,* sporting the royal coat of arms, and produced "with the king"s most gracious privilege." The translator, William Marshall, tells us that in Marsilius" treatise, written two hundred years ago, "thou shall find … the image of these our times most perfectly and clearly expressed and set out." Of particular relevance, Marshall instructs us, is the balancing and curbing of powers whereby "the officers and rulers" and "the multitude or commons" are "each to other established," "both parties keeping themselves within their own right, as it were within a certain limit or bounds," staking claim only to that which "the laws will give them leave." Marsilius of Padua, *Defensor Pacis,* 139.

[17]See my "Two Conceptions of Liberalism," and "Natural Law and Practical Reason."

[18]Lord Acton, "Studies of History," 28.

[19]Lord Acton, "Acton-Creighton Correspondence," 364.

A sense of the importance of the mixed constitution is strong in the historical memory of constitutional liberalism. That said, the mixed constitution is also one of the practices of liberalism that can seem most imperiled. Lacking the glamour of "rights," and because of the inflation of democracy, it is perhaps one of the least understood and valued. One can see the mixed constitution at risk whenever there are appeals to the obvious rightness and urgency of spreading democracy in the Middle East (rather than say good governance, justice and strong institutions); or where it asserted that the judiciary or a non-elected upper house can be easily by-passed because they are not "democratically elected." Political parties and governments cannot always be trusted to protect these constitutional restrictions on their own power, and we find liberalism in danger when "essentially plebiscitarian legitimations"[20]—appeals to the "democratic mandate"—are used to interfere with public associations, or to abolish historical protections and liberties (permitting an extensive period of detention without charge, to take a recent example).

Kantian Liberalism

And now for the final change of gear, into a more philosophical register, which through Kant will give us a line into contemporary Rawlsian construals of liberalism. Kant endorses all of the liberal practices listed at the beginning of the paper. All except one, which he condemns: and that is the mixed constitution. Kant is particularly puzzled at, and sarcastic about, the enthusiasm that the British have for this notion.[21] Understanding why Kant thinks this way provides us with an illuminating springboard, from which we can test my suggestion that liberal practices (bar the mixed constitution in this case) can be capable of very different systematic groundings, where the job of the theologian is to discern and then adjudicate the crucial premises and assumptions. Although Kant has more technical objections to a mixed constitution, to an extent he simply considers the whole palaver to be unnecessary. A mixed constitution seems like a good idea if truth is what we are after, and where the truth is complex and hard to discern, such that we diffract our discernment through a number of consensus seeking channels.

But truth, for Kant, is just not that hard to discern: not once you have the right method. Kant, like many early modern philosophers is enchanted by the paradigm of geometry and mathematics. If only the truths of religion, politics and metaphysics were as transparent and universal as "2+2=4," we would have the key to knowledge and civil peace. So when thinking about political philosophy—the scope and justification of the state's coercive power in relation to the individual—Kant attempts

---

[20]Hirst, "Introduction," 5.
[21]Kant, "On the Common Saying," 82–83, and *Political Writings,* 186–87.

to apply a geometrical method: building up from first principles, using universal laws of reason, which any competent reasoner could employ. Geometers do not arrive at the truths of geometry on the basis of a consensus. They do not need to chew over the properties of a triangle with other geometers in order to come to agreement. Because the structure of reason is universal and transparent, any competent reasoner would arrive at the same truths: there will be consensus, simply because of the universality of reason. Applying the same paradigm to politics- Kant is happy to appoint a monarch with undivided power, just as long as the monarch is a competent reasoner. The monarch represents us because our interests are—obviously—represented by universal reason.

So the way it goes for Kant is something like this. The formal properties of reason itself determine the moral law: where there is universality and necessity, we have a categorical imperative. The mark of the moral law is its universalizability: act only on the maxim that I can at the same time will as a universal law. Among categorical imperatives, Kant creates two sets of distinctions: duties to others and duties to ourselves, and perfect and imperfect duties. Perfect duties (such as telling the truth) are always binding, in contrast to imperfect duties (such as cultivating one's talents, playing the piano and so forth) that can be fulfilled in a finite number of optional ways. The philosophy of political right concerns only perfect duties to others that require external coercion: "right is ... the totality of conditions under which the will of one person can be unified with the will of another under a universal law of freedom."[22] Further, "the theory of right" is the sum of those laws for which an external lawgiving is possible."[23] From here Kant derives the *a priori* founding principles of an ideal constitution: "*freedom* for all members of a society ... the *dependence* of everyone upon a single common legislation ... legal *equality* for everyone."[24] Such an arrangement is "the only constitution which can be derived from the idea of an original contract, upon which all rightful legislation of a people must be founded."[25]

It might seem that here at least, in Kant, we have a properly secular justification for liberal practices (bar the mixed constitution, but a version of that can be put back in without much difficulty, and indeed, Rawls does put it back). Here at least we consult the structure of reason itself, which is conceived as independent of any particular traditional or confessional commitments. Kant of course is the muse behind John Rawls' thought-experiment of the "veil of ignorance," whereby to discern the fundamental laws that ought to govern our life together as citizens we are encouraged to imagine ourselves prior to being embodied in a particular situation, with a particular conception of the good. Those principles that we can agree on,

---

[22]Kant, *Political Writings*, 133.
[23]Ibid., 132.
[24]Ibid., 99.
[25]Ibid.

in this hypothetical pre-born state, without religious convictions and economic interests, are—for Rawls—the ones that should constitute the norms of our political life. What Rawls is doing is to throw us, in a Kantian way, onto the structure of *a priori* reason itself: independent of our particular beliefs, experience, traditions and historicity.

Here at least, it might seem, the theologian faces a proper secular enemy, rather than another strand of theology, with a particular configuration and emphasis of doctrinal themes. This accounts for the whole industry sparked off by Rawls'—some felt rather illiberal—discourtesy to religious believers, when he seemed to insist, in his earlier work at least, that distinctively religious reasons should not be brought into public discussions. So here we have it: a secular versus a theological grounding of liberal practices.

Even this, though, would be much too quick. Rawls' guide here is Kant. Kant is in a tradition of continental rationalism, mediated through Leibniz, Wolff and Baumgarten. When these thinkers talk about God, they have in view a divine mind in two halves: the divine intellect and the divine will. The divine intellect, in this tradition, just *is* the structure of reason as such (it is the storehouse of all possibilities and necessities, some of which are made actual by the divine will). Reason is identical with the divine intellect. Crucially, in this tradition, the divine will can in no way "trump" or override reason: although this is not an external constraint upon God, precisely because reason is identical with the divine intellect. The shape of reason, for this tradition, is the shape of universality as such: which is discerned through *a priori* rules such as the principle of contradiction, of sufficient reason (everything must have a sufficient reason) and of perfection (the most perfect being will do the most perfect thing).

So if we were to ask whether God—when framing political principles, for example—could be permitted to give a "distinctively religious reason," the answer would have to be "no, God could not give a distinctively religious reason," if by that we meant a reason that did not conform to the universal structure of intelligibility as such. The injunction against specifically religious reasons in the Kantian tradition—and nobody tell the Kantians this—arises from an intellectualist doctrine of God: a tradition that identifies God with the structure of reason itself, and subordinates the divine will to the divine intellect. It arises from a theological rationale, where the critique of this rationale will itself be theological, relating to the doctrine of God, creation, fall and eschatology. And there is much to criticize in this tradition, from a theological point of view. The identification of God with mind, and then mind with *a priori* reason, and reason with necessity, would be one starting point. Another would be the disloyalty to the earth, to our creatureliness—our imperfection and sin—that is demanded by the search for a disembodied and absolute perspective on reason and morality. Kantians can be extremely ingenious at denying the accuracy of such an accusation, and in my view they need to be, given Kant's emphatic clarity that our noumenal selves need to be presumed to share God's non-spatial and non-temporal eternity, if the Kantian moral project is to get under way.[26]

Again, we might face the "who cares?" question: even if this is the origin of a particular thought experiment, how does it illuminate, conceptually or practically, the current issue? Well, the surprising presence of theology even here cuts both ways: it opens up a challenge to the secular political philosopher, and then to the theologian. To secular political philosophers who want to continue an unreconstructed Rawlsian line of ruling out "religious reasons" as irrational, there is the lesson that theological traditions can be extremely rational, in a way that even they could not help recognize. Furthermore, it illuminates, I think, a structural feature of any attempt to build up to truth from human consent. This is the way it goes. In the face of a skepticism about arriving at the absolute and transcendent truth, perhaps because of a pluralism about perspectives on such truth, we come up with the promising idea that truth is in fact the product of consent, rather than something independent of the process of consent. But then actual concrete human individuals and groups can arrive at some very uncomfortable decisions: idiotic, unjust or—in hindsight—obviously "of their time." Well then, we must expand our notion of "consent" to mean not just any old consent, but the consent of ideal reasoners: truth is not the product of any old practice, but of an *ideal* practice of discernment. But now a real question arises as to what work is being done by the description of the practice as *"ideal:"* any synonym such as "useful" or "coherent" is likely in the end to collapse into something that looks very like good old-fashioned truth, even if it is not called that. *Why* is something ideal, or useful, or coherent ultimately, except that having *true* beliefs is ideal, and can be very useful and coherent? In other words: the collapsing of truth into reason and will is viable if the subject is the ideal subject. That is, if the subject is God. Anti-realism—the notion that the mind constitutes reality—works for God, because the divine mind does indeed constitute reality. Many secular attempts at anti-realism struggle, I think, because they need the ideal human cognitive subject to become more and more Godlike, when their disbelief in God was precisely one of the founding motivations for the antirealism.[27]

Now that the managers have taken over the university, and theologians are called upon to justify their existence in terms of their non-subject specific "transferable skills," one of these skills at least is this: the ability to sniff out small gods. Theologians are well trained to find the gathering "god concept" around which a particular discourse or practice is oriented: the efficiency of the manager, for example, or the "autonomy" of the Kantian, now stripped of its theological rationalism. Often the gathering concept, rather like the Wizard of Oz, is largely unexamined at close quarters. When finally all

---

[26]For a full treatment, see my *Kant and the Divine Mind*.
[27]For a full treatment of the realism/anti-realism debate see my *Realist Hope*.

the noise stops, and the concept appears, like the Wizard, it can often be exposed as an unimpressive and angry little squirt of a concept.

On the other hand, to put the challenge the other way round, I have sometimes felt that there can almost be a perversity amongst religious believers in the "theology and public reason" debate. It is hard to resist the conclusion that some religious believers find it rather thrilling to be high and mightily offended by the "liberal injunction" against the use of distinctively religious reasons. Rawls in his later works,[28] and some of his followers such as Charles Larmore,[29] have done much to qualify and nuance his earlier more restrictive statements. According to these later developments, all that is actually asked is that believers of all stripes—atheists included—be prepared to attempt to find grounds of mutual reciprocity and intelligibility with their interlocutors, assuming good faith on the other's part and acknowledging the complexity of the burdens of judgment.[30] On this account, we are dealing less with a substantive restriction on metaphysical content or motivation, and much more with an ethic of virtuous communication:[31] with a call for respect, empathy, consideration, and self-interrogation.

Once all these nuances are in, I do think there is at least a question to be put to the determined-to-be-offended religious believer, the "political correctness gone mad" brigade: what sort of religion does one have if the religious reason being offered is so completely incapable of being virtuously communicated? Is not the creator's command intelligible to the creature? Is not the God revealed to us, for us? Or to put it in terms of the germ of truth in rationalist theology, is it not the case, as Aquinas puts it, that God is not just "good" but "goodness" itself, or we might say, not just "reasonable," but "reason" itself. This is part of the mystery of the divine nature tracked by the doctrine of divine simplicity: that is, the mysterious unity and identity in God—which marks out God from any creature—between reason and will, nature and existence. The intellectualism that characterizes continental rationalism involves identifying God primarily with one arc of the mystery only. By making the half-truth the whole truth, even the half is lost: which describes the fate and inadequacy of both "voluntaristic" and "intellectualist" reductions of the divine nature.

Conclusion

To draw things together then. Just by reflecting on one practice, the mixed constitution, we have been able to illumine some of the diverse theological sources—conceptual and

---

[28]See Rawls, *Political Liberalism,* and "Idea of Public Reason Revisited."
[29]Larmore, "Public Reason."
[30]See my *Politics of Human Frailty,* ch. 2.
[31]This emphasis on the Christian virtues required for effective communication is insightfully explored by Biggar, in "Can a Theological Argument Behave?"

historical—of politics, and political philosophy. We hope thereby to turn the behemoth "liberalism" into a more finely grained and diverse concept, which commands attention and care from theologians. In "liberalism," the theologian should not find a theologically neutral and secular politics, but something which is itself a theological tradition of sorts. Not all theological traditions are equally worthy of support. But to judge the truth of something, I must hear properly what is being said. Accordingly, the academic theologian's task in relation to politics can only become distinctively and properly theological—with a proper readiness to make theological judgments about politics—after a process of attention, discernment, historical curiosity and philosophical rigor. I ventured earlier that the opposite of good theology was not no theology, but bad theology. If we are honest about our creaturely embeddedness in the history and culture into which we are thrown, perhaps we could also say that for most of us, the opposite of good liberalism is not no liberalism, but bad liberalism. And we had better make sure that we know the difference.

40. Eric Gregory – Love and Citizenship after Augustine

So now we need not let the question worry us about how much love we should expend on our brother, how much on God.

—*Augustine*, The Trinity 8.5.12

The title of this essay promises a history. But I do not offer a history of the usual sort. By drawing attention to Augustinian themes of love and citizenship, I will not settle a historical question of what, if any, political theory Augustine actually subscribed to, nor the counterfactual questions of what might have been if he had said things he did not say or thought things he could not have thought. The history that most concerns me is roughly the past fifty years of thinking about religion and politics rather than the ecclesial dynamics of fifth-century North Africa.[1] My primary interests are systematic and conceptual, especially in light of the nonstandard defense of liberal political arrangements which was a hallmark of twentieth-century Augustinianism. Augustine himself was no liberal—though scholars credit him with inventing a concept of the "secular" which is crucial to that tradition.[2] Inferences made from

---

[1]Modern scholarship on Augustine and his age has flourished—now to the point of radically deconstructing and resisting Augustine's self-presentation and the familiar terms through which he and his opponents have been read. See, for example, James J. O'Donnell, *Augustine: A New Biography* (New York: HarperCollins, 2005). For overviews of the developments in social-historical scholarship, see *Augustinian Studies* 32:2 (2001).

[2]Robert Markus, *Christianity and the Secular* (Notre Dame: University of Notre Dame Press, 2006). According to Markus, "the sacred and the profane were both familiar in antiquity; but until it was imported by Christianity,

Augustine's writings played a significant role in the formation of the liberal tradition. They also inspired its strongest critics. Today, competing inferences continue to be made in ongoing assessments of Christianity's relation to liberalism. For my part, the tradition of Augustinian liberalism envisions a politics of imperfection which I do not wish to deny. As political counsel for practical deliberation, I have no truck with abandoning its wisdom given the realities of ambiguity, contingency, and hubris. In more Augustinian terms, the *libido dominandi* severely constrains the ability of political communities to pursue the diverse goods of their members. My version of Augustinian liberalism, however, is doubly nonstandard because it makes the virtues that inspire Augustinian *critics* of liberalism central to my case *for* liberalism.

As a way of ordering the conceptual terrain of politics, the heavy and relentless accent on imperfection distorts a liberal Augustinian case for the possibilities of civic virtue. Those possibilities—even of shared goods and loves that might order a just political community—will be my focus. Making room for this sort of liberalism might help free us from the stark alternatives that tend to travel with Augustinian politics. I argue that the challenge for Augustinianism today is to avoid arrogant forms of political perfectionism without adopting essentially negative forms of political liberalism.[3] With this challenge comes a demand to reconstruct a political concept of love that takes account of love's danger and promise. To do so requires distinguishing the aspiration toward perfection from both the prospect of achieved perfectibility and a politics that aims to maximize human excellences in its allotments of rights and responsibilities.

In the twentieth century, anti-totalitarian appeals to Augustine's anthropology and eschatology led to a renaissance of his thought for the morally ambivalent conditions of liberal democracies. These liberal versions of Augustinian politics have become synonymous with sin-oriented, deflationary rhetoric commending the limits of politics and the limits of virtue. This reading strategy now meets serious resistance on many fronts. In theology, for example, Christian critics like Stanley Hauerwas and John Milbank claim that this coalition sacrifices theological orthodoxy in order to make Christianity safe for liberal democracy and market capitalism.[4] On the other hand, non-Christian political theorists like Romand Coles and William Connolly claim that Augustinian theology remains the fertile soil of an anti-liberal politics. They debunk its liberal credentials by linking the tradition with intolerance, scapegoating, and a metaphysics unreceptive to difference. Coles, for example, refers

---

there was no notion of the 'secular' in the ancient world. The word and the concept are both alien to Greco-Roman religion" (4). Moreover, Augustine "was the principal Christian thinker to defend a place for the secular within a religious, Christian interpretation of the world and of history" (10).

[3]For a fuller account of these themes, see Eric Gregory, *Politics and the Order of Love: An Augustinian Ethic of Democratic Citizenship* (Chicago: University of Chicago Press, 2008).

[4]See, for example, Stanley Hauerwas, *With the Grain of the Universe: The Church's Witness and Natural Theology* (Grand Rapids: Brazos Press, 2001); and John Milbank, *Being Reconciled: Ontology and Pardon* (New York: Routledge, 2003).

to the "holocaust" that Augustinian *caritas* has unleashed upon the world.[5] On this view, while Augustinian loving promises freedom through humility, it is always already complicit with ethical and literal violence. Coles identifies a "malignancy at the heart of the loving gift."[6] At the same time, for internal reasons, the tradition is itself in danger of becoming merely a suspicious disposition rather than a vibrant mode of social criticism that might still matter for theology and politics. In particular, loose claims about pessimism and anti-utopianism have distracted the tradition from a potentially fruitful alliance with those who take their inspiration from Aristotle and Aquinas in defense of a virtue-oriented version of "liberal perfectionism." These more ambitious accounts—allegedly in contrast to Augustinianism—are interested in the sorts of virtuous practices that promote human flourishing and discourage those social practices that diminish it. They are neither governed by neutrality nor indifferent to well-being. Yet they remain *liberal* in their recognition of the limited authority of the state and the instrumental quality of political goods. They are attentive to autonomy and self-respect precisely because these goods are valuable components of flourishing. But they also take account of the actual needs of a diverse citizenry and the ways in which political cooperation indirectly enables perfectionist aspirations.[7] I outline what such an alliance might look like in order to show that trumpeting realism and unmasking the pretensions of civic virtue do not exhaust an Augustinian repertoire. This move requires chipping away at some fundamental presuppositions in order to push the Augustinian tradition in a different direction.

For my purposes here, what Augustine actually meant is less central than the ways in which his work has been interpreted and applied to politics. Exegesis and normative theorizing are distinct albeit related tasks. Conceptual analysis of modern Augustinianism can swing free from the quest for the historical Augustine. What is needed, if we are going to understand the recent history of Augustinianism, is a history of reception, not a definitive account of the historical Augustine plus a list of the many mistakes people have made in interpreting him. The twentieth-century revival of political interest in Augustine focused primarily on the realist implications of Book XIX of the *City of God*. I want to

---

[5]Romand Coles, *Rethinking Generosity: Critical Theory and the Politics of Caritas* (Ithaca: Cornell University Press, 1997), 1. Coles is a charitable reader of Augustine, also admiring an Augustine who can disrupt the prideful autonomy of egoism and wondering at the infinite richness of his God. Elsewhere, however, Coles claims that the Augustinianism of someone like Alasdair MacIntyre fosters "the overcultivation of teleological confidence, authority, discipline, pedagogy, and habits in ways that greatly engender cognitive, visceral, and relational invulnerability," in Romand Coles, *Beyond Gated Politics: Reflections for the Possibility of Democracy* (Minneapolis: University of Minnesota Press, 2005), 174.

[6]Romand Coles, *Rethinking Generosity*, 3.

[7]Liberal perfectionists and their accounts of autonomy admit tremendous variety in contemporary political theory. For my purposes, liberal perfectionists include thinkers like Joseph Raz, Joan Tronto, Vinit Haskar, Thomas Hurka, George Sher, John Finnis, Thomas Spragens, and Martha Nussbaum. For helpful reviews as well as independent proposals, see Steven Wall, *Liberalism, Perfectionism, and Restraint* (Cambridge: Cambridge University Press, 1998), and Kimberly A. Yurako, *Perfectionism and Contemporary Feminist Values* (Bloomington, IN: Indiana University Press, 2003).

shift this preoccupation by reconstructing an account of love's relation to citizenship that does not collapse all theology into a never-ending story about politics as a response to sin. Conventional readings of Book XIX too often subordinate the larger framework of a political ethic of *caritas* marked by an Augustinian psychology of enjoyment. In so doing, most Augustinian liberals have focused on the category of vice as an alternative to virtue—a move that undermines the conceptual power of an Augustinian moral psychology that pictures vice as a perpetual danger internal to the practices of virtue.

The first part of this essay distinguishes three types of liberal appropriations of Augustinianism. A first type, popularized by Protestant theologian Reinhold Niebuhr, linked Augustinianism with realist schools in political theory and the virtue of hope. A second type emerged in positive response to the massive influence of John Rawls's theory of justice in the 1970s and 1980s. It built on the first type, but in a distinctive way by emphasizing the significance of fairness as a political virtue for a society marked by conditions of pluralism. Still another type, though less explicit, emerged in the 1990s when suspicions about realism and Rawlsianism lead to a revival of liberal conceptions of civic virtue. In the second and third parts of the essay, I develop and extend this last type as a correction to the more dominant ones. I defend the political implications of an Augustinian theology of love against its many critics, including many Augustinian liberals. By way of conclusion, I suggest that Augustinians offer a neglected resource for contemporary post-Marxist and post-secularist theorizing about a political concept of love.[8]

Types of Augustinian Liberalism

Augustinian liberalism traditionally has been held up as a bulwark against the excesses of democratic optimism and the threats of theocratic authoritarianism. It casts Augustine's *City of God* as the *ur*-text for dethroning mythical ideas of civic greatness. To the pagans, Augustine satirized their prideful claims to have built an empire of virtue. To the Christians, Augustine warned them not to make empire their religion. Any Augustinian liberalism, taking inspiration from this satire, shares a common affirmation of secularity and an accent on the corruptibility of politics. Different proposals, however, stress distinct virtues for a precarious and remedial politics.

The dominant strand of Augustinian liberalism in the twentieth century was Augustinian realism. This type reconstructed Augustine's controversial doctrine of original sin and his dramatic narrative about "two cities" in order to temper the enthusiasm of Enlightenment progress, even as it supported something like

---

[8]The resurgence of "love" in critical theory is helpfully discussed in David Nirenberg, "The Politics of Love and Its Enemies," *Critical Inquiry* 33 (Spring 2007): 573–605, and Richard Beardsworth, "A Note to a Political Understanding of Love in our Global Age," *Contretemps* 6 (January 2006): 2–10.

the "secular" order of liberalism. The term "secular" here trades upon Augustine's own theological meaning—"in this passing age"—rather than the modern sense of secular as nonreligious or atheistic. On this view, Augustine's two cities do not exist in different worlds, but "in this present world mixed together and in a certain sense, entangled with one another."[9] For many citizens in American churches and universities, Reinhold Niebuhr *simply is* Augustinian politics. In fact, given the relative neglect of Augustinianism in twentieth-century Catholic political thought, it is not too much to claim that Niebuhr's Augustine became the Augustine of English-speaking political theology. Under Niebuhr's influence, generations of preachers, pundits, and political theorists have come to learn at least one thing: Augustinians are political realists, not sentimentalists.

Niebuhr's complex fusion of liberal Protestant theology and American democracy is the popular currency of Augustinian politics. He redeemed Augustinianism for the liberalism of the American mind—endowing politics with the religion he thought it needed without giving it too much theology. His retrieval, however, was a truncated Augustinianism. It offered up a limited conception of politics as restraining evil that often accompanied a troubling form of moral consequentialism. Niebuhr's accent on sin, finitude, and paradox could afford love only a shadowy existence in common life. Like many liberals, he came to speak only of competing wills rather than Augustinian loves.[10] Rhetorically positioned as rational and responsible, this account promised the rigor necessary for a more just politics that overcomes the heat of unstable emotions and religious desire.

Modern Augustinian liberalism begins with Niebuhr's realism, and its scholarly counterparts, in ascendancy. This reading, in large part, was governed by pressing questions about secularization, the use of force in a rough and tumble world threatened by fascism and Marxism, and the failure of sentimental responses to these ideologies. It spoke to the hopes and anxieties of American and European scholars in the period from the end of World War II through the Cold War. It continues to attract defenders today, especially those liberal realists who worry that liberalism is no longer willing to "make the tragic choices that defending freedom requires."[11] Political commentators across the spectrum—from David Brooks to Arthur Schlesinger, Jr.—have lamented the absence of another Niebuhr who might rise up with some anti-Pelagian text in

---

[9]*City of God,* translated by R.W. Dyson (Cambridge: Cambridge University Press, 1998), 11.1.

[10]Niebuhr had a recessive voice that might qualify his received pronouncements. This voice emerges in his own criticisms of Augustine's "excessive emphasis upon the factors of power and interest" ("Augustine's Political Realism," in *Christian Realism and Political Problems* [New York: Charles Scribner's Sons, 1953], 127). In this vein, he left the door open for a politics that might avoid the oscillation between "idealist" and "realist" readings of Augustine's famous story of two cities founded upon two loves. But his more dominant tendency to contrast biblical love with rational justice foreclosed such a legacy. Love's dialectical relation to justice was the counterpart of "the general relation of super-history to history," in *The Nature and Destiny of Man,* vol. 2 (New York: Charles Scribner's Sons, 1943), 69.

[11]Peter Beinart, *The Good Fight: Why Liberals—and Only Liberals—Can Win the War on Terror and Make America Great Again* (New York: HarperCollins, 2006), 197.

order to humble the pretensions of imperial hubris or some anti-Donatist text in order to rid the world of romantic assertions of moral purity within a body politic. Appeals to Niebuhr's Augustinianism reveal a continuing presence in the moral and political imagination, even by those who observe its notable absence.[12]

Robert Markus's classic study, *Saeculum,* was the scholarly lodestar of Augustinian liberalism.[13] It was a historical study, but Markus openly had his contemporary society in mind. By highlighting Augustine's mature rejection of the Constantinian establishment, it set the theoretical terms for a realist reading. This view strongly rejects the sacralization of any earthly political community as a vehicle of salvation. There can be no *imperium Christianum* and no *Reichstheologie.* Markus's focus on Augustine's doctrine of sin and homogenization of secular history became the twin conceptual resources for a modern political Augustinianism.

For Markus, the great achievement of this realism is Augustine's *civitas peregrina*: a strange pilgrim city that humbles the ultimate significance of extra-biblical history and extra-ecclesial politics but also creates a this-worldly space for a shared political culture. In contrast to the grand theories of classical politics, the *civitas peregrina* is content to allow a politics restricted to literally mundane tasks, to "those things which are necessary to this mortal life" (*City of God* XIX.17). An updated Augustinian justification of secular politics requires that no single religious vision can presume to command comprehensive, confessional, and visible authority among earthly political communities. The moral of Markus's Augustinian story is clear: beware of communitarianism and the overbearing reach of the coercive state.

Earthly politics cannot fulfill the deepest longings of a human person or community. All is broken and incomplete, and politics cannot heal the rupture. As such, Augustinians should expect less from politics and lower the stakes involved. This is the Augustinianism that Markus finds attractive for a liberal, pluralist society. "In Augustine's mature thought," he writes, "there is no trace of a theory of the state as concerned with man's self-fulfillment, perfection, the good life, felicity, or with 'educating' man towards such purposes. Its function is more restricted: it is to cancel out at least some of the effects of sin."[14] Using standard realist tropes, Markus persistently contrasts Augustine's affirmation of the naturalness of human sociality with an equally emphatic insistence on the fallenness of political community. Earthly politics is a contrivance marked by "tension, strife, and disorder."[15] The Augustinian citizen assumes a "pragmatic posture" and recognizes that politics offers a "lowly form of 'peace.'"[16]

---

[12]For a critical survey of invocations of Niebuhr in the current debate over the "war on terror," see Paul Elie, "A Man for All Reasons," *The Atlantic Monthly* (November 2007): 83–96.

[13]Robert A. Markus, *Saeculum: History and Society in the Theology of St. Augustine* (Cambridge: Cambridge University Press, 1970).

[14]Ibid., 94.

[15]Ibid., 83.

[16]Ibid., 172, 174.

Markus's realism, though always attuned to limits, did not condemn politics itself. Rather, ambivalence about the political is meant to avoid either apocalyptic hostility or sacral identification. One result of this ambivalence is that the focus of the human drama shifts away from political goods and toward the "inner response to the world."[17] Between Incarnation and consummation, history is an "interim" that is "dark in its ambivalence."[18]

Despite an emphasis on the tragic and fleeting character of politics, Markus (like Niebuhr) tried hard to deliver the reader from a gloomy pessimism. By highlighting "eschatology as politics," he even imagined a "politically radical" Augustinianism that is "bound to be unremittingly critical of all and any human arrangements, any actual and even any imaginable forms of social order."[19] Like many theologians in the 1960s and 1970s, he identified *hope* as "the characteristic virtue of the wayfarer: by this he is anchored to his real home."[20] Hope counters the potential defeatism that can follow from the relentless focus on sin and agnosticism about secular history and politics. Hope consoles, but it is not meant to be a cheap deliverance. Hope reflects an "eschatological restlessness" that is not "mere unshaped discontent or unrealistic perfectionism."[21] For Markus, hope provided a psychological location from which the Christian might still critically affirm liberal values. Nevertheless, political engagement remains an externally imposed duty for an exigent circumstance. There is no inner dynamic that might lead one to see citizenship in analogous relation to discipleship.

A second type of Augustinian liberalism shares many characteristics with this first type. But it offers more explicit discussion of moral psychology and the ethics of liberal citizenship because it tracks arguments advanced by philosopher John Rawls. In fact, it finds a common Augustinian cause with Rawls's basic rejection of "the zeal to embody the whole truth in politics."[22] Paul Weithman defends this second type by arguing that liberals and Augustinians share a concern for the political consequences of the vice of pride.

Weithman repeats realist dispositions in his aversion to "perfectionist political projects, projects in which political power would be employed to eradicate sin or to impose on human beings political institutions that their fallen nature makes it impossible to sustain."[23] He is wary of using political power to "coerce belief, to purify

---

[17]Ibid., 63.
[18]Ibid., 23.
[19]Ibid., 166, 168.
[20]Ibid., 83.
[21]Ibid., 170.
[22]John Rawls, "The Idea of Public Reason Revisited," in Samuel Freeman, ed., *John Rawls: Collected Papers* (Cambridge: Harvard University Press, 1999), 574.
[23]Paul Weithman, "Toward an Augustinian Liberalism," in Gareth Mathews, ed., *The Augustinian Tradition* (Berkeley: University of California Press, 1999), 304–322 (314–315). For a similar defense of political liberalism, see Edmund Santurri, "Rawlsian Liberalism, Moral Truth, and Augustinian Politics," *Journal of Peace and Justice Studies* 8:2 (1997): 1–36.

society, or make it more Christian."[24] Liberal democracy is seen as the best way to institutionalize these reservations. Weithman, however, employs an Augustinian account of sin for purposes different from those of traditional realism. He capitalizes on Augustine's moral psychology in order to provide a liberal account of civic virtue. His account is attentive to the needs of political stability as well as to the moral capacities of citizens in a pluralist society. On Weithman's view, Augustine's analysis of pride supports rather than undermines liberalism.

Augustinian theology supports liberal principles of political legitimacy, especially "principles that restrict reasons and values that can be appealed to when justifying the exercise of public power."[25] Given the temptations of politics as an arena for prideful activity, the restraints of political liberalism offer an effective check on human pride that should be attractive to Augustinians committed to humility. Christians who are sympathetic to Augustine's account of sin should be "sensitive to their own undue attraction to the prospect of dominating others and aware of their need to curb it."[26] As with Rawls's approach in *Political Liberalism,* Weithman's account focuses primarily on the epistemic responsibilities of a liberal citizen.[27] The epistemic constraints of liberal civic virtue—like Rawls's idea of public reason—"foster habitual restraint on the desire to dominate others."[28] For Weithman, "pride could be effectively contained by coming to respect other citizens as reasonable."[29] Of course, one could imagine an Augustinian view of sin and pride moving in the opposite direction. Historically, this sort of argument has been put to lamentable effect: given that one's fellow citizens *will not be reasonable,* it is necessary to check their disordered wills through political coercion. Bishop Bossuet's classic defense of divine right absolute monarchy is just one example of an Augustinian praise of universal Christian love which evaporates into a relentless defense of paternalist necessity.[30] But Weithman claims that vigilant Augustinians should endorse liberal concerns about the potential arrogance of religious speech, especially when this speech establishes itself as the true interpreter of the divine will on any given political or legal matter. Respect for justice and fairness promotes civility and consensus-building by recognizing the equal moral capacities of fellow citizens.

---

[24]Weithman, 317.

[25]Ibid., 305.

[26]Ibid., 313.

[27]Rawls's earlier work, *A Theory of Justice,* offered a broader account of moral psychology, including attention to a political concept of love. For an interesting account of this theme, see Susan Mendus, "The Importance of Love in Rawls's Theory of Justice," *British Journal of Political Science* 29 (1999): 57–75. On Rawls's early encounter with religious discussions of love and politics, see Eric Gregory, "Before the Original Position: The Neo-Orthodox Theology of the Young John Rawls," *Journal of Religious Ethics* 35:2 (June 2007): 179–206.

[28]Weithman, 313.

[29]Ibid., 317.

[30]Jacques-Benigne Bossuet, *Politics Drawn From the Very Words of Holy Scripture,* edited by Patrick Riley (Cambridge: Cambridge University Press, 1990).

In laying out these two dominant types of Augustinian liberalism, I have not sought to analyze their merits.[31] Descriptively, they represent interpretations of Augustine interacting with important normative proposals concerning how politics should be conceived and conducted. In fact, when combined with their detractors, I think they show that the debate over modern liberalism has in large part been a debate over the political implications of Augustinian theology. Augustinian critics of liberalism reject both types as pernicious modern reductions of religion to ethics. For my purposes, however, what is striking in both liberal accounts is the unclear role of love in political morality. I could imagine, for example, Weithman linking the virtue of respect to the virtue of love in a way that supports his claims about equality. Respect might be the condition for the possibility of love, or respect might be the form of love in political life. Christians, in fact, may have theological reasons for trying their rhetorical best to communicate about human goods with those who do not share their religious convictions. Robin Lovin, for example, argues that "the best evidence that I have achieved some understanding of what love requires is that I can talk about the good of others in terms they recognize."[32] Markus might also offer an account of love's relation to hope in political engagement.[33] But both types of Augustinian liberalism, at least in these works, do not provide a central political role for love. In this respect, they mirror the conceptual fate of the evasion or rejection of "love" in modern political theory.[34]

A third type of Augustinian liberalism unapologetically moves love to the center of liberal politics. Timothy P. Jackson, for example, advances a morally perfectionist yet politically liberal vision grounded in prophetic Christian love. He defends liberal democracy, but he challenges the preoccupation with stability and contractual justice that he thinks lies behind the attraction of both realism and Rawlsianism. Jackson denies what he considers the anemic notion that citizens *qua* citizens should "prescind as much as possible from judgments about truth, goodness, the meaning of life, and the proper object of love."[35] On his view, more dominant liberalisms offer weak moral

---

[31]For criticism of Markus, see Michael J. Hollerich, "John Milbank, Augustine and the 'Secular,'" in *History, Apocalypse and the Secular Imagination*, ed. M. Vessey, K. Pollmann, and A.D. Fitzgerald (Bowling Green: Philosophy Documentation Center, 1999). For criticism of Weithman, see Michael P. Krom, "Modern Liberalism and Pride: An Augustinian Perspective," *Journal of Religious Ethics* 35.3 (September 2007): 453–477.

[32]Robin Lovin, *Reinhold Niebuhr and Christian Realism* (Cambridge: Cambridge University Press, 1995), 200. Ralph Waldo Emerson makes a similar claim about a "believing love" that democratic citizens adopt in trying to communicate with fellow citizens. One scholar likens Emerson's account of mutual understanding to Augustine's doctrine of charity. See Hans von Rautenfeld, "Charitable Interpretations: Emerson, Rawls, and Cavell on the Use of Public Reason," *Political Theory* 32:1 (2004), 61–84.

[33]In *Christianity and the Secular*, Markus offers a new Augustine who is more attentive to the importance of shared moral vocabularies that bind a society together. He does not abandon the case for Augustinian liberalism, but he distances his reading from those kinds of liberalism associated with proceduralism and state neutrality.

[34]J. David Velleman argues that philosophical attention to love has suffered under the influence of Freud, who "embedded love deep within the tissue of fantasy, thereby closing it off from the moral enterprise," in "Love as a Moral Emotion," *Ethics* 109 (January 1999): 351.

[35]Timothy P. Jackson, "*Prima Caritas, Inde Jus:* Why Augustinians Shouldn't Baptize John Rawls," *Journal of Peace and Justice Studies* 8:2 (1997): 49.

justifications of their own professed commitment to freedom and equality. He locates these failures in a liberal unwillingness to engage moral motivation. Like many Christian critics of modernity, he fears the success of liberalism is parasitic on social structures and moral capacities that it too often undermines or insufficiently affirms. He aims to "protect charity against the corrosive effects of modern contract theory by insisting that love rises above the demands of secular justice."[36] This protection takes the form of what he terms "civic agapism." Civic agapism is a kind of liberalism that recognizes the political need for the charisms of love, sacrifice, and compassion. Jackson offers an attractive vision of a citizen motivated not by "self-referential fear" but "other-regarding love."[37] This view coincides with now common diagnoses of the failures of dominant liberal discourse; namely: (*a*) conceptions of autonomy that find little room for dependency and vulnerability; and (*b*) conceptions of rationality that find little room for affectivity and emotions except as natural energies to be constrained. Nonetheless, Augustinian liberals, perhaps alongside the bourgeois liberals Jackson criticizes, might still worry that this kind of political love exceeds the psychological possibilities of earthly politics. For example, not convinced that arrogance has been abandoned, liberals will rightly ask who is being asked to sacrifice and by what means. This concern motivates objections that agapism as a political ethic jeopardizes the integrity of citizens by encouraging too thick a notion of political responsibility and moral obligation.

Jackson, however, is acutely aware of liberal concerns about an appeal to "love" that "foments dogmatism and aggression."[38] The checkered career of Christian love in political history is a dramatic case in point. Jackson affirms Augustinian notions of fallibility. But, according to Jackson, a response to the paternalist possibility of politicized love must begin by undermining the "overly Platonic vision of love" that he associates with the Augustinian legacy.[39] His agapism, therefore, explicitly rejects Augustinian *caritas* because it trades on a monistic love of the highest good that leads to the idolatry, oppression, and invulnerability identified by critics like Coles and Connolly. But must it?[40] Can Augustinian love be read in a way that might be put in the service of a better kind of liberalism?

---

[36]Timothy P. Jackson, "Is God Just?" *Faith & Philosophy* 12:3 (July 1996): 395.

[37]Timothy P. Jackson, *Love Disconsoled: Meditation on Christian Charity* (Cambridge: Cambridge University Press, 1999), xi.

[38]Timothy P. Jackson, *The Priority of Love: Christian Charity and Social Justice* (Princeton: Princeton University Press, 2003), 41.

[39]Ibid., 52.

[40]I am sympathetic to J. Joyce Schuld's criticism of Connolly and Coles that their attention to the confessing self blurs the distinction between "Augustine's descriptions of the spiritual life of those in the church with a totalizing expectation of political regeneration" (*Augustine and Foucault: Reconsidering Power and Love* [Notre Dame: University of Notre Dame Press, 2004], 215–216). But I fear she says too much in response. There is a contradiction between her criticisms of these authors and her own effort to describe the "political import of the wisdom of sorrow" (218) for a non-arrogant and non-despairing politics. She undermines their fundamentally Augustinian (and Foucauldian) point: theological discourse migrates beyond its own circumscribed borders.

Love, Sin, and Political Morality

Two paradigms of political morality can be found in both Augustinian and non-Augustinian traditions. One places too much confidence in love; the other casts too much suspicion. The error of both views is a failure to relate love and sin to each other in ways that constrain both appeals. Left unconstrained by sin, a first paradigm of politics appeals to love (and related notions of friendship, fraternity, care, community, solidarity, and sympathy). Left unconstrained by love, a second paradigm of politics relies on realist appeals to sin (and related notions of cruelty, evil, and narrow self-interest). Historically, the former theme has justified perfectionist, even theocratic, politics. More recently, the latter theme has justified essentially negative forms of political liberalism. How robustly, then, can Augustinians appeal love or appeal to sin without throwing the relationship between the two out of kilter?

Political Augustinians are rarely accused of sentimentalist naiveté. Augustine's doctrine of love is no quick and easy alternative to his doctrine of sin. Indeed, for Augustine, sin always plays a role in human loving. It finds its mysterious birth in the radical freedom of love itself. Put another way, sin is a species within his internally diverse conception of love. Vice always lurks among the virtues, putting them against pretty tough odds.[41] And love, like cholesterol, can be healthy or deadly. Augustine, in fact, is famous for his ascetic account of the deceptions of love gone wrong. His erotic tales were meant to urge his readers to persevere in the steep ascent of wisdom, even if they now travel with the grim Augustine of most political anthologies and liberal imaginations. This is the Augustine who speaks of disordered love: "have not these trials everywhere filled up human affairs?" (*City of God* XIX.5). For this Augustine, church membership, proper belief, and even right action itself are good as far as they go. But they are no guarantees of good loving. Good works can be motivated by pride or humility, both within and outside the church.

The logic of Augustine's account of love's relation to sin has its share of critics. As I noted above, liberal defenders of Christian love like Jackson distance themselves from Augustine's ostensibly Platonic account of love for God and love for neighbor. Despite a long history of scholarship that rejects this characterization of Augustinian eudaimonism, it remains the site where critics identify an otherworldly and life-denying solipsism fueled by a tournament of loves, human and divine, that is most unwelcome in modern religious and philosophical ethics. Some theological traditions, notably Protestant ones, would become wary of Augustine's language of love, preferring instead the language of faith; other philosophical traditions, notably

---

For an insightful reading of post-Nietzschean political theory in conversation with Augustinianism, see Kristen Deede Johnson, *Theology, Political Theory, and Pluralism: Beyond Tolerance and Difference* (Oxford: Oxford University Press, 2007).

[41]For examples of vice characterized as a counterfeit parody of virtue, see *Confessions* 2.vi.12, and *City of God*, II.21, V.19, 12.7, and XV.22.

Kantian ones, would become wary of the language of love as too fragile and particular, preferring the distance and stability of respect. Love, then, remains one of those words we can use to play out the history of massive theological and philosophical debates. My effort to rehabilitate an Augustinian conception of love in defense of a liberal politics may appear doomed from the start by turning to the most contested feature of Augustinianism.

Moral philosopher Annette Baier, for example, places Augustine against Hume alongside her other misamorists, Plato, Descartes, Spinoza, and Kant. She does so not because of Augustine's refusal to love, but because of his flight from the creaturely temporality of loving. For Augustine, she writes, "love of God will be a sort of live vaccine that will block any riskier loving."[42] Hannah Arendt similarly issued a strong challenge to the politics of Augustinian loving. She claimed Christian eudaimonism leads either to radical inwardness or aggressive intimacy, both of which are world-less. In either case, Augustine's Christian narrative of religious desire makes a "desert out of the world."[43] Many Christian ethicists implicitly agreed with Arendt's assessment. Paul Ramsey, the Christian ethicist most responsible for restoring a concept of love to political ethics, shared this view. According to Ramsey, the religiosity of Augustine's neo-Platonism ensures that "the neighbor too often seems lost in God, love for neighbor in love for God."[44]

Most political liberals worry about the political consequences of any love, whether it is Baier's risky loves or Ramsey's Christian neighbor-love. They would just as soon jettison love from our political vocabulary. Some associate love with the weakness of self-sacrifice or the confusions of benevolence faced with complex circumstances of scarcity and narrow sympathy. Both associations make it a poor cousin to justice. More worrisome for many liberals, however, is love's connection to Homeric *thumos,* Platonic *eros,* organicist *Gemeinschaft,* or a Rousseauian compassion that seeks to "make men free." As Paul Tillich noted more than fifty years ago, love has been "rejected in the name of a formal concept of justice, and under the assumption that community is an emotional principle adding nothing essential to the rational concept of justice—on the contrary, endangering its strictness."[45] Love is something

---

[42]Annette C. Baier, *Moral Prejudices: Essays on Ethics* (Cambridge, MA: Harvard University Press, 1994), 36.

[43]Hannah Arendt, *Love and Saint Augustine*, edited and translated by J.V. Scott and J.C. Stark (Chicago: University of Chicago Press, 1996), 18. Arendt saw appeals to love as themselves unsuitable for politics. She worried that love, religious or not, rendered politics impotent before the exhausting demands of morality and misguided forms of sentimental benevolence. For Arendt, "love, for reasons of its passion, destroys the in-between which relates us to and separates us from others ... Love by its very nature is unworldly, and it is for this reason rather than its rarity that it is not only apolitical but antipolitical, perhaps the most powerful of all antipolitical forces," in *The Human Condition* (Chicago: University of Chicago Press, 1958), 242.

[44]Paul Ramsey, *Basic Christian Ethics* (New York: Charles Scribner's Sons, 1950), 123. Even Reinhold Niebuhr rejected what he claimed were "grave errors in Augustine's account of love," in "Augustine's Political Realism," 130.

[45]Paul Tillich, *Love, Justice, Power: Ontological Analyses and Ethical Applications* (Oxford: Oxford University Press, 1954), 62.

for poets or interpersonal relations, but it is unfit for public virtue and political affirmation. At best, love must wait until liberty and equality have their say. These associations perpetuate liberal assumptions about oppositions between love and respect and between autonomy and compassion. The experience of love may be one of the summit experiences of a human life, but it is perilous for a politics tempted to enforce moral goodness. Love, on this view, not only short circuits the powers of reason: compassionate responsibility also becomes a cover for ideology. This antipathy to love in the public square led to the more impartial, justice-focused understanding of political morality that typifies post-World War II ethics of citizenship.

Given the demoralizing historical connection between love and religious violence, aversion to a love that has a divine referent only exacerbates liberal concerns. As one defender of liberalism puts it, "what makes for poetry in the soul begets fascism in the city."[46] Gary Gutting here paraphrases Richard Rorty's account of the need to separate public and private morality, but it captures the classically liberal claim that religious love may sometimes be beautiful but it is publicly terrifying. Martha Nussbaum, by contrast, commends Augustine for reopening the significance of human emotions and for refusing a Platonic "wish to depart from our human condition."[47] Nevertheless, she concludes that his achievements are not compatible with liberal politics: "the aim of slipping off into beatitude distracts moral attention from the goal of making this world a good world, and encourages a focus on one's own moral safety that does not bode well for earthly justice."[48] For Nussbaum, the austerity of Augustinian love ultimately yields this advice: "instead of taking action as best we can, we had better cover ourselves, mourn, and wait."[49] Augustinian love furnishes a spiritual eroticism unsuitable for this historical world that demands material action against injustice.[50] In effect, Augustinianism makes history a waiting game. The political dramas of the world are to be endured until the Christian self, inwardly related to the eternal, is delivered from this tragedy. Enthusiastic triumphalism or passive quietism is the dialectic of Augustinianism. My reconstruction of the political implications of an Augustinian political ethic of love will dramatically depart from these varied judgments.

On my view, Augustine's original account of Christian love can be seen as navigating between the cultural and philosophical assumptions of "ethically

---

[46]Gary Gutting, *Pragmatic Liberalism and the Critique of Modernity* (Cambridge: Cambridge University Press, 1999), 59.

[47]Martha Nussbaum, *Upheavals of Thought: The Intelligence of Emotions* (Cambridge: Cambridge University Press, 2001), 547.

[48]Ibid., 553.

[49]Ibid., 556.

[50]Nussbaum contrasts Augustinian Christianity with her own understanding of Judaism that "gives the moral sphere considerable autonomy and centrality, seeing the concern of God for man as essentially moral and political, focused on this-worldly concerns and actions, and intelligible from the point of view of this worldly use of intelligence" (549). For a critical interpretation of Nussbaum's understanding of religious ethics, see Martin Kavka, "Judaism and Theology in Martha Nussbaum's Ethics," *Journal of Religious Ethics* 31:2 (2003): 343–359.

responsible" Stoicism and "spiritual" Platonism. An Augustinian account of love that follows Augustine's innovations on these classical traditions is both affective and cognitive, and oriented both to the world and God. Augustinianism motivates and sustains love for the neighbor (even the neighbor as fellow citizen), but it also recognizes the need to discipline our incontinent loves in a world constrained by sin. In fact, to put it crudely, the problem of political morality for an Augustinian is not so much that we love others too little. This is the familiar problem of motivation in contemporary ethical theory that tries to generate other-regard in the face of self-interest. But the deeper problem is that we love too much in the wrong ways. Our motivations and desires are out of whack, not simply lacking. Our affections are distracted and crowded by their very excess not their scarcity. They need ordering, not the pruning or repression of desire.

To reverse traditional readings, Augustinian lovers suffer from plenitude, not poverty. We are overwhelmed by the good things of the world and, in moments of speculative excess, we are tempted to grasp the good as our own rather than to be in relation to it with others.[51] Possessiveness and corruptibility, marked by the failure to acknowledge dependence and vulnerability, are the key terms of Augustinian moral and political psychology. This recognition does not "instrumentalize" the world; rather, it releases political communities from pressures they cannot bear even as it addresses the self-enclosed anxieties about otherness that often generate anti-liberalism and religious persecution.

Under the pressure of his reading of Christian scriptures and his identification of God with the compassion of the crucified Jesus, Augustine sought not to bury but to redeem the moral and political significance of emotions. In particular, by highlighting the summary and the fulfillment of the law in terms of the twofold love commands (Matthew 22:37–40), he would try to *open the cultural space for emotional investment with those who suffer injustice* and accentuate the practical responsibility this entails. The figure of Jesus presented Augustine with the flesh and blood of compassion. Emotions, then, are not simply sentiments or interruptions of the will. In moving us to action, they become instruments of justice in accord with right reason.[52] Augustine's criticism of what he took to be the Stoic ideal of freedom offers a radical break with significant political implications. Indeed, Nussbaum admits that Augustinian Christianity helped move society "toward equal concern for the deprived, the poor, and the different."[53] This effort to undermine the self-mastery of ancient ethics pushes the Christian out into the world. This reading, ironically, shows

---

[51]See, for example, *City of God*, IX.5, XIV.13, *Confessions*, 2.v.10, *On Christian Doctrine*, 1.27.28, and *The Trinity*, 10.27.

[52]John Cavadini helpfully points out that Augustine is careful to distinguish passion (*pertubationes*) from emotion (usually *motus* or *affectus*). Passions can be thought of as pathological emotions. See John Cavadini, "Feeling Right: Augustine on the Passions and Sexual Desire," *Augustinian Studies* 36:1 (2005): 195–217.

[53]Nussbaum, 248.

how Augustinianism can share liberal concerns about self-absorption and the demise of a public realm amidst a plurality of fleeting, fragile, and inauthentic human loves.

Augustine's critics, both secular and religious, have become too enamored by his formative rhetorical contrasts between *amor Dei* (love of God) and *amor mundi* (love of the world) as well as his more technical distinction between *"uti"* love of neighbor ("using" love) and *"frui"* love of God ("enjoying" love). Consider the case of Anders Nygren's classic text, *Agape and Eros*.[54] Augustine's supposedly stark contrast between *uti* and *frui* was Nygren's smoking gun in his indictment of Augustinian *caritas* on behalf of Lutheran theology. Nygren charges that Augustine corrupted the purity of Christian love (gratuitous *agape*) by lodging it within a Platonic structure of acquisitive and egocentric desire to possess the good (*eros*). Jerusalem, as it were, remained merely the ornamental suburb of philosophical Athens, which is the real downtown of Augustinian theology despite its formal protests. Nygren, by contrast, pits the charity of Jerusalem (a decidedly Christian Jerusalem) against the erotics of self-interested Athens. The power of Nygren's antitheses for his philosophical history of religions is not to be denied. His construction of an issue, like Augustine's, powerfully determines the dynamics of heated debate over Christian love and eudaimonism. This debate in many ways parallels secular discussions of love given the influence of Kant's analogous concept of disinterestedness within a kingdom of ends. I want to loosen Nygren's (and Kant's) dichotomous hold in order to show that an Augustinian political theology of love can offer more than mystical absorption into the One and unjust obliteration of the neighbor.

It is difficult to read Augustine without reading *into* him the future of both Christian spirituality and metaphysics, or at least the dualistic future that now dominates modern memory of his legacy. "Using the world" and "enjoying God" may be infelicitous phrases to modern ears who hear in them only manipulation (following Kant) and alienation (following Feuerbach). The difficulty of maintaining the unity yet duality of these double loves is not a uniquely modern one. Hyper-Augustinianism—with its visions of a totalitarian God and worthless humanity or a false "public body" and a true "inner soul" safely locked up and protected from the world—has been the besetting temptation of the Augustinian legacy for some time. Augustine's indulgent rhetorical excess often said as much. He was a culture warrior, and did not want to give an inch to his opponents in an agonistic age when all sorts of ideals were in flux. No doubt his texts, in all of their unsystematic glory, can be pressed into service by all sorts of projects, including my own.

Is there another way to interpret Augustine's account of love from those described above? I think there is a defensible and attractive alternative that does not competitively abandon God for the sake of the human. It involves a shift in perspective from the prevalence of static metaphysical categories of subjects and

---

[54]Anders Nygren, *Agape and Eros*, trans. Philip Watson (Philadelphia: The Westminster Press, 1953).

objects to a more dynamic theological account of moral psychology. Augustine does not separate moral psychology from what we now call ontology. That refusal is part of what makes Augustine a challenging, though interesting, figure for contemporary thought bent on overcoming metaphysics. Augustine does not, like many religious thinkers (including some political Augustinians), reduce theology to anthropology. In fact, the ontological character of love—predicated on a difference between God and creation—is an important feature of Augustine's thought that diverges from modern discussions of love as fellow-feeling or benevolence. In contrast to standard liberal anthropology, Augustinians might follow Augustine in thinking human beings are best understood as bundles of loves. Love is ineliminable, a component of all action and agency. One cannot *not* love. Augustine's intellectual energies, however, are devoted to an exploration of *how* one is to love without desperately trying to possess and consume any good (finite or infinite). As such, he speaks of "using things badly and enjoying them badly."[55] Augustine's own answer involves training in love, learning its appropriate practice. True virtue, for Augustine, is a "rightly ordered love" (*City of God* XV.22). It is tempting to claim that Augustinian political theology is moral, not metaphysical. We might just turn nouns into verbs: the order of love (the "what") into the ordering of love (the "how").[56] But that is a misleading formulation. It pushes the apophatic moments in Augustinian theology over the edge, and fails to account for the way in which the radical transcendence of God is a way of making room for that which is not God. Ontology still matters. To love an eternal and incomprehensible God, for Augustine, stretches the soul to allow for a qualitatively different kind of love which can now include all that is not God. Christ, for Augustine, is God's own sign that signifies itself but also anticipates a fuller disclosure. This God is not an exhaustible or scarce resource, subject to competing claims. In Augustine's God, "our love will know no check" (*City of God* XI.28).

The integrity of loving well is not simply a matter of a faculty called a "will" that can be separated from Augustine's account of non-possessive desire. This theological vision is why Augustine focuses like a laser on the way in which human loving compensates for contingency and mortality by projecting our own little self-referential worlds of fixed meaning. His condemnation of disordered loving is a challenge to fantasies of possession, when we consume others as part of our non-receptive private

---

[55] *The Trinity,* translated by Edmund Hill (Hyde Park, NY: New City Press, 1991), 10.3.13. Hereafter cited as DT. Critics of Augustine's early formulation of *uti* and *frui* often are misled by D.W. Robertons' faulty translation of *On Christian Doctrine* (Upper Saddle River, NJ: Prentice-Hall, 1958). In translating 1.3.3., for example, Robertson neglects the fact that *uti* and *frui* are deponent verbs—passive in form but active in meaning. As such, he highlights the metaphysical status of the objects loved ("there are others to be enjoyed and used") rather than the quality of the loving as using or enjoying.

[56] The early Heidegger's criticism of Augustine seems to move in this direction. See Martin Heidegger, *The Phenomenology of Religious Life*, eds. Matthias Fritsch and Jennifer Anna Gosetti-Ferencei (Bloomington: Indiana University Press, 2004).

world.[57] Augustinians need not engage in abstract metaphysical speculation on *what* one is to safely consider as appropriate objects of love, especially on the model of a subordinationist teleology where proximate goods are only a means to an ultimate good. Augustine's God does not compete with the neighbor for the self's attention, as if God were simply the biggest of those rival objects considered worthy of love. In short, his God is not a particular thing.

For Augustine, God is the very source of love and existence. All things have existence "through Him Who simply *is*" (*City of God* VIII.6). Augustine's God transcends any metaphysical frame of reference that might measure the reality of God in relation to other realities in some hierarchy of ascending goods. This God is not a collection of the maximal set of possible attributes, having qualities like goodness or beauty. As such, rather than being morally paralyzed by the infinite claims of the neighbor or spiritually distracted by the infinite claims of God, the Augustinian self loves the neighbor in God.

To love the neighbor "in God," Augustine's mature formulation, aims to morally protect the neighbor from the self's prideful distortion that the neighbor exists only in terms of one's own ends, or that the neighbor is a threat to the self's relation to this infinite God. Disordered loving (*cupiditas*) grasps at carnal images of divinity and the neighbor, refusing to recognize them as really and inexhaustibly other. It makes them our own and places them under our control (*libido dominandi*). This is the Platonic and Pelagian lust—to grasp what can only be given in the diversity of social life (*City of God* XV.16). Augustinians value individuality and the separateness of plurality, but this kind of atomistic individualism, to borrow from one of his favorite metaphors for sin, would be a kind of theft—robbing the fellow neighbor and the transcendent God of their separate identity beyond our absorbing self-conceptions. *On Christian Doctrine*, the *Confessions*, the *Trinity*, and Augustine's many homilies and letters can best be read as reflections on the dangers of a "thieving" adolescent love that dominates both neighbor and God. This Augustinian love (like Platonism) is couched less in terms of the "will" and primarily in terms of vision and attention—the dynamic perception of the reality of other persons and the obligations this given reality commands.

Augustinians do not love their neighbor "for their own sake," as if any person actually exists independently of a relation to others participating in the goodness of God. To be sure, Augustinians claim to love *them*, as creatures: "not that the creature is not to be loved, but if that love is related to the creator it will no longer be covetousness but charity" (*The Trinity* 9.2.3). Even the "enemy," a highly unstable category for Augustine, is to be loved as a creature of God. An arresting attention to

---

[57]I think this framework offers the best context for reading Augustine's regret at weeping over the death of Dido and his analysis of grief after the unnamed friend in the *Confessions*. The more common reading takes these passages simply as signs of an excessive Platonic spirituality.

individuals and their autonomy—apart from our dangerous projections of worth—is central. In fact, Augustine uses the Latin word *dignitas* over forty times in his corpus. But it is clearly a transformation of heroic Roman "dignity." The dualistic idea of a human nature with a self-generating natural end and an eschatological supernatural end is denied in order to fend off an implicit naturalism that turns both grace and God merely into an addendum to what is already present "naturally." Kierkegaard would accent this Augustinian claim in his presentation of God as the "middle term" in all relationships.[58] This is a striking and potentially scandalous claim for post-Kantian liberals (and some Christian proponents of *agape* who fear a love always looking over the neighbor's shoulder to God). They fear that moral obligation and rational agency are somehow threatened by this appeal to love, unless the other is seen as an unconditioned end *simpliciter*.

Augustinian love is more than either liberal respect or utilitarian benevolence. But that "more" neither denigrates respect for persons nor elevates altruism above self-regard. To love the neighbor "for the sake of something else" (*propter aliud*, Augustine's early phrase in *On Christian Doctrine*)[59] is to love the neighbor "in virtue of" and "in the way that" a loving God also loves any neighbor. To love someone in virtue of another loving that person, even in human relationships, does not eclipse the value of the beloved or deny the importance of mutual recognition. In fact, it aims to protect the neighbor from a human tendency to consume one another, to exhaust others with our enjoyment of them rather than participate with them in the enjoyment of God. Neighbors can really be my neighbors when they are not just *my* neighbors in *my* world. Love overcomes any absolute bifurcation of utility and delight. It attends to the individual person as a wonderful creature participating in the transcendent beauty of God. The neighbor is concretely loved in her own particular identity as a "rational soul," and not simply as a general instance of a common humanity or derivative of a love for God. But a neighbor's *sui generis* identity participates in the differentiated reality of God's creation. For Augustinians, then, the internal and coincident relation between love of God and love of neighbor provides an integrated motivational ideal for human action (*caritas*) that does not place these two loves in principled competition with one another. In fact, Augustine makes a bracing move that has played an important role in modern Christian social ethics: "the two commandments cannot exist without each other" (*The Trinity* 8.5.12).

At a sociological level, this conception of loving another as a fellow creature in God ("for whom Christ has died," Rom. 14:15, 1 Cor. 8:11) has fostered compelling commitments to the equal dignity of persons and the creation of civic institutions that manifest this commitment. It is also likely that this conception of equality before a loving God has encouraged a fearless independence of mind and spirit that is

---

[58]Søren Kierkegaard, *Works of Love*, translated by Howard and Edna Hong (New York: Harper & Row, 1962), 113.
[59]See *Of Christian Doctrine, 1.*

necessary for the self-respect a democratic society requires, especially among those most threatened by cultural constructs that demean them. To know oneself as a beloved "child of God"—"born of the Spirit," "raised with Christ," and called to a distinct vocation of one's own—is perhaps the *ultimate* form of mutual recognition. It may encourage false consciousness, but it can also encourage a certain distance from the assigned social roles of the dominant culture. Augustine makes this very argument against the vanity of the classical citizens beholden to the opinion of others (*On Christian Doctrine* 1.28). To be sure, Augustinians should not ignore ideological abuses of claims about eschatological identity before God that subjugate and pacify the marginalized. Criticism of slave morality is not to be dismissed as out of hand. Augustinian Christianity *can* valorize humiliation (even violent humiliation) as a lesson against pride. But radical deconstructions of the historical reality of Christian resistance to humiliation, to my mind, often adopt the perspective of the comfortable rather than the afflicted in rejecting any role for an eschatological vision.

The faithfulness of radical love for others, even in an eschatological framework, does include consideration of outcomes in a world of complex injustices. Augustine's experience with the intractable yet eroding authority of Roman law and the failure of its political economy placed severe constraints on his imagination for politics as anything other than perpetual response to disorder. He knew little about the distributive capacities of governance. Can love respond to these capacities today? Can love be mediated even through the civic practices and institutions of liberal democracies?

Love and Coercion

Political rhetoric of love can be put to bad use. Augustine, as much as Foucault, knew the pathological dangers as well as the social inevitability of practices that work on the body and the soul. He knew the "tricks that paternalism can play, not only on its victims but on its perpetrators."[60] But he gave in to these tricks when he thought they met with success—the reform of vicious sinners to their true end. His policy of tough love against Donatist schismatics is usually seen as confirmation of the dangers of political love. His violent rhetoric of "seizing," "grasping," and "compelling" the neighbor to her own good is not a usual resource for Augustinian liberals. His words haunt Western theology and politics: "it is God himself who does this through us, whether by entreaty or threat or censure; by fines or by hard work; whether through secret warnings and visitings, or through the laws of the temporal powers."[61] In

---

[60]Eugene TeSelle, "Toward an Augustinian Politics," *Journal of Religious Ethics* 16:1 (Spring 1988): 91.
[61]Augustine, Letter 105, in *Augustine: Political Writings*, ed. E.M. Atkins and R.J. Dodaro (Cambridge: Cambridge University Press, 2001), 169. See also, Letter 104, Letter 173, and *City of God* XIX.16. For textual evidence of how an Augustinian ethic of love was used to motivate religious crusades in the eleventh-century, see Jonathan Riley-Smith, "Crusading as an Act of Love," *History* 65 (1980): 177–192.

fact, Augustine suggests the more severe the coercion, the greater the love. Most Augustinian liberals simply throw up their hands and say Augustine's theology of coercion was a contradiction or an unresolved anomaly. His pastoral and medicinal analogies for political power exercising a "salutary discipline" for fallen humanity are just too much for liberals. They want the realism of Augustine's anthropology without his harsh therapy for dealing with human sinfulness. It is a sad fact that Augustine's appeal to Christian rulers to chastise recalcitrant opponents like a stern father or a caring physician has been a model for many violent "love" crusades.

Is there a way to make better sense of even this Augustine, to engage in a conversation which allows him to be intelligible to us? Recent studies suggest that Augustine's rhetoric is consistent with the violent rhetoric of Roman law and his personal experience of education by punishment. Some have even argued that Augustine's ostensibly reluctant justification of coercion did not rely upon demands for religious conformity. Augustine sought the legal preservation of civil peace in an emergency situation where terrorists threatened the political order.[62] Apart from its obvious connection to today's global security concerns, this argument provides a resolution to the apparent contradiction between Augustine's theology of *saeculum* and his defense of imperial coercion. I am afraid it does not work. It is an anachronistic reading that grants Augustine the distinction between political security and religious conformity. Augustine did not equate being Roman with being Christian. But Augustine was committed to the idea that church schism was an evil that political authority was competent to judge and also to the belief that bodily harm is an effective route to spiritual health. Heresy was a bad habit that sometimes required coercion in order to break it. While he certainly held the view that true faith cannot be coerced, he thought obstacles of habit and passion could be removed to encourage the will's freedom, to make room for the transformative effects of God's grace, even simply the continence that is our best hope in this sad life for the beginning of virtue. Virtue is a matter of doing the right things for the right reasons—so coercion may be necessary but never a sufficient condition of virtue, or so Augustine thought.

John Bowlin, however, has pointed out that the most remarkable feature of Augustine's understanding of coercion is his very effort to both justify and constrain it. He notes: "it is this reason-giving enterprise, this attempt to make sense of a practice that most of his contemporaries consider morally unproblematic, that distinguishes Augustine, not his participation in this or that persecution."[63] The need to give moral reasons may have begun the slow process of coercion being stripped of its normalizing splendor—its capacity to make acceptance of any act of coercion as a natural fact of politics. If Bowlin is right, Augustine is interesting because he does

[62]John Von Heyking, *Augustine and Politics as Longing in the World* (Columbia: University of Missouri Press, 2001), 219.
[63]John Bowlin, "Augustine on Justifying Coercion," *Annual of the Society of Christian Ethics* 17 (1997): 49–70 (53).

not simply abandon coercion to necessity for fear of exacerbating or legitimating its abuse. Rather, Augustine submits it to moral analysis.

The justification of coercion relies on a set of criteria that Bowlin discerns in Augustine's famous letter to Boniface (*Epistle* 185): (*a*) "coercion must be confined to certain role-specific relationships"; (*b*) "coercion must track the truth, its methods must be deployed for the sake of genuine human goods"; and (*c*) "coercion must be tempered with charity, with care for the coerced, and with worry about the negative freedom lost."[64] Augustine's fledgling criteria can be seen as the kernel of ideas and moral practices that lie behind the development of an emergent just war tradition that has come to be significant in liberal politics. For many, it represents the most compelling development of Christian neighbor-love for liberal politics. Love as a civic virtue motivates concern for the vulnerable and afflicted that subsequently justifies (potentially extensive but not unlimited) state coercion on their behalf. When the state acts, it acts on behalf of the vulnerable and for the sake of justice, but it is constrained by love itself. This appeal to love involves the exercise of communal power to meet the needs of others and to protect the best possible conditions for human flourishing—a tradition that might apply just as well to domestic policy as foreign policy.

To be sure, Augustine is more confident than most Augustinian liberals that we can identify such a broad range of goods and that political leaders can effectively promote them. In a passage that sounds strikingly similar to those liberal perfectionists who produce lists of capacities or basic goods, Augustine holds:

> There is indeed such unanimity within the same living and reason-using nature, that while to be sure it is hidden from one man what another man wants, there are some wishes that all have which are known to every single individual. While each man is ignorant of what another man wants, in some matters he can know what all men want. (*The Trinity* 13.2.6)

Liberal society should debate the policies that try to address these wants and needs (for example, poverty relief and provision for health care and education). An Augustinian emphasis on the hiddenness of divine grace will resist political efforts at a full-fledged paternalist reorientation of desire according to a fixed, univocal conception of the human good secured by legal sanction without respect for individual self-determination. That would press anti-anti-perfectionism too far. Some goods are too vulnerable and too rich to be the focus of the state's direct concern.

What matters in moral and political assessment are the details of the coercion and a prudent account of the concrete situation. Good motives are not good enough for social justice, especially when they result in persecutions motivated by moral egoism

---

[64]Ibid., 66–67.

and moral purity. The justification of coercion—of whatever kind (i.e., taxation, compulsory public education, seatbelt laws, banning certain foods, fair housing laws, laws against dueling, gambling regulation)—remains a contestable feature of liberal practice that continually tries to fend off its libertarian critics. These discussions tend to invoke some version of Mill's harm principle as prelude to a registry of liberal rights.[65] Liberal perfectionists affirm these rights alongside their belief that political communities should "enable citizens to search for the good life."[66] Perfectionist arguments, to my mind, make better sense of state activities that sacrifice negative liberties for the sake of positive liberties that would otherwise be unavailable without state intervention. Modes of formalistic respect do not capture the relevant concerns grounded in a shared vision of these goods. These goods are made possible by certain social conditions and political judgments. I am thinking here of legislation against sexual commodification and certain classes of drugs, government funding of the arts and scientific research, and more expansive regulation of financial markets that entrench class divisions and various public goods like the environment and health care. Behavioral economics is increasingly recognizing the fact that human beings suffer from both a lack of self-control and bounded rationality. These economists, perhaps unwittingly, advocate a variety of government programs that try to steer people to make better choices even as they preserve freedom of choice (for example, tinkering with government savings plans and private pension funds so that the default position is automatic enrollment with the opportunity to opt out of the programs).[67] Sometimes perfectionism looks like the slow, boring process of figuring out consumer protection policies and savings plans. Sometimes it looks like the Civil Rights movement's advocacy for coercive measures of federal government action in the face of white Christian supremacists and the brutality of American racism. Indeed, America's great Augustinian liberal, Martin Luther King, Jr., showed that political love is not confined to personal affections without relevance for structures of power.

Conclusion

Augustine, unlike Socrates, does not immediately come to mind as a winsome exponent of the dialogical life for a pluralist society in search of political wisdom. Among modern thinkers, he is more feared than loved. Augustinians are usually identified as leading critics of Enlightenment ideas of progress that are guided by

---

[65]See John Stuart Mill, *On Liberty and other writings*, ed., Stefan Collini (Cambridge: Cambridge University Press, 1989), 13–16.
[66]Martha Nussbaum, *Upheavals of Thought*, 404.
[67]See, for example, Cass R. Sunstein and Richard H. Thaler, "Libertarian Paternalism is Not an Oxymoron," *University of Chicago Law Review* 70:4 (Fall 2003): 1159–1202.

secular principles of rationality. They look to the happy end of the world, not to the ruthless clamor of this grim, dying age of sadness. They favor bounded structures of the ecclesial rather than the wild plurality of a world where individuals freely revised their own plans for life. They long for the transcendent with authoritarian abandon and puritanical anxiety, tending either toward theocratic efforts to hasten its arrival or sectarian withdrawal that subordinates the social role of citizen to that of Christian disciple. In this way, Augustinians are either too preoccupied with goodness or too preoccupied with evil to be of use to liberal politics. Caught not beyond good and evil but between them, the tradition typically delivers a schizophrenic political morality: one otherwordly ("love of God"), another persecutorial ("love of neighbor"), and perhaps several that swing between the two. No doubt those unfamiliar with the tradition of Augustinian liberalism, given their rival stereotypes, may resist this pairing as a categorical mistake. Liberalism, whether by way of Kant or Hume or Locke, is about leaving dreary Augustinianism behind.

Liberals are also supposed to be wary of demanding too much of politics. Some allow this fear to generate an entire political theory, either by carving out a distinct space where "religion" can safely happen or by adopting a religious devotion to liberalism itself. Some celebrate this modern kind of austerity as the welcome separation of spirituality from politics that is thought to be liberating for both. Others fear that by abandoning religious horizons, liberal politics cuts itself off from roots that inspire, sustain, and make sense of its strenuous demands. The eschatological identity of Christians should temper their enthusiasm for revolutionary politics that expect complete intimacy, transparency, and certain progress in an uncertain world. Whether or not this vision is really to be contrasted, as it usually is, with the so-called Greek polis tradition is open to debate. Bernard Yack, for example, argues that Aristotle also knew that "*no* actual political community is well-ordered … all actual political regimes fall short of unqualified justice, and Aristotle's recommendations for improvement would still leave them short of the mark."[68] If a contrast is to be drawn, I think it lies more in Augustine's frustration with the limited ambitions of the classical city. It is not public enough, content to celebrate its immanence and the virtue of the elite few, substituting finite goods for infinite ones. Concerns about self-absorption and the demise of a public realm amidst a plurality of human loves are deeply Augustinian. Indeed, Augustine looks to a heavenly city that is so public there will be no need for coercion or for language itself (*City of God* XXII.6). Augustinians are attracted to a grander style of politics (a *heavenly* city), but they should embrace a liberal one here on earth. There could be worse forms of politics. Deficiency, as it were, might still admit gradation. The practice of moral criticism that still exists within democratic faith—a critical discourse grounded in

---

[68]Bernard Yack, *The Problems of a Political Animal: Community, Justice, and Conflict in Aristotelian Political Thought* (Berkeley: University of California Press, 1993), 6–7.

social movements, virtuous practices, and institutions—cannot be read as simply another kind of nihilism beholden to the hegemonic empire of capitalism. This Augustinian embrace is not whole-hearted—it is more like toleration or endurance than the enthusiasm of belief and commitment. Nevertheless, Augustinian liberals should not abandon love in their patient expectation. Neither justice nor realism demand this much chastity.

Augustinian politics need not compete with visions of imperfection in a tournament of doom and gloom. There is imperfection and there is imperfectionism. Augustinians should not allow their tradition to confirm a spectator's gaze on the tragedy of politics. Horrors there are. Dangers await. But Augustinian politics need not delight in them and acquiesce to the available models of political realism and liberal proceduralism. In particular, as I have argued, they should resist the charge that perfectionist aspiration necessarily abandons liberty and equality. Ethics should be realistic, that is adequate to human creatures, but it should also encourage the transformation of actual practices and the character of citizens.

Most liberal theories sacrifice love on the altar of a restricted conception of justice in order to fend off pathology. Augustinians can offer a liberal politics of love responsive to this concern, but also to abiding theological commitments that too often get buried in the safely constructed discourse of "religion and politics." This offering might intersect with recent calls "to recuperate the public and political conception of love common to the premodern tradition."[69] Some post-secularists are interested in theology precisely for the sake of the secular, a term now transformed by different sorts of naturalisms as much as Augustinianisms. For example, Jacques Derrida's criticism of liberal "knights of good conscience" and his effort to move beyond the predictable liberal economy of "melancholy to triumph and triumph to melancholy," are promising notes for an Augustinianism that wants to be more than a rationalized politics of necessity without going in for nostalgia or idealism.[70] Beyond Derrida, Augustinian liberals might still temper the dreams of more optimistic invocations of post-secular loves. But this temperance need not be governed, as critics claim, by a supposed option for "two theories of value" that splits the material and the divine.[71] Rather, as I have argued, it involves two modes of valuing (using and enjoying) which can coordinate an Augustinian political notion

---

[69]Michael Hardt and Antonio Negri, *Multitude: War and Democracy in an Age of Empire* (New York: Penguin Press, 2004), 351.

[70]Jacques Derrida, *The Gift of Death*, trans. David Wills (Chicago: University of Chicago Press, 1995), 67, 22.

[71]David Nirenberg, "The Politics of Love and Its Enemies," 598. Nirenberg helpfully recognizes that Marx's discussion of exchange and relationship lies deep in the complicated history of Western philosophical and theological reflections on love. For Nirenberg, however, "far from being an antidote to instrumental reason or to relations of possession and exchange, the fantasy that love can free interaction from interest is itself one of the more dangerous offspring of the marriage of Athens and Jerusalem that we sometimes call the Western tradition" (575–576).

of love's danger and promise. These modes offer no guarantees, but the life of virtue does not offer guarantees.

The liberal tradition is in some sense about accepting people as they happen to be. Liberal perfectionists, however, work for a more just society to the extent possible in a world where we tend to fall over, and crash into, one another. Augustinians know about falling and crashing. But we would do well to consider Augustine's insight that how a political society thinks about the directions of its desires and loves has important consequences for the sort of life that members of such a society might lead. Strict observance of non-maleficence as the only way to respect another person risks its own kind of moral failure, both to others and to ourselves. To enjoy liberalism in the Augustinian sense turns on an unhealthy desire to enjoy only ourselves. That is the real danger: not individuality as such, but the tendency to become comfortable in the black hole of one's own privacy. The future of Augustinian liberalism—and so much more—may turn on whether or not we human beings can learn to desire more than ourselves without killing each other or simply forgetting about the shared goods of politics in pursuit of private perfection, aesthetic delight, entertaining distractions, economic security, and even spiritual freedom.

Recent invocations of love by post-Marxist and post-secularist theorists rightly occasion anxieties about its troubled history and false promises. Human beings will abuse the rhetoric of "love" just as much as they abuse the rhetoric of "justice." It will be employed to manipulate and exploit rather than address conditions of manipulation and exploitation. This reality, however, should not mean that liberal democracies (and their philosophers) can proceed as if love is not necessary for a political practice responsive to injustice, persons in need, and the social conditions that frustrate human flourishing.

41. Aristotle Papanikolaou – The Politics of Divine-Human Communion

Since the fall of Communism in the early 1990s, the world's focus has shifted to Islam. There has been much discussion on whether Islam is mutually exclusive with Western liberal democracy. While it seemed that a universal consensus existed, especially after Vatican II, on the compatibility between liberal democracy and Christianity, the post-Communist situation in Eastern Europe provoked some cracks in that consensus. Was Orthodox Christianity similar to Islam in being an obstacle to the implementation of democratic structures in Eastern Europe? Is Orthodox Christianity on the wrong side of the "clash of civilizations"? Added to this was a Western Christian voice emerging over the last few decades that, in one form or another, declared modern liberal democratic principles to be antithetical to Christian understandings of God, community, and the human being. Many of these Christian voices base this claim on the newly revived notion of *theosis,* or "deification," which is especially troubling in the Orthodox world, since those Orthodox who are reflexively anti-Western, who are fighting at all costs for an Orthodox hegemony in traditional Orthodox countries, but who lack the intellectual resources for a rigorous and consistent political theology beyond appeals to the past, can now turn to the thought of, ironically, non-Christian theologians to support their ambivalence to liberal democracy.

The basic claim grounding Christian ambivalence toward modern liberal democracy is that the latter embodies claims about being human that are antithetical to those espoused by Christians. With those who express this ambivalence, I stand in agreement that any consistent Christian political theology must begin with the claim of what it means to be Christian. I have defined what it means to be Christian in terms of *theosis* or, as I prefer to translate it, divine-human communion. It has long been assumed, even by the Orthodox, that the mystical notion of *theosis* has nothing to do with politics, that divine-human communion can only be achieved by fleeing from the "world" to the desert, the monastery, or the forest. And, yet, if we further clarify divine-human communion in terms of fulfillment of the commandment to love God and neighbor, then it becomes clear that the calling to embody the divine presence more fully in the material creation is not simply to those who flee the world, but also to those who remain in the world. *Theosis* was never meant to institute a Gnostic either/or-ness between the divine and the material creation, but affirms material creation as the arena of the divine presence. *Theosis* also does not allow this Gnostic dualism to seep into the various structures that shape our communal spaces; it is not meant to signify an escape from material creation nor an escape from the various structures within which we relate to that material space. It is simply not the case that only those who isolate themselves from family, work, or politics are capable of divine-human communion; it is also a calling for those who either choose or have no other choice but to remain in those structures.

Humans, then, are called from their very birth to communion with God, and their entire lives can be interpreted as one continuous struggle to embody this communion or, otherwise put, to learn how to love. Augustine got this logic straight long ago that if God is love, then our love is simply an indication of God in us, and the marker of that is how we love the other. Love, however, is not automatic; it has nothing to do with being a soulmate. Humans perpetually struggle against those things that seem to get in the way of love—predispositions, fear, low self-esteem, false ego-projections, just to name a few. It may seem that out of love a parent pushes a child in a certain direction, when it is often the case that such a push masks a deep-rooted fear of failing as a parent. What seems like love is often self-referential.

I am of the opinion that the ascetical tradition, in both East and West, understood that fulfilling the love commandment requires ascetical discernment and practices. The best way to look at this tradition is as one of thinking on how to acquire the virtue of love, which is to grow in deeper communion with God. The central question of this ascetical tradition is: what are the practices that one needs to perform in relation to oneself and the other in order to make oneself more available to love both oneself and the other in the way that God does? There is an ascetics to divine-human communion, which is simultaneously the Christian attempt to learn how to love.

Insofar as this ascetics of divine-human communion is performed always in relation to the other, then politics must be reconceived as an ascetical practice. Admittedly, politics was never thought to be such within the ascetical tradition. The ascetical struggle to learn how to love is inescapably in relation to the other(s)—family, friends, and strangers. The encounter with the stranger is simultaneously a challenge and opportunity for the Christian to learn how to love. It's always in relation to the other that the Christian must perform practices that make one more available to be loving, to communing with the divine. Politics are the forms of practices that humans engage in when relating, in Christian language, to the stranger. The type of politics one engages in shapes the way in which one relates to the stranger. Christian relating to the stranger, in other words, Christian politics, must be a performance of practices that either emerge from or attempt to contribute to the Christian struggle to learn to love. There is simply not a space in which the Christian is not to think about the performance of practices that would instantiate the divine presence in the particular relational space in which the Christian is situated.

So much of what passes as Christian politics is counter to a politics of divine-human communion. Christians, as well as those of other religions, often think that since they possess the truth it gives them the authority to engage in a politics of bullying. The "possession" of absolute truth justifies all kinds of politics of demonization and destruction, and of restrictions of certain freedoms, such as religious freedoms. This politics of bullying is part of an ascetics of the demonic. What is ironic is that what often gets paraded as loyalty, fidelity, and commitment to the truth of God simply masks a deeper insecurity that all on which one has staked one's identity, all that one has thought to be true, could simply be wrong. It is using God for the sake of identity politics; it is idolatrous.

Maximus the Confessor warns the monks he is addressing that the vices that get in the way of love are, to name a few, anger, fear, and hatred. It is these very vices that also get in the way of a genuine Christian politics, which is simultaneously an ascetics of divine-human communion. A Christian must be rigorously and vigilantly self-reflexive to make sure that his Christian politics is not motivated by anger, fear, or hatred. A Christian politics must be humble, which does not mean that the Christian is a pushover; to be humble and to be firm in one's convictions is not oxymoronic. A Christian politics, as Mathewes rightly points out, engages the other by not trying to project onto the other, but by listening, conversing, and debating. A Christian politics as asceticism risks losing the debate, but waits patiently for the other to see the wisdom of the Christian vision of divine-human communion. In the end, the politics-as-asceticism that the Christian will perform will contribute to shaping a political space that looks something like a liberal democracy. By liberal democracy, I mean nothing more than a political space shaped by a common good that embodies the principles of equality and freedom, with the former including social and economic equalities, and the latter including religious freedom facilitated by church-state separation.

It is simply nonsense to think that by working for this kind of political space that the Christian is accepting the anthropological baggage of modern liberalism, acquiescing to the modern liberal marginalization of religion, or furthering the modern liberal story of the violence of religion. Those who argue for a mutual exclusivity between any form of liberal democracy and the Christian eucharistic vision of the church are inserting a Gnostic dualism into the Christian theo-political imagination that is simply not consistent with the logic of divine-human communion. While recognizing that the fullness of the Christian vision is a church that exists eucharistically, the Christian attempt to embody a eucharistic mode of being in the world recognizes that the political is not the ecclesial; that how a Christian exists in the world affects the form of the political space; that the political space serves a purpose distinct from but analogous to the eucharistic understanding of the ecclesial. The political space that structures relations in such a way that mirror a eucharistic understanding of the ecclesial, especially in terms of relations that realize the inviolable uniqueness of all human beings, is a liberal democracy. Since, however, the political is not the ecclesial, that political space must structure those relations through human rights language, and, without some notion of the common good, which is revisable and debatable, the principles of freedom and equality embedded in a liberal democracy will simply implode upon themselves.

Although it does not operate according to a nature-grace divide, an ascetics of divine-human communion contributes to a non–natural law understanding of the common good. Indeed, contrary to some understandings, or, perhaps, misconceptions, of natural law, Christian ascetical practices are not simply about the salvation of our soul. They all have political ramifications, insofar as their practice cannot but affect the political space. Even the practices of truth-telling and forgiveness, which are not willed acts as much as they are modes of being, are ascetical practices that affect the political. While understanding forgiveness as an event of communion that is realized through the practice of truth-telling mitigates against any facile understanding of political forgiveness, it is clear that the attempt at forgiveness between nations or groups can facilitate communion-like relations between peoples. Face-to-face forgiveness in the political space between strangers shapes such a space in the form of a liberal democracy.

While I understand the caution behind Christians not easily aligning themselves with modern liberalism, and while I applaud the exhortation that Christians more boldly assert their Christian presuppositions, the vitriolic rhetoric against modern liberalism, which extends to liberal democracy, is dangerous, especially in the hands of an institutional church with real political and cultural power. It is interesting that two of the loudest voices in this antiliberalism rhetoric, Hauerwas and Milbank, come from churches that are institutionally weak. Christians, then, should never forget that the political is not the ecclesial, but they should also remember that the mystical is the political, and that an ascetics of divine-human communion shapes a political space that is liberal democratic.

42. Liberalism and Democracy: Discussion Questions

What is your understanding of the term 'liberalism'?

What kind of role do you think churches and religious bodies should play in public policy in a pluralist society?

What kinds of theological resources does the Christian tradition offer for a critique of liberal modernity?

VII

Oppression, Marginalization and Liberation

Introduction by Amy Daughton

Questions of power have frequently arisen throughout this reader, in connection with themes of authority, of political resistance, of the identity of Jesus. In this section the ways in which power has inflected Christian traditions and practices, including political theology, come under scrutiny. Covering a period from the end of the nineteenth century to today, these collected texts do not trace a genealogy of developing thought. Rather, they display a rising and diversifying attentiveness to the reality and experience of marginalized persons as subjects of theological reasoning. These are critical voices of protest and protection, retrieving and enriching a contextually sensitive evaluation of Christian political theology.

By the end of the nineteenth century, life in Europe and the nations of the North Atlantic had been irreversibly transformed by industrialization and consequent urbanization. This had heralded significant social change as the increasingly landless working class moved to supply labour to new industry, radically changing traditional patterns of life and social relationships. Market crises had their effect as well, and the early 1870s saw the beginning of a global depression, impacting on prices, employment and wages.

It is in this context that *Rerum Novarum* (Of the new things) appeared in 1891. Also referred to as 'On Rights and Duties of Capital and Labour', this papal letter, in this case addressed to Catholic Church leaders, advocated for the just treatment of workers and for mutual protection and spiritual support through mediating associations such as unions. Politically speaking, this navigated a path to reject socialism, while refusing to commit to the contemporary norms of capitalist production and exchange.

In the focus on concrete behaviour and social structures, it was something of a departure for Leo XIII, but what was consistent in the document was the continued reliance on Thomas Aquinas signalled by his earlier *Aeterni Patris* (Eternal Father) in 1879. Readers who have already considered Section I's extracts of Thomas, which focus on his prelapsarian understanding of politics as the lawful working out of human interdependence, will recognize much of the expectations in *Rerum Novarum*: the active theological role of the state in making men (*sic*) better and happier, the role of law as the mechanism of protecting the conditions for that pursuit, and the recognition of private property and public associations as goods for that purpose. In this and subsequent encyclicals these parameters are set in critical contrast to the anthropological assumptions of capitalism, liberalism and socialism.

Many commentators have identified *Rerum Novarum* as an origin point for contemporary Catholic Social Teaching (CST). It is already evident that its roots are necessarily more ancient, yet from this point a clear thread of emphasis on social concerns runs through church documents to the present day. Blossoming into a wider area of thinking for Catholic theologians, CST remains significant for diverse political manifestations of Catholic political thinking; it has been claimed by those committed to Left or Right, while most recent work rejects and subverts those categories of political commitment.

An alternative but related trajectory can be seen in the emergence of liberation theology from the mid-twentieth century. The Second Vatican Council of 1962–65 heralded great changes in how the Church itself was organized, giving weight to episcopal leadership in tackling regional issues. This was important as the Council had seen a concerted push from bishops of impoverished countries to acknowledge global poverty as a frontier in the battle with human sinfulness and a location of radically Christic encounter.

Taken together, this gave greater significance to the Latin American Episcopal Conference meetings at Rio, Medellín, Puebla, which offered increasingly sharpened critiques of the structural dehumanizing of the impoverished in Latin America. Liberation theology developed informing these episcopal events, led by major systematic thinkers, including Gustavo Gutiérrez, Leonardo Boff and Juan Luis Segundo. Like Catholic social thinkers, these liberation theologians owed intellectual and political debts to ancient church sources and added to this the then recent reception in *nouvelle théologie*, as well as social analysis from critical theory.

This last, with its links to Marxist analyses, gave Vatican leadership serious concerns through the 1970s and 1980s as it confronted communism in Europe. All this led to direct hierarchical clashes between liberation theologians and Vatican leaders. However, rather than a straightforward Marxist critique, liberation theology can be characterized as an attempt to rework the whole theological project of understanding God and the world. This is begun with the poor, as the narrative, literal and salvific location of Jesus Christ. The piece we have chosen to represent this complex and wide-ranging school is a relatively late example from Jon Sobrino (2008) that presents the theological project of liberation precisely as a new logic, a new way of reasoning and of imagining for the future, with and led by the reality of the poor.

Sobrino draws on many voices in this pursuit of a true representation of reality, but it must be accepted that these voices themselves are not always from the most marginalized within society. Marcella Althaus-Reid's 2004 piece ¿Bién Sonados? (colloquially described as "we are defeated") gives a cutting edge to liberation theology's vision of the poor not as romanticized saints, but as human persons actively rendered vulnerable by others in society and so directly exploited for profit. In this way Althaus-Reid represents a later generation of commentators on liberation theology, concerned by its clericalism, its patriarchal, and perhaps even colonial viewpoint on poor people, and the consequent erasure of the material reality of poverty for women and queer people from the spirituality it describes.

The voices of challenge to bastions of theological privilege are not limited to recent scholarship. Section IV on political Christology has already introduced the work of James Cone and the accompanying voices of Black theology. To put this movement into context, Cone's A Black Theology of Liberation predates Gutiérrez's 1971 Teología de la liberacíon by a year. Cone's work, alongside that of scholars such as Cornell West, Beverly Harrison, and later Frank Chikane and Robert Beckford, signalled a new generation of academic theologians concerned with the corrupting political shapes that religion had taken on historically and in contemporary society. Black theology confronts churches and theologians with the assessment that the ecclesial and academic reception of Christ's message renders it white, allying it with power and so deforming it into the murderous oppression of people of colour. It is therefore no surprise that Black theology and the political activism of Black power, civil rights and anti-apartheid movements had much to declare mutually. There are powerful examples in the anti-apartheid Kairos document and Martin Luther King Jr.'s statement on Vietnam (Section V, 'Violence and Peace'), both of which are theological assessments of specific government policies.

Vincent Lloyd has recently argued that the subsequent wave of Black theologians made a turn from politics to culture. As contextual theology necessarily became more diversified, Black theology became a voice from and for its particular culture. However, Lloyd argues that this has left the present generation in a precarious position. Cultural diversity can prompt a too flat, uncritical praise for diversity as such, while a rising Afro-pessimism from Black Studies contends that such cultural exposure is pyrrhic, only comodifying Black culture for white consumption. Third-wave Black theology is thus confronted with a specifically metaphysical challenge (that nonetheless has political implications) of a white ideology that rejects Black being.[1] J. Kameron Carter is one of those grappling with the ontology of Blackness, using one of Gregory of Nyssa's homilies (2008). This explores the self-critique to be found in Ecclesiastes and the discovery of universal sovereignty of humankind,

---

[1]Vincent Lloyd, 'Afro-Pessimism and Christian Hope' in Lieven Boeve, Stephan van Erp, Martin Poulsom (eds) Grace, Governance, and Globalization: Theology and Public Life (London: Bloomsbury, 2017).

which for Carter is born paradoxically from Christ's entry into enslavement, giving contemporary bite to Black identity as the image of God.

Working with ancient church sources for the purposes of contemporary protection and shaping of social thought is ultimately characteristic of all the texts collected in this section. What distinguishes them is the level at which that protection prompts critique of established systems. For feminist theology, this included recognizing theological sources *themselves* as necessarily codified and entrenched within particular traditions of reception and practice. For this reason Elisabeth Schüssler-Fiorenza has frequently returned to narrative interpretation, identifying women's voices and interests that have been erased from the reception of scripture, and Mary Daly confronted the perhaps irreparably subjugating character of Christian language and organization as a precursor to post-Christian thinkers for whom the church could not be the place of reform it would need to be for transformation.

The emphasis on androcentric language and narrative continues through much of the succeeding work of feminist theologians up to today. This appeared from the perspective of women theologians who had found purchase in the academy for the first time, largely in the United States where in contrast with Europe fewer theology faculty appointments required an ecclesial *mandatus*. In that academic context, language is the tool by which women make their own claims to humanity, and thus build into the methods by which theology itself is conducted through a broadened, more inclusive lens. In this section, Rosemary Radford Ruether delivers an important critical analysis of Christian traditions as excluding women's experience and ultimately therefore offering a malformed vision of God and the human person as primarily male. This particular extract (1983) also includes a sense of how the intellectual journey towards respect for women's experience might be mapped for individuals.

Such a strategy in the early generation of feminist theology leaves out many facets of global women's experiences. Feminist theology has thereby been rightly critiqued for its own white, straight, Western privilege, resulting in models of feminist thinking grounded in more varied racial, cultural and sociological circumstances of exploitation and exclusion, such as queer, womanist or *mujerista* theology. The critiques raised in these conversations have extended to exploitative assumptions about the natural world, with ecofeminism being a recent and continuing thread of discussion.

However, this historical contribution is not yet concluded; indeed, the so-called contextual phase of theology is ongoing. Straight white feminists still frequently forget to acknowledge what the privilege of our sexuality and skin colour has meant in terms of overpowering the voices of queer people and women of colour. Althaus-Reid's critique of liberation theology is thus live for all theologians today: to acknowledge Christian responsibility for the colonial violence that continues to entrap and kill adults and children across the world. There are multiple indices of vulnerability that intersect and so illustrate the systematic character of global power structures as resting on the poor, the disabled, the stateless and so on.

It would be easy to point to historical instantiations of this: the Constantinian shift of the fourth century; Papally commissioned European expansion from the fifteenth century; or the waves of economic and military imperialism of the twentieth century seen in regime changes and development and trade agreements. Corresponding voices of protest can be identified too in figures like Bartolomé de Las Casas. What sets postcolonial scholarship apart from these historical instances is its assumption that there is an imperial ideology at the heart of Christianity's intellectual commitments that must be subverted and disrupted at the most basic level. Radically different examples could have been included here – Elsa Tamez, Kwok Pui-lan, R. S. Sugirtharajah – but Musa Dube offers a particularly apt example of critique and construction by illustrating the colonizing character of the Gospel of John (2002). She excavates the boundaries of the Johannine community in relation to the Roman and Jewish power struggles on display in the encounter between Christ and the Samaritan woman. That analysis concludes with a new version of the story from novelist Mositi Totontle to reconstruct and reconnect gender, race, land and community of the Gospel in the images of Botswanan storytelling. New stories offer new ideas, new relationships, new opportunities, and the sheer diversity of postcolonial thinking continues to offer this replenishment to political theology.

43. Leo XIII – Extracts from *Rerum Novarum*

Encyclical of Pope Leo XIII on Capital and Labor

To Our Venerable Brethren the Patriarchs, Primates, Archbishops, Bishops, and other ordinaries of places having Peace and Communion with the Apostolic See.

Rights and Duties of Capital and Labor

That the spirit of revolutionary change, which has long been disturbing the nations of the world, should have passed beyond the sphere of politics and made its influence felt in the cognate sphere of practical economics is not surprising. The elements of the conflict now raging are unmistakable, in the vast expansion of industrial pursuits and the marvellous discoveries of science; in the changed relations between masters and workmen; in the enormous fortunes of some few individuals, and the utter poverty of the masses; the increased self reliance and closer mutual combination of the working classes; as also, finally, in the prevailing moral degeneracy. The momentous gravity of the state of things now obtaining fills every mind with painful apprehension; wise men are discussing it; practical men are proposing schemes; popular meetings, legislatures, and rulers of nations are all busied with it – actually there is no question which has taken deeper hold on the public mind.

2. Therefore, venerable brethren, as on former occasions when it seemed opportune to refute false teaching, We have addressed you in the interests of the Church and of the common weal, and have issued letters bearing on political power, human liberty, the Christian constitution of the State, and like matters, so have We thought it expedient now to speak on the condition of the working classes. It is a subject on which We have already touched more than once, incidentally. But in the present letter, the responsibility of the apostolic office urges Us to treat the question of set purpose and in detail, in order that no misapprehension may exist as to the principles which truth and justice dictate for its settlement. The discussion is not easy, nor is it void of danger. It is no easy matter to define the relative rights and mutual duties of the rich and of the poor, of capital and of labor. And the danger lies in this, that crafty agitators are intent on making use of these differences of opinion to pervert men's judgments and to stir up the people to revolt.

3. In any case we clearly see, and on this there is general agreement, that some opportune remedy must be found quickly for the misery and wretchedness pressing so unjustly on the majority of the working class: for the ancient workingmen's guilds were abolished in the last century, and no other protective organization took their place. Public institutions and the laws set aside the ancient religion. Hence, by degrees it has come to pass that working men have been surrendered, isolated and helpless, to the hardheartedness of employers and the greed of unchecked competition. The mischief has been increased by rapacious usury, which, although more than once condemned by the Church, is nevertheless, under a different guise, but with like injustice, still practiced by covetous and grasping men. To this must be added that the hiring of labor and the conduct of trade are concentrated in the hands of comparatively few; so that a small number of very rich men have been able to lay upon the teeming masses of the laboring poor a yoke little better than that of slavery itself.

4. To remedy these wrongs the socialists, working on the poor man's envy of the rich, are striving to do away with private property, and contend that individual possessions should become the common property of all, to be administered by the State or by municipal bodies. They hold that by thus transferring property from private individuals to the community, the present mischievous state of things will be set to rights, inasmuch as each citizen will then get his fair share of whatever there is to enjoy. But their contentions are so clearly powerless to end the controversy that were they carried into effect the working man himself would be among the first to suffer.

They are, moreover, emphatically unjust, for they would rob the lawful possessor, distort the functions of the State, and create utter confusion in the community.

5. It is surely undeniable that, when a man engages in remunerative labor, the impelling reason and motive of his work is to obtain property, and thereafter to hold it as his very own. If one man hires out to another his strength or skill, he does so for the purpose of receiving in return what is necessary for the satisfaction of his needs; he therefore expressly intends to acquire a right full and real, not only to the remuneration, but also to the disposal of such remuneration, just as he pleases. Thus, if he lives sparingly, saves money, and, for greater security, invests his savings in land, the land, in such case, is only his wages under another form; and, consequently, a working man's little estate thus purchased should be as completely at his full disposal as are the wages he receives for his labor. But it is precisely in such power of disposal that ownership obtains, whether the property consist of land or chattels. Socialists, therefore, by endeavoring to transfer the possessions of individuals to the community at large, strike at the interests of every wage-earner, since they would deprive him of the liberty of disposing of his wages, and thereby of all hope and possibility of increasing his resources and of bettering his condition in life.

6. What is of far greater moment, however, is the fact that the remedy they propose is manifestly against justice. For, every man has by nature the right to possess property as his own. This is one of the chief points of distinction between man and the animal creation, for the brute has no power of self direction, but is governed by two main instincts, which keep his powers on the alert, impel him to develop them in a fitting manner, and stimulate and determine him to action without any power of choice. One of these instincts is self preservation, the other the propagation of the species. Both can attain their purpose by means of things which lie within range; beyond their verge the brute creation cannot go, for they are moved to action by their senses only, and in the special direction which these suggest. But with man it is wholly different. He possesses, on the one hand, the full perfection of the animal being, and hence enjoys at least as much as the rest of the animal kind, the fruition of things material. But animal nature, however perfect, is far from representing the human being in its completeness, and is in truth but humanity's humble handmaid, made to serve and to obey. It is the mind, or reason, which is the predominant element in us who are human creatures; it is this which renders a human being human, and distinguishes him essentially from the brute. And on this very account – that man alone among the animal creation is endowed with reason – it must be within his right to possess things not merely for temporary and momentary use, as other living things do, but to have and to hold them in stable and permanent possession; he must have not only things that perish in the use, but those also which, though they have been reduced into use, continue for further use in after time.

7. This becomes still more clearly evident if man's nature be considered a little more deeply. For man, fathoming by his faculty of reason matters without number,

linking the future with the present, and being master of his own acts, guides his ways under the eternal law and the power of God, whose providence governs all things. Wherefore, it is in his power to exercise his choice not only as to matters that regard his present welfare, but also about those which he deems may be for his advantage in time yet to come. Hence, man not only should possess the fruits of the earth, but also the very soil, inasmuch as from the produce of the earth he has to lay by provision for the future. Man's needs do not die out, but forever recur; although satisfied today, they demand fresh supplies for tomorrow. Nature accordingly must have given to man a source that is stable and remaining always with him, from which he might look to draw continual supplies. And this stable condition of things he finds solely in the earth and its fruits. There is no need to bring in the State. Man precedes the State, and possesses, prior to the formation of any State, the right of providing for the substance of his body.

8. The fact that God has given the earth for the use and enjoyment of the whole human race can in no way be a bar to the owning of private property. For God has granted the earth to mankind in general, not in the sense that all without distinction can deal with it as they like, but rather that no part of it was assigned to any one in particular, and that the limits of private possession have been left to be fixed by man's own industry, and by the laws of individual races. Moreover, the earth, even though apportioned among private owners, ceases not thereby to minister to the needs of all, inasmuch as there is not one who does not sustain life from what the land produces. Those who do not possess the soil contribute their labor; hence, it may truly be said that all human subsistence is derived either from labor on one's own land, or from some toil, some calling, which is paid for either in the produce of the land itself, or in that which is exchanged for what the land brings forth.

9. Here, again, we have further proof that private ownership is in accordance with the law of nature. Truly, that which is required for the preservation of life, and for life's well-being, is produced in great abundance from the soil, but not until man has brought it into cultivation and expended upon it his solicitude and skill. Now, when man thus turns the activity of his mind and the strength of his body toward procuring the fruits of nature, by such act he makes his own that portion of nature's field which he cultivates – that portion on which he leaves, as it were, the impress of his personality; and it cannot but be just that he should possess that portion as his very own, and have a right to hold it without any one being justified in violating that right.

10. So strong and convincing are these arguments that it seems amazing that some should now be setting up anew certain obsolete opinions in opposition to what is here laid down. They assert that it is right for private persons to have the use of the soil and its various fruits, but that it is unjust for any one to possess outright either the land on which he has built or the estate which he has brought under cultivation. But those who deny these rights do not perceive that they are defrauding man of what

his own labor has produced. For the soil which is tilled and cultivated with toil and skill utterly changes its condition; it was wild before, now it is fruitful; was barren, but now brings forth in abundance. That which has thus altered and improved the land becomes so truly part of itself as to be in great measure indistinguishable and inseparable from it. Is it just that the fruit of a man's own sweat and labor should be possessed and enjoyed by any one else? As effects follow their cause, so is it just and right that the results of labor should belong to those who have bestowed their labor.

...

19. The great mistake made in regard to the matter now under consideration is to take up with the notion that class is naturally hostile to class, and that the wealthy and the working men are intended by nature to live in mutual conflict. So irrational and so false is this view that the direct contrary is the truth. Just as the symmetry of the human frame is the result of the suitable arrangement of the different parts of the body, so in a State is it ordained by nature that these two classes should dwell in harmony and agreement, so as to maintain the balance of the body politic. Each needs the other: capital cannot do without labor, nor labor without capital. Mutual agreement results in the beauty of good order, while perpetual conflict necessarily produces confusion and savage barbarity. Now, in preventing such strife as this, and in uprooting it, the efficacy of Christian institutions is marvellous and manifold. First of all, there is no intermediary more powerful than religion (whereof the Church is the interpreter and guardian) in drawing the rich and the working class together, by reminding each of its duties to the other, and especially of the obligations of justice.

20. Of these duties, the following bind the proletarian and the worker: fully and faithfully to perform the work which has been freely and equitably agreed upon; never to injure the property, nor to outrage the person, of an employer; never to resort to violence in defending their own cause, nor to engage in riot or disorder; and to have nothing to do with men of evil principles, who work upon the people with artful promises of great results, and excite foolish hopes which usually end in useless regrets and grievous loss. The following duties bind the wealthy owner and the employer: not to look upon their work people as their bondsmen, but to respect in every man his dignity as a person ennobled by Christian character. They are reminded that, according to natural reason and Christian philosophy, working for gain is creditable, not shameful, to a man, since it enables him to earn an honorable livelihood; but to misuse men as though they were things in the pursuit of gain, or to value them solely for their physical powers – that is truly shameful and inhuman. Again justice demands that, in dealing with the working man, religion and the good of his soul must be kept in mind. Hence, the employer is bound to see that the worker has time for his religious duties; that he be not exposed to corrupting influences and dangerous occasions; and that he be not led away to neglect his home and family, or to squander his earnings. Furthermore, the employer must never tax his work people beyond their strength, or employ them in work unsuited to their sex and

age. His great and principal duty is to give every one what is just. Doubtless, before deciding whether wages are fair, many things have to be considered; but wealthy owners and all masters of labor should be mindful of this – that to exercise pressure upon the indigent and the destitute for the sake of gain, and to gather one's profit out of the need of another, is condemned by all laws, human and divine. To defraud any one of wages that are his due is a great crime which cries to the avenging anger of Heaven. "Behold, the hire of the laborers… which by fraud has been kept back by you, crieth; and the cry of them hath entered into the ears of the Lord of Sabaoth" (James 5.4). Lastly, the rich must religiously refrain from cutting down the workmen's earnings, whether by force, by fraud, or by usurious dealing; and with all the greater reason because the laboring man is, as a rule, weak and unprotected, and because his slender means should in proportion to their scantiness be accounted sacred. Were these precepts carefully obeyed and followed out, would they not be sufficient of themselves to keep under all strife and all its causes?

21. But the Church, with Jesus Christ as her Master and Guide, aims higher still. She lays down precepts yet more perfect, and tries to bind class to class in friendliness and good feeling. The things of earth cannot be understood or valued aright without taking into consideration the life to come, the life that will know no death. Exclude the idea of futurity, and forthwith the very notion of what is good and right would perish; nay, the whole scheme of the universe would become a dark and unfathomable mystery. The great truth which we learn from nature herself is also the grand Christian dogma on which religion rests as on its foundation – that, when we have given up this present life, then shall we really begin to live. God has not created us for the perishable and transitory things of earth, but for things heavenly and everlasting; He has given us this world as a place of exile, and not as our abiding place. As for riches and the other things which men call good and desirable, whether we have them in abundance, or are lacking in them – so far as eternal happiness is concerned – it makes no difference; the only important thing is to use them aright. Jesus Christ, when He redeemed us with plentiful redemption, took not away the pains and sorrows which in such large proportion are woven together in the web of our mortal life. He transformed them into motives of virtue and occasions of merit; and no man can hope for eternal reward unless he follow in the blood-stained footprints of his Saviour. "If we suffer with Him, we shall also reign with Him" (2 Tim. 2.12). Christ's labors and sufferings, accepted of His own free will, have marvellously sweetened all suffering and all labor. And not only by His example, but by His grace and by the hope held forth of everlasting recompense, has He made pain and grief more easy to endure; "for that which is at present momentary and light of our tribulation, worketh for us above measure exceedingly an eternal weight of glory" (2 Cor. 4:17).

22. Therefore, those whom fortune favors are warned that riches do not bring freedom from sorrow and are of no avail for eternal happiness, but rather are obstacles (Matt. 19:23–24); that the rich should tremble at the threatenings of Jesus Christ

– threatenings so unwonted in the mouth of our Lord (Luke 6.24-25) – and that a most strict account must be given to the Supreme Judge for all we possess. The chief and most excellent rule for the right use of money is one the heathen philosophers hinted at, but which the Church has traced out clearly, and has not only made known to men's minds, but has impressed upon their lives. It rests on the principle that it is one thing to have a right to the possession of money and another to have a right to use money as one wills. Private ownership, as we have seen, is the natural right of man, and to exercise that right, especially as members of society, is not only lawful, but absolutely necessary. "It is lawful," says St. Thomas Aquinas, "for a man to hold private property; and it is also necessary for the carrying on of human existence". But if the question be asked: How must one's possessions be used? – the Church replies without hesitation in the words of the same holy Doctor: "Man should not consider his material possessions as his own, but as common to all, so as to share them without hesitation when others are in need. Whence the Apostle with, 'Command the rich of this world... to offer with no stint, to apportion largely.'" (*Summa Theologiae*, IIaIIae, 66.2c). True, no one is commanded to distribute to others that which is required for his own needs and those of his household; nor even to give away what is reasonably required to keep up becomingly his condition in life, "for no one ought to live other than becomingly" (*Summa*, IIaIIae 32.6c). But, when what necessity demands has been supplied, and one's standing fairly taken thought for, it becomes a duty to give to the indigent out of what remains over. "Of that which remaineth, give alms" (Luke 11.41). It is a duty, not of justice (save in extreme cases), but of Christian charity – a duty not enforced by human law. But the laws and judgments of men must yield place to the laws and judgments of Christ the true God, who in many ways urges on His followers the practice of almsgiving – 'It is more blessed to give than to receive" (Acts 20.35); and who will count a kindness done or refused to the poor as done or refused to Himself – "As long as you did it to one of My least brethren you did it to Me" (Matt. 25.40). To sum up, then, what has been said: Whoever has received from the divine bounty a large share of temporal blessings, whether they be external and material, or gifts of the mind, has received them for the purpose of using them for the perfecting of his own nature, and, at the same time, that he may employ them, as the steward of God's providence, for the benefit of others. "He that hath a talent," said St. Gregory the Great, "let him see that he hide it not; he that hath abundance, let him quicken himself to mercy and generosity; he that hath art and skill, let him do his best to share the use and the utility hereof with his neighbor" (*Homilies on the Gospels*, 9, n7).

23. As for those who possess not the gifts of fortune, they are taught by the Church that in God's sight poverty is no disgrace, and that there is nothing to be ashamed of in earning their bread by labor. This is enforced by what we see in Christ Himself, who, "whereas He was rich, for our sakes became poor" (2 Cor. 8:9); and who, being the Son of God, and God Himself, chose to seem and to be considered the son of

a carpenter – nay, did not disdain to spend a great part of His life as a carpenter Himself. "Is not this the carpenter, the son of Mary?" (Mark 6.3).

...

31. It cannot, however, be doubted that to attain the purpose we are treating of, not only the Church, but all human agencies, must concur. All who are concerned in the matter should be of one mind and according to their ability act together. It is with this, as with providence that governs the world; the results of causes do not usually take place save where all the causes cooperate. It is sufficient, therefore, to inquire what part the State should play in the work of remedy and relief.

32. By the State we here understand, not the particular form of government prevailing in this or that nation, but the State as rightly apprehended; that is to say, any government conformable in its institutions to right reason and natural law, and to those dictates of the divine wisdom which we have expounded in the encyclical *On the Christian Constitution of the State* (Leo XIII, *Immortale Dei*). The foremost duty, therefore, of the rulers of the State should be to make sure that the laws and institutions, the general character and administration of the commonwealth, shall be such as of themselves to realize public well-being and private prosperity. This is the proper scope of wise statesmanship and is the work of the rulers. Now a State chiefly prospers and thrives through moral rule, well-regulated family life, respect for religion and justice, the moderation and fair imposing of public taxes, the progress of the arts and of trade, the abundant yield of the land – through everything, in fact, which makes the citizens better and happier. Hereby, then, it lies in the power of a ruler to benefit every class in the State, and amongst the rest to promote to the utmost the interests of the poor; and this in virtue of his office, and without being open to suspicion of undue interference – since it is the province of the commonwealth to serve the common good. And the more that is done for the benefit of the working classes by the general laws of the country, the less need will there be to seek for special means to relieve them.

33. There is another and deeper consideration which must not be lost sight of. As regards the State, the interests of all, whether high or low, are equal. The members of the working classes are citizens by nature and by the same right as the rich; they are real parts, living the life which makes up, through the family, the body of the commonwealth; and it need hardly be said that they are in every city very largely in the majority. It would be irrational to neglect one portion of the citizens and favor another, and therefore the public administration must duly and solicitously provide for the welfare and the comfort of the working classes; otherwise, that law of justice will be violated which ordains that each man shall have his due. To cite the wise words of St. Thomas Aquinas: "As the part and the whole are in a certain sense identical, so that which belongs to the whole in a sense belongs to the part" (*Summa*, IIaIIae, 61.1 ad2). Among the many and grave duties of rulers who would do their best for the people, the first and chief is to act with strict justice – with that justice which is called *distributive* – toward each and every class alike.

34. But although all citizens, without exception, can and ought to contribute to that common good in which individuals share so advantageously to themselves, yet it should not be supposed that all can contribute in the like way and to the same extent. No matter what changes may occur in forms of government, there will ever be differences and inequalities of condition in the State. Society cannot exist or be conceived of without them. Some there must be who devote themselves to the work of the commonwealth, who make the laws or administer justice, or whose advice and authority govern the nation in times of peace, and defend it in war. Such men clearly occupy the foremost place in the State, and should be held in highest estimation, for their work concerns most nearly and effectively the general interests of the community. Those who labor at a trade or calling do not promote the general welfare in such measure as this, but they benefit the nation, if less directly, in a most important manner. We have insisted, it is true, that, since the end of society is to make men better, the chief good that society can possess is virtue. Nevertheless, it is the business of a well-constituted body politic to see to the provision of those material and external helps "the use of which is necessary to virtuous action" (Aquinas, *De regimine principum* 1.15, see Section I: 'The Emergence of Political Theology' above). Now, for the provision of such commodities, the labor of the working class – the exercise of their skill, and the employment of their strength, in the cultivation of the land, and in the workshops of trade – is especially responsible and quite indispensable. Indeed, their co-operation is in this respect so important that it may be truly said that it is only by the labor of working men that States grow rich. Justice, therefore, demands that the interests of the working classes should be carefully watched over by the administration, so that they who contribute so largely to the advantage of the community may themselves share in the benefits which they create – that being housed, clothed, and bodily fit, they may find their life less hard and more endurable. It follows that whatever shall appear to prove conducive to the well-being of those who work should obtain favorable consideration. There is no fear that solicitude of this kind will be harmful to any interest; on the contrary, it will be to the advantage of all, for it cannot but be good for the commonwealth to shield from misery those on whom it so largely depends for the things that it needs.

35. We have said that the State must not absorb the individual or the family; both should be allowed free and untrammelled action so far as is consistent with the common good and the interest of others. Rulers should, nevertheless, anxiously safeguard the community and all its members; the community, because the conservation thereof is so emphatically the business of the supreme power, that the safety of the commonwealth is not only the first law, but it is a government's whole reason of existence; and the members, because both philosophy and the Gospel concur in laying down that the object of the government of the State should be, not the advantage of the ruler, but the benefit of those over whom he is placed. As the power to rule comes from God, and is, as it were, a participation in His, the highest

of all sovereignties, it should be exercised as the power of God is exercised – with a fatherly solicitude which not only guides the whole, but reaches also individuals.

36. Whenever the general interest or any particular class suffers, or is threatened with harm, which can in no other way be met or prevented, the public authority must step in to deal with it. Now, it is to the interest of the community, as well as of the individual, that peace and good order should be maintained; that all things should be carried on in accordance with God's laws and those of nature; that the discipline of family life should be observed and that religion should be obeyed; that a high standard of morality should prevail, both in public and private life; that justice should be held sacred and that no one should injure another with impunity; that the members of the commonwealth should grow up to man's estate strong and robust, and capable, if need be, of guarding and defending their country. If by a strike of workers or concerted interruption of work there should be imminent danger of disturbance to the public peace; or if circumstances were such as that among the working class the ties of family life were relaxed; if religion were found to suffer through the workers not having time and opportunity afforded them to practice its duties; if in workshops and factories there were danger to morals through the mixing of the sexes or from other harmful occasions of evil; or if employers laid burdens upon their workmen which were unjust, or degraded them with conditions repugnant to their dignity as human beings; finally, if health were endangered by excessive labor, or by work unsuited to sex or age – in such cases, there can be no question but that, within certain limits, it would be right to invoke the aid and authority of the law. The limits must be determined by the nature of the occasion which calls for the law's interference – the principle being that the law must not undertake more, nor proceed further, than is required for the remedy of the evil or the removal of the mischief.

37. Rights must be religiously respected wherever they exist, and it is the duty of the public authority to prevent and to punish injury, and to protect every one in the possession of his own. Still, when there is question of defending the rights of individuals, the poor and badly off have a claim to especial consideration. The richer class have many ways of shielding themselves, and stand less in need of help from the State; whereas the mass of the poor have no resources of their own to fall back upon, and must chiefly depend upon the assistance of the State. And it is for this reason that wageearners, since they mostly belong in the mass of the needy, should be specially cared for and protected by the government.

38. Here, however, it is expedient to bring under special notice certain matters of moment. First of all, there is the duty of safeguarding private property by legal enactment and protection. Most of all it is essential, where the passion of greed is so strong, to keep the populace within the line of duty; for, if all may justly strive to better their condition, neither justice nor the common good allows any individual to seize upon that which belongs to another, or, under the futile and shallow pretext of equality, to lay violent hands on other people's possessions. Most true it is that by

far the larger part of the workers prefer to better themselves by honest labor rather than by doing any wrong to others. But there are not a few who are imbued with evil principles and eager for revolutionary change, whose main purpose is to stir up disorder and incite their fellows to acts of violence. The authority of the law should intervene to put restraint upon such firebrands, to save the working classes from being led astray by their maneuvers, and to protect lawful owners from spoliation.

39. When work people have recourse to a strike and become voluntarily idle, it is frequently because the hours of labor are too long, or the work too hard, or because they consider their wages insufficient. The grave inconvenience of this not uncommon occurrence should be obviated by public remedial measures; for such paralysing of labor not only affects the masters and their work people alike, but is extremely injurious to trade and to the general interests of the public; moreover, on such occasions, violence and disorder are generally not far distant, and thus it frequently happens that the public peace is imperiled. The laws should forestall and prevent such troubles from arising; they should lend their influence and authority to the removal in good time of the causes which lead to conflicts between employers and employed.

40. The working man, too, has interests in which he should be protected by the State; and first of all, there are the interests of his soul. Life on earth, however good and desirable in itself, is not the final purpose for which man is created; it is only the way and the means to that attainment of truth and that love of goodness in which the full life of the soul consists. It is the soul which is made after the image and likeness of God; it is in the soul that the sovereignty resides in virtue whereof man is commanded to rule the creatures below him and to use all the earth and the ocean for his profit and advantage. "Fill the earth and subdue it; and rule over the fishes of the sea, and the fowls of the air, and all living creatures that move upon the earth" (Gen. 1.28). In this respect all men are equal; there is here no difference between rich and poor, master and servant, ruler and ruled, "for the same is Lord over all" (Rom. 10.12). No man may with impunity outrage that human dignity which God Himself treats with great reverence, nor stand in the way of that higher life which is the preparation of the eternal life of heaven. Nay, more; no man has in this matter power over himself. To consent to any treatment which is calculated to defeat the end and purpose of his being is beyond his right; he cannot give up his soul to servitude, for it is not man's own rights which are here in question, but the rights of God, the most sacred and inviolable of rights.

41. From this follows the obligation of the cessation from work and labor on Sundays and certain holy days. The rest from labor is not to be understood as mere giving way to idleness; much less must it be an occasion for spending money and for vicious indulgence, as many would have it to be; but it should be rest from labor, hallowed by religion. Rest (combined with religious observances) disposes man to forget for a while the business of his everyday life, to turn his thoughts to things

heavenly, and to the worship which he so strictly owes to the eternal Godhead. It is this, above all, which is the reason arid motive of Sunday rest; a rest sanctioned by God's great law of the Ancient Covenant – "Remember thou keep holy the Sabbath day" (Ex. 20.8), and taught to the world by His own mysterious "rest" after the creation of man: "He rested on the seventh day from all His work which He had done" (Gen. 2.2).

42. If we turn not to things external and material, the first thing of all to secure is to save unfortunate working people from the cruelty of men of greed, who use human beings as mere instruments for money-making. It is neither just nor human so to grind men down with excessive labor as to stupefy their minds and wear out their bodies. Man's powers, like his general nature, are limited, and beyond these limits he cannot go. His strength is developed and increased by use and exercise, but only on condition of due intermission and proper rest. Daily labor, therefore, should be so regulated as not to be protracted over longer hours than strength admits. How many and how long the intervals of rest should be must depend on the nature of the work, on circumstances of time and place, and on the health and strength of the workman. Those who work in mines and quarries, and extract coal, stone and metals from the bowels of the earth, should have shorter hours in proportion as their labor is more severe and trying to health. Then, again, the season of the year should be taken into account; for not unfrequently a kind of labor is easy at one time which at another is intolerable or exceedingly difficult. Finally, work which is quite suitable for a strong man cannot rightly be required from a woman or a child. And, in regard to children, great care should be taken not to place them in workshops and factories until their bodies and minds are sufficiently developed. For, just as very rough weather destroys the buds of spring, so does too early an experience of life's hard toil blight the young promise of a child's faculties, and render any true education impossible. Women, again, are not suited for certain occupations; a woman is by nature fitted for home-work, and it is that which is best adapted at once to preserve her modesty and to promote the good bringing up of children and the well-being of the family. As a general principle it may be laid down that a workman ought to have leisure and rest proportionate to the wear and tear of his strength, for waste of strength must be repaired by cessation from hard work.

In all agreements between masters and work people there is always the condition expressed or understood that there should be allowed proper rest for soul and body. To agree in any other sense would be against what is right and just; for it can never be just or right to require on the one side, or to promise on the other, the giving up of those duties which a man owes to his God and to himself.

43. We now approach a subject of great importance, and one in respect of which, if extremes are to be avoided, right notions are absolutely necessary. Wages, as we are told, are regulated by free consent, and therefore the employer, when he pays what was agreed upon, has done his part and seemingly is not called upon to do anything

beyond. The only way, it is said, in which injustice might occur would be if the master refused to pay the whole of the wages, or if the workman should not complete the work undertaken; in such cases the public authority should intervene, to see that each obtains his due, but not under any other circumstances.

44. To this kind of argument a fair-minded man will not easily or entirely assent; it is not complete, for there are important considerations which it leaves out of account altogether. To labor is to exert oneself for the sake of procuring what is necessary for the various purposes of life, and chief of all for self preservation. "In the sweat of thy face thou shalt eat bread" (Gen. 3.19). Hence, a man's labor necessarily bears two notes or characters. First of all, it is personal, inasmuch as the force which acts is bound up with the personality and is the exclusive property of him who acts, and, further, was given to him for his advantage. Secondly, man's labor is *necessary*; for without the result of labor a man cannot live, and self-preservation is a law of nature, which it is wrong to disobey. Now, were we to consider labor merely in so far as it is personal, doubtless it would be within the workman's right to accept any rate of wages whatsoever; for in the same way as he is free to work or not, so is he free to accept a small wage or even none at all. But our conclusion must be very different if, together with the personal element in a man's work, we consider the fact that work is also necessary for him to live: these two aspects of his work are separable in thought, but not in reality. The preservation of life is the bounden duty of one and all, and to be wanting therein is a crime. It necessarily follows that each one has a natural right to procure what is required in order to live, and the poor can procure that in no other way than by what they can earn through their work.

45. Let the working man and the employer make free agreements, and in particular let them agree freely as to the wages; nevertheless, there underlies a dictate of natural justice more imperious and ancient than any bargain between man and man, namely, that wages ought not to be insufficient to support a frugal and well-behaved wage-earner. If through necessity or fear of a worse evil the workman accept harder conditions because an employer or contractor will afford him no better, he is made the victim of force and injustice. In these and similar questions, however – such as, for example, the hours of labor in different trades, the sanitary precautions to be observed in factories and workshops, etc. – in order to supersede undue interference on the part of the State, especially as circumstances, times, and localities differ so widely, it is advisable that recourse be had to societies or boards such as We shall mention presently, or to some other mode of safeguarding the interests of the wage-earners; the State being appealed to, should circumstances require, for its sanction and protection.

46. If a workman's wages be sufficient to enable him comfortably to support himself, his wife, and his children, he will find it easy, if he be a sensible man, to practice thrift, and he will not fail, by cutting down expenses, to put by some little savings and thus secure a modest source of income. Nature itself would urge him to

this. We have seen that this great labor question cannot be solved save by assuming as a principle that private ownership must be held sacred and inviolable. The law, therefore, should favor ownership, and its policy should be to induce as many as possible of the people to become owners.

47. Many excellent results will follow from this; and, first of all, property will certainly become more equitably divided. For, the result of civil change and revolution has been to divide cities into two classes separated by a wide chasm. On the one side there is the party which holds power because it holds wealth; which has in its grasp the whole of labor and trade; which manipulates for its own benefit and its own purposes all the sources of supply, and which is not without influence even in the administration of the commonwealth. On the other side there is the needy and powerless multitude, sick and sore in spirit and ever ready for disturbance. If working people can be encouraged to look forward to obtaining a share in the land, the consequence will be that the gulf between vast wealth and sheer poverty will be bridged over, and the respective classes will be brought nearer to one another. A further consequence will result in the great abundance of the fruits of the earth. Men always work harder and more readily when they work on that which belongs to them; nay, they learn to love the very soil that yields in response to the labor of their hands, not only food to eat, but an abundance of good things for themselves and those that are dear to them. That such a spirit of willing labor would add to the produce of the earth and to the wealth of the community is self evident. And a third advantage would spring from this: men would cling to the country in which they were born, for no one would exchange his country for a foreign land if his own afforded him the means of living a decent and happy life. These three important benefits, however, can be reckoned on only provided that a man's means be not drained and exhausted by excessive taxation. The right to possess private property is derived from nature, not from man; and the State has the right to control its use in the interests of the public good alone, but by no means to absorb it altogether. The State would therefore be unjust and cruel if under the name of taxation it were to deprive the private owner of more than is fair.

48. In the last place, employers and workmen may of themselves effect much, in the matter We are treating, by means of such associations and organizations as afford opportune aid to those who are in distress, and which draw the two classes more closely together. Among these may be enumerated societies for mutual help; various benevolent foundations established by private persons to provide for the workman, and for his widow or his orphans, in case of sudden calamity, in sickness, and in the event of death; and institutions for the welfare of boys and girls, young people, and those more advanced in years.

49. The most important of all are workingmen's unions, for these virtually include all the rest. History attests what excellent results were brought about by the artificers' guilds of olden times. They were the means of affording not only many advantages

to the workmen, but in no small degree of promoting the advancement of art, as numerous monuments remain to bear witness. Such unions should be suited to the requirements of this our age – an age of wider education, of different habits, and of far more numerous requirements in daily life. It is gratifying to know that there are actually in existence not a few associations of this nature, consisting either of workmen alone, or of workmen and employers together, but it were greatly to be desired that they should become more numerous and more efficient. We have spoken of them more than once, yet it will be well to explain here how notably they are needed, to show that they exist of their own right, and what should be their organization and their mode of action.

50. The consciousness of his own weakness urges man to call in aid from without. We read in the pages of holy Writ: "It is better that two should be together than one; for they have the advantage of their society. If one fall he shall be supported by the other. Woe to him that is alone, for when he falleth he hath none to lift him up" (Eccl. 4.9-10). And further: "A brother that is helped by his brother is like a strong city" (Prov. 18.19). It is this natural impulse which binds men together in civil society; and it is likewise this which leads them to join together in associations which are, it is true, lesser and not independent societies, but, nevertheless, real societies.

51. These lesser societies and the larger society differ in many respects, because their immediate purpose and aim are different. Civil society exists for the common good, and hence is concerned with the interests of all in general, albeit with individual interests also in their due place and degree. It is therefore called a public society, because by its agency, as St. Thomas of Aquinas says, "Men establish relations in common with one another in the setting up of a commonwealth" (*Contra impugnantes Dei cultum et religionem,* 2.8). But societies which are formed in the bosom of the commonwealth are styled *private,* and rightly so, since their immediate purpose is the private advantage of the associates. "Now, a private society," says St. Thomas again, "is one which is formed for the purpose of carrying out private objects; as when two or three enter into partnership with the view of trading in common" (Ibid). Private societies, then, although they exist within the body politic, and are severally part of the commonwealth, cannot nevertheless be absolutely, and as such, prohibited by public authority. For, to enter into a "society" of this kind is the natural right of man; and the State has for its office to protect natural rights, not to destroy them; and, if it forbid its citizens to form associations, it contradicts the very principle of its own existence, for both they and it exist in virtue of the like principle, namely, the natural tendency of man to dwell in society.

52. There are occasions, doubtless, when it is fitting that the law should intervene to prevent certain associations, as when men join together for purposes which are evidently bad, unlawful, or dangerous to the State. In such cases, public authority may justly forbid the formation of such associations, and may dissolve them if they already exist. But every precaution should be taken not to violate the rights of individuals

and not to impose unreasonable regulations under pretense of public benefit. For laws only bind when they are in accordance with right reason, and, hence, with the eternal law of God (Summa, IaIIae, 93.3 ad2.).

53. And here we are reminded of the confraternities, societies, and religious orders which have arisen by the Church's authority and the piety of Christian men. The annals of every nation down to our own days bear witness to what they have accomplished for the human race. It is indisputable that on grounds of reason alone such associations, being perfectly blameless in their objects, possess the sanction of the law of nature. In their religious aspect they claim rightly to be responsible to the Church alone. The rulers of the State accordingly have no rights over them, nor can they claim any share in their control; on the contrary, it is the duty of the State to respect and cherish them, and, if need be, to defend them from attack. It is notorious that a very different course has been followed, more especially in our own times. In many places the State authorities have laid violent hands on these communities, and committed manifold injustice against them; it has placed them under control of the civil law, taken away their rights as corporate bodies, and despoiled them of their property, in such property the Church had her rights, each member of the body had his or her rights, and there were also the rights of those who had founded or endowed these communities for a definite purpose, and, furthermore, of those for whose benefit and assistance they had their being. Therefore We cannot refrain from complaining of such spoliation as unjust and fraught with evil results; and with all the more reason do We complain because, at the very time when the law proclaims that association is free to all, We see that Catholic societies, however peaceful and useful, are hampered in every way, whereas the utmost liberty is conceded to individuals whose purposes are at once hurtful to religion and dangerous to the commonwealth.

54. Associations of every kind, and especially those of working men, are now far more common than heretofore. As regards many of these there is no need at present to inquire whence they spring, what are their objects, or what the means they imply. Now, there is a good deal of evidence in favor of the opinion that many of these societies are in the hands of secret leaders, and are managed on principles ill – according with Christianity and the public well-being; and that they do their utmost to get within their grasp the whole field of labor, and force working men either to join them or to starve. Under these circumstances Christian working men must do one of two things: either join associations in which their religion will be exposed to peril, or form associations among themselves and unite their forces so as to shake off courageously the yoke of so unrighteous and intolerable an oppression. No one who does not wish to expose man's chief good to extreme risk will for a moment hesitate to say that the second alternative should by all means be adopted.

55. Those Catholics are worthy of all praise – and they are not a few – who, understanding what the times require, have striven, by various undertakings and

endeavors, to better the condition of the working class by rightful means. They have taken up the cause of the working man, and have spared no efforts to better the condition both of families and individuals; to infuse a spirit of equity into the mutual relations of employers and employed; to keep before the eyes of both classes the precepts of duty and the laws of the Gospel – that Gospel which, by inculcating self restraint, keeps men within the bounds of moderation, and tends to establish harmony among the divergent interests and the various classes which compose the body politic. It is with such ends in view that we see men of eminence, meeting together for discussion, for the promotion of concerted action, and for practical work. Others, again, strive to unite working men of various grades into associations, help them with their advice and means, and enable them to obtain fitting and profitable employment. The bishops, on their part, bestow their ready good will and support; and with their approval and guidance many members of the clergy, both secular and regular, labor assiduously in behalf of the spiritual interest of the members of such associations. And there are not wanting Catholics blessed with affluence, who have, as it were, cast in their lot with the wage-earners, and who have spent large sums in founding and widely spreading benefit and insurance societies, by means of which the working man may without difficulty acquire through his labor not only many present advantages, but also the certainty of honorable support in days to come. How greatly such manifold and earnest activity has benefited the community at large is too well known to require Us to dwell upon it. We find therein grounds for most cheering hope in the future, provided always that the associations We have described continue to grow and spread, and are well and wisely administered. The State should watch over these societies of citizens banded together in accordance with their rights, but it should not thrust itself into their peculiar concerns and their organization, for things move and live by the spirit inspiring them, and may be killed by the rough grasp of a hand from without.

56. In order that an association may be carried on with unity of purpose and harmony of action, its administration and government should be firm and wise. All such societies, being free to exist, have the further right to adopt such rules and organization as may best conduce to the attainment of their respective objects. We do not judge it possible to enter into minute particulars touching the subject of organization; this must depend on national character, on practice and experience, on the nature and aim of the work to be done, on the scope of the various trades and employments, and on other circumstances of fact and of time – all of which should be carefully considered.

57. To sum up, then, We may lay it down as a general and lasting law that working men's associations should be so organized and governed as to furnish the best and most suitable means for attaining what is aimed at, that is to say, for helping each individual member to better his condition to the utmost in body, soul, and property. It is clear that they must pay special and chief attention to the duties of religion and

morality, and that social betterment should have this chiefly in view; otherwise they would lose wholly their special character, and end by becoming little better than those societies which take no account whatever of religion. What advantage can it be to a working man to obtain by means of a society material well-being, if he endangers his soul for lack of spiritual food? "What doth it profit a man, if he gain the whole world and suffer the loss of his soul?" (Matt. 16.26). This, as our Lord teaches, is the mark or character that distinguishes the Christian from the heathen. "After all these things do the heathen seek … Seek ye first the Kingdom of God and His justice: and all these things shall be added unto you" (Matt. 6.32-33). Let our associations, then, look first and before all things to God; let religious instruction have therein the foremost place, each one being carefully taught what is his duty to God, what he has to believe, what to hope for, and how he is to work out his salvation; and let all be warned and strengthened with special care against wrong principles and false teaching. Let the working man be urged and led to the worship of God, to the earnest practice of religion, and, among other things, to the keeping holy of Sundays and holy days. Let him learn to reverence and love holy Church, the common Mother of us all; and hence to obey the precepts of the Church, and to frequent the sacraments, since they are the means ordained by God for obtaining forgiveness of sin and fox leading a holy life.

58. The foundations of the organization being thus laid in religion, We next proceed to make clear the relations of the members one to another, in order that they may live together in concord and go forward prosperously and with good results. The offices and charges of the society should be apportioned for the good of the society itself, and in such mode that difference in degree or standing should not interfere with unanimity and good-will. It is most important that office bearers be appointed with due prudence and discretion, and each one's charge carefully mapped out, in order that no members may suffer harm. The common funds must be administered with strict honesty, in such a way that a member may receive assistance in proportion to his necessities. The rights and duties of the employers, as compared with the rights and duties of the employed, ought to be the subject of careful consideration. Should it happen that either a master or a workman believes himself injured, nothing would be more desirable than that a committee should be appointed, composed of reliable and capable members of the association, whose duty would be, conformably with the rules of the association, to settle the dispute. Among the several purposes of a society, one should be to try to arrange for a continuous supply of work at all times and seasons; as well as to create a fund out of which the members may be effectually helped in their needs, not only in the cases of accident, but also in sickness, old age, and distress.

59. Such rules and regulations, if willingly obeyed by all, will sufficiently ensure the well being of the less well-to-do; whilst such mutual associations among Catholics are certain to be productive in no small degree of prosperity to the State. Is it not rash to

conjecture the future from the past. Age gives way to age, but the events of one century are wonderfully like those of another, for they are directed by the providence of God, who overrules the course of history in accordance with His purposes in creating the race of man. We are told that it was cast as a reproach on the Christians in the early ages of the Church that the greater number among them had to live by begging or by labor. Yet, destitute though they were of wealth and influence, they ended by winning over to their side the favor of the rich and the good-will of the powerful. They showed themselves industrious, hard-working, assiduous, and peaceful, ruled by justice, and, above all, bound together in brotherly love. In presence of such mode of life and such example, prejudice gave way, the tongue of malevolence was silenced, and the lying legends of ancient superstition little by little yielded to Christian truth.

60. At the time being, the condition of the working classes is the pressing question of the hour, and nothing can be of higher interest to all classes of the State than that it should be rightly and reasonably settled. But it will be easy for Christian working men to solve it aright if they will form associations, choose wise guides, and follow on the path which with so much advantage to themselves and the common weal was trodden by their fathers before them. Prejudice, it is true, is mighty, and so is the greed of money; but if the sense of what is just and rightful be not deliberately stifled, their fellow citizens are sure to be won over to a kindly feeling towards men whom they see to be in earnest as regards their work and who prefer so unmistakably right dealing to mere lucre, and the sacredness of duty to every other consideration.

61. And further great advantage would result from the state of things We are describing; there would exist so much more ground for hope, and likelihood, even, of recalling to a sense of their duty those working men who have either given up their faith altogether, or whose lives are at variance with its precepts. Such men feel in most cases that they have been fooled by empty promises and deceived by false pretexts. They cannot but perceive that their grasping employers too often treat them with great inhumanity and hardly care for them outside the profit their labor brings; and if they belong to any union, it is probably one in which there exists, instead of charity and love, that intestine strife which ever accompanies poverty when unresigned and unsustained by religion. Broken in spirit and worn down in body, how many of them would gladly free themselves from such galling bondage! But human respect, or the dread of starvation, makes them tremble to take the step. To such as these Catholic associations are of incalculable service, by helping them out of their difficulties, inviting them to companionship and receiving the returning wanderers to a haven where they may securely find repose.

62. We have now laid before you, venerable brethren, both who are the persons and what are the means whereby this most arduous question must be solved. Every one should put his hand to the work which falls to his share, and that at once and straightway, lest the evil which is already so great become through delay absolutely beyond remedy. Those who rule the commonwealths should avail themselves of the

laws and institutions of the country; masters and wealthy owners must be mindful of their duty; the working class, whose interests are at stake, should make every lawful and proper effort; and since religion alone, as We said at the beginning, can avail to destroy the evil at its root, all men should rest persuaded that main thing needful is to re-establish Christian morals, apart from which all the plans and devices of the wisest will prove of little avail.

63. In regard to the Church, her cooperation will never be found lacking, be the time or the occasion what it may; and she will intervene with all the greater effect in proportion as her liberty of action is the more unfettered. Let this be carefully taken to heart by those whose office it is to safeguard the public welfare. Every minister of holy religion must bring to the struggle the full energy of his mind and all his power of endurance. Moved by your authority, venerable brethren, and quickened by your example, they should never cease to urge upon men of every class, upon the high-placed as well as the lowly, the Gospel doctrines of Christian life; by every means in their power they must strive to secure the good of the people; and above all must earnestly cherish in themselves, and try to arouse in others, charity, the mistress and the queen of virtues. For, the happy results we all long for must be chiefly brought about by the plenteous outpouring of charity; of that true Christian charity which is the fulfilling of the whole Gospel law, which is always ready to sacrifice itself for others' sake, and is man's surest antidote against worldly pride and immoderate love of self; that charity whose office is described and whose Godlike features are outlined by the Apostle St. Paul in these words: "Charity is patient, is kind, … seeketh not her own, … suffereth all things, … endureth all things" (1 Cor. 13.4-7).

64. On each of you, venerable brethren, and on your clergy and people, as an earnest of God's mercy and a mark of Our affection, we lovingly in the Lord bestow the apostolic benediction.

Given at St. Peter's in Rome, the fifteenth day of May, 1891, the fourteenth year of Our pontificate.

44. Jon Sobrino – Extracts from *Extra Pauperes Nulla Salus*: A Short-Utopian Prophetic Essay

The Need for a New Logic to Understand Salvation

Paul exclaimed, "Wretched man that I am! Who will deliver me from this body of death?" (Rom. 7:24). Our times have little room for that type of question, but the terror caused by the world we have described above prompts a similar question: "Who will deliver us from this cruel and inhuman world?"

In the face of such an immense problem, our response must obviously be modest, but we can attempt to offer at least the beginning of an answer. We will do so by understanding salvation in relation to the poor and by seeing in the poor a locus and a potential for salvation. Although it may sound defiant, the formulation *extra pauperes nulla salus* is indeed quite modest. Strictly speaking, we are not saying that with the poor there is automatic salvation; we claim only that without them there is no salvation—although we do presuppose that in the poor there is always "something" of salvation. What we aim to do, ultimately, is to offer hope, in spite of everything. *From the world of the poor and the victims can come salvation for a gravely ill civilization.*

Our way of proceeding will be fundamentally through mystagogy, that is, by trying to enter into a mystery that exceeds our grasp. Even the full knowledge of what a human being is exceeds our grasp, and therefore so also does the full knowledge of what salvation is—although some of its elements are not at all mysterious, such as the eradication of hunger. That very formula exceeds our grasp: *extra pauperes nulla salus.* Of course, concepts and arguments are necessary for entering into the mystery, but they do not suffice. We must also take into account—and make converge with those concepts and arguments—wisdom, reflection, testimony, and experience, and certainly in this case we need the *esprit de finesse* of which Pascal speaks.

The formula defies instrumental reason, and our hubris rebels against it. For that reason it does not appear, as far as I know, in any modern or postmodern texts, for it is not easy to accept that salvation comes from the unenlightened.[1] What prevails is the metaphysical axiom: whether saved or damned, "Reality is us!"

The formula is also a limit statement and therefore acquires meaning only after an analysis of the different contributions of the poor to salvation. And most definitely it is a negative formulation, which does not make it any less, but rather more, important: indeed, it seems to us that the more important things are these days, the more they need to be formulated in negative terms.[2] But even with all these difficulties, we maintain the formula, for it is an expression that is vigorous and is suitable for breaking—at least conceptually—the logic of the civilization of wealth.

---

[1]The formula is present, in a way, in Marx: salvation comes from a social class at the bottom of history. Such is the thought of I. Ellacuría ("El pueblo crucificado," in *Conversión de la Iglesia al reino de Dios* [San Salvador, 1986], 29–31), although we should recall that Marxism does not see salvific potential in the *lumpenproletariat*. To my understanding, the social philosophy that is the basis of democracy does not address the issue either. At the most, it would make poor people citizens with the same rights as others, but it does not place them, either in theory or in practice, at the center of society, nor does it make them, precisely as poor people, the specific bearers of salvation. Neither does the Church do so, either in theory or in practice.

[2]Przywara insists on this. Reality is always greater than our ideas. The bigger reality is, the more deferential our ideas should be. The *via negativa* need not be, then, an expression of lack of knowledge about reality, but may well be an expression of respect and humility in the face of reality—and of a more profound knowledge.

Accepting the formula presents still other difficulties. For some people, the greatest difficulty is the inability of poor people to produce goods on a massive scale. For me personally, the major difficulty lies in the fact that even the world of the poor is invaded with the *mysterium iniquitatis*. There come to mind the evils we see daily among the poor, and we are reminded of this wickedness by those who live and work directly with them. In one way or another they ask us if we are not idealizing the poor or yielding to "the myth of the noble savage," a phrase I heard in Spain during the quincentennial celebration in 1992. And it is not easy to give an answer that soothes the spirit. Seeing the poor in their base communities is one thing: generous and committed to liberation, both their own and others', under the inspiration of Archbishop Romero; it is another thing to see them disenchanted, spoiled by the world of abundance and its offerings, struggling against one another to survive. Then there are the horrors of the Great Lakes region of Africa, or the dozen daily murders in El Salvador. All of these horrors happen in places where poor people live, even though the immediate responsibility is not only, nor always, theirs. We do not even think that the principal responsibility is theirs. And we must also take into account that poor people's reality varies greatly with different times and places.

The theological novelty of this formula also presents difficulties. Some type of relation has always existed between the poor and Christian faith, as we can see in various ways.

1. Our faith allows the poor to move us to extreme indignation, to limitless compassion, and even to radical conversion, which can lead to the "option for the poor" (Medellín) and to living in obedience to "the authority of those who suffer" (J. B. Metz).
2. An ultimate question is raised about whether and why we believe in God (theodicy), when it seems that God cannot or will not eliminate the horrors of our world.
3. Our salvation or damnation depends on our attitude with respect to the poor: "Come, blessed of my Father, because I was hungry and you gave me food.... Depart from me, you cursed ..." (Matt. 25).
4. Finally, since as believers we are "sacraments" of God—representing either God's "presence" or "absence," depending on how we act toward the poor—one way or the other, we will be able to understand what the Scriptures denounce when they repeat five times (three referring to God and two to Christ) that "because of you my name is despised among the nations" (Isa. 52:5, Septuagint version; Ezek. 36:20–22; Rom. 2:24; James 2:7; 2 Pet. 2:2). Or we will make real what Jesus asks of us: "Let your light so shine before men, that they may see your good works and give glory to your Father who is in heaven" (Matt. 5:16).

Medellín gave special importance to the "option for the poor," but we now go a step further, and do so with some novelty: we propose "the option to let salvation come from the poor." Accepting such a proposal is not easy; a new logic is needed. We do not simply add a new concept to an already established mode of thinking. Rather, the new logic is the product of a basic globalizing attitude, with a constitutive caesura: not only is it necessary to be and to act on behalf of the poor (Kant's question, what must I *do*?), but we must also pose the other two Kantian questions: what can I *know*? and what can I *hope for*? We would add two further questions: what can I *celebrate*? and what can I *receive*? And all of this "from among the poor." If in answering these questions poor people become a central theme, then the mode of thinking can be moved by a new and different logic, and we will find reasonable the acceptance and the understanding of the formula *extra pauperes nulla salus*. It is not at all easy, but however that may be, the added dimension of the new logic is necessary.

Such a new way of thinking is what we are trying to offer in this modest essay. In so doing, we are guided by the poetic/creative/prophetic intuition of Bishop Pedro Casaldáliga and by the analytic intuition of Ignacio Ellacuría. The reader will also become aware of how much our thought must wrestle with complexity and uncertainty in treating this topic. The urge to engage in the struggle comes from Rahner's statement, "It just can't be that way!" and from some words of Casaldáliga, who was kind enough to write me: "You say it well, and it needs to be repeated incessantly: outside the poor there is no salvation, outside the poor there is no Church, outside the poor there is no Gospel." And of course we have the hope that others will correct, develop, and complement what we are going to say.

The New Logic of Experience

It happens very often that visitors who arrive from places of abundance find among the poor and the victims a certain "something" that is new and unexpected. That happens when the visitors discover in the world of the poor "something" that is good and positive. They have found "salvation." From Brazil. José Comblin writes:

> The mass media speak of the poor always in negative terms, as those who don't have property, those who don't have culture, those who have nothing to eat. Seen from outside, the world of the poor is pure negativity. Seen from within, however, the world of the poor has vitality; they struggle to survive, they invent an informal economy and they build a different civilization, one of solidarity among people who recognize each other as equals—a civilization with its own forms of expression, including art and poetry.[3]

---

[3]Interview in *Éxodo* 78–79 (2005): 66.

These words affirm that in the world of the poor there are important values; further, they build a civilization of solidarity. This is not an isolated opinion—it is repeated often by others. Many people today seek a more human humanity, and we say this without redundancy, just as Luther was seeking a benevolent God. But people do not find such humanity in the societies of abundance, or in globalization, or even in the democratic order. People do find important elements of humanity in the world of the poor: joy, creativity, patience, art and culture, hope, solidarity. This experience is dialectical, for they have found human life on the "reverse side of the world of the rich." Such experience is salvific, for it generates hope for a more human world. And it is an experience of grace, for it arises where we least expect it.

Chilean theologian Ronaldo Muñoz says something similar in response to the optimistic report of the United Nations Development Program for 2005. He tempers our enthusiasm for the report and recalls the serious ills that still afflict the majority of people. But he insists above all on seeing things in a different way, from a different perspective:

> Rather, we should be amazed at the forbearance and the personal and social development of the women; amazed at the spontaneous solidarity of so many poor people toward their more needy neighbors and companions; amazed at the new organizations of adults and young people, who keep rising up against wind and tide to share in life, to work and celebrate together; amazed at the new dignity of the Mapuche people and their struggle for their rights; amazed at the small Christian communities, Catholic and Evangelical, that keep cropping up and yielding fruits of harmony and hope.[4]

From India, Felix Wilfred, having witnessed what happened during the tsunami, describes both the positive and the negative sides of the world of the poor. And he concludes:

> Facing up to human suffering and responding to it in terms of compassion has developed in the victims some of the values we need in order to support a different sort of world: solidarity, humanity, a spirit of sharing, survival techniques, readiness to assume risks, resistance, and firm determination in the midst of adversities. In the world of the victims, as opposed to the world of empire and globalization, the good is not identified with "success." The good and the just are ideals that the world needs in order to struggle unremittingly to attain something. The cultural resources of the poor, which reflect the values and ideals of a world of the future, help them to confront life with both individual and collective courage.[5]

Let these quotes suffice. Obviously we cannot deduce from them a thesis, but they do express something fundamental: there is "something" to be discovered in the

---

[4]"El poder, ¿para qué?, ¿para quiénes?" *Páginas* 194 (2005): 50–61.
[5]"Golpeando suavemente los recursos locales de la esperanza," *Concilium* 308 (2004): 104.

world of the poor. These people, who do not take life for granted (as we, who are not poor, so often do), these people who die before their time, who have (almost) all the powers of the world against them, still possess "something" that makes them truly live and that they offer to others. That "something" consists of human goods, more than material, and it is therefore "something" humanizing. Those goods are the ones that are not found, or are found only with greater difficulty, in the world of those who are not poor.

The "poor," with all the variety of shades that we will analyze, and above all the "poor with spirit," as Ellacuría called them (thus systematically unifying the beatitudes of Luke and Matthew[6]), are those who humanize and offer salvation, those who can offer inspiration and energy for the creation of a civilization based on solidarity, as opposed to selfishness. For this reason Ellacuría used to speak of "the immense spiritual and human wealth of the poor and of Third World peoples."[7] How many of *those kind* of poor people there are in reality will vary, according to times and places. Obviously not all are like that. In the world of the poor, goodness and evil frequently coexist, especially in times of great crisis. But as regards the healing of a gravely ill society, I believe there are "more than enough" of them. The problem is to take them into account.

Most important of all, in the world of the poor a logic is generated that allows reality to be seen in a different way. Such a logic makes it plain that salvation cannot be identified simply with progress and development—an insight we consider significant. Such a logic makes it plain that salvation comes from the poor. Thus, the experience of grace is for the nonpoor. The option for the poor is not just a matter of *giving to* them, but of *receiving from* them.

The Logic of Salvation in the Christian and Biblical Tradition

What we have just said should come as a total surprise, though it needs some explanation. The nucleus of the logic described is already present—in idealized form—in the biblical tradition concerning Jesus of Nazareth, even though it is ignored by Western culture. The content of salvation fully appears in that tradition, both in symbolic form and in several other dimensions, such as the historical/social dimension of the *reign of God,* the personal dimension of the *heart of flesh,* and the transcendent dimension of the *new heaven.* These dimensions do not offer concrete models or recipes for salvation, but we can find in them basic elements that show us how salvation is produced and expressed.

---

[6]"Las bienaventuranzas, carta fundacional de la Iglesia de los pobres," in *Conversión de la Iglesia al reino de Dios* (San Salvador, 1985), 129–51.
[7]"Misión actual de la Compañía de Jesús," *Revista Latinoamericana de Teología* 29 (1993): 119ff.

For that tradition it is fundamental that salvation comes from the world of the poor, and that it spreads out from there into diverse realms. In the Old Testament Yahweh's option on behalf of a poor, oppressed people is quite evident. We also see, at important junctures of history, that the symbolic bearers of salvation are the small and the weak, and above all—mysteriously—the victims, the servant in his or her individual and collective dimension. Conversely, from the upper strata of society, from the realm of power and abundance, no salvation comes. In fact, the Deuteronomic tradition makes the kings—symbols of power—look pretty bad, with only two exceptions: Josiah and Hezekiah.

From that same perspective are also presented Jesus and the salvation that he brings. Regarding Jesus himself, the savior *par excellence,* there is historically an insistence on his smallness: people say, "We do not know where this fellow comes from" (John 6:14), because he comes from Nazareth, a small and insignificant village from which nothing good can ever come. And transcendentally it is claimed that he became *sarx,* flesh, and assumed the weakness of flesh (John 1:14). But I would like to insist on something that is usually neglected. We ask ourselves where salvation came from for Jesus himself, in his historical form; we ask if something of that salvation came to him also from the world of the poor. I do not know whether, or to what extent, that can be proved from the Gospels, but the matter seems crucial to me. This question should not scandalize us, for it is said also of Jesus, for example, that he went before God with joy and with doubts. As the letter to the Hebrews states, he was like us in all things except sin (Heb. 4:15). He was the firstborn, the eldest brother in the faith (Heb. 12:2).

For that reason we ask not only whether Jesus was salvation for others, but also whether there are indications that others, certainly the heavenly Father and the poor of the earth, were salvation and good news for him. Some indications of that might be in his words: "I give you thanks, Father, for the simple folk have understood and not the wise" (Matt. 11:25). In saying this, was Jesus just overjoyed, or did he feel himself, besides, being evangelized by those simple folk?

We can wonder what Jesus was feeling about the faith of the little ones when he said to the woman with a flow of blood and to the blind Bartimeus (Mark 5:34; 11:52), "Your faith has cured you," and to the sinful woman in the house of Simon the Pharisee, "Go in peace, your faith has saved you" (Luke 7:50); or what he felt when he saw a poor widow throw a few cents into the temple treasury, giving more than the rest, since she was giving all that she had to live on (Mark 12:44); or what he felt before the Canaanite woman, who assured Jesus he was right, "It is true, sir," but who also corrected him movingly, "But it is also true that the dogs eat of the crumbs that the children toss to them." And Jesus declared, "Great is your faith" (Mark 15:28). Without any need to fantasize, we may ask ourselves whether Jesus felt blessed by the faith of these simple folk, whether he would not say within himself—as did Archbishop Romero—"With these people it is not hard to be a good pastor." Our question, then, is whether Jesus experienced salvation coming from the poor.

The most important element for understanding the logic of salvation in this biblical tradition of Jesus of Nazareth is the theologal grounding. The Most High, in order to be the God of salvation, has come down to our history, and he has done so in a twofold manner: he has come down to the human level and, within the human, to what is humanly weak. To express it more precisely, *transcendence* has become *trans-descendence,* benevolent closeness, and thus has become *con-descendence,* affectionate embrace. The same is expressed in the Christological language of the first centuries: *salus autem quoniam caro.* Christ is salvation because he is flesh, *sarx.* That is the new logic.

In principle, grasping that logic is possible anywhere, but it does not normally occur outside the world of the poor. As corroborating evidence, allow me to include some quotes from Jesuits of the Third World; I explain why later. They know well the complexity of salvation. They speak of it in different contexts, but they coincide in their fundamental insight.

From Sri Lanka, Aloysius Pieris writes that the poor are chosen for a salvific mission, not because they are holy but because they are powerless and rejected: "The poor are called to be mediators of salvation for the rich, and the weak are called to liberate the strong."[8] Engelbert Mveng speaks from the context of Cameroon: "The Church of Africa … announces the good news of liberation to those who have succumbed to the temptation of power, wealth, and domination."[9] From El Salvador, we have already heard the proposal of Ignacio Ellacuría: the civilization of poverty is necessary in order to overcome and redeem the evils generated by the civilization of wealth.[10] And from Venezuela, Pedro Trigo writes:

> Against the current position, which holds that the salvation of the poor (some of them) will come about only as an overflow or a redundancy of the health of the economic system, the mission of Jesus (and therefore the Christian mission) proclaims that the salvation of the non-poor will come about only through participation in the salvation of the poor. Nowadays that sounds ridiculous.[11]

The reason for quoting Jesuits in this context is that they may well be influenced by the meditation on the two standards in the *Spiritual Exercises* (nos. 136–48) of

---

[8]"Cristo más allá del dogma. Hacer cristología en el contexto de las religiones de los pobres" (I), *Revista Latinoamericana de Teología* 52 (2001): 16.

[9]"Iglesia y solidaridad con los pobres de África," in *Identidad africana y cristiana* (Estella, 1999), 273ff.

[10]He dedicated much thought to this in his final years. See "Misión actual de la Compañía de Jesús," 115–26 [the text was written in 1981]; "El reino de Dios y el paro en el Tercer Mundo," *Concilium* 180 (1982): 588–96; "Utopía y profetismo desde América Latina: Un ensayo concreto de soteriología histórica," *Revista Latinoamericana de Teología* 17 (1989): 141–84.

[11]"La misión en la Iglesia latinoamericana actual," *Revista Latinoamericana de Teología* 68 (2006): 191. In addition to this, the author insists that the poor are the ones to whom the mission is principally aimed.

St. Ignatius. That meditation presents two "principles" of reality that are dynamic, distinct, and counterpoised. One of them leads to humility and thus to all the virtues; the other leads to pride and so to all the vices. To use our terms, one leads to salvation, and the other to damnation. St. Ignatius also insists that what each principle generates, through successive steps of a process, is in a dialectical relationship with what the other generates: insults versus worldly honors, humility versus pride, all the virtues against all the vices. Most important of all is understanding the origin of the whole process: on the one hand it is poverty, which leads to all the virtues and to salvation; on the other it is wealth, which leads to all the vices and to damnation. There is no reason that this Ignatian intuition should be limited to the path of individual perfection; it can also be historicized. Ellacuría thought that "it is a question … of awakening dynamics that will structure a new world."[12] By starting from (the civilization of) poverty and opposing (the civilization of) wealth, the world can be turned around.

We already stated that this thesis is countercultural, as it was in Bonhoeffer's day: "Only a God who suffers can save us." It is also difficult to defend, for nonsalvation, the *mysterium iniquitatis,* runs wild in the world of the poor. And the biblical basis for supporting the thesis—"the suffering servant brings salvation"—is the supreme scandal for human reason. But the thesis is necessary, for the world of abundance left to itself does not save, does not produce life for all and does not humanize.

What Salvation and What Poor People

We have argued that in the world of the poor there is "something" salvific that is not easily found in other worlds, as we shall explain in short order. First, however, it should be understood what we mean by the terms "salvation" and the "poor."

Forms of Salvation

The salvation of human beings and the need for it can be seen in different spheres of reality. There is *personal* salvation and *social* salvation, there is *historical* salvation and *transcendent* salvation, although we cannot always neatly distinguish these different types. Here we will concentrate on the historical/social salvation of a gravely ill society. We should also distinguish between salvation as a positive state of affairs and salvation as the process by which that state is reached. In both cases salvation is dialectical, and at times it is dual. It takes place in opposition to other realities and processes, and even in conflict with them.

---

[12]"Lectura latinoamericana de los *Ejercicios espirituales* de san Ignacio," *Revista Latinoamericana de Teología* 23 (1991): 132.

As a state of affairs, salvation occurs in diverse forms. Letting ourselves be guided *sub specie contrarii* by the negation of life and the dehumanization that we have analyzed, we may say the following: salvation is *life* (satisfaction of basic vital needs), over against poverty, infirmity, and death; salvation is *dignity* (respect for persons and their rights), over against disregard and disdain; salvation is *freedom*, over against oppression; salvation is *fraternity* among human beings who are brought together as *family,* a conception opposed to the Darwinist understanding of the human race as mere *species*; salvation is *pure air,* which the spirit can breathe in order to move toward that which humanizes (honesty, compassion, solidarity, some form of openness to transcendence), over against that which dehumanizes (selfishness, cruelty, individualism, arrogance, crude positivism).

Salvation is concrete—as is seen in the diverse salvations in the Synoptic Gospels. This concreteness should be recalled in order to counter the danger of "universalizing" in nonhistorical ways the concept of salvation and of the realities that accompany it either positively or negatively, such as poverty or development. That is the way the UNDP understands human welfare, and it has its advantages, but obviously the substance of salvation will be understood differently in different places; one understanding will pertain in the residential suburbs of Paris and the World Bank reports, and perhaps quite another in the refugee camps of the Great Lakes district or in the testimonies of the grassroots communities. From Brazil, Bishop Pedro Casaldáliga wrote that "freedom without justice is like a flower on a corpse." "Freedom" and "justice" are both expressions of salvation, but we must not assume that we, from some supposedly universal space, can understand them adequately and prioritize their need and their urgency.

This leads to the question about the locus from which we theorize about salvation. Such theorizing is a very important task today, since globalization, as ideology, seeks to make people believe that the world's reality is essentially homogeneous and that it is therefore quite unnecessary to ask about the "most appropriate" place for knowing what salvation is or for asking questions about the meaning of being human, or of hope, or of sin, or of God. Liberation theology does not proceed thus; it considers extremely important the determination of the locus that is appropriate for helping us to know the truth about things. That locus is the world of the poor. For that very reason, liberation theology, and not other theologies, has been able to formulate, even if negatively, the locus of salvation: *extra pauperes nulla salus.*

Finally, we must also take into account the diverse forms that the process of salvation takes. Since this process normally takes place against structures of oppression, salvation often takes the form of liberation: "It is necessary to liberate from …" In addition, there is frequently the need not only to struggle against the negative products generated by the structures, but also to yank out their roots; then salvation becomes redemption. For that to happen, according to the Christian biblical tradition, it is necessary to take on the reality of the sin. Thus, inherent in redemption is the struggle against evil, not only from without, but also from within, by taking it on.

Diverse Dimensions of the Reality of Poor People

We need also to determine the diverse dimensions of being poor, for the contribution of poverty to salvation depends on the way it is lived out.[13]

Before classifying the different ways of living poverty, we should recall the basic distinction that Puebla makes when it treats the soteriological dimension of poor people. First of all, poor people, just by what they are, independently of "their moral or personal situation,"[14] "constantly summon [the Church] and call it to conversion"—and such calling to conversion is a great good. Second, the poor evangelize, they save, "since many of them practice in their lives the evangelical values of solidarity, service, simplicity, and readiness to receive the gift of God" (no. 1147), which is the spirit with which they live their poverty. Let us now see who the poor people are.

First, there are the *materially* poor, those who do not take life for granted, those for whom staying alive is their primary task, those for whom the nearness of death, physical or some other type—of their dignity, of their culture—is their normal fate. This is the economic understanding of being poor, the primordial sense, in which the *oikos,* the minimal nucleus of life, is threatened. The poor are "those who die before their time."

Second, there are the *dialectically* poor: not those who are needy simply because nature yields no more, but those who have been impoverished and oppressed. We are speaking of those who are deprived of the fruit of their own labor and who are increasingly excluded from even the opportunity to work. They are likewise deprived of social and political power by the people who, through such plunder, have enriched themselves and have assumed power. This is the sociological understanding of being poor: it denies that the poor can be "associates" or "companions." Besides, they are generally ignored and despised. They are considered nonexistent. They have no name, either in life or in death.

Third, there are the *consciously* poor, those who have achieved an awareness, individual and collective, about the very reality of material poverty and its causes. They have awoken from the dogmatic slumber into which they had been induced;

---

[13]See what we wrote in *Jesucristo liberador. Lectura histórico-teológica de Jesús de Nazaret* (San Salvador, 1991), 220–23 (Madrid, 42001) (English translation: *Jesus the Liberator: A Historical-Theological View* [Maryknoll, NY: Orbis Books, 1992]). In turn, we were inspired by I. Ellacuría, "Pobres," in *Conceptos fundamentales de pastoral* (Madrid, 1983), 786–802.

[14]Puebla mentions this in no. 1142, in speaking of God's option for the poor and the reasons for it, but we believe it is equally valid for describing the potential of poor people to move to conversion.

that is, they have stopped believing that their poverty is natural and inevitable—at times, even desired by God.

Fourth, there are the *liberatively* poor, that is, those who transform that new consciousness into grassroots organization and the practice of liberating solidarity. They have become aware of what they themselves can accomplish and their responsibility toward all poor people. They emerge from their own groups and communities to free others.

Fifth, there are the *spiritually* poor, understanding the "spiritually poor" here in a precise sense: those who experience their materiality, their consciousness, and their activity with gratuity, with hope, with mercy, with fortitude in persecution, with love, and even with that greatest love, which is giving one's life for the liberation of the poor majorities (this is the spirit of the beatitudes for living reality fully). Moreover they live thus with trust in and availability to a Father-God, both at the same time: they confide and rest in a Father, and they are completely available to a God who does not let them rest (the spirit of Jesus before the mystery of God). These are the poor with spirit.

Finally, if we view the reality of the poor from the Christian faith perspective, their poverty possesses both a theologal dimension (God's predilection for them) and a Christological dimension (Christ's presence in them). And this—at least to the extent that believers view the poor this way—renders even more radical the appeal of the poor and their offer of salvation to the nonpoor.

The different dimensions of the reality of poor people—depending on epochs and places—will produce diverse types of fruits of salvation. To put it in synthetic form, by their raw reality they can produce conversion and compassion, and also truth and just practice; and by their multiform spirit they can humanize in various ways the impure air that the spirit breathes.

Historical Forms of Salvation Coming from the World of the Poor

It is not easy to characterize the salvation that comes from the world of the poor. To do so we might be helped by thinking of it in three forms: as an opportunity for overcoming dehumanization, as positive elements for humanizing and attaining goods, and as an invitation to universal solidarity.

Overcoming Dehumanization

We have already said it. By virtue of what they are, poor people can move others to conversion, and if *they* do not do so, one may well ask what ever will. Perhaps this point is what is most directly stressed in the phrase *"extra" pauperes*: apart from the poor there is no easy conversion. The nonpoor can see the immense sufferings of the poor and the world's cruelty toward them. They can compare their own "good life" with the life of the poor, above all if they consider their own situation as a kind of "manifest destiny," and they are able to recognize their sin. None of this is easy, and it does not occur on a massive scale, but the opportunity is always there.

Society may boast of having moved beyond concepts like conversion, but such a belief is a serious error. Other concepts, such as change and desiring a different world do not express the radicality of the shift of direction and way of proceeding that is necessary—and even less do they express the necessary pain, repentance, and purpose of amendment, all of which are implied in conversion. Looked at positively, conversion can lead to truth, to hope, and to praxis. Human beings may find there answers to their most basic questions.

What I can know. The poor are *bearers of truth.* By virtue of what they are, they offer light to the world of abundance, so that this world might see its own truth and thus be able to move toward all truth. Ellacuría used to explain this by using two vigorous metaphors, the inverted mirror and feces analysis. A crucified people is like an inverted mirror in which the First World, on seeing itself disfigured, comes to know itself in its truth, which it otherwise seeks to hide by every means possible. The reality of the crucified peoples appears also by means of copro-analysis: the feces show what the First World produces, its state of health and its truth.[15]

Even if that light of truth is unappealing, disdaining and discarding it is senseless. Science analyzes reality, but in order to see reality as it is, it first needs light. The light that comes from the poor is what makes it possible to overcome voluntary blindness.[16] This light can awaken people from the dogmatic dream to which the West has succumbed: the dream about its own reality. That was how Ellacuría saw it, and in Central American University he recommended that people at least try to "work from the light and in the light that the world's oppressed majorities throw on the whole world, for the blinding of some, but for the illumination of others."[17]

What I am allowed to hope for. Poor people give new life to utopian vision, which was so valued by Ernst Bloch and is now so devalued by postmodernity. Moreover, the poor project such a vision in a precise way. "Utopia" means a dignified and just life for the majorities; it is not the (impossible) ideal of social and political perfection, conceived out of abundance, as in the republics of Plato or Thomas More or Campanella (utopias that are naturalist, theocratic, and aristocratically communist).

---

[15]Adorno says that "it is necessary to set up perspectives in which the world appears disturbed, alienated, showing its cracks and tears, beggarly and deformed" (*Minima Moralia* [Madrid, 1987], 250).

[16]Bonhoeffer says that in the presence of Lazarus a miracle can occur: "what the rich man has not seen, that his world is a world of death," quoted in M. Zechmeister, "Grito y canto," *Revista Latinoamericana de Teología* 69 (2006).

[17]"El desafío," 1076.

The poor transform the very notion of a historical utopia, which is their most important contribution: for them it is not a question of *outopia,* that "no-place" that does not exist, but of *eu-topia,* that "good place" that must exist. What we call the "good life," "quality of life," "welfare state"—prosperity for the minorities—are feats along the road toward the utopia that is conceived out of the abundance of the nonpoor. But of course they are feats with which they are not content, so that they unleash a frantic race for progress. This is the flight forward, despite the presence of a humanity in crisis. In contrast, the utopia of the poor is the *oikos,* the existence and the guarantee of an essential core of basic life and of human family.

Correlatively, from the poor comes hope, *true* hope—that is, the way to hope. In the "world of abundance" there exist expectations, which are extrapolated on the basis of calculations, but there is not a radical break between the present and the future. That's fine, but it is not hope, for, in the Christian sense at least, true hope is hoping against hope. The root of hope is not in objective calculation; neither is it in subjective optimism. Rather it is in love, which bears all. The hope of the poor passes through crises, through epochs of "disenchantment with the immediate," for there do not appear any "immediate and calculable outcomes and victories."[18] But there is a faith that overcomes darkness, and there is a hope that triumphs over disenchantment, as is well shown in poor people's historic patience and their determination to live. It is what we call primordial holiness. That hope is precisely what they offer to the First World. Ellacuría used to say of the First World, comparing it with the hope he saw in Latin America: "The only thing they really have is fear."[19]

What I have to do. The poor mark out the direction and the basic contents of our practice. Let us consider this in what are today two necessary points. The first is that, correlatively to the truth that the poor express and require, they make possible true prophetic condemnation. The profound truth they reveal is that, more than anything else, condemnation is necessary in order to be in tune with reality, that is, in order to be real. For that reason, minimizing the need for prophecy and discrediting it as mere "protest" is a serious error. We must go beyond psychology. By its nature, prophetic condemnation means becoming an echo of a reality that wishes to speak forth. Condemnation means "being the voice of a reality that is oppressed and, moreover, deprived of a voice." If mere protest is something easy, as is sometimes simplistically or cynically supposed, such is not the case with prophetic condemnation. It is costly, for to echo reality you have to be in it (incarnation), you have to see it as it is (honesty with what is real), and above all you have to be moved to mercy and decide to work for

---

[18]P. Casaldáliga, "Del desencanto inmediatista a la utopía esperanzada," *Concilium* 311 (2005): 156.
[19]"Quinto centenario de América Latina: ¿Descubrimiento o encubrimiento?" *Revista Latinoamericana de Teología* 21 (1990): 282.

justice (taking responsibility for the real), by accepting the inevitable consequences of persecution and even of death (bearing the real).[20]

The second point is that the intolerability of poverty requires a dynamic not only for condemning it, but for creating economic, political, and cultural models that overcome it, as Ellacuría used to say. In this sense, "there is no protest without a corresponding proposal." In any case, the poor demand that the new models not be inhumane or dehumanizing.

Signs and Leaven

The poor, as persons and as communities, have remarkable values that are generally ignored: resistance, simplicity, joy in life's basic elements, openness to the mystery of God, and so on; recall the earlier citations of Comblin, Ronaldo Muñoz, and Felix Wilfred. With those values they give new shapes to society, as modest as they may seem to outsiders. In my view, these values are above all in the line of humanization. They are important for living more humanly, but they also facilitate the production of basic goods.

The poor offer models, sometimes small ones, sometimes notable ones—but *their own* models—of grassroots economics, community organization, health care, housing, human rights, education, culture, religion, politics, arts, sports.... In many cultures they possess a great ecological consciousness, and they take care of nature and Mother Earth in ways far superior to the ways of the West.

Furthermore the poor, depending on places and circumstances, organize themselves into people's liberation movements, even revolutionary ones. They accumulate social and/or political power, depending on the issues. They do so to defend their own rights, but also to defend the rights of other poor and oppressed people, and sometimes the rights of a whole people. They seek and sometimes obtain power. Such a victory then makes them run the risk of dehumanization, but often they show a great, humanizing generosity. And they get results.

To put it plainly, the poor have values and produce positive realities and new social forms that, even if not given massive expression, do offer orientations and elements for a new society. At times they do not stay enclosed in their own communities, but appear as a sign for others. Like the lamp in the gospel, they illuminate their surroundings. They can then become the salt that gives flavor and the leaven that makes the dough expand, which means that they produce salvation beyond themselves. This quality is what Ellacuría used to find in poor people's communities, especially in the base communities:

---

[20]To these three reflections of Ellacurían origin we are accustomed to add a fourth: "letting reality bear with us." That happens in the world of the poor.

There are signs that the poor are evangelizers, that they are saviors. The splendid experience of the base communities, as a ferment of Church renovation and as a factor of political transformation, and the frequent example of "poor people with spirit"—who organize in order to struggle in solidarity and in martyrdom for the good of their brothers and sisters, for the most humble and the weakest—already give proof of the salvific and liberating potential of the poor.[21]

The Convocation to the Solidarity of the Human Family

The poor unleash solidarity, which, as has been said so beautifully, is "the tenderness of the peoples." We have defined it as "unequals bearing one another mutually." But we need to analyze the concept in depth and see what poor people contribute to it. Solidarity means poor people and nonpoor people mutually bearing one another, giving "to each other" and receiving "from each other" the best that they have, in order to arrive at being "with one another."[22] Often what is given and what is received are in quite different orders of reality: material aid and human acceptance, for example. And what the nonpoor receive may be, as a humanizing reality, superior to what they give. This kind of solidarity goes beyond mere unilateral aid, with its intrinsic tendency toward imposition and domination. It also goes beyond alliances between those who wish to defend their own common interests over against other people's interests.

Understanding solidarity in the sense of unequals bearing one another mutually is something novel, but such solidarity is necessary in a world of unequals; it can resolve the ambiguity and root out what is harmful in the falsely universalizing concept of globalization. Most importantly, the source of solidarity thus understood and the call to practice it do not come from just anywhere; they come from the poor. Historically such solidarity happens locally, in small ways, through what has happened in places like El Salvador or Nicaragua, but it makes an immense contribution to our understanding of true solidarity, especially now with the proliferation of aid organizations and ideologies, private and governmental, religious and secular. It seems to me most important that such organizations operate according to the objective dynamic of bearing one another mutually, and not according to the self-interested directives of the United Nations, the European Community, and others.

---

[21]"Pobres," 796. Recall also that Puebla (no. 1137) speaks of the effectively political value of the poor: "they have begun to organize in order to live their faith integrally, and therefore also in order to claim their rights." And it comments: "Faith thus makes them a political force for liberation."

[22]We have analyzed this in greater detail in "Bearing with One Another in Faith: A Theological Analysis of Christian Solidarity," in *The Principle of Mercy* (Maryknoll, NY: Orbis Books, 1994), 144–72.

Victims and Redemption

Historically, the poor are victims, and as such they also shape the process of liberation, now in the form of redemption. Archbishop Romero, without pretending to theological precision, said with brilliant insight, "Among the poor Christ desired to place his seat of redemption" (Homily of December 24, 1978).

The term "redemption" is ignored today, as if it explained nothing important about how to heal a sick world; but it explains a lot. In the process of salvation it is necessary to eliminate many evils, and it is necessary to struggle against the structures that produce them. When the evil is profound, enduring, and structural, however, it is necessary to eradicate evils in order truly to heal. This task is so difficult that it has always been thought to require an extraordinary effort, something outside the normal. In metaphoric language this has been expressed by saying that, in order to heal a corrupt world, it is necessary to "pay a price," which is precisely the etymological meaning of "redemption," *redemptio*. In other words, besides the normal labors and sufferings involved in the production of goods, "adding on" something burdensome is a necessity. In more historical language, we might say that to eradicate the roots of evil, we must struggle against evil not only from without, but from within, ready to allow evil to grind us up. Here there appears the "extra" suffering that in history is always related to redemption.

In El Salvador we have often said as much, in the presence of violence. This violence must be combated in diverse ways: from without, as it were, with ideas, negotiations, and even, tragically and in extreme cases, with other violence, making use of it in the most humane way possible. But in order to redeem violence we must combat it also from within, that is, be ready to bear with it. All the martyrs for justice have borne witness to this: Gandhi, Martin Luther King, Archbishop Romero.... Ignacio Ellacuría had just such a premonition on September 19, 1989, two months before becoming a victim of violence himself. In the presence of presidents Óscar Arias of Costa Rica and Alfredo Cristiani of El Salvador, he gave a frankly political speech aimed at moving negotiations forward; he stated, apparently without intending religious overtones:

> There has been much pain suffered and much blood shed, but now the classical *theologoumenon "nulla redemptio sine efussione sanguinis"* reminds us again that the salvation and the liberation of the peoples takes place through very painful sacrifices.[23]

This redemption thesis should be understood well. We are not defending any Anselmian theory, as if suffering were necessary—and effective—for placating the divine

---

[23]"Palabras en el doctorado *Honoris Causa* en Ciencia políticas al presidente de Costa Rica Dr. Óscar Arias," mimeographed text.

wrath and obtaining salvation.[24] In order to save, God does not require a sacrifice that kills his creatures, and therefore there is no need to seek out excellent victims for sacrifice. This would mean that the victims' suffering, by its nature, would "disarm" the power of evil, not magically, but historically. This is a way of trying to explain conceptually the saving element of Christ's suffering on the cross: sin has discharged all its force against him, but in doing so sin itself has been left without force. So it is not that suffering placates God and makes him benevolent; rather what it does is disarm evil. As for God, the cross is proof of his love, since he accepted us precisely at the moment when he could have rejected us, because of the suffering we have inflicted on his Son.

Nor do we seek to defend any kind of sacrificialism, as if suffering in itself were something good for human beings. We do insist on venerating the victims who suffer, because in them there is much of the mystery that is *fascinans et tremens*. And we insist on gratitude, for often such suffering accompanies or follows on great generosity and supreme love. We venerate and give thanks for a positive, primordial reality: in this cruel world, and opposed to it, true love has appeared.

Redemption continues to be a *mysterium magnum*, but sometimes a miracle happens, and the mystery appears visibly as a *mysterium salutis*. Of this we can speak only with fear and trembling, and above all we should speak through our decision to give life to the victims and to pledge our own life in that endeavor. Still, we should not ignore the salvific potential of such a mystery, out of respect for the victims, but also out of a properly understood self-interest, namely, not to impoverish ourselves even more. As we have already seen, the innocent victims save precisely by moving us to conversion, to being honest with reality, to having hope, to practicing solidarity... . And sometimes, even amid horrors, immediate and tangible fruits of salvation are miraculously produced, like leaven that humanizes the dough. It is the miracle of a redemption that is offered and received.

> In Auschwitz, prisoner denies prisoner, but Father [Maximilian] Kolbe breaks with that norm: *prisoner offers his life for another prisoner who is unknown to him.* . . . Although the Enlightenment—so rational and rationalizing—could never comprehend such an act, even in Auschwitz it is possible to live from loving grace in dialogue with the light …, to encourage the hope and remove the despair of the others sentenced to the cell of punishment.[25]

"After Auschwitz we are able to continue praying because in Auschwitz they also prayed,"[26] according to the memorable words of J. B. Metz, one who was not at all given to naive theodicy. And Etty Hillesum put down in writing what she was

---

[24]See what I wrote in *Jesus the Liberator,* 219–32.

[25]C. Díaz, *Monseñor Óscar Romero* (Madrid, 1999), 95–96.

[26]In "Teología cristiana después de Auschwitz," *Concilium* 195 (1984): 214ff. Today the victims of Auschwitz are still remembered, and they are recalled also in order to find in them salvation. Thus do we recall D. Bonhoeffer, E. Stein, E. Hillesum. . . .

hoping for in Auschwitz: "to help God as much as possible."[27] Suffering has wrought redemption.

The Great Lakes region of Africa is the Auschwitz of today, and there also an incredible humanity has been engendered. "It is not difficult to sing and give praise when everything is assured. The marvel is that ... the prisoners of Kigali, who today will receive visits by relatives, who with great travail bring them something to eat, can still bless and give thanks to God. How can they not be the favored ones, those from whom we must learn the meaning of gratuity! Today I received a letter from them. Perhaps they do not realize how much we receive from them and how they save us."[28]

When the Peace Accords were signed in El Salvador in 1992, it was insisted that the peace was an achievement of the martyrs and the fallen. But beyond the great truth of these words, though it is often distorted, there is also the truth that, as in Auschwitz and in the Great Lakes, the "extra" of the victims' suffering has generated redemption, an offer of humanization. In a Salvadoran refugee camp during the war, on the Day of the Dead, some *campesinos* prayed for their murdered relatives and also for the murderers. They said: "You know, we believed that they also, the enemy, should have been on the altar. They are our brothers despite the fact that they kill us and murder us. Of course you know the Bible says: it is easy to love your own, but God asks that we also love those who persecute us."[29] We do not know whether the murderers ever came to receive that offer of salvation that the victims made to them, or whether they accepted it. But with that prayer for the assassins and with other proofs of the victims' love, the world became impregnated with humanity—a capital that should not be squandered, but rather should be put to work, like a great treasure.

That treasure is grace. And if we ask why it should be mentioned in talking about the salvation of a sick society, then we have not understood Jesus of Nazareth, nor human beings, nor the society we live in, which is bursting with sin, but is also teeming with the grace of the victims. We come to be truly human not only by making our own selves—often in Promethean fashion—but by letting ourselves be made human by others. That is the gift dimension of salvation.

But our times don't seem right for talking this way. Society's ideal—comprehensible, but dangerous—is to save only by producing goods, as if all evils will gradually disappear by themselves, without leaving scars and without activating sin's particular dynamic of "returning," of *coming back* to produce more death and inhumanity. For that reason, it is not possible to speak of salvation without keeping present the historical need for redemption.

---

[27]Taken from J. Vitoria, "Una teología de ojos abiertos."
[28]Quote from a nun who has spent many years in the Great Lakes region.
[29]A more detailed account can be found in "América Latina: lugar de pecado, lugar de perdón," *Concilium* 204 (1986): 226.

This point appears quite clearly when we analyze what the martyrs of our time bring about.[30] Today the great entrepreneurs of redemption are the Jesuanic martyrs, taken as a whole; they include both the active martyrs, who live and die like Jesus, and those who are made to die slowly through unjust poverty and/or violence, in massacres, anonymously, in groups and in collective bodies. Strictly speaking, the second are more redeeming than the first, though often no clear dividing line between them is apparent. They all bear the sin of the world, and they weaken the roots of evil, though they never finally eradicate them. Thus do they bring about salvation.

In order to see things this way faith is needed, just as it was in the case of the suffering servant of Yahweh. Sometimes, though, the testimony occurs in verifiable fashion. The case of Archbishop Romero is paradigmatic. A bishop, pursued by the local powers of every sort, murdered innocently and defenselessly by mercenaries in connivance with the empire, generated new hope, fostered new commitment, and called forth an unprecedented universal solidarity.[31] And Archbishop Romero was not just a single individual. Rather, it may well be said that he was the most visible head of a whole people that was struggling against the sin of the world and bearing that sin.

Without making light of the problem of theodicy, on the one hand, or falling into victimology, on the other, we believe that in the immense pain of the victims there is "something" that can heal our world. We approve of Ivan Karamazov's gesture of refusing to enter a heaven to which people must ascend to recover lost harmony. But we do accept entrance into a destroyed earth, to which we must descend in order to find "something" of humanity. Seeking suffering in order to find salvation would be blasphemy.[32] But in the presence of the victims' suffering, it is arrogance to refuse to open up to their salvific power and let ourselves be embraced by them.

Redemption is necessary. "Linking the future of humanity with the fate of the poor has become a historical necessity.... Only the victims can redeem the future."[33] And it is possible. As on the cross of Christ, likewise in history, suffering and total love can be united. Then love saves. As Nelly Sachs says, "They loved so much they made the granite of the night jump and break into pieces."[34]

---

[30]See what we wrote in "Jesuanic Martyrs in the Third World," in *Witnesses to the Kingdom: The Martyrs of El Salvador and the Crucified Peoples* (Maryknoll, NY: Orbis Books, 2003), 119–32.

[31]As regards the salvation the martyrs offer to the Church, see my essay, "The Latin American Martyrs: Challenge and Grace for the Church," in *Witnesses to the Kingdom*, 134–54.

[32]Important is Moltmann's criticism: "It seems to me that it is not correct to speak of the 'crucified people' that 'takes away the sin of the world' and in this way 'redeems' the world. That does nothing more than religiously glorify and perpetuate the people's suffering. The people do not want to save the world with their suffering, but to be finally redeemed from their suffering and to have a humanly dignified life" ("Teología Latinoamericana," in L. C. Susin, ed., *El mar se abrió* [Santander, 2001], 209). The final phrase seems to us correct, but it does not necessarily deny that the poor, by being such, bring salvation into history. Where I would be in agreement with Moltmann is in rejecting any mechanical relation between suffering and salvation.

[33]J. Vitoria, "Una teología de oj os abiertos."

[34]Taken from M. Zechmeister, "Grito y canto."

The Analogy of Being "In the World of the Poor"

So how much salvation can arise in the world of the nonpoor? Undoubtedly, the nonpoor can cooperate in healing a gravely ill society, but on one condition: that they participate really and historically, not just intentionally and spiritually, in the world of the poor.

Many goods are produced among the nonpoor: the science of Pasteur and Einstein; the revolution of "liberty, equality, and fraternity"; the universal declarations of human rights; economic models that can indeed overcome poverty; plus the political power that can make them work. And that can be said as well for the globalization we have already criticized.[35] We are not going to belabor the point.

The nonpoor may also be necessary to make effective the salvation that comes from the poor. They can become prophetic figures who help the poor to recover and maintain confidence in themselves, to develop practices and to spread hope. When such figures do not appear, frustration may increase among the poor, but when they do appear, the community of the poor is empowered and creates an even greater ferment. These prophetic figures may come from among the poor, but also from among the nonpoor. *Archbishop* Romero and *university president* Ellacuría were not from the world of the poor. But as they lowered themselves, they received salvation, and the poor became empowered as saviors.

Left to itself, however, there is no evidence that the world of abundance can bring salvation, and normally the salvation it brings is totally ambiguous: Hiroshima or useful energy? Nourishment and health or individualistic consumerism and spiritless commodification? Universalization or conquest? Such salvation usually arrives mixed with sinfulness: imposition, violence, and the arrogant pretension of beneficence. For salvation to come from this world, it is not enough just to produce goods and heap them on top of the evils; rather it is necessary to purify their ambiguity and cleanse their sinfulness. The world of the nonpoor is capable of attempting both these tasks: it presents proposals that are generally ethical, humanistic, and religious. But the most radical possibility, without which the others are usually not sufficient, consists in lowering ourselves to what is poor in history.

This does not usually happen by our own initiative; it happens only by the encouraging invitation, or by the actual pressure, that comes from the world of the poor. It is difficult, but it can occur, and in diverse ways. The heart of the matter is our participating in some way, analogously, but truly, in the reality of the world of the poor.

This can happen in many forms: by actual, comradely *insertion* in that world, by unequivocal *service* on its behalf, by liberating *praxis* alongside the poor, by running

---

[35]Boff and Casaldáliga have made this point. Even with all the evils it produces, present-day globalization is in fact laying the foundations for a future globalization with great human potential.

risks to defend them, by assuming their *fate* of persecution and death, by sharing *their joys and their hopes.* All this is real and verifiable, not just intentional. And when such participation really takes place, as analogous as it may be, then salvation can come also from the world of abundance. But we must be clear about what analogy does not include: it does not consist in mere intentionality that is unsullied by real poverty. Some people believe that there is no longer any need to participate in that world nowadays; they hold that a well-managed self-interest is sufficient to bring salvation, so that no significant cost is necessarily involved. It's the bargain of our times: in order to save, there is no need for generosity or sacrifice. It recalls the old fallacy: that it is enough to be "poor in spirit," without any sort of participation in real poverty.[36]

45. Marcella Althaus-Reid – *¿Bién Sonados?* The Future of Mystical Connections in Liberation Theology

Bién sonados. A slang expression from South America which means 'disaster struck us', or, 'we have been defeated'. People grow up with the slang expressions of their communities, as I did with the familiar phrase that every so often comes from the lips of people in my country, Argentina. *Soné*, or *me sonaron* may mean 'I lost my job', or, 'I couldn't pay the rent of the boarding house this time.' Or it may mean 'I am pregnant and on my own', or 'I am ill but I cannot afford medicines', or refer to any difficult situation which we may face without many options or hope of improvement. In my own neighbourhood that expression even meant the threatening presence of the police. Although *sonar* (which literally means 'to produce a sound') is an ironic expression of acceptance of the hardness of reality it also recognizes the responsibility of people's actions in the circumstances of their life and does not imply resignation. The life of the poor is a life of struggle against circumstances which cannot be controlled, but which are recognized as carrying no social stigma, precisely because of the deep understanding of structural sin that poor people have. The expression *sonado,* as when facing sudden material losses, refers to that understanding of the web of structural sin and the human sacrifices that it produces where one can just be a casualty.

---

[36]Enrique Álvarez Córdova, a Salvadoran oligarch and landlord, distributed his land to the poor small farmers on the condition that the land be owned and worked in cooperative fashion. He struggled for agrarian reform in his country and entered the ranks of the Democratic Revolutionary Front as a politician, not as a soldier. He was killed in 1979, a brilliant example of analogy.

'Liberation is a Historical and not a Mental Act.'

Karl Marx in Marx and Engels, 1976, p. 38

Is there such a thing as a theology from the poor? Moreover, is there such a thing as an *epistemology from the poor* which could act as the legitimate foundation for a theology from the poor? How do the poor know, and how do knowledge from poverty and faith knowledge relate to each other? Karl Marx, who was a man with the gift of doing philosophy as a second act and epistemology as an action-reflection process, once reflected on the life of London shopkeepers. That was Marx, more than a century ago: the poor man as a philosopher, a man struggling to feed his family on a sack of potatoes per month, reflecting on knowledge, poverty and shopkeepers while sitting in a poor room of a rented house in London. Probably, as the letters he addressed to Engels seem to show, his theory of ideology as historic illusion was nurtured by his life as a poor man; the business of the shopkeepers he needed to pay; his problems with the owner of his rented house and the impossible cost of medicines for his children. It was from that experience of everyday poverty that he recognized the structure of ideology as a methodology, and, by contrast, the fundaments of an epistemology from the poor. Ideology here can be defined as a combination of conceptual frameworks, particular ideas and preassumptions as well as established forms of social representation. However, following Marx, we understand that ideologies are epistemological systems based on social existence, although at some point dislocated from that experience. The main characteristic of ideologies is not that they are not grounded in historical contexts, but the fact that they do not reflect back on their own origins: a sort of Frankestein's monster which remakes its master in its own image; a disowning of origins; a usurpation process.

Liberation Theology joined Marx in doing philosophy as a second act, if by that we mean that the 'reality first' principle is the foundation for doing theology. First, we would say, come people's historical experiences and their needs; the consideration of their struggle for human rights (and the right to eat is the first of these rights), and everyday life should provide the epistemology from poverty as foundational for theology. However, there is a difference between 'epistemologies from poverty' and 'ideologies of poverty'. We have seen these ideologies from poverty in many theological projects from the past, when poverty becomes independent of people's experiences (Marx and Engels, 1976, p. 62), and is configured as a structure made up of values and attributed agency in which the experience of the poor needs to fit. As Marx would say, always when ideas come first, historical experiences do not even come a close second. They are erased and alienated from philosophy, theology and economics, and from the nation's memories too. But ideas and experiences are always in tension in theology. It is the tension of dogma and praxis. It is also the tension between materialism and idealism. Both terms do not need to be exclusive, but the tension is unavoidable because orthodoxy and orthopraxis are not stable terms. Sooner or later dogmas get stabilized and theology tends to impose itself as an ideology. This happens when we grow comfortable with definitions and visions of the world. Even Liberation Theology may have been becoming ideological and losing its foundation of reflecting on the concreteness of life. This may have happened as Liberation Theology kept working as an issue-based theology. There is no argument about the selection of issues such as poverty, globalization processes and exclusion, but the problem may have arisen in the way liberationists developed their reflections methodologically. Once again, a theology from exclusion could become an ideology from exclusion too. Ideology is a method, and if there is something such as a theology based on an epistemology from the poor, it must differ methodologically from other approaches, and not just by a change of issues.

The point is that historically ideologies differ among themselves and may have even been in contradiction to each other, except for one thing that they always keep in common: the methodological process of ideological formation. This process contributes to the structuring of society by systems of ideas originated in historical experience but which later become detached and independent from people. That is precisely Marx's contribution to the understanding of ideology. Ideology for Marx is the methodological process par excellence of human exclusion, what he described in 'The German Ideology' (Marx and Engels, 1976, pp. 51–63) with the phrase *mystical connections*, referring by that to the illusory nature of ideology, and the ghostly authority of its truthful discourses. Truth that is not factual, but of a metaphysical nature is a mystical truth. Mystical truth, even in theology, confirms dogmas as the dictatorship of divine illusions where people tend to disappear in methods and ready-made theological responses to questionings from reality. That may be a hard truth, but no honest theologian can afford to ignore this fact.

Mystical Connections

The process of ideology-making has been organized by Marx in three steps. Marx considers how the process of human exclusion from philosophical thought occurs (separation of ideas from facts).

First of all, Marx acknowledges that ideas are formed by social interactions and people's experiences. Second, that at a certain point in the development of philosophical thought people disappear, without leaving a trace of their concrete human experience. This is the moment of ideas becoming disembodied from human actions, and de-humanized (stripped from the field of experience). Third, Marx considers how, and under which conditions, people seem to reappear again in the philosophical reflection or Grand Idea and in which manner and with which authority they do so. This happens, for instance, at the level of Grand Narratives or discourses of authority. Obviously, Marx also presents us here with an interesting case of what we could consider the death and resurrection of metanarratives, and especially of Christian metanarratives as organized in theological models, including Liberation Theology. For instance, we could consider that people's experiences give birth to a theological reflection, but then, that theology excludes them and organizes itself as dogma; that would be the metanarrative which will need to die in order for people's relation with God to resurrect again. Let us consider this argument from the perspective of exclusion, that is, how people get excluded in theology and what happens thereafter.

Exclusion

The first step to exclude people from epistemological constructs (be they economic or theological) is to redistribute facts and thoughts. That means, to make a separation between the empirical conditions of thoughts and thoughts themselves and to give priority to disembodied ideas over people's experiences (Marx and Engels, 1976, p. 43). It is in this sense that for Marx, following Feuerbach here, theology is a 'belief in Ghosts' (Marx and Engels, 1976, p. 160).

Exclusion as a Dynamic Force

Second, and once ideas have lost all connection to an empirical reality, they must become completely detached from human experience. For that purpose, ideas are represented in a new logical order; a sort of chronology of logical development which is set a-chronologically, that is, after the idea has been selected. This process self-authorizes ideas, creating false genealogies and showing how they fit into accepted imposed patterns of conceptual ordering. This is what Marx specifically calls *mystical connections,* because ideas, in their disconnection from social experiences, acquire metaphysical significance of a social transcendental nature, by attributing them with a divine self-justified origin (as in Androcentric White North Atlantic theology).

The Dynamic of Exclusion Produces Idols

These disembodied ideas become 'persons', while real persons (who have disappeared in the midst of the abstraction process) become inanimate objects, 'things'. These 'persons' have been considered in Liberation Theology to be idols, the product of our hands (or of the hands of ideology). Let us clarify this reversal movement of ideology. Ideas become persons because they are organized as distinct entities and renamed as 'values', 'inherent beliefs', 'rules and norms', 'common sense', and also Systematic Theology, Moral Theology etc. When they work as disembodied theological systems these *persons* also have attributed agency. They are indispensable to sustain an order that they claim to have been originated beyond human circumstances, yet they are necessary for humans to live. People have been reduced to objects as depositories of these person-ideas, their desires and their assumed agency or efficacy. Of course, people are the 'things' of 'person-theologies' too. Unfortunately, and for the sake of honesty, we must admit that theology is not by definition a Freirean process of dialogical processes. Rather, theology tends to behave at certain levels as a banking process. Theology is for domestication and not for transformation when theological methods ask people to fit into them, and not vice versa.

Exclusion and Redistribution of Processes of Knowledge

At the end of this process, these 'person-ideas' that Marx suggests are redistributed in epistemological sub-units in society. They are attributed to sources of authority as being made by the product of historical evolution or as coming from the gospel. And with this, the circle of mystical connections is finished as in a wizardly act of spell-binding. If reality does not match ideas, reality is distrusted. People for theology, and not theology for people. People for God, and not God for people. The challenge here will be to develop a theology, paraphrasing Marx, 'as if people mattered'. 'Person-ideas' are dogmas and theological conceptions which need to be kept, admitting some degree of adaptation even, but seldom a negation.

Was it in this way that Marx said that while shopkeepers were able to distinguish between what somebody professed to be and what the person really was, historiography has not understood? Did Marx refer here to the game of pretences that poor families used to play with shopkeepers, as my own family did, dressing in their finery in order to obtain credit for buying food? The value of products and their prices do not always match. When does theology profess to be what it is not? When objective theological roles appears without actors, then theology appear without people. Theology becomes a mediumistic activity when the discourse begins as in past centuries with phrases such as 'God and Man' [sic]. Or, more fashionably, with discourses ending with the phrase '... and the poor', or, '... and women'.[1] Human experiences become an addendum, or an appendix at the end of a reflection. This is a true example of the marginalization of people's knowledge, to be added to a centre of knowledge which remains normative. Liberation Theology has done this also. The discourses of women theologians in Latin America, and therefore the communities who are supposed to be presented in such discourses, are present as marginal. Reflections from women's theological communities are included in books and symposiums in a couple of identifiable categories such as 'Mariology' or in general as 'Latin American Women' (rereading the Scriptures, or doing liturgy etc.). Liberation Theology has not taken on board Feminist Theology as an integral part of economic reflections,

---

[1]Cf. for this point Dorothy Smith, *The Conceptual Practice of Power* (Boston: Northwestern University Press, 1990), p. 49.

questioning the androcentric construction of economy and politics, and taking non-dualistic insights or a deconstruction of sexuality and gender to the ultimate consequences of analysis. As such, the Liberation Theology in which I was nurtured and trained as a young theologian years ago has ignored at its peril the advances in Feminist Epistemology, concerning the analysis of patriarchy and Economy and also the Althusserian-inspired theories on gender as a performative act in society, for instance. At the beginning of the twenty-first century, the masters of suspicion do not need to be any more Nietzsche, Marx and Freud or at least not exclusively. Names such as Mary Daly, Judith Butler, Luce Irigaray and Sub Comandante Marcos may deserve an even bigger space among our classical 'Mediator Sciences' in the construction of our liberationist hermeneutical circle of suspicion.

This ingrained fetishist process, by which ideologies replaced people, has rendered Liberation Theology incapable of challenging the Latin American patriarchalism lying at the core of its theological, issue-based method. This is the reason why liberation theologians have been repeating themselves so much in recent years, and why so much essentialism is found, even when working on epistemologies from poverty. As a Latin American woman I always felt uncomfortable with theological reflections starting with phrases such as 'women from Latin America', 'the authentic voices of poor Christian women in Latin America' etc. Even from the time that I was a student, Liberation Theology told me *about* myself as if it was a normative discourse behaving as ideologies do, pretending to be a 'natural' or 'a given truth', and 'universal'. How many times have men liberationists said who Latin American women are, and what they need or want, and how they feel and how their desires flow? The structures of sin in theological methods not only exclude women from the corpus of integral liberation theological reflection, but forces many women to adopt a 'theological femininity' which works as a mask. Following Joan Riviere's text 'Femininity as a Mask', Jacques Lacan advances the theory of women using the constructed femininity of their times and religious beliefs as 'a mask to conceal' the presence of masculinity involved in the display of intellectual activities, while avoiding the patriarchal punishments of isolation or derision.[2] Joan Riviere alludes in her article to women who were fulfilling the role of professional women, while responding to the social criteria of idealized femininity as good wives and mothers. Therefore, the structures of sin in theology tend to perpetuate femininity as a mask in women and theology too, and in this way women's theology in Latin America has so often become a 'person'. It is against 'persons' that feminist liberationists struggle. One is what is ideologically constructed as Liberation Theology (with the addendum of women's theology) and the other is women's false consciousness.

---

[2]In 1958 Lacan translated Joan Riviere's article of 1929, 'Femininity as a Mask', and elaborated upon this theme in his seminar of 12 March 1958. See Laura Aschieri's analysis on Lacan and Riviere in 'La Femineidad como Máscara' in *Acheronta*, no. 8, December 1998, http://www.acheronta.org

Women become things to fit the androcentic illusion of the agency of women defined by community and family patriarchal values, heavily invested in patterns of the most abstract and ideological classical theology of all times. Women's epistemology is the most challenging and original epistemology from the poor, because every woman somehow, by the mere fact of being a woman, is ontologically separate from, and materially impoverished by, patriarchal society. However, that epistemology has not informed pastoral reflections or ecclesiology or Christian ethics or church history at the roots of Liberation Theology. Had it done so, we might now be enjoying a theological revolution flourishing like the 'Intergalactic Flowers' of the Zapatistas, who have made of sexual and gender transformations an issue of political revolution. If Liberation Theology could have overcome passé views of social constructions embedded in theological method, a complete alternative and truthful theology may have transformed Latin America and the world, beyond words and declamations of justice.

The epistemology from the poor, which ideology veils, needs to be an epistemology of the struggle and not just a contribution to make theology as ideology picturesque. If not, Liberation Theology cannot become a postcolonial theology, even if it seems to be looking 'more native' than the former theological models we had from the West. There cannot be liberation without decisive departures, but will Liberation Theology reach the point of decisive departures from ideological methods?

Mystical Connections in Liberation Theology

Religion, once formed always contains traditional material . . .

(Engels, 1935, p. 55)

If ideology is a methodology based on a sort of disappearing act or 'escapology', as I say elsewhere,[3] Liberation Theology has not been excepted from that. Mystical connection may be an intrinsic part of the process of doing theology itself, and as such it may be useless, as Marx himself has claimed. Or it may be reformed through a materialist method, as Feuerbach and many liberationists have claimed. That in itself is something still to be resolved. However, theology works by ex-centricity and by eviction, and the challenge to abandon those premises is what will take us far beyond the so-called hermeneutical circle or theological suspicion of the 1970s. It will take us to reconsider the whole basis of our theological enterprise of liberation, but this time the liberation of theology would be costlier than in Segundo's reflection during the 1970s. It could be a liberation which may kill theology, or at least empty theology of ideological methodologies and therefore transform its message deeply.

---

[3] Althaus-Reid treats this in her piece 'Gustavo Gutierrez goes to Disneyland' in the same anthology from which this extract comes: *From Feminist Theology to Indecent Theology* (SCM Press, 2004).

A *kenosis* of theology. Who knows, but perhaps we are only going to know if theology is more than ideology when and if this *kenosis* happens. As a Freirean educator who has worked in conscientization processes even in Scotland, I know that processes of transformation require risk and an acceptance of failure too. However, as a liberation theologian, I also know that theology cannot follow capitalist patterns of production and alienation and the consequent understanding of success. What is theological success? What is the success of Liberation Theology? The fact that Latin American theologians are recognized at certain level of knowledge by the authoritative western centre of theology? A handful of famous names and well-sold books? The support and influence of Liberation Theology in the struggle for people's human rights? The success of Liberation Theology was to establish an epistemology of the *bién sonados* as a foundation for theology. However, two methodological problems occurred. One is theological ex-centricity, the other is eviction. Both are closely related to each other.

The second part of this essay is concerned with the analysis of these two issues.

The Ex-centricity of the Hermeneutical Circle

The concept of theological ex-centricity which is usually seen positively[4] is a negative term, in relation to the hermeneutical circle. This is inspired by Ricoeur's reflection on biblical hermeneutics. By hermeneutical ex-centricity I mean the elements which enter into the Liberation Theology hermeneutical circle of suspicion from outside the sensuous field of theological experience. I define the centre of theology and Liberation Theology by the circle of orthopraxis, and marginalize orthodoxy.

Consider for instance that the starting point of the circle of interpretation is people's historical experience; the material world in motion, or what Lenin called the objective reality which presents itself to humanity via human experience and perception. Consider the hermeneutical circle as a relationship of production, based on community reciprocity of tools (critical reflection, observation as principles of the theological reproductive force), goals (clarified objectives of liberation) and workforce (the community itself as a theological community). In this circle of interpretation, the reading of the Bible and the use of social sciences as mediators (from class theory to the new paradigm shift of language) may be applied in order to know and elucidate the addressee of our theological process. However, it can be proved that the circle of suspicion, as if explained by quantum physics, has brief seconds of parallel existence. This works like the theoretical experiment of Shrödinger's cat, when someone must

---

[4]I have used this term positively in my article, 'Both Indecent and Ex-centric: Teaching Feminist Theology for Articulation or for Exoticism' in M. Grey (ed.), *Liberating the Vision: Papers of the Summer School May 1996* (Southampton: LSU, 1997), pp. 71–7.

decide if the cat in the box is alive or dead or both. The parallel existence of the hermeneutical circle of liberation flicks between the matter of things (via community as the first and primordial element of reflection) and something outside the circle (the church, accepted tradition, theological faith or transcendental 'persons' in the Marxist ideological sense we have referred to above), and patriarchal ideology which is at the base of faith and the church's life. This is why the circle is ex-centric because its claimed 'materialism' needs to decide in milliseconds where it stands: with idealism or with materialism.

Can Christianity ever be the material faith of material prophets and messianic figures such as Jesus and Judith, entering Jerusalem on donkeys with people acclaiming them as true prophets of God while dancing in the streets? Or is Liberation Theology condemned to follow the path of idealism because God cannot be thought of outside structural mystical connections? Deception occurs when ideas are disembodied or attributed to genealogies of grand authority, and all this happens by the laws of reversal between facts and ideas, or peoples' lives and Systematic Theology. Of course, we are talking about a theology whose epistemological locus is the *bién sonadas,* women whose lives are already marked by deception and disillusion at economic, political and religious levels. But how much can Liberation Theology confront itself as a fetish which can and must be questioned beyond the approved traditions of the church and dogmas?

What if some Latin American women cannot approve of the role of Mariology of Liberation, a church which refuses to ordain women and a hierarchical exclusive order of family and ways of being church which apparently cannot be reformed but should be dismantled? This is what has stopped Liberation Theology as a movement: Marcos is miles ahead of us. Mexican women sociologists and writers are miles ahead of us. They do not have respect for patriarchal structures any more. They do not want to adapt them, or reinterpret them as we do in Liberation Theology. They created new ideas, organizations and institutions. Meanwhile, no matter how many Basic Ecclesial Communities have been created and dismantled in recent years, this has only been cosmetic surgery, a face-lifting operation in the life of the church.

If it was not for the ex-centricity of a circle of interpretation which is clinging desperately to systematic western patterns of doing theology and the keeping of church traditions which are irrelevant, nothing could have prevented the militant Latin American church producing a 180-degree turn in ecclesiology and theology by rupture and creativity. But no. We are still putting new patches on old wineskins. To have taken a feminist paradigm could have transformed the lives of millions and produced a deep rethinking of economics and politics. But no, the epistemology of the rebellious poor has been evicted from the circle of interpretation. This has been the case of theological evictions.

On Theological Eviction: People with Suitcases and Furniture on the Pavement of Christianity

I was an adolescent when my family faced eviction. We were given 24 hours to pay overdue rents or leave our house. When the police arrived my mother and myself moved out our few belongings on to the street: some bags of clothes, a box with tea and rice, two chairs. The neighbourhood stood still as if in mourning for yet another eviction; another family put out in the street with a few suitcases and a couple of chairs. Economic mystical connections evicted us. In times of hyperinflation and liberal economic experiments, my mother and myself ceased to be people. Economic theories became people, and evicted us because somehow we became things that did not fit their scheme. The economic system was never evicted; only my mother and myself. As political economic systems evict people so does theology. It is easy, and in the same way as the police in my story did it, theology has literally been putting people out on the pavements of the church for centuries. Of course, these were the poor. Women in theology are the androcentric ontological representation of poverty: poverty of reason; poverty of spirituality; poverty of independence; poverty of divine gender representation. Systematic Theology also made me and my mother and my grandmothers homeless.

However, women are not just evicted from theology, they represent borders, the frontiers between logical theology and what has been called a more 'experiential' theology. Women are expected to work theologically around the domestic, private area of life and they have done so well. No male liberation theologian can write the books that women liberationists do, based on reflecting dialogue among women in community, respecting others' opinions and almost disappearing themselves as theologians in order to allow other voices to come through clear and strong. The problem with that is that women have become ghettoized, and their voices are not heard questioning serious issues on the construction of the Trinity or Christology, as I myself have done. As a consequence of that, Liberation Theology allows the addendum, the women's theological notes on issues considered by men to be women's theological issues. There is no attempt to incorporate these voices into Systematic Theology. It is a complacent liberation of theology indeed that, in this day and age, has not stopped to consider, for instance, whether the Trinity is based in a homosocial conceptualization rooted in conceptions of the economy of family production or whether it is possible to talk about a God who is society, as the late Segundo did, without analysing the patriarchal roots of concepts such as society, community and even solidarity. Is it enough to add to the Trinity the addendum '... and women (or the female *Ruach*)'? Still we are in the realm of ideology, detached from reality because evidently we cannot change our lives by playing with theological imaginary, although we may if we change structures of work and reflection such as churches. If not, Christianity may be considered the doctrine of the Pure Land of Ideology.

People get evicted by theology as a method, but not only people. Do you remember my earlier example? Two women were evicted but also two chairs and a box with rice and tea. Liberation Theology has evicted more than just women in its circle of interpretation; it has evicted non-dualistic patterns of thought; non-hierarchical structures of thought and alternatives to non-reproductive and repetitive male epistemology. That is the real difficulty. Liberation Theology has a colonial nature which works by incorporation or assimilation from the margins to the centre. If that were not the case, Liberation Theology would have rejected the ideological principles of the centres of theology such as those concerning its own production process.

How Liberation Theology Evicted People and Replaced Them with Ghosts

Theological illusions in Liberation Theology may be seen as following Marx's schema of the main characteristics of the process of illusion-building (also referred to by Marx as 'ghosts').

Theological Sources

Theological illusions arise from concrete and well-defined sources of theological production. The sources of production in theology include *capital* (theological traditions, Systematic Theology, Moral Theology) which does not come, as Marx says, referring to German philosophy, 'from heaven', but on the contrary, from earth first, and, second, is promoted to heavenly status.

Theological capital is already the result of exploitation and, of course, of struggles against the market exploitation of souls, such as during the Reformation battles against excommunication for economic debts, or money given for the liberation of souls in heaven. If the invisible exploited people of theology are women, this happened because the objectification of women in certain sexual and gender status was beneficial to keep the deep sexual principles of theology intact. Theology is a sexual subject; obsessively sexual in its interpretation of God's birth and parental relations; of men and women and their sexual ordering in society. The objectification of women is based on the ideological processes which always imply reification, and theological understanding made by those mystical connections. The exploitation of women in history is the invisible basic resource upon which the high sexual content of theology and Liberation Theology is developed, that is, the sexual and gender roles which determine relationships. Economy is just a perspective on human relationships. Liberation Theology stands up for the poor but not beyond these mystical connections; and in any way, not beyond reformism.

Of course, people are the source of theology. So, if women are evicted from theology in the multiple co-ordinates of sexuality, race and gender, so are men too. The ghosts which have been taking the place of the real persons of theology are the constructions of 'the poor', 'the Latin American women', very much abstract categories in which people are expected to fit. From the empty pews and the unpopularity of the popular church we learn that liberationists are confusing the ghosts of systematic theological expectations with the real people. At least I can say that myself and a community of women that I know in Latin America born and bred in Liberation Theology are not there, because the ghosts of women in theology are too narrow, too restrictive and obey patriarchal logic and not that of life.

Theological Un/reflections

The second characteristic of theological illusions is that although they develop from the structures of society, they also remain unreflective on them. Liberation Theology has never produced a reflection on the roots of the sexual exploitation of women in the church and in theology, beyond the already passé paradigm of equality which never asked the 'equal to whom?' question. By exploitation we refer here to what Marx described as 'the merging of all … relationships of people in the one relation of usefulness … [and these] relations are subordinated in practice to the one abstract monetary-commercial relation … namely that I derive benefit for myself by doing harm to someone else' (Marx and Engels, 1976, p. 409). The point is that in a way Liberation Theology still subordinates itself to patriarchal understandings, which are useful for the purposes of keeping hierarchically minded ecclesiologies and a systematic theological thinking in accordance with its own rules of importance. Consider for instance the Basic Ecclesial Communities. BECs have been and still are valuable but peripheral activities, as Leonardo Boff recognizes when he claims that the dismantling of BECs has happened in recent years due not only to the New Right policies of the Vatican, but to the fact that BECs were never included in canon law. This means that to say 'We are the church' is not enough; that this needs to be reflected in the church law too. Also liberationists are subordinating their reflection to western Systematic Theology. Could they not have gone into A-Systematic Theology, and created in community a new legal understanding beyond orthodoxy? Original and inspired thinking such as 'structural sin', 'God in history' and 'structures of human sacrifices' were meant to be the beginning of a new Systematic Theology and not just the refashioning of 'sin', 'grace' or 'the sacraments' in liberation style. Moreover, new themes were meant to be not only new issues, but new points of theological orthopraxis; new starting points for reflections based on a new way of doing things. For instance, instead of 'God the Father', a 'God *La Compañera*' (female comrade), written from the perspective of, for instance, unmarried sexually fulfilled militant women in Latin America (as the *Insurgentes* from Mexico) should have become more legitimate and might have become a foundation theme to develop and supplant that old patriarchal/parental metaphor of god-fathers (which by the way, reinforce a colonial mentality too).

That could have led to a militant theology from the guerrilla women of Latin America, for instance, and not a mystification pretending to be real like the androcentric economy of god-father. A theology of liberation in memory of Tania, who died with Guevara in Bolivia, has more to say about women, compassion and images of God than parental patriarchal ideologies.

Magical Theological Steps

The third aspect which concerns us in Liberation Theology is the ideological step of formation characterized by spontaneous configuration of thought and ideas (Marx and Engels, 1976, p. 61). This constitutes a case of un/reflective theology behaving as ideology: in our example of the god-father metaphor, first comes the centuries-old metaphor for God, second, people must fit into it. Third, theology reclaims people back, reorganizing the experience of the poor into the centuries-old metaphor which has been so destructive for women and colonial in its spirit of dependence related to mother churches. It is also one of the main culprits of women's alienation in politics and economics, by re-presenting their childhood assumed nature once again in sacred laws. Do god-father images have anything positive? Yes, they may have. Even the slaves in their compounds heard that God the Father was compassionate; that is not a novelty for liberationists. Moreover, patriarchy excels in its art of divine contrast: God is meant to be terrible and compassionate; jealous and full of understanding, and similar contradictory metaphors which womanists called 'speaking with forked tongues'. So women in patriarchal Latin America will never be liberated with any reflection based on benign fathers. When theology tries to liberate by putting people back in the existent ideological theological constructs, we are into adaptation processes. In the end, the people are re-absorbed in this process by an interpellative process, and the ideological construct appears as 'natural', 'fresh and new' and almost spontaneous truth. In this way, *Tata Dios* (Father God in Quechua and Spanish) becomes an original and grounded piece of popular theology, when it is simply an ideological interpellation.

The other thing to consider here is that the discourse on the poor as the locus of theological reflection, although grounded in experience, is not exempt from false consciousness. At that point, it is easy for theology of liberation to produce interpellation processes, where people tend to recognize themselves, although the only thing that they are doing is recognizing the internalization of their own oppression. Unfortunately this justifies saying disparate things such as 'Latin

American women only care for their children', or, 'the poor have a simple faith and want to remain in that simple faith'. If these things were true, Christianity would not imply a change of consciousness. Christianity would then be revealed even more clearly as ideology. Ideological reflections create this aura of spontaneous reflection, of ideas not consciously related to their mechanisms of production. It is the same with a popular theology such as Liberation Theology, which enjoys the spontaneity of patriarchalism and never distrusts its own dualistic and androcentric epistemology because it is taken so much for granted.

Theological Inversions

We arrive now at the moment of theological inversion or the *camera obscura* effect produced between theological reflections and life. Theology of liberation has been under the illusion that the best of Christianity expresses people's needs and struggles. In reality, this is an inversion of the fact that the best of the liberationist approach to Christianity is not Christian at all. It is in fact the way that people traditionally live in community, the courage and resistance of Latin Americans under oppression and their intelligence in the strategical consideration of the struggle.

It is interesting to notice that the main task of liberationists has been to remove Christian passivity and attitudes of resignation which were precisely brought to our people's lives by centuries of Christian theology. Therefore, if the world has enlightened the church and not, unfortunately, vice versa, one of the main difficulties with Liberation Theology may lie in the fact of believing in the camera obscura effect. In fact, for a theology which claims to be a theology from the political, one must reflect on the fact that it was Eva Perón who gave women the right to vote in Argentina in full opposition to the church and Christian theology. Since then, the issue-based Liberation Theology which likes to reflect on politics and economy has not advanced into issues of women and politics in Latin America, but perhaps will one day be illuminated by the work of secular thinkers. Many women like myself feel more identified with Latin American feminists than with theologians representing an undemocratic church, whose androcentric consciousness is stagnant. This means that if our struggles could find a point of appropriate theological reflection in Liberation Theology, it would happen only after Liberation Theology, as a second act, learns more about its own androcentric spirituality, and perhaps even then it will not be able to reach many women in our continent. Theology is a limited affair, and only accepting this point, perhaps, we must be able to liberate theology from its ex-centricity, towards a true materialist circle of interpretation. 'Religion, once formed, always contains traditional material', said Engels (Engels, 1935, p. 55), and not even biblical exegesis can save us from the effect of that.

Class-Motivated System of Theological Deception

The fact is that we are always, in one way or another, worshipping systems of production disguised as sacred systems. Liberation theologians struggle for forms of socialism and participatory democracy and therefore try to produce a theological reflection reflecting those ideals. However, the continuous allegiance to church structures which are western inventions, obeying particular economic patterns of exploitation and conceptions of humanity, has damaged or partialized this project. Basic Christian Communities remained as part of the picturesque scene of the Latin American church, in the sense that they were unable to redefine power. It is very romantic to say that 'BECs are the church'. If that was really the case, nobody would have recognized any power or authority outside the BECs, including women's ordination or changes in the hierarchical ruling of the church. In the case of women's historical struggle for liberation, Liberation Theology has become dangerous because it is more of an obstacle than a help in such a struggle. If women in Latin America need to come back to reread their Virgin Mary every so often, their awareness-raising process would not advance very far. Liberation Theology also produces false consciousness among women because of the limitation of its dialectics. Christianity, as in the camera obscura example, needs to present itself as the first and best of the human rights struggles. If women claim their human rights, the same as gays, lesbians or transvestites, we need to find these struggles first of all represented by Christianity, and this cannot be the case. Even the historical Jesus had a limited historical consciousness; he was not outside the context of his time, language and culture. He may have been advanced for *his* time, but not necessarily for ours.

In this last point we reach the core of our questioning process to Liberation Theology. If theology is a second act even in Liberation Theology, then the struggle must have taught liberationists about a Latin American society built upon heavy patriarchal systems of submission and mastery; of violence in the domestic and public realms; of intolerance and authoritative regimes based upon heavy androcentric hierarchies. And liberationists may know by now how the pastoral letters they write every so often in relation to, for instance, family issues, rely on a concept of family which is immoral, since it is still based on property values, and leads to violence and abuse as also to poverty: not only material poverty but the poverty of being which threatens women in patriarchal cultures. For many women like myself, the worship of the Virgin Mary, with all its rereading and energy-wasting process of reinterpretation, stands against the life of many Latin American women. Idealist theologians can be quick rescuing *images,* pictures and historical insights and exegesis here and there in relation to Mary and issues of women and power, but materialist theologians go to life. Rereadings cannot answer for 500 years of women's oppression in Marianist Latin America.

¿Bién sonados?

Probably yes. Probably we are going to be sooner or later *bién sonados* as a church in Latin America if our discourses continue betraying a materialist circle of interpretation and following instead a method of ideology-building. Liberation Theology must avoid the pitfall of becoming the remake of the Jesuitical missions, where Latin Americans, especially women, needed to embrace that childlike quality that colonial discourses adore. That which domesticates and finally evicts us exists in theology as ideology, and as such it is the enemy. Even among the poor communities false androcentric consciousness exists, and its demythification should be a priority for liberationists who fail to see the links between exclusion, globalization processes, neo-Liberalism and patriarchal epistemology. For many faithful Latin American people, the struggle has involved leaving the church and its alliance with the oppressive state. As painful as it is, it seems the only option when theology has become a damaging ideology. For many Latin American women, in search for really alternative political, economic and religious systems apart from old Latin American patriarchy, Liberation Theology may also become the enemy because after 30 years of praxis-orientated reflection the changes produced are too superficial and too slow. It will not do for our daughters.

The Right to Insurrection

Carmen Bullosa, the famous Mexican writer, has a beautiful story in which she contrasts the life and fate of a hill and a centuries-old Roman Catholic cathedral in the middle of Mexico City.[5] Bullosa tells us about their significant location: opposite and facing each other, the Catholic cathedral is falling apart from old age, while the hill keeps growing with animal and natural life. The cathedral, Bullosa points out, is surrounded by contractors propping up its walls and supporting its roof and pillars from the danger of collapse. Meanwhile, the hill which was the site of an old Aztec temple demolished during the *Conquista* has been growing again after the destruction of its trees and life. Growing in size year by year and also growing in life. The hill keeps flourishing, its vegetable nature seems to be unstoppable. Meanwhile life has been leaving the cathedral. People have left and few newcomers are expected. The congregation has been reduced, and there is a feeling of things becoming too old and fragile. However, on the hill, life is bursting out: flowers and birds, and all sorts of insects and animals grow there now. Lovers meet there too. The hill is back with a passion for life that by the justice of time has prevailed against that theological model which came to our continent to kill life and to distort people's quest for the sacred with a modern theological ideology.

---

[5] See Carmen Bullosa, 'El que gira la Cabeza y el Fuego: Historia y Novela' in Kate Duncan and Electra Caridis, *Beyond Solitude: Dialogues between Europe and Latin America* (Birmingham: The University of Birmingham, 1995), pp. 180–96.

This metaphor from Bullosa says in a nutshell why we are going to be *bién sonados* if we keep propping up and introducing cosmetic surgical alterations to the theological monuments of the past. There is an epistemology from the poor, and from the thinking, reflecting and dissident poor. That epistemology, like the Mexican hill, has been flourishing with the disorder and chaos of life that theologians fear so much: the epistemology of women's movements, of lesbian and gay human rights in Latin America, the epistemology of Freire and Sub Comandante Marcos, of Augusto Boal and Marta Lamas, of Pichon Riviere and Alfredo Moffat teaching beggars in Buenos Aires to become psychotherapists and work in their communities under the bridges. Years ago, J. Severino Croatto taught me that the key hermeneutical principle of Liberation Theology was just that, 'liberation'. Now, I would say that it is 'insurrection'. It was Unamuno who claimed that Christianity was a desperate way out towards hope, but without the right to insurrection from Systematic Theology and its ideological methods it becomes another form of escapism. The only way out towards hope in Liberation Theology and in Christianity in general is to recognize and work with an epistemology from the poor as it is presented in feminist epistemology, non-dualistic, non-hierarchical and relational. Only then, when marginal epistemologies become central, do the suppressed margins become central too, and theology becomes marginal in its desire to serve the centre by default. Only then will the real lives of ordinary Latin American women become more important than Mariologies and Trinities. And ideas will become ideas again, and people will return to being people. And this would be a liberation of theology from the false processes of personhood assumed by the idealism often called theology, and the end of mystical connections of theology and politics.

46. J. Kameron Carter – Interlude on Christology and Race

Gregory of Nyssa as Abolitionist Intellectual

If [the human being] is in the likeness of God, and rules the whole earth, and has been granted authority over everything on earth from God, who [can be] his buyer, tell me? who [can be] his seller? To God alone belongs this power; or rather, not even to God himself. For *his gracious gifts,* it says, *are irrevocable* (Rom. 11:29). God would not therefore reduce the human race to slavery, since he himself, when we had been enslaved to sin, spontaneously recalled us to freedom. But if God does not enslave what is free, who is he that sets his own power above God's?

5. —Gregory of Nyssa, Homily IV on Ecclesiastes

In part I of this book, I argue that the modern invention of race or the story of its naturalization is a problem that is pseudotheological or religious in character. More specifically, I argue that behind the modern problem of race is the problem of how Christianity and Western civilization came to be thoroughly identified with each other, a problem linked to the severance of Christianity from its Jewish roots. As Christianity came to be severed from its Jewish roots, it was remade into the cultural property of the West, the religious basis for justifying the colonial conquest that took off in the fifteenth century with the Portuguese and the Spanish, and that reached a zenith both in performance and in intellectual theorization as colonial and intellectual power shifted to France, England, and Germany beginning in the sixteenth century and culminating in the nineteenth century. Remade into cultural and political property and converted into an ideological instrument to aid and abet colonial conquest, Christianity became a vehicle for the religious articulation of whiteness, though increasingly masked to the point of near invisibility.

Thus, with the advent of modernity, the problem is no longer simply Constantinianism or even neo-Constantianism (as John Howard Yoder or others might say).[1] Rather, it is now the problem of what I would like to call the color of Constantinianism. To raise the issue of color or race in the constitution of modernity is to reckon with how modem political power came to articulate itself not merely in religious terms as if abstracted from the body. It is to reckon with how it does so precisely through the protocols of the body (politic), but now conceived as a body (politic) that bears race. That is, it does so through imagining certain bodies as obedient bodies and other bodies as bodies to be obeyed. The frame of obedient bodies in relationship to bodies to be obeyed, a frame which functions through analytics of race is the frame of the modern body politic. To reckon with this problem, as I seek to do in part I with its focus on the late-eighteenth-century maturing of racial discourse, is to reckon with the political economy of whiteness as the perennial, though increasingly invisible, theological problem of our times.

In part II, I offer a reading of the field of African American religious studies as attempting, through its interpretations of black religion, to theorize religion beyond whiteness and theorize black existence beyond the enslaving and otherwise deleterious effects of the "modernity/coloniality" horizon.[2] While the

---

[1]John Howard Yoder, *The Priestly Kingdom: Social Ethics as Gospel* (Notre Dame: University of Notre Dame Press, 1984), 141–44.

[2]Walter Mignolo, *The Darker Side of the Renaissance: Literacy, Territoriality, and Colonization,* 2nd ed. (Ann Arbor: University of Michigan Press, 2003). I am persuaded by Mignolo's claim and the mountain of evidence he presents showing that the "European 'discovery' of a 'New World'" is the constitutive feature of "the emergence of modernity toward the end of the fifteenth century." Modernity, he shows, is inextricably bound to the processes of coloniality. These processes entail "constitution of the Spanish Empire, the expulsion of the Moors, and the success of trans-Atlantic expansion" (xi). Coloniality is the "darker side of the renaissance," the darker side of modernity. As he says, "coloniality is constitutive of modernity. There cannot be modernity, as has been conceived and implemented through the past five hundred years of history, without coloniality" (453). But Mignolo presses further, bolstering claims I make in part I of this book that the colonial difference that underwrites the modern world "has been based on racial classification," which itself is tied to religion (451).

field has made and continues to make important intellectual strides, its efforts in this regard have had mixed—and, indeed, I contend mostly unsuccessful—results, principally because of either inadequate or no engagements at all with the fundamental problem: how white intellectual formation is in fact a religious, cultural, colonializing, and colonizing formation. In other words, whiteness as a theological problem has been insufficiently treated. At its heart is a problematic vision of the human as closed within itself, sealed off from possibilities of cultural intimacy and thus reciprocity. Rather than the site of intimacy, culture becomes the site of closure and containment. Critical in this is how theological discourse itself was deployed in the interests of cultural closure or of European hegemony over the rest of the world. How did theology come to function in this way? A symbiotic discourse of race and of religion, operating under a notion of the universal, became the new inner architecture of theology: the racial-religious discourse of whiteness. Having insufficiently named and treated this problem, black religious intellectuals have unwittingly perpetuated the theological problem of whiteness. That is, in pursuit of liberation (a goal I share) they have tended to submit non-white existence to theological closure precisely through their appreciation of black folks as contained racial-religious objects rather than as theological subjects in relationship to YHWH as God of the covenant.

Naming the Unnameable Problem: On the Theological Interpretation of Scripture

To set up the arguments of the three chapters making up the final part of this book in which I consider how New World Afro-Christianity redirects modern racial discourse precisely by redirecting modern Christianity, this interlude briefly engages an aspect of the thought of the fourth-century theologian—called at the Seventh Ecumenical Council of 787 "the father of the fathers"—Gregory of Nyssa. What interests me are the defining features of Gregory's vision of the just society: his

---

Mignolo has his intellectual finger on the fact that coloniality as linked to raciality is tied to—indeed, is situated within—the theological imagination of Renaissance and subsequent modernist intellectuals, an imagination that, certainly for the Renaissance intellectuals, is tied to their Aristotelian and often Thomist/Roman Catholic sensibilities. For the subsequent intellectuals of the seventeenth through the nineteenth centuries, the religious optic through which coloniality and raciality will come to work (as the center of gravity shifts from the Catholicism of southern Europe in Spain and Portugal to France, England, and Germany in northern Europe) is principally Protestantism.

Mignolo's concern in The *Darker Side of the Renaissance* is not with the Protestant intellectuals of the seventeenth through the nineteenth centuries. His concern is with the Renaissance intellectuals mainly of the fifteenth and sixteenth centuries. His breakthrough, from my perspective as a theologian, is that he grasps that coloniality functions within and is a modulation of theology as a discourse. My qualm with Mignolo's account—and it is a significant one—is that he insufficiently narrates the nature of the shifts that took place within theology itself as a discourse that made colonial conquest amenable to discursive articulation inside of the discourse of theology in the first place. Speaking, to this larger issue must await another day.

unequivocal stance against "the peculiar institution" of slavery and his call for the manumission of all slaves. I am interested in reading Gregory as a fourth-century "abolitionist" intellectual. I speak anachronistically but nevertheless accurately. His antislavery outlook surpassed not only St. Paul's more moderate (but to be fair to Paul, in its own moment, revolutionary) stance on the subject but also those of all ancient intellectuals—pagan, Jewish, and Christian—from Aristotle to Cicero and from Augustine in the Christian West to his contemporary, the golden-mouthed preacher himself, John Chrysostom in the Christian East.

Indeed, the world would have to wait another fifteen centuries—until the nineteenth century, late into the modern abolitionist movement—before such an unequivocal stance against slavery would appear again.[3] And in comparison with the late-modern abolitionist arguments of such luminaries as William Lloyd Garrison, Maria Lydia Childs, and Harriet Beecher Stowe, Gregory of Nyssa's antislavery argument still surpasses. How so? Gregory's abolitionism expresses an exegetical imagination that reads against rather than within the social order. I return to this claim near the end of this interlude. The question I seek to raise now is this: What enabled Gregory to do this? How is his hermeneutical practice as a reader—and, more important, as a pastor and preacher—of the Scriptures able to accomplish many of the ends of a hermeneutics of (feminist, postcolonial, or liberationist) suspicion, while at the same time be more, not less, radical than such reading strategies?

In answering this question, I argue that it was the theological imagination fueling Gregory's exegetical and homiletic practices, and ultimately his orientation as an ascetic thinker of the spiritual life, that enabled his radical theological abolitionism. Moreover, I am suggesting a connection between the theological imagination out of which Gregory operates and the theological imagination that was emerging within certain currents of Afro-Christian faith in its New World dawning. But to return to Gregory, this alone—recognizing that Gregory's abolitionism was tied to his ability to read Scripture theologically and thus interpret reality theologically—is insufficient to explain his historical uniqueness on the issue. I say this because Gregory's Cappodocian contemporaries and fellow champions of Nicene orthodoxy—I am thinking here of his elder brother Basil of Caesarea and his friend Gregory of Nazianzus, who became known simply as "the Theologian"—were also *theological* readers of Scripture and interpreters of reality, who in contrast to Gregory accepted slavery as a part of the social order.

Gregory of Nazianzus advanced a theological position on slavery that was basically identical to the position Augustine in the Christian West develops in his magnum

---

[3]Mason Lowance, ed., *Against Slavery: An Abolitionist Reader* (New York: Penguin, 2000). Lowance says that it was not until late in the modem abolitionist movement (1830–1865) that "'gradualism' was replaced with an aggressive form of protest that led to the abolition of slavery with the Thirteenth Amendment to the [U.S.] Constitution in 1865" (87).

opus, *City of God*: slavery, Gregory of Nazianzus says, is a sinful distinction.[4] It is a distinction that arises because of sin, and therefore—and here is the problem—it is a distinction to be accepted as part of the present reality.[5] The esteemed Basil says the same thing: "In this world, then, it is thus that men are made slaves, but they who have escaped poverty or war, or do not require the tutelage of others, are free."[6] Slavery, Gregory and Basil are saying, is, simply put, just the way things are. But Basil goes even further, for while affirming that "no one is a slave by nature" as a part of the argument he works out in defense of the divinity of the Holy Spirit against the Pneumatomachians (those who fought against the Spirit's codivinity with the Father and the eternal Son), Basil nevertheless says the following in his *theological* interpretation of Noah's statement in Genesis 9:25 ("Curse be Canaan; a servant of servants shall he be unto his brother"):

> Men are either brought under a yoke of slavery by conquest; ... or they are enslaved on account of poverty; ... or, by a wise and mysterious dispensation, the worst children are by their fathers' order condemned to serve the wiser and the better; and this any righteous inquirer into the circumstances would declare to be not a sentence of condemnation but a benefit. For it is more profitable that the man who, through lack of intelligence, has no natural principle of rule within himself, should become the chattel [*ktêma*] of another, to the end that, being guided by the reason of his master, he may be like a chariot with a charioteer, or a boat with a steersman seated at the tiller [an allusion to Plato's *Republic*].[7]

Having said this, Basil then tries to sand down the jagged edges of his statement by enlisting a problematic theology of creation: "Even though one man be called master and another servant," he says, "nevertheless, both in view of our mutual equality of rank and as chattels of our Creator, we are all fellow slaves."[8]

Thus Basil employs a model of mastery and slavery to understand the relationship between the Creator and the creation. Insofar as this is the case, the sociopolitical logic Basil employs, the logic of the body (politic), is, potentially at least, tied to his broader understanding of the identity of the Creator. Basil's vision of the social order, in other words, in which necessarily some are slaves and others are free, functions

---

[4]"Sin," Augustine says, "is the primary cause of servitude, in the sense of a social status in which one man is compelled to be subjected to another man. Nor does this befall a man, save by the decree of God, who is never unjust and who knows how to impose appropriate punishments on different sinners." *De civitate dei* 19.15.

[5]"Such, with Christ who ever elevates my mind, is my best wealth: no tracts of fertile land, no fair groves, no herds of kine, no flocks of fat sheep. Nor yet devoted slaves, my own race who have been separated from me by an ancient tyranny. To people sprung from one land it gave the double name of free and slave. Nay, not from one land, from one God. And so came into being this sinful distinct on." Gregory of Nazianzus, *De rebus suis* 80–82, *Patrologiae cursus completus: Series Graeca* 37.976A; quoted in *St. Gregory of Nazianzus: Three Poems*, trans. Denis Molaise Meehan (Washington, D.C.: Catholic University Press of America, 1987), 27.

[6]Basil, *De spiritu sancto* 20.51, in *Sources chrétiennes* 17.204; *Nicene and Post-Nicene Fathers: Second Series*, 2.8.32.

[7]Ibid.

[8]Ibid.

as a substitute for the doctrine of creation at the same time that Basil maintains an "orthodox" theology of creation. Indeed, his orthodox theology of creation gives him a grammar to articulate and thus read Scripture theologically but yet within the social order.[9] In short, both Basil and Gregory of Nazianzus, as did Augustine in the West, made their peace with the ancient institution of slavery and with "the sinful distinction," as Gregory of Nazianzus calls it, between some persons who are slaves and some who are free, some to be bodies of obedience and others to be bodies to be obeyed.

Gregory of Nyssa as abolitionist intellectual theologically refuses this settlement, whereas his Cappadocian comrades read Scripture in such a way as to *theologically*—yes, *theologically*—accept it. This presents a disturbing situation for those who advocate reading the Scriptures theologically, a situation that can no longer be evaded; namely, that one can read Scripture within the theological grammar of the Christian faith and yet do so in such a way as to read *within* and indeed theologically sanction, if not sanctify, as Michel Foucault says, "the order of things."[10]

This all begs the question that I ultimately want to get at in what follows: What is the deeper moment within Gregory of Nyssa's theological interpretation of Scripture that causes him to read against rather than within the social order? For all theological interpretations of Scripture are not alike—as the formation of modern biblical scholarship from the eighteenth into the nineteenth century, that moment when the modern theological interpretation of Scripture as linked to cultural and nationalist ambitions intellectually took off, makes abundantly clear.[11] What is it about Gregory's practice of reading Scripture theologically that makes him an abolitionist intellectual? What compels him to argue for the unqualified manumission of all slaves, a stance that distinguishes him not only from nontheological readers but also from other would-be theological readers of Scripture? It is this question that must be answered. And so, let me begin answering it with an exploration of Gregory's

---

[9]Daniel F. Strarmara Jr., whose fine essay alerted me to this passage in *On the Holy Spirit,* claims that Basil makes the theological move toward a theology of creation in which God is conceived of as Master because "his Christian conscience must have bothered him" in making the claim that some are necessarily slaves while others are necessarily free, and that this is a good thing. Daniel F. Stramara Jr., "Gregory of Nyssa: An Ardent Abolitionist?," *St. Vladimir's Theological Quarterly* 41, no. 1 (1997): 41. As a conjectural suggestion, this may be the case. However, I am unpersuaded. For it seems to me that Basil's theological claim does not arise from a pricked conscience. Rather, it reveals the theological-intellectual consistency of his conscience.

[10]Michel Foucault, The *Order of Things: An Archeology of the Human Sciences* (New York: Pantheon, 1971; reprint, 1994).

[11]In this regard, see Susannah Heschel, *Abraham Geiger and the Jewish Jesus* (Chicago: University of Chicago Press, 1998); Shawn Kelley, *Racializing Jesus: Race, Ideology and the Formation of Modem Biblical Scholarship* (London: Routledge, 2002); James Pasto, "W. M. L. De Wette and the Invention of Post-Exilic Judaism: Political Historiography and Christian Allegory in Nineteenth-Century German Biblical Scholarship," in *Jews, Antiquity, and the Nineteenth-Century Imagination,* ed. Hayim Lapin and Dale B. Martin (Potomac: University Press of Maryland, 2003); Jonathan Sheehan, *The Enlightenment Bible: Translation, Scholarship, Culture* (Princeton: Princeton University Press, 2005); and George S. Williamson, *The Longing for Myth in Germany: Religion and Aesthetic Culture from Romanticism to Nietzsche* (Chicago: University of Chicago Press, 2005).

exegetical imagination in the *locus classicus* of his position against slavery: Homily IV on Ecclesiastes. From there I look more closely at the theological imagination fueling Gregory's practice of reading Scripture. Central here will be his complex Christological understanding of the image of God, which admittedly is far from exhaustively though I hope adequately dealt with here.

The Exegetical Imagination: Gregory's Fourth Homily on Ecclesiastes

Gregory's homilies *On Ecclesiastes* were a part of the earlier commentaries he wrote on the ascetical and spiritual life of the Christian reader of Scripture.[12] For Gregory, the goal of the ascetical and spiritual life was the same as the goal of the theologico-intellectual life: the contemplation of God's activity in the impoverished, suffering Christ at the cross. As Gregory argues in his *Antirrheticus against Apollinarius* and reaffirmed in his *Catechetical Orations,* it is "the God revealed through the Cross" that is the subject of Christian theology. This God is revealed in the eternal Christ, wounded from the foundation of the world, which includes his temporal wounding, in the economy of redemption.

Mediating the task of theologically contemplating the eternal Christ and the ascetical practice of spiritually contemplating the eternal Christ is the task of exegetically contemplating the eternal Christ. What this means is that through the mediation of exegesis, which is to say, through the scriptural contemplation of Christ—a task, mind you, that comes into full bloom in the work of preaching and the ministry of the sacraments—theological contemplation (or the task of theology) and ascetical contemplation (or the task of sanctification, or living in the Holy Spirit) have, in the end, the same goal: namely, drawing the reader of the Scriptures more deeply into the unfathomable mystery of the eternal Christ. In being drawn into this mystery or in making increasing progress into Christ, the one engaged in theological contemplation and the one engaged in ascetical contemplation—the scholar on the one hand and the layperson on the other; pulpit and pew—are both engaged in the singular task of having their desires shaped and reshaped by the object of their affection. This is accomplished precisely by coming into deeper union with that object, namely, Christ.

In this regard, the believer's existence as a lover of Christ—one's identity, shall we say—is ecstatic (from *ek-stasis*; this theme returns again in the postlude on Maximus the Confessor as "anticolonialist" intellectual). That is, the self is most fully itself only

---

[12]This summary draws on the interpretations of Gregory of Nyssa offered by Jean Daniélou and John Behr, introduction to *From Glory to Glory: Texts from Gregory of Nyssa's Mystical Writings,* ed. Jean Daniélou and Herbert Musurillo (New York: Scribner's, 1961), and John Behr, *The Nicene Faith,* vol. 2 of *The Formation of Christian Theology* (Crestwood, N.Y.: St. Vladimir's Seminary Press, 2004), 458–73.

as it exits the self, only as it exits those modes of identity tied to this worldly order of things, tied to its modulations and modes of power, and tied to the ways this worldly order has structured our loves. The self is most fully itself as it exits that worldly reality—the "cosmos," in Johannine terms; the "totality" as postmodern, critical theorists, might say—so as to enter into a new self, into a new order of love, and thus a new way of being in the world. This new order is the Triune order as "the structure of supreme love."[13] One enters this new mode of existence (*tropos tês huparxeos*), and so dons Christian identity, by entering into the person (*hypostasis*) of the eternal Christ, Jesus of Nazareth. This is the goal, Gregory contends, of both theology (that discourse that reflects on these matters) and the ascetical or spiritual disciplines as carried out in *praktikê,* the life of Christian praxis.

Christian identity, in this respect, then, is leaving behind one mode of identity and ecstatically entering into another. Moreover, this movement by which the Christian is the one who enters into Christ is, according to Gregory of Nyssa, an infinite or unending movement. Referring to Paul's participial usage of the Greek verb *epiktaomai* in Philippians 3:13, he calls it *epektêsis.* While a tome could be written simply on Gregory's fascinating understanding of the Triune God as infinite,[14] what I stress here is actually the flip side of Gregory's notion of an infinite, ecstatic progress or journey into the infinite God; namely, that the infinite movement or ecstasy into the eternal Christ on the part of both the theologian and the ascetic, through the contemplation of the Scriptures, *is* an exiting of the reality of this worldly order of things. It is an exiting of the reality in which love and desire are idolatrously turned back on the creature to become, as Maximus the Confessor says, a structure of tyranny (*turannos*). What the exegetical contemplation of Christ accomplishes, then, is the liberation of the reader of Scripture from tyrannical self-enclosure precisely by reconstituting the reader's identity in Christ. In other words, the exegetical contemplation of Scripture makes readers more than textualists. Contemplative-exegetical reading, as a form of what Paul J. Griffiths calls "religious reading," is in this respect world transforming inasmuch as it reconstitutes the world of the reader by making the reader an inhabitant, as it were, of the world of the religious text.[15] But even here Griffiths must be glossed, for it is all too easy for such "narrative theology" reading strategies to be textualizing strategies and as such fall subject to Gregory's and Maximus's "tyranny" critique. Contemplative-exegetical reading is the reading that is part and parcel of be made *ek-static* to the reigning order of things. Such reading is a feat of asceticism (*askesis*). It is a feat of asceticism with respect to how

---

[13]This phrase comes from Dumitru Staniloae, *Theology and the Church,* trans. Robert Barringer (Crestwood, N.Y.: St. Vladimir's Seminary Press, 1980).

[14]This is what is taken up in David Bentley Hart, *The Beauty of the Infinite: The Aesthetics of Christian Truth* (Grand Rapids, Mich.: Eerdmans, 2003).

[15]Paul J. Griffiths, *Religious Reading: The Place of Reading in the Practice of Religion* (New York: Oxford University Press, 1999), especially 40–41.

one has been positioned in social-space and with respect to how it inculcates one into a different "habitus," as Pierre Bourdieu would say.[16] In other words, such reading remakes, rather than reinscribes, identity. Indeed, in Gregory's case—and in the cases of Briton Hammon (chapter 6), Frederick Douglass (chapter 7), and Jarena Lee (chapter 8) in this book—such reading structures Christian identity and one's relationship to the social order.

If Gregory's later work, especially his massive homiletic commentary on the *Songs of Songs* and his treatise on the *Life of Moses,* reflects on what it means to journey into the luminous darkness of the eternal Christ and so, through him, to progress "from glory to glory" *into* the Triune God, then his earlier homiletic commentary *On Ecclesiastes* explores the flip side of this, which is the opening gesture in the journey into Christ. It explores what it means to *exit* our worldly loves so as to inhabit Christ, or as Paul says to be "in Christ" (*en Christô*) as one's locus of identity and seat of existential orientation. It is in this context that one must situate Gregory's reading of Ecclesiastes generally, and certainly his interpretation of the words found in Ecclesiastes 2:7: "I got me slaves and slave-girls, and homebred slaves were born for me, and much property in cattle and sheep became mine, above all who had been before me in Jerusalem."

On Gregory's reading, Ecclesiastes, the Preacher, has been telling the story of his journey toward wisdom. But that journey has required the Preacher to reorder his loves and thus recognize the proper creaturely status of things. This status is one in which objects disclose God (and thus are theological subjects in their own right) and not merely objects to be owned or possessed. It has required his acknowledgment of his false loves to the social order and that he leave behind those false loves and the worldly order that has structured his loves toward fleeting, creaturely objects. The

---

[16]Bourdieu's notion of habitus does massive work in his theory of sociological knowledge and his understanding of practice, as guided by habitus, in structuring the social order. Key to what Bourdieu means when he speaks of habitus in relationship to practices is this: Practices are constitutive of structures as well as determined by them. Hence, structures are themselves socially constructed through the everyday practices of agents. Bourdieu's concept of habitus points to the integration of practices with structures and how those everyday practices (in this case the academic reading practices of an intellectual class) are both the product of a certain structural domain (i.e., the university) and the reproduction through those very practices of the structure along with the class-consciousness or dispositions of that structural domain. Thus at the core of Bourdieu's notion of habitus (and practice) is a theory, then, of intellectuals or *homo academicus.* Such a theory stresses the specific symbolic interests that shape the cultural production of an intellectual class. In the case we address here, the cultural production at issue is that of scriptural exegesis. With recourse to the notion of habitus, I seek to call attention to the political economy of scriptural exegesis as a particular from of symbolic or cultural capital. Indeed, I seek to redirect that economy in the direction of exegetical contemplation, a contemplation structured by and then filling out the domain of Jewish covenantal life in relationship to YHWH. This "filling out" entails Gentile incorporation into the Jews' relationship to YHWH (cultural intimacy) through the mediation of one from among this people. This one is the Jew Jesus of Nazareth. This is the horizon where exegesis must function. In what follows I offer a reading of Gregory of Nyssa on these matters that supports this contention. Among other writings, Bourdieu explains his notion of habitus in *The Logic of Practice* (Stanford: Stanford University Press, 1990), 54. I have been greatly helped in my understanding of Bourdieu on practice, habitus, and his theory of intellectuals by David Swartz, *Culture and Power: The Sociology of Pierre Bourdieu* (Chicago: University of Chicago Press, 1997).

Preacher's words for doing this, for both acknowledging what he has loved falsely and leaving behind the worldly order of those false loves in pursuit of wisdom, are "All is vanity" (Eccl. 1:2). Gregory interprets the Preacher in Ecclesiastes 2:2–11 as continuing his account of, indeed as confessing, the ways in which he has loved wrongly, how he has loved the creature and ultimately himself over the Creator. Opening the homily, he says, "We still find the occasion for confession controlling [the Preacher's] argument" (*HE*, 74).[17] What is the Preacher now confessing? He is confessing his participation in a slave-owning society by having slaves among his possessions. The Preacher is making a public acknowledgment of how vain and futile he has been in this regard and that he could no longer participate in a social order predicated on slaveholding and at the same time be a follower of YHWH or make progress in wisdom.

Indeed, Gregory reads the Preacher as announcing the most serious indictment of the life he used to live. The Preacher was arrogant and smugly comfortable in that arrogance, perhaps so much so that he was blind to the depths of his own vain sinfulness. "For what is such a gross example of arrogance," Gregory has the Preacher ask, "in the matters enumerated above [that is, in the prior verses of chapter 1 of Ecclesiastes]— an opulent house, and an abundance of vines, and ripeness in vegetable-plots, and collecting waters in pools and channeling them in gardens—as for a human being to think himself the master of his own kind" (*HE*, 74)? Slaveholding, the Preacher comes to see, is the attitude and practice of mastery. It is the very expression and "feeling of Pride" inasmuch as it "turns the property of God into his own property and arrogates dominion to his own kind, so as to think himself the owner of men and women" (73). What does this do, asks Gregory, but lead the one who would be master "[to overstep] his own nature through pride, regarding himself as something different from his subordinates" (73)? It is this acknowledgment or public confession on the part of the Preacher of the vanity entailed in his getting for himself "slaves and slave-girls, and [that] homebred slaves were born for [him]" as part of his concerted campaign to accumulate "much property in cattle and sheep" (Eccl. 2:7) beyond what anyone else "who had been before [him] in Jerusalem" (2:9) had accumulated that opens the way for Gregory's fierce and unparalleled denunciation of slaveholding.

His denunciation begins by calling into question the chief supposition of the slaveholding system: the anthropological distinction between superior and inferior that grounds the logic of mastery and slavery. Drawing perhaps on the argument of his elder brother Basil, Gregory invokes a doctrine of creation that levels all relations within the created order. Since only God is Lord and Master, and therefore everything is subject to God, there can be within the created order no such distinction between human beings as master and slave. What this means for Gregory is that with respect to itself or within the many relations constitutive of it, human nature is free. Human nature is not bound by ownership. This

---

[17]All references to HE are from the translation of 'Homilies on Ecclesiastes' in *Gregory of Nyssa, Homilies on Ecclesiastes: An English Version with Supporting Studies*, ed. Stuart G. Hall (New York: de Gruyter, 1993).

comes out in Gregory's comment on the Preacher's public confession, "'I got me slaves and slave-girls.' What do you mean" in confessing this? Gregory asks (*HE*, 73). Having raised the question, he answers it by beginning his full argument against slavery:

> You condemn man to slavery, when his nature is free and is self-determining [*eleuthera ... kai autexousios*], and you legislate in competition with God, overturning his law for the human species. The one made on the specific terms that he should be the owner of the earth, and appointed to government by the Creator—him you bring under the yoke of slavery, as though defying and fighting against the divine decree. (*HE*, 73)

Gregory's use of the terms *eleutheros* (free) and *autexousios* (self-determining) to describe the condition of human nature is crucial here. In an essay on Gregory's fourth homily on Ecclesiastes, Maria Mercedès Bergadá has argued that *eleutheros* covers freedom in the civil and political arena as opposed to external constraint in these spheres, while *autexousios* refers to that freedom by which the self is not held in internal constraint or bondage to itself, to its own desires.[18]

In employing these terms, Gregory points to human nature's freedom from tyranny on all levels, both external and internal tyranny. This means that human nature evinces a sovereignty that itself is an image and likeness of the sovereign God, who is bound by no constraints, neither "external" in relationship to creation nor "internal" in relationship either to the Triune persons themselves or to the divine nature that the persons in their relations to each other enact.[19] Thus, in the proper sense, God is free; while in the analogical sense, humans are free—that is, in "analogy" to God.[20] This means that human freedom is an analogue of and as such participates in the divine freedom. This begins to come out and do important work for Gregory's argument in the lines following the preceding quotation in which Gregory invokes one of the Genesis stories of creation—highlighting on the one hand its language of the human being as ruler and on the other its language of the human being existing in the image and likeness of God—to bolster his case against slavery. In other words, Gregory begins to read the Scriptures intertextually—Genesis and Ecclesiastes as informing each other— in order to unearth a scriptural grammar for a theological anthropology that makes the case for him against slavery. Given the importance of the passage, I quote it in full:

> You have forgotten the limits of your authority, and that your rule is confined to control over things without reason. For it says *Let them rule over winged creatures and fishes*

---

[18]Maria Mercedès Bergadá, "La Condamnation de l'esclavage dans l'homélie IV," in *HE* 188.

[19]I put "externally" and "internally" in quotation marks here to signal that from God's vantage there is no external or internal. This distinction arises from the vantage of the creature.

[20]I am using "analogy" here in the theologically technical sense of the analogate actually participating in, but within a broader difference from, what it is analogous to. This is precisely what makes it an analogy and not a mere semblance. This is developed in P. Erich Przywara, *Polarity: A German Catholic's Interpretation of Religion*, trans. A. C. Bouquet (London: Oxford University Press, 1935), and more fully in Erich Przywara, *Analogia Entis: Metaphysik—Ur-Struktur und All-Rhythmus*, rev. ed. (Einsiedeln: Johannes-Verlag, 1962).

and four-footed things and creeping things (Gen. 1, 26). Why do you go beyond what is subject to you and raise yourself up against the very species which is free, counting your own kind on a level with four-footed things and even footless things? "You have subjected all things" to man, declares the word through the prophecy, and in that text it lists the things subject, "cattle" and "oxen" and "sheep." Surely human beings have not been produced from your cattle? Surely cows have not conceived human stock? Irrational beasts are the only slaves of humankind. But to you these things are of small account. "Raising fodder for the cattle, and green plants for the slaves of men," it says. But by dividing the human species in two with "slavery" and "ownership" you have caused it to be enslaved to itself, and to be the owner of itself. (*HE*, 73–74)

It is at this point that Gregory unleashes his full invective against, as we moderns might say, "the peculiar institution":

"I got me slaves and slave-girls." For what price, tell me? What did you find in existence worth as much as the human nature? What price did you put on the rationality? How many obols did you reckon the equivalent of the likeness of God? How many staters did you get for selling the being shaped by God? "God said, let us make man in our own image and likeness." If he is in the likeness of God, and rules the whole earth, and has been granted authority over everything on earth from God, who is his buyer, tell me? Who is his seller? To God alone belongs this power. (*HE*, 74)

At this point in Gregory's argument, one might think that he is simply rehashing his elder brother's theology of creation, the key moment of which was Basil's claim that only God is Master. Indeed, does not Gregory himself say as much at the very beginning of his sermon in a reference to Psalm 118:91? "This kind of language [the language of getting slaves and slave-girls for oneself] is raised up as a challenge to God. For we hear from prophecy that *all things are the slaves of the power that transcends all*" (*HE*, 73; italics in original).

Though Gregory sounds a lot like his elder brother, I contend that, in fact, his use of his brother's language is a rhetorical ploy to actually undercut such an interpretation of God as Creator and Lord. By the time Gregory is done, it becomes clear that mastery and lordship are not simply conceptually different from the way we think of and experience earthly mastery and lordship in an unredeemed order. In such an order, mastery and lordship are inflections of sheer power. Gregory's theological undoing of the discourse of power both explodes the logic of earthly lordship *and* disrupts, in Christ, the social imaginary itself by which power sociopolitically displays itself as mastery or as "power/knowledge," again as Foucault might say.[21] In short, YHWH's lordship is of a wholly different order or economic arrangement (*taxis*). Hence Gregory continues the passage above:

---

[21]Michel Foucault, *Power/Knowledge: Selected Interviews and Other Writings, 1972–1977* (New York: Pantheon, 1981).

[To God alone belongs this power;] or rather, *not even to God himself.* For "his gracious gifts," it says, "are irrevocable" [the gift of Israel's election; Rom. 11:29]. God would not therefore reduce the human race to slavery, since he himself, when we had been enslaved to sin, spontaneously recalled us to freedom. But if God does not enslave what is free, who is he that sets his own power above God's? (*HE,* 74; italics mine)

Since the gracious gift of freedom, which for Gregory is the quintessence of human nature, cannot be taken back (as the definition of a gift requires, Jacques Derrida's interpretation of Abraham's binding of Isaac notwithstanding), it follows that human nature cannot be sold.[22] Human nature and its worth are a mirror (*speculum*), and hence "a likeness," of the infinite.[23] "How [then] ... shall the ruler of the whole earth and all earthly things be put up for sale?" Gregory asks:

For the property of the person sold is bound to be sold with him, too. So how much do we think the whole earth is worth? And how much all the things of the earth? If they are priceless, what price is the one above them worth, tell me? Though you were to say "the whole world," even so you have not found the price he is worth. He who knew the nature of humankind rightly said that the whole world was not worth giving in exchange for a human soul [cf. Matt. 16:26–27]. Whenever a human being is for sale, therefore, nothing less than the owner of the earth is led into the sale-room. Presumably, then, the property belonging to him is up for auction too. That means the earth, the islands, the sea, and all that is in them. What will the buyer pay, and what will the vendor accept, considering how much property is entailed in the deal? (*HE,* 74–75)

It has been pointed out by scholars such as Lionel Wickham that Gregory is wrong in his analysis of ancient slavery, for as Roman law had it, the property of the person sold is not sold with him. But Daniel Stramara is correct in his observation that Wickham and others completely miss Gregory's point, which is that the human being is and remains free even if we construct a world order, a society, divided between those who own and those are owned.[24]

This contract or, more accurately for Gregory, this covenant of creation that brings forth the creation in freedom to be a likeness to God and so a likeness to God's freedom is not superseded by the contractual or legal structure of Roman society and law. God's covenant of creation as a covenant with Israel—note Gregory's reference to Romans 11:29—endures. Indeed, slaveholding society, Gregory's argument strongly

---

[22]Jacques Derrida, *The Gift of Death,* trans. David Wills (Chicago: University of Chicago Press, 1995).

[23]I borrow this phrase—the mirror of the infinite—from the brilliant essay by David Bentley Hart, "The Mirror of the Infinite: Gregory of Nyssa on the *Vestigia Trinitatis," Modern Theology* 18, no. 4 (2002): 542–56. For his argument questioning whether a gift can really be given, see Derrida, *The Gift of Death.* For a response to Derrida's argument, see John Milbank, "Can a Gift Be Given? Prolegomena to a Future Trinitarian Metaphysic," *Modern Theology* II (1995): 119–61.

[24]Stramara, "Gregory of Nyssa," 48.

implies, is necessarily super-sessionist and Gnostic (in the sense spoken of here in the prelude on Irenaeus). For it presumes the overcoming of the Old Testament by the New. Therefore, Gregory's exegetical practice calls into question claims that Niceno–Chalcedonian Christianity is necessarily supersessionist against Israel.[25] He recognizes that no "scrap of paper [or] written contract or monetary exchange" can abrogate God's contract, or, better, God's covenant with creation, which is his covenant with the people of Israel (*HE*, 75). It is this covenant that Christ secures and that he draws all of creation into. Thus, though Gregory does not quite put it this way, one can say that to enter into Christ is to journey into YHWH's covenantal guarantee of the freedom of Israel to be YHWH's people and thus into the freedom of creation to belong to YHWH. This path, Gregory notes, is the theological path of equality:

> If you are equal in all these ways, therefore, in what respect have you something extra, tell me, that you who are human think yourself the master of a human being, and say, "I got me slaves and slave-girls," like herds of goats or pigs. For when he said, "I got me slaves and slave-girls," he added that abundance in flocks of sheep and cattle came to him. For he says, "and much property in cattle and sheep became mine," as though both cattle and slaves were subject to his authority to an equal degree. (*HE*, 75)

With these words, Gregory completes his argument against the institution of slavery, calling all Christians by virtue of their identity as Christians, whose domicile is the territory of YHWH's covenantal relationship with creation through Christ–Israel, to manumit all slaves. This call implies (and this would not have been lost on Gregory's auditors) the need to restructure society, particularly a society that would claim to be "Christian."

The Theological Imagination: Christ, the Image of God

Given how he winds up his argument against slavery, one might ask whether the actual engine driving Gregory's vociferous opposition to the institution of slavery and, indeed, his exegetical practice is his theological vision, or whether his abolitionist outlook is driven by a broader "humanist," and thus not necessarily theological, sensibility. Is his vision humanism or not, and if it is theological, what difference does this make? At this point in this interlude, I argue on the basis of the very structure of his own argument that Gregory's abolitionism is based in his theological understanding: more specifically, in his Christological understanding of the Image

---

[25]An example of this kind of claim is R. Kendall Soulen, *The God of Israel and Christian Theology* (Minneapolis: Fortress, 1996). In fairness to Soulen, he has recently modulated such claims considerably. R. Kendall Soulen, "YHWH the Triune God," *Modern Theology* 15. no. 1 (January 1999): 25–54.

of God.[26] It is his vision of Christ himself as the principle Image or Icon of God the Father, the Image *in* whom human beings have been fashioned to themselves be images of God, that gives him the vantage from which to offer his critique of the ancient practice of slavery. For all of its speculative depth and daring, Gregory tethers his Trinitarian and Christological vision of the Image of God to YHWH's irrevocable promises to Abraham and through him to Israel. That is, this vision arises from his theological reading of Scripture. Thus, as it turns out, while to be sure it is Christ who is the Image of God, more accurately it is Christ in his full humanity as Christ–Israel who is the Image of God. He is the "Image" in whom human beings as the "image" have been fashioned. He, as Christ–Israel, is the one into whom human beings are to venture in exiting whiteness and the other racial constructions that whiteness produces.

The Chiastic Structure of Gregory's Argument against Slavery

Gregory employs the familiar rhetorical device of chiasm—from the Greek word *chiazô*—to structure his exegetical argument against slaveholding. Arguments employing this device tend to arrange the clauses constitutive of the argument crosswise. At the center of the chi-structured argument ("χ") is a nonduplicated middle term, which, being the argument's hinge, carries its weight and conveys its crux.[27] Thus, as Nils Wilhelm Lund explains, "the center" of a chiastic argument "is always the turning point."[28] It is the point where "there is often a change in the trend of thought, [the point where] an antithetic idea is introduced." Lund calls this "the law of the shift at the center." Moreover, Lund identifies another important feature of chiastic argumentation that is important for Gregory's specific employment of rhetorical chiasm. He summarizes it under what he calls "the law of shift from center to the extremes."[29] Under this law, "identical terms are often distributed in such a fashion that they occur in the extremes and at the center." Drawing on Lund's analysis of chiasm as a rhetorical strategy in texts of the ancient world, Stramara shows how chiasm structures Gregory's argument against slavery in the fourth homily on Ecclesiastes. He says:

The basic structure is as follows:

---

[26]For clarity's sake, I use Image, with a capital "I," to refer to Christ as the primary Image of God, or as Gregory says, as the "Prototype." I use image, with a lower-case "i," to refer to human beings in their status, as the Genesis stories would have it, as being in the Image. For Gregory, human beings are images in the Image of God. This is amplified in the following discussion.

[27]For more on chiasmus as a rhetorical device in the ancient world, see Stramara, "Gregory of Nyssa," 52 n. 50.

[28]Nils Wilhelm Lund, *Chiasmus in the New Testament: A Study in Formgeschichte* (Chapel Hill: University of North Carolina Press, 1942), 40. Quoted in Stramara, "Gregory of Nyssa," 51–52.

[29]Lund, *Chiasmus in the New Testament,* 41. Quoted in Stramara, "Gregory of Nyssa," 52 n. 50.

a a human being to think himself the master of his own kind
b regarding himself as different from his subordinates
c nature is free, possessing self-determination
d property: irrational creatures
e image and likeness of God: rationality and freedom
d' property: inanimate objects
c' impossible to master the image of God which is free
b' no superiority over subordinates due to title
a' who are you to think yourself the master of a human being?[30]

Drawing on Lund's observation regarding "the law of shift from center to the extremes" in chiastically structured arguments, one can see how Gregory's humanism is radically theological and, therefore, that his abolitionism, lodged within his humanism, is itself radically theological. What enables his abolitionist orientation is how he imagines the key term at the chiastic center of his argument. This is the notion of the "image and likeness" of God, a notion that bears within it a vision of the human as rational and free. Therefore, the conclusion of Gregory's argument is intelligible only from this theological center. Consequently, Stramara is surely correct in concluding that "the main argument for the abolition of slavery occurs not at the conclusion of [the] homily but at [its] center."[31] Indeed, one might go as far as to say simply on rhetorical grounds that the center operates and orients the claims made at the rhetorical periphery.

But because this rhetorical or chiastic center–periphery logic regarding the image of God is also already a logic of theos, a theologic, it must be asked what the theological content of the image of God, which binds the argument together, is. For the notion of the image is what orients Gregory's posture as an abolitionist intellectual: that is, as one who imagines the human being as free, by virtue of one's creation in the likeness of that image (cf. Gen. 1:26).

I reiterate in this context an idea touched on earlier and point to its significance for the argument I am developing in this book and that I press further in part III. That point is this: Gregory's theological abolitionism plays itself out as a vision of Christ's body as killable and indeed as killed flesh that has been resurrected.[32] His abolitionist

---

[30]Stramara, "Gregory of Nyssa," 52.

[31]Ibid.

[32]With this notion of killable flesh, pointing to the theological significance of the insights of some recent critical theorists, see Giorgio Agamben, *Homo Sacer: Sovereign Power and Bare Life,* trans. Daniel Heller-Roazen (Stanford: Stanford University Press, 1995); Abdul R. JanMohamed, *The Death-Bound-Subject: Richard Wright's Archaeology of Death* (Durham, N.C.: Duke University Press, 2005); and Achille Mbembé, "Necropolitics," *Public Culture* 15, no. 1(2003): 11-40. John Milbank also makes an effort to reckon with the theological significance of insights into "homo sacer" and killable flesh in John Milbank, *Being Reconciled: Ontology and Pardon* (New York: Routledge, 2003). There are lacunae in his argument, however. For more on all of this, see J. Kameron Carter, "Race and the Experience of Death: Theologically Dislocating and Relocating American Evangelicalism," in *Cambridge Companion to Evangelical Theology,* Timothy Larsen and Daniel Treier, eds. (New York: Cambridge University Press, 2007), 177–198.

orientation is internal to his Easter outlook on the "Holy Pasch" as the soteriological work of Christ. It is an abolitionism that relocates bodies inside the social space of Christ's wounded flesh.

Now, while one might accept the claim that Gregory's abolitionism, or his account of freedom, is broadly theological or religious in nature, one might yet balk at the claim that his abolitionism is necessarily Christological or, put differently, that his vision of the person and work of Jesus Christ gives specific content to his language of the image of God. After all, there is no mention of Jesus Christ anywhere in the fourth homily except in its benediction where Gregory, as a more or less standard way of concluding a sermon at the time, says, "the grace of our Lord Jesus Christ, to whom be glory for ever" (*HE*, 84). In such an absence of reference to Christ in the homily itself, what warrant is there for the claim that a specifically Christological vision is at work in his abolitionist vision of the human?

The Work of Christ: Easter and the Liberation of Slaves

While it is true that Gregory does not mention Christ explicitly, he does in fact refer to him in an important but implicit way in making his argument against slavery. The implicit reference is to Christ's soteriological work. After saying that only God has the power to buy and sell the human being ("To God alone belongs this power"), Gregory then explains why, in truth, "not even God himself" has this power (*HE*, 74). This power is precluded on the basis of the nature of God's relationship with the human being as the apex of creation. This relationship is not one of necessity. Since God did not create out of necessity, God's relationship to creation is not held together through a master–slave relationship in which bondage and necessity are the central features. Instead, says Gregory with recourse to Romans 11:29, the creature's existence is a gift. It is the product of the sovereignty or freedom of God. It is just this freedom that the human being images as the mirror of the very Being, which is the very act, of freedom that brought it forth. Indeed, should it happen that the creature's freedom, for whatever reason, is effaced and the creature becomes enslaved or falls under mastery to another, the only remedy would be for the God of freedom to freely enter the condition of the enslaved creature and from there, the location of the slave, restore the slave to the wholeness of freedom.

Gregory says that it is precisely this that has happened. The creature has fallen into bondage to itself and now is enslaved to all manner of death, chief being physical death. Indeed, before the judgment seat of death, all are equal. "Your origin," Gregory says to the one who would dare own another human being, "is from the same ancestors, your life is of the same kind, sufferings of soul and body prevail alike over you.... Are not [slave and owner] one dust after death? Is there not one judgment for them?—a common Kingdom, and a common Gehenna?" (*HE*, 75). Yet, Gregory also recognizes that while physical death equalizes at the end of life, the sufferings of this life, tied as they are to the history of nations and to social, economic, political, and even intellectual forces and structures, are unevenly distributed. Thus, "social death," as the contemporary sociologist Orlando Patterson calls it, is a manifestation of the bondage of physical death awaiting us all.[33]

Gregory is concerned with the ultimate enemy that is death. But apparently God is concerned with death understood both physically and socially inasmuch as both modulations of death mutually articulate the other. What is to be paid, as it were, to buy the human being out of the "death contract," the contract of physical and social death, which together efface the image of God (cf. *HE*, 75)?[34] By virtue of the human as a mirror of the Infinite and thus as a participant in the Infinite, only the Infinite God could make such a payment. And moreover, the only thing such a God could pay with—and here Gregory's logic interestingly starts to look like Anselm's of *Cur Deus Homo*—is himself. Indeed, says Gregory, God has paid just such a price, for "he himself, when we had been enslaved to sin, spontaneously recalled us to freedom" (*HE*, 74).

That Gregory is rhetorically alluding here to Easter is another matter that would not have been lost on his auditors, for Gregory preached these homilies during the Lenten season of 379 to prepare his congregation for Easter. Moreover, in a sermon that he once preached during the Easter season (*On the Holy Pasch* [*In Sanctum Pascha*]), Gregory makes the explicit connection between the Easter work of Christ and the abolition of slavery:

> "This day" then "which the Lord made, let us rejoice and be glad in it" (Ps. 117, 24), not with carousing and reveling, not with dancing and drunken mirth, but with divine thoughts. Today the whole world can be seen gathered like one household for the harmony of a single song and neglecting every ordinary business, refashioned as at one signal for earnest prayer.... And truly the present day is well compared with the coming day which it portrays: both are days of human gathering, that one universal, this partial. To tell the absolute truth, as far as gladness and joy are concerned, this day is more delightful than the anticipated one, since then inevitably those in grief will also be seen when their sins are exposed, whereas the present pleasure admits no sorrow. The just man rejoices, and the one whose conscience is not clear awaits the restoration which repentance brings, and every sorrow is put to sleep for the present day, while none is so distressed that relief does not come from the great splendour of

---

[33]Orlando Patterson, *Slavery and Social Death: A Comparative Study* (Cambridge, Mass.: Harvard University Press, 1982).

[34]While alluding to Gregory's language of the "contract" that made the slave system of his day function and the implication that such a contract functions in stark contrast to YHWH's relationship with creation as rooted in an irrevocable covenant, I am also alluding to Abdul M. JanMohamed's recent theorizing (in *Death-BoundSubject*) of the "death contract" as grounding the modem social order, a contract refracted through race. JanMohamed draws heavily on the work of philosophers Giorgio Agamben and Achille Mbembé.

the feast. Now is the prisoner freed, the debtor forgiven, the slave is liberated by the good and kindly proclamation of the church, not being rudely struck on the cheek and released from beatings with a beating, nor being exhibited to the mob on a stand as though it were a show, getting insult and indignity as the beginning of his freedom, but released and acknowledged with equal decency. (*HP*, 7–8)

But as if there were doubts still remaining as to his seriousness about liberating slaves on the basis of the church's proclamation, Gregory says the following to assure his auditors that he is not speaking with mere rhetorical flourish or vacuous fulsomeness:

You masters have heard; mark my saying as a sound one; do not slander me to your slaves as praising the day with false rhetoric, take away the pain from oppressed souls as the Lord does the deadness from bodies, transform their disgrace into honour, their oppression into joy, their fear of speaking into openness; bring out the prostrate from their corner as if from their graves, let the beauty of the [Easter] feast blossom like a flower upon everyone. (*HP*, 8)

And then comes the connection of all of this with Easter and, more specifically, with the one who bears the marks of death-bound or enslaved existence but under the aspect of the resurrection. The resurrection means the liberation of slaves:

If a royal birthday or victory celebration opens a prison, shall not Christ's rising relieve those in affliction? Greet, you poor, your provider; you debilitated and physically disabled, the healer of your sufferings. For through the resurrection hope come zeal for virtue and hatred for vice, since with resurrection removed one saying will prevail with everyone: "Let us eat and drink, for tomorrow we die" (1 Cor. 15, 32). (*HP*, 8)

The Person of Christ: The Deeper Meaning of the Image of God

But there is another dimension to the work that God accomplishes in Christ that drives Gregory's argument against slavery. This is the dimension of the *person* of Christ, which is the identity that the *work* displays or enacts. The person, along with the work of Christ, is also tied to the notion of the image of God. But to grasp the significance of the person of Christ in relationship to Gregory's emphasis on the theological language of the image of God and how it moves him to read Scripture against the social order, one must look to other places in his oeuvre in which he clarifies the connection between the person or identity of Christ, his *hypostasis,* and what he calls the Image of God. The link Gregory makes between the identity or person of Christ and the Image of God helps us see more clearly how his stance against slavery is internal to his theological outlook.

This is displayed most clearly in his minor dogmatic treatise *On the Creation of the Human Being* (*De Hominis Opificio*), which is an extended theological meditation on the Genesis account of creation. It includes a reflection on the very passage that he puts at the chiastic center of his argument against slavery in the fourth homily on Ecclesiastes: Genesis 1:26—"Let us make human beings in our image, after our likeness." The key passage for my purposes is in chapter 22 of *On the Creation*:

> I take up once more in my argument our first text:—God says, "Let us make man in our image, after our likeness, and God created man, in the image of God created man, in the image of God created He him [Gen. 1:26]. Accordingly, the image of God, which we behold in universal humanity, had its consummation then; but Adam as yet was not; for the thing formed from the earth is called Adam, by etymological nomenclature, as those tell us who are acquainted with the Hebrew tongue .... . Man, then, was made in the image of God; that is, the universal nature [*hê katholou phusis*], the God-like thing [*to theoeikelon chrêma*]; not part of the whole, but all the fullness of nature together [*ouchi meros tou holou, all' hapan athroôs to tês phuseôs plêrôma*] was made by omnipotent wisdom.[35]

But Gregory has already made a critically important point earlier in the treatise that must be incorporated into the claims he makes here. It helps us understand why it would be a mistake to see Gregory's distinction between the fullness (*pleroma*) of humanity and its historical unfolding as simply a Christianized Platonism in which the fullness of human nature functions as a Platonic form, the form of the human species. He says:

> We must ... examine the words carefully: for we find, if we do so, that that which was made "in the image" is one thing, and that which is now manifested in wretchedness is another. "God created man," it says; "in the image of God created He him." There is an end of the creation of that which was made "in the image": then it makes a resumption of the account of creation, and says, "male and female created He them." *I presume that every one knows that this is a departure from the Prototype; for "in Christ Jesus," as the Apostle says, "there is neither male nor female."* Yet the phrase declares that man is thus divided.[36]

Together these passages display something crucial about the image of God as Gregory understands it. In the strictest sense, the image of God must be understood on two interrelated levels. It must first be understood on the level of the image as "prototype," the level of what he calls the "God-like thing." And then there is the secondary, but no less real and important, level in which the image of God as prototype is populated, so to speak, or filled out. On this secondary level, the image of God in its prototypical form is given spatiotemporal or geohistorical depth and content precisely by being filled out by actual historical persons, beginning, as the Genesis stories of creation would have it, with male and female. The secondary level of the image of God,

---

[35]*De Hominis Opificio* (hereafter *DHO*) 22 [*Patrologiae cursus completus: Series Graeca* (hereafter *PG*) 44.204D; *Nicene and Post-Nicene Fathers* (hereafter *NPNF*) 5.411B]; translation slightly altered.
[36]*DHO* 16 (*PG* 44.181A; *NPNF* 5.405A); italics mine.

therefore, articulates the prototype in the numerous creaturely inflections and differences making it up, beginning with male and female.

But Gregory has another point to make, and it is with this point that one sees how un-Platonic Gregory is, though he clearly draws on thought forms and modes of rationality indebted to Platonism. Picking up on the Pauline language of Galatians 3:28 about there being in Christ neither male nor female, Gregory links this passage to the Genesis stories of creation, interpreting the statement "God created man ... in the image of God created He him" of Genesis 1:27 to be, in actuality, a reference to Christ himself in whom, according to the Galatians passage, there is neither male nor female. Galatians 3:28 gives Gregory a Christological way of understanding Genesis 1:27. Christ himself is the Image of God the Father, the one who is freedom. As prototype, he images and, indeed, is the Image of the will of the Father, the archetype, and thus the freedom of God. Gregory, in his massive treatise *Against Eunomius (Contra Eunomium),* casts this in Trinitarian terms:

> There is no difference at all between the will of the Son and of the Father. For the Son is the image of the goodness [of God], according to the beauty of the original. It's like when someone looks into a mirror (it is perfectly allowable to explain this by means of material illustrations): the image conforms in every detail to the original, which is the cause of the image in the mirror. The mirror-image cannot move unless the movement originates in the original. When the original moves, the mirror-image of necessity, moves likewise.
>
> Just so is it the case with the Lord, "the image of the invisible God" [Col. 1:15], who is immediately and inseparably united to the Father whose will he obeys in every movement of his own will. If the Father wills something, then the Son, who is in the Father, wills the same as the Father. Indeed, more precisely: He himself is the Father's will [emphasis mine]. For if in himself he possesses all that the Father possesses, then there is nothing of the Father's that he would not possess. Moreover, if he has in himself all that belongs to the Father, or shall we say, if he himself possesses the Father, then, along with the Father and everything that belongs to the Father, he of necessity also possesses the Father's will in toto.[37]

All that the Son is, wills, and does is a translation into the Son's own "indigenous" language as Word (*Logos*), that is, into his own mode of being, all that the Father is, wills, and does. This is Gregory's Trinitarianism (he speaks of the Holy Spirit in the subsequent paragraph). But, what Gregory's claim about Christ the Son, not simply in relationship to the other Trinitarian persons but in relationship to the full complement of human persons (*pleroma*), adds is this: we now see that the translation of the will or freedom of God that the eternal Son is as the Word (*Logos*) of God already contains within itself all of the possible words (*logoi*) of creation. In their creaturely modalities of freedom, all of the words of creation are needed to fully

---

[37]Contra Eunomium (CE) [*Gregorii Nysseni Opera*, ed. Werner Jaeger (Berlin: E. J. Brill, 1921–), hereafter *GNO; Patrologiae cursus completus: Series Graeca*, 45.981D-984A; *NPNF* 5.272A]; translation mine.

articulate or image the eternal Son, who is himself the Image of the will of the God the Father.

But notice what Gregory is saying. He is saying that the historical Jesus Christ—who while being one individuated human person among many is the eternal Son of the Trinity—is, in fact, in his historical concreteness and particularity at the same time the many of human existence. As the One–Many, he is the Image of God in its primacy. This is what Gregory means by designating Christ the prototype. He is the "whole lump of humanity" (*holon to phurama*) itself or the entire plenitude (*plêrôma*) of humankind, which all of humanity fills out as particular inflections or intonations of the prototype.[38] Thus, as David Bentley Hart says in his interpretation of Gregory:

> The "essence" of the human is none other than the plenitude of all men and women, [and therefore] every essentialism is rendered empty: all persons express and unfold the human not as shadows of an undifferentiated idea, but in their concrete multiplicity and hence in all the intervals and transitions belonging to their differentiation; and so human "essence" can be only an "effect" of the whole. Every unlikeness, in the harmonious unity of the body of the Logos, expresses in an unrepeatable way the beauty of God's likeness. The human "original," no longer a paradigm, is the gift and fruit of every peaceful difference and divergence; and only as this differentiating dynamism is the unit of the human "essence" imaginable at all, as the peaceful unity of all persons in the Spirit, who is bringing creation to pass and ushering in the Kingdom. And even in the Kingdom, that essence will not be available to us as a fixed *proprium*. According to Gregory, the final state of the saved will be one of endless motion forward, continuous growth into God's eternity, *epektasis*; salvation will not be an achieved repose, but an endless pilgrimage into God's infinity, a perpetual "stretching-out" into an identity always infinitely exceeding what has already been achieved; there will always be the eschatological within the eschaton, a continuous liberation of the creature … . The eschaton, thus conceived, brings nothing to a halt, returns nothing to its pure or innocent origin … . [It] is … a perpetual venturing away from our world, our totality.[39]

It can thus be said that all particular persons, in the unique and often tragic histories that constitute them as persons, by virtue of their residence in the prototype—or stated differently, by virtue of their histories being embraced from beyond themselves through the incarnation—are of eternal and salvific significance. Christ as prototype frees creation in its fullness—from persons and their histories, to the ecological order, to the animal kingdom—to be a symphonic expression of the freedom of God, for in him the opposition between the universal and particular collapses inasmuch

---

[38]*CE* (*GNO* 2.70; *NPNF* 5.158B).

[39]David B. Hart, "The 'Whole Humanity': Gregory of Nyssa's Critique of Slavery in Light of His Eschatology," *Scottish Journal of Theology* 54, no. 1 (2001): 64–65. What it means that "orthodox" Christian theologians employed theological discourse in justification of a racialized understanding of the modem world as we now know it goes completely unaddressed by Hart. This is a profound lacuna in his otherwise important meditation on Gregory.

as he is the concrete universal (*concretum universale*), the One–Many, that sets all particularity free to exist beyond itself or "to be" in and for God. He is the tune—a jazz or blues tune of suffering divine things—that the symphony of creation, the many, plays.

As "lamb slain from the foundation of the world" (Rev. 13:8) and thus as suffering, killable flesh that culminates Israel's covenant with YHWH as a covenant with creation, Christ's Jewish, covenantal flesh is the harmonic or cadence of creaturely existence. Therefore, according to the theological terms Gregory sets out, human identity must be conceived as an identity constituted in the identity of the prototype himself, Jesus Christ. All particularity articulates the prototype and is an intonation or musical note sounding within the amphitheater of his flesh. As the horizon of all existence, Christ then frees or liberates all beings to, in fact, be and to exist toward the prototype, but within the inflection of creaturely existence.

To be set free in this way is, for Gregory, the very meaning of virtue, which is precisely what Christ restores to humankind. Here is where Gregory's vision of the person or identity of Christ in relationship to the identity of every human being connects to the work of Christ as an Easter work of abolition. He says:

> "He made human nature participant in all good; for if the Deity is the fulness of good [*plêrôma agathôn*], and this is His image, then the image finds its resemblance to the Archetype in being filled with all good." Thus there is in us the principle of all excellence, all virtue and wisdom, and every higher thing that we conceive: but pre-eminent among all is the fact that we are free from necessity, and not in bondage to any natural power, but have decision in our own power as we please [*all' autexousion pros to dokoun echein*]; for virtue [*aretê*] is a voluntary thing [*chrêma… hekousion*], subject to no dominion [*adespoton*]: that which is the result of compulsion and force [*to katênagkasmenon kai bebiasmenon*] cannot be virtue [*aretê*].[40]

In several other places, Gregory reiterates this point about the incongruence between virtue, which turns out to be a way of talking about the image of God, and enslavement. In *On the Soul and the Resurrection (De Anima et Resurrectione)*, Gregory defines freedom in the following way:

> Freedom is likeness [*exhomoiôsis*] to that which is self-determining [*adespoton*] and sovereign [*autokratês*]; it is what we were gifted with from the beginning but what has been tarnished … . Virtue [*aretê*] too is self-determining [*adespoton*] … . But God is the source of all virtue [*aretê*]. Hence, [to be free] is to be united with God so that, as the Apostle says, "God may be all in all."[41]

Or, in the *Catechetical Orations (Catechetica Oratio),* he says the following:

---

40 *DHO* 16 (PG 44.184B–C; *NPNF* 5.405B).
41 *De Anima et Resurrectione (PG* 46.101C–104A, *NPNF* 5.452A–B); translation mine.

He who made humans for participation [*metousia*] in his own [*idiôn*] good, and built into human nature the potentialities for every good thing, so that by them they might be impelled to the corresponding good, would never have deprived them of … the grace [*charitos*] of having no master [*adespoton*] and having one's authority in oneself [*autexousion*].[42]

There are several other passages that reflect the point of these passages or related points. On the basis of the understanding of Christ as the Image of God and of humans existing in the Image, Gregory has theological leverage against the social order at the level of how creation fills out the historical existence of the eternal Word as Jesus of Nazareth. He is able to discern the ways in which bondage to physical death, which has arisen as a result of sin, plays itself out in the sociopolitical order. Indeed, he can discern the ways in which societies structure themselves so as to write various forms of social death, from slavery and poverty (to name two of the big ones for Gregory) to the Holocaust, apartheid, and genocide (to name some atrocities of the twentieth and twenty-first centuries), into the very fabric of the social order. Gregory is clear that the sinful distinctions made between bodies—distinctions that call on some to rule and others to be ruled; some to be killable flesh and others to do the killing—are distinctions rooted in brute but arbitrary power:

It is not nature but power that has divided humankind into servants and masters. For the Lord of the universe has ordained that only the irrational nature should serve man … . Therefore, he who is subject to you by custom and law is yet equal to you in dignity of nature. He is neither made by you, nor does he live through you, nor has he received from you these qualities of body and soul. Why, then, do you get so much worked up to anger against him if he has been lazy, or runs away, or perhaps shown you contempt to your face? You ought to look to yourself instead, how you have behaved to your Lord who has made you and caused you to be born, and has given you a share in the marvels of the world.[43]

What all of this means for Gregory is that God's soteriological action (i.e., Easter) is fundamentally a Christological action (i.e., the covenantal identity of Christ as the Israel of God in relationship to the God of Israel). This soteriological action, its Christological interior, restores the image to its prototype, the Image. I read each of the figures in part III of this book as engaged in a struggle to reclaim this insight reclaims this insight but from the underside of modernity and as turned toward the liberation of dark flesh. Like Gregory, they see that Christ's life as it reaches its apex in Easter restores the image-status of all persons, affirming and positioning all persons in the person of the eternal Christ, the Son of the Trinity, so as to set them free. In so doing, they take up the mandate of the theological ethics of Gregory's thought, but

---

[42]*Catechetical Oratio*5 (*PG* 45.23C; *NPNF* 5.479B); translation mine.
[43]*Gregory of Nyssa: The Lord's Prayer; the Beatitudes*, ed. Hilda C. Graef (Westminster, MD: Newman, 1954), 81–82.

from the vantage of those subject to the violent, racial conquest of modernity, the violence of (pseudo)theological whiteness. And this is the theological mandate: exit the power structure of whiteness and of the blackness (and other modalities of race) that whiteness created, recognizing that all persons are unique and irreplaceable inflections or articulations, not of the power/knowledge nexus of race, but of Christ the covenantal Jew, who is the Image of God, the prototype, and who as such is the fundamental articulation, through the Spirit of God, of YHWH the God of Israel, the one whom Jesus called Father.

I mention the Jewishness of Jesus here because of its significance for understanding the I/image of God. An understanding of Christ as the Image of God and of all human persons existing in the Image, who is Christ, cannot bypass or supersede YHWH's promises to Abraham and thus to Israel, for it is from the history of this people's covenantal interactions with God and thus from God's history that God takes up the history of the world. Moreover, they are the people whose identity, in being a covenantal and thus a nonracial identity, is always eschatologically in front of them. It always exceeds them. After all, it is not until chapter 12 of Genesis and with the call of Abram that Israel's identity is set in motion after he heeds YHWH's call to leave "Ur of the Chaldees" (cf. Gen. 12:1–4). In leaving Ur, he leaves behind the identity that Ur assigned to him as Abram in order eventually to be renamed Abraham. This new name indexes his identity as an identity *in relationship*—to YHWH. And yet, it is still not until several chapters later that "Israel" is actually named (Gen. 32:27–29) and further still before they are a people. But what sets Israel's identity in motion is YHWH's call to Abram to leave "Ur of the Chaldees" in order to enter into his identity as Abraham, covenantal partner of YHWH.

To exist in Christ is to be drawn into such an understanding of identity, into the ecstatic and eschatological identity of Israel's covenantal promises.[44] But it is just such a mode of existence that yields freedom, just such a mode of existence that frees all beings to be unique articulations of Christ the Image, the prototype, so that together human beings across space and time might constitute a jazz ensemble that riffs upon and improvises within the eternal Word. Briton Hammon sees this as lifting off with the birth of Christ; Frederick Douglass, calling this a vision of the "pure and impartial Christianity of Christ," sees it as realized in the death of Christ; and

---

[44]It should be clear from this understanding of Israel's identity that what I am suggesting is not assimilable to a modern "Zionist" understanding of Jewish identity such as one finds in various currents within contemporary American evangelicalism. Such an understanding of Jewish identity in terms of modern Zionism is an articulation of modern racial reasoning, albeit geopolitically situated at the liminal frontier between the so-called Occident and Orient. Here Zionist Jewish identity (as an Occidental construction) needs its Orientalist-Palestinian other. What I am suggesting is just as much a critique of this view as it is of Christianity's severance of itself from its Jewish theological roots. Indeed, what must be grasped is the coherence between modern Zionism and Christianity's severance of itself from its Jewish theological roots. For what one sees with modern Zionism is what happens when Jewish covenantalism is forced onto the Procrustean bed of modern statecraft and nation-state formation, the inner logic of which is racial reasoning.

Jarena Lee sees it as disseminated through time and space by the Spirit of Christ. Together they redirect race, providing a Christian account of New World black existence, an account that follows the itinerary of Christ's life from his birth through his death and resurrection to Pentecost. What they point to is a way of understanding New World Afro-Christian existence as more than a religious-cultural reflex to the Somewhat situation of the Americas in the face of the Somewhat of an opaque human consciousness. To argue this way is paradoxically to argue against freedom. Rather, what I seek to show is how these writers to varying degrees were pointing to a theological reality structuring the dawning moments of Afro-Christian existence in its wandering through the wilderness of modernity.

47. Rosemary Radford Ruether – Extracts from Sexism and God-Talk: Toward a Feminist Theology

Women's Experience and Historical Tradition

It has frequently been said that feminist theology draws on women's experience as a basic source of content as well as a criterion of truth.[1] There has been a tendency to treat this principle of "experience" as unique to feminist theology (or, perhaps, to liberation theologies) and to see it as distant from "objective" sources of truth of classical theologies. This seems to be a misunderstanding of the experimental base of all theological reflection. What have been called the objective sources of theology; Scripture and tradition, are themselves codified collective human experience.

Human experience is the starting point and the ending point of the hermeneutical circle. Codified tradition both reaches back to roots in experience and is constantly renewed or discarded through the test of experience. "Experience" includes experience of the divine, experience of oneself, and experience of the community and the world, in an interacting dialectic. Received symbols, formulas, and laws are either authenticated or not through their ability to illuminate and interpret experience. Systems of authority try to reverse this relation and make received symbols dictate what can be experienced as well as the interpretation of that which is experienced. In reality, the relation is the opposite. If a symbol does not speak authentically to experience, it becomes dead or must be altered to provide a new meaning.

The uniqueness of feminist theology lies not in its use of the criterion of experience but rather in its use of *women's* experience, which has been almost entirely shut

---

[1]See Judith Plaskow, *Sex, Sin and Grace: Women's Experience and the Theologies of Reinhold Niebuhr and Paul Tillich* (Washington, D.C.: University Press of America, 1980), pp. 29–50.

out of theological reflection in the past. The use of women's experience in feminist theology, therefore, explodes as a critical force, exposing classical theology, including its codified traditions, as based on *male* experience rather than on universal human experience. Feminist theology makes the sociology of theological knowledge visible, no longer hidden behind mystifications of objectified divine and universal authority.[2]

The Hermeneutical Circle of Past and Present Experience

A simplified model of the Western theological tradition can illustrate this hermeneutical circle of past and present experience. We must postulate that every great religious idea begins in the revelatory experience. By *revelatory* we mean breakthrough experiences beyond ordinary fragmented consciousness that provide interpretive symbols illuminating the means of the *whole* of life. Since consciousness is ultimately individual, we postulate that revelation always starts with an individual. In earlier societies in which there was much less sense of individualism, this breakthrough experience may have been so immediately mediated through a group of interpreters to the social collective that the name of the individual is lost. Later, the creative individual stands out as Prophet, Teacher, Revealer, Savior, or Founder of the religious tradition.

However much the individual teacher is magnified, in fact, the revelatory experience becomes socially meaningful only when translated into communal consciousness. This means, first, that the revelatory experience must be collectively appropriated by a formative group, which in turn promulgates and teaches a historical community. Second, the formative group mediates what is unique in the revelatory experience through past cultural symbols and traditions. As far back as human memory stretches, and certainly within the history of Biblical traditions, no new prophetic tradition ever is interpreted in a cultural vacuum. However startling and original the vision, it must always be communicated and made meaningful through some transformation of ideas and symbols already current. The hand of the divine does not write on a cultural tabula rasa. Thus the Hebrew prophets interpreted in new ways symbols from Canaanite and Near Eastern religions. Christianity, in successive stages, appropriated a great variety of both Jewish and Hellenistic religious symbols to interpret Jesus. The uniqueness of the vision is expressed by its ability to combine and transform earlier symbolic patterns to illuminate and disclose meaning in new, unexpected ways that speak to new experiential needs as the old patterns ceased to do.

The formative community that has appropriated the revelatory experience in turn gathers a historical community around its interpretation of the vision. This process

---

[2]Sallie McFague, *Metaphorical Theology: Models of God in Religious Language* (Philadelphia: Fortress, 1982), chap. 5.

goes through various stages during which oral and written teachings are developed. At a certain point a group consisting of teacher and leaders emerges that seeks to channel and control the process, to weed out what it regards as deviant communities and interpretations, and to impose a series of criteria to determine the correct interpretive line. The group can do this by defining an authoritative body of writings that is then canonized as the correct interpretation of the original divine revelation and distinguished from other writings, which are regarded either as heretical or of secondary authority. In the process the controlling group marginalizes and suppresses other branches of the community, with their own texts and lines of interpretation. The winning group declares itself the privileged line of true (orthodox) interpretation. Thus a canon of Scripture is established.

Once a canon of Scripture is defined, one can then regard subsequent tradition as reflection upon Scripture and always corrected by Scripture as the controlling authority. In Catholicism and Orthodoxy the notion of the other equally authoritative "apostolic" traditions flowing from early times and existing alongside canonical Scripture does not quite disappear. Creeds, liturgical customs, and oral tradition passed down through apostolic sees also provide access to the original faith of the "primitive community." However much the community, both leaders and led, seek to clothe themselves in past codified tradition that provides secure access to divinely revealed truth, in reality the experience of the present community cannot be ignored.

This contemporary community may consist of many different layers, from the "maximal" leaders to the "ordinary believer." Even an Athanasius or a Leo I, who claim to be merely teaching what has always been taught, are in fact engaged in a constant process of revision of the symbolic pattern in a way that reflects their experience. Received ideas are tested by what "feels right," that is, illuminates the logic of the symbolic pattern in a way that speaks most satisfyingly to their own experience of redemption. It is true that theology can evolve into a secondary and tertiary reflection on the logic of ideas themselves. It continues its vital development only to the extent that such thinking remains in touch with depth experience.

The ordinary believers now have increasingly complex formulas of faith, customs, rituals, and writings proposed to them as the basis for appropriating the original revelatory paradigm as personal redeeming experience. These individuals, in their local communities of faith, are always engaged in making their own selection from the patterns of received tradition that fit or make sense in their lives. There is always an interaction between the patterns of faith proposed by teachers to individuals and the individuals' own appropriation of these patterns as interpretations of experience. But these differences remain unarticulated, held within the dominant consensus about what the revelatory pattern "means."

A religious tradition remains vital so long as its revelatory pattern can be reproduced generation after generation and continues to speak to individuals in the community and provide for them the redemptive meaning of individual and collective experience. Such has been the Exodus-Passover pattern for Jews and the death-resurrection paradigm of personal conversion for Christians. The circle from experience to experience, mediated through instruments of tradition, is thus completed when the contemporary community appropriates the foundational paradigm as the continuing story of its own redemption in relation to God, self, and one another.

Crises of Tradition

Religious traditions fall into crisis when the received interpretations of the redemptive paradigms contradict experience in significant ways. The crisis may be perceived at various levels of radicalness. Exegetical criticism of received theological and Scriptural traditions can bring forth new interpretations that speak to new experiences. This kind of reform goes on in minor and major ways all the time, from individuals making their own private adaptations to teachers founding new schools of interpretation. So long as this is accommodated within the community's methods of transmitting tradition, no major break occurs.

A more radical break takes place when the institutional structures that transmit tradition are perceived to have become corrupt. They are perceived not as teaching truth but as teaching falsehood dictated by their own self-interest and will to power. The revelatory paradigms, the original founder, and even the early stages of the formulation of tradition are still seen as authentic. It seems necessary to go behind later historical tradition and institutionalized authorities and "return to" the original revelation. In the literal sense of the word, there is no possibility of return to some period of the tradition that predates the intervening history. So the myth of return to origins is a way of making a more radical interpretation of the revelatory paradigm to encompass contemporary experiences, while discarding institutions and traditions that contradict meaningful, just, and truthful life. Usable interpretative patterns are taken from Scripture and early community documents to set the original tradition against its later corruption. The original revelation itself, and the foundational stages of its formulation, are not challenged but held as all the more authoritative to set them as normative against later traditions. The Reformation followed this pattern of change.[3]

A still more radical crisis of tradition occurs when the total religious heritage appears to be corrupt. This kind of radical questioning of the meaningfulness of

---

[3]Robert L. Wilken, *The Myth of Christian Beginnings: History's Impact on Belief* (Garden City, N.Y.: Doubleday, 1971).

the Christian religion began to occur in Western Europe during the Enlightenment. Marxism carried the Enlightenment critique of religion still further. Marxism teaches that all religion is an instrument the ruling class uses to justify its own power and to pacify the oppressed.[4] This makes religion not the means of redemption but the means of enslavement. The very nature of religious knowledge is seen as promoting alienation rather than integration of the human person. This kind of ideological critique throws the truth content of religion into radical ethical disrepute. Such an attack on religion is considered "true" by a growing minority of people when they perceive the dominant religious traditions as contradictory to the contemporary experience of meaning, truth, and justice.

Ideological criticism of the truthfulness of the religion may still allow for some residue of genuine insight into the original religious experiences and foundational teachers. The prophets of Jesus may be said to have had truthful insights into just and meaningful life, but this became corrupted and turned into its opposite by later teachers, even within Scripture. Discarding even the truthfulness of foundational teachers, the critic may turn to alternative sources of truth: to recent critical schools of thought against the religious traditions; to suppressed traditions condemned as heretical by the dominant tradition; or to pre-Christian patterns of thought. Modern rationalist, Marxist, and romantic criticism of religion have followed such alternatives in the last two hundred years.

Why seek alternative traditions at all? Why not just start with contemporary experience? Doesn't the very search for foundational tradition reveal a need for authority outside contemporary experience? It is true that the received patterns of authority create a strong need, even in those seeking radical change, to find an authoritative base of revealed truth "in the beginning" as well as a need to justify the new by reference to recognized authority. These needs reveal a still deeper need: to situate oneself meaningfully in history.

The effort to express contemporary experience in a cultural and historical vacuum is both self-deluding and unsatisfying. It is self-deluding because to communicate at all to oneself and others, one makes use of patterns of thought, however transformed by new experience, that have a history. It is unsatisfying because, however much one discards large historical periods of dominant traditions, one still seeks to encompass this "fallen history" within a larger context of authentic and truthful life. To look back to some original base of meaning and truth before corruption is to know that truth is more basic than falsehood and hence able, ultimately, to root out falsehood in a new future that is dawning in contemporary experience. To find glimmers of this truth in submerged and alternative traditions through history is to assure oneself that one is not mad or duped. Only by finding an alternative historical community and

---

[4]For the classic texts of Marxist critique of religion, see *Marx and Engels on Religion,* introd. Reinhold Niebuhr (New York: Schocken, 1964).

tradition more deeply rooted than those that have become corrupted can one feel sure that in criticizing the dominant tradition one is not just subjectively criticizing the dominant tradition but is, rather, touching a deeper bedrock of authentic Being upon which to ground the self. One cannot wield the lever of criticism without a place to stand.

The Critical Principle of Feminist Theology

The critical principle of feminist theology is the promotion of the full humanity of women. Whatever denies, diminishes, or distorts the full humanity of women is, therefore, appraised as not redemptive. Theologically speaking, whatever diminishes or denies the full humanity of women must be presumed not to reflect the divine or an authentic relation to the divine, or to reflect the authentic nature of things, or to be the message or work of an authentic redeemer or a community of redemption.

This negative principle also implies the positive principle: what does promote the full humanity of women is of the Holy, it does reflect true relation to the divine, it is the true nature of things, the authentic message of redemption and the mission of redemptive community. But the meaning of this positive principle — namely, the full humanity of women — is not fully known. It has not existed in history. What we have known is the negative principle of the denigration and marginalization of women's humanity. Still, the humanity of women, although diminished, has not been destroyed. It has constantly affirmed itself, often in only limited and subversive ways, and it has been touchstone against which we test and criticize all that diminishes us. In the process we experience our larger potential that allows us to begin to imagine a world without sexism.

This principle is hardly new. In fact, the correlation of original, authentic human nature (*imago dei*/Christ) and diminished, fallen humanity provided the basic structure of classical Christian theology. The uniqueness of feminist theology is not the critical principle, full humanity, but the fact that women claim this principle for themselves. Women name themselves as subjects of authentic and full humanity.

The use of this principle in male theology is perceived to have been corrupted by sexism. The naming of males as norms of authentic humanity has caused women to be scapegoated for sin and marginalized in both original and redeemed humanity. This distorts and contradicts the theological paradigm of *imago dei*/Christ. Defined as male humanity against or above women, as ruling-class humanity above servant classes, the *imago dei*/Christ paradigm becomes an instrument of sin rather than a disclosure of the divine and an instrument of grace.

This also implies that women cannot simply reverse the sin of sexism. Women cannot simply scapegoat males for historical evil in a way that makes themselves only innocent victims. Women cannot affirm themselves as *imago dei* and subjects of full human potential in a way that diminishes male humanity. Women, as the denigrated half of the human species, must reach for a continually expanding definition of inclusive humanity — inclusive of both genders, inclusive of all social groups and races. Any principle of religion or society that marginalizes one group of persons as less than fully human diminishes us all. In rejecting androcentrism (males as norms of humanity), women must also criticize all other forms of chauvinism: making white Westerners the norm of humanity, making Christians the norm of humanity, making privileged classes the norm of humanity. Women must also criticize humanocentrism, that is, making humans the norm and crown of creation in a way that diminishes the other beings in the community of creation. This is not a question of sameness but of recognition of value, which at the same time affirms genuine variety and particularity. It reaches for a new mode of relationship, neither a hierarchical model that diminishes the potential of the "other" nor an "equality" defined by a ruling norm drawn from the dominant group; rather a mutuality that allows us to affirm different ways of being.

...

Conversion from Sexism: Female and Male Journeys

Consciousness of sexism as evil necessarily begins with females. It is sometimes asked why feminist consciousness has emerged so recently. Why didn't women "revolt" against their subjugation long ago? The intimation behind this question is often that sexist subjugation, in fact, suits women's "nature" and so women have complied with it and supported it. There are several aspects of an answer to this question. There has always been a level of noncompliance or proto-feminist consciousness among women. Women, listening to male ideology against them, have never appreciated this ideology or fully believed it. They have expressed their noncompliance in the networks of communication among women. In every period in which some writings from women have survived, elements of this resistance to male definitions of women can be seen. What men have condemned as female gossip ("bitchiness") is precisely this network of female communication and covert resistance.

This proto-feminist consciousness could not develop into real feminist thought and practice until certain conditions were present. A new cultural ideology had to arise that supported the equal humanity of all persons and called for a new social order that expressed this view. Hierarchicalism, as the established and only possible human order, had to be thrown into question. Only then could feminism, as well as all the modern emancipation movements, begin to arise.

Consciousness is much more of a collective social product than modern individualism realizes. No one can affirm an idea against the dominant culture unless there is at least a subcultural group that gives people both the ideas and the social support for an alternative position. The dominant ideology and social order have to have become weakened and discredited enough that such countercultural groups can build up their position and survive.

Dissenting groups with alternative views on women arose in the Middle Ages and Reformation, but they were soon ruthlessly crushed by the dominant system or else they learned to retreat and accommodate to the dominant culture by suppressing their "heretical" views. Even in the French Revolution, the leading feminist, Olympe de Gouges, was guillotined and her pleas for inclusion of women in the "rights of man" were disregarded in a new Napoleonic code of laws that reinforced female subordination.[5]

The Female Journey

The woman who experiences dissenting thoughts alone, without any network of communication to support her, can hardly bring her own dissent to articulation. Without a social matrix, she will simply be terrorized into submission by the authorities that surround her or acquiesce in their judgment that she is a "witch" or a "madwoman." Only where there is a feminist movement that has been able to survive, to develop networks of communication, and to provide some alternative vision of life is feminist consciousness a real possibility.

Openness to feminist consciousness demands that the ideology and socialization into feminine "virtue" become existentially discredited. All the ways a woman has been taught to be "pleasing" and "acceptable" to men must be recognized as tools of her own seduction and false consciousness. Every woman has bought into some of these roles. We have been the pretty girl-child who is played with and praised for her cuteness; or the sexy lady who manipulates her physical attractiveness; or the good wife who wins praise by her diligent housekeeping and attentive service to male needs — all these prevent a woman from asking herself who she is as a human person.

Much of the strongest feminist consciousness arises not in teenagers or young adults but in older women who have already played out these roles and learned their hollowness. Yet if women comply too long in these traditional female roles, it becomes difficult to break the mold. They have lost so much time. They have missed the chance to develop first-rate skills for a self-defined life. It becomes too painful to face up to one's own years of betrayal. Thus it is the group of women who have already committed ten or twenty years to traditional wifehood that become prime candidates for antifeminist and anti-ERA crusades, particularly if they are supported by their husbands at an affluent economic level.

---

[5]Olympe de Gouges, "Declaration of the Rights of Women and Citizens" (1791), in *Princesses, Ladies and Republicaines of the Terror*, ed. Therese Louis Latour (New York: Knopf, 1930), pp. 175ff.

The cruel fact, which these women know in their bones but dare not articulate, is that they have no skills to support themselves at their present economic level. They are "one man away from welfare." If one does not have the "courage to see," the alternative is to become vehement supporters of female subordination as the only way to shore up one's present mode of survival. Thus the courage of feminist consciousness is always great, but it becomes more difficult or easy depending on one's sexist indoctrination, one's education and skills, and one's place in the life cycle and in class and race hierarchies.

For Christian women, particularly in more conservative traditions, one of the most difficult barriers to feminist consciousness is the identification of sin with anger and pride, and virtue with humility and self-abnegation. Although this doctrine of sin and virtue supposedly is for "all Christians," it becomes, for women, an ideology that reinforces female subjugation and lack of self-esteem. Women become "Christlike" by having no self of their own. They become the "suffering servants" by accepting male abuse and exploitation. Women are made to feel profoundly guilty and diffident about even the smallest sense of self-affirmation. They fear the beginning steps of asking who they are and what they want to do, rather than "putting others first."[6]

In this context, conversion from sexism is truly experienced as a breakthrough, as an incursion of power and grace beyond the capacities of the present roles, an incursion of power that puts one in touch with oneself as a self. *Metanoia* for women involves a turning around in which they literally discover themselves as persons, as centers of being upon which they can stand and build their own identity. This involves a willingness to get in touch with their own anger. Anger is liberating grace precisely as the power to break the chains of sexist socialization, to disaffiliate with sexist ideologies.

Virtue for women demands a new sense of pride, not in the male sense of "lording it over others" but in the sense of basic self-esteem. Without basic self-esteem one has no self at all, as a base upon which to build an identity or to criticize past mistakes. The whole male ideology of pride and humility has to be reevaluated by women. The acceptance of liberating anger and the reclaiming of basic self-esteem allow a woman to look honestly at the situation that has shaped her life. She is able to acknowledge her own compliance with the systems that have diminished her humanity. The shackles of this system on her mind and energy begin to shatter, and she gains the courage to stand up against them.

This breakthrough experience is the basis for the development of consciousness. Women read their own history within the history of patriarchy. They become aware of the depths of the system that has entrapped them and discover a hidden community of women of the past. They reclaim their own history as witnesses to an

---

[6]Judith Plaskow, *Sex, Sin and Grace: Woman's Experience and the Theologies of Reinhold Niebuhr and Paul Tillich* (Washington, D.C.: University Press of America, 1980), pp. 9–50.

alternative possibility and also become increasingly conscious of the complexity of the global socio-economic system that subjugates woman. The difficulty of the task of emancipation becomes clearer. It is no longer just a matter of settling accounts within interpersonal relationships.

This expanded consciousness deepens one's sense of alienation and anger so that one senses oneself ready to "go mad" with alienation and anger. Males take on a demonic face. One begins to doubt their basic humanity. One desires only to be with women, to distance oneself from the whole male world with its myriad games. Most women are deeply afraid of this deeper anger and alienation and stop well short of experiencing it. Their immediate ties of survival and service to men and children are too deep. Moreover, they believe that "loving everyone" and affirming everyone's humanity disallows the experiencing of this anger.

This creates a parting of the ways between feminists — those who are ready and willing to experience this deeper alienation and anger and those who draw back from it. Those who enter into deeper alienation become the "bad feminists," the separatists, lesbians, radicals. Those who take a more moderate stand are tempted to get "brownie points" for not being like those "bad feminists." Yet the depths of anger and alienation to which some women point are not inappropriate. It really has been "that bad." Unless one is willing to take the journey into that deeper anger, even to risk going a bit mad, one really will never understand the depths of the evil of sexism. The great importance of a feminist thinker like Mary Daly is precisely that she insists on taking herself further and further into that journey and insisting that others who wish to be honest follow her. She lays before our eyes the "passion drama" of female crucifixion on the cross of male sexism.[7]

The journey into that deeper anger does not mean that one needs to remain there permanently. There are, as Anne Wilson Schaef points out in her book *Women's Reality*, "levels of truth."[8] One needs to go through a certain level of truth before one can move on to another level. Those who are afraid of anger and alienation always have a tendency to hurry women on to another stage where they become "reasonable" and "gain perspective." But one cannot do that with integrity until one has genuinely faced up to sexism as a massive historical system of victimization of women and allowed oneself to enter into one's anger and alienation. To skip over this experience is to become "reconciling" in a way that is basically timid and accommodating and not really an expression of personal freedom.

Only by experiencing one's anger and alienation can one move on, with real integrity, to another level of truth. One is able, with freedom, to refuse a reversed

---

[7]Mary Daly, *Gyn/Ecology: The Metaethics of Radical Feminism* (Boston: Beacon Press, 1978), pp. 107–312. The concept of Daly's narrative of female victimization as a female "passion drama" is drawn from an unpublished article on Daly's book by Mary Jo Weaver, Religious Studies Department, University of Indiana at Bloomington.
[8]Anne Wilson Schaef, *Women's Reality: An Emerging Female System in the White Male Society* (Minneapolis: Winston Press, 1981), pp. 152–159.

female chauvinism that would cause one to lose touch with the human face of males and to begin to imagine that women alone are human and males are evil and defective. As one experiences women's groups and movements, one recognizes that women too are capable of the corruptions of egoism and power. As a woman breaks the ties that bind her to a relatively powerless world, she needs to acknowledge that she too can become an oppressor of others. One gains "humility" in one's criticism of arrogant egoism in males. Humility here is no longer a tool of timidity and servitude but assumes its rightful meaning as truthful self-knowledge of one's own capacity for oppressive pride. Women must refuse the egoistic self, modeled on male individualism, and affirm instead the "grounded self" which is related to others and to mutual service.

The systems of domination, then, are "male" only in the historical and sociological sense that males have shaped and benefited from them, not in the sense that they correspond to unique, evil capacities of males that women do not share. Women have no guarantees, because of a different "nature," that they will act differently. They do have some different experiences that may help them avoid acting in the same way, but only if they can develop the grounded self that avoids both timidity and reversed egoism. The struggle to shape an alternative system is fundamentally a human struggle, and it demands psychic and social holism. We appropriate into a new, grounded self the suppressed, relational side of our psyches, and we begin to shape new social systems of relationship that allow and support this alternative. One cannot be a grounded self in a vacuum, but only in new, emergent relationships.

The Male Journey

Having seen something of the female conversion journey, one might ask whether there is a comparable male conversion journey from sexism. In principle, one must say that there must be. Sexism is not just a female problem. Indeed, it is primarily a male problem that men have imposed on women. Sexism cannot be solved by women alone. It demands a parallel male conversion. There is ultimately no "new woman" without a new humanity. But I cannot describe the male journey from inside. That has to be done by males, grounded in a male liberation movement. However, as a white that worked in the Black movement for many years, I have some ideas of what conversion is like from the side of the "oppressors." Also, as a woman who has observed males in various stages of response to women's liberation, I have some idea of how that appears to women. On this basis I can suggest some stages of the male journey.

The first stage of male response to women's criticism of sexism is trivialization and ridicule. Men really can't believe that women are an oppressed group. They are convinced of their own benevolence toward women. They individualize the issue and abstract and universalize the situation of relatively privileged wives. They claim that the women they know are "well taken care of" and ought to be happy (grateful). They are unable to see the stresses and vulnerabilities of dependency even in this situation, much less the total system of sexism across classes and history. They laugh off the silliness of "women's lib" (a trivializing diminutive used only for female and homosexual liberation movements).

The second stage of male response is co-optation. Men become aware that the historical polarization of the sexes is a real issue. They leap quickly to the thought that men too have suffered from sexism; indeed, they have suffered "equally." Whole dimensions of their being — their ability to cry, to feel, to relate, to be sensitive — have been repressed in order to shape them for male roles of domination. They too need to be liberated. They need to recover the "feminine" side of themselves. This line is frequently adopted by clergy and other males who belong to the more humanistic disciplines and who find themselves marginalized from the centers of (male-macho) power. Jungian psychology provides the intellectual base for this male "feminism."

Such male feminists often become very dogmatic about what feminism means. They soon imagine that they know more about it than women. In their identification of their own suppressed self with the "feminine," they think they have a handle on women's true "nature." They want women to cultivate this male definition of the "feminine" in order to nurture the "feminine side" of men. They purport to understand and sympathize with women and, no doubt, sincerely think they do. But they tend to become very hostile when women suggest that this definition of the "feminine" is really a male projection and not female humanity. The male ego is still the center of the universe, which "feminism" is now seduced into enhancing in a new way. Such male feminists are sometimes worse enemies of women's emancipation than outright chauvinists.

These two stances are not conversion, but ways of resisting conversion from sexism. Men who are stuck in either of these positions often don't grow out of them. Real conversion from sexism begins to happen only when a man is able to enter into real solidarity with women in the struggle for liberation, often by being involved in a relationship with a particular woman who is pursuing her own liberation. By entering into her struggle, seeing the world of sexism from her eyes, he begins to be able to understand some dimensions of sexism. He attempts to change aspects of his male lifestyle to support her ability to work or go to school. He shares housework and child care. He begins to feel that he too is recovering a more holistic self in the process.

But the vulnerabilities of this type of supportive male are real. If he goes too far in sharing domestic work, so that it interferes with the exclusive male priority of the "job," he soon finds that he loses advancement in the world of male competition. The male who takes paternity leave when his wife has a baby may discover that he is a pariah on the job. He is passed up for promotion, left out of the networks of communication. He learns not to talk about women's rights on the job, much less analyze what women's rights would mean for his own organization. He is tempted to think of his support for "his woman" as a private issue. Sexism is really her problem. He is "helping" her with it, but in a way that can't interfere too much with his own male status.

Deeper male conversion from sexism involves a willingness to enter into risks to himself. He has to recognize his own profound fear of loss of affirmation by the male group ego if he departs from male roles. This may cause him loss of male economic status and privilege as well. But the fear of being repudiated or scorned by other males as "unmanly" is usually his greatest terror. Thus, for men as well as women, conversion means a receiving of a grounded self that not only repudiates male group egoism but also overcomes the passivity that acquiesces to the group ego. Men need to overcome not only their "pride" in masculinity that oppresses women but also their fear of loss of male status by which they oppress themselves and each other. At this point, males are able to recognize, without trying to either co-opt or pander to women, that the struggle against sexism is basically a struggle to humanize the world, to humanize ourselves, to salvage the planet, to be in right relation to God/ess. At this point, men and women can really join hands in a common struggle.

48. Musa Dube – Reading for Decolonization (John 4.1–42)

When the white man came to our country he had the Bible and we had the land. The White man said to us, 'let us pray'. After the prayer, the white man had the land and we had the Bible (a popular African saying).

Modern imperialism was so global and all-encompassing that virtually nothing escaped it; besides, as I have said, the nineteenth-century contest over empire is still continuing today. Whether or not to look at the connections between cultural texts and imperialism is therefore to take a position in fact taken—either to study the connection in order to criticize it and think of alternatives for it, or not to study it in order to let it stand (Edward Said, *Culture and Imperialism*, p. 68).

Introduction: Imperialism(s), Space and Texts

Imperialism is an ideology of expansion that takes diverse forms and methods at different times, seeking to impose its languages, its trade, its religions, its democracy, its images, its economic systems and its political rule on foreign nations and lands.[1]

---

[1]For different types, methods and definitions of imperialism(s), from ancient to contemporary times, see René Maunier, *The Sociology of Colonies: An Introduction to the Study of Colonies*, Vol. 1 (London: Routledge, 1949), pp. 133–260; Robert Delavignette, *Christianity and Colonialism* (New York: Hawthorn Books, 1964), pp. 1–46; Edward Said, *Culture and Imperialism* (New York: Alfred A. Knopf, 1993), pp. 9–13; Ngugi wa Thiong'o, *Decolonising the Mind: The Politics of Language in African Literature* (London: James Currey, 1986), pp. 1–3.

The victims of imperialism become the colonized, that is, those whose lands, minds, cultures, economies and political institutions have been taken possession of and rearranged according to the interests and values of the imperializing powers.[2] Imperialism is, therefore, about controlling foreign geographical spaces and their inhabitants. By its practice and its goals, imperialism is a relationship of subordination and domination between different nations and lands, which actively suppresses diversity and promotes a few universal standards for the benefit of those in power. It involves the colonized and the colonizer, the ruler and the ruled, the center and the periphery, the First World and the Two-Thirds World, relationships which define our current world; and relationships that are closely related to, although not identical to, particular physical places of the earth.

In this introduction, I briefly discuss different imperialist movements and cultural strategies of dominating foreign spaces, the Bible and empire-building before I turn to John 4. Throughout this essay, the term 'imperializing texts' designates those literary works that propound values and representations that authorize expansionist tendencies grounded on unequal international/racial relations. Decolonizing, on the other hand, defines awareness of imperialism's exploitative forces and its various strategies of domination, the conscious adoption of strategies of resisting imperial domination as well as the search for alternative ways of liberating interdependence between nations, races, genders, economies and cultures.

Imperialism is certainly an ancient institution. The Babylonian sovereign Hammurabi, for example, 'gave himself the title of "King of the Four Corners of the World"'[3] to describe his profession of disavowing boundaries. The Babylonian empire had a line of successors in the Assyrian, Hellenistic and Roman Empires. In a tradition that is akin to Hammurabi, Roman emperors were also called 'Saviour(s) of the World'.[4] 'World' in these titles symbolizes the claim to unlimited access to foreign geographical spaces. 'King' and 'Saviour' articulate the claims of power by certain subjects and their followers (races and nations) over unlimited geographical spaces— over the world and its inhabitants. While 'king' implies dominion over space and people—which may be just or unjust—'saviour' also implies power. But it carries an imperial ideology that came to a full-fledged maturity in modern centuries, whereby the violence of imperialism was depicted as a redeeming act for the benefit of the subjugated, or the so-called 'duty to the natives'.

---

[2]V.Y. Mudimbe, *The Invention of Africa: Gnosis, Philosophy and the Order of Knowledge* (Bloomington: Indiana University Press, 1988), pp. 1–2.

[3]René Maunier, *Sociology of Colonies*, Vol. 1, p. 19.

[4]For a more detailed discussion of this title, see Richard J. Cassidy, *John's Gospel in a New Perspective: Christology and the Realities of Roman Power* (Maryknoll, NY: Orbis Books. 1992), pp. 6–16; Craig Koester, 'The Saviour of the World (John 4.42)', *JBL* 109 (1990), pp. 665–80; Charles Talbert, *Reading John: A Literary and Theological Commentary on the Fourth Gospel and the Johannine Epistles* (New York: Crossroad), pp. 118–19.

But it is in Alexander the Great's career that we encounter a well-known and ancient example of what it takes to be a king or saviour of the world. His career makes it evident that military might is as central to empire building as are cultural texts. David Quint's study *Epic and Empire* highlights how Alexander drew his inspiration from the literary characters of *The Iliad*.[5] Alexander reportedly carried *The Iliad* in his conquest journeys and 'kept it under his pillow together with a dagger'.[6] Prior to his attack on Persia and Asia, he visited Troy where he 'honored the memory of the heroes who were buried there, with solemn libations; especially Achilles, whose grave he anointed'.[7] In so doing, Alexander was making the literary character of 'Achilles at Troy a model for the conquests carried out by his armies'.[8] Here a literary text that glorifies military might and conquest comes to legitimate and further imperial agendas in a different history. Conquest in empire building becomes a strategy for becoming king or saviour over the world by annihilating its inhabitants or by initiating a powerful death threat against them.

Quint's extensive study goes on to show that the travel and triumph of epic heroes through untold dangers; the characterization of its heroes as people immensely favored by divine powers; and the characterization of foreigners as either dangerous, evil cyclopes, or women/goddesses desperate to hold on to traveling heroes; have provided imperial travelers of different centuries and empires with a language for representing foreign lands and peoples up until the introduction of the novel. Imperial traveling agents and heroes drew their inspiration from epic characters and plots and so were able to withstand and endure their travel tribulations. Such epic characters and plots inspired them to regard themselves as divinely favored, destined and chosen to survive and conquer against all odds.

Not only do certain values of cultural texts inspire imperialism; the cultures of the empire are also used to maintain power over the colonized. Alexander's empire building project thus entailed an elaborate program of Hellenizing his conquered subjects. Alexander 'established a network of routes from Egypt to India and sprinkled cities throughout out Asia to radiate Greek culture'.[9] He founded Greek cities at 'strategic points, to serve as administrative centers but also to provide a focus as beacon of Greek culture in the alien lands of the Orient'.[10] The three generals who succeeded him 'encouraged solidarity of Greek culture by building cities on the old model, just as Alexander had done'.[11] Even the Roman Empire pursued the program

---

[5]David Quint, *Epic and Empire* (Princeton, NJ: Princeton University Press, 1993), pp. 1–18.
[6]Quint, *Epic and Empire*, p. 4.
[7]Quint, *Epic and Empire*, p. 4.
[8]Quint, *Epic and Empire*, p. 4.
[9]Calvin J. Roetzel, *The World that Shaped the New Testament* (Atlanta: John Knox Press, 1985), p. 2.
[10]David L. Balch and John E. Stambaugh, *The New Testament in its Social Environment* (Philadelphia: Westminster Press, 1986). p. 14.
[11]Balch and Stambaugh, *The New Testament*, p. 14.

of 'instilling a sense of pride in traditional Greek civilization'.[12] These ancient cases indicate that a cultural program serves to tame both the physical and mental space of the colonized. They also indicate that traveling and travelers are not neutral subject.[13] Imperial travelers depart from their familiar places to unfamiliar people and lands with goals of subjugating the later. The colonizing travelers, as indicated by the titles of king and saviour of unlimited spaces, construct themselves in particular fashions to validate their travel and to confront unfamiliar places and people. Physical lands and minds are thus 'spaces' that are subject to remolding through cultural texts and structures such as cities gymnasiums, markets and so on.

In contemporary times, Spain, Belgium, Portugal, Russia, Germany, France and Britain established empires of unparalleled magnitude, leaving little or no part of the earth untouched. Modern empires took different forms and methods from the ancient empires. Their unique strategies assumed the sophistication of dressing military might and economic greed in the guise of evangelical zeal, moral-rhetorical claims, technological, racial and cultural claims of superiority. Modern empires also differed according to each colonizing country as well as according to the particular culture and geographical area of the colonized. Temperatures that were similar or hospitable to the colonizing countries, for example, were much more likely to result in settler colonialism, while areas with non-hospitable temperatures were likely to lead to indirect rule. The struggle for independence has ever since been wedged and won by what largely constitutes the Two-Thirds World countries. Many of the formerly colonized nations are, nonetheless, undergoing new forms of imperialism, neo-colonialism or globalization. Globalization here defines the 'process which has led to the creation of a single, international (global) financial or capital market',[14] and landed most Two-Thirds World economies in huge debts and worse situations than in colonial times. The latest form of imperialism is also evident in ecological control, military muscle, universal media, and economic domination by the former and new imperialist powers.[15] Neo-colonization, in particular, underlines the differences that characterizes imperialist movements, for unlike ancient and modern empires, globalization largely excludes geographical occupation, or colonization proper, and, to some extent, it excludes government as transnational cooperations take the lead.[16]

---

[12]Balch and Stambaugh, *The New Testament*, p. 14.

[13]See Alison Blunt, *Travel, Gender and Imperialism: Mary Kingsley and West Africa* (New York: Guilford, 1994), pp. 15–19.

[14]Ngugi wa Thiong'o, *Moving the Centre: The Struggle for Cultural Freedoms* (London: James Currey, 1993), pp. 12–13; and Christopher Lind, *Something is Wrong Somewhere: Globlization, Community and the Moral Economy of the Farm Crisis* (Halifax: Fernwood, 1995), pp. 26–43.

[15]Lind, *Something is Wrong Somewhere*, p. 31.

[16]See Appadurai in Laura Chrisman and Patrick Williams (eds.). *Colonial Discourse and Postcolonial Theory: A Reader* (New York: Columbia University Press, 1994), p. 273, who has suggested five landscapes that help to highlight the different levels and departments of modern imperialisms: 'ethnoscape(especially groups in movements), technoscape (institutions of technology and its informational flows), "financescape" (the disposition of global capital), "mediascape" (both images produced and the mode of production), "ideoscape" (ideologies)'.

The dominated countries in the globalization era seemingly retain their own political leadership, and appear to be under control. These mutations of empires make it difficult to posit imperialism as a transhistorical institution even with a series of their reoccurrences. Nonetheless, it is hardly debatable that imperialisms of different times, forms, and strategies have affected and continue to affect this world on a global scale. Imperial images and structures of domination continue to affect the lives of billions of men and women, both the subjugated and the subjugator. How the people of the First World and Two-Thirds World perceive each other, how their cultural, economic and political institutions are structured, for instance, is inseparably tied to the imperial movements and the strategies that have been employed to control foreign geographical spaces and its inhabitants.

The above prefatory quotations attest that cultural texts were also central to the strategies of modern imperialism. Elleke Boehmer's study on *Colonial and Postcolonial Literature* indicate that modern imperial agents employed older and familiar narratives to read and to tame the 'new' and strange spaces. A textual strategy assisted the traveling colonial agents to cope and to colonize strange geographical places. As in Quint's findings on epic and empire, writing in modern empires has become an art of tapping

> the energy of metaphoric borrowings and reproductions within the wider tradition of colonial romance and adventure writing. Motifs of shipwreck, resourceful settlement and cultivation, treasure, slaves, and fear of cannibalism resurfaced time and again in boys' stories... [T]he pairing of white master and black slave/servant became an unquestioned commonplace.[17]

Boehmer's analysis further highlights that this web of intertextual reproductions was accompanied by a reproduction of certain cultural symbols and structures in different areas.[18] Architecture, plantations, magic lanterns, foods, clothes and names of European origin were transferred to various parts of the world.[19] Through this uniform transference of a few cultural structures and the reproduction of the same textual representations, different geographical spaces of the world and its inhabitants are homogenized, or colonized.

Both Quint and Boehmer highlight the wide range of imperializing texts, their production and their authors. They are largely written during the peak periods of imperial movements about the colonized and the colonizer, but mostly for and by the colonizing nations. The later are exemplified by the likes of *The Aeneid*, *Heart of Darkness*, *The Tempest* and Kipling's classic poem, 'The White Man's Burden'. They

---

[17]Elleke Boehmer, *Colonial and Postcolonial Literature* (New York: Oxford University Press, 1995), p. 47.
[18]Boehmer, *Colonial and Postcolonial Literature*, pp. 51–59.
[19]See V.Y. Mudimbe, *The Idea of Africa* (Bloomington: Indiana University Press, 1994), pp. 105–53, whose exposition on missionary strategies shows how domesticating both people's physical space and their minds sets up cultural structures such as houses, gardens, and schools that serve as beacons of colonial cultures.

also include literary works that imperial powers bring and give to the colonized. Good examples of these fall within the so-called humanist tradition, which, as Ngugi aptly argues, was a powerful form of colonizing the minds of African students for 'bourgeois Europe was always the center of the universe'.[20] In the latter case, imported texts function as forms of displacing local cultures and colonizing the minds. Imperializing texts, however, take many forms and are written by a variety of people. Sometimes even by the colonized who either collaborate with the dominant forces or yearn for the same power.[21] Regardless of who writes imperializing texts, they are characterized by literary constructions, representations, and uses that authorize taking possession of foreign geographical spaces and people.

One of the strategies of imperializing texts is the employment of female gender to validate relationships of subordination and domination.[22] Quint's study on the genealogy of the epic and its role in the empires, for instance, finds a sustained recall, rewriting, and reproduction of the figure of a fleeing Cleopatra on Aeneas shield in *The Aeneid* and its association with eastern nations. Maunier's sociological study of colonial processes and literature finds that 'native women have often been the first agents of contact', providing what he calls a 'classic literary motif of the tragic romance between the European man and native women'. Thus, Sigmund Freud, speaking within the imperial perspective of his time, could describe a 'woman as the dark continent'.[23] The use of female gender to describe the colonized serves the agendas of constructing hierarchical geographical spaces, races, and cultures,[24] but it also comes to legitimate the oppression of women in societies where these narratives are used.

In sum, texts that legitimate and authorize imperialism include most canonized classics of ancient and contemporary times—regardless of discipline or genre.[25] Classical texts such as the Bible, *The Iliad, The Odyssey* and *The Aeneid* have inspired and participated in different historical processes of imperialism.[26]

---

[20]Ngugi wa Thiong'o, *Decolonising the Mind*, p. 17.

[21]As I will show below, New Testament texts are a good case in point. They were indeed produced by the colonized, yet they subscribe to the ideology of expansion to foreign lands based on relationships of unequal power (Mt. 28.16-20; Jn 4.1–42). Commenting on the tendency of the colonized to assume strategies that befriend the colonizers' methods, David Quint (*Epic and Empire*, p. 18), holds that 'the losers who attract our sympathies today would be—had they only power—victors of tomorrow'.

[22]For further reading on gender roles, representations, and politics of reading in imperializing texts and contexts, see Alison Blunt, *Travel Gender and Imperialism*; Alison Blunt and Gillian Rose (eds.), *Writing Women and Space: Colonial and Postcolonial Geographies* (New York: Guildford, 1994); Laura Donaldson, *Decolonizing Feminisms: Race, Gender, and Empire-Building* (Chapel Hill: University of the North Carolina Press, 1992).

[23]Laura Chrisman and Patrick Williams (eds.), *Colonial Discourse and Postcolonial Theory: A Reader* (New York: Columbia University Press, 1994).

[24]Quint, *Epic and Empire*, pp. 31–41.

[25]See J.M. Blaut, *The Colonizer's Model of the World: Geographical Diffusionism and Eurocentric History* (New York: Guildford, 1993), pp. 1–124, for the construction of hierarchical geographies that legitimate the hierarchical racial constructions accompanying contemporary empires.

[26]See Quint, *Epic and Empire,* for the role of epics.

Contemporary texts range from modern English and French novels, travel narratives, anthropological documentation, and world maps to missionary reports, paintings, tourist photography, museum collections, and intelligence satellite photography.[27] The ensemble of these texts authorize imperialism through assuming various values and strategies: the glorification of military might and conquest; the promotion of travel that characterizes the travelers as authoritatively above foreign lands and their inhabitants; and the construction of foreign people and spaces in specific legitimizing forms. Foreign people are often characterized as inferior, dangerous, diseased, ungodly, kind, lazy and helpless in these texts, while their lands are constructed as empty, feminine, available, harsh, full of evil and profitable for the colonizing powers. These imperializing textual representations depend on sharply contrasting the colonizer's lands and people with those of the colonized. The colonized spaces and inhabitants are basically subjected to the standard of the colonizer, and difference is equated with deficiency.

Because of the centrality of cultural texts to imperialist projects, the struggle for liberation is not limited just to military, economic and political arenas. It necessarily requires and includes a cultural battle of reader-writers who attempt to arrest the violence of the imperializing texts. The centrality of literary texts in imperialism has, therefore, stimulated a literary response from the subjugated at different places and periods of time.[28] The colonized reread the imperializing texts and write new narratives that affirm the adequacy of their humanity, the reality of global diversity, and their right to independence.[29] They write in search of liberating ways that will affirm the interdependence of nations, races, genders and economies, ways which do not depend on oppressive and exploitative relationships.[30] The formerly colonized, who approximate the majority of the Two-Thirds World countries, therefore constitute communities of reader-writers who struggle to decolonize. Their practice challenges the Western or the so-called First World academic cultural texts, exposing and rejecting the literary forms of imperialism, or they admit their acceptance of it. As Said points out, a neutral position is not possible: to read or write for or against imperial domination is an unavoidable position—one that is already taken.[31]

---

[27]See Said, *Culture and Imperialism,* for the role of the novel.

[28]See Bill Ashcroft, Gareth Griffiths, and Helen Tiffin, *The Empire Writes Back: Theory and Practice in Post-Colonial literatures* (New York: Routledge, 1989), pp. 1–109; Barbara Harlow, *Resistance Literature* (New York: Methuen, 1987), pp. 1–75; and Said, *Culture and Imperialism,* pp. 1–150.

[29]See Chinua Achebe, *Hopes and Impediments: Selected Essays* (New York: Doubleday, 1989), pp. 1–20; and Ngugi wa Thiong'o, *Moving the Centre,* pp. 12–25, for their readings of *Heart of Darkness* and the investigation of the function of its constructions.

[30]See Said, *Culture and Imperialism,* pp. 3–43; 303–36, on the concept of interdependence, interconnectedness and the overlapping of territories, histories, cultures and identities. Said holds that interdependence is unavoidable. It is a necessary form of survival sought by both the colonizer and the colonized. The question, therefore, is to seek liberating forms of interdependence since, as he says, survival is about 'connections of things', people, nations, genders, economies rather than independence from one another.

[31]Said, *Culture and Imperialism,* p. 68.

Biblical Texts and Empire-building

The prefatory African saying highlights the Bible as one imperializing text. It emphasizes that for many African nations the success of colonization is inseparably linked with the use of the Bible. Ngugi wa Thiong'o, a Kenyan writer, underscores this experience by holding that the 'English, French, and the Portuguese came to the Third World to announce the arrival of the Bible and the sword.'[32] Ngugi insists that in the modern colonization of Africa, 'both William Shakespeare and Jesus Christ had brought light.'[33] This synoptic paralleling of military might and the biblical text, of Shakespeare with Jesus, does not exempt the Bible from imperialist violence. David Livingstone, for example, is a renowned colonial hero who championed the colonization of Africa and who made it an open secret that in colonization, 'civilization—Christianity and commerce—should ever be inseparable.'[34] In 1820 missionary Pringle could proudly say

> Let us enter upon a new and nobler career of conquest. Let us subdue Savage Africa by justice, by kindness, by the talisman of Christian truth. Let us thus go forth, in the name and under the blessing of God, gradually to extend the territorial boundary also of our colony, until is shall become an empire.[35]

Both Livingstone and Pringle found no contradiction, no secrecy, nor any reason to separate their Christian missions from the imperialist agendas of their countries. Now many people might dismiss the time of Livingstone as a period of church history which has little or nothing to do with the biblical period. Yet the question remains as to whether the travels of Livingstone and others were also sanctioned by Christian texts and whether the mission texts they used advocate liberating ways of interdependence or the suppression of difference. The question remains as to when and where 'the talisman of Christian truth' is located.

If Livingstone and Pringle can be dismissed as zealous church missionaries, figures such as Albert Schweitzer, who acted as a colonial envoy and influenced academic biblical studies in a big way,[36] hardly exempts academic biblical studies, scholars, their interpretations, or indeed, the texts themselves from the violence of imperialism. Modern European and American colonizing powers openly defined their task as a Puritan 'errand to the wilderness', 'a duty to the natives', or 'a mission to civilize'—moral claims derived from Christian texts, which beg to be investigated.[37]

---

[32]Ngugi wa Thiong'o, *Moving the Centre*, p. 31.
[33]Ngugi wa Thiong'o, *Decolonising the Mind*, p. 91.
[34]Norman E. Thomas, *Classic Texts in Mission and World Christianity* (New York: Orbis Books, 1995), p. 68.
[35]Quoted in Mudimbe, *The Invention of Africa*, p. 47, without giving Pringle's second or first name.
[36]Marcus Borg, *Jesus in Contemporary Scholarship* (Valley Forge, PA: Trinity Press International, 1992), pp. 3–4, 18.
[37]See Rudyard Kipling, 'The White Man's Burden'. The poem demonstrates dependency on biblical images: colonizing travelers are portrayed as the light to the heathen and half-devil people. Like Moses, the colonizer is confronted with the complaints of the colonized who wish to return to the night and bondage of Egypt. In short, modern colonizers' projects are equated to the Christian mission.

Reading the Bible and other cultural texts for decolonization is, therefore, imperative for those who are committed to the struggle for liberation. Why the Bible is a usable text in imperial projects and how it should be read in the light of its role are central questions to the process of decolonization and the struggle for liberation. As a Motswana woman of Southern Africa, my reading for decolonization arises from the historical encounter of Christian texts functioning compatibly with colonialism; of the Bible functioning as the 'talisman' in imperial possession of foreign places and people. While history attests to the 'use' of biblical texts, and while the Bible may have been one of the Western texts that helped imperial travel to perceive and to domesticate unfamiliar strange places, my reading seeks to investigate whether its use is supported by the ideology of Christian mission texts. My reading seeks to interrogate the travel/mission texts of the Bible and the power relations between different cultural lands and people that they advocate.

In reading a mission text for decolonization, however, I am not denying that cross-cultural exchanges between races and nations has gone on, still goes on, and must continue to go on outside imperialist contexts. Neither am I equating with imperialism every attempt to spread one's influence to other cultures and lands. Rather, my reading seeks to confront the imperialist projects of biblical texts and to investigate the grounds of their dramatic, historic partnership.[38] Thus I have chosen the story of the Samaritan woman for obvious reasons: it is a mission narrative; one that authorizes its reader-believer to 'go forth', so to speak. Furthermore, my reading will interrogate and highlight the power relations John 4 proposes for international cultural relations and exchanges.

Reading for Decolonization: John 4.1–42

My reading attributes the construction of this story to the Johannine community and their missionary vision, rather than the historical Jesus and his disciples. In reading for decolonization, I will deal with the imperial setting, hidden interests, travelers, geography/lands, expansion, and the construction of the Samaritan woman/people/land. I will conclude by looking at one Two-Thirds World woman's attempt to decolonize the story. Throughout the explication of these factors, I will use particular quotations from the story as subtitles to highlight some of the main

---

[38]Elsewhere I have tabulated the following questions as criteria for identifying imperializing texts: (1) Does this text have a clear stance against the political imperialism of its time? (2) Does this text encourage its readers/hearers/believers to travel to distant lands and how does it justify itself? (3) How does this text construct differences? Is there dialogue and liberating interdependence, or is there condemnation and replacement of all that is foreign? (4) Does this text employ gender and divine representations/claims to construct relationships of subordination and domination? See further, Musa W. Dube, *Postcolonial Feminist Interpretations of the Bible* (St Louis: Chalice, 2000).

imperial ideological constructions of the narrative. Despite my attempt to treat each point independently, the reader will find them closely intertwined.

'The Pharisees had heard Jesus is making and baptizing more disciples than John. . .!' (John 4.1)

The mention of Pharisees, Jesus and John the Baptist highlights an intense struggle for power directly related to imperialist occupation. (Historically, the gospel is written several decades after the Roman Empire had destroyed Jerusalem and the Temple in 70 CE. The destruction of the central Jewish symbols of meaning has contributed to creating an intense inter-group competition for power, characterized by negotiation, collaboration and revolt against the Roman Empire by various national groups. Evidently, in Jn 4.1, three movements/interests groups are vying for power in Palestine: The Pharisees, Jesus and his disciples, and John the Baptist and his disciples. As the first verse clearly indicates Jesus is fleeing from the Pharisees, who have heard he 'is making and baptizing more disciples than John' (v. 1).) I will now briefly explicate these competitions and how they are related to imperialist presence.

First, there is competition for power between the disciples of John the Baptist, a representative of one interest group, and the disciples of Jesus. Thus the text of John rhetorically subordinates John to Jesus. In the prologue, the narrator states that John the Baptist 'was not the light, but he came to testify to the light' (1.6–9). On two other occasions, the Baptist is characterized as devaluing himself to underline the superiority of Jesus. First, he says 'this is he whom I said after me comes a man who ranks ahead of me because he was before me' (1.29–37). Later, he says Jesus 'must increase, but I must decrease' (3.22–30). However, many scholars argue that there is good reason to suggest that John and his disciples were an independent movement. This textual subordination of John to Jesus simplifies the conflicts as one between the Pharisees and Jesus and his disciples, who are, no doubt, the biggest rivals within the Gospel of John.

Second, there is competition between the disciples of Jesus and the disciples of Moses, the Pharisees. In the post-70 CE period the Pharisees were not only another interest group, but were also the officially recognized power in Palestine (3.1, 7.48, 12.42). Therefore, the Pharisees and the Sadducees appear as a united authoritative power in John's gospel (7.32, 45; 11.47, 57), a construction which tries to be faithful to Jesus's times and the author's times. As the gospel attests (7–12.50), competition for power and enmity between the disciples of Jesus and the disciples of Moses (Pharisees) has reached its peak with dire consequences. The disciples of Jesus have lost their influence and have been thrown out of the synagogue (9.22, 35; 12.42). Some may even have died (16.2).

Third, when we enter the story of Jn 4.1–42, we witness the consequences of imperial disruption and inter-group competition at two levels. First, the disciples of Jesus are extending their influence to Samaria because they are losing the national competition to the Pharisees. Second, we enter into centuries of imperial subtexts of disruption, alienation and resistance that strains the relationships of the Samaritans and Jews (4.9, 20–23). This tension goes back to the period of the Assyrian Empire. Through intermarriages and the adoption of some of the religions of their Assyrian colonial masters, Samaritans became what some have termed 'despised heretics' and 'despised half-breeds'. As a result, the Samaritan Jewish ancestors distanced themselves from Samaritans on the grounds of religious impurity. Their strained relationship highlights the extent to which imperial domination has affected and influenced the relationship of different people at different centuries in the world.

In sum, imperial domination is central to the story of the Samaritan woman and to John's gospel as a whole. The local leaders who plan the death of Jesus, for instance, are characterized as in genuine fear that his fame will bring a Roman attack on the nation (11.48–53). At his trial, faithfulness to Roman imperial power is evoked to justify the guilt of Jesus (19.12, 15); and Pilate insists on crucifying Jesus as the awaited political liberator—a Jewish king—despite the chief priests' resistance to the inscription, 'Jesus of Nazareth, the King of the Jews' (19.19–22). All these factors highlight how the Roman imperial expansionist agendas and the imposition of its own cultural symbols and power stimulated a response and led to inter-group competition within Jewish society.[39]

Likewise, Jesus and his disciples' turn to the despised land of Samaritans is linked to the competition for power between the Pharisees and Christian Jews. Both Pharisees and Christian Jews are trying to define Jewish identity during the Roman occupation of Palestine; in particular, after the destruction of their religious symbols—Jerusalem and the Temple. And it is important that this competition for power between local interest groups is not be divorced from the real enemy—from its root cause: the Roman empire. The story of the Samaritan woman illustrates how imperialism affects people in general: it leads the colonized to fight back, to collaborate with the enemy, or to fight among themselves, as in the case of Pharisees and Jesus's disciples.

It seems safe to say that Jesus's disciples are losing (6.66; 12.42–43). They are not making many disciples as other groups (4.1), and so they turn to proselytize the Samaritans. In other words, (the alternative vision of the Johannine community ironically embraces an ideology of expansion, despite the fact that it, itself, is the victim of imperial expansion and is struggling for its own liberation).[40] But as is common in imperial ideologies of expansion, the Johannine search for influence is

---

[39]See Andrew J. Overman, *Matthew's Gospel and Formative Judaism: The Social World of the Matthean Community* (Minneapolis: Fortress Press, 1990), for an illuminating discussion on the impact of imperial forces on first-century Palestine. In particular, how it led to conflict, competition and fragmentation of Jewish society as each interest group attempted to define the cultural boundaries, and how such a competition included collaborating with the imperial powers.

[40]See Craig Koester, 'The Saviour of the World (John 4.42)', *JBL* 109 (1990), pp. 665–80, whose article highlights Jn 4's direct borrowing of imperial ideology to express the Christian identity.

not openly expressed. And so I come to a point in my argument where the hidden interests in the ideology of imperialism can finally be explicitly addressed.

'Look!... See how the fields are ripe for harvesting...!' (John 4.35)

The ideology of imperialism typically conceals its interests and presents its project in rhetorical terms such as the 'duty to the natives', who 'require and beseech domination'.[41] Similarly in John 4, the Johannine community conceals its interests through the literary characterization of Jesus and his disciples. First, the narrator states that Jesus is in transit through Samaria. But his real destination is Galilee. Thus at Sychar, we meet Jesus sitting by the well—notably, outside the village—because 'he is tired out by his journey' to Galilee (vv. 5–6). The refusal to admit to any intention to enter and missionize is further underscored by the fact that Jesus only enters the village when the Samaritans themselves 'asked him to stay with them' (v. 40). Thus the narration of Jesus's journey resists any open acknowledgment of an intention to evangelize Samaria. The story prefers to hold that the Samaritans need Jesus's missionary work (v. 22); they follow Jesus of their own accord (v. 30); and they asked for Jesus's message (v. 40).

The hidden interests are also evident in the characterization of the disciples in the story. First, they appear as a faint background of the story. They have gone to buy food in the city *not* to missionize (v. 9). The dialogue between Jesus and the Samaritan woman takes place in their absence. When they return, she departs, and Jesus begins to speak to them about his food, that is, 'to do the will of him who sent me and to complete his work' (v. 34). In this discussion, they are notably puzzled by Jesus's talk, which turns into a monologue. In general, his disciples remain silent and they never openly question or seem to understand. All these literary constructions distance the disciples from any intention to missionize the Samaritans. The evangelization of Samaritans thus falls squarely on the Samaritans themselves: it is the woman and the villagers who beg Jesus to enter the village and stay with them.

Jesus's response to the disciples in this short scene (vv. 31–38), however, is central to the whole story of the Samaritan woman. The scene provides the disciples with an interpretive grid through which they must understand their food, that is, like Jesus who is sent, they are sent, (vv. 34, 38). They are authorized to go, to enter, and to teach other nations. It is in this scene that the rhetoric of interests and power is aggressively articulated; yet it remains concealed by an ideology of disinterest. Jesus says to them: 'Look around you, and see how the fields are ripe for harvesting... One sows, another reaps. I sent you to reap that for which you did not labor. Others have labored, and you have entered into their labor' (vv. 37–38). Many scholars have wrestled with these sayings.[42] Two factors are pertinent to my reading. First, the fields

---

[41]Said, *Culture and Imperialism*, p. 9.

[42]The main problem lies in the contradictory statements about the sowers. At first, it seems there is equal division of labor and rewards (vv. 36–37), but the concluding verse suggests otherwise (v. 38). While the reapers are disciples, the identity of sowers remains ambiguous. Jesus has been suggested, but since the verse speaks

are ripe for harvest. The statement articulates an evident search for profit and a desire to take possession of something. Regardless of whether the possession is spiritual or material, it involves a will to power which is invested in real people and affects real people. Second, the legitimation of the disciples' power entails frightening values: the disciples are *sent to reap that for which they did not labor*. Such a statement reflects the intensity of competition and struggle for control and, of necessity, depends on unequal relationships.

Consequently, the Samaritans are construed as passive fields to be entered and harvested.[43] Yet, these fields are not limited to Samaria. They include the whole world (v. 42). But once more, this 'global' vision is placed in the mouth of the Samaritans who must proclaim him 'the Saviour of the World'. This characterization distances the disciples from any self-interest and projects an imperial ideology that portrays the colonized as people who 'require and beseech for domination' and the colonizers as people with a moral 'duty to the natives'.

We must remember that historically the story represents a much later vision of the mission (v. 38) arising, as I said, from the Johannine community rather than from the historical Jesus and his disciples. It is therefore striking how the disciples (or the Johannine community) who are most probably the proponents of the missionary vision and authors of the story, present themselves as mute and puzzled by Jesus's talk of ripe fields. Through this literary presentation, the disciples (Johannine community) rhetorically distance themselves from their own vision precisely in order to conceal their interests until the very end. For instance, if the disciples are going to take all the credit for the Samaritan woman's work, the Samaritan people themselves will discredit her importance (v. 42).

Although the rhetoric of concealment pervades the narrative, the story authorizes the Christian disciples/readers/believers to travel, enter, educate and to harvest other foreign lands for the Christian nations. And it does this in a literary fashion that is openly modeled on imperialist values. This is evident both in the saying, 'I have sent you to reap that which you did not labor. Others labored, and you have entered into their labor' and in the title 'Saviour of the World', as a designation of Jesus. Notably, the saying evokes Josh. 24.13, where the Lord God speaks to the Israelites through Joshua saying, 'I gave you a land on which you had not labored, and towns that you had not built, and you live in them; you eat the fruit of vineyards and olive groves that you did not plant'. The book of Joshua is a highly dramatized and idealized capture

---

of many other sowers', other explanations—such as former prophets, Hellenist evangelists, or the Samaritan woman herself have been suggested.

[43]According to Raymond Brown (*The Gospel and Epistles of John* [Collegeville, MN: Liturgical Press, 1988], p.18), 'the disciples must learn to harvest the crop of believers even though they have not sowed the seed'. He goes on to point out that 'in Acts 8.4–25, Phillip the Hellenist evangelizes Samaria, and then the Jerusalem apostles send Peter and John to confirm the conversion'. Although Brown mentions that both the sower and reaper must rejoice together, his interpretation leans toward validating hierarchical structures.

of the Canaan. It is a narrative that glorifies conquest and openly advocates violent colonialism in the name of God.

As noted above, 'Saviour of the World' was a title used to refer to the Roman emperors in the first century. Surprise, surprise! The Johannine Jesus now emerges fully clothed in the emperor's titles.[44] Thus, Jesus also lays claim to unlimited access to all geographical spaces and foreigners. In evoking Joshua's narrative and borrowing the titles of emperors to articulate the Christian mission and to characterize Jesus, John 4 models its vision along imperial goals, strategies and values. The mission is portrayed as a violent entry and domestication of foreign lands and people. It involves reaping fields that one did not plant. This finally brings me to the travelers themselves and their role in the imperialist project. My points will be developed by focusing on Jesus and his disciples as travelers.

'My food is to do the will of him who sent me... I send you...!' (John 4.34, 38)

Imperialism as an ideology of expansion involves superior travelers who reflect the superiority of their origin. Similarly, Jesus and his disciples are the authorized travelers 'from above' (3.34, 8.26; 20.21–23). Their travel is linked with expansion, and it is both locally and 'globally' oriented. First, they are traveling because the expansion of their mission has brought them trouble (v. 1); but soon thereafter, their departure results in further expansion (vv. 30, 39). Jesus's commission to the disciples to harvest the ripe fields, and the Samaritans' declaration that Jesus is the 'Saviour of the World' indicates that their expansion espouses 'global' levels. The disciples of Jesus are 'global travelers', as it were. Like their master, they are authorized from above; hence, they are superior to everyone else.

Jesus and his disciples are travelers invested with high authority far above their hosts. To begin with, Jesus is a very superior traveler. His superiority is communicated through the literary style used for his identification: a gradual unfolding which shows his superiority at every stage of the story. The Samaritan woman, who first thought he was just a simple Jewish man, discovers that Jesus can give her living water which leads to eternal life (v. 10); he is greater than Jacob (vv. 12–14). And he is not only a prophet (v. 19) or a Messiah (v. 26), but the 'Saviour of the World' (v. 42). This gradual unveiling of Jesus's identity characterizes him as an extremely superior traveler who surpasses all other local figures.

The characterization of Jesus in John 4 is consistent with his portrayal in the rest of the gospel of John. For instance, Johannine scholars have noted how Jesus is compared to other Christological figures such as the Word, the Lamb of God, the King of Israel, Moses and the Messiah/Christ. This is a literary device designed to show that he is well above all these figures.[45] The comparison is a rhetorical ladder for

---

[44]Talbert, *Reading John*, p. 118; Koester, 'The Saviour of the World', pp. 665–80, and Cassidy, *John's Gospel*, pp. 6–16.

[45]See Robert Kysar, *John: The Maverick Gospel* (Louisville: John Knox Press, 1976), pp. 22–46; and J.L. Martyn, *The Gospel of John in Christian History: Essays in Interpretation* (New York: Paulist Press, 1978), pp. 9–54.

his elevation: it foregrounds his superiority and almost equates him with God (1.1; 20.28) while it derogates the validity of all others.

While the disciples are rhetorically obscured in the story of the Samaritan woman, they nevertheless travel with Jesus. The story serves to give them the right to travel with authority (v. 38). Their authority is derived from and is closely related to that of Jesus (v. 34, 20.21–23). It is authority from above, from God. However, such authority can only be justified by a negative portrayal of those nations and lands that must be entered, taught and converted. This brings to me to the characterization of the Samaritan woman, or, as some have noted, the Samaritan land.

'If you knew… You worship what you do not know… We worship what we know!' (John 4.10, 22)

Imperialism expounds an ideology of inferior knowledge and invalid religious faith for those who must be colonized. Authoritative travelers depend heavily upon constructions of ignorant natives. There is a sharp division between those who know, the colonizers, and those who know nothing, the colonized. Thus the Samaritan woman is characterized as an ignorant native (v. 10) and in need of help (v. 10). She is constructed as morally or religiously lacking something; that is, she has had five husbands, and the one she has now is not her own (vv. 17–18). Furthermore, she does not know what she worships (v. 22). By way of contrast, Jesus, a superior traveler, is knowledgeable (vv. 10, 22); powerful (vv. 14, 25, 42); sees everything about her past (vv. 17–18, 29); knows and offers answers to her community (vv. 21–26); and teaches her and her people (vv. 21–23). The ignorance of the Samaritan woman is pathetic. Despite all these revelations (v. 26), she remains ignorant to the end. That is, she is still uncertain and asks, 'he cannot be the Messiah, can he?' (v. 29).[46] As Gail O'Day's analysis correctly notes, the Samaritan woman's inability to understand is well above that of the male disciples (vv. 27, 31–33).[47]

Here, ignorance is furthered by employing the feminine gender. In the mission story, a narrative that authorizes traveling to and entering into foreign lands and places, it is significant that she becomes a first point of contact. As in imperializing narratives, this pattern is a statement about the targeted land and its inhabitants. Like the woman who represents them, the foreign land must be entered, won and domesticated. And so the next subtitle highlights the rhetoric of hierarchical geographical spaces.

'Are you greater than our ancestor Jacob, who gave us this well and…drank from it?' (John 4.12)

Authoritative travelers also depend on an ideology of hierarchical geographical spaces. Jesus is the highest authority and the most authoritative traveler in John's

---

[46]See Gail R. O'Day, *Revelation in the Fourth Gospel* (Philadelphia: Fortress Press, 1986), who focuses on the Samaritan woman and gives an extensive analysis of her character.

[47]See Gail R. O'Day, *The Word Disclosed: John's Story and Narrative Preaching* (St Louis: CBP, 1987), pp. 48–49.

gospel. Consequently, a specific geography had to be constructed for him. That is, he has descended from the Father and will ascend to the Father.[48] His origin allows him to become a 'World Saviour' because he is not of the world. However, this also necessitates that the world should be constructed negatively (8.12, 23; 9.39; 12.31; 13.1).

Within the story of the Samaritan woman, hierarchical constructions of geographical spaces are also evident. There are Judea and Galilee, lands that are much holier than Samaria and Sychar; lands which are best avoided (v. 9). Concomitantly, the occupants of Samaria are also of questionable value. The negative characterization of the Samaritans allows Jesus to assert his religious superiority (v. 22), even when he is discrediting both Gerizim and Jerusalem (v. 21). Jacob's well in Samaria (v. 12) pales beside Jesus's spring of superior waters (v. 13). Ripe fields must be entered and harvested by those who did not sow them (vv. 35–38). And, lastly, the world must be saved (v. 42). These hierarchical, geographical constructions authorize travelers of superior origins and values (Jesus and his disciples) to expand, enter and control, at both local and 'global' levels, those geographical areas that are depicted as inferior in their systems of value (Samaria and the world).

'You will worship the Father neither on this mountain nor in Jerusalem…!' (John 4.2)

The imperialist ideology of expansion uses the promotion of its own cultural values to devalue, replace and suppress diversity. Its strategy is characterized by a massive inclusivity, but not equality. Similarly, in Jn 4.1–42 the mission expands from the well to the world. Notably, the expansion declares the cultural centers of Jerusalem and Gerizim as inadequate and replaces them with Spirit and truth.[49] This apparent inclusive replacement maintains the religious/racial superiority of Jesus (v. 22), a characterization that clearly shows that imperialism's universal standards never intend to create relationships of equals, but intend to win devotees. Therefore, the transcendence of both Jewish and Samaritan cultural spaces by the realm of Spirit and truth (vv. 23–24), in fact, installs Christianity in the superior position. And as we now know, this installation proceeds by discrediting all other religious cultures for its own interests. We perceive this unequal inclusion through the discursive use and final dismissal of the only female gendered character in the story.

'They said to the woman, "It is no longer because of what you said that we believe"' (John 4.42)

Imperialist ideologies of subjugation construct extremely gendered discourses. The lands that must be subjugated are equated with women, and narratives about the penetration of distant lands feature women. Ancient epic texts feature numerous

---

[48]See Fernando Segovia, 'Journey(s) of the Word: A Reading of the Plot of the Fourth Gospel', *Semeia* 53 (1991), pp. 23–54, for an extensive treatment of journeys and origins embedded in the plot of John's gospel. For the concept of descending and ascending and its sociological function. See Wayne Meeks, 'The Man from Heaven in Johannine Sectarianism', *JBL* 91 (1972), pp. 44–72.

[49]See Jerome Neyrey, 'Jacob Traditions and the Interpretation of John 4.10–26', *CBQ* 41 (1979), pp. 419–37, on this point.

goddesses and women at the shores of foreign and distant lands. Biblical examples are the stories of the Jericho prostitute (Josh. 2) and the Canaanite woman (Mt. 15.21–28). Like a woman, the target of colonialism is entered, conquered and domesticated. Thus many scholars have noted that the Samaritan woman represents her land. She is the point of entrance, and she is finally domesticated (v. 41). Moreover, those who did not sow, the male disciples, are invited to move in to reap the harvest, while she is dismissed (vv. 37–38).[50]

As previously mentioned, imperialist expansion suggests a massive inclusion of races, lands, genders and religions, but not equality. The inclusion is intended to legitimate control, and control depends on unequal relationships. The unequal inclusivity of this narrative is grounded in the very literary device employed. E. Fuchs's research on the betrothal type-scene is instructive here.[51] Fuchs notes that betrothal type-scenes are a constellation of literary motifs employed to mark the launching of a young patriarch's career. The type-scene begins with a young man's journey to the outside world where he meets his future bride at the well. As the scene proceeds, the status of the woman decreases into obscurity. Men take over to discuss her future and her family's wealth. She marries and departs with her husband. Thus as Fuchs notes, betrothal type-scenes are not about the woman but about the launching of a patriarch's career.

The story of the Samaritan woman is built on the same literary foundation. At first, the narrative leads the reader to celebrate her role (and other relationships involving worship, sowers, and reapers). Yet after she finishes announcing Jesus Christ to her townspeople, she never speaks out again. The discussion of her work and its product is transferred into the hands of Jesus, his male disciples, and the village converts—who, after meeting with Jesus—relegate her work to secondary status (v. 42). Here we perceive the launching of Jesus's career outside his home; that is, the birth of his bride (the church or the Johannine community). Jesus's relationship—and by extension Christianity's relationship to foreign people and lands—is, unfortunately, grounded on a very unequal foundation, as attested by the portrayals of race, gender, and geography in the Gospel of John. Accordingly, what seems to be an inclusive gospel of Spirit and Truth is the reverse. It reflects the installation of Christianity as a universal religion: an installation that proceeds by disavowing all geographical boundaries in order to claim power over the 'world' and relegate all other religions and cultures to inadequacy.

---

[50]Although some readers compare the Samaritan woman's story to John the Baptist or the disciples, who point others to Christ, her story is somewhat different. John the Baptist is at least given a chance to speak for himself and to say that it is his honor to decrease while Jesus Christ increases (3.28–30). The disciples continue to follow Christ and are finally commissioned (20.21–23). The Samaritan woman, however, is never given a chance to say a word after returning from the city. Instead, there is an open dismissal or devaluation of her work (v. 42). If her story represents a later time, when the church began to seriously consider the mission to the Gentiles, then her dismissal is a serious statement on the role of women, rather than just a Johannine pattern of discipleship.

[51]Esther Fuchs, 'Structure and Patriarchal Functions in Biblical Betrothal Type-Scenes: Some Preliminary Notes', *Journal of Feminist Studies in Religion* 3 (1987), pp. 7–13.

Yet as Jeffrey Staley catalogues the uniqueness of the Samaritan woman's story, it is more than just betrothal type-scene.[52] Gary Phillips also notes that 'against the backdrop of the traditional women at the well screen, the Samaritan woman's actions are disturbingly different'.[53] The significant diversion of the Samaritan woman's story points to its wider literary category, one which I have called a type-scene of land possession. For the Samaritan woman and Jesus do not end up married, like in most betrothal stories. The Samaritan woman is not even a marriageable virgin, but a woman who has had five husbands and is living with another one who is not hers. She represents her land. If, as some scholars have noted, her characterization is a statement about Samaria, then Jesus is 'another bridegroom'; another husband. Hence, like other emperors, Jesus is entitled to unlimited access to all the geographical spaces of Samaria and the world, as his new title expressly says. The ideology of this story is that foreign lands are immoral women which await taming by foreign saviours.

In this story, therefore, patriarchal and imperial literary-rhetorical methods of domination are intertwined, making a feminist appropriation of the story a precarious and critically demanding exercise. Undoubtedly, the use of a female figure to articulate relationships of subordination and domination also encourages the oppression of women wherever these texts are used. Therefore, focus on the patriarchal aspect of this narrative, to the exclusion of its imperial aspects, will effect a feminist reading that baptizes colonial oppression and reinscribes the oppression of women.

Given the global experience of imperial and patriarchal domination, its persistence, and the real suffering and exploitation of those who are at its receiving end, how can one read the story of the Samaritan woman for decolonization and for the empowerment of women? How can one foster a new narrative of liberating interdependence that recognizes and nurtures diversity? In searching for the answers to some of these questions, I turn to one Two-Thirds World woman's attempt to rewrite the story for decolonization and the empowerment of women.

One Woman's Decolonizing Reading of John 4.1–42

The Victims' setting is pre-independent to post-independent Botswana and apartheid South Africa. Mositi Totontle's major concerns are the settler colonial practices of the white apartheid regime and their effects on the whole region of Southern Africa;

---

[52]See Jeffrey Staley, *The Print's First Kiss: A Rhetorical Investigation of the Implied Reader in the Fourth Gospel* (Atlanta: Scholars Press, 1988), pp. 95–103, for a detailed comparison between the standard betrothal type-scene and the story of the Samaritan woman.
[53]Gary Phillips, 'The Ethics of Reading Deconstructively or Speaking Face-to-Face: The Samaritan Woman Meets Derrida at the Well', in Edgar V. McKnight and Elisabeth Struthers Malbon (eds.), *The New Literary Criticism and the New Testament* (Valley Forge, PA: Trinity Press International, 1994), p. 303.

in particular, the breakdown of family life due to structurally coerced mine labor immigration. As one of the characters describes it, it 'is a sick land and a broken people' in need of healing, for the 'whole society has been shaken, shattered and scattered'.[54] Within this setting of brokenness, Totontle re-writes the story of the Samaritan woman as follows:

> Mmapula…went down the river to fetch water for her plants. Beside the well sat a still woman dressed in white clothing. Her head was bowed and focused in her open hands. Mmapula trod slowly, wondering who she was and what she was doing at this place and time. Mmapula sat down by the well and began to fill her container with water. Just when she was about to leave, the woman in white looked up and said, 'Samaritan woman, give me a drink'. Mmapula gave her a drink. 'Samaritan woman, go and call your husband', she said retaining Mmapula's gourd without drinking the water. 'I am not a Samaritan woman and I have no husband'. The woman in white closed her eyes for some seconds and said, 'You have spoken well, Samaritan woman. You have no husband. In fact, the husband that you have does not belong to you but to the mines. I have come to give you a drink of living water', she said handing Mmapula the same gourd of water. 'Go back to your village and announce that a prophetess has come bringing healing to the broken hearted'. 'A prophet has come bringing healing to Borolong'. The news spread at the speed of a veld fire through the small village.[55]

Totontle's decolonizing reading of Jn 4.1–42 recognizes and makes attempts to arrest the imperializing aspects of the story. But I wish to show how she arrests the oppressive constructions of gender, race, geography and religion. Lastly, I will discuss the author's use of the Samaritan identity as an ideal space to emphasize interconnections in a world constructed by imperialism.

Central to Totontle's rereading is her attempt to decolonize hierarchical gender and race. First, she arrests gender superiority by featuring a female character in the place of Jesus.[56] Second, the Samaritan woman is explicitly 'sent', and so has the status conferred upon male the disciples in Jn 4.38. There is also a clear attempt to decolonize the construction of racial superiority. For example, when asked for water, Mmapula responds positively without any questions. Mmapula's response challenges and dispenses any claims of cultural purity or impurity; hence, it undercuts the ideology of superior and inferior races that heavily depends on such dichotomies. Her response is subversive with regard to the imperial ideology that heavily depends

---

[54]See Sandra Schneiders, *The Revelatory Text: Interpreting the New Testament as Sacred Scripture* (San Francisco: HarperCollins, 1991), pp. 190–91, for an interpretation that reads the husbands as representations of the different empires of the past. In her reading, the current husband would be the Roman Empire.

[55]Mositi Totontle, *The Victims* (Gaborone: Botsalo, 1993), pp. 57–58.

[56]See Mary Ann Tolbert, 'Protestant Women and the Bible: On the Horns of a Dilemma', in Alice Balch (ed.), *The Pleasure of her Text: Feminist Readings of Biblical and Historical Texts* (Philadelphia: Trinity Press International, 1990), pp. 18–19, who suggests 'imagining Jesus and the twelve as women and a man anointing her head with oil (Mk 14.3–9)' and holds that such a reversal of characters can create a new way of viewing some of these biblical stories.

on the claims of racial superiority and chosenness—as attested by the histories of North American and South African colonization. Yet Mmapula denies her Samaritan identity, while the prophetess insists on it. Her insistence is a point I shall revisit later. Totontle's reading also decolonizes geographical hierarchy by offering the Samaritan woman living water from her own well on her own land. The geographical affirmation of her land serves to affirm its occupants and the adequacy of their cultural values. To accentuate this point, nothing is said about Mmapula's possession of many husbands— although we are informed that she has no husband. Furthermore, prophecy—that is, social criticism and the search for new visions of reconstruction—is preferred over universal salvation. Therefore, the woman in white is notably a prophetess and not a Saviour of the World. She has come to bring healing to the village, and her style of healing affirms that the villagers already have strength and abilities in and among themselves. With regard to religion, Totontle's decolonizing reading avoids any replacement or rejection of other faith orientations. In fact, the prophetess, who is later identified as Mother Mary Magdalene, is also a preacher and a faith-healer. In her preaching, she retells biblical stories from her memory, and in her healing she calls on the African Ancestral Spirits and Jesus to heal the land and bind its wounds.[57] In short, she does not privilege the Christian stories over the religious stories of Africans; she uses them both as she finds them useful. Thus the characterization of Mary Magdalene as a decolonizing interpreter serves to underline and to embrace the identity of Mmapula as despised heretic. The despised heretic becomes the ideal model for a truly post-colonial and inclusive world![58] This latter point brings me to the category/identity of the Samaritan as the ideal space for acknowledging cultural interconnections, as well as for nurturing differences.

Despite Mmapula's denial of her Samaritan identity, Mother Mary Magdalene's insistence on it implies an emphasis on the imperialist setting. Like the biblical Samaritan woman, Mmapula is a despised heretic, an outcaste half-breed; she cannot claim any purity of race or religion, and she has lived through several types of imperialist domination. Various forms of imperialism have affected and constructed Mmapula as well as the Fourth Gospel's Pharisees, John the Baptist, Jesus, and his disciples. The Samaritan identity is, therefore, highlighted as the reality of both the biblical characters of John 4 and Mmapula. Totontle's decolonizing reading shows that imperialism is the reality for those nations and races who claim purity and those who cannot claim it; for those who are consciously aware of imperialism as

---

[57]Mositi Totontle, *The Victims*, pp. 60, 73–76.

[58]Mositi Totontle, *The Victims*, p. 71. Her description of Mother Mary Magdalene's attire depicts her remarkable diversity: She 'was wearing a white turban, a red cape, a rosary, white and red beads on her writs and held a Zion hymn book in her hands. Dineo tried to place her various lines of faith and found that her dress pronounced her a mixture of various things and follower of none.'

a pervasive reality in the world, and for those who are not aware of it. It is indeed a reality for First World biblical readers and for Two-Thirds World biblical readers.

Mmapula's final response underscores the pervasity of imperialism: in the end she does not deny her Samaritan race. In short, she comes to the reality of who she is—a mixture of many different things: a despised heretic and an outcaste half-breed.

Conclusion

Many biblical narratives are imperializing texts insofar as they use history to propound power relations. The mission passages—which can be fairly termed the central Christian narratives that authorize traveling and entering into foreign cultures and lands exemplified by John 4—hardly propose relations of liberating interdependence between races, cultures and genders. Both the prefatory African saying and the words of missionary-colonial agents attest to the participation of biblical texts in colonial projects; they bind the Bible to the history of subjugation and exploitation. This obligates First World and Two-Thirds World communities of reader-writers to interrogate the biblical ideology of travel, expansion, representations of differences, and their various functions.

Because of the historical reoccurrences, the contemporary persistence, and the mutations of imperialisms, imperialism will not be easily bracketed from the critical practice of academic biblical interpretation. Therefore it is imperative that biblical scholars take cognizance of the world that is wedged between imperial domination, collaboration and resistance. It is also imperative that biblical scholars take cognizance of texts that, more often than not, offer models of international relationships which are less than liberating; which have served in different imperialist projects and lift up writing-reading communities which are calling for decolonization. Totontle's decolonizing reading of John 4 challenges biblical readers, hearers, believers and writers to acknowledge and to embrace their Samaritan social spaces of heretics and half-breeds. Similarly, biblical critical practice must be dedicated to an ethical task of promoting decolonization, fostering diversity, and imagining liberating ways of interdependence.

49. Oppression, Marginalization and Liberation: Discussion Questions

Why should theology consider particular contexts?

How is participation in economic life assessed in the diversity of political theology?

What resources do liberation theologies provide to retrieve Christianity from its entrenchment in power?

VIII

Creation, History and Eschatology

Introduction by Elizabeth Phillips

It could be argued that the core of Christian political theology concerns the issues of the church and the political introduced in Section III. It might then be said that the issues introduced in this section (on creation, history and eschatology) provide the broad theological framework within which the specific topics of Sections IV–VII arise from that theological core, and can be approached in various ways as seen in Sections I–II. In other words, (a) the driving and recurring question of Christian political theology has surrounded understanding the sovereignty of God and the kingdom of Christ and the church as the body which represents these realities on earth, in relation to divine and human intentions and structures for the ordering of our common life on earth (Section III); (b) specific issues such as the normativity of Jesus, the use of violence, particular forms and policies of governments, and the realities of and remedies for oppression and marginalization in some sense radiate from these core questions (Sections IV–VII); (c) the larger frame within which all these questions are considered is structured by how we answer questions which are at the same time most basic and most broad of all: What is the purpose and future of creation? What is the meaning and significance of human history and our moment in it? What is the status of creation and history in the time between times, as we await the *eschaton*? (Section VIII); and (d) since its emergence, both within scripture and traditional texts, as well as its emergence as an academic discipline, there has been a broad diversity in approaches to these questions within Christian political theology (Sections I–II).

In a sense we (appropriately) end where we began, because it can be argued that no Christian political theologian has ever given a more compelling account of creation, history, and eschatology than Augustine did in *De Civitate Dei*, widely considered the founding (non-canonical) text of Christian political theology. Reconsiderations of Augustine's politics have flourished recently. One important figure in these conversations has been Charles Mathewes, Professor of Religious Studies at the

University of Virginia. 'The Republic of Grace; or, the Public Ramifications of Heaven' was the concluding chapter in Mathewes's 2007 *A Theology of Public Life.* In it, he closes the argument of the book, which is a theology and an ascetics of Christian citizenship characterized as living eschatologically 'during the world'. Here he focuses on distinguishing his argument for Augustinian eschatology from 'apocalyptic escapism'.

Though it was written long before Mathewes's book and cannot be taken as a reply to it, Oliver O'Donovan's essay on 'The Political Thought of the Book of Revelation' (1985) addresses an assumption which Mathewes shares with many recent and contemporary political theologians: that apocalyptic views of creation and history are escapist, and therefore apocalyptic as a genre and as a mode of theology is ill-suited to normative political theology. O'Donovan takes the reader through the text of Revelation, reading the apocalypse as a political theology of creation and history. As in much of O'Donovan's work, judgement becomes a key theme along the way. O'Donovan has been one of the most important postliberal political theologians in the UK. His Augustinian/Reformed version of postliberalism differs from many other postliberal political theologies which have arisen from the influences of Aristotelian Thomism and/or Anabaptism. Where most US-based postliberals have criticized 'Constantinian' settlements of church and state, O'Donovan embraces a certain form of Christendom.

Whether American or British, postliberal political theologies are decidedly Western, and some of the richest political considerations of creation, history and eschatology have belonged to the East. One of the most important twentieth-century voices in Eastern political theologies has been Sergii Bulgakov, a Russian intellectual at the turn of the century. Having begun seminary education as a teenager, he became disillusioned with the Orthodox faith and committed himself instead to Marxist theory and political activism, only to abandon Marxism and return to the Orthodox Church, becoming a priest. In 1922 he was expelled by the Bolshevik government along with over 150 fellow intellectuals, and he spent the rest of his life in Prague and Paris. 'The Soul of Socialism' was written approximately ten years into his exile as part of his return to social and political writing, after not publishing on such topics for most of the 1920s. Likely inspired by Orthodox social activist Elizaveta Skobtsova (later Mother Maria), he began to return to issues which had interested him previously, treating them in a new light intellectually, spiritually and historically. Much of his important work remains untranslated. In this piece, somewhat unclearly leaving open the question of whether or not there can be a 'Christian socialism', Bulgakov builds an argument about the differing views of history and eschatology in contemporary socialism, in the church as he has known it, and in the church as he believes it should be.

From one of the most important voices in Orthodox political theology we turn to one of the most idiosyncratic interlocutors of recent political theology, a Slovenian philosopher and cultural critic who shuns orthodox Christianity – an atheist who publishes books with John Milbank, famous for his Radical Orthodoxy. Though he sees in orthodox Christianity a feeble ideology, Slavoj Žižek sees in the New Testament Pauline texts, and particularly in Paul's narration of Christ, an incredibly fruitful 'theological' vision. 'Thinking Backwards: Predestination and Apocalypse', from the 2010 book *Paul's New Moment* (one of the books Žižek has written with Milbank), is a characteristically wide-ranging piece which presents types of current apocalypticism, bringing them into conversation with Pascal, Marxism and Chesterton. Žižek characterizes imagination as an apocalyptic way of rethinking history, refusing fatalism about how we arrived at this point in history and leaving open the 'what if' of new possibilities for our common life.

50. Charles Mathewes – The Republic of Grace; or, the Public Ramifications of Heaven

> There we shall be still and see, see and love, love and praise. Behold what will be. in the end to which there will be no end!
>
> Augustine, *de civitate Dei*

What if heaven really were our destiny? What would that mean for how we should live now, during the world? This is the question that this book has tried to answer. It is an intelligible question to us – to all humans – in part because of our intuition that the world as we have it, the world in its simple immanence, is not a fully satisfactory reality, an adequate habitation for our hopes. This intuition begins as a vague discontent, an apprehension that our ordinary experience of the world today is wrong, incomplete. It gains determinate positive content in Christianity's claim that our destiny is gratuitous, that there is life beyond death for us – indeed, that all creation is similarly gratuitous. Heaven, it seems, is not only our destiny, but the world's as well.

How should that conviction shape life during the world? It may seem in tension with this book's argument that Christianity has as its fundamental dynamic a movement towards deeper engagement with the neighbor and creation, as well as with God. But the conflict is more apparent than real. For this dynamic gains its particular determination by Christianity's radically eschatological orientation. The meaning of history itself is determined in Christ, and Christ has come, but his first coming only inaugurated the end times, only began the definitive determination of history; so we await the second coming, the *parousia,* as the ultimate revelation and thus determination of the meaning and significance of history, of our lives, and of God's purposes. Grace, and perhaps especially grace understood as the presence of the Holy Spirit in and among believers, is the true *res publica*, the true "public thing."

Nonetheless, while the conflict is more apparent than actual, a real tension exists here. For in talking about grace, we are tempted to describe it as what lies outside of the structures of cause and effect that constitute creation. It is only a short step from that exteriority to talk that warrants concerns about "otherworldliness." So in talking about the political ramifications of grace, we are brought again back to the tension latent in otherworldliness. Hence the deep roots of this proposal do, in fact, put powerful pressure on the usual understanding of public engagement, pressure of a sort that profoundly shapes Christian public engagement. In truth, this tension lurks at the heart of Christian thought more generally, and not only as a problem, but as a promise of what is to come. Here at the end of this book, I want to see what insights derive from this most fundamental tension. Here we explore how heaven is publicly significant not only in the eschaton but even today; how, that is, a vision of life that is so fundamentally eschatological can also be so profoundly pro-creation as to shape a distinctive and powerful form of public engagement – yet a form of caring about the world that might not make "the world" fully comfortable.

Kairos and Ordinary Time: The Dialectic of Public Life

Christianity does not simply project its hopes for public life upon the world by force of will. It sees intimations of its vision in the tensions between transcendence and mundaneity, revolution and inertia, continuity and discontinuity, that riddle public life. Such tensions are visible to any moderately self-reflective participant in public life. They give public life its dialectical quality.

An example is not hard to find. Much of politics, as it exists today in this impatient, petulant, risibly sin-riddled world, is waiting. We wait at rope lines for candidates to pass; we wait for election returns to arrive late at night, faces pale in the sterile glow of TV screens; we wait while a canvasser reads us his talking points on the phone, or urges us to support her candidate on our doorstep. Less obviously we wait for our friends and family and neighbors and co-workers and new acquaintances to enumerate, in what often seems to us inexplicably, narcissistically meticulous detail, why their chosen candidate or cause is obviously the only right one, wondering all the while where to begin in disputing their whole way of seeing the world. Sometimes we must even wait for our own minds to make up their opinions on issues we feel we need to have a view on *now*, if not yesterday. And always we wait to see – with fear and trembling if we are pious and wise – whether the political causes we supported ultimately turn out the way we hoped they would turn out. (Usually this means waiting to find out how, precisely, we shall be disappointed.) Much of public life is spent enduring interminable time, when time itself drones on.[1]

And then, sometimes suddenly, everything changes. Everything seems to happen all at once: deliberation ends, the ballots are cast, the votes counted, decisions made, the new thing emerges. The old order – which seemed so solid, so firm, so unchanging – is swept away. Public life is a disconcerting concatenation of *kairos* and ordinary time, with jarring shifts from one to the other, a kind of wild oscillation between "now" and "not yet."

Much recent political theory can be seen as a series of attempts to obscure or deny this tension, the dialectical character of public life. The violence of these temporal disjunctions is taken by some to prove that democratic rule is strictly speaking a myth; that elections are too limited, too punctual a device for properly affirming public rule; that the control so exercised by the populace over their government is too flimsy to be described as self-rule. And yet, again and again the people shock their overlords; they vote down referenda urged on them by the governing elites, or approve them in the face of politicians' determined opposition; they elect men or women of the people or throw the bums out of office, upsetting the table at which the cloistered politicians were working out delicate bargains. When this happens, of course, the pooh-poohers of popular rule then suggest that it simply demonstrates that the people have too much power, are too undisciplined, dangerously unconstrained in their political wills – that whimsy and outrage rule the day; that after all what we need is less democratic governance, or less "direct" governance (which comes by and large to the same thing), and more mediation by elites, tempered in the brutal forge of academia. Such is the strategy of much liberal political theory. Still others will say that such experiences demonstrate not that democracy is dangerous but that all power is exercised this way, that "democracy" so understood is really the brute exercise of power, with nothing to do with fairness. From Thrasymachus to Machiavelli to Carl Schmitt, such nihilistic approaches have always been with us.

So it was said 200 years ago; so it is said today; so shall it be said a hundred, a thousand years hence. The very variousness of the charges tells against their veracity. And the antiquity of the accusations suggest that they embody clichéd reactions, running down well-worn rhetorical grooves, rather than actual new thinking on the part of their enunciators.

There are secular critics who recognize this, such as Jeffrey Isaac, William Connolly, and Benjamin Barber. Augustinian Christians share these criticisms, but they also look with sympathetic understanding and even pity upon such secularist animosities at the *saeculum,* and the escapism that these animosities reflect. They understand why public life might make secularists so disturbed at its revolutions. They appreciate the concerns such secularists have about how its vicissitudes can

---

[1]For more see W. H. Vanstone, *The Risk of Love* (New York: Oxford University Press, 1983).

manhandle our plans and break apart our best hopes. They too see how dangerous can be the power of the crowd. But they see these tendencies as dangers and temptations, not inevitabilities, so they think that secularists who fixate on them are thereby blinded to the goods that public life enables, and they diagnose this blindness as expressive of a sort of escapism, the illusion that such engagement can somehow be avoided. Behind and beyond these temptations they see engagement in public life as a refining fire whereby our lives and our communities are hammered into something greater than they would otherwise become. In this way, Augustinians understand the debate about the viability of public life as just one more version of the struggle against escapism, albeit camouflaged in a secular vocabulary, and they respond appropriately thereto.

Apocalyptic Escapism

Escapism is neither a temptation only in public life, nor a temptation only for ingrown secularists. It is at least as palpable, and yet more vigorous, in contemporary religion, particularly in its apocalyptic varieties. In the West, many Christians especially find it tempting. Indeed, a great deal of Christian religiosity today, perhaps especially in America, is possessed by such apocalypticism.

This is presented quite vividly, for example, in the "Left Behind" novels. The "Left Behind" series is the most popular "religious fiction" in America since World War II; indeed, they are among the bestselling novels of any sort in America since World War II. The series has been criticized for its problematic political, cultural, ethical, and religious attitudes.[2] But few recognize how its cultural philistinism, political isolationism and xenophobia, and overall consumerist parochialism are underpinned by what, from this book's perspective, is the most fundamental, and properly theological, problem: a profound and abiding escapism, a confusion or despair about the nature of creation itself and its role in God's salvific providence.

This escapism is manifest in the series title, and is latent in the hostility towards anyone even slightly different than the white, upper-middle-class mentality of its authors. But it appears most profoundly in the Manicheanism beneath the series as a whole – the idea that the world itself is wrong, fundamentally bad, and that our condition as "worldly" is a mark of our fallenness – a Manichean attitude that

---

[2]For critiques of the apocalypticism expressed therein, see Paul Boyer, *When Time Shall Be No More: Prophecy Belief in Modern American Culture* (Cambridge, MA: Harvard University Press, 1992) and 'Biblical Prophecy and Foreign Policy' in Claire Badaracco (ed.), *Quoting God: How Media Shape Ideas about Religion and Culture*, 107–122 (Waco: Baylor Press, 2005); and Martin Cook, 'Christian Apocalypticism and Weapons of Mass Destruction', in Sohail H. Hasmi and Steven P. Lee (eds), *Ethics and Weapons of Mass Destruction: Religious and Secular Perspectives* (New York: Cambridge University Press, 2004). For a different view, see Amy Frykholm, *Rapture Culture: Left Behind in Evangelical America* (New York: Oxford University Press, 2004). Frykholm argues that readers use the books in ways opposed to what their authors seem to intend; but that simply bespeaks the bankruptcy of the series' worldview.

reveals an animus at ineliminable aspects of human life: temporality and materiality. In the series, time is not itself a positive gift to be received; it can only be tolerated, or bulled through, for it is simply a waiting around for something to happen. (One might say that, without the *divertissement* of the ominous antics of the anti-Christ, and the theatricalized hysterics of the Last Days, the series' characters would simply drop dead of boredom.) But the animus is still more palpable in the series' account of damnation, in which hell is wholly a matter of material suffering. Consider the following, from the (almost) climactic encounter of the armies of the anti-Christ with the returned Jesus:

> Tens of thousands of foot soldiers dropped their weapons, grabbed their heads or their chests, fell to their knees, and writhed as they were invisibly sliced asunder. Their innards and entrails gushed to the desert floor, and as those around them turned to run, they too were slain, their blood pooling and rising in the unforgiving brightness of the glory of Christ.[3]

Here, flesh itself seems to have been congealed suffering all along – frozen pain, waiting to thaw into its natural liquid state of agony at the name of Jesus.

The novels' deep animus toward our worldly condition reflects a disappointed recoil from the world, a presumptuous disappointment that the world has let us down, has not met the desires we brought to it. "Left Behind" is not unique in expressing this: pharmacology, our favorite TV shows, all are forms of the oldest technology humans have, the technology of avoidance, *divertissement,* ways of convincing ourselves that we are in control of creation, in charge of time. It may be that apocalyptic temptations are so available to us today just because we are so comfortable in this life, just because we have a hard time appreciating our proper estrangement from it. The root cause of our problem may be, then, a comfort-provoked failure of imagination, reflected in insufficient attention to the otherness of God, and hence to the contingency of our given order. Perhaps we simply cannot imagine a destiny radically better than anything the world, as we find it, can offer.

This failure of imagination lies at the root of our susceptibility to the various escapisms, secular and religious, that confront us, today and every day. But can we offer an alternative?

Augustinian Eschatology against Apocalyptic Escapism

From the outside, this book's proposal may seem sympathetic to the worldview of "Left Behind." After all, it suggests that we should understand ourselves as existing

---

[3]Tim LeHaye and Jerry B. Jenkins, *Glorious Appearing: The End of Days* (Wheaton: Tyndale House, 2001), 226.

during the world, and see this life as a training in suffering and endurance for the next. Is this not just another, albeit more sophisticated, species of apocalyptic escapism?

No. Quite the contrary: this book's Augustinian eschatology and that of "Left Behind" are exact opposites, revealing radically different estimations of worldly life. In the books it is the saints who escape the world, who get to heaven. But for Augustine, it is the sinful who get "raptured" from the church, not the church that is raptured from the sinful; on this view the sinful are the truly escapist.[4] Augustine's own eschatological reflections developed in crucial respects as a critique of the Christian churches' apocalyptic temptations, and the struggle against the human proclivity towards escapism and avoidance – manifest in believers and non-believers alike – has always been one of the fundamental tasks of theology.

We can see this difference displayed in the contrast between the picture of hell in "Left Behind" and Augustine's in Book 21 of the *City of God*. There Augustine argues that while hell is material, it is not hell *because* it is material, but because the damned are attached to their materiality in the wrong way; they make it their absolute, their god. After all, materiality is not a fundamental ontological category, as if the world were fundamentally composed of "matter" and "spirit"; it is simply one stage of the gradual continuum between God's absolute Being and the *nihil* that lies "outside" what God ordains to be. Hence it is not the damned's flesh that is the proper locus of suffering, but their souls (*City of God* 21.3); it is not the world that is the problem but our expectations of it (and by extension of ourselves) – what we demand that it (and we) be.

On an Augustinian reading, then, the eschatology of "Left Behind," and its picture of the world as the locus of sin, simply reveal one more strategy of the sinful soul, longing for evasion. But escapism cannot simply be condemned; it must be replaced, and so this book's strategy has been an indirect one, coming to grips with the disappointment that motivates escapism rather than simply assaulting it. We should not look to have our desires satisfied, but look instead to see what prompts them – to look first not at the world, but at God, and at what God wants for us, proclaimed in and through Christ and the churches he inaugurated. When we have understood God's purposes for us, we can see the world anew, and see it as not ultimately what we think of as "the world" at all, but as part of God's ongoing gratuitous gift of Creation, in and through which (but not from which) we have our being. Our redemption is not found in an escape from our created condition, but a final, full, and endless reception of the gift of Creation itself. Today, during the world, we live east not only of Eden, but of Creation itself – oblique, off-center, eccentric. We must come to see our world as the *old* world, waiting to be transformed into the new, and ourselves – the aged and withered, the

---

[4]See Augustine, *de civitate Dei*, 20.19: "until the mystery of iniquity, which is now hidden inside the church, departs from the church." I thank Kevin Hughes for bringing this to my attention; see K. Hughes, *Constructing Antichrist: Paul, Biblical Commentary, and the Development of Doctrine in the Early Middle Ages* (Washington: Catholic University Press, 2005), 104 n. 52.

tired and cynical – as those who are always being reborn as little children, infants in God's graceful tutelage. As Miroslav Volf puts it, "Unlike the present world, the world to come will not be created *ex nihilo* but *ex vetere*," out of "the old".[5] As in the Incarnation and the Eucharist, there is a continuity, a mystical continuity between old and new – a transubstantiation of creation, if you will, a union of two natures, in which life takes in and redeems death. The resolution of our story comes not most fundamentally by renunciation – the renunciation of escapism or the renunciation of our very temptations toward escapism – but by transfiguration and reception.[6]

This theological claim lies at the base of Augustine's disagreement with both thoroughgoing secularists and thoroughgoing apocalypticism. Against the former, Augustinians affirm the real continuity (and hence relevance) of putatively "otherworldly" concerns with this-worldly ones, and insist that we not suppress or ignore humans' transcendental longings. Against the latter, Augustinians affirm the real continuity (and hence value) of "worldly" matters with otherworldly realities, and insist that we not indulge in our (already too powerful) temptations toward escapism. For Augustinians, this world is pregnant with redemption, groaning in labor, bearing the weight of glory.

This theological vision entails not only a metaphysics of continuity, but more precisely an ontology of natality, wherein beginnings are more fundamental to being than endings. The new, and beginning, is real, yet it implies no rupture with our life before; it has a continuity with our present condition. We have everything backwards – we are moving not towards conclusion but towards truly beginning. As Franz Rosenzweig puts it, the Christian is the "eternal beginner";[7] and for Christians, the fundamental ontology of the world is describable as "being born again" – a form of existence oriented toward an ever deeper beginning. We *are* saved from something, but what we are saved from is fundamentally a bad version of ourselves, our solitude, our isolation. And what we are given is life abundant – life that has properly, at last, begun.

Called to the Feast of the Kingdom of God

The church is that structure wherein we try to live out this habitus of natality. While our inhabitation of it is provisional, we do see in it (or in our understanding of it) some intimations of this most proper mode of our being. The church, as Augustine

---

[5]Miroslav Volf, 'The Final Reconciliation: Reflections on a Social Dimension of the Eschatological Transition', *Modern Theology* 16.1 (January): 92.

[6]See Alexander Schmemann, *For the Life of the World: Sacraments and Orthodoxy* (Crestwood: St. Vladimir's Seminary Press, 1973) and P. Miller, 'Judgment and Joy' in J. Polkinghorne and M. Welker (eds), *The End of the World and the Ends of God: Science and Theology on Eschatology* (Harrisburg: Trinity Press International, 2000), esp. 163–4.

[7]Franz Rosenzweig, *The Star of Redemption*, trans. William W. Hallo (Notre Dame: University of Notre Dame Press, 1985), 359.

says, seeks the end without end (*City of God* 22.30). And it does so fundamentally musically, embodying a musical form of being – in the sense that music is the fundamental experience of receiving the gift of time.[8] The church is the singing society of the redeemed, in pilgrimage during this life, towards that time when it will join in the full choir of the saints, its song finally and fully underway, unrestrained.

How is this *habitus* of natality inhabited today? David Ford gives an important clue when he says that the "Christian vocation can be summed up as being called to the feast of the Kingdom of God. The salvation of selves is in responding to that invitation," so that we have "a responsibility to respond to an invitation into joy".[9] The metaphor of "feast" signals three dimensions of that calling – how we are to relate to ourselves, to our neighbors and creation, and to God.

As regards oneself, here the struggle is to become what Ford calls a "singing self," one capable of "being loved and delighted in" (99). This is a struggle to come to see ourselves as fundamentally public: we are not fundamentally private, isolated, and disconnected monads, but part of a larger harmony, seen and loved by another, God, who in this love wishes us nothing more fundamentally than to be. And this is a struggle, for we fear being seen. To be seen is to be exposed. Too often the gaze is a gaze of judgment or condemnation. But what we do not see is that our "exposure" before God is not fundamentally an exposure to harsh condemnation, but an ennabling love. God's love and judgment are inseparable; God's judgment is rooted in nothing but God's love for us, and so when we seize this judgment without seizing this love, we do not imitate but perversely parody God.[10] We separate them by presumptuously usurping God's right to judge, while dismissing the love that energizes and directs that judgment. And this is our despair. At heart we are self-condemned; we see ourselves, and judge ourselves thereby to have fallen woefully short of where we should be, and so we fear God's judgment as a simple extension of our own. But we must be shriven of this, our most fundamental prejudice, our prejudice against ourselves – a prejudice built on the enormous presumption to be able to see *sicut Deus,* "like God" – and renounce our attempt to seize our inheritance before it is due to us. When we are so shriven, we see that the gaze that we fear is not (as we think it is) the condemning gaze of the judge, but the merciful gaze of God. We see that our panicked activity consists fundamentally in our trying to be God, which means trying to judge ourselves. Instead, we should submit to God's judgment and hence to God's love. We must accept our publicity, our being seen, and through that discern our being loved. Because being loved is an affirmation of our being at all, accepting God's love for us as unmerited by us means accepting our "being begun."

---

[8]See David Ford, *Self and Salvation: Being Transformed* (New York: Cambridge University Press, 1999), 123.
[9]Ibid., 272.
[10]For more see P. Miller 2000, esp. 165: "the encompassing rhetoric for the end [is] *consummation* rather than *judgment.*"

The "singing self" is not alone; we sing with each other, and to each other, as well as to God.[11] The self is part of a choir, so that its being is simultaneously individual and communal. Once our fear of being judged has been named and crucified, living with the neighbor, in the church, we seek genuinely to see and to be seen. This is a phenomenological truth; in loving someone we want to see them exposed to us, we want to see them entire. As with our experiences of love here and now, so paradise will be all of us, with nothing hidden, involving the full disclosure of who we are and how God saved us from ourselves. In this disclosure the practice of confession will turn out to have been all along a practice of presence, of our presence for and before each other. Confession will turn out to be, in part, our proleptic participation in God's kingdom. In our recognition that we will be judged, and the activity of confession that that recognition provokes, we seek to be seen in our desire genuinely to be present. More than that, we seek to see one another, to stand in the warm glow of our neighbors' presences. We shall seek to see by trying, properly speaking, to recognize the neighbor, an act that requires mutual reciprocation. Love and vision regard our relations with others as well; to love someone is to want to see them, to see all of them, to adore them. Indeed, ultimately to see just is to adore; apprehension and adoration finally draw together.

Yet we will not see each other directly but in the refracted and reflected illuminating gaze of God. We will see, that is, through God. To see the neighbor, properly to see them, is to see them as infinitely valuable. As C. S. Lewis said, "There are no *ordinary* people. You have never talked to a mere mortal".[12] This recognition is the basis of the ethical language of "dignity." It is also one crucial, but under-appreciated, source for the political language of democracy. To see our neighbors is the core of democracy; to recognize their value, not their "worthiness," but their value in God.

Naturally the respect for the other's dignity that is endorsed by this adoration is deeper, more profound, than democracy, and hence has a place in other political orders. But democracy can at times be a reinforcing form of Christian witness, because democracy itself can be a partial form of seeing the neighbor, an awesome vision of realizing our ultimate magnitude; it has the advantage of suggesting more distance between a person's position or "station" (in democracy, no one is stationary) and their proper significance. In recognizing the other as a genuine, living other – by seeing the other as the neighbor – we seek truly to see them. This core recognition of the other is what we call "respect," which in German is the far more revelatory word *Achtung* – attention – the way we elicit from one another, if we can hear the call, real

---

[11]See Ford 1999: 122 and P. Miller 2000: 169; for an analogous secular project, see Danielle Allen, *Talking to Strangers: Anxieties of Citizenship since Brown v. Board of Education* (Chicago: University of Chicago Press, 2004), 88–9 on the symbolic expression through singing of a community's "aspiration to wholeness (not oneness)."

[12]C. S. Lewis, *The Weight of Glory and Other Addresses* (New York: Macmillan, 1980), 39.

looking at who we are. And this recognition both warrants our statements about human dignity and generates the political energies of democracy.

This is not an easy task, and it is certainly not what we do in everyday social life; in fact that life may seem to run better if we actually evade it. We so rarely see one another, seeing instead only the masks we place upon one another – stranger, neighbor, friend; child, parent, spouse; colleague, enemy, ally. All these are nothing but forms of cognitive avoidance, ways we negotiate the world in proximity to one another without ever actually asking, "But who, really, *are* you?" So much of our "knowledge" of one another is in this way little more than a technique for avoiding facing each other, confronting the *plenum* that each of us, in our molten quiddity, finally is. So social life can be strangely dissatisfying, even as it grows more efficient; and the dissatisfaction consists fundamentally in this, our tacit recognition that we actually want to see one another – or better, that each of us is worth seeing in ourselves for who we truly are.

Our solicitousness for our neighbor does not rest content in her or his bare thereness. To see the neighbor is to see a mystery that transcends itself and iconically refers to the divine reality beyond it. The dignity of the neighbor is the glow of a divine purpose immanent within her or him, yet also not exhaustively immanent therein. To see the neighbor is to love the neighbor, and to love the neighbor is to be awed by and drawn to the other whose love for the neighbor anchors our own – namely, God. God loves each of us and knows us by name. In light of this, we seek the neighbor out as coparticipant in our proper task of adoring God.

What we are doing, understood as community and as individuals begun by God, is adoring God. But what is that heavenly adoration like What, that is, is this beginning? We have only the slimmest glimpses of it in Scripture and tradition; but what we can say is that our worshipful adoration of God will be endless and infinite – not the bad infinite of ceaselessness, which is really merely temporally extended stasis, but the truly infinite dynamism of everdeepening, ever widening, and ever heightening seeking into (not seeking "out for") God's infinite being. Here, "consummation" entails both achievement and dynamism. Aquinas captured this, in part, in his metaphysics of God as *actus purus*: the idea of God as wholly dynamic, without reserve, willing God's Trinity as love and Creation as the beneficiary of that superabundant love. Yet this dynamism, so complete, is also not a dynamism provoked by some need of something outside of it; in that way the activity is simultaneously a peacefulness, a restful exertion, an exposition of pure gratuity. Such restful dynamism is God's gift to us of self-presence, in the eschaton; as W. H. Vanstone puts it, the glory of God is an activity that leads to passivity, that "destines itself to waiting" in love.[13] God's "completion" is not the cessation of temporal sequence, but its consummation, the fullness of life, of being and time itself.

---

[13]Vanstone, 99.

And a form of this perfection is what God has destined for us as well; as God is, so shall we be when we live fully in God, in God's gratuitous gift to us of Creation. To see Creation for what it truly is, God's Sabbath gift – a restfulness and peace which are not exhaustion but fullness of life and primacy of being – is to begin to live our true lives, to begin the process of living into a beginning without an ending.

At Last, the First Things

In the fusion of stability and dynamism of God as *actus purus* is the core idea of our experience of heaven – both rest and joy, resolution and commencement, the "Sabbath morning without an evening" – and also, unsurprisingly, the core idea of our experience of the presence of God. But the site of this sabbathing is none other than Creation – a new creation, to be sure, but again one born of the old, not a renunciation but a completion, not an annihilation but a resolution. We will see God walk, not in the cool of the day, but in the morning of the new creation.

What will that day, that eschatological morning, look like? What will we feel? What will feeling be, or for that matter understanding? We cannot know here, during the world. The best words we have for it are paradoxical, attempts to communicate the vexation of our comprehension, such as Augustine's claim that "busy idleness (*otioso negotio*) will be our beatitude" (*Ennarationes in Psalmos*, 86.9).[14] But we can affirm now, in faith and hope, that such a beatitude exists; and we can, partially and proleptically, participate in it – in love – even today. C. S. Lewis well describes this faithful, hopeful, and charitable agnosticism:

> At present we are on the outside of the world, the wrong side of the door. We discern the freshness and purity of morning, but they do not make us fresh and pure. We cannot mingle with the splendors we see. But all the leaves of the New Testament are rustling with the rumor that it will not always be so. Some day. God willing, we shall get *in*.[15]

And we shall get in; and then we will, at last, see God as all in all – see the Father, in Christ, through the Holy Spirit, and our neighbor; and through the Father, in Christ, our neighbor, our friend, our other self. Then, at last, shall we be fully joyful; then, at last, shall we be blessed; then, at last, shall we be we; and then, and only then, shall our lives as beginners be fully given to us – not given over, handed over as Jesus was by Judas to the authorities, but truly given, with the giver in the gift, as Jesus gave himself to his disciples, even unto Judas, and through them the world – and our true lives finally begun.

---

[14]See Paul Griffiths, 'Nirvana as the Last Thing? The Iconic End of the Narrative Imagination', in James J. Buckley and Gregory Jones (eds), *Theology and Eschatology at the Turn of the Millennium* (Oxford: Blackwell, 2001) for illuminating work on this.

[15]Lewis, 37.

But in the meantime, during the world, our task is to quicken to that longing, to sharpen our waiting on this advent: to be brave, be strong, stay firm in the faith, do all our work in love, and in so doing to long for the day when – and, best as we can in the here and the now, during the world, to accept the presence of the promise of that day as – we turn to one another, face to face, before the Father, through the Son, in the Spirit, and say: *venite adoremus*.

51. Oliver O'Donovan – The Political Thought of the Book of Revelation

Something rather curious occurs in the final chapter of John Howard Yoder's deservedly celebrated book *The Politics of Jesus*. The chapter is entitled 'The War of the Lamb'; and in it the author, having dealt extensively in the rest of the book with the foundations for Christian political thought in the Gospels and Paul, proposes to 'characterise briefly' the political stance of the Book of Revelation in the course of drawing some conclusions for the whole. The characterisation is indeed brief. It occupies one and a half out of the eighteen pages of the chapter, and attends solely to the image of the slain Lamb in chapter 5. Then, on the concluding page (having found space in the meantime for a four-page exposition of Phil. 2:6) the author returns to Revelation once more, to deplore, with some indignation, what he calls 'the beginning assumption of the irrelevance of apocalyptic, which has so often made it hard to see social meaning in the book of the Apocalypse, even though its entire message has to do with kingdoms and empires'. And finally, like the reluctant schoolboy athlete who breaks into a trot a few yards from the finishing-line, Yoder concludes his book with a rousing Latin quotation: *Vicit agnus noster, eum sequamur*.[1]

We may well sympathise with Yoder's ambivalence. On the one hand it appears that the Book of Revelation must be important for Christian political thought; on the other, the universal prejudice of church and scholarship is against it. The close scholarly attention paid to the general field of apocalyptic during the last quarter-century has elevated a long-standing instinct of caution into an academic orthodoxy. Apocalyptic, we are told, is a flight from the realities of society and history. As Hans Dieter Betz wrote in 1969: 'To the apocalypticist "world history" in its entirety is identical with the "evil eon" and thus falls under that absolutely negative judgment... The apocalyptic view of history is indeed "indicative of a great loss of historical sensitivity" and has, in fact, dispensed with historical thinking. Accordingly,

---

[1]John H. Yoder, *The Politics of Jesus* (Grand Rapids: Eerdmans, 1972) 250. As though sensing the ambivalence in the author's mind, an editor at Eerdmans, with conscious or unconscious irony, decreed that the little Latin peroration should appear in reduced type-face!

history cannot in this view possess any revelatory character.'[2] One response to this orthodoxy, which might prove attractive to someone who was interested not in apocalyptic in general but in this one New Testament example of it, would be to stress the distinctiveness of John of Patmos's book and the many ways in which it defies the generalisations which apocalyptic commonly invites. But this short way with the scholars is not necessarily the best. For the current orthodoxy, in my judgment, gives expression to certain prevalent conceptions which do in fact impede the reading of Revelation and exercise unacknowledged constraints upon what is commonly seen there. Of these I will identify two, taking as a representative sample of the consensus the 1971 article by Paul D. Hanson, 'Old Testament Apocalyptic Reexamined.'[3]

Hanson opposes two views of the world, the mythopoeic and the prophetic. The prophetic view 'recognised…divine activity as involving a movement from promise to fulfilment' and 'embraces the flux and movement of history as the arena of divine activity'; whereas myth 'offers escape from the change of the historical process' (p. 40). The birth of apocalyptic occurs when Deutero-Isaiah reintroduces mythic elements into the prophetic view of history, thereby resolving a difficulty in which the Deuteronomic tradition had become ensnared in the apparent hopelessness of the situation after the fall of Jerusalem. Subsequently apocalyptic moves more and more towards the mythic pole, draws man 'above the flux of the mundane sphere' to 'a salvation won on a timeless, cosmic level… The dialectic between vision and reality began to break down' (p. 50). In classical prophecy, Hanson concludes, 'the realm of human history was the realm within which the covenant relationship between Yahweh and his people was being carried out; historical events were carriers of cosmic significance'. But in apocalyptic events are 'bound to an inevitable progression towards a predetermined end… The dynamic of…history…yields to the inflexibility of a history which becomes a timetable of cosmic events' (p. 57).

The first conception I draw attention to is the opposition of the categories 'mythic' and 'historical', upon which the effectiveness of Hanson's analysis depends. The success of classical prophecy lay in its ability to keep a perfect balance between them; but confronted with the fall of Jerusalem the tradition collapsed into pure history. Deutero-Isaiah tried to restore the balance, but his successors collapsed it in the other direction into pure cosmic myth. Now, it is not a sufficient objection to these categories that they are so plainly a modern version of the idealist polarity of a timeless world of ideas and a changing world of phenomena (a provenance which is strongly underlined when Hanson interchanges the categories of 'myth' and 'history' with those of 'vision' and 'reality'). For the interpretation of texts will always involve the use of concepts foreign to them. But it is important that the text should command the concepts and not the concepts the text; and here, it would

[2]'The Concept of Apocalyptic in the Theology of the Pannenberg Group' in R. W. Funk (ed.), *Apocalypticism* (New York: Herder & Herder, 1969) 201–202. Betz's quotation is from von Rad.
[3]In Paul D. Hanson (ed.), *Visionaries and their Apocalypses* (London: SPCK, 1983) 37–60.

seem, the conceptual apparatus has taken over completely. How else could Hanson fail to admit that for apocalypticists, too, 'historical events were the carriers of cosmic significance'?[4] Biblical apocalyptic inherits (though it treats in a different way) the prophetic problematic of rendering events intelligible in terms of the purposes of God. The justification of history is its recurrent theme. It would seem undeniable, for instance, that the seer of Daniel was fascinated by the meaning of the succession of empires in world-history; but Hanson's way with that undeniable fact is to deny it. The succession of empires, he thinks, 'serves one function only in the vision, that of indicating the point when the cosmic event at the center of the vision would occur' (p. 55).

In Hanson's article we can detect also a second conception, which he has not clearly differentiated from the first though it is in fact quite distinct. History is characterised as 'flux', not only in opposition to the supposedly 'timeless' character of myth but also in opposition to the 'predetermined' character of events in apocalyptic. It is not at all clear to me that one can consistently accuse apocalyptic both of a determinist view of history and of a belief that salvation is timeless. The two charges would seem to exclude each other. But one can certainly maintain together the contradictory of both these positions, and insist both that history is the vehicle of salvation and that it is contingent and directionless. Such a view is easily recognisable, and belongs within the Augustinian mainstream of Western political thought, which, dominated by the image of the two cities, has drawn a clear line between secular and sacred history. Secular history, conforming to no shape and subject to no laws save those which follow from the perennially repeated clash between good and evil, is the locus of those sacred events which reveal the goal of man's existence; but it derives no perspicuous purposiveness from them. This distinction explains what sometimes appears to be almost a self-contradiction in the orthodox criticism of apocalyptic: its insistence *both* upon the meaningfulness of history as the bearer of cosmic significance and upon its character as undetermined flux. There is to be no evading the distinction between the revelatory character of the Christ-event, which declares the purposes of God, and the concealing character of all other events, which leave God's purpose a mystery.

The German scholars who have maintained views similar to Hanson's in the discussion of apocalyptic have been rather more aware than their English-speaking colleagues that their view bespeaks a definite position within a contemporary systematic debate. They are, in fact, acknowledged anti-Hegelians, opposed to the revival of the notion of an embracing world-historical purposiveness, a notion which they see as fundamental to apocalyptic though absent from classical prophecy. Hans

---

[4]I welcome the recognition of this by Christopher Rowland (*The Open Heaven* [London: SPCK, 1982] 38). Rowland seems to me to be on less secure ground when he argues his point from a supposed literal millennium in Revelation 20 (p. 435).

Dieter Betz's article from which I quoted above was written as a shot across the bows of the Hegelian revival led by Pannenberg. An article early in the debate (1961) by Gerhard Ebeling contained an extraordinary four-page quotation from Kierkegaard (a sure sign that Hegel is under fire!) and included the following revealing summary of the position. 'The ground on which we are authorised to think God and history together in the right way (that is, differentiatingly) lies not in apocalyptic, but in the unapocalyptic fact of Jesus... Thinking God and history together in the name of Jesus leads of necessity to a criticism of apocalyptic, certainly not in the sense of a reinterpretation of apocalyptic in terms of a concept of revelation and universal history that is of Hegelian provenance, but in the sense that through his word God manifests his power over history by putting an end to the power of history.'[5] Ebeling brings out as clearly as anyone could the Augustinian secularist terrain on which the objectors stand - the right way to relate God and history is to *differentiate* them, not permitting history to pose as the messenger of the covenant. The one and only place at which history becomes such a messenger is the unapocalyptic fact of Jesus - unapocalyptic in that he does not communicate a general cosmic teleology. The import of the Christ-event for history is not positive but negative, in that it puts an end to its power. The mistake of apocalyptic is to think that it can resolve the opposition of God and history dialectically, and so tame history as God tamed Leviathan, creating a construct of world-historical order which is an 'escape from history' in a different sense - that is to say, that it does not face the scandal which history poses for faith. 'Canst thou', we may imagine Ebeling demanding of John of Patmos, 'draw out Leviathan with an hook?'

The association of Hegel and apocalyptic is instructive. For Hegel is usually seen as the only-begetter of the modern concept of history, which has famously been responsible for the doctrines of Marxism but which also deserves credit for transforming Western liberalism into a creed of progress. But behind Hegel some observers have thought to discern a subterranean channel running back through radical Protestantism, and through the millenarianism of the late middle-ages, to the seminal doctrine of Three Ages promoted by Joachim of Fiore; and Joachim thought that he was interpreting the Book of Revelation.[6] Are we, then, to believe in a counter-cultural tradition of political thought within Christendom, historicist in character, taking its root from John of Patmos and bursting into belated prominence in the nineteenth century, an alternative to the orthodox Augustinian secularism of the West which takes its root from Paul? It is an appealing hypothesis at first glance; but the truth is more complicated. Augustinian secularism, too, is founded on a philosophy of history, albeit a philosophy of *sacred* history. Furthermore, the two-cities concept on which Augustinian political thought rests has no New Testament source more

---

[5]'The Ground of Christian Theology' in Funk (ed.), *Apocalypticism* 64.
[6]See Erich Voegelin, 'Ersatz Religion' in his *Science, Politics & Gnosticism* (Chicago: Regnery, 1968) 81–114.

immediately striking than the Apocalypse of John. We should rather say that the two-cities concept gives rise to two different streams of interpretation – a secularist one which emphasises its negative implications for the teleology of secular history, and an apocalyptic one which understands world-history in terms of the ultimate disclosure of the mystery of evil. But both streams are differentiated from the monist interpretation of society revived by Thomas Aquinas as a result of his rediscovery of Aristotle. The two-cities concept does have a commitment to understand the human good as social, and in this respect stands apart from pure Neo-Platonism; but it is only eschatologically social, and sociality is only eschatologically an unambiguous good, and in this respect it stands apart from Thomist Aristotelianism. Augustine severed the link between historical society and human virtue almost as self-consciously as Thomas stitched the two together again.[7] Placed against this grid, Hegel appears as a historicist variant of the Aristotelian-Thomist tradition. Are we, then, left with a parallelogram of possibilities: John of Patmos sharing historicism with Hegel and the two-cities view with Augustine; Augustine sharing a non-teleological, secularist view of history with Thomas, while Thomas in turn shares a monist optimism with Hegel? Such a schema will serve merely as a hypothesis, to focus the questions.

Within modern Christian political thought the Augustinian secularist stream has yielded a policy of involvement in social and political tasks, which presumes upon the opacity of secular history to ultimate values and hence upon the neutrality, in moral and spiritual terms, of the political realm. For the mainstream Western thinkers politics has been, as it were, an open space, ready to be occupied equally by those who would do evil and those who would do good to mankind. They have developed, therefore, a concept of practical Christian cooperation in the political arena which neither hopes for too much nor fears for too much. In distinction from this we find not only the 'ideological' idolisation of the political realm, of Hegelian inspiration, which understands public history in semi-religious terms, but also the apocalyptic conception of public history as a manifestation of evil. This conception invites the objection, from secularist thinkers who regard themselves as taking history seriously, that it is antihistorical in its stance. It is at least arguable, in reply, that it is to take history no less seriously, and possibly more seriously, if one reckons with its inbuilt structural commitments. But if such a reply is to be made good, there has to be an alternative way of engaging with public affairs which does something better than simply cooperate on the one hand and avert the eyes on the other. *Criticism* is the form of political engagement which emerges as normative within the apocalyptic perspective. Criticism has the advantage, as its proponents see it, of illuminating the course of history by the word of God, yet without pretending to master history or even exploit its supposed neutrality, but pointing to the mystery of the ultimate triumph of the divine word as the object of its hope. The apocalyptic political

---

[7]See R. A. Markus, *Saeculum* (Cambridge: CUP, 1970) 211–230.

thinker calls into question that busy enthusiasm for cooperative endeavour under the shadow of Leviathan, returning the challenge which the Augustinian addressed to him before. 'Wilt thou play with him as with a bird?' The issue between the two approaches can be brought down to this: Is criticism a valid engagement with the public realm, and is any other engagement realistically possible? It is not surprising that where the claims of criticism against cooperation are advanced most strongly, John of Patmos is deemed to be politically significant. This conviction unites such otherwise irreconcilable points of view as those of Jacques Ellul and the liberation theologians of Latin America.[8]

One thing must be made clear, and that is that John's interest in history is by no means simply an interest in particular events that are occurring around him. In my opinion, the number of particular historical references in the Book of Revelation is two. They are found at 13:18 (the number of the beast) and at 17:9–11 (the meaning of its seven heads). If these references were removed, the surrounding material would require little or no editing to preserve its sense, which simply goes to show how little structural weight they carry. John's unfolding of the mystery of evil proceeds not by journalistic documentation but by theological principle. These two definite identifications arise as illustrations of the principle. Compare John's reference to Nero (as I take it to be) with Hegel's famous remark that the universal and homogeneous state would come first into being in America. If that particular prophecy were falsified (or should we say, if it had not been verified?) it would not invalidate Hegel's general reading of political development; the identification merely added to the verisimilitude of the general construction. This is not to deny, of course, that John's understanding of history was influenced by what he saw happening before his eyes. Biblical historians have accumulated a mass of examples, plausible and implausible, of how John's imagery may have been shaped by first-century events. To take an old example: the activity of the false prophet, the beast from the land in chapter 13, may indeed have been suggested by the activities of the Commune of Asia, as commentators, following Sir William Ramsay, have united in affirming. But it would be quite wrong to conclude that the beast from the land *represents* the Commune of Asia. John has nothing definite to say about that body; but he has a great deal to say about the way evil propagates itself as false worship.[9]

---

[8] J. Ellul, *L'Apocalypse: architecture en mouvement* (Paris: Desclée, 1975). For the use of Revelation in the liberationist tradition, see Juan B. Stam, 'El Apocalipsis y el imperialismo', in *Capitalismo Violencia y Anti-vida*, ed. E. Tamez and S. Trinidad (San Jose: Dei-Educa, 1978). I am indebted for this reference to Thomas Hanks.
[9] This distinction, not always well understood by Biblical historians, is nicely made in some lines by Robert Frost:-

Samoa, Russia, Ireland I complain of,
No less than England, France and Italy.
Because I wrote my novels in New Hampshire
Is no proof that I aimed them at New Hampshire.

Before I embark upon exposition, a word is in place about how I judge the Book of Revelation should be read. In recent generations commentators have learned to take John of Patmos seriously as a theological spokesman for first-century Christianity, whose apocalyptic imagery is a disciplined and intelligible theological language.[10] Two features of this language have sometimes proved troublesome to interpreters. One is the use of *sequence* to achieve theological analysis, so that the same phenomenon is presented more than once, each time from a new angle. The core of John's Apocalypse is a sequence of three cycles of seven disasters. Each of these cycles shows us the same thing, the degenerating course of history; but they show us it from different points of view, so that in the last cycle we have come to see how history manifests divine judgment.[11] Another example concerns the notorious 'millennium' of 20:4. John has two last battles, two resurrections, two acts of judgment, the one culminating in the thousand year reign of the saints, the other in the judgment of the great white throne. The first series shows the victory of the true Messiah over the false, the second the victory of the Father over the aboriginal dragon. Everything is shown twice because we must understand that the kingdom of Christ is the kingdom of the Father. It is a kind of reflection on the resumption of the Messianic authority suggested at 1 Corinthians 15:28. I do not believe that John intends to prophesy a this-worldly millennium which is distinct from the reign of God in the new heaven and the new earth; rather he intends to say that the vindication of this-worldly justice and the fulfilment of this-worldly history are included in the reign of God in the new heaven and the new earth.[12] Lest we should conclude that the exercise of Messianic authority is actually confined to a stated number of years, John complements this sequential presentation with another, in which the throne of God and the Lamb is one throne, and in which the servants of God, who were earlier said to reign for a thousand

---

[10]Among those who taught us this lesson, I, like others, must confess a special debt of gratitude to the late George B. Caird, whose commentary (*The Revelation of St. John the Divine* [London: A. & C. Black, 1966]) taught me how to read the Apocalypse.

[11]John M. Court (*Myth and History in the Book of Revelation* [London: SPCK, 1979] 48) invites us to choose between a 'recapitulation theory' which 'asserts that the seven bowls reflect exactly the same events as the seven seals' and a 'chronological theory', in which there is 'a clear distinction between sequences'. I confess that I do not know how to make this choice, since the prophet's concern, as it appears to me, is not with 'events' so much as with the shape of history as a whole.

[12]It is conventional, and not unjustified, to see the origins of the millennium in the need to reconcile two traditional pictures of the end. Thus H. Kraft writes: 'Im apokalyptischen Judentum bestanden nebeneinander zwei Enderwartungen: die nationale, die ein messianisches Reich nach siegreichem Glaubenskrieg erhoffte, und die universale, die meist mit einer Rettung der Gerechten durch Weltuntergang und Neuschöpfung hindurch rechnete. Obwohl diese beiden Auffassungen miteinander und mit der Eschatologie nicht jüdischer Religionen in jeder erdenklichen Weise Verknüpft wurden, empfand man sie doch als grundsätzlich verschieden. Es gehört zur Methode der späteren Prophetie in solchem Fall nicht kritisch zu sichten, sondern zu addieren, und so wurde das Zwischenreich der universalen Auffassung vorgeschaltet' ('Chiliasmus', *RGG*[3] 1.1651). What this account fails to register, however, is that the millennium in Rev. 20:4 is more than a palaeological deposit from a past conflict of apocalyptic expectations, but continues to mediate between two complementary visions, both of which have living significance for the prophet, and which converge in his Christian understanding of the Messianic kingdom as one with God's.

years, now reign 'for ever and ever' (22:5). This illustrates the second feature of John's language of imagery which can prove puzzling: images are *dialectically superimposed* upon one another, without resolution of the tensions that they generate.

With these introductory observations I shall venture upon an account of the political thought of the Book of Revelation.

I

We begin from the question which the prophet articulates decisively at the beginning of his apocalypse proper: why and how does history impugn the excellence of creation? In chapters 4 and 5 he shows us a tableau of creation, in which the throne of God is surrounded by the symbolic representatives of the created order, ceaselessly offering their praise. But their hymns are interrupted by the discovery of a sealed scroll in the hand of the Most High. As a scroll, it represents a history; as a sealed scroll, its contents are unintelligible to us. So the prophet poses his problem: how can the created order which declares the beauty and splendour of its Creator, be the subject of a world-history, the events of which are directionless and contradictory? The goodness of creation is impugned by the meaninglessness of events. Only if history can be shown to have a purpose, can the prophet's tears be wiped away and the praise of the creation be resumed. We can all repeat the words in which the consolation of the Gospel is announced to him: 'Weep not; lo, the Lion of the tribe of Judah, the Root of David, has conquered, so that he can open the scroll and its seven seals.' And then, as the prophet tells us unforgettably: 'I saw a Lamb standing, as though it had been slain' (5:5–6). The sacrificial death of God's Messiah is the event to interpret all events, which alone can offer human existence the cosmic meaning which it demands. It provides the justification of creation in history, and the justification of history in new creation.

With this announcement of his theme the prophet launches into the first of his three cycles of seven: the seven seals, the seven trumpets and the seven bowls, which, as I have said, show us the whole course of history, seen as tragic necessity, three times over, each time from a more profound perspective. In between the second and the third of these cycles John places the central episode of his book, around which all turns, the encounter between the two Christs, the false and the true. The cycles of seven follow a common formal pattern: the Lamb breaks the seven seals, the angel blows the seven trumpets or pours out the seven bowls; and after each something happens. In the first four of each cycle it is always a natural or political disaster. With the fifth and sixth of each cycle the character of the event changes, to expose some aspect of moral or spiritual evil. The seventh of each cycle represents the victory of God over the evils of historical necessity - yet the victory is at the same time the climax of all the evils, because it is the exercise of divine judgment, in which divine wrath overwhelms human wrath (*cf.* 11:18). However, it is not until the third cycle, the cycle of the bowls, that John is ready to show us divine victory emerging immediately out of the historical process, for not until then has he shown us how the course of historical necessity has itself from the beginning been an expression of the divine battle against the emissaries of the primaeval serpent, the devil. In the first two cycles, then, the concluding item of victory has to be presented as it were, through a mirror, as visible only indirectly to faith and not yet fully disclosed. And this is done by a simple structural device which has caused confusion among John's readers, commentators, and even among editors of the biblical text. The content of the seventh seal and the seventh trumpet is placed *before*, not after, the actual breaking of the seal and sounding of the trumpet. So the cycle of the seals ends mysteriously: 'When the Lamb opened the seventh seal, there was silence in heaven for about half an hour' (8:1). And with that silence, the silence of history held back from its tumultuous rush, the silence of a pause imposed before the end should come, the cycle ends. (Not only the traditional chapter division, but also the paragraph divisions of our modern Bibles show how little John's impressive effect has been appreciated!) But that is because the content of that mysterious silence has already been shown to us, in a long vision placed immediately before the breaking of the seventh seal which seemed to interrupt the sequence. The content of that vision explained the form: the four winds were held back, the command was given to restrain the forces of judgment until the servants of God should be sealed on their foreheads (7:1–3). The first cycle, then, shows history concluding in an ambiguous and unearthly hush which (secretly, and as though in a mirror) we are told is the suspension of historical necessity which God has willed for the gathering of the elect. Something similar occurs at the end of the cycle of trumpets.

So much for the common structure of the three cycles of historical necessity. What does John mean to show us through them? And why does history take the form of tragic necessity? Each cycle offers a different answer to this question, of which the first, the answer of the seals, is the most sceptical and the least profound. As each of the first four seals is opened, a horse and rider gallop across the scene: the first horseman carries a bow, and wears a crown of victory; he goes forth, we are told, 'conquering and to conquer' (6:2). The second holds a *hasta longa* and has the power to remove peace from the earth 'so that men should slay one another' (6:4). The third carries in his hand the yoke of slavery, and is accompanied by a voice which complains about the shortage and expense of necessary commodities - 'but do not harm', it adds ironically, 'oil and wine', the luxuries (6:6)! The fourth is named Death and Hades, and causes devastation in the earth through slaughter, famine and plagues of wild beasts. Clearly this sequence of disasters is a progressive sequence, the catastrophe growing worse at each step. And clearly it is intended to be a sequence of events which are politically initiated. War is its starting-point, the confident knightly enterprise of ambitious conquest, for which war is a means of glory and renown; but in its train comes the unleashing of recrimination, civil strife, shortage of supplies, and finally the imperilling of social existence by depopulation and starvation.

One may learn a lot about the character of any tradition of political thought by identifying the activity which it sees as the central paradigm of politics. For Thomas Aquinas it is the founding of cities; for St. Paul and Augustine it is the punishing of wrongdoing. For the prophet John, at this stage of his analysis at least, it is conquest in war. From the adventures of the first horseman who wears the crown there springs an inexorable chain of political and social evil. The fifth seal takes the sequence into the realm of justice by disclosing the unsatisfied cry for vindication which goes up to God from the afflicted righteous; and the sixth evokes the atmosphere of dread and impending disaster which characterises international politics (of the twentieth as well as the first century): kings, potentates and commanders cowering in fear before the judgment that their own ambitions have unloosed, trembling under the weight of responsibility. Yet we would misunderstand John's intentions if we were to think of him as offering us a theodicy of an Augustinian type founded in the fall of the human will. The chain of historical necessity is also a chain of natural necessity. The four horsemen are summoned, not only by the Lamb's breaking of the seal, but by a summons from one of the four living creatures out of the vision of creation. That is to say: it is the forces of nature which have produced this deteriorating spiral of human political strife. The enterprise of conquest, destructive both to nature and to society, has itself arisen from natural impulses and energies. That is the puzzle of nature and history as the prophet conceives it. Nature seems to carry within itself the seeds of its own destruction; and political strife is the fatal overspilling of natural energy which must disrupt nature and bring it to nothing.[13]

In the cycle of seals, therefore, we are left with a simple demonstration of the problem of creation and history: the final stage, the vision of the elect before the heavenly throne, appears rather as a suspension of historical necessity than as a reconciliation of it. But in the cycle of trumpets a new perspective is added: the initiation of the chain of evils lies not with the forces of nature, but with the prayers of the saints which ascend from the altar of sacrifice. The disasters - which in this cycle are natural, not political - are called forth by the demand of outraged justice given

---

[13]Our understanding of the sequence of seven seals departs from the more common interpretation of it as a development of the tradition of 'signs of the end' found also in the synoptic apocalypses (Mk. 13 and par.) (See Court, *Myth* 43–81.) This yields a more church-oriented reading than the one we have followed. The horsemen of the first four seals represent events from the turbulent first-century background of the church's life, the martyrs of the fifth seal become the early Christian martyrs, of whom the synoptic apocalypses speak. Without wishing to deny a measure of formal dependence of John's material upon that of the synoptic tradition, I would pose two questions to those who find this an adequate account of what we read in the sixth chapter of Revelation. Does it do justice to chapter 5, with its carefully delineated setting of the sequence of seals in the context of a cosmic problem? For it is not enough to say, with Court (*Myth* 55), that 'the seer expresses very precisely the fact that his perspective begins with the crucifixion of Christ', when the scroll of history was held in the hand of the enthroned King, and was already a source of anxiety to mortal men before ever the Lamb appeared to open it. And in the second place: has it given a satisfactory account of the climax of the sequence in the vision of the seventh chapter, where the redeemed are carefully identified, first of all, as the faithful of the old Covenant, drawn from the twelve tribes of Israel?

voice through the prayers of the righteous. And then in the cycle of bowls the initiative is transferred again: it comes from God himself, speaking out of his heavenly temple, so that the disasters, which remind us of the plagues of Egypt, are imposed directly by the activity of divine providence. Through the three successive cycles, then, we come progressively to see how divine initiative lies behind the degenerating horrors of history, which appear, at first blush, to be a failure of the created order of nature.

Let us pause over the term 'necessity', which I have used to characterise the tragic history which the cycles of seven disclose to us. Necessity is an appropriate term, because it has traditionally been used by philosophers in an ambivalent way, to point to a distinctive coincidence of good and evil. Necessity is, on the one hand, constraint, which deprives us of the freedom in which our fulfilment in the good is achieved. On the other hand, it is order, which ensures the sovereignty of the good by ruling out randomness and arbitrary meaninglessness. Thus the sequence of cycles contains a part of the answer to the problem posed by the sealed scroll. We are invited to read the inscrutable legend of history by conceiving its tragedy as inexorable constraint; but even in inexorable constraint we can learn to see justice and the hand of God. Already in this conception the threat of sheer arbitrariness is set at a distance, and the good, distinctly, if not unqualifiedly, is present.

This, however, can only be a partial answer. For although order (and so goodness) is vindicated in the act of judgment - so that we can speak of 'satisfaction' in judgment, and can be aware of an existential need for it - nevertheless, where order is imposed at the cost of freedom, then the good of creation is vindicated only negatively: it is not vindicated positively in flourishing and perfection. A universe in which sinful existence is cancelled out by the divine wrath has a kind of formal rightness; yet it is not worthy of a creator to accept such a vindication. (Here, of course, we touch upon the famous 'divine dilemma' which drives the theology of atonement as it was worked out by Athanasius and Anselm.) What place, then, is allowed for freedom in this presentation of historical necessity as divine justice?

In the first place we see freedom exercised in prayer. The afflicted righteous who, at the fifth stage of the first cycle, cry out from beneath the altar, 'How long before thou wilt judge?' (6:10), are told to wait, not merely for the maturation of divine purposes which concern others than themselves, but that their own freedom may be realised in the activity of prayer itself. When we first hear that prayer we hear it only as a cry of impotence. But at the start of the next cycle, we are shown that it is a prayer of power; for it is this prayer, and no other, which the angel mingles with the incense on the altar, so that it rises in the smoke of the incense before God (8:3); and so it is this prayer which, when cast as fire from the altar upon the earth, sets loose the thunder, lightning and earthquake of the seven trumpets. In the second place, freedom is exercised in prophecy. Here we touch on a theme close to John's heart, for it is the theme of his own vocation. The seventh stage of the second cycle - the stage which tells of divine victory, and which precedes, but belongs to, the seventh trumpet

- is a vision of two witnesses who prophesy in God's name with great authority, are slain, and are raised to life again by the power of God. The believer, then, exercises freedom in speech: the speech of prayer which addresses God from the affliction of historical necessity and the speech of prophecy which addresses mankind in the authority of God's word and which triumphs over necessity.

Creation is vindicated in two ways, we conclude: by the immanent judgment of God worked out in the course of historical necessity, and by the overcoming of necessity by the power of the believer's true speech. So much of an answer to the initial question has been given us by the end of chapter 11, the climax of the cycle of seven trumpets. But it is a dialectical answer, which has not been resolved; necessity and freedom have not been reconciled. The realm of politics has been associated with the sphere of necessity, and freedom has been represented in an anti-political way. This impression is reinforced in the vision of the two witnesses by the use John makes of the 'great city, which is allegorically called Sodom and Egypt, where their Lord was crucified' (11:8). The city - that pregnant symbol, which we here meet for the first time in the Apocalypse - is the concrete definition of the human urge to conquer when confronted by the prophetic rebuke of the Word of God. Conquest has assumed a permanent form; it has embodied itself in a political institution, which is opposed to the freedom of the word of truth. Politics is power-against-the-Word. Yet John has not neglected to drop a hint for us (who have not yet reached the conclusion of his vision) that another view of the city is possible. The vision of the two witnesses began with the solemn measurement of the temple of God, which was to be kept safe by divine protection while the city around it, 'the holy city' (11:2), was trampled underfoot by the nations. This 'holy city' is the same as that which is called Sodom and Babylon, and (though John will not grant it the dignity of the name Jerusalem) is the city in which Christ was put to death. The political institution which appears as the embodiment of opposition to the truth may be something else: it may be the holy city given over to desecration. Beneath the phenomenon of power-against-the-Word there is the deeper political reality of a community consecrated to the Word. We are at least permitted to anticipate that the politics of conquest may be countered at the last by an alternative politics of worship.

II

At the beginning of chapter 12, introducing the great central section of the Apocalypse, John presents an allegorical narrative of the birth and triumph of Christ. This is of great importance for our understanding both of what has gone before and of what is to come after. The content of the first two cycles has been enacted, as it were, *ante Christum natum,* or at least *remoto Christo.* The souls of the righteous under the altar were not necessarily the souls of the Christian faithful, but simply the souls of righteous mankind; the two witnesses who prophesied in the great city were not presented as Christian witnesses, but as figures from the Old Testament, the olive-trees and lampstand of Zechariah, 'the two anointed who stand by the Lord of the whole earth' (Zc. 4:14), slain in the appropriate city where every prophet must perish. Of course, it goes without saying that the course of history as seen in these two cycles reaches its climax in 'the kingdom of our Lord and of his Christ' (11:15). We could expect nothing less since it was the Lamb who opened the seals. But only at the seventh stage of each cycle is a distinct reference to Christ introduced - the gentile multitude who 'have washed their robes and made them white in the blood of the Lamb' (7:14), the two prophets slain in the city 'where their Lord was crucified' (11:8). It is the dawning of the kingdom that reveals how the righteous have, in fact, been serving Christ all through the vicissitudes of an oppressive and apparently meaningless history.

But it is equally important that what follows should be understood to belong *post Christum,* in the Messianic age. John's vision proceeds from the taking-up of the Messiah into heaven, to the expulsion and fall of Satan, the persecution of the church, and then to the memorable passage which is most often alluded to by those who wish to characterise his political outlook with a single stroke of the brush, the summoning of the beasts from the sea and the land, which herald the oppressive and idolatrous totalitarian order described in chapter chapter 13.

We should reflect on John's intentions in situating this passage of political criticism at this point. Initially it may surprise us that he should conceive political theory in relation to salvation history. The Western tradition derived from Augustine does not do this: it understands politics in terms of the providential dispensation *post lapsum,* in the light of the covenant with Noah (and, of course, John does not propose to *contest* a relation between politics and providence, as the cycles of seals and trumpets can verify). But he wishes to identify something distinctive about the shape of politics in the Messianic age, between the Ascension and the Parousia of Christ. In this respect his approach will bear comparison with the account of governing authorities given in Romans, 1 Timothy and 1 Peter. For although these passages are important sources for the Augustinian view, they also display (of Romans and 1 Peter at least this can be said) a marked eschatological emphasis. If we are inclined to say that John's interpretation of politics is apocalyptic, while that of the Pauline strand in the New Testament is self-consciously secular, we may do so innocuously - provided that we add that even the secular approach ('every human institution', 1 Pet. 2:13) takes its rise from the expected 'day of visitation' (2:12). The Pauline tradition, too, knows that we stand between the Ascension and the Parousia of Christ, that 'the night is far gone, the day is at hand' (Rom. 13:12), and that our thought about politics begins with the admission that the claim of lordship has been appropriated to himself by the ascended Christ. The implication of this is that believers pray for 'a quiet and peaceable life' under their kings (1 Tim. 2:2); whereas John expects those same prayers to let loose an idolatrous this-worldly empire.

John's image of blasphemous empire is that which was common to Jewish apocalyptic writing from the Book of Daniel onwards. There arises a beast from the sea; the sea, here as elsewhere, represents the abyss of chaos and disorder which was overcome in the divine act of creation. The changes that John introduces into the picture of Daniel chapter 7 are as important as the points of resemblance. John's one beast combines the characteristics of Daniel's four. He is not, like Daniel, propounding a world-history of empires, in which each of the successive great powers, past and present, has a place. He is aware that there is such a history (and will draw upon it later in his treatment of the Great Whore) but he is not concerned to trace it. His interest, rather, is in empire as an eschatological phenomenon, evoked by the diabolical fall which follows upon the triumph of Christ. The order of events in Daniel 7 has thus been turned significantly upon its head. Where the Old Testament prophet saw a sequence of historical empires being brought to a close by the exaltation of the Son of Man, the New Testament prophet sees demonic empire as evoked in a new, though temporarily limited, form precisely by the exaltation of the Son of Man.

John's beast differs from Daniel also in its relation to the dragon, 'that ancient serpent, who is called the Devil and Satan' (12:9). Daniel's four empires emerge in sequence from the abyss of their own accord, whereas John's beast is summoned by a force more primaeval and fundamental than itself, which it resembles not only in the possession of ten horns (which they both share with Daniel's fourth beast) but in the possession of seven heads. The native element of the dragon was heaven. Cast down by the triumph of the Christ, he looks for an earthly form in which to operate, and that form is empire. In various ways the prophet suggests that the relation between the dragon and the beast is a parodic reflection of the relation between God the Father and the Son. The dragon confers upon him 'his power and his throne and great authority' (13:2) in an imitation of the enthronement of the Messiah. We have already remarked that at the end of the Apocalypse evil is overthrown in two stages: the beast by the victorious Messiah and the dragon by the all-judging Father. And now we may also notice the feature of the healed wound, by which the beast parodies the death and resurrection of Christ; it is a symbol of his Messianic status. And we need not invoke Nero Redivivus to explain it; we need look no further than the phenomenon of empire itself, which looks as though it brings life out of death. By imposing order upon chaos empire seems to introduce the promise of resurrection into human affairs. Throughout John's presentation of the beast and its empire we find him absorbed in the pretensions of evil to provide a positive focus for social unity and cohesion. At heart, he believes, evil is simply self-destructive and provides no ontologically secure basis for social life. Yet in the phenomenon of empire it appears to provide a secure basis. And John's criticism of that appearance is that it is parodic and derivative. It achieves what it appears to achieve only by crude imitation and distortion of the good. Thus the authority of the beast is established by the names of blasphemy which it bears, a parody of the one who has authority by bearing the divine name before mankind. The divinity of empire is a borrowed divinity.

Parodic imitation is carried further with the appearance of a second beast, the beast from the land, who is also called the 'false prophet', accompanying the false Christ in literal fulfilment of Mark 13:22. Although the second beast is described in details from Daniel 8:3, its immediate source is in the later apocalyptic tradition (cf. 2 Esdras 6:49ff., 1 Enoch 60:7–8, 2 Baruch 29:4) which speaks of two beasts, Leviathan and Behemoth, one from the sea and one from the land. But John's real interest is in developing a trinitarian account of empire as idolatry. His enlargement of the Father-Son relation into a trinitarian one is quite self-conscious. Although the person of the Holy Spirit is not explicitly mentioned in the Apocalypse proper until almost the last verse, John is continually alluding to the Spirit's role by stressing the place of true prophecy in the church's witness. As he wrote in his introductory letters: 'He who has an ear, let him hear what the Spirit says to the churches' (2:7 etc.). The beast from the land is also the false prophet. Unlike Daniel's he-goat, he speaks. It is his essential *raison d'être* to speak, to act as the ideologist of the empire and to support his speech with miraculous signs, so becoming the prophetic voice which maintains the empire's legitimacy and persuades mankind to adhere to it. John knows that though the essence of empire may be conquest and the denial of true speech, that empire which is falsely Messianic must depend upon the concealment of its essence with a plausible appearance of true speech, which is in fact false speech. The authority of falsehood is of critical importance to the Antichrist's regime; but the only authority which falsehood has, is that which it has borrowed from truth.

The false-prophet maintains the claim of the Antichrist to possess his subjects wholly, as Christ possesses his saints, by a parody of the baptismal seal. In the light of twentieth-century experience, we are fond of seeing here a description of what we call 'totalitarianism', and this is not mistaken. Totalitarianism is the assumption of all independent authority, natural or spiritual, the authority of the parent, of the teacher, of the priest, of the artist, into one authority of the state. But underneath the evil of totalitarianism, as John would show it to us, lies the more fundamental evil of Messianic ideology, the claim to ultimate allegiance. By presenting itself as the emissary of God, and demanding of its members the adherence appropriate only to the church, the empire brings the final condition of Hell into history. It provides a concrete form in which mankind can give himself heart and soul to a community of evil. Thus the mystery of evil serves the divine purpose of final separation.

Here we can only underline the contrast with the Pauline tradition. The state of government for which Christians are commanded to pray is one in which there is space, 'a quiet and peaceable life' (1 Tim. 2:2), space for the question of ultimate allegiance to be raised and answered in the preaching of the Gospel. Such a state is neutral at the ultimate level, however committed it may be at the penultimate. John does not challenge the suggestion that we ought to pray for such a space of freedom and neutrality. Yet he does not expect that prayer to be granted in the form in which it is made, not, at least, for more than intermittent periods. Under the force of the Gospel and of the allegiance to Christ which it evokes, the state comes to demand an opposite and ultimate allegiance. The mutual exclusiveness of the separation of good and evil begins to assume a shape within history. Those who do not worship the beast are thrust out from the market, which (for the first century as for the nineteenth) is the place of morally neutral political relations, the place of commerce without commitment. The closure of the market on ideological lines is a sign of the separation of the communities. Yet even that development, John would tell us, the very opposite of what we have prayed for, the failure of the liberal market to sustain itself under the clash of ultimate claims let loose upon the world by the ascension of Christ, is, though we could never bring ourselves to pray for it as such, God's most direct route towards that day when all our prayers for justice receive their truest answer.

III

It is one of those *prima facie* puzzles with which John confronts his interpreters that he has two dominant images for empire and not just one. After the reign of the beast from the sea and the false prophet, who represent the Messianic pretensions of empire in the Messianic age, we meet in chapter 17, in the first of three major concluding visions of judgment and triumph, the Great Whore. And as though to prevent his interpreters from evading the puzzle which he has set for them, John sets the Whore riding upon a beast which (as we are meant to have no doubt) is precisely the same beast that we have already encountered, still rising from the abyss (17:8), despite the curious feature that it has now acquired a scarlet coloration.

My own suggestion for understanding this dual imagery is that the beast represents empire quite specifically as a phenomenon of the messianic age, evoked by the triumph of the true Messiah and the limited dominion of the devil upon the earth. But empire as such had been a longstanding feature of the Mediterranean world. The prophet had, therefore, to admit a distinction between empire as a permanent feature of world politics and the eschatological heightening of empire - we might say, its demonisation - which marked the age of the church. The representative of world empire in the Old Testament was Babylon; and in introducing the figure of the Whore, whose name is Babylon, John intends to emphasise the continuity between the ancient prophets' experience of empire and the contemporary experience of Christians under the dominion of Rome. It is, of course, absurd to suppose that the name Babylon was merely a device for concealment. When John points out that this Babylon sits upon seven hills, the hint he drops is so heavy that it would surely be sufficient to earn him a further spell on Patmos if it were to come to official notice! The name is theological: it recalls the prophetic understanding of the Mesopotamian empires, and John uses it as an interpretative key to the rise of the Roman empire.

Thus the Whore is not Rome *stricto sensu*. She is human empire as such, which is presently situated at Rome, on the seven hills. Or, more concretely, she is Babylon transferred to Rome. She is an old familiar figure, well known to the reader of the prophets, who has been brought out of retirement by a new patron (of whose demonic origins she is blissfully unaware) and has been set up in a new home, to be used for ends which she cannot begin to understand. Thus John is able to study the political situation of his day from another angle, examining the general features that it shares with the empires of the past, without withdrawing from the particular claims he has made for the apocalyptic character of empire in the Messianic age. And of course he wishes to stress that empire, simply as a secular phenomenon in human politics, has a fate that is due to it, as the prophets of old had said long before. The Great Whore is to be destroyed by her lovers. For the beast himself, however, there is a very different end in store.

Already in chapter 14 John has heard some words recalled from the Isaianic apocalypse (Is. 21:9), proclaimed by one of the three angels entrusted with preaching the 'eternal Gospel' to the earth: "Fallen, fallen is Babylon!' The fulfilment of the prophets' hope for the end of imperial bondage is already a part of the Gospel which the coming of Christ preaches to the world. The particular form of the prophetic quotation at 14:8 deserves close scrutiny. Nowhere is John more careful and subtle in his use of Old Testament material than in his presentation of Babylon. The words from Isaiah 21, 'Fallen, fallen is Babylon!' are immediately followed by others from the Babylon oracle in Jeremiah 51: 'who has made all nations drunk with her wine'. But into this quotation again John weaves some further words, describing the wine as 'the wine of the wrath of her fornication'. Now, when we first hear these words, their bearing seems evident enough. The wrath is the wrath of God, manifest in the sudden growth of the Chaldaean empire, and all nations have been made to experience the impact of divine wrath through Babylon's 'fornication', that is, her indiscriminate conquests. But when the words return, slightly amplified, at 17:2, the reader suddenly awakes to what the author has done. He has woven into the tissue of Babylon quotations an allusion to the prophecy against *Tyre* at Isaiah 23:17. 'At the end of seventy years, the Lord will visit Tyre, and she will return to her hire, and will play the harlot with all the kingdoms of the world upon the face of the earth.' But this immediately puts a very different complexion upon that 'fornication'. For the fornication of Tyre is not indiscriminate conquest, but promiscuous trade. And as we read John's mighty lament over Babylon-Rome which occupies chapter 18 of the Apocalypse, we find that it is composed in about equal parts of allusions to prophetic oracles against conquering Babylon and against trading Tyre. The two major sources are Jeremiah 51 against Babylon and Ezekiel 27 against Tyre. Details of the Babylon prophecy take on a new significance as they are associated with Tyre: the 'many waters' on which the harlot sits, for example, were (in Je. 51:13) a reference to

Babylon's elaborate canal system; but now they are evidently intended to represent the Mediterranean Sea, on which the great commercial city plies her trade.

What are we to make of this? It is possible to see it merely as a happy use of diverse materials in order to characterise more precisely the hold which Rome has upon the nations of her empire, a hold very much rooted in commercial and cultural exchange and by no means merely a matter of military *force majeure*. I cannot help thinking, however, that this would be to underestimate our author. It is not for him a purely circumstantial matter that the new Babylon has learned the arts of old Tyre; nor is his use of the image from Isaiah 23, describing trade as 'fornication', merely decorative. The significance of this marriage of Tyre-and Babylon-motifs is that trade, too, as much as conquest, violates the integrity of communities which become dominated by the cultural influences of the stronger trading power. We have to recall that the tyranny of the beast in chapter 13 was exercised through control of the market. In that sense trade is 'fornication'. It is a cultural promiscuity by which one power exploits and drains the resources from many others. John stands preeminent among those who have seen mercantile enterprise as a tool of empire. He reserves for the very conclusion of his lament on Babylon-Rome a quotation from the Tyre oracle, Isaiah 23:8, to which he gives great prominence: 'Thy merchants were the great men of the earth' (18:22). Less striking to us, perhaps, than to the ancient world is the thought of a society in which the rulers are merchants and the merchants rulers - the paradoxical scene which confronted the astonished Israelite prophet when he looked upon Tyre. Yet he saw nothing so paradoxical as a *world empire* in which this was so. But for John this paradox was the key to the power of the world-empire in which he lived. It ruled over the multitude of nations by exercising commercial and cultural monopoly.

In Ezekiel's lament over Tyre the seafaring classes, who have become rich by Tyre's greatness, wail and weep at her fall; while the 'merchants among the peoples', on the other hand, rather unexpectedly 'hiss' (Ezk. 27:36), presumably because the dominance of international trade by this one power has excluded them from the share of the market to which they felt they had a right. John allows no such division of opinion over the fall of his Babylon-Rome. Without her there would be no commercial endeavour at all; therefore the merchants as well as the seafarers weep at her destruction. Her end means the end of all cultural endeavour: harpists, minstrels, flute-players and trumpeters fall silent. It means the cessation of crafts, and of basic cultural activities such as the grinding of the millstone and the lighting of the lamp. It means (echoing Jeremiah's word of judgment on Jerusalem) the silencing of the voice of the bridegroom and the voice of the bride (18:22–23). But to the list of those who lament the loss of human social culture John adds the 'kings of the earth', the very figures whose independence has been drained away by the fornication which they have committed with this monopolistic cultural force. And this is a point on which we must linger; for the relation between the empire and its client kingdoms is central to the prophet's view of how empire comes to destroy itself.

The beast from the abyss, you will recall, boasts of seven heads and ten horns - a detail which poses an insoluble problem of distribution to the artists of each generation who attempt to depict the *mulier sedens* - and they are explained in chapter 17 as follows. The seven heads represent both the seven hills of Rome and an unfinished series of emperors, of which (John tells us unambiguously) the sixth is now reigning. Beyond this series of seven emperors, the beast is to have a final manifestation as an 'eighth'. The ten horns are ten kings - not, as in the model in Daniel, a series of ten, for they all act together in concert. They must, then, represent the kings of the earth who have committed fornication with the harlot and over whom she exercises dominion. They are the constituent powers on which her extensive empire of trade and conquest is founded. These ten kings, John predicts, are to receive authority for one hour together with the beast (7:12). We are presumably to assume that this one hour is the eschatological climax of the mystery of evil - we see this moment in closer perspective at 19:19 when the two Messiahs meet in battle - the same hour as that in which the beast takes form as the eighth emperor. At this point they will do two things: they will unite with the beast to make war against the Lamb (17:13), and they will turn against the Whore and devour her flesh and burn her up with fire (17:16). And this will be according to the purposes of God, who has 'put it into their hearts to carry out his purpose by being of one mind and giving over their royal power to the beast, until the words of God shall be fulfilled' (17:17).

This is a confusing scenario. The ten kings receive their royal power at the end of history, renounce it to the beast in an act of unanimity, turn upon the empire which has nurtured them, lament the fall which they have themselves encompassed, and then turn blindly and self-destructively against the Lamb. What coherence can we detect in this sequence of acts?

First, we remember that John is offering an analysis of empire which understands it as 'fornication', that is to say, the surrendering of individual integrity in an undisciplined and destructive form of commerce. Empire is not simply an extensive form of unified rule, but one which drains the integrity from all other powers and leaves them improperly dependent and impotent. Thus the ten kings are at once the dependents of empire and the victims of its capacity to arrogate all authority to itself. Their relation to it is that mixture of resentment and need which is characteristic of dependents. Now, the climax of the career of empire, as John sees it, is its dissolution under the force of the resentment which it has engendered. It may appear to have conferred unity on the constituent parts of which it is composed, and so it has. But that unity achieves its paradoxical height in the 'one mind' which unites its dependents in rebellion against the source of their own strength. This final paroxysm of self-destruction is the most complete disclosure of the unity which has been engendered by these means.

But this general thesis about the end of empire is woven together, in John's prediction, with an eschato-logical view of the end of the Messianic pretender. For the beast itself is destined to turn against the empire it has promoted - which is to say that the mystery of evil, though it has taken provisional and penultimate form in an apparently unified, coherent political structure, can achieve its ultimate self-disclosure only as every positive element, borrowed from created goodness, is strained out. The goal of the self-revelation of evil is the vanishing point of unity in pure negativity. The logic of the beast's end and the logic of the whore's end is the same: predatory power collapses in upon itself. And so it is that the two ends are coordinated. It is as the client kings discover and express their unity in turning against its source that they offer the purest worship to the beast; and it is at that point, with the collapse of empire in a furiously united tumult of self-destruction, that the beast can make his final throw of outright war against the Lamb, carrying the force of united negativity against the throne of God himself. But of course it is in vain; for the 'one mind' with which the resentful powers unite to serve the beast and destroy their mistress is also borrowed from the mind of God himself. Its unity is a borrowed unity; the purposefulness of its evil was always a sign of its predatory dependence upon the good which it suppressed. The diabolical project of claiming the throne of lordship was from the beginning a self-contradictory project. The collapse of empire, then, reveals the operation of divine providence; and the future collapse of this Messianic empire will be a revelation of the final rule of God's Messiah over history. The disclosure of the mystery of evil was always at the service of divine providence for the overcoming of evil.

IV

Almost everything we have observed so far has been by way of criticism of political phenomena, suggesting that the stance of the believer must be essentially anti-political. The paradigm of political activity has been imperial conquest; the permanent political institution, the city, has merely served to sustain and develop the exploitation of imperial dominion by commercial means. The exercise of human freedom in response to the Word of God has thrown the believer into irresoluble conflict with the organised community. And in these last days empire has taken on a new significance as the form in which the Antichrist lays claim to wrest mankind's ultimate allegiance from God. Not even in the church can we see a form of social life which qualifies this negative judgment. The faithful believer appears in history as an individual ('him who conquers') or as a pair ('the two witnesses') standing against organised society. The very word 'church' is used by John only to designate the local communities which he addresses in his introductory letters. There is no place for the church catholic on earth. Only when we have lifted our eyes to heaven have we been allowed to see, at the end of history, the reality of a worshipping community: the Jewish and gentile faithful in chapter 7 and the community of first fruits in chapter 14.

For all this there is a reason. The root of any true social order, in which human beings relate to God and to each other lovingly, is the revelation of the conspicuous justice of God. We cannot comprehend how we are to live together until we know that God has shown us his judgments. For the good of social order is founded upon a judgment (*dikaiōma*), a declarative act which establishes righteousness (*dikaiosunē*). In divine judgment the paradoxical conflict between the freedom of the Word of God and the necessity of immanent justice in history is resolved. God's word becomes 'judgment'; its freedom creates the order of a concrete society. And the the necessity of history becomes 'judgment' too; its tragedy is turned into the freedom of the saints' obedience. It is quite clear at what point in the Apocalypse we are permitted to see this coming together of necessity and freedom in divine judgment. It happens in the third cycle of seven, which is introduced by the words of those who have obeyed and conquered the beast, 'Thy judgments have been revealed! (15:4), and is accompanied by a confession of God's justice from the afflicted innocent beneath the altar, 'Yea, Lord God the Almighty, true and just are thy judgments!' (16:7). And it happens at precisely this point because in the preceding section, chapters 12–14, we have seen the Christ revealed and exalted and have heard the angels proclaiming the eternal Gospel, concluding with the vision of the Son of Man coming upon the cloud to judge. We may, then, expect that in the concluding sections of the Apocalypse we shall be shown the outline of a new social existence which is founded upon the judgments of God. This, of course, cannot be a product *of* history, because it is brought about by the judgment of God *upon* history. It is given from heaven, descending like a bride prepared for the bridegroom.

We have observed already that the vision of divine conquest, the central section of the three concluding sections (19:11 - 20:15), presents the victory over evil twice over in two pictures, first as a battle, then as an act of jurisdiction. The Messiah rides out to conquer the beast, and then there is a scene of judgment. Gog and Magog are gathered for battle, and then there is the judgment of the white throne. In the case of the first victory, the victory of the Messiah, the faithful share his judgment, seated on thrones with him, and reign with him for a thousand years (20:4). Those terms 'judgment' (*krima* this time, not *dikaiōma,* which is reserved for the aboriginal constitutive act of God) and 'reign' invite us to consider the promise of an eschatological just order, a sharing in the authority and sovereignty which is given to all members of a true and well-founded community. Such a promise can be realised only by the victory of the true Messiah over the false. The word of truth has first to take form as a sword, issuing from the Messiah's mouth, to defeat those who live by the sword, in order for it then to take form as a judgment, to ennoble and give dignity to those whose social hope has been founded upon it alone. There is, of course, as has been often observed, something highly paradoxical about the picture of the Prince of Martyrs constituting himself the head of an army of conquest. It is an image which negates itself, cancelling, rather than confirming, the significance of the political categories on which it draws.

It is what Aquinas called the merely 'symbolic predication of proportional analogy'. What is less often observed is that the analogy of *judgment* is not merely symbolic, and that here the political imagery does not negate itself. The idea of an ordered social existence under the authority of divine *dikaiōma,* participating in that authority by the activity of human *krima,* is not a purely formal one. It conveys to us a hope that in the life which we are summoned to live with Christ we may experience, as a social reality, that authority of truth and righteousness which our experience of political society on earth has consistently denied us.

We must not fail to observe the implications of this. If it is right to say that the basis for a new order of society is God's word of judgment pronounced in Christ, then it follows that the witnesses who proclaimed that word to challenge the prevailing political order, were not acting anti-politically at all, but were confronting a false political order with the foundation of a true one. We must claim John for the point of view which sees criticism, when founded in truth, as genuine political engagement.

A right ordering of society is realised when mankind in Christ *participates* in the exercise of the Messiah's authority. But the judgment of the saints cannot be the last word about true judgment. When John turns from the triumph of the Messiah to the triumph of the Father, we are shown another act of jurisdiction, which belongs exclusively to God. To be part of an ordered community is to share in the exercise of its proper authority, yes; but more profoundly it is to be subject to the divine authority. For God's authority is not in competition with man's. From God's true speech flows all man's possibility of true speech; from God's judgment flows all man's possibility of judging. Not until we have stood before the great white throne and found ourselves judged there, can we possibly see, enter, or exercise our role in the Holy City, the new Jerusalem. (This is an example of how John's ordering of events is analytical rather than sequential: he proceeds from the judgment of the saints to the judgment of the Father as from an effect to its cause.) We would be well advised, we who love that ecstatic chapter with which John's Apocalypse closes, to remember how carefully and by what steps he has led us up to it.

Part of the impact of this astonishing chapter arises from the fact that we have come all this way, observing nations, races, armies, empires, kings, princes and merchants, simply to see a city - which we might have thought of as the primal form of human society. We have, of course, seen one city before this. Babylon-Rome was the Great City - the epithet distinguishing her from the New Jerusalem, who is the Holy City. John underlines the parallel between the two cities by repeating 17:1 almost verbatim at 21:9. In the tension between these two political symbols the whole conflict between good and evil is worked out: the city is the bride, and the city is the whore. But behind this opposition we will recall that there was a hint of their fundamental identity. In chapter 11 John was commanded to measure the temple but leave the outer court unmeasured, since it was given over to the gentiles who 'will trample over the holy city [note the epithet] for forty-two months' (11:2). In this same city, apparently,

God appointed his two witnesses to prophesy and be slain, and their bodies to lie 'in the street of the great city [note the epithet] which is allegorically called Sodom and Egypt, where their Lord was crucified' (11:8). Here, then, the two epithets are assigned to the one city, which is given on this occasion neither the name Babylon nor the name Jerusalem, though it is associated with the historical Jerusalem by the reference to Jesus' death and by the presence of the temple. What are we to conclude from this? That the city is aboriginally the 'holy city', but has lost its name and its sanctity (apart from the temple in its midst) and is corrupted into a denial of itself? Here is the clearest statement of the aboriginal *unity* of the human community to set against the recurrent emphasis on its *division*. What we see as the two cities is in fact the corruption, and the hope of redemption, of the aboriginal one city.

The details of John's heavenly Jerusalem are drawn primarily from the vision of temple and city which occupies the concluding nine chapters of Ezekiel; but there are significant revisions. Ezekiel's holy city is built around a temple, and is set in the midst of a reorganised Holy Land. John's is a city without a temple, and is set in the midst of a redeemed earth. In a highly significant qualification of Ezekiel 47:12 John says that the leaves of the trees which grow beside the river are for the healing *of the nations*. Thus John points to a universal restoration of the human community as Ezekiel never did. In the light of this we may wonder why, in equipping his guide with a measuring-rod, John did not follow through the implication of Zechariah 2:1–5 (to which he alluded in chapter 11) and declare that the eschatological city should be without walls, since it is protected by God's immediate presence (a logic he will not hesitate to follow when it suggests the abolition of the temple). The answer is, apparently, that he saw the city's walls not simply as a protection, but as a definition. The gates and walls are there not to exclude but to give form: their twelvefold structure confirms the city's continuity both with Israel (of the twelve tribes) and with the church (of the twelve apostles); but the ever-open gates show the elect community in its appointed openness to the world, providing the light by which the nations walk and the shrine to which the kings of the earth bring their glory (21:24).

To the reader who is not attuned to John's dialectical use of images this is an astonishing moment. He is unprepared to entertain the thought of a humanity living and thriving outside of the redeemed Jerusalem. Yet it is highly characteristic of our author to balance complementary aspects of his understanding in this way. As the city of the faithful, the community of the redeemed, the heavenly Jerusalem contains universality in itself. It *is* restored humanity, and 'outside' it there is nothing but rejection (22:15). Yet it is also the *elect* people, whose destiny it is to shed God's light into the whole world. This aspect, too, must be present in the imagery of the final state, especially as it balances and corrects the resentful and destructive relation of the client kings to the imperial city. In this vision of human completeness there must be a symbol of the *mutuality* which was destroyed by empire, which is yet compatible, John believes, with the exclusion of all that is in the service of evil. To ask him to do more than set these two images, the one of universal homogeneity the other of mutuality, alongside one another, is to ask him to be more theoretical than his vision allows him to be - or else to resolve the dialectic of election and universality improperly, by denying one side or the other.

At the heart of the city is the throne of God, which is now also, and eternally, the throne of the Lamb. John's city, like Ezekiel's, is the place where the Lord dwells. But whereas Ezekiel expresses this by making the temple dominate the city, John disposes of the cultic image apophatically: 'I saw no temple' (21:22). He shows himself in this way to be a Hellenistic Christian eschatological thinker, following the lead of the author to the Hebrews, for whom the cultic is the shadow of good things to come, dispelled by the actual form of them in Christ. The presence of God in community is unmediated; it is sheer presence. Therefore the temple 'is' the Lord God Almighty and the Lamb. The temple has been absorbed, we may say, into the throne. But to this observation we must add another: that the throne has become a place of divine speech. At 16:17 we heard God speak 'out of the temple, from the throne, saying, "It is done!"'; but now the voice which was heard through the mediation of the temple speaks immediately, no longer in secret communion with men, but in open settlement of the affairs of the universe. Its words form the goal of the whole Apocalypse, giving a decisive interpretation to the final vision, which is itself the interpretation of all the other visions.

These final words of God are found at 21:3–8. They consist of a declaration of reconciliation, 'Behold, the dwelling of God is with men..', and a declaration of judgment, 'To the thirsty I will give from the fountain of the water of life...but as for the cowardly etc.'. And these two declarations flank three short utterances about the beginning and end of all things: 'Behold, I make all things new.' 'Write this, for these words are trustworthy and true.' 'It is done! I am the Alpha and the Omega, the beginning and the end.' With these three words we stand in the *sanctum sanctorum* of history. Everything is stripped away; even judgment and reconciliation stand to one side. We confront the sheer act and being of God. He who by his mere decision created the heaven and the earth, now by his mere decision makes all things new, conferring upon creation a 'history' and a fulfilment. The words 'I make' and 'All is accomplished' complement one another: there is no futurity about the first, no preterity about the second. History is summoned into being by God's ever-present declarative act, and there and then it is accomplished, reflecting back the glory of the one who summoned it, who can now be known as Alpha and Omega, its source and end.

But in between 'I make' and 'All is accomplished', at the centre of the three utterances, which are the centre of God's final speech, which is from the throne at the centre of the heavenly city, there stands the command to the prophet 'Write!'. An astonishing thing, that the prophet should find his own task at the very heart of the ineffable being and act of God! But in the sovereign decision of God to constitute history, there is implied a decision that history should make him known. He who can declare himself Alpha and Omega, *does* declare himself so in order to make that declaration heard. At the heart of God's self-announcement is the announcement that he is the self-announcing God, not merely self-subsisting but self-communicating. 'In the beginning was the Word; and the Word was with God, and the Word was God.' On that self-communication, mediated to us by prophetic speech, the holy city is founded. At the heart of politics is true speech, divine speech, entering into conflict with the false orders of history, the guarantor of the only true order that the universe can ever attain.

52. Sergii Bulgakov – The Soul of Socialism

I

The life of the nations at the present time is lived under the sign of socialism. Its red star stands in the skies of history like a threatening portent, a sign of judgement or prophecy – but in any case an unavoidable historical reality. We may or may not be in favour of it, we may be crying out for it or cringing before it, we may welcome it or hide ourselves from its presence, but there is no escaping it; it is a sort of fate decreed for the next generation, if not for ourselves. It confronts us like the riddle of the Sphinx, ready to devour anyone who does not give it an answer. And while it stands before the whole world as a threat or at least a sign of crisis, it also contains, as far as the Church is concerned, a question about its religious value and significance. Does it lie under a curse or a blessing, does it belong to the *civitas Dei* or to the *civitas diabolica,* with the Babylon brought low by an angelic hand (Rev. 17–18) or with the City of God coming down from heaven? For the Church is responsible for the life of the humanity to which it belongs, and cannot hold aloof from the spiritual struggles and sufferings of that humanity. The Church's answers will not be offered as dogmatic oracles; they evolve in the process of searching, in the restless struggles of thought and of disturbed conscience, as the agitation of the Spirit of God in human hearts: 'Seek and ye shall find' (Mt 7.7) is a word applicable even to the conciliar harmony [*sobornost'*] of the Church. History causes new shoots to spring out from the evergreen tree of the Church in the self-renewing creativity of its life, a life firmly anchored in ecclesial doctrine and tradition.

Today, then, the ecclesial consciousness faces a fact that poses a religious and dogmatic problem for the Church. For a long time it has been treated with caution and so not perceived in its full particularity, in that it has remained in the sphere of personal ethics or asceticism – which is how social questions have presented themselves in the awareness of the Church from time immemorial. In my opinion, socialism does not represent any problem at all, considered as an ethical issue; rather is it – from time immemorial, indeed – a natural postulate, so to speak, of Christianity's social ethic. Labour must be protected from illicit exploitation, and justice demands that it be rewarded with the fruits of its work, and that these should not be sacrificed to the power of capital. In recent times churchmen of various denominations have attempted to come to terms with socialism, in that they have adopted it from motives of Christian philanthropy (as in the diverse forms of 'Christian socialism' in our day); and they have sometimes joined forces with political parties (such as the Social Democrats) very much at odds with Christianity, without attempting to deal dogmatically with all the questions raised. But we must reckon with socialism as a fundamental and all-embracing fact in contemporary human history, a specific *spiritual* outlook, and we shall do so in so far as we take our stand on firm *dogmatic* and not merely ethical ground – in living communion with the Church, without trying to simplify the question. Just as, in the history of doctrinal definitions that express some distinct experience, any new step forward in the dogmatic awareness of the Church is preceded by a more or less protracted period of 'fermentation' for the questions at issue, so, in relation to socialism, we are still in that period of ferment, of questing, of individual interpretations ('heresies'). This cannot be forgotten or unspoken; but one cannot take any precipitate personal speculations for a comprehensive ecumenical achievement. First there must be a testing of the conformity of such speculations with the spirit of the Church, by connecting them up with the entire ecclesial tradition. But in this process we must never lose sight of the fact that the ecclesial and dogmatic evaluation of socialism and the social question, especially in the Orthodox world, is still at an absolutely elementary stage.

Socialism is not only a socio-economic movement, although it is most directly expressed in such terms. It is also a world-view, a *Weltanschauung*, or, more precisely, a *Lebensgefühl*, a sense and style of life in which different aspects of human nature find expression. It could be said that socialism possesses not only an historical 'body', but also a 'soul' or spirit; and in this sense it can have the significance of a pseudo-religion for its adherents – a world-view with total claims, which is practical as well as theoretical. The *body* of socialism is there for all to see, in the social problems of our day – industrialism, the tyranny of the banks, class hostility, crises in industry and finance, unemployment, the emergence of socialist political parties, communism and the dictatorship of the proletariat – all those subterranean shocks and tremors that constantly threaten the stability of the old world and have already partly destroyed it. Lasalle's defiant motto, *nequeo si superos Acheronta movebo*, has already become reality, as have Carlyle's angry prophecies about Enkelados in chains, or Marx's vengeful foretelling of the dictatorship of the proletariat with its threat of 'expropriating the expropriators'. The 'body' of socialism is like Proteus; it has many forms, always changing. While yesterday it led an illegal, underground existence, today it has become a powerful and sometimes even a dominant reality, above all in my own homeland. But it is now generally true that the human race is dressing itself in more or less socialist garments, and is turning into a socialist anthill; its spread seems to be unstoppable. Economists may have different judgements about the limitations and the non-viability of socialism; and yet it is already impossible to deny or ignore it completely as a characteristic phenomenon of our life today. We can only discuss the different degrees in which the influence of non-socialist factors is manifest in a life fundamentally marked by socialism. Anyone now coming into the world finds him- or herself in a period in which socialism is continually widening its frontiers. Understood simply as a question about poverty and wealth, socialism has always been present in human history, though only as a fact which has hardly ever been historically notable or clearly defined. But now it has become a fact of our inner as well as our outer life, for socialism has a *soul* of its own – a soul that is admittedly wholly pagan – and a *spirit* which has so far been decidedly hostile to God. So let us first spend some time on this question of the 'soul' of socialism.

It is defined by the *anthropology* that is peculiar to socialism. There are two characteristic fundamentals in this doctrine of human nature, sociologism and economism. Both are based on a specific lived experience or vision that is particularly accessible and congenial to our times. *Sociologism* begins from the *collective* character of human existence: already in the Old Testament we encounter the personification of collective 'totalities' – Israel, Amalek, Assur, Ishmael and others, or the beasts of Danielic apocalypse, which also crop up in the New Testament Apocalypse. Today these beasts have imperceptibly transformed themselves into groups or classes, the mythical abstractions of sociology. The telescope and microscope of modern social thought, dictated by statistics and the social sciences in general, bring before everyone's eyes the reality and autonomy of the social corpus, although they have yet to recognise any comparable reality in personal existence; on the contrary, this is swallowed up in the totality of society and even denied in the name of society. In this way, belief in human personhood and its reality comes to be lost; yet it is precisely this that is the first and fundamental datum for religion. More of this later on.

The second fundamental, *economism,* is the general recognition of the dependence of human personhood upon nature – a dependence that is both realised in and overcome by labour, which produces value or wealth – but also, in and with these, the whole of human culture. Economism has its most extreme expression in Marxism, with its so-called 'economic materialism' – better designated as 'materialist economism', in opposition to a *spiritual* (or even spiritualistic) economism. Our age is entirely saturated with this – the development of economic knowledge with its particular, conventional, one-sided and stylised account of human life, the economic trend in historical science, in the press, in society at large. 'The world as economy' and man as *oikonomos* – that is the basic vision of this anthropology. This kind of economism generally sees itself not only as materialistic but as zoological. The economic struggle here becomes a special case of the general struggle for existence which is going on in the whole of the animal world; and furthermore, this social Darwinism is complemented by a crassly materialist perception (or rather misperception) of the economic process. There is no recognition that economy is not only the slavery of mankind under the yoke of elemental nature, but is also a continuing revelation of the human spirit, the triumphant revealing of humanity itself.

In man's economic relation to the world both the greatness of his vocation and the depth of his fall are revealed. It is a *practical* relation to the world, in which man governs and directs nature by humanising it, by making it a 'peripheral body' for himself. Man is a microcosm in the sense that he is the *logos* and the soul of the world. In the economics of labour the fulness of human activity is realised, not simply as the action of a physical worker ('hammer and sickle'), as materialist economism conceives it, but also as the operation of rational will in the world. Natural science and technology display the world to man as a limitless field of possibilities. Matter – dumb, sluggish and formless – becomes transparent and spiritual, a vehicle for human meaning; it becomes 'body' so to speak. It is thus that the cosmic nature of man, his vocation to lordship in the world, appears. In economics the unity of the human species is also graphically displayed and preserved at the external level, since man's labour as an economic agent (a 'transcendental subject of economics') is shaped in history into a unified form, uninterruptedly consistent and integrated. In economic activity the world is dematerialised and becomes a totality of spiritual energies. This is why, incidentally, even the advance of materialist economism is devoted to the process of a wider economic development which increasingly restricts the domain of matter as such by transforming it into *human* energy; the world becomes an 'anthropocosmos'. Yet it is also in the economic relation to the world that the fallenness of man finds expression; his life is mortal, and economics becomes also labour 'in the sweat of his brow' [Gen. 3.19] for the sake of sustaining life and the incessant struggle against death. Human dependence on economic activity is the captivity of death; it is indeed, in a sense, death itself. Economic activity is slavery to death, and so it is both forced and self-interested; it is in relation to this fact that Marxism has its truth, as a kind of halting philosophical recapitulation of the second chapter of Genesis, where God's sentence is passed on man. And yet even in fallenness man still possesses his 'sophianic' nature; his economic life is not characterised only by self-interest but also by the creative and artistic calling of human beings, the service of an ideal, and – like all human enterprise – by the struggle to *grow beyond the self*. This creative, world-embracing impulse in economics is something peculiar to our own age, in which the world has come to be seen as the *work* of man. 'Philosophers have sought long enough to interpret the world, but now it is time to change it'; 'the world is not there to be contemplated, everything must be worked for, nothing is without price' – these are the sayings of two almost contemporary philosophers of economics, expressing the same thought at opposite ends of Europe and in very different ways, Karl Marx and Nikolai

Fyodorov. This massive fact of world history, the fact of the economic subjugation, humanising and, in this sense, transformation (if not yet exactly transfiguration) of the world, has already emerged on the historical stage, though it has yet to reach its consummation. It confronts our religious consciousness and demands a spiritual, even 'dogmatic', understanding of economics. So far this latter has known no dogma other than the pagan one of Epicureanism: any increase in need or demand is a good, the sole criterion in economic life is self-love and the struggle for wealth and so forth. Such is the ingenuous ethic of economic empiricism. Even the wisdom which the Church's consciousness possesses in respect of economics has not wholly escaped the influence of this unprincipled empiricism. As far as personal restraint is concerned, the Church has always had a clearly defined stock of ascetical ideas, firmly rooted in its spiritual tradition. Wealth is here related to in purely negative terms; it is treated as one of the lusts of the flesh in which the power of sin and death is manifested. This introduces an ascetical corrective into economic existence, which controls all economic activity by bringing it before the bar of conscience. But it is still inadequate as a response. According to scripture, work is in itself a religious obligation for human beings, such that the institution of labour is not just a matter of personal self-determination, in so far as economic life is a *social* process. In a certain sense, the sphere of economic work, with its distinctive possibilities, is a kind of destiny for human beings; and this 'destiny' consists in the fact that a complete economic cosmos for us to live in is being constructed out of all our individual economic activities, with all their heterogeneous goals. As far as this destiny and this cosmos are concerned, personal asceticism has no ideas to guide it; it relates to it in a purely empirical way, as to a brute fact. But this unawareness at the level of principle leads to changes at the level of practice – leads, in fact, to the *secularising* of interior and exterior life. A monastery which, spiritually speaking, rests on the foundations of ascetical renunciation of the world and on disinterestedness will still make use of all the achievements of technology and the economic process in meeting its own needs, and will take this quite for granted, since 'there's no stink to money'. Thus the Church ends up sanctifying in principle anything that the world brings out of its treasure-store, though the latter has long since passed beyond its control. It could be said that there has never yet been an epoch in the world's history in which economic life has been secularised and left to itself to such an extent as at the present time. In the pagan world, just as in the Christian Middle Ages, no such secularisation of economic life existed as prevails among Christian nations today (indeed the life of non-Christian peoples – Indian, Chinese, Japanese, Turkish and others – seems at first sight to be a good deal richer than that of Christians). This secularisation finds its ideological expression in materialist economism, which has a certain degree of accuracy where the economic life of our times is concerned, since it is carried on not in the presence but in the absence of God. So the struggle against this materialism cannot remain at the purely apologetic level; we can demonstrate its inadequacy and contradictoriness, but must also react positively, restoring Christian significance to the economic process and ecclesial significance to the elements of economic life. Meanwhile the prevailing attitude to economics is one of pragmatic and unprincipled acceptance of what was for a long time regarded only as one of the 'miracles of Antichrist'.

Where is economic development actually leading us? Does economics have a kind of prophetic office in and of itself, as socialism would have it? Is it perhaps the final and all-embracing time of trial for the whole of history, in the face of which the elect must take refuge in the caves and clefts of the earth (if there are any left)? Is it simply the Christian's fate to be tempted by it without ever understanding it, or is it rather a *necessity*, because the unavoidable road of history towards that eschatological fulfilment that lies beyond history leads through it? History and eschatology, temporal fulfilment and its final end, have for a long time been separated and set in opposition to each other, so that any sort of link between them has been, for all practical purposes, denied: the one must come to an end for the other, like a *deus ex machina,* to begin. In this eschatological transcendentalism, all earthly illumination is quenched and all earthly values destroyed: all that remains is personal merit and personal sin, with their equivalents of reward or punishment, which each individual receives for himself alone, without any regard to the collective work of humanity in history. From such historical and sociological nihilism in the realm of eschatology arises a corresponding nihilism in history. But history has its own *inner* apocalypse, which makes history itself already eschatology fulfilling itself in time: the Lord's Second Coming, of whose day and hour (in the transcendent sense) no-one knows save the heavenly Father, also has times and seasons in the immanent process of historical maturation; and even economics with its achievements must be allowed a place in this historical eschatology. In any event, we are faced with the question: must man's labour and toil under the sun be somehow included in the life of eternity which eschatology opens up, or should it be excluded from it? If the former, how and in what sense? If the latter, why so (since this has yet to be shown)?

History is the self-definition and self-revelation of the *human* – both in Christ and against Christ (since anthropology is also Christology and vice versa). But human life does not exist in some realm beyond that of human economic creativity, which is thus caught up in the ways of God in history. It is only natural that, in this age of economism, the question of the eschatological horizon of economics arises, at the two opposite poles of human thought – the Christian and the anti-Christian, the atheistic. Two names can be mentioned as standing for these two religious tendencies, two names which are in this sense symbols of the age with its two ways, the road to Babylon and the road to the Kingdom of God: they are the names of Karl Marx and Nikolai Fyodorov.

In Marx, the spirit of anti-Christian enmity to God finds a voice of exceptional power; but this spirit is nonetheless bound up with an authentic social pathos and an authentic orientation to the future. There is something in Marx of that outpouring of the Spirit that we find in Israel's prophets, for all the atheistic trappings, the outpouring of the Spirit that conquers the heart. Marx thought of man as a demiurge who, because he was capable of changing the economic and social world, transcended the limits of history ('prehistory' for Marx) and succeeded in passing (by 'a great leap forward') into eschatology ('history'). He transposed the ancient prophecies of the City of God in the messianic kingdom into the atheistic idiom of his materialist economism. Atheism, of course, has and can have no eschatology: eschatology consists, by definition, in God's encounter with the world, the manifestation of the face of God before the whole creation, while Marx's eschatology without God ('history') is generally a great void. 'Prehistory' (i.e. our history), with its dramatic quality and its fulness of content, far exceeds the void that is to come, which remains, as before, the sphere of death and temporality (in this connection Marx must be reckoned, along with other atheistic progressivists, among those who 'deify death', to borrow an expression from some contemporary followers of Fyodorov).

Fyodorov, with his 'project' for transforming the world and triumphing over death by means of the 'regulating of nature', was the first to attempt a religious interpretation of economics, by giving it a place in his eschatology. For him too, man is a demiurge, a builder of the cosmos; but he is also a 'son of man', a 'species being', who has forebears and lives in a universal human 'creation of brethren'. To the extent that he fulfils the will of God, he becomes also a child of God who brings Christ's work to perfection in the world and declares war upon the 'last enemy', death, seeking to achieve, by his own powers, the resurrection of the ancestors. The kingdom of the age to come will be perfected by man through the regulation of nature: history will become eschatology. None of the great thinkers who were Fyodorov's contemporaries and who were personally close to him (Dostoevsky, Soloviev, Tolstoy, Fet, Kozhevnikov) were able to say a decisive 'yes' to his project, despite their personal veneration for him; and the same is true among thinkers of our own time (except for Peterson and certain younger 'Fyodorovians'). But – which is no less remarkable – none of them wanted to say a direct 'no' to it either. It must be admitted that the time has not yet come for a living reception of his system: it is the prophet's fate to be ahead of his time. But in this 'teacher and pastor' there is worked out a real 'movement in Christian thought' (Soloviev); in him we find, for the first time, the Christian consciousness asking the same questions as the whole epoch, asking what God is saying in the revelation of history. Fyodorov understood the 'regulation of nature' as the *common task* of the human race, the sons of men who are called to become sons of God, and as the fulfilment of the destiny prescribed by God. Precisely in this insight, he points to a positive way of overcoming materialist economism, by applying the fundamental dogmas of Christianity to economics in a unique fashion. Materialist economism *can* be conquered by Christian thought. The Church today can still save individual souls from spiritual death, but it will only be strong enough to win this living victory when it makes plain the truth it has to tell about economism, and so cuts the ground from under all the familiar slanders and distortions. But this cannot remain at the level of personal opinion alone: it must become a task for the whole Church, which is 'the pillar and ground of truth' [I Tim. 3.15] because 'the gates of hell shall not prevail against it [Mt. 16.18]'.

II

Logically, materialist economism is bound to lead to fatalism, since what it sees as defining the movement of history is not personality, with its creative struggles, but the impersonal economic process. There is no room here for good or evil or, generally speaking, any notion of ideal value. Yet in practice, quite inconsistently with its doctrine, socialism has, in the modern age, developed an enormous historical dynamic, a 'revolutionary' attitude. The spirit of revolution has been brooding over Europe since 1789, and its pressure is more and more deeply felt as it absorbs more and more social material, so that society in our times is beginning to define itself in relation to revolution, as being for it or against.

Revolution is both a fact and a principle. As *fact,* revolutions are brought about by elemental forces of nature; they are like a volcanic eruption, throwing out lava and ash, or an earthquake that mixes together the different strata under the earth's surface, pushing down one continent and lifting up another. Such elemental forces are evil only in their irrationality; but they are far more evil when man himself becomes a 'natural element'. Animality and madness are aroused, and the memories of ancient injuries stir in the masses, vengeful rage and accumulated hatred – alongside the heroic enthusiasm of particular persons, leaders or groups, of course. The floods of Acheron break through – no limpid stream, but a torrent of water fouled with dirt and mud. The upheavals of history are never a moral idyll such as would satisfy a schoolmaster; Hegel had already remarked as much. As the flood of revolution bursts in, all the vileness in human nature that usually hides itself in shame comes to the fore; the worst elements in humanity surge up – and perhaps the best can manifest themselves as well. The violence and despotism of an oligarchy, the red terror that is always accompanied by such hypocrisy on the part of revolutionaries, demagogy and careerism, all these are a mirror of the wild frenzy that overtakes both the masses and their 'leaders'.

Revolution as a *principle* is the programmatic breaking of the threads of historical tradition, the desire to generate history out of itself. The passion for destruction is here identified with the passion for construction. The consequent barbarisation results not only from the mixing of different social strata but also from the general hostility of revolution towards the culture of the past, even when it actually serves the culture of the future. So it is no accident that the nihilistic revolt against historical tradition is directed equally against faith, and turns into 'militant atheism'. This cannot be explained only by reference to the sins of the ecclesiastical institution, which are unmasked and punished in the revolution. Revolution brings with it a nihilistic hatred for what has been valued, what has been held sacred, and it would be incomprehensible if earthly rebellion were not also revolt against heaven, passing over into enmity towards God.

But granted all this, is not revolution also a normal state of the soul? Cannot a sickness often be welcome, a catastrophe opportune? A sickness, what is more, has its own sufficient causes, usually reaching back broadly and deeply into the past. The executioners too are the victims of history, and all those actively or passively involved in revolution must take responsibility for them and their acts. Revolutions are certainly not made by revolutionaries themselves: in this respect they are overtaken by a quite fallacious historical arrogance. It is more true to say that they – as much as the counter-revolutionaries – are the product of the revolution. Yet it can rightly be said that revolution does have an *idée-force,* an energy deriving from ideas, the explosive material which impels inert matter into movement; and this is not only hatred: it is also *faith* and *passion.* In the idea of revolution the human yearning and striving for the future finds supreme expression, longing for the future, faith in the future: *amor futuri.* It contains a definite ideal of the future and on top of this a specific vision, a projection from the present on to the future. In this sense the soul of revolution is *utopian (ou-topos)* – something that does not yet exist in any identifiable place but which *will* come to exist (the word was coined by Thomas More, the Catholic confessor and martyr of the sixteenth century). There are many different kinds of utopia, but utopia in general is an object of social faith, hope and love, 'the assurance of things hoped for, the conviction of things not seen' (Heb. 11.1). Utopianism is not the direct opposite of realism; it can and must be united with it. Here we have a distinction between means and ends, the task and its fulfilment. Utopia is, in this sense, 'an ideal with a changing content', so that the end belongs to the realm of what will be, and the means to the order of historical teleology. Only when the necessary balance between the two is destroyed does utopianism invade the territory that belongs to realism, and feverish dreams result; or else realism loses its striving for the ideal and becomes an untheoretical pragmatism. The Christian ideal of the Kingdom of God is realised historically in a whole series of alternating historical tasks: at the present time, one of these is the attainment of social justice *along with* personal liberty. These tasks all have corresponding practical means for their attainment; and in this area there may be practical differences of opinion. This is why Christianity, which is called to realise unity in the spirit, cannot identify itself with any particular programme or party. Utopianism is in its essence as much a part of Old Testament messianism as of Christianity itself; but in more recent times it has in practice been monopolised by revolutionary socialism. Although it is fashionable in Marxist circles to dismiss 'utopian socialism' in favour of 'scientific' or realistic socialism, this latter is in no way less utopian than any other vision of utopia. Utopia is always a matter of fable, a story about the future which is still as yet invisible; but it is also a prophecy of the future, since the future is already contained in the present, which offers a foretaste of it. Utopia is the inner nerve in the dynamic of history. 'The heart lives in the future; the present is full of misery' (Pushkin) – that is the law and the dream of the human heart. There may be at times a weakening of this essential dreaming of the heart, but without such a dream man cannot live. History is made by dreamers, not by the hollow men who live by prose; by people of faith, prophets, 'utopians'. For them the present age of 'misery' is only 'prehistory', a prologue to true dialectical history, in which 'contradiction is what leads us forward' as it realises the rational pattern, the *Vernunft*, of history. This is Hegel's 'cunning of reason'. And this dialectic manifests itself, in the nature of things, as revolution in respect of the present which it refuses to accept; it is prepared to sacrifice itself for the future's sake – to sacrifice love of the neighbour for the sake of love for the most remote.

But a faith that has lost its spiritual balance turns into superstition or fanatical fantasy, which is inspired no longer by the vision of the city that is to come but by deceptive mirages. As soon as the utopianism that forms the soul of revolution has lost its religious roots, it ceases to have any spiritual balance. Its social idealism finds itself at odds with the tired positivism with which it has been yoked in the name of an imaginary 'scientific' perspective. Marx's utopianism – like that of other positivists – is wholly irrational, full of contradictions and religiously vacuous. Its conception of history goes no further than 'prehistory' – the epoch of class struggle; Marx's 'history' lacks all real content. Non-religious utopianism within revolutionary socialism (to the extent that it is more than just demagogy) is transmuted into a feverish dream, the *fata morgana* of a fever-stricken soul in the waterless desert. Yet in the name of that love which 'rejoices not in unrighteousness but rejoices in the truth' (I Cor. 13.6), we should recognise here too the expression of an authentic desire, unable to see or to find any religious means for its satisfaction and so failing to understand itself, to be aware of its own inner truth. And so the breach between social idealism, 'progress' and Christianity (especially any kind of faith in a personal God), the sharp reversion to paganism [in modern revolutionary movements], can appear definitive and inevitable. The hysterical blasphemies of the Russian regime, the suffocation of a whole people's religious faith and the development of an anti-religious Inquisition are almost more of a testimony to this than even the bacchanalia of the French Revolution. Social utopians – wild and hysterical in Russia, dim and chilly in other countries – make a religious idol of social revolution. And the other side of the coin is that the Church's representatives see in this only an excellent reason for sitting in judgement on the Revolution, washing their hands in innocence and denying all responsibility. So there develops a total mutual alienation, deafness and incomprehension. The gulf between Christianity and neo-paganism (which thinks it is atheism) certainly does not run along the line of a discernible 'scientific' method. On such grounds, we ought rather to be talking about a reversal of the positions of faith and knowledge; materialism [as a theory] is currently as much obscurantism as nonsense, on the whole. No, the gulf follows the line of an historical dynamic, of diverse relations to social praxis. Of course, it is impossible to minimise the evil will, the familiar and notorious hatred for what is holy in 'militant atheism', especially in its leaders, the generalissimos of the Revolution and their crack troops, who have built their careers on the betrayal of Christ and the spiritual massacre of the innocents. But Satan can assume the guise of an angel of light, in addition to his real and terrible appearance, in the sense that he can wrap himself in the garment of social justice; the atheistic movement is inspired by the deceptions of the Father of Lies, who sets up the pseudo-utopia of a world purged of God, a world that has him as its ruler. Spiritual integrity and simple truthfulness, however, both alike require a careful and patient examination of a situation as it has concretely developed before one makes a final judgement and (so to speak) refers the facts to a higher court. And where there are many people inclined to see this in terms of a spiritual struggle in which the guilt does not lie all on one side, is there perhaps less risk of the misunderstanding that arises not just from spiritual narrowness and evil will [on the part of one side in the struggle] but also through the presence of guilt on the other side as well?

'Repent – *metanoeite* (change your mind, examine yourselves), for the Kingdom of God is at hand' – these words of John the Baptist's, which then become Christ's words as well, have the most comprehensive sense imaginable, especially in the social-historical context. Is this *metanoia* not a summons to new kinds of action, and, above all, to the testing and rethinking of what we imagine to be self-evident, the foundations on which we rest? And do the Church's representatives seek social justice for their age, do they pursue the social utopia that lies at hand in their epoch, in a dynamic way? Or are they happy with a purely static conservatism to which fidelity to tradition can finally be reduced? Is there an historical future, with new tasks to perform, from the Church's point of view, or is the whole Christian philosophy of history exhausted in a simple waiting for the end of the world, in which all that can be looked for is the cancellation of all historical values – 'alles, was entsteht, ist wert, dass es zu Grunde geht' ('The worth of all things now and past/Is that they come to dust at last')? For there is such a thing as a spiritual 'abhorrence of the vacuum'; and we can hardly be surprised if men who can find here no easing of the questions of their conscience set out to seek it in a 'far country'.

Yet it was not always so. No-one could say that the Old Testament lacked an historical sensibility, an awareness of the 'pathos' of history – it is itself a sacred history, striving towards the coming messianic kingdom. But there is still more: the Old Testament takes in the whole of universal history in its pattern (already in Genesis, but equally in the prophets, especially in Daniel, the prototype of later apocalypses). The prophets give us such a sweeping utopian vision (in the positive sense of 'utopian', of course) that there is nothing comparable to them in boldness. What we have here is not just a religious philosophy of history, but also a set of ideal tasks, which lead us beyond our present historical reality. So the preaching of the prophets (Amos, Isaiah,

Hosea) has a social aspect as well as all its other features. Is the New Testament any different? Does it leave behind the prophecies of the Old? This cannot be granted either dogmatically or historically. And yet there is a radical shift of sensibility in the New Testament: 'antinomism', the suspicion of law, comes on the scene, with its wisdom and its attendant problematic. The naivety of Old Testament man gives no place at all to this. And the Kingdom of God is 'at hand' *in* the world, it is 'coming', yet it is not *of* this world. It is *entos hēmōn* – that is to say, first of all, 'within us', but also 'among us'. In relation to the world, there is a tragic polarisation between love for it and (simultaneously) enmity towards it; and because of the complexity of this relationship, Christianity has no room either for the messianic paradise of Jewish apocalyptic or for the earthly paradise of socialism.

The question may thus arise of whether *history* really does exist for Christianity or whether there is only the *empty* time of an indefinite duration, in which there is nothing to be consummated, no 'last times'. This conception of the *last* times means that, if we take seriously the effects of God's incarnation, everything is indeed completed from God's point of view; but for Christian humanity, these 'last times' create their own epoch, with its own consummations and revelations. The New Testament Apocalypse is a revelation about *history*, not only about the end of time, as people so often assume. Here we have the struggle between two opposing principles laid bare in symbolic terms (partly shared with the generality of apocalyptic literature), the two principles that constitute the tragic quality in the pattern of history, with its alternation of victories and defeats. We read here not only of the triumph of the Beast and its false prophets but also of the appearance of the thousand-year reign of Christ on earth. The essential lines of this are filled out in other places in the New Testament; the preaching of the gospel to all nations (Mt 24.14) in connection with various other events, the conversion of Israel, 'life from the dead' [Rom. 11.15], the appearance of the 'adversary' [II Thess. 2.4] – all these mark the boundaries of particular historical epochs. The future is already in essence made clear by the Holy Spirit (Jn 16.13), even though its particularities are still shrouded in ignorance, since it is also the work of human creativity. Thus even in the 'last times' there is a real history; it is not an 'evil infinity', perpetuating for eternity a mixture of good and evil, as in the conceptuality of modern paganism, but has an immanent end or goal, serving as a transition to a higher level, but realised only through the power of God. The end itself, of course, is no longer an historical event, since it transcends history, it does not have a place in the sequence of historical time ('and the angel swore that time should be no more', Rev. 10.6). Although history is internally dependent upon eschatology, it cannot be externally oriented towards it, towards an historical apocalypse, since the end does not lie within but beyond history, outside its horizons, beyond its frontiers. This shift of perspective is often misused: people try to save themselves from historical panic by taking flight into the eschatological realm. Reflection on the end must be constantly echoing in the inner life of man (as must meditation on death and judgement), but it is forbidden for us to determine times and seasons, to utter false prophecies. It is not for this that revelation about the end of history (and about the general resurrection) is given to us; rather it is to reinforce our watchfulness ('Watch, therefore'; Mt 24.42) as a sort of guarantee of the victory of the good, of the positive outcome of history. As experienced in religious terms, history is the apocalypse coming to fruition – apocalypse understood *not* as eschatology but as 'historiosophy', which is something linked with the sense of an orientation towards the future, with the consciousness of obligatory tasks to be performed and of continuing historical labour. Time is measured not in years but in *acts,* and, in view of these obligatory tasks and historical possibilities, only someone for whom the whole of history is nothing but the gradual triumph of Antichrist, who is preparing the way for his personal appearance, can think about the end of history in a purely passive way. In contrast, Christianity demands courage, work and inspiration. Church praises the 'good and faithful servant' who makes use of his talent, and condemns the 'wicked and slothful servant' who buries it. Christian historiosophy reveals the apocalyptic breadth and scale that lies within the struggle to move from the city that now is to the one that is to come, for 'the form of this world is passing away' [I Cor. 7.31]. Thus the revolutionary dynamic that remains blind and unorganised in an atheist context is here acknowledged in its true form. The authentic concept of 'progress', i.e. movement towards a [determinate] goal, towards the Kingdom of God, is to be found only in Christian historiosophy, with its irreconcilable opposition to all that is limited and particularist, to the whole of the bourgeois mentality in history. This is very clear in the springtime of the early Church, when the 'little flock' opposed its heroic detachment to the entire world, and thus (according to Celsus) undermined the foundations of the ancient world and its fundamental values – state and culture. Yet this non-acceptance of the world was closely bound up with an expectation of the imminent end, and with the indifference to history and its concerns that sprang from such an expectation. And of course social quietism followed in its wake. ('Everyone should remain in the state in which he was called' – I Cor. 7.20), along with a distinctive note of conservatism ('There is no authority except from God' – Rom. 13.1); but this is combined with the menacing tones of the Apocalypse. What this amounted to was a peculiar kind of apolitical vision, which accorded significance only to the inner attitude of a man (hence the apparent indifference of Christianity to slavery; yet, historically speaking, it is Christianity that is responsible for exploding slavery from within). The primacy of the inner over the outer is not in dispute here: it forms the spiritual basis of social order. But this *primacy* does not mean social indifferentism or the absence of any value [in the historical world]. The kind of spiritual absenteeism that was not only wise in practical terms but really the sole possible option for early Christianity looked like weakness as soon as Christianity gained any influence in state and society.

In practice, Christianity turned out to be the spiritual leaven of the new social order; it brought to birth a new mode of personal existence, and its practical influence naturally extended far beyond the concrete boundaries of the ecclesiastical organisation itself. Of course, alongside this, it cannot be denied that church communities, like human communities in general, are far from living always on the heights to which they are called. Thus they commonly become a bulwark of conservatism, or at least of the status quo, externally as well as internally. Internal resistance to revolutionism, at least in its nihilistic forms, arises in the Church from its loyalty to *tradition,* by which its entire life is penetrated. This is the living *memory* of the Church, which stands over against the historical amnesia of the children of the Revolution, for whom history begins with themselves. This is a simple human *dignity* that will be constantly dissatisfied with the spiritual bad taste of such a nihilism; there is a more purely historical awareness that will sense this abolition of history to be a wild aberration; and there is, finally, an *ecclesial* awareness for which breaking with tradition as a matter of principle is an intolerable heresy. But at the same time, loyalty to tradition is not loyalty to immobility, to what is outdated or antiquated. Such an understanding is not loyalty to tradition but straightforward secular conservatism; the distinction between them has never yet been adequately drawn. Because of human weakness, alas, there is plenty of unchurchly contraband sailing under the Church's flag; many things that are alien and essentially destructive [to the Church] have gone on adhering to the hull of the ecclesial vessel in its voyage through the centuries, calling forth the *Schadenfreude* of atheists, who are skilled in exhibiting such things in displays and museums. Here the fire of the Revolution turns out to be also a purifying fire for the ecclesial community, however painful its impact may still be.

In any event, the relation of Christianity to the world and its values can never be purely immanent, as in neo-paganism. When the eyes are raised to heaven, they become blind to the immediate environment, and the summons of eternity creates a certain indifference to 'the tedious songs of earth'. There is a proper Christian freedom from the world, which (especially in earlier ages) sought expression in literal external flight from the world around. But such a flight, with its indifference to the question of earthly values, can only be fully realised in the eremitical life; and even there, there is either an aspiration to exercise influence upon the world or a summons to the world to move in the direction of the cloister. It is precisely in the monastic environment that Christian utopian visions have so often been developed, visions that would later become potent forces in the movement of history (the 'third Rome', the sacred empire, the theocratic state). One could even say that the more pure and incandescent in the spiritual struggle in the cloister, the more effective it is in the world (St Francis and his friars, Luther and the Reformation). Not infrequently, however, this world-denying impulse goes with an excessive conservatism in respect of the world, with a conservatism that is itself anything but world-denying. But generally speaking, one could say that in Christianity there is always a fulfilment of the quest for the leading idea within the historical development of the current epoch, and that a conservatism consisting simply in traditional styles of living cannot be considered to be the normal or distinctive mode of Christian social awareness. Between atheistic revolution and a Christian ordering of society there is, of course, a gulf. But does this mean that Christianity, because of its supernatural dimension, knows only a conservative and static vision? Or can it and must it not also acknowledge a practical dynamic? Is a *Christian reformism* possible, inspired by the idea of the Kingdom of God and finding its historical utopia, or, more precisely, utopias, not in any utopian vision of an 'earthly paradise', of course, but in the vision of the triumph of the good in and through the tragic processes of universal history, which lead towards the definitive separation between good and evil?

Here we come up against the fundamental question of Christian life in our times: that of the 'churching' of culture, as it is now expressed. Once again, the sphinx of history puts the question to our understanding, our heart and our freedom – yes or no? Today this question represents an historical watershed, from which the streams flow in divergent directions. The simplest thing is to evade the question under the pretext of a distinction between what belongs to Caesar and what belongs to God (in the individual spirit). That has been the answer of Protestantism, which has put in train the secularisation that is now suffocating the world. Perhaps there was an historical justification for this in the attempt to be free of papal hierocracy; yet the same distinction is not infrequently made in the name of Orthodoxy. Ascetic renunciation of the world, personal pietism, are here treated as a sufficient response – in the spirit of a world renouncing 'apoliticism', in which the dominant structures of society or 'political' passions pure and simple begin to occupy the whole expanse of the battlefield.

Now the Church *is* in fact 'apolitical' – in this sense, that it can never identify its eternal values with any relative or contingent tasks, or any historical institutions (as was once the case in Russia, where only the party supporting unrestricted autocracy counted as truly Orthodox). The Church cannot be a party; it must be *the conscience of a society,* never using humility as an excuse for compromise or indifferentism. But it cannot go along with the secularist disintegration of social order; rather must its spiritual domination struggle towards victory *from within.* This was the ideal of a 'free theocracy' found in the early Soloviev and the later Dostoevsky.

We have lately seen diverse Christian confessions, each in their own way, taking some steps (though as yet still irresolute ones), jointly and for themselves individually, towards a Christian social order. This movement is associated on the worldwide scale with the name of the Stockholm Conference of 1925 (though the Catholic Church, sadly, was not included in this). Representatives of the various Orthodox churches deliberately involved themselves, and thus took on responsibility for educating the nations in the spirit of social Christianity. One of the weaknesses of this movement is what is, to say the least, an inadequate level of clarification of the ideological, or rather the dogmatic, foundations of a movement for the religious conquest of secularisation. The Church is taking on the burden of the ordering of society, in a conscious and principled way, not only *de facto*, as was formerly the case; but for this one needs faith, enthusiasm and a sense of vocation. We must begin to understand God's revelation in history as the apocalyptic reality fulfilling itself, that reality which leads to the full consummation of historical processes and, *in that sense*, to the end of history; and this is something more than a simple cataloguing of events according to their pragmatic significance. A further dimension needs to be in view – a living sense of the incompleteness of history (history as 'prehistory'), which still leaves room for 'utopia', for what *is* not yet but is to come, for the ideal, for hope. Christianity, in its idea of the Kingdom of God, possesses just such a comprehensive and inexhaustible ideal, including in itself all good human goals and achievements. But it also still has its promise, signified in the symbolic language of the Apocalypse as the inauguration of the thousand-year reign of Christ on earth (Rev. 20). This symbol, which is the guiding star of history, was for a long time locked in by a one-sided interpretation, so that the rejection without remainder of this dominant interpretation was immediately reckoned as heresy. But this ultimate manifestation of the Kingdom of God on earth, symbolically rendered in this way, cannot remain a purely passively understood prophecy (worthy of ideological rejection on account of this passivity): it must become an active utopian ideal, a hope. Naturally this symbol in itself is abstract; but it is constantly being filled out with concrete content, in terms of actual advances or achievements in history, of the summons directed by the future towards the present. Pseudo-eschatologism is an expression of panic, spiritual corruption of fatigue, freed from historical responsibility, although as a matter of bare fact (i.e. in a pagan fashion) it does participate in history. But if there is indeed no way of avoiding society, if it is a kind of destiny, then the social order must incorporate into itself the quest for the Christian righteousness associated with the Kingdom of God, for 'Seek, and ye shall find' [Mt. 7.7]. What the Church has to offer cannot be taken away, even when we distance ourselves from it and bury this talent in the earth. But those things that find no adequate response in the Church life of the present day will imperceptibly fall prey to the forces of corruption. Who knows how many 'Sauls' are still trapped in the atheist camp, seduced by its dynamism, because they cannot find among us either attention or response to their questioning? Strength and truth are what will be victorious – not a weakened and compromising apologetic. The tragic experience of our homeland, together with the threats of the storm-clouds now gathering over our world, call us to new ways of living and thinking, '… So that your youth is renewed like the eagle's' (Ps. 103.5): constant renewal is the law and the condition of the spiritual life, as is loyalty to a *living tradition*.

III

Along with economism, *sociologism* is the other determining element of the modern self-consciousness. Man has always had a collective life and a collective consciousness, for example in the immediate organic unity of nation, tribe, family, and so on. Within these limits, the tormenting problems of our own day concerning the relation of personality to society did not arise: the personal and the social were organically bound up with each other, and in the context of this bond, the naive – but prophetic – wisdom of unmediated experience could find expression. Today we have so far lost sight of all this that the independent reality of the two competing elements has come to be doubted and even denied. The idea of the autonomy of society, developed from the work of the social sciences, seems to be something that has no room for the personal principle. Personality dissolves into the social totality and appears as no more than a 'reflex', an ontological illusion, a ripple on the wave of society. Ketle, as he spells out in this 'social physics' the scientific validity of statistical tabulation, objects to any raising of the question about the place of personality, with its free and creative originality, within the framework of this impersonal or supra-personal system of validation. In general though, it is true that social science is frustrated and baffled by its own developments, and attempts to avoid posing the question of personality, in that it capitulates immediately to the principle of a supra-personal rule-governed structure and in practice absorbs personality into the social whole. Popular 'elementary education in politics' (*Polit-gramota*) is no less confident in taking the dismissal of any 'freedom' of personal existence as scientific dogma. In this world of social determinism, the palm must go to Marxism, which declares that the only human reality is that of classes, or groups involved in production. Thus a new social mythology is constructed, in which abstract generalisations are accorded a more significant level of existence than is the concreteness of personal life. In this form, sociologism as an attitude to life and a *Weltanschauung*, lacking any regard for the particularity of its own modes of expression, is fundamentally and essentially a non-Christian, even anti-Christian, worldview, which at the present time is appearing more and more clearly as a rival to Christianity in its negation of personality as a spiritual and creative principle in the name of an impersonal social automatism. The devastation that this superstition causes in souls is not hard to assess (although its effects are limited by practical inconsistencies in its application). It is a distinctive *social atheism*, and the first article of this atheistic creed proclaims that there is no such thing as personal being; from which it follows (incontrovertibly, in its own way) that there is no soul and no God, but only, ultimately, the social Leviathan.

Now Christianity too recognises that there is a real human unity-in-plurality – the *Body of Christ*, which consists of distinct, individual living members (I Cor. 12.12–27) – i.e. personalities; and in this dogma concerning the Church there is sufficient basis for developing the principles of a Christian sociology. Yet for so long, Christian dogmatics has hidden itself in passive silence when faced with pagan sociologism; without taking notice of it, without even once attempting to resist it and set matters to right again. Of course there is no need to fight against the *factual* obviousness of many sociological generalisations. This is as unnecessary as, for example, battling against the factual content of the natural sciences simply on the grounds that arbitrary and ill-thought-out pseudo-philosophical consequences are often inferred from such data. But, up to the present, social problems have been treated in theology only from an ethical point of view, not a sociological one. However, the existence, as a matter of fact, of such regularities in human life as a social body, even if this does not have a fully formative effect on human life, now thoroughly merits a place in theology as well. Christian theology is called to a *broader* view. It must provide an answer for the question before which the resources of sociology fail: how, in life and in thought, can we hold together the equal reality and the equal independence of personality on the one hand and of society as a whole on the other? *De facto* the reality of personality can hardly be contested, even if it is denied in theory: sociology suffers from this impersonalism, and Christian anthropology must be applied to it at this point. But there is also a *de facto* dominance in Christian dogma of an individualistic understanding of society, which is seen as predominantly an aggregate of mutually unconnected personalities – even though this notion does not correspond to its own doctrine of humanity as an organic whole 'in Adam', which is then assumed as a whole in the humanity of Christ. In Christ the whole of humanity exists as a generic reality as well as an ensemble of personalities, as a real unity-in-plurality. The idea of *sobornost'*, which lies at the root of the doctrine of the Church, can also acquire a sociological application, by means of which the lethal doctrine of godless sociologism may be over come. 'You will know the truth and the truth will make you free' [Jn 8.32]. The entire biblical revelation turns upon the notion of a 'Son of Man' who can contain both the personal and the generic principle. And if theology itself has not up to now applied this principle with sufficient seriousness, it is now compelled to do so by the spread of a sociological heresy that violates in the most extreme way the dogma of the Divine Humanity. The history of doctrine shows that the various heresies were in fact *questions* posed to theology, to broaden its awareness of its problematic; and something of this kind is going on today with this heresy of sociologism.

A soulless socialism is of concern to modern life not only in its character as a world-view – an ecclesiological heresy, relating to the sphere of doctrine – but as a heresy in *living* which expresses itself in the processes of secularisation, external socialisation, forced collectivisation, the transformation of the human into a herd or an ant-heap. At the present time, personality (at least in the countries of civilised Europe) is surrounded for the forces of compulsory collectivism and the standardisation of human life. We are talking not only of the Bolshevists, who herd men into the *kolkhoz*, the collective, by physical and economic violence and who in practice transform a godless and godforsaken, impersonal and depersonalised socialism into the militant shape of communism. The entire organisation of modern life is directed towards exactly the same end, even though less open and barbaric compulsion is involved. In a patriarchally ordered style of life, man existed in an *organic* form of sociality, in which his place in life was determined and rendered transparently obvious by a logic that seemed quite sufficient for the existing situation. Even the apostle Paul's injunction, 'Everyone should remain in the state in which he was called … there let him remain with God' (I Cor. 7.20, 24), which to us sounds conservative and quietist, simply presupposes, historically speaking, and apart from its abiding ascetical significance, a patriarchal-organic form of life. For Paul, even so appalling a social institution as slavery had some relative justification, and as such is not condemned by him (Eph. 6.5–9). But this organic style of living has been completely destroyed; and on its ruins has arisen an artificial and rationalised form of life, grounded in technical and economic teleology. There are two aspects to this rationalisation: the revolutionising of life in terms of an atomising of society – so that the process actually leads to greater individualism, in contradiction to the sociologism that negates the reality of personality – and at the same time the forcible uniting of these human atoms in the process of economic and national life – in the factory (industrialisation), in cities (urbanisation), in national institutions (statist centralism), and in general the collectivisation of human life on the basis of the 'general good'. This is what can be designated as the socialism of concrete life, independently of its economic form (so that in this sense the supremely rationalised society of capitalism is perhaps no less 'socialistic' than the coercive regime of communism). Man is by nature incapable of continuing in an atomised condition, and so creates new forms of association; his life is socialised anew – but how, and on the basis of what principles? As a rule, on utilitarian grounds, on the grounds of the *de facto* commonalities of life, practical needs and interests. Hence the development of classes and organisations with their diverse modes of solidarity, governed by the principles of a militant sociologism. Thus the rationalistic form of life sets its seal even on these relationships.

Yet even in the midst of this spiritual decline and fall, man cannot be content simply with the given facts of the situation; he takes up an evaluative stance in respect of these facts and gives them an ideal clothing. He begins to see even forced collectivisation as a peculiar kind of *sobornost'*, which is actually striving towards the true ecclesial form of society. An *active* sociologism develops, something that is already an act of free self-determination: the man who belongs to this or that particular class, in this or that particular condition, begins to assert himself as a generic being with his own distinctive generic life. Modern society represents the ensemble of such vertical group identities, separated from one another, each one constituted as self-sufficient. They move forward in a mutual association, while at the same time, in their reciprocal relations, subordinating themselves to a particular overall standard in assessing their hierarchy of values (the proletarian International, Italian or German fascism, and so on). The general basis for these alliances is the pagan naturalism they share, so that, in this sense, what they share is their 'animality'. This means that what is placed in the highest rank of values or standards is not what has an elevated and autonomous axiological character, but only a subordinate kind of value; and this destroys the entire spiritual hierarchy of values. Of course the unity or solidarity of a class, at least within certain limits, has spiritual worth; likewise national identity as a fundamental principle has a value of its own, though not the supreme value and not an autonomous value that could serve as an ultimate criterion; and the same is true of the state. If any of them lay claim to an absolute status, these principles produce forms of association that really represent a kind of pseudo-Church. They can allow some room within their frontiers even for the Church as a national and historical institution, though one that is always judged by other and higher values than its own. But this kind of relationship to the Church serves only to underline the socio-cultural atheism which, however veiled, is not in any way different from militant atheism. Social life thus offers today a prospect of spiritual desolation and practical atheism. While the Church itself often fell under the state's influence, in the days when the two were united, what we see so clearly today is the 'Beast', the power of social self-legitimation with its automatism and forced collectivism, setting up its own values, causing all men 'to be marked on the right hand or the forehead, so that no-one can buy or sell unless he has the mark' (Rev. 13.16, 17). And 'the number of the Beast ... is a human number' (Rev. 13.18). What we are talking about is the combination of human collectivity at the natural level with the practical atheism of social life. This also introduces into the life of the Church's representative a state of spiritually divided loyalty to two kinds of authority; and the passive retreat into a supposed eremitical reclusion leads in practical terms to enslavement by precisely this lordship of the Beast.

Is the present relation between Church and society the only one possible? Or is it really a matter of handing over to Belial without a struggle what does not belong to him and what therefore cannot be yielded to him? Is there any possibility of a victory from within over this godless social automatism, this cult of the Beast, this 'animality' (in which of course a real *bestiality* is concealed)? *Dogmatically* speaking, this is not only possible but necessary. The Christian doctrine of man as a generically personal being contains also the true conception of what commonality in life might be – a social order in which the personal principle is affirmed as something inseparable from collective or generic life. Thus an individualistic seclusion from the world, an eremitism that cannot distinguish the wilderness [of asceticism = *pustyn*] from the void [*pustota*], is unmasked as a sinfully egotistical self-assertion. Incidentally, monastic solitude and even the hermit life are in fact only an aspect of Christian *service* under particular conditions, whereas egocentricity recognises no call to service, and, in this perspective, is on no higher level than the blatant and deliberate self-love of the Benthamite 'economic man'. Christianity has two commandments on which 'depend all the law and the prophets' – love for God, and in second place, 'like it', love for the neighbour, whereby each and every individual may be such a neighbour. Thus a 'Christian sociology' is possible as an aspect of dogmatic and practical ('moral') theology, which must provide a careful working-out of its problems and goals. This is the task that ecclesial reflection now faces. The ordering of society that rests on natural instinct or on rationalisation and automation must be overcome and dissolved in *ecclesial* life.

Humanity is running out of breath and losing its strength in this hopeless conflict between the egocentricity of individualism and the sadism of communism, between the soullessness of statism and the snarlings of racism. But the Church has thus far had no answer to give; under the pressure of threatened persecution, it has settled for carrying on as one tolerated or licensed state institution among others – or else it has endured, in the communist world, a truly bestial persecution at the hands of the Beast of pagan polity. Yet it is only the Church that possesses the principle of true social order, in which the personal and the collective, freedom and social service can be given equal weight and unified harmoniously. It is itself this very principle – living *sobornost'*. That is also the dogmatic foundation of an ecclesial polity. But to this end there must be an upsurge of fresh inspiration in the members of the Church themselves, a spring of living water which satisfies the thirst of contemporary humanity, for the sake of a new relationship between nations, a new mission to the darkness of social paganism, for the awakening of a new *spirit*. This is not the misplaced utopianism of a 'rose-tinted' Christianity that consigns the tragic character of history, with its necessary schism between good and evil, to oblivion, believing that before the ultimate separation the forces of good are bound to become fully manifest. Still less is this a belated renaissance of clericalism on the Catholic model, which struggle to possess both of the 'two swords', and wants to put the direction of all life into the hands of the ecclesiastical organisation: a life that develops in an ecclesial way, moving outwards from within, has no longer any need of external submission to authority.

No, what we are speaking of is belief in the Church and in its own distinctive living power, activated by the Holy Spirit's life within it. The proclamation of the Kingdom of God, which has never been silenced in the Church, must now make itself heard in those areas of life in which up to now, it has been propounded only in inadequate ways; the dry bones must be vitalised with a new spirit. Even the class struggle in our society of class divisions must not be defined by hatred; it can be defined in terms of class-*conscience* and the awareness of mutual duties. Is this not what the apostle Paul preached even in relation to slaves and slave-owners, in exhorting slaves to be submissive for the sake of Christ, their master, but also reminding slave-owners of their Christian duties towards their slaves? This is the kind of class-conscience that Carlyle devoted his time to developing, calling the 'captains of industry' to be mindful of their service to society. Of course, the class structure of society is, in itself, *not* a phenomenon that sits easily with the Christian conscience, and so is something that has to be overcome; but this overcoming must be something that proceeds from within, not only something that happens at the external level.

The great *sin* of the modern Christian community is its uncreative relationship to social life, a failure which is not made any the less serious by being concealed under the mask of an apparent asceticism. Indifference is not victory, and spiritual absenteeism is not asceticism. In its search for meaning, society is exhausting its powers: it still has no guidance from the Church and has itself lost direction. But in the meantime new projects emerge in the life of society, not only negative ones – the overcoming of that animal principle which has taken the place belonging to holiness – but positive as well, such as the provision of new meaning and motivation for economic work. There is the question, among others, of how rationalised and mechanised labour can have meaning, when, for the worker, it has lost the natural attraction of earlier days, and in a certain sense, lost its aesthetic dimension. Just as Marx's theory has it, such labour has become 'abstract', has drained away working energy. It has no inspiration left and no more delight in *personal* creativity; it has become a mechanical slavery, as much in capitalism as in socialism. There is a curious attempt at rousing some enthusiasm for work in the Soviet idea of *udarnichestvo* [the 'strike troops' or 'forward movement' of industrial construction], in so far as this movement really exists and is not simply cried up for propaganda purposes. Its main significance is that here there is still an attempt being made to give meaning to personal labour in that this is integrated into the common work of 'building socialism'. But it is clear that what is presented here is a pagan substitute for the Kingdom of God as the highest service to which men can dedicate their lives. So we must move away from a passive-quietist, conservative-assimilationist relationship to the work of society, in a direction that is active and practically innovative, and thus take forward the work of Christ. Otherwise the result will be a vacuum; and the spirit's abhorrence of a vacuum will fill it up with evil forces.

There is still one fresh difficulty, one new problematic, which will soon be rearing its head for mankind; a problem which this time arises from the opposite side, not from the burden of labour but from the burden of idleness and leisure. If the view is right which claims that, through 'technocracy', man is approaching a condition in which labour is so organised as to secure a considerable and steadily increasing amount of time for leisure, a new dynasty of technocrats will emerge, who will threaten to turn into a new despotism; and simultaneously the threat grows of increasing inactivity for the masses, with the transformation of their lives into a state of 'diversion', entertainment. The one threat is as great a spiritual danger as the other, and it is only on the spiritual level that they can be averted. The task is to educate the man who has been partially liberated from economic captivity, and who now faces the danger of spiritual repression in the wake of his liberation from the curse – which is also, though, just as much a blessing – of slavery to labour. Faced with a task like this, we may be tempted to protect ourselves by eschatological panic – the end is nigh, humanity is perishing in a universal deluge, except for those saved by the ark.

Can one allow oneself such a logic of historical suicide, if it is not given us to know the time or the hour that the Father has fixed by his own authority [Acts 1.7]?

Not all these questions have already entered into our historical consciousness; but a growing restlessness and a new kind of questioning are emerging in contemporary humanity. *Es irrt der Mensch, solang er strebt*: 'man goes astray as long as he still strives'. But the Spirit of God living in the Church proclaims what is to come, and directs the Church towards that truth. It can only be sought for, as the Kingdom of God can only be sought for. But it is to this longed-for and sought-after social legacy – and also to all other human struggles towards justice – that the Lord's words apply: 'Seek and you will find; knock, and it will be opened to you' [Mt 7.7].

53. Slavoj Žižek – Extracts from Thinking Backward: Predestination and Apocalypse

We effectively live in an apocalyptic time: today, apocalypse is near at many levels: ecology, informational saturation—things are approaching a zero-point, "the end of time is near." Here is Ed Ayres's description: "We are being confronted by something so completely outside our collective experience that we don't really see it, even when the evidence is overwhelming. For us, that 'something' is a blitz of enormous biological and physical alterations in the world that has been sustaining us."[1] At the geological and biological level, Ayres enumerates four "spikes" (accelerated developments) asymptotically approaching a zero-point at which the quantitative expansion will reach its point of exhaustion and will have to change into a different quality: population growth, consumption of resources, carbon gas emissions, the mass extinction of species. To cope with this threat, our collective ideology is mobilizing mechanisms of dissimulation and self-deception that point toward the direct will to ignorance: "A general pattern of behavior among threatened human societies is to become more blindered, rather than more focused on the crisis, as they fall."[2]

Apocalypse is characterized by a specific mode of time, clearly opposed to the two other predominant modes, the traditional circular time (the time ordered and regulated on cosmic principles, reflecting the order of nature and the heavens—the time form in which microcosm and macrocosm resonate with each other in harmony) and the modern linear time of gradual progress or development. The apocalyptic

---

[1]Ed Ayres, *God's Last Offer: Negotiating for a Sustainable Future* (New York: Four Walls Eight Windows, 1999), 98.
[2]Ibid.

time is the "time of the end of time," the time of emergency, of the "state of exception" when the end is near and we are getting ready for it.

There are at least three different versions of apocalypticism today: techno-digital posthuman, New Age, and Christian fundamentalist. Although they all share the basic notion that humanity is approaching a zero-point of radical transmutation, their respective ontologies differ radically: the techno-digital apocalypticism (whose main representative is Ray Kurzweil) remains within the confines of scientific naturalism and identifies at the level of the evolution of human species the contours of its transmutation into "posthumans"; the New Age apocalypticism gives to this transmutation a spiritualist twist, interpreting it as the shift from one mode of "cosmic awareness" to another (usually from the modern dualist-mechanistic stance to the stance of holistic immersion); and, finally, Christian fundamentalists read apocalypse in strict biblical terms—that is, they search (and find) in the contemporary world signs that the final battle between Christ and the antichrist is near, that things are approaching a critical turn. Although this last version is considered the most ridiculous but dangerous as to its content, it is the one closest to the "millenarist" radical emancipatory logic.

Techno-Digital Apocalypticism

Let us first take a look at the techno-digital apocalypticism. If there is, even more than Bill Gates, a scientist-capitalist who perfectly exemplifies the third "spirit of capitalism" with its nonhierarchic and anti-institutional creativity, humanitarian-ethical concerns, and so on, it is Craig Venter, with his idea of DNA-controlled production. Venter's field is synthetic biology, a field that focuses on "life which is forged not by Darwinian evolution but created by human intelligence."[3] Venter's first breakthrough was to develop "shotgun sequencing," a method for analyzing the human genome faster and more cheaply than ever before; he published his own genome, the first time any individual person's DNA had been sequenced. (Incidentally, it revealed that Venter is at risk of Alzheimer's, diabetes, and hereditary eye disease.) Then he announced his next great project: to build an entirely synthetic organism, which could be used to save the world from global warming. In January 2008, he constructed the world's first completely synthetic genome of a living organism: using laboratory chemicals, he recreated an almost exact copy of the genetic material found inside a tiny bacterium. This largest man-made DNA structure is 582,970 base pairs in length; it was pieced together from four smaller (but still massive!) strands of DNA by utilizing the transcription power of yeast, and it is modeled on the genome of a bacterium known as *Mycoplasma genitalium*. (Mycoplasma genitalium is a

---

[3] J. Craig Venter, "A DNA-Driven World" (lecture, BBC One, December 4, 2007, http://www.edge.org/3rd_culture/venter.dimbleby07/venter.dimbleby07_index.html).

bacterium common to the human reproductive tract; it was chosen purely because it has a relatively tiny genome.) The lab-made genome has thus far not resulted in a living microbe that functions or replicates, but Venter has said it is just a matter of time before scientists figure out how "to boot it up" by inserting the synthetic DNA into the shell of another bacterium.[4] This success opens the way for creating new types of microorganisms that could be used in numerous ways: as green fuels to replace oil and coal, to digest toxic waste, or to absorb greenhouse gases, and so on. Venter's dream is effectively to create the first "trillion-dollar organisms"—patented bugs that could excrete biofuels, generate clean energy in the form of hydrogen, and even produce tailor-made foods.

> Imagine the end of fossil fuels: a cessation of ecologically devastating drilling operations, deflation of the political and economic power of neoconservative oil barons, and affordable, low-emission transportation, heating, and electricity. The impact of this technology is profound, and it doesn't stop there. By discovering the details of biochemical and metabolic pathways, we can more closely mimic their elegance and efficiency to solve problems that plague industrial civilization. Maybe we'll engineer a primitive, self-sustaining bio-robot that feeds on CO_2 and excretes O_2. Perhaps we could remove mercury from our water supplies. The limitations are not known, but the possibilities are awe-inspiring.[5]

There are, as Venter admits, also more sinister possibilities: it will also be possible to synthesize viruses like Ebola, or to build new pathogens. But the problem is deeper, as Hope Shand of the ETC Group, a Canada-based bioethics watchdog, points out: "This is extreme genetic engineering that will bring about substantially different organisms and with those comes a new level of unknowns."[6] The problem is our limited understanding of how DNA works: even if we can put together a sequence of synthetic DNA, we cannot predict how this sequence will actually perform, how its components will interact. Jason Chin, who leads a synthetic biology research group in Cambridge, England, says: "DNA communicates with a cell by prompting it to make proteins, but we have a long way to go in understanding the relationship between a given DNA sequence, the proteins it generates and the final properties of an organism."[7]

These dangers are strengthened by the absence of any public control over what goes on in bioethics. As Jim Thomas, another member of the ETC Group, notes, "While synthetic biology is speeding ahead in the lab and in the marketplace …

---

[4]J. Craig Venter Institute, "Venter Institute Scientists Create First Synthetic Bacterial Genome," press release, January 24, 2008, http://www.jcvi.org/cms/research/projects/synthetic-bacterial-genome/press-release/.
[5]Ian Sample, "Frankenstein's Mycoplasma," *The Guardian*, June 8, 2007.
[6]Ian Sample, "Tycoon's Team Finds Fewest Number of Genes Needed for Life," *The Guardian*, June 8, 2007, http://www.guardian.co.uk/science/2007/jun/08/generics.research.
[7]Jonathan Leake, "The Synthetic Genome," *The Sunday Times* (UK), January 27, 2008, http://www.timesonline.co.uk/tol/news/science/article3257051.ece.

there has been no meaningful or inclusive discussion on how to govern synthetic biology in a safe and just way. In the absence of democratic oversight, profiteering industrialists are tinkering with the building blocks of life for their own private gain."[8] Venter has tried to allay the fears of an emerging *Blade Runner* society: "The movie [*Blade Runner*] has an underlying assumption that I just don't relate to: that people want a slave class. As I imagine the potential of engineering the human genome, I think, wouldn't it be nice if we could have 10 times the cognitive capabilities we do have? But people ask me whether I could engineer a stupid person to work as a servant. I've gotten letters from guys in prison asking me to engineer women they could keep in their cell. I don't see us, as a society, doing that."[9] Venter may not see it, but the requests he is bombarded with certainly prove that there is a social demand for the creation of a serving subclass. Kurzweil has offered a different rebuttal of these fears: "The scenario of humans hunting cyborgs doesn't wash because those entities won't be separate. Today, we treat Parkinson's with a pea-sized brain implant. Increase that device's capability by a billion and decrease its size by a hundred thousand, and you get some idea of what will be feasible in 25 years. It won't be, 'OK, cyborgs on the left, humans on the right.' The two will be all mixed up."[10] While this is in principle true (and one can here vary endlessly the Derridean motif of how our humanity always already was supplemented by artificial protheses), the problem is that, with the decrease by a hundred thousand, the prothesis is no longer experienced as such but becomes invisible, part of our immediate organic self-experience, so that those who technologically control the prothesis control us in the very heart of our self-experience.

The paradox is that, insofar as the re-creation of artificial life is the accomplishment of (one of the strands of) modernity, it is Habermas himself who abstains from accomplishing the project of modernity, that is, who prefers modernity to remain an "unfinished project," setting a limit to the unfolding of its potentials. There are even more radical questions to be raised here, questions that concern the very limit of our desire (and readiness) to know: what will prospective parents do when they are informed that their child will have Alzheimer's genes? The recent new buzzword "previvor" (a person who does not have cancer but possesses a genetic predisposition to develop the disease, a "pre-survivor") renders perfectly the anxiety of advance knowledge.

Chinese scientists at the Beijing Genomics Institute have completed the fourth human genome to be sequenced worldwide; they plan to use their genome database

---

[8]ETC Group, "Venter Institute Builds Longest Sequence of Synthetic DNA (That Doesn't Work)," news release, January 24, 2008.
[9]Ted Greenwald, "Q&A: Ridley Scott Has Finally Created the *Blade Runner* He Always Imagined," *Wired Magazine*, September 26, 2007, http://www.wired.com/entertainment/hollywood/magazine/15-10/ff_bladerunner.
[10]Ibid.

to "solve problems related to Chinese-specific genetic diseases," as well as to improve diagnosis, prediction, and therapy.[11] Such phenomena are just the tip of the iceberg of a process going on in China, a process of which not much is heard in a media preoccupied by the Tibet troubles and the like: the expansion of biogenetic revolution. While in the West we are bothered with endless debates on ethical and legal limits of biogenetic experiments and procedures (yes or no to stem cells, questions about how we should be allowed to use the genome, i.e., only to prevent diseases or also to enhance desired physical and even psychic properties in order to create a newborn that fits our desires, etc.), the Chinese are simply doing it without any restraints, and in a model example of the smooth cooperation between their state agencies (say, their Academy of Sciences) and private capital. In short, both branches of what Kant would have called the "private" use of reason (state and capital) have joined hands at the expense of the absent "public" use of reason (a free intellectual debate in the independent civil society about what is going on, how it all infringes on individuals' status as ethically autonomous agents, and so on, not to mention the possible political misuses). Things are proceeding fast on both fronts, not only toward the dystopian vision of the state controlling and steering the biogenetic mass of its citizens, but also toward fast profit-making: billions of US dollars are invested in labs and clinics (the biggest one in Shanghai) to develop commercial clinics that will target rich Western foreigners who, due to legal prohibitions, will not be able to get this kind of treatment in their own countries. The problem is, of course, that, in such a global situation, legal prohibitions are becoming meaningless: their main effect will be the commercial and scientific advantage of the Chinese facilities—to repeat a cliche, Shanghai has all the chances of becoming a dystopian megalopolis like the anonymous city in *Blade Runner*.

How, then, does the digitalization of our lives affect the hermeneutic horizon of our everyday experience? What looms at the horizon of the "digital revolution" is nothing else than the prospect that human beings will acquire the capacity of what Kant and other German Idealists called *intellektuelle Anschauung* (intellectual intuition), the closure of the gap that separates (passive) intuition and (active) production; that is, the intuition that immediately generates the object it perceives—the capacity hitherto reserved for the infinite divine mind. On the one hand, it will be possible, through neurological implants, to switch from our "common" reality to another, computer-generated reality without all the clumsy machinery of today's virtual reality (the awkward glasses, gloves, etc.), since the signals of the virtual reality will directly reach our brains, bypassing our sensory organs: "Your neural implants will provide the simulated sensory inputs of the virtual environment—and

---

[11]Hsien-Hsien Lei, "Beijing Genomics Institute Sequences Fourth Human Genome in the World," Eye on DNA, January 7, 2008, http://eyeondna.com/2008/01/07/beijing-genomics-institute-sequence-fourth-human-genome-in-the-world.

your virtual body—directly in your brain.... A typical 'web site' will be a perceived virtual environment, with no external hardware required. You 'go there' by mentally selecting the site and then entering that world."[12] On the other hand, there is the complementary notion of the "real virtual reality": through "nanobots" (billions of self-organizing, intelligent microrobots), it will be possible to re-create the three-dimensional image of different realities "out there" for our "real" senses to see and enter (the so-called Utility Fog).[13] Significantly, these two opposite versions of the full virtualization of our experience of reality (direct neuronal implants versus the Utility Fog) mirror the difference of subjective and objective: with the Utility Fog, we still relate to the reality outside ourselves through our sensory experience, while the neuronal implants effectively reduce us to "brains in the vat," cutting us off from any direct perception of reality—in other words, in the first case, we "really" perceive a simulacrum of reality, while in the second case, *perception itself is simulated* through direct neuronal implants. However, in both cases, we reach a kind of omnipotence, being able to change from one to another reality by the mere power of our thoughts— to transform our bodies, the bodies of our partners, and so forth: "With this technology, you will be able to have almost any kind of experience with just about anyone, real or imagined, at any time."[14] The questions to be asked here are: Will this still be experienced as "reality"? Is, for a human being, "reality" not *ontologically* defined through the minimum of *resistance*—real is that which resists, that which is not totally malleable to the caprices of our imagination?

As to the obvious counterargument that everything cannot be virtualized—there still has to be the one "real reality," that of the digital or biogenetic circuitry itself that generates the very multiplicity of virtual universes!—the answer is provided by the prospect of "downloading" the entire human brain (once it is possible to scan it completely) onto an electronic machine more efficient than our awkward brains. At this crucial moment, a human being will change its ontological status "from hardware to software": it will no longer be identified with (stuck to) its material bearer (the brain in the human body). The identity of one's self is a certain neuronal pattern, the network of waves, which, in principle, can be transferred from one to another material support. Of course, there is no "pure mind"; that is, there always has to be some kind of embodiment—however, if our mind is a software pattern, it should be in principle possible for it to shift from one to another material support. (Is this not going on all the time at a different level: is the "stuff" our cells are made of not continuously changing?) The idea is that this cutting off of the umbilical cord that links us to a single body, this shift from having (and being stuck to) a *body* to freely floating between different *embodiments* will mark the true birth of the human being,

---

[12]Ray Kurzweil, *The Age of Spiritual Machines* (London: Phoenix, 1999), 182.
[13]Ibid., 183.
[14]Ibid., 188.

relegating the entire hitherto history of humanity to the status of a confused period of transition from the animal kingdom to the true kingdom of the mind.

New Age Apocalypticism

Brought to this extreme, the techno-digital apocalypticism assumes the form of the so-called tech-gnosis and passes over into the New Age apocalypticism. One of the preferred Janus-faced notions mobilized by the New Age spiritualists is the quantum physics notion of synchronicity (the instantaneous link between two events or elements, that is, faster than the time the light needs to travel between the two): the precise quantum notion of synchronicity (two separated particles are interconnected so that a spin of one of the two affects the spin of the other faster than their light connection) is read as a material manifestation/inscription of a "spiritual" dimension that links events beyond the network of material causality: "Synchronicities are the jokers in nature's pack of cards for they refuse to play by the rules and offer a hint that, in our quest for certainty about the universe, we have ignored some vital clues."[15] Here is the New Age spiritualist description of the new social order that is expected to emerge as a secondary effect of the more substantial spiritual shift: "If we are graduating from nation-states to a noospheric state, we may find ourselves exploring the kind of nonhierarchical social organization—a 'synchronic order' based on trust and telepathy—that the Hopi and other aboriginal groups have used for millennia. If a global civilization can self-organize from our current chaos, it will be founded on a cooperation rather than winner-takes-all competition, sufficiency rather than surfeit, communal solidarity rather than individual elitism, reasserting the sacred nature of all earthly life."[16] Does this description—if we scratch away its spiritualist coating—not render a kind of Communism? How, then, are we to get rid of this coating? The best antidote to this spiritualist temptation is to bear in mind the basic lesson of Darwinism: the utter contingency of nature. Why are bees dying massively, especially in the United States, where, according to some sources, the rate of decline has reached up to 80 percent? One of the hypotheses is that the extensive use of fertilizers and insecticides has rendered the plants poisonous for the bees—is this not a nice example of how an ecological catastrophe might look: a break in the weakest link of the chain of natural exchanges derails the entire edifice? The problem here is that one cannot be absolutely sure that all we have to do is to return to natural balance—to which balance? What if the bees in the United States and Western Europe were already adapted to a certain degree and mode of industrial pollution? Or take the recently discovered vast frozen peat bog in western Siberia

---

[15]F. David Peat, *Synchronicity: The Bridge between Nature and Mind* (New York: Bantam Books, 1987), quoted in Daniel Pinchbeck, *2012* (New York: Jeremy P. Tarcher / Penguin, 2007), 395.

[16]Pinchbeck, *2012*, 394.

(the size of France and Germany combined): it started to thaw, potentially releasing billions of tons of methane, a greenhouse gas twenty times more potent than carbon dioxide, into the atmosphere. This hypothesis should be read together with the report, from May 2007,[17] that researchers at the Albert Einstein College of Medicine have found evidence that certain fungi have the capacity to use radioactivity as an energy source for making food and spurring their growth. Their interest was aroused five years ago when a robot sent into the still-highly-radioactive Chernobyl reactor had returned with samples of black, melanin-rich fungi that were growing on the ruined reactor's walls. The researchers then set about performing a variety of tests using several different fungi. Two types—one that was induced to make melanin and another that naturally contains it—were exposed to levels of ionizing radiation approximately five hundred times higher than background levels; both of these melanin-containing species grew significantly faster than when exposed to standard background radiation. Investigating further, the researchers measured the electron spin resonance signal after melanin was exposed to ionizing radiation and found that radiation interacts with melanin to alter its electron structure—an essential step for capturing radiation and converting it into a different form of energy to make food. Ideas already circulate for the radiation-munching fungi to be on the menu for future space missions. Since ionizing radiation is prevalent in outer space, astronauts might be able to rely on fungi as an inexhaustible food source on long missions or for colonizing other planets. Instead of succumbing to terror at this prospect, it is in such cases that one should remain open to new possibilities, bearing in mind that "nature" is a contingent multifaceted mechanism in which catastrophes can lead to unexpected positive results, as in Robert Altman's *Short Cuts,* in which a catastrophic car accident brings about an unexpected friendship.

Such an openness for radical contingency is difficult to uphold—even a rationalist like Habermas was not able to sustain it. His late interest in religion breaks with the traditional liberal concern for the humanist, spiritual, and other content hidden in the religious form; what interests him is this form itself: people who *really* fundamentally believe and are ready to put their lives at stake for it, displaying the raw energy of belief and the concomitant unconditional engagement missing from the anemic-skeptic liberal stance—as if the influx of such unconditional engagement can revitalize our postpolitical drying-out of democracy. Habermas reacts here to the same problem as Chantal Mouffe in her "agonistic pluralism": how to reintroduce passion into politics? Is he, however, thereby not engaged in a kind of ideological vampirism, sucking the energy from naive believers without being ready to abandon his basic secular-liberal stance, so that full religious belief remains a kind of fascinating and mysterious otherness? As Hegel already showed apropos the dialectic of Enlightenment and

---

[17]Kate Melville, "Chernobyl Fungus Feeds on Radiation," Science a GoGo, May 23, 2007, www.scienceagogo. com/news/20070422222547data_trunc_sys.shtml.

faith in his *Phenomenology of Spirit,* such an opposition of formal Enlightenment and fundamental-substantial beliefs is false, an untenable ideologico-existential position. What should be done is to fully assume the identity of the two opposed moments, which is precisely what the apocalyptic "Christian materialism" can do with its unification of the rejection of divine otherness and unconditional commitment.

How are we to combine such radical openness with the apocalyptic certainty of the end of time approaching? It is here that one should bear in mind the properly dialectic reversal of contingency into necessity, that is, of the retroactive nature of the necessity of the forthcoming catastrophe. This reversal was described by Dupuy: "The catastrophic event is inscribed into the future as a destiny, for sure, but also as a contingent accident: it could not have taken place, even if, in *futur anterieur,* it appears as necessary.... . If an outstanding event takes place, a catastrophe, for example, it could not not have taken place; nonetheless, insofar as it did not take place, it is not inevitable. It is thus the event's actualization—the fact that it takes place—which retroactively creates its necessity."[18] Dupuy provides the example of the French presidential elections in May 1995; here is the January forecast of the main polling institute: "If, on next May 8, Ms Balladur will be elected, one can say that the presidential election was decided before it even took place." If—accidentally—an event takes place, it creates the preceding chain, which makes it appear inevitable: *This,* not the commonplaces on how the underlying necessity expresses itself in and through the accidental play of appearances, is *in nuce* the Hegelian dialectics of contingency and necessity. In this sense, although we are determined by destiny, we are nonetheless *free to choose our destiny.* This, according to Dupuy, is also how we should approach the ecological crisis: not to "realistically" appraise the possibilities of the catastrophe but to accept it as destiny in the precise Hegelian sense: like the election of Balladur, "If the catastrophe will happen, one can say that its occurrence was decided before it even took place." Destiny and free action (to block the "if") thus go hand in hand: freedom is at its most radical the freedom to change one's destiny.

So if we are to confront properly the threat of a (cosmic or environmental) catastrophe, we have to introduce a new notion of time. Dupuy calls this time the "time of a project," of a closed circuit between the past and the future: the future is causally produced by our acts in the past, while the way we act is determined by our anticipation of the future and our reaction to this anticipation. This, then, is how Dupuy proposes to confront the catastrophe: we should first perceive it as our fate, as unavoidable, and then, projecting ourself into it, adopting its standpoint, we should retroactively insert into its past (the past of the future) counterfactual possibilities ("If we were to do that and that, the catastrophe we are in now would not have occurred!") on which we then act today.[19] Therein resides Dupuy's paradoxical

---

[18]Jean-Pierre Dupuy, *Petite metaphysique des tsunami* (Paris: Éditions du Seuil, 2005), 19.
[19]Ibid.

formula: we have to accept that, at the level of possibilities, our future is doomed; the catastrophe will take place; it is our destiny—and then, on the background of this acceptance, we should mobilize ourselves to perform the act that will change destiny itself and thereby insert a new possibility into the past. For Badiou, the time of the fidelity to an event is the *futur anterieur*: overtaking oneself toward the future, one acts now as if the future one wants to bring about is already here. The same circular strategy of *futur anterieur* is also only truly efficient when we are confronting the prospect of a catastrophe (say, of an ecological disaster): instead of saying "the future is still open, we still have the time to act and prevent the worst," one should accept the catastrophe as inevitable, and then act to retroactively undo what is already "written in the stars" as our destiny.

One should thus say about the ecological catastrophe: If it will happen, it will be necessary … And is not a supreme case of the reversal of positive into negative destiny the shift from the classical historical materialism into the attitude of Adorno's and Horkheimer's "dialectic of Enlightenment"? While traditional Marxism enjoined us to engage ourselves and act in order to bring about the necessity (of Communism), Adorno and Horkheimer projected themselves into the final catastrophic outcome perceived as fixed (the advent of the "administered society" of total manipulation and end of subjectivity) in order to solicit us to act against this outcome in our present. And, ironically, does the same not hold for the very defeat of Communism in 1990? It is easy, from today's perspective, to mock the "pessimists," from the Right to the Left, from Solzhenitsyn to Castoriadis, who deplored the blindness and compromises of the democratic West, its lack of ethico-political strength and courage in its dealing with the Communist threat, and who predicted that the Cold War was already lost by the West, that the Communist block had already won it, that the collapse of the West was imminent—but it is precisely their attitude that did the most for bringing about the collapse of Communism. In Dupuy's terms, their very "pessimist" prediction at the level of possibilities, of the linear historical evolution, mobilized them to counteract it.

Pascal's Wager

There is thus only one correct answer to the leftist intellectuals who desperately await the arrival of a new revolutionary agent that will perform the long-expected radical social transformation—the old Hopi saying with a wonderful Hegelian dialectical twist from substance to subject: "We are the ones we have been waiting for."[20] Waiting for another to do the job for us is a way of rationalizing our inactivity. However, the trap to be avoided here is the one of perverse self-instrumentalization: "we are the one we are waiting for" does not mean that we have to discover how we are the agent

---

[20]Quoted in Pinchbeck, *2012*, 94.

predestined by fate (historical necessity) to do the task; it means, on the contrary, that there is no big Other to rely on. In contrast to classic Marxism, where "history is on our side" (the proletariat fulfills a predestined task of universal emancipation), in today's constellation, the big Other is *against* us: left to itself, the inner thrust of our historical development leads to catastrophe, to apocalypse, so that what can prevent catastrophe is *pure voluntarism,* that is, our free decision to act against the historical necessity. This is why theology is emerging again as a point of reference for radical politics: the paradox is that it is emerging not in order to supply a divine big Other guaranteeing the final success of our endeavors but, on the contrary, as a token of our radical freedom with no big Other to rely on. It was already Dostoyevsky who was aware of how God gives us freedom and responsibility—he is not a benevolent master steering us to safety but the one who reminds us that we are totally onto ourselves. This paradox is at the very core of the Protestant notion of predestination: predestination does not mean that we are not really free since everything is determined in advance; it involves an even more radical freedom than the ordinary one, the freedom to retroactively determine (change) one's destiny itself.

No wonder Pascal (or, more generally, Jansenism) was the only Catholic thinker who accepted predestination—predestination is a paradoxical supplement to Pascal's notion of wager.[21] The first thing that strikes the eye is that Pascal rejects all attempts to demonstrate the existence of God: he concedes that "we do not know if He is," so he seeks to provide prudential reasons for believing in God: we should wager that God exists because it is the best bet.

> "God is, or He is not." But to which side shall we incline? Reason can decide nothing here. There is an infinite chaos which separated us. A game is being played at the extremity of this infinite distance where heads or tails will turn up. . . .
>   . . . Which will you choose then? Let us see. Since you must choose, let us see which interests you least. You have two things to lose, the true and the good; and two things to stake, your reason and your will, your knowledge and your happiness; and your nature has two things to shun, error and misery. Your reason is no more shocked in choosing one rather than the other, since you must of necessity choose. . . . But your happiness? Let us weigh the gain and the loss in wagering that God is.[22]

Pascal appears to be aware of the immediate objection to this argument, for he imagines an opponent replying: "That is very fine. Yes, I must wager, but I may perhaps wager too much." In short, if I put my wager on God, and God does not exist, then I really do lose something—when one wagers for God, one does stake something, which presumably one loses if God does not exist: truth, the respect for one's worldly

---

[21] Alan Hájek, "Pascal's Wager," *The Stanford Encyclopedia of Philosophy (Fall 2008 Edition),* ed. Edward N. Zalta, http://plato.stanford.edu/archives/fall2008/entries/pascal-wager/. I rely here extensively on this entry.
[22] Blaise Pascal, *Pensées,* trans. W. F. Trotter (1660), sec. 3, no. 233, quoted in Hájek, "Pascal's Wager."

life, and so on. (It is strange how utilitarian-pragmatist Pascal's reasoning is.) There is then a series of other objections:

1. Pascal assumes that the same matrix of decision and reward applies to everybody—but what if the rewards are different for different people? Perhaps, for example, there is a predestined infinite reward for the chosen, whatever they do, and finite utility for the rest.
2. The matrix should have more rows: perhaps there is more than one way to wager for God, and the rewards that God bestows vary accordingly. For instance, God might not reward infinitely those who strive to believe in him only for the utilitarian-pragmatic reasons that Pascal gives. One could also imagine distinguishing belief based on faith from belief based on evidential reasons, and posit different rewards in each case.
3. Then there is the obvious many-Gods objection: Pascal had in mind the Catholic God, but other theistic hypotheses are also live options; namely, the "(Catholic) God does not exist" column really subdivides into various other theistic hypotheses (e.g., the Protestant God exists, Allah exists, there is no God). The obverse of this objection is the claim that Pascal's argument proves too much: its logical conclusion is that rationality requires believing in various incompatible theistic hypotheses.
4. Finally, one can argue that morality requires you to wager against God: wagering for God because of the promise of future profits violates the Kantian definition of moral act as an act accomplished for no "pathological" reasons. It was already Voltaire who, along these lines, suggested that Pascal's calculations, and his appeal to self-interest, are unworthy of the gravity of the subject of theistic belief.

Underlying all this is the basic paradox of belief as a matter of decision: as if to believe something or not is a matter of decision and not of an insight. So, if we read Pascal's wager together with his no-less-known topic of customs—

> You would like to attain faith, and do not know the way; you would like to cure yourself of unbelief, and ask the remedy for it. Learn of those who have been bound like you, and who now stake all their possessions. These are people who know the way which you would follow, and who are cured of an ill of which you would be cured. Follow the way by which they began; by acting as if they believed, taking the holy water, having masses said, etc.[23]

—one can argue that the core of his argument directly concerns not belief but acting: one cannot decide to believe, one can decide only to act *as if* one believes,

---

[23]Pascal, *Pensées*, sec. 3, no. 233, quoted in Hájek, "Pascal's Wager."

with the hope that belief will arise by itself. Perhaps this trust—that if you act as if you believe, belief will arise—is the wager.

Perhaps the only way out of these impasses is what, in his unpublished "secret" writings, Denis Diderot elaborated under the title of the "materialist's credo." In "Entretien d'un Philosophe avec la maréchale de***," he concluded: "Après tout, le plus court est de se conduire comme si le vieillard existait … même quand on n'y croit pas." (After all, the most straightforward way is to behave as if the old guy exists … even if one doesn't believe it.) This may appear to amount to the same as Pascal's wager apropos the custom: even if you don't believe in it, act as if you believe. However, Diderot's point is exactly opposite: the only way to be truly moral is to act morally without regard to God's existence. In other words, Diderot directly turns around Pascal's wager (the advice to put your bets on the existence of God): "En un mot que la plupart ont tout a perdre et rien a gagner a nier un Dieu renumerateur et vengeur." (In a word, it is that the majority of those who deny a remunerating and revenging God have all to lose and nothing to gain.)[24] In his denial of the remunerating and vengeful God, the atheist loses everything (if he is wrong, he will be damned forever) and gains nothing (if he is right, there is no God, so nothing happens). It is this attitude that expresses true confidence in one's belief and makes one do good deeds without regard to divine reward or punishment.

Authentic belief is to be opposed to the reliance on (or reference to) a(nother) subject supposed to believe: in an authentic act of belief, I myself fully assume my belief and thus have no need of any figure of the Other to guarantee my belief—to paraphrase Lacan, an authentic belief *ne s'authorise que de lui-meme*. In this precise sense, authentic belief not only does not presuppose any big Other (is not a belief in a big Other) but, on the contrary, presupposes the destitution of the big Other, the full acceptance of the inexistence of the big Other.

This is also why a true atheist is at the opposite end of those who want to save religion's spiritual truth against its "external" dogmatic-institutional set up. A profoundly religious friend once commented on the subtitle of a book of mine, "The Perverse Core of Christianity": "I fully agree with you here! I believe in God, but I find repulsive and deeply disturbing all the twist of celebrating sacrifice and humiliation, of redemption through suffering, of God organizing his own son's killing by men. Can't we get Christianity without this perverse core?" I couldn't bring myself to answer him: "But the point of my book is exactly the opposite: what I want is all those perverse twists of redemption through suffering, dying of God, and so on, but without God!"

Bee Season (directed by Scott McGehee and David Siegel, based on a novel by Myla Goldberg), one of the better Hollywood melodramas, can be of some help in making clear this crucial point. The film focuses on a modern American family whose picture-perfect surface conceals an underlying world of turmoil. Initially, the

---

[24]Denis Diderot, "Observations sur Hemsterhuis," *Oeuvres*, vol. 1 (Paris: Robert Laffont, 1994), 759.

Naumanns are presented as a harmonious family living in a great Craftsman house outside Oakland. Saul Naumann is an ardent religious studies professor at Berkeley; though he's a bit of a control freak and an intellectual bully, he is also a warm, loving father and husband, a good cook, and a classical violin player. When he realizes that his eleven-year-old daughter, the almost eerily quiet, self-effacing Eliza, is a spelling champion, he takes an aggressive interest in her future wins and starts to coach her: for him, Eliza's triumph is a sign that she possesses a metaphysical gift he may be lacking. Saul's obsessive interest in Eliza (or really, his own success, by proxy) leads him to take over his daughter's training in the secret science of permutation. His once-favored son, Aaron, a socially awkward adolescent, is left to make his own spiritual discoveries. Saul's wife, Miriam, doesn't notice that her husband is turning her daughter into an ancient mystic or that her son is becoming a Hare Krishna, as she is too busy stealing objects from other people's homes to re-create the flawless world shattered years ago by the death of her parents in a car accident.

It is thus as if Eliza's overhuman perfection in spelling triggers a family explosion, disturbing its surface order, compelling all of them to confront the broken pieces of their life. All this takes place against the theological background of *tikkun olam,* the Jewish notion of healing or repairing of the world. According to Kabbalah, God—pure perfection—in his goodness wanted to share his perfection, so he created a receptacle that would receive his gift; however, unable to endure the divine light, the receptacle shattered into thousands of pieces, and it is our duty and universal responsibility to fix what has been shattered, to attempt to restore what has been damaged. In an all-too-obvious metaphor, this is also what the Naumann family needs: the restoring of unity, order, and harmony. With her family disintegrating before her eyes, it's up to Eliza to put the broken pieces of her family's world back together in an unexpected act of selflessness and love.

This act is the movie's final epiphany: the entire film drives toward Eliza's momentous decision, a choice that enables catharsis for the whole family. So how does Eliza order the family chaos? At the climactic moment of the spelling competition, in front of television cameras, when the right answer would make her national champion, she decides to get a word wrong on purpose. While the father is broken, the other two members of the family are relieved, happily, smiling, and even Eliza herself, till now a kind of catatonic monster, manages a spontaneous mischievous smile—what really happens here? Even such a mainstream figure as Roger Ebert got it right: "Eliza's decision [is] to insist on herself as a being apart from the requirements of theology and authority, a person who insists on exercising her free will. This is a stick in the eye of her father. What Eliza is doing at the end of *Bee Season* is Eliza's will. Does that make her God? No. It makes her Eliza."[25] Her act allows her to break out of the enslavement

---

[25]Roger Ebert, "Bee Season," November 11, 2005, http://rogerebert.suntimes.com/apps/ pbcs.dll/article?AID= /20051110/REVIEWS/51019003.

to her father's desire: no longer her father's instrument, she creates a space for herself and for the family to restore its free balance. It is thus the mistake itself, the crack of disharmony, that interrupts the perfect series of her correct answers, which restores harmony.

However, the film gets its theology wrong (or, at least, it presents its highly sanitized version): in Kabbalah, God first withdrew into himself to open up the space for creation; then, he bungled the job of creation, making a deeply flawed and fractured universe—*this* is what we, humans, have to patch up. Happily, the story itself corrects this wrong theology: what if God's mistake was to create a flawless universe, and what if humans patch things up by introducing into it imbalance and disharmony? One might venture here another problematic speculation: this insight goes beyond the limits of Judaism and brings us into the central paradox of Christianity, which concerns the status of freedom: without the notion of a flawed divinity, we have a human subject subordinated to a substantial divinity, which secretly pulls the strings.

Hegel's famous guideline that one should conceive the Absolute not only as substance but also as subject generally conjures up the discredited notion of some kind of "absolute Subject," a mega-Subject creating the universe and watching over our destinies. For Hegel, however, the subject, in its very core, also stands for finitude, cut, the gap of negativity, which is why God becomes subject only through Incarnation: he is not already in itself, prior to Incarnation, a mega-Subject ruling the universe. Consequently, it is crucial not to confuse Hegel's "objective spirit" with the Diltheyan notion of a life-form, a concrete historical world, as the "objectivized spirit," the product of a people, its collective genius: the moment we do this, we miss the point of Hegel's "objective spirit," which is precisely that it is spirit in its objective form, experienced by individuals as an external imposition, constraint even—there is no collective or spiritual super-Subject that would be the author of "objective spirit," whose "objectivization" this spirit would have been. There is, for Hegel, no collective Subject, no Subject-spirit beyond and above individual humans. Therein resides the paradox of "objective spirit": it is independent of individuals, encountered by them as given, preexisting them, as the presupposition of their activity, yet it is nonetheless spirit, that is, something that exists only insofar as individuals relate their activity to it, only as *their* (pre)supposition.[26]

This is why Kierkegaard's critique of Hegel relies on a fatal misunderstanding of Hegel's fundamental insight. The first thing that strikes the eye is that it is based on the (thoroughly Hegelian!) opposition between "objective" and "subjective" thought: "Objective thought translates everything into results, subjective thought puts everything into process and omits results—for as an existing individual he is

---

[26]See Myriam Bienenstock, "Qu'est-ce que 'l'esprit objectif' selon Hegel?" in *Lectures de Hegel*, ed. Olivier Tinland (Paris: Le livre de poche, 2005), 223–67.

constantly in process of coming to be."[27] For Kierkegaard, obviously, Hegel is the ultimate achievement of the "objective thought": he "does not understand history from the point of view of becoming, but with the illusion attached to pastness understands it from the point of view of a finality that excludes all becoming."[28] Here one should be very precise not to miss Kierkegaard's point: for him, only subjective experience is effectively "in becoming," and any notion of objective reality as an open-ended process with no fixed finality still remains within the confines of being. Why? Because any objective reality, "processual" as it may be, is by definition ontologically fully constituted, present as the positively existing domain of objects and their interactions; only subjectivity designates a domain that is *in itself* "open," marked by an *inherent* ontological failure: "Whenever a particular existence has been relegated to the past, it is complete, has acquired finality, and is in so far subject to a systematic apprehension … but for whom is it so subject? Anyone who is himself an existing individual cannot gain this finality outside existence which corresponds to the eternity into which the past has entered."[29] What if, however, Hegel effectively does the exact opposite? What if the wager of his dialectic is not to adopt toward the present the "point of view of finality," viewing it as if it were already past, but, precisely, to *reintroduce the openness of future into the past*, to *grasp what was in its process of becoming*, to see the contingent process that generated to existing necessity? Is this not why we have to conceive the Absolute "not only as substance but also as subject"? This is why German Idealism already explodes the coordinates of standard Aristotelian ontology, which is structured around the vector running from possibility to actuality. In contrast to the idea that every possibility strives to fully actualize itself, one should conceive of "progress" as a move of restoring the dimension of potentiality to mere actuality, of unearthing, in the very heart of actuality, a secret striving toward potentiality. Recall Walter Benjamin's notion of revolution as redemption-through-repetition of the past: apropos the French Revolution, the task of a true Marxist historiography is not to describe the events the way they really were (and to explain how these events generated the ideological illusions that accompanied them); the task is rather to unearth the hidden potentiality (the utopian emancipatory potentials) that were betrayed in the actuality of revolution and in its final outcome (the rise of utilitarian market capitalism). The point of Marx is not primarily to make fun of the wild hopes of the Jacobins' revolutionary enthusiasm, to point out how their high emancipatory rhetoric was just a means used by the historical "cunning of reason" to establish the vulgar commercial capitalist reality; it is to explain how these betrayed radical-emancipatory potentials continue to "insist" as a kind of historical specter and to haunt the revolutionary memory, demanding

---

[27]Søren Kierkegaard, *Concluding Unscientific Postscript* (Princeton, NJ: Princeton University Press, 1968), 86.
[28]Ibid., 272.
[29]Ibid., 108.

their enactment, so that the later proletarian revolution should also redeem (put to peace) all these past ghosts. These alternate versions of the past, which persist in a spectral form, constitute the ontological "openness" of the historical process, as it was—again—clear to Chesterton:

> The things that might have been are not even present to the imagination. If somebody says that the world would now be better if Napoleon had never fallen, but had established his Imperial dynasty, people have to adjust their minds with a jerk. The very notion is new to them. Yet it would have prevented the Prussian reaction; saved equality and enlightenment without a mortal quarrel with religion; unified Europeans and perhaps avoided the Parliamentary corruption and the Fascist and Bolshevist revenges. But in this age of free-thinkers, men's minds are not really free to think such a thought.
>
> What I complain of is that those who accept the verdict of fate in this way accept it without knowing why. By a quaint paradox, those who thus assume that history always took the right turning are generally the very people who do not believe there was any special providence to guide it. The very rationalists who jeer at the trial by combat, in the old feudal ordeal, do in fact accept a trial by combat as deciding all human history.[30]

Why, then, in an apparent contradiction to what we are aiming at, is the blooming genre of what-if histories hegemonized by conservative historians? The typical introduction to such a volume as a rule begins with an attack on Marxists who allegedly believe in historical determinism. Their conservative sympathies become clear as soon as one looks at the tables of contents of the leading what-if volumes: the favored topics oscillate between the "major premise"—how much *better* history would have been if a revolutionary or "radical" event were to be avoided (if King Charles were to win the civil war against the Parliament; if the English Crown were to win the civil war against the American colonies; if the confederacy were to win the U.S. civil war, aided by Great Britain; if Germany were to win the Great War; if Lenin were to be shot at the Finland Station; etc.)—and the "minor premise"—how much *worse* history would have been if history were to take a more "progressive" twist (if Thatcher were to be killed in the Brighton IRA bombing in 1984, if Gore were to win over Bush and be the president on 9/11, etc.).

So what should the Marxist's answer be here? Definitely not to rehash the old boring Georgi Plekhanov ratiocinations on the "role of the individual in history" (the "even if there were no Napoleon, another individual would have to play a similar role, because the deeper historical necessity called for a passage to Bonapartism" logic). One should question the very premise that Marxists (and leftists in general) are dumb determinists rather than entertaining such alternative scenarios.

---

[30]G. K. Chesterton, "The Slavery of the Mind," http://www.cse.dmu.ac.uk/~mward/gkc/books/The_Thing.txt.

The first thing to note is that the what-if histories are part of a more general ideological trend, of a perception of life that explodes the form of the linear-centered narrative and renders life as a multiform flow; up to the domain of the "hard" sciences (quantum physics and its multiple-reality interpretation, neo-Darwinism) we seem to be haunted by the chanciness of life and the alternate versions of reality. Stephen Jay Gould, a Marxist biologist if ever there was one, once remarked that if we were to wind back the film of life and play it again, the storyline of evolution would have been totally different. This perception of our reality as one of the possible—often not even the most probable—outcomes of an "open" situation, this notion that other possible outcomes are not simply canceled out but continue to haunt our "true" reality as a specter of what might have happened, conferring on our reality the status of extreme fragility and contingency, is by no means foreign to Marxism—on it relies the felt *urgency* of the revolutionary act.

Since the nonoccurring of the October Revolution is one of the favored topics of the conservative what-if historians, let us look at how Lenin himself related to it: he was as far as imaginable from any kind of reliance on "historical necessity." (On the contrary, it was his Menshevik opponents who emphasized that one cannot jump over the succession of stages prescribed by historical determinism: first bourgeois-democratic, then proletarian revolution, etc.) When, in his "April Theses" from 1917, Lenin discerned the *Augenblick,* the unique chance for a revolution, his proposals were first met with stupor or contempt by a large majority of his own party colleagues. Within the Bolshevik party, no prominent leader supported his call to revolution, and *Pravda* took the extraordinary step of dissociating the party, and the editorial board as a whole, from Lenin's "April Theses"—far from being an opportunist flattering and exploiting the prevailing mood in the party, Lenin's views were highly idiosyncratic. Many who knew Lenin and his work doubted his state of mind: Alexander Bogdanov dismissed the "April Theses" as the delirium of a madman, while Lenin's wife, Nadezhda Krupskaya, worried that he had gone crazy. Lenin immediately perceived the revolutionary chance that was the result of unique contingent circumstances: if the moment will not be seized, the chance for the revolution will be forfeited, perhaps for decades. So we have here Lenin himself entertaining an alternative scenario: *what if* we do not act now—and it was precisely the awareness of the catastrophic consequences of not acting that pushed him to act.

But there is a much deeper commitment to alternative histories in a radical Marxist view: it brings the what-if logic to its self-reflexive reversal. For a radical Marxist, *the actual history that we live is itself a kind of alternative history realized,* the reality we have to live in because, in the past, we failed to seize the moment and act. Military historians have demonstrated that the Confederacy lost the battle at Gettysburg because General Lee made a series of mistakes totally uncharacteristic of him: "Gettysburg was the one battle, fought by Lee, that reads like fiction. In other words, if ever there was a battle where Lee did not behave like Lee, it was there in southern Pennsylvania."[31] For each of the wrong moves, one can play the game of "what would Lee have done in that situation"—in other words, it was as if, in the battle of Gettysburg, the alternate history had actualized itself.

Thinking Backward

This brings us to the what-if dimension that permeates the very core of the Marxist revolutionary project. In his ironic comments on the French Revolution, Marx opposes the revolutionary enthusiasm to the sobering effect of the "morning after": the actual result of the sublime revolutionary explosion, of the Event of freedom, equality, and brotherhood, is the miserable utilitarian/egotistic universe of market calculations. (And incidentally, is not this gap even wider in the case of the October Revolution?) However, as we have already seen, one should not simplify Marx: his point is not the rather commonsensical insight into how the vulgar reality of commerce is the "truth" of the theater of revolutionary enthusiasm, "what all the fuss really was about." In the revolutionary explosion as an Event, another utopian dimension shines through, the dimension of universal emancipation, which is precisely the excess betrayed by the market reality that takes over "the day after"— as such, this excess is not simply abolished, dismissed as irrelevant, but, as it were, *transposed into the virtual state,* continuing to haunt the emancipatory imaginary as a dream waiting to be realized.[32] The excess of revolutionary enthusiasm over its own "actual social base" or substance is thus literally that of an attribute-effect over its own substantial cause, a ghostlike Event waiting for its proper embodiment. In his less-known *Everlasting Man,* Chesterton makes a wonderful mental experiment along these lines, in imagining the monster that man might have seemed at first to the merely natural animals around him.

> The simplest truth about man is that he is a very strange being; almost in the sense of being a stranger on the earth. In all sobriety, he has much more of the external appearance of one bringing alien habits from another land than of a mere growth of this one. He has an unfair advantage and an unfair disadvantage. He cannot sleep in his own skin; he cannot trust his own instincts. He is at once a creator moving miraculous hands and fingers and a kind of cripple. He is wrapped in artificial bandages called clothes; he is propped on artificial crutches called furniture. His mind has the same doubtful liberties and the same wild limitations. Alone among the animals, he is shaken with the beautiful madness called laughter; as if he had caught sight of some secret in the very shape of the universe hidden from the universe itself. Alone among the animals he feels the need of averting his thought from the root realities of his

---

[31]Bill Fawcett, *How to Lose a Battle* (New York: Harper, 2006), 148.
[32]For a more extensive discussion of what-if histories and the Marxist revolutionary project, see Slavoj Žižek, "Lenin Shot at Finland Station," review of *What Might Have Been,* ed. Andrew Roberts, *London Review of Books* 27, no. 16 (August 18, 2005): 23.

own bodily being; of hiding them as in the presence of some higher possibility which creates the mystery of shame. Whether we praise these things as natural to man or abuse them as artificial in nature, they remain in the same sense unique.[33]

This is what Chesterton called "thinking backward": we have to put ourselves back in time, before the fateful decisions were made or before the accidents occurred that generated the state that now seems normal to us, and the royal way to do it, to render palpable this open moment of decision, is to imagine how, at that point, history may have taken a different turn.

. . .

54. Creation, History and Eschatology: Discussion Questions

What does the doctrine of creation have to do with politics?
Does the narration of history foreclose or open up possibilities for political theology?
How would you describe the *telos* of human politics during history?

---

[33]G.K.Chesterton, *The Everlasting Man*, http://www.cse.dmu.ac.uk/~mward/gkc/books/everlasting_man.html#chap-I-i.

Suggestions for Further Reading

Section I: The Emergence of Political Theology

Atkins, E. M. and R. J. Dodaro (eds.) *Augustine. Political Writings*. Cambridge: Cambridge University Press, 2001.

Cannon, Katie Geneva. 'Slave Ideology and Biblical Interpretation'. In *The Black Studies Reader*, edited by Jacqueline Bobo, Cynthia Hudley, Claudine Michel. New York and London: Routledge, 2004.
Scripture has been drawn on to support particular political practices and ideologies since the earliest roots of political theology. Cannon provides an important example of contemporary critique of such uses specifically as they pertain to the use of white Christian power to enslave people of colour.

Dyson, R. W. (ed.) *Aquinas. Political Writings*. Cambridge: Cambridge University Press, 2002.
In these collections, Dyson gathers more of Augustine's correspondence and more whole elements of Aquinas's thought than this reader can include, contextualizing and analysing the dominant themes.

Holman, Susan R. *The Hungry Are Dying. Beggars and Bishops in Roman Cappadocia*. Oxford: Oxford University Press, 2001.
This includes excellent translations of other Cappadocian texts contemporary with Gregory as well as exploring the social meanings of the poor body.

Rhee, Helen. *Loving the Poor, Saving the Rich: Wealth, Poverty, and Early Christian Formation*. Grand Rapids, MI: Baker Academic, 2012.
A book focusing on patristic sources and early Christian practices to do with money, business, and almsgiving, including their roots in Israelite and Jewish contexts, with a view to the way those ideas shaped community identity, ecclesiology and their most recent reception today.

Rowland, Christopher. 'Scripture'. In *The Cambridge Companion to Christian Political Theology*, edited by Craig Hovey and Elizabeth Phillips, 157–75. Cambridge: Cambridge University Press, 2016.
This chapter is one of the few dedicated explorations of the reception of scripture within Christian political theology.

Silvas, Anna. *The Asketikon of St Basil the Great*. Oxford: Oxford University Press, 2005.
The Asketikon is another fourth-century text, which explores how to shape a
Christian monastic community using questions answered by Basil of Caesarea,
whose own hospital foundation was so large it was described as a 'second city' by
Gregory of Nazianzus.

Section II: Approaches to Political Theology

Graham, Elaine. *Between a Rock and a Hard Place: Public Theology in a Post-secular Age*.
London: SCM Press, 2013.
Graham is one of the foremost authors of the Public Theology approach. Here she
offers a re-envisioning of the tasks of Public Theology in light of the shifts which
have called many of the approach's 'terms of engagement' into question.

Kirwan, Michael. *Political Theology: A New Introduction*. London: Darton, Longman
and Todd, 2008.
This book is an accessible and interesting introduction to the major themes and ideas
which structure contemporary political theology. The author has a particular interest
in Critical Theory, which helps shape the second half of the book.

Milbank, John, and Adrian Pabst. *The Politics of Virtue: Postliberalism and the Human
Future*. London: Rowman and Littlefield, 2016.
An attempt to offer a critique of neoliberalism and an alternative model of virtue
politics that could structure a postliberal future. Draws from and extends the
tradition of Radical Orthodoxy.

Storrar, William, Andrew Morton and Duncan Forrester (eds). *Public Theology for the
21st Century*. London: Continuum, 2004.
A significant summary of the major strands and traditions of public theology as well as
an assessment of the challenges facing this strand of theology in the twenty-first century.

de Vries, Hent, and Lawrence Sullivan (eds). *Political Theologies: Public Religions in a
Post-Secular World*. New York: Fordham University Press, 2006.
Likely best read in a library, this lengthy collection of essays includes many
important contemporary contributors from approaches spanning across the
political–public spectrum on topics of democracy, pluralism and human rights.

Section III: The Church and the Political

Bonhoeffer, Dietrich. *The Collected Sermons of Dietrich Bonhoeffer*, edited by Isabel Best.
Minneapolis: Fortress Press, 2012.

Much attention is (rightly) given to Bonhoeffer's formal theological writings, but it is also worth reading this collection of his sermons delivered in London and Berlin during the early and mid-1930s. Here Bonhoeffer works out his political theology in homiletic form.

Bowman, Cynthia Grant. 'The Development of the Lutheran Theory of Resistance: 1523–1530'. *Sixteenth Century Journal* 4, no.1 (1977).
This seminal piece makes a compelling argument that contrary to the assumption that the German Reformation did not produce a theory of resistance, in fact Luther and later Lutherans were vital transmitters of theories of resistance later developed more fully by Calvinists.

Brady, Thomas A. 'Luther and the State: The Reformer's Teaching in its Social Setting'. In *Luther and the Modern State in Germany*, edited by James D. Tracy, 31–44. Kirkville, MO: Sixteenth Century Journal Publishers, 1986.
This is a piece that sets Luther's theology and his views on the political into the social context of the Reformation.

Kalaitzidis, Pantelis. *Orthodoxy and Political Theology*. Geneva: WCC Publications, 2012.
This text addresses the political theology of Orthodox Churches from an historical and theological perspective, with a view to its implications for life in the church.

Skinner, Quentin. *The Foundations of Modern Political Thought: The Age of Reformation*, 189–349. Cambridge: Cambridge University Press, 1978.
A major introductory text by a historian who seeks to address the political thought of the Reformation, paying particular attention to theories of resistance developed during this period.

Section IV: The Politics of Jesus

Althaus Reid, Marcella. *Indecent Theology. Theological Perversions in Sex, Gender and Politics*. Abingdon, Oxford: Routledge, 2000.
The Christology offered in this collection of Althaus Reid's writings advocates for imprecision, dislocation and ultimately a systematically deviant Jesus.

Amoah, Elizabeth, and Mercy Amba Oduyoye. 'The Christ for African Women'. In *With Passion and Compassion: Third World Women Doing Theology*, edited by Virginia Fabella and Mercy Amba Oduyoye, 35–46. Maryknoll, NY: Orbis, 1988.
A compelling account of grassroots Christology from two Ghanaian theologians.

Baylor, Michael G. (ed.). *The Radical Reformation*. Cambridge: Cambridge University Press, 1991.
This volume in the *Cambridge Texts in the History of Political Thought* series brings together some of the more overtly political texts of sixteenth-century Anabaptists and Reformation radicals.

Cone, James. *God of the Oppressed*. Maryknoll, NY: Orbis, 1997.
    Originally published in 1975, this book sets out Cone's early theology, with 'Jesus Christ as the ground of human liberation' at its core.

Grant, Jacquelyn. *White Women's Christ and Black Women's Jesus: Feminist Christology and Womanist Response*. Atlanta, GA: Scholars Press, 1989.
    A key early voice in the development of Womanist systematic theology, here Grant considers the ways in which feminism has rethought Christology and how it must be thought still differently, through the combined lenses of Black women's experience (race, sex, class) to replenish a fuller meaning of liberation. An important feature of this critical approach is in rejecting too-swift a reconciliation with white feminism, as fundamentally part of the oppressive structures of thinking that exclude Black women's insight into the person of Jesus.

Myers, Ched. *Binding the Strong Man: A Political Reading of Mark's Story of Jesus*. Maryknoll, NY: Orbis, 1988.
    This detailed, landmark work of biblical criticism offers a portrayal of the Jesus of Mark's Gospel in strikingly political and social terms.

O'Donovan, Oliver. *The Desire of the Nations: Rediscovering the Roots of Political Theology*. Cambridge: Cambridge University Press, 1996.
    This is O'Donovan's exploration of the kingship of Christ, which sets the ground for his defence of a version of Christendom.

Section V: Violence and Peace

Cone, James. *The Cross and the Lynching Tree*. Maryknoll, NY: Orbis, 2011.
    In some ways the culminating work of Cone's influential corpus of Black theology, this book explores connections between the violent execution of Black bodies on trees in the American south and the crucifixion of Jesus Christ on a tree in Palestine. Cone critiques white supremacy in Christianity while also drawing on African American resources for Christian proclamation of cross and resurrection which does not deny the continued crucifixion of Black bodies.

Long, Michael G. (ed.). *Christian Peace and Nonviolence: A Documentary History*. Maryknoll, NY: Orbis, 2011.
    This volume includes small but significant writings and excerpts spanning across scripture and Christian history into the twenty-first century.

Reed, Esther. *The Ethics of Human Rights: Contested Doctrinal and Moral Issues*. Waco, TX: Baylor University Press, 2007.
    A theological approach to the problems and promise of human rights through the construction of a Christian theology of 'right' and 'rights'.

Regan, Ethna. *Theology and the Boundary Discourse of Human Rights*. Washington, DC: Georgetown University Press, 2010.
An argument for theological engagement with the discourse of human rights, directly addressing theological critiques of the 'rights' framework.

Stassen, Glen (ed.). *Just Peacemaking: The New Paradigm for the Ethics of Peace and War*. Cleveland, OH: Pilgrim Press, 2008.
An articulation of Just Peacemaking Theory, the interdisciplinary project of twenty-three scholars over six years to develop a set of concrete initiatives for reducing war.

Tolstoy, Leo. *The Kingdom of God Is Within You*. [Available in multiple Tolstoy collections and online.]
In this text, first published in 1884, Tolstoy sets out his vision for a Christianity that eschews both violence and any hope that the state can bring about any kind of socially redemptive action. He views Christianity as necessitating an active resistance to the violence of the state and of government, and a new form of social ethic.

Wink, Walter. *Engaging the Powers*. Minneapolis, MN: Fortress Press, 1992.
In this volume, Wink extended his earlier work on the principalities and powers of the New Testament, constructing a third-way framework for non-violent political action beyond just war and pacifism.

Section VI: Liberalism and Democracy

Bretherton, Luke. *Christianity and Contemporary Politics*. Oxford: Wiley-Blackwell, 2010.
This is an unusual book because it takes as its starting point forms of Christian ecclesial practice (community organizing, welcome of the stranger and fair trade) and seeks to relate these to dynamics in contemporary liberal democracy.

Coles, Romand, and Stanley Hauerwas. *Christianity, Democracy and the Radical Ordinary: Conversations between a Radical Democrat and a Christian*. New York: Wipf and Stock, 2008.
This is a book formed around a dialogue between two radical thinkers. It tries to draw the conversation about liberalism and democracy towards concrete practices and possibilities.

Insole, Christopher. *The Politics of Human Frailty: A Theological Defense of Political Liberalism*. London: SCM Press, 2004.
This book offers a careful reading of a range of liberal thinkers and extends the argument found in Insole's piece in this reader.

Manent, Pierre. *An Intellectual History of Liberalism*. Princeton: Princeton University Press, 1995.
A useful short text that surveys the development of liberal thought about beliefs, practices and institutions. A portrait of the gradual and contested emergence of liberal ideas and of the decline of theological politics.

Song, Robert. *Christianity and Liberal Society*. Oxford: Oxford University Press, 1997.
An assessment of liberal political thought from a Christian theological point of view, addressing the critique of liberalism made by three twentieth-century figures from across the theological spectrum: Reinhold Niebuhr, George Grant and Jacques Maritain.

Weil, Simone. *The Need for Roots*. London: Routledge, 2001.
Simone Weil was a philosopher, political thinker and mystic. In this, her only full book length text, she offered a political-theological vision for the reconstruction of post-War France. Combining an eclectic range of influences she argues against a prevailing turn towards rights-talk and individualism and in favour of a notion of mutual obligation, rootedness and attention to the human other as the grounds of a renewed way of living.

Section VII: Oppression, Marginalization and Liberation

Copeland, M. Shawn. *Enfleshing Freedom: Body*, Race, Being. Minneapolis, MN: Fortress Press, 2010.
Copeland's work summons readers to think in terms of the human flourishing theology might have to offer for the transformation of communities, by way of reckoning with the historical, ideological and concrete realities of Black embodiment.

Jagessar, Michael and Anthony G. Reddie, *Black Theology in Britain*: A Reader. London: Routledge, 2007.
This collection of writings from within and about Black Christianity in Britain introduces readers to the distinctive concerns and sources of British Black theology (e.g. more Caribbean influences than American Black theology) as well as highlighting the least heard voices in British theology: those of Black women.

Kwok, Pui-lan. *Postcolonial Imagination and Feminist Theology*. Louisville, KY: Westminster John Knox Press, 2005.
Giving an overview of postcolonial theology, Kwok offers an introduction to the dominant themes of the discipline today, particularly considering ecology and plurality.

Lloyd, Vincent (ed.). *Race and Political Theology*. Stanford, CA: Standford University Press, 2012.
This collection of essays from scholars in several disciplines explores how Black and Jewish experience might shape political theology while also demonstrating the necessity of taking race into account in any contemporary considerations of religion and politics.

Rowlands, Anna. *Towards a Politics of Communion: Catholic Social Teaching in Dark Times*. London: Bloomsbury, forthcoming.
This book offers an overview of the historical and theological development of the core principles of the Catholic Social Teaching tradition.

Schüssler-Fiorenza, Elizabeth (ed.). *The Power of Naming: A Concilium Reader in Feminist Liberation Theology*. Maryknoll, NY: Orbis, 1996.
A global-ranging collection that offers an entry point to many of the concerns of feminist theologians that have continued to shape theological discourses: work; poverty; environment; all within a broader concern with structures of oppression in contrast with human flourishing.

Sen, Amartya, 'More than 100 Million Women Are Missing'. In *Women's Global Health and Human Rights*, edited by Padmini Murphy and Clyde Lanford Smith, 99–112. London: Jones and Bartlett, 2010; and 'Missing Women – Revisited'. *British Medical Journal* 327, n. 7427: 1297–1298 (2003).
Studies from Nobel economist, Amartya Sen, assessing the mortal impact of neglect and discrimination in health, education and political participation on women's lives across the globe; this is a useful place to begin when considering the impact of context.

Tonstad, Linn Marie. *God and Difference: The Trinity, Sexuality and the Transformation of Finitude*. New York: Routledge, 2015.
This text explores the nature of the Trinity, and concludes with consideration of how diverse queer perspectives on the individual and the community might prompt differing visions of the Trinitarian nature of God.

West, Cornell. *Prophesy Deliverance! An Afro-American Revolutionary Christianity*. 1st edn, 1982. Anniversary edition, Louisville, KY: Westminster John Knox Press, 2002.
Using Marxist resources, West offers an analysis of African American experience that is grounded in an historical critique of race relations as ultimately about the powerlessness of class.

Section VIII: Creation, History and Eschatology

Johnson, Elizabeth. *Ask the Beasts: Darwin and the God of Love*. London: Bloomsbury, 2014.
A fresh look at the doctrine of creation, which rightly attends to plant and animal species as theological subjects in their own right, integrating evolution and theistic creation to argue a case for environmental activism.

Moltmann, Jürgen. *Theology of Hope: On the Ground and the Implications of a Christian Eschatology*. Minneapolis, MN: Fortress Press, 1993.
Originally published in 1965 (in English in 1967), this seminal work of twentieth century was influential for most of early political, Black and liberation theologies.

Phillips, Elizabeth. 'Eschatology and Apocalyptic'. In *The Cambridge Companion to Christian Political Theology*, edited by Craig Hovey and Elizabeth Phillips, 274–296. Cambridge: Cambridge University Press, 2016.

In this chapter, Phillips gives an overview of the centrality of eschatology in political theology and considers whether and how apocalyptic can be normative in Christian political thought.

Portier-Young, Anthea E. *Apocalypse against Empire: Theologies of Resistance in Early Judaism*. Grand Rapids: Eerdmans, 2011.
One of the volumes in a surge of publications on empire in biblical texts, this book is a compelling account of the political settings and functions of early apocalyptic writings.

Williams, Rowan (ed.). *Sergii Bulgakov: Toward a Russian Political Theology*. London: T&T Clark, 1999.
A volume of texts from Bulgakov, edited and extensively introduced by Williams.

[1]*An den Christlichen Adel deutscher Nation (Appeal to the Christian Nobility of the German Nation)*, 1520.

Scripture Index

Biblical works

Genesis

1.26	39, 566, 570, 574
1.27	161, 575
1.28	509
2.2	510
3.19	511, 653
9.25	39, 559
12:1–4	579
14:13–16	186
21:12	175
22.18	48
28	24
32:27–29	579

Exodus

2.12	208
3.8	223
19.5–6	254
20.8	510
20.12	324
20.13	208
21:14	180
21.16	91
22.8	202
22.20	52
25:1–7	16

Leviticus

19.18	57
20.10	91

Numbers

22:28	175

Deuteronomy

1.16	202, 204, 207
5.17	208
6.5	57
7.7–11	254
8.11	25
17.6	207
18.v 21,22	412
22.22	91
27:11–13	345
28.29	219
32.15	25
32.35	215, 255

Judges

3.9	223
15:11	191
21.25	207

1 Samuel

4:3	320
7:8	320
8	1–11
8.7	204
8.11	220
9:16	320
13:14	96
14:45	319
15:32ff.	186
24.6	211
24.11	211
24.7–11	222
26.9	221–2
26.10	222

1 Kings
2.3	209
2.5	208
6.7	184
12.30	224
18:40	186
22.3	207

2 Kings
14.5f.	98

Chronicles
19.6	202, 204

Ezra (or 1 Edras)
6:49ff.	640
15.11	98

Job
4.2-6	28
7.1	55, 60
15:21	96
34.30	219
37:14	149
41:18	197
41:24	123–4

Psalms
2.12	222
6	181
6.7	24
7.9	193
7.10	324
9.9	98
10.3	184
16.2	52
18.8	70
19:1	149
25(24).17	65
33:16	168
45.7	208
62	190
82, 1 and 6	190, 202, 204
82:3,4	207
90:5–6	20
90.10	29
96.5	52
101	207
103.5	665
106	198
109	184
113	195
115(113b). 1	60
118:91	566
144.15	54
147.12ff.	32

Proverbs
3.12	30
30.33	75
6.31–32	91
8.15	75, 205
9.8	66
16.12	209
17.15	209
17.11	209
18.19	513
20.22	191
20.26	209
20.28	209
21:1	98
24.21	217
24.24	209
25.4	209
25.5	209
21.1	222
24.29	191
28.1	221
28:12	96
28:15	96

Ecclesiastes
1.2	564
1.14	44
2:2–11	564
2:7	563–4
2:9	564
4.9-10	513

9:13   95

5.7   62

5:8   88

Wisdom

3.5–6   59

9.15   42, 55

Sirach/Ecclesiasticus

1:2   564

2.1–2   30

2:2–11   564

2:7   563–4

4.9-10   513

Isaiah

2:4   184

3.4   196, 219

9:6   330

9:7   330

10.1–2   222

10.5   219

11:4   197

11:9   184

18:22   643

21   642

21:9   642

23   643

23:8   643

23:17   642

27:1   124

49.23   203

52:5   520

55:10   17

56:6–7   15

58:4   15

Jeremiah

1   193

12:10   88, 94

18:22–23   643

21.12   208

22.3   208

27.17   221

29.7   221

30.21   95

48.10   204

51:13   642

Baruch

3:36   17

29:4   640

Ezekiel

2.37   220

21:22   649

22:27   95

27   642

27:36   642

29.19   220

34.23   95

36:20–22   520

37:24   94

37.25   95

47:12   648

48.21   211

Daniel

2.21   220

5.18   220

6.22   224

8:3   640

9.3–15   40

11:36   125

12:9   639

14:33–39   16

37   220

Hosea

5.11   224

13.11   196, 219

Amos

6.3   23

6.4–6   23

Habakkuk

2.4   43, 53

Malachi

1:6   344

Matthew

3.2   181
5.9   59
5:22ff.   181
5:23   292
5:25, 39–40   178
5:16   520
5.21   208
5:34   524
5:34f.   295
5:37   296
5.39   215–16, 324
5.44   64, 181
5.44,48   190
5:38–9   180
5.38f   524
5:39   182, 184, 189, 216,
                       293, 324
6.12   55, 60
6.21   59
6.32-33   516
6.40   76
8.8–10   58
8:10   325
9.17   75
10.5f   254
10.28   210
10.32, 33   325
10.37   324
10.39   325
11.11   58
11:25   524
11.27   344
13:44–46   318
15.4   324
16.17   254
16:24   294
16.26   64, 149, 550

16:26–27   567
17:27   185
18   192
18:15–17   175
18:15–18   292
18:15–20   290
19:23–24   504
20:25   294–5
22.21   195
22.37, 39   57, 479
22:38   479
22.40   57, 479
23.3   77
23.22   296
24.12   57
24:24   177
25   168, 520
25:31–46   6–13
25.40   505
26.52   180, 324
27:57   310
28:19   292
29:26   295

Mark

1:11   310
1:14–15   310
5:34   524
6.3   506
7.10   324
8.35   325
8.36   64
10:27   295
11:52   524
12.30-1   57
12:44   524
13:22   640
15:24   330
15:28   524
16:6   292

Luke

1:68–79   11–12, 5–12
2:7   309

2:34	296	4.10, 22	606
3.14	58, 180, 210, 325	4.12	606
3.15	187	4.34, 38	605
4:3–12	310	4.35	603
4:19	330	4.42	607
6.24-25	505	5:5–6	633
6.27–8	64	5:17	345
7.6–9	58	6:2	634
7.9	325	6:4	634
7:50	524	6:6	634
9.24	325	6.66	602
9.25	64	6:14	524
10.16	88	7:1–3	634
10.27	57	17:9	174
11.4	60	7:12	644
11.41	505	7:14	638
12.8,9	325	7.32, 45	601
12:13	294	7.48	601
12:20	19	8:1	634
12.34	59	8.12, 23	607
14.10	198	8.26	605
14.26	324	8.34	40
16:19–21	13, 19, 21	9.22, 35	601
18.2	22	9.39	607
18.20	324	10:27	192
21:1–4	16	10.35	202
22.25	205	11.2	637, 647
22.26	205	11:8	637–8, 648
22.32	174	11:18	633
23:33–43	12	11.47, 57	601
23:50	310	11.48-53	602
		12:9	639
John		12.31	607
1.1	606	12.42	601
1.6–9	601	12.42–43	602
1:14	524	13.1	607
1.29–37	601	13:2	639
3.1	601	14–16	290
3:14	141	14:30	125
3.22–30	601	16.2	601
3.29	58	16:11	125
3.34	605	17:1	647
4.1–42	592–612	17:2	642
4.9, 20-23	602	17:13	644

17:16	644	2.4	77
17:17	644	2.15	67
18:33–37	13	2:24	520
18.36ff.	181	5.5	57
19.12, 15	602	5:10	141
19.19–22	602	6.9	60
20:19–23	290	6.22	32
20.21–23	605–6	7:7	182
20.28	606	7:24	518
21:3–8	649	8:30	295
21:9	647	9–11	254
21:22	649	10.12	509
22:15	648	11.15	661
22:5	633	11:29	555, 567, 571
		12	179
Acts		12.8	203
1.7	672	12:19	180, 215
1.8	345	12:4f.	171
2:38	292	12:10	198
2.38ff.	254	12.17	64
3.19–26	254	12:19	215
4	195	12.21	216
5.29	76, 224	13	76
8.27ff.	187	13.1	61, 205, 218, 662
8:36	292	13.1–2	179
10	193, 325	13.3	195
10.1–33	58	13.4	188, 208, 214, 216
10.2	187	13.5	217
10.34ff.	187	13.6	211
10.44	187	13.7	195
13.7, 12	188	13.10	57
15:6	176	13:12	638
16:31ff.	292	14:15	483
19:4	292		
20.35	505	1 Corinthians	
22.1	215	1.17f	286
24.12	215	1.22f	254
25.10	215	2:15	175
28.4	28	6.1ff.	216
		6.7	324
Romans		7.7	58
1.17	43	7:19	187
1.24	72	7.20	662
2.2	91	7.20, 24	668

7.23	224
7.31	662
8:10	325
8:11	483
9:14	294
10.3	186
10.4	24
10:21	292
10.31	21
10.33	80
12.3	344
12:12f	170
12.12–27	666
12.13	187
12.28	203
12.31	103
13.4-7	518
13.5	80
13.6	659
13.9	43
14:30	174
14:33	291
15.24, 28	40
15.28	45, 632
15, 32	573
15.52	325

2 Corinthians

3:17	320
4:4	125
4:13	175
4:17	504
5:6	100
5.6f	38
5.7	55
6:17	293
8:9	505
10.4f	197
10:8	176
13:5	344
13:8	177

Galatians

2	182
2:11	175
2:20	344
3:28	200, 575
5:1	200, 320
5.6	53, 55, 57
6:15	187

Ephesians

2	254
4.29	30
5.4	30
5.21	185
5.25	222
6.5	40
6.5–9	668
6.12	66, 197

Colossians

1:15	573
3.11	200

1 Thessalonians

4.16	325
5.6	25
5.15	64

2 Thessalonians

2:3	125
2.4	661
2:9	125, 177

1–2 Timothy

1.9	182
2.1	218
2.2	54, 61, 203, 638, 640
2.4	24
2:11–14	297
2.12	504
3.1	44
3:7	293
3.15	657
4.4	188
5.8	39
6.17-18	90

Hebrews

2:14ff.	312
4:15	524
10.30	255
11.1	658
12:2	524
12.6	30

James

1.17	60
2:7	520
2.17	55
4.6	55
5.4	504
6:17f.	295

1 Peter

2	181
2:9	170–1
2:12	638
2.13	77, 184, 195, 218, 638
2:13–14	179
2.14	183
2.17	205, 217
2:18f	97
2.19	40
2:21	295
3.7	222
4.11	192

5.5	55, 198
5.8	25
15	172

2 Peter

2:2	520

1 John

1.12	344
2.15–17	63–4
4:18	320
5.7,8	346
6:45	174
14:13	344
17.3	344
19.34	325

Revelation (Apocalypse)

5.9	170
10.6	661
13.4	124
13.8	577
13.16	669
13.17	669
13.18	669
17–18	650
18.4	293
20	123, 665
20.4	632n.12

Subject Index

abolition 555, 558, 560, 568, 577, 663

abortion 424

absolutism 374

abstinence 14–15, 142, 146

active and contemplative lives 144

Acton, Lord 460

actus purus 624–5

Adams, John Quincy 131

Adorno, Theodore 140, 158–60, 530 n.15, 681

The Aeneid 33 n.1, 34, 596–7

Africa 61 n.4, 62 n.6, 63–4, 357, 520, 525, 536, 599

Agamben, Giorgio 435, 570 n.32, 572 n.34

almsgiving 15–16, 21–2, 58–65, 505, 693

Althaus-Reid, Marcella 497–8, 539–55

Althusius, Johann 120, 131

Ambrose of Milan 322, 326–8

Anabaptism 165, 273–4, 321, 323, 614

analogy 47, 82, 105–6, 132, 211, 538–9, 565, 647

Anarchism 269, 299

angels 12–13, 16, 24, 26, 51, 57–9, 66, 148, 336–7, 346, 642, 646

Anglicanism 107, 165–6, 387, 454, 459

anointing (consecration) 23–4, 170, 221–2, 257, 278, 280, 284, 333–7, 341, 411, 594, 610 n.56, 638

Anschütz, Gerhard 114

anthropology 2, 106, 126–7, 138, 389, 453, 467, 481, 485, 565, 652, 655, 667

antichrist 124–5, 173, 176–7, 640, 645, 655, 662, 673

anti-Semitism 241

apartheid 578, 609

apocalypse 614–5, 626, 630, 632–3, 635 n.13, 637, 639–40, 642, 646–7, 649, 652, 655, 661–2, 665, 672–91

apocalyptic 116, 123–6, 132, 141, 152, 273–4, 288–9, 472, 614–5, 618–21, 626–30, 632, 638–40, 642, 661–2, 665, 672, 680

apocalypticism 124, 618, 621, 629 n.5, 673–81

apoliticism 274, 664

Apollo 48–51

Aquinas, Thomas 7, 9–10, 66–103, 163, 322, 375–6, 378–9, 386, 441, 465, 468, 495, 505–7, 513, 624, 630, 635, 647

Arendt, Hannah 374, 388, 477

aristocracy 87, 205–6, 284, 438, 445, 454, 459

Aristotle 10, 66–7, 70–1, 73–4, 79–80, 83–5, 87, 225, 389, 441, 458–9, 468, 488, 490–4, 558, 630

Aristotelianism 630

Aryan Clauses 167, 241–59

ascension 232, 342, 638, 641

Asia 349, 355, 357, 594, 631

atheism 165, 656–7, 669

Atonement 1, 291, 373, 636

Augustine of Hippo 4, 9–10, 31–66, 70–1, 73–6, 91, 100, 102

Augustinianism 274–5, 388, 466–72, 476–80, 488–9

    Augustinian Eschatology 614, 619–21

    Augustinian Liberalism, types of 469–75

Auschwitz 130–7, 535–6

autonomy 157, 424, 455, 464, 468, 475, 478, 483, 652, 666

Babylon 53–5, 186, 221, 223, 229, 637, 641–3, 648, 650, 655

Babylonian empire 593

baptism 164, 170–1, 173, 255, 274, 279, 282, 292–3, 309–10, 325, 332, 338, 342–3, 346

Barion, Hans 123

Barmen Declaration 167

Barth, Karl 109, 118, 133 n.8, 166–7, 241–59, 300, 306

Bartolomé de Las Casas 499

basic ecclesial communities 547, 550

Bellah, Robert 363, 413 n.2

Benjamin, Walter 137 n.23, 158–9, 687

Betz, Dieter 626, 629

Beza, Theodor 117, 117 n.3

bible 7, 17, 261, 361, 371, 412, 536, 546, 560, 592–3, 597, 599–600, 612, 634. *See also* scripture

Bin Laden, Osama 151

Bingen, Hildegard von 141

Bishops 44, 170–3, 176, 178, 192–4, 197–9, 234, 266, 286, 454, 473, 496, 515, 521, 537

Black Christ 275, 313–20

Black church 319

Black power 306, 309, 497. *See also* race

Black revolution 316, 318

Black theology 275, 305–8, 312–14, 316, 319, 323, 497

A Black Theology of Liberation 275, 319, 497

Bloch, Ernst 124 n.19, 159, 530

Bobbitt, Philip 374

Bodin, Jean 111–12, 119

Boehmer, Elleke 596

Boff, Leonardo 496, 550

Böhme, Jacob 143

Bonhoeffer, Dietrich 8, 164, 166, 241–67

Boniface 9, 57, 60–3

Bornkamm, Günther 307–8, 317

Brazil 521, 527

Brutus, Junius 118

Buber, Martin 145, 145 n.2

Buchanan, George 118

Buddha, Gautama 144

Buddhism 276, 364, 367

Bulgakov, Sergii 614, 650–72

Bullinger, Heinrich 120

Bullosa, Carmen 554–5

Bultmann, Rudolf 307–8, 312, 316

Burke, Edmund 386, 455–7, 460

Bush, George W. 373, 435, 688

Cacus 33–4

Caesar, Julius 72

Cain and Abel 180

Calvin, John 199–224

Calvinism 117–18, 121. *See also* Reformed

canon law 171–4, 225, 459, 550

capital and labour 499–518

capital punishment 324, 379, 434

capitalism 153, 228, 350, 357, 365, 373, 385, 387, 420, 425, 432, 439–40, 450, 456, 467, 489, 496, 631 n.8, 668, 671, 673, 687. *See also* market

caritas 468–9, 474–5, 480, 483

Carter, J. Kameron 8, 497, 555–80

Cartesian. *See* Descartes, Rene

Catholic social thought (CST) 496

Catholic Worker Movement 167, 270

Catholicism 449, 557, 582

Cavanaugh, William T. 322–3, 360–73, 450, 452, 460

charity 57, 80, 84, 88, 91, 166, 228, 263, 266, 270, 397, 434, 441, 444–5, 480, 482, 486, 518

chastity 51, 58–9, 61, 489

chiastic structure 569–71

Chomsky, Noam 129

Christendom 8, 138, 164, 168–9, 172, 176, 311, 428 n.37, 460, 614, 629

Christian Commonwealth 409–12

Christian social ethics 413–16, 483
    political liberalism, assumptions of 420–8
    school for virtue 428–32
    secular polity 413–16
    society, critique of 416–20

Christian theology 3, 106, 127, 131, 133, 305, 322, 379, 387, 389, 552, 561, 585, 667

Christology 163, 305, 313, 497, 548, 555. *See also* Jesus Christ

Chrysostom, John 8, 20–31, 558

Church 2–3, 5, 7, 13, 20, 28, 48, 51, 54, 61, 100, 105–8, 118, 120, 123, 127–8, 130–2, 135–9, 142, 163–8, 173, 175, 192–3, 201, 203, 225, 227–32, 234, 240–59, 266, 289, 303–4, 307, 311, 315, 319, 321, 327, 343, 348, 353, 375, 385–87, 410, 413, 415–16, 419, 428–32, 435, 440, 450, 458–9, 476, 485, 493–6, 498, 504, 514, 517, 521, 525, 533, 537, 545, 547, 550–4, 562, 573, 599, 613–14, 620, 622, 638, 641, 645, 648, 650, 654, 656, 662, 664, 669–72

 and government/state 164–8, 172, 182–4, 190–4, 199, 201, 203, 208, 212, 217, 225, 227–32, 234, 238–59, 264, 267

Cicero 45–6, 59, 68, 96, 210 n.3, 211, 322, 558

citizenship 45, 71, 115, 126, 157, 176, 227, 295, 325, 388, 466–90, 614, 676

City of God 9, 31–56, 59, 74, 100, 559

civil religion 106, 135–6, 363, 365, 413 n.2
 burgerliche Religion 135

Civil Rights movement. *See* rights

civil society 101, 160, 166, 226–7, 374, 386, 513, 676

Class struggle 300, 303, 659, 670

Cleage, Reverend Albert 309, 316

coercion 77, 140, 184, 193, 265, 274–5, 288, 299–302, 321, 339–40, 388, 428–9, 462, 473, 484–8

Cold War 146, 362, 470, 681

Coles, Romand 388, 467–8, 475

collectivism 667, 669

colonialism 595, 600, 605, 608. *See also* postcolonialism

coloniality 556, 557 n.2

common good 10, 67–8, 70–1, 74–6, 80, 84–5, 88–9, 93–5, 387, 416 n.9, 417 n.12, 420 n.19, 445, 449, 493, 506–8, 513

Common Law 121

common wealth 390, 401–2, 405, 407–9, 412

communication 115, 376–80, 382, 440, 465, 586–7, 591

communion 316, 318, 377, 389, 490–4, 499, 649, 651

divine-human communion 490–4

communism 233, 264, 299, 357–8, 418 n.18, 432, 438, 456, 490, 496, 651, 667, 670, 681

communitarianism 368, 471

community of goods 90

complaint 92, 94, 98, 189

Cone, James 275, 305–20, 497

Confessing Church 167

Confessions 71, 248, 458 n.12, 476 n.41, 479 n.51, 482

Confucianism 364–5, 367

consensus 80, 163, 381, 422 n.24, 440, 461–2, 473, 490, 582, 627

Constantine 176, 311

Constantinianism 556

constitutionalism 114, 454–6, 459–60

consumerism 141–2, 150, 164, 363, 538

contextual theology 497

contract 82, 106, 118–22, 124, 157, 226, 385–6, 394–401, 436–40, 442, 445, 462, 475, 567–8, 572

contrast model 430

Conzelmann, Hans 307

Cornelius, Peter 58, 187

coronation 146–7. *See also* anointing

counsel 14–15, 25, 70, 185, 247, 252, 295, 304, 330, 356, 411, 467

covenant 115–21, 126–7, 131, 180–1, 187, 240, 254, 256, 330, 338–9, 346, 386, 398–401, 427 n.35, 510, 557, 567–8, 577, 627, 629, 638

creation 613–91

creator 17, 35, 106, 123, 126–7, 147, 161, 232, 243, 329, 333, 345, 364, 382, 387, 389, 403, 406, 465, 482, 559, 564, 566, 633, 636, 690

crime(s) 1–2, 33, 73, 125, 204, 207–8, 210, 213, 215, 223, 262, 326, 434, 504, 511

critical theory 469 n.8, 496

cruelty 22, 26–7, 96, 98, 208, 217, 263, 353, 476, 510, 527, 530

Cynics 44

Daly, Mary 498, 544, 589

Daoism 364

David 24, 58, 94, 184, 186, 195, 203, 206–9,
    211, 274, 315, 322, 327–8, 333, 339, 342,
    347, 378, 470, 633
Day, Dorothy 260–72
de Coligny, Admiral 117
De libero arbitrio 70, 73, 75–6, 102
De partibusanimalium 93
death penalty. *See* capital punishment
debt 331, 423 n.26, 444, 632 n.10
decolonization 592–612
democracy 10, 87, 95, 116, 121, 127, 130–1,
    157, 165, 234, 352, 355, 358–9, 413–14,
    417, 420, 428–31, 433, 437–9, 441, 443,
    446, 447–8, 453, 455–7, 459, 461, 467,
    470, 474, 489–91, 493, 553, 592, 617,
    623, 679
Derrida, Jacques 160, 489, 567 n.22, 609 n.53
Descartes, René 121, 234, 477
Deuteronomic tradition 524, 627
Devil. *See* Satan
discipleship 106–7, 128, 130–1, 139, 163, 472
discipline 2–4, 10, 40, 64, 73–5, 203, 208, 210,
    227, 343, 346, 428, 468 n.5, 479, 485, 508,
    597, 613
divine law 69–70, 74, 76, 91, 102, 246, 324
Donaldson, Laura 597 n.22
doxology 284–8
dualism 156, 377, 453, 491, 493
Dube, Musa 499, 592–612
Durand, Marie 120

Easter 571–3, 577–8
ecclesiology 453–4, 458, 460, 545, 547. *See
    also* church
Eckhart, Meister 147
ecology 672. *See also* feminism
economics 3, 278, 297, 300–2, 311, 382, 387,
    414, 422, 424, 432–4, 439–41, 446, 448,
    463, 490, 493, 499, 525, 548, 553–4, 587–
    9, 592, 595, 612, 653–6, 668, 671. *See also*
    capitalism; collectivism; consumerism;
    socialism
Egypt 11, 186, 220, 240, 258, 293, 366, 594,
    599, 636–7, 648

El Salvador 520, 525, 533–4, 536–7
election 250, 254, 319, 567, 616, 649, 680
empire 163, 179, 225, 269, 441, 443, 469, 489,
    522, 592, 594, 602, 638–45, 663
Enlightenment 122, 134–6, 139, 276, 324,
    381–2, 416, 419, 429, 432, 469, 487,
    584, 679–80
equality 35, 82, 87, 164, 233–34, 302, 305, 324,
    358, 379, 391–2, 430 n.40, 457, 483, 493,
    508, 538, 550, 568, 586
eschatology 163, 460, 467, 613–91. *See also*
    apocalyptic
eschatological restlessness 472
Essenes 277, 284
eternal law 68–70, 75, 212–13, 438, 502, 514
Ethics 66–7, 69, 71, 80–1, 83, 85, 92, 96, 101–2
Eucharist 59 n.3, 170, 271, 389, 445, 621
evangelicalism 570 n.32, 579 n.44
Exsurge Dominine 163

fall, fallen 116, 147, 296, 321, 471, 490, 618,
    627, 635, 643, 653–4
family 13, 34, 80, 86, 94, 234, 238, 266–8, 270–
    1, 277–8, 281–2, 287, 304, 353, 374, 388,
    419, 424–5, 427, 451, 491–2, 506–8, 685
faith and knowledge 151–61, 659
fasting 14, 65, 150, 352
feast 8, 20–1, 23, 95, 150, 334
federal theology 120, 126
feminism 586, 591
    ecofeminism 498
feminist theology 498, 580–92. *See also*
    mujerista theology; womanist theology
Figgis, John Neville 165–6, 225–30
forgiveness 55, 158, 254, 261, 278, 290, 294,
    296, 301, 304, 334, 338, 345, 389, 399, 428
    n.36, 493, 516
Foucault, Michel 484, 560, 566
Fox, Matthew 147
Frankfurt School 108
freedom 36, 39, 45–6, 116–17, 122, 124, 127–
    31, 142, 145, 150, 157, 161, 163, 173, 177,
    191, 195, 200, 209, 218, 225–7, 229, 233,
    244, 254, 291, 298, 312, 314, 319, 323, 351,

355, 368, 371, 382, 387, 415, 417–19, 421–
23, 425, 427, 430, 434, 445, 462, 475, 486,
493, 527, 565, 568, 571, 575–7, 580, 589,
636–7, 646, 663, 670, 680, 682, 686, 690

French Revolution 386, 587, 659, 687, 690

Freud, Sigmund 474 n.34, 544, 597

friendship 95, 397, 476, 679

Fuchs, Ernst 307–8, 608

functionalist approach 363–5

Gandhi, Mohandas 534

Gaudium et Spes 433

gender 165, 499, 544–5, 548–9, 550, 586, 593,
597–8, 606, 608, 610, 612

genetic engineering 151–2, 160–1, 674

Geneva 117, 120, 352, 354

genocide 578

Gentiles 52, 242, 282, 298, 330, 608, 647

gift-exchange 439, 443

globalization 140–3, 152, 522, 527, 533, 538,
541, 554, 595–6

good, goodness 16, 18, 27, 49, 59, 71, 84, 147,
149, 204, 209, 219, 222, 263, 338, 347, 433,
465, 474, 478, 482, 488, 509, 523

Gospels 8, 16, 21, 139, 279, 290, 300, 307–9,
312, 524, 527, 626

government 38–9, 99–111, 119, 127, 131,
163–4, 167, 172, 183, 190–4, 199, 201–3,
205, 226, 269, 271–3, 302, 318, 323, 350–
3, 356, 367, 372, 385, 387, 393, 416–17,
420–2, 434, 437, 440, 447–8, 459, 497,
507, 515, 614, 617, 640

Graham, Elaine 107–8

  Gratian 92

Gregory of Nazianzus 558–60

Gregory of Nyssa 8, 13–20, 77, 99, 555–80

Gregory, Eric 275, 388–9, 466–90

Gutierrez, Gustavo 545 n.3

habeas corpus 434, 438

Habermas, Jürgen 107–8, 133 n.10, 135 n.18,
151–61, 675, 679

Hauerwas, Stanley 109, 323, 387, 413–32, 457,
467, 494

heaven 8–9, 21, 49–50, 57–9, 65, 101–2, 123,
179, 190, 192–3, 195, 220, 223, 228, 262,
295–6, 298, 312, 319, 333, 335, 339, 346,
397, 412, 504, 509, 523, 537, 549, 614,
615–16, 620, 625, 632, 634, 638, 646, 649,
658, 663

Heavenly city 9, 36, 38–9, 42–4, 488, 649

Hegel, G. W. E. 159, 161, 381, 629–30, 657,
679, 686–7

hegemony 281, 389, 491, 557

Heidegger, Martin 160, 481 n.56

Henson, Canon Hensley 229

heresy 61, 197–9, 246–7, 255, 264, 485, 663,
665, 667

hermeneutics 135, 137, 139, 546, 558

Herodias 19

Herodotus 31

Heschel, Abraham 148–9

hierarchy 127, 142, 164, 368, 437, 445–6, 482,
611, 668–9

Hinduism 363, 367

Hitchens, Christopher 361, 363, 365,
370–1

Hitler, Adolf 231, 240–1, 287, 377

Hobbes, Thomas 106, 116, 121–5, 127–9, 131,
285–6, 389–412, 452

Holocaust 105, 107, 130, 158, 287, 468, 578

Holy Land 648

Holy Spirit 20, 31, 57, 77, 100, 174, 179, 181,
183–4, 187, 191, 210, 232, 255, 262, 289,
329, 332–46, 434–5, 442, 559, 560, 575,
616, 625, 640, 661, 670

hope 18, 27, 40, 45, 57–8, 60, 108, 110, 141–3,
158, 166, 231, 240, 245, 262–3, 265, 297,
302, 318, 320, 330, 334, 338, 349, 355, 359,
388, 390, 394, 397, 402, 404, 406, 409,
433, 436, 439, 469, 472, 517, 521–2, 527,
530, 531, 535, 538, 555, 630, 642, 648, 658,
665, 684

Hotman, Francois 117

The Hound of Heaven 262

Huguenots 117–18

human law 68–70, 73–80, 91, 158, 173, 505

human rights. *See* rights

humility 40, 60, 196, 222, 268, 297, 303, 323,
    331, 336, 338–9, 346, 348, 404, 406, 430,
    468, 473, 476, 519, 526, 588, 590
Hundeshagen, Carl Bernhard 118

iconoclasm 131
idealism 134, 136–7, 238, 301, 303–5, 314, 489,
    540, 547, 555, 659, 687
idolatry 76, 131, 208, 258–9, 322, 475, 640
The Iliad 594, 597
image of God 161, 219, 380, 498, 561, 568–8
The Imitation of Christ 262
immanence 488, 615
imperialism 283, 373, 420 n.19, 499, 592–600,
    602–3, 605–7, 610–12
incarnation 159, 287, 329, 441–2, 472, 576,
    621, 661, 686
individualism 234, 368, 425, 427, 432, 482, 527,
    581, 586, 590, 668, 670
inequality 206, 304, 401, 438
inhumanity 8, 22, 26–7, 211, 311, 517, 536
injustice 2, 8, 15, 22, 26–7, 35, 40, 46, 56, 80,
    98, 180, 186, 189, 207, 209–11, 297, 299,
    304, 319–20, 322, 327, 358, 394, 396, 414,
    416, 424, 478–9, 490, 500, 511
Insole, Christopher 387–9, 450–66
interpretation 7–8, 49, 106, 136, 139, 144, 153,
    174, 189, 202, 273, 303, 308, 312, 319, 344,
    387, 410, 412, 415, 498, 546–7, 549, 552,
    554, 557–61, 566, 576, 580–3, 627, 630,
    638, 649, 656, 665, 689
investiture controversy 10
Iraq. See war
Isidore of Seville 74, 79–80, 99
Islam, Muslim 360–1, 363, 365, 370–1, 374,
    389, 440, 490
Israel 10–1, 119–20, 191, 207, 200, 222–3, 245,
    254–6, 278, 296, 318, 320, 345, 371, 403,
    411, 567–9, 578–9, 605, 648, 652

Jacob 17, 24–5, 605–7
Jerusalem 32, 128, 220, 279, 281, 284, 295–6,
    346, 480, 547, 563–4, 601–2, 604, 607,
    627, 637, 643, 647–8

Jesus Christ 8, 12, 15–16, 19–21, 25–6, 31,
    48–51, 57, 60–1, 65, 66, 97, 100–1, 166,
    171, 231, 254, 273, 275, 291–2, 296–7,
    305–6, 309, 311, 314–16, 323, 329, 332,
    334–8, 341, 344, 346, 350, 369, 496, 504,
    571, 576–7, 599, 608
    cross of 8, 15, 106, 128, 150, 216, 244, 259,
        264, 281–3, 288, 290, 294, 299, 312, 330,
        429, 535, 561, 589, 600
    historical Jesus 273, 306–9, 313–14, 320,
        553, 576, 600, 604
Job 28, 149, 191, 197, 260, 268, 403
Johannine community 499, 600, 602–4, 608
John of Salisbury 93, 97
John Paul II 157, 437
Jones, David 378
Jong-Il, Kim 361
Judaism, Jewish 12–13, 23, 48–9, 52, 98,
    127–30, 146, 167, 187, 214, 241, 243–50,
    244–5, 255, 287, 340, 363, 440, 478
    n.50, 556, 577, 579 n.44, 601–2, 607,
    661, 685–6
Judas 14–15, 266, 282, 340, 625
judgment 2, 16, 30, 69, 77, 79, 99, 101, 156,
    174, 236, 247, 255, 289, 294, 309–10, 318,
    342, 358, 386, 448, 451, 454–5, 458, 465,
    571, 587, 622, 626–7, 632–7, 646–7,
    649
Juergensmeyer, Mark 362–4
jurisprudence 105, 113, 368
just war theory 322, 486
justice 2, 10, 15–16, 26, 28, 35, 37, 46–7,
    51–3, 56, 65, 70, 73, 75–6, 80, 82–9,
    95, 98–9, 103, 109, 131, 141–2, 151,
    163, 166, 189–90, 199, 201–2, 204–10,
    212, 218–19, 226–8, 233, 236, 262,
    266, 275, 279, 286, 295, 299, 300–2,
    304, 321–3, 326, 341, 347, 357–9,
    368, 382, 386–8, 394, 399, 404, 409,
    414–15, 426–7, 431, 434, 436–7, 439,
    445–8, 450, 455, 460, 469, 473–5,
    477–9, 486, 488, 498, 501, 503, 505–8,
    511, 516, 527, 534, 545, 554, 585, 632,
    646, 651, 658, 660, 672

Justinian 286

Kairos and Ordinary Time 616–18
Kant, Immanuel 114, 130, 157–8, 453, 461–5,
    477, 480, 488, 676
Käsemann, Ernst 307
Kelsen, Hans 110, 114
kenosis 442, 546
Kierkegaard, Søren 115 n.3, 483, 629, 686–7
King, Martin Luther, Jr., 125–6, 168–77, 177–9,
    275, 323, 347–61, 370, 487, 497, 534
Kingdom of God 126–7, 159, 181–2, 191, 200–
    1, 240, 300, 310–11, 316–20, 516, 621–5,
    655, 658, 660–2, 664–5, 670–2
kingship 7–8, 10, 94, 96, 98, 189, 205, 220–1,
    278, 283, 286, 330
Kipling, Rudyard 599 n.37
Krabbe, Hugo 110
Kuhn, Thomas S. 132, 132 n.2
Kwok Pui-lan 499

labour 96, 134–5, 188, 392, 404, 409–10, 495,
    651–5, 662, 671
Languet, Hubert 118, 118 n.5
Las Casas, Bartoloméde 499
Lazarus and the Rich Man 8, 20–31
Leo XIII 495, 499–518
Leviathan 106–7, 115–31, 330, 385, 389–412,
    629, 631, 640, 666
Liberal Democracy 129, 165, 387–8, 413–33,
    438, 446, 467, 471, 474, 490–1, 493–4
liberalism 4, 110, 275, 324, 364, 370–3, 385–
    494, 496, 554, 629
    constitutional liberalism 451
    postliberalism 109, 614
liberation 319, 495–612
liberation theology 135 n.14, 139, 496–8,
    527, 539–55
liberality 16, 85–6, 387, 432–49
libido dominandi 467, 482
Lincoln, Abraham 119, 372, 417 n.11
Lindbeck, George 109
liturgy 59 n.3, 543
Love 13–20, 466–90

Locke, John 114, 421, 456, 488
Louis XIV 121
Lovibond, Sabina 380
Lund, Nils Wilhelm 569, 569 nn.28–29
Lutheranism 450
luxury 21–2, 25, 29, 31, 311

MacIntyre, Alasdair 109, 323–4, 373–4, 381,
    422 n.24
Macpherson, C. B. 420 n.19, 421 n.21, 425, 425
    n.32, 426 n.33
Madison, James 121, 421
Malcolm X 275
Manent, Pierre 433, 433 n.2, 451 n.2
manifest destiny 530
marginalization 495–612
market 1, 108, 140–1, 157, 161, 364–5, 373,
    420 n.19, 425, 426 n.33, 433–4, 436,
    439, 441, 445–6, 449, 467, 495, 549, 641,
    643, 690
Marpeck, Pilgram 322, 328–47
marriage 42, 62, 66, 165, 189, 219, 229, 337,
    375–6, 425, 489 n.71, 643. *See also* family
Marty, Martin 362, 362 n.3, 369, 369 n. 27,
    420 n.18
martyrs, martyrdom 57, 188, 534, 536–7, 537
    n.31, 635 n.13
Marvin, Carolyn 363, 363 n.10
Marx, Karl/Marxism 140, 159, 318, 445, 519
    n.1, 540–5, 549–50, 653, 655–6, 687, 690
materialism 141, 357, 419, 432, 445, 540, 547,
    652, 654, 659, 681
Mathewes, Charles 275, 492, 613–26
McCoy, Charles 118 n.5, 120 n.10, 121,
    121 n.12
Mendelssohn, Moses 128–9
Mennonite 275 n.1
Merz, Georg 249
Messianism 160, 658
Metaphysics 74, 93–4
Metz, Johann Baptist 105–7, 109, 128 n.24,
    130, 130 nn. 27–28, 132–9, 133 n.9,
    135 n.15, 136 n.22, 137 nn. 24–25, 139,
    164, 535

Milbank, John 109, 323, 387, 432–49, 457, 467, 494, 567 n.23, 570 n. 32, 615
militarism 322–3, 357–8
military 324–5, 356
Milton, John 131
modernity 124, 152–3, 158, 385, 432, 438–9, 475, 556, 556 n.2, 578–80, 675
Moffat, Alfredo 555
Mohl, Robert von 109
'Moloch' 116
Moltmann, Jürgen 105–6, 115–31, 135 n.15, 136 n.21
monarchy 117–18, 298, 386, 433, 435, 437, 454, 473
    constitutional monarchy 435
monks 61, 170–2, 194, 492
Montesquieu 458
moral disclosure 373
Mornay, Philipp Duplessis 116, 118–20, 131
Moses, 16, 25, 128–9, 161, 180, 186, 190, 195, 202–3, 207–9, 212, 214, 222, 256–9, 281, 319, 322, 326, 328, 334, 336–7, 345, 411, 441, 459, 599 n.37, 601, 605
mujerista theology 498
Muñoz, Ronaldo 522, 532
murder 73, 75, 198, 210, 213, 255, 536
Murray, John Courtney 413 n.4, 414 n.4
Mystagogy 442, 519
mysteriuminiquitatis 520, 526
mysticism 107, 139–50, 167
Myth of Religious Violence 323, 360–1, 368–70, 373 n.50

nationalism 283, 351, 362–5, 367, 369, 432, 450
natural law 68–75, 79, 90–1, 111, 114, 117, 120, 125–6, 156, 213, 233, 435, 442, 493, 506
Nazis/Nazism 105, 166–7, 240
neo-Calvinism 449
neo-Platonism 477, 630
Ngugi waThiong'o 599
Niebuhr, Reinhold 274–5, 297–305, 413 n.2, 413 n.4, 414, 414 nn. 4–5, 428 n. 37, 429 n.38, 469–70, 470 n.10, 471, 471 n.12, 477 n.44, 584 n.4

Nietzsche, Friedrich 132 n.1, 228, 230, 358, 544
nihilism 449, 489, 655, 663
Noah 39, 638
nonviolence 131, 269, 273, 293, 353. *See also* pacifism
nouvelle theologie 496
nuclear weapons 146, 358
Nussbaum, Martha 388, 468 n.7, 478, 478 n.47, 478 n.50, 479, 479 n.53, 487 n.66

O'Donovan, Oliver 8, 273, 455, 460, 614, 626–50
oath 190, 223, 292, 295–6, 324–5, 401, 407
obedience 36, 38, 41–2, 47, 61, 118, 120–1, 164–5, 177–99, 202, 208, 214, 218–19, 221–4, 232–3, 293, 298, 343, 351, 375, 377, 401–5, 407, 410, 429–30, 520, 560, 646
of Christ 208, 343
    to God 88, 120–1, 232, 298, 407
The Odyssey 597
Olevian, Caspar 120
O'Neill, Eugene 262
Old Testament 97, 118–19, 152, 186, 254, 459, 524, 638–9, 641–2, 658, 660–1
oppression 8, 97, 138, 210, 227–8, 306, 311–15, 318, 323, 358, 408, 417, 431, 446, 450, 475, 495–612
Orthodoxy 109, 389, 420 n.18, 467, 541, 546, 558, 582, 615, 626–7, 664
Orthodoxy, Eastern 389

pacifism 34, 63, 145, 157, 168, 269, 274, 321–3. *See also* nonviolence
paganism 128, 659, 661, 663, 670
Palestine, Palestinian 280, 601–2, 696
Pannenberg, Wolfhart 306–8, 313, 627 n.2, 629
Papanikolaou, Aristotle 389, 490–4
parliament 112, 121, 124, 448, 688
parousia 615
Pascal's Wager 681–90
Passover 283, 583
paterfamilias 41
patriarchy 286, 544, 551, 554, 588

Paul, St. 170–2, 174–5, 177, 228, 436, 441, 443–5, 518, 558, 635

peace 9, 31–43, 45, 54–6, 59, 65–6, 73, 75, 85–6, 89, 94–6, 102, 108, 111, 122–5, 131, 163, 167, 173, 177, 182–3, 185–6, 188, 196, 201, 207, 209–10, 214, 218, 221, 237, 284, 291, 295, 297, 321–82, 385, 388, 393–5, 400–1, 409, 440, 450–2, 461, 471, 485, 507–9, 536, 560, 625, 634

peacemaking 284, 361

penance 62, 64

Pentecostalism 283

people
  as corporation 226, 266, 270
  of God 54–5
  as legislators 71, 75, 78

perfection
  evangelical 187
  of rational soul 36, 38, 483
  See also good, goodness, Jesus Christ; political society; poverty

Peter, St. 170–2, 174–6, 260, 518

Peterson, Erik 128

Phari *Sees* 216, 260, 284, 340, 601–2, 611

Philosophy from Oracles 48

Physics 66, 71, 74, 99

Plato 46 n.3, 211, 409, 437, 441, 477, 530

Platonism 276, 479, 574–5

pluralism 108, 131, 138, 154, 157, 272, 420 n.18, 430 n.39, 431 n.42, 464, 469

polis 3, 441, 443, 448

political creativity 9, 147, 522, 547, 650, 671

political morality 474, 476–84, 488

political society 490, 647

political theology 107–8, 115–31, 132–9, 323, 386, 388, 455, 460, 480, 491, 495, 613–14

political theory 3, 123, 128, 387, 416, 420–1, 426, 429, 431–2, 466, 469, 474, 488, 617, 638

Politics 70–1, 73, 79, 84, 90, 93–5, 101

pope 123, 125, 169–79, 193–4, 230, 292, 450, 458

postcolonialism 109, 323–4, 499, 545

poverty 7–8, 20, 22, 26, 28, 207, 262, 268–9, 297, 323, 331, 347, 349, 357–8, 438, 479, 486, 496–7, 499, 505, 512, 517, 525–9, 532, 537–41, 544, 548, 553, 559, 578, 652

praxis 2, 159, 530, 538, 540, 554, 562, 660

predestination 672–91

Price, Richard 386

priesthood 170, 258, 283 n.4, 286, 330, 337–8, 346

principalities and powers 150, 218, 272, 288

private property 433, 496, 500, 502, 505, 508, 512

proletariat 240, 264, 266, 651

prophets 47, 52, 57, 95, 119, 147 n.4, 177, 184, 186, 220, 232, 234, 254, 256, 283–5, 288–90, 334–5, 403, 410–11, 547, 581, 584, 638, 641–2, 656, 659–61, 669

Protestant social ethics 274

Protestantism 142, 300, 416 n.9, 429 n.37, 557 n.2, 629, 664

prudence 20, 80–1, 204–5, 322, 328, 391, 516

public morality 374

public theology 107–9

Pufendorf, Samuel von 111

punishment 8, 13, 16, 25, 28–9, 32, 37, 40–1, 48, 56, 63–4, 71, 73, 92, 103, 169, 173, 180–1, 183, 188, 191, 207–8, 213–14, 216, 219, 223, 282, 294, 325, 378–9, 434, 485, 544, 655, 684

Puritanism 121

The Politics of Jesus 273–320

queer 275, 497–8

The Quest of the Historical Jesus 306

quietism 281, 288, 478, 662

Quint, David 594 n.5–8, 596, 597 n.21, 597 n.24, 597 n.26

race 1, 18, 37, 206, 211, 224, 242, 245–6, 255, 257, 259, 265, 301, 304, 318, 327, 329, 351, 358, 397, 433, 499, 502, 514, 517, 527, 531, 550, 555–80

racism 138, 323, 357–8, 487, 670

Radical Orthodoxy 109, 615

Rahner, Karl 133 n.9, 138 n.26, 521

Rauschenbusch, Walter 297

Rawls, John 420, 426–7, 453–4, 461–5, 469, 472–4

realism 2, 274, 381–2, 468–74, 485, 489, 658

reconciliation 245, 635, 649

redemption 42, 147, 224, 231–2, 240, 261, 321, 460, 504, 527–8, 534–7, 561, 582–5, 620–1, 648, 684, 687

Reflections on the Revolution in France 386

Reformation 117, 125, 134, 163–4, 167, 225, 242, 246, 259, 274, 450, 549, 583, 587

Reformed 106, 120, 166, 170, 216, 545, 547, 614

relativism 374

religious freedom 157, 368, 419, 492–3

Renaissance 225, 467, 670

repentance 194, 254, 267, 292, 301, 303, 317, 334–5, 342, 345, 530

representation 131, 165, 315, 388, 446, 451–2, 455, 497, 540, 548, 593, 596–8, 612

Rerum Novarum 495–6, 499–518

resurrection 27, 31, 60, 108, 158, 254, 264, 292, 296, 298, 308, 311–14, 342, 542, 573, 580, 632, 639, 656

revelation 10, 275, 309, 312, 399, 402, 409–10, 412, 581–3, 606, 614–15, 626–50

revolution 125, 156, 228, 302, 306, 314, 316, 318, 351, 356–8, 386, 440, 512, 538, 545, 587, 616, 657–60, 663–4, 676, 687–9

Ricoeur, Paul 546

rights 49, 75–6, 86, 112, 117, 121, 126, 157, 164–5, 217, 224, 226, 241, 244, 259, 299–301, 316, 319, 323–4, 327, 348, 350, 357, 364, 373–82, 386, 388, 409, 412, 421, 424, 435–6, 438, 451–3, 455, 461, 467, 487, 493, 495, 499–518, 532, 538, 587, 592

Civil Rights movement 319, 348, 487, 497

divine rights 473

gay rights 553, 555

human rights 121, 157, 323–4, 373–83, 435–6, 493, 532, 538, 540, 546, 553, 555

natural rights 82, 117, 435, 505, 511, 513

of resistance 106, 116–22, 125

ritual 144, 279, 369

Roman 8, 63–4, 124, 141–2, 165, 215, 223, 227, 276, 282, 434, 459, 483–5, 499, 567, 602

commonwealth 45–6, 53

Empire 8, 63–4, 124, 322, 441, 593–4, 601–2, 641

people 53

Rorty, Richard 478

Rose, Gillian 374

Rousseau, Jean-Jacques 433, 435, 477

Ruether, Rosemary Radford 498, 580–92

rulers 24, 66, 81, 96, 98, 117–19, 125, 164, 167, 179, 194, 197, 203, 207, 209, 217, 280, 283, 318, 379, 450, 454, 460, 485, 500, 506–7, 514, 643

correction of 169, 218, 469

corruption of 24, 43, 169, 355, 583–4, 648, 665

election of 250, 254, 319, 616, 649, 680. *See also* king; people; political authority

Ruston, Roger 375

Sabbath 23, 510, 625

sacrament 167, 171, 175, 255, 259, 286, 325, 445, 449, 516, 520, 550, 561

baptism 164, 170–1, 173, 255, 274, 279, 282, 292–3, 309–10, 319, 325, 332, 342–3, 346

Eucharist 59, 170, 271, 389, 445, 493, 621

Saints 31–2, 45, 186, 286, 328, 331, 334, 338, 342, 344, 347, 403, 430, 497, 620, 622, 632, 635, 640, 646–7

salvation 2, 8, 14, 37, 50, 100, 151, 187, 190, 192, 196, 210, 254, 283, 285, 287, 291, 295, 297, 317–20, 329–33, 343, 345, 445, 458, 471, 493, 516, 518–39, 611, 622, 627–8, 638

Samaritan woman 499, 600, 602–11

Satan 20, 124–5, 152, 177, 277, 638–9, 660

Sattler, Michael 274, 291–7

Schaef, Anne Wilson 589

schism 246–7, 484–5, 670. *See also* heresy; heresies

Schleitheim Confession 274, 321, 490–7

Schmitt, Carl 4, 105–6, 109–15, 121n.13, 123, 124–5, 127–31, 161, 456–7, 617

Schüssler-Fiorenza, Elisabeth 498, 699

Schweitzer, Albert 306–7, 599

Scriptures 3–4, 7, 10–13, 16, 23, 25, 32, 39, 43–4, 52, 54–5, 59, 62–3, 66, 139, 165, 169, 173–7, 179–81, 184, 200, 202–7, 210, 219, 220–1, 254, 271, 292, 295–6, 327, 334, 340–1, 344, 375, 408, 410–12, 479, 498, 520, 543, 557–62, 565, 569, 573, 580, 582–4, 610, 613, 624, 654

sectarianism 229–30, 428 n.37, 607 n.48

secular 151, 361–5

"apocalyptic" events 152

argument uses 368–72

creative destruction 152

fundamentalism 152

history of 368–72

orthodoxies in 152–3

secular 153–4, 157, 362–8, 371, 386

secular nationalism 362

secularization 108, 135 n.17, 152–4, 156, 160, 163, 166, 240, 470

segregation 323

Segundo, Juan Luis 496, 545, 548

Sellars, Wilfrid 155

sexism 580–92

sexuality 498, 544, 550

Seydel, Max 112

Shand, Hope 674

sin(s) 14, 19, 28–9, 32, 37, 39–41, 55, 70, 88, 91, 106, 108, 126, 141, 147, 158, 164, 166, 170, 173–5, 182, 185, 187, 214, 234, 260, 263, 266, 274, 292, 294, 303, 317, 325–6, 329, 331, 334–5, 340–2, 388–9, 393, 433, 458, 463, 467, 469–73, 476–84, 516, 524, 527, 530, 535–7, 539, 544, 550, 555, 559, 572, 578, 585, 588, 616, 620, 654–5, 671

blasphemy 179, 198, 235, 537, 640

idleness 23, 509, 625, 671

mortal 17, 19, 32, 34, 36–8, 42–3, 51, 55, 60, 65, 91, 100, 102, 121–3, 125–6, 129, 201, 204, 214, 224, 260, 334, 342, 504, 653

pride 35, 39–40, 55, 168, 203, 206–7, 223, 260–1, 336–8, 340, 400, 408, 453, 472–3, 476, 484, 518, 526, 564, 588, 590, 592, 595

See also crime; idolatry; tyranny; tyrants

Sinai, 118, 256, 258, 337, 411

Coke, Sir Edward 121

slavery 39–40, 97, 243, 259, 298, 310, 316, 319–20, 324, 375–7, 382, 500, 555, 558–61, 564–74, 576, 578, 634, 653, 662, 668, 671

Smith, Wilfred Cantwell 366

Sobrino, Jon 496–7, 518–39

social contract 106, 120, 385–6

Social Gospel Movement 155, 280, 298, 414, 448–9

social sciences 236, 546, 652, 666

social teaching 135 n.14, 297

socialism 145, 371, 432, 439, 495–6, 553, 614, 650–72

society

household 9, 15, 24, 27, 33, 39, 41, 61, 63, 80, 94, 167, 211, 272, 338, 443, 505

sociality 237, 471, 630, 667

renewal 145, 241, 278, 387, 389, 665

voluntary 128, 142, 246, 301–2, 305, 325, 368, 396, 418, 423, 440, 455, 530

See also Church; common good; community; political society

sociology 3, 113, 563, 581, 592, 652, 666–7, 669

Soelle, Dorothee 106–7, 140–51, 167, 389

solidarity 108, 137, 248, 250, 265, 349, 359, 372, 436, 441, 476, 521–3, 527–9, 533, 535, 537, 548, 591, 594, 668–9, 678

Solomon 93–6, 98, 202, 208–9, 217, 221, 224, 328

Solzhenitsyn, Aleksandr 416–20, 427, 431, 681

Son of Man 12, 16, 315, 331, 342–3, 639, 646, 656, 667

soteriology 285

sovereignty 7, 10, 105, 109–15, 117, 119, 121–2, 126–7, 129, 225, 233, 273, 275, 413, 429, 443, 452, 497, 509, 565, 571, 613, 636, 646

spiritual and temporal powers 163, 321

two swords 123, 282, 386, 670

See also; subjection

Stackhouse, Max 428 n.37

Stahl, Julius Friedrich 128

Stalin, Joseph 361

state 32–3, 35–7, 41–3, 45–6, 53, 55–6, 61, 63, 65, 67, 75, 77, 80–2, 84, 86, 105, 107–18, 121–9, 141, 145, 152, 154–5, 157–8, 165–8, 177, 179, 182, 188–90, 203, 205, 225–9, 231, 233–4, 236, 239, 242–5, 250–1, 261, 265, 269, 271–2, 301, 311–12, 318, 322, 325, 330, 348, 362–3, 366–9, 373–4, 376, 379, 381, 385–7, 390, 394, 400, 409, 413, 415, 419, 425, 429–39, 445, 450–2, 455, 457–8, 460, 463, 468, 471, 486–7, 496, 500–3, 506–9, 511–17, 526–7, 530, 554, 614, 619, 631, 640–1, 648, 658, 662, 668–71, 676, 678

Steiner, George 377

Stoicism 299, 304, 479

Stramara, Daniel 560 n.9, 567, 567 n.24, 569, 569 nn.27–29, 570, 570 n.30

Strauss, Leo 127

subjection 36, 38, 182, 217–18, 222, 231

subsidiarity 269, 387, 437

Suffering Servant of God 315

Sugirtharajah, R. S. 499

supernatural 70, 177, 399, 483, 664

sword 119, 123, 164, 173, 177–91, 197–9, 208–10, 221, 231, 274, 282, 292–4, 324, 326, 328, 333, 339, 386, 599, 646, 670

Tamez, Elsa 499, 631 n.8

Taubes, Jakob 121 n.13, 122–3, 125, 127 n.23

taxation, taxes 76, 168, 185, 195, 211, 218, 268, 270–1, 302, 487, 506, 512

Temple, William 164, 166, 230–41

temples 224, 277, 293, 296, 310, 324, 332–3, 335, 337–9, 344, 346, 524, 554, 636–7, 647–9

terrorism 152–3, 436

Tertullian 322, 324–5

theosis 389, 491

Thompson, Francis 262

Tillich, Paul 308, 477, 477 n.45

toleration 8, 18, 62, 75, 97, 183, 196, 199, 224–5, 229–30, 243, 246, 292, 413 n.3, 431, 450, 489

totalitarianism 234, 361, 371, 374, 439, 456, 640

Totontle, Mositi 499, 609–12

Tracy, David 433 n.1

tragedy 8, 253, 262, 349, 479, 489, 636, 646

transcendence 364, 385, 436–7, 481, 525, 607, 616

transubstantiation 621

Trinity, Trinitarian 436–7, 442, 548, 569, 575–6, 578, 624, 640

triumph 26, 253, 257, 266, 283, 295, 331, 425 n.31, 446, 449, 489, 594, 630, 637, 639, 641, 647, 661–2, 664, 685

Troeltsch, Ernst 142

Turner, Nat 306, 316, 319

tyranny, tyrants 18, 76, 95–8, 118–19, 121, 124–5, 194, 196–8, 205, 220–3, 285, 312, 421, 432–6, 439, 448, 562, 565, 643, 651

United Nations 358, 522, 533

Utopia 116, 121–3, 530–1, 658–60, 664–5

Varro 43–4, 48

Vatican II 138 n.26, 433 n.1, 490

vengeance 178, 180–1, 203–4, 208–9, 214–18, 223, 255, 326, 334–5, 407

Venter, Craig 673, 673 n.3, 674, 674 n.4, 675, 675 n.8

Vietnam 323, 349–51

vice. *See* sin

Vindiciae contra Tyrannos (1574) 116, 118–19

violence 1, 14, 34, 56, 105, 143–6, 150, 152–3, 164, 180, 198, 208–10, 222–3, 237, 265, 273–4, 277, 280–1, 283, 285, 294, 305, 321–83, 385, 392, 417, 430, 433, 450, 468, 478, 493, 498, 503, 509, 534, 537–8, 553, 579, 593, 598–9, 613, 617, 657, 667. *See also* nonviolence; war; pacifism; just war

religious violence 323, 361–2, 368–70, 373, 478
virtue 8, 13–14, 22, 24, 27, 29–31, 46–7, 54–5, 63, 67, 69–71, 73–5, 80–7, 95–7, 101–2, 174, 206–9, 211, 217, 297–8, 305, 322, 327, 335–8, 346, 349, 373, 386, 388, 415, 417–18, 422–3, 425–6, 428–32, 434, 441, 454–5, 457–8, 467–9, 472–4, 476, 478, 481, 483, 485–6, 488, 490, 492, 504, 506–7, 509, 513, 518, 526, 529–30, 568, 570, 572–3, 576–7, 587–8, 630
  clemency 99, 204, 209
  gratitude 176, 298, 403, 535
  humility 40, 60, 196, 222, 268, 297, 303, 323, 331, 336, 338–9, 346, 348, 404, 430, 468, 473, 476, 526, 588, 590, 664
  liberality 85–6
  patience 31, 97, 107, 146, 216–17, 222, 257, 265, 291, 304, 323, 338–9, 346, 396, 522, 531
  piety 13–14, 43, 49, 50, 60–1, 147, 208, 317, 514
Voltaire 683

war 32–6, 40, 42, 56, 59, 85, 111, 121–3, 125, 130, 144, 152, 164, 168–9, 191, 210–11, 213–14, 265, 268–72, 282, 295, 322–4, 326–8, 348–58, 362, 370, 372, 385, 390, 448, 452, 486, 507, 536, 559, 634–5, 644–5, 656, 688
Waynes, John 151

wealth 8–9, 18, 20–31, 57, 59, 64, 87, 90, 95–6, 101–2, 116, 228, 234–5, 266, 278, 297, 311, 335, 357, 438, 512, 517, 519, 523, 525–6, 608, 652, 654
Weber, Max 154
Weithman, Paul 472–4
Wentz, Richard 363
Wickham, Lionel 567
Wilfred, Felix 366, 366 n. 15, 522, 532
Williams, Rowan 324, 373–83, 447
Wink, Walter 321
Winthrop, John 120
wisdom 23, 26–8, 31, 37, 45, 49, 69–70, 135, 168, 202, 205, 212, 233, 240, 283, 286, 330, 335–6, 341, 344, 348, 353, 357, 360, 370, 386, 391, 421, 438, 440–1, 454, 467, 476, 487, 493, 506, 519, 563–4, 654, 661, 666
Witherspoon, John 121
Wolterstorff, Nicholas 380
womanist theology 498
women 580–92
worship 404–5, 407–8

Yoder, John Howard 274, 276–290, 321, 431, 556, 556 n.1, 626

Zealots 273, 277, 279–81, 283–5
Žižek, Slavoj 615, 672–91
Zuckert, Michael 378
Zwingli, Ulrich 274